*Plays, Poems, and Miscellaneous Writings associated with George Villiers, Second Duke of Buckingham*

George Villiers, Second Duke of Buckingham in his thirties. Mezzotint by Isaac Beckett after Simon Verelst. Courtesy of the National Portrait Gallery

# Plays, Poems, and Miscellaneous Writings

associated with

# George Villiers, Second Duke of Buckingham

EDITED IN TWO VOLUMES BY

## ROBERT D. HUME

AND

## HAROLD LOVE

Including *Sir Politick Would-be*

Edited by Wallace Kirsop
and translated by H. Gaston Hall

VOLUME I

## OXFORD
UNIVERSITY PRESS

# OXFORD

UNIVERSITY PRESS

Great Clarendon Street, Oxford OX2 6DP

Oxford University Press is a department of the University of Oxford.
It furthers the University's objective of excellence in research, scholarship,
and education by publishing worldwide in

Oxford  New York

Auckland  Cape Town  Dar es Salaam  Hong Kong  Karachi
Kuala Lumpur  Madrid  Melbourne  Mexico City  Nairobi
New Delhi  Shanghai  Taipei  Toronto

With offices in

Argentina  Austria  Brazil  Chile  Czech Republic  France  Greece
Guatemala  Hungary  Italy  Japan  Poland  Portugal  Singapore
South Korea  Switzerland  Thailand  Turkey  Ukraine  Vietnam

Oxford is a registered trade mark of Oxford University Press
in the UK and in certain other countries

Published in the United States
by Oxford University Press Inc., New York

British Library Cataloguing in Publication Data
Data available

Library of Congress Cataloging in Publication Data
Data available

Printed in Great Britain
on acid-free paper by
Biddles Ltd., King's Lynn, Norfolk

ISBN 978–0–19–812761–1 (Set)
ISBN 978–0–19–920363–5 (Volume I)
ISBN 978–0–19–920364–2 (Volume II)

1 3 5 7 9 10 8 6 4 2

IN MEMORY OF DON MCKENZIE

# Preface

George Villiers, second Duke of Buckingham (1628–87), was one of the most scandalous and controversial figures of the Restoration period. He is now thought of by literary scholars principally as the author of *The Rehearsal* (first performed in 1671), an enormously successful burlesque play that ridiculed John Dryden and, more broadly, the rhymed heroic plays and Cavalier tragedies and tragicomedies of 1660–71. Historians remember Buckingham as an opponent who helped topple Clarendon from power in 1667, as a member of the 'Cabal' ministry (1667–74), and as an ally of the Earl of Shaftesbury in the Whig attempt to debar the Roman Catholic Duke of York from the succession during the political crisis of 1678–83. Modern-day lovers of scandal think of the duke as the rake who lived openly with the Countess of Shrewsbury and killed her husband in a notorious duel in 1668. Buckingham had a prominent place among the 'court wits' (Rochester, Etherege, Sedley, Dorset, Wycherley); he was closely associated with such writers as Butler and Cowley; and he was a conspicuous champion of religious toleration who numbered among his friends such serious thinkers as Martin Clifford, Thomas Sprat, John Wilkins, and William Penn. The extent and variety of the works that constitute the Buckingham canon may surprise many readers.

Scrutiny of the Table of Contents of this edition might suggest that Buckingham was the sole or collaborative author of six plays, nine pamphlets, and squibs of various sorts, plus twenty-two poems, and compiler of a fairly massive commonplace book. The difficulty from an editorial point of view is that there is no way to determine exactly what he contributed to each of these works. Indeed, in an alarming number of cases we have no assurance that even a collaborative attribution can be justified. Many members of the nobility and gentry were averse to print publication. Only two pieces saw print in Buckingham's lifetime in authorized editions with his name attached—*A Short Discourse upon the Reasonableness of Men's having a Religion* (1685) and a sarcastic two-page 'Letter' to the 'Unknown Author' of an attack on that pamphlet. All other printings in the duke's lifetime appeared either anonymously (e.g. *The Rehearsal* in 1672, *The Chances* in 1682) or in overtly clandestine form (e.g. his 'Speech in the House of Lords' of 16 November 1675, published with or without the duke's cooperation under the imprint 'Amsterdam 1675'). No literary holographs survive. Some of the squibs and poems exist in scribal copies, often without date or attribution. No cumulative edition appeared until a two-volume *Miscellaneous Works, Written by His Grace, George, Late Duke of Buckingham* finally came out in 1704–5. Collected and edited by Tom Brown (not a scholarly person), it was more a miscellany than a '*Works*'. Only about a quarter of the contents actually have any connection with Buckingham. The edition was not only posthumous but slovenly and without verifiable authority. It is the only source for a number of Buckingham attributions—which may be accurate, erroneous, or simply fraudulent.

Three of the plays are unquestionably collaborative (*Sir Politick Would-be*, *The Country Gentleman*, and *The Rehearsal*). In the first and third of these cases we can only speculate about the nature of Buckingham's contribution. Two of the plays (*The Chances* and *The Restauration*) are adaptations from the 'Beaumont and Fletcher' canon. The poems exhibit the attribution problems and false ascriptions that plague the canon of Rochester and all others in the court-wit circle who wrote anonymously and circulated scribally. The present edition is a companion venture to Harold Love's *The Works of John Wilmot, Earl of Rochester* (Oxford University Press, 1999) and, like that edition, it makes no claim to being a safety-first enterprise. Following that precedent, we have been cheerfully inclusive rather than exclusive, but without in this case trying to insist upon the probability of Buckingham's authorship. In the absence of a substantial corpus of definitively attributed works (apart from correspondence) we do not possess the basis for quantitative stylometric analysis of authorship in questionable cases. Barring the wholly unexpected appearance of a cache of helpful manuscripts, letters, and diaries, most of the attribution problems surrounding Buckingham will remain insoluble.

The case of the 'Commonplace Book' requires special comment. More than a century ago extracts were published from a MS book in the possession of the then Earl of Jersey, said to have been found in Buckingham's pocket when he died. Virtually all Buckingham scholars have presumed that its contents—chiefly maxims, similes, and philosophical reflections—were composed or excerpted by the duke, and that the original poems it contains were of his composition. Alas, the handwriting is not Buckingham's and a much fuller version of this compilation may be found among the Panshanger MSS in the Hertfordshire Archives and Local Studies—a manuscript miscellany in the hand of Sarah Cowper (1644–1720). She was the wife of the duke's political associate Sir William Cowper, and a close friend and neighbour of the duke's ally and confidant Martin Clifford, to whom she quite explicitly attributed most of the items in the 'Jersey' manuscript. We have concluded that the 'Jersey' version might be Clifford's collection, or a joint enterprise between Clifford and Buckingham, or perhaps the work of an unidentified author. We have included the relevant sections of the Cowper MS in this edition, but make no claim for Buckingham's 'authorship'. The most we can say is that he might have contributed material; the collection comes from his circle and very likely reflects his influence; and he probably owned a copy of the 'Jersey' version.

The net result of a sceptical investigation into Buckingham attributions is sobering. We cannot confidently claim 'sole authorship' for *any* of his works, with the probable exception of the brief reply to the 'Unknown Author' in 1685. One might reasonably ask why this assemblage of 'works' should be published as 'Buckingham's'. We would offer two answers. First, the best of the pieces are very fine indeed, and all of them possess historical significance. Second, 'authorship' was differently understood in the late seventeenth century than it is now, and all this material has plausible associations with the Buckingham circle.

There are essentially two ways to look at the problems of editing 'Buckingham'. The editor may simply despair and abandon the enterprise. Alternatively, the editor may relinquish any claim to being able to identify with confidence the origins of what are often anonymous and misattributed texts. Taking this approach, one does not necessarily expect to be able to discern the authorial intentions of a particular individual who wrote the texts. Seventeenth-century readers were unquestionably interested in attribution, but in a high proportion of cases they found themselves grappling (*sans* introduction and annotation) with anonymous texts. Encountering the works comprised in this edition, the seventeenth-century reader might *sometimes* have associated them with the Buckingham circle and to some degree with the duke himself—but quite often not. What an editor can legitimately claim to present is not so much works 'written personally by George Villiers, Second Duke of Buckingham' as a mélange of disparate texts subsumed for commercial convenience in his own time under an iconic brand name.

Writing as it was practised in the gossipy, libellous, coterie circles in which Buckingham lived was simply not the kind of activity practised by a writer like Dryden—and certainly not the activity conceived by Romantic and post-Romantic individualists. As with playwriting in the time of Shakespeare, the imposition of ahistorical views wreaks havoc on our understanding of what writing meant to those who were doing it. We are aware of no term that conveys the nature of the undertaking. Art historians talk about painting from the 'School of Rembrandt' (for example). What might be dubbed 'contributory authorship' has been practised in many realms but has been studied largely in terms of attempting to distinguish individual contributions—which basically misses the point of the enterprise.

No single concept of authorial responsibility accounts satisfactorily for the heterogeneous set of texts now inextricably entangled with Buckingham's name. He was a contributory author, an adapter, a collaborator, sometimes the sole composer of surviving texts. He was also a patron, respondent, catalyst, and in the case of *An Account of a Conference* perhaps simply the inspiration for another writer. Authorship often fails to reduce to a tidy dichotomy of 'wrote it' vs 'did not write it'. In a context of coterie collaboration, adaptation, and scribal publication we will be wise to accept the inevitability of radically varying and frequently indeterminate degrees of agency for such authors as contemporary rumour and later scholarship have delivered to us. We have inherited a canon of sorts. The best we can do is to disclose the attribution evidence and admit the nature and degree of uncertainty attaching to each text.

Some readers may be disconcerted by 'associated with' in the title of this edition. That phrase was arrived at only after considerable debate and soul-searching. We wanted to signal as precisely as possible the highly unusual authorial status of the contents. 'Plays, Poems, and Miscellaneous Writings' seemed unexceptionable, and 'George Villiers, Second Duke of Buckingham' would be hard to avoid without abandoning the enterprise entirely, but how should the two be yoked? To say 'by' or 'of' would imply a claim for sole authorship that we are very far from making. If we said 'attributed to' we would be directing attention to precisely the issue we cannot solve, and might seem to be presuming attribution of the unthinking kind we wish to put under question. If we were to say 'from the circle of' we would make the contents seem arbitrary—why not include anything we can find of Clifford's, or whatever we fancy of Butler and Cowley? We considered 'by and associated with', but this seemed to imply that we can distinguish the two, which is not true. If some readers are puzzled or irked by *Plays, Poems, and Miscellaneous Writings associated with George Villiers, Second Duke of Buckingham* then perhaps our title has served its function. Far from wanting to feign certainty or to hide the problems, we would like to invite users to recognize that we are dealing here with a concept of authorship radically foreign to the assumptions most of us bring to literary texts.

R. D. H. and H. L.

# Acknowledgements

If the first obligation of editors is to their predecessors, then we must start by naming Thomas Percy, Bishop of Dromore, whose impressive and ambitious edition of the works of Buckingham was begun in the 1760s and typeset, but never published. Most of it survives in fragmentary copies in the British Library, the Bodleian, and the Library of Queen's University, Belfast. We have found Percy's work surprisingly helpful. We are also indebted to two editors of *The Rehearsal*, Montague Summers and D. E. L. Crane, whose editions appeared in 1914 and 1976, respectively, and to James Fowler for his excellent dissertation edition of *The Chances* (1979). We have drawn on Christine Phipps's *Buckingham: Public and Private Man: The Prose, Poems and Commonplace Book of George Villiers, Second Duke of Buckingham (1628–1687)* (1985), while dissenting from a number of its judgements.

This edition was conceived some thirty years ago, and reconceived in the late 1980s when Harold Love embarked upon his *Scribal Publication in Seventeenth-Century England* and *Rochester* and joined this enterprise. It has changed, grown, and surprised the editors considerably since they first thought they had established boundaries and editorial policies. Many friends have generously contributed suggestions, objections, bibliographical hints, and esoteric expertise beyond the realms commanded by either editor. Wallace Kirsop and H. Gaston Hall have provided an edition, translation, introduction, and notes for Buckingham's collaborative play in French. We owe debts of special gratitude to Kathryn Hume, Rosaleen Love, the late D. F. McKenzie, and Judith Milhous. We are no doubt failing to recollect all our debts over the many years we have worked on this project, but want to record particular appreciation to Tony Aspromourgos, Kate Bennett, Ann Blair, Michael Burden, John Burrows, Paul D. Cannan, David and Karen Coke, Jennifer Renee Danby, Pierre Danchin, DeAnn DeLuna, Ian Donaldson, Don-John Dugas, Richard Elias, Paul Harvey, John T. Harwood, Earle Havens, Clement Hawes, J. Philip Jenkins, Paulina Kewes, Matthew J. Kinservik, Peter Lindenbaum, Nancy A. Mace, Nancy Klein Maguire, Ashley Marshall, William Poole, Curtis Price, Scott Sowerby, and Vidhya Swaminathan. Ada Cheung, Felicity Henderson, Diane Heriot, and Meredith Sherlock gave much valued assistance with the transcription and annotation of the 'Commonplace Book'. Felicity Henderson also drafted the initial variant lists used in

xiii

editing *The Chances* and *The Rehearsal* and undertook primary editorial responsibility for our text of *The Restauration*, performing each task with unfailing care and accuracy.

Many librarians in America, Australia, and Great Britain have given us exemplary advice and assistance of many kinds, but we wish to offer particular thanks to Richard Overell, Rare Books Librarian of the Monash University Library, Charles W. Mann, Jr, late Curator of Rare Books at Penn State University, and his successor, Sandra Stelts, William Brockman of Penn State, Fredrick Woodbridge Wilson and Annette Fern of the Harvard Theatre Collection, Bärbel Mund of the Abteilung für Handschriften und seltene Drucke of the Niedersächsische Staats- und Universitätsbibliothek, Dr James Fowler of the Theatre Museum (London), Jean-Pierre Mialon of the Bodleian Library, Dr Stephen Parks of the Osborn Collection, Yale University, C. D. W. Sheppard of the Brotherton Collection, University of Leeds, Amanda Stanton of the Library of the Queen's College, Oxford, Tony Trowles, librarian of Westminster Abbey Library, Heather Wolfe of the Folger, and R. Eugene Zepp of the Boston Public Library. More general thanks to the staffs of the British Library, the Bodleian Library, the Cambridge University Library, the Hertfordshire Archives and Local Studies, the Theatre Museum, the London Metropolitan Archives, Harvard, Yale, Princeton, the University of Texas, and the Folger Shakespeare Library are very much in order. To the library staffs of our home libraries, Penn State and Monash, we owe much for many years of never-failing assistance.

Thomas Minsker of Information Technology Services at Penn State performed the programming wonders that permitted us to do our own typesetting, responding to all crises and problems with unlimited patience and good humour. Bonnie Blackburn was an exemplary copy-editor.

Harold Love would like to thank Mr Simon Woods, Dr Ian Haines, and the nursing staff of Cabrini Hospital, Melbourne, without whose skill and care he would have been unable to complete his work for this edition.

We are grateful to the University of Pennsylvania Press for generous permission to make use (in altered and augmented form) of introductory material and annotations in Sir Robert Howard and George Villiers, Second Duke of Buckingham, *The Country Gentleman*, ed. Arthur H. Scouten and Robert D. Hume (Philadelphia: University of Pennsylvania Press, 1976). For permission to draw on material in

Harold Love, 'How Personal is a Personal Miscellany? Sarah Cowper, Martin Clifford and the "Buckingham Commonplace Book"', in R. C. Alston (ed.), *Order and Connexion: Studies in Bibliography and Book History* (Cambridge: D. S. Brewer, 1997), 111-26, we are indebted to the publisher. For permission to make use of material from Robert D. Hume, 'Editing a Nebulous Author: The Case of the Duke of Buckingham', *The Library*, 7th ser., 4 (2003), 249–77, we are grateful to the editor, Oliver Pickering.

To the Earl of Jersey we are indebted for permission to make use of the 'Jersey' version of the Commonplace Book (which also contains 'Theodorick'), now on deposit in the London Metropolitan Archives, and to the Hertfordshire Archives and Local Studies for permission to publish the Cowper version. Our texts of 'The Larke', 'The Owle', and 'Duke of Bu: of la: Shros:' are published with the permission of the British Library.

For heroic assistance in the final stages of seeing this edition to print we owe special thanks to Tom Minsker and Ashley Marshall.

# *Contents*

## VOLUME I

## VOLUME II

## POEMS

## MISCELLANEOUS WRITINGS

### APPENDICES

# List of Illustrations

## VOLUME I

# *Abbreviations*

Electronic archives are cited as of June 2006.

| | |
|---|---|
| *04mw* | *Miscellaneous Works, Written by His Grace, George, Late Duke of Buckingham* (London, 1704) |
| *04mwb* | *Miscellaneous Works, Written by His Grace, George, Late Duke of Buckingham.* The Second Edition (London, 1704) |
| *05mw* | *Miscellaneous Works, Written by George, Late Duke of Buckingham containing A Key to the Rehearsal, And several Pieces in Prose and Verse, Never before Printed . . . Collected and prepar'd for the Press, by the Late Ingenious Mr. Tho. Brown* (London, 1705) |
| *15wgv* | *The Works Of His Grace, George Villiers, Late Duke of Buckingham*, 2 vols. (London, 1715) |
| AV | accidental variant |
| *BF* | *The Dramatic Works in the Beaumont and Fletcher Canon*, gen. ed. Fredson Bowers (Cambridge: Cambridge University Press, 1966–96) |
| *Biographical Dictionary* | Philip H. Highfill, Jr., Kalman A. Burnim, and Edward A. Langhans, *A Biographical Dictionary of Actors, Actresses, Musicians, Dancers, Managers & Other Stage Personnel in London, 1660–1800*, 16 vols. (Carbondale, Ill.: Southern Illinois University Press, 1973–93) |
| BL | The British Library |
| Chapman | Hester W. Chapman, *Great Villiers: A Study of George Villiers Second Duke of Buckingham 1628–1687* (London: Secker & Warburg, 1949) |
| Child-Villiers | Margaret Elizabeth Child-Villiers, Countess of Jersey, untitled review article quoting extensively from the 'Jersey' version of the commonplace book, *Quarterly Review*, 187 (Jan.–Apr. 1898), 86–111 |
| Crane | George Villiers, Duke of Buckingham, *The Rehearsal*, ed. D. E. L. Crane (Durham: University of Durham, 1976) |
| *CSP* | *Calendar of State Papers* |
| Danchin, *Prologues* | *The Prologues and Epilogues of the Restoration, 1660–1700*, ed. Pierre Danchin, 7 vols. (Nancy: Presses Universitaires de Nancy, 1981–8) |

| | |
|---|---|
| *Dictionary of the Canting Crew* | B. E. Gent., *A New Dictionary of the Terms Ancient and Modern of the Canting Crew* (London, [1699]) |
| *DNB* | *The Dictionary of National Biography*, ed. Leslie Stephen and Sidney Lee, 63 vols. (London: Smith, Elder, & Co., 1885–1900). See also the *ODNB*. |
| Dryden, *Works* | *The Works of John Dryden*, gen. eds. H. T. Swedenberg and others, 20 vols. (Berkeley and Los Angeles, Calif.: University of California Press, 1956–2000) |
| *Encyclopædia Britannica* | *The Encyclopædia Britannica*, 11th edn., 29 vols. (Cambridge: Cambridge University Press, 1910–11) |
| HMC | Historical Manuscripts Commission |
| Hotson | Leslie Hotson, *The Commonwealth and Restoration Stage* (Cambridge, Mass.: Harvard University Press, 1928) |
| HRO | Hertfordshire Archives and Local Studies |
| Hume, *Development* | Robert D. Hume, *The Development of English Drama in the Late Seventeenth Century* (Oxford: Clarendon Press, 1976) |
| *Key* | Anon., *A Key to the Rehearsal* (London: S. Briscoe, 1704), included in Vol. II of the Buckingham *Miscellaneous Works* of 1704–5 |
| Langbaine | Gerard Langbaine, *An Account of the English Dramatick Poets* (Oxford, 1691) |
| LION | Literature Online (lion.chadwyck.com) |
| LMA | London Metropolitan Archives (formerly Greater London Record Office) |
| *London Stage* | *The London Stage, 1660–1800*, 5 parts in 11 vols., ed. William Van Lennep, Emmett L. Avery, Arthur H. Scouten, George Winchester Stone, Jr., and Charles Beecher Hogan (Carbondale, Ill.: Southern Illinois University Press, 1960–68) |
| Love, *English Clandestine Satire* | Harold Love, *English Clandestine Satire 1660–1702* (Oxford: Oxford University Press, 2004) |
| Love, *Scribal Publication* | Harold Love, *Scribal Publication in Seventeenth-Century England* (Oxford: Clarendon Press, 1993); repr. as *The Culture and Commerce of Texts: Scribal Publication in Seventeenth-Century England* (Amherst, Mass.: University of Massachusetts Press, 1998) |
| LV | Line variant |

| | |
|---|---|
| Mizener, 'George Villiers' | Arthur Mizener, 'George Villiers, Second Duke of Buckingham: His Life and a Canon of His Works' (Ph.D. diss., Princeton University, 1934) |
| *New Grove Dictionary of Music* | *The New Grove Dictionary of Music and Musicians*, 2nd edn., 29 vols, ed. Stanley Sadie (London: Macmillan, 2001) (www.grovemusic.com) |
| *ODNB* | *Oxford Dictionary of National Biography*, ed. H. C. G. Matthew and Brian Harrison, 60 vols. (Oxford: Oxford University Press, 2004) (www.oxforddnb.com) |
| *OED* | *Oxford English Dictionary* (www.oed.com) |
| Pepys, *Diary* | *The Diary of Samuel Pepys*, ed. Robert Latham and William Matthews, 11 vols. (London: Bell, 1970–83) |
| Percy | Thomas Percy, unfinished edition of 'The Works of Villiers, Duke of Buckingham'. Partial copies survive in British Library C39.g.18–19 and 643.e.10(2), Bodleian Percy 39 and 92, Bodleian Vet. A5d.1797/1–2, the Northampton Record Office, and the Queen's University Library, Belfast |
| Percy's *New Key* | 'A New Key to the Rehearsal' by Bishop Percy constitutes pages 347–464 of his unfinished edition of Buckingham's 'Works' (see previous item). A slightly truncated copy survives in British Library C39.g.18. The notes themselves are complete, but the list of 'Plays Quoted' breaks off with Green's *Politician Cheated* |
| Phipps | *Buckingham: Public and Private Man: The Prose, Poems and Commonplace Book of George Villiers, Second Duke of Buckingham (1628–1687)*, ed. Christine Phipps (New York: Garland, 1985) |
| *POAS–Yale* | *Poems on Affairs of State: Augustan Satirical Verse, 1660–1714*, gen. ed. George deF. Lord, 7 vols. (New Haven, Conn.: Yale University Press, 1963–75) |
| *PQ* | *Philological Quarterly* |
| PRO | Public Record Office (London) |
| *RES* | *Review of English Studies* |
| Rochester, *Works* | *The Works of John Wilmot, Earl of Rochester*, ed. Harold Love (Oxford: Oxford University Press, 1999) |
| *SB* | *Studies in Bibliography* |
| SD | stage direction |

| | |
|---|---|
| Shakespeare, *Complete Works* | William Shakespeare, *The Complete Works*, ed. Stanley Wells and Gary Taylor (Oxford: Clarendon Press, 1986) [old spelling version] |
| SP | Speech Prefix |
| Summers, *Rehearsal* | George Villiers, Duke of Buckingham, *The Rehearsal*, ed. Montague Summers (Stratford-upon-Avon: Shakespeare Head Press, 1914) |
| *Term Catalogues* | *The Term Catalogues, 1668–1709*, ed. Edward Arber, 3 vols. (London: privately printed, 1903–6) |
| TH | Transmissional history |
| Tilley | Morris Palmer Tilley, *A Dictionary of the Proverbs in England in the Sixteenth and Seventeenth Centuries* (Ann Arbor, Mich.: University of Michigan Press, 1950) |
| TNA | The National Archives [Great Britain] |
| UofPA-1683 | anonymously annotated copy of *Q4* (1683) of *The Rehearsal* now in the Rare Books Room of the University of Pennsylvania Library |
| Weinreb and Hibbert, *London Encyclopædia* | *The London Encyclopædia*, ed. Ben Weinreb and Christopher Hibbert (London: Macmillan, 1983) |
| Wilson, *Court Satires* | *Court Satires of the Restoration*, ed. John Harold Wilson (Columbus, Ohio: Ohio State University Press, 1976) |
| Yardley | Bruce Yardley, 'George Villiers, Second Duke of Buckingham, and the Politics of Toleration', *Huntington Library Quarterly*, 55 (1992), 317–37 |

## Reference policy

For seventeenth-century books we normally give only place and year, though in the bibliographies we give STC or Wing number. Following David Foxon's policy of putting helpfulness above consistency, we include STC and Wing numbers in footnotes where we think this might assist the reader. For eighteenth-century books we normally provide key printer/bookseller information from the title page, as well as city and date, though readers should remember that eighteenth-century conventions in such matters differ considerably from those of later periods.

# General Introduction

George Villiers, second Duke of Buckingham, was revered by many of his contemporaries as a champion of religious toleration and one of the founders of the Whig movement in politics, and hated by at least as many others for exactly the same reasons. Historians have preferred to classify him as a dazzling but unreliable opportunist, wedded to an anachronistic notion of personal glory, and there were certainly elements of instability in both his behaviour and personality; but that judgement is one too much swayed by the exercises in character assassination conducted by his Tory opponents, most famously Dryden in *Absalom and Achitophel* and Pope in the third Moral Essay. His political commitment was consistent throughout his adult lifetime; it was over means and execution that he wavered, sometimes self-defeatingly. Had he lived two years longer to participate in the triumph of his political principles with the Glorious Revolution, history might have been more respectful. One can easily imagine a 61-year-old Buckingham adding a spice of unpredictability to the sober deliberations of the Lords in the Convention parliament and taking his seat as a somewhat disreputable elder statesman in William's privy council—but this was not to be. That he was also a poet, critic, wit, and musician was seen as secondary to his achievements as a politician; yet it is the writer who has lasted: two of his plays, *The Rehearsal* and his revision of John Fletcher's *The Chances*, had long performance histories and are still numbered among the most accomplished theatrical creations of their time. This edition presents all the theatrical and literary writings written by, collaborated on, or plausibly associated with Buckingham. Correspondence, speeches, and purely political writings have been omitted as requiring a different kind of editing for a different readership; but his influential tracts on religious and philosophical questions are included along with a commonplace book which, if not compiled by him personally, is clearly a product of his immediate circle and a reflection of his values.

## LIFE AND CAREER

Buckingham's life has been written with Edwardian urbanity in Lady Burghclere's *George Villiers, Second Duke of Buckingham* (1903); with a novelist's perceptiveness but some straining of evidence in Hester Chapman's *Great Villiers* (1949); and somewhat archly but with scholarly rigour in John Harold Wilson's *A Rake and his Times* (1954), so it will be given here only in its outlines.[1] The son of the glamorous but much-hated favourite of James I, he was born at Wallingford House, Whitehall, on 30 January 1628. In later life his birthday was to coincide with the feast day of the royal martyr Charles I. His father's assiduity in marrying his relatives into the aristocracy meant that Buckingham grew to become the head of an enormously influential extended family: John Maynard Keynes went so far as to claim that the Villiers tribe constituted 'the real blood-royal of England'.[2] On 23 August 1628, the first duke was assassinated at Portsmouth by John Felton. Brought up at court with the children of King Charles I, Buckingham was young enough to see something of the pre-interregnum stage and is said on questionable authority to have met Ben Jonson.[3] He is also likely to have witnessed the court theatricals of the later Caroline years. Following his education by the tutors of the Prince of Wales, under the mentorship of the Marquess, later Duke, of Newcastle, he was sent to Trinity College, Cambridge, where he received an (unearned) MA on the occasion of a visit by the Prince on 21 March 1641. Two future associates, Abraham Cowley and Martin Clifford, became attached to him at this period.

At an early stage in the Civil Wars he and his younger brother, Francis (who was born after their father's death), left Cambridge to join the Royalist army, but were quickly retrieved by their relations and

---

[1] Five important early biographical documents are printed in Appendix I.

[2] J. M. Keynes, *Essays in Biography*, 2nd edn., ed. Geoffrey Keynes (London: Heinemann, 1951), 71. The claim is elaborated on in Violet Powell, *Margaret, Countess of Jersey: A Biography* (London: Heinemann, 1978), 33–42.

[3] *The Rehearsal: a Comedy. Written by . . . George late Duke of Buckingham: To expose some plays then in vogue, and their authors: With a key and remarks, necessary to illustrate the most material passages, of this piece, and to point out the authors, and writings here exposed* (London: H. Hills, 1709), p. viii.

sent on the Grand Tour. His exposure to the sexually liberated ways of the Medici court at Florence and the grandeur and sensuality of the Rome of Bernini were to leave a lasting impression. In Rome he recruited another follower in the mathematician Abraham Woodhead, who encouraged a lifelong interest, shared with the future Charles II, in scientific matters. Chapman (p. 32) has suggested that the absurdities of Italian Baroque stagecraft, quite as much as the heroic plays of the school of Davenant, Orrery, and Dryden, are reflected in *The Rehearsal*. Returning home in 1647 via Venice and Geneva, he was reunited with the Prince in Paris, where he was said by Gilbert Burnet to have instilled him with 'ill principles and bad morals' by bringing him into contact with Thomas Hobbes.[4]

Back in England he was able to regain part of his sequestered estates by pleading his youth at the time of his earlier, abortive military career; however, in July of the following year he was involved in a failed royalist uprising, in which Francis Villiers was killed. The existence of an elegy on this young man, attributed to Andrew Marvell, may mark the beginning of an association with Buckingham that was to be of importance to both men.[5] Buckingham fled to Holland, where, as a member of Charles II's court in exile, he was reunited with his former mentor, Newcastle, and soon earned the enmity of the faction headed by the sober and industrious Clarendon. Burnet wrote about him at this period of his life that

The man then in the greatest favour with the king was the Duke of Buckingham; he was wholly turned to mirth and pleasure; he had the art of turning things into ridicule beyond any man of the age; he possessed the young king with very ill principles both as to religion and morality, and with a very mean opinion of his father, whose stiffness was with him a frequent subject of raillery.[6]

He supported himself during this period by the sale of family jewels and works from his father's art collection; but being wholly unused to economy he was soon in difficulties.

In the Scottish expedition of 1650–1 Buckingham enjoyed his first real taste of authority. From the start he had opposed Clarendon by advocating an alliance with Argyle and the Covenanters, although it

[4] Gilbert Burnet, *Bishop Burnet's History of His Own Time*, 2 vols. (London, 1724–34), i. 100.
[5] For their relationship see *POAS-Yale*, i. 197 and n. 53, and Nicholas Murray, *World Enough and Time: The Life of Andrew Marvell* (New York: St. Martin's Press, 2000), 31, 149, 151, 172.
[6] *History*, i. 52.

would mean the betrayal of the Scottish Royalists and endanger the faithful and heroic Montrose. He apparently saw no problem in the conversion of England to Presbyterianism. Once in Scotland, he forced the unwilling king to continue in this alliance and pursued him on horseback when he made an unavailing break for freedom. During the invasion of England that followed, Buckingham's petulant behaviour on being refused supreme military command antagonized Charles, and, while he fought bravely against the Ironsides at Worcester on 3 September 1651, it was in a doomed enterprise from which he was lucky to be able to escape to the Netherlands. From then on Clarendon possessed so complete an ascendancy that Buckingham sought ways to be reconciled with the parliament. As a step towards this he made the acquaintance in Amsterdam of the Leveller John Lilburne, one of a number of radical sectaries who were to be associated with him then and later. When Lilburne came to trial shortly afterwards in England he praised Buckingham as a benefactor who had protected him from the murder plots of the cavaliers. Another radical encountered during his exile was Lilburne's associate John Wildman, whose connection with Buckingham was to be lifelong.[7]

Protected by a permit from Cromwell, who was said to have envisaged him as a son-in-law, Buckingham made short visits to England before returning permanently in June 1657. However, since a large part of his estates had been granted to the parliamentary conqueror Thomas, Lord Fairfax, a more logical move was to seek the hand of Fairfax's pious only daughter, Mary, whom he married on 15 September 1657.[8] While represented by Clarendon as a betrayal, this alliance turned out to be a positive move for the king in that it brought Buckingham into contact with a large party of former supporters of the parliament who had become disaffected from the regime of Cromwell's Independents, and enabled him to contribute financial and military power when the sentiment of the nation finally turned against the Rump. His respect

[7] For Wildman and his connection with the duke, see Maurice Ashley, *John Wildman: Plotter and Postmaster* (New Haven, Conn.: Yale University Press, 1947).

[8] Mary had been engaged to the Earl of Chesterfield and the bans had been read twice when the marriage was broken off. Twentieth-century commentators have tended to assume that Buckingham was guilty of sharp practice in making off with the heiress, but a Fairfax family letter of 20 Feb. 1656[/7?] contains this passage: 'as a secret I tell you the match is likely to break between Mall [Mary] Fairfax and her lover. The truth is neither shee nor father nor mother like him' (Clements R. Markham, *Life of Robert Fairfax of Steeton . . . compiled from Original Letters and other Documents* (London: Macmillan, 1885), 27).

for Fairfax seems to have been genuine, although the childless marriage to Mary was no more successful than most dynastic unions. He would certainly at this period have encountered Marvell, who had been his wife's tutor; however, Cowley composed the epithalamium for the marriage, a graceful compliment to a noble friend running to eighty-six lines in five stanzas.[9]

The alliance between Fairfax and Buckingham alarmed Cromwell, who, a year after the marriage, had Buckingham committed to the Tower. He was later allowed to go into voluntary seclusion with Cowley at Windsor, but was rearrested briefly when Cromwell was close to death. From then until the Restoration he divided his time between London and the Fairfax estates in Yorkshire. He attended Fairfax during his northern rising in support of Monck, and was soon reconciled with Charles II. His return to ascendency was eased by the fact that his cousin, Barbara, Countess of Castlemaine, had become the king's mistress. Beginning with an appointment as a Gentleman of the Bedchamber, which gave him personal closeness to the king, he was advanced in 1662 to the privy council, where he resumed his settled antagonism to Clarendon and the older generation of the king's advisers. Regional administrative responsibilities as Lord Lieutenant of Yorkshire, for which he was fitted by his association with Fairfax and Newcastle, accompanied this promotion.

Handsome, witty, and the personification of a Restoration 'fine gentleman', Buckingham soon established himself as the most spectacular figure at court. His one-time protégé Sir John Reresby called him 'the finest gentleman of person and witt I thinke I ever see, but could not be long serious or mind business'.[10] Dean Lockier remembered that 'When he came into the presence chamber 'twas impossible for you not to follow him with your eye as he went along—he moved

---

[9] 'Beauty and strength together came, | Even from the Birth of *Buckingham*.' Cowley alludes to his friend's troubles during 'a luckless War', his loss of his estates, and this happy outcome: 'She has ended with this Match thy Tragicomedy . . . Our Poet Fate ends not all Plays so well . . . in the middle Acts, and turnings of the Play | Alas! we gave our Hero up for lost.' *The English Writings of Abraham Cowley*, ed. A. R. Waller, 2 vols. (Cambridge: Cambridge University Press, 1905–6), ii. 462–4.

[10] *Memoirs of Sir John Reresby*, ed. Andrew Browning, 2nd ed. with a new preface and notes by Mary K. Geiter and W. A. Speck (London: Royal Historical Society, 1991), 24. For comments on his unfitness for sustained application to business, see further 71–2. At the time of Buckingham's death, Reresby recorded the opinion that 'He was certainly the most witty man of his time, and the hansomest, as well as the best bred, but wholly addicted to his plesures, and unsteady' (ibid. 453).

so gracefully.'[11] But he was also perceived as an unprincipled hedonist, given to spontaneous reversals of allegiance and conviction. Clarendon wrote of him at this period:

His quality and condescensions, the pleasantness of his humour and conversation, the extravagance and sharpness of his wit, unrestrained by any modesty or religion, drew persons of all affections and inclinations to like his company; and to believe that the levities and vanities would be wrought off by age.[12]

His ability to charm was legendary but seldom exercised longer than the securing of the object at which it was directed. He was also addicted to maligning others, including the king,[13] behind their backs, which did him little good since these remarks were inevitably reported to their victims. He was prone to outbursts of anger expressed through shoving and de-wigging at one extreme and challenges to duels at the other, though actual fighting was usually averted. The Restoration provided him with a vast annual income which he lost little time in squandering. His private life at this period was a mixture of practical debauchery (including at least one rumoured homosexual affair) and romantic infatuations.[14] Among the latter was one for the king's sister, Princess Henrietta: in January 1661 he impulsively followed her back to France from a visit to England, to the great displeasure of her husband-to-be, the brother of Louis XIV. A few years afterwards he was no less scandalously besotted with the married Countess of Shrewsbury. Against numerous glowing eulogies and occasional apologies for his failings as excusable follies, we have to set the dark pictures painted in Samuel Butler's bitter 'Character of a Duke of Bucks' and the singularly repellent portrait left by the Florentine agent Lorenzo Magalotti.[15]

[11] Joseph Spence, *Observations, Anecdotes, and Characters of Books and Men*, ed. James M. Osborn, 2 vols. (Oxford: Clarendon Press, 1966), i. 276.

[12] *The Life of Edward, Earl of Clarendon . . . Written by Himself* (Oxford: Oxford University Press, 1857), ii. 322.

[13] Reresby says 'I myselfe have heard him in his mirth make too bould with his Majesty and his brother' (*Memoirs*, 66).

[14] For accusations of sodomy, see *POAS-Yale*, i. 194 and n. and 223 and n.; however, in the second case, the accusation brought by Le Mar and Loveland was of sodomy with a female, who was afterwards alleged to have been murdered. Buckingham was acquitted and his accusers punished.

[15] Samuel Butler, *Characters*, ed. Charles W. Daves (Cleveland, Ohio: Press of Case Western Reserve University, 1970), 66–7 (printed at ll. 275, below); *Lorenzo Magalotti at the Court of Charles II: His 'Relazione d'Inghilterra' of 1668*, ed. and trans. W. E. Knowles Middleton (Waterloo, Ont.: Wilfred Laurier University Press, 1980), 47–9.

Buckingham's faults of character are largely those that might have been predicted of a fatherless child brought up as a supernumerary member of the royal family. A native of a world in which role-playing was second nature, he lacked any clear role of his own, being neither a genuine royal nor, for many years, an independent nobleman. However, this upbringing also gave him an exceptional talent for those other necessary skills of court life—intrigue, dissimulation, and the ruthless use of blackmail (particularly evident in his relationship with his cousin Cleveland). He was a brilliant mimic, entertaining Charles II with imitations of his ministers that did much to undermine them. Face to face with people who amused him, he could hardly prevent himself from imitating their mannerisms back at them. A love of the stage came naturally to one who was an instinctive actor in real life.

Not always the playboy, Buckingham lost no opportunity to put himself forward as a professional soldier. In addition to his civil-war experience he had served with distinction during his exile under the great French commander Turenne. In 1662–3 he efficiently put down an armed rising in Yorkshire. The clemency he showed on this occasion gained him popularity, which stood him in good stead when he returned there in 1665 to raise a regiment to serve in the second Dutch War. On the outbreak of that war he initially attached himself to the navy before being returned to land by the Duke of York because he insisted on agitating for a seniority for which he was unqualified. The two had never been friendly and Buckingham's future political career was increasingly set in an anti-Yorkist mould. He was briefly at sea again against the Dutch in 1672 but saw no action. Later he fruitlessly sought to serve on the Continent under Schomberg, who refused to accept him. A more successful initiative of his years of prosperity was his establishment of a glassworks at Greenwich for wine glasses and another at Vauxhall for mirrors, an outgrowth of his lifelong interest in the science which at that date was uneasily poised between alchemy and modern chemistry.[16] He was believed to have squandered large sums on a search for the philosopher's stone which would transmute all things into gold. He also took advantage of the building boom that was creating the modern West End. A group of lanes south of the Strand, built over the site of York House (and today once again built over),

---

[16] A 262-page manuscript recording (among other things) the 'Chymical Processes of the Duke of Buckingham' is preserved in Alnwick Castle, Northumberland (MS 609). While this is not, as has been stated, in Buckingham's hand, it may have been prepared for his use.

bore the names of George, Villiers, Duke, and Buckingham Streets and 'Of Alley'. His favourite outdoor recreation was fox hunting with the Bilsdale Hunt in wild country in the Yorkshire dales. The names of the dogs have been passed down by tradition since his time. On 8 October 1677 he wrote to Rochester that he would visit him at Woodstock with 'the best pack of Hownds that euer ran upon English grownd'.[17] The quarry on that occasion would have been deer.

The 'Buckingham faction' that provided his political power base between 1667 and 1674 has been analysed by Alan Marshall.[18] Its centre remained Yorkshire, where Buckingham retained his Lord Lieutenancy and was a substantial landowner. Sir Thomas Osborne, the future Earl of Danby, was one able client recruited through this connection.[19] Sir Thomas Gower, Sir Henry Belasye, Sir William Lowther, Sir Richard Temple, Sir Robert Howard, Sir Charles Sedley, Edward Seymour, and William Garway were allies in the Commons. A further group, acquired in his capacity as a 'gatherer of the strange and willful', included the Rosicrucian and astrologer John Heydon, Colonel Thomas Blood (remembered for his attempt to steal the Crown jewels), and the former republicans Thomas Braithwaite, Sir Charles Wolsely, and, as previously mentioned, John Wildman. John Wilkins was his closest associate on the bench of bishops. His personal entourage included Thomas Sprat as his chaplain, Martin Clifford as his secretary, and an embezzling steward, Edward Christian. Cowley, Waller, and Samuel Butler were among his literary clients. At court influence on the king could be exercised directly through his post as one of the Gentlemen of the Bedchamber, while his charm and talent as a writer drew in two fellow occupants of the position, the Earls of Dorset and Rochester, who were also allies in the Lords.

Buckingham's personal influence with Charles could not be transformed into national political influence until the removal from power of Clarendon. He countered the old lawyer's ingrained gravity with frivolity and unpredictability both in the privy council and the House of Lords, where the occasion of debates on a protectionist bill against the import of Irish cattle earned him a triumph over another elderly

---

[17] *The Letters of John Wilmot, Earl of Rochester*, ed. Jeremy Treglown (Oxford: Blackwell, 1980), 134. The spelling 'ow' for modern 'ou' was invariable with Buckingham.

[18] *The Age of Faction* (Manchester: Manchester University Press, 1999), 41–5.

[19] The close nature of the connection may be deduced from surviving correspondence between the two. See British Library Add. MS 28053, fos. 9–19 and 46, and Egerton MSS 3328, fos. 12, 27, 28, 31, 107, and 23329, fo. 1.

cavalier, Clarendon's ally the Duke of Ormond. Buckingham's levity on this occasion was so extreme as to provoke a challenge from Ormond's son, the Earl of Ossory. (A second challenge by Ossory was to be issued in 1671, when Blood confessed to a plot to assassinate Ormond which some thought had been instigated by Buckingham.) Clarendon regained the initiative in 1667 when Buckingham was accused by a former dependent of having conspired with John Heydon to cast the king's horoscope—a capital offence. A royal proclamation dated 8 March 1666/7 was issued 'For the Discovery and Apprehension of George Duke of Buckingham'.[20] Buckingham, having gone into hiding to escape arrest, eventually surrendered himself and was sent to the Tower, being briefly deprived of his court offices and the patent for his glassworks. Clarendon's intransigence over his release only helped to make Buckingham a hero to the Chancellor's many opponents. Marvell represented him as a human sacrifice offered to Clarendon as a malign god ensconced in his newly built palace:

> This temple of war and of peace is the shrine,
> Where our idol of state sits ador'd and accurs'd,
> And to handsel his altar and nostrils divine,
> Great Buckingham's sacrifice must be the first.[21]

The truth was rather the reverse. Clarendon was finally deprived of his offices on 30 August 1667, inaugurating Buckingham's most important period of political influence.

Typically, he immediately tarnished this public triumph by an act of private imprudence. Having several times demonstrated his valour in war, Buckingham showed bravery of a more reprehensible kind by mortally wounding the Earl of Shrewsbury in a duel fought on 16 January 1668.[22] During the weeks while his opponent lay dying of septicaemia, he gave a speech to the Lords in favour of toleration and attended the premiere of Etherege's *She wou'd if she cou'd*. Afterwards he cohabited with the countess until early in 1674, when the Lords forced them to separate. A satirist supplied an imaginary conversation between the two, following the first performance of *The Rehearsal* on 7 December 1671.

---

[20] A copy of the printed proclamation is in British Library Egerton MS 2882, fo. 263.

[21] 'Clarendon's housewarming', *POAS-Yale*, i. 95.

[22] Contrary to legend, the countess did not hold Buckingham's horse during the duel—she was in France at the time.

> Quoth the *Duke* to the *Countesse*, how like you my Farse
> Not halfe soe well quoth she as I like your Tarse
> Nor I God dam'me like the rehearsall
> Half soe well, As I like the hole next to your Arsehole[23]

In February 1671 the two had a son, styled the Earl of Coventry, who died in infancy.[24] Buckingham's marriage to Mary Fairfax produced no children. The infatuation with Shrewsbury was at the very least a distraction at a stage of his career when he needed all his attention for matters of state and also gave his enemies a ready-made pretext for proceeding against him once his influence began to wane. However, it did not immediately affect his hold on power: Pepys, reporting the jaundiced view of his patron York's secretary, Matthew Wren, noted on 15 November 1668 that 'there is no way to rule the King but by brisknesse, which the Duke of Buckingham hath above all men'.[25] On 14 February 1669 the same authority gave him an account of the duke's shattered finances, claiming 'that he hath about 19600*l* a year, of which he pays away about 7000*l* a year in interest, about 2000*l* in Fee-farm rents to the King, about 6000*l* in wages and pensions; and the rest to live upon, and pay taxes for the whole'.[26] The interest was on borrowings to cover his enormous debts, many of the loans having been negotiated at exorbitant rates or through mortgages which, since they could not be redeemed, were subject to foreclosure. Such extravagance could be sustained only so long as high office continued to offer opportunities for plunder.

The constellation of ministers who advised Charles following the departure of Clarendon was quickly named the Cabal (anagrammatic for Clifford, Arlington, Buckingham, Ashley, and Lauderdale); however, it was never a unified body. Buckingham and Arlington detested each other; Clifford was a crypto-Catholic; Lauderdale concerned himself principally with Scottish affairs, in which he would brook no interference; and Ashley, the most able of them, was only a superficial

---

[23] Yale MS Osborn f b 140, p. 171.

[24] The title was obviously illegal, but Charles II stood godfather to the child and, as Wilson observes, might well have legitimized him in due course (*A Rake and His Times: George Villiers, 2nd Duke of Buckingham* (New York: Farrar, Straus and Young, 1954), 179).

[25] *Diary*, ix. 361.

[26] Ibid. ix. 448. A more accurate estimate of 1671, discussed in Frank T. Melton, 'A Rake Refinanced: The Fortune of George Villiers, Second Duke of Buckingham, 1671–1685', *Huntington Library Quarterly*, 51 (1988), 297–318, estimated Buckingham's potential landed income as £17,951. 14*s*. 0*d*.

convert from the republicanism of his younger years. Whereas Clarendon had successfully promoted harsh punitive measures against Protestants who refused to be reconciled to the Church of England, Buckingham and Ashley worked to reduce the severity of these and were generally trusted by the Nonconformists. At one stage Buckingham went so far as to advise the king to emulate Henry VIII by a second royal seizure of church lands, though this was not proceeded with. However, Charles, playing a double game, was interested in accommodation with the Nonconformists only as an oblique means of advancing the Catholic cause and establishing an alliance with France that would support him in ruling independently of parliament. In the 1650s Buckingham had forced him into an alliance with the Scots which involved a promise to make Presbyterianism the state religion of England. Now in the late 1660s, behind Buckingham's back, the king entered negotiations with Louis XIV over the possibility of a forced conversion of the nation to Catholicism with the assistance of a French army. This duplicity reached its height between July and September 1670, when, following the signing of the secret Treaty of Dover with Louis, Buckingham was sent to France to negotiate a bogus commercial and military treaty. Louis kept up his part in the farce by showering the deluded ambassador with presents and addressing him in letters as 'mon cousin' (presumably on the strength of Buckingham's descent through his mother from Edward IV). Charles was also suitably generous with honours: a new one of 1671 was the Chancellorship of Cambridge University, formerly held by the first duke. In June the leaders of the university trooped to London to instal him and were rewarded with 'a most noble supper consisting of fish, foule, and tarte and custard, and gelly'd and banqueting stuff'. Buckingham replied to the Vice Chancellour's Latin oration 'very handsomely and pertinently'.[27] He was good at such occasions.

Early in 1672, in alliance with Ashley (shortly to become Earl of Shaftesbury), Buckingham promoted the Declaration of Indulgence, which for them was a measure intended to relieve the Nonconformists, but which the king and Clifford privately saw as a means of ameliorating the condition of Catholics. Politically, the issuing of the Declaration involved the dangerous tactic of championing the royal prerogative

[27] Henry More's judgement in *The Conway Letters*, ed. Marjorie Hope Nicolson, rev. edn. ed. Sarah Hutton (Oxford: Clarendon Press, 1992), 334, 335.

in the face of explicit legislation passed by parliament. Buckingham also gave his support to a new war, in alliance with France, against the Dutch, which proved to be both unpopular and unsuccessful as far as England was concerned, though the French made considerable inroads into Dutch territory. His *A Letter to Sir Thomas Osborn* justifies this attack on fellow Protestants on the grounds of their being England's rivals for commercial supremacy. On a visit to Holland in late June 1672 to advise an accommodation with Charles, Buckingham found the young William of Orange determined to resist the French to the death, an attitude difficult for him to comprehend but which alerted him to the problems likely to accrue to Protestant England from a Catholic conquest of the Netherlands. By now Buckingham's position at the head of affairs was itself under threat from an alarmed parliament. On 14 January 1674, in an attempt to exculpate himself from the mismanagement of the previous years, he attacked Arlington during a voluntary appearance before the Commons; however, he was himself the sufferer, as an address by the house to the king in the following month was to lead to his dismissal from all his offices.[28] On 15 January Arlington also appeared before the Commons but was able to defend himself effectively against Buckingham's charges. The king, to whom Buckingham had failed to deliver promised parliamentary support, was glad to have an excuse to dispose of him. The Lords added insult to injury by compelling him to end his liaison with Lady Shrewsbury.[29]

A quatrain written at this time shows how much Buckingham's political standing had been harmed by his private irregularities:

[28] The progress of the case in the House of Lords is summarized in British Library Add. MS 61486, fos. 157$^r$–158$^r$, concluding with the resolution 'That an Address be presented to his Majesty to remove the Duke of Buckingham from all his Employments that are held during his Majesties pleasure And from his Councell and presence for ever.'

[29] Copies of the petition from the relations and trustees of the young Earl of Shrewsbury ('as yet a minor') survive in British Library Stowe MS 182, fo. 36, and Add. MS 29547, fo. 32. The petitioners complain 'of that wicked and scandalous life led by George Duke of Buckingham and with Anna Maria Countesse of Shrewsbury' and the 'shamelesse manner of their cohabiting together'. They say that they would have 'forbourne in respect of the unhappy Lady if Shee and her complice the said Duke of Buckingham had imployed the usuall care of such offenders to cover Actions of shame and Guilt', but they fear that ostentatious provocation would eventually result in the young Earl's challenging Buckingham to a further duel, leading to another 'sad and bloody . . . misfortune'. The petitioners were particularly outraged by the guilty pair's 'haveing buried a base son of theirs in the Abby Church in Westminster by the title of Earle of Coventry with all rites and formallityes'.

On the Duke of B. fall
When Great men fall, their fall makes weeping Eyes
In two or three or four Great familyes
But at this Great man's fall four Cittyes sorrow
Rome & Geneva, Sodom and Gomorrah[30]

A satire called 'A dialogue between the Duke of Buckingham and his father's ghost' (see II. 304), which shows him in transition between power and opposition, expresses the antagonism towards him felt by the Catholics and ex-Clarendonians. In a passage modelled on the address of Cethegus in Jonson's *Catiline* (a play he was known to admire), the ghost urges him to bring the kingdom to ruin and destruction. Buckingham then gives an account of the faction with whom he was rebuilding his parliamentary influence in order to oppose the king who had discarded him:

> *Young D:* The party I have made are brave and strong.
> First *Rochester* next envy'd *Arlington*
> And next *Albermarle*'s Debauched Sonn.
> Next *Buckhurst*<,> *Sidley* and their wenching Traine,
> And *Mulgrave* soe belov'd of *Castlemaine*.
> Our p<ar>ty in the house are numerous,
> Wee hate all those who seeme religious.
> Nay, to make sure wee've gott the Speaker too,
> Then name the thing that wee han't power to doe.
> *Old D.* But I don't remember you have nam'd
> The man who for his partes soe much is fam'd
> Old *Shaftesbury* . . . .[31]

The inclusion of Arlington in the party must rest on memories of their brief alliance against Clarendon, since the two were ancient enemies, and Mulgrave's membership was only temporary; but the others named, including the speaker, Edward Seymour, were all known associates of this period.[32]

---

[30] BL Add. MS 34362, fo. 119r.

[31] Yale University MS Osborn f b 140, p. 98.

[32] Buckingham had of course been forced to work closely with Arlington over the years, which may help account for some of the venom underlying his portrayal of the earl in *The Rehearsal* and so blatantly expressed in 'Aduice to a Paynter, to draw the Delineaments of a Statesman and his Vnderlings'. For eight letters by Arlington to Buckingham written during the political crisis of 1663, see *Miscellanea Aulica: or, a Collection of State-Treatises, Never before*

A curious document from this time is 'The Duke of Buckingham's account of himself in severall matters concerning his private life', an exculpatory narrative, in which he may have been assisted by Thomas Sprat, and which, as was only to be expected, puts the best interpretation possible on a number of incidents raised in parliament to his discredit.[33] His list of these is interesting:

From this Common fame I hear that the cheif Accusations againſt me haue bin these That I am a man of a light mind turning all graue things into ridiculous, That I am of a cruell and insolent Nature, That I contriud the Yorkshire Plott by which many were trepand out of their liues, That some haue bin suspeᶜᵗed to be poisond leaſt they should be witnesses againſt mee, That I emprisond one laſt year without sufficient authority, that I haue leuy'd mony upon the subieᶜᵗ without Aᶜᵗ of Parlement, that I am a Promoter of Popery, And that, I haue spoken reviling words of the King.

Each of these charges is rebutted. His comments on his religious position are of interest for what they do not say as much as for what they do:

. . . I cannot deny, but I haue allways inclind to some moderate way in matters of Conscience, which I proteſt before God has not proceeded from any auersion to the Church of England, but only because I thought that to be the sureſt way to settle the Church and unite the Nation, Perhaps in this I was miſtaken, however I am perfeᶜᵗly convincd that of all the professions of Chriſtianity, this of our Church is the beſt for the true ends of Religion, the rights of Princes, and the juſt freedome of subieᶜᵗs, I beleive it to be the moſt rationall, the moſt Chriſtian, nay the moſt Gentlemanly Religion in Chriſtendome.

Transubstantiation—the great point of dispute between Canterbury and Rome—is dismissed as 'a Doctrine so unnecessary to the Christian Religion, and so contrary to all Sense and Reason' that he had always 'had a conceit' that Catholics themselves secretly disbelieved it. To the 'horrid' accusation of sodomy made against him he replied 'God know's I have much to answer for in the plain way, but I never was so great a Virtuoso in my lust's.'

The loss of office also precipitated a financial crisis, brought about by the double threat of enormous debts and the likelihood that im-

---

*publish'd,* . . . *Faithfully Collected from their Originals, by Mr. T. Brown* (London: J. Hartley et al., 1702), 303–24.

[33] HRO D/EP F49. The full text is printed in Appendix I, item 3.

peachment might render his estates forfeit to the crown. Aware of these dangers, Buckingham, as early as May 1671, had placed his property in the hands of a group of trustees, headed by the experienced bankers Sir Robert Clayton and John Morris and including his old friend and ally John Wildman. This move gave him some protection from seizure (as was proved in February 1673 when the king unsuccessfully tried to overthrow the scheme) and gave him a guaranteed personal income of £5,000 a year. As Frank T. Melton has explained, Buckingham's enormous landholdings had been managed in a highly inefficient manner, inherited from the Middle Ages, in which the individual bailiffs returned income directly to his corrupt chamberlain, Edward Christian, without any proper bookkeeping and with much siphoning off of rents.[34] Clayton and Morris introduced commercial methods of accounting and collection and refinanced the more exorbitant outstanding loans at a much lower rate. Buckingham referred to the arrangement in his 'Defense', of 1674, when he confessed 'I have deliverd up my estate to Honourable Trustees for the sattisfaction of my Creditors, so that I have put it out of my own power to defraud any man of his right, and have provided that my extravagence should be hurtfull to none but my self' (see App. I, ll. 282). The effect of their good management, which may well have been motivated by political sympathy, was to make Buckingham solvent again by 1676 and, in opposition to the general assumption of historians, a wealthy man at the time of his death. The building of his palace at Cliveden, often regarded as symptomatic of wasteful irresponsibility, was carefully financed by sales of unwanted urban land, including that of York House, his old family house in the Strand.[35]

---

[34] Melton, 'A Rake Refinanced', 300–3. See also his 'Absentee Land Management in Seventeenth-Century England', *Agricultural History*, 52 (1978), 147–59.

[35] The principal surviving evidence on the duke's chequered financial history is the twenty-one items in the Osborn shelves/Buckingham box in the Beinecke Library at Yale. Other significant sources include accounts in the Clayton Papers at the Folger (MS X.d. 492, nos. 71–88), British Library Add. MS 5821, fos. 222–3 ('Accompt of the Duke of Buckingham's First Trustees . . . 1673'), and charters and documents in the John Rylands Library cited by Melton. The Osborn Collection documents show that in 1671 the duke's debts stood at £123,140, plus £12,168 4s. in unpaid interest (a sum that had escalated to some £30,773 by 1674). In the summer of 1674 the trustees sold various properties for a total of £97,325 (borrowing money to clear debts to make sale possible in some cases). Loans at as much as 18 per cent were refinanced at 6 per cent. As of 1671 Buckingham's income was calculated by his trustees as £19,306 18s. 2d. They allowed him £5,000 per annum to live on and applied the rest to debt reduction. Sale of property to raise capital unquestionably reduced the income, though an undated calculation among the Osborn Collection papers ('A particular of the yearely Rents

Following his dismissal, Buckingham joined the more able but less charismatic Shaftesbury in the organization of a 'country' parliamentary opposition to the court party, which under the direction of his former client, Danby, had returned to a Clarendonian, pro-Anglican policy hostile to both Nonconformists and Catholics. To further this an alliance needed to be forged with the commercial interests of the City, which was also the principal stronghold of Nonconformity. Buckingham's enthusiasm for this strategy extended to his purchasing a house in Dowgate, where he could entertain and gather information: the king referred to him as 'Alderman George'. Battle was now joined between the Whigs, as the party of Shaftesbury and Buckingham were soon to be known, and the Anglican and Catholic supporters of the Crown. The issue at stake was whether and on what terms the Duke of York, as Charles's heir but a Catholic, might be allowed to succeed to the throne. On 15 February 1677 a premature attempt to force an election over the issue by declaring parliament to have been dissolved by an overlong prorogation led to both Buckingham and Shaftesbury being imprisoned in the Tower.[36] Buckingham remained there until July, when his release was eased through the advocacy of Rochester, Nell Gwyn, and other court friends.[37] Marvell praised his enduring his imprisonment as an assertion of 'the freedom of his own spirit' and 'the

and Revenues of the most noble L. Geo. duke of Buckingham', apparently from late in the duke's life) puts his income (after administrative expenses) at a quite munificent £9,979 2s. 3 1/4d. After the duke's death in 1687 the sale of his Helmsley estate in Yorkshire brought in £86,438 19s. 4d. which the trustees immediately applied to an itemized list of remaining debts. The trustees' accounts continue through the 1690s and appear to imply systematic reduction of remaining liabilities. All protestations to the contrary notwithstanding, Buckingham clearly retained an expendable income of £5,000 per annum throughout his life. The principal on some very substantial debts remained unpaid at the time of his death, but Brian Fairfax appears to have been absolutely correct in claiming that if Buckingham 'was extravagant in spending, he was just in paying his debts, and at his death charged his debts on his estate, leaving much more than enough to pay them' (see App. I, II. 295).

[36] Buckingham's speech in the House of Lords on 15 Feb. 1676/7 caused a major uproar and survives in multiple copies, among them British Library Add. MS 28937, fos. 272$^v$–275$^v$, Add. MS 32095, fos. 6$^r$–15$^v$, Sloane MSS 39, fos. 1$^r$–4$^r$ and 3087, fos. 1$^r$–7$^r$, and Royal Society MS 83, pages 215–25 (Commonplace Book of George Ent). It was printed in the 1704–5 *Miscellaneous Works*, i. 18–32. Buckingham endeavoured to prove that by old statutes parliament was *de facto* dissolved and that the king should call for the election of a new one. A summary of the proceedings in the House of Lords against Buckingham, Salisbury, Shaftesbury, and Wharton 'for proposing, asserting and mainteyning that this Parliament is dissolved' is in Add. MS 32095, fos. 16$^r$–21$^v$.

[37] An undated copy or draft of a letter from Buckingham to Charles II in Add. MS 27872, fos. 20$^r$–22$^v$, speaks of 'The most sensible greife I had in being putt away from your Maiesty' and refers to 'what Mrs Nelly has told me'.

due liberties of the English nation',[38] while Danby was infuriated by the ease with which Buckingham was able to resume his social companionship with the king. But with the outbreak in 1678 of the 'Popish Plot' panic, which he and Shaftesbury actively fomented, their influence grew more threatening. In March 1679 Danby was impeached and in May sent to Tower.[39]

Buckingham's fabled charm was now exercised in popular demagoguery. In a diary entry for 2 November 1677 Anthony Wood noted that 'the duke of Bucks, steward of the citie of Oxon, was entertained with a dinner by the citizens of Oxford at Soladell Harding's in Allsainte parish. There were with him severall country gentlement who ... spoke liberallie at dinner against the University.'[40] He was to return in February 1681 to ensure the election of a right-minded alderman to parliament. On this occasion Wood wrote of the opposition candidate:

He lost it by the means of Bucks and [Lord] Lovelace, who were appointed by the Cabalists to promote this election here, that is, rebellion and discord which the last parliament hath done among the commons and vulgar. (ii. 516)

He further noted that

This is the third time he hath lost it in two yeares' space, purposely by the meanes of B and L who goe from place to place to get in their freinds to be burgesses, purposely to cross the king, raise rebellion and discord in the nation, and to vilifie or make cheap the king, court, and clergy in the minds of the commons. (ii. 523)

The 1677 visit was the subject of 'A proper New Ballad, concerning the Reception of his Grace the Duke of Buckingham, by the right worshipfull the Major and Aldermen off the city of oxon: 1677 . . . To the

---

[38] *An Account of the Growth of Popery, and Arbitrary Government in England* (Amsterdam, 1677), 51–2.

[39] The extreme bitterness of relations between Buckingham and Danby by the end of the decade is evident in a letter of 22 May 1680 from Francis Benson to Ormond: 'Yesterday Philip Le Mar and his mother received their trial at the King's Bench bar, and were both found guilty of being suborned to swear sodomy against the Duke of Buckingham. In the course of the trial some reflections were made upon His Royal Highness, but very severe and frequent ones against the Earl and Countess of Danby; but especially upon the latter, against whom one witness deposed that Le Mar told him the Countess of Danby offered him at her house in the Cockpit £300 if he would give evidence against the Duke of Buckingham upon such a crime.' HMC *Ormonde*, NS v (1908), 324. For an allusion to the Le Mars, see 'A Song on Thomas, Earl of Danby', lines 77–84 and note.

[40] *The Life and Times of Anthony Wood*, ed. Andrew Clark, 5 vols. (Oxford: Oxford Historical Society, 1891–1900), ii. 391.

tune of cuckolds all arow or Tom Tyler' ('Now Listen good Friends and Ile tell you how twas').[41] A similar intervention in a Buckinghamshire poll so annoyed the king that he refused to see Buckingham on his return to court.[42] These occasions give the lie to the accusation that Buckingham was not an effective politician. Today his brilliance as a communicator (an aspect of what Wood called his 'condescension') would have been monitored by a staff of minders whose duty was to save him from the gaffes, moments of impulsiveness, and weak grasp of detail to which he was always prone. Chapman credits him with a hand in the staging of the pope-burnings—grand populist pageants mounted on Queen Elizabeth's birthday by the Whig Green Ribbon Club, of which he was a leading member.[43] In March 1681 he received the freedom of the City and on 24 November shared Shaftesbury's triumph in the public celebration that followed the returning of an *Ignoramus* verdict at his trial for uttering treasonous words. There was even a party, admittedly small, which thought he might be made king in the event of a total exclusion of the Stuarts.[44] But the Britain of his day was not yet ready for the idea that political power should arise from popularity with the electorate; neither can Buckingham's many failings as a statesman be denied, despite his unquestionable talent for demagoguery.

Buckingham never went as far as Shaftesbury in the attempt to undermine the prerogative by asserting parliamentary control of the succession. In the Exclusion crisis of 1678–83 Buckingham supported the placing of constitutional limitations on a Catholic king but declined to vote for making the Duke of York ineligible to succeed, absenting himself from crucial debates in the Lords. While retaining the trust of the Nonconformists, he was forced from his central position in the Whig councils, much as he had earlier been from those of Charles II. Burnet writes of the last years of his life that he was 'sickly, and sunk in his parts',[45] though the holograph letters to William Penn of his last months show no decline in mental powers and he was still

---

[41] Yale Osborn b 54, pp. 1056–9. Text printed in App. II at ll. 314.

[42] J. R. Jones, *The First Whigs: The Politics of the Exclusion Bill Crisis 1678–1683* (Oxford: Oxford University Press, 1961), 99–100.

[43] Chapman, 227–9, 257–60.

[44] See on this subject 'Advice to the painter from a satirical night-muse', ll. 47–8 in *POAS-Yale*, ii. 497.

[45] *History*, 100.

able to endure long days in the hunting field.[46] Having loudly if mis-leadingly advertised his own profligacy, Buckingham retired to his house in York with excursions to a country seat, Helmsley Castle, where he exercised his last post of power as Master of the Bilsdale Hunt.[47] In the summer of 1684 he enjoyed a pleasant yachting trip with the king to Portsmouth. His last grand appearance in London was on 23 April 1685 to take part with his duchess in the coronation of James II.[48] In November 1685 his sister Mary, the 'old' Duchess of Richmond, died, childless like himself.

On 16 April 1687 Buckingham died in an inn at Kirkby Moorside, near Helmsley, from a fever contracted while hunting. His presumably long-suffering wife survived until 1705. His death was seen by most of his own class as the outcome of a life of outrageous excess; yet he was also sincerely mourned by many who respected him as the political heir to Fairfax and Newcastle, the advocate of toleration for Dissenters, and a leader of national resistance to the Catholic heir. While he died before the Glorious Revolution (and, as suggested earlier, might have been more fairly regarded by history had he survived it), he contributed much to the climate of ideas that made it possible. One must also grant that while he lacked many desirable human attributes he had never for a moment been boring or, for very long, bored.

Throughout this entire period Buckingham was the target of per-sonal satires of singular venom and grossness. From 1678 comes 'The Litany of the Duke of Buckingham', a summary of his life in burlesque that brings together pretty well every item of hostile gossip from his long career.[49] 'I sing the praise of a worthy wight' (sung to the old ballad tune 'Sage leaf') is attributed in one early text to Dryden and covers much the same ground. Both these satires are given in full below in Appendix II at ii. 306–311. In 'Rochester's Farewell' (1680), which is not by Rochester, Buckingham is accused of having left no 'Law unbroke of God or Man' and of sins sufficient to 'damn a Nation'.[50]

---

[46] Ibid. The letters are preserved in the National Archives of Scotland and the Historical Society of Pennsylvania. See the introduction to *An Essay upon Reason, and Religion, In a Letter to Nevil Pain* (ii. 80).

[47] The present-day hunt's website lists him as master from 1668 until his death in 1687.

[48] Ironically, the duchess was godmother of James's daughter Mary, who was to succeed to the throne with her husband William of Orange after the revolution of 1688.

[49] Annotated text in *POAS-Yale*, i. 192–9.

[50] *The Gyldenstolpe Manuscript Miscellany of Poems by John Wilmot, Earl of Rochester, and Other Restoration Authors*, ed. Bror Danielsson and David M. Vieth (Stockholm: Almqvist and Wiksell, 1967), 289.

Mulgrave and Dryden's 'An essay on satire' anticipates the gentler policy of the character of 'Zimri' in Dryden's *Absalom and Achitophel* by portraying him as an incorrigible lightweight.

> Let him at business ne'er so urgent sit
> Show him but mirth, and bait that mirth with wit,
> That shadow of a jest shall be enjoy'd
> Though he let all mankind to be destroy'd.[51]

As 'Zimri' he was all too memorably characterized as

> A man so various, that he seem'd to be
> Not one, but all Mankinds Epitome.
> Stiff in Opinions, always in the wrong;
> Was every thing by starts, and nothing long:
> But, in the course of one revolving Moon,
> Was Chymist, Fidler, States-Man, and Buffoon:
> Then all for Women, Painting, Rhiming, Drinking;
> Besides ten thousand freaks that dy'd in thinking.
> Blest Madman, who coud every hour employ,
> With something New to wish, or to enjoy!
> Rayling and praising were his usual Theams;
> And both (to shew his Judgment) in Extreams:
> So over Violent, or over Civil,
> That every man, with him, was God or Devil.
> In squandring Wealth was his peculiar Art:
> Nothing went unrewarded, but Desert.
> Begger'd by Fools, whom still he found too late:
> He had his Jest, and they had his Estate.
> He laught himself from Court, then sought Releif
> By forming Parties, but coud ne're be Chief:
> For, spight of him, the weight of Business fell
> On *Absalom* and wise *Achitophel*:
> Thus wicked but in will, of means bereft,
> He left not Faction, but of that was left.[52]

For posterity, Buckingham was to live chiefly in these lines and the crushing epitaph of Pope's third Moral Essay, ll. 299–314; but we need to remember that both men were opposed to everything that Buckingham stood for both politically and artistically.

---

[51] *POAS-Yale*, i. 406.
[52] 'Absalom and Achitophel', ll. 545–68 in *Works*, ii. 21.

Indeed, the Zimri portrait was in one respect the outcome of literary rivalries that extend beyond retaliation for the earlier insult of *The Rehearsal* to questions involving the relative status of professional and amateur writers.[53] In the 1660s Buckingham had made himself the acknowledged head of a group of young writers with a recognizable programme for the reform of English letters. The group is best known to us from the ways in which it was reflected in the writings of Rochester, especially his account of his 'inner audience' in lines 120–5 of 'An allusion to Horace':[54]

> I loath the Rabble, 'tis enough for me
> If Sydley, Shadwell, Shepheard, Wicherley,
> Godolphin, Butler, Buckhurst, Buckinghame
> And some few more, whome I omitt to name
> Approve my sence, I count their Censure Fame.

What is described here is an alliance of poets and critics which had a lasting influence on the literature and drama of its time. It was court-centred, seeing itself as a continuation of the court culture of Charles I's time, and yet it was also in dialogue with the new voices of the 'town'—that experiment in urban living that was taking shape in the newly built streets and squares between the City and Whitehall. Its model of style was defined by the impromptu conversation of courtiers. In the earlier age, Fletcher had gained praise for the ways that the witty men in his plays imitated that conversation, but the situation would obviously be better if courtiers themselves were doing the writing.[55] Moreover, the style of the ancient wits had come to seem florid and ornate: in Charles II's day the ideal, both in speech and writing, was to be plain, colloquial, and 'easy'—the buzzword that Marvell felt obliged to apply even to *Paradise Lost* in order to recommend it to his contemporaries.[56] This mindset made the court wits instinctively hostile to the baroque complexities and extravagant idealism of Dryden's heroic plays —thus *The Rehearsal*. In comedy and dramatic satire they preferred the tradition of the down-to-earth Jonson to that of the fanciful Shakespeare, though an exception was made for *Timon of Athens*, which

[53] See on this subject Harold Love, 'Shadwell, Rochester and the Crisis of Amateurism', in Judith Slagle (ed.), *Thomas Shadwell Reconsider'd*, pub. as *Restoration*, 20 (1996), 119–34.

[54] *Works*, 74.

[55] Fletcher's validation of courtliness is considered in Robert Markley, *Two Edg'd Weapons: Style and Ideology in the Comedies of Etherege, Wycherley, and Congreve* (Oxford: Clarendon Press, 1988), 56–99.

[56] 'On Paradise Lost', ll. 16, 36.

Buckingham's recommendation encouraged Shadwell to revise in 1677. Among the Restoration writers of comedy Shadwell best conformed to the Jonsonian ideal, and it was he who, in a dedication of 1687 addressed to Sedley, gave the group its most moving elegy:

It is honour enough for me, that I have from my *Youth* Lived in yours, and, as you know, in the *favour* of the *wittiest men of England*, your familiar *friends and acquaintance*, who have encouraged my Writings; and suffer'd my Conversation. I mean not any of the *profess'd Poets*; for I take none of them to be of that *Rank*, and most of 'em *God* knows are far enough from it. But it has happen'd in our time, that some few men of *Quality* have been much the *greatest wits* of the *age*, nor do I think *England* ever produced so great in any *age*, the loss of two of which, the *Earl of Rochester*, and the *Duke of Buckingham*, we who had the honour to be acquainted with them can never bewail enough.[57]

The court wits, as here described, corresponded pretty exactly to the Buckingham faction in court politics. Indeed, as Rochester showed, satire could be as potent a force in demolishing an enemy as parliamentary votes or arguments at council. Buckingham was himself capable of turning council meetings into a form of theatre where the gravity of opponents was burlesqued to their faces with devastating effect. Sedley and Dorset, both talented poets, were Buckingham's followers during his period of influence and glory. They accompanied him on his embassage to France in 1670, followed him into political opposition, and, after his death, contributed to the bringing about of the Revolution. Rochester was always close to Buckingham—when Buckingham was released from the Tower in 1677 he moved straight into the younger man's apartment at court—and towards the end of his life, through the mediation of Burnet, was finding a political and sectarian identity close to that of his mentor. However, it also needs to be said that all four were notorious libertines for at least the earlier parts of their lives, and that their attachment to the Protestant cause in the state does not seem, except latterly in Rochester's case, to have been matched by much in the way of spiritual fervour. For this Buckingham must bear some responsibility as a convinced Erastian and, in the language of the time, Socinian, arguing both directly and by proxy through Martin Clifford that religious truth should always be subject to the test of reason.

---

[57] *The Complete Works of Thomas Shadwell*, ed. Montague Summers, 5 vols. (London: Fortune Press, 1927), v. 291–2.

The Buckingham circle contributed to the development of literature in their time by three means. The first—and the one to which Dryden would have liked to confine them—was as patrons. In the period immediately following the Restoration the leading patron of writers (in effect an unofficial minister of culture) had been the elderly Newcastle, a former member of the Tribe of Ben and a champion of Jonsonian values in drama. As his powers declined with age, Buckingham and Dorset took over his role of patron-in-chief by a kind of lineal succession, and with it his leading protégé in Shadwell. Buckingham's hostility to Dryden may have been sharpened by Newcastle's falling-out with him over which of them was to have the credit for *Sir Martin Mar-all*. Buckingham was a generous patron to Cowley and may have given some assistance to Samuel Butler, though that relationship eventually turned sour. Two letters from Waller, written when Buckingham was co-habiting with the Countess of Shrewsbury, show him cultivating the by then elderly bard, who, however, found their fast ways and late hours too much for him.[58] Generally speaking, Buckingham was too erratic and self-centred and Rochester too poor to be effective as patrons; however, Dorset, rich, generous, and with a love of good writing, was usually prepared to take up the slack.[59]

The second role performed by the group was as models in two separate senses of the world. As Medley and Dorimant they sat for their own portraits to the writers of Restoration comedy; but they also, in real life, embodied a practical ideal of cultured conversation. Accounts of the four leaders and their satellites repeatedly stress the pleasure to be had simply from conversing with them. Pepys found Sedley's talk in the audience at the theatre much more interesting than the play.[60] Shadwell, in addition to the eulogy already quoted, described Buckingham's conversation as 'the most charming in the World'.[61] The essence of this spoken wit, to judge from its representations in Restoration comedy, consisted in quickness of repartee, with one remark demanding to be capped immediately by another, and in the coinage of striking and

---

[58] In the possession of Richard Waller. See Peter Beal, *Index of English Literary Manuscripts*, ii, pt. 2: *Lee–Wycherley* (London: Mansell, 1993), 552, letters 28 and 29.

[59] For his work in this role see Brice Harris, *Charles Sackville, Sixth Earl of Dorset, Patron and Poet of the Restoration* (Urbana, Ill.: University of Illinois Press, 1940), *passim*. Both gentleman and professional writers were welcome to the 'Poets' parlour' at Knole—members of the second group might well find banknotes under their plates.

[60] *Diary*, v. 288 (4 Oct. 1664); viii. 71–2 (18 Feb. 1667).

[61] *Works*, iii. 193.

unusual similes; however, there was also a more sententious aspect, inspired by La Rochefoucauld, which gave birth to pithy encapsulations of a reductive, deeply cynical view of human nature. The witty remark was usually, as in Wycherley's comedies, a deflating one. The philosophy of the group, insofar as it is open to inspection, was grounded in a Hobbesian view of motives as the product of irresistible physiological drives, an Epicurean ethics, and a deep scepticism, born of the experiences of the civil wars, of the possibility for altruism either in the state or the lives of individuals. The Buckingham 'Commonplace Book', which if it is not by Buckingham certainly arose from his circle, is rich in remarks of this tendency. It goes without saying that the spoken wit of courtiers was never merely verbal but always to be accentuated by the arts of graceful self-presentation in which Buckingham, as Lockier has already assured us, was supreme.

The circle also set themselves up to establish models of writing. Clearly Rochester was the most successful in this respect, though the extravagant praise heaped on Dorset and Sedley was prompted by real, if in their cases over-exaggerated, merit. In their chosen domains of lyric and satire of the colloquial kind those three stood at the pinnacle of their generation. They also wrote for the theatre, but it was here that Buckingham, who lagged behind them as a poet, came to excel them, largely because of an inborn understanding of stagecraft possessed by none of his protégés.

*The Rehearsal* was also a means for the disciplining of other writers. This brings us to the Buckingham circle's third role. Through their interjections in the playhouse (often hilarious), their opinions delivered after performances in the Great Withdrawing Room at Whitehall, their parodies, and a body of satires on bad writers and writing, they claimed a right to assess, rank, and, where necessary, reprimand, the work both of fellow amateurs and the emerging class of mercenary writers for bread. Dryden's assertion of the dignity of the professional man of letters (guided by classical principles) in the creation of lasting masterworks was formed in explicit opposition to their calmly assumed entitlement to artistic as well as social superiority. In *Of Dramatick Poesie*, he had introduced Dorset, Sedley, and Buckingham's client Sir Robert Howard, thinly disguised, into a dialogue on critical principles which concluded in the acceptance of his own views on the matter; but there is no suggestion that in real life they acknowledged this eminence. Indeed their attitude towards the Dryden of the 1660s and 1670s is generally supercilious and in Rochester's case arrogantly scornful. A threat made by Rochester in 1676 to have Dryden assaulted by 'Black Will with a cudgel' has led to his being held responsible for the beating administered in Rose Alley on 18 December 1679.[62] Another explanation would have Dorset responsible.[63] A story told in 1712 by Defoe is unlikely to be true but illustrates an attitude that was certainly current:

> A Pasquinade ought to be pointing like a Dart, that should wound Mortally at every cast; the Sting should be so very sharp, that it should kill even all the Resentment of the Persons Satyriz'd: so that the Person pointed at should be asham'd to be Angry; or if he was, he should do as the generous Duke of *Buckingham* did to Mr. *Dryden*, for his Satyr upon him in his *Absalom* and *Achitophel*—when he first Can'd him, and then gave him a Purse of Gold: *That's for your ill Language*, Sir, said the Duke, when he Can'd him: And then giving him the Gold, *here Sir*, said his Grace, *and that's for your Wit.*[64]

Dryden's problem, as they saw it, was primarily that he was not a fluent conversationalist. This meant that the wit of his writings had to be of a secondary order—a painful imitation of what they did spontaneously. The long sequence of Dryden's prefaces, while paying them due respect as noble persons, is unrelenting in its insistence that standards of good writing were created by writers not witty speakers, and that it was knowledge of the great writing of the past not the conversation of the present that was the only reliable foundation of sound taste. Slowly the professionals wore down the amateurs, Buckingham among them, until by the end of all their lives the conversations that mattered in establishing rankings and judgements were not those of the Withdrawing Room but of the professionals' meeting place in the upper room at Will's coffee house. But the role of the Buckingham circle had nonetheless been a very considerable one in creating the styles and standards that were to govern the literary culture of the early eighteenth century.

---

[62] Rochester, *Letters*, p. 20.

[63] See Edward L. Saslow, 'The Rose Alley Ambuscade', *Restoration*, 26 (2002), 27–49.

[64] Defoe's *Review*, 28 March 1712, 151. There is another version of the tale in the number for 17 May 1712, 724, in which the caning takes place in a coffee house and the purse contains 30 guineas.

## PLAYS, POEMS, AND MISCELLANEOUS WRITINGS

Buckingham's literary writings—or to be precise, the works associated with his name—divide into (1) plays, scenes, and revisions designed with one or two exceptions for the public stage; (2) a small body of poems; (3) a group of public letters, prose dialogues, a 'character', and some controversial pamphlets, almost all printed anonymously or posthumously; and (4) a collection of maxims, witty remarks, and short poems collected in a 'commonplace book'. Currently insoluble problems of attribution attend all four classes.

### Plays

We cannot exactly say that Buckingham 'wrote plays', but we may assert that he is convincingly associated with four plays and rather dubiously connected with two others. Each case is unique and requires specifics. The six plays fall into four distinct categories.

*Contributory author.* As early as 1664 (seven years before its stage premiere) *The Rehearsal* was rumoured to be a committee enterprise involving the duke, Martin Clifford, and Thomas Sprat. Later sources name Edmund Waller, Samuel Butler, and Abraham Cowley as participants. Of this group only Cowley is known ever to have written a play, and he died in 1667, well before the first surviving version could have been drafted. Buckingham could imaginably have done the actual drafting of dialogue, or he might have been merely the presiding genius, or he could have served as coordinating editor in addition to contributing any amount of dialogue. The exact nature of the group collaboration is undeterminable. Late rumour holds that the duke was responsible for casting the parody in dramatic form but this cannot be proved. The burlesque proved immensely popular, and in 1675 it was updated to include Dryden's most recent plays. *The Rehearsal* became a repertory staple and was performed regularly for more than a century. The fatuous poet Bayes became a byword, invoked innumerable times in public and private discourse for many decades. Buckingham's reputation as an author derives almost entirely from this one play, frequently reprinted in student editions to the present day.

*Collaborator.* In two cases we have strong evidence for Buckingham's participation in collaborative original composition. *Sir Politick Would-be* was written in French jointly with Saint-Évremond and the Sieur d'Aubigny sometime between *c.*1662 and 1665 (when the former left London and the latter died). The concept may well have been Buckingham's (he was an admirer of Ben Jonson), but what each writer contributed is undeterminable. *The Country Gentleman* failed to reach the stage in March 1669 in circumstances that caused a major public scandal and upheaval in the government (extensively reported by Pepys). According to rumour, the play—a lively London comedy touting 'country' ideology—was written by Sir Robert Howard, but Buckingham was understood to have 'inserted' a scene mocking Sir William Coventry (a fellow member of the privy council). Coventry challenged Buckingham to a duel and was thrown in the Tower of London, amidst which uproar the play died and disappeared. It survived in manuscript, but was not identified and printed until the 1970s. The offensive scene in Act III described by Pepys involves characters present throughout the play, but it does not have the air of a late insertion, and neither does it seem stylistically incongruous. How much hand Buckingham had in the design of the play, or in the writing of the parts of Sir Cautious Trouble-all and Sir Gravity Empty, we see no way to establish.

*Adapter.* An adaptation of Fletcher's *The Chances* (*c.*1617–25) was staged with success in 1664 and printed anonymously in 1682. The knowledgeable Langbaine named Buckingham as the adapter in 1691. The revision is a lively and very early example of 'gay couple' comedy. The changes are mostly minor for three acts, but the last two were radically rewritten in prose and are virtually new work. No one has ever questioned the attribution, but both dramaturgy and dialogue are so good that we are inclined to wonder whether the duke obtained at least some advice and polishing from a veteran professional playwright. *The Chances* remained in the repertory into the nineteenth century, serving as an important vehicle for David Garrick (who twice further adapted the script). An adaptation of Beaumont and Fletcher's *Philaster* (1609) was published under the duke's name in 1715 as *The Restauration, or Right will Take Place*. Since an earlier published prologue and epilogue are certainly his work, we are fairly confident that this is authentically connected with Buckingham, though there is no way of telling whether it is still in the form in which it had been left on his death nearly thirty years earlier. The adaptation is more respectful of the original than is

*The Chances*, but several characterizations and plot elements are modified and the original dialogue is heavily rewritten. The names of the characters have all been changed.

*Putative author.* An untitled fragment of a heroic play in verse about Theodoric, King of the Ostrogoths, has been attributed to Buckingham because it exists in manuscript in the 'Jersey' form of the Commonplace Book. Given the view of heroic drama expressed in *The Rehearsal*, Buckingham would be a decidedly surprising author for this enterprise, and further evidence about the nature of the compilation in which it is found (discussed below) leads us to suspect that it is a product of the 'Buckingham Circle' rather than a text composed by the duke himself.

*Poems*

Among the Restoration court poets, only Mulgrave, Sedley, Waller, and (if he is to be admitted) Wycherley had any pressing interest in the print medium or with the preservation of their verse as an ordered and coherent whole. Buckingham, Dorset, Etherege, and Rochester, with their lesser fellows, were by conscious choice scribally publishing, occasional poets. The first of these terms means that their chosen medium of circulation was manuscript supplemented by oral delivery, the second that their verse was not produced as part of an evolving artistic oeuvre but in response to particular, practical requests for a poem, whether song, eulogy, impromptu, or lampoon, to satisfy a given court occasion. Once the occasion was met, the piece might well be forgotten, or survive only in surreptitious copies; yet it is an undeniable fact that a number of these pieces had an enormous circulation. The power of the scribal medium in an age when most educated individuals kept a private miscellany specifically to serve as a receptacle for such evanescent transmissions is still almost monotonously underestimated. When a poem survives in ten printed copies as against thirty in manuscript, as a number do, it indicates that at least three times as many readers (probably more) encountered it in manuscript form as in print. It is a mistake to assume that because the press produced copies more quickly and in a single act of production, rather than progressively and sequentially, it was more influential as an agency of distribution for texts of this kind.[65]

---

[65] These issues are further discussed in Love, *Scribal Publication*.

Buckingham probably wrote much more verse than the small amount preserved that is associated with his name. He was certainly a gifted artificer of occasional verse but, with one or two exceptions, felt no desire that such productions should outlive the occasions that prompted them. One of these exceptions was his funeral pindaric on his father-in-law Fairfax, which was a political statement as well as an act of sincere homage: appropriately this appeared in printed form as well as being widely circulated in manuscript. Otherwise, the verse attributed to him rarely travelled beyond his own immediate circle: some of the most accomplished pieces were delivered to a wider public only two decades after his death. Others survive in contemporary manuscript copies and two achieved quite wide circulation in this form. One impromptu survives only in a French paraphrase several decades distant. He is at his best in a colloquial, highly personal form of satire which is actually a kind of verbal caricature: of this nature are his attacks on Clarendon in 'The owle', on Arlington in his 'advice-to-a-painter' lampoon, on Danby in the viciously colourful account of the garter ceremony of 1677, and in the shorter pieces burlesquing Monmouth and the king. The parodies of works by Edward and James Howard point enticingly towards the larger accomplishment of *The Rehearsal*. The love elegies and the funeral panegyric, by contrast, do not escape a certain laboured quality: formality did not sit easily upon him. 'A Familiar Epistle to Mʳ Julian Secretary to the Muses' would count as a significant exercise in the genre of the longer, neoclassical satire pioneered by Rochester if we could be sure Buckingham wrote it. The improvisitorial 'Song on Thomas Earl of Danby' is a remarkably effective piece of character assassination, though, once again, we can not be sure how much of it, if any, was his own work. The most we can say is that he would thoroughly have shared its views.

The poems here printed do not constitute a major extension to the Restoration poetic canon; but can all be read with interest and pleasure and suggest something of the conversational wit and talent for mimicry that characterized the living Buckingham.

*Public Letters, A Character, Prose Dialogues, and Controversial Pamphlets*

That Buckingham would write topical ephemera makes good sense. Such things could be knocked off in a few hours of scribbling, circulated scribally, enjoyed, and forgotten. Nine surviving pieces of various sorts have been attached to the duke's name. Only four of them were published in the duke's lifetime (two in authorized editions with his name attached). Five are attributed only in the less than trustworthy *Miscellaneous Works* of 1704–5. One posthumously printed item is said to be merely a secretarial report of a meeting between the duke and a Catholic priest, though several twentieth-century scholars treated it as a work 'by' the duke. We have printed all these items, fully disclosing the basis of attribution in each instance. The pieces fall into four distinct categories:

1. *Public Letters*. Buckingham was a noted contributor in the House of Lords to the political and religious controversies of his day, and his contributions seem occasionally to have extended to print or scribal circulation of his views in 'letter' or pamphlet form. *A Letter to Sir Thomas Osborn* (printed anonymously in 1672) is basically a discreet piece of propaganda in support of the Third Dutch War. *To Mr. Clifford, on his Humane-Reason* (1674?) is an argument for religious toleration launched under the cover of philosophical discourse. We suspect that it was designed for scribal circulation, though no MS copies survive and it was not printed until it was included in the *Miscellaneous Works*.

2. *A Character*. Buckingham's sometime secretary Samuel Butler is among the celebrated seventeenth-century practitioners of this genre— one of his best being his nasty picture of 'A Duke of Bucks' (printed in App. I).[66] A four-page piece entitled *A Hue-and-Cry after Beauty and Vertue* was published without place, date, publisher, or attribution (dated '1685' without explanation by Wing). Two manuscript copies are likewise without date or attribution. The piece was included in the *Miscellaneous Works*, where it is explicitly said to be 'Written by the late Duke of Buckingham, in the Year 1678'. The piece is a vicious attack on a woman who appears to be either a serious confusion of two very different women (Carey Frazier and Lady Saunderson) or perhaps a deliberate composite for purposes of camouflage. It is a splendid example of a viciously misogynist prose libel. Whether Buckingham had any hand in its composition we have no way to determine.

3. *Prose Dialogues*. Two radically different squibs fall under this heading. *The Militant Couple* (date unknown) harshly satirizes a brutal husband and says bluntly that a man who seriously mistreats his wife has only himself to thank if she cuckolds him—and that he deserves it. *The*

---

[66] Butler 'was secretarie to the duke of Bucks, when he was Chancellor of Cambridge' (1671–4). See *'Brief Lives', chiefly of Contemporaries, set down by John Aubrey, between the Years 1669 & 1696*, ed. Andrew Clark, 2 vols. (Oxford: Clarendon Press, 1898), i. 137.

*French Generall* must have been written in July 1685 immediately after the battle of Sedgmoor. It is a scathing depiction of the victorious general, ridiculing the Earl of Feversham's incompetence, pretensions, accent, and pidgin English. Both pieces are included in the *Miscellaneous Works*, but without confirmatory evidence suspicion must still attend their ascription to Buckingham.

4. *Controversial Pamphlets.* The only works printed and publicly acknowledged by Buckingham in his lifetime are *A Short Discourse upon the Reasonableness of Men's Having a Religion* (1685) and the snide two-page reply to the 'Unknown Author' of an attack on that piece. The *Short Discourse* is an argument in favour of formal religious toleration, evidently launched in the hope of enlisting the new king James II in the cause of a change in law that would benefit both Protestant dissenters and Catholics.[67] The piece ignited an intense pamphlet war, with ten writers weighing in, pro and con. A work in an utterly different key is *An Account of a Conference between His Grace George, late Duke of Buckingham, and Father Fitzgerald, an Irish Priest.* It was first published in 1705 in volume 2 of the *Miscellaneous Works*, where the conference is said to have been 'Faithfully taken by one of his Domesticks' when James II sent a priest 'to his Grace in his sickness, to endeavour to pervert him to the Popish Perswasion'. If such an incident occurred, it probably happened in 1686. Buckingham could conceivably have written the thing himself, adopting a third-party standpoint. Alternatively, what the 1705 edition says could be more or less accurate (with the fidelity of the reportage undeterminable). Or perhaps someone with a good understanding of Buckingham's religious views and sense of humour fabricated the whole thing, either in 1686 or at any time up to 1705 when material was needed to fill out a rag-tag edition. We have included *An Account* without claiming that Buckingham wrote it. Very possibly he never saw it, and no such episode may ever have occurred, but the piece is an established part of the corpus of writing associated with Buckingham (much admired by Horace Walpole, for example), and neither attribution nor factuality is really the point.

---

[67] Part of the *Short Discourse* is substantially identical to what was posthumously published as *An Essay upon Reason, and Religion, In a Letter to Nevil Pain*. Clearly Buckingham had been discussing the issues and corresponding about them: how much his final text owed to the advice and assistance of friends or domestics we have no way of guessing.

## Commonplace Book

The so-called 'Buckingham commonplace book' is a remarkable collection of maxims, epigrams, similes, and short poems which this edition presents in a far fuller form than any previously available. But here a problem arises. The version published in extract by Lady Jersey and in full by Christine Phipps, and which has been widely drawn on by scholars for evidence of Buckingham's private opinions, rests on a manuscript in the possession of the Earl of Jersey which contains an unambiguous attribution to Buckingham, but one that is not in the hand of the original scribe.[68] A second and much longer version, which survives in a transcription by Sarah Cowper and was made from papers originally received from Martin Clifford, contains no such attribution: Cowper unquestionably believed the work to be by Clifford. The editors also incline to this view but without being able to exclude the possibility of Buckingham's authorship of all or part of it. This problem is further considered in the introduction to the work, to which the reader is referred. Given, however, that Clifford was one of Buckingham's closest associates, and for some years his secretary, the work has an obvious relevance to any study of his personal attitudes and intellectual influence, and, on that ground alone, could hardly be excluded from this edition.

## TEXTUAL INTRODUCTION

This edition presents a critical, old-spelling text of Buckingham and some crucial Buckinghamia based on a collation of all surviving early editions and manuscripts judged as possessing textual authority. In a disturbing number of instances 'authority' is more *faute de mieux* than an editor could wish. While many holograph letters and documents survive, we have none of a literary work, nor can it be proved that manuscripts in other hands derive from authoritative sources. Most of what was published in Buckingham's lifetime was issued anonymously; whether publication was authorized, let alone supervised by him, is

---

[68] Currently on deposit in LMA. A second manuscript of this version, now in the Princeton University Library, Robert H. Taylor Collection, item no. RTC01, is an 18th-c. copy of the Jersey MS.

doubtful at best. *The Rehearsal* has been edited from the anonymous 1672 and 1675 quartos; *The Chances* from the anonymous 1682 quarto. All later printings derive from these sources, and show no evidence of authorial intervention. *The Restauration* did not appear in print until three decades after his death. The only extant source of *The Country Gentleman* is Folger MS V.b. 228. For some of the pamphlets, squibs, and poems there are anonymous separately printed and scribal copies, as well as the texts published in the 1704–5 *Miscellaneous Works*. The proximity of any of these texts to the presumptive authorial original is usually undeterminable. In such cases the editor has to work with what exists.

The nature of Buckingham's oeuvre, ranging across both printed and manuscript sources of varying degrees of authenticity, has meant that no single editorial method can be applied. With the exception of the poems (some of which present the difficulties usual with scribally transmitted material extant in multiple copies) most of the contents of this edition survive in only one authoritative text. Later editions have been collated for corrections (probably imposed by the printer). Only in the case of *The Rehearsal* does a later lifetime edition contain what *may* be authorial revisions and new material. Where relatively early manuscripts of uncertain origin exist in addition to printed texts (*A Hue-and-Cry*, *The French Generall*) we have had to make choice of copy-text on a case-by-case basis.

### Treatment of Printed Copy-texts

Multiple copies of the editions selected as copy-texts have been compared as a check for type changes made during the printing of the sheets. The edition can be assumed to reproduce the spelling, punctuation, and to a large extent the layout of the copy-texts with the following exceptions:

> Obvious errors of meaning, spelling, and punctuation in the original have been corrected by the editors, drawing in some cases on the readings of later editions. Supplementary materials, such as new scene headings, have been added when essential. Verse set as prose and prose set as verse have been restored to what we estimate was the intended form. In a few cases mislineated verse has been re-lineated to accord with its evident metrical structure. Erroneous speech prefixes have been corrected; however, strict consistency has

not been enforced. All these changes are either recorded in the list of emendations to the copy-text or placed within angle brackets.

Relocations of stage directions in order to clarify meaning are recorded as variants when they would affect a reader's understanding of the relationship of word to action, but minor relocations with no bearing on comprehension are performed silently. (The same principle applies *mutatis mutandis* to marginalia in non-dramatic texts.)

The following additional alterations are also silent. Where verse lines are shared between two or more speakers, the second and any subsequent elements are indented. The long 's' has been replaced throughout by the modern form. Use of italic and/or roman punctuation marks in a way which is inconsistent with the prevailing practice of the copy-text concerned has been regularized. Words other than proper nouns in stage directions have been italicized under this rule. Dashes have been adjusted to consistent lengths of one, two, or four ems depending on the dominant practice in the source text. Single wrong sorts arising from foul case or type depletion are normalized (so '*L*aw' becomes 'Law').

Layout is as close to that of the original as is consistent with modern standards of page design. In the text of *The Rehearsal* decorative arrangements of speech headings have been preserved.

Ligatures (ꜩ and ﬆ) and two-line initial caps used in the main text of this edition are modern typographical features and should not be regarded as corresponding to the practice of the originals, though this will often be the case.

*Apparatus*

The apparatus consists of general and textual introductions to each work, which include an explanation of any special textual policies adopted for that work, together with a list of variant readings, a list or lists of editorial emendations to the copy-text, explanatory notes, and other supplementary lists when appropriate for particular works. The lists of variants cover all sources considered likely to preserve otherwise unrecorded authorial readings; however, only verbal or substantive variants are recorded, except in a few cases where variations in spelling or punctuation were considered significant contributors to meaning or relevant to the establishment of stemmatical relationships. With this qualification, the variants of each source cited are recorded in their entirety, not selectively. The form of the variant record does not allow discrimination between different spellings of the same word in different sources, so, for instance, in a record such as

champion] hero *Q2, Q3*        or        hero?] ~ₐ *Q3*

the form in *Q3* might well be 'heroe'. In this example, the tilde (~) indicates the presence of the same word in *Q3* and the caret (ₐ) indicates the point at which punctuation was omitted in *Q3*. The lists of editorial emendations to the copy-texts cover all changes not previously declared silent, including those to spelling and punctuation.

The special situation of *The Rehearsal*, in which the 1675 additions, although only given in the footnotes, have putative authorial standing and are meant to be read for their own value rather than merely consulted as variants, is discussed in the introduction to that play. Briefly a small number of obvious errors among these passages have been emended and the emendations recorded in a special list. The footnotes to *The Chances* and *The Restauration* record variation between the Fletcherian sources and the respective copy-texts, not the text of the present edition; *thus the lemma will not always be identical with the reading on the page above.* Their aim is to illustrate what the author had in front of him when he made his alteration.

The textual introductions include full bibliographical descriptions of the authoritative sources, including a complete record of press variants; however, only those press variants with a substantive function are relisted in the textual footnotes or the record of emendation. There is a separate discussion of the publication history of the eighteenth-century 'Works' in Appendix III.

### Treatment of Manuscript Copy-texts

The principles outlined above also hold good in many instances for manuscript copy-texts; however, since the copy-texts are neither holographs nor supervised transcripts, a greater liberty of emendation has been taken in order to restore the readings of the lost original, as established from the wider transmissional history. This question is more fully discussed in the introduction to the poems. The principles of textual analysis employed are outlined in Love, *Scribal Publication*, 313–56.

Since manuscripts make far greater use of abbreviated and contracted forms than printed texts of the period, we have silently expanded the most common of these ('yᵉ' for 'the'; & for 'and', and superscript 'd' for final 'ed' or ''d') in both the edition text and the record of variants. The layout and appearance of the copy-text have been respected as far as practicable. In the Commonplace Book, marginal marks of emphasis such as the obelus and the pointing hand have been retained, along with the other marginalia.

# PLAYS

THE

CHANCES,

A

COMEDY:

As it was Acted

AT THE

THEATER ROYAL.

Corrected and Altered by a PERSON
of HONOUR. *D. of Buckingam*

LONDON,

Printed for *A. B.* and *S. M.* and Sold by
*Langley Curtis* on *Ludgate Hill.*, 1682.

Fig. 1. Title page of the first edition of *The Chances* (1682). Courtesy of the Monash
University Library

2

# The Chances

## INTRODUCTION

*The Chances* has a long and complex history. Written by John Fletcher (1579–1625) at an unknown date between 1615 and 1625 (but not published until 1647 when it appeared in the folio *Comedies and Tragedies by Beaumont and Fletcher*), it enjoyed significant success before the closing of the theatres in 1642. It was revived soon after the theatres reopened in 1660 and was—probably by 1664, but definitely by 1667—substantially rewritten by Buckingham, whose adaptation is one of the rare instances in which the new work is generally acknowledged to be a major improvement upon its source. The adaptation was first published in the quarto of 1682. Buckingham's version was itself significantly revamped (most notably twice by Garrick, in 1754 and 1773) and held the stage in various guises into the nineteenth century.[1] It has enjoyed a major revival as recently as 1962, when Sir Laurence Olivier used it as the play that inaugurated the Chichester Festival. Buckingham's adaptation was a vehicle for star actors from Charles Hart through Robert Wilks to David Garrick, John Henderson, and John Palmer. Despite the play's great popularity and high reputation from the seventeenth to the nineteenth century, it received virtually no attention from twentieth-century critics, probably because in its most successful form it was regarded as merely an adaptation.[2]

[1] Following the stage history of the work in its various guises has not been rendered easier by the failure of the editor of the synoptic index to *The London Stage* to discriminate between them. All performances of the Fletcher, Buckingham, and Garrick versions are listed under 'Fletcher' without warning of any kind in the *Index to The London Stage 1660–1800*, ed. Ben Ross Schneider, Jr. (Carbondale, Ill.: Southern Illinois University Press, 1979). The index to Part 1 places performances of the Buckingham version under 'Villiers', while the indexes to Parts 2 and 3 put them under 'Buckingham'. In Part 4 the index puts all performances under 'Villiers' (with a cross-reference under 'Garrick', whose versions were actually being performed). In Part 5 the index puts them all under 'Fletcher' with a note that the piece was 'altered by Garrick' and a cross-reference under 'Garrick' but no hint of any connection under either 'Buckingham' or 'Villiers'.

[2] *The Chances* has been edited with extensive introduction and notes by James Patrick Fowler (Ph.D. thesis, Shakespeare Institute, University of Birmingham, 1978). We have drawn significantly on Dr Fowler's excellent work.

3

## SOURCE AND BACKGROUND

Buckingham's Fletcherian source drew its plot from Cervantes's *La Señora Cornelia*, published in his *Novelas Exemplares* in 1613. The novella appeared in French translation in 1615.[3] Fletcher seems to have relied principally on the translation, though some verbal details suggest that he consulted the Spanish original.[4] Fletcher's use of Cervantes was commented upon in print as early as 1654, and his source was first explicitly identified by Gerard Langbaine in 1691.[5] The date of composition and premiere have been much debated and could fall anywhere from 1615 to the playwright's death in 1625.[6] References to Pope's Bulls and the Duke of Lorraine are now believed to be insertions made to allude to events of 1627 for a revival after Fletcher's death: the surviving prologue refers to Fletcher as dead. There is no hard evidence for any earlier performance, but Bentley is 'inclined to think that this was a revival rather than a first performance of a play left incomplete by Fletcher', since no evidence has been adduced for collaboration.[7] On the basis of the phrase 'The Devil such an Asse' in

[3] *Les novvelles de Miguel de Cervantes Saavedra*, trans. F. de Rosset and Sr d'Audiguier (Paris, 1615).

[4] See Edward M. Wilson, 'Did John Fletcher Read Spanish?', *Philological Quarterly*, 27 (1948), 187–90. The first English translation appeared in *Exemplarie Novells* 'Turned into English by Don Diego Puede-Ser' [James Mabbe] (London, 1640).

[5] Anonymous preface to *Delight in Severall Shapes* (London, 1654), a reissue of the 1640 Mabbe translation of six of the *Novelas Exemplares*, where the reader is informed that Beaumont and Fletcher, described as 'a paire of our best Poets', 'did not scorn to dresse two of these Stories for our English Stage'. See Langbaine, 207–8.

[6] The date controversy and early stage history are conveniently summarized by Gerald Eades Bentley, *The Jacobean and Caroline Stage*, 7 vols. (Oxford: Clarendon Press, 1941–68), iii. 318–23.

[7] In 'The Shares of Fletcher and his Collaborators in the Beaumont and Fletcher Canon (I)', *SB* 8 (1956), 129–46, Cyrus Hoy includes the play in a group whose pronominal and contractional usage 'is enough to set them apart from every other play in the canon' (p. 132) and establish them as the unaided work of Fletcher. His evidence, as it affects the distinguishing habits of Fletcher and Massinger, is summarized in tabular form on p. 145. Hoy's conclusions about solo authorship are endorsed by Bertha Hensman, *The Shares of Fletcher, Field and Massinger in Twelve Plays of the Beaumont and Fletcher Canon*, 2 vols. (Salzburg Studies in English Literature; Salzburg: Institut für Englische Sprache und Literatur, Universität Salzburg, 1974), i. 21–31, though she argues for a composition date at the very end of Fletcher's life. Hoy's attitude towards collaboration has been strongly challenged in recent years, most particularly by Jeffrey Masten in 'Beaumont and/or Fletcher: Collaboration and the Interpretation of Renaissance Drama', *ELH* 59 (1992), 337–56; 'Playwrighting: Authorship and Collaboration', in John D. Cox and David Scott Kastan (eds.), *A New History of Early English Drama* (New York, N.Y.: Columbia University Press, 1997), 357–82; and *Textual Intercourse: Collaboration, Authorship, and Sexualities in Renaissance Drama* (Cambridge: Cambridge University Press, 1997). For the purposes of the present edition, however, we see no reason to

V. ii (which might be an allusion to Ben Jonson's play of 1616 or might be proverbial), Bentley hazards the guess that *The Chances* could well have been produced 'about 1617', two years after the appearance of its source in French.

Performance of Fletcher's play prior to 1627 is strictly conjectural. Evidence from the 1630s, however, suggests that it was a popular stock play, and Bentley terms it 'one of the most successful of Fletcher's comedies'. It was performed at the Cockpit in Court by the King's Men on 30 December 1630 and again on 22 November 1638. It evidently continued to seem valuable to the company, for 'Chances' is among the titles in a list of plays belonging to the King's Men that the Lord Chamberlain forbade any printer to publish without the company's permission (order of 7 August 1641).[8] It was among the large number of titles entered in the Stationers' Register by Robinson and Moseley on 4 September 1646 and was duly published by them as the tenth play in the 'Beaumont and Fletcher' folio of 1647, *Comedies and Tragedies Written by Francis Beaumont and John Fletcher Gentlemen. Never printed before, And now published by the Authours Originall Copies.*[9]

Whether *The Chances* vanished entirely from public view except in printed form during the interregnum period, 1642–60, depends on how one interprets the contradictory evidence surrounding its reduction into a droll entitled *The Landlady*, published in a collection called *The Wits, or, Sport upon Sport* which appeared 'Printed for Henry Marsh . . . 1662'. *The Landlady* is the twenty-third piece in this book, which consists largely of humorous skits extracted from well-known plays (among them *1 Henry IV*, *The Scornful Lady*, *Hamlet*, *The Maid's Tragedy*, and *The Alchemist*). Part II of *The Wits* was published by Francis Kirkman in 1673 with a title page declaring that the drolls and farces 'have been sundry times Acted in Publique, and Private' at Bartholomew Fair, 'In the Countrey at other Faires', in 'Halls' and 'Taverns', and 'On several Mountebancks Stages, At *Charing Cross*, *Lincolns-Inn-Fields*, and other

---

question the long-standing consensus that Fletcher wrote the 1620s *Chances* with no more than the usual amount of advice and revision in the light of comments from friends and actors. Masten is correct in saying that 'collaboration was the Renaissance English theatre's dominant mode of textual production', but in this case no evidence has yet been adduced for more than single-person authorship.

[8] Bentley, *Jacobean and Caroline Stage*, iii. 319.

[9] W. W. Greg, *A Bibliography of the English Printed Drama to the Restoration*, 4 vols. (London: Bibliographical Society, 1939–59), iii. 1013–18.

places' by 'Several Stroleing Players, Fools, and Fidlers, And the Mountebancks Zanies'.[10] Kirkman's introduction says that 'the incomparable *Robert Cox* . . . was not only the principal Actor, but also the Contriver and Author of most of these Farces'. Whether this is true, or true only of the drolls in Part II, is hard to say. Many authorities have assumed that both sets constituted the repertory of a troupe of strollers during the Commonwealth period; John James Elson is more inclined to think that most if not all of them were contrived for readers.[11] *The Landlady* occupies only nine pages of the modern edition. It consists essentially of cut versions of I. ix, III. i, and III. iii of the 1647 Folio text with minor verbal variants, focusing on Don John's turning up with a totally unexpected baby.[12] Elson praises the piece for its racy dialogue but criticizes its lack of action, observing that the principal attraction is the character of the landlady. He is correct in saying that 'The droll ends rather lamely and vaguely, the whole story proving too complicated to be briefly handled' (218 n).

Almost immediately after the King's Company resumed acting in 1660 *The Chances* returned to its active repertory. Sir Henry Herbert records a performance on 24 November 1660, less than three weeks after the company opened its Vere Street theatre.[13] Performance records are radically incomplete at most times prior to *c*.1705, but we know of at least one more performance in the first season after the Restoration because Pepys attended it. On 27 April 1661 he jotted only a brief diary entry, including the comment 'after dinner, with Mr. Creede and Captain Ferrers to the Theatre to see *The Chances*'. Lack of explanation of any sort may merely signify hurry or may suggest that he had already seen or read the play, though as of December 1663 he did not yet own the 1647 Folio (*Diary*, 10 December). He saw the play again on 9 October 1661, when he notes that he found Mrs Pierce and Madam Clifford at home, 'And after dinner took them to the theatre and showed them *The Chances*'.

[10] Both collections are reprinted with introduction and commentary in *The Wits or, Sport upon Sport*, ed. John James Elson (Ithaca, N.Y.: Cornell University Press, 1932).

[11] Cf. Arthur Colby Sprague, *Beaumont and Fletcher on the Restoration Stage* (Cambridge, Mass.: Harvard University Press, 1926), 4; Hotson, 47–9; Elson, 37–8.

[12] See the Elson edition, 210–18 and 388–9.

[13] *The Control and Censorship of Caroline Drama: The Records of Sir Henry Herbert, Master of the Revels 1623–73*, ed. N. W. Bawcutt (Oxford: Clarendon Press, 1996), 266; *London Stage*, Part i, 19–21.

Additional evidence of the place of the play in the King's Company's repertory is the appearance of this title in Dr Edward Browne's list of shows he had seen 'At the Cock Pit in Drewry Lane'.[14] After this there is no record of performance of the unaltered Fletcher play. The records are, however, so sketchy that lack of evidence of performance until the Buckingham version took the stage means almost nothing. Downes lists *The Chances* among twenty-one titles of 'Old Plays' that 'were Acted but now and then; yet being well Perform'd, were very Satisfactory to the Town' (as opposed to fifteen 'Principal Old Stock Plays' for which he gives casts).[15] Whether he made any distinction between the original and the adaptation we have no way to tell. We may note, however, that the original Fletcher play was among 108 titles listed in a Lord Chamberlain's warrant of mid- to late January 1669 concerning 'part of His Majesties Servants Playes as they were formerly acted at the Blackfryers & now allowed of to his Majesties Servants'. This order states that these plays having been the property of the pre-1642 King's Company, exclusive performance rights belong to the company revived on royal authority in 1660.[16] In the case of *The Chances* this was probably only a pro forma matter, since the old play had already been supplanted by Buckingham's adaptation.

## THE BUCKINGHAM VERSION

The play that Buckingham so brilliantly reconceived had some of the 'Spanish romance' features popular in the 1660s but was far removed from the new Carolean modes that were starting to take shape by 1664. Fletcher's comedy—entirely in verse—centres its plot on a high-life contretemps. The Duke of Ferrara has seduced and had a child by 1 Constantia, sister of Petruchio, Governour of Bologna. A rumour of her beauty has reached Don John and Don Frederick, two Spanish youths in search of sexual adventure. Petruchio, advised by his elderly kinsman Antonio, seeks vengeance on the Duke. Intrigue, swordplay, and confusion follow. In the play's most famous scene Don John (mis-

---

[14] See Robert D. Hume, 'Dr. Edward Browne's Playlists of "1662": A Reconsideration', *Philological Quarterly*, 64 (1985), 69–81. The probability seems to be that Browne saw *The Chances* sometime during the spring of 1661, acted by the King's Company during a temporary absence from its Vere Street theatre.

[15] John Downes, *Roscius Anglicanus, or an Historical Review of the Stage*, ed. Judith Milhous and Robert D. Hume (London: Society for Theatre Research, 1987), 24–5.

[16] TNA PRO LC 5/12, pp. 212–13.

taken for someone else) accepts a bundle which turns out to be Constantia's baby, leaving him 'bum-fidled with a Bastard' (I. v. 16). The two amorous young Spaniards later confuse 'Constantia, *a Whore to old Antonio*' with 'Constantia, *Sister to* Petruchio, *and Mistriss to the Duke*' (distinguished in the text as 1 and 2 Constantia).[17] Don John is dispatched by Petruchio to the Duke with a challenge, but the Duke turns out to be eager to marry his Constantia whenever he can find her again. Where Cervantes had ended the search for the missing 1 Constantia with a practical joke played by the Duke on the character corresponding to Petruchio, in Fletcher's version the two closing acts are used to manoeuvre the characters towards a masque-finale in which the missing 1 Constantia is revealed in a supposed vision by Peter Vechio, '*a Teacher of Latine and Musick*', posing as a magician. The outcome could fairly be called vague and muddled. The Duke will marry his lover. Antonio will recover the money his mistress has made off with. The text is singularly unclear about the future of 2 Constantia. She will apparently escape whipping but have to return to keeping with Antonio. A director might choose to suggest otherwise, but textually speaking the future relationship between Don John and 2 Constantia is entirely Buckingham's invention. The romance focus of the play remains firmly on the Duke's commitment to 'the full consummation of my Vow' as he says in the final line of the play. An important part of the appeal of the Buckingham version lies in the character and conversation of the '*Old Gentlewoman, Land-lady to Don* John *and* Fredrick'—a fact duly reflected in the droll extracted from Fletcher's play. What Fletcher left is essentially a romantic intrigue comedy in high life set against a cheerful and unconsummated rakes-pursue-sex plot. The former is seriously lacking in logic, as there is no good reason why the Duke should not have married 1 Constantia already; the latter benefits from the dashing Don John but does not really go much of anywhere. 2 Constantia is a very small part indeed: she has only fifteen lines, all late in the play. Unequal as the parts are, however, the play is left with a strong sense of the '"Bifronted posture" or doubleness' that Gordon McMullan considers 'a key feature of Fletcher's work'.[18]

---

[17] Quotations are from *The Chances*, ed. George Walton Williams, in *The Dramatic Works in the Beaumont and Fletcher Canon*, gen. ed. Fredson Bowers, vol. iv (Cambridge: Cambridge University Press, 1979).

[18] *The Politics of Unease in the Plays of John Fletcher* (Amherst, Mass.: University of Massachusetts Press, 1994), 259.

Virtually all commentators have felt that Fletcher produced three strong acts followed by two rather flabby ones. In the 'Advertisement' to his version of 1773, Garrick says

The three first acts of *The Chances*, originally written by *Beaumont* and *Fletcher*, have been much approved of; but those authors, in this as in many other of their plays, seeming to grow tired of their subject, have finished it with an un-skilfulness and improbability which show, at least, great haste and negligence. The Duke of Buckingham, in his edition of this comedy, gave a new turn and plan to the two last acts, and certainly added interest and spirit to the fable and dialogue; but the play, when it came out of his hands, was still more indecent than before.[19]

Other critics and adapters had long been aware of the tendency of 'Fletcher' plays to lose focus and intensity, or to fail to develop fully and resolve the plot. Langbaine comments as early as 1691

As to his failing in the two last Acts, (a fault *Cicero* sometimes alludes to, and blames in an Idle Poet;) its more to be imputed to his Laziness, than his want of Judgment. I have either read, or been inform'd, (I know not well whether) that 'twas generally Mr. *Fletcher*'s practice, after he had finish'd Three Acts of a Play to shew them to the Actors, and when they had agreed on Terms, he huddled up the two last without that care that behoov'd him. (p. 144)

Contemplating a successful but decidedly flawed play, Buckingham saw several possibilities for improvement.

More might be made of the confusion between the two young women and the implicit contrast between the Landlady and the old Bawd could be effectively developed. Peter Vechio could be dispensed with as a superfluous bit of local colour. Best of all, the dashing Don John could be fleshed out and developed more fully as an incipient rake, and the second Constantia could be expanded from bit part to vehicle for an alluring young actress. Fletcher could do only so much to flaunt the sex appeal of Antonio's whore when enacted by a boy, but after 1660 the part would of course be taken by a comely young woman. There is, in fact, reason to believe that Buckingham may have contrived the role specifically for Nell Gwyn—a possibility to be taken up under 'Stage History and Reception'. The additions necessary for elaborating the sex-game plot would of course be done in the crisp prose of 'Restora-

---

[19] *The Chances. A Comedy*, in *The Plays of David Garrick*, 7 vols., ed. Harry William Pedicord and Fredrick Louis Bergmann (Carbondale, Ill.: Southern Illinois University Press, 1980–2), vi. 203.

tion' comedy, not in verse, save for some end-of-scene couplets such as Don John's at V. iv. 181–2.

Any attempt to reconstruct the process by which the Buckingham adaptation came into being is rendered impossible by lack of information. So far as we are aware, the earliest attribution to Buckingham is Langbaine's statement in his 1691 entry on 'John Fletcher, and Francis Beaumont, Esq;' that '*Chances, a Comedy*' had been 'reviv'd by the late Duke of *Buckingham*' (p. 207). The title page of the 1682 first edition said merely 'Corrected and Altered by a Person of Honour', but the 1692 second edition says explicitly 'By his Grace the Duke of BUCKINGHAM; Author of the REHEARSAL'. We see no good reason to doubt Buckingham's involvement, but we do not know when the alteration was written, or why, or with what assistance.

Evidence from a somewhat problematical manuscript cast that includes Walter Clun (murdered on 2 August 1664) suggests that the new version was added to the King's Company repertory during the 1663–64 season, but probably not earlier than that, since Nell Gwyn was apparently also in that cast and would still have been extremely young. The high degree of technical command exhibited in the plotting and in Acts IV and V (which were virtually written anew in prose) would be quite astonishing from a tyro playwright. Buckingham's only known experience in dramatic composition around this time was with *Sir Politick Would-be* (1662–5?), a comedy written in French in collaboration with Saint-Évremond and Louis Stuart, Sieur d'Aubigny—a work that may pre-date *The Chances* but does not necessarily do so. That he obtained advice from a more practised dramatist seems likely, but any speculation on whom he approached for help can be no more than mere conjecture. Old James Shirley (d. 1666) was still alive, and the young Sir Robert Howard had demonstrated his competence in *The Committee*, staged by the King's Company as early as the autumn of 1662.[20] Cowley, a close associate of the duke, had successfully revamped *The Guardian* (staged at Cambridge in 1642 and published in 1650) for production at Lincoln's Inn Fields as *Cutter of Coleman-Street* (1661). In all likelihood, another helper was Martin Clifford, Buckingham's secretary. Sarah Cowper's commonplace book (Hertfordshire Archives and Local Studies MS D/EP F37) identifies Clifford as the author of variant versions of the prologue and epilogue to *The Chances* (full texts

[20] An argument against Howard's involvement is his reported position as one of the central targets of the early (lost) version of *The Rehearsal*, drafted c.1663–5. See below, p. 339.

at II. 250–2) and he could have assisted with other aspects of the play, as he apparently did with *The Rehearsal*.[21] Even Dryden could have helped.

If the date of the adaptation is as late as February 1667 (as was long believed), then the roster of possible adviser/assistants is far larger—but probably Buckingham's play was on the stage by the spring or summer of 1664. This makes it, in fact, a far more interesting, original, and potentially influential work than any critic could have supposed prior to the discovery of the MS cast in 1979 (discussed under 'Stage History and Reception' below).

Like many post-1660 adaptations of pre-1642 plays, *The Chances* builds up women's parts while remaining very basic in its scenic requirements. After the King's Company moved into its new Bridges Street theatre in May 1663, all its plays were staged with wing-and-shutter changeable scenery, but in all likelihood the company simply pulled standard settings from stock for this play. No fewer than sixteen of the scenes definitely or plausibly take place in the streets of Naples, and some of the short ones may have been played with the proscenium front standing for 'street'. The Landlady's house (Don John and Frederick's lodgings) is the principal interior required. Beyond that the show requires a reasonably grand interior to serve as governor's quarters for Petruchio and a second set of lodgings for scenes involving 1 Constantia (e.g. I. xi and II. ii), and perhaps to serve as Antonio's house for III. ii and III. v, though the latter could be done in a street. A setting appropriate to city outskirts would be good for III. iv (when a hunting party appears). Whether the King's Company bothered with careful distinction of either interior or exterior settings we have no way of telling, but by the middle of the eighteenth century such differentiation was routine.

By the time of the Wilks–Oldfield production of *c.*1704, we are probably safe in assuming a scene plan that required at least six visibly distinct settings.

|  |  |  |
|---|---|---|
|  | Outskirts of City | 2.3 |
|  | Street by Tavern | 2.2 |
|  | Governor's Palace | 2.1 |
| discovery area → |  |  |
|  | Landlady's House | 1.3 |
|  | Antonio's House | 1.2 |
|  | Street | 1.1 |

[21] For the circumstances of Cowper's attributions, which remain open to question, see II. 147–9.

We doubt that the King's Company would have done anything so elaborate in the 1660s. The play could be plausibly staged in a scenic theatre distinguishing only between 'street' (shallow) and 'interior' (deep) settings. The company could differentiate, if it wished, by means of hangings or a bit of furniture, but to a company steeped in the traditions of non-scenic presentation such niceties probably did not seem necessary.

The most particular physical staging demands occur in IV. i–iii. The specificity of setting in Act IV suggests that different scenery was used rather than what had served for earlier street scenes. 2 Constantia's mother goes into a tavern from the street and looks out a practicable window (IV. i. 53.1). A 'Shop' is mentioned at IV. iii. 14. The practicable door and the window to which Don John 'Looks up' (IV. iii. 95, 102.1) could of course just have been the proscenium door and the opening above it.[22] Some of the illustrations from the 1790s and the early nineteenth century imply an effort to suggest Neapolitan scenery and costume, but whether this represents theatrical practice of a later period or just artistic licence we have no way of telling. There is no reason to believe that any attempt was made at visibly 'Italian' settings in the seventeenth century, though the costumes might well have conveyed an Italian-Spanish flavour. Swords were, of course, required aplenty. Beyond that, all we know of staging details comes from two bills for performances by the Drury Lane company on 2 February and 6 April 1716. On both occasions management paid the rather startling sum of 5s. 'For yᵉ Dressing of A Sham Child' (which was clearly more than a bit of straw wrapped into invisibility in a blanket) and 6d. for 'The Use of A Surgeons Box &c' to provide professional trappings for the surgeon in III. ii.[23]

Buckingham stuck extremely close to his source through the first three acts.[24] Words, phrases, and details change occasionally, but as the footnoted folio variants demonstrate, the changes do not interfere with the dramatic action. Buckingham splits I. iii into two scenes (pro-

---

[22] For discussion of the basics of late 17th-c. staging, see Judith Milhous and Robert D. Hume, *Producible Interpretation: Eight English Plays 1675–1707* (Carbondale, Ill.: Southern Illinois University Press, 1985), ch. 2.

[23] The relevant 'Triumvirate bills' are preserved in British Library Egerton MS 2159, fo. 25, and Folger MS W.b. 111, fo. 33.

[24] Buckingham's changes have been sympathetically and skilfully analysed by Arthur Colby Sprague, *Beaumont and Fletcher*, 221–7, and in meticulous detail by Fowler, 'The Chances', ch. 3.

ducing eleven scenes rather than ten in the first act). At the very end of Act II Buckingham replaces the finale with twenty-five lines of crisp prose to set up audience anticipation of the young sparks' pursuit of 'Constantia'. Act III is edited and significantly tightened, with Fletcher's IV. i absorbed as III. vi. The last two acts are written afresh in springy, racy prose, concentrating heavily on 2 Constantia, her mother, and Don John. 'Bawd' becomes mother, and the girl is transmogrified from '*Whore to old* Antonio' to a spirited (and arguably perhaps still virgin) young jillflirt sold by her mother to Antonio—who, fortunately, proved impotent and hence was unable to enjoy her. At the end of the play 1 Constantia and her baby are safely reunited with the Duke (who will marry her forthwith) and in the second plot line Don John and 2 Constantia are left sparring over the terms on which they will get together.

What Fletcher wrote was a kind of romantic almost-tragicomedy of love, attempted assassination, near duels, misunderstandings, and eventual reconciliation. Onto this he tacked an inconclusive subplot involving two rakes, mistaken identity, an old keeper, and a young whore. Buckingham preserves the romantic plot with minimal changes, but develops the second line in a fashion that makes his *Chances* an early step in the evolution of Carolean sex comedy. Don John and 2 Constantia constitute what John Harrington Smith termed a 'gay couple' who engage in a non-marital love duel.[25] Smith never mentions this play (no doubt because it is an adaptation), but Buckingham's characters were probably an important model for such later couples as Dryden's Florimell and Celadon in *Secret-Love* (1667) and his Jacintha and Wildbood in *An Evening's Love* (1668). Smith virtually ignores performers, but we may assume that the availability of Charles Hart and Nell Gwyn at the King's Company was highly influential in the development of a model of comedy featuring a love duel between a dashing rake and a witty, independent woman who do not take love 'seriously' even when on the brink of matrimony.

Among the Fletcher plays Smith cites as pre-1642 instances are *The Scornful Lady* (1613?), *Monsieur Thomas* (1615?), and *The Wild-Goose Chase* (1621?). Early instances after the Restoration include James Howard's *The English Mounsieur* (acted by July 1663) and Sir George Etherege's *The Comical Revenge* (March 1664). Smith sees Dryden's

[25] John Harrington Smith, *The Gay Couple in Restoration Comedy* (Cambridge, Mass.: Harvard University Press, 1948).

*Secret-Love* (March 1667) as particularly important because it balances a 'serious' romantic plot against one featuring 'two lively young people'. This is, obviously, exactly what Buckingham chose to do with *The Chances*. We know also that in 1672 Dryden publicly expressed his admiration for the results. In his 'Defence of the Epilogue. Or, An Essay on the Dramatique Poetry of the last Age' appended to Part 2 of *The Conquest of Granada*, Dryden argues forcefully for the refinement of wit and language in the present day, sharply criticizing Shakespeare, Jonson, and Fletcher. Admitting that *The Chances* constitutes a powerful counter-example, he neatly turns the table by comparing the original with the adaptation.

*Fletcher's Don John* is our onely Bug-bear: and yet, I may affirm, without suspition of flattery, that he now speaks better, and that his Character is maintain'd with much more vigour in the fourth and fifth Acts than it was by *Fletcher* in the three former.[26]

Dryden had two plays premiered by the King's Company in the spring of 1664: *The Indian-Queen* (with Sir Robert Howard) by 25 January, and *The Rival Ladies* by May. If we are correct in assigning *The Chances* to spring or summer 1664, the likelihood seems extremely high that Dryden was familiar with it from that time, and that his 'gay couples' were influenced by it.

Buckingham is careful not to specify exactly what the relationship between Don John and 2 Constantia is going to be. Her mother's having 'sold' her to Antonio for '500 New Pieces' (IV. i. 58) is hardly her fault, and we are told bluntly that he was unable to perform sexually (V. iv. 71-5), so she is technically still innocent, unlike Fletcher's character, who says of herself that she is just 'A plaine whore' when offering her services (*BF*, IV. iii. 80). Buckingham's 2 Constantia is nothing of the sort. She says at IV. i. 52–3 that 'I'l live for ever chast, or find out some handsome young fellow I can love'. In their interchanges in IV. ii Don John assumes that she is 'A mettled Whore' (line 59) and finds himself 'panting for breath already' (61) and 'out of my wits for her' (72). 2 Constantia admits outright that she is 'not worth a groat' but says 'I'll follow ye all the World over; I'll work for ye, beg for you, do

---

[26] *The Works of John Dryden*, xi, ed. John Loftis, David Stuart Rodes, and Vinton A. Dearing (Berkeley, Calif.: University of California Press, 1978), 215. Dryden does not name Buckingham, but probably assumed that informed readers would know that he was the principal contriver of *The Rehearsal*, premiered in Dec. 1671, about two months before publication of Dryden's play was advertised shortly after 7 Feb. 1672. See the *Term Catalogues*, i. 96.

any thing for ye, so you'll promise to do nothing with any body else' (87–90). Don John is charmed, finding her 'made a purpose for me, she is so just of my humour' (91–2). When in V. iv. 13–57 they have a kind of proviso scene, she asks 'whether you can be kind to me', and 'will you always?', and demands that he 'swear'. He says he will do so upon his knees and asks 'what shall I say?' She replies 'what words you please, so they be but hearty, and not those are spoken by the Priest, for that charm seldome proves fortunate'. He swears by her 'fair self' and says 'I'll adore thee to my dying day.' She replies 'the minute thou do'st leave me, I'll . . . kill my self'. In the last lines of the play Don John asks 'when shall we consummate our Joys?' and she replies 'Never; We'll find out ways shall make 'em last for ever.' Don John then closes the play by commenting on the difference ''twixt marry'd Folks and Friends: / Our Love begins just where their Passion ends'. Are we to assume that he is so dazzled by 2 Constantia that he will marry a penniless lower-class girl with a perfectly appalling mother who has tried to whore her? Hardly likely, with the plot in the hands of a 'court wit'. The implication is that 2 Constantia will be wheedled into keeping, and that Don John will enjoy the use of her as long as he cares to. Certainly David Garrick found himself shocked by the implications of the finale and rewrote drastically to enforce marital assumptions, no matter how implausible they are in the setting of this play.[27] A happy ending with marriage is for an upper-class lady like 1 Constantia.

Looking at the Buckingham version in its context, one sees that it is a cleverly engineered combination of what were to be two of the most popular comic forms of the 1660s. The serious plot is along the general lines of the 'Spanish Romance' form popularized by Sir Samuel Tuke's *The Adventures of Five Hours* (January 1663) though Buckingham is, unsurprisingly, much less concerned with chastity, honour, and moral propriety. The tone and ambience of the Duke/1 Constantia plot comes closer to Dryden's *Rival Ladies* (March 1664 or earlier?) and George Digby, Earl of Bristol's *Elvira* (November 1664), with their emphasis on mistaken identity and nocturnal prowlings, though one might point also to Richard Rhodes's *Flora's Vagaries* (c. November 1663) and Thomas

---

[27] A more contemporary response seems to imply an even darker view of Don John. Defending his Nemours in the dedication to *The Princess of Cleve* (1682; pub. 1689), Nathaniel Lee says that when the audience 'expected the most polish'd Hero . . . I gave 'em a Ruffian reeking from *Whetstone's-Park*. The fourth and fifth Acts of the *Chances*, where *Don John* is pulling down; *Marriage Alamode*, where they are bare to the Waste; the *Libertine* and *Epsom-Wells*, are but Copies of his Villany' (part of title italics added).

Porter's lively *The Carnival* (autumn 1663) as even closer in spirit. The contrasting tone of the Don John/2 Constantia plot may be viewed as either ironic commentary or contrastive highlighting of the good and moral, depending on the preferences of the viewer. Etherege built such contrast into his four-plot *Comical Revenge*, and James Howard's split-plot *All Mistaken* (spring 1665?) is another such enterprise. In the latter case Hart and Gwyn provided a madcap love duel, specifically renouncing marriage as the object. Consummated non-marital sex during the course of the play was to be a later development in Carolean comedy, but *The Chances* offers a fairly early and relatively explicit preview of directions to be taken in the next decade.

## STAGE HISTORY AND RECEPTION

What can be deduced or conjectured of the early history of Buckingham's adaptation rests on a manuscript cast published by Ken Robinson in 1979.[28] It was written 'in an early nineteenth-century hand' in a copy of the 1735 edition then in Robinson's possession (current whereabouts not known to us).

| | |
|---|---|
| Duke—Mr Kynaston | Peter—Shatterell |
| Petruchio—Burt | Anthony—Clyn |
| Don John—Hart | 1st Constantia—Mrs Boutel |
| Don Frederick—Mohun | 2nd Ditto—E. G[w]ynn. |
| Antonio—Cartwright | |

This is a deeply disconcerting and problematical piece of evidence, and one's confidence in it is not bolstered by the very late date and complete lack of explanation as to the annotator's source of information. Kynaston, Burt, Hart, Mohun, and Cartwright present no problems: all were members of the King's Company throughout the 1660s. Shatterell was probably Robert Shatterell rather than his brother Edward, the latter being a very minor performer who apparently died before February 1665 after being 'sickely & not well for aboute halfe a yeare before hee Dyed'.[29] The bombshell in this cast is 'Clyn', which virtually has to signify Walter Clun, who was murdered on 2 August 1664. This provides a *terminus ad quem* for Buckingham's adaptation, a date fully two and a half years earlier than had ever been suspected. Thus far

[28] K. Robinson, 'Two Casts Lists for Buckingham's "The Chances"', *Notes and Queries*, 224 (1979), 436–7.
[29] Chancery deposition quoted in the *Biographical Dictionary*, xiii. 287.

there is nothing inherently disturbing about the cast, but the presence of the two women creates all sorts of difficulties. Mrs Boutel would be entirely appropriate as 1 Constantia, but she did not use that name until she married c.1670 and only very recently has lawsuit evidence been found that identifies her with Elizabeth Davenport, who was indeed with the company from fairly early and would almost undoubtedly have been available in the season of 1663–64.[30] The use of her married name six years early is not an insuperable problem: Downes created great confusion by doing precisely that in *Roscius Anglicanus*. We may hypothesize that the nineteenth-century annotator's source was written down after c.1670 by someone who thought of Davenport as Boutel. The apparent presence of Nell Gwyn in the cast, however, raises even greater difficulties.

Unless the cast is a deliberately clumsy fabrication, the only alternative we can find to Nell Gwyn is Anne Marshall Quin, the similarity of whose married name (she gets referred to as Quyn and Guin) frequently led to confusion with Nell.[31] She apparently married Mr Quin 'about 1666–67', but if the annotator used Boutel's married name with reference to a time before the marriage, this could just as well have been done of Mrs Quin as well. Anne Marshall was a principal actress by 1663–64 and could certainly have been cast as 2 Constantia. Manuscript notes by Thomas Killigrew tentatively list her for the courtesan Angelica Bianca in *Thomaso*, planned for production c.1664. On the whole, however, we think Gwyn likelier than Quin as the intended referent. 'E' is right for Nell (Eleanor); the part is better fitted to her 'line' than to Anne Marshall's; and her partnership with Charles Hart in other 'gay couple' plots increases the likelihood that she was cast as 2 Constantia.

The question that then arises is simple: how plausible, or even possible, was this casting in the spring or summer of 1664? Conventional wisdom has long been that Nell Gwyn took no major roles prior to the spring of 1667. This was John Harold Wilson's view,[32] and his position was adopted by the editors of *The London Stage* in their handling of early casts of unknown date. Can we believe a cast that includes both

---

[30] See Judith Milhous, 'Elizabeth Bowtell and Elizabeth Davenport: Some Puzzles Solved', *Theatre Notebook*, 39 (1985), 124–34.

[31] On Anne Marshall Quin, see *Biographical Dictionary*, xii. 242–4.

[32] John Harold Wilson, *All the King's Ladies: Actresses of the Restoration* (Chicago, Ill. University of Chicago Press, 1958), 146–7.

Clun and Gwyn? Robinson is appropriately sceptical and tentative about drawing conclusions, but says that 'It seems extremely unlikely . . . that the lists are the result of guesswork and equally unlikely that someone creating the casts from an intimate knowledge of the Restoration theatre would have misspelt both Nell Gwyn's and Walter Clun's name.'

Information about Gwyn's early career is woefully scanty, with the *Biographical Dictionary* and Wilson differing by eight years on her probable date of birth (1642 vs. 1650). Scrutiny of such early performance evidence as exists, however, seems to lead towards the conclusion that Nell could have begun to take important roles by the spring of 1664 at the age of 14.[33] By 3 April 1665 Pepys was calling her 'pretty witty Nell': she was no shy apprentice at that time. As Butler observes, there is good evidence for Nell's performing in *'The Seege of Urbin, Thomaso, A King and No King, The Indian Emperour,* and *All Mistaken'* during the 1664–65 season, and consequently 'it is entirely possible that she also played Second Constantia . . . during the summer of 1664'. Possible, not proven, must be the verdict, but 2 Constantia is not a very large part, and its effectiveness depends heavily on youthful sex appeal, which no doubt Nell had aplenty.

From the MS cast (probably that of the first production, or close to it) we can get some idea of how the play was conceived and produced in the 1660s. Kynaston would have provided a suave and polished young Duke, Michael Mohun an appropriately gentlemanly, visibly older Don Frederick. Cartwright would have been a decidedly less buffoon-ish Antonio than William Pinkethman made a generation later. Hart as Don John offered a quintessential libertine, a practised ladykiller whose successes could be the envy of all would-be rakes and whose high testosterone reaction to Nell Gwyn was only to be expected. (Gwyn was of course to become Hart's mistress at an unknown date, before graduating to Lord Buckhurst and then to Charles II.) The cast seems ideally calculated to underline the contrast between the two Constantias implied in the text. Elizabeth Bowtell

---

[33] See Douglas R. Butler, 'The Date of Buckingham's Revision of *The Chances* and Nell Gwynn's First Season on the London Stage', *Notes and Queries*, 227 (1982), 515–16, to whose arguments we are indebted. For an argument in favour of the later date of birth, see David Bond, 'Nell Gwyn's Birthdate', *Theatre Notebook*, 40 (1986), 3–9. The *ODNB* gives 2 Feb. 1651 on the basis of a contemporary horoscope.

had very agreeable Features, a good Complexion, but a Childish Look. Her Voice was weak, tho' very mellow; she generally acted the *young, innocent Lady* whom all the Heroes are mad in Love with.[34]

Both Constantias were young and beautiful, and both were to enjoy notable sexual careers—but the different natures of their appeal were perfectly calculated to support Buckingham's characterizations of the two Constantias.[35] The part of the mother falls into one of the lines of the King's Company actress Katherine Corey, and might have been written with her in mind. Thomas Southerne created a similar mother-as-bawd part for Corey in *The Disappointment; or, The Mother in Fashion* (1684). Buckingham's part stands in an ancestral relationship to Lady Wishfort and Mrs Malaprop, though the mother's recondite vocabulary is not incorrectly used.

The first definite performance date known for Buckingham's version of the play is 5 February 1667, when Pepys attended.

I abroad with my wife and little Betty Michell and took them, against my vows but I will make good my forfeit, to the King's house to show them a play, *The Chances*: a good play I find it—and the actors most good in it. And pretty to hear Knipp sing in the play very properly, *All night I Weepe*—and sung it admirably. The whole play pleases me well—and most of all, the sight of many fine ladies; among other, my Lady Castlemaine and Mrs. Middleton; the latter of the two hath also a very excellent face and body I think.

Pepys makes no comment to the effect that the play he saw differed from what he had seen in 1661, but a contemporary letter suggests that the Buckingham adaptation was on stage at this time. On 2 March 1667 an agent sent Lord Ormonde a letter about charges of treason against Buckingham, ending it with a joke:

If I had ye happyness to bee neer yor Grace for an hower or two I could make many pleasant schænes even in this affayr, wch if in Print weer superior to all

---

34 [Edmund Curll and William Oldys?], *The History of the English Stage* (London: E. Curll, 1741), 21.

35 Jennifer Renee Danby points out to us that there is strong presumptive evidence for Rebecca Marshall taking the role of First Constantia in the performance of 5 Feb. 1667. Marshall states in a deposition (TNA PRO SP 29/191, no. 31; printed in facsimile in the *Biographical Dictionary*, vii. 426–7) that she 'acted in the Play that day'. Neither the Second Constantia nor the mother nor the landlady is at all in Marshall's 'line', leaving us to presume that she had (temporarily?) succeeded Davenport/Boutell in the part. See Danby, 'The Faces of Masculinity and Femininity on the Early Restoration Stage: A Study of Five Actors' (Ph.D. thesis; City University of New York, 2004), ch. 4.

yᵉ Ridiculous Caracters My Lᵈ of Bucks described in his Play called yᵉ Fopps.[36]

Following Wilson, Fowler assumes that 'ye ffopps' is *The Chances*, and we agree that this is overwhelmingly likely.

Pepys's comment raises questions about song and singer—and more broadly about songs in general. Buckingham evidently either chose to drop Fletcher's songs or did not have access to them.[37] In theory, 1 Constantia is the singer at Buckingham's II. ii. 10, but as the singing is done offstage there is no reason that it must be done by the performer. 1 Constantia would have been a surprising and atypical role for Mrs Knep (a friend and favourite of Pepys's), but she was a very fine singer and might well have been employed for 'All night I Weepe', sung offstage—its sentiments evidently appropriate to 1 Constantia's circumstances. Our understanding of the music for the play is complicated by the existence of a song for it: 'Wasted with Sighs I sigh'd & pin'd', said to be 'A Song in the Chances Set to Musick by Mr John Eccles sung by Mr Wiltshire and exactly engrav'd by Tho: Cross, the words by Sʳ Robᵗ Howard'.[38] Howard's biographer has assumed that it was written for the original production.[39] Given Howard's known period of literary activity and connection with Buckingham, this is possible—but the extant music is by John Eccles, who was born in 1668 and started writing music for the theatre *c.*1690. If the text was used in the 1660s, then Eccles must have reset it for a revival. But where was it used? The Howard song was not only sung by a man, but expresses male sexual frustration at being refused by a woman: it would be totally inappropriate at II. ii. 10. The only other point in the Buckingham version at which music is explicitly introduced is at IV. ii. 9.1, where lively dance music is called for. 'Wasted with Sighs' could of course have been used as an entr'acte piece late in the play.[40]

[36] Bodleian Library, Carte MS 35, fo. 329ᵛ.

[37] All but one of Fletcher's five songs were omitted in *47ct* but three more were printed in *79fc*.

[38] British Library K.7.i.2, no. 62, pp. 79–80. See Cyrus Lawrence Day and Eleanore Boswell Murrie, *English Song-Books 1651–1702* (London: Printed for the Bibliographical Society at the University Press, Oxford, 1940 for 1937), no. 3575.

[39] H. J. Oliver, *Sir Robert Howard (1626–1698): A Critical Biography* (Durham, NC: Duke University Press, 1963), 137. The music is printed at the end of the text of the play, p. 120.

[40] Oliver, ibid., reports a copy in the Clark Library at UCLA, and a 'possibly unique' copy in the Royal College of Music, London.

The further history of *The Chances* in the repertory of the King's Company is a frustrating blank. In all likelihood it remained a stock play as long as Hart could sustain his part. Commenting on the success of the adaptation, the anonymous editor of the 1711 edition of 'Beaumont and Fletcher' says that 'Mr. *Hart* play'd the Part of *Don John* to the highest Satisfaction of the Audience; the Play had a great run, and ever since has been follow'd as one of the best Entertainments of the Stage'.[41] Lack of known performance dates in the 1670s means merely that Nell Gwyn did not happen to attend, and neither did Charles II. Other than the bills for their attending plays, most recorded performances are of new plays.

A strong argument for the continued success of *The Chances* at Bridges Street and Drury Lane in the 1670s is the play's prompt revival after the union of 1682. It is not among the plays 'that were the Propriety of Mr. *Killigrew*' (i.e. of the King's Company) later mentioned by Downes as 'then Reviv'd' after the union by the 'mixt Company', but it was definitely one of the 'divers others' he did not bother to name.[42] The king and queen attended a performance at a public theatre (not at court) on 30 December 1682. The United Company's bill for the occasion says '[The King] at ye Chances with ye Q: & a box for ye Maides of honor'.[43] The theatre was probably Dorset Garden rather than Drury Lane, if we may trust the usually reliable Langbaine, whose comment on this play (under Fletcher) is

*Chances*, a Comedy, reviv'd by the late Duke of *Buckingham*, and very much improv'd; being acted with extraordinary applause at the Theatre in *Dorset-Garden*, and printed with the Alterations *Lond.* 4° 1682. (p. 207)

Whether the publication of the adaptation in 1682 was directly connected with the United Company production is to be doubted, since there is no cast list and the title page says 'As it was Acted at the Theater Royal' (not 'is Acted', as was customary for current productions). Why and how the play got published at this point will probably remain a mystery.

---

41  *The Works of Mr. Francis Beaumont and Mr. John Fletcher*, 7 vols. (London: Tonson, 1711), I, p. ix. Downes confirms the importance of the role in Hart's repertory, naming Don John as one of three comic parts in which he was extraordinary (*Roscius Anglicanus*, 41).

42  *Roscius Anglicanus*, 82–3. Among the 'divers others' of which we have record of revival between 1682 and 1686 are *Julius Caesar*, *The Northern Lass*, *The Silent Woman*, *A King and no King*, *The Rival Queens*, *The Committee*, *All for Love*, *Mithridates*, and *The Rehearsal*.

43  TNA PRO LC 5/145, p. 120.

Lack of a cast in the editions of 1682 and 1692 is particularly frustrating, since we have one tantalizing hint that Thomas Betterton may have taken over the role of Don John when Hart retired at the time of the union. Writing long after the fact, Theophilus Cibber bitterly criticized Garrick's performance of Don John, arguing that 'he should appear the Rake of Quality . . . we should not lose Sight of the Nobleman.—In this Light, I am informed, did the Character of *Don John* appear, when the great *Betterton* played it; in this Light have I beheld it, when perform'd by that Master of Genteel Comedy, Mr. Wilks.'[44] The testimony is very late and only reported; there is no confirmatory evidence of Betterton's taking the part. We are, none the less, inclined to credit the claim. Dashing rakes in the mode of Etherege's Dorimant and Otway's Beaugard were a Betterton speciality, and however repulsive we may find Theophilus Cibber in moral terms, he was no fool, had intelligent things to say about the theatre, and knew people who had performed with Betterton—his father, for example. Looking at the United Company roster in the 1680s, the obvious alternative to Betterton is his long-time partner William Smith. Unlike Wilks and Mills in the next generation, Betterton and Smith did not adhere to strict division of rakish and sober friends. Smith took Willmore in Behn's *The Rover*, but Betterton was Galliard in her *Feigned Curtizans* and Gayman in *The Luckey Chance*.[45] Betterton is not, however, included in the second (partial) manuscript cast reported by Robinson, which consists merely of a list of five names without specification of roles: Mr Griffin, Goodman, Monfort, Kynaston, Leigh. No women are named. The implied date is presumably between the union and October 1684, when Cardell Goodman left the stage, save for a few guest appearances.

The United Company performed the play at the Middle Temple on 2 February 1683 and at court before James II on 27 January 1686, receiving the usual fee of £20 in both cases. These are the last definite seventeenth-century performance dates, but there is no doubt that *The Chances* remained in the United Company's repertory. Reprints sometimes signal revivals, but not always. However, in the case of the second edition (a quarto published by R. Bently in 1692), the title page expli-

[44] *Two Dissertations on the Theatres* (London: Printed for the Author, 1756), 44–53.

[45] Don John is not among the 183 Betterton parts listed by Judith Milhous in 'An Annotated Census of Thomas Betterton's Roles, 1659–1710', *Theatre Notebook*, 29 (1975), 33–43, 85–94, but it is suggested as a 'questionable' role by Bruce Podewell, 'Thomas Betterton's Roles', *Theatre Notebook*, 32 (1978), 89–90.

citly indicates a connection to current production: 'As it is Acted at the Theater Royal' (as opposed to 'was Acted' in the 1682 edition). Two other pieces of evidence strongly confirm a revival between *c.*1691 and the end of the 1692–93 season. Howard's song for the play was published in *A Collection of Songs set to Musick by Mr Henry Purcell and Mr John Eccles* (*c.*1696). It cannot have been composed earlier than *c.*1690. Wiltshire (Christian name unknown) was a male singer who may have performed with the United Company as early as 1691. A *terminus ad quem* is provided by the identity of 2 Constantia, performed by Charlotte Butler, who is not recorded in London after June 1692 and had decamped permanently to Ireland by 1694.[46] This one piece of casting information comes to us from Colley Cibber, who says

. . . she was a capital and admired Performer. In speaking, too, she had a sweet-ton'd Voice, which, with her naturally genteel Air and sensible Pronunciation, render'd her wholly Mistress of the Amiable in many serious Characters. In Parts of Humour, too, she had a manner of blending her assuasive Softness even with the Gay, the Lively, and the Alluring. Of this she gave an agreeable Instance in her Action of the (*Villiers*) Duke of *Buckingham*'s second *Constantia* in the *Chances*. In which, if I should say I have never seen her exceeded, I might still do no wrong to the late Mrs. *Oldfield*'s lively Performance of the same Character.[47]

Mrs Butler was particularly noted as a singer and could certainly have done the Act II song on behalf of the other Constantia. Nothing else is known about the United Company's productions.[48]

At an unknown date after the actors' rebellion of 1694–95, the Patent Company revived the play, presumably to feature Robert Wilks. No cast is advertised for the performances of 5 February 1704[49] or 22 February 1705, though the latter was Anne Oldfield's benefit and no doubt she took 2 Constantia. The role was to become one of her great successes, and an anonymous biographer said at the time of her death:

[46] *Biographical Dictionary*, ii. 449.

[47] *An Apology for the Life of Mr. Colley Cibber, Written by Himself*, ed. Robert W. Lowe, 2 vols. (London: Nimmo, 1889), i. 163–4.

[48] *The London Stage*, Part 1, 398, reports misleadingly that 'The edition of 1692 restores the role of Peter Vecchio from John Fletcher's original version.' This is untrue. The 1692 edition does, however, print a list of roles lifted from the 1679 Beaumont and Fletcher folio, and the publisher failed to eliminate 'Vecchio' from that list or to make other alterations appropriate to the Buckingham version.

[49] The advertisement in the *Daily Courant* of 4 Feb. 1704 advertises the play 'As newly corrected', but there is no way to determine what this means. Lack of a revised edition implies that the changes were minor.

'Who that has seen her *Constantia* in the *Chances*, but has envy'd *Don John*, and would, like him, have fought an Army to have secured her to himself!'[50] The first advertised cast is for Drury Lane on 24 February 1708: Duke—Barton Booth; Petruchio—John Bickerstaff; Don John—Robert Wilks; Don Frederick—John Mills; Antonio—William Pinkethman; Peter—Jubilee Dicky Norris; Anthony—Richard Cross; 1 Constantia—Lucretia Bradshaw; 2 Constantia—Anne Oldfield (*Daily Courant*). On 13 March 1708 the advertisement reported the same assignments (save for Theophilus Keene taking Petruchio and Norris and Cross apparently swapping parts) and added the two older women's roles: Mother—Mrs Powell; Landlady—Mrs Willis. This is an excellent cast, featuring Wilks and Anne Oldfield but giving them strong support from Booth (a serious, noble Duke) and Mills (Wilks's longtime sidekick) as Frederick. Lucretia Bradshaw should have made a convincingly beautiful and noble 1 Constantia and a fine contrast with the sprightlier Oldfield. An advance puff for a performance on the 29th says that the play

is a true Picture of Life . . . wherein Don *John* and *Constantia* are acted to the utmost Perfection. There need not be a greater Instance of the Force of Action, than in many Incidents of this Play, where indifferent Passages, and such that conduce only to the Tacking of the Scenes together, are enlivened with such an agreeable Gesture and Behaviour, as apparently shows what a Play might be, though it is not wholly what a Play should be.[51]

The production proved popular: the company performed *The Chances* at least once every season from 1707–08 through 1731–32. During this time it gave fifty-seven performances. In forty-three cases the cast was advertised, and Wilks performed Don John in all of them. Of the twenty-four performances with known cast from 1708 through spring 1720, Anne Oldfield took 2 Constantia in at least twenty cases, and probably in twenty-two of them.[52] On 24 October 1717 Hester Santlow played 2 Constantia, and when Oldfield gave up the role in 1720, Sant-

---

[50] *Authentick Memoirs Of the Life of that celebrated Actress Mrs. Ann Oldfield*, 3rd edn. (London: Booksellers and Pamphletsellers of London and Westminster, 1730), 22. The allusion is to V. iv. 54–5.

[51] *The Tatler*, ed. Donald F. Bond, 3 vols. (Oxford: Clarendon Press, 1987), iii. 37 (27–9 June 1710). This issue has usually been ascribed to Steele, but Bond considers the authorship uncertain.

[52] In the advertisements of 5 Dec. 1709 and 1 Jan. 1712 Oldfield is advertised as 1 Constantia, Jane Porter as 2 Constantia instead of vice versa as usual. We suspect that this was an error in advertising copy rather than an experimental role reversal.

low took it over (having meanwhile married Barton Booth). Of the twenty further performances for which a cast was advertised, Mrs Booth played 2 Constantia in all but one of them. Several other roles stayed remarkably stable over nearly a quarter of a century (notably Mills as Don Frederick), but clearly Don John and 2 Constantia were the roles crucial to the play's continued popularity. After Wilks died in 1732 and Hester Booth retired in 1733, *The Chances* fell out of the repertory. Covent Garden mounted a production on 12 April 1738, and Drury Lane tried Henry Giffard and Kitty Clive in the key parts on 23 November 1739—but the Covent Garden revival was abandoned after one night, the Drury Lane revival after two. The 'Scanderbeg' playlist of 1747 says (quite misleadingly) that *The Chances* 'still continues what they call a Stock-Play',[53] but it was not performed again at either theatre until Garrick brought it back with alterations in 1754.

The revival was already planned by 17 August 1751, when Garrick mentions it in a letter.[54] The play may have been brought to his attention by Thomas Sheridan's Dublin production in April of that year. The text published there shows that about 150 lines were cut for the sake of minimizing what was increasingly perceived as indecency, and some obsolete and figurative language was modernized.[55] Another stimulus may have been a hint from above. Thomas Davies reports that

The play of the Chances, as altered from Beaumont and Fletcher, by Villiers Duke of Buckingham, had been thrown out of the common list of plays for above twenty-five years. The King happened to recollect that Wilks and Oldfield had greatly diverted him in that comedy, and he asked one of his courtiers why it was never played. Mr. Garrick, as soon as he learned the King's inclination to see the Chances, immediately set about reforming the play, so as to render it less exceptionable in language and action.[56]

This is possible, though George II would have had to recall a performance in his days as Prince of Wales, since Oldfield gave up her part in

---

53 [John Mottley?], *A Compleat List Of all the English Dramatic Poets*, attached to Thomas Whincop's *Scanderbeg* (London: Reeve, 1747), 110.

54 *The Letters of David Garrick*, ed. David M. Little and George M. Kahrl, 3 vols. (London: Oxford University Press, 1963), i. 172.

55 *The Chances: A Comedy; As it is Acted at the Theatre-Royal in Smock-Alley* (Dublin: J. Esdall, 1751). For analysis, See Fowler, 'The Chances', 106–8. For Sheridan's influence on Garrick's repertory and vice versa, see Esther K. Sheldon, *Thomas Sheridan of Smock-Alley* (Princeton, N.J.: Princeton University Press, 1967), 166 and 354.

56 Thomas Davies, *Memoirs of the Life of David Garrick Esq.*, ed. Stephen Jones, 2 vols. (London: Longman et al., 1808), i. 222–3.

1720. Garrick says in a letter to the Marquis of Hartington that he took exceptional trouble over the revival:

No Care has been wanting on my Part to make ye Reception & Entertainment for his Majesty, as well as I possibly could—I have new dress'd ye Play, put Every Performer I could of Merit in it—nay hir'd Mrs Macklin on purpose for one of ye Characters [the Landlady].[57]

The production was unquestionably a success, enjoying thirteen nights in its first season despite an awkward problem in the casting. Davies reports that

The manager's great difficulty was, how to cast the part of the second Constantia, in such a manner, as that she might bear some resemblance to the first. Mrs. Pritchard was the only actress in the company who had, in a superior degree, much vivacity, variety of humour, and engaging action; but this lady was become so bulky in her person, that she could not be mistaken for Miss Macklin, whose figure was elegant, and who acted the first Constantia. But could Mr. Garrick have surmounted this difficulty, Mrs. Cibber, by a clause in her articles, claimed a right to choose any character she pleased to act in a new or revived play. This actress, whose tones of voice were so expressive of all the tender passions, and was by nature formed for tragic representation, was unaccountably desirous of acting characters of gaiety and humour, to which she was an absolute stranger: she had no idea of comedy, but such as implied a representation of childish simplicity.

Mr. Garrick knew that it was impossible to divert her from the resolution to play Constantia; and therefore determined to give way to her humour, till the want of applause should admonish her to resign the part.

I need not recall to the reader's mind the great delight which Mr. Garrick gave the public in Don John. Mrs. Cibber soon grew tired of a part to which the audience afforded no signs of approbation. Miss Haughton, a young actress, succeeded her for a short time, and merited a good share of applause.[58]

The cast of the 1754 production also featured John Palmer ('Gentleman Palmer', 1728–68) as Don Frederick, Richard Yates as Antonio, the great Kitty Clive as the Mother, and Mrs Macklin as the Landlady. Garrick advertised the production as 'Dress'd after the Old Italian and Spanish Manner'.

---

[57] *Letters*, i. 212–13.

[58] *Memoirs of the Life of David Garrick*, i. 223–4. According to Cross's diary, Mrs Cibber gave up the part after nine nights (*London Stage*, Part 4, 455), a statement confirmed by the playbills.

Exactly what changes Garrick imposed on the text in 1754 is impossible to say with any certainty. The necessity of cleaning it up was manifest, but how thoroughly was it done? No text was published at the time. When the play was revived the next season, it was advertised 'With Alterations' (28 November 1755), as was a performance on 26 January 1757. The editor of Part 4 of *The London Stage* opined that these were presumably the same as those used in 1754, but Garrick's editors have begged to differ, pointing to multiple layers of revision in three hands in the Drury Lane promptbook.[59] The success of the 1754 revival notwithstanding, some members of the audience found the play profoundly distasteful. 'A Gentleman of Oxford' (identity unknown) published a fierce denunciation, evidently written on 4 December 1754:

To-night is to be performed the most barefaced baudry Farce, (for it does not deserve the Name of a Comedy) that ever disgraced the Stage; in which the Manager, who has caused it to be revived, is to perform the principal Part. The Play, Sir, is called *The Chances*, written by the witty and wicked Duke of *Buckingham*, and this is the tenth Night of its Representation to crammed Houses, which have amply rewarded the Manager, for his successful Endeavours to corrupt and deprave the Morals of the People.[60]

This popularity did not last. Drury Lane gave the play three times in 1755–56, twice in 1756–57, and twice in 1757–58. When receipts fell as low as £120 on 13 April 1758, *The Chances* was dropped from the repertory and remained unperformed for fourteen years.

Responses to the 1750s version(s) were decidedly mixed. A reviewer of the performance of 26 January 1757 admired Garrick's performance but expressed qualms about the play:

This Night the *Chances* a Comedy by *Beaumont* and *Fletcher*, and in the Year 1682 revived with Alterations by *Villiers* Duke of Buckingham . . . was acted at this House [Drury Lane]. The Bills of the Day mention further Alterations: we could wish that, when Mr. *Garrick* thought of any Alterations, he had given such as would have rendered it not entirely offensive to all Decency and Virtue. In many Passages we meet with very fine Writing; just Thoughts enlivened by spirited Dialogue, Wit, Humour, and Strokes of Character. The Play

---

[59] Folger Shakespeare Library (shelfmark Prompt C 17). See *The Plays of David Garrick*, vi. 395–6. The hands are those of Garrick himself, Richard Cross (prompter 1747–60), and William Hopkins (prompter 1763–80). This manuscript includes some but not all of the changes introduced in 1773, and we see no way to determine at what date many of them were made.

[60] *The Devil upon Crutches In England, or Night Scenes in London* (London: Philip Hodges, 1755), 32–3.

however, owes its Success principally to quick Turns of Business, a Variety of Incidents, and some diverting Situations. The Plot is very far from being conducted artificially, and in a just subordinancy to the Rules of the Drama; and Vice and Folly are represented in a favourable Light. On the Revival of this Play, a few winters ago, the Connoisseurs were divided about Mr. Garrick, and the late Mr. Wilks, many Persons of Taste who remembered the Latter, prefered the deceased performer; be that as it may, Mr. Garrick's Admirers had great Reason on their Side, because he certainly plays the Part with great Vivacity; and in his Hands Don John is a new created Personage, that will always divert, while our modern Roscius walks the Stage. (*London Chronicle*, 25–7 January 1757)

Baker's very mixed reactions similarly indicate both the appeal of the play and growing audience discomfort with it:

*The Chances.* Com. by the D. of *Buckingham*, 4to. 1682.—This is only the preceding Play alter'd and amended.—It has been frequently performed with great Applause, and indeed, the vast Variety of Business and Hurry of Intrigue, which is actually produced by the Confusion of mistaking two Characters so extremely different as those of the *Constantias*, cannot avoid keeping up the Attention of an Audience, and making the Piece appear, if one may so term it, entirely alive.—Yet notwithstanding the Alterations made in it first by the Duke, and since that in the preparing it for some still later Representations, there runs a Degree of Indelicacy thro' some Scenes, and a Libertinism thro' the whole Character of Don *John*, which, to the Honour of the present Age be it recorded, have for many Years past, experienced a very singular Disapprobation, whenever they have been attempted to be obtruded on the Public.[61]

Garrick was evidently feeling his way towards a concept of rake (and a plot) that would titillate without actually offending. Theophilus Cibber (no friend of Garrick) heaps scorn on his Don John, suggesting that he turned a 'gentleman' into a mere buffoon so that he seemed like '*Ranger* in a *Spanish* Jacket . . . 'Tis no longer the Noble *Don John*,—'tis a little *Jack-a-dandy*.' (For a later depiction of Garrick in this role, see Fig. 2.) 'To personate this noble joyous Voluptuary, there should be Comeliness, Grace, a spirited Dignity, and Ease;—he should appear the Rake of Quality;—not a pert Prig, let loose on a Holiday.—In his most unguarded Frolicks, we should not lose Sight of the Nobleman'.[62] Cibber objects vehemently to a bit of stage business introduced in IV. ii:

---

[61] [David Erskine Baker], *The Companion to the Play-House*, 2 vols. (London: T. Becket et al., 1764), s.v. title. Isaac Reed retained this account in the *Biographica Dramatica* of 1782, as did Stephen Jones in the edition of 1812.

[62] *Dissertations on Theatrical Subjects* (London: Griffiths, 1756), 53.

FIG. 2. David Garrick in the character of Don-John (*The Chances*, I. iii). Engraving by J. Hall after E. Edwards's version of a painting by De Louterbourg (1777). Courtesy of the Harvard Theatre Collection

To point out Particulars, where the whole is absurd, were endless;—One is as good as a Hundred:—Only think of this young *Spanish* Nobleman, because his Ear is caught by the Sound of a Fiddle from the Window of a Tavern, being tempted to give you a Touch of a Hornpipe in the Middle of the Street. Is it in Nature to suppose any Gentleman, in his Senses, could be guilty of so ridiculous an Absurdity?

Cibber's heat is no doubt excessive, but he is probably about right in comparing Garrick's Don John to his Ranger—the pseudo-rake in Hoadly's *The Suspicious Husband* (1747), in which Garrick found one of his most lastingly popular roles. Real rakes were increasingly unacceptable to the mid-century audience.

The return of *The Chances* to the Drury Lane repertory late in Garrick's career was the result of an accident. On 22 April 1772 Samuel Cautherley (not much of an actor) chose to try Don John for his benefit, advertising the play as 'Not acted these 14 years'. The performance was probably regrettable (the prompter Hopkins recorded in his diary, 'Don John Mr Cautherly—la la!'),[63] but Frances Abington was evidently a revelation as 2 Constantia and revived Garrick's interest in the play.

On 21 April 1773 *The Chances* was brought back, performed 'By Command of their Majesties' (George III and Queen Charlotte). Hopkins' wrote in his diary,

This Comedy is reviv'd with great Alterations by Mr G. by particular desire of the Queen. The play went off vastly well Mr. G. Play'd with great Spirit & much Applauded the Alterations are vastly lik'd it will now be a living Play.

Hopkins proved a good prophet: the emended play was to enjoy another generation of popularity. Davies says that 'in Mrs. Abington' Garrick

met with a Constantia who disputed the palm of victory with his Don John. She so happily assumed all the gay airs, peculiar oddities, and various attitudes of an agreeable and frolicksome madcap, that the audience were kept in constant good humour and merriment, which they recompensed by the loudest applause, through all the several scenes in which she acted. The King commanded the Chances, and seemed to enjoy the performance of it.'[64]

---

[63] *The London Stage*, Part 4, 1626.

[64] *Memoirs of the Life of David Garrick*, i. 224–5. Four command performances are recorded in less than two years: 21 Apr. and 17 Nov. 1773, and 13 Apr. and 7 Dec. 1774.

At 56, Garrick was no doubt an increasingly geriatric Don John, but this time his 'alterations' were such as to restore audience comfort. What he did was essentially to castrate Buckingham's play, to use an eighteenth-century critical term.[65] Garrick tightened up many of the scenes, cutting lines, adding lines, and reimporting some scraps of Fletcher's original, but the substantive changes are largely in the interests of decency. Petruchio's account of his sister's seduction and pregnancy is cut very short ('I am ashamed to say the rest').[66] 2 Constantia is made a very wholesome girl ('If any young fellow would but take a liking to me and make an honest woman of me, I would make him the best wife in the world. . . . I do here swear and vow to live forever chaste till I find a young fellow who will take me for better and for worse'). At the end of the play Don John says, 'A match, my girl!' and announces that he will

fix to happiness and one,
Change the wild wanton for the sober plan
And, like my friend, become a modest man.

In short, the rake changes his spots and announces a reform.

Garrick played Don John eleven times in 1773 and 1774, enjoying fat box office returns, as the daily totals printed in *The London Stage* clearly prove: the average gross was a dazzling £244 per night. His new version was duly published in 1773, appeared in a second edition in 1774, and was republished in the New English Theatre series in 1777.[67] Garrick retired in 1776. He was succeeded as Don John by John Henderson, who had taken the role at Bath in 1773, proved himself in it for three nights at the Little Haymarket in August 1777, and first played it at Drury Lane on 4 December that year, teaming with Frances Abington and subsequently with Miss Farren.[68] Henderson apparently modelled

<hr />

[65] For detailed accounts of the changes, see Fowler, 'The Chances', ch. 4 and Appendix C, and *The Plays of David Garrick*, vi. 395–401.

[66] *The Plays of David Garrick*, vi. 233. Following quotations from vi. 250–1 and 269.

[67] A promptbook apparently prepared by Garrick in a copy of the 1774 edition of his revision is preserved in the Beinecke Library at Yale (Im G 193 773Cc). Garrick did not perform the role after 15 Dec. 1774, but on 12 Jan. 1776 the Drury Lane accounts record payment to him of £171 as 'author of the alteration of the Chances and two preludes' (Folger MS W.b. 278). Edward A. Langhans has suggested that Garrick 'probably prepared' this version 'for his successor in the role, John Henderson' but notes that there is no clear evidence that it was ever used. See Edward A. Langhans, *Eighteenth-Century British and Irish Promptbooks: A Descriptive Bibliography* (Westport, Conn: Greenwood, 1987), 56–7. Henderson was not working in London in 1775–76, and we suspect that Garrick made the changes for himself but chose never to try his last version on stage.

[68] What text Henderson used is not clear, but not the one published in 1777 that

his Don John closely on that of his predecessor, for a reviewer comments that 'Mr. Henderson is more *be-Garricked* in Don John than in any character he has before appeared in at the Hay-market Theatre'.[69] In 1779 Henderson jumped to Covent Garden, where Miss Younge became his 2 Constantia in a very popular production. Drury Lane revived the show in 1782 with John Palmer the younger ('Plausible Jack', 1744–98) and Miss Farren. Between Garrick's retirement and the end of the century *The Chances* was performed forty-four times in London. Henderson was featured in twenty-five of those performances before his sudden death in 1785, Palmer in sixteen before his death in 1798. 2 Constantia was taken eighteen times by Farren and eighteen times by Younge.[70] After 1800 neither theatre had any luck recasting the show, and it was never again to be a stock play.[71]

---

masquerades as that of the Drury Lane production at this time. The 'Bell's Edition' says on the title page *The Chances. A Comedy, As altered from Beaumont and Fletcher, by his grace The Duke of Buckingham. Distinguishing also the Variations of the Theatre, as performed at the Theatre-Royal in Drury-Lane. Regulated from the Prompt-Book, by Permission of the Managers, By Mr. Hopkins, Prompter* (London: John Bell, 1777). The frontispiece shows 'Mr Henderson in the Character of Don John', and the cast in the Dramatis Personae is attributed to 'Drury Lane'. However, the cast includes two performers (Mr Jefferson and Miss Platt) who did not return to the company for 1777–78, and the frontispiece is dated 24 Sept. 1777. Clearly the cast was projected rather than actual. The text of the Bell edition, title page notwithstanding, is basically just a reprint of the Buckingham version, *not* any text in use during the time of Garrick. Buckingham's text would, of course, have been totally unacceptable to a London audience in 1777, and Bell's use of it is surprising.

[69] *Whitehall Evening Post*, 19–21 Aug. 1777.

[70] The stage life of the play seems to have outlasted its critical reputation. Commenting on a new edition of the *Tatler*, a writer in the *Gentleman's Magazine* (Supplement for the Year 1786, pp. 1128–9) says: 'The indecency of some scenes in the Chances is here said to have frustrated all attempts to obtrude it upon the public. Is this not a mistake? Henderson, till his death, frequently acted Don John at Covent-garden theatre; and it has been many times played by Palmer at Drury-lane, and once this season.'

[71] What text was used in the last two decades of the eighteenth century is not clear. The Harrison and Wenman reprint of 1780 (a cheap, small-print, double-column affair totalling 21 pages) says on the title page 'As it is Acted at the Theatres-Royal in Drury-Lane and Covent-Garden' and 'Written by Beaumont and Fletcher', but provides no casts and uses the Buckingham text. In 1791 John Bell issued two substantively identical editions, one of eighty-six pages, the other of 103. The title pages both say, ponderously, 'As altered from Beaumont and Fletcher, by his grace The Duke of Buckingham. Adapted for Theatrical Representation, as performed at the Theatres-Royal, Drury-Lane and Covent-Garden. Regulated from the Prompt-Books, By Permission of the Managers. "The Lines distinguished by inverted Commas, are omitted in the Representation."' The ascription is accurate: we are given the Buckingham text. But there are no further alterations and no indication of prompt copy cuts or changes. Current casts are given for both theatres, but we have difficulty believing that they had gone back to the Buckingham text.

Genest reports three performances at Covent Garden in 1806 after a twelve-year hiatus there.[72] The Drury Lane revival of 6 February 1808 failed in four nights, despite having Elliston as Don John (much admired by Elizabeth Inchbald in the part) and the redoubtable Dorothy Jordan as 2 Constantia—admittedly by this time a chubby 46-year-old about to become a grandmother. The problem seems to have lain in changing mores more than in the production. Leigh Hunt's key comment was a question: 'how long will it be, before our managers are persuaded that obscenity is neither humour nor wit?'[73] He asserts that 'The story in short is unfit for comedy. A lady who is seduced by a nobleman, delivered of a child which she is obliged to send away from her, and pursued by the fury of an indignant brother, cannot possibly give rise to any comic feelings.' A reviewer for the *Monthly Mirror* says flatly that 'the cause of its failure' is 'the licentiousness of several scenes, and the whole of the character of *Don John*'. He goes on to deny the efficacy of the bowdlerization:

The play has been praised for its vast variety of business and hurry of intrigue, and the praise is due, if we can but make the business and intrigue square fairly with probability. To these merits is now added the improvement of a text purified from much of its indecency, of which, however, a large lump is left in the very constitution of *Don John*, although he is now certainly made more '*modest to converse with*'.[74]

In other words, even Garrick's domesticated and penitent rake seemed too much of a libertine for the refined inhabitants of the nineteenth century. One more production was apparently mooted but came to naught. Reporting on Edmund Kean's Richard III in February 1814, William Hazlitt said 'We understand, he is shortly to appear as *Don John*, in *The Chances*. We know no character so exactly suited to his powers.'[75]

---

[72] John Genest, *Some Account of the English Stage from the Restoration in 1660 to 1830*, 10 vols. (Bath: Carrington, 1832), viii. 3. For a useful survey of the last phase of the original stage history of the Fletcher canon, see Donald J. Rulfs, 'Beaumont and Fletcher on the London Stage 1776–1833', *PMLA* 63 (1948), 1245–64.

[73] *Examiner*, 14 Feb. 1808.

[74] *Monthly Mirror* (Feb. 1808), 126.

[75] Originally published in the *Morning Chronicle* and reprinted in Hazlitt's *A View of the English Stage; or, A Series of Dramatic Criticisms* (1818) with the passage in which this statement appears omitted. See *The Complete Works of William Hazlitt*, ed. P. P. Howe after the edition of A. R. Waller and Arnold Glover, 21 vols. (London: Dent, 1930–3), v. 182–3 and 402.

The last moderately successful use of *The Chances* on the nineteenth-century stage was made by Frederick Reynolds in a musical version he called *Don John; or the Two Violettas*, which featured Charles Kemble in the title role and enjoyed nineteen performances at Covent Garden in 1821, where it premiered on 20 February. Reynolds preserved little beyond the intrigue-and-confusion story: nothing in the characters or life histories of Don John and 2 Constantia could rouse any moral qualms, though most of the words are taken over from the Garrick version.[76] The Duke turns out to have married the first Violetta already, removing any implied approval of sex before marriage. The second Violetta—a virtuous maiden—gets locked up by her nasty old guardian Fractioso because she refuses to marry him. A reviewer in *The Times* said cheerily that the piece's success 'precludes all remark on the liberty taken with these sterling dramas, and strikes even criticism dumb' (21 February 1821), but Genest refers crossly to 'literary murder' and ridicules some careless details in the changes.[77] The piece seems to have benefitted from some specially advertised new scenes (for example, 'Part of the Bay of Naples, by Moonlight' with 'Vesuvius at a distance—and illuminated Boats passing'—playbill) spectacularly lit by Covent Garden's new gas lights. Reynolds defends the piece as one of a kind with his successful musical alterations of *The Comedy of Errors*, *Twelfth Night*, *The Tempest*, and *The Merry Wives of Windsor*, but admits that despite Bishop's music *Don John* enjoyed only a 'very lukewarm' reception and was 'quietly returned to "the peaceful grave"'.[78]

The next production of any version of *The Chances* on the London stage of which we are aware was of the Buckingham adaptation, mounted by the Phoenix Society for two performances on 29 and 30 January 1922. The professed object of the organization was 'the adequate presentation of the plays of the older dramatists', done with respect for the original texts and performance conditions but not in a spirit of mere antiquarianism. Professional actors were cajoled to participate, usually for two days at times when theatres normally were dark—Sunday night

---

[76] [Frederick Reynolds], *Don John; or the Two Violettas, A Musical Drama, in three acts; founded on Beaumont and Fletcher's Comedy of The Chances* (London: John Miller, 1821). The title page announces music by Bishop and Ware, though the markings in the New York Public Library exemplar copied in MS from the 'L.P. Book' at Covent Garden imply that many of the songs were cut.

[77] Genest, ix. 104–6.

[78] *The Life and Times of Frederick Reynolds. Written by Himself.* 2 vols., 2nd edn. (London: Henry Colburn, 1827), ii. 410–11.

and Monday afternoon.[79] The society's papers long ago disappeared, as has the promptbook, but if Summers is accurate in touting his insistence on sticking to the texts of seventeenth-century editions, then something reasonably close to the 1682 text was used. Reviewers were clearly shocked, though perhaps enjoyably so. The headline for the *Daily Express* review was 'Too Naughty for the Public', and the writer for *The Times* was rather taken with the unconventional views of the Landlady. Clearly, however, reviewers saw the play as no more than a historical curiosity.[80]

Probably almost no one in 1922 imagined that the Buckingham version could be done professionally, but such a revival occurred exactly forty years later when Sir Laurence Olivier opened the first Chichester Festival with it on 3 July 1962, running it in repertory with Ford's *The Broken Heart* and Chekhov's *Uncle Vanya*. The promptbook has vanished from the festival's archives, but Olivier's text was published in *Plays of the Year: 25*.[81] Olivier cuts sixty or seventy lines of Buckingham's text, but reimports about 125 lines from Fletcher's original, restoring Jacobean bluntness to some of the speeches of Antonio and the Landlady. The show was chosen in part 'to show off the amenities of this particular [non-proscenium] theatre'. It was done 'with no sets at all beyond that designed more or less for permanency by the architect'.[82] The festival programme and *The Impossible Theatre* contain production photographs that suggest a flashy period production of melodramatic bent whose aggressive colour choices (Don John in 'shocking' pink, for example) were described by reviewers.[83] The cast was clearly a strong one, with Keith Michell as Don John, and Joan Plowright (Olivier's wife) taking 2 Constantia. Physical action was strongly emphasized,

---

[79] On the Phoenix Society, see Montague Summers, *The Restoration Theatre* (London: Kegan Paul et al., 1934), App. III, where Summers gives a list of the thirty-odd plays mounted under the society's aegis between 1919 and 1925.

[80] Fowler, 'The Chances', 126–30, gives a cogent analysis of surviving materials and commentary. Reviews appeared in *The Times*, *Telegraph*, and *Daily Express* on 31 Jan. 1922, and in the *Observer* and the *Sunday Times* on 5 Feb.

[81] Ed. J. C. Trewin (London: Elek, 1963). How exactly this text matches what was used in performance we cannot be certain. Comparison with a mimeographed actor's script preserved in the Theatre Museum reveals significant cuts and restorations evidently made during rehearsals. The actor's copy itself represents at least one step in revision since some of its pages are labelled 'Revised'.

[82] Sir Laurence Olivier, 'Prologue' to Leslie Evershed-Martin, *The Impossible Theatre: The Chichester Festival Theatre Adventure* (London and Chichester: Phillimore, 1971), p. xii.

[83] We are grateful to James Fowler for permitting us to consult his personal copies of the Chichester programme for *The Chances* and the 1962 Souvenir Programme for the festival.

with actors entering through the audience and racing up and down staircases that connected upper and lower stages. Antonio pursued 2 Constantia in a climactic chase that used a catwalk round the whole auditorium, and Don John made an entry sliding down from a balcony. Most reviewers accepted the bawdy bits cheerfully enough, and Kenneth Tynan openly revelled in it, though they seem to have enjoyed the 'frenetic cavortings', 'Errol Flynnery', and 'flamboyant vulgarity' without much respecting either the play or the production.[84] The play proved unexpectedly popular with the public, and Leslie Evershed-Martin (the founder of the festival) reports that bookings increased rapidly after the premiere (p. 122). The production concept, however, was essentially frivolous. Olivier himself later said that '*The Chances* was a romp and to my mind still a very endearing and pleasant little romp',[85] and he directed it that way. Petruchio and 1 Constantia were played (said *The Times* reviewer) 'with a studied lack of conviction', teased rather than taken straight. And if the setting was not Cloud Cuckoo Land, it might as well have been: any sexual implications might have been imported straight from Feydeau. Neither the romantic plot nor the libertine plot was treated with any seriousness, reducing the play to farce.[86]

## CRITICAL REPUTATION

The play's near total neglect by twentieth-century critics of 'Restoration comedy' notwithstanding, Buckingham's version of *The Chances* has always enjoyed a startlingly high reputation in spite of its dubious

---

[84] Fowler, 'The Chances', 130–8, gives a good account of the production. Reviews appeared in the *Evening Standard*, 4 July 1962; in *The Times*, the *Financial Times*, and the *Guardian*, 5 July; and Tynan in the *Observer*, 8 July. For other commentary, see *Drama Survey*, 2 (Oct. 1962), 178–9; Laurence Kitchin in *Listener*, 68, no. 1743 (23 Aug. 1962), 290; *Theatre World*, 58, no. 451 (Aug. 1962), 18–19; Clive Barnes in *Plays and Players* (Sept. 1962), 12–13; *Theatre Arts*, 46, no. 12 (Dec. 1962), 57–9. For less immediate views, see Zsuzsi Roboz and Stan Gébler Davies, *Chichester 10: Portrait of a Decade* (London: Davis-Poynter, 1975), 71, 93; Evershed-Martin, *The Impossible Theatre*, 122 and 129–35; and Ronald Hayman, *The First Thrust: The Chichester Festival Theatre* (London: Davis-Poynter, 1975), 65–9, 70. Production photographs in the 1962 Chichester Festival Programme (copy in the Theatre Museum, London) and *The Impossible Theatre* reveal a fussy/frilly job of costuming that was probably meant to compensate for the then-disconcerting bareness of the stage.

[85] 'Prologue', *The Impossible Theatre*, p. xiv.

[86] This reconstruction of the 1962 production (by Robert D. Hume from printed sources) turned out to jibe quite well with Harold Love's forty-year-old recollections of the production, which he saw as a postgraduate student in England.

status as a mere 'adaptation'. Langbaine calls it 'reviv'd . . . and very much improv'd'; Gildon says merely 'oftentimes Acted with great Applause of late days at the Theatre in *Dorset Garden*, &c.'[87] Writing at the opening of the eighteenth century, George Granville, Baron Lansdowne, placed his adaptation of *The Merchant of Venice* squarely in what he saw as a distinguished tradition. Granville believed that 'Undertakings of this kind are justify'd by the Examples of those Great Men, who have employ'd their Endeavours the same Way', citing Waller's revision of *The Maid's Tragedy*, Rochester's *Valentinian*, Buckingham's *The Chances*, the Dryden-Davenant *Tempest*, Dryden's *Troilus and Cressida*, Shadwell's *Timon of Athens*, and Tate's *King Lear*, the last being 'the Works of three succeeding Laureats'.[88] More than a century later, Genest's opinion was unequivocal:

. . . the first three acts of the original are excellent, but the last two are very inferiour—the Duke [i.e. Buckingham], by extending the small parts of the 2d Constantia and her mother, has added two acts quite equal to the first three—this is perhaps the happiest *material* alteration of any old play ever made'. (i.67)

A. C. Sprague, still the foremost authority on alterations and adaptations of Fletcher, and by no means an indulgent judge of them, says flatly that 'there can be no doubt that Buckingham left *The Chances* a much better play than he found it'.[89]

Critics are unanimous in agreeing that Fletcher's original fell off badly after the first three acts. Swinburne makes the point as a backhanded compliment in the course of putting down Buckingham's much better-known play:

*The Knight of the Burning Pestle* is at least as superior to *The Rehearsal* at all points as the fifth act of *The Chances* substituted by the author of *The Rehearsal* for Fletcher's original fifth act is superior in dramatic force, character, and humour to that hasty and headlong scrawl of a sketch.[90]

Buckingham extended and improved the intrigues and mistakes, while substantially enhancing the secondary plot and with it the characters of Don John, 2 Constantia, and the character he changed into her mother.

[87] Langbaine, 207; Charles Gildon, *The Lives and Characters of the English Dramatick Poets* (London, [1699]), 57.

[88] 'Advertisement to the Reader', prefixed to *The Jew of Venice* (London: Lintott, 1701), sig. A3[r].

[89] Sprague, *Beaumont and Fletcher*, 221.

[90] Algernon Charles Swinburne, *Contemporaries of Shakespeare* (London: Heinemann, 1919), 152.

Buckingham's outlook was of course that of a Restoration libertine and court wit. The attitude of later eighteenth- and nineteenth-century critics towards his results depends on their degree of moral strictness, or their willingness to tolerate historical difference or to presume that the antics of farce should be exempted from moral judgement. As we have seen, even Garrick's drastic cleansing of 1773 failed to satisfy a pre-Victorian like Leigh Hunt or the critic of the *Monthly Mirror*. By 1800 hardly any critic cared to condone the Fletcher or Buckingham versions, and only a few could swallow even Garrick's. Reprinting the Garrick text in *The British Theatre* in 1808, Elizabeth Inchbald offered some perceptive and tolerant comments:

The reader of this comedy will scarcely conceive the great entertainment which it can bestow in representation. But it requires peculiar powers of comic acting to make it please even on the stage, and therefore it is seldom performed. Don John is the character, which, most of any in the piece, must be assisted with the actor's skill, or the whole drama sinks into insipidity. The second Constantia ranks as a first comic character, but is too little seen to be of any high importance.... The continual bustle, the contrivance, the hurry of intrigue, and the mistakes, in this comedy, are its best claims to the attention of an audience—in these occurrences a reader cannot so well partake; and, as humour is more its quality than wit, of that, again, the reader is denied his equal share with an auditor.[91]

Mrs Inchbald was of the opinion that Henderson's acting kept the play on the stage after the retirement of Garrick, and she was convinced that Elliston ought to have been able to carry the 1808 Drury Lane production.

Among important nineteenth-century critics, Hazlitt is virtually alone in his acceptance of even the Fletcher version without apology or moral discomfort, though he comments on it only in passing. In *Lectures on the English Comic Writers* (1819) he makes the perhaps extravagant claim that

*Rule a Wife and Have a Wife*, the *Chances*, and the *Wild Goose Chase* . . . are superior in style and execution to any thing of Ben Jonson's. . . . They shew the utmost alacrity of invention in contriving ludicrous distresses, and the utmost spirit in bearing up against, or impatience and irritation under them. Don John, in the *Chances*, is the heroic in comedy.[92]

[91] *The British Theatre . . . printed under the authority of the managers from the prompt books. With Biographical and Critical Remarks by Mrs. Inchbald*, 25 vols. (London: Longman et al., 1808), vi, *The Chances*, 'Remarks'.
[92] *Complete Works*, vi. 48–9 (title italics added).

In *Lectures chiefly on the Dramatic Literature of the Age of Elizabeth* (1820) Hazlitt calls 'the *Chances,* the *Wild Goose Chase,* and *Rule a Wife and Have a Wife*' the best of the comedies of 'Beaumont and Fletcher',[93] but *The Chances* is not among the plays to which he devotes detailed commentary.

Writing a generation later in his introduction to *The Works of Beaumont and Fletcher,* the Revd Alexander Dyce, though dealing with the original 1647 text, ranked *The Chances* just below the best of Fletcher's work, and expressed no moral outrage. 'Don John is a good picture of a gay, frank, impetuous, honourable gallant; and his friend, the less mercurial Don Frederick, is equally well delineated. The landlady Gillian is a rich specimen of the grotesque.'[94] Dyce admired the 'throng of incidents' and 'such sprightliness and ease of dialogue', and so lamented the play's disappearance from the repertory:

At the beginning of the present century *The Chances* (as altered by the Duke of Buckingham and Garrick) was still on the list of 'acting plays': somewhat more than twenty years ago, when the rage for musical entertainments had seized the public, it was degraded into a flimsy opera; and most probably, it will never again in any shape 'revisit the glimpses' of the lamps.

In this he guessed wrong, but even in the Garrick version the play was not calculated to sit well with a nineteenth-century audience, and the morals of this particular play were by no means the only problem. As Genest observed in 1832: 'for the last 40 or 50 years 2 only of Fletcher's plays have been on the acting list regularly—latterly even the *Chances* has been laid aside' (vi. 41).

## A NOTE ON THE PRESENTATION OF THE TEXT

For full discussion of textual history and policy, see the Transmissional History (p. 711). Readers should be aware of the somewhat unusual format adopted in this edition. Our main text presents the Buckingham version as it was first published in 1682. At the bottoms of pages we have printed variant readings in the 'Beaumont and Fletcher' Folio edition of 1647 (Buckingham's source), including some passages *in extenso* that were drastically rewritten. The reader may thus see exactly how Buckingham altered the original play. The source notes cease at the end of Act III because the last two acts are independent of Fletcher.

[93] *Complete Works,* vi. 261–2 (title italics added).
[94] *The Works of Beaumont and Fletcher,* ed. Alexander Dyce, 11 vols. (London: Edward Moxon, 1843–6), i, pp. lxiv–lxv.

# The Chances

## PROLOGUE.

*O* *f all men those have reason leaſt to care*
*     For being laugh'd at, who can laugh their share:*
*And that's a thing our Author's Apt to use*
*Upon occasion, when no man can chuse.*
*Suppose now at this inſtant one of you*                                        5
*Were tickled by a Fool, what would you do?*
*'Tis ten to one you'd laugh, here's juſt the case,*
*For there are Fools that tickle with their Face.*
*Your gay Fool tickles with his Dress, and Motions,*
*But your grave Fool of Fools, with silly Notions.*                        10
*Is it not then unjuſt that Fops should ſtill*
*Force one to laugh, and then take laughing ill?*
*Yet since perhaps to some it gives offence,*
*That men are tickled at the want of Sence;*
*Our Author thinks he takes the readieſt way*                              15
*To shew all he has laugh'd at here fair play.*
*For if ill writing be a folly thought,*
*Correcting ill is sure a greater fault.*
*Then Gallants laugh, but chuse the right place firſt,*
*For judging ill is of all faults the worſt.*                                    20

PROLOGUE. *Alternative text at ll. 251. A transcript of the prologue in the commonplace book of*
*George Ent the younger (d. 1679), Royal Society MS 83, p. 92, is virtually identical to the text pub-*
*lished in the 1682 quarto and was presumably derived from a closely related ancestor source.*

## Dramatis Personae*

*Duke of* Ferrara.

Petruchio, *Governour of* Naples.

Don John  ⎫
Don Frederick  ⎬ *two* Spanish *Gentlemen and Comerades.*

Antonio, *an old ſtout Gentleman, Kinsman to* Petruchio.

*Three Gentlemen, Friends to the Duke.*

*Two Gentlemen, Friends to* Petruchio.

Francisco, *a Musician,* Antonio's *Boy.*

Peter *and* Anthony, *two Servants to* Don John *and* Frederick.

*A Surgeon.*

<*Servant to* Antonio.>

<*Shopkeeper.*>

<*Constables and Officers.*>

WOMEN.

1 Conſtantia, *Siſter to* Petruchio, *and Miſtress to the Duke.*

*Gentlewoman, Servant to* 1 Conſtantia.

*Landlady to* Don John *and* Frederick.

2 Conſtantia, *a Whore to old* Antonio.

Mother *of* 2 Conſtantia.

<*Kinswoman* to the Mother of 2 Conſtantia.>

* Not present in Q1682; based on the version in the edition published by
R. Bentley (London, 1692) which was simply copied from the Beaumont and
Fletcher Folio of 1679. For editorial corrections, see the Transmissional History.
The characters in angle brackets have been added by the editors.

# The Chances.

ACT I. SCENE I.

*Enter* Peter *and* Anthony; *two Servingmen.*

*Peter.* Would we were remov'd from this Town (*Anthony*)
That we might taſte some quiet: for mine own part,
I'm almoſt melted with continual trotting
After Enquiries, Dreams, and Revelations,
Of who knows whom or where? serve wenching Soldiers,                 5
I'l serve a Prieſt in Lent firſt, and eat Bell-ropes.
    *Anth.* Thou art the froward'ſt Fool ——
    *Pet.*                              Why good tame *Anthony?*
Tell me but this; to what end came we hither?
    *Anth.* To wait upon our Maſters.
    *Pet.*                              But how *Anthony?*
Answer me that; resolve me there good *Anthony?*                      10
    *Anth.* To serve their Uses.
    *Pet.*                        Shew your Uses *Anthony.*
    *Anth.* To be employ'd in any thing.
    *Pet.*                              No *Anthony,*
Not any thing I take it; nor that thing
We travell to discover, like new Islands;
A salt Itch serve such uses; in things of moment,                    15
Concerning things I grant ye, not things errant,
Sweet Lady's things, and things to thank the Surgeon:
In no such things sweet *Anthony*; put case ——
    *Anth.* Come, come, all will be mended: this invisible Woman
Of infinite report for Shape and Beauty,                             20
That bred us all this trouble to no purpose,
They are determin'd now no more to think on.

0.1 ACT I. SCENE I.] *Actus primus. Scæna prima.*      0.2 *Enter* Peter *and* Anthony; *two
Servingmen*] *Enter two Serving-men*, Peter *and* Anthony      5 Soldiers,] soldiers, | That
know no other Paradice but Plackets:      20 Beauty] vertue      22 on.] on, | But fall
close to their studies.

*Pet.*  Were there ever
Men known to run mad with Report before?
Or wander after that they know not where                    25
To find? or if found, how to enjoy? are mens brains
Made now adays of malt, that their affections
Are never sober? but like drunken people
Founder at every new fame? I do believe
That men in love are ever drunk, as drunken men             30
Are ever loving.
  *Anth.*  Prethee be thou sober,
And know that they are none of those, not guilty
Of the least vanity of love, only a doubt
Fame might too far report, or rather flatter
The Graces of this Woman, made them curious                35
To find the truth, which since they find so
Lock't up from their Searches, they are now resolv'd
To give the wonder over.
  *Pet.*    Would they were resolv'd
To give me some new shooes too: for I'l be sworn
These are e'n worn out to the reasonable souls             40
In their good Worships business: and some Sleep
Would not do much amiss, unless they mean
To make a Bell-man of me: here they come.     [*Exeunt.*

   *Enter* Don John *and* Frederick.

---

23 Were] Was  25 wander] wonder  29 believe] ~ too  36–7 so | Lock't] so
blotted | And lock'd  37 resolv'd] setled  38 over] ever  resolv'd] setled
43 of me:]
        on me: and what now
  Meane they to study, *Anthony*, Morall Philosophy
  After their mar-all women?
   *An.* Mar a fooles head.
   *Pet.* 'Twill mar two fooles heads, & they take not heed,
  Besides the Giblets to 'em.
   *An.* Will you walke Sir,
  And talke more out of hearing? your fooles head
  May chance to finde a wooden night-cap else.
   *Pet.* I never lay in any.   { *Enter Don John*
   *An.* Then leave your lying,  { *and Fredrick.*
  And your blinde Prophesying:
43 here they come.] ~ ~ ~, | You had best tell them as much. | *Pet.* I am no tell-tale.
43.1 SD *marginal in the preceding dialogue before Exeunt in F.*

*Joh.* I would we could have seen her tho: for sure
She muſt be some rare Creature, or Report lies,                              45
All mens reports too.
 *Fred.* I could well wish I had seen *Conſtantia*;
But since she is so conceal'd, plac'd where
No knowledge can come near her; so guarded
As 'twere impossible, tho known, to reach her,                              50
I have made up my belief.
 *Joh.*      Hang me from this hour,
If I more think upon her,
But as she came a ſtrange Report unto me,
So the next Fame shall lose her.
 *Fred.*     'Tis the next way:
But whither are you walking?
 *Joh.*     My old round                    55
After my meat and then to bed.
 *Fred.*     'Tis healthfull.
 *Joh.* Will not you ſtir?
 *Fred.*    I have a little business.
 *Joh.* I'd lay my life this Lady ſtill ——
 *Fred.*      Then you wou'd lose it.
 *Joh.* Pray let's walk together.
 *Fred.*     Now I cannot.
 *Joh.* I have something to impart.
 *Fred.*     An hour hence                 60
I will not miss to meet ye.
 *Joh.*    Where?
 *Fred.*     I'th high ſtreet;
For not to lye, I have a few devotions
To do firſt, then I am yours.
 *Joh.*    Remember.    [*Exeunt.*


[I. ii]     SCENE II.

   *Enter* Petruchio, Antonio, *and two* Gentlemen.

47 Constantia] her   48 plac'd where | No] so beyond venture | Kept and preserv'd
from view, so like a Paradice, | Plac't where no   52 her,] ~, or believe her,
53 strange] strong  54 lose] loose  58 I'd lay] Upon  wou'd lose] will loose
61 ye] you  0.2 Gentlemen] *Gent.*

*Ant.* Cut his wind-pipe, I say.

1. *Gent.*                    Fie *Antonio*.

*Ant.* Or knock his brains out firſt, and then forgive him.
If you do thruſt, be sure it be to th' hilts,
A Surgeon may see throw him.

1. *Gent.*                    You are too violent.

2. *Gent.* Too open, undiscreet.

*Petr.*                    Am I not ruin'd?          5
The Honour of my House crack'd? my Blood poyson'd?
My Credit and my Name?

2. *Gent.*                    Be sure it be so,
Before ye use this violence.  Let not Doubt
And a suspeſting Anger so much sway ye,
Your wisdom may be queſtion'd.

*Ant.*                    I say kill him,          10
And then dispute the cause; cut off what may be,
And what is, shall be safe:

2. *Gent.*                    Hang up a true man,
Because 'tis possible he may be thievish:
Alas, is this good Juſtice?

*Pet.*                    I know as certain
As Day muſt come again; as cleer as Truth,          15
And open as Belief can lay it to me,
That I am basely wrong'd, wrong'd above recompence,
Maliciously abus'd, blaſted for ever
In Name and Honour, loſt to all remembrance,
But what is smear'd and shameful; I muſt kill him,          20
Necessity compells me.

1. *Gent.*                    But think better.

*Pet.*  There is no other Cure left: yet witness with me
All that is fair in man, all that is noble,
I am not greedy of this life I seek for,
Nor thirſt to shed mans blood; and would 'twere possible,          25
I wish it with my soul, so much I tremble
To offend the sacred Image of my Maker,
My Sword could only kill his Crimes; no 'tis
Honour, Honour my noble Friends, that Idol Honour,
That all the World now worships, not *Petruchio*,          30
Muſt do this Juſtice.

*Ant.*          Let it once be done,
And 'tis no matter, whether you or Honour,
Or both be accessary.
     2. *Gent.*          Do you weigh, *Petruchio*,
The value of the Person, power, and greatness,
And what this spark may kindle?
     *Pet.*                    To perform it,                    35
So much I am ty'd to Reputation,
And credit of my House, let it raise wild fires,
And ſtorms that toss me into everlaſting
Ruine, yet I muſt through; if ye dare side me.
     *Ant.*                         Dare?
     *Pet.* Y'are friends indeed, if not.
     2. *Gent.*               Here's none flies from you,     40
Do it in what design you please, we'l back ye.
     1. *Gent.* Is the cause so mortal, nothing but his life?
     *Pet.* Believe me,
A less Offence has been the Desolation
Of a whole Name.
     1. *Gent.*          No other way to purge it?          45
     *Pet.* There is, but never to be hop'd for.
     2. *Gent.*                    Think an Hour more,
And if then ye find no safer road to guide ye,
We'l set up our Reſts too.
     *Ant.*               Mine's up already,
And hang him for my part, goes less than life.
     2. *Gent.* If we see noble Cause, 'tis like our Swords     50
May be as free and forward as your Words.          [*Exeunt.*


[I. iii]          SCENE III.

*Enter* Don John.

     *Joh.* The civil order of this City *Naples*
Makes it belov'd, and honour'd of all Travellers,
As a moſt safe Retirement in all Troubles;

---

37–9 fires, . . . Yet] ~, | That all this Dukedcme [*sic*] smoak, and the stormes that tosse me |
Into the stormes of everlasting ruine, | ~          41 you] ye     ye.] ~ | 1. But then be sure yee
kill him.          42 1.*Gent.*] 2.     cause so] cause | So          49 part, goes] part, | Goes
1 City *Naples*] Towne *Bellonia*

Beside the wholsome Seat and noble temper
Of those Minds that inhabit it, safely wise                    5
And to all Strangers courteous: but I see
My Admiration has drawn night upon me,
And longer to expect my friend may pull me
Into suspition of too late a stirrer,
Which all good Governments are jealous of.                    10
I'l home, and think at liberty: yet certain,
'Tis not so far night, as I thought; for see,
A fair House yet stands open, yet all about it
Are close; and no lights stirring: there may be foul play.
I'l venture to look in: If there be Knaves,                    15
I may do a good Office.                    [*Woman within.*
   *Within.*          *Signior?*
   *John.*                    What? how is this?
   *Within.* Signior *Fabritio?*
   *John.*                    I'l go nearer.
   *Within.*                    *Fabritio?*
   *John.* This is a Womans tongue, here may be good done.
   *Within.* Who's there? *Fabritio?*
   *John.*                    I.
   *Within.*                    Where are you?
   *John.*                    Here.
   *Within.* O come for Heavens sake!                    20
   *John.* I must see what this means.

       *Enter* Woman *with a Child.*

   *Within.* I have stay'd this long hour for you, make no noise,
For things are in strange trouble here, be secret,
'Tis worth your care; be gone now, more eyes watch us,
Than may be for our safeties.
   *John.*                    Hark ye?
   *Within.*                    Peace:                    25
Goodnight.                    [*Exit.*
   *John.* She's gone, and I am loaden; fortune for me;
It weigh's well, and it feel's well; it may chance
To be some pack of worth: by th' Mass 'tis heavy;
If it be Coin or Jewels, It is worth welcome:                    30

---

6  courteous] vertuous          14 play] ~:          16–17 *Signior* . . . *Signior*] Signieur . . .
Signieur          19 there? *Fabritio?*] ~ ? | ~ ?          you] ye          23 trouble here] ~ : ~
24  be gone] begone          27 She's] She is          30 It is] 'tis

I'll ne'r refuse a Fortune: I am confident
'Tis of no common price: now to my Lodging:
If it be right, I'l bless this night.                           [*Exit.*

[I. iv]                      SCENE IV.

*Enter* Don Fredrick.

*Fred.*                          Tis ſtrange,
I cannot meet him; sure he has encounter'd
Some light o' love or other, and there means
To play at in and in for this night. Well *Don John*,
If you do spring a leak, or get an itch,                           5
Till you claw off your curl'd pate, thank your night walks:
You muſt be ſtill a boot-haleing: one round more,
Tho it be late, I'l venture to discover ye,
I do not like your out-leaps.                           [*Exit.*

[I. v]                       SCENE V.

*Enter* Duke *and three* Gentlemen.

*Duke.*   Welcom to Town, are ye all fit?
1. *Gent.*                          To point Sir.
*Duke.*   Where are the Horses?
2. *Gent.*                          Where they were appointed.
*Duke.*   Be private, and whatsoever Fortune
Offer it self, let us ſtand sure.
3. *Gent.*                          Fear us not.
E're you shall be endanger'd or deluded,                           5
We'l make a black night on't.
*Duke.*                          No more, I know it;
You know your Quarters?
1. *Gent.*                          Will you go alone Sir?
*Duke.*   Ye shall not be far from me, the leaſt Noise
Shall bring ye to my Rescue.
2. *Gent.*                          We are counsel'd.                [*Exeunt.*

33 be] hit        0.2 *Enter* Don] *Enter*        6 you] ye        7 boot-haleing] bootehalling
9 [*Exit.*] *not in* F        4 let us] let's        us not] not us        5 you] ye

[I. vi]          SCENE VI.

*Enter* Don John.

*John.*  Was ever man so paid for being curious?
Ever so bob'd for searching out Adventures,
As I am? did the Devil lead me? muſt I needs be peeping
Into mens Houses where I had no business,
And make my self a mischief? 'tis well carry'd;                    5
I muſt take other mens occasions on me,
And be I know not whom: moſt finely handled:
What have I got by this now? what's the purchase?
A piece of evening Arras work, a Child,
Indeed an Infidel: this comes of peeping:                         10
A lump got out of laziness; good white bread,
Let's have no bawling with ye: 's death, have I
Known Wenches thus long, all the ways of Wenches,
Their Snares and Subtilties? have I read over
All their School-learning, div'd into their Quiddits               15
And am I now bumfidled with a Baſtard?
Fetch't over with a card of five, and in my old daies,
After the dire Massacre of a Million
Of maidenheads? caught the common way, ith' night too
Under anothers name, to make the matter                          20
Carry more weight about it? well *Don John*,
You will be wiser one day, when ye've purchas'd
A Beavy of those Butter-prints together,
With searching out concealed Iniquities,
Without commission: why, it would never grieve me,                25
If I had got this Ginger-bread: never ſtirr'd me,
So I had a ſtroke for't: 't had been juſtice,
Then to have kept it; but to raise a Dayry
For other mens Adulteries, consume my self in Candles,
And scouring work, in Nurses, Bells, and Babies,                  30
Only for Charity, for Meer I thank you,
A little troubles me: the leaſt Touch for it,

15 School-learning] Schoole learnings        17 my] mine        22 ye've] ye have
23 those] these        27 I had] ~ ~ had        30 work] works

Had but my Breeches got it, had contented me.
Whose e'r it is, sure 't had a wealthy Mother
For 'tis well cloath'd, and if I be not cozen'd,                    35
Well lin'd within: to leave it here were barbarous,
And ten to one would kill it: a worse sin
Than his that got it: well, I will dispose on't,
And keep it, as they keep deaths Heads in rings,
To cry *Memento* to me; no more Peeping:                           40
Now all the danger is, to qualify
The good old Gentlewoman, at whose House we live,
For she will fall upon me with a Catechism
Of four hours long: I muſt endure all;
For I will know this mother: come good wonder,                     45
Let you and I be jogging: your ſtarv'd trebble
Will waken the rude Watch else: all that be
Curious night walkers, may they find my fee.        [*Exit.*

[I. vii]                     SCENE VII.

                      *Enter* Frederick.

    *Fred.*   Sure he's gone home: I have beaten all the Purlews,
But cannot bolt him: if he be a bobbing
'Tis not my care can cure him: to morrow morning
I shall have further knowledge from a Surgeon ——
Where he lies moor'd to mend his Leaks.

                    *Enter* 1 Conſtantia.

    *Con.*                         I am ready,                      5
And through a world of dangers am flown to ye,
Be full of haſt and care, we are undone else:
Where are your people: which way muſt we travell?
For Heavens sake ſtay not here Sir.
    *Fred.*                     What may this prove?
    *Con.*   Alas, I am miſtaken, loſt, undone,                     10
For ever perish'd, Sir for Heavens sake tell me,
Are ye a Gentleman?

---

37 worse] more        38 Than] Then        4 Surgeon] Surgeons        5a.1 *Enter* 1]
*Enter*            5b I am] I'me        9 Heavens] heave<*turned 'n'*>        11 perish'd,] ~.
Heavens] heaven

*Fred.*          I am.
*Con.*                    Of this place?
*Fred.* No, born in *Spain.*
*Con.*                    As ever you lov'd honour,
As ever your desires may gain their ends,
Do a poor wretched Woman but this Benefit,                          15
For I am forc't to truſt ye.
     *Fre.*                    Y'ave charm'd me,
Humanity and Honor bids me help ye;
And if I fail your truſt ——
     *Con.*                    The time's too dangerous
To ſtay your proteſtations: I believe ye,
Alas, I muſt believe ye: From this place,                            20
Good noble Sir, remove me inſtantly.
And for a time, where nothing but your self,
And honeſt Conversation may come near me,
In some secure place settle me. What I am,
And why thus boldly I commit my credit                               25
Into a Stranger's hand, the fears and dangers,
That force me to this wild course, at more leisure
I shall reveal unto you.
     *Fre.*                    Come be hearty,
He muſt ſtrike through my life that takes you from me.    [*Exeunt.*


[I. viii]                    SCENE VIII.

               *Enter* Petruchio, Antonio, *and two* Gentlemen.

*Pet.* He will sure come.   Are ye all well arm'd?
*An.*                                        Never fear us.
Here's that will make 'em dance without a fiddle.
     *Pet.* We are to look for no weak Foes, my Friends,
Nor unadvised ones.
     *An.*                    Beſt Gameſters make the beſt Play,
We shall fight close and home then.
     I. *Gent.*                    *Antonio,*                          5
You are a thought too bloody.

---

29 takes | You] takes ye          *Exeunt.*] *Exi*          0.2 Gentlemen] *Gent.*
1 ye all] yee          4 Play] game          5 home] handsome

*An.*                    Why? all Physicians
And penny Almanacks allow the opening
Of Veins this Month: Why do ye talk of bloody?
What come we for, to fall to cuffs for apples?
What would you make the Cause a Cudgel-Quarrel?          10
    *Pet.* Speak softly, gentle Cosin.
    *An.*                    I will speak truly;
What should men do ally'd to these Disgraces,
Lick o're his Enemy, sit down, and dance him?
    2. *Gent.* You are as far o' th' Bow Hand now.
    *An.*                         And cry,
That's my fine Boy, thou wilt do so no more Child.          15
    *Pet.* Here are no such cold pities.
    *An.*                    By St. *Jaques*,
They shall not find me one: Here's old tough *Andrew*,
A special Friend of mine, and he but hold,
I'll strike 'em such a Horn-pipe: knocks I come for,
And the best blood I light on; I profess it,          20
Not to scare Costermongers; if I lose my own,
My audit's lost, and farwell five and fifty.
    *Pet.* Let's talk no longer, place your selves with silence,
As I directed ye; and when time calls us,
As ye are Friends, so shew your selves.
    *An.*                    So be it.          [*Exeunt.*   25

[I. ix]                    SCENE IX.

*Enter* Don John *and his* Land-Lady.

    *Land.* Nay Son if this be your regard.
    *Jo.*                    Good Mother.
    *Land.* Good me no goods, your Cousin and your self
Are welcome to me, whilst you bear your selves

10 you] ye    Quarrel?] ~ ?
          On what termes stands this man? is not his honour
          Open'd to his hand, and pickt out like an Oyster?
          His credit like a quart pot knockt together,
          Able to hold no liquor? cleare but this point.
11 I will] Ile          14 try] crie          21 scare] scarre    lose] loose    my] mine
22 My] Mine

Like honeſt and true Gentlemen: Bring hither
To my House, that have ever been reputed                          5
A Gentlewoman of a decent and a fair Carriage,
And so behaved my self?
   *Jo.*                    I know you have.
   *Land.*  Bring hither, as I say, to make my Name
Stink in my Neighbours Noſtrils? Your devices,
Your Brats got out of Alligant and broken Oaths?               10
Your Linsey-wolsey work, your Haſty-Puddings?
I foſter up your filtch'd Iniquities?
Y' are deceived in me, Sir, I am none
Of those receivers.
   *Jo.*            Have I not sworn unto you,
'Tis none of mine, and shew'd you how I found it?             15
   *Land.*  Ye found an easie fool that let you get it.
   *Jo.*  Will you hear me?
   *Land.*  Oaths? What care you for Oaths to gain your ends.
When ye are high and pamper'd? What Saint know ye?
Or what Religion, but your purpos'd lewdness,                   20
Is to be look'd for of ye? nay, I will tell ye,
You will then swear like accus'd Cut-purses,
As far off truth too; and lye beyond all Falconers:
I'm sick to see this dealing.
   *Jo.*                  Heaven forbid, Mother.
   *Land.*  Nay, I am very sick.
   *Jo.*                  Who waits there?
   *Pet.*                    Sir? (*Within.*)               25
   *Jo.*  Bring down the Bottle of *Canary* Wine.
   *Land.*  Exceeding sick, Heaven help me.
   *Jo.*                    Haſte ye sirrah,
I muſt e'en make her drunk; nay gentle Mother.
   *Land.*  Now fie upon ye, was it for this purpose
You fetch'd your Evening walks for your Devotions,            30
For this pretended holiness? no weather
Not before day could hold ye from the Mattins.
Were these your bo-peep Prayers? y'ave pray'd well,
And with a learned Zeal watch'd well too; your Saint
It seems was pleas'd as well: Still sicker, sicker.            35

---

6 and a] and          7 you] ye          9 devices] Devises          16 it.] ~, | She had better
have worne pasternes.          17 you] yee          18 care you] doe you care          23 off] of
25c *Pet.*] *Ant.*          30 Devotions] digestions          34 Zeal] ~:

*Enter* Peter *with a Bottle of Wine.*

*Jo.*  There is no talking to her till I have drench'd her.
Give me: Here Mother, take a good round draught,
'Twill purge Spleen from your Spirits: deeper Mother.
  *Land.*  I, I, Son; you imagine this will mend all.
  *Jo.*  All, I faith Mother.
  *Land.*                    I confess the Wine                    40
Will do his part.
  *Jo.*           I'll pledge ye.
  *Land.*                    But Son *John.*
  *Jo.*  I know your meaning Mother; touch it once more.
Alas you look not well, take a round draught,
It warms the blood well, and restores the colour,
And then we'll talk at large.
  *Land.*                    A civil Gentleman?                    45
A stranger? one the Town holds a good regard of?
  *Jo.*  Nay I will silence thee there.
  *Land.*  One that should weigh his fair name? oh a Stitch!
  *Jo.*  There's nothing better for a stitch, good Mother,
Make no spare of it you love your health;                         50
Mince not the matter.
  *Land.*           As I said a Gentleman,
Lodge in my House? now Heaven's my comfort *Signior!*
  *Jo.*  I look'd for this.
  *Land.*  I did not think you would have us'd me thus:
A woman of my credit: one, heaven knows,                          55
That loves you but too tenderly.
  *Jo.*                    Dear Mother,
I ever found your kindness and acknowledg it.
  *Land.*  No, no, I am a fool to counsel ye. Where's the Infant?
Come, let's see your workmanship.
  *Jo.*                    None of mine Mother;
But there 'tis, and a lusty one.
  *Land.*                    Heav'n bless thee,                    60
Thou hadst a hasty making; but the best is,
'Tis many a good man's fortune; as I live,
Your own eyes *Signior*; and the nether Lip

35.1 Peter] Anthony      40 I faith] y'faith      47 silence thee] silence      56 loves]
lov'd

As like ye, as ye had spit it.
   *Jo.*            I am glad on't.
   *Land.*  Bless me, what things are these?
   *Jo.*                  I thought my labour     65
Was not all loſt, 'tis Gold, and these are Jewels,
Both rich, and right I hope.
   *Land.*              Well, well, Son *John*,
I see ye're a Wood-man, and can chuse
Your Deer, though it be i'th' dark, all your discretion
Is not yet loſt; this was well clap'd aboard:          70
Here I am with ye now, when as they say
Your pleasure comes with profit; when you muſt needs do,
Do where you may be done to, 'tis a wisdom
Becomes a young man well: be sure of one thing,
Lose not your Labour and your time together,        75
It seasons of a Fool, Son, time is precious,
Work wary whilſt you have it: since you muſt traffick
Sometimes this slippery way, take sure hold *Signior*,
Trade with no broken Merchants, make your Lading,
As you would make your reſt, adventurously,        80
But with advantage ever.
   *Jo.*            All this time, Mother,
The Child wants looking to, wants meat and Nurses.
   *Land.*  Now blessing o' thy heart; it shall have all,
And inſtantly; I'l seek a Nurse my self, Son,
'Tis a sweet Child: ah my young *Spaniard*,        85
Take you no further care Sir.
   *Jo.*                Yes of these Jewels,
I muſt by your good leave Mother: these are yours,
To make your care the ſtronger: for the reſt
I'l find a Maſter; the gold for bringing up on't
I freely render to your charge.
   *Land.*             No more words,        90
Nor no more Children, (good Son) as you love me.
This may do well.
   *Jo.*          I shall observe your Morals,
But where's *Don Fredrick* (Mother?)

68 ye're] ye are     71 ye] you     72 you] ye     73 you] ye     75 Lose] Loose
77 you . . . you] ye . . . ye     82 to] too     83 heart] care     87 your good] your
93 *Fredrick*] *Ferdinand*

*Land.*                    Ten to one
About the like adventure: he told me
He was to find you out.                    [*Exit.*
    *Jo.*                    Why should he ſtay thus?            95
There may be some ill chance in't: Sleep I will not,
Before I have found him: now this Woman's pleas'd,
I'le seek my Friend out, and my care is eas'd.            [*Exit.*


[I. x]                    SCENE X.

                    *Enter* Duke *and three* Gentlemen.

    1. *Gen.*  Believe Sir, 'tis as possible to do it,
As to remove the City; the main Faction,
Swarm through the Streets like *Hornets*, and with angers
Able to ruine States, no safety left us,
Nor means to die like men, if inſtantly            5
You draw not back again.
    *Du.*                    May he be drawn,
And quarter'd too, that turns now; were I surer
Of death than thou art of thy fears, and with deaths
More than those fears are too!
    1 *Gen.*                    Sir, I fear not.
    *Du.*  I would not break my vow, ſtart from my honor,            10
Because I may find danger; wound my Soul,
To keep my body safe.
    1 *Gen.*                    I speak not Sir,
Out of a baseness to ye.
    *Du.*                    No, nor do not
Out of a baseness leave me: what is danger
More than the weakness of our apprehensions?            15
A poor cold part o'th' Blood? who takes it hold of?
Cowards and wicked livers: valiant minds
Were made the Maſters of it, and as hearty Sea-men
In desperate ſtorms, ſtem with a little Rudder
The tumbling ruins of the Ocean,            20


0.2 *three* Gentlemen.] *Gent.*   3 and] arm'd   8 than] then   deaths] death   9 than] then
10 break] crack   13 ye] you   15 than] then

So with their cause and Swords do they do dangers.
Say we were sure to die all in this venture,
As I am confident again&t it: is there any
Among&t us of so fat a sense, so pamper'd,
Would chose luxuriously to ly abed,                            25
And purge away his Spirit, send his Soul out
In *Sugar*-sops , and Syrops? give me dying,
As dying ought to be, upon mine enemy,
Parting with mankind, by a man that's manly:
Let 'em be all the world; and bring along                      30
*Cain*'s Envy with 'em, I will on.
   2 *Gen.*                    You may Sir,
But with what safety?
   1 *Gen.*                Since 'tis come to dying,
You shall perceive, Sir, that here be those among&t us
Can die as decently as other men,
And with as little Ceremony: On brave Sir.                     35
   *Du.*  That's spoken heartily.
   1 *Gen.*                And he that flinches
May he die louzy in a ditch.
   *Du.*                No more dying,
There's no such danger in't: What's a clock?
   3 *Gen.*  Somewhat above your hour.
   *Du.*                        Away then quickly,
Make no noise, and no trouble will attend us.      [*Exeunt.*  40


[I. xi]                  SCENE XI.

*Enter* Frederick *and* Anthony *with a Candle.*

   *Fre.*  Give me the Candle: So, go you out that way.
   *An.*  What have we now to do?
   *Fre.*                    And o' your life sirrah,
Let none come near the door without my knowledge,
No not my Landlady nor my Friend.
   *An.*                    'Tis done Sir.
   *Fre.*  Nor any serious business that concerns me.              5
   *An.*  Is the wind there again?

25 chose] chuse    abed] a bed    33 Sir, that] sir,    38 in't] in it    0.2 Anthony]
Peter [*and until 'Exit'*]

*Fre.*                    Be gone.
*An.*                              I am Sir:                    [*Exit*
*Fre.*    Now enter without fear ——

Enter 1. Conſtantia *with a Jewel.*

And noble Lady

That safety and civility ye wish'd for
Shall truly here attend you: no rude tongue
Nor rough behaviour knows this place, no wishes                    10
Beyond the moderation of a man,
Dare enter here: your own desires and innocence,
Joyn'd to my vow'd obedience, shall proteſt ye.
　　*Con.*   Ye are truly noble,
And worth a womans truſt: let it become me,                       15
(I do beseech you Sir) for all your kindness,
To render with my thanks this worthless trifle;
I may be longer troublesome.
　　*Fre.*                    Fair Offices
Are ſtill their own rewards: Heaven bless me Lady
From selling civil courtesies: may it please ye                   20
If ye will force a favour to oblige me,
Draw but that Cloud aside, to satisfie me
For what good Angel I am engag'd.
　　*Con.*                    It shall be.
For I am truly confident ye are honeſt:
The piece is scarce worth looking on.
　　*Fre.*                    Truſt me,                          25
The abſtraſt of all beauty, soul of sweetness,
Defend me honeſt thoughts, I shall grow wild else.
What eyes are there, rather what little Heavens,
To ſtir mens contemplations? what a Paradise
Runs through each part she has? Good Blood be temperate:          30
I muſt look off: too excellent an objeſt
Confounds the Sense that sees it. Noble Lady,
If there be any further service to caſt on me,
Let it be worth my life, so much I honour ye,
Or the engagement of whole Families.                             35

---

7a.1  *SD follows 6c in F*    *Enter 1.*] *Enter*        13  ye.] you, | Were dangers more then
doubts.

*Con.* Your service is too liberal, worthy Sir,
Thus far I shall intreat.
 *Fre.*    Command me Lady.
You make your power too poor.
 *Con.*    That presently
With all convenient haſt you would retire
Unto the Street you found me in.
 *Fre.*    'Tis done.     40
 *Con.* There if you find a Gentleman oppreſt
With force and violence, do a mans office,
And draw your Sword to rescue him.
 *Fre.*    He's safe.
Be what he will, and let his Foes be Devils,
Arm'd with your beauty, I shall conjure 'em.    45
Retire, this Key will guide ye: all things necessary
Are there before ye.
 *Con.*   All my prayers go with ye.   [*Exit.*
 *Fre.* Ye clap on proof upon me: men say Gold
Does all, engages all, works through all dangers:
Now I say beauty can do more: The King's Exchequer,   50
Nor all his wealthy *Indies*, could not draw me
Through half those miseries this piece of pleasure
Might make me leap into: we are all like Sea-Cards,
All our endeavours and our motions,
(As they do to the North) ſtill point at beauty,   55
Still at the faireſt: for a handsom Woman,
(Setting my soul aside) it should go hard,
But I would ſtrain my body: yet to her,
Unless it be her own free gratitude,
Hopes ye shall dye, and thou tongue rot within me,   60
E're I infringe my faith: now to my rescue.   [*Exit.*


[II. i]    ACT II.  SCENE I.

 *Enter* Duke *pursu'd by* Petruchio, Antonio, *and that Faƈtion.*

 *Duke.* You will not all oppress me?
 *An.* Kill him i'th' wanton eye: Let me come to him.

45 beauty] pitty  57 aside] a side  0.1 ACT II. SCENE I.] *Actus Secundus. Scæna prima.*

*Duke.* Then you shall buy me dearly.
*Petr.*                                    Say you so Sir?
*An.* I say cut his Wezand, spoil his peeping:
Have at your love-sick heart Sir.

*Enter* Don John.

*Jo.*                          Sure 'tis fighting.                    5
My Friend may be engag'd: Fie Gentlemen,
This is unmanly odds.            ⌠Duke *falls*: Don John
                                 ⌡*beſtrides him.*
*An.*              I'll ſtop your mouth Sir.
*Jo.* Nay then have at thee freely:
There's a Plumb Sir to satisfie your longing.
*Petr.* Away: I hope I have sped him: here comes rescue.    10
We shall be endanger'd: where's *Antonio?*
*An.* I muſt have one thruſt more Sir.
*Jo.*                              Come up to me.
*An.* A mischief confound your fingers.
*Petr.*                              How is it?
*An.*                                    Well:
'Has given me my *Quietus eſt*; I felt him
In my small guts, I'm sure 'has feez'd me:              15
This comes of siding with you.
2 *Gent.*                    Can you go Sir?
*An.* I should go man, and my head were off,
Never talk of going.
*Petr.*          Come, all shall be well then.    ⌠*Trampling*
I hear more rescue coming.                        ⌡*within.*

*Enter the* Duke's *Faĕtion.*

*An.*                    Let's turn back then;
My scull's uncloven yet, let me but kill.              20
*Petr.* Away for heaven's sake with him.
*Jo.*                          How is it?
*Duke.*                              Well, Sir,
Only a little ſtagger'd.
*Du. Faĕt.*          Let's pursue 'em.

3 you] yee        7a.sd *SD marginal at 8 in F    falls*] ~ *down*        13 is it] is't
16b you] ye        17 off] of        18 {*Trampling* | *within.*] *Not in F*        19a.1 *SD*
*marginal at 18.1 in F*        21 heaven's] heaven        is it] is't

*Duke.* No not a man I charge ye: thank's good Coat,
Thou haſt sav'd me a shrew'd welcome: 'twas put home too,
With a good mind I'm sure on't.
    *Jo.*                 Are you safe then?        25
    *Duke.* My thanks to you brave Sir, whose timely valour,
And manly courtesie came to my rescue.
    *Jo.* Ye had foul play offer'd ye, and shame befall him
That can pass by oppression.
    *Duke.*          May I crave Sir,
But thus much honor more, to know your name?      30
And him I am so bound to?
    *Jo.*           For the Bond Sir,
'Tis every good man's tye: to know me further
Will little profit ye; I am a ſtranger,
My Country *Spain*, my name *Don John*, a Gentleman
That came abroad to travell.
    *Duke.*          I have heard Sir,        35
Much worthy mention of ye, yet I find
Fame short of what ye are.
    *Jo.*          You are pleased Sir,
To express your Courtesie: may I demand
As freely what you are, and what mischance
Caſt you into this danger?
    *Duke.*          For this present        40
I muſt desire your pardon: you shall know me
E're it be long Sir, and a nobler thanks,
Than now my Will can render.
    *Jo.*             Your Will's your own Sir.
    *Duke.* What is't you look for Sir, have you loſt any thing?
    *Jo.* Onely my hat i'th' Scuffle; sure these fellows      45
Were night-snaps.
    *Duke.*      No, believe, Sir: pray use mine,
For 'twill be hard to find your own now.
    *Jo.*             No Sir.
    *Duke.* Indeed ye shall, I can command another:
I do beseech you honor me.
    *Jo.*          Well Sir then I will,
And so I'll take my leave.

---

25 you] ye      35 came abroad to travell] lyes here for my study      43 Than] Then
44 you] yee      46 pray] ~ ye      49 you] ye    Well Sir then I will] I will sir

*Duke.*                    Within these few daies                    50
I hope I shall be happy in your knowledge.
Till when I love your memory.          [*Exit cum suis.*
    *Jo.*                    I yours.

                    *Enter* Frederick.

This is some noble fellow.
    *Fre.*                    'Tis his Tongue sure.
*Don John?*
    *Jo.*    Don Frederick?
    *Fre.*                    Y'are fairly met Sir?
I thought ye had been a Bat-fowling: prethee tell me,          55
What Revelations haſt thou had to night,
That home was never thought of?
    *Jo.*                    Revelations?
I'll tell thee *Frederick.*  But before I tell thee,
Settle thy underſtanding.
    *Fre.*                    'Tis prepared Sir.
    *Jo.*  Why then mark what shall follow. This night *Frederick,*          60
This bawdy night.
    *Fre.*          I thought no less.
    *Jo.*                    This blind night,
What doſt thou think I have got?
    *Fre.*                    The Pox it may be.
    *Jo.*  Would 'twere no worse: ye talk of Revelations,
I have got a Revelation will reveal me
An errant Coxcomb whil'ſt I live.
    *Fre.*                    What is't?          65
Thou haſt loſt nothing?
    *Jo.*                    No, I have got I tell thee.
    *Fre.*  What haſt thou got?
    *Jo.*                    One of the Infantry,
A Child.
    *Fre.*  How?
    *Jo.*          A chopping Child, man.
    *Fre.*                    Give you joy Sir.
    *Jo.*  A lump of lewdness *Frederick* that's the truth on't:
This Town's abominable.

---

52a.sd *cum suis*] *Duke, &c*    54 Y'are] Ye' are    62 dost thou] dost    65 errant]
arrant    whil'st] while    68 you] ye

*Fre.*                    I ſtill told ye *John*          70
Your whoring muſt come home; I councell'd ye:
But where no grace is ——
　　*Jo.*                    'Tis none of mine, man.
　　*Fre.*    Answer the Parish so.
　　*Jo.*                    Cheated introth.
Peeping into a house, by whom I know not,
Nor where to find the place again: no *Frederick*          75
'Tis no poor one,
That's my beſt comfort, for 't has brought about it
Enough to make it man.
　　*Fre.*                    Where is't?
　　*Jo.*                    At home.
　　*Fre.*    A saving Voyage: But what will you say *Signior*,
To him that searching out your serious worship,          80
Has met a ſtranger fortune?
　　*Jo.*                    How good *Frederick?*
A militant Girle to this Boy would hit it.
　　*Fre.*    No mine's a nobler venture: what do you think Sir
Of a diſtressed Lady, one whose beauty
Would over-sell all *Italy?*
　　*Jo.*                    Where is she ——          85
　　*Fre.*    A Woman of that rare behaviour,
So qualify'd, as Admiration
Dwells round about her: of that perfeƈt Spirit ——
　　*Jo.*    I marry Sir.
　　*Fre.*                    That admirable Carriage,
That sweetness in discourse; young as the Morning,          90
Her blushes ſtaining his.
　　*Jo.*                    But where's this Creature?
Shew me but that.
　　*Fre.*                    That's all one she's forth-coming.
I have her sure Boy.
　　*Jo.*                    Heark ye *Frederick*,
What truck betwixt my infant?
　　*Fre.*                    'Tis too light Sir,
Stick to your charge good *Don John*, I am well.          95
　　*Jo.*    But is there such a Wench?

---

72 of ] o'          76 'Tis] Had I but kist the ring fort; 'tis          82 Girle] ~ now
95 charge] charges

*Fre.*                              First tell me this,
Did you not lately as you walk'd along,
Discover People that were armed and likely
To do offence?

*Jo.*           Yes marry, and they urg'd it
As far as they had spirit.

*Fre.*                          Pray go forward.                    100

*Jo.*   A Gentleman I found engag'd amongst 'em,
It seems of noble breeding, I'm sure brave mettal,
As I return'd to look you I set in to him,
And without hurt (I thank Heaven) rescu'd him.

*Fre.*   My work's done then:                                105
And now to satisfie you there is a Woman,
Oh *John*, there is a Woman ——

*Jo.*                          Oh where is she?

*Fre.*   And one of no less worth than I told ye;
And which is more, faln under my protection.

*Jo.*   I am glad of that; forward sweet *Frederick*.      110

*Fre.*   And which is more than that, by this nights wandring,
And which is most of all, she is at home too Sir.

*Jo.*   Come let's be gone then.

*Fre.*                          Yes, but 'tis most certain,
You canot see her *John*.

*Jo.*              Why?

*Fre.*                      She has sworn me,
That none else shall come near her: not my Mother        115
Till some doubts are clear'd.

*Jo.*                  Not look upon her?
What Chamber is she in?

*Fre.*              In ours.

*Jo.*                      Let's go I say:
A Woman's Oaths are wafers, break with making,
They must for modesty a little: we all know it.

*Fre.*   No I'll assure ye Sir.

*Jo.*                      Not see her?                   120
I smell an old dog trick of yours, well *Frederick*, Ye talk'd to me of
whoring, let's have fair play,
Square dealing I would wish ye.

---

97 you . . . you] ye . . . ye        99 marry] mary        104 him,] ~, And came my selfe off
safe too.        108 than I told] then *I* assure        111 than] then        116 some] ~ few
120 ye] you

*Fre.*                    When 'tis come
(Which I know never will be) to that issue,
Your Spoon shall be as deep as mine Sir.
    *Jo.*                    Tell me,                              125
And tell me true, is the cause honourable?
Or for your ease?
    *Fre.*          By all our friendship, *John*,
'Tis honeſt and of great end.
    *Jo.*                    I am answer'd:
But let me see her though: leave the door open
As you go in.
    *Fre.*          I dare not.
    *Jo.*                    Not wide open,                       130
But juſt so, as a jealous Husband
Would level at his wanton Wife through.
    *Fre.*          That courtesie,
If ye desire no more, and keep it ſtriſtly,
I dare afford ye: come, 'tis now near Morning.          [*Exeunt.*   135


[II. ii]                    SCENE II.

            *Enter* Peter *and* Anthony.

*Peter.*   Nay, the old Woman's gone too.
    *Anth.*                    She's a Catterwauling
Amongſt the Gutters; but conceive me, *Peter*,
Where our good Maſters should be?
    *Peter.*                    Where they should be,
I do conceive, but where they are, good *Anthony* ——
    *Anth.*   I, there it goes: my Maſter's bo-peep with me,          5
With his sly popping in and out again,
Argu'd a Cause.                              [*Lute sounds.*

128 I] *Ioh.* ~          130 you] yee          2 Amongst] Among          7a.SD *Lute sounds*] ~ ~ |
*within*          7 Cause.]
           ~, a frippery cause.
        *Pet.*  Beleeve me,
      They bear up with some carvell.
        *Ant.*  I doe believe thee,
      For thou hast such a Master for that chase
      That till he spend his maine Mast—
        *Pet.*  Pray remember , <*cont.*>

                        Hark.
*Peter.*            What?
*Anth.*                    Doſt not hear a Lute?
Agen?
    *Peter.*   Where is't?
    *Anth.*            Above, in my Maſter's Chamber.
    *Peter.*   There's no Creature: he hath the key himself man.
    *Anth.*   This is his Lute: let him have it.     [*Sing within a little.*   10
    *Peter.*   I grant ye; but who ſtrikes it?
    *Anth.*   An admirable Voyce too, hark ye.
    *Peter.*                         *Anthony,*
Art sure we are at home?
    *Anth.*                Without all doubt *Peter.*
    *Peter.*   Then this muſt be the Devil.
    *Anth.*                          Let it be.
Good Devil sing again: O dainty Devil,                         15
*Peter,* believe it, a moſt delicate Devil,
The sweeteſt Devil ——

                *Enter* Frederick *and* Don John.

    *Fred.*                If you would leave peeping.
    *Jo.*   I cannot by no means.
    *Fred.*                Then come in softly,
And as you love your Faith, presume no further
Than ye have promised.
    *Jo.*                *Basco.*                          20
    *Fred.*   What make you up so early Sir?
    *Jo.*   You Sir, in your Contemplations.
    *Peter.*   O pray ye peace Sir.
    *Fred.*                Why peace Sir?
    *Peter.*                          Do ye hear?
    *Jo.*   'Tis your Lute.  She's playing on't.
    *Anth.*                The House is haunted Sir,
For this we have heard this half year.
    *Fred.*                     Ye saw nothing?                25

        Your courtesie good *Anthony,* and withall,
        How long 'tis since your Master sprung a leak,
        He had a sound one since he came.
    11 ye] you        14 be.] ~. *Sing agen.*        17 you would] ye could        19 you] ye
    20 Than] Then    *Basco*] *Basto*        23c ye] you        24 Lute. She's] ~. | *Fred.* Pray yee
    speak softly. | ~

*Anth.*  Not I.
*Peter.*          Nor I Sir.
*Fred.*               Get you our Breakfaſt then,
And make no words on't; we'll undertake this Spirit,
If it be one.
*Anth.*    This is no Devil *Peter.*
Mum, there be Bats abroad.                    [*Exit ambo.*
*Fred.*               Stay, now she sings.
*Jo.*  An Angels Voyce I'll swear.
*Fred.*               Why did'ſt thou shrug so?          30
Either allay this heat; or as I live
I will not truſt ye.
*Jo.*          Pass: I warrant ye.          [*Exeunt.*

                *Enter* 1. Conſtantia.

*Conſt.*  To curse those Stars that men say govern us,
To rail at Fortune, to fall out with my Fate,
And tax the general World, will help me nothing:          35
Alas, I am the same ſtill, neither are they
Subjeɛt to helps, or hurts; our own desires
Are our own Fates, and our own Stars, all our Fortunes,
Which as we sway 'em, so abuse or bless us.

            *Enter* Frederick, *and* Don John *Peeping.*

*Fred.*  Peace to your Meditations.
*Jo.*                    Pox upon ye.          40
Stand out o'th' Light.
*Conſt.*          I crave your mercy Sir;
My mind o'r charg'd with care made me unmannerly.
*Fred.*  Pray ye set that mind at reſt, all shall be perfeɛt.
*Jo.*  I like the Body rare; a handsome Body,
A wondrous handsome Body; would she would turn:          45
See, and that spightful puppy be not got
Between me and my light again.
*Fred.*               'Tis done,
As all that you command shall be: the Gentleman
Is safely off all danger.

---

26 you] us          28 *Peter.*] ~. *Sing.*          29.sd *Exit ambo*] *Exeunt Servants*
32.1 *Enter* 1.] *Enter*          34 Fortune, to] fortune,          35 tax] taſke          38 Fates, and]
*fates,*

*Jo.*                    Rare Creature!
*Conſt.*  How shall I thank ye Sir? how satisfie?                 50
*Fred.*  Speak softly gentle Lady, all's rewarded,
Now does he melt like Marmalad.
  *Jo.*                              Nay, 'tis certain,
Thou art the sweeteſt Woman that eyes e'r look'd on.
  *Fred.*  None diſturb'd ye?
  *Conſt.*  Not any Sir, nor any sound came near me,           55
I thank your care.
  *Fred.*            'Tis well.
  *Jo.*                        I would fain pray now,
But the Devil, and that Flesh there, o'th' World,
What are we made to suffer?
  *Fred.*                            He'll enter;
Pull in your head and be hang'd.
  *Jo.*                              Hark ye *Frederick*,
I have brought you home your Pack-Saddle.
  *Fred.*                                Pox upon ye.        60
  *Conſt.*  Nay, let him enter: fie my Lord the Duke,
Stand peeping at your Friends.
  *Fred.*                      Ye are cozen'd Lady,
Here is no Duke.
  *Conſt.*        I know him full well *Signior.*
  *Jo.*  Hold thee there Wench.
  *Fred.*                    This mad-brain'd fool will spoyl all.
  *Conſt.*  I do beseech your Grace come in.
  *Jo.*                                My Grace,              65
There was a Word of Comfort.
  *Fred.*                    Shall he enter,
Who e'r he be?
  *Jo.*          Well follow'd *Frederick*.
  *Conſt.*  With all my heart.

                *Enter* Don John.

  *Fred.*                      Come in then.
  *Jo.*                              Bless ye Lady.
  *Fred.*  Nay, ſtart not, though he be a Stranger to ye.
He's of a Noble ſtrain, my Kinsman, Lady,                       70

49 Rare Creature!] *O de dios.*      53 that eyes] I    on.] ~: | I hope thou art not honest.
60 you] ye      68a.1 *SD at* 68b *in* F

My Country man, and Fellow-Traveller,
One bed contains us ever, one purse feeds us,
And one Faith free between us; do not fear him,
He's truly honeſt.
 *Jo.*   That's a lie.
 *Fred.*      And truſty:
Beyond your wishes: valiant to defend,     75
And modeſt to converse with, as your blushes.
 *Jo.* Now may I hang my self; this commendation
Has broke the neck of all my Hopes; for now
Muſt I cry, no forsooth, and I forsooth, and surely,
And truly as I live, and as I am honeſt    80
'Has done these things for nonce too; for he knows,
Like a moſt envious Rascal as he is,
I am not honeſt, this way: h'as watch'd his time,
But I shall quit him.
 *Conſt.*   Sir, I credit ye.
 *Fred.* Go, salute her *John.*
 *Jo.*     Plague o' your Commendations. 85
 *Conſt.* Sir, I shall now desire to be a trouble.
 *Jo.* Never to me, sweet Lady; thus I seal
My Faith, and all my Service.
 *Conſt.*    One word *Signior.*
 *Jo.* Now 'tis impossible I should be honeſt.
What points she at? my Leg I warrant, or   90
My well-knit Body: sit faſt *Don Frederick.*
 *Fred.* 'Twas given him by that Gentleman
You took such care of; his own being loſt i'th' Scuffle.
 *Conſt.* With much joy may he wear it: 'tis a right one
I can assure ye Gentlemen; and right happy  95
May he be in all fights for that Noble Service.
 *Fred.* Why do ye blush?
 *Conſt.*    'T had almoſt cozened me,
For not to lye, when I saw that, I look'd for
Another owner of it; but 'tis well.   *[Knock within.*
 *Fred.* Who's there? Stand ye a little close: come in Sir. 100

---

83 honest, this] honest, nor desire to be, | Especially this  85 salute] kisse 88 *Signior*]
Signeur  89–90 honest. | What] honest, | She kisses with a conjuration | Would make
the devill dance: what  90 at? my] at? | My  90–1 or | My] or my  91 Body:
sit] body: | Sit  95 Gentlemen] Gentleman  96 he] you  Noble] faire
99 owner] Master

*Enter* Anthony.

Now what's the News with you?

   *Anth.*   There is a Gentleman without, would speak
With *Don John.*

   *Jo.*   Who Sir?

   *Anth.*   I do not know Sir, but he shews a man          105
Of no mean reckoning.

   *Fred.*             Let him shew his Name,
And then return a little wiser.          [*Exit* Anthony.
How do you like her *John?*

   *Jo.*            As well as you *Frederick,*
For all I am honeſt; you shall find it too.

   *Fred.*   Art thou not honeſt?

   *Jo.*            Art thou an Ass?          110
And modeſt as her blushes? What a blockhead
Would e'r have popp'd out such a dry Apology,
For his dear Friend? and to a Gentlewoman,
A Woman of her Youth, and Delicacy,
They are Arguments to draw them to abhor us.          115
An honeſt moral man; 'tis for a Conſtable:
A handsome man, a wholesome man, a tough man,
A liberal man, a likely man, a man
Made up like *Hercules,* unslack'd with Service:
The same to night, to morrow night, the next night,          120
And so to perpetuity of pleasures,
These had been things to hearken to, things catching;
But you have such a spiced consideration,
Such Qualmes upon your Worship's Conscience,
Such Chilblains in your blood, that all things prick ye,          125
Which Nature, and the liberal World makes Cuſtom,
And nothing but fair Honour, O sweet Honour,
Hang up your Eunuch Honour: That I was truſty,
And valiant, were things well put in; but modeſt!
A modeſt Gentleman! O wit where waſt thou?          130

   *Fred.*   I am sorry *John.*

   *Jo.*          My Lady's Gentlewoman
Would laugh me to a School-boy, make me blush

---

100.1 *SD marginal at 100 (after* 'there?') *in F.*      107 wiser.] ~. | *Ant.* Well Sir.
109 it] ~ so    119 unslack'd] unslak'd    122 to] too    125 prick] pinch

With playing with my Cod-piece-point: fie on thee,
A man of thy discretion.
 *Fred.*    It shall be mended;
And henceforth ye shall have your due.

    *Enter* Anthony.

 *Jo.*     I look for't:   135
How now, who is't?
 *Anth.*   A Gentleman of this City,
And calls himself *Petruchio.*
 *Jo.*    I'll attend him.

    *Enter* Conſtantia.

 *Conſt.* How did he call himself?
 *Fred.*     *Petruchio,*
Does it concern ye ought?
 *Conſt.*   O Gentlemen,
The hour of my deſtruction is come on me,  140
I am discover'd, loſt, left to my ruine:
As ever ye hay pity ——
 *Jo.*   Do not fear,
Let the great Devil come, he shall come through me firſt:
Loſt here, and we about ye?
 *Fred.*   Fall before us?
 *Conſt.* O my unfortunate eſtate, all angers  145
Compar'd to his, to his ——
 *Fred.*    Let his, and all mens,
Whil'ſt we have power and life, ſtand up for Heavens sake.
 *Conſt.* I have offended Heaven too; yet Heaven knows ——
 *Jo.* We are all evil:
Yet Heaven forbid we should have our deserts.  150
What is a?
 *Conſt.* Too too near to my offence Sir:
O he will cut me piece-meal:
 *Fred.*    'Tis no Treason?
 *Jo.* Let it be what it will: if a cut here,
I'll find him cut-work.

136 City,] towne  137b.1 *SD at 137a in* F  139 ye] you  142 hay] had
143 me: first] me:  147 Heavens] heaven

*Fred.*                    He muſt buy you dear,
With more than common lives.
   *Jo.*                    Fear not, nor weep not:                    155
By Heaven I'll fire the Town before ye perish,
And then the more the merrier, we'll jog with ye.
   *Fred.*   Come in, and dry your eyes.
   *Jo.*                    Pray no more weeping:
Spoyl a sweet Face for nothing? my return
Shall end all this I warrant ye.
   *Conſt.*                    Heaven grant it may.                    [*Exeunt.*   160


[II. iii]                    SCENE III.

*Enter* Petruchio *with a Letter.*

   *Petr.*   This man should be of Quality and worth
By *Don Alvaras* Letter, for he gives
No slight recommendations of him:
Ile e'en make use of him.

*Enter*  Don John.

   *Jo.*                    Save ye Sir: I am sorry
My business was so unmannerly, to make ye                    5
Wait thus long here.
   *Petr.*                    Occasions muſt be serv'd Sir:
But is your name *Don John?*
   *Jo.*                    It is Sir:
   *Petr.*                    Then,
Firſt for your own brave sake I muſt embrace ye:
Next, for the credit of your noble Friend
*Hernanda de Alvara*, make ye mine:                    10
Who lays his charge upon me in this Letter
To look ye out, and
Whil'ſt your occasions make you resident
In this place, to supply ye, love and honor ye;
Which had I known sooner ——

160 ye] you    it may] it    1–4 Quality . . . use of him.]
               speciall rank:
      For these commends carry no common way,
      No slight worth with 'em:
      A shall be he.
9 for] from    10 *Hernanda*] *Hernando*    12 and] ~ for the goodnesse in yee,
13 you] yee

*Jo.*                    Noble Sir,                                    15
You'll make my thanks too poor: I wear a Sword Sir,
And have a Service to be ſtill dispos'd of
As you shall please command it.
    *Petr.*  That manly curtesie is half my business: Sir,
And to be short, to make ye know I honor ye,                           20
And in all points believe your worth like Oracle,
This day *Petruchio*,
A man that may command the ſtrength of this place,
Hazard the boldeſt Spirits, hath made choice
Only of you, and in a noble Office.                                    25
    *Jo.*  Forward, I am free to entertain it.
    *Petr.*                    Thus then:
I do beseech ye mark me.
    *Jo.*                    I shall Sir.
    *Petr.*  *Ferrara*'s Duke, would I might call him worthy,
But that he has raz'd out from his Family,
As he has mine with Infamy, This man,                                  30
Rather this powerful Monſter, we being left
But two of all our House, to ſtock our Memoires,
My Siſter *Conſtantia* and my self; with Arts and Witchcrafts,
Vows, and such Oaths Heaven has no mercy for,
Drew to dishonour this weak Maid, by ſtealth,                          35
And secret passages I knew not of,
Oft he obtain'd his wishes, oft abus'd her,
I am asham'd to say the reſt: This purchas'd,
And his hot blood allay'd, he left her,
And all our Name to ruine.
    *Jo.*                    This was foul play,                       40
And ought to be rewarded so.
    *Petr.*                    I hope so;
He scap'd me yeſternight:
Which if he dare again adventure for ——
    *Jo.*  Pray Sir what Commands have you to lay on me?

19 That] Gentle sir, | ~    business: Sir,] Businesse:        21–2 Oracle, | This] ~, |
              And how above my friends, which are not few,
              And those not slack, I estimate your vertues,
              Make your selfe understand, ~
27 Sir] doe it            32 Memoires] memories            33 Sister *Constantia*] Sister,
35 stealth] stealthes      39 allay'd, ] ~ as friends forsake us | At a miles end upon our way,
42–3 yesternight: | Which . . . againe] yester-night: which . . . | Againe        43 for ——] ~,
heaven pardon him, | I shall with all my heart.      44 *line var.*] For me, brave Signior, |
What do yee intend?

*Petr.*   Only thus; by word of mouth to carry him                 45
A Challenge from me, that so (if he have honor in him)
We may decide all difference between us.
   *Jo.*   Fair, and noble,
And I will do it home: when shall I visit ye?
   *Petr.*   Please you this afternoon, I will ride with ye;        50
For at a Caſtle six mile hence, we are sure
To find him.
   *Jo.*          I'll be ready.
   *Petr.*                    My man shall
Wait here, to conduĉt ye to my House.
   *Jo.*   I shall not fail ye Sir.                    [*Exit* Petruchio.

                  *Enter* Frederick.

   *Fred.*                     How now?
   *Jo.*   All's well, and better than thou could'ſt expeĉt, for this    55
Wench here is certainly no Maid; and I have hopes she is the same
that our two curious Coxcombs have been so long a hunting after.
   *Fred.*   Why do ye hope so?
   *Jo.*   Why? because firſt she is no Maid, and next because she's
handsome; there are two Reasons for you: now do you find out a       60

45–6  Only . . . him | A]
          Onely, faire sir, this trust,
          Which from the commendations of this Letter,
          I dare presume well placed, nobly to beare him
          By word of mouth a single
46  me, that so] me, | That man to man,            47  difference between us] difference
52–3  My man . . . House.] To attend ye, | My man shall wait: with all my love'       54  I]
My service      ye Sir] yee       54a  *SD at 53 in* F            55–68  well, and better . . . for all
this:]
          well: who dost thou think this wench is?
          Ghesse, and thou canst?
             *Fred.* I cannot.
             *Iohn.* Be it knowne then,
          To all men by these presents, this is she,
          She, she, and only she, our curious coxcombs
          Were errant two moneths after.
             *Fred.* Who, *Constantia?*
          Thou talk'st of Cocks and Bulls.
             *Ioh.* I talke of wenches,
          Of Cocks and Hens *Don Frerdick* [*sic*]; this is the Pullet
          We two went proud after.
             *Fred.* It cannot be.
             *Iohn* It shall be;
          Sister to *Don Petruchio*: I know all man. <*cont.*>

third, a better if you can. For take this *Frederick*, for a certain
Rule, since she loves the sport, she'll never give it over. And
therefore (if we have good luck) in time may fall to our shares.
    *Fred.* Very pretty Reasons indeed. But I thought you had known
some particular that made you conclude this to be the Woman.          65
    *Jo.* Yes, I know her name is *Constantia.*
    *Fred.* That now is something; but I cannot believe her
dishonest for all this: she has not one loose thought about her.
    *Jo.* It's no matter, she's loose i'th' hilts by Heaven. There has
been stirring, fumbling with Linnen, *Frederick.*                     70
    *Fred.* There may be such a slip.
    *Jo.* And will be *Frederick*, whil'st the old Game's afoot. I fear
the Boy too will prove hers I took up.
    *Fred.* Good circumstance may cure all this yet.
    *Jo.* There thou hit'st it *Frederick*, come let's walk in, and comfort   75
her; that she is here is nothing yet suspected. Anon I shall tell
thee why her Brother came, (who by this light is a noble Fellow)
and what honor he has done to me, a Stranger, in calling me to
serve him. There be Irons heating for some on my word *Frederick.*
                                                        [*Exeunt.*

        *Fred.* Now I beleeve.
        *Iohn* Goe to, there has been stirring,
    Fumbling with Linnen *Fredrick.*
        *Fred.* 'Tis impossible,
    You know her fame was pure as fire.
        *Ioh.* That pure fire
    Has melted out her maiden-head: she is crackt:
    We have all that hope of our side, boy.
        *Fred.* Thou tell'st me,
    To my imagination, things incredible:
68 she has not] I see no    about] in    69 It's no matter, she's] That's all one, | She is
69–70 There has ... *Frederick*] but the world must know | A faire way, upon vow of
marriage    72 *Frederick*, whil'st] *Fredrick*, | Whil'st    afoot] a foot    73 too will]
too | Will    hers] ~ too    74 circumstance may] circumstance | May    75 *Frederick*,
come] *Fredrick*: | Come,    76 that she is] her being    here is] here | Is    I shall] Ile
77 thee why] thee | Wherefore    light is] light | Is    a] ~ brave    78 honor he has]
honour | H'as    Stranger, in calling me to serve him.] stranger:    79 Irons heating]
Irons | Heating    on my word *Frederick.*] will hisse into their heart blouds, | 'Ere all be
ended; so much for this time. | *Fred.* Well sir‸

[III. i]                    ACT III.  SCENE I.

                        *Enter* Landlady *and* Anthony.

*Land.*  Come Sir, who is it keeps your Maſter Company?
*Anth.*  I say to you, *Don John.*
*Land.*                     I say what woman?
*Anth.*  I say so too.
*Land.*                 I say again I will know.
*Anth.*  I say 'tis fit you should.
*Land.*  And I tell thee he has a Woman here.                           5
*Anth.*  I tell thee 'tis then the better for him.
*Land.*  Was ever Gentlewoman
So frumpt off with a Fool? well sawcy Sirrah,
I will know who it is, and to what purpose;
I pay the Rent, and I will know how my House                            10

0.2 Anthony] *Peter* [*and until* '*Exit*']      1 Come Sir, who]
              CCome [*sic*] ye doe know.
        *Pet.*  I do not by this hand Mistris.
      But I suspect.
        *Land.*  What?
        *Pet.*  That if egges continue
      At this price, women wil ne're be sav'd
      By their good works.
        *Land.*  I will know.
        *Pet.*  Yee shall, any thing
      Lyes in my power: The Duke of *Loraine* now
      Is seven thousand strong: I heard it of a fish-wife,
      A woman of fine knowledge.
        *Land.*  Sirrah, sirrah.
        *Pe.*  The Popes Buls are broke loose too, and 'tis suspected
      They shall be baited in England.
        *Lan.*  Very well sir.
        *Pet.*  No, 'tis not so well neither.
        *Lan.*  But I say to yee,
      Who
4 you] yee      5 thee he] thee | He      6 I] And ~      thee 'tis] thee | 'Tis      him.] ~.
        *Lan.*  You are no Bawd now?
        *Pet.*  Would I were able to be call'd unto it:
      A worshipfull vocation for my elders;
      For as I understand it is a place
      Fitting my betters farr.
9 to] for

Comes by these inflammations: if this geer hold,
Beſt hang a sign-poſt up, to tell the *Signiors*,
Here ye may have lewdness at livery.

*Enter* Frederick.

*Anth.* 'Twould be a great ease to your age.
*Fred.*                              How Now?
Why what's the matter Landlady?
*Land.*                        What's the matter?                15
Ye use me decently among ye, Gentlemen.
*Fred.*  Who has abus'd her, you Sir?
*Land.*                          Od's my witness
I will not be thus treated, that I will not.
*Anth.*  I gave her no ill Language.
*Land.*                        Thou lieſt lewdly.
Thou took'ſt me up at every word I spoke,                      20
As I had been a Mawkin, a flirt Gillian;
And thou think'ſt, because thou canſt write and read,
Our Noses muſt be under thee.
*Fred.*                        Dare you Sirrah?
*Anth.*  Let but the Truth be known Sir, I beseech ye,
She raves of Wenches, and I know not what Sir.               25
*Land.*  Go to, thou know'ſt too well, thou wicked Varlet,
Thou Inſtrument of evil.
*Anth.*  As I live Sir, she's ever thus till Dinner.
*Fred.*  Get ye in, I'll answer you anon Sir.        [*Exit* Anthony.
Now your grief, what is't? For I can guess ——               30
*Land.*  Ye may, with shame enough,
If there were shame amongſt ye; nothing thought on,
But how ye may abuse my house: not satisfied
With bringing home your Baſtards to undo me,
But you muſt drill your Whores here too; my patience          35
Because I bear, and bear, and carry all,
(And as they say am willing to groan under)

28 Sir, she's] Sir, | She is    29 in, I'll] ~, | ~    29–30 Sir. [*Exit* Anthony. | Now]
                            sir.
        *Pet.* By this hand
        Ile break your Possit pan.        [*Exit.*
        *Lan.* Then by this hood
        Ile lock the meat up.
        *Fr.* Now
30 is't? For] ~? | ~    36 Because] (~    37 (am] ∧am

Muſt be your make-sport now.

   *Fred.* No more of these words,
Nor no more murmurings Lady; for you know          40
That I know something. I did suspeƈt your anger,
But turn it presently and handsomly,
And bear your self discreetly to this Woman,
For such a one there is indeed.

   *Land.*                'Tis well Son.

   *Fred.* Leave off your Devil's Matins, and your Melancholies,   45
Or we shall leave our Lodgings.

   *Land.*             You have much need
To use these vagrant ways, and to much profit:
Ye had that might content
(At home within your selves too) right good Gentlemen,
Wholesome, and ye said handsome. But you Gallants,     50
Beaſt that I was to believe ye ⸺

   *Fred.*            Leave your suspition:
For as I live there's no such thing.

   *Land.*            Mine honor;
And 'twere not for mine honor.

   *Fred.*           Come, your honor,
Your house, and you too, if you dare believe me,
Are well enough: Sleek up your self, leave crying,      55
For I muſt have ye entertain this Lady
With all civility, she well deserves it
Together with all service: I dare truſt ye,
For I have found ye faithful: when you know her
You will find your own fault; no more words, but do it.   60

   *Land.* You know you may command me.

*Enter* Don John.

   *Jo.*                Worshipful Lady,
How does thy Velvet Scabbard? by this hand
Thou lookeſt moſt amiably: now could I willingly
(And 'twere not for abusing thy *Geneva* print there,)
Venture my Body with thee. ⸺

   *Land.*           You'll leave this ropery,     65

---

45 Leave off] Leaving     51 Beast] Boast     55 *SD marginal 'Bowle of wine | ready' in*
F     58 service] secresie

When ye come to my years.

*Jo.*                    By this light,
Thou art not above fifteen yet, a meer Girle,
Thou haſt not half thy teeth ——

    *Fre.*                    Prethee *John*
Let her alone, she has been vext already:
She'l grow ſtark mad, man.

    *Jo.*                    I wou'd fain see her mad,                    70
An old mad Woman ——

    *Fre.*                    Prethee be patient.

    *Jo.*  Is like a Millers Mare troubled wi'th' Tooth ache.
She makes the rareſt faces.

    *Fre.*                    Go, and do it,
And do not mind this fellow.

        *Exit Landlady and comes back again presently.*

    *Jo.*                    What, agen!
Nay, then it is decreed: though hills were set on hills,                    75
And Seas met Seas, to guard thee, I would through.

    *Land.*  Od's my witness, if ye ruffle me,
I'l spoil your sweet face for you, that I will.
Go, go to the door there's a Gentleman there would speak with ye.

---

66 ye] you    68 teeth] ~: come    70 wou'd fain] would    72 wi'th'] with
73 She makes] Shee'll make    74a.1–84 *Exit Landlady . . . be gone:*]

        *Lan.* Well Don Iohn.
    There will be times agen; when O good Mother,
    What's good for a carnosity in the Bladder?
    O the green water, mother.
        *Ioh.* Doting take yee,
    Doe ye remember that?
        *Fr.* She has payd ye now sir.
        *La.* Clarry, sweet mother, Clarry.
        *Fr.* Are ye satisfied?
        *Lan.* Ile never whore againe; never give Petticoats
    And Wastcoats at five pound a peece; good Mother,
    Quickly Mother: now mock on Son.
        *Ioh.* A devill grinde your old chaps.    *[Exit Land.*
        *Fr.* By this hand wench
    Ile give thee a new hood for this.
    Has she met with your Lordship?
    Touch-wood rake her.    *[Enter Anthony.*
    Shee's a rare ghostly mother.
        *Ant.* Below attends yee
    The Gentlemans man sir that was with yee.
        *Joh.* Well Sir;
    My time is come then:

*Jo.* Upon my life *Petruchio*; good dear Landlady carry him into          80
the dining-Room, and I'll wait upon him presently.

*Land.* Well *Don John*, the time will come that I shall be even
with you.                                                                [*Exit*

*Jo.* I muſt be gone: yet if my projeƈt hold,
You shall not ſtay behind: I'l rather truſt                               85
A Cat with sweet milk *Frederick*; by her face

                        *Enter* Conſtantia.

I feel her fears are working.

*Con.*                              Is there no way,
I do beseech ye think yet, to divert
This certain danger.

*Fre.*                       'Tis impossible:
Their Honors are engag'd.

*Con.*                         Then there muſt be murder,                90
Which Gentlemen, I shall no sooner hear of,
Then make one in't: you may, if you please Sir,
Make all go less.

*Jo.*                  Lady, wer't mine own cause,
I could dispence: but loaden with my Friends truſt,
I muſt go on though general Massacrees                                    95
As much I fear ——

*Con.*                       Do ye hear Sir; for Heavens sake
Let me requeſt one favour of you.

*Fre.*                              Yes any thing.

*Con.* This Gentleman I find is too resolute,
Too hot, and fiery for the cause, as ever
You did a virtuous deed, for honor's sake                                100
Go with him and allay him, your fair temper
And noble disposition, like wish'd showers,
May quench those eating fires, that would spoil all else.
I see in him deſtruƈtion.

*Fre.*                       I will do it.
And 'tis a wise consideration,                                           105
To me a bounteous favour: Hark ye *John*,
I will go with ye.

---

86.1 *SD at 84 in F*        93 less] ~ yet        96 sake] pittie        97 favour] love
98 find is] find        104b I] *Fred.* ~        105 *Fre.* And] And

*Jo.*          No.
*Fre.*          Indeed I will,
Ye go upon a hazard; no denyal;
For as I live I'll go:
     *Jo.*          Then make ye ready,
For I am ſtrait a Horse-back.
     *Fre.*                    My Sword on, and          110
I am as ready as you: what my bleſt Labour,
With all the art I have can work upon 'em,
Be sure of, and expeƈt fair end: the old Gentlewoman
Shall wait upon ye, she is discreet and secret,
Ye may truſt her in all points.
     *Con.*                    Ye are noble;          115
And so I take my leave.
     *Jo.* I hope Lady, a happy issue for all this.
     *Conſt.* All Heavens care upon ye, and my prayers.
     *Jo.* So, now my mind's at reſt.
     *Fred.*                    Away, 'tis late *John.*          [*Exeunt.*


[III. ii]          SCENE II.

*Enter* Antonio, Surgeon, *and a* Gentleman.

*Gent.* What Symptoms do ye find in him?
*Sur.* None, Sir, dangerous, if he'd be rul'd.


110 on, and] on,          111 blest] best          114 ye] you          discreet and secret] both grave and
private          115 Ye] And yee          116 take my leave] kisse your hand          117 *line var.*]
          That seale for me too,
          And I hope happy issue Lady.
III.ii. [*Scene has been shortened, and freely rewritten in prose*]
          *Enter* Antonio, *a Surgeon, and* 2. Gent.
          *1 Gent.* Come sir be hearty: all the worst is past.
          *Ant.* Give me some Wine.
          *Sur.* 'Tis death Sir.
          *Ant.* 'Tis a horse sir.
          'Sbloud, to be drest to the tune of Ale onely,
          Nothing but sawces to my sores.
          *2 Gen.* Fie *Antonio,*
          You must be govern'd.
          *Ant.* Has given me a dam'd Glister,
          Only of sand and snow water, gentlemen, <*cont.*>

*Gent.* Why! what does he do?

*Sur.* Nothing that he should. Firſt, he will let no Liquor down but Wine, and then he has a fancy that he muſt be dreſt always to the Tune of *John Dory.*  5

*Gent.* How? to the Tune of *John Dory?*

*Sur.* Why? he will have Fidlers, and make them play and sing it to him all the while.

> Has almost scour'd my guts out.
>   *Surg.* I have giv'n you that sir
> Is fittest for your state.
>   *Ant.* And here he feeds me
> With rotten ends of rooks, and drown'd chickens,
> Stewd Pericraniums, and Pia-maters;
> And when I goe to bed, by heaven 'tis true gentlemen,
> He rolls me up in Lints, with Labels at 'em,
> That I am just the man ith' Almanack,
> In head and face, is *Aries* place.
>   *Surg.* Wilt please ye
> To let your friends see ye open'd?
>   *Ant.* Will it please you sir
> To let me have a wench: I feele my body
> Open enough for that yet?
>   *Surg.* How, a wench?
>   *Ant.* Why look yee gentlemen; thus I am us'd still,
> I can get nothing that I want.
>   *1 Gent.* Leave these things,
> And let him open ye.
>   *Ant.* De'ye heare Surgeon?
> Send for the Musick, let me have some pleasure
> To entertaine my friends, beside your Sallads,
> Your green salves, and your searches, and some wine too,
> That I may onely smell to it: or by this light
> Ile dye upon thy hand, and spoyle thy custome.
>   *1 Gen.* Let him have Musick.           *Ent. Rowl. with wine.*
>   *Surg.* 'Tis ith' house, and ready,
> If he will aske no more: but wine—            *Musick.*
>   *2 Gent.* He shall not drink it.
>   *Sur.* Will these things please yee?
>   *Ant.* Yes, and let 'em sing
> *John Dorrie.*
>   *2 Gent.* 'Tis too long.
>   *Ant.* Ile have *John Dorrie,*
> For to that warlike tune I will be open'd.
> Give me some drinke, have yee stopt the leakes well Surgeon,
> All will runne out else?
>   *Surg.* Feare not.
>   *Ant.* Sit downe Gentlemen:
> And now advance your plaisters.        *Song of Joh. Dorry.*
> Give 'em ten shillings friends: how doe ye finde me? *<cont.>*

*Gent.* An odd fancy indeed.                                                    10
*Ant.* Give me some Wine.
*Sur.* I told you so. —— 'Tis Death Sir.
*Ant.* 'Tis a Horse Sir. Doſt think I shall recover with the help
of Barley water only?
*Gent.* Fie, *Antonio*, you muſt be govern'd.                                   15
*Ant.* Why Sir? he feeds me with nothing but rotten Roots, and
drown'd Chickens, ſtew'd *Pericraniums* and *Pia-maters*, and when
I go to bed, (by Heaven 'tis true Sir) he rowls me up in lints with
Labels at 'em, that I am juſt the man i'th' Almanack, my head and
face is *Aries* place.                                                          20
*Sur.* Will't please ye to let your Friends see you open'd?


What Symptomes doe you see now?
   *Sur.* None Sir, dangerous:
But if you will be rul'd—
   *Ant.* What time?
   *Surg.* I can cure ye
In forty dayes, so you will not transgresse me.
   *Ant.* I have a dog shall lick me whole in twenty:
In how long canst thou kill me?
   *Surg.* Presently.
   *Ant.* Doe it; there's more delight in't.
   *1 Gent.* You must have patience.
   *Ant.* Man, I must have busines; this foolish fellow
Hinders himselfe: I have a dozen Rascalls
To hurt within these five dayes: good man mender,
Stop me up with Parsley, like stuft Beefe,
And let me walke abroad.
   *Surg.* Ye shall walke shortly.
   *Ant.* For I must finde *Petruchio*.
   *2. Gent.* Time enough.
   *1 Gent.* Come lead him in, and let him sleep: within these three dayes
Wee'll beg yee leave to play.
   *2 Gent.* And then how things fall,
Wee'll certainly informe yee.
   *Ant.* But Surgion promise me
I shall drinke Wine then too.
   *Surg.* A little temper'd.
   *Ant.* Nay, Ile no tempering Surgion,
   *Surg.* Well, as't please ye,
So ye exceed not.
   *Ant.* Farewell: and if ye finde
The Mad slave, that thus slasht me, commend me to him,
And bid him keep his skin close.
   *1 Gent.* Take your rest sir.                              *Exeunt.*

*Ant.* Will't please you, Sir, to give me a brimmer? I feel my
body open enough for that. Give it me, or I'll die upon thy hand,
and spoil thy custom.

*Sur.* How, a brimmer?                                          25

*Ant.* Why look ye Sir, thus I am us'd still; I can get nothing
that I want. In how long time canst thou cure me?

*Sur.* In forty days.

*Ant.* I'll have a Dog shall lick me whole in twenty.
In how long canst thou kill me?                                30

*Sur.* Presently.

*Ant.* Do't that's the shorter, and there's more delight in't.

*Gent.* You must have patience.

*Ant.* Man I must have business; this foolish Fellow hinders
himself; I have a dozen Rascals to hurt within these five days. Good   35
Man-mender stop me up with Parsley like stuff'd Beef, and let
me walk abroad.

*Sur.* Ye shall walk shortly.

*Ant.* I will walk presently Sir, and leave your Salads there, your
green Salves and your Oyls, I'll to my old dyet again, strong Food,   40
and rich Wine, and try what that will do.

*Sur.* Well, go thy ways, thou art the maddest old fellow I e'r
yet met with.                                          [*Exeunt.*


[III. iii]          SCENE III.

*Enter* Constantia *and* Landlady.

*Const.* I have told ye all I can, and more than yet
Those Gentlemen know of me; but are they
Such strange Creatures say you?

1 than] then          2–3 but . . . you? | *Land.* There's]
                              ever trusting
          Your Councell and concealement: for to me
          You seem a worthy woman; one of those
          Are seldome found in our sex, wise and vertuous,
          Direct me I beseech ye.
               *Land.*  Ye say well Lady,
          And hold yee to that poynt; for in these businesses
          A womans councell that conceives the matter,
          (Doe ye marke me, that conceives the matter Lady)
          Is worth ten mens engagements: She knows something
          And out of that can worke like wax: when men
          Are giddy-headed, either out of wine,
          Or a more drunkennesse, vaine ostentation, <*cont.*>

*Land.*                    There's the younger,
*Don John,* the errant'ſt *Jack* in all this City:
The other, time has blaſted, yet he will ſtoop,                    5
If not o'rflown, and freely on the Quarry;
H'as been a Dragon in his days. But *Tarmont,*
*Don Jenkin* is the Devil himself, the dog-days,
The moſt incomprehensible Whoremaſter,
Twenty a night is nothing; the truth is,                    10
Whose chaſtity he chops upon, he cares not.
He flies at all; Baſtards upon my conscience,
He has now in making multitudes: The laſt night
He brought home one; I pity her that bore it,
But we are all weak Vessels, some rich Woman                    15

Discovering all: there is no more keep in 'em,
Then hold upon an Eeles taile: nay 'tis held fashion
To defame now all they can.
    *Con.* I, but these gentlemen—
    *Land.* Doe not you trust to that: these gentlemen
Are as all Gentlemen of the same Barrell:
I, and the selfe same pickle too. Be it granted,
They have us'd yee with respect and faire behaviour,
Yet since ye came: doe you know what must follow?
They are Spaniards, Lady, Gennets of high mettle,
Things that will thrash the devill, or his dam,
Let 'em appeare but cloven.
    *Con.* Now heaven blesse me.
    *Lan.* Mad Colts will court the wind: I know 'em Lady
To the least haire they have; and I tell you,
Old as I am, let but the pinte pot blesse 'em,
They'll offer to my yeares—
    *Con.* How?
    *Lan.* Such rude gambolls—
    *Con.* To you?
    *Lan.* I, and so handle me, that oft I am forc'd
To fight of all foure for my safety: there's

4 errant'st] arrantst        7 H'as] Has        10 nothing;] ~:

Beggers, Broom-women,
And those so miserable, they look like famine,
Are all sweet Ladies in his drink.
    *Con.* He's a handsome Gentleman.
Pitty he should be master of such follies.
    *Land.* Hee's ne're without a noise of Sirrenges
In's pocket, those proclaim him; birding pills,
Waters to coole his conscience, in small Viols;
With thousand such sufficient emblemes:

(For wise I dare not call her) was the Mother,
For it was hung with Jewels; the bearing cloath
No less than Crimson Velvet.
    *Conſt.*              How?
    *Land.*                 'Tis true Lady.
    *Conſt.*  Was it a Boy too?
    *Land.*             A brave Boy; deliberation
And judgment shew'd in's getting, as I'll say for him,                    20
He's as well pac'd for that sport ——
    *Conſt.*              May I see it?
For there is a Neighbour of mine, a Gentlewoman,
Has had a late mischance, which willingly
I would know further of; now if you please
To be so courteous to me.
    *Land.*            Ye shall see it:                              25
But what do ye think of these men now ye know 'em?
Be wise,
Ye may repent too late else; I but tell ye
For your own good, and as you will find it Lady.
    *Conſt.*  I am advis'd.
    *Land.*          No more words then; do that,        30
And inſtantly, I told ye of, be ready:
*Don John,* I'll fit ye for your frumps.
    *Conſt.*             I shall be:
But shall I see this Child?
    *Land.*            Within this half hour,
Let's in, and there think better.             *[Exeunt*


[III. iv]          SCENE IV.

*Enter* Petruchio, Don John, Frederick.

    *Jo.*  Sir, he is worth your knowledge, and a Gentleman
(If I that so much love him, may commend him)
That's full of honor; and one, if foul play
Should fall upon us, (for which fear I brought him)
Will not fly back for phillips.

18 than] then      27 Be] And of the cause *I* told ye of ? ~      34 better.] ~; she that's
wise, | Leapes at occasion first; the rest pay for it.      3 That's full of honor] Of free and
vertuous parts

*Petr.*                    Ye much honor me,                    5
And once more I pronounce ye both mine.
  *Fred.*  Stay, what Troop
Is that below i'th' Valley there?
  *Jo.*                    Hawking I take it.
  *Petr.*  They are so; 'tis the Duke, 'tis even he Gentlemen,
Sirrah, draw back the Horses till we call ye,                    10
I know him by his Company.
  *Fred.*                    I think too
He bends up this way.
  *Petr.*                    So he does.
  *Jo.*                    Stand you ſtill,
Within that covert, till I call: he comes
Forward; here will I wait him: to your places.
  *Petr.*  I need no more inſtruct ye?
  *Jo.*                    Fear me not.                    15
                    [*Exit* Petruchio *and* Frederick.

                    *Enter* Duke *and his Faċtion.*
  *Duke.*  Feed the Hawks up,
We'll fly no more to day: O my bleſt Fortune!
Have I so fairly met the man?
  *Jo.*                    Ye have Sir,
And him ye know by this.
  *Duke.*                    Sir, all the honor,
And love ——
  *Jo.*          I do beseech your Grace ſtay there, and          20
Dismiss your Train a little.
  *Duke.*                    Walk aside,
And out of hearing I command ye: now Sir
Be plain.

8 it] ir          13-14 he comes | Forward; here] you *Fredrick*, | By no meanes be not seen,
unlesse they offer | To bring on odds upon us; he comes forward, | Here          14 him] ~
fairly          places] Cabins          15 not] ~, | I'le give it him, and boldly          19 ye]
you          20 there, and] there, | (For I know you too now) that love and honour | I come
not to receive; nor can you give it, | Till ye appeare faire to the world; I must beseech ye
22-3 Sir | Be plain] ~,
          *Iohn* Last time we met, I was a friend.
          *Duke* And Nobly
     You did a friends office: let your businesse
     Be what it may, you must be still— <*cont.*>

*Jo.*  I will, and short;
Ye have wrong'd a Gentleman, beyond all Justice,                          25
Beyond the Mediation of all Friends.
    *Duke.*  The man, and manner of wrong?
    *Jo.*                                         *Petruchio*;
The wrong, ye have dishonour'd his Sister.
    *Duke.*  Now stay you Sir,
And hear me a little: This Gentleman's                                    30
Sister that you nam'd, 'tis true I have long lov'd,
As true I have enjoy'd her: no less truth
I have a Child by her.  But that she, or he,
Or any of that Family are tainted,
Suffer disgrace, or ruine, by my pleasures,                               35
I wear a Sword to satisfie the World no,
And him in this Cause when he pleases; for know Sir,
She is my Wife, contracted before Heaven,
(Witness I owe more tie to, than her Brother)
Nor will I fly from that Name, which long since                           40
Had had the Churches approbation,
But for his Jealous Nature.
    *Jo.*  Your pardon Sir; I am fully satisfi'd.
    *Duke.*  Dear Sir, I knew I should convert ye; had we
But that rough man here now too ——
    *Jo.*                                    And ye shall Sir.             45
What hoa, hoo.
    *Duke.*      I hope ye have laid no Ambush?

*Enter* Petruchio.

       *Iohn*  Your pardon,
    Never a friend to him, cannot be friend
    To his own honour.
       *Duke*  In what have I transgress'd it?
    Ye make a bold breach at the first Sir.
       *Iohn*  Bolder,
    You made that breach that let in infamy
    And ruine, to surprize a noble stocke.
       *Duke* ~ ~ Sir

25 Gentleman] ~ | Little behind your selfe    26 Beyond the] Beyond    28 dishonour'd]
whord    Sister.] ~. | *Duke* What's his will in't? | *Iohn* His will is to oppose you like a
Gentleman, | And single, to decide all.          30 a little] with the like beliefe
Gentleman's] Gentleman          31 Sister] His ~    lov'd,] ~, | Nor was that love lascivious,
as he makes it;          37 pleases] please          39 than] then          42 Nature] danger
43 *line var.* Sir, your pardon, | And all that was my anger, now my service.          44 Dear]
Faire          46 What] Whoa

*Jo.*   Only Friends.
*Duke.*          My noble Brother welcome:
Come put your anger off, we'll have no fighting,
Unless you will maintain I am unworthy
To bear that Name.
*Petr.*          Do you speak this heartily?          50
*Duke.*   Upon my Soul, and truly; the firſt Prieſt
Shall put you out of these doubts.
*Petr.*          Now I love ye;
And I beseech ye pardon my suspicions,
You are now more than a Brother, a brave Friend too.
*Jo.*   The good man's over-joy'd.

*Enter* Frederick.

*Fred.*          How now, how goes it?          55
*Jo.*   Why, the man has his Mare again, and all's well:
The *Duke* professes freely he's her Husband.
*Fred.*   'Tis a good hearing.
*Jo.*          Yes, for modeſt Gentlemen.
I muſt present ye: May it please your Grace
To number this brave Gentleman, my Friend,          60
And noble Kinsman, amongſt the reſt of your Servants.
*Duke.*   O my brave Friend! you shower your Bounties on me:
Amongſt my beſt thoughts *Signior*, in which number
You being worthily dispos'd already,
May freely place your Friend.          65
*Fred.*   Your Grace does me a great deal of honor.
*Petr.*   Why, this is wondrous happy: But now Brother,
Now comes the bitter to our sweet: *Conſtantia.*
*Duke.*   Why, what of her?
*Petr.*          Nor what, nor where do I know:
Wing'd with her fears, laſt night, beyond my knowledge,          70
She quit my house, but whither ——
*Fred.*          Let not that ——
*Duke.*   No more good Sir, I have heard too much.
*Petr.*          Nay sink not,
She cannot be so loſt.

53 ye] you          54 than] then          56 well:] ~ₐ *Fredrick,*          58–9 Gentlemen. I . . .
ye: | May] ~. | ~ . . . ~: ~          61 the rest of] those          65 May freely] May          Friend] ~
to honour me          66 *line var.*] My love sir, | And where your Grace dares trust me, all my
service.          69 know:] ~?          71 whither] whether

*Jo.*                   Nor shall not Gentlemen;
Be free again, the Lady's found; that smile, Sir,
Shews you diſtruſt your Servant.
    *Duke.*                   I do beseech ye.                              75
    *Jo.*   Ye shall believe me, by my Soul she's safe.
    *Duke.*   Heaven knows I would believe Sir.
    *Fred.*                              Ye may safely.
    *Jo.*   And under noble usage: this Gentleman,
Met her in all her Doubts laſt night, and to his Guard
(Her fears being ſtrong upon her) she gave her Person,                 80
Who waited on her, to our Lodging; where all reſpeſt,
Civil, and honeſt Service now attend her.
    *Petr.*   Ye may believe now.
    *Duke.*                   Yes I do, and ſtrongly;
Well, my good Friends, or rather my good Angels,
For ye have both preserv'd me; when these virtues                 85
Die in your Friends remembrance ——
    *Jo.*                   Good your Grace
Lose no more time in Complements, 'tis too precious,
I know it by my self, there can be no Hell
To his that hangs upon his hopes.
    *Petr.*                   He has hit it.
    *Fred.*   To Horse again then, for this night I'll crown                 90
With all the Joys ye wish for.
    *Petr.*                   Happy Gentlemen.                 [*Exeunt.*

           *Enter* Francisco, *and a Man.*

    *Fran.*   This is the maddeſt mischief, never Fool
Was so fub'd off as I am, made ridiculous,
And to my self, to my own Ass; truſt a Woman,
I'll truſt the Devil firſt, for he dares be                 95
Better than his word sometimes. Pray tell me,
In what observance have I e'r fail'd her?
    *Man.*   Nay, you can tell that beſt your self.
    *Fran.*                   Let me
Consider.

75 you] ye      76 she's] she is      78 this] ~ faire      87 Complements] complement
89 hopes] ~; especially | In way of lustly pleasures      91b.1 Francisco, *and a Man*] *Francisco*
92–7 *as prose in Q; F lineation restored*      94 self, to my] selfe, mine      95 dares] dare
96 than his] then's      96–8 sometimes. Pray ... self.] sometime: what faith have I
broke? | In what observance failed?

*Enter* Don Frederick *and* Don John.

*Fred.*   Let them talk, we'll go on before.

*Fran.*   Where did'ſt thou meet *Conſtantia*, and this Woman?     100

*Fred.*   *Conſtantia!* what are these Fellows? Stay by all means.

*Man.*   Why Sir, I met her

In the great Street that comes from the Market-place,

Juſt at the turning by a Gold-smith's Shop.

*Fred.*   Stand ſtill *John.*

*Fran.*          Well, *Conſtantia* has spun     105

Her self a fair thred now: what will her beſt

Friend think of this?

*Fred.*        *John,* I smell some jugling, *John.*

*Jo.*   Yes, *Frederick,* I fear it will be prov'd so.

---

99 Consider] consider, | For this is monstrous usage     99a.1 *line var.*] *Enter Don Iohn and Fred.*     99b talk, we'll go on before] talke, | Wee'll ride on faire and softly     [*ll. 100–20 freely rewritten*]

> *Fran.* Well *Constantia,*
> *Fred. Constantia,* what's this fellow? stay by all means.
> *Fran.* Ye have spun your selfe a faire thred now.
> *Fred.* Stand still *Iohn.*
> *Fran.* What cause had you to fly? what feare possest ye?
> Were you not safely lodg'd from all suspition?
> Us'd with all gentle meanes? did any know
> How ye came thether, or what your sin was.
> *Fred. Iohn,*
> I smell some juggling *John.*
> *John* Yes, *Fredrick,* I feare it will be found so.
> *Fran.* So strangely,
> Without the counsell of your friends; so desperatly
> To put all dangers on ye?
> *Fred.* 'Tis she.
> *Fran.* So deceitfully
> After a strangers lure?
> *John* Did ye marke that *Fredrick?*
> *Fran.* To make ye appeare more monster; and the Law
> More cruell to reward ye? to leave all,
> All that should be your safegard, to seeke evils?
> Was this your wisedome? this your promise? well
> He that incited ye—
> *Fred.* Marke that too.
> *John* Yes Sir.
> *Fran.* 'Had better have plough'd farther off; now Lady,
> What will your last friend, he that should preserve ye,
> And hold your credit up, the brave *Antonio,*
> Thinke of this slip? he'll to *Petruchio,*
> And call for open justice. <*cont.*>

*Fran.*  But what should the reason be doſt think of this
So suddain change in her?
*Fred.*                         'Tis she.
*Man.*                                    Why, truly                    110
I suspeᘯt she has been entic'd to it by a Stranger.
*Jo.*  Did you mark that *Frederick?*
*Fran.*                              Stranger? who?
*Man.*  A young Gentleman that's newly come to Town.
*Fred.*  Mark that too.
*Jo.*              Yes Sir.
*Fran.*                      Why do you think so?
*Man.*  I heard her grave Conduᘯtress twattle something    115
As they went along that makes me guess it.
*Jo.*  'Tis she *Frederick.*
*Fred.*              But who that he is *John.*
*Fran.*  I do not doubt to bolt 'em out, for they
Muſt certainly be about the Town. Ha! no more words;
Come, let's be gone.              [*Exeunt* Fran. *and* Man.
*Fred.*          Well.
*Jo.*                Very well.
*Fred.*                            Discreetly.               120
*Jo.*  Finely carri'd.
*Fred.*            Ye have no more of these Tricks?
*Jo.*  Ten to one Sir, I shall meet with 'em if ye have.
*Fred.*  Is this fair?
*Jo.*              Was it in you a Friends part to deal double?
I am no Ass *Don Frederick.*
*Fred.*                      And, *Don John,*
It shall appear I am no Fool: Disgrace me              125
To make your self thus every Woman's courtesie;
'Tis boyish, 'tis base.

*John* 'Tis she *Fredrick.*
*Fred.* But what that he is *John.*
*Fran.* I do not doubt yet
To bolt ye out, for I know certainly
Ye are about the Towne still: ha, no more words.    *Ex.*

121 Ye] You        122 Sir, I] ~, | ~            123 fair] honest      124–5 *John,* It] ~, | ~
125 Fool: Disgrace] ~; | ~        126 self thus] self        126–7 every Woman's courtesie;] a
lecher?

*Jo.*          'Tis false: I privy to this Dog-trick?
Clear your self, for I know well enough
Where the wind sits, or as I have a life ——          [*Trample within.*
   *Fred.*   No more, they are coming, shew no discontent,          130
Let's quietly away; If she be at home
Our Jealousies are over, if not, you
And I muſt have a farther parly *John.*
   *Jo.*   Yes, *Don Frederick*, ye may be sure we shall:
But where are these Fellows? Pox on't,          135
We have loſt them too in our Spleens, like Fools.

             *Enter* Duke *and* Petruchio.

   *Duke.*   Come Gentlemen, Let's go a little faſter;
Suppose you have all Miſtresses, and mend
Your pace accordingly.
   *Jo.*          Sir, I should be
As glad of a Miſtress as an other man.          140
   *Fred.*   Yes, o' my Conscience would'ſt thou, and of any
Other man's Miſtress too; that I'll answer for.          [*Exeunt.*

127 false: I] ~, and most unmanly to upbraid me,
        Nor will I be your bolster Sir.
        *Fred.* Thou wanton boy, thou hadst better have been Eunuch,
        Thou common womans curtesie, then thus
        Lascivious, basely to have bent mine honour.
        A friend? I'le make a horse my friend first!
        *Iohn* Holla, holla,
        Ye kicke to fast sir: what strange braines have you got,
        That dare crow out thus bravely? I better been a Eunuch? | ~
128 self, for] selfe, | For     128–9 know well enough | Where] know where     129 sits,
or] sits, and most nobly, | Or     *Trample within*] *A noyse within* | *like horses* (*marginal over 2
lines at 131 in F*)     130 they are coming,] they'r horses. | Nor     130–1 discontent,
let's] discontent: to morrow comes; | Let's     131–2 home our] home, | Our     132–3 over,
... parly *John*] put off     134–6 Yes ... Pox on't, we] The fellow | We     136 them
too] him     136.1 *SD marginal over 2 lines at 135–7 in F*     137–8 Gentlemen, Let's go
a little faster; | Suppose] Gentlemen, | Now set on roundly: suppose     138 you] ye
Mistresses, and] mistresses, | And     138–9 mend | Your] mend your     139 accordingly]
according     139–42 *Jo.* Sir ... answer for.] *Pet.* Then have at ye.

[III. v]                    SCENE V.

*Enter* Antonio *and his* Man.

*Ant.* With all my Gold?
*Man.* The Trunk broke open, and all gone.
*Ant.* And the Mother in the Plot?
*Man.* And the mother and all.

III. v. [*from Fletcher, IV. ii.*]
              Scæne 2. *Enter Antonio and his Servant.*
    *Ant.* With all my jewels?
    *Ser.* All Sir.
    *Ant.* And that money
I left i'th' trunke?
    *Ser.* The Trunke broke, and that gone too.
    *Ant.* *Franscisco* of the plot?
    *Ser.* Gone with the wench too.
    *Ant.* The mighty poxe go with 'em: belike they thought
I was no man of this world, and those trifles
Would but disturbe my conscience.
    *Ser.* Sure they thought Sir,
You would not live to persecute 'em.
    *Ant.* Whore and Fidler,
Why, what a consort have they made? Hen and bacon?
Well my sweet Mistris, well good Madam martaile?
You that have hung about my neck, and lick't me,
I'le try how handsomely your Ladyship
Can hang upon a Gallowes, there's your Master-piece;
But harke ye Sirrah, no imagination      *Bawd ready above.*
Of where they should be?
    *Ser.* None Sir, yet we have search'd
All places we suspected; I beleeve Sir,
They have taken towards the Ports.
    *Ant.* Get me a conjurer,
One that can raise a water devill, I'le port 'em;
Play at duck and drake with my money? take heed Fidler;
I'le dance ye by this hand, your Fidle-sticke
I'le grease of a new fashion, for presuming
To medle with my degamboys: get me a Conjurer,
Enquire me out a man that lets out devils:
None but my C. Cliffe serve your turne?
    *Ser.* I know not—
    *Ant.* In every street, Tom foole, any bleare-eyd people
With red heads, and flat noses can performe it;
Thou shalt know 'em by their half gowns & no breeches:
Mount my mare Fidler? ha boy? up at first dash? <*cont.*>

*Ant.* And the Devil and all: the mighty Pox go with 'em: belike          5
they thought I was no more of this World, and those trifles would
but diſturb my Conscience.

*Man.* Sure they thought, Sir, you wou'd not live to diſturb them.

*Ant.* Well, my sweet Miſtress, I'll try how handsomely your
Ladiship can hang upon a pair of Gallows, there's your Maſter-          10
piece. No imagination where they should be?

*Man.* None Sir: yet we have search'd all places we suspeĉted; I
believe they have taken towards the Port.

*Ant.* Get me then a Water-Conjurer, one that can raise Water-
Devils, I'll port 'em, play at Duck and Drake with my money?          15
Get me a Conjurer I say, enquire out a man that lets out Devils.

*Man.* I don't know where.

*Ant.* In every Street *Tom Fool*, any blear-ey'd people with red
heads, and flat noses can perform it. Thou shalt know 'em by their
half gowns, and no breeches. Find me out a Conjurer, I say, and          20
learn his price, how he will let his Divils out by the day. I'll have
'em again if they be above Ground.                              [*Exeunt.*


[III. vi]                    SCENE VI.

*Enter* Duke, Petruchio, Frederick, *and* John.

*Petr.* Your Grace is welcome now to *Naples*; so ye are all,
Gentlemen.

> Sit sure, I'le clap a nettle, and a smart one,
> Shall make your filly firck: I will find Fidler,
> I'le put you to your plundge boy: Sirrah meet me
> Some two houres hence at home; In the meane time
> Find out a conjurer and know his price,
> How he will let his devils by the day out,
> I'le have 'em, and they be above ground.          *Exit Ant.*
>    *Ser.* Now blesse me,
> What a mad man is this? I must do something
> To please his humour: such a man I'le aske for,
> And tell him where he is: but to come neare him,
> Or have any thing to do with his don devills,
> I thanke my feare, I dare not, nor I will not.          *Exit.*

III. vi. [*from Fletcher, IV. i.*]          1 Your . . . are all,]
> Now to *Bollonia*, my most honoured brother,
> I dare pronounce ye a hearty, and safe welcome,
> Our loves shall now way-lay ye; welcome

*Jo.* Don Frederick, will you ſtep in, and give the Lady notice who comes to visit her?

*Petr.* Bid her make haſte, we come to see no curious Wench, a night-gown will serve turn. Here's one that knows her nearer. 5

*Fred.* I'll tell her what you say Sir. [*Exit.*

*Petr.* Now will the sport be to observe her alterations, how betwixt fear and joy she will behave her self.

*Duke.* Dear Brother, I muſt entreat you —— 10

*Petr.* I conceive your mind Sir, I will not chide her.

*Enter* Frederick *and* Peter.

*Jo.* How now?

*Fred.* You may Sir: not to abuse your patience longer, nor hold ye off with tedious circumſtance; for ye muſt know ——

*Petr.* What? 15

*Duke.* Where is she?

*Fred.* Gone Sir.

*Duke.* How?

*Petr.* What did you say Sir?

*Fred.* Gone: by Heaven remov'd. The Woman of the house too. 20

*Petr.* What, that reverend old Woman that tir'd me with Complements?

*Fred.* The very same.

*Jo.* Well, *Don Frederick.*

*Fred.* *Don John,* it is not well. But —— 25

3 *Don Frederick*, will] The same to you brave Sir; *Don Fredrick* | Will  you] ye  notice who] notice | Who  4 visit] honour  5 make haste, we] be suddain, | We 6 night-gown will] night-gowne | Will  serve] ~ the  7 you] ye  *Exit.*] ~ *Fred.* | *Duke* My deare brother, | Ye are a merry Gentleman.  8 be to] be | To  9 betwixt . . . self.]

like wildfire
She'll leap into your bosome; then seeing me,
Her conscience, and her feares creeping upon her
Dead as a fowle at souse, she'll sinke.
10 Dear Brother, I] Faire brother, | I  11 Sir, I] ~, | ~  her.] ~:
yet ten duckets Duke,
She falls upon he [*sic*] knees, ten more she dare not—
*Duke* I must not have her frighted.
*Pet.* Well you shall not·
But like a summers evening against heate,
Marke how I'le guild her cheekes?
13 You] Ye  Sir: not] Sir: | Not  longer, nor] noble friends, | Nor  14 circumstance; for ye] circumstance, | For you  20 remov'd. The] ~. | ~  20–3 too. | *Petr.* What . . . very same.] too.

*Petr.* Gone?

*Fred.* This Fellow can satisfie I lie not.

*Peter.* A little after my Maſter was departed, Sir, with this Gentleman, my Fellow and my self being sent on business, as we muſt think on purpose.      30

*Petr.* Hang these Circumſtances, they always serve to usher in ill ends.

*Jo.* Now could I eat that Rogue, I am so angry. Gone?

*Petr.* Gone?

*Fred.* Direꝸly gone, fled, shifted, what would you ha' me say?      35

*Duke.* Well, Gentlemen, wrong not my good opinion.

*Fred.* For your Dukedom, Sir, I would not be a Knave.

*Jo.* He that is, a Rot run in his blood.

*Petr.* But hark ye Gentlemen, are ye sure ye had her here? Did ye not dream this?      40

*Jo.* Have you your nose Sir?

*Petr.* Yes Sir.

*Jo.* Then we had her.

*Petr.* Since ye are so short, believe your having her shall suffer more conſtruꝸion.      45

*Jo.* Well Sir, let it suffer.

*Fred.* How to convince ye Sir, I can't imagine, but my life shall juſtifie my innocence, or fall with it.

27 Fellow can] fellow | Can    satisfie] testifie    28 A little after my] Some foure houres after | My    departed, Sir,] departed    29 Gentleman, my] Gentleman, | My on business, as] of businesse, | (As    30 think on] thinke) of    31 always serve to usher in] appeare like owles, to    33 eat that Rogue] eate | The devil in his own broath angry. Gone?] tortur'd. | Gone?    35 ha'] have    36 Gentlemen, wrong] Gentlemen, | Wrong    37 Dukedom, Sir, I] Dukedome | I    would] will    Knave] ~ Sir    38 is, a] is | A    39 Gentlemen, are] Gentlemen, | Are    44 ye] you her shall] her | Shall    [*ll. 46–62 freely rewritten*]

       *Iohn* Let it suffer,
But if I be not cleere of all dishonour,
Or practice that may taint my reputation,
And ignorant of where this woman is,
Make me your Cities monster.
       *Duke* I beleeve ye.
       *John* I could lye with a witch now, to be reveng'd
Upon that Rascall did this.
       *Fred.* Only thus much
I would desire your Grace, for my minde gives me
Before night yet she is yours: stop all opinion,
And let no anger out, till full cause call it,
Then every mans owne work's to justifie him,
And this day let us give to search: my man here <cont.>

*Duke.* Thus then —— for we may be all abus'd.

*Petr.* 'Tis possible.                                                                50

*Duke.* Here let's part until to morrow this time; we to our way,
to clear this doubt, and you to yours. Pawning our honors then to
meet again? when if she be not found ——

*Fred.* We ſtand engag'd to answer any worthy way we are call'd
to.                                                                                  55

*Duke.* We ask no more

*Petr.* To morrow certain.

*Jo.* If we out-live this night Sir.          [*Exit* Duke *and* Petru.

*Fred.* Come, *Don John*, we have somewhat now to do.

*Jo.* I am sure I would have.                                                        60

*Fred.* If she be not found, we muſt fight.

*Jo.* I am glad on't, I have not fought a great while.

*Fred.* If we die ——

*Jo.*                         There's so much money sav'd in Lechery.

                                                              [*Exeunt.*


[IV. i]                    ACT IV.  SCENE I.

                    *Enter* 2. Conſtantia *and her* Mother.

*Mo.* Hold *Cons*, hold, for goodness hold, I am in that deser-
tion of Spirit for want of breath, that I am almoſt reduc'd to the
necessity of not being able to defend my self againſt the inconven-
ience of a fall.

2. *Conſt.* Dear Mother let us go a little faſter to secure our selves      5
from *Antonio*; for my part I am in that terrible fright, that I can
neither think, speak, nor ſtand ſtill, till we are safe a Ship-board,
and out of sight of the Shore.

            Tels me, by chance he saw out of a window
            (Which place he has taken note of) such a face
            As our old Landladies, he beleeves the same too,
            And by her hood assures it: Let's first thether,
            For she being found, all's ended.
                *Duke* Come, for heavens sake,
            And Fortune, and thou beest not ever turning,
            If there be one firme step in all thy reelings,
            Now settle it, and save my hopes: away friends.          [*Exeunt.*

[*The remainder of the play is independent of Fletcher.*]

*Mo.* Out of sight o'the Shore? why, do ye think I'll depatriate?

2. *Conſt.* Depatriate? what's that?          10

*Mo.* Why, ye Fool you, leave my Country: what will you never learn to speak out of the vulgar road?

2. *Conſt.* O Lord, this hard word will undo us.

*Mo.* As I am a Chriſtian, if it were to save my honour (which is ten thousand times dearer to me than my life) I would not be          15
guilty of so odious a thought.

2 *Con.* Pray Mother, since your honour is so dear to ye, consider that if we are taken, both it and we are loſt for ever.

*Mo.* Ay Girle, but what will the world say, if they should hear so odious a thing of us, as that we should depatriate?          20

2 *Con.* Ay, there's it, the world; why, Mother, the world does not care a pin if both you and I were hang'd; and that we shall be certainly, if *Antonio* takes us, for running away with his Gold.

*Mo.* Proteſt I care not, I'll ne're depart from the demarches of a person of Quality; and let come what will, I shall rather choose          25
to submit my self to my fate, then ſtrive to prevent it by any deportment that is not congruous in every degree to the ſteps and measures of a ſtrict practitioner of honor.

2 *Con.* Would not this make one ſtark mad? Her ſtile is not more out of the way, then her manner of reasoning; she firſt sells me          30
to an ugly old fellow, then she runs away with me and all his gold, and now like a ſtrict practitioner of honor, resolves to be taken, rather then depatriate, as she calls it.

*Mo.* As I am a Chriſtian, *Cons*, a Tavern, and a very decent Sign; I'l in I am resolv'd, though by it I should run a Risco of          35
never so ſtupendious a Nature.

2 *Con.* There's no ſtopping her: what shall I do?

*Mo.* I'l send for my Kins-Woman and some Musick, to revive me a little; for really, *Cons*, I am reduc'd to that sad imbecility by the injury I have done my poor feet, that I'm in a great incer-          40
titude whether they will have liveliness sufficient to support me up to the top of the ſtairs or no.          [*Exit.*

2 *Con.* This sinning without pleasure I cannot endure; to have always a remorse, and ne'r do any thing that should cause it, is intolerable. If I lov'd mony too, which (I think) I don't, my          45
Mother she has all that; I have nothing to comfort my self with but *Antonio's* ſtiff Beard, and that alone, for a Woman of my years, is but a sorry kind of entertainment. I wonder why these old fumbling fellows should trouble themselves so much, only to

trouble us more. They can do nothing, but put us in mind of our    50
graves. Well, I'll no more on't; for to be frighted with Death and
Damnation both at once is a little too hard. I do here vow I'l live
for ever chaſt, or find out some handsome young fellow I can love;
I think that's the better; [*Mother looks out at the Window.*

   *Mo.*  Come up, *Cons*, the Fiddles are here.             55
   2 *Con.*  I come. ——        [*Mother goes from the Window.*
I muſt be gone, though whither I cannot tell; these Fiddles, and
her discreet Companions will quickly make an end of all she has
ſtollen, and then 500 New Pieces sells me to another old fellow.
She has taken care not to leave me a farthing; yet I am so,         60
better than under her conduct: 'twill be at worſt but begging for
my life;

And ſtarving were to me an easier Fate     { *Goes up to her*
Than to be forc'd to live with one I hate.    { *Mother.*


[IV. ii]                      SCENE II.

*Enter* Don John.

   *Jo.*  It will not out of my head but that *Don Frederick* has sent
away this Wench, for all he carries it so gravely: yet methinks he
should be honeſter than so; but these grave men are never touch'd
upon such occasions: mark it when ye will, and you'll find a grave
man, especially if he pretend to be a precise man, will do ye forty   5
things without remorse, that would ſtartle one of us mad Fellows to
think of. Because they are familiar with Heaven in their prayers,
they think they may be bold with it in any thing: now we that are
not so well acquainted, bear greater Reverence.

                      [*Musick plays above.*
What's here, Musick and Women? would I had one of 'em.               10
            [*One of 'em looks out at the Window.*
That's a Whore; I know it by her smile. O' my conscience take a
Woman masked and hooded, nay covered all o're so that ye cannot
see one bit of her, and at 12 score diſtance, if she be a whore as ten to
one she is, I shall know it certainly; I have an inſtinct within me
never fails.                   [*Another looks out.*   15
Ah Rogue! she's right too I'm sure on't.

   *Mo. above.*  Come, come let's dance in t'other room, 'tis a great
deal better.

*Jo.* Say you so? what now if I should go up and dance too? It is a
Tavern. Pox o' this business: I'l in I am resolv'd, and try my own    20
fortune; 'tis hard luck if I don't get one of 'em.

*As he goes to the door* 2 Conſtantia *enters.*

See, here's one bolted already: fair Lady whither so faſt?
2. *Con.* I don't know Sir.
*Jo.* May I have the honor to wait upon you?
2 *Con.* Yes, if you please Sir.    25
*Jo.* Whither?
2 *Con.* I tell ye I don't know.
*Jo.* She's very quick. Would I might be so happy as to know you
Lady.
2. *Conſt.* I dare not let you see my face Sir.    30
*Jo.* Why?
2. *Conſt.* For fear you should not like it, and then leave me, for to
tell you true, I have at this present very great need of you.
*Jo.* If thou haſt half so much need of me, as I have of thee Lady,
I'll be content to be hang'd though.    35
2. *Conſt.* It's a proper handsome Fellow this; if he'd but love me
now, I would never seek out further. Sir, I am young, and unexper-
ienced in the World.
*Jo.* Nay, if thou art young, it's no great matter what thy face is.
2. *Conſt.* Perhaps this freedom in me may seem ſtrange; but Sir,    40
in short, I'm forc'd to fly from one I hate, if I should meet him, will
you here promise he shall not take me from you?
*Jo.* Yes, that I will, before I see your face, your shape has charm'd
me enough for that already; if any one takes ye from me, Lady, I'll
give him leave to take from me too —— (I was a going to name    45
'em) certain things of mine, that I would not lose, now I have you in
my arms, for all the Gems in Chriſtendom.
2. *Conſt.* For Heaven's sake then conduċt me to some place
where I may be secured a while from the sight of any one whatsoever.    50
*Jo.* By all the hopes I have to find thy face as lovely as thy
shape, I will.
2. *Conſt.* Well Sir, I believe ye, for you have an honeſt look.
*Jo.* 'Slid I am afraid *Don Frederick* has been giving her a charaċter
of me too. Come, pray unmasque.    55
2. *Conſt.* Then turn away your face; for I'm resolv'd you shall
not see a bit of mine till I have set it in order, and then ——

*Jo.* What?

2. *Conſt.* I'll ſtrike you dead.

*Jo.* A mettled Whore, I warrant her; come if she be now but    60
young, and have but a nose on her face, she'll be as good as her
word: I'm e'en panting for breath already.

2. *Conſt.* Now ſtand your ground if you dare.

*Jo.* By this light a rare creature! ten thousand times handsomer
than her we seek for! this can be sure no common one: pray Heaven    65
she be a Whore.

2. *Conſt.* Well Sir, what say ye now?

*Jo.* Nothing; I'm so amaz'd I am not able to speak. I'd beſt fall to
presently, though it be in the Street, for fear of losing time. Prethee
my dear sweet Creature go with me into that corner, that thou and    70
I may talk a little in private.

2. *Conſt.* No Sir, no private dealing I beseech you.

*Jo.* 'S Heart, what shall I do? I'm out of my wits for her. Hark
ye, my dear Soul, canſt thou love me?

2. *Conſt.* If I could, what then?    75

*Jo.* Why, you know what then, and then should I be the
happieſt man alive.

2. *Conſt.* I, so you all say till you have your desires, and then you
leave us.

*Jo.* But, my dear Heart, I am not made like other men; I never    80
can love heartily till I have ——

2. *Conſt.* Got their Maidenheads; but suppose now I should be
no Maid.

*Jo.* Prethee suppose me nothing, but let me try.

2. *Conſt.* Nay, good Sir hold.    85

*Jo.* No Maid? why, so much the better, thou art then the more
experienc'd; for my part I hate a bungler at any thing.

2. *Conſt.* O dear, I like this Fellow ſtrangely: hark ye Sir, I am
not worth a groat, but though you should not be so neither, if you'l
but love me, I'll follow ye all the World over; I'll work for ye, beg    90
for you, do any thing for ye, so you'll promise to do nothing with any
body else.

*Jo.* O Heavens, I'm in another World, this Wench sure was
made a purpose for me, she is so juſt of my humour. My dear, 'tis
impossible for me to say how much I will do for thee, or with thee,    95
thou sweet bewitching Woman; but let's make haſte home, or I
shall never be able to hold out till I come thither.        [*Exeunt.*

[IV. iii]                SCENE III.

*Enter* Frederick *and* Francisco.

*Fred.* And art thou sure it was *Conſtantia*, say'ſt thou that he was leading?

*Fran.* Am I sure I live Sir? why, I dwelt in the house with her; how can I chuse but know her?

*Fred.* But did'ſt thou see her face?                                    5

*Fran.* Lord Sir, I saw her face as plainly as I see yours juſt now, not two Streets off.

*Fred.* Yes, 'tis e'en so: I suspeċted it at firſt, but then he forswore it with that confidence —— Well, *Don John*, if these be your praċtices, you shall have no more a Friend of me, Sir, I          10 assure you. Perhaps though he met her by chance, and intends to carry her to her Brother and the Duke.

*Enter* Don John, *and Second* Conſtantia.

A little time will shew. —— Gods so, here he is; I'll ſtep behind this Shop, and observe what he say's.

*Jo.* Here, now go in, and make me for ever happy.                      15

                                        <*Exit* 2 Conſtantia.>

*Fred.* Dear *Don John*.

*Jo.* A pox o' your kindness, how the Devil comes he here juſt at this time? Now will he ask me forty foolish Queſtions, and I have such a mind to this Wench, that I cannot think of one excuse for my life.                                                                 20

*Fred.* Your Servant Sir: pray who's that you lock'd in juſt now at that door?

*Jo.* Why, a Friend of mine that's gone up to read a Book.

*Fred.* A Book? that's a queint one i'faith: prethee *Don John* what Library haſt thou been buying this Afternoon? for i'th'          25 Morning to my knowledge thou had'ſt never a Book there, except it were an Almanack, and that was none of thy own neither.

*Jo.* No, no, it's a Book of his own he brought along with him. A Scholar that is given to reading.

*Fred.* And do Scholars (*Don John*) wear Petticoats now adays?      30

*Jo.* Plague on him, he has seen her. —— Well *Don Frederick*, thou know'ſt I am not good at lying, 'tis a Woman I confess it, make your beſt on't, what then?

*Fred.* Why then, *Don John,* I desire you'll be pleas'd to let me see her. 35

*Jo.* Why, faith *Frederick,* I should not be againſt the thing, but ye know a man muſt keep his word, and she has a mind to be private.

*Fred.* But *John* you may remember when I met a Lady so before, this very self same Lady too, that I got leave for you to see 40 her *John.*

*Jo.* Why, do ye think then that this here is *Conſtantia?*

*Fred.* I cannot properly say I think it *John,* because I know it; this Fellow here saw her as you led her i'th' Streets.

*Jo.* Well, and what then? who does he say it is? 45

*Fred.* Ask him Sir, and he'll tell ye.

*Jo.* Sweet heart, doſt thou know this Lady?

*Fran.* I think I should Sir, I ha' liv'd long enough in the House with her to know her sure.

*Jo.* And how do they call her prethee? 50

*Fran. Conſtantia.*

*Jo.* How! *Conſtantia?*

*Fran.* Yes Sir, the Woman's name is *Conſtantia;* that's flat.

*Jo.* Is it so Sir? and so is this too. [*Strikes him.*

*Fran.* Oh, Oh. [*Runs out.* 55

*Jo.* Now Sirrah, you may safely say you have not born false witness for nothing.

*Fred.* Fie, *Don John* why do you beat the poor Fellow for doing his Duty, and telling truth?

*Jo.* Telling truth? thou talk'ſt as if thou had'ſt been hir'd to 60 bear false witness too: ye are a very fine Gentleman.

*Fred.* What a ſtrange confidence he has? But is there no shame in thee? nor no consideration of what is juſt or honeſt, to keep a Woman thus againſt her will, that thou know'ſt is in love with another man too; do'ſt think a Judgment will not follow this? 65

*Jo.* Good dear *Frederick,* do thou keep thy Sentences and thy Morals for some better opportunity, this here is not a fit Subjeċt for 'em: I tell thee she is no more *Conſtantia* than thou art.

*Fred.* Why won't you let me see her then?

*Jo.* Because I can't: besides she is not for thy turn. 70

*Fred.* How so?

*Jo.* Why, thy *Genius* lies another way; thou art for flames, and darts, and those fine things: now I am for the old plain down-right way; I am not so curious *Frederick* as thou art.

*Fred.* Very well Sir; but is this worthy in you to endeavour to     75
debauch ——

*Jo.* But is there no shame? but is this worthy? what a many
buts are here? If I should tell thee now solemnly thou haſt but one
eye, and give thee reasons for it, would'ſt thou believe me?

*Fred.* I think hardly Sir, againſt my own knowledg.                 80

*Jo.* Then why doſt thou, with that grave face, go about to per-
swade me againſt mine? You should do as you would be done
by *Frederick.*

*Fred.* And so I will Sir, in this very particular, since there's no
other remedy; I shall do that for the *Duke* and *Petruchio,* which I    85
should expect from them upon the like occasion: in short, to let
you see I am as sensible of my honour, as you can be careless of
yours; I muſt tell ye Sir, that I'm resolv'd to wait upon this Lady
to them.

*Jo.* Are ye so Sir? Why I muſt then, sweet Sir, tell you again, I    90
am resolved you shan't. Ne'r ſtare, nor wonder, I have promis'd to
preserve her from the sight of any one whatsoever, and with the
hazard of my life will make it good; but that you may not
think I mean an injury to *Petruchio,* or the *Duke,* know *Don
Frederick,* that though I love a Wench perhaps a little better, I    95
hate to do a thing that's base, as much as you do. Once more
upon my honor this is not *Conſtantia*; let that satisfie you.

*Fred.* All that will not do. ——          [*Goes to the Door.*

*Jo.* No? why then this shall. (*Draws*) Come not one ſtep
nearer, for if thou do'ſt, by Heaven it is thy laſt.                 100

*Fred.* This is an insolence beyond the temper of a man to
suffer; —— thus I throw off thy friendship, and since thy folly has
provok'd my patience beyond its natural bounds, know it is not in
thy power now to save thy self.

*Jo.* That's to be try'd Sir, though by your favour.                 105
          [*Looks up to the window.*
Miſtress what you call 'em, —— prethee look out now a little,
and see how I'll fight for thee.

*Fred.* Come, Sir, are you ready?

*Jo.* O Lord, Sir, your Servant.          [*Fight.*

[IV. iv]                   SCENE IV.

*Enter* Duke, *and* Petruchio.

*Petr.* What's here fighting? let's part 'em. How? *Don Frederick* against *Don John?* how came you to fall out, Gentlemen? What's the Cause?

*Fred.* Why Sir, it is your quarrel, and not mine, that drew this on me: I saw him lock *Constantia* up into that house, and I desir'd    5
to wait upon her to you; that's the Cause.

*Duke.* O, it may be he design'd to lay the obligation upon us himself. Sir, we are beholden to you for this favour, beyond all possibility of ——

*Jo.* Pray, Sir, do not throw away your thanks before you know    10
whether I have deserv'd 'em or no. O, is that your design? Sir you must not go in there.                    [Petruchio's *going to the Door.*

*Petr.* How, Sir, not go in?

*Jo.* No Sir, most certainly not go in.

*Petr.* She's my Sister, and I will speak with her.    15

*Jo.* If she were your Mother Sir, you should not, though it were but to ask her blessing.

*Petr.* Since you are so positive, I'll try.

*Jo.* You Shall find me a man of my word Sir.                    [*Fight.*

*Duke.* Nay pray Gentlemen hold, let me compose this matter.    20
Why do you make a scruple of letting us see *Constantia?*

*Jo.* Why, Sir, 'twould turn a man's head round to hear these Fellows talk so; there is not one word true of all that he has said.

*Duke.* Then you do not know where *Constantia* is?

*Jo.* Not I, by Heavens.    25

*Fred.* O monstrous Impudence! upon my life Sir, I saw him shut her up into that house, and know his temper so, that if I had not stop'd him, I dare swear by this time he would have ravish'd her.

*Jo.* Now that is two Lies: for first he did not see her, and next the Lady I led in is not to be ravish'd, she is so willing.    30

*Duke.* But look ye Sir, this doubt may easily be clear'd; let either *Petruchio* or I but see her, and if she be not *Constantia,* we engage our Honors (though we should know her) never to discover who she is.

*Jo.* I, but there's the point now, that I can ne'r consent to.    35

*Duke.* Why?

*Jo.* Because I gave her my word to the contrary.

*Duke.* And did you never break your word with a Woman?

*Jo.* Never before I lay with her; and that's the case now.

*Petr.* Pish, I won't be kept off thus any longer: Sir, either let   40
me enter, or I'll force my way.

*Fred.* No pray Sir, let that be my Office, I will be reveng'd on
him for having betray'd me to his friendship.

Petruchio and Frederick offer to fight with John.

*Duke.* Nay ye shall not offer him foul play neither.
Hold Brother, pray a word; and with you too Sir.   45

*Jo.* Pox on't, would they would make an end of this business,
that I might be with her again. Hark ye Gentlemen, I'll make ye a
fair Proposition, leave off this Ceremony among your selves, and
those dismal threats againſt me, phillip up cross or pile who shall
begin firſt, and I'll do the beſt I can to entertain ye all one after   50
another.

Enter Antonio.

*Ant.* Now do my fingers itch to be about some bodies ears for
the loss of my Gold. Ha! what's here to do, Swords drawn? I muſt
make one, though it coſt me the singing of ten *John Doryes* more.
Courage brave Boy, I'll ſtand by thee as long as this Tool here   55
laſts; and it was once a good one.

*Petr.* Who's this? *Antonio?* O Sir, you are welcome, you shall
be e'en Judge between us.

*Ant.* No, no, no, not I Sir, I thank ye; I'll make work for others
to judge of, I'm resolv'd to fight.   60

*Petr.* But we wo'n't fight with you.

*Ant.* Then put up your Swords, or by this hand I'll lay about
me.

*Jo.* Well said old *Bilbo* i'faith.       [*They put up their Swords.*

*Petr.* Pray hear us though: this Gentleman saw him lock up my   65
Siſter into that house, and he refuses to let us see her.

*Ant.* How Friend? Is this true?

*Jo.* Nay good Sir, let not our friendship be broken before it is
well made. Look ye Gentlemen, to shew ye that you are all mistaken, and that my formal Friend there is an Ass.   70

*Fred.* I thank you Sir.

*Jo.* I'll give my consent that this Gentleman here shall see her,
if his information can satisfie you.

*Duke.* Yes, yes; he knows her very well.

*Jo.* Then Sir, go in here if you please; I dare truſt him with her,    75
for he is too old to do her either good or harm.

*Fred.* I wonder how my Gentleman will get off from all this.

*Jo.* I shall be even with you Sir another time for all your
grinning.

*Enter a* Servant.

How now? where is he?                                                  80

*Ser.* He's run out o'the back door Sir.

*Jo.* How so?

*Ser.* Why Sir, he's ran after the Gentlewoman you brought in.

*Jo.* 'S death, how durſt you let her out?

*Ser.* Why Sir, I knew nothing.                                       85

*Jo.* No thou ignorant Rascal, and therefore I'll beat something
into thee.                                                [*Beats him.*

*Fred.* What, you won't kill him?

*Jo.* Nay come not near me, for if thou doſt by Heavens I'll give
thee as much; and would do so however, but that I won't lose time    90
from looking after my dear Sweet —— a pox confound you all.
                       [*Goes in and shuts the Door after him.*

*Duke.* What? he has shut the Door.

*Fred.* It's no matter, I'll lead you to a private backway by
that corner, where we shall meet him.                      [*Exeunt.*

[V. i]            ACT V. SCENE I.

*Enter* Antonio's Servant, Conſtables *and* Officers.

*Ser.* A Young Woman say'ſt thou and her Mother?

*Man.* Yes, juſt now come to the house. Not an hour ago.

*Ser.* It muſt be they, here Friend, here's money for you; be sure
you take 'em, and I'll reward you better when you have done.

*Conſt.* But Neighbour how — hup — shall I now — hup —               5
know these these Parties? for I would — hup — execute my
Office — hup — like — hup — a sober Person.

*Man.* That's hard; but you may easily know the Mother, for
she is — hup — drunk.

*Conſt.* Nay — hup — if she be drunk, let — hup — me alone           10
to maul her, for — hup — I abhor a Drunkard — hup — let it be
man — Woman, or — hup — Child.

*Man.* Ay Neighbour, one may see you hate drinking indeed.

*Conſt.* Why Neighbour — hup — did you ever see me drunk?
answer me that Queſtion: did you ever — hup — see me drunk?          15
*Man.* No, never, never: come away, here's the house. [*Exeunt.*

[V. ii]          SCENE II.

*Enter* 1. Conſtantia.

1. *Conſt.* Oh, whither shall I run to hide my self! The Conſtable has seiz'd the Landlady, and I'm afraid the poor Child too.
How to return to *Don Frederick's* house, I know not; and if I
knew, I durſt not, after those things the Landlady has told me of
him. If I get not from this drunken Rabble, I expose my honour;          5
and if I fall into my Brother's hands, I lose my life: you Powers
above, look down and help me, I am faulty I confess, but greater
faults have often met with lighter punishments:

*Then let not heavier yet on me be laid,*
*Be what I will, I am ſtill what you have made.*          10

*Enter* Don John.

*Jo.* I'm almoſt dead with running, and will be so quite, but I
will overtake her.

1. *Conſt.* Hold *Don John*, hold.

*Jo.* Who's that? Ha? is it you my Dear?

1. *Conſt.* For Heaven's sake Sir, carry me from hence, or I'm          15
utterly undone.

*Jo.* Phoo pox, this is th' other: now could I almoſt beat her, for
but making me the Proposition: Madam, there are some a coming
that will do it a great deal better; but I am in such haſte, that I
vow to Gad Madam ——          20

1. *Conſt.* Nay pray Sir ſtay, you are concern'd in this as well as
I; for your Woman is taken.

*Jo.* Ha! my Woman?          [*Goes back to her.*
I vow to Gad Madam, I do so highly honor your Ladyship, that I
would venture my life a thousand times to do you Service. But          25
pray where is she?

1. *Conſt.* Why Sir, she is taken by the Conſtable.

*Jo.* Conſtable! which way went he?          [*Rashly.*

1. *Conſt.* I cannot tell, for I run out into the Streets juſt as
had seiz'd upon your Landlady.          30

*Jo.* Plague o'my Landlady, I meant t'other Woman.

1. *ConS.* Other Woman Sir! I have seen no other Woman never since I left your house.

*Jo.* 'S heart, what have I been doing here then all this while? Madam, your moſt humble —— 35

1. *ConS.* Good Sir, be not so cruel, as to leave me in this diſtress.

*Jo.* No, no, no; I'm only going a little way, and will be back again presently.

1. *ConS.* But pray Sir hear me; I'm in that danger ——

*Jo.* No, no, no, I vow to Gad Madam, no danger i'the World; let 40 me alone, I warrant you.                          [*Exit.*

1. *ConS.* He's gone, and I a loſt wretched, miserable Creature, loſt for ever.

                    *Enter* Antonio.

*Ant.* O, there she is.

1. *ConS.* Who's this, *Antonio?* the fierceſt Enemy I have.          45
                                                    [*Runs out.*

*Ant.* Are ye so nimble-footed Gentlewoman? If I don't over-take you for all this, it shall go hard —— She'll break my wind with a pox to her. A plague confound all Whores.          [*Exit.*


[V. iii]                    SCENE III.

        *Enter* Mother *to the second* ConStantia, *and* Kinswoman.

*Kins.* But, Madam, be not so angry, perhaps she'll come again.

*Mot.* O *Kinswoman*, never speak of her more, for she's an odi-ous Creature, to leave me thus i'th' lurch. I that have given her all her breeding, and inſtructed her with my own Principles of Edu-cation.          5

*Kins.* Proteſt, Madam, I think she's a Person that knows as much of all that as ——

*Mot.* Knows, *Kinswoman?* There's ne'r a Woman in *Italy* of thrice her years knows so much the procedures of a true gallantry, and the infallible Principles of an honourable friendship as she does.          10

*Kins.* And therefore, Madam, you ought to love her.

*Mot.* No, fie upon her, nothing at all, as I am a Chriſtian: when once a Person fails in Fundamentals, she's at a period with me. Besides, with all her wit, *ConStantia* is but a Fool, and calls all the Meniarderies of a bonne mine, affectation.          15

*Kins.* Indeed I muſt confess, she's given a little too much to the careless way.

*Mot.* Ay, there you have hit it *Kinswoman*, the careless way has quite undone her. Will ye believe me *Kinswoman?* as I am a Chriſtian, I never could make her do this, nor carry her body thus, but juſt when my eye was upon her; as soon as ever my back was turn'd, whip, her elbows were quite out again: would not you ſtrange now at this? 20

*Kins.* Bless me sweet goodness! But, pray Madam, how came *Conſtantia* to fall out with your Ladiship? Did she take any thing ill of you? 25

*Mot.* As I'm a Chriſtian I can't resolve you, unless it were that I led the dance firſt; but for that she muſt excuse me, I know she dances well, but there are others who perhaps underſtand the right swim of it as well as she; 30

*Enter* Don Frederick.

And though I love *Conſtantia* ——

*Fred.* How's this? *Conſtantia?*

*Mot.* I know no reason why I should be debarr'd the priviledge of shewing my own parts too sometimes.

*Fred.* If I am not miſtaken that other Woman is she *Don John* and I were directed to, when we came firſt to Town, to bring us acquainted with *Conſtantia*. I'll try to get some Intelligence from her. Pray Lady, have I never seen you before? 35

*Kins.* Yes, Sir, I think you have, with another Stranger, a Friend of yours, one day as I was coming out of the Church. 40

*Fred.* I'm right then. And pray who were you talking of?

*Mot.* Why Sir, of an inconsiderate inconsiderable Person, that has at once both forfeited the honor of my concern, and the concern of her own honor.

*Fred.* Very fine indeed. And is all this intended for the beauti- 45
ful *Conſtantia?*

*Mot.* O fie upon her Sir, an odious Creature as I'm a Chriſtian, no Beauty at all.

*Fred.* Why, does not your Ladiship think her handsome?

*Mot.* Seriously, Sir, I don't think she's ugly, but as I'm a Chris- 50
tian, my Position is; That no true Beauty can be lodg'd in that Creature, who is not in some measure buoy'd up with a juſt sence of what is incumbent to the devoir of a Person of Quality.

*Fred.* That Position, Madam, is a little severe, but however she has been incumbent formerly, as your Ladyship is pleas'd to say; now that she's marry'd, and her Husband owns the Child, she is sufficiently justifi'd for all she has done. 55

*Mot.* Sir, I must blushingly beg leave to say you are there in an error. I know there has been passages of love between 'em, but with a temperament so innocent, and so refin'd, as it did impose a negative upon the very possibility of her being with Child. 60

*Fred.* Sure she is not well acquainted with her. Pray Madam, how long have you known *Constantia?*

*Mot.* Long enough I think Sir; for I had the good fortune, or rather the ill one, to help her first to the light of the World. 65

*Fred.* Now cannot I discover by the fineness of this Dialect, whether she be the Mother or the Midwife: I had best ask t'other Woman.

*Mot.* No Sir, I assure you, my Daughter *Constantia* has never had a Child: a Child! ha, ha, ha; O goodness save us, a Child! 70

*Fred.* O then she is the Mother, and it seems is not inform'd of the matter. Well Madam, I shall not dispute this with you any further; but give me leave to wait upon you to your Daughter; for her Friend I assure ye is in great impatience to see her.

*Mot.* Friend Sir? I know none she has; I'm sure she loaths the very sight of him. 75

*Fred.* Of whom?

*Mot.* Why, of *Antonio* Sir, he that you were pleas'd to say had got my Daughter with Child. Sir — ha — ha — ha —

*Fred.* Still worse and worse; 'Slife cannot she be content with not letting me understand her, but must also resolve obstinately not to understand me because I speak plain? Why, Madam I cannot express my self your way, therefore be not offended at me for it; I tell you I do not know *Antonio*, nor never nam'd him to you: I told you that the *Duke* has own'd *Constantia* for his Wife, that her Brother and he are Friends, and are both now in search after her. 80

85

*Mot.* Then as I'm a Christian, I suspect we have both been equally involv'd in the misfortune of a mistake. Sir I am in the derniere confusion to avow that though my Daughter *Constantia* has been lyable to several Addresses, yet she never has had the honour to be produc'd to his Grace. 90

*Fred.* So then you put her to bed to ——

*Mo. Antonio* Sir, one whom my ebb of fortune forc'd me to enter into a negotiation with, in reference to my Daughter's Per-

son; but as I'm a Chriſtian with that candor in the action, as I was 95
in no kind deny'd to be a witness of the thing.

 *Fred.* So, now the thing is out. This is a damn'd Bawd, and I
as damn'd a Rogue for what I did to *Don John*: for o' my conscience, this is that *Conſtantia* the Fellow told me of. I'll make
him amends what e'r it coſt me. Lady, you muſt give me leave not 100
to part with you, till you meet with your Daughter, for some
reasons I shall tell you hereafter.

 *Mot.* Sir, I am so highly your Obligee for the manner of your
Enquiries, and you have grounded your Determinations upon so
juſt a Basis, that I shall not be asham'd to own my self a Votary to 105
all your Commands.           [*Exeunt.*

[V. iv]     SCENE IV.

*Enter second* Conſtantia.

 2. *Conſt.* So, I'm once more freed from *Antonio*; but whither to
go now, there's the queſtion; nothing troubles me, but that he was
sent up by that young Fellow, for I lik'd him with my Soul, would
he had lik'd me so too.

*Enter* Don John, *and a* Shopkeeper.

 *Jo.* Which way went she?              5
 *Shop.* Who?
 *Jo.* The Woman?
 *Shop.* What Woman?
 *Jo.* Why, a young Woman, a handsome Woman, the hand-
someſt Woman thou ever saw'ſt in thy life: speak quickly Sirrah, 10
or thou shalt speak no more.
 *Shop.* Why, yonder's a Woman: what a Devil ayls this Fellow?
                    [*Exit.*
 *Jo.* O my dear Soul, take pity o' me, and give me comfort, for
I'm e'en dead for want of thee.
 2. *Conſt.* O you're a fine Gentleman indeed, to shut me up in 15
your  house, and send another man to me.
 *Jo.* Pray hear me.
 2. *Conſt.* No, I will never hear you more after such an Injury,
what would ye have done if I had been kind to ye, that could use
me thus before?                    20
 *Jo.* By my troth that's shrewdly urg'd.

2. *Conſt.* Besides, you basely broke your word.

*Jo.* But will ye hear nothing? nor did you hear nothing? I had three men upon me at once, and had I not consented to let that old Fellow up, who came to my rescue, they had all broken in     25
whether I would or no.

2. *Conſt.* Faith it may be it was so, for I remember I heard a noise; but suppose it was not so, what then? why then I'll love him however. Hark ye Sir, I ought now to use you very scurvily, but I can't find in my heart to do it.     30

*Jo.* Then God's blessing on thy heart for it.

2. *Conſt.* But a ——

*Jo.* What?

2. *Conſt.* I would fain ——

*Jo.* I, so would I: come let's go.     35

2. *Conſt.* I would fain know whether you can be kind to me.

*Jo.* That thou shalt presently; come away.

2. *Conſt.* And will you always?

*Jo.* Always? I can't say so; but I will as often as I can.

2. *Conſt.* Phoo! I mean love me.     40

*Jo.* Well, I mean that too.

2. *Conſt.* Swear then.

*Jo.* That I will upon my knees: what shall I say?

2. *Conſt.* Nay, use what words you please, so they be but hearty, and not those are spoken by the Prieſt, for that charm sel-     45
dome proves fortunate.

*Jo.* I swear then by thy fair self, that look'ſt so like a Deity, and art the only thing I now can think of, that I'll adore thee to my dying day.

2. *Conſt.* And here I vow, the minute thou do'ſt leave me, I'll     50
leave the World, that's kill my self.

*Jo.* O my dear heavenly Creature! —— [*Kisses her.*
That kiss now has almoſt put me into a swoon, for Heaven's sake let's quickly out of the Streets for fear of another scuffle. I durſt encounter a whole Army for thy sake; but yet methinks I had better     55
try my courage another way; what think'ſt thou?

2. *Conſt.* Well, well; why don't you go then? [*As they are going
out,*

Enter 1. Conſtantia, *and juſt then* Antonio *seizes upon her.*

*Jo.* Who's this, my old new Friend has got there?

*Ant.* O have I caught you Gentlewoman at laſt?
Come, give me my Gold.     60

1. *Con𝔰t.* I hope he takes me for another, I won't answer, for I had rather he should take me for any one than who I am.

*Jo.* Pray Sir, who is that you have there by the hand?

*Ant.* A Person of Honor Sir, that has broke open my Trunks, and run away with all my Gold; yet I'll hold ten pound I'll have it whip'd out of her again.

2. *Con𝔰t.* Done, I'll hold you ten pounds of that now.

*Ant.* Ha! by my troth you have reason; and Lady I ask you pardon; but I'll have it whip'd out of you then Gossip.

*Jo.* Hold Sir, you mu𝔰t not meddle with my Goods.

*Ant.* Your Goods? how came she to be yours? I'm sure I bought her of her Mother, for five hundred good pieces in Gold, and she was abed with me all night too; deny that if you dare.

2. *Con𝔰t.* Well, and what did you do when I was abed with you all night? confess that if you dare.

*Ant.* Umh, say you so?

1. *Con𝔰t.* I'll try if this Lady will help me, for I know not whither else to go.

*Ant.* I shall be sham'd I see utterly except I make her hold her peace. Pray Sir by your leave; I hope you will allow me the Speech of one word with your Goods here, as you call her; 'tis but a small reque𝔰t.

*Jo.* I Sir, with all my heart. How, *Con𝔰tantia!* Madam, now you have seen that Lady, I hope you will pardon the ha𝔰te you met me in a little while ago; if I committed a fault, you mu𝔰t thank her for it.

1. *Con𝔰t.* Sir, if you will for her sake, be perswaded to prote𝔠t me from the violence of my Brother, I shall have reason to thank you both.

*Jo.* Nay Madam, now that I am in my wits again, and my heart's at ease, it shall go very hard but I will see yours so too; I was before di𝔰tra𝔠ted, and 'tis not 𝔰trange the love of her should hinder me from remembring what was due to you, since it made me forget my self.

1. *Con𝔰t.* Sir, I do know too well the power of Love, by my own experience, not to pardon all the effe𝔠ts of it in another.

*Ant.* Well then, I promise you, if you will but help me to my Gold again, (I mean that which you and your Mother 𝔰tole out of my Trunk) that I'll never trouble you more.

2. *Con𝔰t.* A match; and 'tis the be𝔰t that you and I could ever make.

*Jo.* Pray Madam fear nothing; by my love I'll ſtand by you,
and see that your Brother shall do you no harm.

2. *Conſt.* Hark ye Sir, a word; how dare you talk of love, or
ſtanding by any Lady, but me Sir?                                     105

*Jo.* By my troth that was a fault; but I did not mean it your
way, I meant it only civilly.

2. *Conſt.* I, but if you are so very civil a Gentleman we shall not
be long friends: I scorn to share your love with any one whatsoever; and for my part, I'm resolv'd either to have all or nothing.    110

*Jo.* Well my dear little Rogue, thou shalt have it all presently,
as soon as we can but get rid of this Company.

2. *Conſt.* Phoo, y' are always abusing me.

*Enter* Frederick *and* Mother.

*Fred.* Come, now Madam, let not us speak one word more, but
go quietly about our business; not but that I think it the greateſt    115
pleasure in the World to hear you talk, but ——

*Mot.* Do you indeed Sir? I swear then good wits jump Sir; for
I have thought so my self a very great while.

*Fred.* Yo've all the reason imaginable. O, *Don John*, I ask thy
pardon; but I hope I shall make thee amends, for I have found out    120
the Mother, and she has promis'd me to help thee to thy Mistress again.

*Jo.* Sir, you may save your labour, the business is done, and I
am fully satisfi'd.

*Fred.* And doſt thou know who she is?                                125

*Jo.* No faith, I never ask'd her name.

*Fred.* Why, then, I'll make thee yet more satisfi'd; this Lady
here is that very *Conſtantia* ——

*Jo.* Ha! thou haſt not a mind to be knock'd o'r the pate too,
haſt thou?                                                           130

*Fred.* No Sir, nor dare you do it neither; but for certain this is
that very self same *Conſtantia* that thou and I so long look'd after.

*Jo.* I thought she was something more than ordinary; but shall
I tell thee now a ſtranger thing than all this?

*Fred.* What's that?                                                 135

*Jo.* Why, I will never more touch any other Woman for her
sake.

*Fred.* Well, I submit; that indeed is ſtranger.

2. *Conſt.* Come Mother, deliver your Purse; I have deliver'd my
self up to this young Fellow, and the bargain's made with that old    140
Fellow, so he may have his Gold again, that all shall be well.

*Mot.* As I'm a Chriſtian Sir, I took it away only to have the honour of reſtoring it again; for my hard fate having not be-ſtow'd upon me a Fund which might capacitate me to make you Presents of my own, I had no way left for the exercise of my gen- 145 erosity, but by putting my self into a condition of giving back what was yours.

*Ant.* A very generous design indeed. So, now I'll e'en turn a sober Person, and leave off this wenching, and this fighting, for I begin to find it does not agree with me. 150

*Fred.* Madam, I'm heartily glad to meet your Ladyship here; we have been in a very great disorder since we saw you. —— What's here, our *Landlady* and the Child again?

        *Enter* Duke, Petruchio, *and* Landlady *with the Child.*

*Petr.* Yes, we met her going to be whip'd, in a drunken Con-ſtables hands that took her for another. 155

*Jo.* Why, then, pray let her e'en be taken and whip'd for her self, for on my word she deserves it.

*Land.* Yes, I'm sure of your good word at any time.

1. *Conſt.* Hark ye dear *Landlady.*

*Land.* O sweet Goodness! is it you? I have been in such a peck 160 of troubles since I saw you; they took me, and they tumbled me, and they hall'd me, and they pull'd me, and they call'd me painted *Jezebel,* and the poor little Babe here did so take on. Come hither my Lord, come hither; here is *Conſtantia.*

1. *Conſt.* For Heaven's sake peace, yonder's my Brother, and if 165 he discovers me I'm certainly ruin'd.

*Duke.* No, Madam, there is no danger.

1. *Conſt.* Were there a thousand dangers, in those Arms, I would run thus to meet them.

*Duke.* O my Dear, it were not safe that any should be here at 170 present, for now my heart is so o'erpress'd with joy, that I should scarce be able to defend thee.

*Petr.* Siſter, I'm so asham'd of all the faults, which my miſtake has made me guilty of, that I know not how to ask your pardon for them. 175

1. *Conſt.* No, Brother, the fault was mine, in miſtaking you so much, as not to impart the whole truth to you at firſt; but having begun my love without your consent, I never durſt acquaint you with the progress of it.

*Duke.* Come, let the Consummation of our present joys, blot 180 out the memory of all these paſt miſtakes.

*Jo.* And when shall we consummate our Joys?
  2. *Conſt.* Never;
We'll find out ways shall make 'em laſt for ever.
  *Jo.* Now see the odds 'twixt marry'd Folks and Friends:    185
Our Love begins juſt where their Passion ends.

*FINIS.*

# EPILOGUE.

*Perhaps you Gentlemen, expeɫ to day*
*    The Author of this fag end of a Play*
*According to the Modern way of Wit*
*Shou'd ſtrive to be before-hand with the Pit,*
*Begin to rail at you, and subtly to*                              5
*Prevent th' affront by giving the firſt blow.*
*He wants not Presidents, which often sway*
*In matters far more weighty than a Play:*
*But he no grave admirer of a Rule,*
*Won't by Example learn to play the fool.*                        10
*The end of Plays should be to entertain,*
*And not to keep the Auditors in pain.*
*Giving our price, and for what trash we please,*
*He thinks the Play being done, you should have ease.*
*No Wit, no Sence, no Freedom, and a Box,*                        15
*Is much like paying money for the Stocks.*
*Besides the Author dreads the ſtrut and meen*
*Of new prais'd Poets, having often seen*
*Some of his Fellows, who have writ before,*
*When* Nel *has danc'd her Jig, ſteal to the Door,*               20
*Hear the Pit clap, and with conceit of that*
*Swell, and believe themselves the Lord knows what.*
*Moſt Writers now adays are grown so vain,*
*That once approv'd, they write, and write again,*
*Till they have writ away the Fame they got;*                     25
*Our Friend this way of writing fancies not,*
*And hopes you will not tempt him with your Praise,*
*To rank himself with some that write new Plays:*
*For he knows ways enough to be undone*
*Without the help of Poetry for one.*                             30

## FINIS.

EPILOGUE. *Alternative text at 11. 250. A transcript of the epilogue in the commonplace book of*
*George Ent the younger (d. 1679), Royal Society MS 83, pp. 92–3, is virtually identical to the text pub-*
*lished in the 1682 quarto and was presumably derived from a closely related ancestor source.*

# A Song in The Chances

FIG. 3. *A Song in The Chances Set to Musick by Mr John Eccles Sung by Mr Wiltshire.* The words by Sir Robert Howard. Transcribed from the version 'exactly engraved by Tho. Cross' (London, *c.*1700). Source: British Library K.7.i.2, no. 62. Accidentals have been modified to conform to modern practice.

pride to use Re - venge

Rea-son pride Sum-mon'd their for - ces to my Aid, but

found those life - gards those life - gards were af - fraid

Rea-son en-slav'd cou'd not pre-vail, pride shrunk and feirce re-venge grew pale so

sev'-rall sev'-rall ways so sev'-rall sev'-rall ways the Squar - dron

flyes at the first at the first vol-ley of her Eyes at the

first at the first vol-ley of her Eyes I then re-solv'd to take my

flight for e - ver for e - ver from her dang' - rous Sight but then in dreams in

dreams she wou'd ap - pear as full of Charmes of Charmes and as se-

- vere at length at length I found at length at length I found I found I must I

found I must I must I must en - dure what she what She or death cou'd on - ly

cure at length I found I found I must I must I must en - dure what she what she or

Death cou'd on - ly cure at length I found I found I must I must I must en - dure what she or

Death cou'd on - ly cure what she or Death cou'd on - ly cure.

# Sir Politick Would-be

COMEDIE A la maniere des Anglois.

Edited by Wallace Kirsop

## INTRODUCTION

### By H. Gaston Hall and Wallace Kirsop

*Sir Politick Would-be* remains almost totally unknown to English-language readers and critics and its connection with Buckingham has gone almost unmentioned by scholars. It was composed *c.*1662–5 but the earliest surviving text is the one published in Charles de Saint-Denis, Sieur de Saint-Évremond's *Œuvres meslées* of 1705. Bishop Percy included the play in his edition of Buckingham (drafted and mostly printed in the 1760s), and had that edition been published *Sir Politick* would probably have attracted more attention and more esteem than it has hitherto enjoyed outside of France. The play is a complex and witty satire whose significant Jonsonian components suggest that Buckingham had a more than casual part in its conception, if not necessarily in its composition. A translation has been supplied below in Volume II, Appendix V.

## THE PROBLEM OF AUTHORSHIP

Whereas there is a continuing discussion about the collaboration of Saint-Évremond with the Count d'Ételan in the writing of *La Comédie*

Wallace Kirsop expresses his pleasure in and gratitude for the invaluable collaboration of his old friend and colleague Gaston Hall in this new version and first translation of *Sir Politick Would-be*. The enterprise has benefited greatly from the skill and experience of Meredith Sherlock in preparing old-spelling critical editions of seventeenth-century texts for publication. The help of Robert D. Hume and Harold Love in providing materials and guidance has been unfailing. Thanks are also due to Roger Stoddard and to Angus Martin for obtaining copies of documents and for seeking out information. Many libraries on three continents have played a part in granting access to, or answering questions about, original editions of Saint-Évremond. The impeccable service offered by the staff of these various institutions is much appreciated. Special mention should be made of Donald Kerr, curator of the Esmond de Beer collection at the University of Otago Library.

*des Académistes*,[1] the claimed joint authorship of *Sir Politick Would-be* has received little commentary. In practice the work is included in the French author's œuvre, but the affirmation in the first shoulder note of the 1705 edition, '*Le dernier Duc de* Buckingham *& Mr. d'*Aubigny *ont eu beaucoup de part à la Composition de cette Piéce*',[2] has gone largely unchallenged and unelaborated. The most circumstantial account of the affair is contained in Pierre Des Maizeaux's biographical account of Saint-Évremond, itself suspect in various respects in the eyes of modern scholars:

> My Lord *d'Aubigny* having been sent into *France* at Five Years of Age, was educated at the College of *Port-Royal*; went young into Holy Orders, and was made a Prebendary of *Nôtre-Dame* in *Paris*. After the Restoration, he return'd into *England*, and the King having married the *Infanta* of *Portugal*, My Lord *d'Aubigny* was made Lord-Almoner to the Queen. He was a Man of great Abilities, and frank easy Nature, which made the Duke of *Buckingham* and Mr. *de St. Evremond* extremely fond of his Conversation. Being often together, they discours'd about all manner of Subjects, but chiefly about the Dramatick Pieces of several Nations. Mr. *de St. Evremond* not understanding the *English* Tongue, those Gentlemen acquainted him with the best Strokes in our most celebrated Plays; of which he retain'd a clear Idea to the very last; and from these ingenious Conversations resulted his *Reflections on the* English *Stage*, which are extant in his Works. To the same *Witty Triumvirate* we owe also the Play call'd SIR POLITICK WOULD-BE, towards which each of them *clubb'd* part of the Characters, which Mr. *de St. Evremond* reduc'd into Form. Those who shall find that Play a little too long, must consider, that 'twas written after the *English* Way; and besides, it is to be observ'd, that as it never was design'd to be presented on the Stage, they made it rather their Business to draw full Characters, than to animate the Action by a variety of surprizing Intrigues, and an unexpected unravelling of the Plot: Which those who peruse that Play ought to consider, before they pass their Judgment upon it.[3]

The latest research on Ludovic Stuart, Seigneur d'Aubigny (1619–65), plays down the extent of his involvement with and commitment to the Port-Royal movement.[4] What is more important in this context is his interest in court culture.

  [1] See *La Comédie des Académistes* & *Les Académiciens*, ed. Paolo Carile (Milan: Cisalpino-Goliardica; Paris: Nizet, 1976), *passim*, and Quentin M. Hope, *Saint-Evremond and his Friends* (Geneva: Droz, 1999), 91–100.

  [2] *Œuvres meslées* (London, 1705), i. 253.

  [3] Des Maizeaux, *The Life of Monsieur de St. Evremond* (London, 1714), p. xl.

  [4] Antony McKenna, 'Aubigny, Ludovic Stuart, seigneur d'', in *Dictionnaire de Port-Royal*, ed. Jean Lesaulnier and Antony McKenna (Paris: H. Champion, 2004), 127–8.

Whether or not *Sir Politick Would-be* was ever performed privately for Charles II or Buckingham is not known. Saint-Évremond's connection with the latter is well attested,[5] but much else remains pure speculation. As a result the inclusion of Saint-Évremond's play in an edition of Buckingham has to be a gesture towards a strongly claimed tradition rather than an incontrovertible proof of collaborative dramatic writing based on a documented interest in English theatre.[6] However, it is worth noting that Bishop Percy voiced no doubts about the joint authorship in his projected edition of Buckingham, which included *Sir Politick Would-be*.[7] Buckingham's enthusiasm for Ben Jonson is well documented and the probability is good that he was the source of Saint-Évremond's interest in writing a Jonsonian comedy. Buckingham's French was unquestionably excellent; whether he could have contributed to the actual composition of the text (or tried to do so) is unknowable. *Sir Politick* is quite unlike *The Chances*, *The Country Gentleman*, *The Rehearsal*, or *The Restauration*, but this is no argument against Buckingham's participation in the present enterprise. All four of those plays are adaptive and/or collaborative, and as a group they present singularly few parallels in design or execution.

### THE COLLABORATIVE BACKGROUND AND SETTING OF THE PLAY

*Sir Politick Would-be* owes its title role and setting in Venice to Ben Jonson's *Volpone*, but the politics of the new Sir Politick and the evocation of Venice differ significantly. Sir Politick and his wife may seem no older; but this play, written between 1662 and 1665, is set at least a generation later: around 1628, the year in which the first Duke of Buckingham was assassinated and the second duke was born.

---

[5] See *Lettres*, ed. René Ternois, 2 vols. (Paris: M. Didier, 1967–8), i. 262–70.

[6] See Saint-Évremond, *Œuvres en prose*, ed. René Ternois, 4 vols. (Paris: M. Didier, 1962–9), iii. 32–60.

[7] See 'Appendix I: The history of Percy's edition of Buckingham', in *The Percy Letters*, iii: *The Correspondence of Thomas Percy and Thomas Warton*, ed. M. G. Robinson and Leah Dennis (Baton Rouge, La.: Louisiana State University Press, 1951), 148–67. The date at which Percy decided to include *Sir Politick* must be regarded as questionable. Most of the edition was completed, and typeset by Tonson before 1767. However, the surviving proofs of *Sir Politick* date from the 1790s and were apparently typeset by Nichols. Robinson floats the theory that Percy made the decision to include the French play at that time when he realized that he could not complete the extensive biography that he had intended to include in volume ii (p. 164). This is a plausible hypothesis, but must be regarded as speculative on present evidence.

The latter's collaborator and the principal author of the comedy, Charles de Saint-Denis, Sieur de Saint-Évremond (1613–1703), was at that time around 15. He had an active military career throughout the French War with Spain (1636–59); that is, from late in the reign of Louis XIII through the Regency of Anne of Austria and the French civil war known as the Fronde. He served the free-thinking Duke d'Enghien, later Prince de Condé (the Grand Condé), and—after Condé's defection to Spain—Cardinal Mazarin, who governed what and when he could for Anne of Austria during the Fronde. As war was seldom waged in winter at that time, Saint-Évremond was free to spend his winters with the royal court and/or in Paris, where he was an active observer of court politics and entertainments, especially theatre and court ballet. As a young man he had frequented the company of the sceptic Pierre Gassendi, whom he regarded as the most enlightened and the least presumptuous of philosophers. In 1659 he followed the court to the Spanish border for the signing of the Peace of the Pyrenees, which ended the Spanish War with a treaty that included Louis XIV's marriage to the Infanta of Spain. Saint-Évremond expressed doubts in private correspondence which later brought about his third disgrace—he had twice in the 1650s spent months in the Bastille for satirical comments on men in a position to punish them—and his exile. In October of the following year he accompanied the Count de Soissons on the great French diplomatic mission to London to congratulate Charles II on his restoration, and he remained for nearly six months, perhaps on a secret mission for Mazarin's rival, the Surintendant des Finances Nicolas Foucquet. He returned to a new political world in Paris following Mazarin's death on 9 March 1661: the beginning of Louis XIV's personal reign, an early manifestation of which, the dramatic arrest of Foucquet on 5 September, precipitated Saint-Évremond's return to London towards the end of November as an asylum seeker.

Rather less is known of the third alleged participant in the genesis of the comedy, Ludovic Stuart (1619–65), a younger son of the Duke of Lennox and thus related to Charles II. Brought up as a Catholic in France, he had taken holy orders; and on the deaths of his elder brothers he inherited the land and title of Aubigny. Following the Restoration, he went to London and, after the king's marriage to the Infanta of Portugal, became her Almoner. In his biographical preface to the 1705 edition of Saint-Évremond's *Œuvres meslées,* Silvestre states that

Saint-Évremond 'vécut sur tout dans une grande liaison avec Mr d'Aubigny'—that he was especially close to M d'Aubigny.[8] That is, closer than to the other known prominent members of Saint-Évremond's circle in London, which included not only the second Duke of Buckingham, but also James Butler, first Duke of Ormond (Lord Lieutenant of Ireland from 1662), Henry Jermyn, Earl of Saint Albans (rumoured to have been secretly married to Henrietta Maria after the execution of Charles I), Henry Bennet (from 1665 Earl of Arlington), and Lord Crofts. It was not d'Aubigny's death on 3 November 1665 which broke up the circle, but the court's move in July 1665—on the outbreak of plague—first to Hampton Court, then to Oxford. Preparations for the Second Dutch War were also a factor. Holland was then allied with France. Saint-Évremond considered it impolitic to remain in a country which might soon be at war with France and departed for Holland, probably also in July. Thus it would seem reasonable to posit early 1662 as a *terminus a quo* for the collaboration on *Sir Politick* and July 1665 as the *terminus ad quem*. I do not know whether it was later revised for a performance of which there is no record or for any other reason before its posthumous publication forty years later.

As the future Lord Arlington seems to have remained on good terms with the members of this circle throughout the period in which it was written, and with Saint-Évremond even after the break with Buckingham, he is unlikely to have been satirized in the role of Sir Politick, as is sometimes suggested.

There seems little doubt, however, that comic or satirical reference in the play is not limited to Venice, but includes allusions to affairs current at the beginning of the Restoration of a more or less constitutional monarchy in England and also of Louis XIV's efforts to make the recently shaken monarchy in France absolute. The ancient elective constitutional monarchy of Venice, with its own claim to sovereignty rooted in divinity—the Doge delivered decrees from a throne in the great Basilica of St Mark—is not without interest in that connection; and doubtless it is not an accident that at the end of the play the German Traveller suggests travel to three other great free-trading ports—the Hanseatic cities of Hamburg, Lübeck, and Danzig. Like Venice, the Hanseatic League was in decline in 1662–5. But these city-states contrast sharply with the great Asian monarchs involved in the Circulation

---

[8] *Œuvres en prose*, i, pp. xxxii–xxxiii.

scheme: the Great Mogul, the Shah of Persia, and the Ottoman Sultan. It is pertinent to Venetian reactions to the Circulation and pigeon-post projects in *Sir Politick* that in 1628 the Sultan of Turkey was at war with the Shah of Persia and the pressure of Turkish expansion on the Venetians consequently reduced. By the time it was being written, the Venetians were faced with renewed Turkish advances in Europe and were defending Candia (modern Herakleion) in Crete against the longest siege in European history, finally successful in 1669, which is also the last year in which an Assembly of the Hanseatic League took place and fourteen years before the Turkish advance into Europe was defeated by the Polish army near Vienna in 1683. Understandably, at the French court there is a considerable difference between the role of the Grand Turk danced by Desmarets in *Le Grand Bal de la Douairière de Billebahaut—The Grand Ballet of the Dowager of Bilbao*—in 1626 and the elaborate reception of the Turkish diplomatic mission to France led by Suleiman-Aga in 1669, the immediate inspiration of Molière's *Le Bourgeois Gentilhomme* and associated *Ballet des nations* (1670).

By the seventeenth century, Venice had expanded landwards to include Verona since the turbulent times evoked in *Romeo and Juliet*, but had lost to the advancing Ottoman Empire the island of Cyprus, where the latter part of *Othello* is set, and other territories that had once made it the master (as they said) of three-eighths of the Roman Empire. Nor was Venetian commerce flourishing in the years following production of *The Merchant of Venice*. The loss of such ports as Nauplia, the shift of world trade to the Atlantic, competition with the ocean-going fleets of Holland and England even in the Mediterranean, and an aversion to innovation, among other things, had seriously reduced its competitiveness. Venetian politics was firmly focused on preserving what was left of the *status quo ante*, and any sort of speculation—let alone schemes like Circulation and a pigeon post—was antithetical to the prevailing ethos. In 1602 a law was introduced restricting Venetian merchants to the uncompetitive home fleet—good news in the short term perhaps for shipowners, but a further loss of competitiveness for the merchants of Venice. And it was not only at sea that the city-state was threatened.

From 1494 onwards French and later Spanish invasions of Italy, their occupations of previously independent regions, their rivalries, and at the same time the doctrinal demands of successive popes put Venetian independence under pressure and at risk. *Venice Preserved* may have been based on a fiction not published by Saint-Réal until 1674, but in 1628 the Spanish threat was also real. A great deal—of consequence to Venice and the rest of Europe—would depend upon the outcome of the Thirty Years War (1618–48). In various publications the Venetian Paolo Sarpi, whose *History of the Council of Trent* was published under a pseudonym in London in 1619, defended the sovereignty of Venice; and his correspondence shows that he envisaged defensive alliances, not only with France and Holland, but even with the Turks. 'It causes sorrow here, people fearing the Turk in Italy', he wrote to Groslot on 23 October 1611–12, 'but it would be a universal salvation'.[9] The Catholic Sarpi also had a sceptical tolerance of religious differences; an aversion to persecution; a willingness to defy Papal bans and to collaborate with Lutherans, Calvinists, and Anglicans; and a concept of the Church as a *convocatio fidelium*, an aggregation of individuals—none of whom as mere humans could be considered intellectually competent to determine which of them were heretic and which orthodox.[10] In *Sir Politick* one notes the word *humanité* (humanity) in the sense of the human race in general or mankind independently of national or religious affiliation, a sense not implicit in the Latin word from which it is derived and long considered new in Molière's *Dom Juan*, III. ii (1665).

In foreign affairs the elected Doge may have been as sovereign as any divine-right prince or ruler, but in internal affairs his freedom was severely curtailed, originally by a Great Council and in the seventeenth century by an oligarchy, the Senate. Of interest in relation to Sir Politick's projects and the action of this play are restrictions placed on the Doge's ability to meet foreigners in private or to correspond even with his wife without official scrutiny. In 1628 the first two stages of Sir Politick's projected pigeon post, Istria in the north-east Adriatic and Dalmatia (now coastal Croatia), were still Venetian territory; but Bosnia was Turkish. Dominico's role as eavesdropping spy doubtless mocks (amongst other things) a cultural climate in which ordinary citizens were encouraged to denounce in writing anything they regarded as suspicious. One of the reasons why there were so many curiosities for the German Traveller to see is that, quite apart from the products of Venetian art and industry, there had been a long tradition requiring Venetian travellers to return with ornaments for St Mark's.

---

[9] William Bouwsma, 'Venice, Spain, and the Papacy: Paolo Sarpi and the Renaissance Tradition', in Eric Cochrane (ed.), *The Late Italian Renaissance, 1525–1630* (London: Macmillan, 1970), 366–7.

[10] Ibid., 371–2.

There is, however, one thing that perhaps had not changed very much from the time when Peregrine realizes in *Volpone* (1605) that the lady

> [who] Lies here, in Venice, for intelligence
> Of tires, and fashions, and behaviour
> Among the courtesans

is Lady Politick (II. i). Dress, fashion, and behaviour are all important in the comedy, sometimes between the Venetians and their foreign visitors, and often between the visitors themselves. In relation to Lord Tancred's exchanges with Antonio in I. iv, the plans of Mme de Riche-Source and Sir Politick's wife to free the wives of Venice (from III. iii on), and the masquerade in Act IV, remarks on Venetian wives and courtesans in Thomas Coryat's *Crudities* (1611) may be noted. Commenting on the large number of courtesans, and doubtful about the 'ungodly' toleration 'of such licentious wantons in so glorious, so potent, so renowned a city', Coryat observes that Venetians

> thinke that the chastity of their wives would be the sooner assaulted, and so consequently they should be capricornified, (which of all the indignities in the world the Venetian cannot patiently endure) were it not for these places of evacuation. But I marvaile how that should be true though these Cortezans were utterly rooted out of the City. For the Gentlemen do even coope up their wives always within the walles of their houses for feare of these inconveniences, as much as if there were no Cortezans at all in the City. So that you shall very seldome see a Venetian Gentleman's wife but either at the solemnization of a great marriage, or at the Christning of a Jew, or late in the evening rowing in a Gondola.[11]

In essence Coryat's account is borne out by the findings of historians over the past century on the situation of women in Renaissance and post-Renaissance Venice, although it is clear that note has to be taken of nuances and complexities that hardly belong in a comedy.[12]

---

[11] Quoted in Ben Jonson, *Volpone*, ed. Philip Brockbank (London: Benn, 1968), 162–3.

[12] See, e.g. Heinrich Kretschmayr, *Geschichte von Venedig*, 3 vols. (Gotha and Stuttgart, 1905–34; repr. Aalen: Scientia Verlag, 1964), iii. 204–10; Federica Ambrosini, 'Toward a Social History of Women in Venice from the Renaissance to the Enlightenment', in John Martin and Dennis Romano (eds.), *Venice Reconsidered: The History and Civilization of an Italian City-State, 1297–1797* (Baltimore, Md. and London: Johns Hopkins University Press, 2000), 420–53; Patricia Fortini Brown, *Private Lives in Renaissance Venice: Art, Architecture, and the Family* (New Haven, Conn. and London: Yale University Press, 2004).

## Sir Politick Would-be: A French 'Comedy in the Manner of the English'

Robert Finch and Eugène Joliat, editors of *Sir Politick Would-be* (Geneva, 1978), relate the play to the origins of the eponymous Sir Politick in *Volpone* and generally to the seven other comedies Saint-Évremond mentions in his brief reflections on English theatre: Jonson's *Every Man in his Humour*, *Every Man Out of his Humour*, *Epicœne*, *The Alchemist*, *Bartholomew Fair*, and *The Devil is an Ass*, as well as Middleton's *Michaelmas Term*. Finch and Joliat also provide a few suggestions on Saint-Évremond's connections in the years 1662–5 (when *Sir Politick* was written) with the second Duke of Buckingham, the Sieur d'Aubigny, and Henry Bennet, later Lord Arlington, together with the pertinent information that members of the group indulged in satirical mimicry, as discussed elsewhere. Indeed mimicry was a habit for which Saint-Évremond went to prison in 1653. Three years later he wrote to the Count d'Olonne describing a comic, almost violent dispute between Guillaume de Bautru, Count de Serrant, and his younger brother Count de Nogent over the recent abdication of Christina of Sweden. The more or less illiterate Nogent maintained that erudition had ruined her because, had she remained a monoglot, she would not have been tempted to leave Sweden, arguing that nobility and manners on the one hand and knowledge on the other are more or less incompatible— comments contextual to the Marquis's attitude towards ignorance in his debate with the German in Act III of *Sir Politick* and evidence of Saint-Évremond's interest in the comic potential of contrasted personalities long before he reached England. Academician and no mean personal satirist, Bautru—but for his gout, writes Saint-Évremond— might have added blows to the insults to ignorance he delivered in defence of Christina's learning. Each brother maintained his position so fiercely, Saint-Évremond implies, because he did so as it were in self-defence: 'Bautru ayant peu d'obligation à la nature de son genie, et Nogent pouvant dire, sans estre ingrat, qu'il ne doit son talent ni aux Arts ni aux Sciences.'[13] It was satirical remarks on Cardinal Mazarin— discovered in Saint-Évremond's *Lettre sur la Paix* (*Letter on the Peace of*

[13] 'Bautru being little obliged to nature for his genius and Nogent being able to say without ingratitude that he owes his talent neither to the arts nor to the sciences.' Saint-Évremond, *Lettres*, i. 67–72.

*the Pyrenees*) during the Foucquet affair, thus after Mazarin's death—that prompted his flight back to England in November 1661. In preparation for the court's departure for Anjou and Brittany, apparently after the arrest of Foucquet had been decided, Saint-Évremond had left a *cassette*—a box containing money, letters, and papers including the *Lettre sur la Paix*—in the care of Mme de Plessis-Bellière, a friend of Foucquet's and the mother-in-law of Saint-Évremond's great friend the Marquis de Créqui. It was seized after the arrest of Foucquet, all of whose known close supporters were also investigated. Amongst writers who had collaborated on the great *fête* at Vaux-le-Vicomte earlier in the year, Paul Pellisson, the historian of the French Academy, was sent to the Bastille for five years; and Jean de La Fontaine, the future poet of the *Fables*, was exiled to Limoges. Molière alludes to a potentially incriminating *cassette* left with a friend in *Tartuffe*, IV. viii and V. i. The allusion may well have been to this one.

On the English context I would add two further comments. First, although it is unnecessary to see an allusion to Jonson's *Catiline* in Agostino's speech in V. ii, the possibility might be mentioned, since Act V is the only act that seems to me more Jonsonian than French. Its themes, on the other hand, strike me as very French, as I shall later elaborate. Second, I would mention Dryden, not as a playwright, but as the poet of *Annus Mirabilis*. Ternois[14] cannot contextualize M. de Riche-Source's project for the circulation of gold in the global economy on the analogy of the circulation of blood in humans by which Saint-Évremond replaces in II. iv Peregrine's inventions in *Volpone*, IV. i. That the fantasy is not entirely isolated is suggested, however, by the second quatrain of *Annus Mirabilis*, attacking Holland's trading policies:

> Trade, which like blood shoud circularly flow,
> Stop'd in their Channels, found its freedom lost:
> Thither the wealth of all the world did go,
> And seem'd but shipwrack'd on so base a Coast.

Coincidence perhaps, but more likely evidence: either of 'circulation' as an idea in the air (whether or not arising from a specific source), or that *Sir Politick* was known in English literary circles, which included Dryden by 1667, the year when he wrote *Annus Mirabilis* in retrospection of the dreadful events of 1666. The world would have to wait a few years for John Law's paper circulation project.

14 In Saint-Évremond, *Œuvres*, iii. 36.

Far from being 'a collection of etiolated Jonsonian humours', as Montague Summers describes *Sir Politick* in a phrase rejected by Finch and Joliat (p. 10), it fits snugly into a series of remarkable French comedies first performed between 1635 and 1673, whatever the more remote debt of folly on the French stage may be to Ariosto (notably in court ballet), to Erasmus, and to Cervantes (through a number of dramatizations from *Don Quijote*, the deluded eponymous hero of which could be persuaded to do almost anything, provided it was presented as the duty of a knight errant or a chivalric lover). If, from the eight or so English plays of whose action Saint-Évremond was apprised by his friends, he chose to develop a new cast around the Sir Politick of *Volpone*, it seems likely in the context of contemporary French comedy that this was because—like Don Quijote—Sir Politick is a 'would-be' with whom other 'would-bes' could be associated. Indeed Lord Tancred's testimony to the Senators in V. iii: 'There is an English knight, whom books on politics have driven mad', reads like an allusion to Don Quijote if not to the two female Quijotes of *Les Précieuses ridicules*, all three of whom the reading of romances had made mad.

Ternois might have paid more attention to Act V ('The last act is long and lacks life').[15] It could have helped him, not only to a deeper understanding of the themes of *Sir Politick*, but to the connection of this thoughtful act, relatively English in its dramaturgy, with the numerous comic lunatics of the mid-seventeenth-century French stage. There one may meet a few lunatics locked up and laughed at and others portrayed as out and about on the street. The foregoing indicates that such characterization is not limited to France; but its development in French culture in the seventeenth century may not be unrelated to phenomena which, two centuries later, would be termed local colour and realism. Nor will it escape the notice of the careful reader that alongside Sir Politick, properly speaking the only English 'would-be' other than his wife, Saint-Évremond presents two Venetians, only one German, and no fewer than three French 'would-bes'. Antonio, three of the four Senators, and the Madam with her girls all play roles within their roles, but seem to know exactly what they are doing and thus are not 'would-bes'. Or one might prefer to separate such conscious 'would-bes' who deliberately play roles within their roles from the unconscious, obsessional, metaphysical 'would-bes' like Sir Politick who seem unaware that the roles they imagine they play are not effec-

---

[15] *Œuvres*, iii. 38.

tively the basic roles in which they are cast as imagined by the play-wright. Lord Tancred, the practical joker and tease, relates to the French comic role of the *railleur*, particularly from III. vi. If (as sup-posed) Saint-Évremond began work on his first comedy, *Les Acadé-mistes*, in 1638, then he probably knew André Mareschal's comedy *Le Railleur, ou La Satyre du temps* (*The Tease, or The Satire of the Times*), performed in the 1635–6 season and published in 1638. In any case he must have known Desmarets's comedy *Les Visionnaires* (*The Visionaries* or *The Obsessed*), performed and published in 1637, in which one of the visionaries is also a *railleur*. But I anticipate.

When, in the last speech of *Sir Politick*, Lord Tancred looks back upon the mad and the ridiculous characters in the play, 'les Foux et les Ridicules', Saint-Évremond himself might have been looking back upon a series of French plays running from Charles Beys's *L'Hospital des fous* (1635) to Molière's *Les Précieuses ridicules*, the first new play that he wrote for Paris on his return in 1658 and one that Saint-Évremond would appear to have seen. It is one of the plays specifically mentioned in his commentaries on theatre. The two bourgeois girls of its title are ridiculous because they are, as suggested above, female Quijotes who have read too many romances: in other words, would-be *précieuses*, as-piring to the elegance of a world from which they are excluded by birth and fortune and of which they ape the vocabulary in a manner paral-leled today only by the lunatic fringes of political correctness, but with something of the silliness, *mutatis mutandis*, of Antonio's highfalutin greetings to Lord Tancred in *Sir Politick*, I. iv. The rejected suitors of the two *précieuses* avenge themselves by sending them their two valets extravagantly disguised as noblemen, allegedly attracted by the fame of the two *précieuses*. As the valets themselves also 'would-bes', all four roles involve both showing off and showing one another up, until the valets are unmasked at the denouement—the whole action, inciden-tally, played within doors, unusual still as a setting for comedy in Paris at that time. The somewhat comparable burlesque masquerade in Act IV of *Sir Politick* also indicates the interior of a modest home, perhaps with something like the 'scene area' of a Restoration London theatre envisaged, but contrasting with the neoclassical urban outdoor setting implied in the first three acts.

Saint-Évremond probably also saw Molière's next successful com-edy, *Sganarelle, ou le Cocu imaginaire* (*Sganarelle, or the Imaginary Cuck-old*), performed and published in a pirated edition in 1660. The title role of this one-act farce is the role that Molière was destined to perform himself more times than documented for any other role, a fact which along with piracy of the first edition and other evidence indicates a huge stage success. Curiously, in its list of actors Sganarelle's wife is listed simply as *Sa femme* and named *la Femme de Sganarelle* (Sganarelle's Wife) in her speech prefixes. Perhaps 'Somebody's Wife' is commonplace in *Dramatis personae*; but I know only of *la Femme de Sganarelle* and *la Femme de Sir Politick* (Sir Politick's Wife), which contrasts with 'Fine Madame Would-be, the Knight's wife' amongst 'the Persons of the Play', and 'Lady Would-be' as a speech prefix in *Volpone*. Repetition of Molière's formula is unlikely to have been coincidental.

*Sganarelle*, however, is more suggestive for the implications of its subtitle. *The Imaginary Cuckold* opens the series of 'would-be' dominant roles played by Molière until his fatal haemorrhage on stage as Argan, the imaginary invalid of his last play, *Le Malade imaginaire* (*The Hypochondriac*) (1673). Earlier, in *Les Précieuses ridicules* the valet Mascarille played by Molière enters disguised as a nobleman, the ridiculous imaginary 'Marquis de Mascarille'; but that is not a dominant role. In *L'École des femmes* (*The School for Wives*) Arnolphe assumes the title 'M. de la Souche' as an imaginary nobleman. Likewise the well-off farmer Georges Dandin in the comedy of that title suffers as the would-be nobleman M. de la Dandinière, while the oxymoron of the title *Le Bourgeois Gentilhomme* (*The Bourgeois Nobleman*) certifies M. Jourdain as a *gentilhomme imaginaire*. One might say that Orgon in *Tartuffe* is similarly a 'would-be' man of piety or an *imaginaire* as far as the piety he professes is concerned, and thus the more easily deceived by the conscious hypocrite Tartuffe, who skilfully plays upon Orgon's self-deception.

Saint-Évremond could not have met Molière's later plays before completing *Sir Politick*, and some he may never have known. But the plays he came to know caused him to revise his impression of French comedy:

Nôtre Molière, à qui les Anciens ont inspiré le bon esprit de la Comedie, égale leur Benjanson à bien representer les diverses humeurs et differentes manieres des hommes, l'un et l'autre conservant dans leurs peintures un juste raport avec le genie de leur Nation.[16]

---

[16] *Œuvres*, iii. 60. 'Our Molière, in whom the Ancients inspired the good spirit of comedy, equals the Ben Jonson of the English in properly representing the contrasting humours and different manners of men, the one and the other preserving in their depictions a proper

This comment and the partial sketch of Molière's 'would-bes' are offered to suggest that *Sir Politick*, with its comedy based on self-deception, delusion, and obsession as well as on contrasted national manners, is in the mainstream of French court ballet and comic theatre, or dare I say 'would have been' had it not missed performance in Paris because it was written in England by a *persona non grata* at the French court.

An important tributary to that mainstream in the early 1660s was *Les Visionnaires*, a five-act comedy in verse written for the first, smaller theatre in Cardinal Richelieu's Palace in Paris by Jean Desmarets, later Sieur de Saint-Sorlin. Even more than in *Sir Politick*, the plot in *Les Visionnaires* is subordinate to character and situation; and the situations mostly juxtapose obsessional characters who show each other off and show each other up. In the 'Argument' or preface to the play, Desmarets observes:

Dans ceste Comedie sont representez plusieurs sortes d'esprits Chimeriques ou Visionnaires, qui sont attaints chacun de quelque folie particuliere: mais c'est seulement de ces folies pour lesquelles on ne renferme personne; et tous les jours nous voyons parmy nous des esprits semblables, qui pensent pour le moins d'aussi grandes extravagances, s'ils ne les disent.[17]

Three daughters are promised in marriage that very day to four different men by a father who nonetheless comes perhaps a little nearer to sanity than anyone else in the play other than a relative with a minor utility role. The seven obsessional or visionary roles involved in the various betrothals are (1) a captain in the tradition of Plautus' *miles gloriosus*, a type renewed a year earlier on that very stage in Corneille's *L'Illusion*; (2) an extravagant poet whose diction burlesques Pléiade poetics; (3) an *amoureux en idée* in love with the idea of love; (4) an imaginary millionaire who describes as his palace one that he does not own (and Richelieu did); (5) a girl in love with Alexander the Great; (6) her sister who believes everyone is in love with her; and (7) another sister besotted with theatre. The plot involves not much more than the arrangement of one too many betrothals and their annulment, because the betrothed are all too obsessed with their chimeras or too self-obsessed to marry. The action, adds Desmarets, 'n'est sousten que des connection with the genius of his nation.'

[17] 'In this comedy are represented several sorts of chimerical or visionary *humours*, who are afflicted each with some individual madness: but it is only those follies for which no one is locked up; and every day we see amongst us comparable people who at least think such ridiculous things even if they do not say them.'

extravagances de ces Visionnaires qui se meslent encore ensemble en quelque sorte, pour faire mieux parestre ces folies les unes par les autres'.[18]

Not surprisingly, although *Sir Politick* may have features of Jonsonian plot lacking in *Les Visionnaires*, its dramatic structure in the first three acts scarcely differs from what Desmarets indicates here. (The humours were thought to influence outlook and action through the rise of animal spirits, Desmarets's *esprits*, to the brain; and Molière wrote several melancholic roles for himself, not least the title role of *Le Misanthrope*, once subtitled *L'Atrabilaire amoureux—The Melancholic in Love*.) A similar set is implied in Acts I to III, suggesting neoclassical unity of place, which (on one interpretation) is not violated even by the change of scene to a place easily reached in a day, such as the indoor scenes of Acts IV and V in *Sir Politick*. There is unity of action because there is no real subplot in either play; and some of the same tags emphasizing unity of time are used in both plays, e.g. 'pour le soir' ('early evening', as indicated somewhat unusually in *Les Visionnaires*, I. iv) and the more commonplace 'dez ce soir', suggesting that everything will be done within the twenty-four hours of the notional unity of time. Nor is it difficult to notice some of the special 'visionary' vocabulary of *Les Visionnaires* in *Sir Politick*, V. ii, to cite only Azaro's phrases 'extravagance de ses visions' and 'en idée' (of Sir Politick's correspondence with Constantinople), recalling Desmarets's 'poète extravagant' and 'amoureux en idée', to say nothing of Pamfilino's 'chimères' and 'chimériques'.

Desmarets's comment that in *Les Visionnaires* we meet 'only those follies for which no one is locked up' probably refers not only to the secular debate on the treatment of various manifestations of lunacy reflected in the final act of *Sir Politick* but also to another, earlier play: Beys's tragicomedy *L'Hospital des fous*, adapted from one of Lope de Vega's many plays known under more than one title and published in 1636 following performance somewhat earlier. One of Lope's titles, *Los Locos de Valencia*, links it to the great lunatic asylum in the Spanish city of Valencia once held by El Cid; but of interest here is Beys's adaptation for the French stage and in particular a visit made by his tragicomic characters to an asylum. Without counting the keeper, or the poets and lovers who receive only a mention, six lunatics are locked up in the asylum: the Philosopher, the Musician, the Litigant, the Astrol-

---

[18] 'is sustained only by the ridiculousness of these obsessionals who still mix with one another somehow to highlight one another's foolishness'.

oger, the Soldier, and the Alchemist. All of them are egocentric meg-alomaniacs whose delusions highlight those of their companions; and 'le plus fou de céans veut corriger les autres' ('the maddest one here wants to set the others straight'). The Philosopher's contribution to the wider debate is the suggestion that, whereas the mentally ill should be pitied more than the victims of physical deformities and mutilations, the public comes to laugh at them as if they were on stage. But the sugges-tion is not accepted with respect to those whose lunacy is deemed their own fault.

In the context of the comic dramaturgy of madness, Beys's prelimi-nary remarks to the reader are of particular interest:

Si les Fous que je mets dans cét Hospital te semblent scavans, tu diras qu'il s'en trouve de pareils, et que j'ay voulu prendre les meilleurs. Toutes leurs images ne sont pas brouillées, ils ne sont blessez qu'en un endroit. Ils sont fous, en ce qu'ils s'estiment plus qu'ils ne sont, et dans cette opinion ils parlent d'eux, comme tu voudrois parler des choses qu'ils estiment estre.[19]

Desmarets adapts this notion to the roles of some of his *visionnaires*: his imaginary millionaire, for example. Phalante describes as his own the new Château de Richelieu in Poitou of which Desmarets would later become Steward and the poet of *Les Promenades de Richelieu* (1653). Nor is the notion unhelpful with respect to certain roles in *Sir Politick*, especially the *récits*—accounts of what various characters have done, claim to have done, or say they will do off stage.

The master of fictional *récits* of this sort, however, is Pierre Corneille in his comedy *Le Menteur* (*The Liar*), performed in the 1643–4 season and probably known to Saint-Évremond if only because it was highly successful and in the repertory of plays Molière brought back to Paris in 1658. *Le Menteur*, too, was adapted from a Spanish comedia: Alar-cón's *La Verdad sospechosa* (*Suspect Truth*). Dorante, the liar of the title, differs from some of the other compulsives and obsessionals found in seventeenth-century theatre to the extent that he lies deliberately. In-deed, his lies may be taken as metaphors for the creativity of writers and actors and as such set against the fantasies of demented roles in other plays, illusions also suggestive of literary and other creativity. In

---

[19] 'If the lunatics that I put in this asylum seem to you learned, you will say that there are some like that and that I wished to select the best. All of their fantasies are not muddled; they are only flawed in one respect. They are crazy in that they imagine that they are more than they are; and having that opinion, they speak about themselves as you would like to speak about the things they imagine they are.'

any case the imaginary *cadeau* or entertainment described by Dorante in I. v makes an ideal comparison with the entertainment proposed by Mme de Riche-Source in *Sir Politick*, III. v.

Pierre Nicole's *Lettres imaginaires* and *Lettres visionnaires* and the *Satires* of Nicolas Boileau-Despréaux from the mid-1660s damaged Desmarets's reputation in something of the way that familiar lines in Dryden's *Absalom and Achitophel* and Pope's *Epistle III* damaged the second Duke of Buckingham's. So let me repeat here (after my *Richelieu's Desmarets and the Century of Louis XIV*[20] and earlier edition of *Les Visionnaires*[21]) that, at the time Saint-Évremond was writing his *Académistes*, Desmarets was perhaps the leading founder-member of the new French Academy. His novel *Ariane* (1632) is the earliest book recorded as having been read during a meeting of the pre-academic group. When later the Academy was officially inaugurated, it first met in Desmarets's home in Paris. He was its first and is still its longest-serving Chancellor. It was the Bautru mentioned above who introduced Desmarets into Cardinal Richelieu's personal service in 1634 and who, in a dialogue published eleven years earlier, shares with Desmarets detailed remarks on numerous court personalities. *Les Visionnaires* was his second comedy. His first comedy, *Aspasie*, written earlier for Cardinal Richelieu's new proscenium-arch theatre, is to some extent a Neoplatonic allegory of the new Academy and its nationalist rhetorical objectives. He was also one of the three members of the Academy delegated to execute its first commission, the evaluation of Corneille's famous tragicomedy (as it then was), *Le Cid*. But this first Chancellor of the French Academy was also the famous Marets of court ballet, the last official French court jester, the *Bouffon du roi* who had begun to appear in court entertainments some twenty years earlier and soon danced regularly with King Louis XIII, including *Le Ballet de la merlaizon* (*Ballet of the Blackbird Hunt*) (1635), which Saint-Évremond evidently saw and enjoyed. The king devised the ballet and danced the role of a lure-merchant's wife in drag. He clearly took delight in dancing in drag with Desmarets as well as singing psalms paraphrased for him by the same. It is worth adding that the bird hunted was the European blackbird *turdus merula*, since the nursery rhyme recalling 'four and twenty blackbirds baked in a pie' refers not only to this

---

[20] (Oxford: Clarendon Press, 1990).
[21] 2nd edn. (Paris: Société des Textes Français Modernes, 1995).

species, but to the special sort of pastry from which a number of birds fly forth as evoked by Antonio in I. iv of *Sir Politick*.

In 1639 Desmarets devised the great *Ballet de la félicité* to celebrate the long-awaited birth of the Dauphin, the future Louis XIV. In January 1641 it was Desmarets, and not the Cardinal's original 'five authors' including Corneille, who wrote and staged *Mirame* for the grand opening of a great new proscenium-arch theatre in the Palais-Cardinal with perspective sets and scene-shifting machinery designed by Bernini on a commission from Richelieu's delegate in the matter, Cardinal Mazarin. A few weeks later Desmarets staged in the same new theatre his *Ballet de la prospérité des armes de la France* to celebrate the marriage of Clémence de Maillé-Brézé, Cardinal Richelieu's niece, to the Duke d'Enghien, future Prince de Condé, into whose company of guards Saint-Évremond entered in 1642.

Saint-Évremond could scarcely have failed to notice the new theatre or Desmarets's connection with it. Left to the Crown on Richelieu's death and then to decay during the civil war of the Fronde, this theatre is better known with new installations as the Palais-Royal where Molière's troupe performed from 1661 until his death, and then as the theatre where Lully produced the operas satirized three years later in Saint-Évremond's third and last comedy, *Les Opéra* (1676). The dramaturgy of *Mirame* combined for the first time in France the changing spectacles familiar in court ballets with neoclassical unity of place and time because, with Bernini's help, a way had been found to alter the sets by means of lighting and of machinery which moved, among other things, images of the sun and moon symbolizing not only the passing of twenty-four hours, but the king and queen, present at the performance. Louis XIII was, of course, a Sun King long before his more famous and more pompous son.

Reactions to *Mirame* varied. Several commentators, such as Tallemant des Réaux in his *Historiettes*, interpreted its allegory as referring to a scandalous relation between the queen, Anne of Austria, and the first Duke of Buckingham. Such an allusion is as improbable as it would have been untimely and unwise, but there had been the scandals of Buckingham's attempt to kiss the queen in a riverside garden in Amiens in June 1625 and his abortive effort to relieve the siege of La Rochelle a couple of years later. I do not know whether there is an allusion to the incident of the kiss in the Marquis's comic query in *Sir Politick*, IV. i, and Sir Politick's startled rejoinder: 'Kiss in Venice! Kiss a Dogesse!' However, there is published evidence that in 1625 (thus two

years before the siege) Desmarets, acting in another capacity and doubtless as Deputy for Fortifications, visited La Rochelle and reported the
execution of a merchant from Bordeaux for trading illicitly with Spain.
In France there were serious restraints on trade. Reorganization of international commerce as part of a general settlement of the European
nations and their colonies is the subject of Desmarets's last play, *Europe*,
an allegory thought to embody Richelieu's plans, in the year of his
death 1642, for an overdue settlement of the Thirty Years War. It
appears, incidentally, to have been as the title of this play that the word
*Europe* (vice *Chrétienté* or similar = *Christendom*) first appears in the
title of a separate publication.

Neither Desmarets's political activities nor *Les Visionnaires* had been
forgotten when, twenty years later, Saint-Évremond began work on *Sir
Politick*. There were nine editions of *Les Visionnaires* before Saint-
Évremond's exile, a publishing success at the time; and Molière's troupe
brought it back to Paris with five performances in 1659 and another
sixteen in the period 1660–6. Nor did Molière exploit it solely for his
roles written for himself. In *Les Fâcheux (The Importunates)*, his first
comedy written as part of a ballet-comedy, the action is limited to successive comic encounters between a young lover in a hurry and a series
of egocentric importunates with whom he is incompatible, particularly
at the moment of the meeting. Although the plot is largely linear, the
series of encounters between incompatibles constitutes the dramatic
action much as, *mutatis mutandis*, such encounters do in *Les Visionnaires* and in the first three acts of *Sir Politick*. From *Les Fâcheux* Saint-
Évremond may have picked up the idea, not simply to link such incompatible characters as the Marquis and the German in mutual incomprehension, but to give the latter added scope for miming irritation
and impatience by supposing him in a hurry. Saint-Évremond's comments on *Les Fâcheux* show that he knew it; and he must have known
that it had been devised for Nicolas Foucquet's splendid festival at Vaux-
le-Vicomte, the splendours of which precipitated the Surintendant's
disgrace and, with it, his own exile. He might not have guessed that
*Les Fâcheux* would be followed by a series of collaborations between
Molière and Jean-Baptiste Lully on ballet-comedies leading directly to
the operas he would satirize in *Les Opéra*.

At this point I propose some preliminary conclusions: that in addition to the eight English plays identified as related in various ways to
*Sir Politick*, we add a short list of eight French plays no less meaning-
fully related; that these include Molière's *Les Précieuses ridicules*, *Sgana-*

*relle ou Le Cocu imaginaire*, *Les Fâcheux*, and (for reasons to be adduced) *La Critique de l'Ecole des femmes*, together with Beys's *L'Hospital des fous*, Mareschal's *Le Railleur ou La Satyre du temps*, Desmarets's *Les Vision-naires*, and Corneille's *Le Menteur*, and that various aspects of Saint-Évremond's stagecraft in this comedy 'in the manner of the English'—characterization, themes, and dramatic structure—are in fact more in the manner of the French. Even the propensity to satirical mimicry of associates and superiors which he shared with his friends in England is well attested before his exile. Pierre Silvestre and Pierre Des Maizeaux record that with various friends—Silvestre mentions in particular the Marshal de Clérambaut, Des Maizeaux the Count de Miossens—Saint-Évremond covertly mimicked and mocked the Prince de Condé while in his service. When in 1646 the Prince got wind of it, he was more than a little annoyed. Apparently the hero of Rocroi, the Grand Condé, enjoyed a bit of mimicry himself, but not at his own expense. He preferred being compared with Alexander the Great, not always to the latter's advantage.

Against the suggestion that in the role of the Marquis de Bousignac there may be discovered characteristics of Philibert de Gramont, a great friend of Saint-Évremond who was also at the royal court in London when *Sir Politick* was written, may be set the possibility that the latter had learned to mock Gascon mannerisms during his years of service down around Bordeaux if not at another time elsewhere. What seems indisputable is that the Marquis had become a comic type at the French court. Witness the first scene of Molière's rehearsal comedy, *L'Impromptu de Versailles* (1663):

> *Molière, parlant à de la Grange*: Vous, prenez garde à bien représenter avec moi votre rôle de marquis.
> *Mlle Molière*: Toujours des marquis!
> *Molière*: Oui, toujours des marquis. Que diable voulez-vous qu'on prenne pour un caractère agréable de théâtre? Le marquis aujourd'hui est le plaisant de la comédie; et comme dans toutes les comédies anciennes on voit toujours un valet bouffon qui fait rire les auditeurs, de même dans toutes nos pièces de maintenant, il faut toujours un marquis ridicule qui divertisse la compagnie.[22]

---

[22] '*Molière, speaking to La Grange*: You, be careful to act your role as marquis with me well.
*Mlle Molière*: Always marquis!
*Molière*: Yes, always marquis. What the devil do you want me to take for a character amusing on stage? Nowadays the marquis is the funny character in comedy; and just as in all

Such, for example, are the *petits marquis* of *Le Misanthrope* (1666), Acaste and Clitandre, who admire themselves and swear euphemistically very much as the Marquis de Bousignac does. Meanwhile, if there is a single point of view from which the various roles in *Sir Politick* may be seen as satirical, it is arguably the following exactly contemporary one, expressed at the French court by the Duke de La Rochefoucauld in his *Maximes* (1664): 'Le vrai honnête homme est celui qui ne se pique de rien' ('The true gentleman is the one who has no pretensions about anything') (no. 203).

It is hardly surprising that a Frenchman who had been interested for decades in the theatre of his own country and who, after one earlier visit, had only recently arrived in England and is said to have known very little English at the time, should write a play in French more in keeping with French than with English conventions and themes.

In *Sir Politick* Saint-Évremond may also be more concerned with affairs at the French court than previously suspected. Even if he remained ignorant of the matters I am about to mention, in their deliberations on madness and on the fate of the prisoners in V. ii, the Senators discard sentences similar to those obtained by Desmarets in the prosecution of two lunatics, Charpy de Sainte-Croix, sentenced to solitary confinement in the Bastille on 9 June 1661, and Simon Morin, burnt alive in Paris on 13 March 1663. Both men were fanatics who had been secretaries in the Extraordinaire des guerres, a branch of government concerned with military finance of which Desmarets was Controller-General from 1634 to *c.*1661, when the office may have been called in as Louis XIV began his personal reign. In both cases Desmarets worked with ecclesiastical members of the Conseil de conscience. Charpy had been the secretary of a seditious favourite of Louis XIII, the Marquis de Cinq-Mars, executed in 1642; and his book of strange biblical exegesis had attracted a number of disciples as far away as Bordeaux, doubtless a matter of concern for the court. Judged dangerous to the state, the book was burnt by the public executioner and Charpy imprisoned—Azaro's recommendation 'that one deprive of liberty scandalous lunatics who treat serious matters in exorbitant ways', rejected in *Sir Politick*, V. ii.

The arrest of Morin arranged by Desmarets was his fifth. Over the previous twenty years Morin had been first imprisoned and released as

the old comedies one sees a clownish valet who makes the audience laugh, so in our plays of the present day, there must be a ridiculous marquis to entertain the public.'

a lunatic, then, following further disturbing prophecies, sent to the asylum —the Petites-Maisons—at Charenton and released again in 1656. Illness and death had reduced the Conseil de conscience to four active members in 1661: François Hardouin de Péréfixe, Bishop of Rodez (later Archbishop of Paris); Henri de La Mothe-Houdancourt, Bishop of Rennes; François Annat, Louis XIV's Jesuit confessor; and the king himself. On various charges Morin's followers were whipped, branded, banished, or imprisoned. Charged with sorcery, heresy, and threatening regicide, Morin himself was convicted of 'human and divine lese-majesty' and burnt in the Place de Grève—a punishment too inhuman even for Agostino, who recommends only strangling in *Sir Politick*, V. iii.

In a verse letter to the Duchess of Longueville (the Prince de Condé's sister, the famous former *frondeuse*, and earlier the Mlle de Bourbon for whose court debut Desmarets had written lyrics to sing in a masquerade), Jean Loret refers on 17 March 1663 to the executed Morin as

> Un Imposteur, un téméraire,
> Un mal-heureux Vizionnaire . . .

However, as Amelino warns in *Sir Politick*, V. ii, over-zealous reaction to madness is not without risk, since 'the most zealous for vengeance will not perhaps be unexposed to punishment'. Nor was it long before Nicole and others were publishing that Desmarets, the poet of *Les Visionnaires*, was himself a dangerous *visionnaire*.

Apart from all the political and other references that set *Sir Politick* in a French context of the early 1660s, it is worth reflecting on what the play demonstrates of Saint-Évremond's capacity to view some of his own cherished attitudes with a certain irony. In Jean-Marc Chatelain's recent and acclaimed study *La Bibliothèque de l'honnête homme: Livres, lecture et collections en France à l'âge classique*[23] Saint-Évremond is almost the witness of choice for the stance of the *honnête homme*, the champion of urbane conversation and of reading consonant with it against the sort of brutish pedantry represented by the German. Yet Bousignac's creator can laugh at him and hence a little at himself as well as at Gramont. It is ultimately a measure of *Sir Politick*'s quality that things are not simply black and white.

                                                        H. G. H.

---

[23] (Paris: Bibliothèque Nationale de France, 2003).

## Textual Introduction

Since the Second World War a great deal has been achieved to bring order and accuracy to the complex legacy of texts, both printed and manuscript, bearing the name of Saint-Évremond. Sorting out a bewildering canon enshrined in numerous seventeenth- and eighteenth-century separate and collected editions, some more or less authorized, others unashamedly pirated, is not unlike the task facing anyone attempting to cope with the Buckingham corpus. Thanks in particular to the Société des Textes français modernes and to the late René Ternois we now have at our disposal careful and reliable versions of the prose works and of the letters, the most substantial part of the output of their diffident and aristocratic author.[24] Similarly the two redactions of Saint-Évremond's earliest play, under the titles *La Comédie des Académistes* and *Les Académiciens*, have been intelligently and meticulously brought to modern readers by Paolo Carile.[25] Even the other two theatrical texts, *Sir Politick Would-be* and *Les Opéra*, neither of them published in any surviving form before their émigré writer died in 1703, have been included in the Droz series Textes littéraires français.[26] There are good reasons, however, to look more closely at what was accomplished in following a familiar and well-tried formula for annotated critical editions.

There are no known manuscripts of *Sir Politick Would-be*, despite the fact that there is a forty-year gap between its composition and its first printing in the grand quarto Tonson edition of 1705. Consequently we are altogether reliant on the text prepared by Pierre Silvestre (1662–1718)[27] and Pierre Des Maizeaux (1673–1745),[28] two Huguenot refugees who came to know and collaborate with Saint-Évremond in his old

24 *Œuvres en prose*, ed. Ternois; *Lettres*, ed. Ternois. See also Denys Potts, *Saint-Evremond: A Voice from Exile. Newly Discovered Letters to Madame de Gouville and the Abbé de Hautefeuille (1697–1701)* (Oxford: Legenda, 2002).

25 *La Comédie des Académistes* & *Les Académiciens* (1976).

26 *Sir Politick Would-be*, ed. Robert Finch and Eugène Joliat (Geneva: Droz, 1978); *Les Opéra*, ed. Robert Finch and Eugène Joliat (Geneva: Droz, 1979).

27 On Silvestre see *Œuvres en prose*, i, pp. xii–xlv (including the preface to the 1705 edition) and *Lettres*, ii. 356–78.

28 Des Maizeaux figures frequently in Anne Goldgar, *Impolite Learning: Conduct and Community in the Republic of Letters, 1680–1750* (New Haven, Conn. and London: Yale University Press, 1995), where the essential references will be found.

age. Finch and Joliat follow the normal practice of giving priority to the 'vulgate' of 1705. Indeed they reproduce its version of the play in facsimile, a little incongruously given the modest dimensions of the Droz pages compared with Tonson's. Without explanation they omit the errata list containing four necessary corrections to the text.[29] It is convenient for modern readers to have access to the play in the form in which it was first widely available, but we have no guarantee that the accidentals—spelling or punctuation—reflect the author's own habits. On the contrary, noting Silvestre's claims about Saint-Évremond's utter carelessness about punctuation,[30] we can be sure of fairly decisive intervention by the editors. There is thus no overwhelming reason to prefer a text strongly influenced by English usage of the time, for example in the capitalization of common nouns.

Des Maizeaux was to be actively involved in three later editions of Saint-Évremond's works—Amsterdam in 1706, Paris in 1711, and Amsterdam in 1726. The preface to the last-named denounces various intervening reprints and piracies and stresses the fact that emendations have been made after renewed consultation of manuscripts or of copies corrected by the author:

Il paroit par ce que je viens de dire, qu'il n'y a que l'Edition de Londres de 1705, celle de Hollande de 1706, & celle de Paris de 1711, qui ayent été dignes de l'attention du Public. Mais cette quatriéme Edition est preferable à divers égards.

Je l'ai revûë sur les Manuscrits de Mr. de St. Evremond, & sur les Corrections qu'il avoit faites à diverses reprises dans mon exemplaire d'une vieille impression. Cette Revision m'a donné lieu de rétablir quelques passages qui avoient été omis. On y trouvera aussi quatre ou cinq petits Ouvrages qui n'étoient pas dans les Editions precedentes.[31]

The duodecimo *Œuvres* of 1726 have to be considered, therefore, as a sort of 'Ausgabe letzter Hand', at a remove insofar as we are dealing

---

[29] See *Œuvres meslées* (London, 1705), i. sig. d4ᵛ. Or was an errata slip lost from the copies they had seen?

[30] *Œuvres meslées*, i. sig. a4ʳ and *Œuvres en prose*, i, pp. xvi–xvii.

[31] *Œuvres* (Amsterdam, 1726), i, p. xvi. 'It is apparent from what I have just said that only the editions of London (1705), Holland (1706), and Paris (1711) are worthy of general attention. But this fourth edition is preferable in several ways. I have revised it on the basis of M. de Saint-Évremond's manuscripts and the corrections he made from time to time in my copy of an old edition. This revision has enabled me to restore various passages which had been omitted. One will also find included four or five short works which were not in the earlier editions.'

perforce with Des Maizeaux and not with Saint-Évremond himself. The distance already noted between the author and the accidentals of 1705 precludes any recourse to Greg's 'rationale of copy-text'. Once one decides for 1726, an edition whose spelling in particular is more obviously modern, one should reproduce it faithfully.

Since *Sir Politick Would-be* is being included in a resolutely old-spelling edition within the Anglo-American tradition, there is no room for the compromises that are habitual in French procedures. The only normalization undertaken concerns the space usually preceding colons, semicolons, exclamation marks, and question marks, which has not been preserved, and the conversion of long ſ to s. Otherwise the spelling and the punctuation of the 1726 copy-text are reproduced punctiliously.

Whether or not one shares Ternois's misgivings about Des Maizeaux as a biographer and as an editor (a judgement tempered a little as his own enterprise neared its end),[32] we have no other way at present of recovering Saint-Évremond's words. This does not mean that 1726 has to be followed slavishly. Some corrections of literals and absurdities are made and duly noted among the textual variants, which otherwise record substantive changes only from the 1705 edition. Because the 1726 revision was slight for this work, these are not very numerous.[33] Again, in contradistinction to much French practice the apparatus is not cluttered with variants of no authority.

The circumstances in which the edition was prepared made it impossible to do a thorough preliminary bibliography of Saint-Évremond. This is all the more regrettable since libraries and booksellers not infrequently own or wish to sell sets made up of volumes from authorized and pirated editions side by side. No Australian library owns the 1726 *Œuvres* at present, so collations had to be done from photocopies of sets held in North America. Physical examination was done of sets of the 1726 edition in British libraries, and the Clifford copy of the 1705 Tonson quarto in the National Library of Australia was a useful supplement to the Finch and Joliat facsimile. No evidence of stop-press correction was found, nor were there any indications of cancellation. The editor, fully aware of his own criticisms of work based on inadequate examination of the physical evidence, is of necessity hesi-

---

[32] Compare *Œuvres en prose*, i, pp. xlvi–lxvii with *Œuvres en prose*, iv, pp. vii–xi.

[33] Some of them attenuate—a little arbitrarily—the Gascon character of the Marquis de Bousignac's expressions and pronunciation. An example of eyeskip in I. iii is corrected.

tant about advancing conclusions with too great a show of certainty. However, he, his assistant, and his colleagues have done their best and have laid out their textual observations as clearly and as comprehensively as possible.

W. K.

# Sir Politick Would-be

## *ACTEURS.*

Sir Politick Would-be, *Chevalier Anglois, Politique ridicule.*

Mr. de Riche-Source, *Homme d'Affaires François, Chimérique en Projets.*

La Femme de Sir Politick, *grave & sottement capable.*

Me. de Riche-Source, *Coquette & Bourgeoise.*

Le Marquis de Bousignac, *Gascon brillant, avec un faux air de la Cour de France.*

Un Voyageur Allemand, *exact & régulier, qui voit jusqu'aux dernieres Epitaphes des Villes où il passe.*

Mylord Tancrede, *homme d'esprit, qui connoît le ridicule de tous les autres.*

Une Entremetteuse *faisant la* Dogesse, *& ses* Demoiselles *faisant les* Femmes de Senateurs.

Dominico, *Venitien mysterieux, faisant l'Espion.*

Le Signor Antonio, *Diseur de Concetti, Ami de* Tancrede.

|  | |
|---|---|
| Quatre Senateurs | Agostino; *faux Caton, & ridiculement grave.* |
|  | Azaro, *beau Discoureur.* |
|  | Amelino, *du même esprit.* |
|  | Pamfilino, *Homme de bon-sens.* |

Un Valet *du Signor Antonio.*

Un Valet *de Sir Politick.*

Un Huissier.

La Scene est à VENISE.

FIG. 4. Ballroom scene in IV. iv.of *Sir Politick Would-be*. Reproduced from the 1726 edition in Saint-Évremond's *Œuvres*. Courtesy of the Harry Ransom Humanities Research Center, The University of Texas at Austin

# SIR POLITICK WOULD-BE,

## *COMEDIE.*[1]

## ACTE PREMIER.

## SCENE PREMIERE.

### Mr. DE RICHE-SOURCE, SIR POLITICK WOULD-BE.

#### Mr. DE RICHE-SOURCE.

MONSIEUR, le bruit de vôtre réputation en général, & les graces que ma maison a reçûës de vous en particulier, m'obligent à vous assurer du respect que j'ai pour vôtre personne, & de la reconnoissance que j'ai de vos faveurs.

#### SIR POLITICK.

Permettez que je sache vôtre nom.                                    5

#### Mr. DE RICHE-SOURCE.

Je suis ce François, dont la femme a reçu chez vous tant de courtoisie.

#### SIR POLITICK.

Beaucoup d'honneur à vôtre bien humble serviteur de lui avoir rendu quelque service. Le pouvoir est petit, mais la bonne volonté est grande.                                                          10

#### Mr. DE RICHE-SOURCE.

Nous connoissons par nôtre propre expérience la bonne volonté & le crédit: trop heureux d'avoir rencontré l'une & l'autre dans nôtre mauvaise fortune.

#### SIR POLITICK.

J'ai bien cru qu'à vôtre âge, & en famille, vous ne voyagiez pas sans cause. Possible quelque stratagême de Cour vous a obligé d'en      15
sortir.

---

[1] Le Duc de Buckingham, & Mr. d'Aubigny ont eu beaucoup de part à la composition de cette piece. Voyez la VIE de Mr. de St. Evremond, sur l'année 1662.

MR. DE RICHE-SOURCE.

J'ai toûjours eu assez de prudence pour me garantir des stratagêmes de Cour: mais on se trouve enveloppé dans des malheurs
publics, que la prudence ne peut éviter.

SIR POLITICK.

La France est la grande mer, où s'élevent les tempêtes.            20

MR. DE RICHE-SOURCE.

Chaque pays a ses tempêtes: la vertu a des envieux par tout; &
la vôtre assurément n'en a pas été exemte.

SIR POLITICK.

J'ai vu quelques orages en ma vie; mais j'ai su m'accommoder
aux vents, & me servir assez bien des voiles. Graces à la Politique,
je pense être arrivé au port présentement.            25

MR. DE RICHE-SOURCE.

Vous devez compte au public de vos talens: & à Dieu ne plaise
que vous appellassiez être au port, de vous tenir en repos.

SIR POLITICK.

Ma vie n'est pas tout-à-fait oisive: nous avons de quoi nous
donner toûjours un peu d'occupation.

MR. DE RICHE-SOURCE.

Vôtre capacité vous attire tous ceux qui ont besoin de conseil: &            30
quoi que vous n'ayiez point de poste ici, je m'assure que vous ne
laissez pas d'avoir grande part aux affaires de la République.

SIR POLITICK.

On m'a toûjours dit que j'avois quelque talent pour les Affaires.
Les années du moins ont dû me donner de l'expérience: mais la
République est bonne & sage; elle n'a pas besoin d'autre conseil            35
que du sien.

MR. DE RICHE-SOURCE.

C'est en quoi paroît sa sagesse, de consulter une personne aussi
éclairée & aussi capable que vous.

SIR POLITICK.

J'avouë qu'on se trompe dans la bonne opinion qu'on a de moi.
A la verité, beaucoup de Sénateurs viennent ici chercher des lu            40
mieres que je n'ai pas.

MR. DE RICHE-SOURCE.

Je croi qu'ils rendront justice à la fin à vôtre mérite; & le Senat
vous mettant dans son corps, fera par interêt ce qu'il fait quelquefois à des Etrangers par honneur.

SIR POLITICK.

Vous n'êtes pas le premier qui m'en a voulu flater. Si la Répu-   45
blique nous en juge dignes, nous tâcherons de répondre le mieux
qu'il sera possible à son choix. Mais vous, Monsieur, vous avez
quitté le Pays orageux, pour chercher celui où regne le calme.

MR. DE RICHE-SOURCE.

Ha! Monsieur, je ne hai rien tant que le repos, & tiens à grand
malheur pour moi, d'avoir quitté la France. C'est le Pays des affaires   50
& de la fortune. Néanmoins on ne s'abandonne pas; il faut agir
selon l'état où l'on se trouve, & voir ce qu'il y a à faire en ce pays-ci.

SIR POLITICK.

Monsieur, si le peu de talent que Dieu m'a donné, vous peut
être utile à quelque chose, comme je vous l'offre avec franchise,
vous pouvez en disposer sans cérémonie.   55

MR. DE RICHE-SOURCE.

On est trop heureux de rencontrer à Venise un secours si
necessaire: & en quelque lieu que ce soit, l'honneur de vôtre connoissance peut être compté entre les meilleures fortunes. Mais,
Monsieur ......

SIR POLITICK.

Permettez-vous qu'on en use avec liberté? Je vais dire un mot à   60
un Sénateur, qui m'avoit chargé de quelque projet Politique.

MR. DE RICHE-SOURCE.

C'est à moi de vous demander pardon d'en avoir usé incivile-
ment. Je saurai prendre mon tems, si vous le trouvez bon, pour
jouïr quelquefois d'une conversation si profitable.

SIR POLITICK.

Vous en serez toûjours le maître, & pouvez commander à toute   65
heure à un serviteur particulier. Si toutefois vos affaires vous per-
mettoient de demeurer ici un moment, je reviendrois vous trouver.

MR. DE RICHE-SOURCE.

Vous pouvez demeurer tant qu'il vous plaira; j'attendrai avec
plaisir vôtre retour.

## SCENE II.

### Mr. DE RICHE-SOURCE, Me. DE RICHE-SOURCE.

##### Mr. de Riche-Source.
AH! ma femme, que je viens d'entendre un habile-homme!

##### Me. de Riche-Source.
Ne vous l'avois-je pas bien dit? C'est le premier homme que j'aye vu de ma vie.

##### Mr. de Riche-Source.
Je ne m'entête pas facilement; mais je ne m'y connois point, ou Sir Politick est une personne bien capable. 5

##### Me. de Riche-Source.
Capable! au delà de tout ce que vous pouvez penser, & le meilleur ami qu'on vit jamais. Si nous en avions eu un en France fait comme lui, nous ne serions pas à Venise.

##### Mr. de Riche-Source.
Il faut regarder les choses comme elles sont. Sir Politick étoit à Venise quand nous étions à Paris: présentement nous sommes tous 10 deux en même lieu, & j'entrevois des choses qui pourroient bien nous consoler de la disgrace où nous sommes.

##### Me. de Riche-Source.
Vous ne sauriez vous imaginer le secours que vous en pouvez tirer: & ne craignez point de lui communiquer vos lumieres, (en cas qu'il vous communique les siennes, cela s'entend;) il est homme-d'honneur, & aussi sûr qu'il est habile. C'est un trésor que d'avoir Sir Politick pour ami. 15

##### Mr. de Riche-Source.
C'est bien mon dessein de faire une bonne liaison avec lui: mais me conseilleriez-vous de lui découvrir nôtre grande affaire?

##### Me. de Riche-Source.
Quoi? la Circulation? 20

##### Mr. de Riche-Source.
Oui, la Circulation, qui est, comme vous savez, le plus beau projet du monde.

##### Me. de Riche-Source.
Vous ne sauriez mieux faire: aussi-bien est-il impossible de le conduire seul.

Mʀ. ᴅᴇ Rɪᴄʜᴇ-Sᴏᴜʀᴄᴇ.

Vous avez raison, & je le ferai. Je veux néanmoins avoir encore     25
une conversation avec lui auparavant; non pas que je m'en défie,
de la sorte que vous m'en parlez: mais un si bon Politique pourroit
prendre quelque méchante impression de moi, si je lui communi-
quois d'abord une si grande pensée.

Mᴇ. ᴅᴇ Rɪᴄʜᴇ-Sᴏᴜʀᴄᴇ.

Ce n'est pas à nous autres femmes d'entrer en de telles affaires:     30
vous en userez comme il vous plaira.

Mʀ. ᴅᴇ Rɪᴄʜᴇ-Sᴏᴜʀᴄᴇ.

Le voici déja de retour. Allez-vous-en; je me trompe, ou nous
allons entamer bien des choses.

## SCENE III.

Mʀ. DE RICHE-SOURCE, SIR POLITICK,
DOMINICO, *qui les écoute.*

Mʀ. ᴅᴇ Rɪᴄʜᴇ-Sᴏᴜʀᴄᴇ.

MOnsieur, nous nous sommes assez observés. Il est de la prudence
d'un homme sage de ne se fier pas légérement aux inconnus: mais
puis que les hommes ne font pas les affaires seuls, & qu'il est impossible de rien executer de beau, sans entrer en confiance; je vous
supplie, Monsieur, de ne me refuser pas la vôtre, & vous ne vous     5
repentirez jamais de me l'avoir donnée.

Sɪʀ Pᴏʟɪᴛɪᴄᴋ.

Vous êtes tombé dans ma pensée: mais il n'étoit pas, ce me
semble, de la dignité de ma Politique de m'ouvrir le premier.

Mʀ. ᴅᴇ Rɪᴄʜᴇ-Sᴏᴜʀᴄᴇ.

La France est assez considerable dans l'Europe, pour ne pas né-
gliger un homme qui en connoît parfaitement les interêts.     10

Sɪʀ Pᴏʟɪᴛɪᴄᴋ.

Madame vôtre femme m'en a averti plus d'une fois; & je ne suis
pas à apprendre vôtre mérite & vos qualités: mais puis que vous
êtes étranger ici, trouvez bon que je vous fasse part de quelques
observations que j'ai faites. Chaque Pays a ses usages; c'est pourquoi je vous recommande ces choses: Premierement, le pas grave,     15
& la contenance composée: cela sent son personnage. Pour vos Discours, ne dites jamais rien que vous croyiez; & ne croyez jamais

rien de ce qu'on vous dira: que toutes vos actions soient reglées par les Loix, dont je porte un *Compendium* sur moi. De Religion, vous vous accommoderez à celle du pays en apparence, & pourrez en 20 effet en avoir une autre, si vous n'aimez mieux n'en avoir point du tout; ce que je laisse purement à vôtre choix.[2]

#### Mr. de Riche-Source.

Il faudroit que je fusse mal-habile-homme, si assisté comme je suis de vos conseils, je ne pouvois me conduire. Mais je vous supplie, Monsieur, de me donner quelques lumieres de la constitution 25 de cet Etat.

#### Sir Politick.

Vous pouvez juger de la bonté de ses Loix par sa durée. Vous savez néanmoins que rien n'est parfait en ce monde, & je pense que le gouvernement pourroit être encore plus accompli. Je vous dirai en dernier secret, que les Législateurs ont manqué lourde- 30 ment à l'interêt de la République, quand ils n'ont fait qu'un seul Doge.

#### Dominico, *qui vient sur le Théatre, les écoute à ces mots de* République *& de* Doge, *& dit à part.*

Qu'entens-je de Secret, de République, de Doge! Il y a quelque mystére ici dessous: écoutons.

#### Sir Politick.

Le Doge est une espéce de Consul. Les Romains en avoient 35 deux: moi, j'en voudrois quatre. En voici la raison. Un Doge a toûjours soixante & dix ans, & quelquefois plus: ce qui lui reste de vie, n'est qu'infirmité: tantôt il garde le lit, tantôt la chambre. S'il y en avoit quatre, quand un seroit couché, trois seroient debout; si deux malades, deux en santé; si trois, il en resteroit toûjours un 40 pour vaquer aux affaires, & se trouver à tous les Conseils.

#### Dominico, *tout bas.*

Voici des gens mal-intentionnés, qui cherchent à profiter des défauts du Gouvernement.

#### Sir Politick.

Autre raison, tirée de la Politique. C'est une maxime fonda- mentale d'Etat, que toutes les parties du gouvernement doivent 45 avoir de la convenance. Or, à Venise, unité de Doge est absurde, comme chose qui sent son air monarchique.

---

[2] Cela est imité de la Comedie de *Ben. Johnson* intitulée: Volpone, or the Fox; (c'est-à-dire, le Renard) Act. IV. Sc. I.

### Mr. de Riche-Source.

Je n'ai jamais rien entendu de si juste. La derniere raison est d'un vrai homme d'état. La premiere est de ces choses que l'on croit naturelles, & que tout le monde pense, aussi-tôt qu'elles sont trouvées.          50

### Sir Politick.

Naturelles tant qu'il vous plaira: mais il y a douze cens ans que dure la République, sans que personne s'en soit jamais avisé. J'avouë bien qu'il y a des projets plus profonds; & vous en allez entendre un qui est bien d'une autre spéculation. Il regarde les af-          55
faires étrangéres. Vous devez savoir que la République a de grands interêts à la Porte, & qu'il lui est necessaire d'être bien informée de cette Cour-là: mais si nôtre Ambassadeur en donne la moindre connoissance, il y va de sa tête pour le moins. J'ai trouvé le moyen de lui faire tenir des nouvelles en deux jours, & de recevoir des          60
siennes en aussi peu de tems, sans aucun danger.

### Mr. de Riche-Source.

Comment, Monsieur; il faut être Magicien pour cela!

### Sir Politick.

Si vous appellez magie ce qui n'est pas dans le cours ordinaire des choses, je l'avouë; il n'y a pourtant rien de surnaturel; écoutez seulement. J'ai des relais de pigeons chez mes correspondans ....          65

### Mr. de Riche-Source.

De Pigeons!

### Sir Politick.

Cela vous surprend? Oui, de Pigeons. Je voi bien que vous n'êtes pas profond dans les affaires du Levant; écoutez. J'ai à Venise des Pigeons de l'Istrie, à qui j'attache une lettre pour l'Am-
bassadeur: mon correspondant de l'Istrie la prend, & l'attache au          70
pigeon de Dalmatie: celui de Dalmatie l'attache au pigeon de la Bosnie: un autre Venitien dépêche ce dernier, qui porte ma lettre à l'Ambassadeur. Voilà des nouvelles de Venise à Constantinople en deux jours: cela est-il extraordinaire & utile?

### Mr. de Riche-Source.

Rien au monde ne le sauroit être plus.          75

### Sir Politick.

Je pourrois vous dire beaucoup d'autres choses de cette nature; mais j'ai quitté les projets politiques, pour travailler en Speculation militaire; & je vous dirai, comme à mon ami, que j'ai trouvé de beaux secrets pour la Guerre. Beaucoup de gens en ont pour les

siéges; ce qui fait que je m'y applique moins: j'en ai plusieurs pour   80
les retraites, & un principalement pour les batailles, qu'un Empereur ne sauroit trop acheter.

DOMINICO, *bas.*
Je ne doute point qu'il n'ait vendu ce dernier au *GRAND-
SEIGNEUR*, & il sera peut-être employé contre la République.

SIR POLITICK.
Dites-moi, Monsieur, n'avez-vous pas cru que pour devenir   85
grand homme de guerre, il falloit être aux armées?

MR. DE RICHE-SOURCE.
Je l'ai cru jusqu'ici; & je vous avouë que je le crois encore.

SIR POLITICK.
Erreur populaire: il n'y a rien de si opposé au grand Capitaine,
que de se trouver aux occasions; & je vais vous le faire toucher au
doigt & à l'œuil.   90

MR. DE RICHE-SOURCE.
Cependant, c'est contre une opinion générale, & reçûë de toute
éternité.

SIR POLITICK.
Il faut avoir de la réverence pour nos peres; mais ils étoient
hommes comme nous. Si en toutes choses on s'en étoit tenu à ce
qu'ils ont trouvé, on feroit la guerre encore avec des fléches, & il   95
n'y auroit aujourd'hui non plus d'Antipodes, qu'il y en avoit de leur
tems. Monsieur, dépouillez-vous de toute prévention pour eux, &
pour moi.

MR. DE RICHE-SOURCE.
Puis que vous le trouvez bon, je vais examiner la chose avec une
pleine liberté d'esprit.   100

SIR POLITICK.
Vous me ferez plaisir: ça, m'avouërez-vous pas qu'à l'approche
d'une armée ennemie, il n'y a point d'homme qui ne soit retenu
par la peur, ou emporté par le courage?

MR. DE RICHE-SOURCE.
C'est très-bien raisonné.

SIR POLITICK.
Si vôtre Général est sujet à la crainte, il laissera perdre l'occa-   105
sion de défaire les ennemis.

MR. DE RICHE-SOURCE.
Il est vrai.

SIR POLITICK.

S'il ne craint rien, il combat mal-à-propos, & se fait défaire lui-même.

MR. DE RICHE-SOURCE.

Il n'y a rien à repliquer là-dessus.                                    110

SIR POLITICK.

Dans le Cabinet, on conduit une guerre de sang froid: on fait la supputation des deux armées, on considere quelques autres circonstances.

MR. DE RICHE-SOURCE.

Mais il me semble qu'on prendroit des mesures bien plus justes, en voyant les troupes?                                            115

SIR POLITICK.

Point du tout: à un homme d'esprit, voyez-les, ne les voyez pas, c'est la même chose. C'est toûjours une armée, des gens de pied, & des gens de cheval, des canons, des mousquets, des piques, des pistolets. La Spéculation militaire fait tout.

MR. DE RICHE-SOURCE.

J'avouë qu'elle y fait beaucoup.                                      120

SIR POLITICK.

Or ma supputation faite, j'envoye ordre à un Lieutenant de donner bataille, je défais les ennemis, & voilà un pays que j'ai conquis. Si je me trouve foible, je donne ordre de demeurer dans les retranchemens; l'armée ennemie se dissipe, & voilà un pays que j'ai sauvé.                                                            125

MR. DE RICHE-SOURCE.

Je commence à voir clair présentement, & vous ne me laissez pas le moindre doute dans l'esprit.

SIR POLITICK.

Philippe II, Prince militaire au dernier point, connut de bonne heure ces maximes, & s'en est toûjours fort bien servi.

MR. DE RICHE-SOURCE.

Philippe II! Vous m'étonnez. Il a toûjours passé pour un grand    130
Politique, & jamais pour un Guerrier.

SIR POLITICK.

Autre erreur populaire. Il a toûjours eu dans la tête d'être plus grand Capitaine que son pere; & voyant l'erreur où Charles-Quint étoit tombé, de se trouver aux occasions, il prit le parti de faire la guerre du Cabinet. Qu'en arrive-t-il? Philippe II. projette une ba-    135

taille; le Duc d'Albe la donne: à vôtre avis, qui la gagne? Philippe
II. assurément, & n'en doutez pas. On peut dire la même chose
sur le Duc de Parme. Le Duc assiege Anvers, & Philippe prend la
Ville. Oui, je tiens Philippe le plus grand Capitaine de nos jours,
& peut-être de l'antiquité, si vous en exceptez Périclès.                   140

MR. DE RICHE-SOURCE.

Monsieur, tous les hommes que j'ai vus jusques ici; je dis les
plus habiles, n'ont que de la superficie: vous seul approfondissez
les matieres; l'esprit demeure convaincu de vos raisons.

SIR POLITICK.

On a peut-être un peu plus de méditation qu'un autre, & on
digere les choses.                                                          145

MR. DE RICHE-SOURCE.

Oserois-je esperer une grace?

SIR POLITICK.

Vous avez tout pouvoir.

MR. DE RICHE-SOURCE.

C'est être bien incivil; mais je ne saurois m'en empêcher.
Auriez-vous la bonté de me donner quelqu'un de vos Secrets pour
la guerre? Il n'y a rien que je ne donne pour faire étudier mon fils en   150
spéculation militaire. Le plaisir que j'aurois de le voir plus Capitaine que ces petits Messieurs, qui font les entendus, pour avoir
fait cinq ou six campagnes! Monsieur, je ne suis pas importun;
mais je vous demande en grace quelqu'un de vos secrets pour la
guerre.                                                                      155

SIR POLITICK.

Quant à cela, vous m'en dispenserez, s'il vous plaît. Vous êtes
François, & je suis Anglois. Nos nations ont eu autrefois de
grands differens; ils peuvent recommencer, & je ne vous donnerai
pas des armes pour nous battre.

MR. DE RICHE-SOURCE.

Nos deux nations sont en bonne intelligence.                                160

SIR POLITICK.

Peut-être ne durera-t-elle pas long-tems. Un Politique doit tout
prévoir.

MR. DE RICHE-SOURCE.

Je vous assure qu'il ne me reste aucune amitié pour un pays, où
mon mérite a été si mal reconnu.

SIR POLITICK.

Le chagrin passe, & l'amitié peut revenir. Bref, Monsieur, 165
n'esperez pas que je vous donne rien, qui puisse aller un jour
contre le bien de ma Patrie. En toute autre chose, faites état que
personne n'est plus à vous que Sir Politick. *Ils sortent.*

DOMINICO, *seul.*

Gens dangereux à la République! Attaquer les Législateurs! Se
prendre à la constitution de l'Etat! Multiplier jusques à quatre un 170
Magistrat unique! Mutation de gouvernement appuyée sur
l'exemple de deux Consuls, & rafinée par la méditation d'un spé-
culatif! Comme j'ai voué beaucoup de service au Doge, il n'y a rien
que je ne fasse pour ruiner un projet, qui va à lui donner trois
compagnons. Je veux l'en avertir lui-même; & si je ne puis lui 175
parler (car il est souvent indisposé,) je dirai tout à un Sénateur de
mes amis, qui en informera le Sénat.

## SCENE IV.

### LE SIGNOR ANTONIO, MYLORD TANCREDE,
*qu'il avoit connu à Londres.*

ANTONIO.

QUe vois-je! bon Dieu! Le ciel favorable à Venise, envoye ici
l'Etoile du Nord briller parmi nous.

TANCREDE.

Je ne suis ni Astre, ni Etoile, & je viens d'un pays où vous savez
qu'on ne brille pas. Je suis de vos amis il y a long-tems, ravi de me
trouver dans un lieu où nous puissions renouveller nôtre connois- 5
sance.

ANTONIO.

Vous venez donc faire rougir nos jasmins du vermeil de vos roses.

TANCREDE, *bas.*

Ce n'est plus le même homme que j'ai connu autrefois; & quel
langage est ceci? Voyons pourtant jusqu'au bout. *Haut.* Il est vrai
que nous avons des roses en abondance; & puis, ce sont les armes 10
d'Angleterre.

ANTONIO.

Les armes d'Angleterre sont des roses en peinture; mais en effet
des tonnerres si redoutables sur les ondes, que les foudres de terre-
ferme en comparaison à peine sont des éclairs.

TANCREDE.

Monsieur, je ne sai que répondre là-dessus. 15

ANTONIO.

Les rivieres les plus profondes font le moins de bruit, & les petits torrens nous étourdissent: de même les esprits vains & legers
ont plus de langage; les solides moins de paroles & de discours.

TANCREDE.

Vous êtes obligeant pour ma nation & pour moi.

ANTONIO.

Excusez, si l'humilité de mes pensées, & la bassesse de mes 20
termes ne peuvent s'élever à la grandeur de mon zele; & agréez, je
vous prie, la dévotion de mes services, dont vous pouvez disposer
uniquement.

TANCREDE.

Je me suis toûjours attendu que vous me conserveriez quelque
part dans l'honneur de vos bonnes graces. 25

ANTONIO.

La même difference que je trouve dans les Arts, entre la théorie
& la pratique; la même se rencontre en fait de services, entre
l'offre & l'execution. Venons donc à la réalité des effets. Les
Dames ont-elles le même ascendant sur vos inclinations, que vous
avez sur leurs ames? 30

TANCREDE.

Je les ai toûjours fort aimées.

ANTONIO.

Si vous aimez ces grandes beautés fatales au repos des humains,
nous avons des Helenes & des Cléopatres.

TANCREDE.

Laissons-les pour les Rois & les Empereurs: j'en veux qui bien
loin de troubler l'Univers, ne puissent pas me troubler moi-même. 35

ANTONIO.

Vous n'en voulez donc pas qui fassent les tourmens des cœurs,
comme les délices des yeux?

TANCREDE.

Je veux trouver du plaisir sans peine.

ANTONIO.

Ah! je le comprens. Il vous faut de ces beautés innocentes, dont
les traits sont doux, & de qui les charmes n'ont rien de cuisant:          40
semblables à ces beaux jours, où le soleil adoucit ses regards, &
désarmé de ses brûlantes ardeurs, laisse joüir les hommes d'un
tems agréable & serain.

TANCREDE, *bas*.

Quelque impertinent que soit devenu mon ami, je veux voir s'il
m'est bon à quelque chose. *Haut*. Vous m'entendrez mieux, si vous          45
comprenez que je veux de belles Putains.

ANTONIO, *bas*.

Expression du Nord! *Haut*. Vous voulez dire des Courtisanes:
personnes officieuses, qui rappellant une image des premieres Loix
de la nature, s'affranchissent de la tyrannie des nôtres, pour le plaisir commun des deux sexes.          50

TANCREDE.

Voilà justement mon fait.

ANTONIO.

Nous vous conduirons quand il vous plaira chez des Flores &
des Laïs. Vous ne désagréerez pas que j'y fasse trouver un concert,
où les Sirénes, d'enchanteresses qu'elles sont, pourroient devenir
enchantées.          55

TANCREDE.

Vous ne sauriez m'obliger davantage.

ANTONIO.

Je ne prétens pas que si peu de chose m'aquitte envers vôtre
Seigneurie de toutes les obligations que je lui ai; & peut-être
aurons-nous le bonheur de lui donner un Repas assez curieux.

TANCREDE.

Je recevrai avec joye tout le plaisir que vous me voudrez faire.          60

ANTONIO.

Je n'ose pas tout-à-fait vous le promettre; car c'est un Repas
d'invention, & j'ai besoin d'officiers ingénieux, qui puissent bien
représenter la gentillesse de l'artifice.

TANCREDE.

De quoi me parlez-vous-là, de Gentillesse & d'Artifice dans un
repas? Les viandes les plus naturelles sont les meilleures.          65

ANTONIO.

Vôtre Seigneurie parle encore selon la coutume grossiere de
France & d'Angleterre, où l'on convie ses amis à un repas pour
boire & manger. Nôtre nation a des manieres plus épurées. Vous
mangerez chez vous auparavant, ou à vôtre retour, comme vous le
jugerez à propos. Nos festins se font ici pour le charme de la vûë.          70

TANCREDE.

Et pour le goût, rien?

ANTONIO.

Le goût n'est que pour les repas vulgaires: ce sont ici des illusions agréables.

TANCREDE.

Je commence à vous entendre; il faut venir là comme curieux,
& sans appetit.                                                              75

ANTONIO.

*Si, si*; vous comprenez.

TANCREDE.

Vous me donnez une grande curiosité. Quand puis-je esperer
cette fête?

ANTONIO.

Je ne puis pas répondre du tems. J'ai bien un homme admirable
pour plier le linge, qui représente toutes sortes de poissons, &          80
divers oiseaux.

TANCREDE.

C'est déja une assez grande merveille.

ANTONIO.

Ah! j'ai plus. J'ai un pâtissier, qui peut faire un service de pâtés,
à l'ouverture desquels sortiront mille oiseaux, qui voltigeront dans
la sale, au grand contentement des curieux, ravis d'une chose si          85
surprenante.

TANCREDE.

Quels Officiers vous manquent donc, après tout cela?

ANTONIO.

Un homme bien necessaire; un certain Sculpteur, rare & ex-
quis, qui sait travailler une rave en Siréne, d'un artifice sans égal.
C'est un ouvrage excellent, dont nous faisons l'ornement de nos          90
Salades.

TANCREDE.

Ce seroit un assez grand inconvénient que de ne l'avoir pas.

ANTONIO.

Il m'en faut encore un autre, plus important mille fois.

TANCREDE.

Qui peut être ce rare Officier?

ANTONIO.

C'est un Ingénieur, qui travaille miraculeusement en sucre.          95

TANCREDE.

Un Confiturier, voulez-vous dire?

ANTONIO.

Un Ingénieur, qui fait un château de sucre avec des tours &
d'autres fortifications si bien entenduës, que la régularité des meilleures places n'en approche pas.

TANCREDE.

Cela vaut une leçon de Mathématique.          100

ANTONIO.

Mieux sans doute. C'est-là particulierement que j'ai appris l'Art
militaire.

TANCREDE.

Je suis charmé de toutes vos raretés. Voilà dîner délicatement;
non comme nos brutaux, qui ne trouvent au repas que le plaisir de
manger.          105

ANTONIO.

En ce pays, tout est esprit, gentillesse, invention. S'il faut manger, par une necessité naturelle que nous avons commune avec les
bêtes, on mange chacun chez soi, pour cacher les imperfections où
la nature nous assujettit: mais en public, ce ne sont que subtiles
apparences, figures ingénieuses, & délicates représentations; car          110
vous devez savoir que tout dépend du bel art, & de la belle cérémonie.

TANCREDE.

Je ne suis déja plus si grossier que j'étois, & j'espere de me
rendre digne un jour de vôtre table. En attendant ce repas, que vous
me promettez, vous trouverez bon que suivant vôtre conseil, j'aille          115
cacher mes imperfections naturelles à mon logis.

ANTONIO, *seul.*

Quelque effort que fasse nôtre bon Anglois, il a de la peine à
s'élever aux choses sublimes. Quand j'étois en Angleterre, j'accom-

modois mes pensées & mes discours au génie de son peuple. J'ai
voulu faire ici l'honneur de ma nation, & régaler ce Mylord de 120
*Concetti* très-beaux, & très-relevés: mais je me suis apperçu par
des reponses vulgaires, que j'allois au delà de sa portée. Je hai les
esprits bas & rampans, je ferois bien de n'avoir plus de commerce
avec un homme si commun.

*Fin du premier Acte.*

## ACTE II.

### SCENE PREMIERE.

### LE VOYAGEUR ALLEMAND, LE MARQUIS DE BOUSIGNAC, MYLORD TANCREDE.

L'ALLEMAND.

NE perdons point de tems, je vous prie, & voyons aujourd'hui
quelque chose de curieux.

LE MARQUIS.

Et moi, promenons-nous, je vous prie, nous n'aurons que trop
de loisir à Venise pour voir ce qu'il y a de curieux. Un peu de conversation.                                                          5

L'ALLEMAND.

Qu'appellez-vous Conversation? s'amuser à discourir! Je ne suis
pas venu d'Allemagne pour ne faire que parler.

LE MARQUIS.

Toutes vos curiosités ne valent pas un quart-d'heure d'entre-
tien. Mais qui est cet étranger qui vient vers nous?

L'ALLEMAND.

C'est un Mylord avec qui je loge, cousin du Duc de Buckingham: 10
voulez-vous faire connoissance avec lui?

LE MARQUIS.

Cousin, dites-vous, du Duc de Buckingham; & si je veux faire
connoissance?

L'ALLEMAND.

Je ne sai pas si vous le voulez connoître: nous autres ne recher-
chons la connoissance de personne.                                  15

LE MARQUIS.
Après les obligations que j'ai au Mylord-Duc, je négligerois la connoissance de son parent! Tout mon déplaisir est de l'aborder par rencontre: mais puis que l'occasion s'offre à nous, il ne la faut pas perdre. Présentez-moi, je vous prie.

L'ALLEMAND.
Mylord, voici un Gentilhomme François, qui desire de vous con-     20
noître.

LE MARQUIS.
Monsieur, ce n'est pas ici un lieu propre à vous rendre mes respects: j'irai chez vous, si vous l'avez agréable, pour vous dire que je
dois tout au parent de Monsieur le Duc de Buckingham.

TANCREDE.
L'honneur que j'ai d'appartenir à Monsieur de Buckingham     25
m'est avantageux en tout, & particuliérement à me donner celui de
vôtre amitié.

LE MARQUIS.
C'est peu de chose, Monsieur, que mon amitié: mais j'ai tant
d'obligation au Mylord-Duc, qu'assurément vous pouvez disposer
de mon bien & de ma vie.     30

TANCREDE.
On est heureux, Monsieur, de pouvoir obliger un homme de
mérite, & vous êtes trop reconnoissant de quelque plaisir médiocre.

LE MARQUIS.
Appellez-vous un plaisir médiocre l'honneur que j'ai reçu de
lui? Je vous dirai la chose comme elle est, sans manquer d'un mot.
Monsieur de Montmorency, l'honneur de nôtre nation, (cela se     35
peut dire,) ayant su que j'allois en Angleterre, me donna une lettre
pour Mylord-Duc, vôtre parent, & me chargea de lui témoigner la
joye qu'il avoit de l'heureux accouchement de Madame sa femme,
& de la naissance de Monsieur son fils. C'étoit une pure civilité.
Monsieur de Montmorency étoit Amiral de France, Monsieur de     40
Buckingham Amiral d'Angleterre: d'Amiral à Amiral il n'y a que
la main. Le Royaume de France est plus grand que celui d'Angleterre, la flote Angloise plus considérable que la nôtre; tous deux
Ducs, grands-Seigneurs, bien-faits, libéraux, généreux. Ce n'est
pas à moi de décider; & il me semble que toutes choses étoient     45
assez égales entr'eux. Enfin, Monsieur de Montmorency me chargea de ce compliment, dont je vous ai parlé. Je prens la poste
aussi-tôt. J'arrive à Calais, & m'embarque avec le vent & la marée:

mais la mer étoit si grosse, & la tempête si furieuse, qu'à la dam- 50
nation de mon ame les vagues venoient quelquefois à un pied du
bord du bateau. Nous fûmes cinq grosses heures à passer, qui
furent cinq années pour moi. Mon nom n'est pas inconnu dans les
armées. J'ai vu quelques batailles en ma vie, & me suis trouvé à
quelques logemens. C'est-là qu'on connoît les braves. J'ai ouï dire
à Monsieur de Vignoles[3] qu'il n'y avoit pas une action plus péril- 55
leuse dans la guerre. Ce n'est pas trop ma coutume de parler de
moi; mais je puis dire sans vanité, que j'ai fait d'assez beaux com-
bats, & de toutes sortes. Avec cela, Monsieur, mon passage a été
la plus grande, & peut-être la seule peur que j'aye jamais euë.

TANCREDE.

Cela ne se doit pas appeller Peur, c'est manque d'habitude. Vos 60
yeux n'étoient pas accoutumez à ce danger-là.

LE MARQUIS.

Je me suis mépris aux termes: ce n'étoit pas Peur, Mylord, vous
avez raison; cependant j'aimerois mieux cent perils de terre qu'un
de mer. J'admirois la brutalité de quelques Anglois, de ces marauts
sans doute, qui tirent au billet pour un teston à qui sera pendu. 65
Monsieur! ils fumoient nonchalamment dans un si grand danger,
tandis que je me recommandois à Dieu, & songeois tout de bon à
ma conscience. Fumer dans une tempête! vous m'avouërez que ce
n'est pas courage: car comment se défendre contre des vagues?
Cela ne laisse pas de choquer un homme de cûr, qui n'est pas ac- 70
coutumé à ces sortes de dangers, de voir des couquins faire les in-
trépides mal-à-propos. J'aurois donné la moitié de mon bien, pour
tenir ces brutaux à une sortie, ou à quelque assaût. Nous eussions
vu, morbleu ...... Mais, Monsieur, je crains de vous ennuyer.

TANCREDE.

Ah! Monsieur, il faudroit être de méchante humeur, pour ne 75
prendre pas plaisir à un récit si agréable.

LE MARQUIS.

Enfin, me voilà passé. Je compte la poste pour rien, excepté que
les maîtres des postes rançonnent les François. J'arrive à Londres,
où le soir je fais mettre un habit à l'air, pour lui ôter les méchans
plis, que la male lui avoit donné, & pour y attacher une garniture. 80
Le lendemain je me mis le mieux que je pus; non pas magnifique-

[3] Vieux Maréchal de camp sous le regne de Louïs XIII, à qui on se remettoit
ordinairement du soin de l'Infanterie.

ment: mais les gans, le collet, les plumes, les rubans, avoient ce je
ne sai quoi, qu'il ne faut pas disputer aux François. Les autres Nations nous veulent imiter: mauvais singes, ou Dieu me damne.
En cet état, je m'en vais chez Mylord-Duc. Ah, Monsieur, quel     85
visage! quel air! quelle mine! Il n'avoit rien d'étranger, & jamais
François n'a eu la mine plus Françoise que lui. Voici le compliment, que je lui fis le plus court qu'il me fut possible. On est assez
de la Cour, pour savoir que les longues harangues y sont mal re-
çuës. *Monsieur*, lui dis-je, *Monsieur de Montmorency m'a chargé de*     90
*vous assurer de la part qu'il prend à la naissance de Monsieur vôtre fils.*
Je ne parlai point des couches de la femme, de peur d'allonger le
compliment: je crus que la naissance du fils comprenoit tout.
*Mais*, continuai-je, *de tous ceux, Monsieur, qui s'interessent à ce qui*
*vous touche, il n'y en a point qui soit plus vôtre serviteur que lui.*     95
J'ajoutai cela de moi, pour montrer qu'on n'est pas un miserable.
Cela fait effet. Tant que je parlai, Mylord-Duc eut toûjours son
chapeau hors de la tête; & après que j'eus fini, il me répondit en
ces termes, que je n'oublierai jamais: *Je suis bien obligé à Monsieur*
*de Montmorency de sa civilité: je me tiendrois heureux de lui en pou-*     100
*voir témoigner mon ressentiment, & en vôtre particulier, Monsieur, de*
*vous servir.* Par-Dieu, cela est bien civil!

TANCREDE.
Monsieur de Buckingham n'avoit garde de vous traiter moins
civilement; & je m'assure qu'il ne fut pas long-tems sans vous faire
ces petits plaisirs, dont vous nous avez parlé.     105

LE MARQUIS.
C'est-là le Plaisir dont je vous parlois: un homme d'honneur,
bien Gentilhomme, en peut-il recevoir d'autres? Je ne puis comprendre comment la plupart des gens ont le cûr fait: je sai bien
pour moi que ces choses-là sont les seules qui me touchent. Peut-
être auroit-il voulu m'oubliger d'une autre maniere, si j'avois de-     110
meuré plus long-tems à Londres. Je n'y fus rien que trois jours.

TANCREDE.
Quelque affaire importante vous rappella sans doute à Paris.

LE MARQUIS.
Nulle affaire: nous étions alors dans la paix.

TANCREDE.
Les Dames ne laissent pas un homme de vôtre humeur en repos, quand la Guerre ne l'occupe pas.     115

LE MARQUIS.

Je ne pensois pas avoir l'honneur d'être connu de vous, Mylord.
Il est vrai que je n'ai guére été sans quelque Amourette en ma vie.
En ce tems-là j'aimois une Dame, aussi-bien faite qu'il y en eût à
la Cour, & je n'étois pas seul à la trouver aimable. Ces Messieurs,
qui font un métier de la galanterie, les faiseurs de siéges, attaque-    120
rent cette place, & furent repoussez. Un des plus renommez parmi
les galans, ne put souffrir sans chagrin d'être chassé de chez elle,
& fit à la Reine quelque conte d'elle & de moi. Je ne sai; il y eut
une affaire entre nous, où il ne fut pas heureux. Voilà de l'éclat,
comme vous pouvez penser, & aussi-tôt martel en tête au mari,    125
qui sous prétexte d'affaires domestiques, l'emmena à la campagne.
Ne pouvant me consoler de ce fracas, je pris le tems de son absence pour voyager, & j'allai en Angleterre, dans le dessein d'y
faire quelque séjour: mais ......

TANCREDE.

Mais ces résolutions-là ne se tiennent point. Quand on a goûté    130
une fois des plaisirs de France, on s'accommode aux nôtres mal-
aisément.

LE MARQUIS.

Point du tout, vôtre pays me paroît agréable; outre que la guerre
tantôt deçà, tantôt delà, m'a appris à vivre par tout. Voulez-vous
que je vous parle franchement: les Anglois n'aiment pas nôtre    135
nation: nos bons Vins de Grave les font toûjours souvenir de la
perte de la Guienne; ils ne sauroient nous le pardonner.

TANCREDE.

Nous garderions long-tems nôtre ressentiment. Je vous assure
qu'on a beaucoup de civilité en Angleterre pour les François,
quand ils sont honnêtes-gens; & je suis fâché qu'un plus long sé-    140
jour ne vous ait donné moyen de l'éprouver.

LE MARQUIS.

Vous me parlez des gens de qualité! il n'y a rien de si civil: mais
le peuple, qu'en dites-vous? Avoüez qu'il est furieux. Comment! je
ne pouvois faire deux pas dans la ruë, sans entendre à mes oreilles:
*Francheman*: c'est un *Francheman*. Ah! Monsieur, qu'on nous haït!    145

TANCREDE.

Monsieur, je me rens, puis que cela vous est arrivé à vous-
même: jusques-là, je n'avois pas remarqué une animosité si extraordinaire.

LE MARQUIS.

Si j'avois l'honneur d'être connu de vous, vous croiriez que je ne
suis pas menteur. Sur la perte de mon salut, j'entendois *Franche-*   150
*man* à droit, *Francheman* à gauche, *Francheman* par tout. En quelque lieu que j'aye été, Dieu merci, on ne m'a dit guére d'injures.
Aussi, de se fâcher sottement, & de se commettre avec un peuple,
il faut être fou. Je pris le parti de repasser la mer, & ensuite de voir
l'Italie.   155

TANCREDE.

Je vous trouve un homme fort avisé. Il y a grande difference de
l'Angleterre à l'Italie, pour contenter la curiosité d'un Voyageur.
Mais je ne m'apperçois pas que j'empêche ici vôtre conversation: je
me retire, & rens graces à Monsieur, de m'avoir donné l'honneur
de vôtre connoissance.   160

LE MARQUIS.

C'est à moi de le remercier, Mylord. Il aura, s'il lui plaît, la
bonté de me mener chez vous, où je prétens vous rendre mes respects, & vous assurer de mon obéïssance. *Parlant à* l'Allemand.
Ami, je vous remercie de m'avoir donné la connoissance de ce
Mylord. Il est Par-Dieu fort honnête-homme, & il se connoît en   165
gens. On ne peut pas en user plus civilement qu'il a fait avec moi.
Il a été long-tems en France assurément.

L'ALLEMAND.

Et à Strasbourg, à Francfort, à Nuremberg. Il a fort voyagé.

LE MARQUIS.

Quand me menerez-vous chez lui?

L'ALLEMAND.

Quand vous voudrez. Mais retirons-nous d'ici. Voilà deux   170
Venitiens qui approchent de nous, avec lesquels vous feriez peut-
être connoissance, & je n'ai pas de tems à perdre.

## SCENE II.

### DOMINICO, LE SENATEUR AGOSTINO.

DOMINICO.

VOtre Excellence ne pouvoit pas arriver plus heureusement. Je
m'en allois chez elle, pour l'avertir d'une chose, que la bonne fortune de la République m'a fait entendre sans y penser.

AGOSTINO.

J'ai impatience d'entendre une chose qui doit regarder le salut public.                                    5

DOMINICO.

Me promenant tantôt dans la place, j'ai entendu deux étrangers parler de la République. Leur qualité d'Etrangers: leur mine sérieuse, leur mystére m'a donné envie de les écouter; & heureusement j'ai ouï ce que je m'en vais dire à Vôtre Excellence.

AGOSTINO.

On m'a déja donné quelques avis sur ces deux étrangers, & on          10
me les a dépeints comme des gens capables de remuer bien des choses. Poursuivez.

DOMINICO.

Il se passoit entr'eux divers discours tendant à former une grande liaison, quand tout d'un coup ils ont baissé le ton de la voix.

AGOSTINO.

N'avez-vous point eu la curiosité de vous informer de leurs          15
noms?

DOMINICO.

Je ne les ai point quittés de vûë qu'ils ne soient entrés dans leur maison; & m'étant informé autant que j'ai pu, de la qualité de ces personnages, j'ai su qu'il y a un Chevalier Anglois, nommé *Sir Politick*, par sa capacité en Politique; & un François, dont on n'a su          20
me dire le nom, grand faiseur de Projets pour les affaires d'argent.

AGOSTINO.

Voilà mes deux hommes. Le premier consommé dans la Politique, n'est-ce pas?

DOMINICO.

Le même.

AGOSTINO.

Je sai quels ils sont, & de quoi ils sont capables. Qu'avez-vous          25
ouï?

DOMINICO.

Tout d'un coup Sir Politick a baissé le ton de la voix; mais le bon génie de la République a rendu sa précaution inutile, & rien n'a empêché que je n'aye entendu distinctement ce qu'il disoit. *Les Législateurs ont manqué lourdement à l'interêt de la République,*          30
*quand ils n'ont fait qu'un seul Doge. Le Doge est une espece de Consul.*
*Les Romains en avoient deux; moi j'en voudrois quatre.*

AGOSTINO.

De quel déréglement n'est point capable l'esprit de l'homme,
puis qu'on ose trouver des défauts dans la constitution de nôtre
gouvernement! Mais, dites-moi, n'avez-vous rien ouï, qui vous      35
fasse soupçonner quelque Conspiration?

DOMINICO.

J'ai bien connu par leurs discours que ce sont des gens tout propres à conspirer...... Dans la verité, je n'ai rien entendu par où l'on
puisse voir une Conspiration formée.

AGOSTINO.

On m'a dit plus que cela. Songez un peu, & rappellez dans vôtre      40
esprit ce que vous pourrez de leur conversation.

DOMINICO.

Ils ont parlé de *grands Capitaines*.

AGOSTINO.

Mes avis portent qu'ils ont intelligence avec certains Généraux.
Vous souvient-il point du nom de ces *Capitaines?*

DOMINICO.

*Charles-Quint, Philippe II*, le *Duc d'Albe*, le *Duc de Parme*.      45

AGOSTINO.

Ce sont noms empruntés, qui font leur Chifre.

DOMINICO.

Cela pourroit bien être.

AGOSTINO.

Dites hardiment que cela est: il n'y a pas à douter.

DOMINICO.

Il est vrai qu'ensuite de ces *Capitaines*, ils ont discouru long-
tems de *troupes*, de *gens de pied*, de *gens de cheval*, de *canons*, de      50
*mousquets*, de *piques*, de *pistolets*; ce qui n'avoit point de rapport à
*Philippe II:* car il me paroissoit qu'ils parloient de choses présentes;
ajoûtant une particularité qui me surprit fort: "Que pour devenir
grand Capitaine, on n'avoit pas besoin d'aller à l'armée; que la
guerre se conduisoit mieux du cabinet; & que la spéculation mili-      55
taire faisoit tout."

AGOSTINO.

Ils ont raison. Je voi bien que ce sont gens profonds dans
l'Algebre. Avec l'Algebre on fait tout: ils ont raison. Je n'étois pas
mal averti, & vous aviez oublié justement ce qu'il y a de plus important. C'en est assez pour ce qui regarde la guerre. N'avez-vous      60
point découvert quelque intelligence dans les Cours étrangeres?

DOMINICO.

Vous en jugerez vous-même par leur conversation, que sur ce point je pense avoir fort bien retenuë. *J'ai un projet*, dit Sir Politick, *qui est bien d'une autre spéculation: il regarde les affaires étrangeres.*  65

AGOSTINO.

C'est-là qu'il falloit bien écouter.

DOMINICO.

Je puis assurer Vôtre Excellence que je n'en ai pas perdu un mot. *J'ai trouvé un moyen*, poursuivit Sir Politick, *de faire tenir des nouvelles de Venise à Constantinople en deux jours, & d'en recevoir en deux autres.*  70

AGOSTINO.

Malheur à la Chrétienté, & particulierement à la République.

DOMINICO.

Il a parlé de certains *relais de pigeons* établis chez des *correspondans* en *Istrie* & en *Dalmatie*, dans la *Bosnie*, &c.

AGOSTINO.

Cela est extraordinaire: mais il n'est pas impossible; & j'ai ouï parler autrefois de quelque chose d'approchant. Ce seroit un coup  75
d'Etat de savoir leurs correspondans: n'en ont-ils nommé aucun?

DOMINICO.

Vôtre Excellence peut bien juger qu'ils n'avoient garde d'en nommer. Je n'ai rien entendu de plus, excepté qu'il se vantoit d'avoir de merveilleux *Secrets pour la guerre.* Voilà tout.

AGOSTINO.

L'affaire est plus importante encore que vous ne pensez. Je vais  80
en informer le Sénat, & je n'oublierai pas de faire valoir le service que vous rendez. La République vous est obligée: elle n'en sera pas ingrate. DOMINICO *sort.*

AGOSTINO, *seul.*

Cet homme est bien intentionné: mais si je ne m'étois aidé de quelque industrie, j'en aurois tiré fort peu de lumiere. Je lui ai fait  85
accroire que j'avois déja eu les mêmes avis; ce qui l'a rendu plus docile à répondre à mes questions. Sans cela, il m'alloit débiter des choses mal disposées, & qu'assurément il n'avoit pas bien entenduës. C'est ainsi que je suis parvenu à la connoissance de la verité.
Je voi nettement où l'affaire va: ces gens sont gagnés du Turc, qui  90

se prépare à une grande guerre contre nous: il a choisi déja ses *Capitaines*, que Sir Politick nous cache sous de faux noms: il a fait ses *troupes*, tant de *pied*, que de *cheval*, & tiré de ses magazins toutes les armes, & les machines necessaires pour son dessein. La guerre se fera par les avis de ces mêmes gens, qui la *conduiront du cabinet* 95 avec beaucoup de prévoyance & de secret. C'est ainsi qu'ils prétendent faire de si grandes choses, sans être à l'armée. Voilà, si je ne me trompe, l'explication de tous leurs discours. Au reste, il ne faut pas s'endormir dans une chose qui regarde le salut de l'Etat. Je vais employer tous mes soins, pour en avoir l'éclaircissement 100 entier; & si la bonne conduite peut assurer du succès, j'ose esperer de garantir la République d'un grand danger.

## SCENE III.

### DOMINICO, AGOSTINO.

#### Dominico.

JE reviens trouver Vôtre Excellence, pour lui dire, que ces deux Etrangers, dont je lui ai parlé, vont à la rencontre l'un de l'autre. Il sera facile de les écouter.

#### Agostino.

Menez-moi où ils sont, & trouvons quelque endroit commode, où nous puissions nous cacher. 5

#### Dominico.

Les voici tout proche de nous, mettons-nous ici derriere.

## SCENE IV.

### Mr. DE RICHE-SOURCE, SIR POLITICK: AGOSTINO, & DOMINICO, *qui les écoutent*.

#### Mr. de Riche-Source.

MOnsieur, jamais homme n'a porté la Politique au point où vous l'avez mise. La Spéculation militaire, & les Secrets pour la guerre, seroient des choses inconnuës sans vous: mais, Monsieur, à quoi bon vôtre Politique, toute excellente qu'elle est, si vous n'avez de l'Argent pour en faire mouvoir les ressorts, & exécuter les projets? 5 Que vous servira la spéculation militaire, & comment pouvoir conduire une armée du cabinet, si vous n'avez de l'argent pour

composer cette armée, & la faire subsister? Vos secrets pour la
guerre demeurent inutiles faute d'argent: car, comme vous le savez, l'argent est le nerf de la guerre.                                    10

SIR POLITICK.

Monsieur, si les Etats où je me trouve, veulent m'employer,
c'est à eux de faire la dépense qu'il conviendra. S'ils ne la font pas,
il y va plus de leur interêt que du mien.

MR. DE RICHE-SOURCE.

Je l'avouë, & il n'y a rien de si certain: mais outre le service du
public, qui touche les gens de bien, un homme d'honneur est bien        15
aise de voir ses talens mis en usage. Or, Monsieur, faites les plus
belles propositions du monde, si elles doivent coûter de l'argent,
on vous traite de chimerique, ou d'imposteur.

SIR POLITICK.

Vôtre discours est solide, & j'en suis persuadé: mais je vous dirai
librement ce que dit nôtre Plutarque de Cheronée:                       20

Onc ne furent à tous toutes graces données.

Tous les dons sont départis diversement. Comme je vous ai fait
voir avec confiance ceux que je puis avoir, je vous confesserai avec
franchise, que je n'ai pas grand mérite pour les affaires d'Argent.

MR. DE RICHE-SOURCE.

Et moi, Monsieur, (vous ne me soupçonnerez pas de vanité,) je        25
suis peut-être en cela le plus extraordinaire homme qu'ait produit
ma Nation. Je ne borne pas ma science à un métier méchanique
d'augmenter les Revenus, de retrancher des Dépenses superfluës, de
mettre un ordre exact en toutes choses, de bien regler les affaires
du Prince, & celles de la Nation en même tems: j'ai un Projet qui    30
va au bien général de tous les peuples.

SIR POLITICK.

Vous me donnez l'idée d'une grande affaire; & si vous la con-
duisez avec une bonne politique, il en réussira quelque chose de
merveilleux. Je dis merveilleux pour les hommes du commun; car
rien ne surprend les génies extraordinaires.                           35

MR. DE RICHE-SOURCE.

Le projet est grand; mais un homme comme vous le concevra aisément. Je l'ai découvert quelquefois à des esprits médiocres, qui ne
le pouvoient comprendre.

SIR POLITICK.

C'est le malheur des grands personnages. Leurs conceptions passent la portée presque de tout le monde. Achevez.     40

MR. DE RICHE-SOURCE.

Il y a des endroits où la Politique me fera besoin; & là vos talens seront employez. Ecoutez, je vous prie; car il faut quelque explication de mon côté, & de l'attention du vôtre.

SIR POLITICK.

Je suis tout préparé; & j'espere que je ne perdrai rien de vôtre discours.     45

MR. DE RICHE-SOURCE.

Mon dessein est d'établir la Circulation: tout mon projet aboutit à cela; & voici ce que c'est. Vous connoissez le prix de l'Or, communicable entre les hommes, qui doit couler par des canaux libres; &, suivant un mouvement qui ne soit jamais interrompu, maintenir son cours, jusqu'à ce qu'il ait accompli sa circulation. Je n'aurai pas de peine à vous persuader qu'il enrichira tous les pays par     50
où il passe; qu'il n'y a rien d'ingrat, rien de sterile chez les nations où l'on en connoît l'usage. L'affaire est que cet Or si necessaire au monde, n'a plus son passage libre. Ma circulation est empêchée; trouvons le moyen de déboucher les canaux, & je verrai bientôt la     55
fin de mon ouvrage. C'est en ceci, Monsieur, que j'ai besoin de vôtre Politique.

SIR POLITICK.

Vous pouvez croire qu'elle ne vous manquera pas: faites-en état comme d'un secours assuré.

MR. DE RICHE-SOURCE.

Les Princes de l'Orient, le Grand-Seigneur, le Roi de Perse, le     60
Mogol, sont ceux qui par un interêt particulier, préjudiciable au bien général, ont bouché les canaux dont je vous parle. Mais il faut reprendre la chose de plus loin.

SIR POLITICK.

J'appellerois ceci la *Science de la Circulation*, & la *Doctrine des Canaux*.     65

MR. DE RICHE-SOURCE.

Je l'ai prise sur la considération du corps humain; & à vous dire le vrai, la circulation du sang nouvellement découverte m'a beaucoup servi à former l'idée de mon projet.

SIR POLITICK.

Reprenez vôtre matiere.

MR. DE RICHE-SOURCE.

Autrefois les Orientaux trafiquoient avec nous par échange de    70
denrées, & souvent nous tirions d'eux des choses rares & précieuses pour des bagatelles. Détrompés à la fin, ils ont pris plus
d'avantage sur nous que nous n'en avions sur eux; car ils ont établi
le trafic de l'Or: & comme leurs marchandises sont inépuisables,
& nôtre luxe infini; il arrive que le fond de nôtre métail ne l'étant    75
pas, c'est une necessité que tout l'Or de l'Occident passe en
Orient, & que l'Asie soit maîtresse un jour de toutes les richesses
du monde.

SIR POLITICK.

Elle l'étoit autrefois sous Darius: mais Alexandre sut vanger la
pauvreté de l'Europe; & nôtre fer, c'est-à-dire, la guerre, pourra    80
nous en faire raison.

MR. DE RICHE-SOURCE.

Je vous ai fait voir clairement en quel état sont les choses; c'est à
vous maintenant de déboucher nos Canaux. Si cela se fait par né-
gociation, voilà un beau champ ouvert à vôtre Politique. Si les
Traités ne servent de rien, alors vous pourrez mettre en usage la    85
Spéculation militaire, & employer quelqu'un de vos Secrets pour
la guerre. Celui des Batailles, à mon avis, suffira, ces peuples-là
commettant tout au hazard d'une journée.

SIR POLITICK.

L'affaire n'est pas aisée: elle est grande de mon côté, & plus que
du vôtre: je l'entreprens néanmoins, & j'espere d'en venir à bout.    90
Voulez-vous que je rende l'Europe maîtresse de l'Asie?

MR. DE RICHE-SOURCE.

Vous en ferez ce qu'il vous plaira.

SIR POLITICK.

Hé bien donc! je ferai mon plan sur l'expédition d'Alexandre.
Les Romains n'ont été qu'aux bords de l'Asie. Quand ils ont voulu
aller plus avant, ils n'ont eu que de la mauvaise fortune, & j'en sai    95
les raisons. Je veux d'abord, voyez-vous, je veux ..... Mais si nous
nous contentions de lever les obstacles de la Circulation?

MR. DE RICHE-SOURCE.

Je pense que ce seroit le mieux.

SIR POLITICK.

En ce cas, il faut unir quelques Cités principales. Faisons un
Triumvirat de Paris, de Londres, & de Venise.                    100

MR. DE RICHE-SOURCE.

Avec qui pourrions-nous traiter cela?

SIR POLITICK.

Il doit se traiter avec le Maire de Londres, avec le Prevôt des
Marchands de Paris, & avec les Procurateurs de St. Marc.

MR. DE RICHE-SOURCE.

J'admire comme sur le champ, & si à propos, vous savez trouver
les veritables gens avec qui vous avez à négotier.              105

SIR POLITICK.

Un Politique, j'entens un Politique consommé, doit avoir la
connoissance de tous les Etats, & savoir les differens Ministres
ausquels il faut s'adresser. Mais un si grand dessein que le nôtre ne
souffre pas une longue digression. Voilà donc mon Triumvirat
établi. Aussi-tôt je dépêche une Ambassade solemnelle, qui répré-   110
sente à ces Rois que la Circulation est du droit des gens; que vouloir l'empêcher, c'est interesser les Nations, & aller contre la
liberté naturelle de tous les peuples.

MR. DE RICHE-SOURCE.

Apparemment ils vous donneront satisfaction.

SIR POLITICK.

Ou ils me la donnent, ou ils ne me la donnent pas. S'ils me font   115
justice, je me remets dans le plein & libre exercice de la Circulation. S'ils reçoivent mes Ambassadeurs avec l'orgueil des Princes
de l'Orient, & que mesdits Ambassadeurs reviennent sans rien
faire, alors Paris, Londres, & Venise joignent leurs forces, & ces
trois Puissances unies envoyent une armée navale brûler tous les   120
vaisseaux de l'Orient, pour réduire ces peuples injustes à la raison.
J'ai fait ce qui étoit de moi: vos canaux sont débouchés; c'est à
vous de faire le reste.

MR. DE RICHE-SOURCE.

Les canaux étant ouverts, mon or à l'instant reprend son cours,
& repassant d'Orient en Occident, ma circulation se fait sans em-   125
pêchement pour le bien de l'Univers. Voyez comment la chose ira.
Tout l'argent qui va de Marseille dans les coffres du Grand-
Seigneur, passera dans ceux du Roi de Perse; de la Perse dans ceux
du Mogol, où ne s'arrêtant plus comme il avoit accoutumé, il

repassera en Europe par le moyen des Anglois & des Hollandois       130
qui trafiquent aux Indes: d'Angleterre & de Hollande il retournera
en France, où après une petite Circulation particuliere, il reviendra
à Marseille, d'où il est parti, par le moyen du canal qui joint les
deux Mers. Chaque Nation a ses Canaux; & il suffit de savoir que
les obstacles étant levés, l'Or & l'Argent auront un tour & un       135
retour éternel.

### Sir Politick.

Je n'ôte jamais l'honneur à personne, & j'avouë sans envie que
le projet est grand & beau: mais sans moi vos Canaux seroient encore à déboucher; & partant ce grand ouvrage de la Circulation
seroit demeuré long-tems une belle idée.                            140

### Mr. de Riche-Source.

Je vous ai déclaré d'abord que j'aurois besoin de vous; & il est
certain que nous nous sommes necessaires l'un à l'autre.

### Sir Politick.

De cela j'en demeure d'accord volontiers; & si nous allons tous
deux de bon pied, nous sommes les maîtres de nôtre affaire.

### Mr. de Riche-Source.

On ne sauroit commencer trop tôt. Voulez-vous que j'écrive au       145
Prevôt des Marchands de Paris?

### Sir Politick.

Nous avons à faire ici à des gens soupçonneux & jaloux, qu'il
faut ménager délicatement. Laissez-moi un peu sonder les Procurateurs de St. Marc. Pour le Maire de Londres, j'en répons.

### Mr. de Riche-Source.

Et moi, du Prevôt des Marchands de Paris.                           150

### Sir Politick.

Voilà une partie de ce que nous pouvons souhaiter. Gardons
seulement le secret.

### Mr. de Riche-Source.

Permettez que je vous accompagne à vôtre logis.

### Sir Politick.

Les gens qui ont d'aussi grandes affaires que nous dans la tête,
ne doivent pas s'amuser aux cérémonies. Trouvez-vous, s'il vous    155
plaît, à mon logis sur le soir.

## SCENE V.

AGOSTINO, & DOMINICO, *qui les écoutoient.*

### Agostino.

JE rends graces au bon génie de la République, de m'avoir conduit
ici à propos. J'ai entendu tout ce que je pouvois desirer. Je ne vous
demande plus qu'une chose: en quel quartier de la ville est leur
maison?

### Dominico.

Tout proche d'ici. C'est celle que vous voyez au bout de la ruë,     5
un peu plus petite que les autres.

*Fin du second Acte.*

## ACTE III.

## SCENE PREMIERE.

## L'ALLEMAND, LE MARQUIS.

### L'Allemand.

VOus avez dit tantôt bien des paroles oisives avec le cousin du
Duc de Buckingham: n'étoit-ce pas assez de le saluer? Si vous
vouliez faire plus de connoissance, il falloit boire les uns avec les
autres. C'est ainsi qu'on fait des amitiés, & non pas dans les places
publiques à babiller. Sans vous, j'aurois vu plus de quatre Eglises,     5
& plus de vingt Tombeaux avec les Epitaphes.

### Le Marquis.

Vous m'en contez bien; & n'aimai-je pas mieux avoir eu commerce avec un honnête-homme, que d'avoir vu tout l'Arsenal de
Venise! Je dis l'Arsenal; car si je puis avoir quelque curiosité, c'est
pour les choses qui regardent la guerre. A vous voir, vous autres     10
Messieurs les Allemands, graves & sérieux comme vous êtes, on
vous prendroit pour des Catons; & vous êtes cent fois plus fous
que nous, ou Dieu me danne. Venir de deux cens lieuës charger
un registre d'Inscriptions & d'Epitaphes! belle curiosité! Je ne vous
en ai rien dit; mais il y a long-tems que vous m'importunez avec     15
vos Horloges. Je me moque, Messieurs, de vos petits chefs-
d'œuvre, & tiens même au dessous d'un galant-homme toutes les

raretés d'Italie. Il m'importe bien de savoir l'Original, la Copie; l'Antique, le Moderne; & cent autres fadaises de cette nature-là? Serai-je mieux à la Cour, quand je saurai quel est le plus grand 20 maître de *Michaël*, ou d'*Angelo*; de *Raphaël*, ou d'*Urbin?* Si je revenois à Paris avec une science de pareilles Couyouneries, Dieu n'ait jamais pitié de moi, si les Dames ne me chassoient des ruelles, & les Courtisans des Cabinets. C'est un pays délicat que le nôtre: on n'y sauroit être savant en quoi que ce soit, sans passer 25 pour un Pedant; je dis parmi les honnêtes-gens.

L'ALLEMAND.

Je vous dirai, moi, que vous êtes plus entêté de vos Cabinets, que je ne le suis de mes Horloges. Ce n'est pas que je prenne en mauvaise part la correction, pour ce qui me regarde en particulier: mais pour les Allemands, Mort-nom-sang-Dieu,⁴ taisez-vous, & 30 ne parlez pas de ma nation.

LE MARQUIS.

Et moi, je vous abandonne la mienne. Parlez des François tant qu'il vous plaira, pourvu que vous me teniez honnête-homme, & vôtre serviteur.

L'ALLEMAND.

J'en croirai ce que je voudrai: mais ne pensez pas être de mes 35 amis, quand vous médirez de mon pays. Dire que les *Allemands* sont des *fous*, qui *viennent de deux cens lieuës charger un registre d'Inscriptions & d'Epitaphes!* S'il ne me souvenoit d'avoir bu avec vous .....

LE MARQUIS.

Touchez-là: nous boirons encore ensemble, & je vous prie de 40 croire que si vôtre maniere de voyager ne me plaît pas, j'ai du moins en vénération la gloire des armes, qui est commune à nos deux Nations. La conduite que vous tenez dans vos voyages me déplaît, je l'avouë, aussi ne faites-vous pas grand cas de la mienne. Remettons nôtre different au jugement de quelque personne espi-45 rituelle. La femme de Sir Politick, femme de grand esprit, comme vous savez, l'en voulez-vous croire?

L'ALLEMAND.

Je ne demande pas mieux.

LE MARQUIS.

La voilà, ce me semble.

---

⁴ Serment ordinaire du Maréchal de Rantzau, qui étoit Allemand.

L'ALLEMAND.

C'est elle sans point douter.                                                50

## SCENE II.

## LE MARQUIS, LA FEMME DE SIR POLITICK,
## L'ALLEMAND.

### LE MARQUIS.

MAdame, vos deux bons amis ont failli à se brouiller. La colere est
passée présentement; mais le sujet de la dispute ne l'est pas: nous
allons vous l'exposer, & décidez, je vous prie; car nous sommes
convenus l'un & l'autre d'acquiescer à vôtre jugement.

### LA FEMME DE SIR POLITICK.

Sans doute qu'un bon ange a conduit ici mes pas, pour finir le          5
different qu'un démon, auteur de la discorde, a fait naître. Mon
zele, Messieurs, pourra suppléer au défaut de la prudence; car
pour le métier de bien juger, c'est une chose fort difficile. Il faut
qu'un bon Juge possede necessairement la Jurisprudence. En second lieu, il faut ...... il faut enfin bien des choses. C'est un métier   10
très-difficile que de bien juger!

### LE MARQUIS.

Tout un Parlement ensemble ne sait pas ce que vous demandez
à un Juge seul; & puis, il n'y va ni du bien, ni de la vie.

### LA FEMME DE SIR POLITICK.

Ah! Monsieur, il y va de plus que vous ne pensez: il y va de la
Concorde & de l'Amitié, deux choses bien précieuses. Mais puis     15
que vous avez honoré vôtre humble Servante de ce choix, elle
n'oubliera rien pour vous rendre une sentence équitable.

### LE MARQUIS.

La question est de savoir quelle est la meilleure maniere de
voyager, de celle de Monsieur, ou de la mienne?

### LA FEMME DE SIR POLITICK.

Question fort épineuse! où la connoissance de la Géographie     20
me servira bien.

### LE MARQUIS.

Ecoutez, s'il vous plaît, il ne faut qu'un peu de sens commun
pour nôtre affaire; & la femme de Sir Politick sait toutes choses.

#### La Femme de Sir Politick.

Nous avons un peu voyagé: peut-être savons-nous mieux que
beaucoup d'autres, le devoir d'un Voyageur. Il faut premierement    25
savoir les Loix & les Coutumes des pays où l'on passe: je l'entens
toûjours dire à Sir Politick.

#### Le Marquis.

Laissons cela à Sir Politick: nous sommes de simples Voyageurs, qui ne voulons pas nous embarrasser l'esprit de choses fort
difficiles.    30

#### La Femme de Sir Politick.

Difficiles! Si vous aviez trois conversations avec Sir Politick, il
oseroit bien se vanter de vous apprendre plus d'affaires d'Etat en
ce peu de tems, que n'en sait le plus vieux Sénateur de la République.

#### Le Marquis.

Pour moi, je ne veux d'affaires d'Etat, ni à Venise, ni à Paris,    35
quand j'y serai de retour. Je me verrois bien étonné parmi des sacs,
& dans les papiers jusqu'aux oreilles; sans plumes, sans rubans,
n'osant faire galanterie, ni me trouver à une belle action.

#### L'Allemand.

Si vous vous amusez à l'écouter, nous perdrons le reste de la
journée. Voulez-vous m'entendre?    40

#### La Femme de Sir Politick.

Je vous donne une oreille, & garde l'autre pour Monsieur.

#### L'Allemand.

C'est une coutume générale en Allemagne que de voyager: nous
voyageons de pere en fils, sans qu'aucune affaire nous en empêche
jamais. Si-tôt que nous avons appris la Langue Latine, nous nous
préparons au voyage. La premiere chose dont on se fournit, c'est    45
d'un Itineraire, qui enseigne les voyes. La seconde, d'un petit
Livre, qui apprend ce qu'il y a de curieux en chaque païs. Lors que
nos Voyageurs sont gens de Lettres, ils se munissent en partant de
chez eux d'un livre blanc, bien relié, qu'on nomme Album Amicorum, & ne manquent pas d'aller visiter les Savans de tous les    50
lieux où ils passent, & de le leur présenter, afin qu'ils y mettent
leur nom: ce qu'ils font ordinairement, en y joignant quelques
propos sententieux, & quelque témoignage de bienveillance en
toutes sortes de langues. Il n'y a rien que nous ne fassions pour
nous procurer cet honneur; estimant que c'est une chose autant    55

curieuse qu'instructive, d'avoir connu de vûë ces gens doctes, qui font tant de bruit dans le monde, & d'avoir un *specimen* de leur Ecriture.

LA FEMME DE SIR POLITICK.

Est-ce là tout l'usage que vous faites de cet ingenieux Livre?

L'ALLEMAND.

Il nous est aussi d'un très-grand secours dans nos débauches:      60
car lors que toutes les Santés ordinaires ont été bûës, on prend
l'ALBUM AMICORUM, & faisant la revûë de ces grands hommes, qui
ont eu la bonté d'y mettre leurs noms, on boit leur santé copieuse-
ment. Nous avons aussi un JOURNAL, où nous écrivons nos
remarques, à l'instant même que nous les faisons. Rarement nous      65
attendons jusqu'au soir; mais jamais Voyageur Allemand ne s'est
couché, sans avoir mis sur le papier ce qu'il a vu durant la journée.
Il n'y a point de montagne renommée qu'il ne nous soit necessaire
de voir. Qu'il y ait de la neige ou non, il n'importe; il faut aller au
haut, s'il est possible. Pour les Rivieres, nous en devons savoir la      70
source, la largeur, la longueur du cours, combien elles ont de
ponts, de passages, & particulierement où elles se déchargent dans
la mer. S'il reste quelque chose de l'Antiquité, un morceau d'un
ouvrage des Romains, la ruine d'un Amphithéatre, le débris d'un
Temple, quelques arches d'un Pont, de simples Pilliers; il faut tout      75
voir. Je n'aurois pas fait d'ici à demain, si je voulois vous compter
tout ce que nous remarquons en chaque ville. Il n'y a point
d'Edifice, point de Monument ......

LE MARQUIS.

Qu'appellez-vous *Edifice* & *Monument?*

L'ALLEMAND.

Ce sont les Ouvrages publics.      80

LE MARQUIS.

Y comprenez-vous les Eglises?

L'ALLEMAND.

Les Eglises, les Abbayes, les Convents. Il y a bien d'autres
choses; les Places publiques, les Hôtels-de-Ville, les Acqueducs,
les Citadelles, les Arsenaux.

LE MARQUIS.

Eh! dites-moi, Monsieur, quel tems avez-vous pour dîner, vous      85
autres qui aimez les longs repas?

### L'Allemand.

Dans nos voyages, nous ne dînons point. La nuit est faite pour
la débauche: mais dîner ou non, il n'y a point de belle Maison, de
beau Bois, de belles fontaines, de beaux Jardins, que nous ne
soyons obligés de voir.                                                90

### Le Marquis.

Beau Devoir, à ma fantaisie! belle obligation!

### L'Allemand.

La plus belle que sauroit avoir un Voyageur. Je ne dis rien des
Tombeaux, & des Epitaphes: on sait bien que c'est par-là qu'il
faut commencer. Je n'oublierai pas les Clochers & leurs Carillons,
ni les Horloges, qui font passer les douze Apôtres avant que de      95
sonner; non plus que le Paradis terrestre, & l'Arche de Noé, où
tous les animaux se remuënt comme par magie. Mais c'est en Allemagne qu'il faut venir voir ces Chefs-d'œuvres-là; & je n'avois
que faire d'en sortir pour de pareilles inventions. Il ne sera pas
hors de propos de vous apprendre certaines coutumes que les          100
Voyageurs observent sans manquer. Par exemple, nous sommes
fort curieux des Maisons Royales, & pourtant nous ne les voyons
jamais quand les Rois y sont. Dans mon voyage de France, je vis le
Louvre l'été, quand le Roi étoit à Fontainebleau; & Fontainebleau
l'hiver, quand la Cour fut revenuë à Paris.                          105

### Le Marquis.

Voilà une coutume fort bizarre, ce me semble: les Maisons des
Rois ne paroissent jamais si belles, que lors que la Cour y est.

### L'Allemand.

Chaque chose a sa raison; & celle-ci est très-considerable.
Nous ne sortons pas de nôtre pays pour faire la cour. Si un Allemand vouloit être Courtisan, il le seroit de son Souverain, ou de    110
ses Magistrats. Nous cherchons chez les étrangers les Raretés que
nous n'avons pas chez nous; & vous jugez bien qu'il seroit impossible de les considerer dans les Maisons Royales parmi les Gardes
du Prince.

### La Femme de Sir Politick.

Cette raison est profonde. Les Allemands n'ont pas le brillant       115
des François: mais ils sont judicieux & solides. Monsieur, avez-
vous vu l'Angleterre?

### L'Allemand.

J'y ai demeuré long-tems.

LA FEMME DE SIR POLITICK.
Et qui avez-vous connu là?
L'ALLEMAND.
Personne. Ce n'est pas nôtre coûtume de connoître les gens du     120
pays où nous sommes, hors un Maître, qui nous apprend la
Langue par les regles de la Grammaire; & en voici la raison. Les
Naturels méprisent les Voyageurs. Tout au contraire les étrangers
se cherchent, & font amitié ensemble; car ils ont un même interêt,
& il y a plaisir d'être avec des gens qui peuvent parler des pays les     125
uns des autres. Ainsi nous voyons les François en Angleterre, les
Anglois en France, les Flamands en Italie, & les Italiens à
Bruxelles, ou ailleurs.
LA FEMME DE SIR POLITICK.
Mais, Monsieur, au moins, vous avez bien vu les Raretés de nôtre
Royaume?     130
L'ALLEMAND.
Je les ai toutes vûës, & elles sont fort belles à voir. Vous avez les
Tombeaux de Westminster, & sur tout l'Epitaphe de Talbot,[5] le
Portrait de Henri VIII, à White-Hall avec la Procession entrant
dans Boulogne. Vous avez les Lions de la Tour, & le Combat des
Ours & des Taureaux contre les Dogues, qui sont pieces fort     135
curieuses.
LA FEMME DE SIR POLITICK.
Ce sont des choses de très-grande curiosité: vous pouviez néan-
moins y ajoûter beaucoup d'autres Merveilles.
L'ALLEMAND.
J'estime fort le Combat des Cocqs, la Course des hommes, celle
des Chevaux, les Harangues des pendus, & la Cérémonie de My-     140
lord Maire. Je ne dois pas oublier les Enseignes des Cabarets, &
autres, dont j'ai cent fois admiré la magnificence. Il y a pourtant
une chose que je n'approuve pas: c'est la coutume que vous avez en
Angleterre de n'y point mettre d'Inscriptions, comme on fait à
Paris & ailleurs: *AU LION NOIR, A L'OURS, &c*; au grand dé-     145
triment de nos Compatriotes amateurs de vôtre Langue, qui en
considerant les Enseignes, pourroient apprendre plusieurs Mots
necessaires.

---

[5] Jean Talbot premier Comte de Shrewsbury, la terreur des François. Il fut
emporté d'un coup de Canon devant Châtillon près de Bourdeaux, en 1453.

## La Femme de Sir Politick.

Cet inconvenient est certainement fâcheux, & je ne doute point
que le Parlement n'y remediât, si vous vouliez bien le pétitionner.        150

## L'Allemand.

Il y a encore bien des choses curieuses en Angleterre; les Ro-
chers que le Diable a assemblés en pleine campagne;[6] les fossés
faits par le Diable pareillement à New-Market. Oxford & Cambridge sont pleins de Raretés. J'ai remarqué sur tout à Oxford la
Lanterne du déloyal Gui Faux, qui devoit mettre le feu aux pou-        155
dres, & qu'on garde soigneusement. On peut voir encore les
Eglises de Cantorbery & de Salisbury.

## La Femme de Sir Politick.

Je suis pleinement satisfaite. Il ne se peut rien désirer de plus.
C'est un beau métier que celui d'un Voyageur, quand on le fait
comme vous. Il est vrai qu'il est pénible.        160

## L'Allemand.

Nul bien sans peine. Ce n'est pourtant pas là nôtre plus grand
travail. Les choses qui arrivent extraordinairement, & où nous
sommes obligés de nous trouver, sont les plus rudes. Par exemple,
je suis à Turin, je suis à Genes, je suis prêt d'entrer à Rome; si
j'entens parler de l'Election de l'Empereur, du Sacre du Roi de        165
France, du Couronnement d'un Roi d'Angleterre, d'un Mariage,
d'un Traité de Paix, d'une Entrée; il faut prendre la poste où l'on
se trouve, & arriver à tems pour voir la cérémonie.

## La Femme de Sir Politick.

Vous m'apprenez-là de grands mystéres. De toutes les manieres
de voyager, il n'y en a point de si admirable, après celle de Sir Po-        170
litick, qui travaille à réformer le Gouvernement des Pays par où il
passe.

## Le Marquis.

Suspendez vôtre jugement, Madame, & vous souvenez que
vous m'avez promis une oreille: peut-être changerez-vous de sentiment.        175

## La Femme de Sir Politick.

Dites vos raisons.

## Le Marquis.

Les voici, mes raisons. Je ne sai si vous aurez la bonté de les
écouter: j'ai vu que les honnêtes-gens se donnoient la peine de
m'entendre.

---

[6] Le *Stone-henge*, dans la Plaine de Salisbury.

L'ALLEMAND.

A quoi bon tant de babil?                                       180

LE MARQUIS.

Je ne fais pas le métier de Voyageur; mais il me prend quelquefois envie de l'être, dans l'inutilité de la Paix, dans l'absence d'une
Maîtresse, dans une Disgrace qui arrive à la Cour pour une belle
action. La curiosité de voir des Marbres, des Tombeaux, des Statuës, ne fut jamais le sujet de mes Voyages. On cherche à connoî-   185
tre les Cours étrangeres, pour voir si on y peut faire quelque chose;
on cherche à pratiquer les honnêtes-gens, & les Dames. Vous êtes
Angloise, Madame; & vous, Monsieur, vous avez vu l'Angleterre?

L'ALLEMAND.

Je l'ai vûë.

LE MARQUIS.

Posons le cas que j'y veuille demeurer quelque tems; voici la   190
maniere que j'y tiendrois.

LA FEMME DE SIR POLITICK.

Vous avez choisi l'Angleterre avantageusement pour nous, qui
la connoissons. C'est proceder avec franchise.

LE MARQUIS.

Je vais d'abord chez nôtre Ambassadeur, que je connois, s'il est
homme de Cour; & aussi-tôt mille amitiés. *Comment avez-vous pu*   195
*vous résoudre à quitter la Cour? il faut bien qu'une Affaire d'impor-*
*tance vous amene ici?* & cent autres choses que sait dire un galant-
homme à son ami. Vous pouvez croire que je ne demeure pas en
arriere de complimens: & après mille civilités, je lui dis quelque
chose de mes avantures; ni trop, ni trop peu. Remarquez: car il me   200
souvient toûjours qu'il est Ambassadeur, & qu'il faut ménager
mon secret avec lui.

LA FEMME DE SIR POLITICK.

Quand vous auriez étudié sous Sir Politick, vous n'en sauriez
guere davantage.

LE MARQUIS.

La Cour n'est pas une mauvaise école: on y apprend quelque   205
chose. Si l'Ambassadeur est un vieux Politique, qu'on ait vu rarement chez le Roi, je lui apporte des Lettres de recommendation
de ses amis; & à peine les a-t-il lûës, que j'en reçois beaucoup de
civilité. Après l'avoir assuré de mon très-humble service, je répons
à diverses questions qu'il me fait, assurément bien: puis quittant   210

les affaires générales, je lui dis des particularités de ses connois-
sances; ajoûtant adroitement quelque chose de la satisfaction
qu'ont les Ministres de son Ambassade. Enfin, je n'oublie rien
pour m'insinuer dans ses bonnes graces, & m'acquerir une grande
liberté dans sa maison. La Table d'un Ambassadeur est bonne; c'est          215
une retraite, s'il vous arrive une affaire, un combat, l'enlevement
d'une fille de qualité qu'on aime, ou quelque autre action d'honneur. Cela fait, je cherche un Anglois, qui me présente au Roi.

LA FEMME DE SIR POLITICK.

N'y auroit-il pas plus de convenance de vous faire présenter par
vôtre Ambassadeur?          220

LE MARQUIS.

Qui en doute, s'il est homme de Cour? Il diroit galamment au
Roi: *SIRE, voici Monsieur le Marquis de Bousignac, qui sera bien
connu de VOTRE MAJESTÉ par sa réputation, s'il n'a l'honneur de
l'être par sa personne*; & le Roi répondroit: *Je ne suis pas si peu informé des affaires des pays étrangers, que je ne sache la qualité & le*          225
*mérite du Marquis de Bousignac.*

LA FEMME DE SIR POLITICK.

Mais si vôtre Ministre est seulement homme d'état?

LE MARQUIS.

Quoi? de ces formalistes! qui croyent toûjours représenter *le Roi
leur Maître:* je ne m'accommode pas de ces gens-là. Vous creveriez
plutôt que de leur arracher le mot de *MARQUIS*, à moins qu'ils          230
ne soient assurés du Marquisat.

LA FEMME DE SIR POLITICK.

Vous n'avez donc point de Marquisat?

LE MARQUIS.

Vous venez de l'autre monde. Apprenez que les Marquisats ne
sont bons que pour les vieux Seigneurs de Province, qu'on ne voit
pas dans les Cabinets. Pour nous autres Marquis de Cour, (BEAU          235
PRIVILEGE DE LA NOBLESSE FRANÇOISE!) nous faisons nous-mêmes
nôtre qualité, sans avoir besoin du Roi pour cela, comme en ont
vos Anglois pour être *MYLORDS*. Mais pour éviter tout embarras
avec les Ambassadeurs, j'ai recours à l'industrie, & voici mes machines. Je regarde l'Ordinaire le plus proche de White-Hall, qui          240
soit bon, & où viennent les plus honnêtes-gens: j'y vais dîner trois
ou quatre fois, pour en rencontrer quelques-uns, & lier avec eux
un peu d'amitié.

L'ALLEMAND.

Comment un étranger *liera-t-il* avec eux ce *peu d'amitié* aux
Ordinaires? On dîne, on paye, & on s'en va.                    245

LE MARQUIS.

Il y a mille choses à faire, que vous n'entendez pas.

L'ALLEMAND.

Je voudrois bien les savoir, ces choses.

LE MARQUIS.

Je boi durant le repas à leur santé, sans oublier la Civilité Angloise, après avoir bu. Si on parle de la bonté des viandes, je tranche
tout net pour le Bœuf d'Angleterre contre celui de Paris; les    250
viandes rôties au beurre, me semblent meilleures que les lardées; je
me creve de *Poudin*, contre mon Cûr, pour gagner celui des autres;
& s'il est question de fumer au sortir de table, je suis le premier à
faire apporter les Pipes. A la fin, on se sépare. Les uns cherchent à
jouër; les autres vont à White-Hall: je sui les derniers, & quand le   255
Roi passe, je m'approche le plus que je puis de sa personne.
Ecoutez ma maniere, Madame, elle est assurément fort noble. Si-
tôt que sa Majesté parle à quelqu'un, je me mets de la conversation: cela n'a-t-il point d'effet? j'éleve le ton de la voix. Tout le
monde me regarde. J'entens qu'on se demande à l'oreille: *Qui est ce*   260
*François-là? Le Marquis de Bousignac,* dis-je assez haut pour être
entendu. Ce beau procedé les étonne; & je me rens maître géné-
reusement de la Conversation.

LA FEMME DE SIR POLITICK.

On a bien raison de dire que la Noblesse Françoise a quelque
chose que celle des autres pays n'a pas.                          265

LE MARQUIS.

Le même soir je vais chez la Reine, où j'en fais autant. On ne
parle pas la Langue; mais on fait une réverence de certain air, qui
attire les yeux des Belles: & sans vanité, on a je ne sai quoi de galant, qui ne leur déplaît pas. Familier en moins de rien avec tous
les grands Seigneurs: *Mylord, Mylord, Mylord - Duc.* Je ne sai que   270
dire après; mais il n'importe: la familiarité s'établit toûjours. Je
rens visite à toutes les Dames qui parlent François, & dis en passant quelque méchant mot Anglois aux autres. La *Mylédy* soûrit
pour le moins: & quelquefois il se fait de petites Conversations,
où l'on ne s'entend point, fort agréables. Voilà, Monsieur, ce qu'il   275
nous faut de l'Angleterre pour nos Courtisans, & pour nos Dames:
non pas des Tombeaux de Westminster; non pas Oxford &

Cambrige. Cela est-il bien pensé, Madame? décidez présentement
en faveur des merveilles que Monsieur vous a fait entendre.

### La Femme de Sir Politick.

Certes, je suis confuse de ces differentes Merveilles; & mon es-       280
prit embarrassé ne sait où se prendre pour former le jugement que
vous attendez. Quand je songe à cette Curiosité infinie, qui ne né-
glige pas la moindre chose de toute une Nation, je suis prête à
décider en faveur de l'Allemand. Si je pense au gentil François,
l'Alcibiade de nos jours, je suspens mon jugement, & dis en moi-       285
même: O! la chose arduë, que de bien juger! D'autre part, c'est
une pensée judicieuse à l'Allemand de ne point voir les naturels du
pays où il se trouve, pour en éviter le mépris; & il n'y a rien de si
sage que de remettre à les pratiquer en d'autres lieux, où le nom
commun d'Etrangers fait leur amitié. Mais qui n'admirera la Ci-       290
vilité du François à l'Ordinaire proche de White-Hall; sur tout,
quand il *se creve de Poudin contre son cœur, pour gagner celui des
autres.* Cette pensée des Ordinaires me surprend, & je ne sai comment elle a pu tomber dans l'esprit d'un Etranger. Cela est d'un
homme consommé dans les affaires de nôtre pays: c'est ce que Sir       295
Politick entendoit admirablement, & là où il faisoit ses plus beaux
Projets.

### Le Marquis.

On a des vûës comme un autre, & on pense quelquefois ce que
pensent les gens d'esprit: non pas que je veuille me comparer à Sir
Politick. A Dieu ne plaise que j'aye cette vanité-là!                   300

### La Femme de Sir Politick.

Assurément mon Mari a quelque chose d'extraordinaire; je le
puis dire sans vous offenser: mais finissons la digression, & repre-
nons nôtre sujet. *Voir le Louvre en été, quand le Roi est à Fontainebleau, & Fontainebleau en hiver, quand la Cour est revenuë à Paris;*
c'est une prudence Allemande, qui ne peut venir que d'un très-       305
grand sens: car l'Allemand cherche la Maison du Roi, & non pas
le Roi dans la Maison. Le François, au contraire, cherche les Rois,
& ne se soucie pas de leurs Maisons. Or après avoir employé tous
les moyens que l'esprit humain peut fournir, il a recours à cette
hardiesse Françoise, qui le fait parler au Roi, sans que le Roi lui       310
parle, & qui *le rend maître genereusement de la conversation,* au
grand étonnement de nos Anglois. Plus je considere la chose, plus
je suis irrésoluë, & ne sai qui des deux je dois couronner. Bien

dirai-je que dans la maniere Allemande, vous êtes, Monsieur, le
premier homme de vôtre Nation; & que nul des François n'est        315
comparable à celui-ci dans la sienne.

### LE MARQUIS.

Je suis content, Madame, & les autres Nations ne me donnent
point de jalousie.

### L'ALLEMAND.

Je vous suis trop obligé de vos loüanges.

### LA FEMME DE SIR POLITICK.

J'ai fait seulement mon devoir.        320

## SCENE III.

## ME. DE RICHE-SOURCE, LA FEMME DE SIR POLITICK.

### ME. DE RICHE-SOURCE.

TAndis que nos Maris songent au bien des Etats, il m'est venu
une chose dans la pensée, où il n'y auroit pas moins de mérite qu'à
ce qu'ils font, si on en pouvoit venir à bout: mais en cela, Madame, j'aurois besoin de vôtre secours.

### LA FEMME DE SIR POLITICK.

Madame, sans savoir ce que vous voulez me communiquer,        5
j'oserois affirmer que la pensée est considerable; & si pour l'execution de quelque projet, vous avez besoin de mon assistance, vous
en pouvez disposer entierement.

### ME. DE RICHE-SOURCE.

Mon Dieu, Madame, n'avez-vous point pitié de ces pauvres
Esclaves, que la jalousie des maris tient si cruellement enfermées?        10
Le cœur me saigne toutes les fois que je songe à la misere de leur
condition.

### LA FEMME DE SIR POLITICK.

Les esclaves de Tunis & d'Alger sont libres, si on compare leur
captivité aux fers de ces miserables femmes; & depuis que je réside
à Venise, c'est la seule chose qui ait donné à mon ame des at-        15
teintes douloureuses.

### ME. DE RICHE-SOURCE.

J'admire la cruauté de ces méchans hommes, qui tyrannisent de
pauvres Dames sans aucun fruit: car j'ai assez bonne opinion de

nôtre sexe, pour croire qu'elles ne laissent pas de faire l'amour, tant bien gardées qu'elles puissent être. 20

### La Femme de Sir Politick.

*L'Amour*, comme dit à propos un Ancien, *a les clefs de toutes les portes:* non pas que ce soit de veritables clefs. L'Auteur mystérieux a voulu nous faire entendre sous un langage figuré, que l'esprit subtil des Amoureux trouvoit l'invention d'entrer par tout.

### Me. de Riche-Source.

A ce compte, voir & jouïr n'est qu'une même chose. Dieu me 25 garde de blâmer la jouïssance; j'estime que c'est le vrai but de toutes sortes d'amitiés: mais c'est toûjours un grand malheur à des personnes bien nées de se passer du Beau-Procedé & de la Belle-Galanterie.

### La Femme de Sir Politick.

En ce point, Madame, mon opinion n'a pas de conformité avec 30 la vôtre. A quoi bon toutes ces cérémonies amoureuses? Je suis d'avis en fait d'Amour, qu'on retranche les choses superfluës, & que sans s'amuser à l'inutilité des prémisses, on vienne solidement à la conclusion.

### Me. de Riche-Source.

Cependant, il est bien rude de n'avoir ni Jeu, ni Promenades, ni 35 Collations, ni Assemblées: j'aimerois autant mourir pour moi, que de ne jouïr pas de tous les divertissemens que peut donner un honnête-homme.

### La Femme de Sir Politick.

Frivoles amusemens de personnes oisives! Je ne plaindrois pas, moi, celles qui pourroient employer solidement certaines heures 40 sans danger: mais j'ai horreur des accidens déplorables que nous voyons arriver ici journellement; & il n'y a rien que je n'entreprenne pour sauver des fureurs de la jalousie ces innocentes victimes.

### Me. de Riche-Source.

Madame, sans nous effrayer des difficultés que nous trouverons, 45 n'y a-t-il point moyen de les mettre dans le commerce du Beaumonde? Comme elles n'ont jamais rien vû, elles ont assurément un fort méchant Air, & ce seroit un grand plaisir de leur pouvoir apprendre la Belle-Maniere.

### La Femme de Sir Politick.

Tout beau, Madame; changeons de discours: voilà Mylord Tan- 50 crede avec un homme qui me paroît être Venitien.

Me. de Riche-Source.
Laissez-moi faire: je vais les engager dans une conversation où ils ne s'attendent pas, & qui nous éclaircira de bien des choses.

La Femme de Sir Politick.
Mais prenez garde de vous découvrir.

Me. de Riche-Source.
Ne vous en mettez pas en peine: je ferai la chose si délicate-    55
ment qu'ils n'en auront pas le moindre soupçon.


SCENE IV.
TANCREDE, LA FEMME DE SIR POLITICK,
ANTONIO, Me. DE RICHE-SOURCE.

Tancrede.
MEs Dames, je vous amene un honnête-homme de mes amis, qui souhaite d'avoir l'honneur d'être connu de vous.

La Femme de Sir Politick.
Nous sommes trop obligées à sa civile curiosité, & à sa civilité curieuse: bien fâchées de ne pouvoir répondre par mérite condigne à la courtoise envie qu'il a euë de nous voir.    5

Antonio.
Madame, la modestie sied bien aux personnes, dont les bonnes qualités sont aussi connuës que les vôtres.

Me. de Riche-Source.
Je suis d'un pays où l'on parle avec franchise: j'ose dire que vous nous trouverez certain Air, & des Manieres qu'il ne faut pas cher-cher à vos Dames Venitiennes: mais où les auroient-elles prises,    10
les pauvres femmes? C'est le Beau-Monde qui les donne, & elles ne voyent que des Maris. Helas! elles sont bien à plaindre!

Antonio.
Je vous assure, Madame, que j'en ai plus de compassion que vous: jusques-là que ne n'ai pas voulu me marier, pour n'être pas obligé, selon la coutume du pays, à rendre une femme malheu-    15
reuse.

Me. de Riche-Source.
Paris est le Paradis des femmes. Quand un Honnête-homme se marie, il sait bien que sa femme ne peut pas vivre sans quelque petite inclination, & qu'autre chose est un Epoux, autre chose un

Galant. S'il y a un Bal, un Balet, quelque Assemblée, où il faille     20
paroître & se faire des Amans, le mari va chercher par tout les
pierreries, connoissant bien que ce n'est pas pour lui qu'on se pare:
mais comme je viens de dire, il est Honnête-homme. Dame aussi,
les femmes vivent à peindre avec leurs maris. Elles les caressent,
elles les flatent, elles les baisent, elles leur témoignent tant d'ami-     25
tié; ce n'est que douceur d'un côté, & complaisance de l'autre.
C'est un si bon ménage!

ANTONIO.

L'heureuse vie dont vous me parlez! Tous les maris jouïssent-ils
de ce bonheur-là?

ME. DE RICHE-SOURCE.

Quasi tous. Il en faut excepter quelques malheureux qui ont     30
épousé des Prudes.

ANTONIO.

Qu'appellez-vous des Prudes?

ME. DE RICHE-SOURCE.

Ces femmes incommodes, fâcheuses, de méchante humeur.

ANTONIO.

Cela est trop général: je ne connois point encore les Prudes.

ME. DE RICHE-SOURCE.

Des personnes sauvages, retirées, qu'on nomme fort ridicule-     35
ment *femmes-de-bien:* des vertueuses de profession, que les
honnêtes-gens n'abordent pas, & qu'on laisse dans les familles
pour faire enrager les maris.

TANCREDE.

Ces accidens-là sont heureusement fort extraordinaires: car c'est
une vraye damnation d'épouser de ces femmes qui croyent qu'on     40
leur doit tout, parce qu'elles ne font point l'amour.

ANTONIO.

Voyez le méchant goût de nos Sénateurs: ils n'estiment que ces
femmes-là dans les maisons.

ME. DE RICHE-SOURCE.

Grand abus: c'est de-là que viennent tous les désordres de vos
familles.     45

ANTONIO.

J'en demeure d'accord avec vous.

ME. DE RICHE-SOURCE, *à la* FEMME DE SIR POLITICK, *bas.*
Madame, je le tiens homme-d'honneur.

LA FEMME DE SIR POLITICK, *bas.*
Et moi pareillement.

ME. DE RICHE-SOURCE, *bas.*
J'en répons. *Haut.* Monsieur, je ne me suis jamais trompée en
Physionomie: je jurerois que vous êtes un homme sûr, un homme     50
à qui on se peut fier de toutes choses.

ANTONIO.
Jusques ici on ne m'a pas reproché d'avoir trompé personne.

TANCREDE.
Il a plus d'honneur qu'homme du monde.

ME. DE RICHE-SOURCE.
Eh! bien; c'en est assez: nous vous recommandons le secret. Sachez que nous avons fait le dessein, Madame & moi, de soulager     55
la pitoyable condition de vos pauvres Dames.

ANTONIO.
Voilà justement mon projet.

ME. DE RICHE-SOURCE.
Quel bonheur de nous rencontrer dans la même pensée! Après
cela, je ne désespererai jamais de ma bonne fortune.

TANCREDE.
Mais encore où aboutit ce projet?     60

ANTONIO.
D'établir à Venise la douceur des bons ménages.

ME. DE RICHE-SOURCE.
Et pour y parvenir de mettre ces pauvres femmes dans le commerce du Beau-Monde.

TANCREDE.
Voyons un peu par où il faut commencer.

ME. DE RICHE-SOURCE.
Je n'y voudrois pas tant de finesse: prions-les à un Bal dès ce     65
soir. Un impromptu réussit mieux quelquefois qu'une chose pré-
méditée.

LA FEMME DE SIR POLITICK.
Il faut pourpenser les choses avec loisir & méditation: & puis,
les Dames de Venise ne vont pas au Bal chez les étrangers.

##### Me. de Riche-Source.

Je l'ai pensé d'abord comme vous: mais j'ai cru que la considera-    70
tion qu'on a pour Sir Politick en pouvoit ôter toute la difficulté.

##### Tancrede.

Ne cherchez plus rien après cela: c'est la seule chose qu'il y
avoit à trouver.

##### La Femme de Sir Politick.

Il faut avouër que la grande opinion qu'on a de mon mari, peut
applanir bien des choses.                                            75

##### Me. de Riche-Source.

Nous ne sommes plus en peine que de l'expédient qu'il faut
prendre pour les faire prier.

##### Tancrede.

Il faut s'en remettre à Monsieur: personne au monde n'y peut
réussir si bien que lui.

##### Antonio.

Je m'en charge volontiers, & vous répons de vous en amener    80
cinq ou six des principales.

##### La Femme de Sir Politick.

Ce seroit un grand coup d'y pouvoir faire venir la Dogesse: telle
Gravité que la sienne autoriseroit fort l'assemblée.

##### Tancrede.

Il gouverne tout dans sa maison.

##### Antonio.

C'est celle qui me donnera le moins de peine. Mais voulez-vous    85
que cela se fasse bien-tôt?

##### Tancrede.

Le plutôt, est le mieux.

##### Me. de Riche-Source.

Dès ce soir: pourquoi differer?

##### La Femme de Sir Politick.

Sans en parler à nos Maris?

##### Me. de Riche-Source.

On ne les consulte jamais sur les affaires de cette nature-là. Trop    90
d'honneur pour eux d'avoir si bonne compagnie.

##### La Femme de Sir Politick.

Ce sera donc pour ce soir, puis que Madame l'a résolu.

Me. de Riche-Source.
Songeons à disposer toutes choses pour le Bal.

Antonio.
Fort bien: de mon côté je m'en vais disposer les Dames à venir
honorer vôtre fête.                                                    95

## SCENE V.

### Me. DE RICHE-SOURCE, LA FEMME DE SIR
### POLITICK, TANCREDE, LE MARQUIS, L'ALLEMAND.

Me. de Riche-Source.
ALlons, Madame, travaillons un peu à nôtre affaire: ces Messieurs
auront la bonté de nous y aider.

Le Marquis.
Nous serions peu civils aux Dames de leur refuser nos services
dans une chose galante comme celle-ci.

Tancrede.
Commandez seulement, vos ordres seront executés.              5

L'Allemand.
Je suis prêt à tout.

Me. de Riche-Source.
Voici de quelle maniere il faut disposer les siéges: Un grand
fauteuil pour la Dogesse sur une estrade; des chaises à dos pour les
femmes des Senateurs; puis des siéges plians pour les étrangers &
pour nous, comme on a coutume de les ranger.                  10

La Femme de Sir Politick.
Madame, il faut excuser une Françoise, qui ne connoît que les
usages de son pays: j'ose vous dire néanmoins que vôtre ordonnance n'a pas la gravité requise pour une telle occasion.

Me. de Riche-Source.
Madame, en toute autre chose je vous cederai volontiers: mais
je puis vous dire que depuis l'âge de huit ans que j'étois *la petite*   15
*Suzon*, il ne s'est fait Bal, ni Assemblée à la ville, où je n'aye été.
J'en ai vu même au Louvre assez souvent; car mon mari étoit
comme de la Cour, par les amis que nous y avions. J'en ai vu chez
Madame la Comtesse, chez Madame la Princesse de Conti, où j'ai
fort bien observé comme les choses devoient aller; & il n'y a point   20
d'année que je n'aye donné moi-même quelques Fêtes fort jolies,
qui valoient bien les grandes assemblées.

### Le Marquis.

Quand on parle des choses qu'on a vûës, & de celles qu'on a
faites, on mérite d'être écouté.

### La Femme de Sir Politick.

Achevez, Madame, ce que vous avez à représenter.     25

### Me. de Riche-Source.

Le dernier Carnaval (nous avions le cœur bien en joye) je don-
nai les violons aux Dames de ma Cotterie, d'une maniere aussi
galante que chose qui se fût passée de tout l'hiver. Je commençai
par un Souper-collation, qui étoit un Ambigu, où il n'y avoit pas
l'abondance des Cadeaux; mais tout y étoit excellent: des viandes  30
prises si à propos, qu'un quart-d'heure plutôt elles eussent été un
peu dures, un quart-d'heure plus tard, elles auroient commencé à
se passer. On n'en trouve point de même ailleurs; & mon mari &
moi les avions fait apprêter devant nous. La Sale étoit éclairée
comme en plein jour, pas un siége qui passât l'autre, & la place  35
pour danser à ravir. Des Suisses à la porte, qui ne laissoient entrer
que les gens priés; l'élite de la Cour & de la Ville, avec la parenté,
cela s'entend, & les amis particuliers de la maison. Au milieu du
Bal, je me dérobai finement, pour me déguiser, & faire une Mascarade entre nous, rien que de la famille. Nous la dançâmes sans  40
que personne nous reconnût, & si-tôt que je fus deshabillée, je
pris une place froidement, comme si de rien n'eût été. Chacun se
tuoit à deviner, sans en approcher de mille lieuës: c'est le plus
grand plaisir d'une Mascarade; & je vous avouë que ç'a été le plus
heureux soir de toute ma vie.     45

### La Femme de Sir Politick.

Madame, pour ce qui se fait à vôtre Cour, je n'en parle pas,
mais sachez qu'un Bal de République demande un peu plus de
mesure; & quand vous songerez qu'une Dogesse & des femmes de
Sénateurs seront tantôt ici, vous changerez, à ce que j'estime, vôtre
ordonnance.     50

### Me. de Riche-Source.

Dites vôtre sentiment.

### La Femme de Sir Politick.

Mon sentiment est qu'on place la Dogesse & les Sénatrices en
telle sorte, qu'elles représentent un petit Senat: la Dogesse comme
dans un trône, & les Sénatrices aux deux côtés sur des bancs. Ce
leur sera une chose agréable de tenir la place de leurs Maris, &  55
courtoise à nous de leur faire avoir cet honneur-là.

L'ALLEMAND.

Je suis de l'opinion de Madame: mais je voudrois qu'il y eût au trône de petites figures en bosse fort bien taillées, & de beaux feuillages au dos des bancs.

TANCREDE.

Que peut-on dire contre la proposition de Madame? Y a-t-il     60
rien de mieux pensé?

LE MARQUIS.

Qui doute que pour le sérieux elle n'ait plus de sens que toutes les femmes ensemble? La pensée est judicieuse, je l'avouë; mais je ne me dédis pas: nôtre maniere Françoise est plus galante; & il est fort suffisant à Madame la République de ne prendre pas les     65
modes de Paris, quand tout le monde court après. Je ne suis, morbieu, point homme de République: d'un pays où il n'y a point de Cour, ne m'en parlez pas.

ME. DE RICHE-SOURCE.

Je sai fort bien que tout ce qu'a dit Madame seroit ridicule à Paris; & personne ne m'apprendra rien en fait de Bal & d'As-     70
semblée: mais s'il faut observer de telles cérémonies dans une République, Dame, je m'en rapporte; elle connoît cela mieux que moi.

LA FEMME DE SIR POLITICK.

Dans la suite de la fréquentation, vous pourrez leur inspirer vos Galantises: pour la premiere fois, il faut de la gravité.     75

ME. DE RICHE-SOURCE.

Je sai me rendre à la raison, ne me plût-elle pas. Allons, Madame, disposer toutes choses comme vous le jugez à propos.


SCENE VI.

TANCREDE, ANTONIO.

TANCREDE.

NOus avons donné bien des affaires à nos folles: elles ont été je ne sai combien de tems à disputer sur la maniere dont il faut recevoir la Dogesse, quelle place, quels siéges il faut avoir; & à la fin elles sont convenuës d'un appareil le plus ridicule du monde.

ANTONIO.

Je me suis bien douté que nôtre conversation auroit produit  5
quelque chose de fort extravagant.

TANCREDE.

Mais, dites-moi, que ferons-nous de ceci, & comment finir la
comédie?

ANTONIO.

J'irai leur faire les excuses de la Dogesse, sur quelque indisposition imaginaire.  10

TANCREDE.

Cela ne me contente pas.

ANTONIO.

Que voudriez vous davantage?

TANCREDE.

Je voudrois que vous leur menassiez une Entremetteuse, &
quelques filles, qui réprésentassent la Dogesse, & des femmes de
Senateurs.  15

ANTONIO.

Vous m'inspirez-là une pensée fort plaisante, & fort aisée à
executer; car je viens de laisser à cent pas d'ici justement la compagnie qu'il nous faut. Allez préparer toutes choses pour nous recevoir, & laissez-moi le soin du reste.


## SCENE VII.

### ANTONIO, LE SENATEUR PAMFILINO.

ANTONIO.

JE suis fort en peine de ce que pensera Vôtre Excellence d'un dessein de divertissement que nous avons fait le Mylord & moi; ce
Mylord qui a eu l'honneur de vous voir, & que vous estimez assez.

PAMFILINO.

Quand vous m'aurez dit quel est ce divertissement, je vous dirai
ce qui m'en semblera. Parlez.  5

ANTONIO.

Ayez donc la patience de m'écouter, s'il vous plaît. Il y a ici deux
Etrangeres assez accommodées, à ce qu'il me paroît, mais assurément les plus ridicules personnes que j'aie jamais vûës. La premiere
est une Angloise, grave, composée; fausse en discours, en poli-

tique; en prudence sottement mystérieuse. L'autre est une petite   10
Françoise, d'un esprit tout opposé. Elle n'aime que le *Beau-*
*Monde*, ne parle que du *Bel-Air*, de la *Belle-Maniere*, se croit déli-
cate, galante, polie; & veritablement elle est plus Bourgeoise que
ne sont les femmes de Marchands les plus grossiéres.

PAMFILINO.

Que voulez-vous faire de ces deux femmes? Il est tems de les   15
mettre à quelque usage. Achevez.

ANTONIO.

C'étoit une necessité de vous en faire la peinture. Ces deux
femmes, plus ridicules encore que je ne vous les dépeins, se sont
mis dans la tête de tirer les Dames Venitiennes de la déplorable
captivité où l'on les retient, & de leur inspirer les coutumes, l'air,   20
la maniere, le procedé des femmes les plus galantes.

PAMFILINO.

Je ne voudrois pas jurer que cela n'arrivât quelque jour; mais
j'espere que le dessein de vos Dames ne réussira pas aujourd'hui.

ANTONIO.

Ce n'est rien encore. Apprenez jusqu'où va leur extravagance.
La petite Françoise veut donner le Bal ce soir à vos femmes; &   25
l'Angloise voudroit que la Dogesse y fût; disant gravement que
telle Gravité autoriseroit fort l'assemblée. Le Mylord, pour s'en
divertir, a juré que j'avois tout pouvoir dans leurs maisons, & qu'il
n'y avoit rien de si facile pour moi que de les amener. J'y ai con-
senti; & me voilà chargé de faire venir la Dogesse, & cinq ou six   30
femmes de Senateurs chez nos deux folles.

PAMFILINO.

Comment vous acquitterez-vous de cette commission-là?

ANTONIO.

Le Mylord voudroit que je leur menasse .... Oserois-je dire le
mot devant Vôtre Excellence?

PAMFILINO.

Dites hardiment.   35

ANTONIO.

Une Entremetteuse & des Filles, pour représenter la compagnie qu'elles demandent: mais ......

PAMFILINO.

Mais que rien ne vous en empêche: cela se peut faire avec des
Etrangers. Il me souvient qu'étant à Paris fort jeune, on me faisoit

essuyer souvent de ces tours-là: on me produisoit des Princesses,      40
qui se trouvoient des filles de la même nature que celles-ci. Ne
quittez pas une entreprise si heureusement commencée; je prens la
chose sur moi.

#### Antonio.
Avec un si bon garent que Vôtre Excellence, nous travaillerons
sans scrupule à nous donner ce divertissement-là.                      45

*Fin du troisiéme Acte.*


# ACTE IV.
## SCENE PREMIERE.
*Toutes choses sont préparées pour le Bal.*

## SIR POLITICK, Mr. DE RICHE-SOURCE, LA FEMME
## DE SIR POLITICK, Me. DE RICHE-SOURCE,
## TANCREDE, LE MARQUIS, L'ALLEMAND,
## UN VALET DU SIGNOR ANTONIO.

#### Sir Politick.
MA femme, que voi-je? Le Senat doit-il se tenir ceans aujour-
d'hui?

#### La Femme de Sir Politick.
Monsieur, vous verrez quelque chose d'assez extraordinaire,
dont vous ne serez pas fâché.

#### Me. de Riche-Source, *à* Sir Politick.
Vous parlez mieux que vous ne pensez. Oui, le Senat doit se te-     5
nir ceans aujourd'hui. Remerciez vos femmes, Messieurs, remer-
ciez-les de l'honneur que vous allez recevoir.

#### Mr. de Riche-Source.
Mais encore, quel peut être cet honneur-là?

#### Me. de Riche-Source.
On ne gagne jamais rien à être curieux. Tu sais que je ne m'informe pas de tes actions, ne t'informe pas des miennes. C'est le    10
moyen d'être toûjours bien ensemble.

#### Sir Politick.
Dans les Familles, comme dans les Etats, il importe à celui qui
gouverne de savoir tout ce qui s'y passe.

Me. de Riche-Source.

Oh bien! il faut donc vous en instruire. Apprenez que la Dogesse va venir à un Bal que nous lui donnons.          15

Sir Politick.

La chose en soi nous est grandement honorable: mais je veux en savoir le Projet, & par quels instrumens elle s'est faite.

Me. de Riche-Source.

Par une rencontre admirable. Le Seigneur Antonio nous est venu voir avec le Mylord; & après plusieurs discours sur la captivité des Dames de Venise, enfin nous sommes demeurés d'accord          20
qu'elles ne laissoient pas d'aller au Bal, & que même il ne seroit pas difficile de les obliger à venir ceans. Là-dessus le Seigneur Antonio s'est fait fort d'y amener la Dogesse, & quelques Nobles Venitiennes avec elle.

Tancrede.

Il gouverne tout dans leurs maisons.          25

Sir Politick.

C'est la premiere affaire de hazard qui soit jamais entrée dans la mienne: je n'aime pas les présens de la fortune, & je ne sai comment je recevrois un Royaume, qui me viendroit sans Projet & sans Politique.

Tancrede.

Permettez-moi de vous dire que jamais affaire ne fut moins de          30
hazard que celle-ci; & n'en déplaise à vos Dames, la part qu'elles y ont est fort médiocre. Sans la haute opinion qu'on a de vôtre gravité & de vôtre sagesse, nous ne verrions ceans ni Dogesse, ni femmes de Senateurs. C'est l'effet de vos Projets & de vôtre grande Politique, exercée depuis si long-tems.          35

Sir Politick.

La chose avoit besoin d'être expliquée. Oui, vous me faites comprendre facilement que nous ne devons rien au hazard: on fait plus d'estime de moi que je ne vaus, je le confesse, mais rendons honneur pour honneur, & songeons à bien recevoir une si auguste Compagnie. Je n'ai pas oublié nos rangs d'Angleterre, & n'ignore          40
pas ce que doit un *CHEVALIER* à un *LORD*: néanmoins, comme nous sommes à Venise, & que la Fête se fait dans ma maison, vous ne trouverez pas mauvais que je porte la parole.

TANCREDE.

J'honore trop vôtre vertu, pour manquer jamais à vous rendre
ce qu'on vous doit ici, & ailleurs; outre que personne n'est capable        45
de s'aquitter de cet emploi-là si bien que vous.

LE MARQUIS.

Monsieur Politick, saluë-t-on la Dogesse?

SIR POLITICK.

Oui vraiment, on saluë la Dogesse, avec des inclinations
profondes, & des révérences bien basses.

LE MARQUIS.

Je demande si on baise?                                                      50

SIR POLITICK.

Baiser à Venise! baiser une Dogesse! Ma femme, vôtre gentil
François demande si on baise la Dogesse?

LE MARQUIS.

Je ne sai pour qui on me prend: vous diriez qu'on n'a jamais
baisé des femmes de qualité. J'ai baisé deux Duchesses en ma vie,
qui le portoient bien haut, sur ma parole; & des Maréchales de           55
France, quantité.

UN VALET DU SIGNOR ANTONIO.

Le Seigneur Antonio m'a envoyé ici pour vous dire que la Dogesse va venir. Elle est en chemin à l'heure que je vous parle.

SIR POLITICK.

Allons, Messieurs, allons la recevoir avec l'ordre & la dignité
qu'il convient garder en telle cérémonie. Comme je dois porter la        60
parole, on trouvera bon que je marche le premier: les deux femmes
suivront, pour faire les honneurs du logis: Madame fera, s'il lui
plaît, un compliment à la Françoise: Mylord & le mari de Madame suivront après, & ces deux Messieurs ensuite.

LE MARQUIS, à l'ALLEMAND.

Je ne suis point un trouble-fête; je veux ce qu'on veut: mais je         65
voi bien ce que je voi. On nous traite, vous d'Allemand, & moi de
miserable. Aller derriere un Bourgeois à la cérémonie, sont les
graces qu'on nous fait ceans. Ce n'étoit pourtant pas la même
chose à Paris: car, sans vanité, ces petites gens de ville ne mettoient pas le pied au Louvre, que j'étois dans les Cabinets. Pour le     70
Mylord, je lui cede; non pas en qualité de Mylord, fût-il Duc; un
Marquis François, brave, & bien vêtu ne cede à personne; mais
après les obligations que j'ai au Duc de Buckingham, je ne dispu-
terai rien à ceux qui lui appartiennent.

Sir Politick.

Nous avons fait ces rangs ici sans consequence, pour le présent:     75
ne troublez pas, je vous prie, un personnage qui va faire une
grande action à la tête de cette compagnie.

Mr. de Riche-Source.

Prenez-vous garde à un Impertinent?

Le Marquis.

Bourgeois, remerciez le lieu où nous sommes: sans le respect de
la Dogesse, qu'il faut recevoir, & la considération de ces Mes-     80
sieurs, je vous apprendrois à parler.

Me. de Riche-Source.

Allez, petit Suivant; c'est bien à vous de faire comparaison avec
mon Mari.

Tancrede.

Eh! Messieurs, voilà la Dogesse: remettez vos querelles à une
autre fois, & laissez parler Sir Politick.     85

Sir Politick.

Le *Primordium* m'a donné bien de la peine; le reste ne m'a rien
coûté.

Tancrede.

Silence, Messieurs, silence.


## SCENE II.

L'ENTREMETTEUSE *prise pour* DOGESSE, LES
DEMOISELLES *se disant* FEMMES DE SENATEURS,
ANTONIO, SIR POLITICK, LA FEMME DE SIR
POLITICK, TANCREDE, LE MARQUIS,
L'ALLEMAND, Mr. DE RICHE-SOURCE,
Me. DE RICHE-SOURCE.

Sir Politick, *haranguant* la Dogesse.

SI la bonne réception se mesuroit par la grandeur, & la décoration
des bâtimens, par les lambris dorés, & les riches tapisseries, Vôtre
Serenité, Madame, & vous, très-excellentes Senatrices, seriez
aujourd'hui mal reçûës dans la petite & simple maison de cettui
vôtre plus qu'humble serviteur: mais si vous cherchez à loger dans les     5
cœurs, plutôt que dans les palais, vous trouverez les nôtres enrichis
de zele, garnis de fidelité, remplis d'affection, revêtus de services

& de devoirs pour la République en général; pour VÔTRE SERENITÉ, & Vos EXCELLENCES en particulier. Ne croyez pas, s'il vous plaît, en voyant ce peu que nous sommes, recevoir seulement l'offre de nos 10 vœux: figurez-vous de voir ici les Députés des plus belliqueuses Nations, qui viennent vous en rendre leurs hommages. Mylord, ma femme, & moi, mettons à vos pieds l'Angleterre, l'Ecosse & l'Irlande: ces deux Messieurs & Madame vous offrent la France, grand & puissant Royaume, s'il en fut jamais; & Monsieur, qui 15 réunit en soi mille interêts differens, vous presente les vastes Provinces de la Germanie. Voilà, très-Serene Dogesse, & très-excellentes Senatrices, tout ce que je puis dire en public: mais VÔTRE SERENITÉ me permettra de confier à son oreille quelque chose de particulier, dont ces Messieurs & ces Dames ne seront pas scan- 20 dalisés, s'il leur plaît. *Bas.* Je vous dirai en confidence, Madame, que nous allons établir, Dieu aidant, la Circulation: projet merveilleux, qui par des canaux, inconnus au reste des hommes, fera venir une abondance de Richesses dans cet Etat.

LA DOGESSE.

La République vous est fort obligée; je dis fort; & le Doge mon 25 mari, mon mari le Doge, vous en remerciera en son particulier, comme nous faisons au nôtre. *Bas.* Quant à ce que vous m'avez dit à l'oreille, vous m'obligerez de mettre à part quelque chose pour moi, quand vous ferez venir tant de biens dans cet Etat.

SIR POLITICK, *à part.*

Voici de la Corruption jusques dans la maison du Doge! Cela 30 n'arriveroit pas, s'il y en avoit quatre, comme j'ai dit: ils s'observeroient les uns les autres. *A LA* DOGESSE. Cette réïteration des obligations que nous veut bien avoir la République, nous assure d'une double reconnoissance, dont l'une nous regarde, comme personnes publiques, & Députés de ces grandes Nations, l'autre comme des 35 particuliers affectionnés à son service.

LE MARQUIS.

J'admire cet homme; il torne toutes choses comme il lui plaît.

SIR POLITICK.

Pour la répétition de *Doge*, qui ne voit, Madame, qu'elle marque deux fois vôtre dignité, pour nous faire comprendre doublement l'auguste honneur de vôtre présence. 40

LE MARQUIS.

Autre version excellente, qui vaut la premiere, pour le moins.

SIR POLITICK, *à part.*

Puis qu'elle est interessée, il faut la gagner politiquement par l'Interêt. *A* LA DOGESSE. Un mot à l'oreille de vôtre Serenité. Nous aurons soin de vôtre maison: ce n'est rien dérober au public; car vôtre rang a besoin d'être soutenu. Il se fera pour vous une petite   45
Circulation particuliere; je n'en dis pas davantage.

LA DOGESSE, *bas.*

Vous avez raison, Monsieur Politick, nous sommes obligés à beaucoup de dépense.

LE MARQUIS.

J'enrage, morbieu, quand il parle bas; je voudrois ne pas perdre un mot de tout ce qu'il dit.   50

ME. DE RICHE-SOURCE, *à la* DOGESSE.

Vous aurez la bonté, Madame, d'excuser des personnes mal préparées à vous recevoir: car enfin ....... c'est qu'après tout ....... effectivement, nous ne nous attendions pas à cet honneur-là. Pour ces jeunes Dames, elles auront un peu moins d'excuses: j'espere de leur faire voir quelques manieres assez galantes, qui ne leur dé-   55
plairont pas.

LA DOGESSE.

Point d'excuses entre amies: nous venons vous voir sans façon.

LE MARQUIS.

Voilà, Madame, ce qu'a dit Sir Politick dans sa harangue: Vôtre Serenité veut se *loger dans les cûrs.*

LA FEMME DE SIR POLITICK, *à son Mari.*

Monsieur, voici le Signor Antonio, à qui vous avez l'obligation   60
de tant d'honneur.

SIR POLITICK *au* SIGNOR ANTONIO.

Le respect que j'ai pour la Présence Serene, ne me permet pas de vous témoigner assez combien je sai connoître & reconnoître la grande Faveur que ce m'est.

ANTONIO.

L'envie que j'avois de meriter quelque part dans l'honneur de   65
vôtre amitié, m'a fait entreprendre une chose assez extraordinaire: mais je me tiens assez heureux si j'ai réussi.

LA FEMME DE SIR POLITICK, *à la* DOGESSE.

Madame, je crains que VÔTRE SERENITÉ ne soit amusée ici trop long-tems. Ne vous plaît-il pas d'aller à la Sale où se doit faire le Bal?   70

## SCENE III.

### TANCREDE, LE MARQUIS.

#### TANCREDE.

LAissons-les aller prendre leurs places, & demeurons ici un moment. Avez-vous jamais ouï si bien parler?

#### LE MARQUIS.

De ma vie. J'ai ouï mille Sermons; & de si hauts, qu'il faloit
être bien savant pour les entendre: j'ai ouï des Ouraisons Funébres
ammirables; je dis ammirables: mais, à la dannation de mon ame,     5
je n'ai jamais rien entendu de si relevé.

#### TANCREDE.

Il y a beaucoup de choses relevées, & j'y en ai trouvé aussi de
fort agréables.

#### LE MARQUIS.

J'ai remarqué un joli trait. La Maison de Sir Politick n'est pas
grande, ni bien meublée: il a donné le change à la Dogesse adroite-   10
ment, la faisant *loger dans nos cûrs, plutôt que dans un Palais.*
Là-dessus il fait merveille: il *enrichit nos cûrs de zele,* les *garnit de
fidelité,* les orne, les pare, & fait tant enfin, qu'elle se trouve am-
mirablement logée. C'est un tour d'adresse, Mylord, & j'avouë qu'il
m'a plu extrémement.                                                  15

#### TANCREDE.

Je m'assure que peu de gens y ont pris garde.

#### LE MARQUIS.

J'avois une inclination merveilleuse pour les Sciences, mais je
n'ai osé lire que des Romans & des Comédies à la Cour, de peur
qu'on ne me prît pour un Pédant. Avec cela, le naturel demeure
toûjours; & quand j'entens de belles choses, je les connois aussi-   20
tôt.

#### TANCREDE.

Qu'avez-vous trouvé de tous ces Etats, que nous avons *mis aux
pieds* de la Dogesse?

#### LE MARQUIS.

Ah! rien de plus grand, de plus magnifique; & trop: il m'en
reste un escrupule, qui m'inquiete, je le confesse.                  25

#### TANCREDE.

Quelle inquietude en pouvez-vous avoir?

LE MARQUIS.
Qu'on ne l'écrive à la Cour, Mylord.

TANCREDE.
Qui diable s'en donneroit la peine?

LE MARQUIS.
Ce ne seront pas des gens considérables: mais il y a de petits
écriveurs dans les pays étrangers, qui ont des correspondances os-        30
cures, par où ils font tout savoir au Cardinal de Richelieu. Ce
Ministre sait tout.

TANCREDE.
Et quand il sauroit ceci, que pourroit-il vous en arriver?

LE MARQUIS.
Que pourroit-il m'en arriver! Eh! rien; rien qu'une disgrace!
Privation de cabinet, Exil de Cour: je dis tout au moins. Com-        35
ment? faire ici le Député de la France, qui offre le Royaume de
son chef. Cela ne vaut pas la peine d'en parler.

TANCREDE.
Ce sont de simples Civilités.

LE MARQUIS.
Des Civilités! d'offrir un Etat?

TANCREDE.
Sir Politick a fait la même chose de l'Angleterre.        40

LE MARQUIS.
Peut-être en a-t-il la commission. Un vieux Politique comme
lui ne fait rien mal-à-propos. Sur ma parole, il sait bien par où en
sortir.

TANCREDE.
Il est vrai que cet homme-là ne s'engage à rien légerement.

LE MARQUIS.
J'en suis sûr: mais il a tort d'embarquer les autres: c'est avoir bien        45
peu de considération pour ses amis.

TANCREDE.
L'affaire est faite: il faut empêcher qu'elle ne produise de méchans effets en France.

LE MARQUIS.
Il n'y a plus de remede, que celui de garder le secret.

TANCREDE.
Je vous promets de n'en ouvrir pas la bouche.        50

LE MARQUIS.
Insinuez, je vous prie, la même discrétion aux autres: sans rien
dire de mon appréhension toutefois. Vous savez, mon Maître,
comment il faut servir ses Amis.

TANCREDE.
Laissez-m'en le soin: je vais faire un interêt commun du secret;
& j'ose vous assurer qu'on n'en parlera point.                          55


## SCENE IV.

*On leve un Rideau, & on voit la Sale du Bal, où l'*ENTREMETTEUSE
*se disant* DOGESSE, *est dans le Trône, & les* DEMOISELLES,
*qu'on prend pour les Nobles Venitiennes, sur des Bancs.*

L'ENTREMETTEUSE *prise pour* DOGESSE, LES
DEMOISELLES *se disant* FEMMES DE SENATEURS,
SIR POLITICK, LA FEMME DE SIR POLITICK,
ANTONIO, TANCREDE, LE MARQUIS,
L'ALLEMAND, Mr. DE RICHE-SOURCE,
ME. DE RICHE-SOURCE.

LA DOGESSE, *bas.*
ME voici comme une vraye DOGESSE: quarrons-nous dans ce
trône, & faisons un peu de NÔTRE SERENITÉ. *Haut.* Mes filles
....... *Bas.* J'oubliois déja ..... *Haut.* Senatrices, tenez bien la place
de vos Maris.

*Une des prétenduës* FEMMES DE SENATEURS.
Nous saurons fort bien tenir notre rang.                                 5

LA FEMME DE SIR POLITICK, *à* ME. DE RICHE-SOURCE.
Hé bien, Madame, êtes-vous convaincuë? Vos fauteuils & vos
chaises à dos auroient-elles fait le même effet? Ces pauvres Dames
sont si transportées de joye, qu'elles ne sauroient se contenir.

ME. DE RICHE-SOURCE.
Il faut excuser une étrangere: mais avouëz que je me suis renduë
de bonne heure à vos raisons.                                           10

SIR POLITICK *à* LA DOGESSE.
Madame, VÔTRE SERENITÉ voudroit-elle entendre un Air
harmonieux avant de commencer la Danse?

LA DOGESSE.
Un peu de Mélodie: j'aime la Mélodie.

SIR POLITICK.

Musique, une Piéce harmonieuse.

*On jouë une Piéce ridiculement grave.*

Ceci est profond, & grandement cromatique. Il suffit. Signor    15
Antonio, sachez de SA SERENITÉ, si elle voudroit me faire l'honneur
de danser une Pavane avec le très-humble & très-dévouë Serviteur
de la République.

ANTONIO.

Je vais le savoir. *A* LA DOGESSE, *bas.* Il faut danser une Pavane
avec Sir Politick.                                                20

LA DOGESSE, *bas.*

Je ne la sai pas.

ANTONIO, *bas.*

Il n'importe.

LA DOGESSE, *bas.*

Comment ferai-je?

ANTONIO, *bas.*

Comme lui: regardez ce qu'il fera, & faites de même.

SIR POLITICK.

Madame, je prens la liberté de danser une Pavane avec VÔTRE    25
SERENITÉ, d'autant plus hardiment; que cette Danse grave me semble
convenir à la Dignité de DOGESSE.

LA DOGESSE.

Vous avez raison, Monsieur Politick: me voilà prête, dansons
quand il vous plaira.

SIR POLITICK.

J'ai lu beaucoup de Traités de la Danse, & j'ai trouvé dans tous    30
qu'il appartenoit à l'homme de mener la femme: mais avec vous,
Madame, ce privilege honorable n'a point de lieu. C'est à VÔTRE
SERENITÉ de mener, & à moi de me laisser conduire.

LA DOGESSE.

Signor Antonio, Monsieur Politick veut que je prenne la place
de l'homme: cela est extrémement civil; que me conseillez-vous?    35

ANTONIO.

Je vous conseille, Madame, de laisser toutes choses dans l'ordre
accoutumé: VÔTRE SERENITÉ n'est pas venuë ici pour ôter aucun
avantage à Sir Politick.

Sir Politick *mene: elle danse la Pavane ridiculement,*
*faisant tout ce que fait Sir Politick, qui danse aussi*
*ridiculement qu'elle, avec sa gravité ordinaire.*

Sir Politick, *après avoir dansé.*

Cette Danse est politique extrémement, & convenable à l'occasion présente. Si j'étois à un Bal où il y eût un Genéral d'Armée,     40
je danserois la Pyrrhique, Danse militaire.

Tancrede *au* Marquis.

Le rafinement de respect étoit ingénieux à Sir Politick, de vouloir se laisser mener par la Dogesse.

Le Marquis.

Cet homme trouve ce que les autres ne trouvent point. Cela ne
s'est pourtant jamais fait à Danse du monde; & il n'y a point     45
d'homme de Cour à qui la tête ne torne dans ces Républiques, à
voir ce qu'on y voit. J'en ferai de bons countes aux Créquis & aux
Bassompierres à mon retour.

Tancrede.

Tandis que vous êtes ici, il faut s'accommoder aux manieres du
pays.     50

Le Marquis.

Je le voi de reste: mais retournons à la Danse. Signor Antonio,
Madame la Dogesse ne veut-elle pas qu'on danse les Branles?
C'est proprement ce qui fait un Bal.

Antonio.

Que voulez-vous dire par vos *Branles?*

Le Marquis.

Vous ne savez ce que c'est?     55

Antonio.

Non.

Le Marquis.

Vous êtes le seul Gentilhomme de l'Europe qui ne sache pas
son *Branle simple*, le *Gai*, le *Poitou*, & le *Montirandé.*

Antonio.

Aussi peu les uns que les autres.

Le Marquis.

Et les Courantes: vous les ignorez?     60

Antonio.

Non pas les Courantes.

#### Le Marquis.

Parbieu, je vais les danser avec vos Dames; aussi-bien ne garde-
t-on aucune regle à vôtre Bal. N'attendons pas qu'on nous donne
un rang à l'ordinaire avec l'Allemand, & faisons-nous raison nous-
mêmes. Je veux attaquer cette brune: elle me plaît. Madame,      65
voulez-vous me faire l'honneur de danser une courante avéque moi?

#### La Dame.

De tout mon cœur.

#### Le Marquis.

Place, place à Madame. La Courante, violons, & de mesure, je
vous prie: je ne prendrois pas plaisir à me voir hours de cadence.
Cette révérence est assez cavaliere, ce me semble; elle ne sent pas      70
le baladin. Battons du pied pour prendre le tems. J'ai parti trop
tôt. Revenons. Il faut refaire la révérence. Voilà partir à propos,
cela! mais ces couquins de violons m'ont déja mis hours de cadence: rentrons-y malgré eux. Le plus court est de recommencer.
Vous ne savez ce que vous faites, violons: je croi que vous dormez.      75
Encore une fois la révérence, & partons. Pour ce coup, si vous me
faites manquer, je vous le pardonne.

*Quand la Courante est dansée*

A la fin j'en suis venu à bout; mais avec bien de la peine. Il faut
une oreille de Diable avec ces maudits violons. J'ai dansé tout un
hiver à Paris (chacun le sait) sans avoir jamais sourti de cadence. Il      80
faut tout dire; c'étoit les vingt-quatre.

#### Tancrede.

Je ne sai ce que vous avez fait à Paris: mais ici, c'est danser
admirablement.

#### Le Marquis.

Non pas cela: assez en homme de qualité. Je voudrois vous
pouvoir regaler d'une *Vignone*, & d'une *Belleville:* il n'y a pas      85
moyen. Ce n'est qu'à la Cour qu'on peut danser les figurées.

#### Tancrede.

Ne dansez-vous pas encore avec quelque autre Dame?

#### Le Marquis.

Je ne veux, morbieu, pas perdre ma réputation: j'en suis bien
sourti; danse qui voudra. Mylord, je veux vous faire une confidence. Cette belle, avec qui je viens de danser, elle m'aime, & ce      90
sont des œillades! il n'y a rien de pareil.

TANCREDE.
Toute femme qui n'a point de liberté, est prête à faire l'amour,
quand elle en trouve l'occasion.

LE MARQUIS.
Ce n'est pas ce que vous pensez: le cûr est pris sur ma parole.

TANCREDE.
Je commence à m'en appercevoir. Tenez; elle vous regarde.                95

LE MARQUIS.
Ne faites pas semblant de rien voir, & soyez discret, je vous
prie. Ce n'est pas un jeu à Venise, que d'être aimé de la femme
d'un Senateur.

TANCREDE.
Je vous en répons: mais je sai me taire; soyez assûré de ma discrétion.                                                                 100

LE MARQUIS.
Je me fie à vous, Mylord; & c'est m'y fier de ma vie.

ME. DE RICHE-SOURCE.
Allons, ça: aquittons-nous de nôtre promesse. J'ai promis à ces
Dames de leur faire voir des choses, & des manieres: enfin, je vais
faire pour l'amour d'elles ce que je n'ai pas fait il y a quinze ans.

MR. DE RICHE-SOURCE.
Elle va danser la *Sarabande:* c'est une merveille. Quand nous    105
nous mariâmes, on se mettoit à genoux devant elle, pour la voir
danser.

ME. DE RICHE-SOURCE.
Qui est-ce qui se souvient ici de *la petite Suzon?* Mon ami, t'en
souviens-tu?

MR. DE RICHE-SOURCE.
Oui, mamie, & je souhaite que tu donnes autant de plaisir à la    110
compagnie, que tu en donnois en ce tems-là.

ME. DE RICHE-SOURCE.
Voici donc la petite Suzon, qui va danser la Sarabande. Des
castagnettes?

MR. DE RICHE-SOURCE.
Des castagnettes? des castagnettes?

TANCREDE.
On n'en trouve point.                                                   115

ME. DE RICHE-SOURCE.

Il y a remede: mes doigts m'en serviront: essayons. Cela ne va pas mal.

MR. DE RICHE-SOURCE.

Prenez garde, Messieurs, je vous prie.

ME. DE RICHE-SOURCE, *en dansant.*

Ce balancement de corps vous plaît-il? Parlez, Mesdames.

LA DOGESSE.

A ravir.                                                                  120

ME. DE RICHE-SOURCE.

Et ce mouvement de bras; qu'en dites-vous? Cet air est-il Espagnol?


SCENE V.

UN VALET DE SIR POLITICK,
L'ENTREMETTEUSE *prise pour* DOGESSE, LES
DEMOISELLES *se disant* FEMMES DE SENATEURS,
ANTONIO, SIR POLITICK, LA FEMME DE SIR
POLITICK, TANCREDE, LE MARQUIS,
L'ALLEMAND, MR. DE RICHE-SOURCE,
ME. DE RICHE-SOURCE.

UN VALET DE SIR POLITICK, *à son Maître,*
*& à* MR. DE RICHE-SOURCE.

ON vous demande de la part du Senat.

SIR POLITICK.

Ouais! que veut dire ceci? Nous demander à l'heure qu'il est! il faut que ce soit une affaire bien pressante.

MR. DE RICHE-SOURCE.

On aura eu quelque grande Nouvelle, sur quoi on veut nous consulter.                                                        5

SIR POLITICK.

Ce ne peut être autre chose.

MR. DE RICHE-SOURCE.

Mais pourquoi moi?

SIR POLITICK.

Il y a quelque fonds à trouver, ou quelque dépense à faire.

MR. DE RICHE-SOURCE.

Ce seroit m'employer pour peu de chose. Je croirois plutôt qu'on a eu vent de nôtre Projet.　　　　　10

SIR POLITICK.

Ne raisonnons pas davantage, & allons apprendre ce qu'on veut de nous. *A* LA DOGESSE. Madame, vous nous excuserez, Monsieur & moi, de quitter VÔTRE SERENITÉ. La République desire de nous quelque service, que nous allons lui rendre avec respect & affection. Ces Dames auront la bonté de nous pardonner pareillement.　　15

LA DOGESSE.

Revenez bien-tôt, Messieurs, nous vous attendons.

ME. DE RICHE-SOURCE.

Ne laissons pas de continuer nôtre Bal. Voyez ce second pas de Sarabande; il est tout-à-fait à l'Espagnole.

LE MARQUIS, *qui avoit suivi* SIR POLITICK,
& MR. DE RICHE-SOURCE, *rentre.*

Savez-vous, Mesdames, qui demandoit vos maris de la part du Senat?　　　　　20

ME. DE RICHE-SOURCE.

Et qui?

LE MARQUIS.

Des Archers, qui les ont menés en prison.

TANCREDE.

Vous avez vu quelques Gardes, qu'on leur a envoyés par honneur, ou pour leur sureté.

LE MARQUIS.

Des Archers, vous dis-je, qui les ont fait Prisonniers d'Etat. Je　25
m'y connois: j'en ai vu mener plus de trente à la Bastille.

ME. DE RICHE-SOURCE.

Quelle infamie! quelle trahison! tandis que nous faisons tout ce qu'il nous est possible pour honorer leurs femmes, ces traîtres font arrêter nos maris. Qu'on ferme les portes: la Dogesse ne sortira point, qu'on ne nous les ait rendus.　　　　　30

ANTONIO *à* TANCREDE, *bas.*

Si cette femme-ci fait ce qu'elle dit, nous nous trouverons en quelque embarras. *Haut à la* FEMME DE SIR POLITICK. Madame, il faut pardonner à vôtre amie l'excès de son ressentiment: mais vous êtes trop sage pour le suivre, & faire arrêter une Dogesse dans vôtre maison. Ce seroit le comble de la douleur pour vôtre mari,　35
de vous voir si peu politique, & un grand reproche à sa suffisance,

que vous eussiez si mal profité de ses instructions.

LA FEMME DE SIR POLITICK.

Certes le coup est grand & imprévu; mais il n'est pas au-dessus de nôtre prudence. Je projette de renvoyer ces Dames avec tout honneur, sans manquer en rien de ce que veut de nous en cette oc-   40
casion la Politique.

TANCREDE.

Voilà ce qui s'appelle une Femme forte & prudente, à qui la tête ne tourne point dans le malheur, & qui prend le seul parti qui lui reste.

LA FEMME DE SIR POLITICK, *à* LA DOGESSE.

Madame, VÔTRE SERENITÉ est trop équitable, pour ne pardon-   45
ner pas à mon amie l'excès de son ressentiment. S'il y a peu de Politique, c'est l'effet d'une affection conjugale, qui mérite d'être excusée auprès d'une personne aussi vertueuse que vous. Je vous supplie donc, Madame, d'ensevelir tout dans l'oubli, & de nous être propice envers vôtre mari, pour le recouvrement des nôtres.   50

LA DOGESSE.

Laissez-moi faire; je m'en vais bien laver la tête au Doge.

UNE SENATRICE.

Et nous à nos Maris.

ANTONIO.

Dépêchons-nous de servir les malheureux, dans la chaleur de l'affaire: il n'y a point de tems à perdre.

LA DOGESSE.

Nous ne voulons pas être amusées. Adieu, laissez-nous aller.   55

UNE SENATRICE.

Allons vîte, allons.

LA FEMME DE SIR POLITICK.

Rien ne nous peut empêcher de rendre à VÔTRE SERENITÉ nos respectueuses observances.

*La* DOGESSE, *& les* SENATRICES *sortent avec précipitation.*

TANCREDE.

Au désordre où vous voyez ces bonnes Dames, elles me parois-sent aussi affligées de l'affront, que vous-mêmes. Il est vrai que si   60
elles avoient été en vôtre place, elles auroient perdu l'esprit; & si vous aviez été Dogesse, vous auriez conservé toute une autre dignité.

La Femme de Sir Politick.
Certes, nous aurions gardé plus de décence.

*Fin du quatriéme Acte.*

## ACTE V.

## SCENE PREMIERE.

### AGOSTINO, AZARO, AMELINO, PAMFILINO, SIR POLITICK, Mr. DE RICHE-SOURCE.

Agostino.

VOici, Messieurs, ces Miserables, qui vivant dans le sein de la République, sous la douce protection de nos Loix, ont entrepris de les renverser. Voici des Furieux, qui s'étant fait un degré de ce premier attentat, pour monter aux plus noires Trahisons, ont enfin consulté avec le Turc la ruine de la République. Parlez, 5
méchans: parlez, execrables; & dites la verité: je vous le commande.

Sir Politick.

Je l'ai toûjours dite, & je la dirai toûjours; si ce n'est en matiere d'Etat: en ce cas, je tiens qu'on peut mentir pour le Bien de la chose publique.

Agostino.

Si les remors de la conscience ne vous la font pas dire, les tour- 10
mens sauront bien vous l'arracher. Parlez: De quel pays êtes-vous?

Sir Politick.

Je suis Anglois, pour l'honneur, & pour la vie.

Agostino.

De quelle profession?

Sir Politick.

Politique: & il n'est pas que vous n'en ayez ouï parler. C'est moi qui ai su joindre la veritable Science des Projets avec les maximes 15
de Nicolas Machiavel, & de François Bodin.

Agostino.

De quelle qualité?

SIR POLITICK.

Chevalier de pere en fils, depuis la Reine Bodicea, qui fit tuer
tant de Romains.

AGOSTINO.

Vous devriez mourir de honte devant vos Juges, d'avoir des-          20
honoré une si longue suite d'ayeux.

SIR POLITICK.

J'ai reçu beaucoup d'honneur de mes devanciers: mais nous en
laisserons un peu à nos successeurs; & la postérité nous fera justice, quand vous ne nous la ferez pas.

AGOSTINO.

Sauriez-vous nier que vous n'ayiez accusé nos Législateurs, &          25
voulu établir chez nous quatre Doges?

SIR POLITICK.

Par quelque moyen que vous l'ayez pu savoir, je le confesse.

AGOSTINO.

*Habemus confitentem reum.*

SIR POLITICK.

Je l'ai voulu, il est certain; & je le veux encore: mais c'est pour le
soulagement de la vieillesse du Doge, & pour la dignité de la Ré-          30
publique.

AGOSTINO.

*Habemus non modò confitentem, sed contumacem.* Ces *relais de pi-*
*geons* établis de Venise à Constantinople: cette invention quasi
surnaturelle, vous a donné le moyen de lier vos commerces avec le
Turc. C'est sur vos bons avis qu'il a fait le projet d'une Guerre          35
contre nous, que vous devez *conduire du cabinet,* & voilà comment
se doit entendre vôtre *Spéculation militaire,* & vos *Secrets pour la*
*Guerre.* Il n'est plus tems de dissimuler: vous voyez que nous savons tout.

SIR POLITICK.

Vôtre Excellence ne sait pas tout, puis qu'elle ignore nos bonnes          40
intentions. J'ai trouvé une invention admirable d'établir mes
commerces à Constantinople; mais certes pour le Bien de cet Etat,
& pour le Salut de vôtre Ambassadeur. Si j'entens la *Spéculation*

*militaire*; si j'ai quelques *Secrets pour la Guerre*, le fruit de mes veilles ne regardoit que vous. Je prétendois apprendre à un Senateur d'aller au Senat, & de conduire une armée en même tems. Je voulois vous enseigner l'Art de défaire vos ennemis, sans vous exposer aux coups: *ars belli perfectissima*. C'est une grande qualité à un Général d'Armée de savoir faire combattre toutes les troupes avant que de combattre lui-même. C'est la derniere science du Capitaine de savoir faire combattre l'armée sans y être.

ᴀɢᴏꜱᴛɪɴᴏ.

Nous savons où nous en tenir pour ce qui vous regarde. *A* Mʀ. ᴅᴇ Rɪᴄʜᴇ-Sᴏᴜʀᴄᴇ. Et vous, malheureux, d'où êtes-vous?

Sɪʀ Pᴏʟɪᴛɪᴄᴋ.

Il ne répondra pas. Vôtre Excellence doit savoir que c'est moi qui porte la parole en toutes choses: il trouvera bon que je réponde pour lui.

Mʀ. ᴅᴇ Rɪᴄʜᴇ-Sᴏᴜʀᴄᴇ.

Je demeure d'accord de tout ce qu'il dira.

ᴀɢᴏꜱᴛɪɴᴏ.

Nous avons bien affaire de vos conventions. Parlez: de quel pays êtes-vous?

Sɪʀ Pᴏʟɪᴛɪᴄᴋ.

Il est François, vous dis-je.

ᴀɢᴏꜱᴛɪɴᴏ.

Il me contraindra de l'écouter! De quelle profession?

Sɪʀ Pᴏʟɪᴛɪᴄᴋ.

Circulateur général & particulier.

ᴀɢᴏꜱᴛɪɴᴏ.

Il seroit inutile de les interroger davantage. Qu'on les ramene en prison.

*Ils sortent.*


# SCENE II.
## LES QUATRE SENATEURS, UN HUISSIER.

ᴀɢᴏꜱᴛɪɴᴏ.

NOus sommes heureux en ce point, Messieurs, d'avoir la confession de leurs Crimes, par leurs propres bouches. Ils n'avouent pas seulement leurs entreprises contre nos Loix; ils les soutiennent; ils demeurent d'accord de leurs intelligences avec le Turc: mais

c'étoit, disent-ils, pour le salut de nôtre Ambassadeur. Qui leur a          5
demandé des soins si officieux? Qui les a employés? A qui ont-ils
communiqué leurs bons desseins? *Constat de facto.* Du reste il faut
s'en rapporter à de bonnes intentions, qu'on n'a pas connuës.
Voici, Messieurs, voici le fin du Projet, aussi politique qu'exe-
crable. Après avoir concerté avec le Turc cette expédition impie,          10
ils font je ne sai quelle conféderation, entre Paris, Londres, &
Venise, pour nous engager dans l'Orient, & porter nos armes
contre la Perse. Il arrive de-là, Messieurs, que le Grand Seigneur
trouve la République dépourvûë, & que le Persan occupé par nous
dans ses propres États, ne peut entrer dans ceux de nôtre ennemi          15
commun. Catilina, ce conspirateur célébre, ce grand & renommé
scelerat, étoit un homme de bien, & un bon citoyen, au prix de ces
gens abominables: c'étoit un Romain, qui vouloit se rendre maître
des Romains. S'il avoit résolu de tuer le Consul, & de se défaire
du Senat, au moins laissoit-il à Rome ses Dieux, ses Loix, ses          20
Mœurs, & sa Langue. Dans la servitude qu'on nous avoit pré-
parée, on ne laissoit à Venise ni Religion, ni Loix, ni Coutumes;
on ne laissoit peut-être aucun vestige de la Nation. Qui cherche-
roit, Messieurs, un supplice égal à leur forfait, n'en trouveroit
point chez les plus ingénieux tyrans: mais je ne puis, je le confesse,          25
me dépouiller des sentimens de l'humanité, *quamquam fortasse
inhumanum sit humanum esse erga eum qui hominem exuerit.* Qu'on
les étrangle seulement, Messieurs; & pour une marque éternelle
de la benignité de nos jugemens, punissons du supplice le plus
commun le crime le plus extraordinaire & le plus barbare.          30

### Azaro.

Mon sentiment est tout contraire à celui de l'Excellentissime
Seigneur qui vient de parler. Il conçoit ces gens-ci comme des
personnes extraordinaires, ennemies de nôtre gouvernement, capables de grands & pernicieux desseins; qui concertent enfin avec
le Turc la ruine de la République: pour moi, Messieurs, je pense          35
que ce sont des foux: mais il y a de deux sortes de *Folie*; l'une, qui
vient de *privation de Sens*; l'autre, d'une *Imagination déréglée.* La
première toute imbécile nous fait plaindre en elle la misere de la
condition humaine: la seconde, toûjours agitée, agite le monde par
l'extravagance de ses visions, & excite la haine des gens raison-          40
nables, qui aiment l'ordre & le repos. Il n'est pas mal-aisé de
connoître laquelle de ces deux folies possede nos Conspirateurs
prétendus, puis que leur imagination les porte au-delà de toutes
les choses les mieux établies. Ils se donnent la liberté de créer

chimériquement des Magistrats: ils se font en idée des Corres- 45
pondances à Constantinople: ils forment des Ligues imaginaires,
& reglent, en un mot, toutes nos affaires de paix & de guerre à
leur fantaisie. Je voudrois savoir, Messieurs, de quelle autorité ils
agissent, avec quel ordre, quelle mission? Certes la Folie a un grand
avantage sur la Sagesse, si les paroles & les actions des sages sont 50
punies, aussi-tôt qu'elles sortent de la regle; tandis que les foux
ont le privilege de tout dire, & de tout faire impunément. Quelle
punition prendre, dira-t-on, de ces Prisonniers? Mon avis n'est pas
qu'on les condamne à la mort, comme a voulu cet Excellentissime
Seigneur, par un excès de zele pour la République: mais qu'on ôte 55
la liberté à des foux scandaleux, qui traitent extravagamment les
matieres serieuses, réservées à la prudence des sages.

### Amelino.

Peu de gens s'étonneront, Excellentissime Seigneur, de vôtre
emportement contre la Folie, dans l'attachement inviolable que
vous avez toûjours eu à la Sagesse. Comme les opinions des hom- 60
mes sont differentes, j'ai cru qu'il m'étoit permis d'avoir un autre
sentiment; & vous serez surpris, Messieurs, que la seule considération des gens sensés, m'inspire aujourd'hui de l'indulgence & de
l'humanité pour les foux. Oui, Messieurs, le sujet de ma douceur
est une pitié interessée, qui fait que je m'oppose à leur punition en 65
faveur des sages. En effet, il y a un si grand mélange de Sagesse &
de Folie dans les personnes raisonnables, qu'on ne peut assez admirer l'inégalité qui nous fait voir si divers & si contraires à nous-
mêmes. Celui qui a su gagner nôtre jugement, & assujettir nôtre
raison par la supériorité de la sienne, a besoin de nôtre facilité 70
peut-être le même jour pour faire excuser son mauvais sens. Tel
est le plus sage du monde en une chose, qui est extravagant dans
une autre. Ces grands hommes, dont nous honorons la memoire,
n'étoient pas exemts de folie: les esprits extraordinaires de tous les
tems ont eu la leur: c'est aux imaginations déréglées que nous de- 75
vons l'invention des Arts: le *Caprice* des Peintres, des Poëtes, des
Musiciens, n'est qu'un nom civilement adouci, pour exprimer leur
*Folie*, sans leur déplaire. Laissons, Messieurs, laissons les foux en
repos, s'ils y peuvent être: il y a trop de gens interessés à leur protection. Que s'ils viennent à faillir contre nos Loix, ordonnons de 80
leur châtiment selon leur crime: mais si on veut les punir pour
l'interêt du bon sens, & pour l'honneur de la raison; qu'on se sou-
vienne que cette raison a sujet de se plaindre de beaucoup de gens,
& que les plus zelez pour la vangeance, ne seront peut-être pas à
couvert de la punition. 85

### Pamfilino.

Depuis que j'ai l'honneur d'entrer au Senat, j'ai observé que
l'envie de faire voir nôtre esprit, & la vanité de bien parler, nous
tirent souvent hors du sujet dont il est question, pour nous jetter
en des choses générales, dont il ne s'agit pas. Je connoissois, Messieurs, comme le reste des gens, qu'il y avoit des Foux dans le          90
monde: mais d'en savoir les ordres, les rangs, les distinctions; de
connoître ces differences délicates qu'il y a de folie à folie, les
affinités & les alliances qui se trouvent entre la sagesse & cette
même folie, c'est, Messieurs, ce que je ne savois point, & ce que je
viens heureusement d'apprendre de vos beaux discours. Pour l'af-          95
faire présente que nous avons à traiter, vous l'avez jugée indigne
de vos réflexions; & tout ce que je puis recueillir de vos avis, se ré-
duit à châtier des foux serieux, qui font le métier des sages, ou de
pardonner aux extravagans, en faveur de ces mêmes sages, qui
sortant de leur assiéte, ne font que trop souvent le métier des foux.          100
Beau motif de punition, ou de grace! Jugeons, Messieurs, jugeons
Sir Politick & son compagnon, par eux-mêmes; sans les charger
du crime des imaginations déréglées, s'ils sont innocens; & sans
appeller les grands hommes à leur secours, sans interesser les
Peintres, les Poëtes, les Musiciens à leur salut, s'ils sont criminels.          105
Mais, Messieurs, c'est nous-mêmes qui donnons corps à une chose
purement chimérique: n'allons pas plus loin qu'il ne faut: retran-
chons la moitié de nôtre esprit; il ne nous paroîtra aujourd'hui ni
d'innocens, ni de coupables: nous verrons seulement des foux ridicules, plus propres à nous divertir qu'à nous nuire. Chercher du          110
sens aux chimeres; travailler son intelligence, où rien ne peut être
entendu, c'est encherir sur les chimériques, & se faire une folie
mystérieuse, qui passe la naturelle.

### Agostino.

Arrêtez-là. Vous prétendez avoir vos lumieres, & j'ai les miennes,
qui ne sont point fondées sur de simples conjectures: je parle *ex*          115
*visu & auditu*. Il faut avouër que vous avez l'esprit bien en repos,
*cum agitur de summa rerum*. Le Senat Romain, en de moindres
perils, chargeoit les Consuls de prendre garde *ne quid detrimenti*
*Respublica caperet* ...... Mais qui frappe à la porte, quand nous
déliberons sur une affaire de telle importance?          120

*Il tire la sonnette, & l'*HUISSIER *entre.*

### L'Huissier.

Excellentissimes Seigneurs, un Anglois, un Mylord souhaite de
vous parler.

AGOSTINO.

Qu'on le mette en prison.

L'HUISSIER.

Il demandoit à entrer, pour vous dire une chose de conse-
quence.                                                                            125

PAMFILINO.

Faites-le entrer.


## SCENE III.

### TANCREDE, LES QUATRE SENATEURS.

TANCREDE.

JE vous demande pardon, Messieurs, de la liberté que je prens: je
sai que c'est manquer au respect qui vous est dû; mais ayant appris
que vous êtes assemblés extraordinairement, pour juger deux Miserables, que vous avez fait arrêter, j'ai cru que vous ne trouveriez
pas mauvais que je vous informasse d'une chose qui peut contri-          5
buer à leur salut.

AGOSTINO.

Taisez-vous, Monsieur le Mylord: vous êtes bien effronté de
venir ici de la sorte, & plus encore de vouloir éclairer les Senateurs
de Venise.

PAMFILINO.

Ceci est veritablement contre les formes; mais la bonne inten-        10
tion doit faire excuser toutes choses. Parlez, Mylord, qu'avez-vous
à dire pour le salut de ces Prisonniers?

TANCREDE.

Je viens dire à vos Excellences que ces pauvres Prisonniers n'ont
point d'autre crime que leur Folie.

PAMFILINO.

Les connoissez-vous?                                                        15

TANCREDE.

On ne peut pas les connoître davantage.

PAMFILINO.

Et qui sont-ils?

TANCREDE.

Il y a un Chevalier Anglois, que les Livres de Politique ont
rendu fou, & qui a servi dix ans de divertissement à la Cour
d'Angleterre. Pour l'autre, je ne le connois que depuis que je suis à        20

Venise: c'est un François chimérique, qui veut établir la Circulation de l'Or, & le faire revenir au même lieu d'où on le transporte,
après avoir fait le tour du Monde.

PAMFILINO.

En avois-je bien jugé, Messieurs? Prenons garde, je vous prie,
qu'au lieu de nous garentir d'un danger au-dedans, nous ne per-    25
dions la réputation au déhors; & que le Senat, qui a donné
jusqu'ici une si grande opinion de sa sagesse, ne s'expose à la rail-
lerie Françoise, & au mépris des Anglois, quand on saura que
nous traitons si gravement leurs Ridicules publics, & leurs Chimériques déclarés. Je suis d'avis, Messieurs, qu'on les mette aussi-    30
tôt en liberté: nous ferons voir nôtre discernement à séparer les
choses dont on doit se moquer, d'avec celles qu'on doit veritablement craindre.

AZARO.

Si j'ai été d'une autre Opinion, je me rens presentement à la
vôtre, comme à la seule raisonnable.    35

AMELINO.

J'avois bien cru qu'il falloit pardonner aux insensés; mais vous
me faites connoître qu'il faut se moquer de ceux-ci: je suis de vôtre
avis en toutes choses.

PAMFILINO..

Qu'on ramene les Prisonniers, & donnons-leur nous-mêmes la
liberté.    40

AGOSTINO.

N'allons pas si vîte, Messieurs: la précipitation est la mere du
repentir.

PAMFILINO.

C'est trop discourir sur une affaire si ridicule.

AGOSTINO.

Je persiste en mon opinion, quoi que seul de mon avis; & plaise
à Dieu que le vôtre ne soit pas funeste à la République.    45


SCENE IV.

*On fait rentrer les Prisonniers.*

LES QUATRE SENATEURS, TANCREDE,
SIR POLITICK, MR. DE RICHE-SOURCE.

PAMFILINO.

VEnez, scelerats; venez, gens dangereux à la République; venez
recevoir le pardon de tous vos crimes. Politique, Circulateur, allez
établir des *Relais de Pigeons*, & mettre la *Circulation* en pratique où
il vous plaira.

SIR POLITICK, *à* MR. DE RICHE-SOURCE.

Ouais! du ton que parle ce Senateur, on diroit qu'il veut se mo-      5
quer de nous, quand il nous donne la liberté. Traiter de foux deux
si grands personnages que vous & moi, c'est une chose que je ne
comprens pas! Il y va de la réputation de ma Politique, & de
l'honneur de vôtre Circulation: je ne souffrirai jamais l'infamie de
ce jugement-là. *Aux* SENATEURS. Messeigneurs, retournez aux avis      10
tout de nouveau: je vous déclare que nous aimons mieux être
pendus, comme Conspirateurs, que d'être sauvés comme foux.

MR. DE RICHE-SOURCE.

Tout-beau, Monsieur Politick, si vous avez envie d'être pendu,
je ne l'ai pas, moi: Fou, ou Sage, pourvu qu'on me sauve, je suis
content.                                                              15

PAMFILINO.

Mylord, où sont les Femmes de ces Messieurs?

TANCREDE.

Les voilà qui entrent.


## SCENE V.

### LES QUATRE SENATEURS, TANCREDE, SIR POLITICK, MR. DE RICHE-SOURCE, LA FEMME DE SIR POLITICK, ME. DE RICHE-SOURCE, LE MARQUIS, L'ALLEMAND.

PAMFILINO.

SOyez les bien-venuës, Mesdames; je suis chargé de grands remer-
cimens pour vous de la part des Femmes de Venise. Leur *captivité*
vous donne de la compassion: leur *méchant air* vous fait pitié: vous
les voulez mettre dans le *commerce du beau-monde:* elles vous en
sont infiniment obligées; mais leur bonheur est réservé pour un      5
autre tems, & il doit arriver un jour par des personnes plus considérables que vous. Adieu, belle & honorable compagnie.

*Les* SENATEURS *sortent.*

### Sir Politick.

Adieu de bon cœur, petits Politiques: vous ne vous connoissez guere en grands personnages; & Venise n'est pas digne de nous posseder. 10

### Me. de Riche-Source.

On ne sait ce que c'est ici du bel-air; du beau procedé; de la belle maniere. Les femmes n'y voyent que des maris. Sortons le plutôt que nous pourrons.

### La Femme de Sir Politick à Tancrede.

Mylord, si vous demeurez en cette ville après nous, je vous supplie de faire mes complimens à la Dogesse. Cette honnête Dame 15 n'a point de part à nôtre disgrace, assurément.

### Le Marquis.

Pour moi, je n'ai de complimens à faire à personne. Qui me ratrapera dans une République, sera bien fin: on n'y sauroit être aimé d'une femme, sans courir hazard de sa vie. Cette Noble Venitienne avec qui j'ai dansé, m'a témoigné quelque passion, il est 20 vrai; mais rien de concluant; & j'ai déja reçu dix avis qu'on vouloit m'assassiner. Vive la France pour les Galans; j'en ai toûjours été quitte pour un combat avec le mari, ou avec un rival: ici, le poignard, ou le poison; le tout avec honneur, & dans les formes. Adieu, Messieurs & Mesdames; très-humble & très-obéïssant 25 serviteur. *Il sort.*

### L'Allemand.

Laissons aller Bousignac en France, & allons tous de compagnie à Hambourg, à Lubec, à Dantzic: ce sont des Cités d'un riche trafic, où il sera facile d'établir la Circulation.

### Tancrede.

Pour moi, je ne demeure pas un moment ici, quand vous en se- 30 rez sortis: j'irai à Rome, ce grand théatre du monde, pour faire connoître l'ingratitude de la République, & le bonheur du Pays qui vous possedera.

### Sir Politick.

Mylord, en quelque lieu que nous soyons, disposez de nôtre Politique, & de nôtre Circulation, comme de choses qui sont au- 35 tant à vous, qu'à nous-mêmes.

### Tancrede, *après qu'ils sont tous partis.*

Il faut avouër que j'ai une plaisante étoile, de me faire tomber entre les mains les Foux & les Ridicules de toutes les Nations: ils

divertissent quelque tems; mais à la fin ils ennuyent, & Dieu
merci, m'en voilà défait.                                    40

*Fin du cinquiéme & dernier Acte.*

# The Country Gentleman

## INTRODUCTION

*The Country Gentleman* was suppressed before it was performed, and it was not published. The political uproar it caused in 1669 was extensively reported by Pepys and others, but beyond such reports almost nothing was known of the play itself until a scribal copy surfaced in 1947, was identified in 1973, and was published in 1976.[1] Here we will recount the suppression and scandal, discuss the play itself in its generic context, briefly analyse the political and ideological content, and survey what is known of the manuscript's origins and provenance.

### SUPPRESSION AND SCANDAL

The principal satiric target of the play was Sir William Coventry (an important Treasury official), and because Samuel Pepys worked closely with Coventry and was appalled and frightened by what happened, the diarist heard the ongoing story directly from the victim as it unfolded, and recorded what he was told. He was to conclude his diary on 31 May 1669: had he done so three months earlier the episode would remain a great deal more obscure.

The play had been scheduled for production by the King's Company at their Bridges Street playhouse on Saturday, 27 February 1669. The imbroglio began some time before that, but Pepys first heard of the matter on Monday, 1 March:

I was most of all surprized this morning by my Lord Bellasses, who . . . tells me of a Duell designed between the Duke of Buckingham and my Lord Halifax or Sir W. Coventry—the challenge being carried by Harry Savill, but prevented by my Lord Arlington and the King told of it. And this was all the dis-

---

[1] Sir Robert Howard and George Villiers, Second Duke of Buckingham, *The Country Gentleman*, ed. Arthur H. Scouten and Robert D. Hume (Philadelphia, Pa.: University of Pennsylvania Press, 1976). We are grateful to the University of Pennsylvania Press for permission to adapt material from the introduction and notes to that edition.

course at Court this day.[2] But I meeting Sir W. Coventry in the Duke of York's chamber, he would not own it to me, but told me that he was a man of too much peace to meddle with fighting, and so it rested. But the talk is full in the town of the business.

By Tuesday, 2 March more details were circulating about the town. In a newsletter to Sir Willoughby Aston, John Starkey wrote:

There was a challenge lately intended for the Duke of Buckingham upon S$^r$ William Coventrys account, which was discovrd by a Letter sent to him from M$^r$ Henry Savil to know when he would be certainly at home and might be spoake with, which with some other items may be understood to be the forerunner of a chalenge. The occasion this, there was a new play to be acted on Saturday last called the Country gentleman, said to be made by the Duke & S$^r$ Robt Howard, wherein tis said that the Earle of Clarendon, Sr W: Coventry and some other Courtiers are plainly personated, but especially S$^r$ William in the midst of his table of Writings, this he (or some of his relations) would not brooke, but whether he or the L$^d$ Hallifax was to fight the Duke is not knowne. But the King hath prevented all; and the play is not acted. (British Library Add. MS 36916, fo. 128)

On Wednesday the 3rd Pepys discussed business with Coventry and his ally Sir John Duncomb, but found them 'more then usually busy'. On this day John Nicholas wrote to his father, Sir Edward Nicholas:

We have had much discourse about a Challenge & a Duell ... the whole busines seemes a Mystery. ... It seemes some more sagatious then ordinary acquainted the King w$^{th}$ their suspitions & so the designe if there were any was prevented. The world will have it that its occasioned by a new Play made by Sir Rob: Howard called the Country Gentl in w$^{ch}$ y$^e$ Duke of Bucks hath incerted a part to personate S$^r$ W$^m$ Coventry sitting in the midst of a Table w$^{th}$ papers round him to w$^{ch}$ he can easily turne himself round on his chaire as he pleases, such an one it seemes he hath, but there are other circumstances in y$^e$ part likewise more abusive. there are others personated also in that Play as i heare, my L$^d$ Chanc$^r$ [Clarendon], S$^r$ Jo: Duncomb. It hath not yet been acted, & the King they say hath forbidden it. (British Library Egerton MS 2539, fos. 327$^v$–328)

Nicholas is correct in saying that Coventry's colleague Duncomb is satirized, but both he and Starkey are quite wrong in reporting that Claren-

---

[2] The persistent but erroneous reports that Lord Halifax was involved probably stemmed from three facts: he was a friend, ally, and uncle of Coventry; he was Henry Savile's brother; and his kinsman the Earl of Shrewsbury had been killed by Buckingham in a duel a year earlier.

don was among the objects of satire, though the rumour was natural enough. Buckingham's loathing for the former Lord Chancellor was notorious—so people naturally assumed that Clarendon would be the butt of any political satire by Buckingham.

As early as 1 March, Colbert de Croissy (the wily French ambassador) reported that:

The divisions of this Court increase every day. . . . Coventry . . . has the honour of being of feelings opposed to the duke of Buckingham, who thought to make him the butt of ridicule by having a scene added to a comedy, a scene in which he introduces a state counsellor who appears on the stage next to a table all full of drawers, one of which has for a sticker: affairs of *Spain*, the other: affairs of *Holland*, and so on for the others; and he has this counsellor, who is to be made as like Lord Coventry as possible, say stupid things. (Colbert to de Lionne, 1/11 March)[3]

Louis XIV was deeply interested in English politics, and as usual he was kept well informed.

Until 3 March the whole affair must have seemed mysterious indeed to outsiders, for the principals kept their mouths shut as long as possible. On that day, however, a warrant was issued 'to James Beck, serjeant-at-arms, to apprehend Sir William Coventry, and convey him to the Tower for having sent a challenge to the Duke of Buckingham'. And on Thursday Sir John Robinson, Lieutenant of the Tower of London, duly reported that he had 'received Coventry by the hands of Beck . . . according to his Majesty's order'.[4] By this time, attempted concealment was futile, and Pepys was able to piece together the whole story—on which Coventry gradually filled in missing details. On Thursday, 4 March Pepys reports:

I did meet Sir Jere. Smith, who did tell me that Sir W. Coventry was just now sent to the tower about the business of his challenging the Duke of Buckingham. . . . This news of Sir W Coventry did strike me to the heart; and with reason, for by this and my Lord of Ormond's business, I do doubt that the Duke of Buckingham will be so fleshed, that he will not stop at anything but be forced to do anything now, as thinking it not safe to end here; and Sir W. Coventry being gone, the King will have never a good counsellor, nor the Duke of York any sure friend to stick to him.

---

[3] French diplomatic archives in the Quai d'Orsay, 'Affaires Étrangères', letters of 11, 14, 18, and 20 Mar. 1669 (N.S.). Translations by Annick Scouten-Rouet.

[4] *CSP Domestic*, 1668–9, 222.

Later that day, Pepys heard more details from Lord Bellases (Belasyse):

he told me the perticulars of this matter; that it arises about a quarrel which Sir W. Coventry had with the Duke of Buckingham about a design between him and Sir Rob. Howard to bring him into a play at the King's House [the Bridges Street Theatre]; which W. Coventry not enduring, did by H. Savill send a letter to the Duke of Buckingham that he had a desire to speak with him—upon which, the Duke of Buckingham did bid Holmes (his champion ever since my [Lord] of Shrewsbury's business) go to him to know the business; but H. Savill would not tell it to any but himself, and therefore did go presently to the Duke of Buckingham and told him that his Uncle Coventry was a person of honour, and was sensible of his Grace's liberty taken of abusing him and that he had a desire of satisfaction and would fight with him. But that here they were interrupted by my Lord Chamberlains coming in, who was commanded to go to bid the Duke of Buckingham to come to the King, Holmes having discovered it.

In short, Buckingham had his second tattle to the king, who thereupon intervened. Belasyse told him

that the King did last night at the Council ask the Duke of Buckingham, upon his honour, whether he received any challenge from W. Coventry; which he confessed that he had. And then the King asking W. Coventry, he told him that he did not owne what the Duke of Buckingham had said, though it was not fit for him to give him a direct contradiction. But, being by the King put upon declaring upon his honour the matter, he answered that he had understood that many hard questions had upon this business been moved to some lawyers, and that therefore he was unwilling to declare anything that might from his own mouth render him obnoxious to his Majesty's displeasure, and therefore prayed to be excused—which the King did think fit to interpret to be a confession, and so gave warrant that night for his commitment to the Tower.

'Very much troubled' at this news, Pepys hastened to the Tower 'to give him comfort and offer my service to him; which he kindly and cheerfully received, only owning his being troubled for the King his master's displeasure'.

From the 4th of March until the 20th (when Coventry was released), Pepys visited him in the Tower nearly every day. In the course of a long talk on the 6th Pepys heard Coventry's own account of the satire:

He told me the matter of the play that was intended for his abuse—wherein they foolishly and sillily bring in two tables like that which he hath made, with a round hole in the middle, in his closet, to turn himself in; and he is to be in one of them as maister, and Sir J. Duncomb in the other as his man or imitator—and their discourse in those tables, about the disposing of their books and papers, very foolish.

What had actually prevented public performance of the play was evidently a direct threat made by Coventry against the performers.

> But that that he is offended with, is his being made so contemptible, as that any should dare to make a gentleman a subject for the mirth of the world; and that therefore he had told Tom. Killigrew [principal owner and manager of the King's Company] that he should tell his actors, whoever they were, that did offer at anything like representing him, that he would not complain to my Lord Chamberlain, which was too weak, nor get him beaten, as Sir Ch. Sidly is said to do,[5] but that he would cause his nose to be cut.

The king would presumably have forbidden the play or ordered the removal of the table scene if it had been present in the copy he was shown—but what actually stopped public performance was a direct physical threat by the victim.[6]

Together with Colbert de Croissy's code dispatches to Louis XIV, Pepys's reports of his conversations with Coventry allow us to reconstruct the train of events fairly exactly. Coventry apparently heard of the play while it was being rehearsed and complained to the king, who then demanded a copy from the actors and inspected it personally. Care had been taken, however, to remove the key scene, and Coventry was denied the injunction he sought—so says Colbert in his letter of 1/11 March. Coventry then took matters into his own hands, preventing performance by announcing that he would have the impersonator's nose cut, a threat which evidently reduced the actors' enthusiasm for the play to the vanishing point. Just a month earlier, Edward Kynaston had been severely beaten for personating Sir Charles Sedley, and Coventry was proposing to do far worse.

With the play stopped, why then challenge Buckingham? Here we can only speculate, but we can do so with some assurance. Gossip evi-

---

[5] On the previous 1 Feb., a month earlier, Pepys recorded: 'to the King's playhouse, thinking to have seen *The Heyresse* . . . but when we came thither, we find no play there—Kinaston, that did act a part therein in abuse to Sir Charles Sidly, being last night exceedingly dry-beaten with sticks by two or three that assaulted him—so as he is mightily bruised, and forced to keep his bed.' The play is lost and the details of the personation are unknown. See Milhous and Hume, 'Lost English Plays', *Harvard Library Bulletin*, 25 (1977), 5–33, no. 34.

[6] Spurr is thus not quite right in saying that 'the lampooning of . . . Coventry . . . was enough to get the play banned before performance' (John Spurr, *England in the 1670s: 'This Masquerading Age'* (Oxford: Blackwell, 2000), 113).

dently began to run wild even before 1 March—and Coventry was both a proud and humourless man and a Cavalier gentleman. The affront could not be tolerated, and so he sent his nephew Henry Savile to 'speak' to Buckingham. This placed the duke in an awkward position. He was an expert swordsman and could probably have skewered Coventry with ease, but a year earlier (21 January 1668) Buckingham had killed the Earl of Shrewsbury in an extremely scandalous six-man duel (and Lady Shrewsbury continued to be his mistress). He had obtained the king's pardon only with difficulty; another duel might ruin him politically, especially since public satire on a fellow member of the gentry and a government functionary was outrageous by the standards of the time and public sympathy was almost entirely with the aggrieved Coventry. (Pepys reported on 7 March that 'not less then 60 coaches' had brought indignant visitors to Coventry in the Tower the previous day.) The sensible course of action was to leak word of the challenge to the king and let higher authority intervene.

Charles II was probably not pleased with Buckingham, but he took the opportunity to get rid of a minister he did not like. On 7 March Charles wrote to his sister, 'I am not sorry that S$^r$ Will: Coventry has given me this good occasion, by sending my L$^d$ of Buckingham a chalenge, to turne him out of the Councill. I do intend to turn him allso out of the Tresury. The truth of it is, he has been a troublesome man in both places, and I am well rid of him.'[7] Coventry was certainly very harshly treated. As he had apparently been warned would happen, the king's lawyers dug up an ancient statute to use against him for issuing the challenge. A newsletter reports: 'it was by the Statute of 3 Hen: 7th found to be felony for any to conspire the Death of a privy Counsellour', for which Coventry was imprisoned and 'turnd out of the Counsell and suspended . . . of all his places of profitt and trust'.[8] Coventry spent nearly three weeks in the Tower, though the confinement itself was probably quite comfortable. Indeed his second, Henry Savile, likewise incarcerated there, seems to have indulged in some serious partying with friends. On the night of the 9th some of his visitors very nearly fought a duel right in the prison:

On Tuesday night there was a quarrel between the Duke of Richmond and Mr. James Hamilton, after they had dined at the Tower with Sir [*sic*] Henry

---

[7] See Julia Cartwright, *Madame: A Life of Henrietta, Daughter of Charles I and Duchess of Orleans* (New York: Scribner's, 1894), 283.

[8] Add. MS 36916, fo. 129.

Savile. they had chosen their seconds, but the Lord General sent for the principals, and put them on their honours not to prosecute it. The Earl of Rochester was one of the party. . . . (HMC Report XII, Part 7, 62)

The dour Coventry was presumably not living it up with the Earl of Rochester.

Even after his release, Coventry remained in deep disgrace. On 31 March, Pepys 'walked out with him into St. James's park; where being afeared to be seen with him (he having not leave yet to kiss the King's hand, but notice taken, as I hear, of all that go to him)[9] I did take the pretence of my attending Tanger Committee to take my leave; though to serve him, I should I think stick at nothing'. Coventry's career was completely wrecked; he lived on until 1686, a notable speaker in Parliament, but one lacking influence within the government, despite his competence and honesty.[10] Buckingham's attack seems to have been a coldly calculated piece of deliberate destruction. Coventry told Pepys that 'the Duke of Buckingham did himself some time since desire to join with him, of all men in England, and did bid him propound to himself to be Chief Minister of State, saying that he would bring it about; but that he refused to have anything to do with any faction' (6 March). Coventry was of course (like Pepys) a stout Yorkist, and one cannot readily imagine him allying himself with the Duke of York's bitterest enemies. Buckingham evidently did not realize how little use the king had for Coventry, and having decided that if Sir William would not join Buckingham's party he should be squashed, the duke hit on a highly effectual means of achieving this end.[11]

The suppression of the play and the scandal of the challenge were a one-month wonder. Colbert tells us that during the week of 1 March Coventry's friends flocked to the Bridges Street Theatre to take immediate vengeance if the actors tried to stage the satire: 'the most consid-

[9] 'Men ruined by their prince are like thunder strucken places, it is counted unlawfull to approach 'em' (Commonplace Book, 145: 5).

[10] The biographer of Buckingham's friend and second Sir Robert Holmes has this to say of Coventry. 'No one who has read an instruction or a minute or a note drafted by William Coventry can ever quite escape the fascination of that brilliant intelligence, that incisiveness of expression and that handwriting, at once exquisite and unaffected, in which they are recorded. Never obscure, never crabbed, never irrational, he seems to personify civilisation and efficiency.' Richard Ollard, *Man of War: Sir Robert Holmes and the Restoration Navy* (1969; London: Phoenix Press, 2001), 81.

[11] To judge from the numerous comments on Coventry in books by Pincus and Spurr, he was a sober, sensible, competent, and fair-minded civil servant of considerable experience, and in no way deserving of the king's dislike or Buckingham's ridicule.

erable people at the court have offered Coventry their help and all his friends were loudly threatening to ill treat the comedians on the stage if they were daring enough to put on the comedy that caused the quarrel. On the contrary the Duke's house was practically deserted' (letter of 4/14 March). As soon as the audience was satisfied that no performance would be attempted, the play was promptly forgotten. Naturally it was not published: Coventry's friends would have dealt harshly with any printer who tried to bring it out. Only the chance preservation of a late copy (most likely made in the 1690s to satisfy the curiosity of one of Coventry's relations by marriage) allows us to see what the satire actually consisted of, and to analyse it in the context of the play in which it was embedded.

## THE PLAY AND ITS GENERIC CONTEXT

*The Country Gentleman*, unseen and unread in its own time, proves to be an interesting and highly unusual document in the history of the evolution of early Carolean comedy. We need to view it as Sir Robert Howard's last play (albeit not a solo effort), as a text in its own right, as an ideological/satiric document, and as a problem in collaboration.

Sir Robert Howard (1626–98) is remembered today largely as John Dryden's brother-in-law. He was unquestionably one of the foremost English dramatists of the 1660s, and by 1669 he was also one of the more prominent political figures of his day, a wealthy and talented man who was a rising power in the government.[12] By 1666 Howard had emerged as a leading figure in the House of Commons, a loyal supporter of the king who was nonetheless a conspicuous defender of the rights of the Commons. In 1667 he drew critical attention in Andrew Marvell's *Last Instructions to a Painter*. Howard was a brilliant financial specialist who was to become Secretary to the Treasury in 1671 and went on to hold high (and lucrative) Exchequer offices. He remained a major figure in the government for some thirty years.

Sir Robert's initial relations with Buckingham cannot have been cordial. The Howard brothers engaged in a disgraceful public brawl with the duke when he led a faction to disrupt Henry Howard's play *The United Kingdoms* (c.1663?)—a fracas reported in the 1704 *Key to the Rehearsal* (see II. 338). As 'Bilboa', Sir Robert was rumoured to be among

---

[12] The standard biography is H. J. Oliver, *Sir Robert Howard*.

the principal targets in the lost 1665 version of *The Rehearsal*. But by 1667 Howard was delivering fiery speeches against Lord Clarendon and describing Buckingham as 'a great man'.[13] On 28 June that year, while in hiding on account of a fabricated charge of treason, Buckingham entrusted Howard with a crucial letter to the king,[14] and in the next few years they worked closely together as fellow 'Undertakers' in the government.[15]

His political career notwithstanding, Howard found time during the 1660s to become a prominent and fairly prolific writer. Indeed, in 1669 Edward Phillips (Milton's nephew) hailed him as one of the three most distinguished living dramatists, ranking him after the Earl of Orrery but ahead of Dryden.[16] Howard's first literary production, published in 1660, was a book of *Poems*, also containing translations and *The Blind Lady*, an unperformed play—a volume of no great merit. His second play, *The Surprisal* (April 1662), is a competent, melodramatic tragi-comedy that anticipates many of the features of the 'Spanish romance' genre which Sir Samuel Tuke's popular *The Adventures of Five Hours* formally inaugurated a year later. In his third play, *The Committee* (November 1662), Howard scored a hit, which held the stage for a century and a half and long remained among the enduring favourites from the Carolean period. The play combines a lively if decorous double love plot with savage satire on Cromwell's sequestration committee. The vigorous action, lively intrigue, and memorably ugly characterizations of the puritans add up to a highly enjoyable play. Its most memorable feature is the Cavaliers' faithful Irish servant Teague, a lovable bungler who does his best, usually with catastrophic results. The real warmth and loyalty with which Howard invests this seventeenth-century soldier Schweik made the character a favourite vehicle for actors from John Lacy in the Restoration to John Moody at the end of the eighteenth century.

After this triumphant foray into Jacobean-style city comedy, Howard turned with surprising success to rhymed heroic drama. *The Indian-*

---

[13] See Oliver, 134.

[14] Winifred, Lady Burghclere, *George Villiers, Second Duke of Buckingham, 1628-1687: A Study in the History of the Restoration* (London: John Murray, 1903; repr. New York: Kennikat Press, 1971), 179.

[15] Howard disliked and resented this characterization. See Oliver, 149–51.

[16] See R. G. Howarth, 'Edward Phillips's "Compendiosa Enumeratio Poetarum"', *Modern Language Review*, 54 (1959), 321–8. It was published with the 17th edn of Johannes Buchler's *Sacrarum Profanarumque Phrasium Poeticarum Thesaurus* (London, 1669).

*Queen* (January 1664) is now usually treated as Dryden's work. In fact, Dryden claimed (in his prefatory matter to *The Indian Emperour*) merely to have contributed a 'part' to the earlier piece, which was published in Howard's *Four New Plays* (1665) and was first printed as Dryden's in 1717, long after both men were dead. Howard's next dramatic venture was *The Vestal-Virgin* (1664), a bloodbath tragedy for which he devised an alternative tragicomic ending with only the villain killed. His last performed play, *The Great Favourite, or The Duke of Lerma* (February 1668) is a brilliant dramatic tour de force, regarded by many twentieth-century critics as among the finest 'serious' plays of the later seventeenth century. It was probably written with a hostile eye on the Earl of Clarendon. Since the play was apparently an adaptation of a lost tragedy by John Ford we have no way of telling how much of the credit rightly belongs to Howard.[17]

Sir Robert Howard is now most often cited for his appearance as the cranky and classics-oriented Crites in Dryden's *An Essay of Dramatick Poesie* (written in 1665–6, published in 1668)—a work snidely commented upon in *The Country Gentleman* (III. i. 25–34). Howard's commonsensical preface to *Four New Plays* had criticized Orrery's inflation, stasis, and rhyme. Dryden (an enthusiast for rhyme and 'Nature wrought up to an higher pitch . . . exalted above the level of common converse' (*Works*, xvii. 74)) put Howard down rather unkindly in his *Essay*. Howard replied fairly politely in his preface to *The Duke of Lerma* in 1668, maintaining that rhyme is less natural than blank verse and criticizing the unities of place and time. Dryden's angry and intemperate reply in 'A Defence of an Essay of Dramatique Poesie' accuses Howard of plagiarism in *Lerma* and belabours him with classical authorities. From a present-day vantage point, however, Howard emerges from this row as the more sensible if less sophisticated theorist.

As of 1669 Sir Robert Howard was neither an obscure amateur nor a hopeful dilettante. His poem *The Duel of the Stags* (1668) had excited ridicule from some of the court wits (Dorset and Saville's 'The Duel of the Crabs' is a particularly telling riposte) and he had been effectively lampooned as 'Sir Positive At-all' by Shadwell in *The Sullen Lovers* (May 1668), but he was an experienced playwright of exceptional versatility. He had anticipated the boom in Spanish romance, tried city intrigue comedy, participated in the creation of a rhymed heroic play

---

[17] See Alfred Harbage, 'Elizabethan-Restoration Palimpsest', *Modern Language Review*, 35 (1940), 287–319.

(somewhat reluctantly), tried genuine tragedy, and experimented in two forms of tragicomedy. He had eschewed split-plot tragicomedy and farce. Where next? Comedy was definitely heading towards farce and foolery in the later 1660s. Dryden himself felt compelled to try his hand at the lighter form of Spanish romance in *An Evening's Love* (1668), much against his own inclinations. Farcical debasements of Molière were becoming increasingly popular: the Newcastle–Dryden *Sir Martin Mar-all* (1667) and Lacy's *The Dumb Lady* (spring 1668?) were soon to be followed by versions of *Tartuffe* by Shadwell and Medbourne (1669 and 1670) and Caryll's *Sir Salomon* (1670). We now know that Etherege's *She wou'd if she cou'd* (February 1668) and Betterton's *The Amorous Widow* (c.1669) foreshadow the great 1670s boom in sex comedy—but that boom could not have been predicted in 1668–69.

What mode would Howard choose to work in? One might expect him to try his hand at high-flown pseudo-heroic comedy of the sort to be pioneered by his brother Edward in *The Womens Conquest* (1670) and by Dryden (in double-plot guise) in *Marriage A-la-Mode* (1671). Contrariwise, a return to the 'low' London comedy of *The Committee* would have been a reasonable choice. In the event, Howard chose to try something altogether more difficult, and he produced a play generically almost unique in its time.

*The Country Gentleman* definitely has a place in the flurry of plays personating recognizable individuals in real life *circa* 1670. Whatever Howard felt about his appearance as Sir Positive At-all, the experience does not seem to have put him off personal satire. Sir Positive is an insufferably arrogant bore who lays down the law to everyone on every imaginable occasion. At the end of Shadwell's play he is married off to someone else's pregnant whore but is made to conclude (when he discovers the truth of the situation) that he has done well: 'He's a wise man that marry's a harlot, he's on the surest side, who but an Ass would marry at uncertainty?' (Act V, *Complete Works*, i. 91.). Pepys reports the howling success of Shadwell's caricature:

But Lord, to see how this play of *Sir Positive Att all*, in abuse of Sir Rob. Howard, doth take, all the Duke's and everybody's talk being of that, and telling more stories of him of the like nature, that it is now the town and country talk; and they say is most exactly true. The Duke of York himself [said] that of his <playing at> trapball is true, and told several other stories of him. (8 May 1668)

Edward Howard was also unlucky enough to make an appearance in this play—as the egregious poet, Ninny.

In the two months before the *Country Gentleman* imbroglio a pair of spectacularly conspicuous personations reached the public stage. Kynaston's dressing up to mimic the foppery of Sir Charles Sedley in a performance of Newcastle's *The Heiress* has already been mentioned—the upshot being a severe beating administered by hired thugs. Probably there was no point to Kynaston's ill-fated prank beyond getting the goat of a noted dandy. The second case was an outcropping of court intrigue. Pepys heard the story (coincidentally) from Sir William Coventry:

> ... he told me of the great factions at Court at this day, even to the sober engaging of great persons and differences. ... It is about my Lady Harvy's being offended at Doll Common's [Katherine Corey's] acting of Sempronia [in Jonson's *Catiline*] to imitate her—for which she got my Lord Chamberlain, her kinsman, to imprison Doll; which my Lady Castlemayne made the King to release her, and to order her to act it again worse then ever the other day where the King himself was. And since, it was acted again, and my Lady Harvy provided people to hiss her and fling oranges at her. (15 January 1669)

Colbert de Croissy recounts the same story, with even more detail. Vicious personal caricatures were starting to flood the stage early in 1669, and *The Country Gentleman* belongs to this movement. Kynaston's beating and the banning of the Howard–Buckingham play took the steam out of the fad.

Whether the attack on Coventry was planned before Howard designed his play (presuming the basic outline to be his) we do not know, but on the basis of internal evidence we would judge that the key scene in Act III could indeed have been 'incerted', as John Nicholas reports. Act III is much the longest (256 lines longer than Act I, 95 lines longer than Act IV, the next longest): subtracting the 120-odd lines of the 'table' scene would still leave it longer than Acts I, II, and V. The table scene fits the characters perfectly and adds a touch of festivity and a needed climax to an otherwise rather sedate satire on pompous asses. But the scene is not crucial to the plot and could have been inserted as an afterthought.

No major sources for *The Country Gentleman* have ever been identified. The play is built around sharply etched pairs of characters—as was Howard's custom. We are given three sets of suitors (Worthy and Lovetruth, Sir Cautious Trouble-all and Sir Gravity Empty, and the fops Slander and Vapor), two pairs of attractive young women (Sir Richard's daughters Isabella and Philadelphia, and Trim's daughters

Lucy and Kate), and the warring servant figures (the barber Trim and the landlady Mrs Finical). Standing alone above these six pairs is Sir Richard Plainbred, presented as a normative standard of judgement who is really only an amused observer of the action. As a wise and kindly father, he is almost unique in comedies of the time, which tend to treat youth as good and older people as irrelevant and generally unpleasant anachronisms.[18] Not until the 1680s does the 'good' father figure become at all common, as in Shadwell's *The Lancashire Witches* (1681) and *The Squire of Alsatia* (1688).

The action of the play is extremely slight, though its short, rapid-fire speeches give an impression of more motion than the plot actually contains. Technically the play might be called an 'intrigue comedy', but there is no real attempt to maintain even pro-forma suspense about the outcome. There is no 'blocking figure' (which is highly unusual): Sir Richard offers no opposition whatsoever to his daughters' marrying Worthy and Lovetruth, and neither we nor they imagine that he will. The bulk of the play presents a very decorous version of the 'gay couple' love game and some intrigues and counter-schemes carried on mostly for fun. The pompous asses and the fops are duly punished for their pretentions, the former married off to the barber's daughters and the latter to a pair of boys disguised as women in the fashion of Jonson's *Epicœne*. The men of business, the fops, and the two trickster servants are fiercely serious about their plotting, but the audience can watch with amused indifference, knowing that matters are entirely under control. Indeed, Isabella and Philadelphia deliberately toy with the fops, leading them on as they plan to humiliate them. And their father delights in their trick and crows over it. In a more normal 'Restoration comedy' he would have been threatening to immure them in the country if they did not instantly marry the foolish knights, setting a gimlet-eyed old duenna to spy on them, and so forth. The change is refreshing.[19]

The introduction of the love game between romantic couples is definitely an innovation for Howard. In *The Committee* Arbella tells the bashful Colonel Blunt, 'I'le save you the labour of Courtship, which Shou'd be too tedious to all plain and honest natures: It is enough I

---

[18] On this trope, see Elizabeth Mignon, *Crabbed Age and Youth: The Old Men and Women in the Restoration Comedy of Manners* (Durham, NC: Duke University Press, 1947).

[19] Derek Hughes points out that the romantic couples' 'developing love is repeatedly represented in imagery of judicial process, as is the lovers' punishment of the fops Vapor and Slander. It is these improvised games of justice that chiefly facilitate the final harmony' (*English Drama, 1660–1700* (Oxford: Clarendon Press, 1996), 115).

know you love me' (1665; 130). But a witty love-duel in the Beatrice-
and-Benedick tradition can have great attractions. In such plays as
James Howard's *All Mistaken* (1665?) and Dryden's *Secret-Love* (1667)
both man and woman rail against marriage and its limitations, though
in the latter case love finally conquers wanderlust and witty antagonism
is abandoned in favour of the deeper satisfactions of living happily ever
after. Sir Robert Howard evidently believed in romantic marriage, so
his love game is quite strictly a game, played with affection and amusement by the participants, not an expression of genuine ambivalence
about marriage. Howard's bantering proviso scene (II. i. 427–76) mixes
the joking and the serious, but leaves us in no doubt of the genuineness
of the couples' love. Decorous as the play is, however, Howard is by no
means indulging in the old *précieuse* conventions of Caroline drama,
which had carried over into the post-1660 heroic drama. These ladies
are not drooping flowers of chaste insipidity. Rather, they are saucy
schemers who deliberately cozen the fops, affecting love to lure them
into mock marriages. Disgusted by the fops' lies and pretensions, the
girls determine on revenge: 'lets marry 'em to stinking feet' says Philadelphia (V. i. 222)—not the sort of crack to be looked for from the
heroines of the kinds of plays that had pleased Queen Henrietta Maria
in the previous reign. There are no 'killing eyes' and sighing, platonic
lovers here, though Howard is aware of these conventions and mocks
them, as when Isabella says to her sister, 'lets give 'em looks apeece'
(III. i. 686–7).

The two most vivid characters in the play are the scheming servants.
Mistress Finical is an aging affecter of gentility who adores French
words, food, and fashion. Roger Trim the barber is more complicated.
He is a former servant of Sir Richard's, and he never works against the
interests of the Plainbreds, but he is always out for himself. Selfish and
ambitious, Trim is deferential to his social betters, but arrogant and
nasty in his treatment of others. He means to rise in the world, and he
forces his unhappy daughters to marry Sir Cautious and Sir Gravity,
much against their judgement and inclination. Lucy says 'For my part,
I had rather have an honest fellow, though he cryd smal coal, and I fain
to wash him evry night, before he came to bed' (II. i. 288–90). And she
tells her father 'Troth Sir we had rather have plain honest men of our
own size, honest Tradesmen, or Farmers.' To which Trim replies: 'No
more I say, be obedient, we may be all advanc't, you both Ladies' (II. i.
297–301). The continuing lamentations of Trim's daughters give a
genuine ugliness to his social climbing and add a considerable element
of complexity and human feeling to the play. The girls' preference for

decent men of their own class is essentially without parallel in early Restoration drama. Lucy and Kate are not fully enough developed to become objects of distressingly serious pity, but as we see them badgered into accepting the fate their father designs we should realize that Howard is giving us a real and sobering social critique. Unpleasant as Trim is, he makes a distinguished addition to a long line of tricky servants who manipulate comic plots. A figure like Jonson's Brainworm in *Every Man in His Humour* (1598) is a rough analogue. Trim is, however, more than just a 'vice' or a 'clever servant': he is much too real, unpleasant, and nastily self-serving to be categorized that way. Howard was probably aware of the tricky or comical barbers in such plays as Jonson's *The Silent Woman* (1609) and *The Staple of News* (1626), Marston's *The Dutch Courtesan* (1603–5), and most particularly Haircut in Shirley's *The Lady of Pleasure* (1635), who pretends to be a courtier. Trim's complexity, however, makes one look ahead to the culmination of the barber-intriguer in the familiar Figaro of Beaumarchais, Mozart, and Rossini.

Without the table scene, *The Country Gentleman* would probably have enjoyed a good run. The pace is brisk, the tone light, the persiflage amusing. Mistress Finical and Trim would have given their performers (e.g. Katherine Corey and John Lacy) fine vehicles for vividly unattractive characters. Howard presumably wrote with the talents of particular actors in mind: experienced playwrights almost always did so, and all five of Howard's earlier plays had been staged by the King's Company, in which he was a shareholder. *The Country Gentleman* is both somewhat old-fashioned and almost revolutionary. In its romantic view of marriage, the play seems far from *au courant*, and Howard's experimentation with the gay couple is so cautious as to be almost invisible save by contrast with his earlier work. The amount of reliance placed on verbal badinage is quite exceptional for this date. Howard seems to be following the lead of plays like Etherege's *She wou'd if she cou'd* and Sedley's *The Mulberry-Garden*, both staged with mediocre success in the spring of 1668—plays that stress character and language at the expense of action. What is revolutionary is the ideology of the play: the exemplary father and the championing of country against city are astonishing in the 1660s. Howard went his own way, insisting on exemplary morals and incorporating a kind of satire that uses positive as well as negative examples. More clearly than all but a handful of other late seventeenth-century comedies, *The Country Gentleman* embodies a full and clear set of positive values.

In the years 1668 to 1672 English playwrights were vigorously debating the proper nature of comedy. Critical pleas in favour of other types notwithstanding, farce and sex comedy proved most viable in the theatre. In retrospect, we can see *The Country Gentleman* as a potential contribution to a debate. Dryden and Edward Howard were championing 'heroic' comedy; Etherege was moving towards a 'refined' comedy of wit and manners; Shadwell was upholding a more satiric form of 'London' comedy. Sir Robert Howard, we discover, was looking to combine elements of Etherege's witty conversation with Shadwell's sharper, lower-life satire. To these elements he added his own positive norms in a remarkably effective and enjoyable combination.

At this point, we need to address the troublesome issue of attribution. Who conceived the play and who wrote it? No direct evidence survives concerning either Howard or Buckingham other than reports of the challenge and the resulting public uproar. Starkey's newsletter says the play is 'said to be made by the Duke & Sr Rob$^t$ Howard'. John Nicholas is more specific: 'a new Play made by Sir Rob: Howard . . . in w$^{ch}$ y$^e$ Duke of Bucks hath incerted a part to personate S$^r$ W$^m$ Coventry sitting in the midst of a Table w$^{th}$ papers round him'. Colbert de Croissy says almost the same thing: Buckingham 'added' a 'scene . . . to a comedy'. We have no good reason to disbelieve the general attribution to Howard, and Buckingham's involvement seems beyond reasonable doubt. One piece of linguistic evidence for Buckingham's involvement only in the table scene is that from line 27 to 174 Sir Gravity's customary expression, 'I' (that is, 'Aye') abruptly changes to 'y Gad', which is a phrase much favoured by Bayes in *The Rehearsal*. Nothing except the table seems to connect Sir Cautious to Sir William Coventry, which inclines us to believe that the personation was a late inspiration rather than a part of the original design of the play. Given that exuberant burlesque farce was something Buckingham excelled in, and that Howard is not known ever to have indulged in it, we would suppose that Buckingham was the composer of the table scene. This does not, however, negate the possibility that Buckingham could have advised and assisted Howard in conceiving the thrust and ideology of the play. However late and incidental the personation of Coventry, the ideas that are systematically expressed in the play are part of a joint political agenda on which Howard and Buckingham were hard at work in 1669.

## IDEOLOGY AND POLITICS

*The Country Gentleman* contains two radically different sorts of satire. One—specific personation—is concentrated solely in the table scene in Act III; the other—a consistent and provocative ideological position—is diffused throughout the whole of the play. What led to scandal, the challenge to a duel, and the ultimate non-performance of the play was the table scene, but, as Annabel Patterson has shown, the satiric and political objects of the play are all of a piece throughout.[20]

The table scene, presumptively written by Buckingham, was unquestionably intended as personal ridicule of Sir William Coventry. Coventry had designed a desk for his personal office, and liked to show it off to visitors. On 4 July 1668 Pepys says 'Up, and to see Sir W. Coventry. . . . He showed me his closet, with his round table for him to sit in the middle, very convenient.' The concept was clearly that one could put papers relating to different subjects at different points in the circle, and spin oneself to the right pile in a trice. Probably only a very small number of people in the audience would have known about Coventry's desk, but just as word of mouth served to inform Pepys that Sir Robert Howard was the target in *The Sullen Lovers*, so it could have been used to inform all and sundry that Coventry was the original of Sir Cautious Trouble-all. Doubling the desk and having a spinning competition was a brilliant farcical touch of a sort no doubt particularly irritating to the proud and humourless Coventry.

Colbert de Croissy informs us that without this particular scene, a manuscript of the play had been reviewed by Charles II and found unobjectionable (letter of 1/11 March). It was, however, very far from being apolitical. To understand its ideological slant, one needs to understand some things about the context in which it was written and intended to be staged. What we now know as the Second Dutch War (1665–7) had severely strained the king's relations with an increasingly fractious and unhappy Parliament. Plague and the Great Fire of London had done nothing to improve the mood of the public. Wars are expensive, and paying for unsuccessful wars is particularly galling. The defeat of a major tax bill in Parliament on 8 November 1666 marked a

---

[20] See Annabel Patterson, '*The Country Gentleman*: Howard, Marvell, and Dryden in the Theater of Politics', *Studies in English Literature*, 25 (1985), 491–509. The following discussion is indebted to Patterson's excellent political analysis.

political turning point. Just two days later, Dryden's dedication of *Annus Mirabilis* to Sir Robert Howard loudly recommends submission to the king and his policies. Shortly thereafter we get a very different perspective from Marvell in *Last Instructions to a Painter*, stressing Howard's key part in the opposition to the excise. The 'country' party that was forming in opposition to the administration headed by the Earl of Clarendon was by no means tidy or homogeneous.[21] Steven Pincus describes them as

a loose and very angry grouping based on ideological discontent. The Duke of Buckingham facilitated cooperation and encouraged connections among many disparate groups and interests, all of which were becoming concerned about the increasingly intolerant and absolutist direction of the government's activity. This coalition included former Presbyterians and proponents of greater religious liberty like Lord Ashley, Sir Robert Howard—who had become 'no small man in that house, of which he is a member'—and Sir Richard Temple. . . . These men were not held together by common political or religious backgrounds—they had fought on different sides in the 1640s . . . but had come to fear and despise the tenets of Anglican Royalist governance. . . . They agreed with men like Buckingham and Sir Robert Howard that an intolerant baroque monarchy could not fight and win the war they thought they were fighting, that it was not a truly English style of government. Buckingham attracted support precisely because he was perceived to be sympathetic to religious liberty and to oppose irresponsible and arbitrary government. (*Protestantism and Patriotism*, 372–3)

As Pincus demonstrates, Buckingham enjoyed enormous (and broadly based) popularity in the later 1660s.

The heterogeneity of the loose alliance that gathered around Buckingham is obvious from its inclusion of both Andrew Marvell and Sir Robert Howard—though they had far more in common than one might imagine. Patterson observes that 'For Marvell, the proper role of the country gentleman was not one of unquestioning loyalty' to the king (p. 497), and he had no patience with the kind of determined idealization of unsatisfactory events that Dryden displays so tenaciously in *Annus Mirabilis*. Both Marvell and Howard were deeply concerned with what we would now call public accountability. On 7 December 1666 the Commons passed an unprecedented 'proviso' drafted by How-

---

[21] On the gradual formation of the 'country party', see Steven C. A. Pincus, *Protestantism and Patriotism: Ideologies and the Making of English Foreign Policy, 1650–1668* (Cambridge: Cambridge University Press, 1996), ch. 23 ('The rise of political opposition').

ard concerning a new tax bill, requiring accountability. Pepys was horrified, writing in his diary that 'this Proviso in Parliament is mightily ill taken by all the Court-party, as a mortal blow and that strikes deep into the King's prerogative' (8 December 1666). Marvell, contrariwise, wrote to his constituents in Hull that it would be 'of very good service to the publick'.[22] In the year following, Clarendon was hounded out of office and into exile, a set of events that left the government deeply shaken. As Ronald Hutton summarizes the state of affairs, the king's ministers 'were divided and frightened. He had an enormous debt, a regular revenue which had always been inadequate, and a Parliament which did not believe in the problem. He had been defeated by foreign powers and remained without allies.'[23] What followed, as we now well know, was the emergence of the Cabal government (in which Buckingham was to play a decidedly inglorious part) and Charles's decision to strike a secret bargain with Louis XIV. This was of course all in the future: during the summer and autumn of 1668 Sir Robert Howard was evidently spending his leisure time in composing a new play chock-full of topical relevance.

Viewed in ideological terms, *The Country Gentleman* comprises at least five sharply contrasted dichotomies: (1) Court and London versus Country; (2) landed gentry versus new-money upstarts; (3) English patriots versus foreigners and those apeing the foreign; (4) public debate of national business versus secrecy and 'cabals'; (5) plain English versus fancy verbiage. As Howard constructs the ideological positioning of the play, what emerges is a systematic idealization of a cultural nationalism based on valorization of Old English values. This is signalled up front when Worthy suggests jokingly but quite seriously that Trim can distract Sir Richard Plainbred with talk of 'Queen Elizabeth, or deep mouthd hounds or fat lands' (II. i. 416–17).

Starting with its title, *The Country Gentleman* takes a truly radical position vis-à-vis the London/country dichtomy to be found in a large number of the city comedies of the Carolean period.[24] In almost all these plays, 'country' is to be equated with butt, booby, rustic simpli-

---

[22] *The Poems and Letters of Andrew Marvell*, 2 vols., ed. H. M. Margoliouth, rev. Pierre Legouis and E. E. Duncan-Jones (Oxford: Clarendon Press, 1971), ii. 47.

[23] Ronald Hutton, *Charles the Second, King of England, Scotland, and Ireland* (Oxford: Oxford University Press, 1989), 253.

[24] Whether *The Country Gentleman* bears any relation to Edward Howard's *The London Gentleman* (lost) there is no way to tell. Nothing is known of that play save the entry of the title in the *Stationers' Register*, 7 Aug. 1667. See Milhous and Hume, 'Lost Plays', no. 24.

city, lack of social polish, boredom, and so forth. Even where foreign affectation is mocked—as for example in James Howard's *The English Mounsieur* (1663)—rustics are looked on with amused condescension at best. Readers will remember Margery Pinchwife in Wycherley's *The Country-Wife* (1675) and the horror with which the principals in Etherege's *The Man of Mode* regard being stuck in the country, but dozens of examples could be cited. *The Country Gentleman* startlingly reverses all normal expectations in this regard. Isabella and Philadelphia consider London dirty, boring, affected, and altogether a place to get away from at the first opportunity (I. i. 421–2). Sir Richard would not even come to London save for the necessity of settling his brother's estate (I. i. 183–4). How the courtier part of the London audience would have responded we will, unfortunately, never know. At a guess, a gauntlet was being flung down. Certainly a point was being made.[25]

Land versus other sources of income was a division with very practical implications. Country landowners hated raising taxes in order to deal with expensive foreign complications that arose from the need to protect English trade interests abroad. The play loudly trumpets what we would now call an isolationist/protectionist position. Foreign goods are expensive and a waste of the money made from English farming. The king's debts upset almost everyone, and the play bluntly preaches economy. In the speech that ends the play Sir Richard says 'we'l to the Countrey with our wifes; where we'l cheerfully spend what we have, and wast nothing, that our Ancestors left us' (V. i. 480–2). There was a lesson here for Charles II, if he would only attend to it. But he was never one for spending only what he had and wasting nothing. Given the play's association with Buckingham, this preachment takes on some unintentional irony, though we now know that in 1671 Buckingham actually did decide to live within his income, and in 1685 he retired to the country to enjoy hounds, hunting, and domestic economy.

---

[25] How the contemporary audience would have reacted to the party divisions implicit in the ideology projected in *The Country Gentleman* is an interesting question. Spurr observes that 'There was a "court party" within parliament, but the pretence was that no partisanship ever disturbed the pure consciences of those debating the nation's business. A charade was played out in 1673 when Henry Coventry attacked Sir Thomas Meres for distinguishing "between the country gentlemen and the courtiers, whereas there was none, nor ought to be none". Meres may not have used the precise terms "court" and "country", but many of his contemporaries did so without turning a hair' (p. 226).

The English/foreign dichotomy is presented throughout the play with humour, but not merely in a spirit of fun. The scene in Act I in which Mistress Finical offers Sir Richard his choice of a long list of fancy imported wines and he curses the lot of them and demands 'well boyld ale' (an *English* product) is a comic emblem for a serious point (I. i. 404–16). Back on 22 November 1667, Sir Robert Howard had risen in the Commons to denounce a customs scandal in which importers of French wines had engaged in bribery to get large quantities into England without paying the proper duty.[26] In February and March 1668 Howard argued in the Commons for additional excise duties to be levied on foreign wines.[27] The argument—both in Parliament and in this play—is that spending a lot of money on expensive foreign luxuries damages the domestic economy and wastes the country's money.

The English view of France and the French is always conflicted in the late seventeenth century. France was a large, rich, powerful, dangerous neighbour, both feared and envied.[28] A writer like Dryden resists, apes, envies, and filches from the French. Mistress Finical is systematically mocked as one who slavishly imitates French fashion and adopts French words. She is, naturally, vastly taken with the fops, Vapor and Slander, whose dress and fancy language seem to her the height of elegance. The play thoroughly trashes the fops. The satire is, however, actually rather careful. The fops are not identified with anyone in particular, and nowhere does the play imply that they are courtiers. Wycherley says outright that Sparkish has the run of the court and is on familiar terms with the king (or claims to be); here the audience is left to draw any such conclusions for itself. Very likely, it was meant to do so and would have done so. Dressed in the showy fashion of Sir Charles Sedley and others, they would instantly have been identified with French fashions and the court. The play very bluntly brands them cowards when they run away from a duel, which gives the lie to their loud boasts about serving heroically in the English

---

[26] See Oliver, *Sir Robert Howard*, 149; Anchitell Grey, *Debates of the House of Commons, From the Year 1667 to the Year 1694*, 10 vols. (London: D. Henry et al., 1763), i. 46–7; and Marvell, *Poems and Letters*, ii. 47.

[27] Grey, *Debates*, i. 98–101, 109–10.

[28] Buckingham has generally been regarded as pro-French, but Pincus calls this seriously into question, arguing that the duke's fear of French power and ambition made him deeply hostile to France (*Protestantism and Patriotism*, 437). Pincus also points out (p. 358) the excoriation of the French in *Observations of Monsieur de Sorbier's Voyage into England* (1665) by Buckingham's friend and ally Thomas Sprat.

fleet against the Turkish pirates in 1668 (III. i. 439–67). The implication
is that the court dandies who had populated the fleet against the Dutch
were cowards who contributed to the naval disasters of 1667. Marvell's
more direct comment was very much to this effect:

> Monk from the bank the dismal sight does view.
> Our feather'd *Gallants*, which came down that day
> To be Spectators safe of the *new Play*,
> Leave him alone when first they hear the Gun;
> (*Cornbry* the fleetest) and to *London* run.[29]

Howard has no use whatever for Frenchified gallants, and even less for
pseudo-gallants. His hostility goes beyond the economic and political
into realms of cultural linguistics and national character. To what extent this was Howard's own view and to what extent it was merely a
convenient political position is impossible to say.

Sir Richard Plainbred, Worthy, and Lovetruth represent a cultural
and political ideal. Juxtaposed against them on one side are the effemin-
ate, Frenchified fops; on the other are the fanatic politicians, likewise
bent on marrying Sir Richard's daughters (and their vast fortunes). Sir
Cautious Trouble-all and Sir Gravity Empty are not, so far as we can
see, specifically identified with Sir William Coventry and Sir John
Duncomb outside the table scene, but as Annabel Patterson observes,
they are 'from their first entrance . . . established as caricatures of the
scheming Machiavellian statesmen who make the very name of "politician" suspect' (pp. 502–3). They are constantly scheming and plotting,
and they see plots everywhere. Patterson has argued—plausibly, we believe—that their 'function . . . is to dramatize the contemporary debate
over the role of the Privy Council, by representing, in caricature, a style
of government that privileged secrecy' (p. 503). Parliament could be
indefinitely prorogued, and if the business of the Privy Council was
kept well out of the public view, who knew what dirty deals might be
done behind the scenes? Marvell inveighs against the 'close Cabal' as
early as 1667 (*Last Instructions*, line 121). Howard was promoting what a
later century would call open covenants, openly arrived at. Exactly what
social backgrounds Sir Cautious and Sir Gravity come from we are
never told. They are called rich 'merchants' at II. i. 137, and by the logic
of the play they ought to be city merchants who have become wealthy

---

[29] *Last Instructions*, lines 596–600 (*Poems and Letters*, i. 162). Cornbury was the eldest son
of the Earl of Clarendon.

by trade, got themselves elected to Parliament, and are now dabbling dangerously and incompetently in matters of state. But either the authors chose not to make them merchants, or the identification with Coventry and Duncomb compelled them to blur the politicians' background.

A surprising amount of space in the play is devoted to matters of language, and this turns out to be no accident. From the outset, Sir Richard is strongly associated with linguistic plainness. Trim tells Mistress Finical that 'he loves few words, and those of the plainest sort' (I. i. 17–18) and Act I ends with his insistence upon 'words as naked as Truth ought to be'. Vapor and Slander are great liars, more social pests than national dangers, but Lovetruth says disgustedly, 'Why I hate a lye naturally, and am disturb'd at such things, as I am at spiders, and cobwebs, that they are not swept away, and make the nation a litle cleaner' (II. i. 405–7). Sir Cautious and Sir Gravity represent a much greater socio-political danger, substituting names and papers for reality and imagining that their private colloguing will allow them to deal effectively with affairs of state.[30]

The ideological argument of the play is very simply that landed gentry, English patriots, and all upholders of open political debate and plain dealing should unite against corrupt placeholders, new-money upstarts, foreign sympathizers, and self-serving plotters. Loyalty to the king is loudly proclaimed ('we'l love our King, and be true to our Countrey' says Sir Richard in the final lines of the play), but the deeply embedded values of the play are directly hostile to the world of courtiers and the London society that constituted a major part of the theatre audience. Patterson characterizes *The Country Gentleman* as 'a displacement into dramatic fiction of issues otherwise incapable of public discussion' (p. 506). Whether some part of the audience would have found the play thought-provoking one can only guess. Many theatregoers would probably have found the trumpeting of country styles and values purely ridiculous. Even if the critique of London and government were understood, how seriously would it have been taken? Commenting on Charles's approval of a script from which the table scene had been removed, Patterson observes that

---

[30] Derek Hughes comments that 'Inverted order is everywhere to be seen. Whereas Sir Richard unfailingly desires a straightforward correspondence of word and thing, the language of London has been corrupted by "new coin'd words", and is less a means of communication than a support for the pretensions of the false or degenerate gentry, whose very names suggest insubstantial sound and air: Slander, Vapor, Fart' (*English Drama*, 114).

this would suggest that its criticism of his government was sufficiently oblique that he could have let it go forward for production. He might, of course, have read it as an innocuous comedy, of no political significance; though given Howard's recent activities, one doubts that Charles would have been so naive. More probably he saw it as an ingenious and amusing reproach to him and his minsters, tactful enough that it would cause less trouble to ignore than to suppress it. (p. 507)

The uproar created by the attempted personation in the table scene took the play right out of the realm of drama-of-ideas and ideological provocation. Our best guess is that the direct attack on Sir William Coventry was a late inspiration. Even unstaged, the table scene put paid to Sir William's political career, so in that sense it certainly worked. The lack of performance history is frustrating: one would love to know what Pepys and others would have made of the serious ideas floated in a comic setting.

## THE MANUSCRIPT AND TEXTUAL POLICY

*The Country Gentleman* survives as Folger Shakespeare Library manuscript V.b. 228.[31] Physically, the manuscript comprises twenty-five sheets laid one on top of another and sewn as one gathering, covered in a marbled paper. Thus there are fifty leaves (31.8 × 20 cms.). The text occupies fo. $2^r$ through to fo. $45^r$. The first leaf, leaf $45^v$, and the last five leaves are blank. The manuscript is written in a late seventeenth-century English mixed hand with residual italic features, partly cursive but with individual graphs within a word, especially 'i', 'd', 'f' and 'y', often separate. The secretary 'e' is used throughout. The writing is in the hand of one scribe (though two corrections have been written in another contemporary hand). The watermark on the paper is the familiar horn and baldric in an ornamented cartouche found by both Churchill and Heawood in numerous English documents from 1675 to 1695. In Labarre's *Dictionary*, Heawood reproduces a watermark closely resembling that of V.b. 228 and comments: 'An example of a mark found more often in MSS. than in printed books of the 17th C. is that of the Horn in an ornamented cartouche (Fig. 194) England. 1683.'[32]

[31] For bibliographical advice we are indebted to Mrs Laetitia Yeandle of the Folger Shakespeare Library.

[32] E. J. Labarre, *Dictionary and Encyclopædia of Paper and Paper-Making* (London: Oxford University Press, 1952), 352.

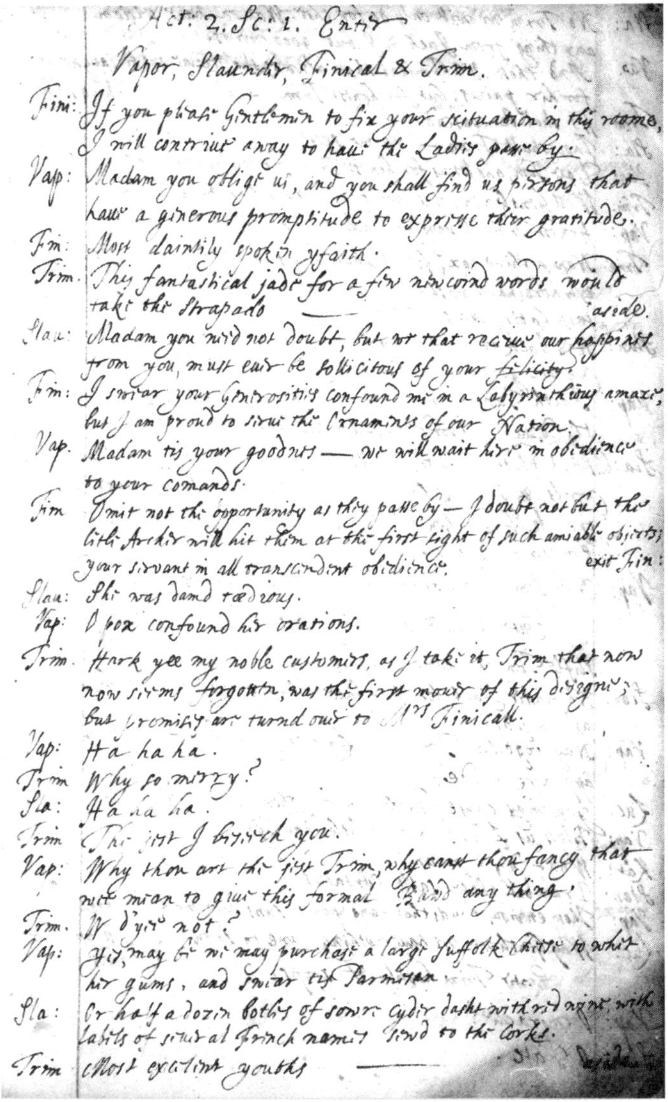

Act: 2. Sc: 1. Enter
Vapor, Slaunder, Finical & Trim.

Fini: If you please Gentlemen to fix your situation in this roome, I will contrive a way to have the Ladies passe by.

Vap: Madam you oblige us, and you shall find us persons that have a generous promptitude to expresse their gratitude.

Fin: Most daintily spoken yfaith.

Trim. This fantastical jade for a few newcoind words would take the Strapado — aside.

Slau: Madam you need not doubt, but we that receive our happinesse from you, must ever be sollicitous of your felicity.

Fin: I swear your Generosities confound me in a Labyrinthine amaze, but I am proud to serve the Ornaments of our Nation.

Vap. Madam tis your goodnes — we will wait here in obedience to your comands.

Fin Omit not the opportunity as they passe by — I doubt not but the litle Archer will hit them at the first sight of such amiable objects; your servant in all transcendent obedience. exit Fin:

Slau: She was damd tedious.

Vap: A pox confound her orations.

Trim. Hark yee my noble customers, as I take it, Trim that now now seems forgotten, was the first mover of this designe; but promises are turnd over to Mrs Finicall.

Vap: Ha ha ha.

Trim Why so merry?

Sla: Ha ha ha.

Trim The jest I beseech you.

Vap: Why thou art the jest Trim, why canst thou fancy that wee mean to give this formal Bawd any thing.

Trim. W'dyee not?

Vap: Yes, may be we may purchase a large Suffolk cheese to whet her gums, and swear tis Parmisan.

Sla: Or half a dozen botles of sowre Cyder dasht with red wine, with labels of several French names tied to the corks.

Trim Most excelent youths — aside.

Fig. 5. The first page of Act II of the manuscript of *The Country Gentleman*. Courtesy of the Folger Shakespeare Library. MS V.b. 228

The paper is extremely similar to that being made by J. Villeray in France at this time. The manuscript has no title, date, or attribution, though '["The Country Gentlemen"], anon.' has been printed on fo. 1$^r$ in pencil in a modern hand—a title deduced from the last line of the play. Many seventeenth-century playwrights had the habit of introducing a play's title into its text, usually at or near the end.[33]

The manuscript was spotted by Dr James G. McManaway (of the Folger) on 28 July 1947 in the Museum Street bookshop of Raphael King in London. He initiated the purchase by cable, and the manuscript was duly dispatched to Washington, DC. King did not say where or how he had acquired it. He clearly did not know that it was valuable, but he apparently did know the title, since the purchase correspondence names 'The Country Gentleman'. When the MS arrived at the Folger it was studied by McManaway and by Dr Giles Dawson, then Curator of Books and Manuscripts and a specialist in bibliography and palaeography. They dated the MS 1670–1700 but failed to identify it. This is not surprising, for they had nothing to go on beyond a dubious title. Had they looked in Montague Summers's *The Playhouse of Pepys* (1935) under that title the index would have led them straight to Pepys and John Starkey's newsletter. Without the help of the title and knowledge of the table scene, identifying the play would be a pretty hopeless business.

The provenance remains a puzzle, as does the origin of the surviving manuscript. The copy is scribal and both hand and paper suggest a date closer to 1690 than to 1670. Another manuscript bought by the Folger from Raphael King at the same time offers a fortuitous hint about its derivation. Folger MS V.b. 227 is a terrible amateur verse translation of Corneille's *Rodogune* (1644). The translator was Arthur Somerset (?–1743), fifth son of Henry Somerset, first Duke of Beaufort. This dismal effort, the sort of thing tutors made their teenage charges produce, was presented by young Somerset to his sister Anne (duly inscribed), whom he terms 'Lady Anne Coventry'. Anne, fourth daughter of the Duke of Beaufort, was born 22 on July 1673 and died at nearly 90 on 14 February 1763. She would have been called Lady Anne Somerset until 4 May 1691, when she married Sir Thomas Coventry. His father was created first Earl of Coventry on 26 April 1697, a title to which he succeeded on

---

[33] Robert Stanley Forsythe reports more than a hundred instances from the earlier part of the century. See *The Relations of Shirley's Plays to the Elizabethan Drama* (1914; repr. New York: Blom, 1965), 93–4.

his father's death on 15 July 1699. His wife should thereafter have been termed the Countess of Coventry. Indeed, between 1697 and 1699 she should technically have been termed Lady Deerhurst (her husband's courtesy title between the time of the creation of the earldom and his father's death). We may hypothesize that *Rodogune* was presented to her in the 1690s, most probably between 1691 and 1697. Exactly what connection the two manuscripts have is not certain. They are on similar (but not identical) paper, and they are bound in similar marbled paper. *Rodogune* is an elegant fair copy, so the handwriting is unrelated. Their turning up together two hundred and fifty years later strongly suggests, but does not prove, a relationship. A plausible hypothesis is that Lady Anne Coventry, curious about a celebrated scandal in the past of a deceased uncle by marriage, either took a family copy or found an opportunity to have one made from an unknown source. The family connection and the similarity of paper do give a hint towards possible provenance. Unhappily, no record of what is now Folger V.b. 228 has been found either at Badminton (the seat of the Dukes of Beaufort) or at Longleat, the seat of the Marquesses of Bath. The possible connection with Longleat is that Sir William Coventry's sister Mary was to become the grandmother of the first Marquess of Bath. The Coventry Letter-Book from the 1670s is full of paper with the horn and baldric in an ornamented cartouche watermark: the family certainly had such paper available. Where Raphael King found the manuscript remains unknown, and the records of his firm were long ago destroyed. Many English country houses were of course put on sale after the Second World War; their furnishings and libraries were often sold at auction and dispersed. Probably King got the two manuscripts for next to nothing at one of the many country auctions, shuddered at the quality of *Rodogune*, and sold them cheap ($50 for both of them). In all likelihood, there are no surviving records to show where V.b. 228 was between 1700 and 1947.

In preparing a text of V.b. 228 for publication we have adopted a more conservative editorial policy than that followed by the 1976 editors. Original spelling and punctuation have been retained with almost all inconsistencies preserved. Abbreviations in the text and stage directions have been silently expanded (with the exception of 'Mrs' in stage directions). Thus 'Gentm.' becomes 'Gentleman'; 'Lāp' becomes 'Ladyship'; '&' becomes 'and'; 'conversacon' becomes 'conversation', and so forth. U silently becomes V as appropriate in modern usage (the scribe is quite inconsistent). Oddly placed apostrophes have been retained as the scribe wrote them (e.g. 't'were'). The first word of a speech by a new speaker is silently capitalized; so is the initial word of what is clearly a new sentence within a speech. Speech tags have not been expanded or regularized, though we have used a full stop as the terminal punctuation (the copyist uses full stop and colon interchangeably). Abbreviations in stage directions have been silently expanded but we have not imposed capitalization or punctuation. Stage directions have been placed consistently on the page: entrances centred; exits full right. 'Aside' and indicators of movement or gesture have been situated logically in relation to the speeches they accompany, though with as little departure from the practice of the manuscript as clarity permits. Following the pattern of other plays, we have set stage directions in italic type with the exception of character names. Many stage directions are set off with a bracket in the manuscript, and we have tried to preserve the character of each bracket, whether simple, decorated, or square. A few close-brackets have been silently supplied where the layout of this edition demanded them. Some editorially interpolated stage directions have been set in angle brackets and recorded in the list of emendations in the Transmissional History. We have ignored most of the scribe's corrections in the manuscript, almost all of which are simply wrong words or words started wrongly that were crossed out when the scribe realized his or her error. All emendations of obvious scribal errors (e.g. 'they' for 'the') have been listed in the Transmissional History. We have not added missing terminal punctuation in speeches. 'Then' has been allowed to stand where the modern sense is 'than', and 'I' has not been altered to 'aye'. Because Folger V.b. 228 is a scribal copy of unknown origin and definitely of later date than the original, we have felt freer to depart from it in some format incidentals than in the case of the Commonplace Book, but our intention has been to reproduce the verbal and visual effect of the manuscript without going to the extreme of a diplomatic text.

# The Country Gentleman

## Persons in the Play[1]

*Roger Trim*. A scheming barber, formerly a servant to Sir Richard Plainbred; determined to arrange a profitable marriage for his daughters.

*Mistress Finical*. A scheming landlady, a middle-aged pretender to gentility who affects French words and fashions.

*Jack Vapor and Tom Slander*. Two lying fops, scheming cowards who hope to marry Isabella and Philadelphia for their money.

*Sir Cautious Trouble-all* [Sir William Coventry] and *Sir Gravity Empty* [Sir John Duncomb]. Two grave 'men of business'; caballing fools; also courting Isabella and Philadelphia for their money.

*Worthy and Lovetruth*. Two country gentlemen of wit and sense; in love with Isabella and Philadelphia.

*Sir Richard Plainbred*. An exemplary country gentleman, wise and witty, who detests city fashions and believes in old-fashioned country virtues.

*Isabella and Philadelphia*. Sir Richard's witty daughters; heiresses; in love with Worthy and Lovetruth.

*Kate and Lucy*. Trim's daughters.

*Ned and Will*. Boys in Sir Richard's household.

*John*. A servant.

*A Maid*. Servant to Mrs Finical.

*The scene is Mistress Finical's house in London.*

---

[1] This list has been supplied by the editors.

## Act: 1: Scene 1.

*Enter* Trim *and* Mrs Finicall

*Trim.* Nay nay is your house ready Mrs Finicall?

*Fini.* Mr Trim I am a person that seldome give permission to my affairs to be in disorder.

*Trim.* Well well Mrs Finicall, half these words had suffic'd, my trade is to clip superfluities.                                                    5

*Fini.* I'de have you to know Mr Trim I am a person.

*Trim.* Enough good Mrs Finical, your guests will be here immediatly, I'le assure you. I did a neighbors part to help you to such Lodgers.

*Fini.* Why truly neighbor Trim I have had persons of the best     10
quality, that have bin pleasd to think my accomodation as to point of Lodgings very sufficient—and me

*Trim.* Very sufficient too without question.

*Fini.* Yes sir, as to point of conversation I have not bin a stranger to the best breeding; my father was kild—                           15

*Trim.* No history now I beseech you: Sir Richard Plainbred is an honest Countrey Gentleman: he loves few words, and those of the plainest sort. Had it not bin for an extraordinary occasion, this Town had not had Sir Richards company.

*Fini.* Why does he hate this Town, the place of such refind and   20
transcendent conversation?

*Trim.* Yes, for he swears he lives here in ignorance, and the plainest dealing he usd to find was among the Lyons, for he knew when they were angry by their roaring: he never understood what fine people meant, either by what they said or did.                       25

*Fini.* Blesse me, I shall hardly affect such Company.

*Trim.* And tis odds but he will have as litle kindnes for yours. for he had as leive you should spit at him, as sputter new coynd words, he'l pay for what he has, here's one there's tother, promise litle perform more, vexes no body, but apt to be vext and angry at  30
other mens faults, and has few of his own.

*Fini.* Now I swear I have lodgd two persons here in my back lodgings, one Mr Worthy, and Mr Lovetruth just of this Knights humour. I cannot expresse myself with a bonne mine, but they fall upon me with a most unbred audaciousnes.                                35

*Trim.* Well no more grievances Mrs Finical, but get your lodgings ready: I sent my man to the Townsend to conduct 'em to your house: burn sweets in the chambers, and be ready to receive your guests with your best endearment.

*Fini.* Must their dyet be drest in my house?                    40

*Trim.* Nay, that let them resolve you—begon good Landlady, and dispatch—                                    {*exit* Finical

now methinks I long to see my old Master: he bound me prentice I thank him, and I am bound to him for what I have—Trim thou art witty—ha—                                    45

*Enter* Vapor *and* Slaunder.

*Vap.* Honest Trim thou man of unshaken faith, we were to enquire for thee at thy own house; but saw thee enter the premises, and come to bespeak to new perriwigs.

*Trim.* I know not Gallants whether you shake my faith or no, but by my troth you make me tremble to hear you talk of new    50
perriwigs; you know how sharp the last Bill was, and to whet it a litle more, when perchance the edge may be turnd against my self were to be Felo-de-se.

*Slaun.* Trim be not so witty to thy own destruction, no more but so—                                    55

*Vap.* If you persist in want of faith at this present, no salvation to be expected from us, and that ready money that you might have, shall be transferd for a fundation of new credit to another Clipster.

*Trim.* At this rate Gentlemen your poor Creditors must be forc't to maintain you, while you walk with our ruins about you.    60

*Slaun.* Not so Trim we consider your several abilities.

*Trim.* And tax us in a subsidy way, but you namd some ready money.

*Vap.* Some there shall be to refresh Trim.

*Trim.* Well you shall have two new periwigs.                    65

*Slaun.* But d'hear Trim the hair of our last dropt off like the wool of a rotten sheep.

*Vap.* Nay tis very true Trim, therfore no more waiting at Tyburn there Slaunder and I one execution day saw our beloved Trim attend the hangman with a bag under your coat: we find    70
now we are put off with dead haire.

*Trim.* Why Gentlemen if ever their Ghosts come to demand their hair, you shal pay nothing for it, that's fair, but for your live hair, I justify it.

*Slau.* Live hair from dead men?    75

*Trim.* Yes Sir, for if cut off while they are warm, it retains its spiritual vivacity: This is true Philosophy, as the hangman told me who is a great searcher into nature.

*Vap.* S'life Tom I shall never hear a noise in my chamber, but I shal think a ghoſt is coming for his locks.    80

*Trim.* You need not apprehend Sir, for tis all womens hair, the mens is to short, and those that pay that fatal visit to Tiburn are moſt commonly bawds and whores, whose wel known images cannot fright your Worships.

*Slaun.* Witty Trim, but prithee what doſt thou do here? these    85
are hansome Lodgings.

*Trim.* Why Gentlemen I have taken these Lodgings up—for

*Vap.* Wenches

*Trim.* No Sir, honeſt women, and those that may easily continue so.    90

*Slaun.* And be women.

*Trim.* Yes Sir, being rich women.

*Vap.* How rich Trim D' mee thou art the honeſt fellow.

*Trim.* But they are richer then I am honeſt, Sir Richard Plainbreds daughters, and heirs, and the richeſt that the Weſt of Eng-    95
land ever bragd of, and the sweeteſt—Well I am in haſt, you shall have your perriwigs.

*Slau.* Nay nay a word dear Trim.

*Trim.* By my troth they are ready to come.    *<aside>*

*Vap.* Nay dear Trim, really Tom, Trim is a very worthy fellow.    100

*Trim.* But in horrible haſt.

*Slau.* Nay but Trim be but assiſting, and we will—

*Trim.* What? speak out.

*Slau.* Why make thee flourish for ever, thy basons shall be converted into silver.    105

*Vap.* And all the sawcers thou letſt bloud in.

*Slau.* Thy box of inſtruments of beaten silver, and a case for thy Citterne of the same.

*Vap.* Thy shop shall be painted in fresco, and thy Pole a massy wedge of silver.    110

*Trim.* And if I can procure opportunity.

*Vap.* Enough enough Trim for thy part, we are not usd, to be refusd.

*Slau.* Refusd, Jack Vapor and I know the trouble of that willing sex, S'life their importunities are so insupportable, that we    115 muſt marry for a refuge: D'mee t'were a very great pleasure to be shown a woman that would refuse.

*Trim.* Well Gentlemen you'l secure my reward.

*Vap.* To thy own liking.

*Trim.* Well then there's another party muſt be made (viz) the    120
Landlady Mrs Finical.

*Slaun.* But how shal we dispose her.

*Trim.* O you need not fear, she admires a Bo Garson as you call it, I'le call her to you, and give her a whisper by the way.

*Vap.* Doe honeſt Trim.                                      *exit* Trim.    125
Slife Tom I fancy this jade fortun begins to smile upon us, rich heirs as it were caſt upon us.

*Slau.* That we could but see these wealthy as Indian Vessels come sayling this way

*Vap.* The divell take me Tom wee'l clap 'em aboard quickly, me-    130
thinks Tom we look like Privateers mand out by Trim, who goes no purchas no pay.

*Enter* Trim *and* Finical *whispering.*

See where he coms inspiring the Lanlady—and how they eye us.

*Trim.* Your reward shall be sure, procure you opportunity, and these be the Gallants that will procure them.                    135

*Fini.* Procure them, procure them say—or any woman breath-ing; goodnes, goodnes; what gentile persons they are, how their periwigs sit, how fragrantly they smell, what a prodigious fancy they have in their garnitures.

*Trim.* The Landlady is won—approach          {*aside to them.*    140

*Vap.* Madam.

*Fini.* O blesse me here's breeding.

*Vap.* We are persons that are sensible of an obligation, and we have an humble requeſt to implore from your faire Gentlenes.

*Fini.* O moſt ravishing—procure em—I warrant you—I {*aside.*    145

*Slau.* We hope Madam our friend Mr Trim has renderd you some account of our requeſt, and realy Madam we would not have thirſted for the honor of your friendship; but that we were well informd that you were a person that underſtood honor.

*Trim.* Very good.                                             150

*Fini.* O sweet Gentlemen I find a correspondent pleasure to serve you and shall perform my part punctualy, for I assure you that although I am now reduc't to let Lodgings, yet I am a person that have seen the world, and my father was a person—

*Trim.* Nay good Mrs Finical no Heraldry, nor hiſtory at this     155
time, your gueſts will be with us before we are aware.

*Fini.* In fine then be secure Galants of my devotions; for you
shall find me a person—

*Trim.* Nay good Miſtress no more—Gentlemen begon, you know
where I live, and here you may privatly lay your designs with Mrs     160
Finicall; begon now, and as soon as they come you shall have
notice.

*Vap.* Thanks honeſt Trim, Madam we kisse your hands and
live your creaturs.

*Slau.* My beſt services attend your Ladyship.     165

{*exeunt* Vapor *and* Slaunder

*Fini.* O me the fineſt sweeteſt, the moſt delicate (*Finical curtsies very low.*) spoken men, that ever saluted my eyes; procure
kyther; yes neighbor Trim the Ladyes are their own at firſt sight—
they scatter the sweeteſt charms.

*Trim.* How she neighs after the hobby-horses.     170

*Enter* Sir Cautious Trouble-all *and* Sir Gravity Empty
*looking about.*

*Fini.* Neighbor Trim, who are these?

*Trim.* Peace, great men that traffique in buisnes.

*Cau.* Very fair lodgings.

*Emp.* Yes very fair Lodgings; O Mr Trim are you acquainted
here?     175

*Trim.* Please your honors I have known my neighbor Mrs Finical and her Lodgings which I have now taken for a noble Maſter
of mine.

*Cau.* Truly Mr Trim you have prevented us: we came with a
designe to have taken 'em for some friends of ours.     180

*Trim.* Had I known your honors intentions, I should have
accomodated my Maſter Sir Richard Plainbred elswhere, who is
now juſt at the Townsend, with his two daughters his heires, who
is brought up by the death of his brother; whose faire eſtate now
joynd to his makes his daughters the richeſt heires, that ever the     185
Weſt of England bragd of.

*Cau.* Sir Gravity, this may be worthy of our consultation, the
subjeĉt matter of our debate muſt be rich heires.

*Emp.* Yes, that's clear, it muſt be of rich heirs.

*Cau.* But our designs muſt     190

*Empt.* I sir our designs muſt

*Caut.* What Sir Gravity

*Empt.* Why Sir Cautious as you were a saying.

*Caut.* Your pardon Sir Gravity I supposd you were offering somwhat, but since you command me, I'le lay it downe for a rule: ther's no going through a designe without Caballing.    195

*Empt.* No Sir, nothing to be don without Caballing.

*Fini.* I do not like these dull men neighbor. ⎫
*Trim.* O they are men of wisedom.    ⎬ *aside*

*Caut.* And—therfore—Parties muſt be disposd.    200

*Empt.* No doubt on't

*Caut.* And their Father muſt know

*Empt.* Without queſtion

*Caut.* What Sir Gravity?

*Empt.* Why their father muſt needs know somthing.    205

*Caut.* Right, what we are, what men of power and buisnes.

*Empt.* Without doubt.

*Caut.* And Trim, and the Landlady muſt be usd.

*Empt.* By all means.

*Caut.* And break their power with Sir Richard that oppose us.    210

*Empt.* Without queſtion.

*Caut.* And give 'em out for undertaking fellows, and spoile their credit.

*Empt.* I, I, undertakers by all means.

*Caut.* Sir Gravity, let us divide our negotiations; discourse you    215
with the Lanlady, while I transaĉt with Trim—Mr Trim a word I take it you said rich heires.

*Trim.* Yes Sir the glory of the Weſt, their land reaches to the sea, and their Royalty of fishing to the Ocean.

*Caut.* Why Mr Trim I have heard of Sir Richard Plainbred    220
and his Eſtate, tis large, and in short Mr Trim if you will be assiſting to us in the getting of these fortunes, yours shal be made; you know who we are, and what we can doe.

*Trim.* I know your honors can make me at any time.

*Caut.* Let me see—there are Clarks places—many and I sup-    225
pose you can write a faire hand.

*Trim.* And flourish a letter, I thank my good Maſter Sir Richard.

*Caut.* Or there are places that may be executed by a Deputy.

*Trim.* O good Sir your honors may depend upon me.    230

*Caut.* Enough, within an houre wee'l call at your house, and consult, but what is this Landlady?

*Trim.* I doubt Sir but a crosse humoursom jade, and I fear engag'd for some others, but your honors shall be better informd.

*Caut.* If it be so Trim, destroy her credit with Sir Richard as   235
soon as ever he comes; Trim thou shalt learn policy—Well—thou maist be fit for buisnes in Time.

*Trim.* O Lord Sir.

*Caut.* Sir Gravity no more till I inform you: how d'you find her.

*Empt.* Why faith a man may say upon consideration of the   240
first time, and according to what might be expected as to the point of a woman.

*Caut.* Come I shall inform you more fully—farewell Mistress.

                                                    *Exeunt*

*Fini.* Marry come up to these persons of honor—onely to cry farewell Mistress; marry come up, Breeding—I swear the other   245
two were angels to these honorable clowns: they would have said at least Madam your Ladyship's servant.

*Trim.* But these are men of buisnes.

*Fini.* Men of buisnes, it may be they put on busy faces, and look like dull harefinders: Pray let me be troubled no more with   250
these dull men of buisinesse.

*Trim.* Nay but Mrs Finical.

*Fini.* Nay but Mr Trim, I'le hear no more of their dull honors —Mistress marry come up.

                    *Enter* Worthy

*Trim.* But one word Mistress                                    255

*Fini.* Not half—let me alone I say—Mistress forsooth—

*Worth.* How now my belovd in wrath? who has stird my tinkling cymbal

*Trim.* Sure this is one of her Countrey guests—          *aside*

*Fini.* Pish Mr Worthy pray stand off—Lord how you smell of   260
ale.

*Worth.* Ale, why thou person of a Madam so cald; my forefathers begot one another upon the strength of ale, and drew a dreadfull long bow, and were terrible to their foes, and wou'd hit the marke as certainly, as by its inspiration I thus ayme at thy   265
flanting pinner.

*Trim.* S'life this is the maddest blade—                 *aside*

*Fini.* As I am a living woman I'le cry out; I was bewitched when I took such a rude unbred fellow into my Lodgings, I that have bin estimd by persons of quality for my converse, and those   270

that underſtand breeding and the mode, and to entertaine according to the fashion, to be thus affronted.

*Worth.* Vomit no more then in the dispraise of ale, true English liquor, for the sake of those modish things thou talkeſt of. I gratify my revenge upon thee, as one of the wel-bred apparitions, and would have all the fashionable spirits conjurd out of the nation, that men of subſtance may walk unterrifyd: Leave jarring my sweet Jewes harp—and d'heare, are not you a Barber?

*Trim.* Yes Sir, my name's Trim at your service.

*Worth.* Wipe of those pearly drops with thy soft checquerd apron.

*Fini.* If thy friends were living, they would be sorry to see how they had caſt away education upon thee, thou art e'en now paſt breeding.

*Worth.* That's all our faults, for I suppose by the reverend promimises of thy countenance thou should be paſt breeding too.

*Fini.* Neibor Trim as ever you will believe me, I am not thirty yet and he belies me basely—to be abusd thus in the sight of my neighbor—knock and be hangd another night, I'le ne'r rise in my smock more to let thee in to be abusd thus for my good will.

(*weeps*

*Worth.* D'heare Mr Trim, do you shave my Landlady?

*Trim.* What do you mean Sir?

*Worth.* Why I mean Sir she has a beard, you may see her tears like drops of the tankard hang upon it.

*Trim.* There will be no losse Sir, she'l lick 'em up, and keep 'em in ſtore for the next crying.

*Worth.* Moſt ingenious Trim, from this jeſt thou shalt commence my barber.

*Trim.* I shall be glad to serve your worship, and you shall find me a person.

*Worth.* Make a fine speech to me Sir, and I'le begin to shave your crown—Come, come—Nay good Landlady no more eruptions S'life evry sob raises the divellisheſt belch—come clear up, and we'l dine together, and be all made friends with luſty ale, and thou as Maudlin.

*Fini.* Hands off, help neighbour.

*Enter* Lovetruth.

*Lov.* Why how now my Landlady imboſt—Nay prithee Worthy —prithee now—doſt not remember the catterwauling the other

275

280

285

290

295

300

305

night without doors; and haſt thou a mind to have as much within?

*Fini.* Thou art as rude as he for thy life—Pray neighbor Trim    310
help me; I swear one time or other when they are a litle fluſterd,
they'le endanger my chaſtity, for if you'l believe, I swear these two
ruffianlike youths came in the other night posseſt with ale, and
toſt me upon the bed, and then went away like raskals as they
were, and did no more.      315

*Enter a maid running*

But for my part—

*Maid.* Miſtress Miſtress there's a coach at the dore and company in it abusd by some Gentlemen that paſt by, Offended it
seems with the coachmans driving so near 'em; indeed there may
be hurt don.      320

*Wort.* Slife Lovetruth we'l see what tis—

                               *exeunt Worthy and Lovetruth*

*Trim.* On my conscience Sir Richard—          *runs after*

*Fini.* Have you burnt sweets in the chamber?

*Maid.* Yes forsooth.

*Fini.* How rudenes?      325

*Maid.* Madam I crave your pardon.

*Fini.* You will needs be a clown—(*clashing of swords*) blesse me
there's a noise of swords—hark, prithee wench run out and bring
me word what tis

*Enter* Trim

*Trim.* Slid Miſtress your Lodgers are whipſters, twas Sir Rich-    330
ards coach, and two perfumd offended Gallants were beating
the coachman, and the two Ladies crying out, but in a twinkling
of an eye your two merry countrey blades took away their swords
as easily as a man could a switch from an oſtler—ale—gether—
s'life tis a moſt admirable fighting liquor—come Landlady and meet    335
your gueſts.

     Trim *runs out, and comes back ushering* Sir Richard Plainbred,
       Isabella *and* Philadelphia *led by* Worthy *and* Lovetruth.

*Sir Rich.* Gentlemen I thank you now by my troth heartily; I
see the fine men may be medled with: and I am glad I owe the
kindnes to my worthy country friends; I know your father Mr
Worthy, and yours Mr Lovetruth; they had good eſtats and good    340
names; and it joyes me that you inherit both.

*Wort.* We are doubly pleasd when we can do a faire office to a worthy friend.

*Isa.* Be pleasd to receive my thanks Sir.

*Phil.* And mine.        345

*Lov.* Wou'd we could give you cause to thank us always.

*Sir Rich.* And how Mr Trim; you are well thrivd I heare—you have taken hansom Lodgings for us.

*Trim.* I hope Sir they are convenient—this is your Landlady Sir.

*Sir Rich.* I cry you mercy Mistress, we shall trouble you till the        350
end of the Terme.

*Fini.* I shall estime my self fortunat to serve you, and these faire Ladies.

*Sir Rich.* She has borrowd a printed curtesie.

*Trim.* He begins to find her.        <*aside*>        355

*Fini.* Will it please your worship to have any dinner?

*Sir Rich.* By al means Landlady; we country people have good stomaks; yet we came but from Branford this morning—what may we have?

*Fini.* You may have what you please from Jerro's, Shatlings, or        360
La frondes.

*Sir Rich.* What are these?

*Fini.* Persons that dresse according to the mode, and will dispatch your soop, cotelets, ragous, fricaces, amlets, deserts—and

*Sir Rich.* Why Mistress d'you think we can live upon names;        365
here's not one word of beef or mutton.

*Fini.* Beef and Mutton—o Lord!

*Sir Rich.* O Lady.

*Fini.* I swear I scarce understand that language; there's no person of quality now, but scorns to have his Hall stink of beef.        370

*Sir Rich.* Why then a pox of your persons of ill qualities—no marvell we cannot sell our beef—it seems they eat no English meat here, but send into France for victuals and Cooks, as well as clothes and taylors—pox on your raggi, your supos, and your Catlotti—stink of beef—        375

*Isa.* My father's angry.

*Wor.* O let him beat her by al means.

*Fini.* I swear there is no person that understands eating.

*Sir Rich.* Understand eating, hey day—understand eating what a divell is there any trick in it besides a good stomach        380

*Phil.* My father's vext.

*Lov.* He has found his fashionable Landlady

*Trim.* Gentlemen we muſt ſtave and tale.

*Sir Rich.* Underſtand eating, I hope tis a fashionable art &c.

*Fini.* Why is your worship so incenſt? I onely informd your wor-      385
ship the manner of living; for I have heard many persons of quality, and of transcendent converse say that our Anceſtors—

*Sir Rich.* What of them?

*Fini.* Did not underſtand eating, but livd upon naſty beef and
heavy ale.      390

*Sir Rich.* S'life Miſtress Finical Fart, the slaves that said so, had
no anceſtors but such as they were ashamd of, Coblers, smal-coal
men and kennell rakers.

*Fini.* I swear Sir

*Sir Rich.* Prithee doe swear, rather then say thou wilt with that      395
fashionable mumpe; what do you hang your pretty underlip for?
wou'd it be thought a pretty fine young thing?

*Fini.* I am sure I was never thus abusd by a ſtranger.

*Sir Rich.* What does it cry for? begon and get me a great peece
of beef, a luſty leg of mutton, and a large fat capon with white legs      400
and spurs; my countrey servants muſt eat. I hear your Pages and
Lackyes are kept here with the smell of meat and cabige-porrige:
no more words but about it.

*Fini.* Will your Worship have any wine?

*Sir Rich.* If there be a glasse of good sack.      405

*Fini.* There are other wines now more in vogue.

*Sir Rich.* What be they?

*Fini.* Why there is your Bourdeaux, Burgundie, Bourgoigne,
vin de Champaigne, Sillery, Hermitage, O Brian, Piedmont, Port a
Port, Peralta Escevas vin d'Ay      410

*Sir Rich.* Vin divell, and a pox of him that taught thee these
hard names: Pox on your Bourdeaux, Burgundie, Champaigne,
Sillery, sullery, Hermitage, Piedmont sciveses Ribble Rabble, hark
you Miſtress, no more of these vogue names, but inſtead of all
without a murmur get me some ale, well boyld ale, and not too      415
feeble: no more replications, but begon and dispatch {*exit* Finical

*Wor.* I hope Sir my Landlady has not offended you.

*Sir Rich.* Such a fashionable jade is a terrible plague; new coind
words ſting me like so many wasps—but I am glad Gentlemen we
shall have your company. How now Girles, weary?      420

*Isa.* No Sir, but I suppose we shall be, if we ſtay long in this
Town.

*Wor.* Here is nothing worthy of such women.

*Isa.* Pray Sir take our opinion for that.

*Lov.* Wou'd we knew how to be convinc't.     425
*Phil.* If we had not met you, possibly we had thought so too.
*Trim.* I have an humble request to your worship.
*Sir Rich.* What may that be good Mr Trim?
*Trim.* That you would be pleasd to give my two daughters
leave to attend my Mistresses; I have bestowd good breeding, and     430
good clothes on 'em, and I hope they know how to behave themselvs.
*Sir Rich.* No question they can make the new fashionable
hip shotten curtsie, with faces coverd with nothing but paint and
patches.     435
*Trim.* No Sir, I did not forget your worships principles; they
go always veild as much as Spanish Ladies.
*Sir Rich.* Well Mr Trim they shall be welcom: Gentlemen you
are my guests today; nay no excuses.
    Once more plain hearty thanks receive from me,     440
    In words as naked as Truth ought to be.

*Finis actus primi.*


Act: 2. Scene 1.

*Enter* Vapor, Slaunder, Finical *and* Trim.

*Fini.* If you please Gentlemen to fix your scituation in this
roome, I will contrive a way to have the Ladies passe by.
*Vap.* Madam you oblige us, and you shall find us persons that
have a generous promptitude to expresse their gratitude.
*Fin.* Most daintily spoken yfaith.     5
*Trim.* This fantastical jade for a few new coind words would
take the Strapado—                       *aside.*
*Slau.* Madam you need not doubt, but we that receive our
happines from you, must ever be sollicitous of your felicity.
*Fin.* I swear your Generosities confound me in a Labyrinth-     10
ious amaze, but I am proud to serve the Ornaments of our
Nation.
*Vap.* Madam tis your goodnes—we will wait here in obedience
to your comands.
*Fin.* Omit not the opportunity as they passe by—I doubt not     15
but the litle Archer will hit them at the first sight of such
amiable objects; your servant in all transcendent obedience.
                                   *exit* Finical

*Slau.* She was damd tœdious.

*Vap.* O pox confound her orations.

*Trim.* Hark yee my noble cuſtomers, as I take it, Trim that     20
now seems forgotten, was the firſt mover of this designe; but
promises are turnd over to Mrs Finicall.

*Vap.* Ha ha ha.

*Trim.* Why so merry?

*Sla.* Ha ha ha.                                                 25

*Trim.* The jeſt I beseech you.

*Vap.* Why thou art the jeſt Trim, why canſt thou fancy that
wee mean to give this formal Bawd any thing.

*Trim.* What d'yee not?

*Vap.* Yes, may be we may purchase a large Suffolk Cheese to     30
whet her gums, and swear tis Parmesan.

*Sla.* Or half a dozen botles of sowre cyder dasht with red wine,
with labels of several French names sewd to the Corks.

*Trim.* Moſt excelent youths—                            *aside*

*Sla.* No Trim we will only do for thee. Women have seldom       35
any thing from Jack and I but good words.

*Vap.* And those Miſtress Finical shall alwaies receive and be
laught at for her paines; but for honeſt Trim—      *{hugs him*

*Trim.* He shal be cousend.                           *<aside>*

*Sla.* Thou shalt Trim—let me see                               40

*Vap.* Peace Tom, and let us for honeſt Trim outdoe expressions

*Trim.* Well Gentlemen, Ile ſtep out and try what may be don.

*Vap.* Honeſt Trim I vow to Gad tis on thee we depend.

*Trim.* *<aside.>* Now a third pox (for they have had two already)
mark these for extraordinary raskals—Ile keep my young Ladies    45
from such Caterpillars—                                    *exit*

*Slan.* Now Jack to our fortuns, I fancy we look so sillily now
we are going to court honeſt women.

*Vap.* Faith Tom, I muſt not fancy them honeſt; if I doe the
divell a word I shall get out.                                   50

*Sla.* Pish these countrey whitepots will so gape at fine words,
and gay clothes; that we shall have no more trouble but when they
make us low curtsies, to take 'em up and kiss 'em.

*Vap.* Nay Tom I think as for our persons—our mines—and

*Enter* Lucy *and* Kate *with hoods over their faces.*

Slife Tom they come, but veild.                                  55

*Slan.* No matter Jack for their faces, their eſtats are the beauties—at 'um Jack.

*Vap.* Nay together Tom—Ladies I hope we shall not appeare
rude.

*Luc.* You may chuse Gentlemen whether you will or no.          60

*Vap.* Bless us Ladies with a litle day light.

*Kat.* What d'yee mean?

*Slan.* Draw but those sable curtains.

*Vap.* Those envious clouds that hang upon your suns and make
it night.          65

*Luc.* Why Gentlemen we have nothing rare to show

{*pull up their hoods*

*Enter* Trim *haſtily and ſtops.*

*Vap.* O miracle!

*Slan.* O Fate.

*Trim.* How is this————          *over heares*

*Luc.* What's the matter?          70

*Kat.* Some revelation sure.

*Vap.* The same Tom.

*Slan.* My heart misgave me Jack the very same.

*Luc.* Prithee lets ſteal away.

*Slan.* Ladies if you go, we dye—we had free hearts, till we saw          75
you.

*Kat.* Saw us, where?

*Vap.* Alas! as you alighted from your coach.

*Luc.* Alighted from our coach.

*Vap.* Yes Madam as you alighted with your worthy father it          80
seemd to us as if two deities had descended; no mortal ever
appeard so divine.

*Sla.* Our passions urg'd us to gaze once more upon such more
then charming objeƈts.

*Kat.* What may this meane?          85

*Luc.* Sure they abuse us.

*Vap.* We beg Madam but the permission to breath our passions to you.

*Slan.* And to assure you, that though your fortuns might tempt
mean durty souls; we only dote upon your persons.          90

*Luc.* Our fortunes: you are pleasant Gentlemen; sure you
presume upon your good clothes.

*Kat.* Or upon the fashion, to say nothing that's true.

*Vap.* We beseech you Madam wrong not our sincer hearts.

*Sla.* We are persons that never professe any thing, but what is      95
real.

*Luc.* And you have told us truth.

*Vap.* By all that's good, by your fair selves, and by our honor.

*Trim.* The leaſt Oath of all—                                    *aside*

*Kat.* You saw us light out of the Coach.                          100

*Sla.* By all thats good we did, and beg permission to receive
the same happines to see you often.

*Luc.* As much as you did then, t'were no reason to deny you.

*Sla.* You blesse us divine Ladies, wee'l retire, and ruminate on
our unexpeĉted captivity, leaſt we appear guilty of ill manners, by   105
pressing at firſt time too much upon your gentlenes.

*Vap.* Pitty our flames you faire Divinities and let 'em not consume hearts that adore you; We humbly take our leaves leaſt we
should add to the trouble of your journy, and kisse your hands
fair Goddesses.                                                   110

*Sla.* Moſt divine Ladies.

*Vap.* S'life they are gon Tom, poor love-sick fools.

*Sla.* Lets retire Jack with dying eyes—and thus chaldese 'em           ·
                                                  {*exeunt making faces.*

Trim *peeps after them.*

*Luc.* What may this frippery mean—our fortuns might tempt
meane durty souls, sure they meant old rasors, and washbals.         115

*Kat.* And talkt of our journey, and lighting out of a coach; they
are a very impudent sort of Lyars.

*Enter* Trim

*Luc.* See my father—did you not meet two fine puppets Sir.

*Trim.* Yes, and know the miſtake; they took you two for Sir
Richard Plainbred's daughters—I could fit these hot lovers—but     120
I am a rogue if I would throw any thing upon 'em but caſt
whores.

*Luc.* If I miſtake not, these kind of Gentlemen make no more
of what they say, then of a tradesman bill, never examine either.

*Kate.* I believe they are all slime within like snailes in painted   125
shells.

*Trim.* They owe me money, and pay me with nothing but lyes.

*Enter* Sir Cautious Trouble-all *and* Sir Gravity Empty.

Sir Cautious Trouble all, and Sir Gravity Empty—wou'd these
would miſtake so—they look this way—Girles pull up your coun-
tenances, be grave, and seem what the others took you for—obay—     130
while I pay reverence to your Ladyships—they eye them ſtill
{ *Trim makes legs to them.*
*Caut.* These are the Ladies certainly—Whiſt Mr Trim—are
these—
*Trim.* These are they Sir—advance
*Caut.* You muſt present us Trim.     135
*Emp.* By all means present us.
*Trim.* Ladies here are two honorable persons rich merchants
that desire to kisse your hands; you muſt know 'em by fame, when
I tell you this is Sir Cautious Trouble-all, and this Sir Gravity
Empty, men of parts, and buisnes.—Dispatch. Mr Vapor and     140
Mr Slander have bin here.
*Caut.* Enough, we are warnd—Ladies, though affairs are ur-
gent for dispatch, they muſt give way to our expressing our selvs
your admirers.
*Empt.* Yes Ladyes, affairs muſt ſtay.     145
*Luc.* We are obliged to your honors.
*Empt.* We imagind you muſt needs underſtand matters right;
for buisnes being a weighty matter, and for all that, let it be as it
will, we let you perceive that it muſt be, as it may be.
*Caut.* Ladies you shall find our services real, and it may be use-     150
full without many words.
*Empt.* Nay that's true, few words are beſt.
*Kat.* You counsell well Sir.
*Caut.* For counsell you shall not want it, and in the firſt place
have a care of your Landlady.     155
*Luc.* Why Sir?
*Empt.* Why the reason is plain, I say as Sir Cautious said, have
a care of your Landlady by all means.
*Caut.* Ladies she is a woman of contrivances.
*Emp.* That is of tricks.     160
*Kat.* A moſt admirable explanation.
*Caut.* And of small credit with her neighbors
*Empt.* Of litle or none at all.
*Caut.* She's a seller
*Emp.* Yes she is one that sells.     165
*Luc.* What Sir?
*Emp.* Sir Cautious, Lady, can tell you, as he was saying.

*Caut.* Yes Ladies, she sels other peoples credits.

*Luc.* She is a dangerous woman it seems.

*Caut.* Tis not wise to truſt her.                    170

*Emp.* By no means, as Sir Cautious wisely intimates

*Luc.* S'life Kate these are Scoolmaſters inſtead of lovers.

*Kat.* As I live, I am afraid of correction.

*Caut.* You may see, Ladies, our concern for your good.

*Emp.* That you may easily; for we intending that your concerns    175
shal be our concerns, and so of consequence our concerns muſt
be your concerns, that matters may be in the way of prudential intrigues.

*Enter* Isabella *and* Philadelphia.

*Trim.* How now young Ladies—what shall I do, {*ſteps to them*
Ladies come own your selvs my daughters, or poor Trims hopes are    180
fled

*Caut.* What are these Ladies?

*Trim.* An't please your honors they are my daughters, come to
see their neighbor Miſtress Finicall.

*Caut.* Sir Gravity, they muſt not visit uninſtructed.            185

*Emp.* No, by no means without inſtruction.

*Caut.* For here may grow a Caball.

*Emp.* A thousand to one else.

*Caut.* Gentlewomen we perceive you are daughters to Mr Trim.

*Isa.* Who are these?                                            190

*Trim.* I have undon all—                          *aside.*

*Caut.* And we are friends to Mr Trim.

*Emp.* Yes, Ladies friends to Mr Trim, as Sir Cautious mature-
ly ſtates the queſtion

*Isa.* It may be so; and what then?                              195

*Trim.* Why will you undoe me?              {*ſteps to the ladies.*

*Caut.* We therfore thought fit to advise you to have no intimacy with Miſtress Finicall.

*Empt.* No intimacy by any means.

*Trim.* I muſt be bold and venture—              *aside*  200

*Caut.* For as Sir Gravity advises, if you truſt Miſtress Finicall
you will prejudice your own reputation.

*Isa.* You expect no fee.

*Caut.* How Miſtress?

*Kat.* Nor you Sir, doe you?                                     205

*Emp.* Why truly, Ladies, as for my part, as to the point of
expectation, let it be more, or lesse, prudence muſt govern.

*Trim.* Nay, nay Girles their honours give good advise
*Isa.* In pitty to our Father Trim we        {*aside and curtsy to him.*
forbeare        210
*Trim.* Begon good Ladies or you will not long
*Isa.* We thank your honors for our good advise.
*Phil.* And hope we shall have the grace to remember.
*Isa.* Your servants, Ladies, wee'l wait upon you, when you are
disingag'd from company        *exeunt* Isabella *and* Philadelphia.        215
*Caut.* Trim you put in seasonably, but you muſt carry a more
severe hand over these wenches.
*Emp.* By all means Mr Trim, a more severe hand over these
girles
*Trim.* I hope by time, and your honors advise I shall be able to        220
manage an affaire—I'le follow them, and improve in them what
has bin said—and give thanks for my deliverance.        *exit* Trim
*Luc.* Now for us heires again.
*Caut.* Ladies, wee ask your pardon—somthing appertaining to
your service cald us aside, Plots muſt be crosseplotted; mines        225
countermind: I sow jealousie, and hinder all harveſts, and by
several wayes I ſtudy all humours, and conſtitutions, the sanguine,
the phlegmatique, the bold, the fearfull; the easy, the wilfull, the
rash, the sober, the crafty, the foolish, the vaine, the proud, the
ponderous, the prodigal, the plain, the dissembler; the true man        230
and the lyar, and accordingly fit my designs and inſtruments.
*Lu.* To what end is all this?
*Caut.* To make 'em all need me, and conjure power within my
circle.
*Emp.* There's policie for you Ladies, on my conscience the beſt        235
you ever heard.
*Kat.* We admire Sir.
*Emp.* Ne'r ſtirre, you may well enough.
*Caut.* Ladies I beg your pardon, I had almoſt forgot a neces-
sary matter—I hear you were waited on by one Mr Vapor, and        240
one Slaunder—for I have intelligence of evry thing—Ladies, you
doe not know 'em.
*Empt.* No Ladies, you are ignorant of them.
*Luc.* They are at their politiques again—        *aside.*
*Caut.* Ladies it's true, they are of our acquaintance.        245
*Emp.* Yes we know 'em,—but pish—they are—
*Caut.* Ladies, as Sir Gravity was a saying.
*Kat.* Nothing.
*Caut.* They are shadows, mere trifles of men.

*Emp.* Yes Ladies, shadows of men, that was it, I was going to   250
have told you; I suppose you know what shadows are.

*Luc.* Are they such things?

*Caut.* They are mere duſt ſtird by evry thing, and fowle every
thing they light upon

*Luc.* But why doe your Honors allow such acquaintance?   255

*Caut.* Why as spyes, and informers.

*Empt.* No, no for nothing else Ladies but to bring newes, and
intelligence of such things as may possibly come to passe.

*Caut.* But Ladies if you please to accept of our loves, and counsels you shall want neither.   260

*Emp.* No Ladies, you shall have 'em both.

*Luc.* He takes his Cues singularly well—      *aside.*

*Kat.* We muſt in spight of our blushes acknowlege an obligation to your honors.

*Luc.* And hence forward shall have a care of our conversation   265
according to your honors directions

*Caut.* Sweet Ladies we doat on your prudence, as much as your
beauties.

*Emp.* Every whit Ladies, for as to the point of prudence, we
are usd to it.   270

*Luc.* Alas! I fear we are not worthy.

*Caut.* Nay I beseech you Ladies wrong not our jugements.

*Emp.* Ladies we are judicious, else the world miſtakes that
eſteems us so.

*Kat.* We submit, as in prudence we ought.   275

*Caut.* Ladies our admiration is compleat—at this time wee'l
take our leaves, and give you no further trouble, but beg leave to
attend you often with our loves and counsels—so your servants
Ladies

*Emp.* I realy Ladies, your servants truly     *{exeunt ambo*   280

*Luc.* Was there ever such things; how true their names are, one
troubles all things.

*Kat.* And the other like his name, as empty as an Eccho.

*Luc.* That Cautious is as malitious as a hurt titmouse, he snaps
at every thing.   285

*Kat.* As I am a living woman my father will help us to the
worſt on't.

*Luc.* For my part, I had rather have an honeſt fellow, though
he cryd smal coal, and I fain to wash him evry night, before he
came to bed.   290

*Kat.* And good reason, for nothing can wash away their foulnes.

*Enter* Trim *haſtily.*

*Trim.* How now my Girles? what do the fish bite?

*Luc.* Yes moſt eagerly, but by my troth Sir I think they are hardly worth the pulling up.

*Trim.* Pish, hamper 'em I say, and then hold hook and line, and Trim is made for ever.    295

*Luc.* Troth Sir we had rather have plain honeſt men of our own size, honeſt Tradesmen, or Farmers that could but ſtuff us up with bacon and pudding.

*Trim.* No more I say, be obedient, we may be all advanc't, you both Ladies; and I for ought I know, more then I'le speak of.    300

*Luc.* Why father?

*Trim.* Why daughter, into the ladies, and be ruld—or—no more—so—                          *exeunt* Lucy *and* Kate
Succesfull Trim hitherto as I may say; ha Trim thou maiſt live    305
to leave waiting upon lowsy cuſtomers all saturday night, and mowing of briſtly beards, that turn razors to hand sawes.

*Enter* Miſtress Finical *running.*

*Fin.* Where, where where Mr Trim?

*Trim.* Here, here, here Miſtress Finicall.

*Fin.* The Gentlemen I mean, the Ladies are coming.    310

*Trim.* And the Gentlemen are gon.

*Fin.* Gone.

*Trim.* Yes gone.

*Fin.* How gone?

*Trim.* How gone? why upon their legs; troth Miſtress Finical I    315
told the Gentlemen, that I thought you could not effeſt matters.

*Fin.* Did you so Mr Trim, you might have spard your opinion Mr Trim, and talkt of your own trade—gon—thus.

*Trim.* Goodnes, goodnes if you fume so, you will waſte into exhalations.    320

*Fin.* Shall I so Snapfinger, pray meddle no more with my matters.

*Trim.* But be advisd good Tinder.

*Fin.* Advise how to make cheating wash bals of nothing but soap and ashes—you advise a person that knowes how—    325

*Trim.* To out scold Billingsgate Corporation.

*Enter* Worthy

*Fin.* Sirrah Shaver I'de have you know.

*Wor.* How now Landlady inſtruſting Trim in fury?

*Trim.* O Sir take heed, she shoots case-shot at her next sput-
tering volley, tis ten to one but she hits you with a brace of teeth     330
like a chain bullet.

*Wor.* By this light then she shall mumble pap the remaining
part of her welbred days, come clear up this December weather,
and dry thy twincklers.

*Fin.* Hands off you rude Countrey Bumkin.                                335

*Wor.* That sowre look of thine would turn milk beyond runnet
come wipe &c

*Fin.* Let me alone or Ile thruſt my bodkin in your Chops.

*Trim.* O good Sir, the moon's in Cancer, as an antient Poet
observes, and she'l run horn mad.                                        340

*Wort.* Why what wind blew up this ſtorme?

*Trim.* Why Sir here were two Gallants.

*Fin.* Hold thy tongue thou Varlet, or ile ſtop thy mouth with
my glove                         {*goes to ſtop his mouth with her glove.*

*Trim.* Oh, oh help Mr Worthy oh, oh, she has {*spits*} almoſt    345
poysond me with the ambergrease of her palmes.

*Fin.* He lyes basely upon my honor, smell Mr Worthy, they
are as sweet as a nut.

*Wort.* Away with your ſtaind sheepskin, and hear me and mark
me; if you continue the trick of scolding, I'le take an old joynt      350
ſtool, and fix it upon Trim's Pole, and thus compose a cucking
ſtoole for thee, and baptize thee for a scold in kennell water.

*Fin.* I was never so uncivilly usd in all my life, I have livd in
this ſtreet these ten years, and with credit, and regard among my
neighbors; and to be thus flowted—                    {*weeps.*  355

*Trim.* She melts.

*Wort.* O the showre layes the ſtorme, and I grow gratious; go
in poor Landlady, and compose thy totterd pinner by thy broad
brass andiron, for I broke thy fraile lookinglasse set in cedar, the
laſt unhappy night, but I'le buy thee a better, my poor girle of   360
forty and so all friends; go in—go in and drye those pearly drops

*Fin.* But to be so usd.

*Wort.* No more, no more looshe, looshe        *exit* Finical
Why what the Divell inspird this Fury Trim.

*Trim.* On my conscience your worship is a very honeſt Gentle-   365
man.

*Wor.* Faith Trim as the world goes, I am so, so.

*Trim.* May I truſt your Worship.

*Wort.* That thou maiſt Trim.

*Trim.* And will you lend your helping hand.                    370

*Wort.* If it be honeſt Trim.

*Trim.* Why then Sir the matter is Miſtress Finical is ingag'd in assiſting Mr Vapor and Mr Slander to help them to Sir Richards daughters.

*Wort.* How by this light I'le go drown the jade in one of her    375
own washing tubs.

*Trim.* Nay good Sir have patience—These fierce gallants at their firſt entrance by good fortun met my daughters, and taking them for the young ladies, immediatly made an onset with a volley of oaths.                                              380

*Wort.* And thou wouldſt continue the miſtake, and drive it into matrimony.

*Trim.* No Sir, not to them, for truly I should count my wenches caſt away upon 'em; but presently after in came others of more profound purses, Sir Cautious Trouble all and Sir Gravity   385
Empty; and they fell upon the same miſtake (with some small assistance of mine) and courted my daughters with many good words of themselvs, and more ill ones of all others.

*Wort.* O, and these should be the parties—enough I have thee to a haire.                                                    390

*Trim.* A very pretty conceit Sir considering my trade.

*Wort.* Well Trim, moſt happy notions, and contrivances begin to inspire thee—Thy daughters shall be the heires—and Miſtress Finicals Galants shall be disposed of.

*Enter* Love-truth

*Lov.* How now Worthy are our Lodgings hanted with ribbands?  395

*Wort.* I never heard of walking ribbands.

*Love.* Nay they were born about by a couple of images of men.

*Trim.* O Sir those were they.

*Lov.* I ſtayrd upon 'em, heard 'em tell 5 or 6 to their foot boyes, and came away.                                             400

*Wor.* Lyes to their foot boys.

*Lov.* Why they sent so many howd'yees to several persons, and to every one swore they were her servants before al the world.

*Wort.* And art thou diſturbd at such misdemeanors?

*Lov.* Why I hate a lye naturally, and am diſturbd at such    405
things, as I am at spiders, and cobwebs, that they are not swept away, and make the nation a litle cleaner.

*Wort.* Trim Lovetruth is an honeſt fellow, wee'l take him in to help contrive.

*Trim.* I commit myself wholy to your worship. 410

*Wort.* Lovetruth you muſt enter into a designe with Trim, and me concerning those fine rascals.

*Lov.* Enough, I am ready—but where are the Ladies Worthy?

*Wort.* S'life wel remembred, wee'l send Trim to entertain Sir Richard, and try for a look or two. D'hear Trim, find out Sir 415 Richard, and entertain him a litle while with the praises of Queen Elizabeth, or deep mouthd hounds or fat lands, while we vent our working thoughts to the Ladies.

*Trim.* With utmoſt diligence. *Exit*

*Wort.* Now Lovetruth if we could but finish this adventure, 420 and enter these caſtles of treasure.

*Lov.* To see the luck o'nt, that our firſt loves should be brought after us, tis a good omen.

*Wort.* The coach that brought them was an inchanted vessell directed by Organda the unknown—blesse my eysight, they come 425 Lovetruth.

*Enter* Isabella *and* Philadelphia.

*Lov.* I had a pretty saying in my head, tis gon; how shall we begin after Madam?

*Wort.* Follow man, and I will lead the way to the breach; the boldeſt always enter—Save you Ladies, this is a happines above 430 our merits.

*Isa.* Why truly if you speak as you think, you deserve very litle.

*Lov.* But we are willing to merit.

*Phi.* What Gentlemen?

*Wort.* Why you faire Ladies. 435

*Isa.* And what then?

*Wort.* Why we would have our deseres.

*Isa.* That is us, as you would have us underſtand.

*Wort.* Nay I think you knew that before.

*Isa.* Yes, I think you talkt some fuſtian ſtuff to me at my 440 fathers house in the Countrey.

*Phi.* And this Gentleman mumbled over a few prayers to me.

*Lov.* And am as devout as ever.

*Phi.* I warrant you have chang'd your religion twenty times since you came to London. 445

*Isa.* Sinners you are without queſtion.

*Wo.* Why forgive us, and take us into Paradise, and prevent our future transgressions.

*Isa.* And when you have us, then—

*Wor.* We are happy.                                                                 450

*Isa.* For a moneth.

*Phi.* Or till the firſt ill humour we shew.

*Isa.* Then if we kick the litle dog, we shal be cald froward.

*Phi.* Or if we laugh, wanton.

*Isa.* A lac't hankerchef will be thought profusenes.                    455

*Phi.* And at laſt be turnd to look after the poultry in red morning waſtcoats and petticoats.

*Isa.* And our Coach horses turnd to Plow.

*Phi.* And—

*Wor.* Hold, hold we desire to be heard a word for the Defend-    460
ants, we will grant a lease of love with honeſt and sufficient covenants, which shal not expire till after our deaths.

*Lov.* We will never let you be out of humour.

*Wo.* For you shal never have so much time out of our arms.

*Lo.* We will keep you alwais pleasd.                                         465

*Wo.* And be ourselvs as cheerful as larks in glasing mornings.

*Lov.* We wil save our Eſtats, and spend our revenues.

*Wo.* And leave poſterity an easy example.

*Lov.* You shall always be obayd.

*Wo.* And your Commission shall not be taken from you after    470
mariage, but always command in chief.

*Lov.* Go abroad when you please.

*Wo.* And we ask leave to ride with you in the Coach.

*Isa.* Enough, enough.

*Wo.* Nay these are joynt and several answers, we give em upon    475
oath, and we hope the Court will judge 'em sufficient.

*Lo.* Peace man—Sir Richard as I live.

*Enter* Sir Richard Plainbred, Lucy *and* Kate, *and* Trim *following
at a litle diſtance scratching his head.*

*Wo.* How this slave Trim has negleƈted his duty.

*Sir Rich.* Here Girles, here are Mr Trims daughters come to see
you, and as fine as both their hands can make 'em.                        480

*Trim.* I did what man could doe—          *aside to Worthy.*

*Wo.* Rogue you should have hung about his legs.

*Sir Ri.* And how is't my good neighbors, shal we be merry this
ev'ning?—ho—Trim call the boys          *exit* Trim

I want breath in this town, it grows fuſty for want of air, ha,     485
neighbor that we might depart to our country peace.

*Enter* Trim *and* Boyes *with their hats tuckt up.*

—here boys—how now with your hats tuckt up? what jumpt into
the fashion before you are an houre old here; Down with 'em I
say—Or—S'life your friends shall know you when they see you—
here carry these notes, this to my counsell Mr Plodwell, and the     490
other to Smithfield about my returns for money, and make haſt
back.

*Boyes.* I, we will Sir                                   *exeunt boys*

*Enter* Mrs Finicall.

*Fin.* May it please you Sir Richard your Atturney waits you
without.                                                    495
*Sir Ri.* I go, I go, Gentlemen Ile be for you presently     *exit*
*Wo.* Now the blessing upon my deare Landlady.
*Fin.* Hands of, Sir Rude be in troth I am not so quickly
friends.
*Wo.* Why so hot have you eaten onyon porridge to day.     500
*Fin.* I'de have you to know, my breath's as sweet as yours: I
swear Ladies I have severe apprehensions that this boyſtrous
Gentleman offends your modeſties.
*Isa.* No Landlady he assaults none but yours.
*Fin.* But I shall preserve my chaſtity.                   505
*Wo.* From bore cats, and monkies.
*Fin.* I have had as good men as thy self present their addresses
to me, and I would have thee to know
*Wo.* Trim carry the magpye to her cage, Trim away with her.
*Fin.* Let me alone Sirrah, or I'le                        510
*Trim.* Nay Miſtress Finicall but one word.
*Lo.* Trim away with her
*Fin.* I am abusd thus always Ladies.
*Trim.* But Miſtress Finicall, Mr Vapor and Mr Slaunder have
sent word they are coming, and if you should not be in the way,     515
matters may go ill.
*Fin.* Uds my life I go, I go, your servant Ladies.  <*exit* Finical>
*Wo.* After her Trim, and dam up the floud, that it overflow
here no more,                                        *exit* Trim
now Ladies if you please to reply we'l rejoyne.           520

*Isa.* And what then?

*Wo.* Proceed to tryal.

*Isa.* You are too haſty for chancery suits, it is enough we have received your Depositions: come Miſtress Lucy, and Miſtress Kate I swear Mr Trim may be proud of two such pretty daughters.    525

*Wo.* Nay Madam you muſt needs ſtand for Esquire Trims daughters a litle while.

*Isa.* The meaning?

*Wo.* A designe we have, which you shall know within, as soon as Trim can get from his duty, tis honeſt, and you may be charit-   530 able.

*Isa.* When we deny such a thing we are neither.

*Lo.* Some pitty leave for us.

*Wo.*                        —unles you doubt us.

*Isa.* Perhaps you ask more, then we have about us.

*Finis Aĉtus secundi.*

Aĉt 3. Scene 1.

*Enter* Sir Cautious *and* Sir Gravity

*Caut.* You see now Sir Gravity what advantage it is to be thought men of buisnes; every man will be pretending to it, nay and are angry if they cannot be eſteemd so.

*Emp.* Yes men will be angry, but let 'em, I say buisnes muſt be don by men of buisnes.    5

*Cau.* Right Sir Gravity, but there are but few such; some are conceited and haſty, others wity and uncertain, some grave and ignorant others formal and Lazie, some violent and shallow, others deep and treacherous, some busy and malitious, others quiet and silly; a sound Politition Sir Gravity muſt be better composd.    10

*Emp.* You have spoken admirably Sir Cautious, and a man of buisnes muſt be well composd, very well composd as to point of abilities in relation to matters and debates &c.

*Enter* Trim.

*Caut.* O Mr Trim you are punĉtual, what newes?

*Trim.* Newes, why your honors are admired sufficiently, the La-   15 dies talk of nothing but the wonderful things of wisedom.

*Caut.* That's good Sir Gravity, I told you what would happen.

*Emp.* That you did Sir Cautious, and I'le take my oath o'nt I thought as much.

*Trim.* I will go trye to windlesse 'em this way, when I but hint   20
by the by that your honors are here, they will bee creeping this way.

*Caut.* Doe so good Trim, while we peruse some papers, leaſt any time may be imprudently loſt              *exit* Trim
Sir Gravity I have of late contrivd a way to debate a matter or a   25
buisnes all alone, and yet by way of Dialogue.

*Emp.* How by Dialogue, and yet alone, Gad that would bee very pretty.

*Caut.* Yes Sir Gravity, by Dialogue and yet alone, as thus to intimate in my self; I thus propose a queſtion, and firſt Sir   30
Cautious he speaks to't, and gives his sense of it, Then Trouble-all answers, and so debate alternative: Then joyning Sir Cautious to Trouble all, Cautious and Trouble all summe up the debate and determine the queſtion

*Emp.* Would I may never ſtir now, it is very pretty, I have it,   35
for though I say it, I am as quick as another, as for example, I propose a thing, you answer it, and thereupon I and you—no Gad that's not right.

*Caut.* I have thought of another projeƈt Sir Gravity, will settle us in the opinion of the world for ever, as to what wee pretend to,   40
the dispatch of buisnes, for tis that you know we are made for.

*Emp.* I gad, and so we are.

*Caut.* It is my main projeƈt, and if I am not miſtaken will nick 'em all.

*Emp.* Y gad, and so it will; what i'ſt?                45

*Caut.* Have you ever seen an oyſter Table.

*Emp.* Yes I have, there's one I take it

*Caut.* U'ds so I have another at my lodging hard by, I'le send for it, and do it to the life before you—d'heare John

*Enter* John

John fetch me my oyſter Table at home, be here in a minute.   50

*exit* John

*Emp.* I pray Sir Cautious explain a litle, y gad I am ſtrange-ly taken with it, though I d'ont know what 'tis.

*Caut.* You muſt know Sir Gravity, that upon the modell of an Oyſter table, I have plodded out a Table for buisnes.

*Emp.* How Sir, a Table for buisnes? y gad that's very pretty.   55

*Caut.* Why Sir thus, to your hole in the midle, which you know is antient, I have added a modern passage into't.

*Emp.* Very good y Gad: and what then?

*Caut.* This same passage I open and shut at pleasure, now Sir as soon as I am in, I fix my self upon a ſtool made for the nonce,          60
which turns upon a swivell, and place my papers about me—See here I have my Spanish papers, here my Dutch papers, here my Italian papers, here my French papers, and so round. Now Sir in a trice dispatch to what part of the world you please, I am ready for you.          65

*Emp.* Admirable good y Gad, and this table may also serve for domeſtique affaires.

*Caut.* No, there shall be two, one for domeſtique, the other for forreigne; and in the forreigne there is somthing more consider-able yet then all this.          70

*Emp.* Very fine; what I pray?

*Cau.* Why the thing you know, that we men of buisnes ought to be moſt currant in, as to affairs abroad is the position of the several intereſts of forreign Potentates, how they ſtand in amitie or animosity toward us, and with one another.          75

*Emp.* Very good.

*Caut.* This coſt a world of paines and expence by intelligence, and such like; wheras by the modell and direćtions of my for-reigne Table, you have all that intrigue laid before you at one dash.

*Emp.* Y gad thats very neat, what modell can this bee?          80

*Caut.* Why Sir the modell is not tœdious neither, 'tis only thus: if enemies opposite, one here tother there, if friends—close touch—So I never trouble my self with reading newes books or Gazets, but go into my chamber, look upon my Table, and snap presently; Ile tell you how the whole world is disposd.          85

*Emp.* Sookers what would I have given to have found out this firſt, Let us discusse this a litle farther; for this thing is new, and therfore give me leave to ask some queſtion, what wood muſt this Table be made of?

*Caut.* Any you please, why do you ask?          90

*Emp.* Nay tis not for any great moment, but only I love to be exaćt in matters of concern—Shall I tell you a ſtrange thing? if you had not found out this invention juſt as you did, Gad I dare almoſt be hangd, if I had not light upon't myself; it jumps so right with my Genius.          95

*Enter* John *with a Table.*

*Caut.* O here it coms, wel don John—withdraw     *exit* John
come, come to our buisnes, which Table will you have?
*Emp.* This.
*Caut.* Remember then tis the domeſtique: here are the domes-
tique papers; you furnish that as I do this—get in—so—well Sir,     100
this I'le boldly say before we begin: Whoever knowes the use of
this Table, forbears the use of wine, rises at six, and goes to
dinner precisely at twelve: give me leave for to tell you, is more
then amply provided to set up in any part of Chriſtendom for a
man of buisnes —So are you ready?     105
*Emp.* Yes, and y Gad tis the notableſt thing that ever yet was
thought on.
*Caut.* Why then for experiment, name me any place abroad.
*Emp.* Paris.
*Caut.* Here I am, now I name you a place at home—Putney.     110
*Emp.* Well what muſt I do now?
*Caut.* Why turn about the Whife—as I did.
*Emp.* O I cry you mercy, here tis—y'gad now I begin to under-
ſtand it; now call to me agen.
*Caut.* Well—Kingſton.     115
*Emp.* Sooks I cant find it, are you sure tis here?
*Cau.* I, I look, look.
*Emp.* I have it, very fine y gad.
*Cau.* Now call to me.
*Emp.* No, no call to me once more, that I may be perfeɕt.     120
*Caut.* Well then Islington.
*Emp.* Here I have it at my fingers ends, now I will Lay you an
embroyderd pair of gloves, that I do it as well as you.
*Caut.* With all my heart, wee'l name only Towns, and as faſt as
we can.     125
*Emp.* A match, the faſter the better, I'le begin—Venice.
*Caut.* Pendennis.
*Emp.* Roan.
*Caut.* Marybone
*Emp.* The Brill.     130
*Caut.* Harrow oth' Hill
*Emp.* Orleans.
*Caut.* Petty France
*Emp.* Peru.
*Caut.* There you are out, tis no Town Cue.     135
*Emp.* Oſtend.

*Caut.* Gravesend.
*Emp.* The Vly.
*Caut.* Rye.
*Emp.* Grand Caire.                                                 140
*Caut.* Ware.
*Emp.* Rome.
*Caut.* Combe.
*Emp.* Rotterdam.
*Cau.* Cam.                                                         145

*Both*  ⎰ Naples
        ⎱ Chelsey
          Hague
          Highgate
          Brussels                                                  150
          Briſtow
          Cullen
          Gilford

*Enter* Sir Richard *and admires.*

*Empty.* Hold, hold; who is this?
*Caut.* Sir Richard, I am confident, get out Sir Gravity.           155
*Sir Rich.* How now, what are these Juglers?
*Caut.* Save you worthy Sir, you may perceive—
*Emp.* Your help Sir Cautious, I beseech you.
*Caut.* Immediatly Sir Gravity.
*Emp.* Sookers my papers; I have loſt a Town or two y'gad.          160
*Caut.* As I was saying Sir, you may perceive wee are men of
buisnes, and contriving a quick method of dispatches; for affaires
presse us.
*Sir Ri.* O, cry you mercy, troth I took you for Conjurers; I ask
you pardon for interrupting you—proceed, proceed.                  165
*Caut.* Sir we ought firſt to advise you, that one Vapor and
Slaunder.
*Sir R.* Those are two Sir.
*Caut.* But they make up but one ill man; so I salve that objeƈtion.
*Emp.* I made haſt Sir to tell you as much; that objeƈtion's       170
cleard.
*Sir R.* Tis very well, I intend not to trouble you with another.
*Caut.* But Sir, I beseech you one word by way of counsell.
*Emp.* I sir, as to Counsell.
*Sir R.* No sir; I need no counsell.                               175

*Caut.* But by your favor, as to your own good.

*Emp.* I sir, your own good; mind that.

*Sir R.* Why? what a pox are you rude or mad?

*Caut.* But Sir, as to those persons Vapor and Slaunder—give us leave to warne you                                                                    180

*Emp.* Take warning Sir, as Sir Cautious advises.

*Sir R.* I am warnd, and will avoid men of buisnes evermore.

*Enter* Trim *before* Lucy *and* Kate.

pray begon leaſt I be uncivill to your wisedoms.

*Trim.* How Sir Richard—now invention, or all is spoild
                      {*they whisper with* Sir Richard *and he shakes 'em of*
Sir your daughters desire a word with you, and a man that cals      185
about the return of money.            {Trim *whispers to* Sir Richard.

*Sir R.* I go, I go Trim.

*Caut.* But Sir, to prove what we have said to you, favour us a word—we perceive these are your daughters.

*Sir Rich.* D'yee so Sir?—alas poor Gentlemen! I see they are      190
mad now.

*Empt.* But in cases of these natures, when matter of faſt offers it self, upon the exorbitancy of the occasion

*Sir R.* Good exorbitant Sir, your friends are to blame, they put you not into a dark roome.                                                    195

*Cau.* Why Sir?

*Sir R.* And yours too to blame indeed.                                *exit*

*Caut.* This is the ſtrangeſt thing.
                      {Trim *goes to follow him and ſteps back.*

*Emp.* A countrey Gentleman ignorant of Politiques, he's no man of buisnes.                                                                      200

*Trim.* Your honors had like to have spoyld all; win the Ladies firſt; he's a teſty old man; make all sure, I'le give the Ladies a whisper too shal frighten them from venturing to delay their preferment.

*Cau.* Honeſt Trim, and thou shalt find thy preferment; I will      205
not name the place now.

*Emp.* No, leave that to us.

*Trim.* Your honors Creature—
                      {*makes mouths at 'em and goes to his daughters*
I see these may be made Chaldeans—{*to them aside*} Dispatch,
wind up matters for fear we are discoverd, you are made for ever      210
—your servant Ladies—Charge 'em they are your own    *exit* Trim

*Cau.* Ladies, you have seen that we have love, and I suppose you know that we are in buisnes. Love muſt be obayd, buisnes muſt be dispatcht. You command our affeċtions; The Nation our service; Love contends with buisnes, and buisnes disputes   215
with Love. One's private, tother publique: Ones natural, the other prudential; Therfore summing up all, we move you to unite the private and publique concerns, leaſt one impede the other.

*Luc.* Alas Sir we should be unhappy to prejudice the Publique.

*Emp.* Nay Ladies, you were very unhappy, should you doe so;   220
there Sir Cautious I think I nickt her.

*Kat.* But Sir?

*Caut.* But what Ladies? I know what you would say, for prudence may conjeċture.

*Emp.* Nay Ladies, prudence will conjeċture.   225

*Kat.* What Sir?

*Emp.* As Sir Cautious was saying concerning what you wou'd say, and as your saying concerning what I would say.

*Caut.* Why Ladies, as Sir Gravity intimates, I was a saying that you might objeċt these particulars.   230

*Emp.* Nay Ladies, you shall hear all you can say, I warrant you.

*Luc.* Why truly Sir it may save our blushes.

*Cau.* Why Ladies you may say men are not to be truſted, you scarce know us, tis too soon, your fathers consent, what time, what place, who shall marry you.   235

*Emp.* This is all that can be objeċted, give me leave to tell you Ladies.

*Cau.* To these I answer, we are men of buisnes, and may be truſted; the nation knowes us, if you don't; Never too soon to do wisely, your father's teſty, the time now, the place Coventgarden   240
Church; and Mr Trim fetch the Parson

*Emp.* Look you there Ladies; what's to be don, I would fain know.

*Luc.* Alas we can say but litle; we are plainly bred.

*Kate.* But we are fearfull.   245

*Caut.* Of what Ladies? of disposing your selvs wisely, why though your father be apt to be out of humour, yet he will be well enough pleasd, when he sees his intereſt increaſt, respeċted in the Town and feard in the Countrey.

*Emp.* Ladies, there's no more to be sought for, then fear and   250
respeċt.

*Luc.* Alas; we know not what to say, what shall we doe Sister?

*Kat.* Nay Sister, you are the eldest.

*Luc.* Truly Sister, I think these are honorable persons.

*Kat.* Nay, and wise ones without question.                              255

*Luc.* Sure then we ought to be directed by their sage counsell.

*Caut.* Ladies, your prudent debates make us admire you more, and more.

*Emp.* Truly Sir Cautious, as you say, their debate does make us admire 'em.                                                              260

*Caut.* Well Ladies, we dare promise you, that the whole nation shall judge you happy.

*Emp.* I Madam, every man, woman, and child I warrant you.

*Kat.* Well at this time tis not discreet for your honors to stay longer for fear of suspition—Mr Trim will contrive further oppor-   265
tunity.

### *Enter* Slaunder

I see strangers Sister, lets begon—we trust your honors

*Cau.* You may safely deare Ladies.                    *exeunt Ladies*

*Emp.* The most discreet Ladies that I have known.

*Caut.* What does Slaunder here? we must be wise Sir Gravity.    270

*Emp.* By all means wise, Sir Cautious

*Slan.* Sir Cautious Trouble all, and Sir Gravity Empty no person is more yours then Tom Slaunder; nor is possest with a greater admiration of your parts and eloquence; ne'r stir Sir, tis an harmonious pleasure to heare you speak to a buisnes.                    275

*Caut.* Your servant Mr Slaunder—but what buisnes brings you hither—what; the rich heiresses?

*Slan.* O you railly Sir, you know my temper too well to look after honest women—but as I take it, some Ladies went from your honors.                                                              280

*Caut.* Women Mr Slander, we understand not what you meane.

*Emp.* No, upon our honors we are so far from understanding you, that really we are wholy ignorant.

*Caut.* Your servant Mr Slaunder—you are only fit to approach Ladies; we are dull men of buisnes, your servant Mr Slaunder.    285

*Emp.* No Sir we are not fit for love matters, your servant

*exeunt*

*Slan.* Your honors most obedient servant—umh—there is somthing in the wind—these Politicians had such odd counten-

ances; one piece of their faces spoke gravity, and the other at the
same time a ridiculous gayetie: They are grave, formal, false fel-    290
lowes, they will promise one thing to five people and forsweare it
to six more.

Enter Vapor

We may fitt 'em; what a Divell made you ſtay so long?

*Vap.* Why, I was dund by the way by a company of impertinent Tradesmen: they were so thick, that twas a good while be-    295
fore I could break battalion, and made such damd dull harangues,
that the slaves ought to loose their debts in equitie. One had a
wife that was in the ſtraw, and was willing the poor foole should
have tendance, another had a child to chriſten, and was desirous
the litle ape should be made a Chriſtian: another was to pay that    300
day for some commodities, or his credit was crackt: At laſt (for
between you and I Tom I had warmd my soule with a glasse of
wine) I briskly cryd pox of your wifes, and children, and credits;
so the slaves shook with the thundring of my brow shrunk into
absence.    305

*Slan.* Your expressions swell Jack.

*Vap.* From wine my fancy borrows feathers, and mounts above
comon gazing.

*Slan.* But heark you Jack, here was Sir Cautious Trouble all
and Sir Gravity Empty; And I saw women goe from 'em.    310

*Vap.* Hang 'em dull porers in scribled papers.

*Slan.* Why Jack, thou despiseſt all things now.

*Vap.* Pish we are fool'd by grave looks, and dull hiſtorie;
There's your Alexander, and your Cæsar; that same Alexander
never durſt fight, but when he was drunk: and that same Cæsar    315
won a chance battell at—I have forgot the name of the place; but
that's all one, and I can demonſtrate, that I could have beaten
him that day to a ratcatcher, if I had commanded tother army:
for that Pompey was a pitifull fellow. The Romans were a
company of huffing coxcombs, and observe one thing Tom, you    320
never heard of one of 'em, that ever fought a duell, a company of
crowd fighting fellowes—but

*Slan.* But Jack, you forget the buisnes—what say you about
the grave Knights?

*Vap.* Why, I say if I had met 'em I'de have beſtowd kicks o'th    325
arse apeece upon 'em.

*Enter* Mrs Finical

O Madam your faithfull servant.

*Fin.* No complements now Galants, but quickly, quickly,
quickly to a room that I'le shew you where you shall not misse the
Ladies.                                                                330

*Vap.* We obay you Mam.                                    *exeunt.*

*Enter* Trim *peeping.*

*Fin.* Lord what a fine movement they have, o how charming's
their behaviour, blesse me, blesse me Goodnes.

*Trim.* D'heare neighbor, who are those?

*Fin.* Good Mr Trim what need you be so inquisitive?          335

*Trim.* What are you the privat Lady?

*Fin.* No matter whether I am, or no.                        *exit*

*Trim.* Tis so; they are my fine Gallants, besides I know 'em by
their su saw manner of going—they have rich women, and
honeſt women to waſt their fames and fortunes.              340

*Enter* Worthy, Lovetruth, Isabella, Philadelphia,
Lucy *and* Kate.

Gentlemen a discovery.

*Wor.* Of what Trim?

*Trim.* Of the enemy Vapor and Slander, who are lodgd in am-
bush by our Lanlady Bawd Finicall, and as soon as these Ladies
are discoverd, they will certainly be attaqued.               345

*Wor.* S'life Ladies let Mr Trims daughters ſtand forward, and
when they appear, wee'l confirm their coxcombships in their mistake, by paing reverence to the supposed heires.

*Trim.* Ladies you are beholding to Lucy, and Kate, they ſtand
between you, and trouble.                                     350

*Wor.* Thus then advance your selvs; and we thus to our
poſtures.

*Isa.* And thus wee'l begin to praɕtise our humiliation,—your
Ladyships moſt humble servant

*Phil.* —Your servant Mam.                                   355

*Enter* Finicall *peeping.*

*Fin.* By my life they are here, I'le send 'em such as shall dazle
'em yfaith.                                            {*runs out*

*Wor.* How now, that was Scout-Miſtress generall Finical the
enemy will immediatly have intelligence

*Trim.* Let me counterspie          {*peeps out and runs in.*  360
To arms, to arms, be in readines, the enemy approaches with
flying colors all about their clothes—I'le retire for a reserve.   *exit*
*Wor.* Thus we bow to our feignd altars.
*Lov.* Peace, peace they come.

*Enter* Vapor *and* Slaunder.

*Vap.* Divine Ladies, your moſt humble servants      {*to Lucy*  365
*Slan.* Madam I am the faithfull adorer of your vertues {*to Kate*
*Vap.* What are these Gentlemen?
*Luc.* Some—
*Vap.* What pretenders?—Gentlemen, we serve these Ladies.
*Slan.* And we admit no rivals.                             370
*Wor.* Nay Gentlemen be not angry; rather then make a quar-
rell, or a clutter wee'l retire to Mr Trims daughters.
*Love.* We hope you will be pleasd to admit of our addresses to
them.
*Vap.* Yes, go say dull things to 'em, fuſtian speeches ſtoln out  375
of the schoole of Complements—but really Ladies I am extremly
surprizd, that you could indure such unbred conversation.
*Luc.* Why Gentlemen would you not have us civill?
*Slan.* Madam tis a miſtaken civility to endure wrong things; as
ill company, ill smels, ill meat, and ill drink.            380
*Kate.* But when we have no daintyes, course meat muſt be en-
durd.
*Vap.* We therfore Madam present you with the feaſts of our
passions; we underſtand how to nourish pure flames, which cannot burn, but where the fuell is a sublimd resentment.      385
*Luc.* Indeed Sir—
*Sla.* Tis that Lady perhaps, has warmd the hearts of many of
your sex; really you can hardly imagine how many persons of
quality are now in languishing condition—realy I could find in my
heart to discover a person, that—                           390
*Kat.* What Sir?
*Slan.* Why Lady a person of quality, that is now dying for that
rogue Jack there—and some others, that begin to fall away—ha
Jack, do you blush rogue?
*Vap.* Nay prithee Tom hold thy tongue, fy, fy—no such     395
thing Ladies, if you discover any more Tom, realy I shal be even
with thee; and discover the invitations, and treats, that I have to
bring you to certain places, and certain persons, that shall be
nameles, y'gad you had beſt begin Tom.

*Slan.* Nay, nay quarter Jack, fye, fye.      400

*Lov.* How I kindle at these lyes—      {*aside*

*Wor.* Sweet Ladies, wee'l only ſtep out, and give 'em kicks apeece—they'l take no notice of it

*Isa.* Be quiet, or—

*Phil.* I have much adoe to hold my bull dog too.      405

*Vap.* Well, well honeſt Tom no more impeachments—faith Madam we confess this makes us laugh somtimes to see the beaus eus, that the Ladies caſt upon us, and if they can but faſten any discourse upon us; they fall presently upon hermitages, and willow-garlands, and shades, and groves, and Elysian fields, and      410 treading forsaken paths with folded arms.

*Slan.* And then Madam, what d'yee think we doe?

*Kat.* What Pray Sir?

*Slan.* Why go presently, and laugh at 'em for persons ridicule.

*Lov.* What's that?      }  *aside*    415

*Wor.* Why the rogues talk of the Divell.

*Luc.* You are cruel to our sex.

*Kat.* Nay, and abuse 'em too.

*Vap.* No, no Mam, a litle mirth for diversion

*Luc.* Tis wonder none of their friends, or relations dont make      420 it a quarrell

*Vap.* How a quarrell—they know us too well.

*Slan.* They know, if they but look awry, they muſt fight.

*Vap.* We count a duell without fooling a good mornings exercise.      425

*Wor.* Dambd Rogues.      {*aside*

*Slan.* We had as lieve fight a duell, as fence, the exercise is the same to us.

*Vap.* Do you remember Tom the laſt duell we fought, what I told thee, when I was going to draw my sword.      430

*Slan.* Very well Jack.

*Luc.* Pray what was it Sir?

*Slan.* Nay realy Madam let the rogue tell you himself, if he please.

*Vap.* Why since your Ladyship is pleasd to command me, Ile      435 confesse a fault—why I swear I was so pleasd, when I was going to engage, that the D'evl take me, but I had a mind to a wench.

*Sla.* You may think now that Jack Vapor does not tell true; but to convince you, I swear wee were both in such an extasie; when the sea-fight began againſt the Turk.      440

*Kat.* O me, the noise should rather have terrifyd you.

*Luc.* Blesse me, the great guns are terrible things.

*Wor.* The wenches perform rarely.                        {*aside*

*Vap.* Noise Madam, why the noise was no more to us, then the crackling of bay leafs in the fire; and yet the bullets flew so thick, that I toſt up my hat for an experiment, and really it was carryd away into another ship.                        445

*Luc.* Methinks Sir another bullet should have bin so civil, as to have brought you another hat back in its place.

*Slan.* You are witty Lady—but really to shew you that Jack Vapor tells you nothing but Truth, as I was combing my periwig (for I was careles of the impertinent bullets) one took my combe out of my hand.                        450

*Kat.* And broke the teeth, I am confident

*Slan.* Why Madam for all that, the bullets were the leaſt of danger, for realy we were so near, that at the same time, the fire of the guns burnt my haire, which then lay in curls upon my shoulders; and ever since I was forc't to weare a periwig.                        455

*Kat.* I thought Sir, you had said, that it then burnt your periwig.                        460

*Slan.* Your pardon Madam, I miſtook, and but a litle; for twas Jack Vapors periwig; and he ſtood so near me, that twas in a manner the same thing.

*Luc.* It seems, it was a periwig.

*Vap.* Yes Madam, it was, and burnt to nothing; but it was no wonder; for at the same time, I went to settle my Cravat, and really I puld away a handfull of ashes.                        465

*Luc.* Now Kate they lye warmly to one another.    { *both*

*Kat.* What are they contriving now? sure they are    { *aside*
not so immodeſt, as to hope to invent greater lyes.                        470

*Wor.* If you please Ladies, One, but one kick.

*Isa.* Peace.

*Vap.* You see Ladies we are here yet; and really it seems, as if by miracle we were preservd for you.

*Luc.* But can such brave men famd for duells, and battels love such plain countrey things, as we are?                        475

*Kat.* What say you to those Gentlewomen, Mr Trims daughters, with their advantages of city breeding.

*Isa.* Admirable wenches.                        {*aside*

*Lu.* If it were not for our eſtats you would swear more oaths to them.                        480

*Vap.* Those.

*Sla.* Who those.

*Phil.* Now, have at us.

*Vap.*  ⎫
       ⎬  *Ha, ha, ha.*                                        485
*Slan.* ⎭

*Vap.* Those? what those pusses, with complexions like the sea-coal they sit over.

*Slan.* Which mixt with their painting gives 'em a murray cheeke.

*Vap.* Alas Ladies, Tom and I are no ſtrangers to 'em, and to        490
shew you your error; their father is our Barber, and those wenches usd to light us down ſtairs.

*Enter* Finical, *and sees them courting.*

*Slan.* Dear Lady.

*Vap.* We dye without your pity moſt divine Ladies.

*Enter* Trim

*Trim.* How Finical! then all will out.                              495

*Fin.* Wha, wha, what doe you court them?

*Trim.* Hold your tongue, or I'le ſtop up your bung hole
                                          {*ſtops her mouth.*

*Fin.* You are miſta- ken- mis- taken, taken taken, let me alone, they are.

*Trim.* Peace blatant Beaſt.                                         500

*Vap.* Now, now Sir let her alone.

*Isa.* Stand ſtill; never such sport.

*Fin.* Stinking, scurvy, impudent Jackanapes, I had a tooth that was in some measure loose, and o' my conscience the raskall has thruſt it down my throat.                                       505

*Slan.* But what's the matter Miſtress? why miſtaken?

*Fin.* Nay tis gon down, and let it e'en go, and gnaw its way out; I care not if I were dead.

*Vap.* But what's the matter

*Fin.* You are bewitchd, abusd, betrayd, cheated, foold, fubd        510
cozend by that rogue, cheat, pimp, wash ball, cittern-fac'd slave.

*Vap.* But how? what do they all laugh at so          {*all laugh.*

*Fin.* Laugh at; they may laugh well enough, you have made love all this while to the shavers baſtards—the others are the heirs: O; o, o, I shall run mad.          *exeunt* Mrs. Finical *and* Trim    515

*Wor.* She roars ſtatelely                              {*all laugh*

*Vap.* Tom.

*Slan.* Jack.

*Vap.* We are undon.

*Slan.* I dare no more look behind me, then a pursued Cutpurse.      520

*Vap.* What's to be don Tom? I do not use to be out of countenance, when I have got a cup in my pate.

*Wor.* The counsell is disorderd.

*Isa.* No doubt the debate is weighty.

*Slan.* To be now forsaken of impudence, when tis so needfull.      525

*Luc.* Ladies, tis time to relieve us.

*Isa.* Come Phil wee'l advance—            ⎰ *to Worthy*
nay, nay you muſt continue upon duty.      ⎱ *and Lovetruth.*

*Phi.* Or you shall be disbanded, if you mutiny.

*Isa.* Save you noble Galants, why so confusd? miſtake's no rob-      530
bery.

*Phi.* Ignorance excuses great offences.

*Vap.* Tom all's well, they are smitten for all this, lets be confident.                                                      {*aside*

*Slan.* Why faith Madam we love divertisments, we complyd      535
with your designe.

*Isa.* How?

*Vap.* Why Ladies I warrant, you think we were miſtaken; confesse now—did you not think that we had miſtook you ha, ha, ha.

*S.* Were you so deceivd? now faith speak ha, ha.                540

*Isa.* Hey day.

*Phi.* Now for some back-hand lyes.

*Vap.* Why Ladies then—S'life Tom, what shall we say? thou wert
wont to be witty.

*Slan.* Why swear twas—                                          545

*Vap.* Ladies, I swear twas—what Tom?

*Slan.* Why that—S'life, I know not what.

*Isa.* The Galants are in labour.

*Phi.* And will be deliverd of luſty lyes, and all twins.

*Wor.* May we march now?                                         550

*Isa.* Not a foot.

*Lov.* Wou'd I were in the Stocks, to excuse my patience.

*Phil.* Your love will not doe it, it seems.

*Vap.* Why Tom let us swear, it was to trye—to try

*Slan.* Their humours Jack.                                      555

*Vap.* Gramercy Tom—well Ladies I warrant you have bin
ghessing; faith we gave you a litle time: but since you cannot, we'l

tell you, ne'r ſtir we did it to trye your humors, Tom and I laid the designe.

*Slan.* I really Ladies twas our device, we beg your pardon for 560 our seeming rudenes, but we doat upon good humor.

*Luc.* Now they lie backward.

*Vap.* Troth Ladies you ought to pardon us, mariage is a knot for ever; and it ought to be tyed with circumspeƈtion.

*Phi.* Why pray Gentlemen whom are you to marry? 565

*Isa.* Let us see the Ladies, and give our opinions.

*Vap.* Tom, the poor Souls are jealous— {*aside* Why dear ladies, we'l wait upon you to your lookinglasses, and there you shall looke, and see their divine images.

*Slan.* The saints, we pray to 570

*Isa.* Nay, no hand upon't

*Phi.* Tis not so near a bargain

*Wor.* Lovetruth, we will advance, though we are disbanded.

*Luc.* Kate, how pale our Galants look. {*aside*

*Wor.* Stand off, fine gay nothings—I take it, you gave us leave 575 to court these Ladies.

*Lov.* Nor did we abuse your goodnes, we told 'em all truth.

*Isa.* We are apt to think so

*Phi.* Nay we'l be depoſd on't, to the beſt of our knowlege.

*Vap.* What might the famous truths, you told be? 580

*Wor.* One was, that you were raskals.

*Isa.* Yes, that was one, we'l be juſt.

*Lov.* The other was, that you durſt not fight.

*Phi.* Twas so I remember very well; nay we'l be juſt to you.

*Vap.* Poor fellows you are dead men for this. 585

*Phi.* Then ring their knells, ding, dong, bell.

*Slan.* You'l give us satisfaƈtion. {*as in secret.*

*Vap.* We'l have it Sir; yes we will.

*Wor.* O sir, you are he, that with a glasse in your pate fancy yourself Heƈtor, and once an hour defend Troy ten years at a time. 590

*Lov.* And you Sir suck toads, and spiders, and with your poysonous breath talk of honeſt men, and women.

*Vap.* Ladies, we laugh at these fellows; when we have the honor to catch 'em out of your sight, no more but so.

*Wor.* Why t'wil be no more but so; Such moths, as you are, 595 should be ſtifled, that eat as faſt into the fame of honeſt and brave minds, as the others into a cloth bed

*Vap.* Tom. {*whispers*

*Slan.* Enough.
*Vap.* Gentlemen a word.                                                    600
*Phi.* A quarrel on my life; I am afraid Sister.
*Isa.* Pish Phil lets never love such men, that will feare such
butterflies can hurt.
*Lov.* Be punctual, and doe not fool us                        {*aside*
*Vap.* We'l be there before you.                                          605
*Wor.* Shall I bring a cudgell, for feare you should be squeamish
at a sword.
*Vap.* By this hand, which I kisse in fury, we'l be reveng'd.
*Slan.* And speedily.
*Love.* Nay if you be so furious, shall we bring a wench to   610
entertain you before you begin.
*Vap.* Tis well: come Tom—follow us if you dare.

*Enter* Sir Richard *and meets 'em.*

*Sir R.* How now, what are you?
*Vap.* Persons Sir, that have a value for your daughters.
*Slan.* We should be proud Sir.                                          615
*Sir R.* Y'are proud enough of all conscience—depart good,
fine, perfumd Gentlemen; They are too plaine for such holyday
outsides.
*Vap.* I but Sir.
*Sir R.* No but Sir                                                          620
*Slan.* Be pleasd Sir.
*Sir R.* I am not pleasd, nor will not be pleasd, without you'l be
pleasd Sir.
*Vap.* We shall be happy.
*Sir R.* So shall I sir, if you'l begon Sir.                              625
*Sla.* This strange rudenes.
*Vap.* Well Sir at this time some affaires call for us. You re-
member Gentlemen—
*Wor.* Trust our memories Sir, for we have but litle wit.
                                        {*exit* Vapor *and* Slander.
*Sir Rich.* Why, how now Daughters, are these your suitors?   630
*Isa.* In a manner Sir.
*Sir R.* Pray be plain forsooth.
*Phi.* There was but a litle mistake betwixt us and home.
*Sir R.* Heyday, what ridle is this?
*Wor.* Why Sir your daughters by honest Mr Trim being in-   635
formd of the approach of these two glorious suitors; for fear of

their being dazled, interposd Mr Trims fair daughters between
them, and their brightnes, and they have bin courted, and courted
with such flames and such devotions, as was fit for such rich
heires.                                                                                          640
   *Sir R.* Is this truth?
   *Lov.* Yes, and the plain truth.
   *Sir R.* Ha my Girles, my own Girles, my own honeſt true countrey Girles, come hither and hug me, hug me agen: have you han-
dled your puppets so neatly?                                                                 645
   *Wor.* The ſtory Sir is worth hearing.
   *Sir R.* And we'l have it at my chamber over a bottle.

*Enter* Trim.

ha Trim, my honeſt Trim, I bound thee Trim and I found thee
faſt Trim.
   *Trim.* What's the matter now?                                          650
   *Sir R.* Come along with me Trim, fetch out some sparkling
canary and some smiling ale: we'l drink the girles, the victorious
girles health; come Gentlemen, we'l be merry Trim, and drink thy
girles health too; they are the rich heirs Trim, ha ha ha.
   *Trim.* Now I find it.      *Exeunt* Sir Richard *and* Trim.   655
   *Wor.* So there's your fine suitors condemd—but whats our
sentence?
   *Isa.* Ask our father.
   *Wor.* But if he should deny us.
   *Phi.* What should we doe then?                                         660
   *Lov.* Why, you may chuse whether it shall be put to the venture,
or no.
   *Wor.* Now I think on't Lovetruth we'l ask no more queſtions,
then needs muſt.
   *Isa.* You are afraid you shall be denyed                           665
   *Wo.* And you two may be—but I have another more sober rea-
son, why we will not ask him.
   *Isa.* That I would know, give eare siſter.
   *Wor.* Why if the old Gentleman should cry—no—these two
fine raskals had not courage enough to cut our throats.               670
   *Lov.* And then shall not we tell how to dye hansomly.
   *Isa.* Umh, that was a bug's word; d'heare Gentlemen, tis well
remembred: you shan't fight.
   *Phi.* Not a passe; we shall be in the news books.
   *Wo.* Why then we wont ask your father.                            675

*Isa.* Choose.

*Lov.* You might tell us, if you wou'd.

*Phi.* Come Sister our father will misse us.

*Isa.* Come Mistress Lucy and Kate we ask your pardon for the trouble you have received. 680

*Luc.* We rather thank your Ladyships for our share in the sport.

*Wor.* And shall we part thus?

*Lov.* But one kind word.

*Wo.* Or a speaking look. 685

*Isa.* Nay, if you are so reasonable, have at you, come Sister, lets give 'em looks apeece. {*they look at 'em*}

*Wor.* Umh, so it goes through and through; Lovetruth prithee look behind me, and see where the look comes out.

*Lov.* No man, tis but got to thy heart yet—and now. 690

*Phi.* Nay, if you encroach.

*Wor.* Nay sweet Gentlewomen lend us but these hands a litle—dear worthy Ladies.

*Lov.* Best of women.

*Isa.* Fy, fy you spoyle our Gloves. 695

*Wor:*   Upon these premises we'l kisse for ever,
       and signe, and seal, and seale till you deliver.

*kisse their hands at each word*

*Finis Aɛtus Tertij*

## Aɛt: 4  Scene: i.

### Isabella, Philadelphia.

*Isa.* Thou lovst revenge Phil.

*Phi.* I were no woman else.

*Isa.* They are not worth it.

*Phi.* As much to say, a man may be so bad, that he's not worth the hanging. 5

*Isa.* Nay, the raskals are bad enough.

*Phi.* But yet we have not usd 'em bad enough; there's my trouble.

*Isa.* Lets but resolve we will use 'em scurvily; and trust to a womans wit to help us, that never fails at a mischievous designe. 10

*Phi.* To be rayld at by such slaves; such belyars of themselvs and all others.

*Isa.* Rogues, that proſtrate all women to their imaginations.

*Phi.* Slaves, that can't counterfeit honeſt men.

*Isa.* And yet tractable apes of the worſt sort of men.          15

*Enter* Lucy *and* Kate

O my rich heirs, how fare you?

*Luc.* Well Ladies, we were ever true friends.

*Phi.* By my life our noble seconds, who thruſt your smal vessels between us and the fireships moſt kindly: would we could do you as good a turn.          20

*Kat.* Alas, my father designs to bury us alive.

*Isa.* Forefend Wench!

*Lu.* He had as good, as marry us to two such grave fellows: we muſt never smile agen.

*Kat.* If we do, we muſt ſteal a laugh, as carefully as a shrewd   25
turne.

*Isa.* Come, come t'wil doe well enough: they'l cheat others, and you may cousen them.

*Enter* Trim.

*Trim.* My beſt Ladies, be pleasd to retire: my grave Knights are ready to approach; and Lucy and Kate muſt once more be the   30
rich heyresses.

*Isa.* Nay Mr Trim we'l ſtay, and see some sport, and behave ourselvs as formerly before the other coxcombs.

*Trim.* Nay good Ladies by no means: Trims hopes lye at ſtake; it may not passe so well upon the grave.          35

*Isa.* Nay, prithee Trim lets see their formal wisdoms play their tricks too.

*Phi.* Good Trim let us; 'twil be excelent diversion, and full of variety to see apes dance firſt, and Elephants caper after.

*Trim.* Nay Ladies, as ever you'l do good to Trim, retire.          40

*Luc.* Troth Ladies you ought to ſtay, and ſtand for us now.

*Enter* Finicall

*Fin.* Are you there, you treacherous Varlet?

*Isa.* We shall see some sport yet.

*Trim.* Why what's the matter my sweet Walloon, bordering upon a Frenchifyd Lady?          45

*Fin.* Sirrah look to'ot; I may chance spoyle your designs, or intrigues to speak more intelligibly.

*Trim.* How's that?

*Fin.* Yes sirrah, Ile shave you yfaith.

*Trim.* Ladies, I am undon if you do not ſtick to me          {*aside*          50

*Fin.* Your grave Gentlemen are attending: I'le do your buisnes treacherous snapfinger.

*Trim.* Ladies, own me for a friend to the Gallants, or I am ruind          {*aside*

*Isa.* Nay, and more too—but for our own designs.          55

*Fin.* Playing double Jackanapes?

*Trim.* Why Mrs Finicall, now your choler is a litle vented, hearken to your miſtake: I was dealing with these Ladies for your friends, and more then that—heare me          {*whispers*

*Fin.* How shall I believe thee? thou art as slippery, as one of          60
thy washbals.

*Trim.* Nay, let the Ladies speak for my part, if I am thus rewarded for my honeſt care—

*Isa.* Mrs Finical you may believe him, he hath bin assiduary in the service of Mr Vapor, and Mr Slander, and not unsuccesfully          65
neither; I blush to say so; but in an honeſt mans vindication tis no shame.

*Fin.* Your Ladyship overjoyes me I swear; I dare say it with much assurance they are the sweeteſt, fineſt, jentieſt Bo-garsons that do illuſtrat this age.          70

*Isa.* Well Miſtress Finicall, since you know so much, I shall not scruple to tell you, you may find 'em out, if you please, and if you say we are not unwilling to see 'em, you shal not be chid.

*Fin.* I fly sweet Ladies: Mr Trim I ask your pardon for this grand miſtake          {*exit*          75

*Trim.* The grand pox take thee: Ladies may never wish of yours grow cold before tis fulfild. D'yee hear Girles?

                                        {*whispers to his daughters.*

*Phi.* What did you mean Siſter, to invite these raskals.

*Isa.* Alas! the quarrell came juſt then into my head, and I employd her bu-si-nes to try to ſtop some of 'em.          80

*Ph.* O me, I underſtand you.

*Isa.* Mr Trim, did you see Mr Worthy and Mr Lovetruth?

*Trim.* They are gon forth Madam.

*Isa.* How Phil! what shall we do? gon to fight as sure as we live.

*Phi.* If those Rogues should dare fight!          85

*Isa.* Lets send after 'em.

*Phi.* But how, if we cant find 'em?

*Isa.* Then we'l go cry by ourselvs. 　　　　　 {*exeunt*

*Trim.* They are gon in some disorder.

*Luc.* You may guesse the Gentlemen. 　　　　　90

*Trim.* Nay if that be all, good fortun and a Prieſt send 'em to a proper place. Now Girles be witty, and knit up matters, appoint time and place, and me to provide the Prieſt, take right aym, whilſt I fetch the markes 　　　　　 {*exit*

*Luc.* Since it muſt be so Kate, who can help it? 　　　　　95

*Kat.* Did ever we think to turn honorable?

*Luc.* When we quarter our Coat with their honors, I think it muſt be three razors rampant, and three washbals argent in a field sables.

*Kat.* They'l have pretty hansome conveniencies with us, if not 　　100 portions: in the firſt place they'l be trimd for nothing.

*Luc.* If they be'nt ashamd to be trimd, after they have askt blessing.

*Enter* Trim *whispering with* Sir Cautious Trouble-all
*and* Sir Gravity Empty.

*Kat.* Peace, they come, and whispering with their Lord father.

*Trim.* Your honors may perceive how carefull I have bin: I 　　105 have removd all scruples: the way is plain, and to tell you true, the country Ladies do so long to be complemented, and are so tickled that the men of buisnes will addresse, and bow, and cringe to them, and present, or so, that there's nothing wanting but the Prieſt. 　　　　　110

*Caut.* And that Mr Trim I will counsell you, how to contrive.

*Emp.* Yes Mr Trim, you shal receive counsell, which may improve you.

*Trim.* For that Sir I am prepard, and the church yard joynes to the back door; every thing shall be ready; and the Parson has a 　　115 swift trowling voice, that in a trice will chop up the matter; nay your honors shall see how Ile prepare the Ladies.

　　　　　 {*ſteps to the Ladies*
Sweet Ladies tis but a blush the more, the Parson shall be ready, and the back door open to let you into hapines.

*Luc.* I but so suddenly Mr Trim. 　　　　　120

*Trim.* Why can you make too much haſt to be happy? why its true, you have great eſtats, and they honor, let 'em meet, let 'em meet; hang formal delay.

*Kate.* But if—

*Trim.* But pish—your honors may venture, there's nothing to     125
be removd, but a But, and an If.                          <*exit* Trim>

*Cau.* Ladies, we are friends and have bin succesfull in many intrigues, and doubt not, but we shall in this: Persons of buisnes will
honor you, and make their way by you, and all will eſtime you
for disposing your selvs to sober—                             130

*Empt.* O sobriety carries a great ſtroke—y gad all in all.

*Luc.* But Sir we are scarce acquainted with you.

*Cau.* Why Ladies, fame hath brought us acquainted, there's an
answer as to that.

*Emp.* Why thus Ladies, we use to answer matters, as matters     135
happen to ſtart up before us; and Ile warrant fame has bin pratling
of us, Ile warrant you.

*Kat.* Indeed we have heard much of you.

*Emp.* O have you so Ladies? and yet not acquainted with us?
that's very good yfaith; there we caught you.                  140

*Lucy.* —Yet—                                          {*sighs*

*Cau.* What d'you sigh for Lady?

*Luc.* For fear Sir:—Women have bin abusd.

*Caut.* Never Lady by men of sobriety, and buisnes, but by
light fellows such as Vapor and Slander: we beseech you Madam,    145
give us leave to call in Mr Trim, and let him take order to make
us fortunat as to you, and to ourselvs.

*Emp.* Fortunat on all sides, or y'gad I would not give a pin
for't.

*Enter* Trim *haſtily.*

*Trim.* Dispatch, dispatch; Sir Richard, Sir Richard—speak     150
quickly, is it don? is it don?

*Cau.* Sweet Ladies believe us and speak, for buisnes lyes in a
word.

*Luc.* I am ashamd to say—

*Trim.* What? speak out.                                  155

*Luc.* Nay Mr Trim you are such a man: do you speak siſter.

*Kat.* Nay indeed you are the eldeſt siſter.

*Trim.* Come, come, kisse their hands, and seal the bargain.

*Luc.* Fye Mr Trim.

*Kat.* You make us ashamd.                               160

*Cau.* Thus with our hands Ladies we seal our hearts ⎰ *kisse their*
*Emp.* Ygad hearts and hands all go together         ⎱ *hands.*

*Luc.* Well, well.

*Emp.* Twill be as well as your Sister sayes, I warrant you Mistresse. 165

*Kat.* Away, away you men are such things.

*Trim.* So, so all's well, go in Ladies least we be discoverd.

*{exeunt* Lucy *and* Kate

*Cau.* Now honest Trim Speak to thy self preferment.

*Emp.* Yes Mr Trim, you shall have a place certainly, we never faile. 170

*Caut.* But what must we do? is Sir Richard coming?

*Trim.* No, no twas but a trick of mine; for I knew, when the Ladies were driven to a pinch, they would declare like a shop keeper who when his customer is departing tells his lowest price.

*Caut.* Excelent Trim. 175

*Trim.* But however now begon, and stay at the lodging I shewd you over against the Church; and let me alone to bring to the rendevouz the licence, Priest, and Ladies; so farewell.

*Caut.* Yes, there we'l stay, and pray put the Ladies in mind, we are men of buisnes, and desire 'em to make hast. 180

*Emp.* I, I make hast, that we may dispatch

*{exit* Cautious *and* Empty.

*Trim.* Farewell to—your sharpsighted honors, I cannot chuse but smile to think how gravely their honors will look upon their Brides, when they know them to be the issues of Roger Trim.

*Enter* Isabella *and* Philadelphia *sad.*

Why how now my sweet pretty Ladies—what melancholy? did ever 185 Trim think he should live to see you sad: why what's the matter?

*Isa.* Nay, no great matter Trim, but—

*Trim.* But what? dare you not trust me?

*Phil.* Nay tis no great matter.

*Trim.* Why then you may the easier tell it. 190

*Isa.* This fighting may bring our names in question.

*Phi.* Yes indeed, the Gentlemen are not to be heard of.

*Trim.* O, is this the matter? sits the wind there about? why Ladies are you afraid that such galant fellows as Mr Worthy, and Lovetruth are to be hurt by flye-blowes. 195

*Isa.* Nay we are not afraid of any in particular—but of—

*Trim.* But of those two; come n'er blush for the matter; they deservd to be lovd; they hurt by such things as onely look like men by the help of me and Frisk theyr Taylor?

*Phi.* But you are mistaken Trim. 200

*Trim.* But I am not mistaken, nor will not be mistaken; yet I'le

get two licences ready; and the Parson will be piping hot, for he
will be ready warmd upon my service.

*Isa.* Nay, fye Trim.

*Trim.* That fye may be better beſtowd: Ladies I muſt leave     205
you a litle I shal be happy for ever so; and you shall be happy; so:
Ile but order matters, and make my appearance in a trice

{*exit* Trim

*Isa.* But if these Rogues should hurt 'em basely?

*Phi.* Or murder 'em?

*Isa.* By all that's good we'd revenge 'em.     210

*Ph.* Prithee how?

*Isa.* Why, I would bribe a Jury to hang one, though 'twere with
my eſtate.

*Phi.* And I'de hang tother, though I marryd the foreman o'nt.

*Enter* Vapor *and* Slaunder *laughing.*

*Isa.* How now? hey day.     215

*Phi.* The jeſt my merry men all?

*Vap.* Now, w'oud I may never ſtir Ladies: ha, ha     {*laughs*

*Sla.* Your pardon dear Ladies.

*Isa.* Why Gentlemen, are you to laugh for a wager?

*Phi.* And I warrant, we are to judge, whom it becoms beſt.     220

*Vap.* Really Ladies we ask your pardon, but it was so pretty an
accident, I swear I cant tell it without laughing     ha, ha, prithee
Tom tell it     ha, ha.

*Sla.* As I live Jack I have laughd so much, that I have scarce
breath     ha, ha.     225

*Vap.* Nay faith Tom you shall help.

*Isa.* Pray Gentlemen if it be so pretty tell it us in parts.

*Sla.* N'er ſtir Jack tis wittily thought on.

*Phi.* Come then, begin in a right key.

*Vap.* You know Ladies, there paſt some certain whispers ha ha ha.     230

*Isa.* Now Sir you should answer in a base voice ha ha ha.

*Phi.* Begin agen good Treble.

*Vap.* Nay Ladies, you interrupt us.

*Isa.* Peace Siſter.

*Vap.* Why as I was a saying, according to the cuſtom of such     235
whispers, we agreed to fight.

*Sla.* And a place was appointed.

*Vap.* And as I was going along, a fancy came into my head,
that these were pittiful fellows; Sayes I Tom—

*Sla.* No Jack, tw'as I said Jack.     240

*Vap.* By your pardon Tom.

*Sla.* By your favor twas I said Jack, by the same token, 'twas at the backside of the red Lyon in Holburn; I muſt not be over born Jack.

*Vap.* And I as litle as any man Tom; I ſtand to'ot, that 'twas I 245 said Tom, when we came in sight of Lambs Conduit.

*Sla.* I grant you that Jack, when we came to Lambs conduit.

*Isa.* We rejoyce Gentlemen at this right underſtanding.

*Vap.* Madam, honor is jealous, but by this you may perceive that Lambs conduit was the place appointed: I cannot hold laugh 250 ing      ha, ha prithee Tom speak      ha ha.

*Sla.* Why being there Ladies and walking a long time up and down, and beginning to suspeƈt the Gentlemen were full of peace upon second thoughts, upon a suddain—really I cannot speak for Laughing      ha, ha, help Jack      ha, ha, ha. 255

*Vap.* We saw two peep out of a ditch, and perceived they were our enemies but—      ha, ha, ha,      help me Tom

*Sla.* As soon as they spyd us they fell a running with such speed, that I shall dye with laughing.

*Isa.* Why, what needed they to have come thither? 260

*Vap.* O Madam tis common, very common: some to get a name, wil get a quarrell, and hide by the appointed place, till the enemy is gon, and then appear, or if he do'nt come swear out his own reputation.

*Phi.* Upon my life these two raskals have bin at this hide and 265 seek, and lay their baſtard-fears to wrong Fathers.      {*aside*

*Isa.* And what's becom of your enemies?

*Vap.* Why Madam, since they dare not fight with English Gentlemen, I suppose they'l match themselvs with Irish footmen ha ha ha; for they are damd fleet. 270

*Sla.* Faith Jack that was witty.

*Enter* Worthy *and* Lovetruth *whilſt they are laughing.*

*Isa.* Now Phil for a ſtorm, the clouds gather.

*Wor.* So merry Gentlemen?

*Lov.* Whats here, a puppet play?

*Phil.* They begin to fall to signes. 275

*Isa.* We shall have ſtill musique.

*Sla.* Jack, what's to be don?

*Vap.* Take no notice Tom, but salute 'em and creep away; Ladies we kiss your hands: Gentlemen your servants.

*{sing going out in a coranto movement*

*Sla.* Your Servant Ladies.                                              280

*Wor.* Nay, my fine Gentlemen a word I beseech you.

*Vap.* Well Sir, your buisnes.

*Lov.* Nay Sir, you muſt to the book too.

*Isa.* How they look Phil like lewd prentices cald for the
accompt of the Cash by sowr maſters                    *{aside*   285

*Sla.* Well Sir, the matter, we have buisnes.

*Wor.* You shall have more, pray what discourse have you had
with these Ladies.

*Vap.* That's very pretty yfaith: your servants, your servants.

*Wor.* Stir a foot, and you shall be ſtrangled in your own ribands.   290

*Isa.* Slid, we'l tell em Phil, second me in my way          *{aside*
why Gentlemen, we dare own, what they said to us.

*Wor.* How's this?

*Phi.* We do not fear who knows, what we permit to be said to us.

*Lov.* Hey-day                                                         295

*Vap.* Cheer up Tom: *{aside}* by all that's good you ought to be
adord.

*Sla.* Realy your juſtice is as sublime as your beauty.

*Isa.* The matter's not much Gentlemen; tis only that—

*Vap.* Nay Madam, Ile swear you'l injure yourselvs to give such   300
fellows the leaſt satisfaction.

*Phi.* I, but for our own honors.

*Sla.* Pish, despise 'em, Ile tell your Ladyship a pretty jeſt.

*Isa.* Nay, nay they shall know it: why Gentlemen these Galants
waited for you at the appointed place with their swords.        305

*Phi.* And you made a passe with your heels.

*Lov.* Was this the Romance of your adventures Gentlemen?

*Wor.* Pretty raskals; scavengers of lyes; do you come to lay down
your filth here?

*Vap.* A Ladies chamber is no place.                                   310

*Sla.* No, that's your protection.

*Lov.* If you urge us, it sh'ant be yours Raskall.

*Wor.* I have thought of an expedient, Lovetruth (since we muſt
not violat the sanctuary of a Ladies chamber) for I have not a farthing worth of patience left about me. S'life the rogues smile: I   315
heard of some Baylifs, that not daring to arreſt a man in Grays
inn walks, toſt him over the wall, and arreſted him on tother side,
and so prithee lets thruſt the rogues out of the room, and cut their
throats without.

*Lov.* A reasonable motion, come.                                    320

*Isa.* Hold: why, how now Gentlemen, are you angry?

*Wor.* If your Ladyship will please to give us leave, we are very angry.

*Isa.* At what?

*Wor.* At lyes.                                                      325

*Isa.* What lyes?

*Wor.* At those, that were told you by these Mandrakes, things gotten by hangmen.

*Vap.* Ha, ha Madam we despise 'em, and therfore we are not concernd.                                                            330

*Sla.* Not we faith                                        {*sings.*

*Wor.* Why d'hear you brace of impudences? did we not find you two in a ditch? and did you not rouze like frightd deer?

*Lov.* And did not you make your ribands fly like ſtreamers on a ship under sayle.                                                   335

*Wor.* And did you tell your own shames under our names?

*Vap.* Ha, ha Tom didſt ever hear the like?

*Wor.* Wonderfull impudence! what thinks your Ladyship of these Knights errant.

*Isa.* Think Sir? why we think that you injure them, I judge,       340
as I should, of a cause never the better for a crosse Bill.

*Phi.* A Parrat ſtory, juſt as you are taught.

*Vap.* Now, wou'd I may ne'er ſtir, if nature ever framed such generous persons

*Wor.* Why, tis well: what rogues were we to love these women    345
that like outsides.

*Lov.* And to pay devotion to those that believe in lyes.

*Isa.* And why muſt we believe in you Gentlemen, sooner then in persons bred in the Nurseries of honor.

*Phi.* And who in the higheſt sphear of breeding have bin lights    350
to others.

*Isa.* Who underſtand punɛtilios.

*Wor.* Good.

*Phi.* And weigh their breath

*Lov.* Excellent.                                                   355

*Isa.* Know Grandeur.

*Phi.* Underſtand equipage.

*Isa.* The beſt essences.

*Phi.* The choiceſt powders.

*Isa.* To match ribands.                                            360

*Phi.* Mount feathers.

*Isa.* Make legs.

*Phi.* Kisse the Ladies litle dogs.

*Isa.* Dance.

*Phi.* Sing.                                                                    365

*Wor.* Dissemble, swear, jeer, lie, theeve, hang—I shall be mad: come Lovetruth; Ladies your servants: we are the cowards, damd cowards, and fools too, damd fools.

*Vap.* Truth will out Tom; they confesse, and we forgive 'em.

*Sla.* I, I Jack, moſt divine Ladies really Jack.                                370

*Isa.* Nay, nay Gentlemen: you have a pretty good repute in your countrey; but it may be twas only for thumping it at Cudgels; or fighting with Keepers at QuarterStaff; but sharpes is another matter I promis you.

*Phi.* And a rapier with a nimble french thruſt La, la.                           375

*Wor.* Its very true Ladies; and any thing els is true that you have a mind to say, and as true as any thing these Gentlemen ever did say, or ever will say. So farewell Kind Ladies.

*Isa.* Nay, pray ſtay, it may be you may be wrongd.

*Phi.* Tis possible.                                                             380

*Isa.* By my troth now tis againſt Magna Charta not to bring an Englishman to a faire Tryall.

*Vap.* Tom, these are witches.

*Sla.* Wou'd we were in the ditch agen.                            {*aside*

*Isa.* Come Gentlemen, for matter of faƈt?                                        385

*Wor.* What turn now?

*Isa.* We'l lend you our chamber for the ſtage; Come for the Prize.

*Phi.* Nay to'ot Gentlemen, out with your direful ſteels, your rods of correƈtion.                                                        390

*Vap.* What does your Ladyship mean?

*Isa.* Why that you should fight: draw Gentlemen: we have bin usd to see bloud; not a feaſt at our Town, but there are abundance of bloudy skonces.

*Wor.* Be but so good as to tell us honeſtly, don't you abuse us?                 395

*Lov.* Speak quickly.

*Isa.* Upon our words we d'ont

*Wor.* Lovetruth, kisse their feet quickly, and to our matters,
Come my perfumd ſtinkards, as to try the title of the ditch {*draw*

*Lov.* Dispatch, or—                                                            400

*Vap.* What in a Lady's chamber? pretty breeding yfaith.

*Isa.* Nay Sir, we give leave.

*Phi.* Nay, I beseech you Gentlemen be not so modeſt.

*Sla.* Really Madam not in your chamber for a world.

*Isa.* But Sir t'woud be an obligation by way of diversion to     405
your injurd Miſtresses, a pass or two for our sakes.

*Vap.* Really Madam neither Tom nor I have our pumps here,
and we are so usd to fence in 'em, that it were a dishonorable
disadvantage: To shew you now realy, there is no loonging in high
heel shoes                                          {*try to loong*   410

*Wor.* Lovetruth, lets break their legs, that they may be carryd
about no more by those rotten engines.

*Isa.* Stay Gentlemen, no more, they are unmasqut; and your
honor preservd by us, that ever did eſtime it.

*Wor.* Lovetruth, lets kisse their hands.                        415

*Lov.* And never let them go.

*Phi.* But what shall the Gentlemen do the while?

*Wor.* Well remembred Lady, why as we found 'em so we'l
leave 'em. Come Gentlemen to your To—roy—

*Vap.* Why, if it be in complaisance to shew you the movement   420
of a Courant, we are not nice; come Tom—

*Lov.* Nay come Gentlemen, bee not so long a ſtarting.

*Sla.* Nay faith we love a Frolique come Jack—

*Wor.* And as you tender your shin bones, give not over, till the
Ladies permit you.                                               425

*Vap.* I, I we shall be so civill.

*Enter* Sir Richard *as they dance and sing.*

*Sir R.* How now! whats here to do? hey, hey one follow tother;
what here's Chicken a Chicken a trayn-tro.

*Wo.* We came but juſt in Sir as you did.

*Isa.* Enough Gentlemen.                    {Isabella *ſteps to him.*   430

*Vap.* Your Ladyships servant.                    {*as out of wind.*

*Wor.* I hope they have crackt their winds.

*Sir R.* Pray Gentlemen, what exercise was this?

*Sla.* Dancing Sir.

*Sir R.* Do you cal this dancing To—roy—To—roy              435
                                           {Sir Richard *imitates.*

*Vap. and Sla.* Ladies, your servants.

*Sir R.* Dancing with all my heart: pray ſtay a litle Gentlemen;
without there; cal my beef eating ſlaves, to dance their Chriſtmas
gambol, dispatch—Tis an imitation of foot ball playing; twas an

exercise that in my time I have lovd, and given many a tall fellow    440
the trip upon the Go-by-hey: an ingenious servant of mine, and
a good foot bal-player one Chriſtmas presented my old exercise in
a Dance: come away with it nimbly.

*The Dance*

*Sir R.* Now my fine Galants, how do you like it?
*Vap.* Why it would serve in the dull countrey, but here it    445
would seem ridicule.
*Sir R.* Ridicule! as I take it that's a plain word finely spoild:
troth Gentlemen, wee had beſt part, for I see our diversions can-
not please one another.
*Vap. Sla.* Your servants.                                           450
*Sir R.* Nay pray Gentlemen in your To-roy, to-roy.
*Wor.* You hear Gentlemen.
*Vap.* Well, well To-roy, To-roy.                    *{they go out kickt*
*Wor.* Lovetruth the rising kick.
*Sir R.* Pray Ladies, what's the meaning of all this?                455
*Wor.* If you please Sir, in the parlor you shall have all the
ſtory; your Daughters have made coxcombs of 'em once more.
*Sir R.* Then once more come hug me Girles; come lets go in
and hear the ſtory: prithee Girle, think of somthing, that I may
give you.                                                            460
*Isa.* We want nothing Sir.
*Sir R.* Did I think I should ever so much as smile in this
Towne: come Gentlemen, one laughing bout more. I have something come from the Country, you shall see it, and taſt it, and
over it our Story                                    *{exeunt.*       465

*Enter* Trim *and puls back* Isabella *and* Philadelphia.

*Trim.* What mad work have you made Ladies?
*Isa.* How now man! why doſt thou look so ghoſtly? are the
beacons fird?
*Trim.* Yes, the chief is, Miſtress Finical flames out, set afire by
Vapor and Slander: she swears she'l be revengd, and tell your    470
father, you love Worthy and Lovetruth.
*Phi.* What shall we do?
*Isa.* This may be troublesome.
*Trim.* Come, come, dispatch matters: if you have a mind, you
underſtand me.                                                       475
*Isa.* But this jade may be quicker, then we can be.

*Phi.* Lets shut her up in the room, where she keeps cold meat.

*Isa.* Hang her, she'l rumble there like an earthquake. {*she ſtudyes*} I have it—go you and tell Miſtress Finical I ſtay to speak with her, quickly man.                                                        480

*Trim.* And what then?

*Isa.* Trouble not yourself, you shall have notice how to aĉt your part—nay begon, tell her tis earneſt buisnes.

*Trim.* Well, I goe—The Parson is at hand.

*Isa.* Well, well                                        {*exit* Trim    485

*Phi.* Now Siſter, whats your Plot?

*Isa.* Why we muſt collogue with this Finical, and pretend to have these raskals, or she may spoyle—

*Phi.* What?

*Isa.* A buisnes I suspeĉt you have a mind to.                      490

*Phi.* And not you?

*Isa.* Nay, I'le do as thou doſt: in plain English shall we venture upon 'em.

*Phi.* If ever trafique with a man, we muſt venture.

*Isa.* And better with these, then others.                          495

*Phi.* Mariage is a long voyage.

*Isa.* And apt for ſtorms; but thither we are bound,
we are not reveng'd enough; hark you Phil.              {*whispers*

*Phi.* I underſtand you.

*Isa.* Be ready, and now withdraw befor Finicall appears.          500

Enter Finical.

she comes; vanish.                              {*exit* Philadelphia.

*Fin.* Did you send to speak with me Madam?

*Isa.* I did Miſtress Finicall.

*Fin.* What may your pleasure be?

*Isa.* Why, I am so ashamd.                                    505

*Fin.* Perhaps you may have reason.

*Isa.* I wou'd desire—I doe so blush.

*Fin.* Tis not an ill signe; the heart will speak—
I have found her                                          {*aside*

*Isa.* Pray do you know where Mr Vapor is?                      510

*Fin.* Why d'yee ask?

*Isa.* I wou'd be willing to speak with him.

*Fin.* I swear Madam I cannot be a person that ought to pretend to underſtand friendship, but I muſt assure your Ladyship, hee's full of resentments, and his friend too.                      515

*Isa.* But—

*Fin.* Nay Madam, no Buts—they know breeding, no more but so.

*Isa.* I believe it.

*Fin.* Whether you believe it, or no, I know it.                    520

*Isa.* But—

*Fin.* Nay, I'le tell you, there is no But in the case, the world allows 'em without a But for moſt accomplisht persons.

*Isa.* It may be, I think so too.

*Fin.* They care not for may be's: there's no may be's in the case    525 neither.

*Isa.* But pray hear me I desire but to speak one poor word with Mr Vapor.

*Fin.* I'le assure you he's highly incenſt; and I hold my self dis-oblig'd                    530

*Isa.* Nay, good sweet dear Land Lady.

*Fin.* Now you can give fine words: to put such an affront on persons of such value, such regard, such breeding, such parts, such bon mines.

*Isa.* We were forc't to do it, to conceal our inclinations for 'em,    535 since so contrary to my fathers humor.

*Fin.* May this be reality?

*Isa.* Help me but to speak with him, and I'le make him full reparations—if he loves me.

*Fin.* Nay, fy upon him; he loves you but too much: well tis    540 doubtfull, but Ile try what may be don, I have some influence.

*Isa.* I shall so long to hear from you: I'le requite you, dear honey, sweet Land Lady, I am so ashamd.          {*exit*

*Fin.* O the wind is changd; I did imagine such perfeƈtions muſt at laſt scatter charms.                    545

*Enter* Philadelphia.

Umh, here's tother Lady bird, as sure as I live sick of the same disease: I'le seem reservd.          {*she walks gravely*
I underſtand the manner of an intrigue.

*Phi.* Miſtress, Miſtress Finical.    {*Finical looks over her shoulder.*

*Fin.* Humh.                    550

*Phi.* I have a requeſt to you.

*Fin.* To me Lady? no, no, no sure I am too inconsiderable.

*Phi.* Nay Landlady, if you be unkind I shall cry.

*Fin.* Tis so: what's the buisnes that your Landladies now in

requeſt? I thought Mr Trim had bin the person: he's witty and   555
truſty.

*Phi.* Nay good Landlady, doe me but one kindnes.

*Fin.* Kindnes, what kindnes?

*Phi.* I would fain speak—

*Fin.* With Mr Slaunder—nay never blush.   560

*Phi.* And will you be so good?

*Fin.* Well, well get you in; I am good naturd, and be sure you
make him reparation

*Enter* Trim.

*Trim.* Miſtress your father cals earneſtly for you.

*Phi.* I go Mr Trim—        Remember        {*to* Finical   565

*Fin.* Pish, away—so fond        {*exit* Philadelphia.

*Trim.* Why how now Miſtress Finical? what privat with the
Ladies?

*Fin.* No crafty Mr Trim, you are the man, you are Hee.

*Trim.* Why that politique smile, or rather grin?   570

*Fin.* Get you about your buisnes neat Sir, there are fourpenny
cuſtomers wayting at your shop, or the fellow to grind old razors.

*Trim.* Very good, and I am thrown out of the Caball: tis well.

*Fin.* No good Mr Trim, you are for the honorable grave men
of matters, I am but a foolish woman that admire outsides.   575

*Trim.* And why that mump? has your Ladyship a thiſtle in
your chops.

*Fin.* No Sir Jackanapes, I compose my mouth to as much be-
seeming advantage, as the beſt woman in this, or the next parish.

*Trim.* Nay sure now you have a nettle under your tayle, you   580
winch so.

*Fin.* When I winch Sirrha it shal be to give you a kick o'th
chops, and beat out more teeth, then thou haſt drawn this
fort'night

*Trim.* Indeed—la?   585

*Fin.* Yes Sir, for as to that art your cuſtom is spoyld, ever since
you tyed a fellow by the tooth with a ſtring to the cieling, and
snatching away the ſtool made the beam draw it.

*Trim.* That, I take it, was the time, when you firſt ſtrook a
ground in these parts, and by two Pimps were given out for a rich   590
widow, till fame cracking by the weight of the matter, you were
reduc'd to let lodgings, to buy brown bread, small beere, and
lac'd pinners.

*Fin.* Sirrah, sirrah if I had not buisnes—

*Trim.* Nay, come Landlady, faith we'l be friends come—tell    595
me a litle—

*Fin.* I'le see thee hangd firſt: shift for thy self Varlet: tell
thee? ha, ha, ha: tell thee? ha, ha                              {*exit*

*Trim.* She's workt, finely workt; how I love these Ladies—twill
all do, my mind gives 'twill, and then Trim's made for ever; now  600
to my buisnes—and

   That I may see my matters how to handle,
   Come Hymen and light up thy farthing candle.

     *Aƈtus quarti finis.*


## Aƈt: 5. Scene 1.

*Enter* Isabella

*Isa.* No newes yet? sure I shall heare tidings: here Miſtress Finicall gravely direƈted me to wait my doom: she will be aƈtive sure,
for as soon as she had the commission, she fell a hunting like a
new uncoupled spaniell: Ile make use of a book, as if melancholy,
and to keep my self from laughing: now will we work these raskals    5
to forswear friends and Miſtresse, and yet make 'em think they
have us too—

    *Enter* Mrs Finicall.

*Fin.* How now sweet Lady, at your meditations? what melancholy?

*Isab.* Not very merry.                                             10

*Fin.* But how, if I cannot compass matters?

*Isa.* Then—

*Fin.* Come, come never despair: Ile produce one that shall help
your meditations.                                        {*exit* Finical

*Isa.* It takes.                                          {*reads*    15

   *Enter* Finical *with* Vapor

*Fin.* Now the God of love be propitious.       <*exit* Finical>

*Vap.* In your meditations Madam?

*Isa.* I was reading Sir Somthing of the power of love.

*Vap.* Madam, cou'd you read my heart, you might be there
better informd.                                                     20

*Isa.* I could hardly find there so much of its power: here 'tis said it overcoms all things.

*Vap.* By your pardon Madam, to give you an evidence what power it hath over me, it has overcome all my juſt sentiments for my laſt injury; since Miſtress Finical (by your permission) has    25
told me that so severe a treatment proceeded from your designe, not aversion.

*Isa.* Alas Sir, you know my father.

*Vap.* I do Madam, and pitty those severe chains he puts upon you: but by the crowning of my passions you may receive a happy    30
libertie

*Isa.* Alas Sir, you miſtake, my buisnes is not for my self.

*Vap.* How Madam! what d'yee mean?

*Isab.* Alas Sir, tis anothers concern, and not my own that gives me and you this trouble.    35

*Vap.* I beseech you Madam, be plain.

*Isa.* Why Sir, I will not abuse you, nor your patience: you have bin pleasd to profess a passion for me.

*Vap.* By all that's good Madam—

*Isa.* Nay, no oaths: hear me out: and your friend Mr Slaunder    40
has profeſt love to my Siſter.

*Vap.* And (I swear) burns for her in pure flames.

*Isa.* From these two fountains flow all our misfortuns.

*Vap.* That's very ſtrange Madam.

*Isa.* Tis too true; Sir I know where you professe you love truly.    45

*Vap.* Moſt devoutly Madam.

*Isa.* And you make an idol of friendship.

*Vap.* Madam I am juſt: what should this mean?    {*aside*

*Isa.* Why then consider the unhappines of an infortunat person.    50

*Vap.* Who Madam?

*Isa.* My poor siſter, who saw, and lov'd, and muſt dye for you, if you can't love, or cant be to your friend injuſt.    {*weeps*

*Vap.* Madam do not weep.

*Isa.* I could weep sooner for a dying friend, then for one quite    55
dead: there's more pitty due to one that languishes in torment which—
then unto those whose cares dye with their death.    {*weeps*

*Vap.* Really Madam my heart mourns to see you weep.

*Isa.* Were it for myself, I'de dye unpittyd, rather then tell my    60
blushing folly; but for my poor siſter—I have counseld her, and

counseld her, but she's no more capable of advice, then people in
high feavor fal'n to raving.

*Vap.* I swear I pitty her.

*Isa.* I am more happy, if I durſt truſt you.                         65

*Vap.* By my honor Madam you may, as your own soule.

*Isa.* Why then Sir know I have disposd of my affeƈtions, to one
I wish that you might call your friend and brother: him I resolve
to marry: would our nuptials might be kept at one moment, that I
might see my poor siſter sav'd.                                        70

*Vap.* Madam, I muſt wish you happy and him you love; but in
point of honor your love to another has releaſt me from all obligations, which by my juſt professions to you, I layd upon my self.

*Isa.* He nibles, and will bite.                           {*aside*

*Vap.* Yet Madam, will you believe a truth: may I perish, if all    75
this while, I did not love your siſter, and was divided in my
flames.

*Isa.* Burnt at both ends—pure slave!                     {*aside*

*Vap.* But I thought fit to suppresse that passion: This Madam
is a truth by all that's good, and your siſter shal live, and live   80
belovd of me.

*Isa.* But for your friend Sir, will it not be an injury to him.

*Vap.* Friend! who Tom Slander my friend?

*Isa.* Is he not Sir?

*Va.* Friend Madam? I find you doe not know me.                      85

*Isa.* Why sir?

*Va.* My friend! its true I give him permission to receive the
advantage of my company: he diverts me: the fellow has some
smattering of wit, and somtimes launces out a fourth-rate jeſt. He
has learnd to dance and fence; speaks the french tongue (though   90
not correƈtly) and has some advantage from my Taylor, which
sets him out, and can make a noise, but for a friend Madam.

*Isa.* O me! how I was miſtaken.

*Va.* Why Madam, do you think I wou'd have sufferd your
siſter to have marry'd Tom Slander, and not have told her, what a   95
fop he was.

*Isa.* This is a firſt-rate rogue                          {*aside*

*Va.* No Madam, I would not have seen your siſter unhappy,
and now will make her happy.

*Isa.* I joy in my successe—umh          {*ſteps to the door and cals.*  100

*Enter* Worthy

here Sir is the man, that muſt immediatly be mine: to his
conduct I commit you; but firſt embrace.

*Va.* Noble Mr Worthy, may I be eternally—

*Wo.* No oaths good Sir, I embrace your friendship

*Isa.* How does my siſter, Mr Worthy?                                    105

*Wor.* Languishing till she hears your successe.

*Isa.* She shal be happy Mr Worthy: now take your new friend
and brother, and ſtay where I appointed you, till I bring my siſter:
she'l be so ashamd, she'l not be able to look upon you, till the
Prieſt has warranted the confidence: go begon: poor Siſter, I long    110
to bring her comfort

*Vap.* Beſt Lady, ever yours.

*Isa.* Are the boys ready                                           {*aside*

*Wor.* To a pin—I shall be—

*Isa.* You don't know what: tis as it hits: {*exit* Worthy *and* Vapor.   115
now for my Siſter to act her as charitable part for me; then let
these fine fellows laugh at us.

### *Enter* Mrs Finicall

*Fin.* Madam, your father cals.

*Isa.* I go Miſtress Finical; what a bawdy politique look she has.
                                                                   {*exit*

*Fin.* Now for my other sick Lady—I think the coaſt is clear      120
{*peeps at the doors*} really I cannot but gratify my self with the
approbation of my abilities, to manage a design that is feminine;
I'le give the signe—Whiſt—whiſt                  {*she goes to each door*

### *Enter* Slander *and* Philadelphia *at several doors.*

now I shall prudently retire.                        <*Exit* Finical>

*Phi.* Now Sir, what do you conceive in your good breeding,       125
that I desire to speak with you about?

*Sla.* Nay faith Madam I cannot imagine.

*Phi.* Yes, yes I warrant, you fancy tis to beg your pardon, weep,
then whine, and then sigh, and ſtill whine, and prettily confess
my passion.                                                         130

*Sla.* I hope Madam you did not send for me, to abuse me agen.

*Phi.* No Sir, nor to be abusd by your opinion.

*Sla.* Really Madam I have no such thought

*Phi.* It mads me to be put upon such a whining employment: if
I were in love with a man, that I thought did not love me, I wou'd   135
use my garters, and hang before I would confess, and drown my
self in shame.

*Sla.* Madam, I underſtand you not.

*Phi.* And I am ashamd you shou'd, but nature has that power—                                                                   140

*Sla.* I beg your Ladyship not to speak so darkly.

*Phi.* If I durſt truſt you.

*Sla.* By my life you may.

*Phi.* By my blushes I am asham'd to do't—but I muſt, or she muſt to Bedlam.                                                         145

*Sla.* Who Madam?

*Phi.* My siſter, my foolish Siſter, bewitcht by you.

*Sla.* O Lord Madam I am not the person, that have the vanity to affeᶜt such a blessing.

*Phi.* How foolishly you smile? with what triumph in your jeer-     150
ing chaps? why Sir she's not the firſt woman that has bin in love.

*Sla.* Nor I the firſt man.

*Phi.* Who! you in love, with whom?

*Sla.* Why faith Madam with your siſter.

*Phi.* O raskall!                                          {*aside*     155
with my siſter Sir? I thought it had bin with me.

*Sla.* Madam I honor you, and beg your pardon: I pretended that onely out of design; and Miſtress Finicall will swear it.

*Phi.* Like enough.                                        {*aside*

*Sla.* Therfore never hearts burnt with such equal flames.            160

*Phi.* This is very happy for my siſter, if it be true.

*Sla.* It is Madam by my good name.

*Phi.* As a Cutpurse, or bawd may swear.                   {*aside.*
But Sir, you will have one scruple.

*Sla.* None by this light.                                             165

*Phi.* Your friend pretended to my siſter.

*Sla.* Who Madam?

*Phi.* Your dear friend Mr Vapor.

*Sla.* My dear friend! who Jack Vapor? your pardon Madam;
you very much miſtake the measurs I have of persons, and friend-     170
ships.

*Phi.* Is he then not your friend?

*Sla.* A friend! a property, or my motion rather: faith Madam,
I had as lief bin told, that I had contraᶜted a friendship with
one of Punchionello's puppets.                                         175

*Phi.* Treacherous slave.                                  {*aside*
But Sir I thought he had bin a fine Gentleman.

*Sla.* As ever was painted: why now to discover all to you; he
lives upon me, I pay for his Ordinaryes.

*Phi.* But how came you to be so familiar with him?                    180

*Sla.* Why faith Madam, he had a Sister, that was a pretty wench, and some kindnes there was betwixt us, which Jack knew of, and therfore—I need say no more.

*Phi.* Knew of! why was he a pimp to his own sister?

*Sla.* Not so Madam, but formerly he has not bin a stranger to     185
my pleasures.

*Phi.* Why he talks high.

*Sla.* When he gets a glasse in his pate, he makes me smile, and diverts me with his Rodomontados greater then any Gascoignes: once he swore he was big with honor, and must be     190
deliverd in a battle: he's as abusive as a city carter, and will be beaten as easy as a schoolboy: I have had so many quarrels for him, that realy I was upon the point of discarding him my company.

*Phi.* Wo'nt the Earth swallow this raskall?                    {*aside*  195
I am glad Sir you are so free, to make my sister happy: but tell me Sir can you love the poor creature?

*Sla.* Above my soul.

*Phi.* That's easy.                                            {*aside*
And once more may I trust you?                                         200

*Sla.* By my love to your dear Sister you may.

*Phi.* Then Sir I'le shew you one, must be your friend and brother

*Sla.* What does she mean?                         {*exit* Philadelphia.

*Enter again with* Lovetruth.

*Phi.* No words, but embrace brothers and friends.              205

*Sla.* Your perpetual slave.

*Lov.* You oblige me Sir.

*Phi.* Time is pretious: this Gentleman will conceal you, till I bring my sister: you must not expect she will dare look upon you til the Priest makes you hers, she ought so much to blush at this     210
fondnes; but I will attend you, that you may be sure—so begon —no complements, nor words, time wasts.—
                    (*exit* Lovetruth *and* Slander)
That the earth should breed such fellows: why should they not go with crosses upon their breasts, like infected houses, that wholsom people may have warning of 'em.                    215

*Enter* Isabella

O sister very good success, thy lover hath yielded.

*Isa.* And thine is a pitifull lover: at leisure we'l compare their examinations, and see which is the most felonious raskall. Worthy has lockt up your true lover.

*Phi.* And Love-truth yours.                                            220

*Isa.* Hang 'em, lets keep 'em there, they're safe.

*Phi.* Nay, now lets marry 'em to stinking feet.

*Isa.* Proceed then, for I am full of revenge.

*Phi.* I can assure thee, thy lovers a pretty fellow, and full of compassion, and untruths.                                            225

*Isa.* Thine has an excellent character: he can forswear a friend, and a Mistresse in a breath.

*Phi.* I wonder how they can pick up so many lies.

*Isa.* Why as the hedgehogs do crabs by rowling in 'em.

*Enter* Worthy

*Wor.* My admir'd Ladies, I come to know your pleasures.          230

*Isa.* What concerning our Prisoner?

*Wor.* There's somthing more.

*Isa.* Why I think you had best turn him out, and laugh at him.

*Wor.* And what's your pleasur for the Parson?

*Isa.* Give him a couple of shillings, or if you will half a crown,   235
and tell him, as you wou'd an expecting creditour, that he shall come another time.

*Wo.* You'l not make payment now then.

*Isa.* I am not now provided.

*Wo.* By your favor Madam, you have always enough about you.     240

*Phi.* But how, if we han't a mind to pay, will you arrest us?

*Wor.* If I could get you to the black spiritual Baylif, he should have an execution on you.

*Isa.* Then to Goale, that's mariage.

*Wo.* Thither you must go one time or other: the only benefit,    245
you can expect, is to chuse your Keeper.

*Isa.* We shall think ont.

*Wo.* Will you give security, that you will satisfy the debt.

*Isa.* No, no we'l grant no incumbrances.

*Enter* Lovetruth.

*Lov.* Best Ladies I have securd my prisoner, and am come to      250
know

*Wor.* Hold thy peace man, they'l not marry: they have orderd us to discharge the Parson, and give him twelve pence a piece.

*Lo.* Dearest Ladies, is this your sentence?

*Phi.* In troth, now it is just come too't, wee are afraid to ven-    255
ture.

*Isa.* An unlucky mariage is such a sin, that repentance never recovers it.

*Wo.* And to be damn'd to an unlucky love, is as hopeles: Love-truth, how like asses we behold each other?    260

*Lo.* We'l e'vn restore the Galants to their liberty, and present 'em again to the Ladies.

*Wor.* And let 'em kick us before 'em, to afford 'em al the sport imaginable.

*Lo.* Nay, I begin to believe I could endure a beating.    265

*Wo.* Or I to have my brains knockt out—Sweet Ladies, will you give us leave to cut one anothers throats before you?

*Isa.* Why, if you have a mind to divert us with a passe, or two.

*Wo.* Draw Lovtruth, we can never do one another such a cur-tesie.    270

*Lov.* They are kind in somthing yet          {*draw*

*Isa. Phi.* Hold.

*Isa.* What! are you mad, or drunk?

*Wo.* Sober, as your self, witnes this action: we will be mad or drunk, when we live without you.    275

*Isa.* Phil, begin, I can hold no longer.

*Phi.* But you are uncivill though, that you are.

*Lo.* I hope we may be bold with our selves.

*Phi.* But you are rude to the Parson, to make a man of his rev-erend coat wait thus.    280

*Isa.* And may be, catch cold, by walking in one of the allies, where the wind plays with his cassock, till he gets a hoarsnes, that will make him whisper his next daies exercise.

*Wor.* The meaning Ladies?

*Isa.* Are you so dull? come lead on.    285

*Wo.* Lovetruth, shall we venture to take their hands?

*Isa.* You'd best stay, 'till we take yours

*Lo.* May our loves last—

*Phi.* As long as mens, and womens use to doe.

*Isa.* Enough: fetch each of us our Sister, that we may furnish    290
our prisoners—make hast: no expressions: dispatch

{*exit* Worthy *and* Lovetruth

*Enter* Trim

*Trim.* O my dear Miſtress—for ever, for ever.

*Isa.* What Trim?

*Trim.* All's sure: don, don; I have two honorable daughters, and the grave Knights, bringing their supposed co-heyrs, to ask     295
blessing of Sir Richard Plainbred; but they shall receive it of Sir Roger Trim; for knighted I shall be.

*Enter* Worthy, *and* Lovetruth *with the two Boyes dreſt like women.*

How now what are these?

*Isa.* Two rich heyrs Trim; nothing but heyers in this place.

*Trim.* I underſtand.     300

*Isa.* Come Mr Worthy, you and I muſt take one: Siſter you, and Mr Lovetruth know how to dispose of yourselvs, and that Gentlewoman: by my troth the boyes look well: come, come tw'ill do well enough: you muſt answer in a soft voice.

*1.* We warrant you, Madam     305

*Phi.* Remember to give the sign when you are dispatcht.

*Isa.* What you long to be finisht.

*Phi.* Nay, fye Siſter.

*Isa.* Farewell Trim, wish us well, and watch my father.

*Trim.* Fear no pursuits—          {*exeunt all but* Trim     310
happy Trim, thou shalt have thy name mingled with honor, be worship of the neighbours, and become known to the Heralds: my pewter shall be changd, and the Barber's Arms (of three rasors and a rose) turnd into a Lyon, and some gentiler flower.

*Enter* Mrs Finicall *haſtily.*

How! Miſtress Finical? I'le have some sport with her however:     315
whether so faſt Miſtress?

*Fin.* What's that to you? I am in haſt.

*Trim.* O what a busy face you have: I will know somthing.

*Fin.* Know how to ſtring your Cittern: marry come up.

*Trim.* Come, come; where are the Ladies, and your Galants?     320

*Fin.* Prithee go look: I know? a silly woman: am I fit to know, or contrive? fy, fy.

*Trim.* How thou doſt smile thy face into a new-cut Brawn.

*Fin.* How Brawn Sirrha?

*Trim.* Yes, juſt like Brawn, when tis cut in riggles; it seems to     325
smile as scurvily as thou doeſt.

*Fin.* Ha, ha, art thou angry? come, come you conceal your plots from me; I am useles: you'l be mighty rich, if your designs take.

*Trim.* Very good. 330

*Fin.* The firſt I would advise you for your Credit, is to purchase another hat, that you may not fear of a showr walk agen in the rain, as I met you once with your Bason on your head.

*Trim.* You are wondrous witty and wanton: young things will be pleasant. 335

*Fin.* Uds my life! I forget my matters.

*Trim.* Nay, one word more.

*Fin.* As I live, I muſt fetch a thing out of my closet: I pro-teſt I am in haſt: Let me alone Sirrah—        {*exit* Finical.

*Trim.* How the jade swels upon hopes; when the bladder's 340 prickt, how she'l sink.

*Enter* Sir Richard.

Now to entertain Sir Richard—good luck pursues thee Trim.

*Sir R.* Trim, was my Atturney here to day?

*Trim.* No a'nt please your worship.

*Sir R.* These Lawyers are like so many limetwigs; if one touches 345 'em he ſticks.

*Trim.* I hope your worships buisnes will not hold you long: I know your worship is not affeɧed to this place.

*Sir R.* No Trim, tis as good for me to swallow a pin and a cruſt, as to live long here: 'tis a certain choking 350

*Trim.* Your worship has a sweet place in the Countrey.

*Sir R.* Tis quiet Trim, and wholsome: here's no peace of any kind, the ayr itself is infeɧed with foule breath, and smoke of charcoal.

*Trim.* But your Worship has not bin here so long to know the 355 worſt of this place. Tis shrewdly alterd since your worship was here.

*Sir R.* But I wanted not a true description from an worthy and honeſt friend, whose misery it is to be here: I do abhorr a place, where the moſt eſtimed crafts are cheating; and the moſt admir- 360 able policy word-breaking: where moſt people spend all they have, and some more then, theyr own: Greatnes is now to be judgd by outside, and intereſt changd for grandeur: Your Countrymen scarce know theyr Landlords, and are grown to poor to care for 'em. Fy upon't Trim, in former times we liv'd by one another, and 365 now we live upon one another.

*Trim.* Sir I cannot but remember, when I was but a ſtripling, how your honeſt Tenants and neighbors would rejoyce, to shew their good wills: here Sir is nothing but your servant, and a mouth made.                                                                    370

*Sir R.* Talk no more Trim, before I'de ſtay long here, I wo'ud loose my Brothers eſtate.

*Enter* Mrs Finical *haſtily with a posset-pan under her apron.*

How now Miſtresse? whether so faſt?

*Fin.* About some occasions, that are importunat for dispatch.

*Sir R.* And why so many fine words? what's that under your     375
apron?

*Trim.* Let Sir Richard see Miſtress.

*Fin.* Stand off Sirrah.

*Trim.* S'life it rings: tis the silver warming-pan or the great Posset-pot.                                                                        380

*Sir R.* Nay, pray Miſtress Finicall lets see your treasure.

*Fin.* Well Sir, I am not ashamd to shew it; nor sha'nt be ashamd of the use of it.

*Sir R.* The use of it! why those smiles sweet Miſtress?

*Fin.* You shall perceive.                                                        385

*Trim.* She's big with the secret.                              {*aside*

*Fin.* It may conteyn a Sackposset, but I know nothing: no more but so.

*Enter* Sir Cautious Trouble all *with* Lucy;
*and* Sir Gravity Empty *with* Kate.

*Kneel to* Sir Richard.

*Sir R.* Hey day! what's the matter?

*Caut.* Your blessing Sir.                                              390

*Emp.* I sir your benediction.

*Sir R.* Are you marry'd to this Lady?

*Caut.* Yes Sir.

*Sir R.* And you Sir to this?

*Emp.* No doubt on't Sir—Sir Cautious and I mannage together.   395

*Sir R.* Why then down upon your marrow bones agen: Trim ſtand forth and showr down thy blessings—ha, ha, ha.

*Cau.* How! are not you Sir Richard's daughter?

*Luc.* I never sayd, I was.

*Emp.* Nay, I warrant you are not Sir Richards daughter neither.   400

*Kate.* If my Siſter be not, how should I be?

*Caut.* Sir Gravity Empty, this matter is worthy of our debate; never men were so nigh the sullying our reputations for ever.

*Emp.* Y'gad very nigh; lets debate.

*Enter* Worthy *with* Isabella, *and* Vapor
*with a Boy in womans clothes*        {*kneel.*

*Sir R.* How more kneeling?        405

*Wor.* One blessing more added to what I have, in your Isabella.

*Sir R.* What! is she yours now?

*Isa.* And yours Sir ſtill, I hope.

*Sir R.* Fy Isabella not so kind, to let me give thee to Worthy? Thats all thy fault: thou haſt chosen with my heart, as well as thy        410
own.

*Isa.* And will you let me Sir be yours ſtill?

*Sir R.* Come, come y'are a fond fool: Mr Worthy, I will not bid you use her well: she's safe in thy true worth, and she'l deserve it, she's a good Girle—ha—what wou'd you have Sir?        415

*Trim.* Now for my Triumph.        {*aside*

*Vap.* I beg your blessing also for Philadelphia.

*Sir R.* My blessing! I'le give it to a Musk cat assoon. My Philadelphia, did not one mother bring 'em, and one father beget 'em.

*Vap.* Sir, since there is a fate.        420

*Sir R.* Sir, since there is a Fart: can you look me in the face you Gipsie        {*puls of her hoods*
howe's this! O sweet Sir take your Philadelphia, and ask her, if she knowes, who's her father, if she does, she is a wise child.

*Vap.* By this hand I am basely abusd.        425

*Fin.* How, how, how!

*Trim.* Nay Miſtress Finicall, you are the Inginer.

*Enter* Lovetruth *with* Philadelphia,
*and after* Slaunder *with the other Boy in womens clothes.*

{*Kneel.*

*Sir R.* How now! more devices?

*Lov.* Your pardon, and blessing for me and your Philadelphia ſtill.        430

*Sir R.* Now by my life, my heart's easd: blesse me Girle; thou haſt chosen with my eyes: but you should have askt my consent child; but I am too well pleasd, to chide.

*Lov.* She bargaind Sir, that I should never take her from you.

*Sir R.* You have marry'd an asse: I have bred 'em fondly come,    435
I mu&t hug you both.                                   {*embraces 'em*
*Sla.* Uds life, what are you then? Jack Vapor what the divell
have you and I marryd?
*Vap.* Why Tom, I believe (as we deserve) two whores, and it
may be ca&t ones to those Gentlemen.                        440
*Isa.* Nay Gentlemen, I engage my credit, they are not whores.
*Sir R.* Nay, then they are too good for 'em.
*Phi.* Do you not know 'em Sir? look well.
*Sir R.* How! my two Boyes Ned and Will? ha, ha, ha. I shall
split with laughing; But your favour Gentlemen; you have such   445
fames, that Ile not tru&t your brides with you to night: you may
spoyle my Boyes.
*Ned.* Nay, I prote&t, my husband woud 'a bin kissing.
*Will.* And mine was going to search by virtue of his juris-
di&ction.                                                 450
*Vap.* Your Servant Gentlemen; laugh on: Tom tis well we scapd
so.
*Sir R.* Nay Gentlemen, I beseech you &tay; and give your
friends joy, and Mr Trims sons in law.
*Sla.* S'life Jack we are repayrd: Sir Cautious Trouble all, hap-    455
pines attend your Nuptials.
*Vap.* Sir Gravity Empty, Juno smile upon your Mariage bed.
*Caut.* Gentlemen, we despise you, and Fortune.
*Emp.* Yes Gentlemen, you and Fortune we despise.
*Cau.* Heark you Mr Trim, things pa&t there's no speaking of:    460
but upon debate we have concluded, you mu&t leave of your
checquerd Apron.
*Emp.* Y'gad we have debated, and debated agen, and therfore
leave off you mu&t.
*Trim.* I shall obay your honors, as your mo&t obedient Father:    465
Sir Richard I hope you'l be pleasd to thank this Lady of intrigues:
she plotted, and designd.
*Fin.* You Jackanapes Slave, I'le hit thee a flap o'th chaps if
thou jeer&t me
*Sir R.* No wrath my fine fashionable Landlady, but pursue thy    470
intentions, and make the Sack-posset; and let a good Supper be
provided: you shall be all my gue&ts, and lea&t there should be no
dancing at your Weddings, come Isabella, lets see what you can
doe.

*A Dance.*

And now for you Mr Vapor, and Mr Slander, Ile ease you of your     475
wifes, and leave you to get rich Heyres, if you can: <*To Cautious
and Empty*> For you my honorable grave Friends, you are wise,
and need no counsell: you shall have my good wishes, and
opinion that your wifes may be very honeſt. For my self, Worthy,
and Lovetruth, we'l to the Countrey with our wifes; where we'l     480
cheerfully spend what we have, and waſt nothing, that our Ancestors left us: We'l not expose our content to noise, nor our fortunes
to crowds: we'l doe good to all, that desire, and hurt to none
that deserve it: we'l love our King, and be true to our Countrey,
wish all well: in particular                                       485

      This noble Company, and in return agen
      With smiles reward the Countrey Gentlemen.

                        *Exeunt omnes.*

# The Rehearsal

## INTRODUCTION

A Comedy, which is so perfect a Master-Piece in it's Way, and so truly an Original, that notwithstanding it's prodigious Success, even the Task of Imitation . . . has appear'd as too arduous to be attempted with Regard to this, which through an whole Century still stands alone, notwithstanding the very Plays it was written expressly to ridicule are forgottten, and the Taste it was meant to expose totally exploded. (David Erskine Baker, 1764)[1]

Originally drafted before the closure of the theatres in 1665 on account of plague, *The Rehearsal* was revised and staged in December 1671 and first published in 1672. Significant topical additions were inserted by the time of the third edition in 1675, though whether Buckingham and his collaborators had any part in those revisions cannot be determined.

*The Rehearsal* was unique in its time and it held the stage steadily for more than a century, which is extraordinary for such a radically topical satire. Not until the appearance of Sheridan's *The Critic* in 1779 was it supplanted in the London repertory. The brilliance and importance of Buckingham's piece would be difficult to deny, but the play presents both historical and interpretative puzzles for which no satisfactory answers have ever been found. Exactly who wrote it and how remain subjects for speculation and debate. The degree to which it attacks particular individuals (especially John Dryden) is hard to say. Whether the play has a political subject (or subtext) along with its obvious literary satire continues to be disputed. Its particular importance lies in the mordant view it gives us of new plays in the period 1660 to 1675—a time when dramatic criticism was barely in its infancy and journalistic commentary on plays and theatrical performance was functionally non-existent. As a critical document the play may be considered 'obvious' or 'opaque' depending on the assumptions of the commentator.[2]

---

[1] *The Companion to the Play-House*, ii, s.v. 'Buckingham'.
[2] An Introduction of this sort is not the proper venue for a critical analysis. What seem to us the most important literary analyses of *The Rehearsal* include Dane Farnsworth Smith, *Plays about the Theatre in England from* The Rehearsal *in 1671 to the Licensing Act in 1737* (New York: Oxford University Press, 1936), ch. 2; V. C. Clinton-Baddeley, *The Burlesque Tradition*

With the benefit of hindsight, one may see *The Rehearsal* as a trenchant satire on what Buckingham and his friends considered pretentious claims to authorial autonomy and the right of the author to
control the meaning of his or her text.[3] Dryden asserts such claims in
his early criticism, and Sir Robert Howard's fiercely sceptical denials of
such authorial control of textual meaning brought about their celebrated clash in prefatory essays *c*.1668. Dryden's enormous reputation led
most nineteenth- and twentieth-century critics to see him as undispu-
ted victor in this duel, but in fact Howard's reader-response approach
is probably closer to present-day critical norms. Dryden stridently proclaimed the control of the text by the author, whereas (like Howard)
Buckingham saw text and author as subject to the judgement of the
man of taste—himself and his friends, as embodied in the Smith and
Johnson of his play. Critical attitudes towards the play over the past
two centuries have tended to fall into two groups. Some critics revel in
the demolition of the silliness of the heroic play, whereas others dislike
the rubbishing of Dryden. The underlying critical issues, however, are
timeless.

## COMPOSITION AND AUTHORSHIP

The early history of *The Rehearsal* is murky and likely to remain so. Although it was first performed in December 1671, there is good reason to
believe that it had been started and possibly even completed as early as
the spring of 1665 in a form now lost. No one has ever doubted

in the *English Theatre after 1660* (1952; repr. New York: Blom, 1971), esp. 31–7; Peter Lewis,
'*The Rehearsal*: A Study of its Satirical Methods', *Durham University Journal*, NS 31 (1970), 96–
113; Sheridan Baker, 'Buckingham's Permanent *Rehearsal*', *Michigan Quarterly Review*, 12
(1973), 160–71; Robert F. Willson, 'Bayes versus the Critics: *The Rehearsal* and False Wit', in
'*Their Form Confounded': Studies in the Burlesque Play from Udall to Sheridan* (The Hague:
Mouton, 1974), ch. 4; John H. O'Neill, *George Villiers, Second Duke of Buckingham* (Boston,
Mass.: Twayne, 1984), ch. 4. For important readings from a political angle, see the articles by
McFadden and Stocker discussed below. *The Rehearsal* has often been considered 'important'
for the wrong reasons by critics who imagine that it drove heroic drama off the stage. As a
work virtually *sui generis* it is sometimes ignored (despite its enormous popularity and omni-
presence on the stage for more than a century) by critics whose generic presuppositions it
does not suit. The play does not even appear in the indexes to Laura Brown's *English
Dramatic Form, 1660–1760* (1981) or J. Douglas Canfield's *Tricksters and Estates: On the Ideology
of Restoration Comedy* (1997) and *Heroes and States: On the Ideology of Restoration Tragedy*
(2000).

[3] For such a reading, see Paul D. Cannan, *The Emergence of Dramatic Criticism in England:
From Jonson to Pope* (New York: Palgrave, 2006).

FIG. 6. Title page of the first edition of *The Rehearsal* (1672). Collection of Robert D. Hume

Buckingham's involvement in the writing of the piece, but how many helpers he had, who they were, and how much they contributed we will never know for certain, barring the discovery of new evidence.

## The Ur-Rehearsal of circa 1665

Almost everything known about the origins of the play derives from the Briscoe *Key* of 1704:

When his *Grace* began it, I cou'd never learn . . . we may certainly gather from the Editions of the Plays reflected on in it, that it was before the end of 1663; and finish'd before the end of 1664; because it had been several times *Rehears'd*, the Players were perfect in their Parts, and all things in Readiness for its Acting, before the *great Plague*, in 1665; and that then prevented it.

But what was so ready for the Stage, and so near being Acted, at the breaking out of that *Terrible Sickness*, was very different from what you have since seen in Print. In that he call'd his Poet *Bilboa*; by which Name the Town generally understood Sir *Robert Howard* to be the Person pointed at. . . . The Acting of this *Farce* being thus hindered, it was laid by for several Years, and came not on the publick Theatre, till the Year 1671.

During this interval, many great Plays came forth, writ in Heroick Rhyme; and, on the Death of Sir *William D'Avenant* 1669, Mr. *Dryden*, a new *Laureat* appear'd on the Stage, much admir'd, and highly Applauded; which mov'd the Duke to change the name of his Poet from *Bilboa*, to *Bayes*.[4]

We cannot verify every part of this account—the players 'perfect in their Parts' may be a flight of fancy—but overall it rings true. The numerous explicit hits at plays on the stage around 1663 (some not known to have been revived after 1665) are a potent argument for the existence of a lost Ur-*Rehearsal* written *c.*1664. That Dryden was not the primary and obvious target of this satire is self-evident: at that time he was known only as the author of a pair of flops (*The Wild Gallant* and *The Rival Ladies*), though he had worked with his brother-in-law Sir Robert Howard on *The Indian-Queen* (January 1664), and his *The Indian Emperour* was to prove a success in the spring of 1665. The most prominent writers of successful heroic plays were Sir Robert Howard; Roger Boyle, Earl of Orrery; and Sir William Davenant. For a work written in the context of 1664 to succeed in 1671—by which time Dryden was far and away the most prominent active playwright—major

---

[4] *A Key to the Rehearsal* (London: S. Briscoe, 1704), which constitutes pages i–xv and 1–32 of Volume ii of the 1704–5 *Miscellaneous Works*. Quotation at pp. xi–xii. The whole of the preface is printed in App. IV.

changes would plainly have been necessary, and from the number of references to plays produced between 1667 and 1671 we may infer that if the Ur-*Rehearsal* was ever completed, the play underwent drastic alterations before it was staged in the form preserved in the quarto of 1672.

A play such as *The Rehearsal* is in its very nature liable to late changes and topical insertions. That Buckingham—or perhaps someone associated with the King's Company—remained on the lookout for new material during rehearsals or even during the first run is clear from some hits at Dryden's *Marriage A-la-Mode*. Most of the gibes at that play make their first printed appearance in the 1675 quarto of *The Rehearsal*, but the presence of allusions in *Q1* of 1672 is beyond dispute. This has caused some confusion, especially since *Marriage A-la-Mode* has traditionally been dated *c.*April 1672, which seemed to imply that the 1672 text of Buckingham's farce might represent a version that had evolved over a period of several months. However, prologue and epilogue references have led to a widely accepted redating of *c.* December 1671 for *Marriage A-la-Mode*.[5] This greatly simplifies the state of affairs: the King's Company actors were evidently rehearsing both plays at about the beginning of December 1671, and nothing would have been easier than the insertion of a few jokes at the expense of the one in the acting script of the other. Nothing was sacred about the version performed in December 1671, and the accretion of further additions after the current text went to press in the spring of 1672 is in no way surprising,[6] though there is no hard evidence of new material aimed at targets later than Dryden's *Assignation* (*c*. November 1672). Whatever their date, all known addenda appeared in *Q3* when it was published in 1675. The stability of the printed text after that date may be unexpected but is a fact.

### The Problem of Authorship

Lack of information about the Ur-version notwithstanding, the compositional history through its three phases is a good deal clearer than the question of authorship.[7] *The Rehearsal* was published anonymously

[5] See Robert D. Hume, 'The Date of Dryden's *Marriage A-la-Mode*', *Harvard Library Bulletin*, 21 (1973), 161–6.

[6] The title was entered in the *Stationers' Register* on 19 June 1672 and advertised in the *Term Catalogues*, i. III, the same month.

[7] This discussion draws on Judith Milhous and Robert D. Hume, 'Attribution Problems in English Drama, 1660–1700', *Harvard Library Bulletin*, 31 (1983), 5–39.

throughout Buckingham's lifetime, yet his involvement in the authorship must have been common knowledge even during the first run, for
Evelyn ascribes it to him without hesitation as early as 14 December
1671.[8] No one has ever challenged Langbaine's assertion: 'ascribed to
the Late Duke of *Buckingham*'.[9] The difficulty lies in determining what
assistance he had from friends and dependents. Martin Clifford, Thomas Sprat, Samuel Butler, Edmund Waller, and Abraham Cowley have
all been suggested as possible contributors.[10] The evidence for Clifford
and Sprat is principally stanzas 4 and 5 of the '1668' version of 'The
Session of the Poets':

> Intell'gence was brought, the court being sat
> That a play tripartite was very near made,
> Where malicious Matt Clifford and spiritual Spratt
> Were join'd with their Duke, a peer of the trade.
>
> Apollo rejoic'd, and hop'd for amends,
> Because he knew it was the first case
> The Duke e're did ask the advice of his friends,
> And so wish'd his play as well clapp'd as his Grace.[11]

Clifford was apparently Buckingham's secretary for much of the 1660s;
Thomas Sprat (1635–1713) was his personal chaplain (and later became
Bishop of Rochester). Both men were wits, and their providing advice
and assistance to their patron is *ipso facto* likely enough. We know that
Clifford was definitely involved in a related pamphlet attack in his
*Notes upon Mr. Dryden's Poems in Four Letters*, not published until 1687,
but the fourth letter of which is dated 1 July 1672. For what value the
evidence may have, the anonymous 'Curll' biography of Sprat states
that 'As to his Taste in *Poetry*, it was equally skilful, of which his own
Works, and the great share it is well known he had in the *Rehearsal*, are

---

[8] *The Diary of John Evelyn*, 6 vols., ed. E. S. de Beer (Oxford: Clarendon Press, 1955), iii. 599.

[9] Langbaine, *An Account of the English Dramatick Poets*, 546. Presumably because the work continued to be published without title page ascription, Langbaine placed the work under 'Unknown Authors', but his attribution is unequivocal.

[10] *Annals of English Drama, 975–1700*, ed. Alfred Harbage, rev. S. Schoenbaum (London: Methuen 1964), 168. The third edition, ed. Sylvia Stoler Wagonheim (London: Routledge, 1989), 174, replaces Waller and Cowley with 'and others', but without explanation.

[11] *Poems on Affairs of State*-Yale, i. 328. This poem was probably written not in 1668 but by the end of 1664—further evidence for the composition of the Ur-*Rehearsal* by that time. See Gillian Fansler Brown, "'The Session of the Poets to the Tune of Cook Lawrel": Playhouse Evidence for Composition Date of 1664', *Restoration and Eighteenth-Century Theatre Research*, 13, no. 1 (May 1974), 19–26, 62. The nasty pun at the end of stanza 5 is representative of the tone of the piece.

lasting Monuments: The Duke of *Buckingham* being often heard to say, *That he never thought any of his Compositions perfect, till they had received Mr. Sprat's Approbation.*[12] Two aspects of the 1672 printed text—the fact that its Act/scene headings and a number of stage directions were in Latin and its repeated use of the 'inkhorn' spelling 'papyr' for 'paper' (cf. papyrus)—suggest that the manuscript may have been prepared by Sprat, who was a formidable classical scholar.

The case for Waller and Cowley seems to derive from the anonymous 'Life' of Waller prefaced to the 1711 edition of his *Poems, &c. Written upon Several Occasions*: 'It is said he [Waller] had a Hand in the *Rehearsal*, with Mr. *Clifford*, Mr. *Cowley*, and some other Wits.'[13] Cowley and Waller were both intimates of Buckingham's, but on the evidence of their other work neither seems likely to have been especially helpful with *The Rehearsal*. Cowley died in 1667, so he could not have been involved beyond the early version. Butler is named, together with Clifford and Sprat, by Anthony à Wood, and his association with Buckingham makes his participation in a group enterprise plausible.[14] As the author of *Hudibras* Butler had plenty of experience in burlesque, though none that we know of in drama.

Our best guess is that ideas were contributed by a group of Buckingham's associates and that he himself did much of the actual composition of the play. The 1711 'Life' of Waller says that 'it was at first written like a Comment on several Plays' (perhaps in the fashion of *The Censure of the Rota*) 'but the Duke thinking the Method was too grave, and the Raillery not piquant enough, took his Hints from thence, and turn'd the Comment into a Comedy' (p. xlvii).[15] The appearance of III. ii. 203–24 among the 'British Princes' satire group may be a relic of this phase of the work's genesis. The contemporary testimony of the 'Ses-

---

[12] *Some Account of the Life and Writings of the Right Reverend Father in God, Thomas Sprat, D.D. Late Lord Bishop of Rochester, and Dean of Westminster* (London: E. Curll, 1715), p. xiv.

[13] (London: Tonson, 1711), p. xlvi.

[14] Anthony a Wood, *Athenæ Oxonienses*, 4 vols., ed. Philip Bliss (London: F. C. and J. Rivington et al., 1813–20), iv. 209. Allardyce Nicoll is, however, alone in his peculiar and unsubstantiated assertion that 'Butler probably took more than an equal share' with Buckingham in the writing of the piece (*A History of English Drama, 1660–1900*, rev. edn., 6 vols. (Cambridge: Cambridge University Press, 1952–1959), i. 248).

[15] *The Censure of the Rota* (Oxford, 1673), attributed to Richard Leigh, was a twenty-page pamphlet attack on Dryden and in particular on *The Conquest of Granada*. It was followed by another such piece, ironically titled *The Friendly Vindication of Mr. Dryden From the Censure of the Rota by His Cabal of Wits* (Cambridge, 1673). Both quote (and harshly criticize) particular phrases, lines, and passages from Dryden's plays.

sion' makes the involvement of Clifford and Sprat highly probable. That Cowley and Waller were more than peripherally concerned seems unlikely, given their known work. On biographical grounds, such involvement as Butler had is likely to have come c.1671 when the version we know was prepared for the stage. Obviously any number of people could have contributed ideas to the project. All in all, the description of composition in a nasty anonymous ballad seems likely enough:

> Yet gathring from Plays, Pimps, and Table chatt
> With the help of his owne Canonicall Spratt,
> And his Family Scribe Antichriſtian Matt,
> > With a fa, la, etc.

> With Transcribeing of that, and Transversing of those
> With Transmuteing of Rhyme, and Transfuseing of Prose
> He has dreſt up his Farce, with other Mens Cloths.
> > With a fa, la, etc[16]

Barring the discovery of fresh evidence, we will never have any certainty about who did exactly what in concocting *The Rehearsal*. We offer the hypothesis that Buckingham was primarily responsible for the shaping of the final artefact—with substantial assistance from Clifford and Sprat, and ideas contributed by his literary circle.[17]

The great popularity of *The Rehearsal* naturally led to topical updatings in the course of the first couple of years after its premiere. The success of *Marriage A-la-Mode*, the publication of *The Conquest of Granada*, and the performance of Dryden's *The Assignation* offered opportunities too good to pass up. Whether Buckingham gleefully carried out these updatings himself, or supervised them, or merely acquiesced in someone at the theatre putting together insertions, or had nothing whatever to do with the additions, we have no way to determine. For what the claim is worth, *Q3* asserts that the play is printed 'With amendments and large Additions by the Author'. Virtually all scholars have assumed that Buckingham himself was responsible in some fashion for the additions, but we are aware of no proof beyond the title

---

[16] Osborn b 105 (Yale University). This passage is usually quoted in its more familiar form in *Poems on Affairs of State*, vol. ii (London, 1703), 216–17. For the full text of the poem, see Appendix II, ll. 306, below.

[17] Collaborative playwriting had of course gone severely out of fashion by the 1630s (see Paulina Kewes, *Authorship and Appropriation: Writing for the Stage in England, 1660–1710* (Oxford: Clarendon Press, 1998), App. A), but among amateurs from the nobility and gentry it was still occasionally practised, as for example in *Pompey the Great*, translated by Filmer, Godolphin, Sackville, Sedley, and Waller, and performed c. December 1663.

page.[18] Buckingham could not have stopped the actors from tinkering with the text, and there is no reason to think he would have wanted to. The years 1672–5 were stormy ones for the duke (though less so after his removal from office in the spring of 1674), but no more than a few days would have been required for the necessary research and rewriting. He could certainly have participated actively in the revision and approved anything he did not write himself, but this is mere supposition.

The stability of the text after 1675 is testimony to its effectiveness as general rather than specific satire. That *The Rehearsal* contains personal satire and direct parodies is beyond question, but the theatrical viability of the play does not depend on the recognition of particular hits. Consequently the managers soon realized that further topical interpolations were not necessary. As we shall see, however, a certain number of quasi-improvisational additions were nonetheless to become customary.

### BUCKINGHAM'S TARGETS AND THE THE NATURE OF THE SATIRE

What inspired Buckingham and his friends to write *The Rehearsal*? What models might have been of use to them? The author of the 1704 *Key* recounts a lurid tale of Buckingham's life being endangered by angry friends of the Howards when he led a faction to damn Henry Howard's *The United Kingdoms*—a play apparently staged *c.*1663, not printed, and now lost.[19] Buckingham is said then to have turned to 'Writing, to expose the *Follies* of these new-fashion'd Plays in their proper Colours. . . . And so set himself to the Composing of this *Farce.*' This may be true or partly true, but the form of *The Rehearsal* is radically original and Buckingham or his coterie deserve credit for constructing a truly imaginative satiric vehicle.

In discussing background and inspiration for the play, critics almost always point to Molière's *L'Impromptu de Versailles* (staged in Paris in October 1663) and Davenant's *The Playhouse to be Let* (staged at Lincoln's Inn Fields about two months earlier). The Buckingham circle was unquestionably familiar with the latter: *The Rehearsal* contains di-

---

[18] Arthur Mizener, 'George Villiers' (394), is virtually alone in questioning the attribution, which he calls 'a dangerous one in the light of Buckingham's habits', made 'for no better reason than that he was still alive'. Mizener is absolutely correct in saying that there is 'no direct evidence on this point one way or the other'.

[19] For this story, see App. IV, ll. 338. Howard's play was reportedly being performed at 'the *Cock-pit*', which implies either a much earlier date or a performance at court.

rect and explicit hits at some of its component pieces, especially those derived from Davenant's *Sir Francis Drake* and *The Cruelty of the Spaniards in Peru*. Davenant's medley, however, seems remote in technique from Buckingham's enterprise. Molière's *Impromptu*, though similar in its use of a stage setting, is utterly different in aims and perspective, being a defence by Molière against Edmé Boursault's attack on him in *Le Portrait du peintre*. We cannot agree with Crane that 'The form of the play was very likely suggested by Molière's' piece' (p. vii).[20] Among earlier English works proposed as a model, Beaumont's(?) *The Knight of the Burning Pestle* (1607? pub. 1613) is often given a nod, though it appears not to have been revived until 1667 or later, and Summers has denied (rightly, we believe) 'any real connection with *The Rehearsal*, beyond the broadest common ground of burlesque' (*Rehearsal*, p. xxi).

What seems to us the most obvious source of possible inspiration has been ignored by almost all critics: Ben Jonson's *Poetaster*, a 'Comicall Satyre' acted in 1601. Dissimilar as Jonson's play unquestionably is in many respects, it contains systematic satire on bad plays and sets out to ridicule pretentious and incompetent playwrights. We would point particularly to the 'king Darivs dolefull straine' passage (III. iv. 208–26), the 'meere spunge' passage (IV. iii. 104–29), the plagiary trial, the stuttering-vomit sequence, and the verdict (V. iii).[21] The structure and commentary technique adopted by Buckingham and his friends are radically different, but the determination to punish bad (and recognizable) playwrights without naming them and to excoriate bombast is very similar. Like his character Johnson (who seems aptly named, especially since Jonson's name was usually so spelt at the time), Buckingham was a champion of 'the old plain way' (I. ii. 9 and 85). Jonson's *Works* were readily available in folio to any moneyed person in the early 1660s,[22] and Buckingham might well have found in *Poetaster* (or perhaps in something like 'The Induction on the Stage' in *Bartholomew Fair*) encouragement to take up cudgels against pretentious playwrights of

---

[20] John Wilcox, in *The Relation of Molière to Restoration Comedy* (New York, N.Y.: Columbia University Press, 1938), 187, sees no relationship at all, finding *The Rehearsal* 'completely independent . . . from Molière'.

[21] *Ben Jonson*, ed. C. H. Herford and Percy Simpson, 11 vols. (Oxford: Clarendon Press, 1932), iv. The play was controversial. For Jonson's defence of his satiric practice ('My Bookes haue still beene taught / To spare the persons, and to speake the vices') see p. 320.

[22] Pepys, for example, considered buying 'Johnson' on a visit to his bookseller on 10 Dec. 1663 (*Diary*, iv. 410) at just about the time Buckingham might have been starting his satire. The Jonson Folio *Works* was reprinted in three volumes in 1640–1.

his day. Another potential source of inspiration with which he could well have been familiar is Georges de Scudéry's *Comédie des comédiens* (1635), though it is more a picture of 'actors behind the scenes' than a literary satire.[23]

We might at this point raise a practical question. When, *circa* late 1663, Buckingham decided to write a dramatic satire instead of leading a hostile party to hiss at performances of works of which he disapproved, which theatre did he think would produce his play? No scholar seems to have raised the point heretofore, but if the Ur-*Rehearsal* was aimed simultaneously in a double-barrelled way at the Howard family on one side and Sir William Davenant on the other, might Buckingham not have had a problem of venue? Sir Robert Howard was one of the major shareholders in the King's Company, and if the *Key* is to be believed, his family and friends had threatened Buckingham with physical violence at the time of *The United Kingdoms*. Would the company have welcomed and staged his further attack some eighteen months later? As principal owner and manager of the Duke's Company, Sir William Davenant (a vain and pretentious man) was surely in a position to refuse satires on himself, even if he were prepared to offend the numerous and influential Howards. Perhaps one of the companies did accept the piece and put it in rehearsal, and perhaps only the closure of the theatres on account of plague on 5 June 1665 kept it off the stage. But we have to wonder whether it actually got as far as rehearsal at this time. The play as we know it is another matter.

Insofar as the Ur-*Rehearsal* was an essentially literary attack, it was aimed to puncture what Buckingham and some of his friends clearly considered an obnoxious fad for rhymed heroic drama.[24] Dryden's Neander boasts in the *Essay of Dramatick Poesie* that 'no serious Playes written since the Kings return have been more kindly receiv'd . . . then the *Seige of* Rhodes, the *Mustapha*, the *Indian Queen*, and *Indian Emperour*'.[25] By the early 1670s Dryden felt able to say in his 'Of Heroique Playes' that 'Whether Heroique verse ought to be admitted into

---

[23] In his notorious *Observations sur le Cid* (1637) Scudéry denounced Corneille as thoroughly as Buckingham was to attack Dryden, but he did so in a critical examen devoid of all humour.

[24] Some evidently disagreed. Dorset and Sedley contributed to *Pompey the Great* (Lincoln's Inn Fields, Dec. 1663). Rochester contributed a couplet scene to Sir Robert Howard's unfinished *The Conquest of China* (see *Works*, 124–32) and there are rhymed sections in *Lucina's Rape*.

[25] *Works*, xvii. 73–4.

serious Playes, is not now to be disputed: 'tis already in possession of the Stage: and I dare confidently affirm, that very few Tragedies, in this Age, shall be receiv'd without it.'[26] Whatever the nature and targets of the earlier draft, Buckingham definitely intended to trash Dryden (along with rhymed heroic drama, and a variety of particular targets and popular devices) in the 1671 version of *The Rehearsal* that finally reached the stage.

Annotation of the text was first published in 1704–5. Each successive annotator has grappled with intractable problems concerning the degree of specificity of source targets and satire. But how purely literary is the satire? One of the few substantive pieces of testimony about *The Rehearsal* that survives from the seventeenth century is from Dryden himself, admittedly writing more than twenty years after the fact:

> I answer'd not the *Rehearsall*, because I knew the Author sate to himself when he drew the Picture, and was the very *Bays* of his own Farce: Because also I knew, that my Betters were more concern'd than I was in that Satire: And lastly, because Mr. *Smith*, and Mr. *Johnson*, the main Pillars of it, were two such Languishing Gentlemen in their Conversation, that I cou'd liken them to nothing but to their own Relations, those Noble Characters of Men of Wit and Pleasure about the Town.[27]

What exactly did Dryden mean when he said that his 'Betters' were 'more concern'd' as targets of satire than he was? This statement has been variously puzzled over, discounted, or derided; not until 1974 did any scholar mount a systematic attempt to substantiate the claim. *The Rehearsal* is a potent literary satire, but it is arguably at least in intention a serious political satire as well.

## Literary Allusions

A great deal of scholarly attention has been devoted to the identification of Buckingham's particular targets in *The Rehearsal*. This is in no way surprising: the play unquestionably contains numerous specific hits and parodies, and the annotated copies and popularity of 'Keys' in the

---

[26] *Works*, xi. 8.

[27] 'Discourse concerning the Original and Progress of Satire' (1693), *Works*, iv. 8–9. The comment about Smith and Johnson resembling 'Noble Characters ... of Wit and Pleasure about the Town' suggests a much more acerbic view of the 'court wits' than Dryden usually permitted himself in public during the Carolean period. The views expressed in the dedication of *All for Love* to Danby (pub. 1678) are exceptional.

eighteenth century prove that readers have long wanted to pinpoint the plays and passages Buckingham attacked. To seek a footnote identification for each gibe is understandable, but in our view unwise. There are four sorts of satire operating in *The Rehearsal*, and the reader needs to be aware of the distinctions.

1. Explicit parody of easily recognizable scenes in contemporary plays. Examples are Mr Comely's 'going out of town' in James Howard's *The English Mounsieur* (*Rehearsal*, III. ii. 139) and the song in dialogue in Stapylton's *The Slighted Maid*, which is actually named in Buckingham's text (V. i. 245). In fact, there is no great number of such obvious hits. Significantly, a majority of them seem to derive from the Ur-*Rehearsal*; most of the rest concern Dryden and particularly *The Conquest of Granada*. Several of the definite targets are obscure plays that were probably no longer in the repertory by 1671, so very few members of the audience would have recognized them.

2. Parodies of particular lines or passages. Examples are the reference to a winding-sheet in *The Conquest of Granada* (IV. i. 82), or the 'Morning pictur'd in a Cloud' in *The Siege of Rhodes* (III. ii. 190). In such instances the scholar may feel reasonably certain that he or she has pinpointed a specific origin and stimulus for Buckingham's text, but the chances of any one member of the original audience drawing the connection are very small. To point out such allusions is useful in helping us see how Buckingham and his allies constructed the play, but is if anything a distraction when one is trying to imagine its effectiveness in the theatre.

3. Swipes at individuals, some of them easily recognizable, others probably discernible only to differing groups of insiders. Bayes/Dryden as the proud parent of Drawcansir/Almanzor must have been instantly obvious to almost everyone. Contrariwise, that 'top his part' and '*Pit Box and Gallery*' were favourite expressions of Edward Howard (as the 1704 *Key* informs us) was probably known to very few people even in 1671. How many members of the original audience would have picked up on and enjoyed the Anne Reeves passages one can only speculate. Something like the Gresham College reference (II. i. 87:26) works on one level as general mockery of the Royal Society, on another as a dig at Dryden's short-lived association with it—but how many people can have known or cared about the latter? The chances that more than a few audience members caught the personal allusion seems slight. There is, however, a very real possibility that individual actors were teased or

satirized long before we can document this tradition in eighteenth-century performances.

4. Generalized burlesque of a sort requiring no specific application for enjoyment. A surprisingly large proportion of Buckingham's farce falls under this heading. Parallels of action, character, or phrase are easy to discover in contemporary drama, but one can rarely say with any assurance that Buckingham had a particular author or passage in view, much less that he supposed that members of his audience would make the connection.

The lasting popularity of *The Rehearsal* throughout most of the eighteenth century, long after practically all its specific targets were forgotten, is proof that even the particular hits could work as generalized burlesque. Drawcansir, for example, is unquestionably a take-off on Dryden's Almanzor, but he remains entertaining regardless of whether the reader or viewer is familiar with the sources of Buckingham's inspiration. Much the same could be said of Bayes. That he was a composite figure, originally grounded in Davenant and Sir Robert Howard rather than Dryden, can scarcely be disputed. That the 1672 and 1675 versions are heavily freighted with particular mockery of Dryden is likewise clear. But Bayes's babbling of stewed prunes, persons of quality, fame, power in writing, and so forth, remains deliciously preposterous whether one knows anything about Dryden or not. The many parallels between Dryden's published criticism and Bayes's arrogant pronouncements cannot be coincidental, but Bayes's fatuousness stands very nicely by itself, even though it gains a special relevance and sting when read with its applicability to Dryden in mind.[28] Certainly Bayes's play was long to serve as a universally accepted example of pretentious, incompetent, ridiculous 'tragedy'. Thus, attacking Arthur Murphy's bombastic *The Orphan of China*, a pamphleteer calls it 'a monstrous Farce, to be equalled by none in Absurdity, except by that of Poet *Bays* in the *Rehearsal*'.[29]

---

[28] Virtually all critics have read the play as a demolition of Bayes and everything that his play stands for. An exception is Kristiaan P. Aercke, 'An Orange Stuff'd with Cloves: Bayesian Baroque Rehearsed', *English Language Notes*, 25/4 (1988), 33–45, who considers Bayes 'a Baroque artist who is interested . . . in creating a unity out of disunity' and is therefore terribly misunderstood by Smith, who 'does not understand the author's concepts and intentions'.

[29] *A Letter from Mons. de Voltaire to the Author of the Orphan of China* (London: I. Pottinger, 1759), 24. There is an earlier slighting reference to 'the Style of Poet *Bays*' on p. 21. The author of this diatribe was evidently an English hack writer, not Voltaire. Such references are legion in 18th-c. English dramatic criticism.

The number of plays definitely and specifically attacked is quite small, but parallels can be adduced to a great many plays. Buckingham fires direct salvos at *The Wild Gallant*, *The Siege of Rhodes*, *Ormasdes*, *The English Mounsieur*, *The Slighted Maid*, *The Villain* (all probably part of the Ur-*Rehearsal*). He works in extensive allusions to *Tyrannick Love* and *The Conquest of Granada* plus a few jabs at *Marriage A-la-Mode* in the *Q1* version; and he (or someone) adds a swipe at *The Assignation* and some more digs at *Marriage A-la-Mode* and *The Conquest of Granada* in the *Q3* version of 1675. Roughly ten additional plays seem to have given Buckingham particular ideas; beyond that he was working with the kinds of language and situations common in drama of the 1660s and early 1670s.

Whether Buckingham was doing more than amusing himself may be doubted. The conventions of so artificial a genre as heroic drama are easy to mock, and Buckingham was a scoffer and derider by nature. Many scholars have assumed that *The Rehearsal* was written out of genuine indignation and in the hope of driving heroic drama off the London stage. Whatever Buckingham may have hoped it would do, we cannot suppose that the actors who performed it had any such object in view. We can scarcely emphasize too strongly that *The Rehearsal* was produced by the King's Company. Dryden was not only their principal playwright but a shareholder in the venture. They had scored great and profitable successes with *Tyrannick Love* and *The Conquest of Granada*. We cannot suppose that the managers would have staged *The Rehearsal* if they had thought that it would damage the popularity of these valuable stock plays, let alone drive them off the boards. There is good reason to believe that different parts of the original audience responded very differently to heroic bombast. The sentiment that John Evelyn's wife admired uncritically clearly struck the Buckingham circle as ludicrous. We must also reckon with the more complex reaction sketched by Cibber in his discussion of how tragedy may 'admit of a *Laugh of Approbation*' where the sentiments 'blaze even to a ludicrous Lustre, and doubtless the Poet intended to make his Spectators laugh while they admir'd them'.[30]

---

[30] For Mrs Evelyn's rhapsodic admiration of *The Conquest of Granada*, see her letter to Mr Bohun, *c.* Jan. 1670/1, quoted in *The London Stage*, Part i, 177. Cibber's discussion of appreciative laughter at heroic bombast (instancing *Macbeth* and *Richard III*, as well as several of Dryden's protagonists) is in his *Apology*, i. 121–4.

To suppose that enjoyment of parody—even of travesty—is necessarily inimical to enjoyment of the original is critically simple-minded. Many a twentieth-century lover of Wagner has relished Anna Russell's account of *Der Ring des Nibelungen*, and seventeenth-century audiences were evidently no less flexible and sophisticated. Langbaine remarks that he had seen Katherine Philips's translation of Corneille's *Pompey* 'acted with great applause, at the Duke's Theatre; and at the End was acted that Farce [*Mock-Pompey*] printed in the fifth Act of *The Play-house to be Let*.[31] In fact, we have no evidence that *The Rehearsal* damaged the popularity of the plays it attacked. A generation or two later critics began to fall into the easy assumption that Buckingham had triumphantly stemmed the tide of tosh. As early as 1693 Thomas Rymer, a ferocious proponent of common sense, declared in his *A Short View of Tragedy* that 'We want a law for Acting the *Rehearsal* once a week, to keep us in our senses, and secure us against the Noise and Nonsense, the Farce and Fustian which, in the name of Tragedy, have so long invaded, and usurp our Theater.'[32] Rymer seems not to have understood how totally ineffectual the satire was in damaging the popularity of the object of its attack. Likewise John Dennis asserts flatly in 1696 that 'the Rehearsal almost alone reform'd the taste of the Age. So great an influence had the Ridiculum in that Play joyn'd with good Sense, upon the minds of the People, and consequently upon the practice of those who Writ.'[33] Writing some thirty years later, Dennis is even more extravagant:

When The Town too lightly gave their aplause, to Half a Dozen Romantick, Ryming, whining Blustring Tragedies, allurd by their novelty and by their glare, then Villers Duke of Buckingham writt the *Rehearsall*, which in a little Time opend their eyes, and taught them to Despise what before They rashly admird.[34]

All this, however, was so much wishful thinking. As early as 1718 Charles Gildon pointed out that the very plays attacked, or others full 'of all the Absurdities exploded in that pleasant Criticism', were not less thronged.[35] The many later commentators who have praised Buck-

[31] *An Account of the English Dramatick Poets*, 405.
[32] *The Critical Works of Thomas Rymer*, ed. Curt A. Zimansky (New Haven, Conn.: Yale University Press, 1956), 170.
[33] *Remarks on a Book Entituled, Prince Arthur*, in *The Critical Works of John Dennis*, ed. Edward Niles Hooker, 2 vols. (Baltimore, Md.: Johns Hopkins Press, 1939–43), i. 49–50.
[34] 'The Causes of the Decay and Defects of Dramatick Poetry' (1725?), ibid. ii. 277.
[35] *The Complete Art of Poetry*, 2 vols. (London: Charles Rivington, 1718), i. 202–3.

ingham for driving heroic drama off the stage have written in ignorance of the facts: far more rhymed heroic plays were written and staged after the production of *The Rehearsal* in 1671 than had been before it, as the list of titles in the *Annals of English Drama* clearly shows. Heroic drama was a fad, and it would have run its course much as it did with or without *The Rehearsal*. Buckingham capitalized on the fad more than he discouraged it.

## Political Allusions and Implications

If Buckingham had a serious purpose, it is more likely to have been political than literary. The picture of monarchy that emerges from his mocking representation of the heroic play certainly has suggestive points. Writing a generation ago, A. H. Scouten said that 'If it were not for our knowledge that the royalist Butler aided the duke, we might put a different intepretation on the whole work. . . . By 1671 Buckingham may have been deliberately satirizing Dryden's reverential praise of monarchy.'[36] Perhaps surprisingly, no scholar picked up on various hints and seriously endeavoured to explore the possibilities until George McFadden's pioneering article of 1974.[37] At least three issues are involved: kingship in general, the post-1660 Stuart monarchy in particular, and the policies of the restored government. A persuasive case can be made that Buckingham was targeting all of them. The heart of the case for political application may be summed up in six points:

1. Dryden's comment in 1693 (quoted above) is odd: 'I answer'd not the *Rehearsal*, because . . . I knew, that my Betters were more concern'd than I was in that Satire.' Who are these 'betters'? Perhaps Davenant, but in December 1671 he had been dead three and a half years, and there is not much in *The Rehearsal* as it has come down to us to connect Bayes to him. No other writer is so centrally and obviously in Buckingham's sights, and by 1671 no playwright in England could plausibly be thought Dryden's equal, let alone his better. The suggestion that Dryden is alluding to something outside the literary realm must therefore be taken seriously.

---

[36] John Loftis, Richard Southern, Marion Jones, and A. H. Scouten, *The Revels History of Drama in English*, v: *1660–1750* (London: Methuen, 1976), 250.

[37] George McFadden, 'Political Satire in *The Rehearsal*', *Yearbook of English Studies*, 4 (1974), 120–8. We are indebted to McFadden's discussion.

2. The brown paper applied to Bayes's broken nose at the beginning of Act III, Scene i is illustrated in ways strikingly similar to the black nose patch affected by Buckingham's political rival and bête noire, Henry Bennet, Earl of Arlington. Arlington's patch is referred to by numerous contemporary commentators (for example, in Buckingham's own 'Aduice to a Paynter, to draw the Delineaments of a Statesman'),[38] and is clearly depicted in contemporary portraits.[39] Laurence Echard's *History of England* tells us that in 1674/5 'it became a common Jest for some Courtier to put a black Patch upon his Nose, and strut about with a White-Staff in his Hand' in mockery of Arlington.[40] At the time *The Rehearsal* was first staged, Arlington was Buckingham's principal political opponent, and if illustrations of Bayes's nose patch are accurate, we may presume that it would have called Arlington to mind. Probably 'Arlington' should be understood as representing not just himself but also as standing as a proxy for a variety of Buckingham's political enemies.

3. So, in another way, might the principal usurping king, the Gentleman-Usher. The title refers to a pompously rigged-out major-domo whose task was to process gravely before persons of rank at their public appearances. The real-life Arlington had none of Bayes's sprightliness but was characterized by 'a taste for rich clothes and ponderous dignity, the latter enhanced by his heavy figure and the frown imposed by frequent headaches'.[41] These habits had been acquired in Spain, meaning that the merest hint of Spanish dress would have been enough to suggest an identity. His companion, King Phys., may well by the same logic have suggested the royal physician Sir Alexander Frazier, whose great influence at court is commented on by Pepys ('he can do what he please with the King'—*Diary*, v. 275).

4. Writing in 1691 Gerard Langbaine says that 'There are some who pretend to furnish a *Clavis* to it; my Talent not lying to Politicks, I know no more of it, than that the Author lashes several Plays of Mr. *Dryden*.'[42] This testimony dates from twenty years after the premiere,

[38] *Miscellaneous Works*, 1704–5, ii. 81. Printed at 11. 15, below.

[39] See his portrait in the National Portrait Gallery, reproduced in Maurice Lee, Jr., *The Cabal* (Urbana, Ill.: University of Illinois Press, 1965), after 150. For Bayes's wearing of such a patch, see the frontispiece to *The Rehearsal* in the 1715 *Works* (ii. following 32), reproduced opposite p. 34 in D. F. Smith, *Plays about the Theatre*.

[40] (London: Tonson, 1720), ii. 911.

[41] Hutton, *Charles the Second*, 193.

[42] *An Account of the English Dramatick Poets*, 546.

but if anything the persistence of rumours of political meanings gives credence to the possibility. By 1691 Charles was dead, James was in exile, and the broils of the early 1670s were very ancient history. That Buckingham 'lashes several Plays of Mr. *Dryden*' is undoubtedly true, but might the very conspicuousness of this assault serve as cover for a second set of meanings?

5. The 1704 *Key* glosses 'Two Kings of *Brentford*' with the explanation that they are 'Supposed to be the two Brothers, the King and the Duke' (2)—i.e. Charles II and the Duke of York—an obvious enough parallel. One might ask, 'If so, what then?' Perhaps a passing swipe at James and his supporters was intended by Buckingham and enjoyed by those hostile to the king's probable successor, though this need not imply any larger political meaning. But if one looks to the larger picture of governmental chaos contained in Bayes's version of Dryden's Stuart propaganda, then one might wonder if some stern advice to the royal brothers has been cleverly camouflaged with heaps of glaringly obvious literary trimmings. By this reading the play is not a parody of the usurpation and Restoration of 1649–60, but of a more recent one in which Arlington and Frazier had appropriated the direction of affairs while the king and duke danced and dawdled.[43]

6. Within months of the first performance of *The Rehearsal*, Andrew Marvell, a political associate of Buckingham, had used the title and principal character of the play as the basis of an attack, conducted through *The Rehearsal Transpros'd* (September 1672; second part licensed May 1673), on state repression of dissenters. Mr Bayes in this transformation becomes the Anglican anti-tolerationist Samuel Parker. This is not an issue specifically alluded to by Buckingham but suggests that the play's discourse was read by Marvell as intrinsically oppositional.

This may seem no very overwhelming case for a political subtext, but then had the satire been systematic or flagrant, Buckingham's play would certainly have been suppressed—as *The Country Gentleman* was in 1669. We may wish that an early-day Earl of Egmont had attended a performance and gone home to write a terse political exegesis in his diary, the sort of comment we are fortunate enough to possess for

---

[43] Derek Hughes comments that 'the play of restoration never reaches any kind of conclusion. ... The multiple kings divide and discredit the received iconography of authority.' *English Drama*, 85. The division of authority is of course innately comic. W. S. Gilbert's two kings of Barataria in *The Gondoliers* could be read as a Victorian version of Buckingham's joke.

Fielding's *Historical Register for the Year 1736*. But if Buckingham was to get away with such dangerous stuff, it would have had to be well hidden amidst literary burlesque. Buckingham could risk only the sort of satire that could not be proven. This leaves us less certain than we would like to be about the political satire, but if we consider the broader implications of Bayes's play in conjunction with the glancing allusion to Arlington, the ideology seems entirely conformable with Buckingham's political position and sympathies. As McFadden states the case, in the two Kings of Brentford

> Buckingham established the basic donnée of his satire . . . and . . . he also incorporates his fundamental objection to the regime of Charles II: that it brought confusion, divided the loyalty of the country, undermined its own ministers, and condemned the nation to inaction. Since Charles was unwilling to divorce his barren queen, the Duke of York, who was officially recognized as his successor, had a greatly enhanced status. . . . [Buckingham's] attitude toward the brothers struck contemporaries as one of ill-concealed contempt.' (p. 125)

The ineffectiveness of the two-headed government, the court intrigues, and the swipes at military mismanagement add up to a picture of a kingdom in total disarray.

McFadden's political interpretation has been politely acknowledged by most subsequent critics, but never seriously reckoned with. It is short and simple, more a sketch of a possibility than a systematic attempt to build a serious case. Fourteen years later, Margarita Stocker published a more fully developed political-ideological reading, but it has attracted virtually no commentary from scholars, who have dismissed it by ignoring it.[44] Stocker argues that 'in *The Rehearsal* political and literary satire are analogous, mutually reinforcing, and effectively inseparable. . . . [It] offers a logical political analysis of its time, precisely by diagnosing the ideology implicit in its literary target, the heroic drama' (p. 11). Buckingham was not in open opposition and could not afford openly to denounce the duplicity and incompetence of his king. As Stocker observes, 'The literary burlesque is a very distracting cover for political ideas' (p. 13), and equally important, the target of the literary ridicule is a systematic embodiment of the Stuart kings' divine-right theory of monarchy. To rubbish Dryden was to lay

---

[44] Margarita Stocker, 'Political Allusion in *The Rehearsal*', *Philological Quarterly*, 67 (1988), 11–35.

waste to his propaganda on behalf of Charles II. Buckingham systematically builds a parallel between the State and Bayes's poetic kingdom, and the hostile commentary of Johnson and Smith on the latter applies equally to the former. Dryden's heroic plays, particularly *The Conquest of Granada*, represent 'exempla' of the 'political theory and action' that Buckingham wanted to attack: they therefore provide a perfect dual target in which one of the items attacked both invokes the other and provides camouflage. Bayes's play projects—on his part unintentionally—a mordant picture of chaos, incompetence, and instability. The central thrust of Stocker's case is essentially that if we allow 'Buckingham's frivolous reputation' to dictate our reading of his play, then it seems no more than an 'enjoyable trifle', a mocking *jeu d'esprit* at the expense of Dryden's literary pretensions and a fad for inflated heroic drama. But if we look at the content of the mock-play and its relationship to current events and Stuart ideology, then perhaps we see a radically different enterprise.

*The Rehearsal* is certainly not a systematic political allegory, but its persistent preoccupation with government and kingship is by no means necessitated by the literary satire that provides its overt *raison d'être*. If both Arlington and Charles II were too wise to cry 'That was levell'd at me' (as Gay has it in Air 30 of *The Beggar's Opera*), this may simply be proof that Buckingham managed to make his point without giving anyone a handle against him. Buckingham regarded Arlington as an upstart nonentity, a vain pedant who was incompetent to manage public affairs. McFadden argues the satiric parallel as he believes it would have been perceived 'among insiders at court: Bayes, a bookish onlooker upon the world of affairs, directs a cast of actors in a senseless charade of political action. Arlington, equally an outsider, was pretending to direct affairs in Charles's court' (p. 123). The even more natural identification of Arlington with the Gentleman Usher would, if accepted, be an expression of the same prejudice. To view the literary satire as merely a cover for political satire would certainly be wrong. The stuff and substance of *The Rehearsal* is derived from literary elements. But to ignore all the statecraft and the swipe at Arlington would be equally misguided, for *The Rehearsal* is a kind of distillation of Buckingham's ideology and hostilities, a slashing commentary on literature and government alike. It does not really add up to anything; one might fairly say that the political satire is visibly the patchy product of one who was everything by starts and nothing long—chemist, fiddler, statesman, and buffoon—but the buffoonery is brilliant.

One must not forget, in the excitement of ingenious interpretation, to ask whether there is any solid historical evidence to confirm one's reading. How many people who attended the play in the early 1670s made this sort of 'application' to Arlington, Charles II, and the world of government? We will never know. Unlike the newspaper world of the 1730s when people were satirizing Sir Robert Walpole, the 1670s did not generate the kind of documentation that permits a scholar to prove this sort of case. Serious covert satire is always easier to imagine than to prove, and in cases of possible allegory where there is definitely a direct, literal, and obvious 'meaning' who is to say that the additional meaning is 'really there'?[45] The more careful the author is to avoid unmistakeable clarity and reprisals, the harder to be sure that the text 'means' what we might like to think it does. Did Buckingham want more than a coterie faction of the audience to make the (dangerous) application he seems to invite? Was he making a serious political argument with a call to action? Or was he merely amusing himself? He neither toppled Arlington nor got himself in public trouble. We are left in a position of no great certainty, but Dryden's odd comment about his 'Betters' and Langbaine's mention of those who would 'furnish a *Clavis*' suggest that there were those at the time who saw more than a simple literary burlesque in *The Rehearsal*.

## STAGE HISTORY

The performance history of *The Rehearsal* falls into two sharply distinct phases. Little is known of the first production, of reception, or of revivals until *c*.1705, when both theatres consistently start to place advertisements in the *Daily Courant*. Before that we are almost entirely in the realm of fragmentary evidence and guesswork; after that we have essentially complete documentation of the play's extensive performance history in London. A quite fantastic number of allusions to Bayes, and to the characters and episodes in the play, are to be found in eighteenth-century letters, newspaper articles, and pamphlets. Frequent offhand allusions in such places as the *Spectator* and the letters of Horace Walpole suggest the degree to which Buckingham's creation had attained

---

[45] For a discussion of the problems associated with 'multeity' ('those characteristics of a text that give it intrinsic author-designed multiple meanings'), see Robert D. Hume, 'The Politics of Opera in Late Seventeenth-Century London', *Cambridge Opera Journal*, 10 (1998), 15–43, esp. 28–35.

iconic status in the cultural imagination of later generations—a status sustained by numerous reprintings and by its remaining a 'stock play' in the London theatres.

## Seventeenth-Century Performances and Reception

The extreme scantiness of performance records prior to the establishment of daily newspapers in London makes our knowledge of *The Rehearsal*'s early history on stage sketchy in the extreme. Anthony à Wood states that the premiere occurred on 7 December 1671,[46] and this must be close to correct, for on the 14th John Evelyn wrote in his diary: 'At the R: *Society*, whence to see the *Duke* of *Buckinghams* ridiculous farce & Rhapsody called the *Recital*, bouffoning all Plays yet prophane enough.'[47] About this production we have virtually no information. Writing a century later, Thomas Davies offers us a speculation and a very dubious anecdote.

The original actor of Bayes was the celebrated John Lacy. . . . How this character was dressed by Lacy it is not now to be known. Dryden, it was said, was fond of wearing black velvet; and we may suppose the player endeavoured to resemble him, as near as possible, in dress and deportment. I have heard, indeed, that the Duke of Buckingham and the Earl of Dorset prevailed on Dryden to accompany them, in the boxes, on the first night of acting the Rehearsal; and placed the poet between them to enjoy the feelings of his mind during the exhibition of his own picture. The peculiarities of Dryden, when he [Bayes?] instructed the players, seem to be strongly marked through the whole piece.[48]

From this and similar 'evidence', nineteenth- and twentieth-century scholars erected an interpretative theory that rested on the presumption that *The Rehearsal* was a systematic satire on Dryden's personal appearance, dress, speech, behaviour, habits, and medical quirks.[49] Montague

---

[46] *Athenæ Oxonienses*, iv. 209.

[47] *Diary*, iii. 599. Because Evelyn drastically rewrote his diary, one must beware of putting too much faith in his dates. His attendance is a bit surprising, for he took a sour view of Buckingham. Some three weeks earlier, on 19 Nov., he had written: 'Leaving *Euston*, I lodged this night at Newmarket, where I found the jolly blades, Racing, Dauncing, feasting & revelling, more resembling a luxurious & abandon'd rout, than a Christian Court: The *Duke* of *Buckingham* was now in mighty favour, & had with him here that impudent woman, the Countesse of *Shrewsbery*, with his band of fidlars &c.' (iii. 596).

[48] Thomas Davies, *Dramatic Miscellanies*, 3 vols. (London: For the Author, 1784), iii. 289–90.

[49] For a sceptical demolition of this tissue of supposition and extrapolation, see O'Neill,

Summers says in the introduction to his extremely influential edition of
1914 that 'John Lacy . . . who created Bayes, was most carefully instructed in all his business and rehearsed by Buckingham himself. Dryden's voice, his mode of dressing, his gait and manners, were all carefully imitated, so that in representation there must have been a thousand touches now lost to us' (p. xi). The basis for this fine tale is Francis Lockier (1667–1740), Dean of Peterborough, who had met Dryden
many years earlier. According to Spence, he reported in 1730 that ''Tis
incredible how much pains he [Buckingham] took with one of the
actors [i.e. Lacy] to teach him to speak some passages in Bayes's part in
the *Rehearsal* right.'[50] This might be correct, but Lockier does *not* say
that Bayes was made to resemble Dryden in personal details. Such
claims were extrapolated by later critics. A century after Lockier,
Genest paraphrases Malone as follows:

> Much of the success, which the Rehearsal met with, was, doubtless, owing to
> the mimickry employed—Dryden's dress and manner, and usual expressions,
> were all minutely copied, and the Duke of Buckingham took incredible pains
> in teaching Lacy to speak some passages in the part of Bayes—in these he
> probably imitated Dryden's mode of recitation, which was by no means excel-
> lent. (*Malone*)[51]

So thoroughly has Bayes been identified with Dryden that biographers
have often assumed that Bayes's characteristics and identifying quirks
can safely be attributed to Dryden. This is bad methodology: even if we
did not have evidence that Buckingham's playwright started out as a
composite of at least two other people, we have no reason to suppose
that Buckingham felt compelled to restrict his characterization to biographical fact. Bayes *might* have been dressed and coached to 'take off'
Dryden in a recognizable and mean-spirited way, but we agree with
O'Neill that the King's Company is unlikely to have 'taken part in a
scheme to humiliate him' (p. 107). That he could have been persuaded
unwittingly to sit with Buckingham and Dorset at the premiere and
been taken by surprise seems totally implausible. Dryden ought, after

---

*George Villiers*, 102–7.

[50] Spence, *Anecdotes*, i. no. 667. Spence's editor Osborn notes that the 'earliest manuscript'
of the anecdote reads 'to make him enter into Bay's character'. Lockier's stories are judged by
Osborn to be 'more memorable for gusto than accuracy' (i. 273).

[51] Genest, i. 114. His source was Edmond Malone's 'Some Account of the Life and
Writings of John Dryden', in *The Critical and Miscellaneous Works of John Dryden*, ed.
Edmond Malone, 4 vols (London: Cadell and Davies, 1800), i. 99–100. See also Harold Love,
'Roger L'Estrange's Criticism of Dryden's Elocution', *Notes and Queries*, 246 (2001), 398–400.

all, to have been in the theatre every day for rehearsals of his own *Marriage A-la-Mode* at just this time, and he must have been cognizant of what was going on—whatever that was. By all accounts, Buckingham was a brilliant mimic, and we may presume that a vital part of the performance impact of *The Rehearsal* derives from body language and miming, whether personally aimed at Dryden or not. There is strong evidence for a performance tradition handed down from Lacy to Hayns to the Cibbers and Garrick. Buckingham might well have coached Lacy, even if he took no responsibility for rehearsing and staging the play.

That Buckingham travesties several of Dryden's plays in glaringly obvious ways cannot be denied. That Bayes is given many of Dryden's published critical opinions is likewise beyond dispute. Whether John Lacy made up as Dryden and personated him in ways recognizable to at least a knowledgeable part of the audience is a totally different question, and one on which virtually no seventeenth-century documentation exists. If a major (though covert) part of the play's design was political, then identifying Bayes personally with Dryden might be taken either as a distraction from the message about Lord Arlington or as wonderfully good cover for a dangerous message that needed to be well disguised. O'Neill is inclined to feel that the handsome compliments Dryden pays Buckingham's version of *The Chances* in 1672 are evidence against his having been personally travestied. Contrariwise, one might argue that Dryden was clever and self-controlled enough to put up a good show of being untouched and unmortified. Davies's view is at least as plausible: 'Dryden put the best face on the matter . . . [but] The revenge he took, in the character of Zimri, in his *Absalom and Achitophel* . . . is a proof that he was thoroughly angry' (iii. 288). Then again, one might counterargue that Dryden's devastating depiction of Buckingham in 1681 was driven by political motives, not personal hurt. Lacking evidence, one should perhaps refrain from speculation that cannot be validated. That Dryden enjoyed *The Rehearsal* seems unlikely, but it appears to have done him little or no real harm. Neither immediately nor in the long run is there any ground for believing that the popularity of Dryden's plays was damaged—and however ready the actors may have been to wound him personally, they seem extremely unlikely to have been ready to jeopardize the appeal of plays which had been tremendous commercial successes. If Buckingham wrote with genuine animus and a desire to drive rhymed heroic drama off the stage, he must have been extremely disappointed in the results.

We have no evidence as to the length of the initial run (ten days would have been quite exceptional at this time), and despite the play's apparent popularity Charles II did not attend a performance until 21 December 1674.[52] Only a sprinkling of other seventeenth-century performances are known. King James, Mary of Modena, and the maids of honour attended one on 6 May 1686.[53] On 3 January 1687 Lord Ashburnham wrote in his diary: 'I went to the play (the Rehearsal) where there was a great deal of company.'[54] A performance occurred in April 1689 with Jo Hayns playing Bayes (discussed below). Music survives from a revival c.1692 (also discussed below). A reprint of *The Rehearsal* in 1683 may reflect an otherwise unrecorded revival. This small total—seven definite performances—is no real indication of the popularity of Buckingham's play. Since it became a stock piece, we are probably safe in supposing that it was performed more than fifty times before the advent of daily newspaper advertisements, and the total could easily be twice that or more.

Almost no evidence survives to tell us what early audiences made of the play. The appearance of a second edition in 1673 implies a brisk market for the first, and the substantial textual additions (of unknown date) printed in the third edition in 1675 suggest lively public interest and concern for keeping the show topical. Some public currency soon after the original production is suggested by a reference to 'two good kings . . . at Brentford town' in 'Nostradamus' Prophecy' (1672), a non-theatrical satire.[55] The only substantive response we have discovered to *The Rehearsal* in the 1670s is a poem of thirty-four lines which has not, so far as we are aware, been previously published.[56]

> To the Illustrious Author his Grace the
> Duke of Buckingham vpon his Play called the Rehearsall.
>
> Thy fam'd and arbitrary Farse I saw,
> Where all that's witt's condemn'd without a Law
> 'Twere meane for thee thy reason to prevent,

---

[52] TNA PRO LC 5/141, p. 116.

[53] TNA PRO LC 5/147, p. 125. The performance is confirmed by the diary of General Patrick Gordon (see *The London Stage*, Part 1, 349). The king, queen, and maids of honour attended again on 20 January 1687 (LC 5/147, p. 361).

[54] *The London Stage*, Part 1, 355.

[55] See *POAS-Yale*, i. 187.

[56] The apparently unique source is Yale University, Beinecke Library, MS fb 140 (formerly Chest II, no. 3; formerly Phillips MS 8303), pp. 96–7. See Transmissional History, II. 551.

Who Claym'st in witt to bee Omnipotent.
As inst! the name *Rehearsall* seems to bee,     5
Since for Eight yeares[57] 'thas beene rehears'd by thee;
And did more pretious time with thee devide,
Then all Mankind, and businesse could beside:
Thou scorns't to write after the common rate,
Things to compose, that are but things create;     10
Yet in this Chaos there is shew'n by you
Something that would seeme great, and would bee new.
Soe have I seen where the Calme Thames doth glide,
In a fam'd house[58] not far from the Banke side.
Where People swarme to see the roaring Bears     15
More bayted then great Statesmen with theire Peers:[59]
There the disorderly and ill gazing Rout,
From vnseene Cause doe giddily fall out;
And vnprovok't, theire fury still repeate,
Yet all this while there's something new and great.     20
Wee see in thy *Rehearsall*, who dares fight,
As carelesly and boldly as you write.
Which shewes you the Drawcansir of all witt,
Since, far as thy Poetique Rage can hitt.
Thou with thy mighty and Impartiall blow,     25
Hurl'st equall fates vpon thy freind and foe.
In all thy mighty Actions still wee find,
That witt and Judgment are below thy mind.
Since wee perceive, all is despis'd by you,
That man can write or what men ought to doe.     30
Each Play to thy *Rehearsall's* but a foile,
Then who dares praise that in an humble stile;
'Tis thy owne word alone, must speake thy praise,
Thou art Drawcansir, thou art onely Bayes.[60]

The anonymous author is clearly hostile to Buckingham, but the poem is more pointed than abusive. We see no evidence for a particular date, but it was written after *The Rehearsal* had enjoyed a very considerable success. The reference to 'Eight yeares' in line 6 shows the writer's

[57] Referring to the long gestation of *The Rehearsal*, on which see p. 336 ff.

[58] The bear garden, which was still in business on the Bankside site it had occupied in Shakespeare's time.

[59] This may refer to the incident in Jan. 1674 when Arlington and Buckingham were successively interrogated before the Commons. For an account of this episode, see British Library Add. MS 61486, fos. 152–8; on Buckingham see fos. 157ʳ–158ʳ.

[60] Implying that the play is complicit with the high baroque theatrical procedures that it ostensibly satirizes; and that it is therefore not a rational but an extravagant criticism of extravagance.

awareness that the play had been started *c*.1664, helping to confirm both internal and external evidence to that effect. The literary thrust of the poem is against Buckingham's blanket condemnation of 'all that's witt' (2), his hurling 'equall fates vpon thy freind and foe' (26), and his claim 'in witt to be Omnipotent' (4). The real point of the poem, however, seems to be more political than literary. Buckingham is derided for the time he has spent on literary satire at the expense of serious business. Lines 13–19 imply a parallel between what goes on in Parliament and the bear-baiting to be found a little further down the Thames—presumably a cut at Buckingham's prowess as a debater in the House of Lords. Indeed, says the anonymous critic, the duke shows us 'who dares fight, / As carelesly and boldly' as he writes (ll. 21–2): Buckingham is the model for his own Drawcansir. The message of the poem seems to be that Buckingham is just as open to ridicule and condemnation as Drawcansir—or Bayes.[61]

About early casts of *The Rehearsal* we know almost as little as we do of early reception. The seventeenth-century quartos name no actors on the Dramatis Personae page, and contemporary commentary is little help. From the 1671 prologue we learn that John Lacy (d. 1681) apparently created the part of Bayes.[62] Certain deductions from the text are possible. Amarillis was presumably played by Anne Reeves (I. ii. 23), or the references to Esperanza (her role in *The Conquest of Granada*) would make no sense. William Cartwright is addressed by name at I. ii. 161 when Bayes corrects his delivery of 'I am the bold *Thunder*'. Since Bayes's play cannot begin without Abraham Ivory (named at I. ii. 190), we may deduce that he acted either the Gentleman-Usher or the Physician. George Shirley is named at II. iv. 36.2; Jo Hayns and Shirley are called upon to dance at the end of the play (V. iii. 31–2). According to a contemporary doggerel poem in Bodleian Wood 417 Hayns was responsible for arranging the various dances:

> I confesse the Dances, were very well writt,
> And the Tune, and the Time, by Hains as well hitt,
> And Littlewood's motion, and Dresse had much Witt.[63]

---

[61] Dryden echoes this opinion in his *Vindication of the Duke of Guise* (1683) when he says 'Much less am I concern'd at the noble name of *Bayes*; that's a *Brat* so like his own *Father*, that he cannot be mistaken for any other body' (*Works*, xiv. 327).

[62] The deduction is confirmed by Downes (*Roscius Anglicanus*, 40), who broke into verse:

> For his *Just Acting*, all gave him due Praise,
> His Part in the *Cheats*, Jony Thump, Teg *and* Bayes,
> In these Four Excelling; The Court gave him the Bays.

[63] 'A New Ballad to an Old Tune Call'd Sage Leafe' (printed in full in Appendix II, ii.

John Littlewood (fl. 1668–71) was a minor actor; we cannot guess from this allusion whether he took a part or merely danced.[64] The huge gaps in our knowledge of all seventeenth-century casts leave us no way even of speculating about production concepts and impact. Were the parts of Smith and Johnson taken by (say) Charles Hart and Michael Mohun? Their scorn could have been devastating. But suppose Mohun was used as Prince Pretty-man opposite Kynaston's Volscius? Were the lady loves of Bayes's heroes enacted by (for example) Elizabeth Boutell and Rebecca Marshall? Casting company principals in the 'interior' play would give it a more plausible spin. But if the principal parts were taken by company nonentities and travestied, a very different impression would be conveyed. Did the company put its best personnel into what it saw as a major production, or was this initially conceived as a sort of Christmas-season one-off? Most frustratingly, we have no idea who took the part of Drawcansir. Dryden's Almanzor had been played by the great Charles Hart, and casting him in the satiric version of the ranting superhero could have been hilarious—but would Hart have revelled in the joke or refused to stoop to such buffoonery? We simply do not know.

No performance is recorded between 1674 and 1686. By then Lacy was dead, and there is no record of Hayns performing with the United Company in 1685–86. Probably this was the period in which Susanna Percival Mountfort (later Verbruggen) took the part of Bayes *en travestie* with success. This we know from Colley Cibber, who tells us that 'while her Shape permitted, she was a more adroit pretty Fellow than is usually seen upon the Stage. . . . People were so fond of seeing her as a Man, that when the Part of *Bays* in the *Rehearsal* had for some time lain dormant, she was desired to take it up, which I have seen her act

306). A broadside version is in Bodleian Wood 417, no. 25. The Wood version is dated '1680' on the verso in ink, but annotated 'published in Jan. or Feb. 1673'. The date is evidently before January 1674 because the poem contains the phrase 'keepes the Adultresse' (l. 102 of the version in Yale MS Osborn b 105).

[64] Montague Summers states in *Playhouse of Pepys* (London: Routledge and Kegan Paul, 1935), 284 and 328 n. 28, that Kynaston took the part of Volscius, citing Bodleian MS Eng. Poet e.4 as his source. This MS contains a group of mock commendatory poems mostly aimed at Edward Howard (see 11. 8, below). Item 83 (198–9) is a copy of some twenty lines of Volscius's speech (correctly ascribed to Buckingham) said to be 'On the humour in Mr [blank] Howard's play where Mr Kinaston disputes his staying in or going out of town, as he is pulling on his boots. In imitation of the Earl of Orrery.' We take this to imply that Edward Kynaston took the part of Comely in Howard's play. See *The English Mounsieur* (pub. 1674), intro. by Robert D. Hume (Los Angeles, Calif.: Augustan Reprint Society, 1977), pp. x–xi. Kynaston could also have played Volscius, thus adding to the humour of the satire, but this is pure speculation.

with all the true coxcombly Spirit and Humour that the Sufficiency of
the Character required.'[65]

In April 1689 Jo Hayns took over the part of Bayes after returning to
England from Rome. The 1701 *Life* of Hayns tells the story as though
he first took the part as far back as the premiere in 1671, but given the
dubious reliability of the source, this seems unlikely:

*Hayns* betakes himself to the Kings Play House in *Drury-Lane*, is entertain'd,
at which time the Rehearsal writ by his Grace the Duke of *Buckingham*, was to
be Acted, The Famous *Lacy*, whose Part was that of *Bays*, unseasonably falls
sick of the Gout, and consequently is incapable of appearing on the Theatre,
*Hayns* is look'd upon as the fittest Person to supply the place of the Distem-
per'd, His Grace himself being pleased to instruct him in the Nature of the
Part, and Mr. *Lacy* by his Grace's command, took no small pains in teaching it
him; nor did *Lacy* gain less Reputation by this his Suffragan and Schollar, then
if he had Acted himself. So well did *Hayns* perform it, that the Earl of
*R[ochester]* Lord *B[uckhurst]* Sir *Charles S[edley]* and several of the most Ingenious Men, ever after held him in great esteem, which encreased more and
more with his Conversation; with which the Duke was so extremely pleased,
that going immediately after on an Embassy in *France*, his Grace thought
*Hayns* worthy of the Honour of going along with him.[66]

Be this as it may, we have convincing evidence that Hayns performed
the part of Bayes at the time of his return to London. On 23 April 1689
Narcissus Luttrell bought a copy of *Jo. Haines in Pennance: Or, his Re-
cantation Prologue, at his acting of Bayes in the Duke of Buckingham's Play,
call'd, The Rehearsal. Spoken in a white Sheet, with a burning Taper in his
Hand, upon his Admittance into the House, after his Return from the
Church of Rome.*[67] Hayns apparently took the part frequently in the
early 1690s. In his note 'To the Reader' prefaced to *A Fatal Mistake*
(unacted; pub. 1692) Hayns says 'I have Acted Mr. *Bays* so often, and
so feelingly.' The appearance of *Q6* in 1692 may well signal continued
revival at this time. The scantiness of the late seventeenth-century performance records notwithstanding, the popularity of *The Rehearsal*

[65] *Apology*, i. 167.
[66] Tobyas Thomas, *The Life Of the Late Famous Comedian, Jo. Hayns* (London: J. Nutt,
1701), 5. This account may contain a substantial amount of fact, but the implied chronology is
at least somewhat muddled, and perhaps drastically so. Hayns went to France with Buckingham in July 1670—more than a year before the play was performed. If he took the role of
Bayes in Lacy's lifetime he seems more likely to have done so later in the 1670s than at the
time of the premiere. If John Lacy coached Hayns in the part, he must have done so prior to
his death in 1681.
[67] See *The London Stage*, Part 1, 370, and Danchin, *Prologues*, iv. 721–3.

seems amply proved by the string of new editions and particularly by the publication of the *Key* printed in the *Miscellaneous Works* of 1704–5. This conclusion is confirmed by Gildon's statement in 1699 that the play 'is frequently acted of late Days'.[68]

### Eighteenth-Century Production History

The eighteenth-century stage history has been studied by Emmett L. Avery, whose work has since been verified and supplemented by *The London Stage*.[69] Nearly three hundred performances in London are known between 1704 and 1777, potent testimony to the more than topical appeal of the play. In 1778 it was cut down to three acts, and the appearance of Sheridan's *The Critic* in 1779 permanently eclipsed it.

By 1700 hardly any of the plays directly travestied in *The Rehearsal* remained in the repertories of the two London companies. Part II of *The Conquest of Granada* (three times) and *Marriage A-la-Mode* (once) were performed in the first decade of the eighteenth century, but few members of the audience save obsessive readers of play quartos would have recognized particular hits unless they used the 1704 *Key* as a guide.[70] We may guess that by the 1690s the theatrical life of *The Rehearsal* had come to depend on its intrinsic wit and humour—and perhaps increasingly on extra-textual additions—not on audience application to literary or political targets.

The first performance after 1700 of which we have record was advertised at Drury Lane in the *Daily Courant* of 18 November 1704 with Richard Estcourt (newly arrived from Dublin) featured as Bayes. No other performer was named, and the play was said to be 'Not Acted these five Years'—a claim that did not necessarily apply to the rival Lincoln's Inn Fields theatre, though no production there is known. Further performances were given on 21 November, 1 December, 4 January, and 2 February, again with only Estcourt named. He was the first great eighteenth-century Bayes, remaining a particular favourite in the

---

[68] *Lives and Characters*, 167.

[69] 'The Stage Popularity of *The Rehearsal*, 1671–1777', *Research Studies of the State College of Washington*, 7 (1939), 201–4.

[70] The growing need for annotation is signalled on the title page of the seventh edition (1701), which adds the phrase 'With some Explanatory Notes'. In fact, the publishers added only three marginal notes (signalled with asterisks). Against II. iii. 0.1 and 26.1 they added 'Prince in Marriage Al'amode'; against II. v. 0.1, 'To Ridicule the Dance of the fat Spirits in the Tempest, and the Angels Dance in H. 8th when it was first Play'd'; against III. ii. 0.1 'The two Kings in Granada'.

part until his death in 1712. He was famous as a mimic, but what or whom he mimicked (if anyone) in this role is not clear. The likeliest target was other performers. No other actor was advertised as Bayes until after his death, and the likelihood is that he took the part at all performances.

We do not have anything approaching a full cast for the play until 18 January 1709 at Drury Lane, when the following performers were advertised: Bayes—Estcourt; Johnson—Wilks; Smith—Mills; Prettyman —Powell; Volscius—Cibber; 'comical parts' by Johnson, Pinkethman, Bullock, Norris, Leigh, and Fairbank. On 18 November the same year the two Kings of Brentford were advertised as Bullock and Bowen, Physician—Cross; Gentleman Usher—Pinkethman; Tom Thimble— Doggett; Thunder—Johnson. We may deduce that the gentlemen commentators were played straight by principals, but that otherwise the play was mostly a romp for low comedians, which is certainly what one would expect. The implications of the advertised casts at this time are that Bayes's play was presented as low burlesque rather than performed 'seriously' over the top.

After Estcourt's death in 1712 the play fell out of the repertory until it was revived on 7 February 1717 at the command of the Prince of Wales.[71] From that time, it was almost always performed at least once or twice each season. No cast members were advertised until 15 November 1721 when Cibber was Bayes, Booth was Johnson, and Mills was Smith, roles they repeated on 15 January 1722 when the company also advertised William Pinkethman as Sol and Benjamin Johnson as Luna. These actors probably took their parts for most of the performances given during the 1720s, though the majority of the advertisements contain no cast information.

From Colley Cibber's later account of the 1717 revival we learn some interesting details:

The Play of the *Rehearsal*, which had lain some few Years dormant, being by his present Majesty (then Prince of *Wales*) commanded to be revived, the Part of *Bays* fell to my share. To this Character there had always been allow'd such ludicrous Liberties of Observation, upon any thing new, or remarkable, in the state of the Stage, as Mr. *Bays* might think proper to take. Much about this

[71] A promptbook started by W. R. Chetwood is probably connected to this production, though it contains different layers of prompt markings, some of them possibly in the hand of Richard Cross, who succeeded Chetwood as prompter at Drury Lane in 1741–42. The promptbook is now in the William Andrews Clark Memorial Library at the University of California, Los Angeles (*PR3328 B5 R3 1692 cop. 2). For discussion see Langhans, *Eighteenth-Century Promptbooks*, 213–14.

time, then, *The Three Hours after Marriage* had been acted without Success; when Mr. *Bays*, as usual, had a fling at it, which, in itself, was no Jest, unless the Audience would please to make it one: But however, flat as it was, Mr. *Pope* was mortally sore upon it. This was the Offence. In this Play, two Coxcombs, being in love with a learned Virtuoso's Wife, to get unsuspected Access to her, ingeniously send themselves, as two presented Rarities, to the Husband, the one curiously swath'd up like an *Egyptian* Mummy, and the other slily cover'd in the Paste-board Skin of a Crocodile: upon which poetical Expedient, I, Mr. *Bays*, when the two Kings of *Brentford* came from the Clouds into the Throne again, instead of what my Part directed me to to say, made use of these Words, viz. 'Now, Sir, this Revolution, I had some Thoughts of introducing, by a quite different Contrivance; but my Design taking air, some of your sharp Wits, I found, had made use of it before me; otherwise I intended to have stolen one of them in, in the Shape of a *Mummy*, and t'other, in that of a *Crocodile*.' Upon which, I doubt, the Audience by the Roar of their Applause shew'd their proportionable Contempt of the Play they belong'd to. . . . But this . . . was so heinously taken by Mr. *Pope*, that, in the swelling of his Heart, after the Play was over, he came behind the Scenes, with his Lips pale and his Voice trembling, to call me to account for the Insult.[72]

The tradition of interpolating current allusions was clearly an important part of *The Rehearsal*'s appeal for eighteenth-century audiences. Unfortunately, hardly any of them were recorded, so we know the tradition, but not the particulars.

What little we know of Cibber's characterization of Bayes comes from Davies, who reports (accurately) that he succeeded Estcourt in the part and says that 'In acting Bayes, Colley Cibber was dressed like a smart coxcomb. In the delineation of the character, he made him sufficiently ridiculous; but I thought he rather exhibited the laughter at Bayes's extravagances than the man that was enamoured of them' (iii. 302–3). Davies, who was born *c*.1712, implies that he had seen Cibber perform the part, which is biographically possible. The distinction he draws is an important one for a production's performance concept: is Bayes's fatuousness to be flaunted and relished or is it to be travestied and ridiculed? From internal evidence, one may deduce that Buckingham intended the former: Johnson wants to display Bayes for Smith's delectation.

When Colley Cibber ceased to perform Bayes in 1736, *The Rehearsal* dropped temporarily out of the repertory. All forty-seven performances

---

[72] *A Letter from Mr. Cibber, to Mr. Pope* (London: W. Lewis, 1742), 17–19. *Three Hours after Marriage* by Pope, Gay, and Arbuthnot ran seven nights at Drury Lane in Jan. 1717. *The Rehearsal* was performed on 7 and 8 Feb.

since its revival in 1717 had been at Drury Lane and, as Avery observes, Cibber may well have taken the principal part in all of them. When the play reappeared on the London stage on 10 October 1739, it did so at Covent Garden with Theophilus Cibber as Bayes. This was not merely a routine revival. It ran ten straight nights (extraordinary for an 'old' play), totalled twenty-two by the end of December, and amassed an astounding thirty-eight performances by the end of the season in June, including the last three nights—a virtually unique occurrence in the eighteenth century. There is some evidence that Theophilus tarted the play up for this revival, but we know little about the production. Thomas Davies says, rather tantalizingly, that

Theophilus ... displayed more vivacity in Bayes than his father; by the invention of new-raised troops, or hobby-horses, and other novelties, with some fresh jokes upon the actors, he drew the public to it for three weeks successively.—But Theophilus mixed too much grimace and false spirit in his best-acted parts. (iii. 303).[73]

The advertisement for the first performance gives Bayes—[T.] Cibber; Johnson—[Lacy] Ryan; Smith—[Dennis] Delane; and 'other parts by Hippisley; Bridgewater, Rosco, Hale, Hallam, Stephens, Roberts, Arthur, James, Neale, Mullart, Bencraft, Mrs Cross, Miss Burgess, Miss Norman'. Vocal parts by Leveridge, Legar [Laguerre], Salway, Bencraft, Mrs Lampe, and Miss Young were advertised; dancing by Poitier and Mlle Roland. How integral the song and dance was we cannot tell. The advertisement specifies 'With all the Music, Songs, Dances, Scenes, Machines, Habits, and other Decorations proper to the Play'.[74] The usual implication of such notices is that nothing customary would be omitted, but in the advertisement of 31 October (the twelfth night) there is a small addendum: 'With an Additional Re-Inforcement of Mr Bayes's new-rais'd Troops', which seems to imply more variety-show attractions. No text for this production has ever been discovered. In theory, the alterations should have meant that a licence needed to be applied for, and hence that there ought to be a Larpent manuscript among the censor's papers. In practice, the Covent Garden management evidently figured that no one would make a fuss

[73] Theophilus Cibber may have multiplied or otherwise emphasized the hobby horses, but they are of course in the original 1671 text at V. i. 281.1–2.

[74] One indication of special musical effects is that the Drury Lane account books often note a special addition of 10s. in the 'incident charge' for the play to pay for '2 extra hautboys' for the night (e.g. 31 Mar. 1772, paid on 15 May—Folger W.b. 274).

over a repertory staple, alterations or no. Our guess is that this was an acutely farcicalized production, but the audience obviously loved it.

The Covent Garden production ran another fifteen times in 1740–41 and its continued success led to a revival at Drury Lane on 21 November 1741, when Theophilus Cibber returned to that company. The playbill for that day says, inaccurately and misleadingly, 'Not acted these 7 years' and advertises 'Songs, Dances, New Scenes, Machines, Habits and other proper decorations. The Music New—compos'd by Mr Arne.' It specifies Delane and Mills as the two gentlemen, lays stress on additional music ('Vocal Parts by Beard, Lowe, Johnson, Ray, Raftor, &c'), and most interestingly adds 'Particularly the Representation of a Battle of the Two Operatical Generals Per gli Signori Giovanni and Tomasino detti Beard and Lowe'. The operatical generals are clearly a topical revamping of the Act V battle scene in which General and Lieutenant General enter, each with 'a Lute in his hand' (V. i. 185.1ff.), done in mockery of the Italian opera company that had opened on 31 October at the King's Theatre Haymarket with *Alexander in Persia* (a pasticcio arranged by Galuppi). John Beard was a noted operatic singer himself and had worked extensively for Handel; Thomas Lowe was likewise a popular singer. Thomas Augustine Arne's music apparently does not survive, but he was one of the foremost English theatre composers of the century and quite capable of either imitating or burlesquing battle music for *opera seria*. In the original play, the reduced scale of the battle was meant to ridicule *The Siege of Rhodes*. With the satiric target off the stage for many decades, Theophilus Cibber seems to have made the sensible decision to expand the combat into a grand frolic. One hint of the possible nature of the new-raised soldiery is a cartoon published in 1745, 'A New Muster of Bays's Troops'.[75] (See Figure 7, overleaf.) The cartoon was occasioned by a request for 'leave to raise 200 men in defence of his Majesty's person and government' by James Lacy (the Drury Lane patentee) at the time of the Jacobite invasion.[76] Some of the characters depicted hardly seem suitable for Mr Bayes's battle (Garrick as Richard III, Neale as Abel in *The Committee*, Macklin as Shylock, Delane as Othello), but Harlequin, Pierrot, Punch, and Ancient Pistol might conceivably have been pressed into service, as might the costumes, the baggage wagon, and paraphernalia of battle. Whatever the 'Additional Reinforcement' consisted of, it was clearly a

[75] This suggestion is made by the editors in *The Plays of David Garrick*, v. 307–10.
[76] *General Advertiser*, 28 Sept. 1745.

Fig. 7. *A New Muster of Bays's Troops*. By an unknown engraver, 'Sold at the Print and Pamphlet-Shops, 1745'. Courtesy of the Folger Shakespeare Library

success, for it became an advertised feature of all future London productions both at Drury Lane and elsewhere.

Theophilus Cibber's Drury Lane production of 1741 enjoyed nine performances, but had to be dropped when it encountered ruinous competition. Henry Giffard had illegally opened the Goodman's Fields Theatre in the autumn of 1741, giving 'concerts' with plays thrown in gratis. David Garrick gave his first public performance in London on 19 October as Richard III and quickly proved sensationally popular. On 3 February 1742 Goodman's Fields opened an alternative production of *The Rehearsal* with Garrick as Bayes. The two ran head to head on 6 February, after which Drury Lane threw in the towel.

The Goodman's Fields production ran thirteen times in February and once each in March, April, and May. It was clearly a personal triumph for Garrick, and when he jumped to Drury Lane near the end of the season, Bayes was the role he chose for his debut (26 May 1742). Garrick was to be the last great exponent of the role, and he dominated it completely for the rest of its stage life.

Garrick played the part of Bayes some ninety times between his first essay at Goodman's Fields and his final performance of the role on 7 December 1772. Exactly what constituted the 'Garrick version' of *The Rehearsal*, however, cannot be specified with any confidence. From marked copies, promptbooks, and editions printed after Garrick's retirement we may deduce that he continued to tinker with the script, cutting, restoring, and emending. Contemporary critical testimony proves that he did a fair amount of ad-libbing (some of which may not have been at all spontaneous).[77]

If the personal copy preserved at the Folger represents Garrick's acting version early in his career (and perhaps specifically what was given at Goodman's Fields), then the textual alterations were fairly minimal, consisting mostly of cuts to dispose of obsolete material and reduce running time. These are summarized in Table 1, overleaf.

---

[77] We have consulted two performance-related copies that have a connection with Garrick: (1) Folger Prompt R 12. This is evidently a personal copy of the 1683 quarto with Bayes's speeches flagged and some substantial cuts indicated, especially in the latter part of the play. Langhans suggests that 'perhaps' it reflects performance in 1742 at Goodman's Fields or Drury Lane or both, though we can see no definite evidence on the date or venue. (2) Herefordshire Museum and Art Gallery (not known to Langhans)—a similar personal copy of the 1687 quarto, without 'restorations' marked. We offer the hypothesis that (1) represents an earlier version of Garrick's text than (2), which seems more precisely and carefully crafted.

Garrick continued to perform Bayes with great regularity throughout the 1740s and 1750s and with reduced frequency through the 1760s. The copy text selected by Pedicord and Bergmann for *The Plays of David Garrick* was the Bell edition of 1777—an odd choice, given that

TABLE 1. *Garrick's cuts and changes in* The Rehearsal *early in his career as recorded in Folger Prompt R 12 and the Herefordshire Museum and Art Gallery personal copy*

| Act | Folger copy | Herefordshire copy |
|---|---|---|
| I.i | | 10–20 |
| | | 46–54 |
| I.ii | | 10 and those → 15 |
| | | 16 I . . . but *cut* |
| | 34:4–34:14 | 34:4–34:14 |
| | 130–1 | 130 I'm sure → 131 Dialogue? and |
| II.i | | 86:26 Gresham College → the Royal Society |
| II.ii | | 37 |
| | | 48:2–3 replaced by: *Smith falls asleep. Bayes.* ay sir—& if you'll keep yourself awake I shew you a good Reason for it. |
| II.iii | | added before 22.1: *Bayes.* Igad had there been another line I could not have stood it |
| III.i | | 80:9–80:24 |
| | | 80:25 this *changed to* such a |
| III.ii | 198:6 | |
| | 200–2 | |
| | 229:2 as I → 229:26 | 229:2 as I → 229:25.1 |
| | 232–43 | 232–43 |
| IV.i | 6 and he → 64 be so | 10–64 be so |
| | 85–7 | |
| | 98–158 [but marked 'stet'] | 98 Zookers → 154 yet passionate |
| | 196:1–3 | |
| V.i | 38–96 | 37.1–96.2 |
| | | 109.1 and foll. sp. tags: *two Heralds* [replaced by] *Soldier* |
| | | 124–6 |
| | 144 at door → 213 (incl. 167 1–3, 185:1–2) | 158–213 |
| | | 219 that shall be nameless [replaced by] who told it me |
| | | 240–244:1 |
| | | 245 Ah *through* a— [replaced by] Easily |

Garrick had given up the role five years earlier, and that it is evidently not especially close to what he did for much of his career. By Pedicord and Bergmann's count, some seventeen passages are marked for deletion in the prompt and personal copies known to them (ranging 'from part of a sentence to thirty-five and a half speeches'—v. 305). Garrick seems to have reinstated a number of passages he had previously cut, though no dates can be given with any confidence. Even Folger Prompt R 12, generally taken to represent an early phase of the text's history under Garrick, has one long cancelled passage against which 'stet' has been written. No published text from Garrick's active career represents his current theatrical practice at any point, even though the 1761 edition expressly claims to present the play as it 'was Acted on Monday, September 14, 1761, by Command, and before Their Majesties, the King and Queen, and Most of the Royal Family'. The text is in fact merely the standard derivation from *Q3* of 1675. Garrick's text was probably more cut than altered, but as Pedicord and Bergmann rightly say, 'Much of what went on during presentations of the Garrick period can only remain conjecture' (v. 311).

Despite our uncertainties about the exact state of Garrick's text at any time, we know quite a lot about the nature and impact of his productions. Thomas Davies gives us a vivid picture of his costume (see Fig. 8, overleaf) and distinguishes his concept and presentation of Bayes from that of his predecessors:

Mr. Garrick, when he first exhibited Bayes, could not be distinguished from any other gay well-dressed man; but he soon altered it to a dress he thought more suited to the conceit and solemnity of the dramatic coxcomb. He wore a shabby old-fashioned coat, that had formerly been very fine; a little hat, a large flowing brown wig, high-topt shoes with red heels, a mourning sword, scarlet stockings, and cut-fingered gloves.

The difference, between Garrick and his immediate predecessors, was very conspicuous. They, by their action, told the spectators that they felt all the ridicule of the part; he appeared quite ignorant of the joke that [the play?] made against him. They seemed to sneer, at the folly of Bayes, *with* the audience; the audience laughed loudly *at* him. By seeming to understand the satire, they caught at the approbation of the pit; he gained their loudest plaudits, without letting them know he deserved it. They were in jest; he was in earnest. (*Dramatic Miscellanies*, iii. 303–4)

Few actors save low comedians like to portray boobies. Colley Cibber was accustomed to taking obnoxious fop parts, but seemingly did not relish the idea of seeming oblivious to Bayes's fatuity. Not everyone

Fig. 8. 'Mr Garrick in the Character of Bayes'. By an unknown engraver. Published by Wenman, 1777. Courtesy of the Harvard Theatre Collection

preferred Garrick's playing the part straight (Horace Walpole, for one, liked Cibber's characterization better),[78] but it displays an interesting willingness to enter into the part rather than mock it. The peculiar costume, manifestly injurious to Bayes's pretentions, seems designed to invite a ridicule to which Garrick was determined to keep his Bayes impervious, playing the part deadpan throughout, as Stone and Kahrl observe.[79] Charles Lamb records another aspect of the performance through the recollection of an elderly playgoer named Lovel:

I saw him [Lovel] in his old age and the decay of his faculties, palsy-smitten, in the last sad stage of human weakness . . . yet even then his eye would light up upon the mention of his favourite Garrick. He was greatest, he would say, in Bayes—'was upon the stage nearly throughout the whole performance, and as busy as a bee'.[80]

The comment conveys the amazing energy of Garrick's portrayal that had remained for half a century with this witness.

Garrick was not yet 25 and in his first season in London when he took the part. He found the audience particularly responsive: 'I have ye Greatest Success immaginable in ye Part of Bayes, & instead of clapping Me they huzza wch is very uncommon approbation.'[81] An important element of Garrick's appeal in the role—at least early in his career, and probably later as well—was mimicry of the performance styles of prominent actors of his own day. Davies says that

In Bayes he introduced an imitation of several celebrated actors, particularly Delane, Bridgewater, Mills, Hale, and Giffard. He represented their voice and manner so perfectly, that the theatre ecchoed with repeated shouts of applause. It was observed that several of the players enjoyed the jest very highly, till it became their own case; they then gave as evident signs of uneasiness and disgust as they had before of pleasure and satisfaction. This unjustifiable method of depreciating the abilities of his fellow-comedians, by pointing out their pe-

---

[78] Walpole found Garrick's Bayes 'entertaining—but it was a garreteer-bard—Old Cibber preserved the solemn coxcomb; and was the caricature of a great poet, as the part was designed to be'. *The Yale Edition of Horace Walpole's Correspondence*, ed. W. S. Lewis, et al., 48 vols. (New Haven, Conn.: Yale University Press, 1937–83), xxxiii. 88.

[79] *David Garrick, A Critical Biography* (Carbondale, Ill.: Southern Illinois University Press, 1979), 477. For analysis of Garrick as Bayes and discussion of his 'tendency to explain or to ingratiate himself through self-ridicule', see Leigh Woods, *Garrick Claims the Stage* (Westport, Conn.: Greenwood, 1984), 129–35.

[80] 'The Old Benchers of the Inner Temple', in *Elia* (London: Taylor and Hessey, 1823), 201.

[81] *The Letters of David Garrick*, i. no. 22 (to Peter Garrick, 6 Feb. 1741[/2]).

culiarities, he continued two or three years, and then dropped it as an unfair and cruel practice. It has been since resumed by some actors of great and general merit, and by others who have nothing else to recommend them to public notice.[82]

We are sceptical as to the accuracy of Davies's claim that in 1741–42 Giffard (the manager at Goodman's Fields) was so offended by Garrick's spoof of him at a rehearsal that he challenged Garrick to a duel and wounded him in the arm.[83]

Arthur Murphy's account of Garrick's early productions of *The Rehearsal* suggests that with the targets long obsolete he saw the play as a vehicle for satire on acting styles:

To the Duke of Buckingham's admirable satire, Garrick was able to make a considerable, and indeed, requisite addition ... he seized the opportunity to make the *Rehearsal* a keen and powerful criticism on the absurd stile of acting that prevailed on the stage. In the character of *Bayes* he exhibited to the life the vain coxcomb, who had the highest conceit of himself, and thought the art of dramatic poetry consisted in strokes of surprise and thundering versification. The players of his day he saw were equally mistaken. In order, therefore, to display their errors in the most glaring light, he took upon him occasionally to check the performers, who were rehearsing his plays, and teach them to deliver their speech in what he called the true theatrical manner. For this purpose, he selected some of the most eminent performers of the time, and, by his wonderful powers of mimickry, was able to assume the air, the manner, and the deportment of each in his turn.[84]

Murphy goes on to name Hale and Ryan (both of Covent Garden) as among those mocked, but reports that James Quin was spared this treatment because his style fitted the characters he enacted. Murphy says that in declaiming 'So boar and sow' Garrick as Bayes 'retired to the upper part of the stage, and drawing his left arm across his breast, rested his right elbow on it, raising a finger to his nose, and then came forward in a stately gait, nodding his head, as he advanced, and, in the exact tone of Delane', spoke the lines. He then imitated the 'plaintive'

---

[82] Thomas Davies, *Memoirs of the Life of David Garrick*, 4th edn., 2 vols. (London: for the Author, 1784), i. 47–8 (passage not in the first edition or the 1808 edition).

[83] Davies, *Memoirs of the Life of David Garrick*, ed. Stephen Jones, i. 42. Davies's assertion that the play had to be 'put off for a fortnight longer, *on account of the sudden indisposition of a principal performer*' is disproved by the performance calendar in *The London Stage*. Garrick was definitely performing.

[84] Arthur Murphy, *The Life of David Garrick, Esq.*, 2 vols. (London: J. Wright and J. F. Foot, 1801), i. 51–3.

voice of Hale in another ridiculous speech in the text, and the 'tremulous raven-tone' of Ryan in a third.[85] That Garrick 'took off' performers of his day is indisputable; whether he mimicked those who were on stage with him is questionable. In any case, Stone and Kahrl state that 'Garrick soon abandoned the personal mimicry' of fellow actors,[86] but he continued to include personal allusions. A critic in the *Universal Museum* of March 1762 says:

Great part of the humour lies in Bayes's taking off the other actors.—When Yates speaks a little Latin falsly, he says, 'and you, Mr. Yates, you that was bred an attorney, not to speak it right!' Blakes, who acts Prince Prettyman, comes on with his usual gait, and Bayes mimicks him, saying, 'Now enter Mr. Blakes—not Prince Prettyman.' It is easily supposed how small these gentlemen must appear, on such occasions, but to the no small entertainment of the audience. (p. 170)

The same critic records that at the point at which Lardella's coffin opens to disclose a banquet (IV. i. 168.1), Garrick added a triumphant line for Bayes: 'Where's your Shakespear now, Smith!' Pedicord and Bergmann are of the opinion that 'Garrick's additions were extemporaneous' and that 'very likely these additions changed with almost every performance' (v. 313). Some were perhaps spontaneous and topical. The prompter Richard Cross records Garrick saying to Ned Shuter (who had just engaged to move to Covent Garden) 'you are a good Actor & I am sorry you have left me', which drew some applause.[87] We suspect, however, that many of Garrick's extra-textual comments were planned and repeated, or at least that occasions for them could be utilized as he saw fit. He was certainly prepared to take advantage of current events. When Garrick revived the play in 1766 for a command performance he said as Bayes, when informed that the actors had gone off to dinner, 'I'll *Rosciad*, I'll *Thespis* ye, I'll make ye tremble'—and drew a hand from the audience.[88]

Not everyone approved Garrick's put-downs of fellow actors. The author of a pamphlet published in 1758 says flatly that 'the introducing

[85] Murphy, *Life of Garrick*, i. 53–4.
[86] *David Garrick*, 478.
[87] Folger MS Wa. 104 (2) (21 May 1753).
[88] Folger scrapbook, cited in Stone and Kahrl, *David Garrick*, 480. Charles Churchill's *The Rosciad* (1761) was a savage satire on the actors (though praising Garrick); Hugh Kelly's *Thespis* (1766) was 'a Critical Examination into the Merits of all the Principal Performers Belonging to Drury-Lane Theatre'—which was likewise kind to Garrick, but gave some others their lumps.

private characters upon a stage can never be justified',[89] and Theophilus Cibber delivered himself of a huffy reproof for such 'artful Spleen', claiming that '*Garrick's Bayes* (not *Buckingham's*)' was

no longer consider'd as a witty Satyr on the Foibles, and Faults, of Authors,— and a Reproof of the Town for their false Taste of the Drama:—It became a motley Medley of Buffoonery, to explode the Actors.—But, where did he attack 'em?—On their weak Side, indeed,—where they cou'd not be on their Guard: Instead of critically pointing out their Want of Taste, or Judgment,— he cruelly turn'd the whole Artillery of his Mockery against their natural Defects, or such Particularities of Voice, which did not misbecome them; nor met with Reproof 'till his Vice of taking off, as it is call'd, became the foolish Fashion;—and taught School-Boys to be Critics.[90]

Cibber was, to be sure, bitterly envious of Garrick, and his assertion that Garrick's mimicking Dennis Delane contributed to Delane's drinking himself to death seems extravagant.

With the literary targets of *The Rehearsal* long vanished from the repertory the play needed invigoration from other sources. For the company's low comedians it became a frolic. For Garrick it could be made to serve as a personal showpiece, but also as a vehicle for mocking what Garrick regarded as bad acting. This was a conscious and avowed aim throughout his career. 'E.F.', the author of *Mr. Garrick's Conduct, As Manager of the Theatre-Royal in Drury Lane, considered*, refers to 'the Pleasure You frequently gave the Town in the Character of *Bayes*' and justifies his mimickry of fellow performers: 'To do You Justice, the ridiculous Light in which You exposed the Mistakes of your Brother Comedians . . . though attended with some Degree of Cruelty, deserved the Applause You gained at *Good-man's Fields* House.'[91] Some three decades later, after he had played Bayes for the last time, Garrick wrote a curtain-raiser called *The Meeting of the Company; or, Bayes's Art of Acting* (premiered 17 September 1774). The prompter Hopkins noted in his diary that 'it is full of fine Satyr & an Excellent Lesson to all performers'.[92] We suspect that in Garrick's hands *The Rehearsal* became much less a literary satire and much more an exhibition of and dissertation upon bad acting.

The astonishing stage popularity of *The Rehearsal* in the eighteenth century clearly owes a great deal to the excellence of the vehicle that it

[89] *A Letter to Mr. Garrick on the Opening of the Theatre* (London: J. Coote, 1758), 17.
[90] *Two Dissertations on the Theatres* (1756), 44–5.
[91] (London: C. Corbett, 1747), 15.
[92] *The London Stage*, Part IV, iii. 1833.

offers a performer of Bayes. Among them, Colley Cibber, Theophilus Cibber, and David Garrick collectively played the role more than two hundred times. The younger Cibber and Garrick were not, however, the only mid-century actors to take the role. The management of Goodman's Fields found the play important enough as a repertory piece that it attempted to replace Garrick with 'A Gentleman' (James Dance, later known as James Love) for a number of performances in 1745. When he tried the role at Covent Garden on 2 May 1746 the *Daily Advertiser* offered him some 'advice' two days in advance:

Let not any Success you might meet with at one End of the Town where the Audience must be composed of a different Class of People from what you may expect at Covent Garden, tempt you to think of mimicking an Actress [identity unclear] whom the Town doats upon; and particularly avoid Puffing; a Scheme long ago worn threadbare, but lately quite demolish'd by an enterprizing Genius [Garrick]. Not even an Epilogue from the Gods would be of any Service now; and therefore if you have anything that's new, any fiery Flights of Fancy, and all that, let them lie dormant till the Time of Action and then endeavour to elevate and surprise. Value these Hints.

When Garrick went to Dublin in 1745–46, Drury Lane tried to replace him with the young Samuel Foote (13 December, 24 January), and Foote shared the role with Theophilus Cibber at Covent Garden in 1747–48, but not until nearly thirty years after he first essayed the part did Foote mount his own production. John Lee tried the part as a benefit piece at Covent Garden in 1758. Tate Wilkinson attempted it ('with imitations') at the Haymarket in the summer of 1764, and Ned Shuter in the summer of 1765. Between 1739 and 1769 the only calendar year without a performance in London was 1751. Garrick apparently lost his enthusiasm for the role by the mid-1750s, but took it occasionally through to 1767. In 1771 Thomas King assumed the part at Drury Lane, though Garrick did three final performances in 1772. Henderson attempted it at both the Haymarket and Drury Lane in 1777, after which Drury Lane dropped the play entirely, its place in the repertory filled by *The Critic*.

Comments on James Love as Bayes in Edinburgh in the 1750s shed some light on performance style and practice. Deriding 'the Deficiency, nay palpable Absurdity of Mr. *Love* . . . a mere Burlesque on Burlesque', an anonymous critic opined:

We cannot help thinking, that this Character is most egregiously mistaken by Mr. *Love*. Every Body knows, that it was drawn by the Duke of *Buckingham*, in Ridicule of a certain great Poet; and whoever reads it over with an unbiassed

Attention, will easily perceive that he is a stiff, self-conceited, pragmatical Fellow: One of your Buckram Gentlemen, who, being fully persuaded that he is the most wise and ingenious Man alive, would not yield the smallest Point to any Person whatever. Instead of this, we see Mr. *Love* looking through a heavy, clownish Fellow most fantastically dressed, speaking and acting with all the Grimace and Buffoonery of a *Jack Pudding*; and, with a foolish Face of Satisfaction, raising a hoarse Laugh at his own Jests. We would not be understood by this, as if we meant to arraign the Judgment of the Town, who frequently *seem* to applaud him in *Bayes*; so far from this, we are of the Number of those who give what he thinks Marks of Approbation; for we defy any Man to keep his Gravity, at seeing such shrugging of Shoulders, so many wry Faces, and uncouth Gesticulations. By these strangely-mechanical Means we are extreamly diverted, and naturally fall a clapping, altho', upon cool Reflection, we are very much ashamed of our Merriment. We have heard People say, that all they wanted of a *Bayes*, was to make them shake their Sides: Such we would wish Joy, on having found a Performer more than able for the arduous Task. Others have blindly affirmed, that Mr. *Love* plays it exactly in the Manner of Mr. *Garrick*, and perhaps as well, if not better: These we would pity, and give to understand, that they are vainly comparing what are literally as opposite as Light and Darkness.[93]

Bayes as buffoon and Bayes as solemn pretender to wit and dignity are vastly different conceptions of part and play.

The last production of any significance was Samuel Foote's at the Haymarket, produced with himself as Bayes on 18 June 1773. The lack of a text is most unfortunate, for Foote seems to have departed drastically and successfully from what he inherited. Thomas Davies describes the production thus:

The Bayes of Foote was an odd mixture of himself and the Duke of Buckingham; the old building was new-faced with a modern front. He contrived to adapt, as well as he could, his new superstructure to the old ground-work. His fancy was so exuberant, his conceptions so ready, and his thoughts so brilliant, that he kept the audience in continual laughter. Public transactions, the flying follies of the day, debates of grave assemblies, absurdities of play-writers, politicians, and players, all came under his cognizance, and all felt the force of his wit; in short, he laid hold of every thing and every body that would furnish merriment for the evening. Foote could have written a new Rehearsal equal to the old. (*Dramatic Miscellanies*, iii. 304–5)

Foote clearly saw the show as a chassis on which to hang a whole farrago of topical jokes and allusions. How much he cut is impossible to

---

[93] 'A Society of Gentlemen' [James Boswell?], *A View of the Edinburgh Theatre during Summer Season, 1759* (London: A. Morley, 1760), 33–5.

guess, but probably quite a lot. Where Garrick kept most of the text and added stylistic burlesque and some interior playhouse allusion, Foote seems to have changed the text itself wholesale. The audience expected some humorous additions and topical references, just as audiences now expect 'I've got a little list' to depart from W. S. Gilbert's set text in *The Mikado*. When Covent Garden revived the play in the autumn of 1774 with John Lee as Bayes, a reviewer commented ascerbically:

Never did we see the part of *Bayes* attempted by a performer so entirely destitute of spirit, taste, and pleasantry. The sallies of wit (pretended to be *extempore*) usually thrown out by the Actors in this play, were so very sparingly sprinkled this evening, that we remember but one apparently manufactured by *Bayes* himself, though delivered by another performer. Mr. *Lewes*, the Harlequin, being reprehended by the author for introducing pantomimical tricks into his character, replies, that 'he was told by the *Bayes* of the other House, that a part in Tragedy was good for nothing without a Start or a Tumble.'[94]

As Tate Wilkinson was to say very late in the century, 'Bayes is always *ad libitum*'—and this was clearly a part of the play's appeal.[95]

At the very end of the play's stage life it was chopped down to three acts to serve as an afterpiece. Its last London performance as a mainpiece was at Covent Garden on 20 January 1778. Just two weeks later, on 2 February, the company offered it as an afterpiece with a special note of explanation in their bill: '*The Rehearsal* having been found too tedious in Representation, and Part of the Dialogue between Bayes and the two Gentlemen wholly obsolete, it has been thought advisable to . . . reduce the Piece to Three Acts'. The afterpiece version was used again at Covent Garden on 18 March 1782 (a benefit) and three times in September and October 1785.[96] The last appearance of the play on the

---

[94] *Westminster Magazine* (Oct. 1774). Lee Lewes specialized in Harlequin characters, and performed them in various shows. For an illustration of his costume in a Harlequin part, see *Biographical Dictionary*, ix. 271. Roles were not specified in the newspaper advertisements, but we deduce that Lewes took one of the 'tragic' parts and hammed it up.

[95] Tate Wilkinson, *The Wandering Patentee; or, A History of the Yorkshire Theatres, from 1770 to the Present Time*, 4 vols. (York: For the Author, 1795), i. 279. Wilkinson reports this in connection with a compliment to himself by Mr Wroughton, who said he was the only person to act Bayes 'like a gentleman'—'Meaning that . . . Mr. W. acted that character well, and without taking any rude liberties with the performers in their profession'.

[96] The text of the Covent Garden afterpiece version was not printed as such. Two related prompt copies of the 1768 edition in the British Library (841.b.55 and 841.e.79) with the text cut down to three acts might conceivably connect to this production, though we see no clearcut evidence for attribution of venue. On these promptbooks, see Langhans, *Eighteenth-Century Promptbooks*, 214–15.

eighteenth-century London stage was as the middle offering in a triple-bill at the Haymarket on 9 August 1792. On that occasion it served as a benefit piece for Richard Wilson, who featured in the playbill 'a Grand Review of Bayes's Troops, with a Sham Battle of Horse and Foot'. Wilson's text had probably been performed at Edinburgh and perhaps elsewhere in the provinces. It had already been published in volume 6 of *A Collection of the most esteemed Farces and Entertainments performed on the British Stage*.[97] The Wilson version is drastically lopped and sometimes awkward in its compressions and juxtapositions, but what remains is surprisingly close to the 1675 text. Wilson did not even clean up the sexual allusions to Bayes's mistress and his serving as gigolo to a 'woman in the city' (p. 348). He does substitute 'Shakespeare' for 'Suckling' at II. i. 62 as the poet Bayes claims to outdo (p. 354). But all considered, Wilson remained astonishingly faithful to the language, tone, and particulars of the original.

Genest reports a performance at Covent Garden as late as 22 June 1819 (reduced to one act), with Farren as Bayes (ix. 6).[98] Montague Summers' edition (p. xvii) records a single performance on 20 November 1912 under the auspices of the Sheffield Playgoers' Society (reportedly a success) and two performances at the Regent Theatre, London, on 5 and 6 July 1925.[99] Probably there have been a number of college and amateur productions. Robert D. Hume saw one such effort at an American Society for Eighteenth-Century Studies meeting at Bethany College (West Virginia) in October 1982, enjoyed it, and found that it proved entertaining even to those members of the audience who were totally unacquainted with the literary targets.

## *Staging* The Rehearsal

Little is known about the stage presentation of the play, even after 1700. An effective performance could be given on a bare stage. Since we are supposed to be seeing what would now be called a dress rehearsal, however, we may guess that technical effects and scenery were supplied in the changing fashions of the times. Probably the 1671 pro-

[97] (Edinburgh: C. Elliot, 1788), 343–66.

[98] A playbill preserved in the Dartmouth College Library says 'for the first time these thirty years' and describes it as by Buckingham, altered by Garrick, 'with additions by a celebrated dramatist' (unidentified), given as an afterpiece for *The Clandestine Marriage*.

[99] *Playhouse of Pepys*, 286.

duction was a great deal simpler than the one of 1717, and by 1739 there is reason to suppose that presentation had become far flashier. By way of evidence we have only two significant sources: the very minimal stage directions included in *Q1* and *Q3* and the William Andrews Clark Memorial Library promptbook (*PR3328 B5 R3 1692 copy 2) associated with productions at Drury Lane between 1717 and the early 1740s. This prompt copy has at least one major gap (pp. 17–26 are missing), but does supply some important particulars and hints. Illustrations of particular scenes are sometimes suggestive, but the degree of faithfulness to theatrical practice in such pictures is often impossible to judge.

*Act I.* The play opens in the street outside the King's Company's Bridges Street Theatre. In the 1671 production this could conceivably just have been played against the proscenium (a standard convention), but by 1717 (and perhaps from the start) a wing-and-shutter painted scene of a 'street' was shown. For Scene ii the action moves to the stage of the theatre. Lacking any indication to the contrary in the Clark promptbook, we may guess that action took place on a bare stage, exposing the guts of the theatre as a novelty. A cryptic notation '3 chair O:D' means (we would guess) that three chairs were provided on the opposite prompt side.[100] At line 38 Bayes says 'let's sit down', which he and his guests then presumably do. The Thunder and Lightning prologue requires no scenery and seemingly got none.

*Act II.* For the start of Bayes's play the promptbook specifies 'Palace 3d Carpet'. No scenic notes are given for the rest of the act, but 'Put on 2 Gr[eat] Chairs' at II. iii. 44.1 (by the first line of Bayes's last speech) means that the 'two great chairs upon the Stage' occupied by the usurpers at II. iv. 30.1–2 were set in place at the start of Act II, Scene iv.

*Act III.* The promptbook fails us here. The palace setting could be used for most of Scenes i and ii, but at III. ii. 148.1 a street scene (different from that used for I. i) is definitely needed for Prince Volscius going out of town. When he 'sits down' at III. ii. 205.1, what does he sit on? Perhaps he just (comically) sits right down in the road. We cannot tell.

*Act IV.* The promptbook says (very confusingly) 'T̶e̶m̶p̶l̶e̶ Continues' (evidently an error) and specifies 'Table & 3 Chairs'. At IV. i. 68.1 we

---

[100] Langhans suggests that 'O:D' is an error for O:P. He interprets the '3' as 'the groove number' (an indication of placement depth), but we doubt that they would have been set so far upstage and three chairs are needed for Bayes and the two gentlemen to sit.

get *'Enter a Funeral'*, which implies that the coffin and appurtenances are carried on in full view, but the promptbook says 'NH' [New Hall] and 'Funeral Discd.' [Funeral Discovered], implying a change of scene with the 'discovery' of the funeral accomplished by drawing the shutters apart to reveal it already on stage. The latter is the better way of staging the scene: at a guess the original production did not make full use of changeable scenery capacity at Bridges Street. A much reproduced illustration appears to show Pallas dispensing wine from the trick lance, Bayes (patch on nose prominent), and the two gentlemen standing.[101] The action is depicted as occurring in a vaulted walkway with numerous columns—not a very plausible setting for the feast that follows (broken up by Drawcansir): we are inclined to doubt the theatrical veracity of the picture. Scene ii with Volscius and Pretty-man takes place in a scene described as 'c:c' (perhaps 'chimney chamber'?). For reasons not clear to us, the promptbook specifies a brief change to 'Wood thro'', which Langhans interprets as 'a cut wood setting through which could be seen the deeper reaches of the scenic area'. This was probably used as a transition to the dropping of the curtain at the end of Act IV (IV. ii. 81).

*Act V.* Bayes and the two gentlemen start on the forestage. 'The Curtain is drawn up' at 6.1, grandly revealing usurpers 'in State', cardinals, princes, ladies, heralds, et al. The promptbook specifies 'H. [high?] Palace' as the setting. At V. i. 37.1–4 the 'two right Kings' and three fiddlers 'descend in the Clouds' (that is, appear in a cloud machine large enough to hold five people that comes down out of the flies and eventually lands on the stage). It is signalled by a 'C:B:' (cloud bell). The promptbook also implies an extra-textual addition at this point: a 'T:B:' (trap bell) rings to signal the emergence of 'Spirits', apparently to sing with the kings. The promptbook indicates a switch to the 'C' chamber setting and a dance (not in the text). The battle takes place in an exterior setting specified as 'sh: wood', which Langhans takes to

---

[101] This illustration is reproduced by Smith in *Plays about the Theatre* opposite p. 34 without a stated source, and as the frontispiece to vol. xi of Dryden's *Works*, where it is said to show 'Bayes Explaining That He Wrote the Part of "Armarillis" for His Mistress: Act I, Scene I, *The Rehearsal.*' The source is vol. ii of the 1715 *Works* ('Adorn'd with Cuts'), facing the title page of the play. As we interpret the engraving, the scene depicted is not I. ii. 23–30 but rather IV. i. 184–6 where Pallas fills bowls of wine out of her lance. Her huge belly is probably a joke at the expense of 'big bellied' (pregnant) actresses performing inappropriate roles. In the spring of 1713, for example, Anne Oldfield had played Cato's virgin daughter in a state of advanced pregnancy.

means 'short wood' and interprets as 'a downstage forest setting (probably a drop)'. We presume that this relatively limited space for the battle represents staging for the original, small-scale battle and that by the 1741 Drury Lane production more of the stage would have been used. A likely indication of the elaboration of the battle at both theatres by this time is an entry in John Rich's Covent Garden scene inventory of 1744: 'the bridge in the Rehearsal 3 peices', indicating staging that required a special setting, presumably for hobby horses and soldiers to charge over.[102] At the end of the promptbook is a marking (which we interpret as a late addendum by Hopkins) suggesting a bell or whistle signal for dropping the curtain 'When the horses are all off'—that is, after cleaning up the results of the battle, which ends when 'Drawcansir *comes in, and kills 'em all on both sides*' (V. i. 287.2-3). No new setting is specified for Bayes's last interchanges with the actors.

A promptbook preserved in the Harvard Theatre Collection (shelfmark TS 2568.100) offers some insight into the play's late history in cut-down form. The maker of the promptbook used the printed edition of 1768, interleaved and with about twenty pages removed in their entirety. Numerous large and small additional cuts drastically reduced running time: the result is essentially a two-act version. The precise function of this copy is not clear. Bayes's speeches are flagged; PS and OP entrances and exits are marked early in the script, as are scene changes and 'warnings' that are evidently keyed by number to a separate list used by the call boy. A few MS additions and directions are added. At I. i. 130 we learn that 'after much ceremony Bayes goes of[f] first'. At I. ii. 34:1-2 Bayes is made to deny having 'had' his mistress by replacing 'for I have talkt bawdy . . . how was that' with

*John*. O yes you have
*Bayes*. No no upon my soul.
*Smith*. Come, come Confess
*Bayes*. No, no upon my Honor, but I shall.

thus imposing moral cleansing of a sort. At I. ii. 51 Bayes improves his explanation of his plot by saying 'now we'll suppose these two Thumbs the Two Kings and these fingers the People (you see Ive got the story at my fingers ends)'. Small updates are made: 'ifackins' becomes 'upon my soul' at I. ii. 34:18; Cartwright's name gets cut at I. ii. 161; 'Tyring-room' becomes 'Green-room' at II. i. 29. Adopting Garrick's change at II. i. 62, 'Sir John Suckling' becomes 'Shakespear'. At II. iv. 2 there is

102 British Library Add. MS 12201, fo. 62r.

an addition: 'Did you ever hear of a Polititian [reading of word doubtful] having any Brains'. At IV. ii. 72 Bayes is asked 'but why clear the stage' and replies 'Because the Troops [have?] a Propensity to Blow up a Redoubt—and ecod if you dont look sharp they may mistake you for a Couple of straw figures & Pop you into it'. At V. i. 3 Bayes says 'Now I'll shew you a sham fight'. During the great battle (V. i. 287.1–5) Bayes says smugly, 'did you see any thing like that at Bagshot Heath'.[103] We suspect that this copy reflects provincial performance around the end of the eighteenth century. The only internal hint of a date is the name 'Incledon' written at the start of II. ii in the complete text. The name is, however, written in a totally different hand from the prompt annotations. Charles Incledon—a noted actor and singer—could have been plausibly cast as one of the two kings of Brentford, and might have taken the part almost any time between the mid-1790s and 1820. In any event, there is no particular reason to associate this promptbook with performance in London. What is surprising about it is the degree of fidelity to the original text. Cuts aside, remarkably little was changed.

Aside from the problematical illustration already mentioned, not much is to be learnt from eighteenth-century engravings of scenes from *The Rehearsal*. Engravings of Garrick (separately) and Henderson (in an edition of 1777) as Bayes (both without background) were published by Bell's British Theatre in 1777. Bell also published one of Richard Suett as Bayes walking down an eighteenth-century street fronted with fancy railings and lamps in an edition of 1796.[104]

We should raise a question that we cannot answer with much confidence. How accurately does *The Rehearsal* represent actual theatre production practice c.1670?[105] In a useful compilation of surviving informa-

---

[103] Bagshot Heath in Surrey, not far from the later site of Sandhurst. Bagshot and Hounslow Heaths were both long associated with highwaymen (hence Farquhar's use of those names in *The Beaux Stratagem*), but both also offered excellent terrain for military manoeuvres. Weinreb and Hibbert report that the latter was used 'as a Review Ground from 1686, when James II's standing army was encamped' there (*London Encyclopedia*, 397).

[104] All three are reproduced in black and white in Kalman A. Burnim and Philip H. Highfill, Jr., *John Bell, Patron of British Theatrical Portraiture: A Catalog of the Theatrical Portraits in his Editions of Bell's Shakespeare and Bell's British Theatre* (Carbondale, Ill.: Southern Illinois University Press, 1998), nos. 159, 187, and 317. The original watercolour of the Garrick portrait is in the British Museum (LB. 69). A full-length oil version of the Suett portrait is in the Theatre Museum (London). Whether it has any connection to theatrical practice in London or anywhere else is questionable. Suett is not known to have taken the part in London.

[105] What we are shown in *The Rehearsal* depicts, of course, a fairly late stage in the production process. Bayes presumably read the script to the actors before rehearsals began,

tion about rehearsal in the seventeenth- and eighteenth-century London theatre, Tiffany Stern has argued at some length that Buckingham's play is not a reliable source and should not be taken as any kind of indication of historical reality.[106] Caution is certainly indicated, as there is no corroborating evidence about a lot of points, and of course the play is a burlesque satire that ridicules a pretentious and incompetent playwright attempting to stage a terrible play. We must presume considerable comic distortion. The question is whether a playwright of the 1670s—let us say Thomas Shadwell or Elkanah Settle—did the sorts of things Bayes attempts to do. Was the author in fact in charge (e.g. IV. ii. 72)? Was the author expected to be able to explain meaning and motivation (I. ii. 1–8)? Suggest, correct, and illustrate line delivery (e.g. II. i. 153–5)? Presume—company dancing master notwithstanding—to direct, criticize, and correct the dancing (II. v. 13–15)? However comically badly Bayes does these things, we suspect that there would be little point in mocking them if playwrights did not customarily do them. Stern's denial of these things rests in part on her predetermined notion (explained in her 'Introduction') of what constituted mid-seventeenth-century norms and partly on some serious misunderstandings of both Buckingham and his play. She repeatedly insists that Bayes is an 'amateur' playwright who has never had a play staged, which misses the whole point. Buckingham is not satirizing an incompetent amateur whose previous work has been refused and whose present play will not in fact be performed. Bayes has had a play refused (II. ii. 26), but his last play (a clear reference to *The Conquest of Granada*) was a tremendous success (I. i. 63–4). Stern makes much of Buckingham's knowledge of French theatre and his friendship with Saint-Évremond, but the idea that Buckingham was showing (via Bayes) what performance rights an amateur author *ought* to have in England strikes us as perverse: Bayes is far from being a positive exemplar of anything. Buckingham and his circle almost undoubtedly had entrée to rehearsals at both theatres in the later 1660s if they wanted it, and they

and his trying to communicate some very basic points is clearly meant to be evidence of the badness of the play and its author's incompetence. Whether Buckingham read the script aloud and exercised directorial functions we have no way of telling. The well-known anecdotes about his instructing James Lacy in the part of Bayes may or may not have any foundation in fact, and such instruction could have been done privately rather than in public rehearsals in the theatre.

[106] Tiffany Stern, *Rehearsal from Shakespeare to Sheridan* (Oxford: Clarendon Press, 2000), esp. 128–39.

must have known quite well what went on there, both at routine work-ups supervised by the managers and at author-supervised rehearsals of new plays. We agree that Buckingham 'never parodied "rehearsal" it-self' and that what he shows represents what was done for 'important' new plays.[107] What one simply cannot be certain of is the degree of comic exaggeration.[108]

## RECEPTION AND INFLUENCE

*The Rehearsal* made an immediate splash, its success apparently fuelled in part by rumours of its exalted authorship. A letter reports as early as 16 December 1671:

> I am told the fame of the Duke of Buckingham's new play has reached the French Court, and that that King asked Mons[r.] Colbert when he would write him a play, who excusing his want of talents that way to serve him; the King told him he would be out of fashion for the Chief Minister of State in Eng-land had gotten a great deal of honour by writing a farce.[109]

Buckingham's position in the English government was shakier than it seemed in public view, but we may fairly say that no hit play in London before or since has ever been written by so great a nobleman and so eminent a member of a ruling administration. A heroic tragedy would undoubtedly have been more in keeping with the dignity of his rank and eminence.

Without daily performance records (lacking until *c.*1705) and with dramatic criticism not yet even in its infancy, we can make only a rough estimate of the visibility and impact of *The Rehearsal* in its first three decades. An indication of the play's immediate impact and popularity is Marvell's appropriations for the purpose of politico-religious satire in *The Rehearsal Transpros'd* (1672). One hint of the magnitude of its continuing success is the six editions it enjoyed before 1700. Looking at other manifestly successful and popular plays of the sixties and seventies (including some of Buckingham's targets), we may see that Dryden's *The Conquest of Granada* and *Tyrannick Love* man-aged five editions each; Wycherley's *The Plain-Dealer* (1676) six, the 1667 and 1674 versions of the Dryden-Davenant-Shadwell(?) *Tempest* a

---

[107] Stern, 138, 139.
[108] See Milhous and Hume, *Producible Interpretation*, ch. 2, esp. 59–69.
[109] *Historical Manuscripts Commission*, Sixth Report (1877), 368b.

total of six, Wycherley's *The Country-Wife* five, Dryden's *Marriage A-la-Mode* four, and Etherege's celebrated *The Man of Mode* three. By this admittedly rough index, *The Rehearsal* was among the most popular plays of its time, a conclusion borne out by the very large number of performances it ran up between 1704 and 1778. Farce it might be, but it enjoyed both popularity in the theatre and a serious critical reputation. Bayes rapidly became a proverbial figure, used both as a casual reference and more systematically as a satiric tool. An instance of the former is Settle's statement that 'Popery was to pop into the Throne, like the Kings of *Brentford* out of the *Clouds*; without either Noise or Tumult, and a Pox of all these unnecessary Tools call'd Armies to introduce it.'[110] A good example of the latter is 'An Ironical Panegyric from Poet Bayes to King Phys in his Irish Pilgrimage' (British Library Harl. MS 7319, fos. 326$^r$–328$^v$) in which Bayes (representing Dryden) sourly reviews the dismal career of James II up to the time of his invasion of Ireland in 1690. More broadly, the critical power of *The Rehearsal* is acknowledged by Charles Leslie in his preface to the four-volume reprint of his political newspaper of this title:

> *I borrow'd the* Title *of that most* Humorous *and* Ingenious *of our* Plays, *call'd, The* Rehearsal, *which is indeed a* Satyr *upon the other* Plays *and* Lew'd *Poems of those Times, and Exposes the* Blasphemous *BOUNCE of their* Heroes, *and their* Madrical *LOVE* Scenes, *as very* Ridiculous, *and the* WIT Frothy *and* Lean. *This seem'd something like the Task I was about to Undertake, to Unravel the more Pernicious* Papers *and* Pamphlets *of this Age, which Aim'd at* Wit *too, and to Gratify the* Corrupt Passions *of Mankind.*[111]

We should view direct compliments with some scepticism. Shadwell's dedication of his *Timon of Athens* (1678) to Buckingham says rather fulsomely

> I am extremely sensible what honour it is to me that my Writings are approved by your Grace; who in your own have so clearly shown the excellency of Wit and Judgment in your Self, and so justly the defect of 'em in others, that they at once serve for the greatest example, and the sharpest reproof. And no man who has perfectly understood the *Rehearsal*, and some other of your Writings, if he has any *Genius* at all, can write ill after it.[112]

---

[110] Elkanah Settle, *A Supplement to The Narrative* (London, 1683), 9.

[111] *The Rehearsal* (title varies) appeared from 1704 to 1709 and was reprinted as *A View of the Times* by 'Philalethes' in 1708–9.

[112] *Complete Works*, iii. 193.

But writing in 1691 with no possibility of personal advantage, the per-
nickety Langbaine said flatly that Buckingham's satire 'will ever be valued by Ingenious Men'.[113] Revising Langbaine in 1699, Charles Gildon
retains the attribution and maintains the praise while depersonalizing:

> This being an excellent Farce, and ascribed to the late Duke of *Buckingham*, as
> Author, has bore several Impressions, and is frequently acted of late Days.
> This Play lashes the ridiculous Model of our modern Tragedies.[114]

To what effect, he did not at this time say. As we have noted, Gildon
himself was aware that the plays ridiculed by Buckingham retained
their popularity for some years, but Dennis and others contributed to a
myth of the power of the satire. By the 1720s the actual impact of
Buckingham's play was essentially impossible to evaluate, especially in
the absence of newspaper archives or the sort of performance calendar
that various antiquaries (notably Frederick Latreille) later tried to con-
struct and which John Genest finally brought to print in 1832.

By 1714 virtually all the writers and plays attacked in *The Rehearsal*
were functionally a dead issue, but the play long retained both its theatrical popularity and the high critical reputation that we find as early as
Langbaine. In 1714 Gildon uses Buckingham's reputation as a platform
from which to launch his hostile examen of Rowe's tragedies in *A New
Rehearsal, or Bays the Younger*. Though written in dialogue form and divided into acts and scenes, this piece is simply a biting close analysis of
Rowe's tragedies, carried out in conversation among Freeman and
Truewit (gentlemen of wit and taste), Sir Indolent Easie ('pleas'd with
every Thing and every Writer'), Sawny Dapper ('A Young Poet of the
Modern stamp'), and Mr Bays ('A Pedantic, Reciting Poet, admir'd by
the Mob and himself, but justly contemn'd by Men of Sense and
Learning'). A passage in Act III addresses the objects of Buckingham's
satire and its impact on audiences.

> *Truewit.* Did you ever read the *Rehearsal* Mr. *Bays?* Methinks all Dramatic
> Poets shou'd be Master of that Farce.
> *Bays.* I have made my Advantage of it I assure you, Sir, for I have con-
> sider'd what is there ridicul'd pleas'd at that time, and by Consequence will
> please again.
> *Truewit.* So instead of being taught by *Smith* and *Johnson*, you are in-
> structed by *Bays*.

---

[113] *An Account of the English Dramatick Poets*, 546.    [114] *Lives and Characters*, 167.

*Bays.* Right, Sir, and I have Copied my most taking things from this *Brentford* Tragedy: I write to please the Town, Sir, and if I do that, 'tis more than any of the Critics can do. You find that the Town at the same Time they went to the *Rehearsal*, went to see those very Plays that were ridicul'd in it, and applauded their Rants and Rhime, and all that.

*Freeman.* But, Mr. *Bays*, 'tis as certain, that upon this Dramatic Criticism the Poets alter'd their Method, and left off their Rants and their Rhimes, and endeavour'd to come more into Nature.[115]

Gildon here asserts the reformative power of dramatic criticism, but perhaps without much conviction.

The continuing high critical reputation of *The Rehearsal* is manifest in the glowing encomia bestowed on it in the 1764, 1782, and 1812 versions of the *Biographia Dramatica*, where it is said to be 'the truest and most judicious Piece of Satire that ever yet appear'd'.[116] Not every critic was so rapturous. Samuel Johnson considered Bayes 'a mighty silly character' and found the specificity of the satire limiting: 'If it was intended to be like a particular man, it could only be diverting while that man was remembered.'[117] In a grumpier mood he opined that 'The greatness of Dryden's Character is even now the only principle of Vitality which preserves that Play from a State of Putrefaction.'[118] Horace Walpole was similarly bothered by his sense of the particularity of targets. Having been to see Sheridan's play, he wrote on 13 January 1780 to Lady Ossory: '*The Critic*, I own, was not so new as I expected; and then my being ill versed in modern dramas, most of the allusions must have escaped me. Does not half the merit of *The Rehearsal* depend on the notes?'[119] No, in fact, it does not. An antiquarian bibliophile can use the *Key* to relish the hits, but what kept the play viable for some 300 performances after its targets had vanished from the stage is the

---

[115] [Charles Gildon], *A New Rehearsal, or Bays the Younger* (London: J. Roberts, 1714), 84.

[116] Baker, *Companion to the Play-House*, I, s.v. 'Rehearsal'.

[117] James Boswell, *Boswell's Life of Johnson*, ed. George Birkbeck Hill, rev. L. F. Powell, 6 vols. (Oxford: Clarendon Press, 1934–50), ii. 168. Boswell adds, 'I maintained that it had merit as a general satire on the self-importance of dramatick authours. But even in this light he held it very cheap.'

[118] *Dr Johnson by Mrs Thrale*, ed. Richard Ingrams (London: Chatto & Windus, 1984), 23. In *Thraliana*, ed. Katharine C. Balderston, 2 vols. (Oxford: Clarendon Press, 1942), i. 172, this opinion is reported as part of a denial by Johnson that Buckingham's satire 'hurt the Reputation' of Dryden. Cf. Boswell's reportage from June 1784, where Johnson is said to have opined that 'It has not wit enough to keep it sweet', and then 'caught himself, and pronounced a more rounded sentence': 'It has not vitality enough to preserve it from putrefaction' (*Boswell's Life of Johnson*, iv. 320).

[119] *Walpole's Correspondence*, xxxiii. 159.

brilliance of the vehicle it offers the performer of Bayes. He is, of course, the butt, quite unconscious of his fatuity, but to a connoisseur like Buckingham's suavely ironic Johnson, Bayes is a pretender to relish rather than abominate. *The Rehearsal* is not an angry satire but a complacently sardonic one, and no doubt its fizzy tone is a large part of what made it so attractive for so many decades.

The impact of *The Rehearsal* on later 'plays about the theatre' is difficult to assess precisely.[120] The tutor in Joseph Arrowsmith's *The Reformation* (Duke's Company, sometime in 1672?) is a direct hit at Dryden that suggests some lessons learnt. Thomas Duffett's brilliant series of travesties (*The Empress of Morocco*, *The Mock-Tempest*, and *Psyche Debauch'd*), staged by the King's Company in 1673, 1674, and 1675, are wonderful demolitions of flashy Duke's Company shows, but have little direct connection to Buckingham's satire. Much the same may be said of Colley Cibber's neglected *The Rival Queans* (*c.*1699?).[121] *The Female Wits* (anon.; staged 1696; pub. 1704) comes much closer as a genuine rehearsal play, but its target is really the female playwrights of the day: it is more personal smear than literary criticism. Some of Buckingham's techniques are cleverly utilized by Richard Estcourt in *Prunella*, a spoof on pre-Handelian Italian opera. It was staged just one night in 1708 as a benefit afterpiece to a performance of *The Rehearsal* with Estcourt performing Bayes.[122] Unfortunately, the music is lost. From the text one might guess that Estcourt's piece was a worthy forerunner of Carey and Lampe's marvellous *The Dragon of Wantley* (1737). Another piece of anti-operatic satire, explicitly conceived as a descendant of Buckingham's play, is Thomas Durfey's *The Two Queens of Brentford: or, Bayes no Poetaster: A Musical Farce or Comical Opera*, never staged but published in 1721.[123] Durfey employs Smith and Johnson (making the latter 'A Severe Critical Satyrist') and adds Chanter (another 'Witty Gentle-

[120] On such plays the standard study remains Dane Farnsworth Smith's *Plays about the Theatre*.

[121] On this work, see Cheryl Wanko, 'Colley Cibber's *The Rival Queans*: A New Consideration', *Restoration and Eighteenth-Century Theatre Research*, 2nd ser., 3, no. 2 (1988), 38–52, and *The Plays of Colley Cibber*, ed. Timothy J. Viator and William J. Burling, i (Madison, N.J.: Fairleigh Dickinson University Press, 2001), 419–77.

[122] 12 Feb. 1708. For the little known of this charming work, see Roger Fiske, *English Theatre Music in the Eighteenth Century*, rev. edn. (London: Oxford University Press, 1986), 49–50.

[123] Published as part of *New Opera's* (London: Chetwood, 1721). Durfey says that the piece 'was once very near being acted, as being Rehears'd upon the Stage, but afterwards was laid by, some Accidents happening in the Playhouse' (Preface).

man of the Town'). He retains Pretty-man, Volscius, 'Armorilis', and Parthenope from the play-within-a-play, but adds several others (e.g. Firebrand Belrope, a publisher of news; Tokay, 'A Foreign Spy'; Thimblessa, 'An old Mistress' of Prince Prettyman; and Fleabitten, 'Attendant and Favourite' to the two Queens of Brentford). The rather ponderous satire is quite general, and is in fact not really even aimed at Bayes. Durfey says in his preface that the piece was 'not design'd so Satyrical upon Poetry as that was against Mr. *Dryden*, but intended rather against the Criticks, the Poet *Bayes* giving it all along a cast of Banter, and at last makes himself open in the Rank of a deserving Author'. John Gay's *The Rehearsal at Goatham* (*c*.1731; not performed; pub. 1754) has traditionally been connected with English versions of *Don Quixote* (whose puppet play it dramatizes) and with Fielding's wildly popular *The Author's Farce* (1730). However, recently published notes on Swift imply a relationship to both Buckingham and Swift. 'Dr. Swift wrote 3 Acts of a Play called the Players Rehearsal in the manner of the Rehearsal wrote by the D. of Buckingham which he gave to Mr. Gay to finish about a Year before Gay died.'[124] Elias observes that since the piece is only one act, two or three 'scenes' must be what Swift allegedly wrote, but he is correct that the 'expanded satiric commentary and interruptions' that are interpolated are 'more in the style of Buckingham's *The Rehearsal*' than Fielding's romp. A play that proclaims its relationship to Buckingham is Kitty Clive's *Bays in Petticoats* (staged as a benefit piece at Drury Lane in 1750 and published in 1753). A slight piece, it enjoyed fourteen performances between 1750 and 1762. Clive portrayed Mrs Hazard, a temperamental society lady whose very bad pastoral burletta (actually written by a man) is in rehearsal at Drury Lane. Anti-feminist ridicule of her as an authoress is of course misdirected: 'Clive ridicules not women who seek to write for the stage, but the knee-jerk reaction against female authors.'[125] The last and most important instance of *The Rehearsal*'s influence on eighteenth-century playwrights is the work which decisively supplanted it in the repertory: Sheridan's *The Critic* (1779). Summers dismissed Sheridan's confection out of hand: 'The water of *The Critic* is a mean thing to

---

[124] A. C. Elias, Jr., 'Swift's *Don Quixote*, Dunkin's *Virgil Travesty*, and other New Intelligence: John Lyon's "Materials for a Life of Dr. Swift," 1765', *Swift Studies*, 13 (1998), 27–104 at 71–2.

[125] Matthew J. Kinservik, 'Garrick's Unpublished Epilogue for Catherine Clive's *The Rehearsal: or, Bays in Petticoats* (1750)', *Études anglaises*, 49 (1996), 320–6 at 323.

place beside the strong wine of *The Rehearsal'* (p. xxv), and indeed it is
a simpler, more obvious, more accessible piece. The one is a satire, the
other merely a spoof, but both are a lot of fun.[126]

### PRINCIPLES OF ANNOTATION

In annotating *The Rehearsal* our object has been to provide the reader
with as much assistance as we can in identifying satiric hits and
possible hits while not simply burying the text in a flood of remote
parallels. We are convinced that the play can be read or staged virtually
without knowledge of its particular targets, and that it is effective and
enjoyable that way. Yet between 1704 and the present time vast
amounts of editorial effort and ingenuity have been expended in target
identification, and one of the functions of an edition such as this one
must be to present the findings of our predecessors as well as to add
what we can ourselves.

In preparing these notes we have drawn freely on annotated copies
of early quartos,[127] on the two principal 'Keys', and on the two major

---

[126] On the rich 18th-c. tradition of rehearsal plays, see Smith's *Plays about the Theatre* (for
the period 1671–1737) and Dane Farnsworth Smith and M. L. Lawhon, *Plays about the Theatre
in England, 1737–1800* (Lewisburg, Pa.: Bucknell University Press, 1979). The genre has
continued to flourish, a particularly popular late 20th-c. exemplar being Michael Frayn's
*Noises Off*.

[127] Particularly the University of Pennsylvania copy of Q1683. There is, of course, no
guarantee that what someone scribbled in the margins is accurate or that it possesses
authority of any kind. Annotations in the margins of 'old' copies are not uncommon, but a
surprising number of them turn out to derive from the oft-reprinted *Key* of 1704. The copy of
Q1701 at Yale, for example, richly annotated at more than fifty points in the text, turns out to
be nothing more than a somewhat careless replication of the *Key* in the margins of the play,
as does British Library copy C.34.i.1 of Q1672. Narcissus Luttrell's annotated copy (Boston
Public Library, Mass., shelfmark G.3967.19) presents a special set of problems. He bought a
copy of *Q3* for 3d., dated it merely '1682', signed it as was his custom, and wrote 'ye Duke of
Buckingham' on the title page. A cataloguer for the Boston Public Library in 1915 noted the
'close resemblance' between some of the target passage identifications and those in the 1704
*Key*—and jumped to the conclusion that Luttrell was the author of that key. This seems
highly implausible. Of the sixty-four notes in the *Key* Luttrell semi-duplicates twenty-four,
but he adds two others (thereby anticipating identifications later made by Percy and Summers). His quotations are sufficiently different that he manifestly did not simply copy from
the printed source after it became available in 1704, but if Luttrell himself was the author of
the *Key*, then why were two notes not used, what accounts for the difference in quotations,
and where did the other forty notes come from? Luttrell's annotations are purely literary
(almost all involve quotations and page references to printed sources) and seventeen of the
twenty-six concern Dryden. Anyone familiar with Dryden, Davenant, and Stapylton's *Slighted Maid* would have come up with much the same identifications. Almost exactly the same
passages are annotated in Folger 5325 (copy 2 of *Q3*), attributed to 'the Late Lord Marquis of

modern editions—those by Summers (1914) and Crane (1976).[128] All
MS identifications that we have found in contemporary copies are
reported (sceptically in some cases). The excellence of the 1704 *Key*
published by Briscoe is such that we have reproduced its commentary
almost verbatim. This *Key* was of course reprinted many times in the
eighteenth century (for example in 1717 with the misleading title, *The
New Key*),[129] but its substance remained unchanged. The first full-dress
attempt at an annotated edition was made by Bishop Percy in his
*Works of George Villiers, Duke of Buckingham*, an edition set in type but
never actually published and distributed. According to Nichols, most of
the impression was destroyed in a warehouse fire in 1808.[130] We know
of only three substantially complete copies: British Library C.39.g.18–
19, Bodleian Vet. A5.d.1797/1–2, and Bodleian Percy 39. Percy's
extensive notes are valuable, but lacking in discrimination. He cites
great numbers of remote parallels as though they were clear-cut
sources, and without trying to ascertain whether the plays at issue were
performed (or even printed) after 1660. To reproduce his notes
verbatim would be both monstrously wasteful of space and seriously
misleading. We have therefore adopted the policy of summarizing his
suggestions succinctly, indicating those cases in which we find his
parallels exceptionally strained or remote. In every case where our note
is indebted to one of our predecessors we have indicated that debt by
name or short title and page number. Silent appropriation of notes has
been something of a tradition: Percy borrowed liberally from the
original *Key*, Summers from both, and Crane from all three. We
believe that we have improved significantly on our predecessors in a
number of ways, but we do not wish to try to minimize our very considerable debt to them.

In adding notes to the already bulky compilations of earlier editors
we have concentrated upon allusions and parallels of the sort that
would have been reasonably obvious to a theatregoer or reader of the

---

Hallifax' in an annotation dated 1730.

[128] We have also made good use of David Womersley's student edition in *Restoration
Drama: An Anthology* (Oxford: Blackwell, 2000).

[129] *The New Key to the Rehearsal* (London: Printed for S. Briscoe and Sold by J. Morphew
and A. Dod, 1717), Price 6*d*. The title page proudly states that it is 'Presented to his Royal
Highness the PRINCE', but the pamphlet is merely a reprint of the *Key* included in the
*Miscellaneous Works* of 1704–5 and 1715.

[130] John Nichols, *Literary Anecdotes of the Eighteenth Century*, iii (London: Printed for the
Author, 1812), 161. On the Percy edition, see App. III, ii. 332–3, below.

1670s who happened to be familiar with such works as Dryden's *Essay of Dramatick Poesie* or *Tyrannick Love*. As Bishop Percy's notes amply demonstrate, one may pile up long lists of possible sources of inspiration and remote parallels without adding significantly to our comprehension of *The Rehearsal* or our enjoyment of it. To read Buckingham's play with one eye on the text and the other on footnotes about sources is to rob the play of its vitality. Unlike Fielding's *The Tragedy of Tragedies* (1731), written to be read and full of mock-scholarship, *The Rehearsal* is first and foremost a stage vehicle designed to amuse a theatre audience. A substantial proportion of our new notes, therefore, are devoted to verbal issues and contextual allusions rather than to speculation about particular literary targets or the compilation of parallel passages from other plays.

## Publication History and Textual Policy

No manuscripts survive, and the Ur-*Rehearsal* of *c*.1665 is lost. The revised and drastically updated version first performed in December 1671 was published in June 1672 by Thomas Dring without attribution, express or implied. The popularity of the play is indicated by the prompt appearance of the second edition, published in 1673. It was a resetting of the first with scattered corrections and some minor additions. In 1675 Dring brought out the third edition, again unattributed but with several major textual additions and numerous verbal changes.[131] Most of the latter appear to be the result of either deliberate stylistic revision or careful recording of line evolution established in performance. Almost all later editions until the present one have reproduced the 1675 edition or one of its derivatives.[132] Further editions in Buckingham's lifetime were published in 1683 (fourth) and 1687 (fifth—in the year of his death) but they are without substantive change or authority.

For this edition we have chosen to adopt *Q1* (1672) as copy-text while presenting the additions and variants of *Q3* (1675) at the bottom of the page in smaller type. Major additions have been emboldened to make them stand out. The version performed in 1671 has its own interest and integrity. Trying to envisage that artefact from notes indicating changes and absences when reading the third edition text is exceedingly

---

[131] Advertised 15 Feb. 1675. See the *Term Catalogues*, i. 199.
[132] The principal exception is Edward Arber's 'English Reprints' edition of 1868.

difficult, but contrariwise readers should have little trouble understanding what was added or altered when looking at the apparatus attached here to the *Q1* text. We are not trying to cast special doubt on the possibility of authorial origin of the 1675 changes, merely attempting to render both versions easy to visualize and comprehend.

In using the foot-of-page apparatus for this play, readers need to understand the policies and conventions within which we have worked. The material in smaller type below the main text presents the *Q3* additions and variants so that the reader may reconstruct the 1675 version. To reduce clutter and confusion, anomalous italic/roman punctuation has been silently regularized in this apparatus, and missing stops supplied after speech prefixes. A few obvious misprints in extended passages when the *Q3* variant becomes an alternative reading text have also been corrected and recorded in a supplementary list in the Transmissional History at the back of the volume. Line numbers with colons (e.g. 24:5) refer to new material first published in the 1675 third edition. In this example, '24' refers to the insertion point in the original 1672 text, and '5' denotes the fifth line of added material. For additions of five lines or more a line number is supplied every five lines (5, 10, 15), as in the main text. For shorter additions, a line number is supplied against the first added line. All Explanatory Notes for lines with colons are to material added in 1675.

# The Rehearsal

## PROLOGUE.

*We might well call this short Mock-play of ours*
*A Posie made of Weeds instead of Flowers;*
*Yet such have been presented to your noses,*
*And there are such, I fear, who thought 'em Roses.*
*Would some of 'em were here, to see, this night,*      5
*What stuff it is in which they took delight.*
*Here, brisk, insipid Blades, for wit, let fall*
*Sometimes dull sence; but oft'ner, none at all:*
*There, strutting Heroes, with a grim-fac'd train,*
*Shall brave the Gods, in King* Cambyses *vain.*      10
*For (changing Rules, of late, as if men writ*
*In spite of Reason, Nature, Art, and Wit)*
*Our Poets make us laugh at Tragœdy,*
*And with their Comedies they make us cry.*
*Now, Critiques, do your worst, that here are met;*      15
*For, like a Rook, I have hedg'd in my Bet.*
*If you approve; I shall assume the state*
*Of those high-flyers whom I imitate:*
*And justly too; for I will shew you more*
*Than ever they vouchsaf'd to shew before:*      20
*I will both represent the feats they do,*
*And give you all their reasons for 'em too.*
*Some honour to me will from this arise.*
*But if, by my endeavours, you grow wise,*
*And what was once so prais'd you now despise;*      25
*Then I'l cry out, swell'd with Poetique rage,*
*'Tis I,* John Lacy, *have reform'd your Stage.*

---

Prologue
7 *Blades*] *Rogues Q3*     10 *vain*] *vein Q2, Q3*     19 *shew*] *teach Q3*     20 *vouchsaf'd to shew*] *would let you know Q3*     21 *both represent*] *not only shew Q3*     22 *And*] *But Q3*     23 *to me will*] *may to me Q3*     *this*] *hence Q3*     25 *was*] *you Q3*     *you*] *shall Q3*

## The Actors Names.

*Bayes.*
*Johnson.*
*Smith.*
Two Kings of *Brentford.*                          5
Prince *Pretty-man.*
Prince *Volscius.*
Gentleman Usher.
Physician.
*Drawcansir.*                                      10
General.
Lieutenant General.
*Cordelio.*
*Tom Thimble.*
Shirley.                                           15
Fisherman.
Sun.
Thunder.
Players.
Souldiers.                                         20
Two Heralds.
Four Cardinals.
Mayor.
Judges.
Serjeants at Arms.                                 25

   *Women.*

*Amaryllis.*
*Cloris.*
*Parthenope.*
*Pallas.*                                          30
Lightning.
Moon.
Earth.

  Attendants of Men and Women.

   Scene *Brentford.*                35

The Actors Names
 15 Shirley *Added in Q4*  22–5 Four . . . Arms.] *Identified by brace as* 'Mutes.' *Q3*

# THE

## REHEARSAL.

[I. i]               ACTUS I. SCÆNA I.

Johnson *and* Smith.

*Johns.* Honeſt *Frank!* I'm glad to see thee with all my heart:
how long haſt thou been in Town?

*Smi.* Faith, not above an hour: and, if I had not met you here,
I had gone to look you out; for I long to talk with you freely, of all
the ſtrange new things we have heard in the Country.                    5

*Johns.* And, by my troth, I have long'd as much to laugh with
you, at all the impertinent, dull, fantaſtical things, we are tir'd out
with here.

*Smi.* Dull and fantaſtical! that's an excellent composition. Pray,
what are our men of business doing?                    10

*Johns.* I ne'er enquire after 'em. Thou know'ſt my humour lyes
another way. I love to please my self as much, and to trouble
others as little as I can: and therefore do naturally avoid the company of those solemn Fops; who, being incapable of Reason, and
insensible of Wit and Pleasure, are always looking grave, and troub-    15
ling one another, in hopes to be thought men of Business.

*Smi.* Indeed, I have ever observed, that your grave lookers are
the dulleſt of men.

*Johns.* I, and of Birds, and Beaſts too: your graveſt Bird is an
Owl, and your graveſt Beaſt is an Ass.                    20

*Smi.* Well; but how doſt thou pass thy time?

*Johns.* Why, as I use to do; eat and drink as well as I can, have
a She-friend to be private with in the afternoon, and sometimes
see a Play: where there are such things (*Frank*) such hideous,
monſtrous things, that it has almoſt made me forswear the Stage,    25
and resolve to apply my self to the solid nonsence of your pretenders to Business, as the more ingenious paſtime.

*Smi.* I have heard, indeed, you have had lately many new Plays,
and our Country-wits commend 'em.

I. i.

19  is an] is and *Q3*          26–7 pretenders to] Men of *Q3*

*Johns.* I, so do some of our City-wits too; but they are of the    30
new kind of Wits.

*Smi.* New kind? what kind is that?

*Johns.* Why, your Blade, your frank Persons, your Drolls:
fellows that scorn to imitate Nature; but are given altogether to
elevate and surprise.    35

*Smi.* Elevate, and surprise? pr'ythee make me underſtand the
meaning of that.

*Johns.* Nay, by my troth, that's a hard matter: I don't underſtand that my self. 'Tis a phrase they have got among them, to
express their no-meaning by. I'l tell you, as well as I can, what it    40
is. Let me see; 'tis Fighting, Loving, Sleeping, Rhyming, Dying,
Dancing, Singing, Crying; and every thing, but Thinking and
Sence.

*Mr.* Bayes *passes o'er the Stage.*

*Bayes.* Your moſt obsequious, and moſt observant, very servant, Sir.    45

*Johns.* Godso, this is an Author: I'l fetch him to you.

*Smi.* Nay, pr'ythee let him alone.

*Johns.* Nay, by the Lord, I'l have him.       [*Goes after him.*
Here he is. I have caught him. Pray, Sir, for my sake, will you do
a favour to this friend of mine?    50

*Bayes.* Sir, it is not within my small capacity to do favours,
but receive 'em; especially from a person that does wear the
honourable Title you are pleas'd to impose, Sir, upon this.——
Sweet Sir, your servant.

*Smi.* Your humble servant, Sir.    55

*Johns.* But wilt thou do me a favour, now?

*Bayes.* I, Sir: what is't?

*Johns.* Why, to tell him the meaning of thy laſt Play.

*Bayes.* How, Sir, the meaning? do you mean the Plot.

*Johns.* I, I; any thing.    60

*Bayes.* Faith, Sir, the Intrigo's now quite out of my head; but
I have a new one, in my pocket, that I may say is a Virgin; 't has
never yet been blown upon. I muſt tell you one thing, 'Tis all new
Wit; and, though I say it, a better than my laſt: and you know
well enough how that took. In fine, it shall read, and write, and    65
aɛt, and plot, and shew, ay, and pit, box and gallery, I gad, with

33 Blade] Virtuosi *Q3*   frank] civil *Q3*   34 scorn] scorns *Q3*   40 well] near *Q3*   47 Nay]
No *Q3*     49 Sir,] ~, now *Q3*

any Play in *Europe*. This morning is its laſt Rehearsal, in their habits, and all that, as it is to be acted; and if you, and your friend will do it but the honour to see it in its Virgin attire; though, perhaps, it may blush, I shall not be asham'd to discover its nakedness unto you.—I think it is o' this side. 70

[*Puts his hand in his pocket.*

*Johns.* Sir, I confess I am not able to answer you in this new way; but if you please to lead, I shall be glad to follow you; and I hope my friend will do so too.

*Smi.* I, Sir, I have no business so considerable, as should keep 75 me from your company.

*Bayes.* Yes, here it is. No, cry you mercy: this is my book of *Drama Common places*; the Mother of many other Plays.

*Johns. Drama Common places!* pray what's that?

*Bayes.* Why, Sir, some certain helps, that we men of Art have 80 found it convenient to make use of.

*Smi.* How, Sir, help for Wit?

*Bayes.* I, Sir, that's my position. And I do here averr, That no man yet the Sun e'er shone upon, has parts sufficient to furnish out a Stage, except it be with the help of these my Rules. 85

*Johns.* What are those Rules, I pray?

*Bayes.* Why, Sir, my firſt Rule is the Rule of Transversion, or *Regula Duplex:* changing Verse into Prose, or Prose into verse, *alternative* as you please.

*Smi.* How's that, Sir, by a Rule, I pray? 90

*Bayes.* Why, thus, Sir; nothing more easie when underſtood: I take a Book in my hand, either at home, or elsewhere, for that's all one, if there be any Wit in't, as there is no Book but has some, I Transverse it; that is, if it be Prose, put it into Verse, (but that takes up some time) if it be Verse, put it into Prose. 95

*Johns.* Methinks, Mr. *Bayes*, that putting Verse into Prose should be call'd Transprosing.

*Bayes.* By my troth, a very good Notion, and hereafter it shall be so.

*Smi.* Well, Sir, and what d'ye do with it then? 100

*Bayes.* Make it my own. 'Tis so alter'd that no man can know it. My next Rule is the Rule of Record, and by way of Table-

Book. Pray observe.

*Johns.* Well, we hear you: go on.

*Bayes.* As thus. I come into a Coffee-house, or some other          105
place where wittie men resort, I make as if I minded nothing;
(do you mark?) but as soon as any one speaks, pop I slap it down,
and make that, too, my own.

*Johns.* But, Mr. *Bayes*, are not you sometimes in danger of their
making you reſtore, by force, what you have gotten thus by Art?          110

*Bayes.* No, Sir; the world's unmindful: they never take notice
of these things.

*Smi.* But pray, Mr. *Bayes*, among all your other Rules, have
you no one Rule for Invention?

*Bayes.* Yes, Sir; that's my third Rule that I have here in my          115
pocket.

*Smi.* What Rule can that be?

*Bayes.* Why, Sir, when I have any thing to invent, I never
trouble my head about it, as other men do; but presently turn o'er
this Book, and there I have, at one view, all that *Perseus*,          120
*Montaigne, Seneca's Tragedies, Horace, Juvenal, Claudian, Pliny,
Plutarch's lives*, and the reſt, have ever thought, upon this ſubject:
and so, in a trice, by leaving out a few words, or putting in others
of my own, the business is done.

*Johns.* Indeed, Mr. *Bayes*, this is as sure, and compendious a way          125
of Wit as ever I heard of.

*Bayes.* I, Sirs, when you come to write your selves, o' my
word you'l find it so. But, Gentlemen, if you make the leaſt
scruple of the efficacie of these my Rules, do but come to the Play-
house, and you shall judge of 'em by the effects.          130

*Smi.* We'l follow you, Sir.          [*Exeunt.*


[I. ii]          *Enter three Players upon the Stage.*

1 *Play.* Have you your part perfeſt?

2 *Play.* Yes, I have it without book; but I do not underſtand
how it is to be spoken.

---

104 Well, we] We *Q3*     you] ~ Sir *Q3*     109 not you] you not *Q3*     117 be] ~, I
wonder *Q3*     119 o'er] over *Q3*     127–8 I, Sirs, when you ... Gentlemen] Sirs *Q3*
I. ii.
2 do not] don't *Q3*

*3 Play.* And mine is such a one, as I can't ghess for my life what humour I'm to be in: whether angry, melancholy, merry, or in love. I don't know what to make on't.          5

*1 Play.* Phoo! the Author will be here presently, and he'l tell us all. You muſt know, this is the new way of writing; and these hard things please forty times better than the old plain way. For, look you, Sir, the grand design upon the Stage is to keep the Auditors      10 in suspence; for to ghess presently at the plot, and the sence, tires 'em before the end of the firſt Aɕt: now, here, every line surprises you, and brings in new matter. And, then, for Scenes, Cloaths and Dancing, we put 'em quite down, all that ever went before us: and these are the things, you know, that are essential to a Play.    15

*2 Play.* Well, I am not of thy mind; but, so it gets us money, 'tis no great matter.

*Enter* Bayes, Johnson *and* Smith.

*Bayes.* Come, come in, Gentlemen. Y 'are very welcome Mr. ——a——Ha' you your Part ready?

*1 Play.* Yes, Sir.          20

*Bayes.* But do you underſtand the true humour of it?

*1 Play.* I, Sir, pretty well.

*Bayes.* And *Amarillis*, how does she do? Does not her Armor become her?

*3 Play.* O, admirably!          25

*Bayes.* I'l tell you, now, a pretty conceipt. What do you think I'l make 'em call her anon, in this Play?

*Smi.* What, I pray?

*Bayes.* Why I'l make 'em call her *Armarillis*, because of her Armor: ha, ha, ha.          30

*Johns.* That will be very well, indeed.

*Bayes.* I, it's a pretty little rogue; she is my Miſtress. I knew her face would set off Armor extreamly: and, to tell you true, I writ that Part only for her. Well, Gentlemen, I dare be bold to say, without vanity, I'l shew you something, here, that's very ridi-    35 culous, I gad.          [*Exeunt Players.*

*Johns.* Sir, that we do not doubt of.

7 1 *Play.*] Q2 Q3 1. *Q1*          9 than] then *Q3*          14 Dancing] Dances *Q3*    quite] quiet *Q3*          15 these] those *Q3*          29 I'l] I *Q3*          32 I] Ay *Q3*    rogue; she is my Mistress.] rogue; *Q3*          33 writ] write *Q3*          34–8 her. Well, . . . Pray, Sir] her. You must know she is my Mistress

*Johns.* Then, I know another thing, little *Bayes*, that thou hast had her, I gad.
*Bayes.* No, I gad, not yet; but I'm sure I shall: for I have talkt bawdy to her already.
*Johns.* Hast thou, faith? Pr'ythee how was that? <*cont.*>

*Bayes.* Pray, Sir, let's sit down. Look you, Sir, the chief hindge of this Play, upon which the whole Plot moves and turns, and that causes the variety of all the several accidents, which, you          40
know, are the thing in Nature that make up the grand refinement of a Play, is, that I suppose two Kings to be of the same place: as, for example, at *Brentford*; for I love to write familiarly. Now the people having the same relations to 'em both, the same affec- tions, the same duty, the same obedience, and all that; are div-          45
ided among themselves in point of devoir and intereſt, how to behave themselves equally between 'em: these Kings differing sometimes in particular; though, in the main, they agree. (I know not whether I make my self well underſtood.)
*Johns.* I did not observe you, Sir: pray say that again.          50
*Bayes.* Why, look you, Sir, (nay, I beseech you, be a little curi- ous in taking notice of this, or else you'l never underſtand my notion of the thing) the people being embarraſt by their equal tyes to both, and the Soveraigns concern'd in a reciprocal regard, as

*Bayes.* Why, Sir, there is, in the French Tongue, a certain Criticism, which, by the variation of the Masculine Adjective instead of the Fœminine, makes a quite different          34:5
signification of the word: as, for example, *Ma vie* is my life; but if, before *vie* you put *Mon* instead of *Ma*, you make it bawdy.
*Johns.* Very true.
*Bayes.* Now, Sir, I, having observ'd this, set a Trap for her, the other day in the Tyring-Room; for this said I, *Adieu bel Esperansa de mavie*; (which I gad is very          34:10
pretty) to which she answer'd, I vow, almost as prettily, every jot; for said she, *Songes a mavie Mounsieur*; whereupon I presently snapt this upon her; *Non, non, Madam*—— *Songes vous a mon*, by gad, and nam'd the thing directly to her.
*Smi.* This is one of the richest Stories, Mr. *Bayes*, that ever I heard of.
*Bayes.* I, let me alone, I gad, when I get to 'em; I'l nick 'em, I warrant you: But I'm          34:15
a little nice; for you must know, at this time, I am kept by another woman, in the City.
*Smi.* How kept? for what?
*Bayes.* Why, for a *Beau Gerson:* I am, ifackins.
*Smi.* Nay, then we shall never have done.
*Bayes.* And the Rogue is so fond of me, Mr. *Johnson*, that I vow to gad, I know not          34:20
what to do with my self.
*Johns.* Do with thy self! no; I wonder how thou canst make a shift to hold out, at this rate.
*Bayes.* O Devil, I can toil like a Horse; only, sometimes, it makes me melancholy: and then I vow to gad, for a whole day together, I am not able to say you one good          34:25
thing if it were to save my life.
*Smi.* That we do verily believe, Mr. *Bayes*.
*Bayes.* And that's the only thing, I gad, which mads me, in my Amours; for I'l tell you, as a friend, Mr. *Johnson*, my acquaintances, I hear, begin to give it out that I am dull: now I am the farthest from it in the whole World, I gad; but only, forsooth, they          34:30
think I am so, because I can say nothing.
*Johns.* Phoo pox, That's ill natur'dly done of 'em.
*Bayes.* Ay gad, there's no trusting o' these Rogues; but——a——Come *Q3*

38 you, Sir] you, Sirs *Q3*          41 thing] things *Q3*          that] which *Q2*

well to their own intereſt, as the good of the people; may make a          55
certain kind of a———you underſtand me———upon which, there
does arise several disputes, turmoils, heart-burnings, and all
that———In fine, you'l apprehend it better when you see it.

*[Exit, to call the Players.*

*Smi.* I find the Author will be very much oblig'd to the Players,
if they can make any sence of this.                                        60

*Enter* Bayes.

*Bayes.* Now, Gentlemen, I would fain ask your opinion of one
thing. I have made a Prologue and an Epilogue, which may
both serve for either: (do you mark?) nay, they may both serve
too, I gad, for any other Play as well as this.

*Smi.* Very well. That's, indeed, Artificial.                            65

*Bayes.* And I would fain ask your judgements, now, which of
them would do beſt for the Prologue? For, you muſt know, there
is, in nature, but two ways of making very good Prologues. The
one is by civility, by insinuation, good language, and all that, to—
—a———in a manner, ſteal your plaudit from the courtesie of the         70
Auditors: the other, by making use of some certain personal
things, which may keep a hank upon such censuring persons, as
cannot otherways, A gad, in nature, be hindred from being too
free with their tongues. To which end, my firſt Prologue is, that I
come out in a long black Veil, and a great huge Hang-man           75
behind me, with a Furr'd-cap, and his Sword drawn; and there tell
'em plainly; That if, out of good nature, they will not like my Play,
why I gad, I'l e'en kneel down, and he shall cut my head off.
Whereupon they all clapping———a———

*Smi.* But, suppose they do not.                                        80

*Bayes.* Suppose! Sir, you may suppose what you please, I have
nothing to do with your suppose, Sir, nor am not at all mortifi'd at
it; not at all, Sir; I gad, not one jot. Suppose quoth a!———

*[Walks away.*

*Johns.* Phoo! pr'ythee, *Bayes,* don't mind what he says: he's a
fellow newly come out of the Country, he knows nothing of        85
what's the relish, here, of the Town.

---

60 sence] ~ out *Q3*          63 either] ~: that is, the Prologue for the Epilogue, or the
Epilogue for the Prologue *Q2, Q3*          73 otherways] other ways *Q2*          77–8
Play, why] Play, *Q3*          80 But,] I, ~ *Q3*          do not] don't *Q3*          83 jot] ~, Sir *Q3*
a!———]~!———ha, ha, ha. *Q3*          84 he's] he is *Q3*

*Bayes.* If I writ, Sir, to please the Country, I should have
follow'd the old plain way; but I write for some persons of
Quality, and peculiar friends of mine, that understand what
Flame and Power in writing is: and they do me the right, Sir, to     90
approve of what I do.

*Johns.* I, I, they will clap, I warrant you; never fear it.

*Bayes.* I'm sure the design's good: that cannot be deny'd. And
then, for language, I gad, I defie 'em all, in nature, to mend it.
Besides, Sir, I have printed above a hundred sheets of papyr, to     95
insinuate the Plot into the Boxes: and withal, have appointed two
or three dozen of my friends, to be readie in the Pit, who, I'm
sure, will clap, and so the rest, you know, must follow; and then
pray, Sir, what becomes of your suppose? ha, ha, ha.

*Johns.* Nay, if the business be so well laid, it cannot miss.        100

*Bayes.* I think so, Sir: and therefore would chuse this for the
Prologue. For if I could engage 'em to clap, before they see the
Play, you know 'twould be so much the better; because then they
were engag'd: for, let a man write never so well, there are, now-
a-days, a sort of persons, they call Critiques, that, I gad, have no   105
more wit in 'em than so many Hobby-horses; but they'l laugh
you, Sir, and find fault, and censure things that, A gad, I'm sure
they are not able to do themselves. A sort of envious persons, that
emulate the glories of persons of parts, and think to build their
fame, by calumniating of persons that, I gad, to my knowledge, of     110
all persons in the world are, in nature, the persons that do as
much despise all that, as——a——In fine, I'l say no more of 'em.

*Johns.* I, I, you have said enough of 'em in conscience: I'm sure
more than they'l ever be able to answer.

*Bayes.* Why, I'l tell you, Sir, sincerely, and *bona fide*; were it   115
not for the sake of some ingenious persons, and choice female
spirits, that have a value for me, I would see 'em all hang'd before
I would e'er more set pen to papyr; but let 'em live in ignorance
like ingrates.

*Johns.* I marry! that were a way to be reveng'd of 'em indeed:       120
and, if I were in your place, now, I would do it.

*Bayes.* No, Sir; there are certain tyes upon me, that I cannot be
disingag'd from; otherwise, I would. But pray, Sir, how do you
like my hang-man?

*Smi.* By my troth, Sir, I should like him very well.                           125
*Bayes.* I, but how do you like it? (for I see you can judge)
Would you have it for the Prologue, or the Epilogue?
*Johns.* Faith, Sir, it's so good, let it e'en serve for both.
*Bayes.* No, no; that won't do. Besides, I have made another.
*Johns.* What other, Sir?                                                        130
*Bayes.* Why, Sir, my other is *Thunder and Lightning.*
*Johns.* That's greater: I'd rather ſtick to that.
*Bayes.* Do you think so? I'l tell you then; though there have
been many wittie Prologues written of late, yet I think you'l say
this is a *non pareillo:* I'm sure no body has hit upon it yet. For    135
here, Sir, I make my Prologue to be Dialogue: and as, in my
firſt, you see I ſtrive to oblige the Auditors by civility, by good
nature, and all that; so, in this, by the other way, *in Terrorem*, I
chuse for the persons *Thunder* and *Lightning*. Do you apprehend
the conceipt?                                                                    140
*Johns.* Phoo, pox! then you have it cock-sure. They'l be
hang'd, before they'l dare affront an Author, that has 'em at that
lock.
*Bayes.* I have made, too, one of the moſt delicate, daintie
*Simile's* in the whole world, I gad, if I knew but how to applie it.   145
*Smi.* Let's hear it, I pray you.
*Bayes.* 'Tis an alusion to love.

> So Boar and Sow, when any ſtorm is nigh,
> Snuff up, and smell it gath'ring in the Skie:
> Boar beckons Sow to trot in Cheſtnut Groves,                          150
> And there consummate their unfinish'd Loves.
> Pensive in mud they wallow all alone,
> And snort, and gruntle to each others moan.

How do you like it now, ha?
*Johns.* Faith, 'tis extraordinary fine: and very applicable to         155
*Thunder* and *Lightning*, methinks, because it speaks of a Storm.
*Bayes.* I gad, and so it does, now I think on't. Mr. *Johnson*, I
thank you; and I'l put it in *profecto*. Come out, *Thunder* and
*Lightning*.

Enter Thunder and Lightning.

---

126 I, but] But *Q3*    it] ~ Sir *Q3*        127 for the] for a *Q3*        128 it's] 'tis *Q3*
138 nature,] ~, good language, *Q3*      142 dare] ~ to *Q3*        150 Chestnut] *Q2, Q3*;
Chesnunt *Q1*        153 snort,] snore *Q3*        157 on't.] ~ˌ *Q3*

*Thun.* I am the bold *Thunder*.                                              160
*Bayes.* Mr. *Cartwright*, pr'ythee speak a little louder, and with
a hoarser voice. I am the bold *Thunder?* Pshaw! speak it me in a
voice that thunders it out indeed: I am the bold *Thunder*.
*Thun.* I am the bold *Thunder*.
*Light.* The brisk *Lightning*, I.                                           165
*Bayes.* Nay, you muſt be quick and nimble. The brisk *Light-*
*ning*, I. That's my meaning.
*Thun.* I am the braveſt *Hector* of the Skie.
*Light.* And I, fair *Helen*, that made *Hector* die.
*Thun.* I ſtrike men down.                                                   170
*Light.* I fire the Town.
*Thun.* Let the Critiques take heed how they grumble,
          For then begin I for to rumble.
*Light.* Let the Ladies allow us their graces.
          Or I'l blaſt all the paint on their faces,                         175
          And dry up their Peter to soot.
*Thun.* Let the Critiques look to't.
*Light.* Let the Ladies look to't.
*Thun.* For *Thunder* will do't.
*Light.* For *Lightning* will shoot.                                         180
*Thun.* I'l give you dash for dash.
*Light.* I'l give you flash for flash.
          Gallants, I'l singe your Feather.
*Thun.* I'l *Thunder* you together.
*Both.* Look to't, look to't; we'l do't, we'l do't: look to't, we'l do't.    185
                              [*Twice or thrice repeated.*
                              [*Exeunt ambo.*
*Bayes.* That's all. 'Tis but a flash of a Prologue: a Droll.
*Smi.* 'Tis short, indeed; but very terrible.
*Bayes.* Ay, when the *simile* is in, it will do to a Miracle, I gad.
Come, come; begin the Play.

### Enter firſt Player

1 *Play.* Sir, Mr. *Ivory* is not come yet; but he'l be here pre-            190
sently, he's but two doors off.
*Bayes.* Come then, Gentlemen, let's go out and take a pipe of
Tobacco.                                                       [*Exeunt.*

### Finis Actus primi.

161 speak] ~ that *Q3*     and] an *Q2*     162 hoarser] hoarse *Q3*     *Thunder?*] ~! *Q3*
186 That's all] There's no more *Q3*     187 'Tis] Yes, ~ *Q3*     188 *simile* is] *similes Q3*

[II. i]                 ACTUS II. SCÆNA I.

Bayes, Johnson *and* Smith.

*Bayes.* Now, Sir, because I'l do nothing here that ever was done
before——                                                    [*Spits.*
   *Smi.* A very notable design, for a Play, indeed.
   *Bayes.* Inſtead of beginning with a Scene that discovers some-
thing of the Plot, I begin this with a whisper.                    5
   *Smi.* That's very new.
   *Bayes.* Come, take your seats. Begin, Sirs.

*Enter Gentleman-Usher and Physician.*

   *Phys.* Sir, by your habit, I should gheſs you to be the Gentleman-
Usher of this sumptuous place.
   *Ush.* And, by your gait and fashion, I should almoſt suspeſt you   10
rule the healths of both our noble Kings, under the notion of
Physician.
   *Phys.* You hit my Funſtion right.
   *Ush.* And you, mine.
   *Phys.* Then let's imbrace.                                     15
   *Ush.* Come then.
   *Phys.* Come.
   *Johns.* Pray, Sir, who are those two so very civil persons?
   *Bayes.* Why, Sir, the Gentleman-Usher, and Physician of the
two Kings of *Brentford*.                                         20
   *Johns.* But how comes it to pass, then, that they know one an-
other no better?
   *Bayes.* Phoo! that's for the better carrying on of the Intrigue.
   *Johns.* Very well.
   *Phys.* Sir, to conclude,                                      25
   *Smi.* What, before he begins?
   *Bayes.* No, Sir; you muſt know they had been talking of this a
pretty while without.

II. i.
2–4 before—— . . . Instead] before, instead *Q3*        5 this] ~ Play *Q3*        6 That's]
Umph! *Q3*        new] ~, indeed *Q3*    16 Come then] Come *Q3*    18 those two] those *Q3*
19 Physician] *Q2*, *Q3*; Physicians *Q1*    21 But] ~, pray then, *Q3*    pass, then] pass *Q3*
23 Intrigue.] Plot? *Q3*

*Smi.* Where? in the Tyring-room?

*Bayes.* Why ay, Sir. He's so dull! Come, speak again.                    30

*Phys.* Sir, to conclude, the place you fill, has more than amply
exacted the Talents of a wary Pilot, and all these threatning Storms
which, like impregnant Clouds, do hover o'er our heads, (when
they once are grasp'd but by the eye of reason) melt into fruitful
showers of blessings on the people.                                       35

*Bayes.* Pray mark that Allegory. Is not that good?

*Johns.* Yes; that grasping of a Storm with the eye is admirable.

*Phys.* But yet some rumours great are Stirring; and if *Lorenzo*
should prove false, (as none but the great Gods can tell) you then
perhaps would find, that——                         [*Whispers.*    40

*Bayes.* Now they whisper.

*Ush.* Alone, do you say?

*Phys.* No; attended with the noble——               [*Whispers.*

*Ush.* Who, he in gray?

*Phys.* Yes; and at the head of——                   [*Whispers.*    45

*Bayes.* Pray mark.

*Ush.* Then, Sir, moSt certain, 'twill in time appear
These are the reasons that induc'd 'em to't:
FirSt, he——                                         [*Whispers.*

*Bayes.* Now t'other whispers.                                            50

*Ush.* Secondly, they——                             [*Whispers.*

*Bayes.* He's at it Still.

*Ush.* Thirdly, and laStly, both he, and they——     [*Whispers.*

*Bayes.* There they both whisper.          [*Exeunt Whispering.*
Now, Gentlemen, pray tell me true, and without flattery, is not          55
this a very odd beginning of a Play?

*Johns.* In troth, I think it is, Sir. But why two Kings of the same
place?

*Bayes.* Why? because it's new; and that's it I aim at. I despise
your *Johnson*, and *Beaumont*, that borrow'd all they writ from | 60
Nature: I am for fetching it purely out of my own fancie, I.

*Smi.* But what think you of Sir *John Suckling*, Sir?

*Bayes.* By gad, I am a better Poet than he.

*Smi.* Well, Sir; but pray why all this whispering?

33 impregnant] impregnate *Q3*    Clouds, do] Clouds, *Q3*    heads,] ~, will *Q3*    39 as] which
*Q3*    41 they whisper] he whispers *Q3*    43 *Whispers.*] ~. | *Bayes.* Again. *Q3*    47 appear]
~. *Q3*    48 induc'd 'em] have mov'd him *Q3*    50 t'other] the other *Q3*
52 He's at] at *Q3*    54 There] Now *Q3*    62 you] ~, Sir, *Q3*    *Suckling,* Sir?]
*Suckling. Q3*

*Bayes.* Why, Sir, (besides that it is new, as I told you before)    65
because they are suppos'd to be Polititians; and matters of State
ought not to be divulg'd.

*Smi.* But then, Sir, why——

*Bayes.* Sir, if you'l but respite your curiosity till the end of the
fifth Act, you'l find it a piece of patience not ill recompenc'd.    70

[*Goes to the door.*

*Johns.* How dost thou like this, *Frank?* Is it not just as I told
thee?

*Smi.* Why, I did never, before this, see any thing in Nature,
and all that, (as Mr. *Bayes* says) so foolish, but I could give some
ghess at what mov'd the Fop to do it; but this, I confess, does go    75
beyond my reach.

*Johns.* Why, 'tis all alike: Mr. *Wintershull* has inform'd me of
this Play before. And I'l tell thee, *Frank*, thou shalt not see one
Scene here, that either properly ought to come in, or is like any
thing thou canst imagine has ever been the practice of the World.    80
And then, when he comes to what he calls good language, it is,
as I told thee, very fantastical, most abominably dull, and not one
word to the purpose.

*Smi.* It does surprise me, I am sure, very much.

*Johns.* I, but it won't do so long: by that time thou hast seen a    85
Play or two, that I'l shew thee, thou wilt be pretty well acquainted with this new kind of Foppery.

---

77 Why, 'tis] It is *Q3*    alike] a like *Q3*    78 before] already *Q3*    79 that either . . . in]
worth one farthing *Q3*    or is] or *Q3*    84 I am] I'm *Q3*    87 Foppery.] ~.

*Smi.* Pox on't but there's no Pleasure in him: he's too gross a fool to be laugh'd at.

*Enter Bayes.*

*Johns.* I'l swear, Mr. *Bayes* you have done this Scene most admirably; tho, I must
tell you, Sir; it is a very difficult matter to pen a Whisper well.

*Bayes.* I, Gentlemen, when you come to write your selves, O' my word, you'l find it so.

*Johns.* Have a care of what you say, Mr. *Bayes*, for Mr. *Smith* there; I assure you,    87:5
has written a great many fine things already.

*Bayes.* Has he, ifackins? Why then Pray, Sir, how do you do, when you write?

*Smi.* Faith, Sir, for the most part, I am in pretty good health.

*Bayes.* I but I mean, what do you do, when you write? *<cont.>*

[II. ii]              SCÆNA II.

*Enter the two Kings, hand in hand.*

*Bayes.* These are the two Kings of *Brentford*; take notice of their ſtile: 'twas never yet upon the Stage; but, if you like it, I could make a shift, perhaps, to shew you a whole Play, written all juſt so.

  1 *King.* Did you observe their whisper, brother King?     5
  2 *King.* I did; and heard besides a grave Bird sing
      That they intend, sweet-heart, to play us pranks.

*Bayes.* This, now, is familiar, because they are both persons of the same Qualitie.

  *Smi.* 'Sdeath, this would make a man spew.               10
  1 *King.* If that design appears,
      I'l lug 'em by the ears
      Until I make 'em crack.
  2 *King.* And so will I, i'fack.
  1 *King.* You muſt begin, *Mon foy.*                      15
  2 *King.* Sweet, Sir, *Pardonnes moy.*

*Bayes.* Mark that: I Makes 'em both speak *French*, to shew their breeding.

  *Johns.* O, 'tis extraordinary fine.

   *Smi.* I take Pen, Ink, and Paper, and Sit down.                    87:10
   *Bayes.* Now, I write standing; that's one thing: and then, another thing is, with what do you prepare your self?
   *Smi.* Prepare my self! what, the Devil, does the fool mean?
   *Bayes.* Why, I'l tell you, now, what I do. If I am to write familiar things, as Sonnets to *Armida*, and the like, I make use of Stew'd Prunes only; but, when I have a grand     87:15
design in hand, I ever take Phisic, and let blood: for, when you would have pure swiftness of thought, and fiery flights of fancy, you must have a care of the pensive part. In fine, you must purge the Belly.
   *Smi.* By my troth, Sir, this is a most admirable Receipt for writing.
   *Bayes.* Ay, 'tis my Secret; and, in good earnest, I think, one of the best I have.     87:20
   *Smi.* In good faith, Sir, and that may very well be.
   *Bayes.* May be, Sir? I gad, I'm sure on't: *Experto crede Roberto.* But I must give you this caution by the way, be sure you never take snuff, when you write.
   *Smi.* Why so Sir?
   *Bayes.* Why, it spoil'd me once, I gad, one of the sparkishest Playes in all *England*.     87:25
But a friend of mine, at *Gresham Colledge*, has promis'd to help me to some spirit of Brains, and, I gad, that shall do my business. *Q3*

II. ii.
1 These] Oh, These now *Q3*     3 written] writ *Q3*     6 sing] ~. *Q3*     8 This,
now, is] This is now, *Q3*

2 *King.* Then, spite of Fate, we'l thus combined ſtand;　　　20
And, like true brothers, walk ſtill hand in hand.
　　　　　　　　　　　　　　　　*[Exeunt Reges.*

*Johns.* This is a very Majeſtick Scene indeed.

*Bayes.* Ay, 'tis a cruſt, a laſting cruſt for your Rogue Critiques,
I gad: I would fain see the proudeſt of 'em all but dare to nibble at
this; I gad, if they do, this shall rub their gums for 'em, I promise　　25
you. It was I, you muſt know, writ the Play I told you of, in this
very Stile: and shall I tell you a very good jeſt? I gad, the Players
would not aᷓt it: ha, ha, ha.

*Smi.* That's impossible.

*Bayes.* I gad, they would not, Sir: ha, ha, ha. They refus'd it, I　　30
gad, the silly Rogues: ha, ha, ha.

*Johns.* Fie, that was rude.

*Bayes.* Rude! I gad, they are the rudeſt, uncivileſt persons, and
all that, in the whole world: I gad, there's no living with 'em. I
have written, Mr. *Johnson,* I do verily believe, a whole cart-load of　　35
things, every whit as good as this, and yet, I vow to gad, these insolent Raskals have turn'd 'em all back upon my hands again.

*Johns.* Strange fellows indeed.

*Smi.* But pray, Mr. *Bayes,* how came these two Kings to know
of this whisper? for, as I remember, they were not present at it.　　40

*Bayes.* No, but that's the Aᷓtors fault, and not mine; for the
Kings should (a pox take 'em) have pop'd both their heads in at
the door, juſt as the other went off.

*Smi.* That, indeed, would ha' done it.

*Bayes.* Done it! Ay, I gad, these fellows are able to spoil the　　45
beſt things in Chriſtendom. I'l tell you, Mr. *Johnson,* I vow to gad,
I have been so highly disoblig'd, by the peremptoriness of these
fellows, that I am resolv'd, hereafter, to bend all my thoughts for
the service of the *Nursery,* and mump your proud Players, I gad.

21 true] two *Q2*　　26–31 writ . . . Rogues:]
that have written a whole Play just in this very same stile; but it was never Acted yet.
　*Johns.* How so?
　*Bayes.* I gad, I can hardly tell you, for laughing (ha, ha, ha) it is so pleasant a story:
ha, ha, ha.
　*Smi.* What is't?　　　　　　　　　　　　　　　　　　　　　　　　26:5
　*Bayes.* I gad, the Players refus'd to act it, Ha, ha, ha.
　*Smi.* That's impossible.
　*Bayes.* I gad they did it, Sir, point blank refus'd it, I gad, *Q3*
33 Rude!] ~! *Q3*　　34 world] ~, I gad *Q3*　　39 came] come *Q2*　　41 for
the] ~ ~ two *Q3*　　48 I am] I'm *Q3*　　bend all] bend *Q3*　　thoughts] ~ wholly *Q3*
49 gad.] ~.　*<cont.>*

[II. iii]                    SCÆNA III.

                        *Enter Prince* Pretty-man.

*Pret.*  How ſtrange a captive am I grown of late!
         Shall I accuse my Love, or blame my Fate?
         My Love, I cannot; that is too Divine:
         And againſt Fate what mortal dares repine?

                        *Enter* Cloris.

         But here she comes.                                    5
         Sure 'tis some blazing Comet, is it not?     [*Lyes down.*
*Bayes.*  Blazing Comet! mark that. I gad, very fine.
*Pret.*  But I am so surpris'd with sleep, I cannot speak the reſt.
                                                        [*sleeps.*
*Bayes.*  Does not that, now, surprise you, to fall asleep juſt in
the nick? His spirits exhale with the heat of his passion, and all   10
that, and swop falls asleep, as you see. Now, here, she muſt make
a *simile.*
*Smi.*  Where's the necessity of that, Mr. *Bayes?*
*Bayes.*  Because she's surpris'd. That's a general Rule: you muſt
ever make a *simile* when you are surpris'd; 'tis the new way of     15
writing.
*Cloris.*  As some tall Pine, which we, on *Ætna,* find
         T' have ſtood the rage of many a boyſt'rous wind,
         Feeling without, that flames within do play,
         Which would consume his Root and Sap away;                  20
         He spreads his worſted Arms unto the Skies,
         Silently grieves, all pale, repines and dies:
         So, shrouded up, your bright eye disappears.
         Break forth, bright scorching Sun, and dry my tears.
                                                         [*Exit.*

So; now Prince Pretty-man comes in, and falls a sleep, making love to his Mistress,   49:1
which, you know, was a grand Intrigue in a late Play, written by a very honest
Gentleman: a Knight. *Q3*

II. iii.
9 asleep juſt] a sleep *Q3*      24.1 *Exit.*] ~.
     *Johns.* Mr. *Bayes,* Methinks, this *simile* wants a little application too. <*cont.*>   24.1:1

*Bayes.* I am afraid, Gentlemen, this Scene has made you sad;       25
for I muſt confess, when I writ it, I wept my self.

*Smi.* No, truly, Sir, my spirits are almoſt exhal'd too, and I am
likelier to fall asleep.

*Prince* Pretty-man *ſtarts up, and says*——

*Pret.* It is resolv'd.                                          [*Exit.*

*Smi.* Mr. *Bayes,* may one be so bold as to ask you a queſtion,    30
now, and you not be angry?

*Bayes.* O Lord, Sir, you may ask me what you please. I vow
to gad, you do me a great deal of honour: you do not know me, if
you say that, Sir.

*Smi.* Then, pray, Sir, what is it that this Prince here has re-    35
solv'd in his sleep?

*Bayes.* Why, I muſt confess, that queſtion is well enough ask'd,
for one that is not acquainted with this new way of writing. But
you muſt know, Sir, that, to out-do all my fellow-Writers, whereas they keep their *Intrigo* secret till the very laſt Scene before the    40
Dance; I now, Sir, do you mark me——a——

*Smi.* Begin the Play, and end it, without ever opening the Plot
at all?

*Bayes.* I do so, that's the very plain troth on't: ha, ha, ha; I do, I
gad. If they cannot find it out themselves, e'en let 'em alone for    45
*Bayes,* I warrant you. But here, now, is a Scene of business: pray
observe it; for I dare say you'l think it no unwise discourse this,
nor ill argu'd. To tell you true, 'tis a Debate I over-heard once
betwixt two grand, sober, governing persons.


[II. iv]                        SCÆNA IV.

*Enter Gentleman-Usher and Physician.*

*Ush.* Come, Sir; let's ſtate the matter of faȼt, and lay our heads
together.

*Phys.* Right: lay our heads together. I love to be merry sometimes; but when a knotty point comes, I lay my head close to it,

---

*Bayes.* No, faith; for it alludes to passion, to consuming, to dying, and all that; which, you
know, are the natural effects of an Amour. *Q3*

25 *Bayes.* I am afraid, Gentlemen] But I'm afraid *Q3*       27 too] to *Q3*       28 asleep] a
sleep *Q3*          29 *Exit.*] ~. | *Bayes.* That's all. *Q3*       32 me] ~ any thing; *Q3*
48 Debate] Discourse *Q3*

with a pipe of Tobacco in my mouth, and then I whew it away,          5
i'faith.

*Bayes.* I do juſt so, I gad, always.

*Uſh.* The grand queſtion is, whether they heard us whisper?
which I divide thus: into when they heard, what they heard, and
whether they heard or no.                                            10

*Johns.* Moſt admirably divided, I swear.

*Uſh.* As to the when; you say juſt now: so that is answer'd.
Then, for what; why, what answers it self: for what could they
hear, but what we talk'd of? So that, naturally, and of necessity,
we come to the laſt queſtion, *Videlicet*, whether they heard or no?   15

*Smi.* This is a very wise Scene, Mr. *Bayes.*

*Bayes.* Yes; you have it right: they are both Polititians. I writ

---

II. iv.
5 pipe . . . mouth] snuff box in my hand *Q3*     whew] fegue *Q3*        9 thus:] ~.
    *Phys.* Yes, it must be divided so indeed.
    *Smi.* That's very complaisant, I swear, Mr. *Bayes,* to be of another man's opinion,
before he knowes what it is.
    *Bayes.* Nay, I bring in none, here, but wel-bred persons, I assure you.
    *Uſh.* I divided the question *Q3*                                        9:5
13 Then,] ~, as *Q3*
17 Yes;] Ay, *Q3*          17–18 Politicians. . . . world] Politicians.
    *Uſh.* Pray then to proceed in method, let me ask you that question.
    *Phys.* No, you'l answer better, pray let me ask it you.
    *Uſh.* Your will must be a Law.
    *Phys.* Come then, what is it I must ask?
    *Smi.* This Politician, I perceive, Mr. *Bayes,* has somewhat a short memory.    17:5
    *Bayes.* Why, Sir, you must know, that t'other is the main Politician, and this is but
his pupil.
    *Uſh.* You must ask me whether they heard us whisper.
    *Phy.* Well, I do so.
    *Uſh.* Say it then.                                                       17:10
    *Smi.* Hey day! here's the bravest work that ever I saw.
    *Johns.* This is mighty methodical!
    *Bayes.* Ay, Sir; that's the way: 'tis the way of Art; there is no other way, I gad, in
business.
    *Phys.* Did they here us whisper?                                          17:15
    *Uſh.* Why, truly, I can't tell; there's much to be said upon the word Whisper: to
whisper, in Latin is *Susurrare,* which is as much as to say, to speak softly; now, if they
heard us speak softly, they heard us whisper: but then comes in the *Quomodo,* the how;
how did they hear us whisper? Why, as to that, there are two wayes; the one, by
chance, or accident: the other, on purpose; that is, with design to hear us whisper.    17:20
    *Phys.* Nay, if they heard us that way, I'll never give 'em Physic more.
    *Uſh.* Nor I e'er more will walk abroad before 'em.
    *Bayes.* Pray mark this; for a great deal depend upon it, towards the latter end of the
Play.
    *Smi.* I suppose, that's the reason why you brought in this Scene Mr. *Bayes?* <cont.>   17:25

this Scene for a pattern, to shew the world how men should talk of business.

*Johns.* You have done it exceeding well, indeed. 20

*Bayes.* Yes, I think this will do.

*Phys.* Well, if they heard us whisper, they'l turn us out, and no bodie else will take us.

*Ush.* No bodie else will take us.

*Smi.* Not for Polititians, I dare answer for it. 25

*Phys.* Let's then no more our selves in vain bemoan:
We are not safe until we them unthrone.

*Ush.* 'Tis right:
And, since occasion now seems debonair,
I'l seize on this, and you shall take that chair. 30

> *They draw their Swords, and sit down in
> the two great chairs upon the Stage.*

*Bayes.* There's now an odd surprise; the whole State's turn'd quite topsi-turvy, without any puther or ſtir in the whole world, I gad.

*Johns.* A very silent change of a Government, truly, as ever I heard of. 35

*Bayes.* It is so. And yet you shall see me bring 'em in again, by and by, in as odd a way every jot.

> [*The Usurpers march out flourishing their swords.*

*Enter* Shirley.

*Shir.* Hey ho, hey ho: what a change is here! Hey day, hey day!
I know not what to do, nor what to say. [*Exit.*

*Smi.* But, pray, Sir, how came they to depose the Kings so 40
easily?

*Bayes.* Why, Sir, you muſt know, they long had a design to do it before; but never could put it in practice till now: and, to tell you true, that's one reason why I made 'em whisper so at firſt.

*Smi.* O, very well: now I'm fully satisfi'd. 45

---

*Bayes.* Partly, it was, Sir; but, I confess, I was not unwilling, besides, to shew the world a pattern, here, *Q3*

24 *omitted Q3* 39 *Exit.*] ~.

*Johns.* Mr. *Bayes*, in my opinion, now, that Gentleman might have said a little 39:1
more, upon this occasion.

*Bayes.* No, Sir, not at all; for I under writ his Part, on purpose to set off the rest.

*Johns.* Cry you mercy, Sir. *Q3*

*Bayes.* And then, to shew you, Sir, it was not done so very easily neither; in this next Scene you shall see some fighting.

*Smi.* Oh, ho: so then you make the ſtruggle to be after the business is done?

*Bayes.* Aye.                                                                    50

*Smi.* O, I conceive you: that is very natural.


[II. v]                    SCÆNA V.

*Enter four men at one door, and four at another, with their swords drawn.*

1 *Soldier.* Stand. Who goes there?

2 *Sol.* A friend.

1 *Sol.* What friend?

2 *Sol.* A friend to the House.

1 *Sol.* Fall on.               [*They all kill one another. Musick ſtrikes.*   5

*Bayes.* Hold, hold.               [*To the Musick. It ceaseth.*

Now here's an odd surprise: all these dead men you shall see rise up presently, at a certain Note that I have made, in *Effaut flat*, and fall a Dancing. Do you hear, dead men? remember your Note in *Effaut flat.* Play on.                          [*To the Musick.*   10

Now, now, now.           | *The Musick play his Note, and the dead*

O Lord, O Lord!           | *men rise; but cannot get in order.*

Out, out, out! Did ever men spoil a good thing so? no figure, no ear, no time, no thing? you dance worse than the Angels in *Harry the Eight,* or the fat Spirits in *The Tempeſt,* I gad.          15

1 *Sol.* Why, Sir, 'tis impossible to do any thing in time, to this Tune.

*Bayes.* O Lord, O Lord! impossible? why, Gentlemen, if there be any faith in a person that's a Chriſtian, I sate up two whole nights in composing this Air, and apting it for the business: for,   20 if you observe, there are two several Designs in this Tune; it begins swift, and ends slow. You talk of time, and time; you shall see me do't. Look you now. Here I am dead.

[*Lyes down flat on his face.*

51 that] ~, I swear, *Q3*

II. v.

5 1 *Sol.*] 2 *Sol. Q3*          14 thing?] ~? Udzookers, *Q3*          than the] than []he *Q3* [*Correctly in catchword*]

Now mark my Note in *Effaut flat*. Strike up Musick.

Now.  [*As he rises up haſtily, he tumbles and falls down again.*  25
Ah, gadsookers, I have broke my Nose.

*Johns.* By my troth, Mr. *Bayes*, this is a very unfortunate Note
of yours, in *Effaut flat*.

*Bayes.* A plague of this damn'd Stage, with your nails, and your
tenter-hooks, that a man cannot come to teach you to Act, but he  30
muſt break his nose, and his face, and the divel and all. Pray, Sir,
can you help me to a wet piece of brown papyr?

*Smi.* No indeed, Sir; I don't usually carry any about me.

2 *Sol.* Sir, I'l go get you some within presently.

*Bayes.* Go, go then; I'l follow you. Pray dance out the Dance,  35
and I'l be with you in a moment. Remember you four that you
dance like Horsemen.  [*Exit* Bayes.

*They dance the Dance, but can make nothing of it.*

1 *Sol.* A Devil! let's try this no more: play my Dance that Mr.
*Bayes* found fault with.  [*Dance, & Exeunt.*

*Smi.* What can this fool be doing all this while about his nose?  40

*Johns.* Pr'ythee let's go see.  [*Exeunt.*

*Finis Actus secundi.*

[III. i]  ACTUS III. SCÆNA I.

Bayes *with a papyr on his Nose, and the two Gentlemen.*

*Bayes.* Now, Sir, this I do, because my fancie in this Play is to
end every Act with a Dance.

*Smi.* Faith, that fancie is very good, but I should hardly have
broke my nose for it, though.

*Johns.* That fancie, I suppose, is new too.  5

*Bayes.* Sir, all my fancies are so. I tread upon no mans heels;
but make my flight upon my own wings, I assure you. As, now,

24 Note in] Note *Q2, Q3*    25 he tumbles and] he *Q3*    28 *Effaut flat*] *Effaut Q3*
30 man] Gentleman *Q3*    35 I'l] I *Q3*    36 you four that you] you *Q3*
37 Bayes.] ~.
      *Smi.* Like Horsemen! what, a plague, can that be? *Q3*    37:1
38 more] longer *Q3*    39 with] ~ so *Q3*
III. i.
1 Sir] Sirs *Q3*    7–12 you. As, . . . acted:] you. *Q3* [*Cf.* +24.1:1–2 below]

this next Scene some perhaps will say, It is not very necessary to
the Plot: I grant it; what then? I meant it so. But then it's as full of
Drollery as ever it can hold: 'tis like an Orange stuck with Cloves,          10
as for conceipt. Come, where are you? This Scene will make you
die with laughing, if it be well acted: it is a Scene of sheer Wit,
without any mixture in the world, I gad. [*Reads——*] Enter
Prince *Pretty-man*, and *Tom Thimble* his Taylor. This, Sirs, might
properly enough be call'd a prize of Wit; for you shall see 'em come          15
in upon one another snip snap, hit for hit, as fast as can be. First
one speaks, then presently t'other's upon him slap, with a Repartee; then he at him again, dash with a new conceipt: and so
eternally, eternally, I gad, till they go quite off the Stage.
                                        [*Goes to call the Players.*
    *Smi.* What a plague, does this Fop mean by his snip snap, hit          20
for hit, and dash?
    *Johns.* Mean? why, he never meant any thing in's life: what
dost talk of meaning for?

                            *Enter* Bayes.

    *Bayes.* Why don't you come in?

            *Enter Prince* Pretty-man *and* Tom. Thimble.

    *Pret.* But pr'ythee, *Tom Thimble*, why wilt thou needs marry?          25
If nine Taylors make but one man; and one woman cannot be
satisfi'd with nine men: what work art thou cutting out here for
thy self, trow we?
    *Bayes.* Good.
    *Thim.* Why, an't please your Highness, if I can't make up all          30
the work I cut out, I shan't want Journey-men to help me, I warrant you.
    *Bayes.* Good again.
    *Pret.* I am afraid thy Journey-men, though, *Tom*, won't work
by the day, but by the night.          35
    *Bayes.* Good still.

---

12 it is] Now, here comes in *Q3*          13 the] ~ whole *Q3*          13–14 gad. [*Reads* . . . Sirs,]
gad, between Prince Pretty-man and his Taylor: it *Q3*          15 be call'd] becall'd *Q3*
24.1 Thimble.] ~.
This Scene will make you dye with laughing, if it be well Acted; for 'tis as full of Drollory          24.1:1
as ever it can hold: 'tis like an Orange stuffd with Cloves, as for conceit. *Q3* [*Cf. 9–11*
*above*]
28 trow we] trow *Q3*          31 Journey-men] ~ enough *Q3*

*Thim.* However, if my wife sits but cross-leg'd, as I do, there will be no great danger: not half so much as when I trufted you for your Coronation-suit.

*Bayes.* Very good, i'faith. 40

*Pret.* Why, the times then liv'd upon truft; it was the fashion. You would not be out of time, at such a time as that, sure: A Taylor, you know, muft never be out of fashion.

*Bayes.* Right.

*Thim.* I'm sure, Sir, I made your cloath in the Court-fashion, 45 for you never paid me yet.

*Bayes.* There's a bob for the Court.

*Pret.* Why, *Tom*, thou art a sharp rogue when thou art angry, I see: thou pay'ft me now, methinks.

*Thim.* I, Sir, in your own coyn: you give me nothing but words. 50

*Bayes.* Admirable, before gad.

*Pret.* Well, *Tom*, I hope shortly I shall have another coyn for thee; for now the Wars come on, I shall grow to be a man of mettal.

*Bayes.* O, you did not do that half enough.

*Johns.* Methinks he does it admirably. 55

*Bayes.* I, pretty well; but he does not hit me in't: he does not top his part.

*Thim.* That's the way to be ftamp'd your self, Sir. I shall see you come home, like an Angel for the Kings-evil, with a hole bor'd through you. [*Exeunt.* 60

*Bayes.* That's very good, i'faith: ha, ha, ha. Ha, there he has hit it up to the hilts, I gad. How do you like it now, Gentlemen? is not this pure Wit?

*Smi.* 'Tis snip snap, Sir, as you say; but, methinks, not pleasant, nor to the purpose, for the Play does not go on. 65

*Bayes.* Play does not go on? I don't know what you mean: why, is not this part of the Play?

*Smi.* Yes, but the Plot ftands ftill.

*Bayes.* Plot ftand ftill! why, what a Devil is the Plot good for, but to bring in fine things? 70

*Smi.* O, I did not know that before.

*Bayes.* No, I think you did not: nor many things more, that I am Mafter of. Now, Sir, I gad, this is the bane of all us Writers:

38 you] ~, Sir, *Q3*     45 cloath] Cloaths, *Q3*     48 *Tom*, thou art] *Tom*, thou ar *Q2*
49 methinks.] ~.

    *Bayes.* There's pay, upon pay! as good as ever was written, I gad! *Q3*     49:1
53 come] are coming *Q3*     61 *Bayes.* That's...ha, ha, ha.] *Bayes. Q3*     66 you] yon *Q2*

let us soar never so little above the common pitch, I gad, all's
spoil'd; for the vulgar never underſtand us, they can never con-     75
ceive you, Sir, the excellencie of these things.

*Johns.* 'Tis a sad fate, I muſt confess: but you write on ſtill?

*Bayes.* Write on? I, I gad, I warrant you. 'Tis not their talk
shall ſtop me: if they catch me at that lock, I'l give 'em leave to
hang me. As long as I know my things to be good, what care I     80
what they say? What, they are gone, and forgot the Song!

*Smi.* They have done very well, methinks, here's no need of one.

*Bayes.* Alack, Sir, you know nothing: you muſt ever interlard
your Plays with Songs, Ghoſts and Idols, if you mean to——a——

*Johns.* Pit, Box and Gallery, Mr. *Bayes.*     85

*Bayes.* I gad, Sir, and you have nick'd it. Hark you, Mr. *John-*
*son*, you know I don't flatter, a gad, you have a great deal of Wit.

*Johns.* O Lord, Sir, you do me too much honour.

---

74 soar] ~ but *Q3*   75 us] it *Q3*     77 still] ~; for all that *Q3*     80 to be] are *Q3*
81–2 they are gone, . . .

one.] are they gone, without singing my last new Song? 'Sbud, would it were in their
Bellies. I'll tell you, Mr. *Johnson*, if I have any skill in these matters, I vow to gad, this
Song is peremtorily the very best that ever yet was written: you must know, it was
made by *Tom Thimble's* first wife after she was dead.

    *Smi.* How, Sir? after she was dead?     81:5

    *Bayes.* Ay, Sir, after she was dead. Why, what have you to say to that?

    *Johns.* Say? Why, nothing: he were a Devil that had any thing to say to that?

    *Bayes.* Right.

    *Smi.* How did she come to dye, pray Sir?

    *Bayes.* Phoo! that's no matter; by a fall: but here's the conceit, that upon his knowing     81:10
he was kill'd by an accident, he supposes, with a Sigh, that she dy'd for love of him.

    *Johns.* I, I, that's well enough: let's hear it, Mr. *Bayes.*

    *Bayes.* 'Tis to the Tune of Farewel, fair *Armida*, on Seas, and in battels, in Bullets,
and all that.

SONG.

    In swords, Pikes, and Bullets, 'tis safer to be,     81:15
       Than in a Strong Castle, remoted from thee:
    My deaths-bruise pray think you gave me, tho a fall
    Did give it me more, from the top of a wall;
    For then if the Moat on her mud would first lay,
    And after before you my body convey:     81:20
    The blew on my brest when you happen to see,
       You'l say, with a Sigh, there's a True blew for me.

Ha, Rogues! when I am merry, I write these things as fast as hops, I gad; for, you must
know, I am as pleasant a Debauchtee, as ever you saw: I am ifaith.

    *Smi.* But Mr. *Bayes*, how comes this song in here? for, methinks, there is no     81:25
great occasion for it. *Q3*

84 Idols] Dances *Q3*     86 gad, Sir] gad *Q3*

*Bayes.* Nay, nay, come, come, Mr. *Johnson*, Ifacks this muſt not
be said, amongſt us that have it. I know you have wit by the judge-       90
ment you make of this Play; for that's the measure I go by: my
Play is my Touch-ſtone. When a man tells me such a one is a person of parts; is he so, say I? what do I do, but bring him presently
to see this Play: If he likes it, I know what to think of him; if not,
your moſt humble Servant, Sir, I'l no more of him upon my word,       95
I thank you. I am *Clara voyant*, a gad. Now here we go on to our
business.

[III. ii]                          SCÆNA II.

*Enter the two Usurpers, hand in hand.*

*Ush.*  But what's become of *Volscius* the great?
        His presence has not grac'd our Court of late.
*Phys.*  I fear some ill, from emulation sprung,
        Has from us that Illuſtrious *Hero* wrung.
*Bayes.* Is not that Majeſtical?                                              5
*Smi.*  Yes, but who a Devil is that *Volscius*?
*Bayes.* Why, that's a Prince I make in love with *Parthenope*.
*Smi.*  I thank you, Sir.

*Enter* Cordelio.

*Cor.*  My Leiges, news from *Volscius* the Prince.
*Ush.*  His news is welcome, whatsoe'er it be.                                10
*Smi.*  How, Sir, do you mean that? whether it be good or bad?
*Bayes.* Nay, pray, Sir, have a little patience: Godsookers you'l
spoil all my Play. Why, Sir, 'tis impossible to answer every imper-
tinent queſtion you ask.
*Smi.*  Cry you mercie, Sir.                                                  15
*Cor.*  His Highness Sirs, commanded me to tell you,
        That the fair person whom you both do know,
        Despairing of forgiveness for her fault,
        In a deep sorrow, twice she did attempt
        Upon her precious life; but, by the care                             20
        Of ſtanders-by, prevented was.

89 Ifacks] I faith *Q3*        96 a] I *Q3*
III. ii.
2 Court] Courts *Q3*         11 mean that?] mean *Q3*

*Smi.* 'Sheart, what ſtuff's here!

*Cor.* At laſt,

    *Volscius* the great this dire resolve embrac'd:

    His servants he into the Country sent,           25

    And he himself to *Piccadillè* went,

    Where he's inform'd, by Letters, that she's dead.

*Ush.* Dead! is that possible? Dead!

*Phys.* O ye Gods!                        [*Exeunt.*

*Bayes.* There's a smart expression of a passion; O ye Gods! That's    30
one of my bold ſtrokes, a gad.

*Smi.* Yes; but who is the fair person that's dead?

*Bayes.* That you shall know anon.

*Smi.* Nay, if we know it at all, 'tis well enough.

*Bayes.* Perhaps you may find too, by and by, for all this, that she's    35
not dead neither.

*Smi.* Marry, that's good news: I am glad of that with all my
heart.

*Bayes.* Now, here's the man brought in that is suppos'd to have
kill'd her.                    [*A great shout within.*    40

    *Enter* Amarillis *with a Book in her hand and Attendants.*

*Ama.* What shout Triumphant's that?

              *Enter a Souldier.*

*Sol.* Shie maid, upon the River brink, near *Twick'nam* Town,
the assassinate is tane.

*Ama.* Thanks to the Powers above, for this deliverance.

    I hope its slow beginning will portend            45

    A forward *Exit* to all future end.

*Bayes.* Pish, there you are out; to all future end? No, no; to all
future end; you muſt lay the accent upon end, or else you lose the
conceipt.

*Johns.* Indeed the alteration of that accent does a great deal,    50
Mr. *Bayes.*

*Bayes.* O, all in all, Sir: they are these little things that mar, or
set you off a Play.

*Smi.* I see you are very perfeᏟ in these matters.

26 *Picadillè*] *Peccadille* Q2, *Q3*      31 a] I *Q3*      33 anon] ~ Sir *Q3*      37 news] ~
indeed *Q3*      40 *within.*] ~. | SCÆNA III. *Q3*      42 Town, the] ~, ~ false *Q3*
50–3 *lines omitted in Q3*

*Bayes.* I, Sir; I have been long enough at it to know something.      55

     *Enter Souldiers dragging in an old Fisherman.*

*Ama.* Villain, what Monſter did corrupt thy mind
    T'attaque the nobleſt soul of humane kind?
    Tell me who set thee on.
*Fish.* Prince *Pretty-man.*
*Ama.* To kill whom?                                                   60
*Fish.* Prince *Pretty-man.*
*Ama.* What, did Prince *Pretty-man* hire you to kill Prince
*Pretty-man?*
*Fish.* No; Prince *Volscius.*
*Ama.* To kill whom?                                                   65
*Fish.* Prince *Volscius.*
*Ama.* What, did Prince *Volscius* hire you to kill Prince *Volscius?*
*Fish.* No; Prince *Pretty-man.*
*Ama.* So, drag him hence,
    Till torture of the Rack produce his sence.      [*Exeunt.*   70
*Bayes.* Mark how I make the horror of his guilt confound his
intelleᶜts; for that's the design of this Scene.
*Smi.* I see, Sir, you have a several design for every Scene.
*Bayes.* I; that's my way of writing: and so I can dispatch you,
Sir, a whole Play, before another man, I gad, can make an end of   75
his Plot. So, now enter Prince *Pretty-man* in a rage. Where the
Devil is he? Why *Pretty-man?* why when, I say? O fie, fie, fie, fie;
all's marr'd, I vow to gad, quite marr'd.

     *Enter* Pretty-man.

Phoo, pox! you are come too late, Sir: now you may go out again,
if you please. I vow to gad Mr.——a——I would not give a button   80
for my Play, now you have done this.
*Pret.* What, Sir?
*Bayes.* What, Sir? 'Slife, Sir, you should have come out in
choler, rous upon the Stage, juſt as the other went off. Muſt a
man be eternally telling you of these things?                         85
   *Johns.* Sure this muſt be some very notable matter that he's
so angry at.

55 it] ~, one would think, *Q3*      72 for] ~ he's out at one and t'other: and *Q3*
74 so] ~ Sir, *Q3*      74–5 you, Sir,] you *Q3*      76 Plot. So,] ~. | SCÆNA IV. | ~ *Q3*
79 too] to *Q3*

*Smi.* I am not of your opinion.

*Bayes.* Pish! come, let's hear your Part, Sir.

*Pret.* Bring in my Father, why d'ye keep him from me? 90
    Although a Fisherman, he is my Father,
    Was ever Son, yet, brought to this diſtress,
    To be, for being a Son, made fatherless?
    Oh, you juſt Gods, rob me not of a Father.
    The being of a Son take from me rather. [*Exit.* 95

*Smi.* Well, *Ned*, what think you now?

*Johns.* A Devil, this is worſt of all. Pray, Mr. *Bayes*, what's the meaning of this Scene?

*Bayes.* O, cry you mercie, Sir: I purteſt I had forgot to tell you. Why, Sir, you muſt know, that, long before the beginning of this 100 Play, this Prince was taken by a Fisherman.

*Smi.* How, Sir, taken Prisoner?

*Bayes.* Taken Prisoner! O Lord, what a queſtion's there! did ever any man ask such a queſtion? Taken Prisoner! Godsookers, he has put the Plot quite out of my head, with this damn'd ques- 105 tion. What was I going to say?

*Johns.* Nay, the Lord knows: I cannot imagine.

*Bayes.* Stay, let me see; taken: O 'tis true. Why, Sir, as I was going to say, his Highness here, the Prince, was taken in a Cradle by a Fisherman, and brought up as his Child. 110

*Smi.* Indeed?

*Bayes.* Nay, pr'ythee hold thy peace. And so, Sir, this murder being committed by the River-side, the Fisherman, upon suspi- cion, was seiz'd; and thereupon the Prince grew angry.

*Smi.* So, so; now 'tis very plain. 115

*Johns.* But, Mr. *Bayes*, is not that some disparagement to a Prince, to pass for a Fishermans Son? Have a care of that, I pray.

*Bayes.* No, no, no; not at all; for 'tis but for a while: I shall fetch him off again, presently, you shall see.

*Enter* Pretty-man *and* Thimble.

*Pret.* By all the Gods, I'l set the world on fire 120
    Rather than let 'em ravish hence my Sire.

*Thim.* Brave *Pretty-man*, it is at length reveal'd,
    That he is not thy Sire who thee conceal'd.

*Bayes.* Lo' you now, there he's off again.
*Johns.* Admirably done i'faith. 125
*Bayes.* Ay, now the Plot thickens very much upon us.
*Pret.* What Oracle this darkness can evince?
  Sometimes a Fishers Son, sometimes a Prince.
  It is a secret, great as is the world;
  In which, I, like the soul, am toss'd and hurl'd. 130
  The blackeſt Ink of Fate, sure, was my Lot,
  And, when she writ my name, she made a blot.

*[Exit.*

*Bayes.* There's a bluſt'ring verse for you now.
*Smi.* Yes, Sir; but pray, why is he so mightily troubled to find
he is not a Fishermans Son? 135
*Bayes.* Phoo! that is not because he has a mind to be his Son,
but for fear he should be thought to be nobodies Son at all.
*Smi.* I, that would trouble a man, indeed.
*Bayes.* So, let me see. Enter Prince *Volscius*, going out of Town.
*Smi.* I thought he had been gone to *Piccadillé*. 140
*Bayes.* Yes, he gave out so; but that was onely to cover his
design.
*Johns.* What design?
*Bayes.* Why, to head the Army, that lies conceal'd for him in
*Knights-bridge*. 145
*Johns.* I see here is a great deal of Plot, Mr. *Bayes*.
*Bayes.* Yes, now it begins to break; but we shall have a world
of more business anon.

  *Enter Prince* Volscius, Cloris, Amarillis, *and* Harry *with*
  *a Riding-Cloak and Boots.*

*Ama.* Sir, you are cruel, thus to leave the Town,
  And to retire to Country solitude. 150
*Clo.* We hop'd this Summer that we should at leaſt
  Have held the honour of your company.
*Bayes.* Held the honour of your Company! prettily expreſt!
Held the honour of your company! Godsookers, these fellows will
never take notice of any thing. 155

124 Lo'] Lo *Q3*    130 I,] ~ₐ *Q2, Q3*    131 Lot,] *Q2, Q3*; ~. *Q1*    134 but pray,]
but *Q3*    137 nobodies] no bodies *Q2, Q3*    138 I] Nay *Q3*    139 see. Enter . . .
Town] see. | *Enter Prince* Volscius, *going out of Town Q2*; see. | SCÆNA V. | *Enter Prince*
Volscius, *going out of Town.* [*Reads Q3*    141 gave] ~ it *Q3*    146 here is] here's *Q2, Q3*

*Johns.* I assure you, Sir, I admire it extreamly; I don't know
what he does.

*Bayes.* I, I, he's a little envious; but 'tis no great matter. Come.

*Ama.* Pray let us two this single boon obtain,
    That you will here with poor us ſtill remain.        160
    Before your Horses come pronounce our fate,
    For then, alas, I fear 'twill be too late.

*Bayes.* Sad!

*Vols.* *Harry*, my Boots; for I'l go rage among
    My Blades encamp'd, and quit this *Urban* throng.      165

*Smi.* But pray, Mr. *Bayes*, is not this a little difficult, that you
were saying e'en now, to keep an Army thus conceal'd in *Knights-
bridge.*

*Bayes.* In *Knights-bridge?* ſtay.

*Johns.* No, not if the Inn-keepers be his friends.      170

*Bayes.* His friends! Ay, Sir, his intimate acquaintance; or else,
indeed, I grant it could not be.

*Smi.* Yes, faith, so it might be very easily.

*Bayes.* Nay, if I do not make all things easie, I gad, I'l give you
leave to hang me. Now you would think that he is going out of    175
Town; but you shall see how prettily I have contriv'd to ſtop him
presently.

*Smi.* By my troth, Sir, you have so amaz'd me, I know not
what to think.

Enter Parthenope.

*Vols.* Bless me! how frail are all my beſt resolves!      180
    How, in a moment, is my purpose chang'd!
    Too soon I thought my self secure from Love.
    Fair Madam, give me leave to ask her name
    Who does so gently rob me of my fame?
    For I should meet the Army out of Town,      185
    And, if I fail, muſt hazard my renown.

*Par.* My Mother, Sir, sells Ale by the Town-walls,
    And me her dear *Parthenope* she calls.

*Vols.* Can vulgar Veſtments high-born beauty shrowd?
    Thou bring'ſt the Morning pictur'd in a Cloud.      190

---

173 easily] easie *Q2, Q3*      178 me,] ~, that *Q3*      188 calls.] ~.
*Bayes.* Now that's the *Parthenope*, I told you of.      188:1
*Johns.* I, I: I gad you are very right. *Q3*

*Bayes.* The Morning pictur'd in a Cloud! A, Gadsookers, what
a conceipt is there!

*Par.* Give you good Ev'n, Sir.                    [*Exit.*

*Vols.* O inauspicious Stars! that I was born
    To sudden love, and to more sudden scorn!                195

*Ama. Cloris.* How! Prince *Volscius* in love? Ha, ha, ha.
                                        [*Exeunt laughing.*

*Smi.* Sure, Mr. *Bayes*, we have loſt some jeſt here, that they
laugh at so.

*Bayes.* Why did you not observe? He firſt resolves to go out of
Town, and then, as he is pulling on his Boots, falls in love. Ha,   200
ha, ha.

*Smi.* O, I did not observe: that, indeed, is a very good jeſt.

*Bayes.* Here, now, you shall see a combat betwixt Love and
Honour. An ancient Author has made a whole Play on't; but I
have dispatch'd it all in this Scene.                       205

            Volscius *sits down.*

*Vols.* How has my passion made me *Cupid*'s scoff!
    This haſty Boot is on, the other off,
    And sullen lyes, with amorous design
    To quit loud fame, and make that Beauty mine.
    My Legs, the Emblem of my various thought,             210
    Shew to what sad diſtraction I am brought.
    Sometimes, with ſtubborn Honour, like this Boot,
    My mind is guarded, and resolv'd to do't:
    Sometimes, again, that very mind, by Love
    Disarmed, like this other Leg does prove.              215

194 inauspicious] in auspicious *Q3*          200 love] ~ with her *Q3*          201 ha.] ~.
    *Smi.* But pray, Sir, where lies the jest?
    *Johns.* In the Boots.
    *Bayes.* Gad, you're i'th' right, it does lie in the Boots; your friend and I know where
the jest lies, though you don't. *Q2*          201–2 ha. . . . jest.] ha.
    *Smi.* Well, and where lyes the jest of that?
    *Bayes.* Ha?                                       [*Turns to Johnson.*
    *Johns.* Why; In the Boots: where should the jest lie?
    *Bayes.* I Gad, you are in the right: it does          [*Turns to Smith.*
Lie in the Boots——Your friend, and I know where a good jest lies, tho you don't, Sir.   201:5
    *Smi.* Much good do't you, Sir. *Q3*
203 now] ~, Mr. *Johnson Q3*          205.1 down.] ~ *to pull on his Boots:* Bayes *Stands by and
over acts the Part as he speaks it. Q3*          209 mine.] ~.
    *Smi.* Pr'ythee mark what pains Mr. *Bayes* takes to Act this speech himselfe!          209:1
    *Johns.* Yes, the fool, I see, is mightily transported with it. *Q3* [*Version of 216–18*]
210 My] *Vols.* ~ *Q3*

*Johns.* What pains Mr. *Bayes* takes to act this speech himself!

*Smi.* I, the fool, I see, is mightily transported with it.

*Vols.* Shall I to Honour or to Love give way?
Go on, cryes Honour; tender Love says, nay:
Honour, aloud, commands, pluck both boots on;                    220
But softer Love does whisper, put on none.
What shall I do? what conduct shall I find
To lead me through this twy-light of my mind?
For as bright Day with black approach of Night
Contending, makes a doubtful puzzling light;                     225
So does my Honour and my Love together
Puzzle me so, I can resolve for neither.
          [*Exit with one Boot on, and the other off.*

*Johns.* By my troth, Sir, this is as difficult a Combat as ever I
saw, and as equal; for 'tis determin'd on neither side.

*Bayes.* Ay, is't not, I gad, ha? For, to go off hip hop, hip hop,    230
upon this occasion, is a thousand times better than any conclusion
in the world, I gad. But, Sirs, you cannot make any judgement of
this Play, because we are come but to the end of the second
Act. Come, the Dance.                                          [*Dance.*

216–17 *lines omitted in Q3* [*Cf.* +209:*1–2*]     218 *Vols.* Shall] Shall     227.1 *Exit*] *Goes out
hopping Q3*     230 not] ~ now *Q3*     232–4 gad. . . . *Dance.*] gad.

*Johns.* Indeed, Mr. *Bayes*, that hip hop, in this place as you say, does a very great
deal.

*Bayes.* O, all in all Sir; they are these little things that mar, or set you off a Play:
as I remember once, in a Play of mine, I set off a Scene I gad, beyond expectation,
only with a Petticoat, and the Belly ake.                                       232:5

*Smi.* Pray, how was that, Sir?

*Bayes.* Why, Sir, I contriv'd a Petticoat to be brought in upon a Chair, (no body
knew how) into a Prince's Chamber, whose Father was not to see it, that came in by
chance.

*Johns.* God's my life, that was a notable Contrivance indeed.                  232:10

*Smi.* I but, Mr. *Bayes*, how could you contrive the Belly-ake?

*Bayes.* The easiest ith' World, I Gad: I'l tell you how, I made the Prince sit down
upon the Petticoat, no more than so, and pretended to his Father that he had just
then got the Belly-ake: whereupon, his Father went out to call a Physician, and his
man ran away with the Petticoat.                                               232:15

*Smi.* Well and what follow'd upon that?

*Bayes.* Nothing, no Earthly thing, I vow to Gad.

*Johns.* O, my word, Mr. *Bayes*, there you hit it.

*Bayes.* Yes I gave a world of content. And then I paid 'em away besides, for I
made 'em all talk baudy; ha, ha, ha: beastly, downright baudry upon the Stage, I gad;  232:20
ha, ha, ha; but with an infinite deal of wit, that I must say.

*Johns.* That, I that, we know well enough, can never fail you. <*cont.*>

Well, Gentlemen, you'l see this Dance, if I am not miſtaken, take  235
very well upon the Stage, when they are perfeċt in their motions,
and all that.

*Smi.* I don't know 'twill take, Sir; but I am sure you sweat
hard for't.

*Bayes.* Ay, Sir, it coſts me more pains, and trouble, to do these  240
things, than almoſt the things are worth.

*Smi.* By my troth, I think so, Sir.

*Bayes.* Not for the things themselves, for I could write you,
Sir, forty of 'em in a day; but, I gad, these Players are such dull
persons, that, if a man be not by upon every point, and at every  245
turn, I gad, they'l miſtake you, Sir, and spoil all.

*Enter a Player.*

What, is the Funeral ready?

*Play.* Yes, Sir.

*Bayes.* And is the Lance fill'd with Wine?

*Play.* Sir, 'tis juſt now a doing.  250

*Bayes.* Stay then; I'l do it my self.

*Smi.* Come, let's go with him.

*Bayes.* A match. But, Mr. *Johnson*, I gad, I am not like other
persons; they care not what becomes of their things, so they can
but get money for 'em: now, I gad, when I write, if it be not juſt  255
as it should be, in every circumſtance, to every particular, I gad, I
am not able to endure it, I am not my self, I'm out of my wits, and
all that, I'm the ſtrangeſt person in the whole world. For what
care I for my money? I gad, I write for Fame and Reputation.

*[Exeunt.*

*Finis Aĉtus Tertii.*

---

*Bayes.* No, I Gad can't it come bring in the Dance　　　　　*[Exit. to call 'em.*
*Smi.* Now, the Devil take thee for a silly, confident, unnatural, fulsom Rogue.

*Enter* Bayes *and* Players.

*Bayes.* Pray Dance well, before these Gentlemen: you are commonly so lazy; but  232:25
you should be light and easie, tah, tah, tah.

*All the while they Dance,* Bayes *puts 'em out with teaching 'em.* Q3

235 mistaken] deceiv'd  *Q3*　　238 know] ~ how  *Q3*　　245 by] ~ 'em  *Q3*
257 not] no more *Q3*　　259 my money? I gad,] mony? *Q3*　　for Fame and] for *Q3*

[IV. i]               ACTUS IV. SCÆNA I.

*Bayes, and the two Gentlemen.*

*Bayes.* Gentlemen, because I would not have any two things alike in this Play, the laſt Aċt beginning with a witty Scene of mirth, I make this to begin with a Funeral.

*Smi.* And is that all your reason for it, Mr. *Bayes?*

*Bayes.* No, Sir; I have a precedent for it too. A person of Hon-   5
our, and a Scholar, brought in his Funeral juſt so: and he was one (let me tell you) that knew as well what belong'd to a Funeral, as any man in *England*, I gad.

*Johns.* Nay, if that be so, you are safe.

*Bayes.* I gad, but I have another device, a frolick, which I think   10
yet better than all this; not for the Plot or Charaċters, (for, in my Heroick Plays, I make no difference, as to those matters) but for another contrivance.

*Smi.* What is that, I pray?

*Bayes.* Why, I have design'd a Conqueſt, that cannot possibly,   15
I gad, be aċted in less than a whole week: and I'l speak a bold word, it shall Drum, Trumpet, Shout and Battel, I gad, with any the moſt warlike Tragœdy we have, either ancient or modern.

*Johns.* I marry, Sir; there you say something.

*Smi.* And pray, Sir, how have you order'd this same frolick   20
of yours?

*Bayes.* Faith, Sir, by the Rule of Romance. For example: they divide their things into three, four, five, six, seven, eight, or as many Tomes as they please: now, I would very fain know, what should hinder me, from doing the same with my things, if I   25
please.

*Johns.* Nay, if you should not be Maſter of your own works, 'tis very hard.

*Bayes.* That is my sence. And therefore, Sir, whereas every one makes five Aċts to one Play, what do me I, but make five Plays to   30
one Plot: by which means the Auditors have every day a new thing.

IV. i.
5 too.] besidesₐ *Q3*      23 divide] divided *Q3*      29 therefore, Sir, whereas] then, Sir, this contrivance of mine has something of the reason of a Play in it too; for as *Q3*
30 makes] ~ you *Q3*

*Johns.* Moſt admirably good, i'faith! and muſt certainly take, because it is not tedious.

*Bayes.* I, Sir, I know that, there's the main point. And then, 35 upon *Saturday*, to make a close of all, (for I ever begin upon a *Monday*) I make you, Sir, a sixth Play, that sums up the whole matter to 'em, and all that, for fear they should have forgot it.

*Johns.* That consideration, Mr. *Bayes*, indeed, I think, will be very necessary. 40

*Smi.* And when comes in your share, pray Sir?

*Bayes.* The third week.

*Johns.* I vow, you'l get a world of money.

*Bayes.* Why, faith, a man muſt live: and if you don't, thus, pitch upon some new device, I gad, you'l never do it, for this Age 45 (take it o' my word) is somewhat hard to please. There is one prettie odd passage, in the laſt of these Plays, which may be executed two several ways, wherein I'ld have your opinion, Gentlemen.

*Johns.* Well, what is't? 50

*Bayes.* Why, Sir, I make a Male person to be in Love with a Female.

*Smi.* Do you mean that, Mr. *Bayes*, for a new thing?

*Bayes.* Yes, Sir, as I have order'd it. You shall hear. He having passionately lov'd her through my five whole Plays, finding at laſt 55 that she consents to his love, juſt after that his Mother had appear'd to him like a Ghoſt, he kills himself. That's one way. The other is, that she coming at laſt to love him, with as violent a passion as he lov'd her, she kills her self. Now my queſtion is, which of these two persons should suffer upon this occasion? 60

*Johns.* By my troth, it is a very hard case to decide.

*Bayes.* The hardeſt in the world, I gad; and has puzzled this pate very much. What say you, Mr. *Smith?*

*Smi.* Why, truly, Mr. *Bayes*, if it might ſtand with your juſtice, I should now spare 'em both. 65

*Bayes.* I gad, and I think——ha——why then, I'l make him hinder her from killing her self. Ay, it ſhall be so. Come, come, bring in the Funeral.

*Enter a Funeral, with the two Usurpers and Attendants.*

---

46 There is] But There's *Q3*     48 two] *Q3*; to *Q1*, *Q2*     50 Well, what is't] What is't, Sir *Q3*  54 hear] here *Q3*  64 justice] ~ now *Q3*  65 should now] would *Q3*

Lay it down there: no, here, Sir. So, now speak.

*K. Ush.*    Set down the Funeral Pile, and let our grief          70
          Receive, from its embraces, some relief.

*K. Phys.*    Was't not unjuſt to ravish hence her breath,
          And, in life's ſtead, to leave us nought but death?
          The world discovers now its emptiness,
          And, by her loss, demonſtrates we have less.          75

*Bayes.* Is not that good language now? is not that elevate? It's my *non ultra*, I gad. You muſt know they were both in love with her.

*Smi.* With her? with whom?

*Bayes.* Why, this is *Lardella*'s Funeral.

*Smi. Lardella!* I, who is she?          80

*Bayes.* Why, Sir, the Siſter of *Drawcansir*. A Ladie that was drown'd at Sea, and had a wave for her winding-sheet.

*K. Ush.*    *Lardella*, O *Lardella*, from above,
          Behold the Tragick issue of our Love.
          Pitie us, sinking under grief and pain,          85
          For thy being caſt away upon the Main.

*Bayes.* Look you now, you see I told you true.

*Smi.* I, Sir, and I thank you for it, very kindly.

*Bayes.* Ay, I gad, but you will not have patience; honeſt Mr.

——a——you will not have patience.          90

*Johns.* Pray, Mr. *Bayes*, who is that *Drawcansir?*

*Bayes.* Why, Sir, a fierce *Hero*, that frights his Miſtriss, snubs up Kings, baffles Armies, and does what he will, without regard to good manners, juſtice or numbers.

*Johns.* A very prettie Charaɛter.          95

*Smi.* But, Mr. *Bayes*, I thought your *Heroes* had ever been men of great humanity and juſtice.

*Bayes.* Yes, they have been so; but, for my part, I prefer that one quality of singly beating of whole Armies, above all your moral vertues put together, I gad. You shall see him come in pres-    100
ently. Zookers, why don't you read the papyr?          [*To the Players.*

*K. Phys.* O, cry you mercie.          [*Goes to take the papyr.*

*Bayes.* Pish! nay you are such a fumbler. Come, I'l read it my self. [*Takes a papyr from off the coffin.*] Stay, it's an ill hand, I muſt use my Speɛtacles. This, now, is a Copie of Verses, which I make    105

---

69 no] ~, no *Q3*       76 Is not that] Is not this *Q3*    It's] 'Tis *Q3*       84 issue] issues *Q3*       89 Mr.] M. *Q2, Q3*          94 good manners, justice or numbers] numbers, good manners, or justice *Q3*

*Lardella* compose, juſt as she is dying, with design to have it pin'd on her Coffin, and so read by one of the Usurpers, who is her Cousin.

*Smi.* A very shrewd design that, upon my word, Mr. *Bayes.*

*Bayes.* And what do you think I fancie her to make Love like, here, in the papyr?    110

*Smi.* Like a woman: what should she make Love like?

*Bayes.* O' my word you are out though, Sir; I gad you are.

*Smi.* What then? like a man?

*Bayes.* No, Sir; like a Humble Bee.    115

*Smi.* I confess, that I should not have fancy'd.

*Bayes.* It may be so, Sir. But it is, though, in order to the opinion of some of your ancient Philosophers, who held the transmigration of the soul.

*Smi.* Very fine.    120

*Bayes.* I'l read the Title. *To my dear Couz, King* Phys.

*Smi.* That's a little too familiar with a King, though, Sir, by your favour, for a Humble Bee.

*Bayes.* Mr. *Smith*, for other things, I grant your knowledge may be above me; but, as for Poetry, give me leave to say, I under    125
ſtand that better: it has been longer my practice; it has indeed, Sir.

*Smi.* Your servant, Sir.

*Bayes.* Pray mark it.

> Since death my earthly part will thus remove    *[Reads.*
> I'l come a Humble Bee to your chaſte love.    130
> With silent wings I'll follow you, dear Couz;
> Or else, before you, in the Sun-beams buz.
> And when to Melancholy Groves you come,
> An Airy Ghoſt, you'l know me by my Hum;
> For sound, being Air, a Ghoſt does well become.    135

*Smi.* [*After a pause.*] Admirable!

*Bayes.*
> At night, into your bosom I will creep,
> And Buz but softly if you chance to sleep:
> Yet, in your Dreams, I will pass sweeping by,
> And then, both Hum and Buz before your eye.    140

*Johns.* By my troth, that's a very great promise.

*Smi.* Yes, and a moſt extraordinary comfort to boot.

*Bayes.*
> Your bed of Love, from dangers I will free;
> But moſt, from love of any future Bee.

---

107 on] upon *Q3*    110 you think] yon think now *Q3*    124 for] in *Q3*
136 *(After a pause.)*] *Q3*; After a pause. [*printed as if dialogue in Q1, Q2*]    140 and] an *Q3*

And when, with pitie, your heart-ſtrings shall crack,                    145
With emptie arms I'l bear you on my back.

*Smi.* A pick-a-pack, a pick-a-pack.

*Bayes.* Ay, I gad, but is not that *tuant* now, ha? is it not *tuant?*
Here's the end.

Then, at your birth of immortality,                    150
Like any winged Archer, hence I'l fly,
And teach you your firſt flutt'ring in the Sky.

*Johns.* O rare! it is the moſt natural, refin'd fancie this, that
ever I heard, I'l swear.

*Bayes.* Yes, I think, for a dead person, it is a good enough way                    155
of making love: for being diveſted of her Terreſtrial part, and all
that, she is only capable of these little, pretty, amorous designs
that are innocent, and yet passionate. Come, draw your swords.

*K. Phys.* Come sword, come sheath thy self within this breſt,
That only in *Lardella*'s Tomb can reſt.                    160

*K. Ush.* Come, dagger, come, and penetrate this heart,
Which cannot from *Lardella*'s Love depart.

*Enter* Pallas.

*Pal.*          Hold, ſtop your murd'ring hands
At *Pallases* commands:
For the supposed dead, O Kings,                    165
Forbear to aƈt such deadly things.
*Lardella* lives: I did but try
If Princes for their Loves could dye.
Such Cœleſtial conſtancie
Shall, by the Gods, rewarded be:                    170
And from these Funeral obsequies
A Nuptial Banquet shall arise.
          [*The Coffin opens, and a Banquet is discover'd.*

*Bayes.* Now it's out. This is the very Funeral of the fair person
which *Volscius* sent word was dead, and *Pallas*, you see, has turn'd
it into a Banquet.                    175

---

145 your] *Q3*; you *Q1*, *Q2*          153 it] This *Q3*          fancie this,] fancy *Q3*          158 your] you
*Q3*          160 That only] That *Q2*; Which only *Q3*          173 *Bayes.*] ~. So, take away the
Coffin. *Q3*          175 Banquet.] ~.
          *Smi.* Well, but where is this Banquet?
          *Bayes.* Nay, look you, Sir, we must first have a Dance, for joy that *Lardella* is not
dead. Pray, Sir, give me leave to bring in my things properly at least.
          *Smi.* That, indeed, I had forgot: I ask your pardon. <*cont.*>

*Johns.* By my troth, now, that is new, and more than I expeſted.

*Bayes.* Yes, I knew this would please you: for the chief Art in Poetry is to elevate your expeſtation, and then bring you off some extraordinary way.

*K. Uſh.* Resplendent *Pallas*, we in thee do find 180
   The fierceſt Beauty, and a fiercer mind:
   And since to thee *Lardella*'s life we owe,
   We'l supple Statues in thy Temple grow.

*K. Phys.* Well, since alive *Lardella*'s found,
   Let, in full Boles, her health go round. 185
   [*The two Usurpers take each of them a Bole in their hands.*]

*K. Uſh.* But where's the Wine?

*Pal.* That shall be mine.
   Lo, from this conquering Lance,
   Does flow the pureſt wine of *France:* |*Fills the Boles*
   And, to appease your hunger, I  |*out of her Lance.* 190
   Have, in my Helmet, brought a Pye:
   Laſtly, to bear a part with these,
   Behold a Buckler made of Cheese.  [*Vanish* Pallas.

     *Enter* Drawcansir.

*K. Phys.* What man is this that dares diſturb our feaſt?

*Draw.* He that dares drink, and for that drink dares die, 195
   And, knowing this, dares yet drink on, am I.

*Johns.* That is as much as to say, that though he would rather die than not drink, yet he would fain drink for all that too.

*Bayes.* Right; that's the conceipt on't.

*Johns.* 'Tis a marveilous good one, I swear. 200

*K. Uſh.* Sir, if you please, we should be glad to know
   How long you here will ſtay, how soon you'l go.

---

*Bayes.* O, d'ye so, Sir? I am glad you will confess your selfe once in an error, Mr. 176:5
Smith.

     *Dance. Q3*

176–79 *Johns.* By . . . way.] *Moved down to precede Drawcansir's entrance at 193.1* Q3
182 since to thee] since Q2   193 Pallas.] ~.
 *Bayes.* There's the Banquet. Are you satisfi'd now, Sir? Q3 [*Followed by 176–79*] 193:1
197 is] ~, Mr. *Bayes,* Q3   200 swear.] ~.
 *Bayes.* Now there are some Critics that have advis'd me to put out the Second 200:1
*Dare,* and print *Must* in the place on't; but, I gad, I think 'tis better thus a great deal.
 *Johns.* Whoo! a thousand times.
 *Bayes.* Go on then. Q3

*Bayes.* Is not that now like a well-bred person, I gad? So modeſt, so gent!

*Smi.* O, very like.                                                          205

*Draw.* You shall not know how long I here will ſtay;
But you shall know I'l take my Boles away.

> *Snatches the Boles out of the Kings*
> *hands, and drinks 'em off.*

*Smi.* But, Mr. *Bayes,* is that (too) modeſt and gent?

*Bayes.* No, I gad, Sir, but it's great.

*K. Ush.* Though, Brother, this grum ſtranger be a Clown,          210
He'l leave us, sure, a little to gulp down.

*Draw.* Who e'er to gulp one drop of this dares think
I'l ſtare away his very pow'r to drink.

> *The two Kings sneak off the Stage,*
> *with their Attendants.*

I drink, I huff, I ſtrut, look big and ſtare;
And all this I can do, because I dare.          [*Exit.*          215

*Smi.* I suppose, Mr. *Bayes,* this is the fierce *Hero* you spoke of.

*Bayes.* Yes; but this is nothing: you shall see him, in the laſt Aƈt, win above a dozen battels, one after another, I gad, as faſt as they can possibly be represented.

*Johns.* That will be a sight worth seeing, indeed.          220

*Smi.* But pray, Mr. *Bayes,* why do you make the Kings let him use 'em so scurvily?

*Bayes.* Phoo! that is to raise the charaƈter of *Drawcansir.*

*Johns.* O' my word, that was well thought on.

*Bayes.* Now, Sir, I'l shew you a Scene indeed; or rather, indeed,          225
the Scene of Scenes. 'Tis an Heroick Scene.

*Smi.* And pray, Sir, what is your design in this Scene?

*Bayes.* Why, Sir, my design is *Roman* Cloaths, guilded Truncheons, forc'd conceipt, smooth Verse, and a Rant: In fine, if this Scene does not take, I gad, I'l write no more. Come, come in, Mr.          230
——a——nay, come in as many as you can. Gentlemen, I muſt desire you to remove a little, for I muſt fill the Stage.

*Smi.* Why fill the Stage?

*Bayes.* O, Sir, because your Heroick Verse never sounds well, but when the Stage is full.          235

---

207 my] your *Q3*          219 possibly be represented] possible come upon the Stage *Q3*
220 worth] ~ the *Q3*          225 Sir,] Sirs *Q3*          227 what is] what's *Q3*          228 is
*Roman* Cloaths,] is *Q3*          230 does] do *Q3*

[IV. ii]                          SCÆNA II.

*Enter Prince* Pretty-man, *and Prince* Volscius.

Nay, hold, hold; pray by your leave a little. Look you, Sir, the drift
of this Scene is somewhat more than ordinary: for I make 'em
both fall out because they are not in love with the same woman.

   *Smi.* Not in love? you mean, I suppose, because they are in
love, Mr. *Bayes?*                                                                              5

   *Bayes.* No, Sir; I say not in love: there's a new conceipt for you.
Now speak.

   *Pret.* Since fate, Prince *Volscius*, has found out the way
      For our so long'd-for meeting here this day,
      Lend thy attention to my grand concern.                             10

   *Vols.* I gladly would that ſtory of thee learn;
      But thou to love doſt, *Pretty-man*, incline:
      Yet love in thy breaſt is not love in mine.

   *Bayes. Antithesis!* thine and mine.

   *Pret.* Since love it self's the same, why should it be                    15
      Diff'ring in you from what it is in me?

   *Bayes.* Reasoning; I gad, I love reasoning in verse.

   *Vols.* Love takes, *Cameleon*-like, a various dye
      From every Plant on which it self does lye.

   *Bayes. Simile!*                                                                     20

   *Pret.* Let not thy love the course of Nature fright:
      Nature does moſt in harmony delight.

   *Vols.* How weak a *Deity* would Nature prove
      Contending with the pow'rful God of Love?

   *Bayes.* There's a great Verse!                                                    25

   *Vols.* If Incense thou wilt offer at the Shrine
      Of mighty Love, burn it to none but mine.
      Her Rosie-lips eternal sweets exhale;
      And her bright flames make all flames else look pale.

   *Bayes.* I gad, that is right.                                                       30

   *Pret.* Perhaps dull Incense may thy love suffice;
      But mine muſt be ador'd with Sacrifice.
      All hearts turn ashes which her eyes controul:
      The Body they consume as well as Soul.

IV. ii.

      8 has found out] now has found *Q3*          11 of] from *Q3*

*Vols.* My love has yet a power more Divine;                    35
    Victims her Altars burn not, but refine:
    Amid'st the flames they ne'er give up the Ghost,
    But, with her looks, revive still as they roast.
    In spite of pain and death, they're kept alive:
    Her fiery eyes makes 'em in fire survive.                    40
*Bayes.* That is as well as I can do.
*Vols.* Let my *Parthenope* at length prevail.
*Bayes.* Civil, I gad.
*Pret.* I'l sooner have a passion for a Whale:
    In whose vast bulk, though store of Oyl doth lye,          45
    We find more shape more beauty in a Fly.
*Smi.* That's uncivil, I gad.
*Bayes.* Yes; but as far a fetch'd fancie, though, I gad, as ever
you saw.
*Vols.* Soft, *Pretty-man*, let not thy vain pretence          50
    Of perfect love, defame loves excellence.
    *Parthenope* is sure as far above
    All other loves, as above all is Love.
*Bayes.* Ah! I gad, that strikes me.
*Pret.* To blame my *Cloris*, Gods would not pretend.         55
*Bayes.* Now mark.
*Vols.* Were all Gods joyn'd, they could not hope to mend
    My better choice: for fair *Parthenope*,
    Gods would, themselves, un-god themselves to see.
*Bayes.* Now the Rant's a coming.                              60
*Pret.* Durst any of the Gods be so uncivil,
    I'ld make that God subscribe himself a Devil.
*Bayes.* Ah, Godsookers, that's well writ!
*Vols.* Could'st thou that God from Heav'n to Earth translate,
    He could not fear to want a Heav'nly State.                 65
    *Parthenope*, on Earth, can Heav'n create.
*Pret.* *Cloris* does Heav'n it self so far excel,
    She can transcend the joys of Heav'n in Hell.
*Bayes.* There's a bold flight for you now! 'Sdeath, I have lost
my peruke. Well, Gentlemen, this is that I never yet saw any one    70
could write, but my self. Here's true spirit and flame all through, I
gad. So, So; pray clear the Stage.

*[He puts 'em off the Stage.*
*Johns.* But, Mr. *Bayes,* pray why is this Scene all in Verse?
*Bayes.* O, Sir, the subject is too great for Prose.
*Smi.* Well said, i'faith; I'l give thee a pot of Ale for that an-     75
swer: 'tis well worth it.
*Bayes.* Come, with all my heart.
        I'l make that God subscribe himself a Devil.
That single line, I gad, is worth all that my brother Poets ever
writ. So, now let down the Curtain.          *[Exeunt.*     80

        *Finis Actus Quarti.*


ACTUS V. SCÆNA I.

        Bayes, *and the two Gentlemen.*

*Bayes.* Now, Gentlemen, I will be bold to say, I'l shew you the
greatest Scene that ever *England* saw: I mean not for words, for
those I do not value; but for State, shew, and magnificence. In
fine, I'l justifie it to be as grand to the eye every whit, I gad, as
that great Scene in *Harry* the Eight, and grander too, I gad; for,     5
instead of two Bishops, I have brought in two other Cardinals.
> *The Curtain is drawn up, and the two usurping
> Kings appear in State, with the four Cardi-
> nals,* Prince Pretty-man, *Prince* Volscius,
> Amarillis, Cloris, Parthenope, *&c. before
> them, Heralds and Serjeants at Arms with
> Maces.*

*Smi.* Mr. *Bayes,* pray what is the reason that two of the Cardi-
nals are in Hats, and the other in Caps?
*Bayes.* Why, Sir, because——By gad, I won't tell you.
*Smi.* I ask your pardon, Sir.          10

72.1–73 *Stage.* | *Johns.* But . . . pray] *Stage.*
   *Johns.* I wonder how the coxcomb has got the knack of writing smooth Verse thus.
   *Smi.* Why there's no need of brain for this: 'tis but scaning—the labour's in the
finger; but where's the sence of it?
   *Johns.* O', for that, he desires to be excus'd: he is too proud a man to creep servily
after Sense, I assure you. But pray, Mr. *Bayes, Q3*          73:5
74 too] to *Q2*          80 So, now let] Let *Q3*
V. i.
6 have brought] bring *Q3*          two other] here four *Q3*          6.1 *up, and*] *up, Q3*
9–10 you . . . . Sir.] you. Your Country friend, Sir, grows so troublesome. *Q3*

*K. Ush.*    Now, Sir, to the business of the day.

*Vols.*      Dread Soveraign Lords, my zeal to you,
             Muſt not invade my duty to your Son;
             Let me intreat that great Prince *Pretty-man*
             Firſt do speak: whose high preheminence,                    15
             In all things that do bear the name of good,
             May juſtly claim that priviledge.

*Pret.*      Royal Father, upon my knees I beg
             That the Illuſtrious *Volscius* firſt be heard.

*Bayes.*  Here it begins to unfold: you may perceive, now, that he      20
is his Son.

*Johns.*  Yes, Sir; and we are very much beholden to you for that
discovery.

*Vols.*      That preference is only due to *Amarillis*, Sir.

*Bayes.*  I'l make her speak very well, by and by, you shall see.        25

*Ama.*       Invincible Soveraigns——              [*Soft Musick.*

*K. Ush.*    But ſtay, what sound is this invades our ears?

*K. Phys.*   Sure 'tis the Musick of the moving Spheres.

*Pret.*      Behold, with wonder, yonder comes from far
             A God-like-Cloud, and a triumphant Carr:                    30
             In which, our two right Kings sit one by one,
             With Virgin Veſts, and Laurel Garlands on.

*K. Ush.*    Then, Brother *Phys*', 'tis time that we were gone.
             | *The two Usurpers ſteal out of the Throne,*
             | *and go away.*

*Bayes.*  Look you now, did not I tell you that this would be as
easie a turn as the other?                                               35

*Smi.*  Yes, faith, you did so; though, I confess, I could not believe you; but you have brought it about, I see.
             | *The two right Kings of* Brentford *descend*
             | *in the Clouds, singing in white gar-*
             | *ments; and three Fidlers sitting before*
             | *them, in green.*

*Bayes.*  Now, because the two Right Kings descend from above,
I make 'em sing to the Tune and Stile of our modern Spirits.

1 *King.*  Haſte, brother King, we are sent from above.                  40

---

    *K. Phys.* **Speak** *Volscius.* *Q3*                                                    11:1
20–3 *follow 17 in Q3*    22 beholden] beholding *Q2, Q3*    32 Virgin] Virgins *Q3*    33 that we
were gone] we should begon *Q3*        35 turn] change *Q3*

2 *King.*          Let us move, let us move:
                Move to remove the Fate
                Of *Brentfords* long united State.
1 *King.* Tara, tara, tara, full East and by South,
2 *King.* We sail with Thunder in our mouth,                    45
          In scorching noon-day, whil'st the traveller stayes,
          Busie, busie, busie, busie, we bustle along.
          Mounted upon warm *Phœbus* his Rayes,
          Through the Heavenly throng,
                Haste to those                                  50
          Who will feast us, at night, with a Pigs Petty-toes.
1 *King.*          And we'l fall with our pate
                In an *Ollio* of hate.
2 *King.* But now supper's done, the Servitors try,
          Like Souldiers, to storm a whole half-moon-pye.       55
1 *King.* They gather, they gather hot Custard in spoons,
          Alas, I must leave these half-moons,
          And repair to my trusty Dragoons.
2 *King.* O stay, for you need not as yet go astray;
          The Tyde, like a friend, has brought ships in our way,  60
                And on their high-ropes we will play.
                Like Maggots in Filberds, we'l snug in our shell,
                We'l frisk in our shell,
                We'l firk in our shell,
                And farewel.                                    65
1 *King.* But the Ladies have all inclination to dance,
          And the green Frogs croak out a Coranto of *France*.
*Bayes.* Is not that pretty, now? The Fidlers are all in green.
*Smi.* I, but they play no Coranto.
*Johns.* No, but they play a Tune, that's a great deal better.    70
*Bayes.* No Coranto quoth a! that's a good one, with all my heart.
Come, sing on.
2 *King.*          Now Mortals that hear
                How we Tilt and Carrier,
                With wonder will fear                           75
                The event of such things as shall never appear.
1 *King.* Stay you to fulfil what the Gods have decreed.
2 *King.* Then call me to help you, if there shall be need.

---

44 Tara, tara, tara] Tarra, tan tara *Q3*        46 scorching] scorning *Q2*        50 Haste]
Hasting *Q3*        57 Alas] But ~ *Q3*        74 Carrier] Carreer *Q2, Q3*

1 *King.* So firmly resolv'd is a true *Brentford* King
   To save the diſtressed, and help to 'em bring,       80
   That ere a Full-pot of good Ale you can swallow,
   He's here with a whoop, and gone with a holla.
        [Bayes *phillips his finger, and sings after 'em.*

*Bayes.* He's here with a whoop, and gone with a holla. This, Sir,
you muſt know, I thought once to have brought in with a Conjurer.

*Johns.* I, that would have been better.       85

*Bayes.* No, faith, not when you consider it: for thus 'tis more
compendious, and does the thing every whit as well.

*Smi.* Thing! what thing?

*Bayes.* Why, bring 'em down again into the Throne, Sir; what
thing would you have?       90

*Smi.* Well; but, methinks, the Sence of this Song is not very
plain.

*Bayes.* Plain? why, did you ever hear any people in Clouds speak
plain? They muſt be all for flight of fancie, at its full range, without the leaſt check, or controul upon it. When once you tye up   95
spirits, and people in Clouds to speak plain, you spoil all.

*Smi.* Bless me, what a Monſter's this!

   | *The two Kings light out of the Clouds, and*
   | *ſtep into the Throne.*

1 *King.* Come, now to serious counsel we'l advance.

2 *King.* I do agree; but firſt, let's have a Dance.

*Bayes.* Right. You did that very well, Mr. *Cartwright.* But firſt,   100
let's have a Dance. Pray remember that; be sure you do it always
juſt so: for it muſt be done as if it were the effeċt of thought, and
premeditation. But firſt, let's have a Dance. Pray remember that.

*Smi.* Well, I can hold no longer, I muſt gag this rogue; there's
no induring of him.       105

*Johns.* No, pr'ythee make use of thy patience a little longer:
let's see the end of him now.       [*Dance a grand Dance.*

*Bayes.* This, now, is an ancient Dance, of right belonging to
the Kings of *Brentford*; and since deriv'd, with a little alteration, to
the Inns of Court.       110

      *An Alarm. Enter two Heralds.*

1 *King.* What sawcie Groom moleſts our privacies?

1 *Her.*  The Army's at the door, and in disguise,
     Desires a word with both your Majesties:
2 *Her.*  Having, from *Knights-bridge*, hither march'd by stealth.
2 *King.*  Bid 'em attend a while, and drink our health.          115
*Smi.*  How, Mr. *Bayes*, the Army in disguise?
*Bayes.*  Ay, Sir, for fear the Usurpers might discover them that
went out but just now.
*Smi.*  Why, what if they had discover'd them?
*Bayes.*  Why then they had broke this design.                   120
*Smi.*  That's true, indeed. I did not think of that.
1 *King.*  Here, take five Guineys for those warlike men.
2 *King.*  And here's five more; that makes the sum just ten.
1 *Her.*  We have not seen so much the Lord knows when.
                                    [*Exeunt Heralds.*
1 *King.*  Speak on, brave *Amarillis.*                           125
*Ama.*  Invincible Soveraigns, blame not my modesty,
     If at this grand conjuncture——
                   [*Drum beats behind the Stage.*
1 *King.*  What dreadful noise is this that comes and goes?

     *Enter a Soldier with his Sword drawn.*

*Sold.*  Haste hence, great Sirs, your Royal persons save,
     For the event of war no mortal knows:                     130
     The Army, wrangling for the gold you gave,
     First fell to words, and then to handy-blows.  [*Exit.*
2 *King.*  O dangerous estate of Soveraign pow'r!
     Obnoxious to the change of every hour.
1 *King.*  Let us for shelter in our Cabinet stay:               135
     Perhaps these threat'ning storms may pass away.
                                     [*Exeunt.*
*Johns.*  But, Mr. *Bayes*, did not you promise us, just now, to
make *Amarillis* speak very well?
*Bayes.*  Ay, and so she would have done, but that they hinder'd
her.                                                             140
*Smi.*  How, Sir? whether you would or no?
*Bayes.*  Ay, Sir; the Plot lay so that, I vow to gad, it was not to
be avoided.
*Smi.*  Marry, that was hard.
*Johns.*  But, pray, who hinder'd her?                           145

120 this] the *Q3*    121 omitted *Q3*    127.1 beats] beat *Q3*    132 Exit.] ~.
  *Bayes.* Is not that now a pretty kind of a Stanza, and a handsome come off ? *Q3*    132:1

*Bayes.* Why, the battel, Sir, that's juſt coming in at door. And I'l tell you now a ſtrange thing: though I don't pretend to do more than other men, I gad, I'l give you both a whole week to ghess how I'l represent this Battel.

*Smi.* I had rather be bound to fight your Battel, Sir, I assure you.                                                                    150

*Bayes.* Why, there's it now: fight a Battel? there's the common error. I knew presently where I should have you. Why, pray, Sir, do but tell me this one thing, Can you think it a decent thing, in a battel before Ladies, to have men run their Swords through one    155 another, and all that?

*Johns.* No, faith, 'tis not civil.

*Bayes.* On the other side; to have a long relation of Squadrons here, and Squadrons there: what is that but a dull prolixity?

*Johns.* Excellently reason'd, by my troth!                             160

*Bayes.* Wherefore, Sir, to avoid both those Indecorums, I sum up my whole battel in the representation of two persons only, no more: and yet so lively, that, I vow to gad, you would swear ten thousand men were at it, really engag'd. Do you mark me?

*Smi.* Yes, Sir; but I think I should hardly swear, though, for all    165 that.

*Bayes.* By my troth, Sir, but you would, though, when you see it: for I make 'em both come out in Armor, *Cap-a-pea*, with their Swords drawn, and hung, with a scarlet Ribbon at their wriſts, (which, you know, represents fighting enough) each of 'em    170 holding a Lute in his hand.

*Smi.* How, Sir, inſtead of a Buckler?

*Bayes.* O Lord, O Lord! inſtead of a Buckler? Pray, Sir, do you ask no more queſtions. I make 'em, Sir, play the battel in *Recitativo*. And here's the conceipt. Juſt at the very same inſtant that    175 one sings, the other, Sir, recovers you his Sword, and puts himself in a warlike poſture: so that you have at once your ear entertain'd with Musick, and good Language; and your eye satisfi'd with the garb, and accoutrements of war. Is not that well?

*Johns.* I, what would you have more? he were a Devil that    180 would not be satisfi'd with that.

150 Battel, Sir] Battle *Q3*          151 you] ~, Sir *Q3*          152 Why,] Whoo! *Q3*
156 another] a nother *Q3*      158 *Bayes.*] ~. Right *Q3*      159 that but a] it but *Q3*
170 enough)] ~.)

    *Johns.* I, I; so much, that, if I were in your place I would mak 'em go out again    170:1
without ever speaking one word.
    *Bayes.* No; there you are out; for I make *Q3*
171 holding] hold *Q3*          179–81 war. . . . that] war *Q3*

*Smi.* I confess, Sir, you ſtupifie me.

*Bayes.* You shall see.

*Johns.* But, Mr. *Bayes*, might not we have a little fighting for I
love those Plays, where they cut and slash one another, upon the          185
Stage, for a whole hour together.

*Bayes.* Why, then, to tell you true, I have contriv'd it both ways.
But you shall have my *Recitativo* firſt.

> *Enter, at several doors, the General, and Lieutenant General,*
> *arm'd Cap-a-pea, with each of them a Lute in his hand,*
> *and his sword drawn, and hung, with a scarlet*
> *Ribbon at his wriſt.*

*Lieut. Gen.* Villain, thou lyeſt.

*Gen.* Arm, arm, *Gonsalvo*, arm; what ho?                                 190
    The lye no flesh can brook, I trow.

*Lieut. Gen.* Advance, from *Aĉton*, with the Musquetiers.

*Gen.* Draw down the *Chelsey* Curiasiers.

*Lieut. Gen.* The Band you boaſt of, *Chelsey* Curiasiers,
    Shall, in my *Putney* Pikes, now meet their Peers.        195

*Gen.* *Chiswickians*, aged, and renown'd in fight,
    Joyn with the *Hammersmith* Brigade.

*Lieut. Gen.* You'l find my *Mortlake* Boys will do them right,
    Unless by *Fulham* numbers over-laid.

*Gen.* Let the left-wing of *Twick'nam* foot advance,                      200
    And line that Eaſtern hedge.

*Lieut. Gen.* The Horse I rais'd in *Petty-France*
    Shall try their chance.
    And scowr the Medows, over-grown with Sedge.

*Gen.* Stand: give the word.                                              205

*Lieut. Gen.* Bright Sword.

*Gen.* That may be thine,
    But 'tis not mine.

*Lieut. Gen.* Give fire, give fire, at once give fire,
    And let those recreant Troops perceive mine ire.           210

*Gen.* Pursue, pursue; they fly
    That firſt did give the lye.                *[Exeunt.*

184 fighting] ~? *Q2, Q3*          188 first.] ~.

*Johns.* I, now you are right: there is nothing then can be objected against it.          188:1
*Bayes.* True: and so, I gad, I'l make it, too, a Tragedy, in a trice. *Q3*
198 *Lieut. Gen.*] *Lieut. Gent. Q3*          205 *Gen.*] *Gent. Q3*          207 *Gen.*] *Gent. Q3*

*Bayes.* This, now, is not improper, I think, because the Spectators know all these Towns, and may easily conceive them to be within the Dominions of the two Kings of *Brentford.* 215
*Johns.* Most exceeding well design'd!
*Bayes.* How do you think I have contriv'd to give a stop to this battel?
*Smi.* How?
*Bayes.* By an Eclipse: Which, let me tell you, is a kind of fancie 220 that was yet never so much as thought of, but by my self, and one person more, that shall be nameless. Come, come in, Mr.——a ——.

*Enter Lieutenant General.*

*Lieut. Gen.* What mid-night darkness does invade the day,
 And snatch the Victor from his conquer'd prey? 225
 Is the Sun weary of this bloudy sight,
 And winks upon us with his eye of light?
 'Tis an Eclipse. This was unkind, O Moon,
 To clap between me, and the Sun so soon.
 Foolish Eclipse! thou this in vain hast done; 230
 My brighter honour had Eclips'd the Sun.
 But now behold Eclipses two in one.  [*Exit.*
*Johns.* This is an admirable representation of a Battel, as ever I saw.
*Bayes.* I, Sir. But how would you fancie now to represent an 235 Eclipse?
*Smi.* Why, that's to be suppos'd.
*Bayes.* Suppos'd! Ay, you are ever at your suppose: ha, ha, ha. Why, you may as well suppose the whole Play. No, it must come in upon the Stage, that's certain; but in some odd way, that may 240 delight, amuse, and all that. I have a conceipt for't, that I am sure is new, and, I believe, to the purpose.
*Johns.* How's that?
*Bayes.* Why, the truth is, I took the first hint of this out of a Dialogue, between *Phœbus* and *Aurora*, in the *Slighted Maid*: 245 which, by my troth, was very pretty; though, I think, you'l confess this is a little better.
*Johns.* No doubt on't, Mr. *Bayes.*

*Bayes.* But, Sir, you have heard, I suppose, that your Eclipse
of the Moon, is nothing else, but an interposition of the Earth,      250
between the Sun and Moon: as likewise your Eclipse of the Sun is
caus'd by an interlocation of the Moon, betwixt the Earth and
Sun?

*Smi.* I have heard so, indeed.

*Bayes.* Well, Sir; what do me I, but make the Earth, Sun, and      255
Moon, come out upon the Stage, and dance the Hey: hum? And,
of necessity, by the very nature of this Dance, the Earth muſt be
sometimes between the Sun and the Moon, and the Moon
between the Earth and Sun; and there you have both your Eclipses. That is new, I gad, ha?      260

*Johns.* That muſt needs be very fine, truly.

*Bayes.* Yes, there is some fancie in't. And then, Sir, that there
may be something in it of a Joque, I make the Moon sell the
Earth a Bargain. Come, come out Eclipse, to the Tune of *Tom
Tyler.*      265

*Enter* Luna.

*Luna.   Orbis,* O *Orbis,*
        Come to me thou little rogue *Orbis.*

*Enter the Earth.*

*Orb.* What calls *Terra firma,* pray?
*Luna. Luna* that ne'er shines by day.
*Orb.* What means *Luna* in a veil?      270
*Luna. Luna* means to shew her tail.

*Enter* Sol.

*Sol.* Fie, Siſter, fie; thou mak'ſt me muse,
        Dery, dery down,
    To see thee Orb abuse.
*Luna.* I hope his anger 'twill not move;      275
    Since I did it out of love.
        Hey down, dery down.

249  But,] Ah dear Rogue: but——a—— *Q3*                254  so,] some such thing *Q3*
255  Sir;] ~, then *Q3*          259–60 Eclipses. That . . . ha?] Eclipses, by demonstration. *Q3*
262  there is some] it has *Q3*          263  in it] in't *Q2;* in't too *Q3*      I] ~ bring 'em in all
singing, and *Q3*          268 What] Who *Q3*          271  tail.] ~.
    *Bayes.* There's the bargain, *Q3*
271.1 Sol] ~, *to the Tune of* Robin Hood *Q3*      274  thee] the *Q3*      276  did] shew'd *Q3*

*Orb.* Where shall I thy true love know,
  Thou pretty, pretty Moon?
*Luna.* To morrow soon, ere it be noon,      280
  On Mount *Vesuvio.*       [*Bis.*
*Sol.* Then I will shine.
*Orb.* And I will be fine.
*Luna.* And we will drink nothing but Lipary wine.
*Omnes.* And we, *&c.*         285
*Bayes.* So, now, vanish Eclipse, and enter t'other Battel, and
fight. Here now, if I am not miſtaken, you will see fighting enough.

> *A battel is fought between foot and great Hobby-*
> *horses. At laſt,* Drawcansir *comes in, and kills*
> *'em all on both sides. All this while the Battel is*
> *fighting,* Bayes *is telling them when to shout, and*
> *shouts with 'em.*

*Draw.* Others may boaſt a single man to kill;
  But I, the bloud of thousands, daily spill.
  Let petty Kings the names of Parties know:   290
  Where e'er I come, I slay both friend and foe.
  The swifteſt Horsmen my swift rage controuls,
  And from their Bodies drives their trembling souls.
  If they had wings, and to the Gods could flie,
  I would pursue, and beat 'em, through the skie:   295
  And make proud *Jove,* with all his Thunder, see.
  This single Arm more dreadful is, than he.  [*Exit.*
*Bayes.* There's a brave fellow for you now, Sirs. I have read of
your *Hector,* your *Achilles,* and a hundred more; but I defie all your
Hiſtories, and your Romances too, I gad, to shew me one such 300
Conqueror, as this *Drawcansir.*
*Johns.* I swear, I think you may.
*Smi.* But, Mr. *Bayes,* how shall all these dead men go off? for I
see none alive to help 'em.
*Bayes.* Go off! why, as they came on; upon their legs: how 305
should they go off? Why, do you think the people do not know

282 shine.] ~. [*To the Tune of* Trenchmore. *Q3* 284 we] I *Q3* 285 *&c.*] ~.
     [*As they Dance the Hey,* Bayes *speaks.*
  *Bayes.* Now the earth's before the Moon; now the Moon's before the Sun: there's 285:1
the Eclipse again.
  *Smi.* He's mightily taken with this I see.
  *Johns.* I, 'tis so extraordinary, how can he chuse? *Q3*
298 I have read] You may talk *Q3*  299 *Hector,* your] *Hector,* and *Q3* a hundred
more] I know not who *Q3*  300 too, I gad] too *Q3*  306 do not] here don't *Q3*

they are not dead? He is mighty ignorant, poor man; your friend here is very silly, Mr. *Johnson*, I gad, he is. Come, Sir, I'l show you go off. Rise, Sirs, and go about your business. There's go off for you. Hark you, Mr. *Ivory*. Gentlemen, I'l be with you presently.          310
                                                                 [*Exit.*

   *Johns.* Will you so? then we'l be gone.

   *Smi.* I, pr'ythee let's go, that we may preserve our hearing. One Battel more would take mine quite away.          [*Exeunt.*


[V. ii]                    *Enter* Bayes *and Players.*

   *Bayes.* Where are the Gentlemen?

   1 *Play.* They are gone, Sir.

   *Bayes.* Gone! 'Sdeath, this laſt Aɕt is beſt of all. I'l go fetch 'em again.          [*Exit.*

   3 *Play.* Stay, here's a foul piece of papyr of his. Let's see what     5
'tis.

[*Reads.*]              *The Argument of the Fifth Aɕt.*

*Cloris,* at length, being sensible of Prince *Pretty-man*'s passion, consents to marry him; but, juſt as they are going to Church, Prince *Pretty-man* meeting, by chance, with old *Joan* the Chand-     10
lers widow, and remembring it was she that firſt brought him acquainted with *Cloris:* out of a high point of honour, break off his match with *Cloris*, and marries old *Joan*. Upon which, *Cloris*, in despair, drowns her self: and Prince *Pretty-man*, discontentedly, walks by the River side.          15

   1 *Play.* Pox on't, this will never do: 'tis juſt like the reſt. Come, let's be gone.          [*Exeunt.*

308 is] ~. ha, ha, ha *Q3*    you] ~ how they shall *Q3*       309 Rise] ~, rise *Q3*
310 you. Hark . . . *Ivory*] you now. Ha, ha, ha. Mr. *Ivory*, a word *Q3*       313 would] will *Q2, Q3*

V. ii.
4 *Exit.*] ~.
   1 *Play.* What shall we do, now he is gone away?          4:1
   2 *Play.* Why, so much the better; then let's go to dinner. *Q3*
6 'tis.] ~.
   3 or 4 *Play.* I, I; come let's hear it. *Q3*          6:1
8 *Cloris,*] 3 *Play.* ~ *Q3*       16 1 *Play.* Pox on't, this] <*no line break*> This *Q3*       17 be
gone] begone *Q3*    *Exeunt.*] ~.
   *Most of the Play.* Ay, pox on't, let's go away. *Q3*          17:1

[V. iii]                    *Enter* Bayes.

*Bayes.* A plague on 'em both for me, they have made me sweat,
to run after 'em. A couple of senceless rascals, that had rather go
to dinner, than see this Play out, with a pox to 'em. What comfort
has a man to write for such dull rogues? Come Mr.——a——
Where are you, Sir? come away quick, quick.                         5

                    *Enter Player.*

*Play.* Sir, they are gone to dinner.
*Bayes.* Yes, I know the Gentlemen are gone; but I ask for the
Players.
*Play.* Why, an't please your worship, Sir, the Players are gone
to dinner too.                                                      10
*Bayes.* How! are the Players gone to Dinner? 'Tis impossible:
the Players gone to dinner! I gad, if they are, I'l make 'em know
what it is to injure a person that does 'em the honour to write for
'em, and all that. A company of proud, conceited, humorous, cross-
grain'd persons, and all that. I gad, I'l make 'em the moſt con-    15
temptible, despicable, inconsiderable persons, and all that, in the
whole world, for this trick. I gad, I'l be reveng'd on 'em; I'l sell
this Play to the other House.
*Play.* Nay, good Sir, don't take away the Book; you'l disappoint the Town, that comes to see it acted here, this afternoon.    20
*Bayes.* That's all one. I muſt reserve this comfort to my self, my
Book and I will go together, we will not part, indeed, Sir. The
Town! why, what care I for the Town? I gad, the Town has us'd
me as scurvily, as the Players have done: but I'l be reveng'd on
them too; I will both Lampoon and print 'em too, I gad. Since they 25
will not admit of my Plays, they shall know what a Satyriſt I am.
And so farewel to this Stage for ever, I gad.          [*Exit.*
    1 *Play.* What shall we do now?

V. iii.
3 than] then *Q3*        5.1 *Player*] ed.; *Players again Q1, Q2; Stage-keeper Q3*        6 *Play.*]
*Stage. Q3*        9 *Play.*] *Stage. Q3*        12 'em] ~ to *Q2*        19 *Play.*] *Stage. Q3*        good]
*Q3*; ~, *Q1*        20 Town,] company *Q3*        22 Book] Play *Q3*        will] shall *Q3*        Sir.]
~. | *Stag.* But what will the Town say, Sir? | *Bayes. Q3*        25 I will both] for I'l *Q3*        and
print . . . gad.] 'em all And *Q3*        27 for ever, I gad] I gad, for ever *Q3*        27–8 *Exit.* .
. . now?] *Exit Bayes.* | *Enter* Players. *Q3*

2 *Play.* Come then, let's set up Bills for another Play: We shall lose nothing by this, I warrant you.                                                    30

1 *Play.* I am of your opinion. But, before we go, let's see *Haynes* and *Shirley* practise the last Dance; for that may serve for another Play.

2 *Play.* I'l call 'em: I think they are in the Tyring-room.

*The Dance done.*

1 *Play.* Come, come; let's go away to dinner.                                    35

[*Exeunt omnes.*

29 2] 1 *Q3*        Play: We] ~: | 2 *Pay.* I, I; ~ *Q3*        32–3 for another Play] us
another time *Q3*        34 2 *Play*] *Q2, Q3*; 2 *Bayes Q1*        'em] ~ in *Q3*        are] ~ but *Q3*

# Dance in The Rehearsal

Anon.

Fɪɢ. 9. A dance tune in *The Rehearsal*. Transcribed from Royal College of Music MS 1172, fo. 19. Dances are called for at II. v. 11 and 39, III. ii. 234, V. i. 107, and V. iii. 34.1

# EPILOGUE.

*The Play is at an end, but where's the Plot?*
*That circumstance our Poet* Bayes *forgot,*
*And we can boast, though 'tis a plotting Age,*
*No place is freer from it than the Stage.*
*The Ancients Plotted, though, and strove to please*      5
*With sence that might be understood with ease;*
*They every Scene with so much wit did store*
*That who brought any in, went out with more:*
*But this new way of wit does so surprise,*
*Men lose their wits in wond'ring where it lyes.*      10
*If it be true, that Monstrous births presage*
*The following mischiefs that afflicts the Age,*
*And sad disasters to the State proclaim;*
*Plays, without head or tail, may do the same.*
*Wherefore, for ours, and for the Kingdoms peace,*      15
*May this prodigious way of writing cease.*
*Let's have, at least, once in our lives, a time*
*When we may hear some Reason, not all Rhyme:*
*We have these ten years felt its Influence;*
*Pray let this prove a year of Prose and Sence.*      20

*FINIS.*

Epilogue

12  afflicts] afflict *Q2, Q3*

# The Restauration

## INTRODUCTION

*The Restauration* presents us with a set of currently insoluble problems. We will set forth such facts as are known, but they leave us, unfortunately, pretty much at an impasse.

Beaumont and Fletcher's *Philaster, or Love lies a Bleeding* was popular both before and after the Interregnum.[1] Edmund Waller states in the prologue to his alteration of *The Maid's Tragedy* that 'Of all our elder Plays, | This and *Philaster* have the lowdest fame'.[2] It was regularly performed by the King's Company between 1660 and 1676. In 1695 the Patent Company staged an adaptation by Elkanah Settle, which appears to have failed and disappeared from the stage.[3] The first we know of any earlier adaptation is the publication in volume 1 of Buckingham's *Miscellaneous Works* (1704) of 'A Prologue to *Philaster*' explicitly said to be '*By the Duke of* Buckingham'. The same volume contains 'The *Epilogue*, to be spoken by the Governour in *Philaster*', likewise '*By the Duke of* Buckingham' (i. 9–13). Internal evidence in the epilogue points to spring 1683 as the date. All unconfirmed attributions in the *Miscellaneous Works* must be regarded as suspect, but none can be ignored.

In 1711 the anonymous author of the 'Preface' to the seven-volume edition of *The Works of Mr. Francis Beaumont, and Mr. John Fletcher* states that 'after' the success of *The Chances* (pub. 1682)

His Grace . . . bestow'd some time in altering another Play of our Authors, called *Philaster*, or *Love lies a Bleeding*; He made very considerable Alterations

---

[1] The best version of the Beaumont and Fletcher text for reading purposes is the generously introduced and annotated Revels edition, *Philaster or, Love Lies a–Bleeding*, ed. Andrew Gurr (1969; repr. Manchester: Manchester University Press, 2003).

[2] Edmund Waller, *The Maid's Tragedy Altered. With some other Pieces* (London, 1690), sig. B2ʳ (misprinted F2). Waller's prologue probably dates from the mid-1660s.

[3] On the Settle version, see Sprague, *Beaumont and Fletcher*, 195–202.

in it, and took it with him, intending to finish it the last Journey he made to *Yorkshire* in the Year 1686. I cannot learn what is become of the Play with his Grace's Alterations, but am very well inform'd it was since the Revolution in the Hands of Mr. *Nevil Payn*, who was Imprison'd at *Edinburgh* in the Year 1689.[4]

The text of an adaptation of *Philaster* was published in the third edition of Buckingham's *Works* in 1715. The publishers of the 1704 edition may have intended to include it: that edition has a gap in numbering of 72 pages following p. 144 that is suspiciously close to the 80 pages used for the play in 1715. The correspondence in size is even closer if we remember that *15wgv* includes the prologue and epilogue, which are located separately in *04mw*. If this hypothesis is correct, the most likely reason for the play's non-appearance in 1704 would have been failure to reach agreement with the owners of the copyright of *Philaster*. The adaptation is the first piece in volume 1, and all we know of it comes from the separate title page: '*The Restauration: or, Right will take Place. A Tragicomedy. Written by George Villiers, late Duke of Buckingham.* From the Original Copy, never before Printed. London: Printed in the Year MDCCXIV.' No hint is given as to the history of the enterprise or when and how the publishers obtained the manuscript. Four years later Giles Jacob listed the title in his section of 'Plays Written by Anonymous Authors' with a terse comment: 'Injuriously father'd upon the Duke of *Buckingham*. Never acted.'[5] This opinion, possibly founded on no more than lack of stated provenance and a negative qualitative judgement, was echoed in later playlists, as for example David Erskine Baker's *The Companion to the Play-House* (1764), Isaac Reed's *Biographia Dramatica* (1782), Stephen Jones's *Biographia Dramatica* (1812), Genest, and other authorities.

Some obvious questions need to be addressed. When published in 1704, the prologue and epilogue are said to be for '*Philaster*': could they have been written (by Buckingham or anyone else) for a revival of the old Beaumont and Fletcher play? The answer is clearly 'No'. The epilogue is 'to be spoken by the Governour', and this character appears in the text printed in 1715 but not in the original play. Another issue is Buckingham's plausibility as author of the prologue and epilogue. The

---

[4] (London: Tonson, 1711), i, p. ix. The Cambridge *Dramatic Works*, i. 103, calls this edition *L*, on the assumption that it was edited by Gerard Langbaine the younger.

[5] *The Poetical Register: or, the Lives and Characters of the English Dramatick Poets* (London: E. Curll, 1719), 326.

prologue alludes rather intimately (without naming the duke) to his prodigality with money and his political career—but only those in the know could realize this, and the piece makes little sense without that knowledge. Would Buckingham have indulged in this sort of self-display, and would rumour-mongering in the pit have rendered the meaning comprehensible to the audience?[6] Perhaps. The epilogue is also somewhat problematical, with its cutting comments on the Earl of Shaftesbury (who died on 21 January 1683). Buckingham had parted political company with his old Whig ally some three years earlier, and he may not have believed in *de mortuis nil nisi bonum*. Would he have used Dryden's name for the earl from *Absalom and Achitophel*? Perhaps he would.

How plausible is the suggestion (made as late as 1711) that a copy was in the possession of Henry Nevil Payne? Entirely so. Buckingham and Payne were friends in the 1680s. The duke sent Payne a partial draft of his 1685 essay on religion and toleration; he also gave him the use of a yacht in 1686 and had some financial dealings with him at that time. Payne wrote a pamphlet in support of Buckingham's essay, and a letter from him to one of the duke's 'domestics' is printed in the 1704 *Miscellaneous Works* (i. 71–4).[7] Payne could certainly have had a copy of a draft manuscript by Buckingham. How seriously should we take Giles Jacob's blunt dismissal of the attribution? At a guess, not very seriously. He was writing a generation after the duke's death and he offers no evidence. The unreliable nature of the Buckingham *Works* and the uneven quality of the interpolated passages are not to be denied, but they are insufficient evidence for disattribution, especially for a writer whose solo work is as thinly documented as Buckingham's.

Was Buckingham responsible for the 1715 text? We have no overwhelming reason to believe the attribution—or to disbelieve it. The dramaturgical design of the adaptation is competent enough. Arthur Colby Sprague dismisses Jacob's statement as 'not in itself of much value', but says 'What does throw doubt on the Duke's authorship is the indifferent quality of the alteration itself, and particularly the nerveless mediocrity of the verse.'[8] He finds the discrepancy between 'the vigor which characterizes the two pendant compositions' and some of

---

6 Prior to 1699 playwrights' names were never used in playbills in London. See *The Letters of John Dryden*, ed. Charles E. Ward (Durham, NC: Duke University Press, 1942), 112–13.

7 On Payne and his relations with Buckingham, see below, II. 79–80.

8 Sprague, 189.

the clunkier lines of the playscript seriously discordant. Then again, we have no way of knowing how much help Buckingham received in polishing them. The style of the verse in the adaptation takes us into unknown territory: beyond a couple of competent but conventional poems, and (perhaps) *Theodorick*, the duke had no known experience in writing high-flown verse. Whether the extant text was worked up a bit by a ghost helper we have no way to determine.[9] The possibility should be acknowledged that Payne (author of three plays) could be the adapter or unacknowledged assistant. The adaptation could of course be by another person, identity unknown. Is the surviving text wholly or largely Buckingham's work? Not proven—but certainly not disproven —is the best verdict we can offer.

Despite the uneven quality of the writing (which may be the result of the revision being incomplete at Buckingham's death), *The Restauration* has many positive virtues when regarded as a creation for the stage rather than a work of literature. It also contains much fascinating evidence for changes in literary and theatrical taste between the 1610s and the 1680s and for the historical evolution of both spoken and literary English. For these reasons, and because dramaturgical issues arise from every aspect of the rehandling, a complete record of variations between the 1715 *Works* (*15gvw*) and the version of *Philaster* in the Beaumont and Fletcher second folio (*79fc*) has been given in the footnotes, including the text of omitted passages and scenes. Certainly the verbal reworking was remarkably thorough. Archaic words and syntax were ruthlessly modernized. Flowery Jacobean verbiage and intricate imagery was pruned back whenever it threatened to hinder the forward movement of the action or would be difficult for an audience of the 1680s to comprehend. When new speeches were supplied they were of a kind suitable for the specialized talents of the United Company's leading actors and actresses and the reigning practice of declaiming lines to a 'tone'.[10] They also reflected the emergence of a new kind of

---

[9] On the subject of the kind of assistance expected by an aristocratic author, see Timothy Raylor, 'Newcastle's Ghosts: Robert Payne, Ben Jonson, and the "Cavendish Circle"', in Claude J. Summers and Ted-Larry Pebworth (eds.), *Literary Circles and Cultural Communities in Renaissance England* (Columbia, Mo.: University of Missouri Press, 2000), 92–114, in which he reproduces a Newcastle MS worked over by a revising ghost and tries to establish what the conventions for this kind of work might have been. Buckingham was close to Newcastle and could well have imbibed some attitudes from him.

[10] For a recent discussion of this practice, see Harold Love, 'Vocal Register in Behn's *Love-Letters between a Nobleman and his Sister*', *English Language Notes*, 41 (2003), 44–53.

management based on an incipient star system and the cultivation of
specific 'lines' in place of the older sharer organization with its extensive doubling of roles and stress on versatility. The careful reworking of
five parts written in the original for boy actors so that they could be
played by women is of great interest. One of those parts—Galatea/
Melesinda—has been severely curtailed. Megra/Alga has been given
greater force and venom as a villainess, perhaps with an eye to the
emerging talent of Elizabeth Barry. Araminta and Endymion have
been simplified, both in respect of language and motivation, to accom-
modate them to a more passionate, less poetic style of performance.
Women actors did not need to mediate female sexuality through the
use of ornate language, since they could do it directly with their voices
and their bodies. Among the men the most severely treated is
Pharamond/Thrasomond, who finds himself reduced from a flawed
but believable prince to a priapic buffoon who could be played by a low
comedy specialist such as James Nokes. The two comic exchanges that
follow Philaster's exit at II. i. 60 and the woodsmen's scenes at the beginning of IV. i have been lopped in obedience to neoclassical principles, because they do nothing to advance the action. While all these
changes will disappoint admirers of *Philaster*, they are the outcome of a
coherent theatrical vision. As one would expect from the author of *The
Rehearsal*, the adapter frowns on Beaumont and Fletcher's fondness for
surprises. When he gives the 'Clown' a brief entrance prior to his intervention in the rescue scene of IV. i and Philander and Araminta their
dialogue at V. i. 42–92 before their marriage, he is preparing the audience for events that the original introduces as wholly unexpected peri-
peteia. As the second of these passages shows, however, he shares their
fondness, and that of Massinger and Orrery after them, for strained
points of honour—another subject of satire in *The Rehearsal*.

Was *The Restauration* ever performed? No record of performance
survives, but this means very little.[11] The existence of the prologue and
epilogue strongly suggest an intention to perform the work. Their topi-
cality implies a date soon after Shaftesbury's death in Holland on 21
January 1683. This was the first season of the United Company, whose
managers were seizing the opportunity to mount productions of fav-

---

[11] The editors of *The London Stage*, Part 1, 319, enter *The Restauration* under Feb. 1683
with the comment that neither authorship nor performance is certain. They worked solely
from knowledge of the prologue and epilogue. Their statement that 'The adaptation was
apparently never printed' is, obviously, wrong.

ourite plays out of the old King's Company's repertory. Several by 'Beaumont and Fletcher' were among those revived, notably *Rule a Wife and have a Wife*, *The Scornful Lady*, *The Beggars Bush*, *Rollo*, *The Humorous Lieutenant*, and *The Double Marriage*.[12] By February 1684 the company had produced Rochester's version of Fletcher's *Valentinian*. That the United Company would want to mount *Philaster* makes excellent sense; so does the proposition that they might want to remove some of its more obvious dramaturgical blemishes. If Buckingham, whose *Chances* remained a repertory staple, offered them an 'improved' *Philaster*, the company would probably have jumped at the chance to produce it. Whether this happened we simply do not know. Lack of publication means almost nothing, and performance records are desperately thin in the 1680s. If produced, the adaptation was apparently not much of a success.

The source play was an obvious candidate for adaptation. It had been highly successful for nearly three-quarters of a century, but it suffered from some glaring (albeit curable) defects. Beaumont and Fletcher wrote it *c.*1608–10, and it was first published as *Phylaster* in the quarto of 1620. *Q2* of 1622 contains a radically different beginning and ending, utilized in all subsequent printings.[13] Eight quartos had appeared by 1661 (including a piracy). Like other separately published plays, *Philaster* was added to the 1679 Beaumont and Fletcher folio; a ninth quarto edition appeared in 1687.

The play was performed at the Red Bull in the summer of 1660, and produced by the King's Company at Vere Street as early as 13 November that year.[14] Pepys, who as a boy had learned the part of Arethusa for a projected amateur performance, saw it for the first time on 18 November 1661 (finding it 'far short of my expectation'). He found a visit of 30 May 1668 more rewarding. Between 1662 and 1676 seven further performance dates are known—a large number for an era in which we are able to assign a play to fewer than one tenth of likely performing days. *Philaster* was among the plays selected for performance 'all by women' after the Bridges Street Theatre burnt in 1672, and it was performed on 1 November that year at the Inner Temple—a sign

---

[12] See Downes, *Roscius Anglicanus*, 82–3.

[13] For a good textual history of *Philaster*, see *The Dramatic Works in the Beaumont and Fletcher Canon*, Fredson Bowers, gen. ed., vol. 1 (Cambridge: Cambridge University Press, 1966). *Philaster* was edited by Robert K. Turner. The textual history occupies pp. 369–97.

[14] Performance information drawn from *The London Stage*, Part 1, pp. 12, 20, 42, 46, 49, 124, 137, 189, 200, 223, 244.

of its being a favourite. The play appears to have retained its popularity (probably in the original version) through the 1680s. Langbaine says that *Philaster* 'has always been acted with Success; and has been the diversion of the Stage, even in these days' (p. 213). By 1699, however, Gildon says more tepidly, 'A Play often Acted formerly, and sometimes of late Years', though admitting that it 'is accounted one of the best our Authors have Published'.[15] Performances are recorded at Drury Lane in 1711, 1712, and 1714–16.[16] After two performances in 1722 there was a hiatus until Drury Lane revived the play, adapted by George Colman the Elder in 1763 as a vehicle for the debut of William Powell.

As early as 1672, however, critics were starting to rear their heads, and the favourites of yore were getting subjected to sceptical scrutiny. In Dryden's 'Defence of the Epilogue' ('Or, An Essay on the Dramatique Poetry of the last Age'), appended to *The Conquest of Granada* when it was published in 1672, he mounted a direct attack on Fletcherian practice:

*Fletcher* . . . neither understood correct Plotting, nor that which they call *the Decorum of the Stage*. I would not search in his worst Playes for examples: he who will consider his *Philaster* . . . and many others which I could name, will find them much below the applause which is now given them: he will see *Philaster* wounding his Mistriss, and afterwards his Boy, to save himself: Not to mention the Clown who enters immediately, and not only has the advantage of the Combat against the Heroe, but diverts you from your serious concernment with his ridiculous and absurd Raillery. (*Works*, xi. 206)

Writing five years later in *The Tragedies of the Last Age*, Thomas Rymer excoriates Arbaces in *A King and No King* for exactly the same reason: 'If nothing else in the character of *Arbaces*, the drawing his Sword against a *Woman*, was enough in Poetry to damn him. After that *outrage*, he could make no pretensions to ought that is good or honourable.'[17] This notion of decorum may strike the twenty-first-century reader as quaint, but if both Dryden and Rymer were appalled and contemptuous at what had come to be considered a violation of dram-

---

[15] Gildon, *Lives and Characters*, 60.

[16] John Harold Wilson states that 'After 1695' *Philaster* 'was seen upon the stage under its own name, but with [Settle's] alterations'. *The Influence of Beaumont and Fletcher on Restoration Drama* (Columbus, Ohio: Ohio State University Press, 1928), 47. We can find no evidence to substantiate this claim.

[17] *Critical Works*, 47. On such strictures, see Gunnar Sorelius, *'The Giant Race before the Flood': Pre-Restoration Drama on the Stage and in the Criticism of the Restoration* (Studia Anglistica Upsaliensia, 4; Uppsala: Almqvist & Wiksell, 1966), esp. 138, 170–1.

atic propriety, then probably the theatre managers would have felt that some discreet fixing was in order.

As our record of the verbal differences between the original and the adaptation suggests, a great deal of detailed adjustment was done, but the changes to plot and action are clearly driven by principle.[18] The adapter (presumptively Buckingham) has neatly met Dryden's objections. Philaster (now dubbed Philander) duly triumphs over the rustic clown in combat ('*Clown* falls'—IV. i. 204.1) and he does not deliberately wound his beloved. Instead Philander, finding Araminta together with Endymion and misinterpreting the situation, rushes at them to attack the boy and accidentally wounds the woman (IV. i. 152.1). Likewise the adapter reworks the embarrassing passage (IV. vi. 23–5 in Beaumont and Fletcher) in which Philaster deliberately wounds the sleeping page in the hope that he will be identified as the assailant who hurt Arethusa. The result, in Sprague's words, is that 'Philaster never intends to harm Arethusa, and in wounding Bellario has no thought of saving his own skin, but only of doing an act of justice. Moreover, nearly two pages [some forty lines] are added to the later scene in which he begs forgiveness' (V. i. 42–92).[19]

Quite a bit of incidental cutting and tightening is done throughout the play (almost all of the Act IV hunting scene vanishes, for example), but the other principal change in what remains comes in the character of Philaster/Philander's rival, the Spanish prince Pharamond/Thrasomond. In the original the prince is a pompous fool, but not completely implausible as a nobleman and suitor. The adapter turns him into a clown and a butt ('a complete buffoon throughout', as Sprague says). Though 24 years old, he requires a 'Governour' who directs and prompts him as necessary ('You must be angry, Sir'—I. i. 177). Beaumont and Fletcher's Pharamond is a womanizing lout whose liaison with Megra is contemptible, but Thrasomond is entirely deprived of stature and dignity, exhibited sneaking off 'in Drawers' when their fornication is interrupted (II. i. 159.1). The resulting play is shorter, tighter, more focused. We agree with Sprague that some clarity of motivation is lost, along with a considerable amount of richness in detail and complexity of character. Philander is a very sanitized version of Philaster, and Araminta is a coy and conventionalized version of the decisive and outspoken Arethusa. Dryden's objections are met, but the adaptation is

[18] Sprague's excellent analysis, pp. 187–95, remains standard, and we are indebted to it.
[19] Sprague, 191.

not as interesting a play as the original, flawed though that original certainly is. So far as we can see, the 'Buckingham' version exercised no influence on Settle's adaptation of 1695. Of course it was not available in print, but if it had been performed c.1683 then a prompt copy ought to have been available in the Patent Company's library. Writing in 1691, Langbaine exhibits no awareness of the 'Buckingham' version. Writing in 1699, Gildon is totally silent about both the Buckingham and the Settle adaptations.

Did the 1683 adapter have anything in mind beyond improving de-corum and cutting running time? Is the new title, for example, a hint of a political agenda? In terms of the content of the play itself, *The Restauration: or, Right will take Place* refers to Philander's regaining the throne of Sicily, from which his father was toppled by the incumbent king. Restorations and the deposition of usurpers had of course been a favourite theme of 1660s playwrights, but *if* the adaptation was written and staged (or intended to be staged) *c.* spring 1683, was an application of some sort being invited? Derek Hughes interprets the play as a dec-laration of loyalty: 'Loyalist triumphalism received support even from the Duke of Buckingham, who had quarrelled with Shaftesbury and drifted away from the Exclusionists.'[20] A more thoroughgoing political reading is offered in brief by Nancy Klein Maguire, who identifies Phil-ander with James, Duke of York:[21]

Mary and William had been singled out for succession during the Crisis, and Buckingham glances at this possibility. In the play, a usurper is forcing the English [*sic*] princess to marry a foreign prince who is prince only in name, and Buckingham goes to pains to make him appear an oaf. Philander, the rightful heir whose father's throne has been usurped, still has friends, but, like James, he is wronged, broken in fortune, and overcome by grief. The play resonates with the divisions of the Exclusion Crisis.

In the heated atmosphere of 1683 a so-minded viewer of the play might have made such an 'application', but the parallels seem fairly remote. James's father had indeed been ousted by a usurper, but his brother was on the throne and stubbornly insisting on maintaining the succession as it stood. Equating Araminta and her clown of a Spanish suitor with Mary and her husband William seems a stretch. Buckingham had ul-

---

[20] *English Drama, 1660–1700*, 310–11.
[21] 'Tragicomedy', in Deborah Payne Fisk (ed.), *The Cambridge Companion to English Restoration Theatre* (Cambridge: Cambridge University Press, 2000), 86–106 at 99–100.

timately refused to back the exclusionists, but as he told the French ambassador, Barillon, he and the Duke of York had always been enemies.[22] A hagiographic allegory in favour of James would come very oddly from Buckingham, and any audience aware of his involvement in the adaptation would have been most unlikely to read a positive message about James into it. Not too much should be made of the putative date. Allusions in the prologue and epilogue are powerful evidence for dating them *c.* February 1683, but there is no way of knowing when the adaptation itself was made, or when the 1715 title was applied—or by whom. The new title might certainly have been taken in 1683 as 'loyalist triumphalism', but the adaptation itself seems to us to make a very awkward and unsatisfactory allegory of anything apart from the event specified in its title—the Restoration of 1660.

More tentatively, we raise the possibility that Buckingham may have identified both psychologically and politically with Philander. Having been brought up by Charles I as a surrogate member of the royal family, he was himself a kind of disinherited prince, while his passion for the Duchess of Orleans was symmetrical, except in its outcome, with the Philander–Araminta relationship. At the time of the Exclusion crisis there was even some support for him, in preference to Monmouth or William, as a possible elective king. In July 1679 Barillon, the French ambassador, reported to Louis XIV that Buckingham was promoting the notion that he had a hereditary claim to the throne, as a descendant of Edward IV, that was better than that of the illegimate Monmouth, adding that the 'notion closely resembles a chimera . . . however, in this country chimera are not so absurd as elsewhere'.[23] One wonders too how a follower of Monmouth would have responded to the play had it reached the stage in the early 1680s. The possibility of such an interpretation being made could be one reason why the adaptation may never have been performed. In the year of publication, 1715, a new identification must have been made by some readers by which Philander was equated with the Old Pretender and the King with the newly installed George I.

We are left with a theatrically and linguistically interesting script that Buckingham *may* have adapted or had a hand in, and which *may* have been staged by the United Company in the spring of 1683. In all probability the attribution problem will remain permanently unre-

[22] Chapman, 255.     [23] Burghclere, 367.

solved. All puzzles aside, however, *The Restauration* possesses considerable interest as an example of the application of the Carolean critical principles that had evolved in the 1670s.

Readers should note that the footnotes are a record of the verbal differences between *15wgv* and *79fc* and not between our edited text and *79fc*. For this reason wherever *15wgv* has been emended the lemma will differ from the reading of the edition text, as at I. i. 4 Gentleman] Gentlemen, where this edition reads 'Gentlemen'. Editorial changes are recorded in the Transmissional History at pages 711ff. Errors in *79fc* are accepted as substantive readings and neither corrected nor commented on. The copy used is British Library C. 45. i. 7, since it is available for further reference on the EEBO database. It should also be noted that changes to capitalization have been recorded whenever they are significant for indicating alterations to verse lineation but otherwise ignored. Differences in verse lineation between the sources are recorded in the footnotes, while those introduced by the editors are listed in the Transmissional History. The reviser's modifications to versification are more than trivial in that they embody a totally changed way from Fletcher's of hearing and constructing the stage pentameter line, though one that still falls short of Augustan ideals of regularity.

# The Restauration

Text prepared by Felicity Henderson

## THE PROLOGUE.

### By the Duke of BUCKINGHAM.

*N*othing is harder in the World to do,
 Than to quit what our Nature leads us to.
*As this our Friend here proves, who, having spent*
*His Time and Wealth for other Folks Content;*
*Tho' he so much as Thanks could never get,*      5
*Cann't, for his Life, quite give it over yet;*
*But, striving still to please you, hopes he may,*
*Without a Grievance, try to mend a Play.*
*Perhaps he wish'd it might have been his Fate*
*To lend a helping Hand to mend the State:*      10
*Tho' he conceives, as things have lately run,*
*'Tis somewhat hard at present to be done.*
*Well, let that pass, the Stars that rule the Rout,*
*Do what we can, I see, must whirl about:*
*But here's the Devil on't, that, come what will,*     15
*His Stars are sure to make him Loser still.*
*When all the* Polls *together made a Din,*
*Some to put out, and others to put in,*
*And every where his Fellows got and got*
*From being nothing to be God knows what:*      20
*He, for the Public, needs would play a Game,*
*For which he has been trounc'd by public Fame;*
*And to speak Truth, so he deserv'd to be*
*For his dull clownish Singularity:*
*For when the Fashion is to break ones Trust,*      25
*'Tis Rudeness then to offer to be Just.*

0.1 THE PROLOGUE] A Prologue to *Philaster* 04*mw*    2 what] that 04*mw*

## Dramatis Personæ.

### MEN.

*The King.*
Philander, *true Heir to the Crown.*
Thrasomond, *Prince of* Spain.
Cleon, *A Lord.*
Agremont,  ⎱
          ⎰ *Gentlemen his Confederates.*
Adelard,    ⎰
*A* Spaniard, *Governour to Prince* Thrasomond.

### WOMEN.

Araminta, *The King's Daughter.*
Melesinda, *A modest Lady attending on the Princess.*
Alga, *A wanton Court Lady.*
*Two other Court Ladies.*
Euphrosyne, *Daughter to* Cleon, *but disguised like
   a Page, under the Name of* Endymion.

### SCENE *Sicily.*

*79fc*
*The Scene being in* Cicilie.
Persons Represented in the Play.

*The* King.
Philaster, *Heir to the Crown.*
Pharamond, *Prince of* Spain.
Dion, *a Lord.*
Cleremont ⎱ *Noble Gentlemen his*
Thrasiline ⎰ *Associates.*
Arethusa, *the Kings Daughter.*
Galatea, *a wise modest Lady
   attending the Princess.*
Megra, *a lascivious Lady.*

*An old wanton Lady, or Croan.*
*Another Lady attending the Princess.*
Eufrasia, *Daughter of* Dion, *but disguised
   like a Page, and called* Bellario.
*An old Captain.*
*Five Citizens.*
*A Countrey fellow.*
*Two Woodmen.*
*The Kings Guard and Train.*

# The Restauration, &c.

## ACT I. SCENE I.

### Cleon, Agremont *and* Adelard.

*Agr.* Here's no Body come yet.

*Cleon.* They had Orders from the King to attend here. Besides it has been published, that no Officer should deny Admission to any Gentlemen that desire to attend and hear.

*Agr.* Can you ghess the Cause of this Ceremony?                5

*Cleon.* That's plain, Sir, the foreign Prince that's come to marry *Araminta*, Heiress to this Kingdom.

*Adel.* Your diving Politicians, and those who would seem to have deep Intelligence, give out that she does not like him.

*Cleon.* O, Sir, the Multitude speak what they would have. But    10 her Father has sent this Prince so many Assurances of the Match before his coming over, that I think she's resolved to be ruled.

*Agr.* And will this foreign Prince enjoy both the Kingdoms of *Sicily* and *Calabria*, Sir?

*Cleon.* That it is so intended is moſt certain; but it will sure be    15 very troublesome and difficult for him to enjoy them both in Safety, the Right Heir to one of them being now living, and of so noble and virtuous a Character, especially when the People are possessed with an Admiration of the Bravery of his Mind and Pity of his Injuries.                20

I. i. 0.1 *Cleon*] *Enter* Dion        1 no . . . yet] not Lords nor Ladies        2 They . . . Orders] Credit me Gentlemen, I wonder at it. They receiv'd strict charge        3 has been] was boldly        deny Admission to] forbid        4 Gentleman] Gentlemen        5 Cause . . . Ceremony] cause        6 That's . . . foreign] Sir, it is plain about the *Spanish* 7 *Araminta* . . . Kingdom] our Kingdoms Heir, and be our Soveraign        8–9 Your . . . him] Many (that will seem to know much) say, she looks not on him like a Maid in Love        10 Multitude] multitude (that seldom know any thing but their own opinions)        what] that 10–12 But . . . over] but the Prince, before his own approach, receiv'd so many confident messages from the State        13 And . . . Prince] Sir, it is thought, with her he shall        the] these        14 *Calabria*, Sir?] *Calabria*.        15–16 That . . . in] Sir, it is (without controversie) so meant. But 'twill be a troublesome labour for him to enjoy both these Kingdoms, with        17–18 being . . . Character] living, and living so vertuously 18–19 when . . . Admiration of] the people admiring        20 Pity of] lamenting

*Agr.* You mean *Philander.*

*Cleon.* I mean the same. His Father, we all know, was unjuſtly driven by our late King of *Calabria* from his fruitful *Sicily*: I wish the Blood I drew my self in those accursed Wars were well wash'd off.

25

*Agr.* My Ignorance of the Affairs of *Sicily* will not let me know how it comes to pass that *Philander* (being Heir to one of these Kingdoms) the King should suffer him to go abroad so much at Liberty.

*Cleon.* Your Temper is more fortunate, I find, than to busy your self in enquiring after State News; but I muſt tell you that lately the King risqu'd both his Kingdoms for offering to imprison *Philander*. For the City rose in Armes, nor could be quell'd by any Threats or Force till they saw the Prince ride thro' the Streets unguarded; and then throwing up their Caps with loud Huzza's and Bonfires, they laid aside their military Appointments. This Reason Politicians give for the Marriage of his Daughter to a foreign Prince, that he may be able to keep his own People in Awe by his Forces.

30

35

*Agr.* Who is this Prince's Father?

40

*Cleon.* A Person of mean Extraction, but by Wiles and Arts obtaining Power, usurp'd the Kingdom where he reigns, and keeps it under by a ſtanding Army, which our King intends to copy.

*Enter* Melesinda, Alga, *a Lady and a* Spaniard.

*Adel.* See the Ladies, what's the firſt?

*Cleon.* A worthy Lady that attends the Princess.

45

*Adel.* The other that follows her?

---

21 You . . . *Philander*] Who, *Philaster?* 22 I . . . His] Yes, whose 22–3 was unjustly driven] was 23 *Calabria*] ~, unrighteously deposed 23–5 I . . . off] My self drew some blood in those Wars, which I would give my hand to be washed from 26 *Agr.*] *Cle.* Sir, of the . . . *Sicily*] in State-policy 27 how . . . that] why 28 go] walk so much at] with such free 30–43 Your . . . copy] Sir, it seems your nature is more constant than to enquire after State news. But the King (of late) made a hazard of both the Kingdoms, of *Cicilie* and his own, with offering but to imprison *Philaster*. At which the City was in arms, not to be charm'd down by any State order or Proclamation, till they saw *Philaster* ride through the streets pleas'd, and without a guard; at which they threw their Hats, and their arms from them; some to make bonefires, some to drink, all for his deliverance. Which (wise men say) is the cause, the King labours to bring in the power of a Foreign Nation, to aw his own with 43.1 *a Lady* . . . Spaniard] *and a Lady* 45 worthy Lady] wise and modest Gentlwoman 46 other . . . her] second

*Cleon.* She is one that loves to try the several Conſtitutions of Men's Bodies, and indeed has deſtroyed her own by making Experiments upon them, for the good of the Commonwealth.

*Agr.* Of which she is certainly a very profitable Member.    50

*Adel.* And pray what odd grave Fellow's that who follows alone?

*Cleon.* One of Prince *Thrasomond*'s Train, and his Governour.

*Agr.* Why is that Prince a Boy?

*Cleon.* Yes, he's a pretty forward Boy about four and twenty.

*Adel.* That is a forward Boy indeed, when will he be a Man?    55

*Cleon.* Never; he'll live a Boy till threescore, and then turn Child again.

May you have your Desires, Ladies!

*Alga.* Then you muſt sit down by us.

*Adel.* With all our Hearts, Ladies.    60

*Gover.* I will sit near this Lady.

*Mel.* Not near me, Sir, but there's a Lady loves a Stranger, and you appear to me a very ſtrange Fellow.

*Agr.* Madam, how ſtrange soever he is, he will not be so long, for I perceive he can quickly be acquainted.    65

*Adel.* Peace, the King.

*Enter King,* Thrasomond, Araminta, *and Train.*

47 that] ~ may stand still discreetly enough, and ill favour'dly Dance her Measure; simper when she is Courted by her Friend, and slight her Husband.
    *Cle.* The last?
    *Di.* Marry I think she is one whom the State keeps for the Agents of our confederate Princes: she'll cog and lie with a whole Army before the League shall break: her name is common through the Kingdom, and the Trophies of her dishonour, advanced beyond *Hercules* pillars. She

48 her own] the worth of ~ ~ body    48–9 Experiments] experiment    49 them] it
50 Of . . . very] She's a    51–8 *Adel.* And . . . Desires,] *La.* Peace, if you love me: you shall see these Gentlemen stand their ground, and not Court us.
    *Gal.* What if they should?
    *Meg.* What if they should?
    *La.* Nay, let her alone; what if they should? why, if they should, I say, they were never abroad: what Foreigner would do so? it writes them directly untravel'd.
    *Gal.* Why, what if they be?
    *Meg.* What if they be?
    *La.* Good Madam let her go on; what if they be? Why if they be I will justifie, they cannot maintain discourse with a judicious Lady, nor make a Leg, nor say Excuse me.
    *Gal.* Ha, ha, ha.
    *La.* Do you laugh Madam?
    *Di.* Your desires upon you
59 *Alga*] *La*    down by] beside    60–1 *Adel.* With . . . *Gover*] *Di*    61 will] shall this] you then    62 *Mel.* Not] *La.* Sir] perhaps    loves a] indures no    63 you . . . me] to me you appear    64–5 *Agr.* . . . can] *Meg.* Me thinks he's not so strange, he would

*King.* To give a stronger Testimony of Love
Than only Promises (which commonly
In Princes find at once both Birth and Burial)
We've drawn you by our Letters, noble Prince                    70
To make here your Addresses to our Daughter,
And your self known and lov'd by all our Subjects.
As for this Lady Maid, whose Sex and Innocence
Yet teach her nothing but her Fears and Blushes;
I hope her Modesty so recommends her to you for a Wife,        75
Were she not fair enough to be a Mistress.
Lastly, my noble Son, (for so I now must call you)
That I have done this publickly, is not
To add a Comfort in particular
To you or me, but all, and to confirm                          80
The Nobles and the Gentry of these Kingdoms
By Oath to your Succession; this shall be
Within a Week at most.
        *Adel.* This will be hardly done.
        *Agr.* It must be ill done whensoever it is done.        85
        *Cleon.* At least it will be but half done whilst so brave a Man
is thrown off and living.

68 only] sickly          69 find at once] find          70 We've] In one breath we have
by . . . Prince] worthy Sir,          71 here . . . our] your fair indearments to your
72–3 your . . . Innocence] worthy services known to our subjects,
Now lov'd and wondered at. Next, our intent,
To plant you deeply, our immediate Heir,
Both to our Blood and Kingdoms. For this Lady,
(The best part of your life, as you confirm me,
And I believe) though her few years and sex
75–7 I . . . my] Desires without desire, discourse and knowledge
Only of what her self is to her self,
Make her feel moderate health: and when she sleeps,
In making no ill day, knows no ill dreams.
Think not (dear Sir) these undivided parts,
That must mould up a Virgin, are put on
To shew her so, as borrowed ornaments,
To speak her perfect love to you, or add
An Artificial shadow to her nature:
No Sir; I boldly dare proclaim her, yet
No Woman. But woo her still, and think her modesty
A sweeter mistress than the offer'd Language
Of any Dame, were she a Queen whose eye
Speaks common loves and comforts to her servants.
Last,
78 That] What     this publickly] thus publick     not] ~ only     82 this] which     83 a
Week] this month          85 whensoever it is] if it be          86 At . . . will] When 'tis at
best, 'twill     done whilst] done, | Whilst          86–7 Man . . . living] Gentleman's wrong'd
and flung off

*Enter* Philander.

*Officer.* Make room there for the Lord *Philander*.
*Adel.* Mark but the King how pale he looks with Fear.
*King.* What brings him here? You're curious I find          90
To see this Interview.
    *Phil.*                The Wonders, Sir,
Your Majeſty has often spoken in Praise
Of *Thrasomond*, makes me desire to hear
What he can say himself.
    *Gover.*                Come, now begin.
*Thras.* Kissing your white Hand, Miſtress, I take leave,     95
To thank your Royal Father, and thus far
To be my own free Trumpet: Then observe,
Great King, and these your Subjeɕts, mine that muſt be,
For so deserving you have spoke me, Sir,
(And so deserving I dare speak my self;)                      100
To a Person of what Eminence,
What Expeɕtation, what Faculties,
Manners and Virtues you will wed your Kingdoms;
You have in me all you can wish. This Country
By more than all my Hopes, I hold moſt happy              105
In their dear Memories, that have been Kings
Both great and good; happy in yours, that is,
And from you (as a Chronicle to keep
Your noble Name from eating Age,) do I
Opine my self of all moſt happy, Sir.                         110
Believe me in a Word, a Prince's Word,
There shall be nothing to make up a Kingdom
Mighty and flourishing, both fenc'd and fear'd,
But thro' the Travels of my Life I'll find it,
And tie it to this Country: And I vow                         115

---

87.1 *Enter* Philander] *follows l. 124.2 in 79fc*      88–94 Make . . . begin] *Thra*. I fear.
      *Cle*. Who does not?
      *Di*. I fear not for my self, and yet I fear too:
Well, we shall see, we shall see: no more
97 Then observe] Understand        101 To] ~ what        102 What Expectation]
Ripe expectation of        103 will] would        104 have . . . wish.] in me have your
wishes. Oh        105–6 most happy | In] it | Happy, in        106–7 been Kings | Both]
been | Kings        110 self of all] self        happy, Sir.] happy. Gentlemen        113 both . . .
fear'd,] defenced, fear'd, | Equall to be commanded and obey'd,

My Reign shall be so easie to the Subjects,
That every Man shall be his Prince himself,
And his own Law, yet I his Prince and Law.
And, dearest Lady, to your dearest Self;
Dear in the Choice of him, (whose Name and Lustre          120
Must make you more and mightier,) let me say,
You are the blessed'st living: For, sweet Princess,
You shall enjoy a Man to be your Servant,
And you shall make him yours, for whom great Queens
Must die and sigh.——

    *Phil.*             Thou ugly silly Rogue.          125

    *Cleon.* I wonder what's his Price, for one may see
He has a mind to sell him self by his Praises.

    *Agr.* Would I might die if I see any thing
In him to raise him but to a Constable.

    *Adel.* Now do I fancy that this Speech was made by the Gover-          130
nour.

    *Agr.* O' my Conscience I think so too, for by his Action you
might see the Fool did not understand what he said.

    *Cleon.* Well, we shall see more of it anon.

    *Phil.* May I beg leave, Sir, of your Majesty          135
To speak a Word or two with this strange Prince?

---

116 Subjects] subject    123 Man] man of men    be your] be | Your    123–4 Servant,
| And you] servant; you    124 whom great] whom | Great    124–5 Queens | Must]
Queens must    125 die . . . Rogue] die. *Thra.* Miraculous.
    *Cle.* This speech calls him *Spaniard*, being nothing but
A large inventory of his own commendations.
                        *Enter* Philaster.
126–40 one . . . *Aside.*] certainly he'll tell himself he has so prais'd his shape: But here comes
one more worthy those large speeches, than the large speaker of them? let me be swallowed
quick, if I can find, in all the Anatomy of yon mans vertues, one sinew sound enough to
promise for him, he shall be Constable. By this Sun, he'll ne're make King unless it be for
trifles, in my poor judgment.
    *Phi.* Right Noble Sir, as low as my obedience,
And with a heart as Loyal as my knee,
I beg your favour.
    *King.* Rise, you have it Sir.
    *Di.* Mark but the King how pale he looks with fear. [*at l. 88 in 15gvw*]
Oh! this same whorson Conscience, how it jades us!
    *King.* Speak your intents Sir.
    *Phi.* Shall I speak 'um freely?
Be still my royal Soveraign.
    *King.* As a subject
We give you freedom.
    *Di.* Now it heats.
    *Phi.* Then

*King.* I give it you, but ſtill remember that you are
A Subjeᣔ.
    *Phil.* Yes, Sir, I am so: And more a Slave to *Araminta*,
And in spight of thee and Fate will be so ever.      [*Aside.*  140
Thus—I turn my self to you, big foreign Man,
Ne'er ſtare, nor put on Wonder, for you muſt
Endure me, and you shall. This Earth you tread on
(A Dowry, as you hope, with this fair Princess,
Whose very Name I bow to) was not left        145
By my dead Father (O! I had a Father!)
To your Inheritance; and I up and living,
Having my self about me and my Sword,
These Arms, and some few Friends besides the Gods,
To part so calmly with it, and sit ſtill;       150
And say I might have been! I tell thee, *Thrasomond*,
When thou art King, look I be dead and rotten,
And my Name loſt: Hear, hear me, *Thrasomond*,
This very Ground thou go'ſt on, this fat Earth,
My Father's Friends made fertile with their Faith,    155
Before that Day of Shame shall gape, and swallow
Thee and thy Nation, like a hungry Grave,
Into her hidden Bowels; Prince, it shall,
By *Nemesis* it shall.
    *Cleon.* Here's a Fellow has some Fire in his Veins. The Out-  160
landish Prince looks like a Tooth-drawer.
    *King.* You do displease us; you're now too bold.
    *Phil.* No, Sir, I am too tame;
Too much a Dove, a thing born without Passion;
A very Shadow, that each drunken Cloud      165
Sails over, and makes nothing.
    *King.*            What means this?
Call our Physicians; sure he's somewhat tainted.
    *Adel.* I do not think 'twill prove so.

---

141 turn my self ] turn | My language    big] Prince, you    143 on] upon    145 very
Name] memory      148 Sword,] sword, | The souls of all my name, and memories,
153 lost: Hear] ashes; For    155 Faith] faiths    159 shall.] ~. | *Pha.* He's mad
beyond cure, mad.    160 in his] in's    161 Tooth-drawer.] ~. | *Phi.* Sir, Prince of
Poppingjayes, I'le make it well appear | To you I am not mad.    162 You do] You    us;
you're now] us. | You are    164 Dove] Turtle    165 very] faint    each]
every    165–6 Cloud | Sails] cloud sails    166 over, and] over, | And    What
. . . this?] I do not fancy this,    167 he's] he is

*Cleon.* 'Has given him a general Purge already, and now he
means to let him Blood. Be conſtant, Gentlemen, by these Hilts    170
I'll run his Hazard, tho' I run my Name out of the Kingdom.
    *Thras.* Muſt I speak now?          [*To his Governour.*
    *Gov.*            Ay, ay, and do it home.
    *Thras.* What you have seen in me to ſtir Offence
I cannot tell, except it be this Lady,
Whom the King offer'd me without my seeking.    175
And I expeɔt he will secure her to me.
    *Gov.* You muſt be angry, Sir.
    *Thras.*         Well then I will. ——
I value not whose Branch you are, my Blood
And Person do deserve her well, and I
Therefore assure you that she shall be mine.    180
    *Phil.* If thou wert sole Inheritor to him
That once subdu'd the World, and could'ſt see no Sun
Shine upon any thing but thine; were *Thrasomond*
As truly valiant as I feel him cold,
And ring'd among the choiceſt of his Friends,    185
Such as would blush to talk such serious Follies,
Or back such bellied Commendations——
    *King.* Sir, you wrong the Prince, I gave you not
The Freedom here to brave our beſt of Friends;
You deserve our Frown. Go to, —— and be better temper'd.    190
    *Phil.* It muſt be, Sir, when I am nobler us'd.

169 already,] ~, for all the right he has,    171 tho'] although    172 *Thras.* Must . . .
home] *Cle.* Peace, we are one soul    174 tell, except] find, unless    175–80 Whom
. . . mine.] Offer'd into mine arms, with the succession,
Which I must keep though it hath pleas'd your fury
To mutiny within you; without disputing
Your *Genealogies*, or taking knowledge
Whose branch you are. The King will leave it me;
And I dare make it mine; you have your answer.
182 once . . . World] made the world his    183 any thing] any    187 Commendations.]
                               commendations,
And from this present, spight of all these bugs,
You should hear further from me.
188 Prince, I] ~: | ~    188–9 not | The] not this    189 Freedom here] freedom
best of ] best    190 to, —— and] to,    191 us'd.] ~.
    *Gal.* Ladyes,
This would have been a pattern of succession,
Had he ne're met this mischief. By my life,
He is the worthiest the true name of man
This day within my knowledge. <*cont.*>

*King.* Tell me what you aim at in your Riddles.

*Phil.* Had you my Eyes, Sir, and my Sufferings,
My Griefs upon you, and my broken Fortunes,
My Wants great, and now naught but Hopes and Fears,                195
My Wrongs would make ill Riddles to be laugh'd at.

*King.* Give me your Wrong in private.

*Phil.*                                   Take 'em then, [*Whisper.*
And ease me of a Load would bow ſtrong *Atlas.*

*Agr.* He dares not ſtand the Shock.

*Cleon.* I cannot blame him, there's Danger in it; every Man in     200
this Age has not a Breaſt of Chriſtal for all Men to read their
Thoughts through. Mens Hearts and Faces are so far asunder, that
they hold no Intelligence. Do but view your Stranger well, and
you shall see a Fever thro' all his Bravery. If he give not back his
Crown again on the Report of an Elder Gun, I have no Augury.       205

*King.* Go to: Be more your self, as you expeĉt
Our Favour, else you will ſtir our Anger:
I muſt have you know you are and shall be at
Our Pleasure: Smooth your Brow, or by the Gods—

*Phil.* I'm dead, Sir, you're my Fate: It was not I                210
Said I was wrong'd: I carry all about me
My weak Stars lead me to; all my weak Fortunes.
Who now, in all this Presence, dares (that is
A man of Flesh, and is but mortal) tell me
I do not moſt entirely love this Prince,                           215
And honour his full Virtues?

*King.*                       He's posseſt.

*Phil.* Yes, with my Father's Spirit. 'Tis here O King!


*Meg.* I cannot tell what you may call your knowledge,
But the other is the man set in mine eye;
Oh! 'tis a Prince of wax.

*Gal.* A Dog it is.

192 Tell me what] *Philaster,* tell me, | The injuries      193 Had you] If you had      my
Sufferings] sufferance      195 Wants] want's      196 at.] ~. | Dare you be still my King
and right me not?      197 Wrong] wrongs      private.] ~. [*They whisper.*      197-8 'em
. . . And] Take them, and      200 in it] in't      201 Breast] soul      202 Thoughts]
actions      203 your] yon      204 Bravery.] bravery, and feel him shake like a true
Tenant;      205 on] upon      206 to: Be] ~: | ~      206-7 expect | Our] respect our
207-8 Favour, else . . . Anger: | I] favour: | You'l stir us else: Sir, I      208 know you are]
know | That y'are      208-9 at | Our] at our      209 Pleasure: Smooth] pleasure, what
fashion we | Will put upon you: smooth      210 I'm] I am      211 was] was not
212 lead] led      to;] ~ₐ      213 now . . . dares] dares in all this presence speak      214 A]
But      is but] may be      216 He's] Sure he's      217 'Tis] It's

A dangerous Spirit, now he tells me King,
I was a King's Heir, bids me be a King,
And whispers to me these are all my Subjects:                    220
'Tis strange he will not let me sleep, but dives
Into my Fancy, and there gives me Shapes,
That kneel, and do me Service, call me King;
But I'll suppress him, 'tis a Factious Spirit.
    *King.* I do not like this;                          225
I'll make you tamer, or I'll dispossess
You both of Life and Spirit: For this Time
I pardon your wild Speech, without so much
As your Imprisonment.   [*Exeunt King,* Thrasomond *and Train.*
    *Cleon.* I thank you, Sir, you dare not for the People.        230
See how his Fancy labours: Has he not
Spoke home and bravely? What a dangerous Train
Did he give Fire to! How he shook the King!
Made his Soul melt within him, and his Blood
Run into Whey! It stood upon his Brows                           235
Like a cold Winter's Dew, Let's speak to him.
    *Agr.* How do you, worthy Sir?
    *Phil.*                   Well, very well;
So well, that if it please the King, I may live
Many Years.
    *Cleon.*    The King must please,
Whilst we know what you are, and who you are,                    240

220 are] be      223 call] cry     224 'tis] he's  Spirit] spirit, | And will undo me: noble
Sir, hour hand, I am your servant      225 *King.*] ~. Away,      226–7 dispossess
| You both] dispossess you | Both    229.sd *Train*] Are.    230 People.] people.

    *Gal.* Ladies, what think you now of this brave fellow?
    *Meg.* A pretty talking fellow, hot at hand; but eye yon stranger, is not he a fine compleat
Gentleman? O these strangers, I do affect them strangely: they do the rarest home things,
and please the fullest! as I live, could love all the Nation over and over for his sake,
    *Gal.* Pride comfort your poor head-piece Lady: 'tis a weak one, and had need of a Night-
cap.

231–32 not | Spoke home] not spoke | Home    235 Brows] brow    236 Winter's . . .
him.] winter dew.

    *Phi.* Gentlemen,
You have no suit to me? I am no minion:
You stand (methinks) like men that would be Courtiers,
If you could well be flatter'd at a price,
Not to undo your Children: y'are all honest:
Go get you home again, and make your Country
A vertuous Court, to which your great ones may,
In their Diseased age, retire, and live recluse.

238 So] And so    it . . . I] the King please, I find | I    238–9 live | Many] live many

Your Wrongs and Merits. Shrink not, noble Sir,
But think still of your Father, in whose Name
We'll waken all the Gods, and conjure up
The Rods of Vengeance; th' abused People,
Who like to raging Torrents shall swell high,                    245
And so begirt the Dens of these Male Dragons,
That thro' the strongest Safety they shall beg
For Mercy at your Sword's Point.
    *Phil.*               Friends, no more:
Our Ears may be corrupted: 'Tis an Age
We dare not trust our Wills to: Do you love me?                  250
    *Cleon.* Do we love Worth and Honour?
    *Phil.*              I thank you, Sir;
My Lord, pray is your Daughter living?
    *Cleon.*           Yes;
And for the Penance of an idle Dream
Has undertaken a tedious Pilgrimage.

              *Enter a Lady.*

    *Phil.* Is it to me you come?
    *Lady.*          To you, brave Lord.                    255
The Princess would intreat your Company.
    *Phil.* The Princess send for me? Sure you're mistaken.
    *Lady.* If you are called *Philander.*
    *Phil.* If she but now will love or kill me I am happy.
I will this Moment attend thee to her.        [*Exit with Lady.*  260

---

241 Merits] juiuries   noble] worthy   242 think . . . Father] add your Father to you
249 Ears] years   251 *Cleon*] *Thra*   Worth] Heaven   251–2 I . . . Yes] My Lord
*Dion,* you had
A vertuous Gentlewoman, call'd you Father;
Is she yet alive?
    *Di.* Most honour'd Sir, she is
253 Penance] penance but   254 undertaken] undertook   255 me] ~, or any of
these Gentlemen   255–6 Lord. | The] Lord; the   256 intreat your] intreat | Your
resent   257 Sure you're] y'are   258 are] be   *Philander*] *Philaster*, 'tis to you
259–60 If . . . *Lady.*] Kiss her hand, and say I will attend her.
    *Di.* Do you know what you do?
    *Phi.* Yes, go to see a woman.
    *Cle.* But do you weigh the danger you are in?
    *Phi.* Danger in a sweet face?
By *Jupiter* I must not fear a woman.
    *Thra.* But are you sure it was the Princess sent?
It may be some foul train to catch your life. &lt;*cont.*&gt;

*Cleon.* Go on, and be as truly happy as th' art fearless.
Come, Gentlemen, let us make our Friends acquainted.
Left the King prove false.                    [*Exeunt.*

Enter *Araminta* and Lady.

*Ara.* Will *Philander* come?
*Lady.* Dear Madam, you were wont to credit me at first.          265
*Ara.* But didst thou tell me he would come?
How look'd he when he told thee he would come?
*Lady.* Why well.
*Ara.*                    And was he not a little fearful?
*Lady.* How! fearful! sure he knows not what that is.
*Ara.* You are all of his Faction, the whole Court          270
Is bold in Praise of him!
*Lady.* Madam, his Looks methought did shew much more
Of Love than Fear.
*Ara.*                    Of Love! To whom? To you?
*Lady.* Madam, I mean to you.
*Ara.* Of Love to me! Alas! Thy Ignorance          275
Let's thee not see the Crossness of our Births.
Nature that loves not to be questioned

*Phi.* I do not think it Gentlemen: she's noble,
Her eye may shoot me dead, or those true red
And white friends in her face may steal my soul out:
There's all the danger in't: but be what may, [*Ex.* Phil.
Her single name hath arm'd me.

261 on, and] on: | And     th' art] thou art          262 let us] let's          263 *Exeunt*] *Ex.*
*Gentlemen*          263.1 *Lady.*] *a* Lady.
    *Are.* Comes he not?
    *La.* Madam?
265 wont to] wont | To     266 he . . . come?] so?
I am forgetful, and my womans strength
Is so o'recharg'd with danger like to grow
About my Marriage that these under-things
Dare not abide in such a troubled sea:
268 And . . . he] And          269 How! fearful!] Fear Madam?     that] it          271 him!] ~,
                    whilst I
May live neglected: and do noble things,
As fools in strife throw gold into the Sea,
Drown'd in the doing: but I know he fears.
272 Madam . . . much] Fear? Madam (me thought) his looks hid          273 you?] ~?
Did you deliver those plain words I sent,
With such a winning gesture, and quick look
That you have caught him?
276 Crossness] crosses

Why she did this or that, but has her Ends,
And knows that she does well; never gave the World
Two things so opposite, so contrary                              280
As he and I am.
    *Lady.*  Madam, I think I hear him.
    *Ara.*                          Bring him in.
Ye Gods! that will not have your Dooms withſtood,
Whose holy Wisdom, at this Time it is
To make the Passion of a feeble Mind                             285
The Way to your great Juſtice. I obey.

*Enter* Philander.

    *Lady.*  Here is my Lord *Philander.*
    *Ara.*                          'Tis well. ——
What shall I say?
    *Phil.*          Madam, your Messenger
Made me believe you sent to speak with me.
    *Ara.* 'Tis true, *Philander,* but the Words are such,      290
So unbecoming of a Virgin's Mouth,
That I could wish 'em said by any other Body.
Can you not ghess what 'tis that I would say?

279 knows that] knows          281 am.] ~: If a bowl of blood
Drawn from this arm of mine, would poyson thee,
A draught of his would cure thee. Of love to me?
283 Ye] You    will] would          284 Wisdom] wisdoms          285 Mind] maid          286 to
your great] unto your          287–8 'Tis . . . say?] Oh! 'tis well: | Withdraw your self.
289 sent] wisht          291–310 So . . . Say] I have to say, and do so ill beseem
The mouth of woman, that I wish them said,
And yet am loth to speak them. Have you known
That I have ought detracted from your worth?
Have I in person wrong'd you? or have set
My baser instruments to throw disgrace
Upon your vertues?
    *Phi.* Never Madam you.
    *Are.* Why then should you in such a publick place,
Injure a Princess and a scandal lay
Upon my fortunes, fam'd to be so great:
Calling a great part of my dowry in question.
    *Phi.* Madam, this truth which I shall speak, will be
Foolish: but for your fair and vertuous self,
I could afford my self to have no right
To any thing you wish'd.
    *Are. Philaster,* know
I must enjoy these Kingdoms,
    *Phi.* Madam, both?
    *Are.* Both or I die: by Fate I die *Philaster,* ‹*cont.*›

*Phil.* When I behold
That heav'nly Frame, I find such Sweetness there,                    295
I cannot think you guilty of a Thought
Which has a Harshness in it, much less a Cruelty.
But then, when I consider who you are,
And what your Father is, how can I chuse
But fear you muſt intend my utter Ruin.                    300
    *Ara.* You are not well acquainted with my Thoughts,
Tho' they are such as make me blush as oft
As I would fain discover them to you;
Yet for my Life I cannot think them ill,
Nor wish them other, than what juſt they are.                    305
    *Phil.* Why won't you tell them then?
    *Ara.* Because I dare not tell them.
    *Phil.*                 Yes you may:
Let them be ne'er so cruel, I will hear
My Doom with Patience, and obey it too.
Say you would have my Life, I'll give it you;                    310
For 'tis of me a Thing so loath'd, and of

If I not calmly may enjoy them both.
    *Phi.* I would do much to save that Noble life:
Yet would be loth to have posterity
Find in our stories, that *Philaster* gave
His right unto a Scepter, and a Crown,
To save a Ladies longing.
    *Are.* Nay then hear:
I must, and will have them, and more.
    *Phi.* What more?
    *Are.* Or lose that little life the gods prepared,
To trouble this poor piece of earth withall.
    *Phi.* Madam, what more?
    *Are.* Turn then away thy face.
    *Phi.* No.
    *Are.* Do.
    *Phi.* I cannot endure it: turn away my face?
I never yet saw enemy that lookt
So dreadful, but that I thought my self
As great a Basilisk as he; or spake
So horribly, but that I thought my tongue
Bore Thunder underneath, as much as his:
Nor beast that I could turn from: shall I then
Begin to fear sweet sounds? a Ladies voice,
Whom I do love? Say

310 Life, I'll] life, | Why, I will    310–11 you; | For 'tis] you; for it is    311 me a] me
 | A        311–13 of . . . me, | That] unto you that ask | Of so poor use, that

So small a Use to you, who ask it of me,
That I shall make no Price if you would have it.
    *Ara.* Why then it is your Life that I muſt have,
Your whole entire Life, or lose my own.    315
    *Phil.* I gladly thus resign it to you: Here
Draw this and kill me; I shall thank you for it:
For since my cruel Fortune has decreed,
That you muſt never, Madam, give Consent
To what alone can make me live with Ease,    320
The dying by your Hand is all I covet.
    *Ara.* Oh! 'tis not so, *Philander*, that I mean;
Kill you! no, I'd sooner die my self
Than offer you but once the leaſt Offence.
Why I would rather kill my self than live,    325
If be my Fate that you would have it so.
By all the holy Powers I would. Good Gods!
Cannot you ghess my meaning yet.
    *Phil.*                    Oh Heavens!
What is't she means! It cannot sure be Love;
And yet she is too full of noble Thoughts    330
To lay a Train for this contemned Life,
Which she might have for asking: Madam, you
Perplex my Mind so much with what you say,
I know not what to think; I know well what
To wish for; I so earneſtly do wish it    335

313 Price . . . it] price | If you intreat, I will unmov'dly hear    314–30 *Ara.* Why . . . is]
    *Are.* Yet for my sake a little bend thy looks.
    *Phi.* I do.
    *Are.* Then know I must have them and thee.
    *Phi.* And me?
    *Are.* Thy love: without which, all the Land
Discovered yet, will serve me for no use,
But to be buried in.
    *Phi.* Is't possible?
    *Are.* With it, it were too little to bestow
On thee: Now, though thy breath doth strike me dead
(Which know it may) I have unript my breast.
    *Phi.* Madam, you are

332 she might] you may        332–57 Madam . . . him.] to suspect
Were base, where I deserve no ill: love you!
By all my hopes I do, above my life:
But how this passion should proceed from you
So violently, would amaze a man, that would be jealous.

That indeed I can think of nothing else.
'Twas not the Fear of losing of a Crown
That gave my Tongue such Rage before you
This Day.
The Crown's a thing of which I feel no Want,                    340
But that I have it not to offer you.
There is another Fear lies deeper here,
The Fear of losing that on which my Life
Depends; and which I ne'er shall tamely part with:
For, Madam, know, while poor *Philander* lives,                345
'Tis but in vain your Father shall pretend
To marry you to any but ——
    *Ara.* But to whom?
    *Phil.* But to him who wants the Impudence to hope
So great a Blessing: One who harbours Thoughts            350
Of what he is so mean and humble in
Respect of you, that were his Council ask'd
Whether or no you ought to make him happy,
He fears he hardly could advise you to it;
Who is however still resolved to die,                          355
Before he sees you given to another,
And therefore on his Knees begs you to kill him.
    *Ara.* Another Soul into my Body shot,
Could not have warm'd my Heart with more new Life
Than these your Words have done; had you but staid        360
A little longer I had vow'd the same;
But I am wretched now, unless you love me.
    *Phil.* Love you!
My Soul adores you with so strong a Zeal,
So far above the Rate of common Love,                         365
That mine deserves a more exalted Name,
If any more exalted I could find.
    *Ara.* I have then no more to ask of Heav'n;
And sure our Love will meet the greater Blessing,
In that the greatest Justice of the Gods                      370

359–69 warm'd . . . And] fill'd me with more strength and spirit,
Than this thy breath: but spend not hasty time,
In seeking how I came thus: 'tis the gods,
The gods, that make me so; and
369 Love will] love | Will    meet . . . Blessing] be the nobler, and the better blest
370 greatest] secret

Is blended with it: But you muſt not ſtay,
Leſt some unwelcome Gueſt should find you here.
Think how we may continue a secret Way
To keep Intelligence betwixt us, that
On all Occasions we may both agree,                                    375
Which Path is beſt to tread.
    *Phil.*             I have a Boy
Sent by the Gods, I think, for this Intent,
Not yet seen in the Court. Hunting the Buck,
I found him sitting by a Fountain side,
Of which he borrow'd some to quench his Thirſt,                        380
And paid the Nymph again as much in Tears:
A Garland by him lay, made by him self,
Of many several Flowers he'd in the Bay
Stuck in that myſtick Order, that the Rareness
Delighted me; but ever when he turn'd                                  385
His tender Eyes upon them, he would weep,
As if he meant to make them grow again.
Seeing such pretty helpless Innocence
Dwell in his Face, I ask'd him of his Story.
He told me that his Parents lately dy'd,                               390
Leaving him to the Mercy of the Field,
Which gave him Roots, and of the Chriſtal Springs,
Which did not ſtop their Streams; and of the Sun,
Which ſtill, he thank'd him, yielded him his Light.

371 blended] mingled    But . . . stay] Let us leave and kiss    372–6 find . . . Which]
fall betwixt us,
And we should part without it.
    *Phi.* 'Twill be ill
I should abide here long.
    *Are.* 'Tis true, and worse
You should come often: How shall we devise
To hold intelligence? That our true lovers,
On any new occasion may agree, what
376–7 Boy | Sent] boy sent    377 think, for] hope to    382 by him lay] lay him
by    383 he'd] bred    386 them] 'um    387 them] 'um    389 of] all
390 lately] gentle    391 Field] fields    393 Streams; and of] courses: and
394–5 Light. | I]
                    light,
Then took he up his Garland and did shew,
What every flower as Country people hold,
Did signifie: and how all ordered thus,
Exprest his grief: and to my thoughts did read &lt;*cont.*&gt;

I gladly entertain'd him, who was as glad to follow;     395
And I've got the truest and most faithful Boy alive,
Him will I send to bear our hidden Love.

*Enter Lady.*

*Lady.* Madam, the Prince is come to kiss your Hands.
*Ara.* For Heaven's Sake, dear *Philander*, hide your self.
*Phil.* Hide me from *Thrasomond!* when Thunder roars,     400
Which is *Jove's* Voice, tho' *Jove* I do revere,
I hide me not; shall then a foreign Prince
Have leave to brag to any foreign Nation,
That he did make *Philander* hide himself?
*Ara.* Why then say nothing to him.
*Phil.*                                   I'll obey.     405

*Enter* Thrasomond.

*Thras.* My Princely Mistress, as true Lovers ought,
I came to kiss those fair Hands, and to shew,
In outward Ceremonies, the dear Love,
Writ here within my Heart.

The prettiest lecture of his Country Art
That could be wisht: so that, me thought, I could
Have studied it. I

395 him, who] him, | Who    was as] was          395–7 follow; . . . to] follow; and have got
The trustiest, loving'st, and the gentlest boy,
That ever Master kept: Him will I send
To wait on you, and
397.1 *Lady*] ~. | *Are.* 'Tis well, no more.
398 kiss your Hands] do his service      399 For . . . self ] What will you do *Philaster* with
your self ?
    *Phi.* Why, that which all the gods have appointed out for me.
    *Are.* Dear, hide thy self. Bring in the Prince
400–4 *Thrasomond*! . . . make] *Pharamond*!
When Thunder speaks, which is the voice of *Jove*,
Though I do reverence, yet I hide me not;
And shall a stranger Prince have leave to brag
Unto a forreign Nation, that he made
405 Why . . . obey] He cannot know it.
    *Phi.* Though it should sleep for ever to the world,
It is a simple sin to hide my self,
Which will for ever on my conscience lie.
    *Are.* Then good *Philaster*, give him scope and way
In what he saies: for he is apt to speak.
What you are loth to hear: for my sake do.
    *Phi.* I will.
407 came] come    those] these      409 here within] in

*Phil.* If I can have no other Answer                                    410
I am gone.
　*Thras.* To what would he have Answer?
　*Ara.* To his Claim, as he pretends, to his Father's Crown.
　*Thra.* Sir, I did let you alone to day before the King.
　*Phil.* Sir, do so ſtill, I would not talk with you.
　*Thras.* But now the Time is fit. Do but name                          415
The leaſt Pretence or Title to a Crown.
　*Phil.* Peace, *Thrasomond,* —— if thou ——
　*Ara.*                               *Philander,* hold. ——
　*Phil.* I have done.
　*Thras.*          You're gone, I'll fetch you back again.
　*Phil.* You shall not need.
　*Thras.*                 What now?
　*Phil.*                         Know, *Thrasomond,*
I loath to brawl with such a Blaſt as thou,                              420
Who art nothing but a valiant Voice: But if
Thou shalt provoke me farther, Men shall say,
Thou wert, and not lament it.
　*Thras.* Do you slight my Greatness so?
And in the Chamber of the Princess?                                      425
　*Phil.* It is a Place, to which I muſt confess,
I owe a Reverence. But wer't in a Church,
Nay, at an Altar; there's no Place so safe,
Where thou dar'ſt injure me, but I dare kill thee;
And for your Greatness know, Sir, I can grasp                            430
You and your Greatness thus, thus into nothing:
Give me not a Word back. —— farewell.          [*Exit.*
　*Thras.* 'Tis an odd Fellow this as e'er I saw.
I'll ſtop his Mouth hereafter with some Office.

410 can . . . Answer] shall have an answer no directlier,       411 have] ~ an       412 as
. . . Crown] unto the Kingdom      413 Sir . . . day] Sirrah, I forbear you      414 *Phil.*]
*Phi.* Good
415 fit] fitter      415–16 name . . . Crown.] offer
To make mention of right to any Kingdom,
Though it be scarce habitable.
　*Phi.* Good Sir, let me go.
　*Pha.* And by my sword.
417 *Philander,* hold] Leave us *Philaster*      418 You're] You are      gone] ~ by heaven
back again] back      421 nothing] nought      422 farther] further      424 slight my]
slight | My      424–5 so?  | And] so, and      427 in a] the      428 Nay] I      an] the
432 me] not a word,      *Exit*] ~ Phi      433–4 this . . . Office] Madam, we must stop
His mouth with some Office, when we are married

*Ara.* You had beſt to make him your Councellor.                    435
  *Thras.* I think he would discharge it well. But Madam,
I hope our Hearts are knit; but yet so slow
The Ceremonies of State are, that 'twill be long
Before our Hands be so, therefore now,
Without expeċting farther Ceremonies,                              440
Let us enjoy some ſtoln Delights together.
  *Ara* Since you dare utter this I muſt withdraw.          [*Exit.*
  *Thras.* Nay, if you are so squeamish thank your self,
If I should try elsewhere.

*The End of the Firſt Aċt.*

ACT II. SCENE I.

*Enter* Philander, Endymion.

  *Phil.* And thou shalt find her honourable, Boy,
Full of Regard unto thy tender Youth,
For thy own Modeſty, and for my Sake,
Apter to give than thou wilt be to ask.
  *End.* Sir, you did take me up when I was nothing;          5
And only yet am something by being yours;
You truſted me unknown; and that which you
Were apt to conſtrue Innocence in me,
Might have been Craft; the Cunning of a Boy
Harden'd in Lies and Theft; yet ventur'd you          10
To part my Miseries and me; for which,

---

435 had best to] were best    Councellor] Controuler      437 but] and      439–44 therefore
. . . elsewhere] If then you please,
Being agreed in heart, let us not wait
For dreaming for me, but take a little stoln
Delights, and so prevent our joyes to come.
    *Are.* If you dare speak such thoughts,
I must withdraw in honour.                                        *Exit* Are.
    *Pha.* The constitution of my body will never hold out till the wedding;
I must seek elsewhere.                                            [*Exit* Pha.
444.1 *The . . . Act.*] Not in *79fc.*

II. i. 0.1 Philander] Philaster *and*      3 thy] thine      4 ask] ~, I, or deserve      7–8 you
| Were] you are      8 apt to construe] apt | To conster a simple      9 Might] Perhaps,
might

I never can expect to serve a Lady
That bears more Honour in her Breaſt than you.
    *Phil.* But, Boy, it will prefer thee, thou art young,
And bear'ſt a childish overflowing Love           15
To them that speak thee fair; when thy Age
And Judgment once shall end those Passions,
Thou wilt remember beſt these careful Friends
That plac'd thee in the nobleſt Way of Life;
She is a Princess I prefer thee to.           20
    *End.* In that small Time that I have seen the World,
I never knew a Man haſty to part
With Servants he thought truſty: I remember
My Father would prefer the Boys he kept
To greater Men than he; but did it not           25
Till they were grown too saucy for himself.
    *Phil.* Why, gentle Boy, I find no Fault at all
In thy Behaviour.
    *End.*        Sir, if I have made
A Fault of Ignorance, inſtruct my Youth,
I shall be willing, if not apt to learn;           30
Age and Experience will adorn my Mind
With larger Knowledge; and if I have done
A wilful Fault, think me not paſt all Hope
For once; what Maſter holds so ſtrict a Hand
Over his Boy, that he will part with him           35
Without one Warning? Let me be corrected
To break my Stubborness, if it be so,
Rather than turn me off, and I shall mend.
    *Phil.* Thy Love doth plead so prettily to ſtay,
That, truſt me, I could weep to part with thee.    40
Alas! I do not turn thee off; thou know'ſt
It is my Business that doth call thee hence,
And when thou art with her, thou dwell'ſt with me:
Think so, and 'tis so: and when Time is full,
And thou haſt well discharg'd this heavy Truſt    45
Laid on so weak a one, I will again
With Joy receive thee; as I live I will:

---

16–17 speak . . . end] clap thy cheeks, and speak thee fair yet: | But when thy judgment comes
to rule     18 these] those     23 Servants] a servant     27–8 all | In] all in
45 And] That

Nay, weep not, gentle Boy, 'tis more than Time
Thou did'ſt attend the Princess.
    *End.*                   I am gone;
But since I am to part with you, my Lord,                          50
And none knows whether I shall live to do
More Service for you, take this little Pray'r;
Heav'n bless your Loves, your Fights, all your Designs;
May sick Men, if they have your Wish be well;
And Heav'n hate those you curse, tho' I be one.         [*Exit.*   55
    *Phil.* The Love of Boys unto their Lords is ſtrange,
I have read Wonders of it; yet this Boy,
For my Sake (if a Man may judge by Looks
And Speech) would outdo their Story: I may see
A Day to pay him for his Loyalty.                        [*Exit.*   60

*The Buckingham text continues on page 490.*

55 Heav'n] Heavens        59 outdo their] out do        60 *Exit.*] ~ Phi.
                             *Enter* Pharamond.
    *Pha.* Why should these Ladies stay so long? They must come this way; I know the Queen
imployes 'em not, for the Reverend Mother sent me word they would all be for the Garden.
If they should all prove honest now, I were in a fair taking; I was never so long without sport
in my life, and in my conscience 'tis not my fault: Oh, for our Country Ladies! Here's one
boulted, I'le hound at her.
                           *Enter* Galatea.
    *Gal.* Your Grace!
    *Pha.* Shall I not be a trouble?
    *Gal.* Not to me Sir.
    *Pha.* Nay, nay, you are too quick; by this sweet hand.
    *Gal.* You'l be forsworn Sir, 'tis but an old glove. If you will talk at distance, I am for you:
but good Prince, be not bawdy, nor do not brag; these two I bar, and then I think, I shall
have sence enough to answer all the weighty *Apothegmes* your Royal blood shall manage.
    *Pha.* Dear Lady, can you love?
    *Gal.* Dear, Prince, how dear! I ne're cost you a Coach yet, nor put you to the dear
repentance of a Banquet; here's no Scarlet Sir, to blush the sin out it was given for: This wyer
mine own hair covers: and this face has been so far from being dear to any, that it ne're cost
penny painting: And for the rest of my poor Wardrobe, such as you see, it leaves no hand
behind it, to make the jealous Mercers wife curse our good doings.
    *Pha.* You mistake me Lady.
    *Pha.* [*sic*] Lord, I do so; would you or I could help it.
    *Pha.* Do Ladies of this Country use to give no more respect to men of my full being?
    *Gal.* Full being! I understand you not, unless your Grace means growing to fatness; and
then your only remedy (upon my knowledge, Prince) is in a morning a Cup of neat White-
wine brew'd with *Carduus*, then fast till supper; about eight you may eat; use exercise, and
keep a Sparrow-hawk, you can shoot in a Tiller; but of all, your Grace must flie *Phlebotomie*,
fresh Pork, Conger, and clarified Whay; They are all dullers of the vital spirits.
    *Pha.* Lady, you talk of nothing all this while.
    *Gal.* 'Tis very true Sir, I talk of you. <*cont.*>

*Pha.* This is a crafty wench, I like her wit well, 'twill be rare to stir up a leaden appetite, she's a *Danae*, and must be courted in a showr of gold. Madam, look here, all these, and more, than ——

*Gal.* What have you there, my Lord? Gold? Now, as I live 'tis fair gold; you would have silver for it to play with the Pages; you could not have taken me in a worse time; But if you have present use my Lord, I'le send my man with silver and keep your gold for you.

*Pha.* Lady, Lady.

*Gal.* She's coming Sir behind, will take white mony. Yet for all this I'le match ye.

[*Exit* Gal. *behind the hangings.*

*Pha.* If there be but two such more in this Kingdom, and near the Court, we may even hang up our Harps: ten such *Camphire* constitutions as this, would call the golden age again in question, and teach the old way for every ill fac't Husband to get his own Children, and what a mischief that will breed, let all consider.

*Enter* Megra.

Here's another; if she be of the same last, the Devil shall pluck her on. Many fair mornings, Lady.

*Meg.* As many mornings bring as many dayes,
Fair, sweet, and hopeful to your Grace.

*Pha.* She gives good words yet; Sure this wench is free.
If your more serious business do not call you,
Let me hold quarter with you, we'll take an hour
Out quickly.

*Meg.* What would your Grace talk of?

*Pha.* Of some such pretty subject as your self.
I'le go no further than your eye, or lip,
There's theme enough for one man for an age.

*Meg.* Sir, they stand right, and my lips are yet even,
Smooth, young enough, ripe enough, red enough,
Or my glass wrongs me.

*Pha.* O they are two twin'd Cherries died in blushes,
Which those fair suns above, with their bright beams
Reflect upon, and ripen: sweetest beauty,
Bow down those branches, that the longing taste,
Of the faint looker on, may meet those blessings,
And taste and live.

*Meg.* O delicate sweet Prince;
She that hath snow enough about her heart,
To take the wanton spring of ten such lines off,
May be a Nun without probation.
Sir, you have in such neat poetry, gathered a kiss,
That if I had but five lines of that number,
Such pretty begging blanks, I should commend
Your fore-head, or your cheeks, and kiss you too.

*Pha.* Do it in prose; you cannot miss it Madam.

*Meg.* I shall, I shall.

*Pha.* By my life you shall not.
I'le prompt you first: Can you do it now?

*Meg.* Methinks 'tis easie, now I ha' don't before;
But yet I should stick at it.

*Pha.* Stick till to morrow.
I'le ne'r part you sweetest. But we lose time,
Can you love me?

*Meg.* Love you my Lord? How would you have me love you? <cont.>

*Enter* Araminta *and a Lady.*

*Ara.* Where is the Boy?

*Lady.* I think within, Madam.

*Ara.* But are his Cloaths made yet?

*Lady.* He has 'em on.

*Ara.* 'Tis a pretty sad talking Boy this, is 65
He not? I would fain know his Name.

*Lady. Endymion,* Madam.

*Pha.* I'le teach you in a short sentence, cause I will not load your memory, this is all: love me, and lie with me.

*Meg.* Was it lie with you that you said? 'Tis impossible.

*Pha.* Not to a willing mind, that will endeavour; if I do not teach you to do it as easily in one night, as you'l go to bed, I'le lose my Royal blood for't.

*Meg.* Why Prince, you have a Lady of your own, that yet wants teaching.

*Pha.* I'le sooner teach a Mare the old measures, than teach her any thing belonging to the function; she's afraid to be with her self, if she have but any masculine imaginations about her; I know when we are married, I must ravish her.

*Meg.* By my honour, that's a foul fault indeed, but time and your good help will wear it out Sir.

*Pha.* And for any other I see, excepting your dear self, dearest Lady, I had rather be Sir *Tim* the Schoolmaster, and leap a Dairy-maid.

*Meg.* Has your Grace seen the Court-star *Galatea*?

*Pha.* Out upon her; she's as cold of her favour as an apoplex? she sail'd by but now.

*Meg.* And how do you hold her wit Sir?

*Pha.* I hold her wit? The strength of all the Guard can not hold it, if they were tied to it, she would blow 'em out of the Kingdom, they talk of *Jupiter,* he's but a squib cracker to her: Look well about you, and you may find a tongue-bolt. But speak sweet Lady, shall I be freely welcome?

*Meg.* Whither?

*Pha.* To your bed; if you mistrust my faith, you do me the unnoblest wrong.

*Meg.* I dare not Prince, I dare not.

*Pha.* Make your own conditions, my purse shall seal 'em, and what you dare imagine you can want, I'le furnish you withal: give two hours to your thoughts every morning about it. Come, I know you are bashful, speak in my ear, will you be mine? keep this, and with it me: soon I will visit you.

*Meg.* My Lord, my Chamber's most unsafe, but when 'tis night I'le find some means to slip into your lodging: till when——

*Pha.* Till when, this, and my heart go with thee. [*Ex. several ways.*

*Enter* Galatea *from behind the hangings.*

*Gal.* Oh thou pernicious Petticoat Prince, are these your vertues? Well, if I do not lay a train to blow your sport up, I am no woman; and Lady Towsabel I'le fit you for't. [*Exit* Gal.

61 Where is] Where's    62 I think within] Within    63–4 But . . . on] Gave you him gold to buy him cloaths?

*La.* I did.

*Are.* And has he don't?

*La.* Yes Madam

65–6 this . . . know] is it not? | Askt you    67 *Endymion*] No

*Enter* Melesinda.

*Ara.* Oh, you are welcome: What good News?
*Mel.* As good as any one can tell your Highness,
That says she has done that you would have wish'd.          70
*Ara.* Haſt thou discover'd?
*Mel.*          Yes, I have ſtrain'd a Point
Of Modeſty for you.
*Ara.*          I prithee how?
*Mel.* In liſt'ning after Baudry. I perceive
Let a Lady live never so modeſtly,
She will be sure to meet one Time or other          75
With Opportunities of hearing that.
Your Prince, brave *Thrasomond*, has been so amorous,
And in so excellent a Stile!
*Ara.*          With whom?
*Mel.* Why with the Lady that I did suspeƈt.
I am inform'd both of the Time and Place.          80
*Ara.* O when! and where!
*Mel.*          To Night: Her Chamber.
*Ara.*                    Run
Thy self into the Presence; mingle there
With other Ladies, leave the reſt to me.
If Deſtiny (to whom we dare not say
Why thou did'ſt this) have not decreed it so,          85
In laſting Leaves, (whose smalleſt Charaƈters
Were never alter'd) then this Match shall break.
Where is the Boy?
*Lady.*          Here, Madam.

*Enter* Endymion.

*Ara.*                    You are sad,
I see, to change your Service, is't not so?
*End.* Madam, I have not chang'd; I wait on you          90
To do him Service.

69 Highness] Grace          70 has] hath          71 Yes, I] I          71-2 Point | Of] point of
73-4 perceive | Let] see, let          74-5 modeſtly, | She will] modestly, she shall          75-7 meet
. . . Your] find a lawful time, to harken after bawdery; your          77-8 has . . . Stile] was so
hot on't          79-80 that . . . of] I suspect: I can tell          81 Her Chamber] his Lodging
81-2 Run | Thy] Run thy          82 there] ~ again          87 then] yet          88 Where
is] Where's          You] Sir, you          88-9 sad, | I see, to] sad to

*Ara.*              Thou disclaim'st me then?
*Philander* told me thou canst sing and play.
   *End.* If Grief will give me leave, Madam, I can.
   *Ara.* Alas, what kind of Grief can thy Years know?
Was't a curst Master that thou hadst at School?                95
Thou art not capable of other Grief.
Thy Brows and Cheeks are smooth as Waters be,
When no Breath troubles them; believe me, Boy,
Care seeks out wrinkled Brows and hollow Eyes,
And builds himself Caves to abide in them.                     100
Come, Sir, pray, tell me truly, does your Lord
Love me?
   *End.* I know not, Madam, what Love is.
   *Ara.* Canst thou know Grief, and never yet knew'st Love?
Thou art deceiv'd, Boy; does he speak of me
As if he wish'd me well?
   *End.*              If it be Love                            105
To lose the Memory of all things else,
To forget all Respect of his own Friends,
In thinking of your Face; if it be Love
To sit cross-arm'd, and sigh away the Day,
Mingled with Starts, crying your Name as loud                  110
And hastily as Men i'th' Streets do Fire:
If it be Love to weep himself away,
When he but hears of any Lady dead
Or kill'd, because it might have been your Chance;
If when he goes to rest, (which will not be)                   115
'Twixt ev'ry Prayer he says, to name you once,
As others drop a Bead, be any Sign
Of Love, then, Madam, I dare swear he loves you.
   *Ara.* O y' are a cunning Boy, and taught to lie
For your Lord's Service: But thou know'st a Lie                120
That bears this Sound is welcomer to me,
Than any Truth, that says he loves me not.
Lead the Way, Boy; do you attend me too;
'Tis thy Lord's Business hastes me thus away.        [*Exeunt.*

91–2 me ... thou] in me; | Tell me thy name.
     *Bell. Bellario.*
     *Are.* Thou
95 Was't ... at] Hadst thou a curst master, when thou went'st to        98 Breath] dreath
101 Sir, pray] Sir,        101–2 Lord | Love] Lord love        102 I ... Love] Love Madam?
I know not what it        105–6 Love ... else,] love,        117–18 any ... then] to be in
love; | Then        120 Service] credit        124 thus away] thus; Away

*Enter* Cleon, Agremont, Adelard, Alga, Melesinda.

*Cleon.* Come, Ladies, shall we talk a Round? As Men          125
Do walk a Mile Women should talk an Hour,
After Supper 'tis their Exercise.
   *Mel.* 'Tis late.
   *Alga.* 'Tis all
My Eyes will do to lead me to my Bed.          [*Exeunt.*   130

*Enter King,* Araminta, *and a Guard.*

124.1 Alga,] Megra *and*          125 talk] take          127 Supper 'tis] supper:
'Tis          130 *Exeunt.*] *Gal.* I fear they are so heavy, you'l scarce find
The way to your lodging with 'em to night.
                         *Enter* Pharamond.
   *Thra.* The Prince.
   *Pha.* Not a bed Ladies? y'are good sitters up;
What think you of a pleasant dream to last
Till morning?
   *Meg.* I should choose, my Lord, a pleasing wake before it.
                         *Enter* Arethusa *and* Bellario.
   *Are.* 'Tis well my Lord y'are courting of Ladies.
Is't not late Gentlemen?
   *Cle.* Yes Madam.
   *Are.* Wait you there.                         [*Exit* Arethusa.
   *Meg.* She's jealous, as I live; look you my Lord,
The Princess has a *Hilas,* an *Adonis.*
   *Pha.* His form is Angel-like.
   *Meg.* Why this is he, must, when you are wed,
Sit by your pillow, like young *Apollo,* with
His hand and voice, binding your thoughts in sleep;
The Princess does provide him for you, and for her self.
   *Pha.* I find no musick in these boys.
   *Meg.* Nor I.
They can do little, and that small they do,
They have not wit to hide.
   *Di.* Serves he the Princess?
   *Thra.* Yes.
   *Di.* 'Tis a sweet boy, how brave she keeps him!
   *Pha.* Ladies all good rest; I mean to kill a Buck
To morrow morning, ere y'ave done your dreams.
   *Meg.* All happiness attend your Grace, Gentlemen good rest,
Come shall we to bed?
   *Gal.* Yes, all good night.                         [*Ex.* Gal. *and* Meg.
   *Di.* May your dreams be true to you;
What shall we do Gallants? 'Tis late, the King
Is up still, see, he comes, a Guard along
With him.
130.1 *and a*] *and*

*King.* You Gods, I see, that who unrighteously
Holds Wealth or State from others, shall be curſt
In that which meaner Men are bleſt withal:
Ages to come shall know no Male of him
Left to inherit, and his Name shall be                                135
Blotted from Earth; if he have any Child,
It shall be crossly match'd: The Gods themselves
Shall sow Division 'twixt her Lord and her.
Yet, if it be your Wills, forgive the Faults
Which I have done; let not your Vengeance fall               140
Upon this undeserving Child of mine:
She has not broke your Laws; but how can I
Look to be heard of Gods, who muſt be juſt,
Praying upon the Ground I hold by Wrong?

*Enter* Cleon.

*Cleon.* Sir, I have ask'd her Women, but they, I think, are Bauds:   145
I told them I muſt speak with her; they laugh'd, and said their
Miſtress lay speechless: I said my Business was important; they
said their Lady was about it: I grew hot, and cry'd my Business
was a Matter that concern'd Life and Death; they answer'd, so
was that which their Miſtress was a doing. Answers more direct I    150

131 *King.*] ~. Look your intelligence be true.
  *Are.* Upon my life it is: and I do hope,
Your Highness will not tye me to a man,
That in the heat of wooing throws me off,
And takes another.
  *Di.* What should this mean?
  *King.* If it be true,
That Lady had been better have embrac'd
Cureless Diseases; get you to your rest,                    [*Ex.* Are. *and* Bel.
You shall be righted: Gentlemen draw near,
We shall imploy you: Is young *Pharamond*
Come to his lodging?
  *Di.* I saw him enter there.
  *King.* Haste some of you, and cunningly discover,
If *Megra* be in her lodging.
  *Cle.* Sir,
She parted hence but now with other Ladies.
  *King.* If she be there, we shall not need to make
A vain discovery of our suspicion.

138 Division 'twixt] wild strife betwixt    139 Faults] sin    140 Which . . . Vengeance] I
have committed, let it not    143 who] that    145 ask'd] asked, and    Women]
women swear she is within    146 them] 'em    147 Mistress] Lady    150 that
which . . . doing.] sleeping, at which their Lady was; I urg'd again, she had scarce <*cont.*>

could not get: In short, Sir, I conceive she is very well employ'd.

   *King.* 'Tis then no time to dally: You o'th' Guard,
Wait at the Back-door of *Alga*'s Lodgings,
And see that none pass thence upon your Lives,
But bring them to me whosoe'er they be:         155
Knock, Gentlemen, knock louder, louder yet:
What has their Pleasure ta'en away their Hearing?
   *Maid.* Who's there that knocks so at the dead of Night?
   *Cleon.* Some Friends that are come here to pay you a Visit.

    *Enter the Guard, bringing in* Thrasomond, *in Drawers,*
       *muffled up in a Cloak.*

   *Guard.* Sir, in obedience to your Commands,       160
We ſtopt this Fellow ſtealing out of Doors.

time to be so since last I saw her; they smil'd again, and seem'd to instruct me, that sleeping
was nothing but lying down and winking:

151 conceive . . . employ'd] think she is not there     153 *Alga*'s Lodgings] the Princes
lodging      154–5 Lives, . . . be:] lives.     156 knock louder] knock loud
157 ta'en away] taken off     157–71 Hearing? . . . will.] hearing?

I'le break your meditations? knock again:
Not yet? I do not think he sleeps, having this
Larum by him; once more, *Pharamond*, Prince.
                          Pharamond *above.*
   *Pha.* What sawcy groom knocks at this dead of night?
Where be our waiters? By my vexed soul,
He meets his death, that meets me, for this boldness.
   *K.* Prince, you wrong your thoughts, we are your friends,
Come down.
   *Pha.* The King?
   *King.* The same Sir, come down,
We have cause of present Counsel with you.
   *Pha.* If your Grace please to use me, I'le attend you
To your Chamber.          [*Pha. below.*
   *King.* No, 'tis too late Prince, I'le make bold with yours.
   *Pha.* I have some private reasons to my self,
Makes me unmannerly, and say you cannot;
Nay, press not forward Gentlemen, he must come
Through my life, that comes here. Enter.
   *King.* Sir be resolv'd, I must and will come.
   *Pha.* I will not be dishonour'd;
He that enters, enters upon his death;
Sir, 'tis a sign you make no stranger of me,
To bring these Renegados to my Chamber,
At these unseason'd hours.
   *King.* Why do you
Chafe your self so? you are not wrong'd, nor shall be;
Onely I'le search your lodging, for some cause
To our self known: Enter I say.
   *Pha.* I say no.          [*Meg. Above.*

*[They pull off his Cloak.*

*Agr.* Who's this, the Prince?

*Cleon.* Yes; he's *incognito.*

*King.* Sir, I muſt chide you for this Looseness:
You've wrong'd a worthy Lady; but no more.            165

*Thras.* Sir I came hither but to take the Air.

*Cleon.* A witty Rogue, I warrant him.

*Agr.* I, he's a Devil at his Answers.

*King.* Conduct him to his Lodgings.
Come, Sirs, break open the Doors.            170

*Maid.* You shall not enter here.

*Agr.*                    We muſt, and will.

*Alga.* Nay, let 'em enter; I am up, and ready;
I know the Business they come hither for,
'Tis the poor breaking of a Lady's Honour
They hunt so after; let 'em have their Wills.            175
My Lord, the King, this is not noble in you,
To publish thus the Weakness of a Woman.

*King.* Come down.

*Alga.* I dare, my Lord, for all your Whispers;
This your base Carriage shall not ſtartle me:            180
But I have Vengeance ſtill in Store for some,
That shall, in Spight of this your great Design,
Be Joy and Nourishment to all the Nation.

*King.* Will you come down?

*Alga.*                    I will to laugh at you.
I'll vex you to the Heart, if my Skill fail not.            185

*Cleon.* 'Tis ſtrange that a Lady cannot ride a Heat or two to
breath her self, but she muſt be ruin'd for't. If this Geer holds,

172 Nay, let] Let 'em enter Prince, | Let            172–3 ready; . . . for] ready; I know their
business            175 so] ~ hotly            have . . . Wills] enjoy it. | You have your business
Gentlemen, I lay here.            176 My] O my            177 publish thus] make publick
179–80 for . . . me] your whootings and your clamors,
Your private whispers, and your broad fleerings,
Can no more vex my soul, than this base carriage;
181 still] yet            182 That . . . Design] Shall in the most contempt you can have of me
183 Nourishment . . . Nation] nourishment            184–5 I . . . if] Yes, to laugh at your worst:
but I shall wrong you, | If            185 fail] ~ me            not.] ~. |
   *King.* Sir, I must dearly chide you for this looseness,
You have wrong'd a worthy Lady; but no more, [*these are at 164–5 in 15wgv*]
Conduct him to my lodging, and to bed.
   *Cle.* Get him another wench, and you bring him to bed in deed.
186 that . . . Lady] a man            Heat or] Stagg |  Or            187 her self] himself            but . . . If]
without a warrant: | If            holds] hold

that Lodgings be search'd thus, Pray Heav'n we may lye with our
own Wives quietly.

*Enter* Alga.

*King.* Good Madam *Alga,* where's your Honour now?          190
No Man can fit your Pallat but the Prince:
Thou moſt ill-shrouded Rottenness, thou Piece
Made by a Painter and Apothecary,
Had'ſt thou none to allure unto thy Luſt,
But he that muſt be wedded to my Daughter?                  195
By all the Gods, all these, and all the Pages
Shall whoot you thro' the Court; what do you laugh?
    *Alga.* Faith, Sir, your Majeſty muſt pardon me,
I cannot chuse but laugh to see you merry.
If you do this, O King, or dare to think on't,              200
By all those Gods you swore by, and as many
More of my own, I will have Fellows with me,
Such Fellows as shall make you noble Mirth:
The Princess, your dear Daughter, shall ſtand by me,
She shall be whooted at as well as I.                       205
Urge me no farther, Sir, I know her Haunts,
Her Layes and Leaps, and will discover all;
Nay, will dishonour her: I know the Boy
She keeps; a handsome Boy about eighteen;
Can tell what she does with him; where and when.            210

---

188 thus, Pray] ~, | ~          189 quietly] in safety, | That they be not by some trick of State
mistaken          189.1 *Enter*] ~ *with*          190 Good . . . *Alga*] Now Lady of
honour          193 Apothecary] a Pothecary          194-5 Had'st . . . to] Thou troubled sea
of lust; thou wilderness,
Inhabited by wild thoughts; thou swoln cloud
Of Infection; thou ripe Mine of all Diseases;
Thou all Sin, all Hell, and last, all Devils, tell me,
Had you none to pull on with your courtesies,
But he that must be mine, and wrong
197 Shall . . . laugh] And all the Court shall hoot thee through the Court,
Fling rotten Oranges, make ribald Rimes,
And sear thy name with Candles upon walls:
Do you laugh Lady *Venus*
198 your Majesty] you          200 or . . . on't] nay, if you dare do it;          201 those]
these          202-3 with . . . Fellows] and such | Fellows in it,          203 make you] make
205 She . . . I] On walls, and sung in ballads, any thing          206 farther, Sir] more     her]
~, and her          207 and Leaps] leaps, and outlayes          210 Can tell] Know

Come, Sir, you put me to a Woman's Madness,
The Glory of a Fury; and if I
Don't do it to the Height ——
    *King.*                What Boy is this?
    *Alga.* Good-minded Prince, alas Sir, you know nothing;
I'm loth to utter more. Keep in this Fault,                                      215
As you would keep your Health, from the hot Air
Of the corrupted People; or by Heav'n
I will not fall alone: What I have known
Shall be as publick as a Print; nay, as
Your Counsels, and by all as freely laught at.                                   220
    *King.* Has she a Boy?
    *Agr.*             I think I've seen one, Sir,
That waits upon her.
    *King.*          Get you to your Quarter;
For this Time I will ſtudy to forget you.
    *Alga.* Do you ſtudy to forget me, and I'll ſtudy to forget you.
                       [*Exeunt King,* Alga *and Guard.*
    *Agr.* Why here's a Male Spirit for *Hercules!* If ever there be nine   225
Worthies of Women this Wench shall ride aſtride, and be their
Captain.
    *Cleon.* Sure she has a Garrison of Devils in her Tongue; she
utter'd such Balls of Wild-fire, that all the Doctors in the Country
will scarce cure him: That Boy was a ſtrange found out Antidote     230
to cure her Infection, That Boy, that Princess's Boy, that brave,
chaſte, virtuous Lady's Boy, and a fair Boy, a well-spoken Boy:
All these considered can make nothing else

---

212–13 I . . . do] I do not | Do        213 this] ~ she raves at        214 Good . . . nothing]
Alas! good minded Prince, you know not these things        215 I'm] I am     utter . . . in]
reveal 'em. Keep        219–20 nay . . . at] all tongues
Shall speak it as they do the language they
Are born in, as free and commonly; I'le set it
Like a prodigious star for all to gaze at,
And so high and glowing, that other Kingdoms far and Forreign
Shall read it there, nay travel with it, till they find
No tongue to make it more, nor no more people;
And then behold the fall of your fair Princess
221–2 I . . . her] So please your Grace I have seen a boy wait
On her, a fair boy
222 Get] Go get        223 I will] I'le        224 I'll study to] I'le study | To        228 has]
hath        229 utter'd] uttereth        fire] ~. She has so netled the King,        231 Princess's]
Princess        232 Lady's] Ladies

—— But there I'll leave you, Gentlemen.
*Adel.* Nay, we'll go wander with you.                    235
                                        [*Exeunt.*

*The End of the Second Act*


ACT III. SCENE I.

*Enter* Cleon, Agremont, Adelard.

*Agr.* Nay, doubtless it is true.
*Cleon.*                    I and the Gods
Have rais'd this Punishment to scourge the King
With his own Issue: Is it not a Shame
For us that should be Freemen, to behold
A Man that is the Bravery of his Age,                     5
*Philander*, preſt down from his Royal Right
By this regardless King; and only look
And see the Scepter ready to be caſt
Into the Hands of that lascivious Lady,
That lives in Luſt with a smooth Boy, now to be           10
Marry'd to yon' ſtrange Prince, who, but that People
Please to let him be a Prince, is born a Slave
In that which should be his moſt noble Part,
His Mind.
    *Adel.* That Man that will not ſtir with you
To aid *Philander*, let the Gods forget                   15
That such a Creature walks upon the Earth.
    *Agr. Philander* is too backward in't himself;
The Gentry all wait for him, and the People,
Againſt their Nature long to be in Arms;
And like a Field of ſtanding Corn, that moves             20
With a ſtiff Gale, their Heads bow all one Way.

234 I'll] I          235.1 *Exeunt . . . Act*] *Exeunt*          235.2 *The . . . Act.*] *Not in 79fc.*
III. i. 0.1 Cleon, Agremont] Cle. Di. *and*          1 it is] 'tis    and] ~ 'tis          2 Have]
That          3 Shame] shame | For us, that should write noble in the land;          14 will]
would          18 all . . . him] do await it          19 long . . . Arms] are all bent for him
20 that moves] that's mov'd

*Cleon.* The only Cause that draws *Philander* back
From this Attempt is the fair Princess, whom
I fear he loves.
    *Adel.*      He'll not believe it then.
    *Cleon.* Why, Gentlemen, 'tis without Queſtion so.     25
    *Agr.* 'Tis moſt true, she lives dishoneſtly;
But how shall we, if he be doubtful, work
Upon his Faith.
    *Adel.*      Every one knows 'tis true.
    *Cleon.* Since 'tis so, and tends to his own good,
I'll make this new Report to be my Knowledge.     30
I'll say I knew it; nay, I'll swear I saw it.
    *Agr.* It will be beſt.
    *Adel.*            Yes sure, it muſt needs move him.
    *Cleon.* Nothing but this will force him into Aċtion.

Enter Philander.

See, here he comes. Good morrow to your Grace;
We have been waiting for you.
    *Phil.*           Worthy Friends,     35
You that can keep your Memories to know
Your Friends in Miseries, and cannot frown
On Men disgrac'd for Virtue; a good Day
Attend you all: What Service may I do,
Worthy your Expeċtation?
    *Cleon.*        My good Lord,     40
We come to urge that Virtue (which we know
Lives in your Breaſt) forth; rise, and make a Head:
The Nobles and the People are all dull'd
With this usurping King; and not a Man
That ever heard or knew of such a Thing     45
As Virtue, but will second your Attempts.
    *Phil.* How honourable is this Love in you
To me that have deserv'd none? Know, my Friends,

23–4 Princess, . . . loves] Princess love, | Which he admires and we can now confute  24 He'll] Perhaps he'l    it then] it    26 'Tis . . . true] I 'tis past speech    27 doubtful] curious    28 Every . . . true] We are all satisfied within our selves    29 'tis so] it is true    31 knew] know    32 Yes . . . needs] 'Twill    32–3 him. | *Cleon.* Nothing . . . Action] him    34 See, here] *Di.* Here    Grace] honour    35 been . . . for] spent some time in seeking    Worthy] My worthy    37 Friends] friend 39–40 do, | Worthy] do worthy    40 Expectation] acceptation    45 heard] ~ the word    knew of] knew

(You that were born to shame your poor *Philander*
With too much Kindness) know I could afford                    50
To melt my self in Thanks; But my Designs
Are not yet ripe: Let it suffice, e'er long
I shall employ you; but the Time's not come.
   *Cleon.* The Time is fitter some than you expeсt;
That which hereafter hardly will be reach'd                    55
By Violence, may now be caught with Ease.
As for the King, you know the People long
Did hate him; but the Princess now ——
   *Phil.*                Why, what
Of her, I pray?
   *Cleon.*     Is loath'd as much as he.
   *Phil.* By what ſtrange Means?
   *Cleon.*          She's known a Whore.
   *Phil.*              Thou ly'ſt,    60
                [*Offers to draw; is held.*
And thou shalt feel thou doſt; I thought thy Mind
Was full of Honour; thus to rob a Lady
Of her good Name is an infeсtious Sin
Not to be pardon'd; be it false as Hell,
'Twill never be redeem'd if it be sown                         65
Among the People, fruitful to increase
All Evil they shall hear. Let me alone,
That I may cut off Falshood while it springs:
Set Hills on Hills betwixt me and the Man
That utters this, and I will scale them all,                   70
And from the utmoſt Top fall on his Neck
Like Thunder from a Cloud.
   *Cleon.*         This is moſt ſtrange.
Sir, though you love her ——
   *Phil.*     No, Sir, I love Truth;

50 Kindness) know] courtesie)        52 Let it suffice] suffice it, that        53 you . . .
come] your loves: but yet the time is short of what I would        54 fitter some] fuller Sir
55 hardly will] will not perhaps     56-7 caught with Ease. | As] caught; As     57 King,
you] King, | You     57-8 long . . . now ——] have long hated him; | But now the
Princess, whom they lov'd.     58-9 what . . . pray] what of her     60 Whore.] ~
    *Phi.* Thou lyest.
    *Di.* My Lord——
60.1 *draw*;] ~ *and*        61 thou dost; I] it; I had        62 Was full] Had been
66 Among] Amongst        68 while] whilst        73 Sir, though you] Sure he does    No
. . . love] I do love fair

She is my Miſtress; and who injures her
Draws Vengeance from me: Sirs, let go my Arms.                    75
   *Adel.* Nay, good my Lord, be patient.
   *Agr.*                              Sir, remember
This is your honour'd Friend, the good Lord *Cleon*,
That comes to do you Service, and will shew
You why he utter'd this.
   *Phil.*                    I ask your Pardon;
My Zeal to Truth made me unmannerly:                             80
Should I have heard Dishonour spoke of you
Behind your Back, untruly, I had been
As much diſtemper'd and enrag'd as now.
   *Cleon.* But this is true.
   *Phil.*                    O, good Sir, say not so.
Is it then true all Woman-kind is false.                         85
Urge it no more; it is impossible;
Why should you think the Princess could be light?
   *Cleon.* Because, Sir, she was taken in the Faĉt.
   *Phil.* 'Tis false; Oh Heav'n! 'tis false: It cannot be;
Can it? Speak, Gentlemen, for the Love of Truth;                 90
Is't possible all Women should be damn'd?
   *Cleon.* Why no, my Lord.
   *Phil.*                    Why then it cannot be.
   *Cleon.* And she was taken with her Boy.
   *Phil.*                              What Boy?
   *Cleon.* A Page; a Boy that serves her.
   *Phil.*                              Oh, Good Gods!
A little Boy!
   *Cleon.*    Ay; Know you him, my Lord?                    95
   *Phil.* Sin and Hell: Know him! Sir, you are deceiv'd:
I'll reason it a little coldly with you:
If she were luſtful, would she take a Boy
That knows not yet Desire? She would have one
Should meet her Thoughts, and know the Sin he aĉts,              100
Which is the great Delight of Wickedness:
You are abus'd, and so is she and I.

75 me: Sirs] me Sirs    76–7 remember | This] remember this    77 Friend . . . *Cleon*]
friend    78 you] his    78–9 shew | You why] shew you | Why    79 your
Pardon] you pardon Sir    84 is true] my Lord is truth   good . . . not] say not so, good
Sir forbear to say    85 Is . . . true] 'Tis the truth that   Woman-kind] womenkind
87 Princess could be] Princess    88 Because, Sir] Why   in the Fact] at it    90 for
the] for   Truth] truth speak    91 all Women should] can women all    94–5 Gods!
| A] gods, a    96 Sin and Hell:] Hell and sin    100 know] knows

*Cleon.*  How you, my Lord?
*Phil.*                    Why, all the World's abus'd
In an unjuſt Report.
    *Cleon.*            Your Virtues, Sir,
Cannot look through the subtile Thoughts of Woman:    105
In short, my Lord, I took 'em; I, my self.
    *Phil.*  Now all the Devils, thou did'ſt! Fly from my Rage:
Would thou had'ſt taken Fiends ingendring Plagues,
When thou did'ſt take 'em; hide thee from my Eyes:
Would thou had'ſt taken Thunder on thy Breaſt    110
When thou did'ſt take 'em, or been ſtrucken dumb,
That so this Deed for ever might have slept
In Silence.
    *Adel.*  Have you known him so ill temper'd?
    *Agr.*  Never before.
    *Phil.*                The Winds that are set loose
From the four several Corners of the World,    115
And spread themselves all over Sea and Land,
Kiss not a chaſte one. What Friend bears a Sword
To run me through?
    *Cleon.*            Why are you mov'd at this?
    *Phil.*  When any falls from Virtue I am mad;
I am diſtracted; I've an Intereſt in't.    120
    *Cleon.*  But, Good my Lord, recall your self, and think
What's to be done.
    *Phil.*            I thank you: I will do't.
Please you to leave me, I'll consider on't:
To-morrow I will give you all my Answer.
    *Cleon.*  The Gods direct you.    [*Ex. Cleon. Adel. Agr.*    125

---

104 Your Virtues, Sir] Oh noble Sir your vertues    105 through] into    106 'em] them
108 taken] ta'ne   Fiends] devils    109 'em] them    111 'em] them
112 That . . . ever] For ever: that this foul deed    112–13 slept | In] slept in    114 set]
let    115 World] earth    118 Why] ~, my Lord   you] ~ so    119 mad] distract
120 am . . . I've] have    121 self, and] self | And    121–2 think | What's] think
what's best    122 do't] do it    123 on't] of it    124 give . . . Answer] find your
lodging forth,
And give you answer
The readiest way.
125 The] All the    you.] ~
    *Thra.* He was extream impatient.
    *Cle.* It was his vertue and his noble mind.
125.SD Adel.] Cle. *and*

*Phil.* I had forgot to ask him where he took 'em:
I'll follow him. O that I had a Sea
Within my Breaſt, to quench the Fire I feel!
More Circumſtances will but fan this Fire:
It more afflicts me now to know by whom          130
This Deed is done, than simply that 'tis done:
And he that tells me this is honourable,
As far from Lies, as she is far from Truth.
O that, like Beaſts, we could not grieve our selves
With that we see not! Bulls and Rams will fight     135
To keep their Females ſtanding in their Sight;
But take them from 'em, and you take at once
Their Spleens away, and they will fall again
Unto their Paſtures, growing fresh and fat,
And taſte the Waters of the Springs as sweet        140
As 'twas before, finding no Start in Sleep:
But miserable Man,—See, see, you Gods!

*Enter* Endymion.

He walks ſtill, and the Face you let him wear
When he was innocent, is ſtill the same!
Not blaſted! Is this Juſtice? Do you mean           145
T'intrap Mortality, that you allow
Treason so smooth a Brow? I cannot now
Think he is guilty.
    *End.*          Health to you, my Lord:
The Princess doth commend her Love, her Life,
And this unto you.
    *Phil.*         Oh, *Endymion,*             150
Now I perceive she loves me; she doth shew it
In loving thee, my Boy; she has made thee brave.
    *End.* My Lord, she has attir'd me paſt my Wish,
And paſt my Merit, fit for her Attendant,
Tho' far unfit for me who do attend.               155
    *Phil.* Thou art grown courtly, Boy, O let all Women,
That love black Deeds, learn to dissemble here;
Here, by this Paper, she does write to me,
As if her Heart were Mines of Adamant

126 'em] them     137 them] 'em   'em] them     146 T'intrap] To intrap    151 doth] does    154 And . . . Merit] Past my desert, more

To all the World besides, but unto me                    160
A Maiden Snow, that melted with my Looks.
Tell me, my Boy, how doth the Princess use thee?
For I shall ghess her Love to me by that.
    *End.* Scarce like her Servant, but as if I were
Something ally'd to her, or had preserv'd              165
Her Fame or Life, with Hazard of my own;
As Mothers fond do use their only Sons;
As I'd use one that's left unto my Truſt,
For whom my Life should pay if he met harm.
    *Phil.* Why this is wondrous well, *Endymion*; but      170
What Language, preethee, doth she feed thee with?
    *End.* Why, she doth tell me, she will truſt my Youth
With all her loving Secrets, and does call me
Her pretty Servant; bids me weep no more
For leaving you, she'll see my Services                175
Rewarded; and such Words, of that soft Strain,
That I am nearer weeping when she ends,
Than e'er she does begin.
    *Phil.*              So, so! This is
Much better ſtill.
    *End.*          Are not you well, my Lord?
    *Phil.* Well! Yes, *Endymion*.
    *End.*                    Methinks your Words      180
Fall not from off your Tongue so evenly,
Nor is there in your Looks that Quietness
That I was wont to see.
    *Phil.*              Thou art deceiv'd,
My Boy. And she does ſtroke thy Head?
    *End.*                      Why, yes.
    *Phil.* And she does kiss thee? Ha?
    *End.*                      How's that, my Lord?      185
    *Phil.* She kisses thee, my Boy.

166 Fame . . . own] life three times by my fidelity      169 harm] ~, | So she does use me
170-1 well . . . What] well: | But what      171 Language, preethee] kind language
doth] does      172 doth] does      176 Rewarded] Regarded      178 does begin]
spake      178-9 So . . . Much] This is much      179 not you well] you ill      180 Well!
Yes] Ill? No      183-4 deceiv'd, . . . And] deceiv'd boy: | And      184 does stroke]
stroakes      Why, yes] Yes.
    *Phi.* And she does clap thy cheeks?
    *Bell.* She does my Lord
185 thee] ~ boy    How's that] How      186 thee, my Boy] thee

*End.*                        Not so, my Lord.
*Phil.* Come, come, I know she doth.
*End.*                        No, by my Life.
*Phil.* Why then she does not love me; come she does,
I bade her do it; I charg'd her by all Charms
Of Love between us, by the Hope of Peace                        190
We should enjoy, to yield thee all Delights,
Naked, as to her Bed: I took her Oath
Thou should'ſt enjoy her: Tell me, Boy, is she
Not far above compare? Is not her Breath
Sweet as *Arabian* Winds, when Fruits are ripe?                        195
Are not her Breaſts two liquid Ivory Balls?
Is she not all a laſting Mine of Joy?
*End.* I, now I see why my diſturbed Thoughts
Were so perplex'd; when firſt I went to her
My Heart held Augury: You are abus'd,                        200
Some Villain has abus'd you; I do see
Whereto you tend: Fall Rocks upon his Head
That put this in you; 'tis some subtil Train
To bring that noble Frame of yours to nought.
*Phil.* Thou think'ſt I will be angry with thee; come,                        205
Thou shalt know all my Drift; I hate her more
Than I love Happiness, and plac'd thee there
To pry with narrow Eyes into her Deeds.
Haſt thou discover'd? Has she fall'n to Luſt,
As I would wish her? Speak some Comfort to me.                        210
*End.* My Lord, you did miſtake the Boy you sent:
Had she the Luſt of Sparrows or of Goats;
Had she a Sin that way hid from the World,
Beyond the Name of Luſt; I would not aid
Her base Desires; but what I came to know,                        215
As Servant to her, I would not reveal,
To make my Life laſt Ages.
*Phil.*                        Oh my Heart!
This is a Salve worse than the main Disease.
Tell me thy Thoughts, for I will know the leaſt
That dwells within thee, or will rip thy Heart                        220

187 doth] does        189 bade] bad        193–4 Boy . . . compare] gentle boy, | Is she not
paralleless        203 in] to        209 Has] Is        216–17 reveal, | To] reveal, to
217–18 Heart! | This] heart; this

To know it: I will see thy Thoughts as plain
As I do now thy Face.
    *End.*          Why, so you do.
She is (for ought I know) by all the Gods,
As chaſte as Ice; but were she foul as Hell,
And I did know it thus; the Breath of Kings,          225
The Points of Swords, Tortures, nor Bulls of Brass,
Should draw it from me.
    *Phil.*          Then it is not time
To dally with thee; I will take thy Life,
For I do hate thee: I could curse thee now.
    *End.* If you do hate me, you can't curse me worse:    230
The Gods have not a Punishment in Store
Greater for me, my Lord, than is your Hate.
    *Phil.* Fie, fie, so young, and so dissembling too!
Tell me both when and where thou didſt enjoy her,
Or Plagues fall on thee if I kill thee not.         235
    *End.* Heav'n knows I never did: And when I lie
To save my Life, may I live long and loath'd.
Hew me asunder, and I'll love the Limbs
Which you cut off, better than those that grow:
And kiss them dead, because you made 'em so.      240
    *Phil.* Fear'ſt thou not Death? Can Boys contemn that?
    *End.*                            Oh,
What Boy is he, can be content to live
To be a Man that sees the very beſt
Of Men thus passionate, thus without Reason?
    *Phil.* Oh, but thou doſt not know what 'tis to die.    245
    *End.* Yes but I do, my Lord, I know it well:
'Tis less than to be born; a laſting Sleep,
A quiet reſting from all Jealousie,
A thing we all pursue: I know besides,

222 now] know    227–8 it . . . To] 'tis no time to    228 thee; I] ~; | ~    228–9 Life,
| For] life, for    230 me, you can't] you could not    232 me, my Lord] me
233 dissembling too] dissembling    234 me both] me   didſt] dist    235 Or] ~ let
thee] me   kill] destroy    238–40 I'll . . . because] whilst I can think
I'le love those pieces you have cut away,
Better than those that grow: and kiss these limbs,
Because
241 Death? Can] death? | Can    241–2 Oh, | What] Oh, what    242 he, can] he | Can
242–3 live | To] live to    243 Man that] man | That   the very] the   243–4 best
| Of] best of    246 but . . . well] Yes, I do know my Lord

'Tis but the giving up a Game which muſt be loſt.                    250
    *Phil.* But there are Pains, false Boy, for perjur'd Souls;
Think but on them, and then thy Heart will melt.
    *End.* May they fall all upon me whilſt I live,
If I be perjur'd, or have ever thought
Of that you charge me with; if I be false,                    255
Send me to suffer in those Punishments
You speak of: Kill me.
    *Phil.*            Oh, what should I do?
Why, who can but believe him? He does swear
So earneſtly, if it were not true,
The Gods would not endure him. Rise *Endymion*,                    260
Thy Proteſtations are so deep, and thou
Doſt look so truly when thou utter'ſt them,
That, tho' I know 'em false as were my Hopes,
I cannot urge thee farther: But thou wert
To blame to injure me; for I muſt love                    265
Thy honeſt Looks, and never take Revenge
Upon thy tender Youth: A Love from me to thee
Is firm, whate'er thou doſt. It troubles me
That I have call'd the Blood out of thy Cheeks,
That did so well become them; but, good Boy,                    270
Let me not see thee more; something is done
That will diſtract me; that will raise a Storm
Within my Breaſt too great for me to quell,
If thou com'ſt near me.
    *End.*          I will fly as far
As there is Morning, e'er I give diſtaſte                    275
To that moſt honour'd Mind. But thro' these Tears,
Shed at my hopeless parting, I can see
A World of Treason practic'd upon you,
And her, and me. Farewel for evermore;
If you shall hear that Sorrow ſtruck me dead,                    280

250 'Tis . . . up] It is but giving over of    which] that    251 Boy, for] boy, | For
251–2 Souls; | Think] souls; think    252 them] these    then thy] then | Thy    melt] ~,
and thou wilt utter all    256–7 Punishments | You] punishments you    259 earnestly,]
~, that    263 know] known    264 farther] further    266 never take] take no
266–7 Revenge | Upon thy] revenge upon | Thy    270 them] thee    272–4 raise
. . . me] make me mad,
If I behold thee: if thou tender'st me,
Let me not see thee
275 e'er] ere

And after find me loyal, let there be
A Tear, at least, shed by you for me; and
I then shall rest in Peace.                    [*Exit.*
    *Phil.*                    Blessings be with thee,
Whatever thou deserv'st. Oh where shall I
Go bathe this Body? Nature too unkind,                    285
That made no Med'cine for a troubled Mind.                    [*Exit.*

*Enter* Araminta.

    *Ara.* I marvel my Boy comes not back again;
But that I know my Love will question him
Over and over, how I slept, wak'd, talk'd;
How often his dear Name was mentioned by me;                    290
How I sigh'd, wept, and sung, and thousand more
Such things; I should be angry at his Stay.

*Enter* King.

    *King.* What at your Meditations? Who is with you?
    *Ara.* None but my single self; I need no Guard:
I do no wrong, nor fear none.
    *King.*                    Have you not a Boy?                    295
    *Ara.* Yes, Sir.
    *King.*          What kind of Boy?
    *Ara.*                    A waiting Boy.
    *King.* A handsome Boy?
    *Ara.*                    A very handsome Boy.
    *King.* He talks and sings, and plays?
    *Ara.*                    I think he does.
    *King.* About eighteen?
    *Ara.*                    I never ask'd his Age.
    *King.* Pray, is he full of Service?
    *Ara.*                    Why do you ask?                    300
    *King.* Put him away.

282–3 at . . . then] shed from you in my memorie. | And I    283 in] at    *Exit*] ~ Bel
Blessings] Blessing    285 bathe this] bath thy    286 *Exit*] ~ Phi    290–1 often
. . . How] I remembred him when his dear name | Was last spoke, and how, when
291–2 and sung . . . things] sung, | And ten thousand such    293 at] are    is with]
attends    295 Have] Tell me: have    296 A] ~ Page, a    297 A . . . Boy] I
think he be not ugly:
Well qualified, and dutiful, I know him,
I took him not for beauty
298 talks] speaks    I . . . does] Yes Sir    300 Pray, is] Is    Why] By your pardon why

*Ara.*                How, Sir?
*King.*                                Put him away.
'Has done you that good Service, I'm asham'd
To speak of.
    *Ara.*        Good Sir, let me underſtand you.
    *King.* If you fear me, shew it in Duty; put
Away that Boy.
    *Ara.*        Let me have reason for it,                    305
And then your Will to me shall be a Law.
    *King.* Do not you blush to ask it? Caſt him off,
Or I shall do the same to you: Y' are one
Shame with me, and so near unto my self,
That, by my Life, I dare scarce tell my self               310
What you have done.
    *Ara.*                What have I done, my Lord?
    *King.* It is a Language that all love to learn;
The common People speak it well already:
They need no Grammar; underſtand me well,
There be foul Whispers ſtirring; caſt him off,            315
And suddenly I charge you do't, Farewel.            [*Exit.*
    *Ara.* Where may a Maiden live securely free,
Keeping her Honour safe? Not with the living,
They feed upon Opinions, Errors, Dreams,
And make 'em Truths: They draw a Nourishment              320
Out of defaming, grow upon Disgraces,
And when they see a Virtue fortify'd
Strongly, above the Batt'ry of their Tongues,
Oh, how they caſt about to ruin it!

*Enter* Philander.

    *Phil.* Peace be to your fair Thoughts, my deareſt Miſtress.     325
    *Ara.* O dear *Philander*, I've a War within me.

---

301 How, Sir] Sir          301–2 away. | 'Has] away, h'as          302–3 Service . . . To] service,
| Shames me to          304–5 put | Away] put away          305–6 it . . . Law] it Sir, and then
| Your will is my command          310 scarce] not          311 you] ~, my self          312 It is
a] 'Tis a new          316 I . . . do't] do it     *Exit*] ~ King          321 defaming] defamings
324 about . . . it!] to sink it; and defeated
(Soul sick with Poyson) strike the Monuments
Where noble names lie sleeping: till they sweat,
And the cold Marble melt.
325 Peace be] Peace     fair Thoughts, my] fairest thoughts          326 dear *Philander*, I've]
my dearest servant I have

*Phil.* He muſt be more than Man that makes these Chryſtals
Run into Rivers: Sweeteſt Fair, the Cause?
And as I am your Slave, ty'd to your Goodness,
Your Creature made again from what I was,                    330
And newly spirited: I'll right your Honour.
 *Ara.* Oh, my beſt Love, that pretty Boy ——
 *Phil.*         What Boy?
 *Ara.* The pretty Boy you gave me.
 *Phil.*       What of him?
 *Ara.* Muſt be no more mine.
 *Phil.*     Why?
 *Ara.*      They're jealous of him.
 *Phil.* Who's jealous?
 *Ara.*    The King is.
 *Phil.*      Oh my Fortune!                    335
Then 'tis no idle Story. Let him go.
 *Ara.* Oh cruel! what are you hard-hearted too?
Who now shall bring you word how much I love you?
Who now shall weep to you the Tears I send?
Who now shall give you Letters, Rings, and Bracelets?        340
Waſte tedious Nights in Stories of your Praise?
And throw away his Health in serving you?
Who shall take up his Lute, and singing to it,
Charm me asleep, making me dream, and cry
Oh my dear, dear *Philander?*
 *Phil.*      Oh my Heart!                    345
Would he had broken thee, that made thee know
This Lady was not true. Madam, forget
This Boy; I'll get you one a great deal better.
 *Ara.* Oh, never, never such a Boy again
As my *Endymion* is.

331 Honour] honours  332 that pretty] that  334 They're] They are  335 Who's
jealous] Jealous, who  King is] King  336 Story] jealousie  337 cruel! what]
cruel,  338 now . . . word] shall now tell you  love] lov'd  339 now . . . you]
shall swear it to you, and weep  340 now shall give] shall now bring  Rings, and] Rings,
341 Waſte] Lose his health in service? wake [*Cf. l. 342*]  Nights in] nights | In
341–2 Praise? . . . you?] praise? Who shall sing
Your crying Elegies? And strike a sad soul
Into senseless Pictures, and make them mourn?
343–4 singing . . . making] touch it, till
He crown a silent sleep upon my eye-lid,
Making
344–5 cry | Oh] ~, ~  347 true. Madam] Loyal. Mistress  348 This] The  you
. . . deal] thee a far  349–50 again . . . is] again, as my *Bellario*

*Phil.*                'Tis but your Fancy.                                350
*Ara.* With thee, my Boy, farewel for evermore
All Secrecy in Servants; farewel Faith,
And all Desire to do well, for it self:
Let all that shall succeed thee, for thy Wrongs,
Betray chaſte Love.
    *Phil.*          And all this Passion for                       355
A Boy?
    *Ara.* He was your Boy; you put him to me:
The Loss of such a one requires a Mourning.
    *Phil.* Oh, thou forgetful Woman!
    *Ara.*                How, my Lord?
    *Phil.* False *Araminta*; thou haſt quite undone me.
Haſt thou a Med'cine to reſtore my Wits                      360
Again, when I have loſt 'em? Oh you Gods!
Give me a worthy Patience: Have I ſtood
Alone the Shock of all the worſt Misfortunes?
Have I seen Mischiefs numberless and mighty
Grow like a Sea upon me? Have I taken                        365
Dangers as ſtern as Death into my Bosom,
And laugh'd upon 'em, made 'em but a Mirth,
And flung 'em off? Do I live under this
Usurping King, like one, who languishing,
Hears his sad Bell, and sees his Mourners by?               370
Do I bear all this bravely, and muſt sink
At length under a Woman's Falshood? O,
That Boy, that cursed Boy! None but a Boy
To ease your Luſt?
    *Ara.*          Why, did he tell you so?
    *Phil.* It may be he did.

350 *Phil*] *Bell*    Fancy] fond affection        351 evermore] ever        355 Betray] Sell and
betray          355–6 for | A] for a        356 Boy] ~, and        357 The] And the    a
. . . Mourning] must have a mourning for      359 *Araminta* . . . me.] *Arethusa!*      361 Again,
when] When    'em?] ~ ? If not, leave to talk, and do thus.
    *Are.* Do what Sir? would you sleep?
    *Phi.* For ever *Arethusa.*
363 Alone] Naked, alone    all . . . Misfortunes] many fortunes        365 like] live
366 Dangers] Danger      367 'em . . . 'em] it . . . it      368 'em off] it by      368–9 under
. . . who] now like him, | Under this Tyrant King, that      370–1 Mourners . . . bear]
Mourners? Do I | Bear        371–2 sink | At] sink at        372 length under] length |
Under        372–3 O, | That] Oh that        373 Boy, that] boy, | That        373–4 Boy
| To] villain boy, to        374–5 Why . . . undone] Nay, then I am betray'd

*Ara.*                    Alas, then I'm undone:                    375
I see the Plot caſt for my Overthrow.
    *Phil.* Now you may take that little Right I have
To this poor Kingdom; give it to your Joy,
For I have no Joy in it. Some far Place,
Where never Womankind durſt set her Foot,                    380
I'll seek to curse you in.
    *Ara.*                    Oh, I am wretched!
    *Phil.* There dig a Cave, and preach to Birds and Beaſts,
What Woman is, and help to save 'em from you:
How Heav'n is in your Eyes; but in your Hearts
More Hell than Hell has; how your Tongues like Scorpions,    385
Both heal and poison; how your Thoughts are woven
With thousand Changes in one subtil Web,
And woven so by you: How that foolish Man
That reads the Story of a Woman's Face,
And dies believing it, is loſt for ever.                    390
How all the good you have is but a Shadow;
I'th' morning with you, and at night behind you,
Paſt and forgotten. How your Vows are Froſts,
Faſt for a Night, and with the next Sun gone.
How you are, being taken all together,                    395
A meer Confusion, and so dead a *Chaos*,
Truth's Love can diſtinguish nothing in you. These
Sad Texts till my laſt Hour I'm bound to utter.
So farewel all my Woe, all my Delight.          [*Exit.*
    *Ara.* Be merciful, you Gods, and ſtrike me dead;    400
What way have I deserv'd this? Make my Breaſt
Transparent as pure Chriſtal, that the World,
Jealous of me, may see the fouleſt Thought
My Heart does hold. Where shall a Woman turn
Her Eyes to find out Conſtancy? Save me!                    405

              *Enter* Endymion.

How black, methinks, that guilty Boy looks now!

376 see] feel    Overthrow] overthrow; Oh I am wretched [*Cf. l. 381b*]    381–2 I'll . . .
*Phil.*] For bursting with her poisons, must I seek, | And live to curse you;    383 'em]
them        388 woven] worn        397 Truth's . . . you] That love cannot distinguish
397–8 These | Sad] These sad    398 Texts till] Texts [ Till    I'm] I am    utter] ~ of you
399 *Exit*] ~ Phi    400 you] ye    404 does hold] holds    404–5 turn | Her]
turn her    405 Eyes to] eyes, | To    405–6 me! . . . How] me, how
406 black . . . guilty] black, [*Enter* Bell.
And guilty (me thinks) that

Oh, thou Dissembler! that before thou spak'st
Wer't in thy Cradle false! sent to make Lies,
And betray Innocents: Thy Lord and thou
May glory in the Ashes of a Maid,                             410
Fool'd by her Passion; but the Conquest is
Nothing so great as wicked. Fly away,
Let my Command force thee to that, which Shame
Should do without it. If thou understood'st
The loathed Office thou hast undergone,                       415
Why, thou would'st hide thee under Heaps of Hills,
Lest Men should dig, and find thee.
    *End.*                   Oh, what God,
Angry with Men, hath sent this strange Disease
Into the noblest Minds? Madam, this Grief
You add unto me, is no more than Drops                        420
To Seas, for which they are not seen to swell:
My Lord hath struck his Anger through my Heart,
And let out all the Hopes of future Joys.
You need not bid me fly; I came to part,
To take my latest Leave: Farewel for ever.                    425
I durst not run away, in Honesty,
From such a Lady, like a Boy that stole,
Or made some grievous Fault; the Pow'r of Gods
Assist you in your Suff'rings; hasty Time
Reveal the Truth to your abused Lord,                         430
And mine: That he may know your worth; whilst I
Go seek out some forgotten Place to die.          [*Exit.*
    *Ara.* Peace guide thee, thou hast overthrown me once,
Yet if I had another *Troy* to lose,
Thou or another Villain, with thy Looks,                      435
Might talk me out of it, and send me with
My Hair dishevel'd, through the fiery Streets.

                *Enter a Lady.*

    *Lady.* Madam, the King has sent for you in haste,
To go abroad with him.
    *Ara.*            Whither, d'ye know?
    *Lady.* A Hunting, Madam.

414 Should] Would    422 hath] had    423 Hopes] hope    432 *Exit*] ~ Bell
433 thou hast] th'ast    436 with] naked    438–40 has . . . Madam] would hunt,
and calls for you | With earnestness.

*Ara.*                    I'm in tune to Hunt.                    440
*Diana*, if thou canſt rage with a Maid,
As with a Man, let me discover thee
Bathing, and turn me to a fearful Hinde,
That I may die, pursu'd by cruel Hounds,
And have my Story written in my Wounds.          [*Exeunt.*  445

*The End of the Third Aɛt.*


## Act IV. Scene I.

*Enter* Philander.

*Phil.* Oh that I had been nourish'd in these Woods
With Milk of Goats and Acorns, and not known
The Right of Crowns, nor the dissembling Trains
Of Women's Looks; but dig'd my self a Cave,
Where I my Fire, my Cattle and my Bed                    5

---

440 I'm] I am        445 *Exeunt . . . Act*] Exeunt        445.1 *The . . . Act.*] Not in *79fc.*
IV. i. o.1 *Enter* Philander] *Enter* King, Pharamond, Arethusa, Galatea, Megra, Dion, Cleremont, Thrasilin, *and Attendants.*
    *K.* What, are the Hounds before, and all the woodmen?
Our horses ready, and our bows bent?
    *Di.* All Sir.
    *King.* Y'are cloudy Sir, come we have forgotten
Your venial trespass, let not that sit heavy
Upon your spirit; none dare utter it.
    *Di.* He looks like an old surfeited Stallion after his leaping, dull as a Dormouse: see how he sinks; the wench has shot him between wind and water, and I hope sprung a leak.
    *Thra.* He needs no teaching, he strikes sure enough; his greatest fault is, he Hunts too much in the Purlues, would he would leave off Poaching.
    *Di.* And for his horn, has left it at the Lodge where he lay late; Oh, he's a precious Lime-hound; turn him loose upon the pursuit of a Lady, and if he lose her, hang him up i'th' slip. When my Fox-bitch Beauty grows proud, I'le borrow him.
    *King.* Is your Boy turn'd away?
    *Are.* You did command Sir, and I obey you.
    *King.* 'Tis well done: Hark ye further.
    *Cle.* Is't possible this fellow should repent? Me thinks that were not noble in him: and yet he looks like a mortified member, as if he had a sick mans Salve in's mouth. If a worse man had done this fault now, some Physical Justice or other, would presently (without the help of an Almanack) have opened the obstructions of his Liver, and let him bloud with a Dog whip.
    *Di.* See, see, how modestly your Lady looks, as if she came from Churching with her Neighbour; why, what a Devil can a man see in her face, but that she's honest?
    *Pha.* Troth no great matter to speak of, a foolish twinkling with the eye, that spoils her Coat; but he must be a cunning Herald that finds it. <*cont.*>

Might have been shut together in one Shed;
And then have taken me some Mountain Girl,
Beaten with Winds, chaſte as the hardned Rocks
Whereon she dwells; that might have ſtrew'd my Bed
With Leaves and Reeds, and with the Skins of Beaſts,                    10
And born at her big Breaſts my large course Issue.
This had been a Life free from Vexation.

*Enter* Endymion.

*End.* Oh wicked Men! an Innocent may walk
Safe among Beaſts; nothing assaults me here.

*Di.* See how they Muster one another! O there's a Rank Regiment where the Devil carries the Colours, and his Dam Drum major, now the world and the flesh come behind with the Carriage.

*Cle.* Sure this Lady has a good turn done her against her will: before she was common talk, now none dare say, Cantharides can stir her, her face looks like a Warrant, willing and commanding all Tongues, as they will answer it, to be tied up and bolted when this Lady means to let her self loose. As I live she has got her a goodly protection, and a gracious; and may use her body discreetly, for her healths sake, once a week, excepting Lent and Dog-days: Oh if they were to be got for mony, what a great sum would come out of the City for these Licences?

*King.* To horse, to horse, we lose the morning, Gentlemen.                    [*Exeunt.*

*Enter two* Woodmen.

*1 Wood.* What, have you lodged the Deer?
*2 Wood.* Yes, they are ready for the Bow.
*1 Wood.* Who shoots?
*2 Wood.* The Princess.
*1 Wood.* No she'l Hunt.
*2 Wood.* She'l take a Stand I say.
*1 Wood.* Who else?
*2 Wood.* Why the young stranger Prince.
*1 Wood.* He shall Shoot in a Stone-bow for me. I never lov'd his beyond-sea-ship, since he forsook the Say, for paying Ten shillings: he was there at the fall of a Deer, and would needs (out of his mightiness) give Ten groats for the Dowcers; marry the Steward would have had the Velvet-head into the bargain, to Turf his Hat withal: I think he should love Venery, he is an old Sir *Tristram*; for if you be remembred, he forsook the Stagg once, to strike a Rascal Milking in a Medow, and her he kill'd in the eye. Who shoots else?
*2 Wood.* The Lady *Galatea.*
*1 Wood.* That's a good wench, and she would not chide us for tumbling of her women in the Brakes. She's liberal, and by my Bow they say she's honest, and whether that be a fault, I have nothing to do. There's all?
*2 Wood.* No, one more, *Megra.*
*1 Wood.* That's a firker I' faith boy; there's a wench will Ride her Haunces as hard after a Kennel of Hounds, as a Hunting-saddle; and when she comes home, get 'em clapt, and all is well again. I have known her lose her self three times in one Afternoon (if the Woods had been answerable) and it has been work enough for one man to find her, and he has sweat for it. She Rides well, and she payes well. Hark, let's go.                    [*Exeunt.*

*Enter* Philaster.

7 have] had                    11 And] Our Neighbours; and have        Breasts my] breasts | My
11–12 Issue. | This] issue. This        13 Men! an] men! | An        Innocent] innocent man
13–14 walk | Safe] walk safe        14 Beasts; nothing] beasts, | Nothing                    14–15 here.
| See! there] here. See,

See! there my troubled Lord sits, as his Soul    15
Were searching out a way to leave his Body.
It grieves me that I'm forc'd to disobey
His laſt Commands; but 'tis not in my Pow'r
To forbear speaking, when I look on him.
I'll make as if I wanted, tho' Heav'n knows    20
I can't, because I do not wish to live.
You that are griev'd can pity; hear, my Lord.
    *Phil.* Is there a Creature yet so miserable
That I can pity?
    *End.*    Oh, my noble Lord,
View my ſtrange Fortune, and beſtow on me    25
Out of good Nature (if my Services
Can merit nothing) so much as may help
To keep this little piece I hold of Life
From Cold and Hunger.
    *Phil.*    Is it thou? Go sell,
For shame, those misbecoming Cloaths thou wear'ſt,    30
And feed thy self with them.
    *End.*    Alas, my Lord,
I can get nothing for them; People here
Think it were Treason for them but to touch
Such gay, fine things.
    *Phil.*    Now, by my Life, this is
Unkindly done to vex me with thy Sight;    35
Thou'rt fallen back to thy dissembling Trade.
How should'ſt thou think to cozen me again?
Remains there yet a Plague untry'd for me?
Ev'n so thou wept'ſt when firſt I took thee up;
Wretch that I was to do so; if thy Tears    40
Can work on any other, use thy Art,

15 troubled Lord sits] griev'd Lord | Sits    15–16 Soul | Were] soul were    16 way
to] way, | To    16–21 Body . . . live] body. Pardon me that must
Break thy last commandment; For I must speak
26 Out . . . Nature] According to your bounty    Services] service    27 help] serve
28 this] that    29–30 Go . . . shame] be gone | Go sell    30 misbecoming]
misbeseeming    31–2 Lord, | I] ~, ~    32–4 them . . . fine] them: | The silly
Country people think 'tis Treason | To touch such gay    36 back] again    39 wept'st]
~ and spok'st    first I] ~ | ~    39–40 up . . . so] up; curse on the time    40–1 thy
Tears | Can] thy | Commanding tears can    41 other, use] other, | Use    41–
2 Art, | I'll] art, I'le

I'll not betray it. Which Way wilt thou take?
That I may shun thee? for thy Eyes to mine
Are Poison; and I'm loth to grow in Rage:
Say, which way wilt thou take?
  *End.*       Which way you please:   45
Since I can't go with you, I have no Choice;
But I'm resolv'd where'er I go to have
That Path in chase which leads unto my Grave. [*Exeunt severally.*

     *Enter* Cleon, *and the Woodmen.*

 *Cleon.* This is the strangest sudden Change! You Woodmen.
 *1 Wood.* My Lord *Cleon.*           50
 *Cleon.* Saw you a Lady come this Way on a sable Horse, and
stubb'd with Stars of white?
 *2 Wood.* Was she not young and tall?
 *Cleon.* Yes. Rode she to the Wood or to the Plain?
 *2 Wood.* Faith, my Lord, we saw none.   [*Ex. Woodmen.* 55

      *Enter* Agremont.

 *Cleon.* Pox o' your Questions then. What is she found?
 *Agr.* Nor will be, I think.
 *Cleon.* Let him seek his Daughter himself! she cannot stir
about a little necessary Business, but the whole Court must be in
Arms; when she has done, we shall have Peace.     60
 *Agr.* There's already a thousand fatherless Tales amongst us;
some say her Horse run away from her; some a Wolf pursu'd her;
others it was a Plot to kill her; and that arm'd Men were seen in
the Wood; but questionless she rode away willingly.

     *Enter King and* Adelard.

 *King.* Where is she?
 *Agr.*     Sir, I cannot tell.
 *King.*       How's that?   65
If thou dost answer so ——
 *Agr.*    Sir, shall I lie?

---

42 Way wilt] way | Wilt   42–3 take? | That] take, that   43 thee? for thy] thee;
| For thine   43–4 to . . . I'm] are poyson to mine; and I | Am   44–5 Rage . . .
take] rage. This way, or that way   45–6 Which . . . go] Any will serve. But I will chuse
48 which] that  *Exeunt*] ~ Phil. *and* Bell.   49 Woodmen] *Woodman*   51 Horse,
and] horse   55 *Ex. Woodmen.*] *Exeunt* Wood.   58 stir] stray   59 necessary]
~ natural   62 from] with   65-6 How's . . . so] How is that? Answer me so again

*King.* Yes, and be damn'd, rather than tell me that;
I say again, where is she? Mutter not;
Sir, speak you where she is.
   *Cleon.*           I do not know.
   *King.* Speak that again so boldly, and by Heav'n      70
It is thy laſt; you, fellows, answer me;
Where is she? Mark me all, I am your King;
I wish to see my Daughter, shew me her,
I do command you all, as you are Subjeſts,
To shew her me: What am I not your King?           75
And are you not t' obey what I command.
   *Cleon.* Yes; if the thing be possible and honeſt.
   *King.* Be possible and honeſt? Hear me, thou,
Thou Traytor, that confin'ſt thy King to what
Is possible and honeſt; shew her me.             80
   *Cleon.* Indeed I can't, till I know where she is.
   *King.* You have betray'd me; you have loſt my Life,
The Jewel of my Life; go, bring her me,
And set her here before me; 'tis the King
Will have it so; whose Breath can ſtill the Winds,      85
Uncloud the Sun, charm down the swelling Seas,
And ſtop the Floods of Heav'n: Can't it? Speak.
   *Cleon.* No.
   *King.*      No? Cannot the Breath of Kings do this?
   *Cleon.* No; nor smell sweet it self, if once the Lungs
Be but corrupted.
   *King.*        Is it so? Take heed.          90
   *Cleon.* Sir, take you heed you do not dare the Pow'rs
That muſt be juſt.
   *King.*        Alas, what are we Kings?
Why do you, Gods, place us above the reſt
To be serv'd, flatter'd, and ador'd, till we
Believe we hold within our Hands your Thunder;     95
And when we come to try the Pow'r we have,

67 and be damn'd] lie and damn      69 she is] is she    I] Sir, ~     73 me her] her
me     76 And . . . command] If I, then am I not to be obeyed?     77 the thing be]
you command things     78 Be] Things     79 confin'st] darest confine
79–80 what | Is possible] things | Possible     80 me] ~, | Or let me perish, if I cover not
all *Cicily* with bloud     81 can't . . . know] cannot, unless you tell me     82 you . . .
Life] y'have, let me lose     84 her here] her     86 Seas] Sea     87 Can't it?
Speak] speak, can it not     91 you do not] how you

There's not a single Leaf shakes at our Threatning?
I've sinn'd, 'tis true, and here stand to be punish'd;
Yet would not thus be punish'd: Let me chuse
My Way, and lay it on.                                    100
    *Cleon.* He articles with Heav'n; would somebody would draw
the Bonds for the Performance of Covenants betwixt them.

          *Enter* Thrasomond, Melesinda, *and* Alga.

    *King.* What, is she found?
    *Thras.*                    No; we have ta'en her Horse,
He gallop'd empty by.
    *King.* You, *Melesinda*, rode with her into          105
The Wood: Why left you her?
    *Mel.*                    She bid me do't.
    *King.* What if she did? You should not have obey'd.
    *Mel.* 'Twould ill become my Fortunes and my Birth
To disobey the Daughter of my King.
    *King.* Y'are willing to obey us for our Hurt;        110
But I will have her.
    *Thras.*            If I have her not,
There shall be no more *Sicily* by Heav'n.
    *Cleon.* Why, what will he carry it away in's Pocket?
    *King.* I see the Injuries I've done must be
Reveng'd.
    *Cleon.* But this will never find her out.            115
    *King.* Run all; disperse your selves; whoe'er he be,
That can but bring her to me shall be happy.
    *Thras.* Come, let us seek.
    *Cleon.*                    Each Man a several Way.   [*Exeunt.*

97 a single] a    Threatning] threatnings      98 I've] I have      101 Heav'n] the gods
somebody] some body      101–2 draw the] draw      104–5 by. | *King.* You] by: there's
some Treason; | You      105–6 into | The] into the      106 bid me do't] did command
me      107 What . . . obey'd] Command! you should not      110 willing] all cunning
112 There . . . Heav'n] By this hand there shall be no more *Cicily*      113 Why, what]
What      away] to *Spain*      Pocket?] pocket?
    *Pha.* I will not leave one man alive, but the King,
A Cook and a Taylor.
    *Di.* Yet you may do well to spare your Ladies Bed fellow, and her you may keep for a
Spawner.      114 I've] I have      114–15 be | Reveng'd] be reveng'd      115 But . . .
never] Sir, this is not the way to      116–17 whoe'er . . . happy] the man that finds her,
Or (if she be kill'd) the Traytor; I'le may him great.
    *Di.* I know some would give five thousand pounds to find her
118 *Cleon*] *King*      Way] way, here I my self. <*cont.*>

*Enter a* Country Fellow.

*Clown.* I'll see the King if he be in the Forest; I have hunted him
these two Hours; if I should go home, and not see him, my Sister       120
would laugh at me. I can meet with nothing but People better
hors'd than my self, that outride me; nor can I hear any thing but
shouting: These Kings had need of good Brains? this whooping is
able to put a mean Man out of his Wit. Well, I'll about it again.
                                                                    [*Exit.*

*Enter* Araminta.

*Ara.* Where am I now? Feet, find me out a Way,                       125
Without the Counsel of my troubled Head;
I'll trust you boldly amidst all these Woods;
O'er Mountains, thorough Brambles, Pits, and Floods.
Heaven I hope will ease me: I am sick.

*Enter* Endymion.

*End.* Yonder's my honour'd Lady, fast asleep:                        130
I fear she faints; the lovely red is gone
To guard her Heart: She breaths not. Madam,
Open once more those rosie Twins, and send
To my dear Lord your last Farewel. She stirs.
How is it, Madam, pray?
*Ara.*                    'Tis not well done                          135
To put me in a miserable Life,
And hold me there: I pray thee let me go;
I shall do best without thee: I am well.

*Enter* Philander.

*Phil.* I was to blame to be so much in Rage;
I'll tell her truly when and where I heard                            140

*Di.* Come Gentlemen we here.
*Cle.* Lady you must go search too.
*Meg.* I had rather be search'd my self          118   *Exeunt*] ~ *omnes*

118.1–124 Enter . . . Wit.] *Precedes 195a in 79fc. See below.*          120 go] come          Sister]
Sisters          121 meet with] see          122 nor can I] I can          any thing] nothing          124 Wit]
wits          127 trust] follow          amidst all] about          130–1 honour'd . . . lovely] Lady;
Heaven knows I want nothing;
Because I do not wish to live, yet I
Will try her Charity. O hear, you that have plenty,
From that flowing store, drop some on dry ground; see,
The lively
131–2 gone | To] gone to          132 Heart: She] heart; | I fear she faints. Madam look up,
she          not. Madam] not          134 To my dear] Unto my          last] latest          She] Oh, she
135 pray] Speak comfort          well] gently          139 was] am          140 truly] coolely

This killing Truth; I will be temperate
In speaking, and as juſt in hearing too.
Oh monſtrous! Tempt me not, you Gods; good Gods,
Tempt not a frail Man: What's he that has a Heart,
But he muſt ease it here?                                            145
    *End.* Are you not better yet?
    *Ara.*                              I'm well forbear.
    *Phil.* Let me love Lightning, let me be embrac'd
And kiss'd by Vipers rather than bear this.
Despair dwell with you; what before my Face?
Nature invent a Curse, and throw it on you:                          150
May Poison grow between your Lips, Diseases
Be your Brood: I'll part you once at leaſt.
               [*Runs at* Endymion, *and hurts* Araminta.
    *Ara.* Oh, dear *Philander*, leave to be inrag'd,
And hear me.
    *Phil.*         I have done; not the calm Sea,
When *Æolus* locks up his windy Crew,                                155
Is less diſturb'd than I: Thus you shall know it;
Dear *Araminta*, do but take this Sword,
And feel how temperate a Heart I have;
Then you, and this your Boy, may live and reign
In Luſt, without controul. Wilt thou, *Endymion*?                    160
I prithee kill me: Thou art poor, and may'ſt
Nourish ambitious Thoughts; were I but dead
There would be nothing then to hinder thee.
Am I mad now? Pray speak: I'm sure I were

---

142 hearing too] hearing    143 you] ye    146 Are . . . yet] My Lord, help the Princess
   I'm] I am    148 Vipers . . . this] Scorpions, or adore the eyes
Of Basilisks, rather than trust to tongues,
And shrink these veins up; stick me here a stone
Lasting to ages in the memory
Of this damn'd act. Hear me you wicked ones,
You have put the hills on fire into this breast,
Not to be quench'd with tears, for which may guilt
Sit on your bosoms; at your meals, and beds
149 dwell with] await    150–152.1 Nature . . . Araminta] Poyson of Aspes between your
lips; Diseases
Be your best issues, Nature make a Curse
And throw it on you
153 Oh, dear] Dear    leave to] leave | To    153–4 inrag'd, | And] enrag'd, and
154 done] done; | Forgive my passion    calm] calm'd    155 Crew] brood    156 Thus
you shall] I'le make you    158 feel] search    162–6 were . . . live:] when I am dead:
This way were freer; Am I raging now?<*cont.*>

If after all the Wrongs I have receiv'd,                    165
I should desire to live: You will not kill
Me then?
  *End.*  Not for a World.
  *Phil.*                    I blame not thee,
*Endymion,* thou haſt done but that which Gods
Would have transform'd themselves to do: Be gone;
Leave me without Reply. This is the laſt          [*Exit* End.  170
Of all our Meetings; come then, kill me with
This Sword; be wise, leſt worse might follow; one
Of us muſt die.
  *Ara.*          Indeed I think I muſt;
My Wound begins to make me faint already.


If I were mad I should desire to live;
Sirs, feel my pulse; whether have you known
A man in a more equal tune to die?
  *Bel.* Alas my Lord, your pulse keeps madmans time,
So does your tongue. *Phi.*

166–7 kill | Me] kill me          167 then] ~? | *Are.* Kill you          170 *Exit* End.] *Not in 79fc*
171 Meetings . . . then] meeting          171–2 with | This] with this          172 Sword; be]
sword; | Be    lest worse might] or worse will          172–203.1 one . . . *Fight*] we are two
Earth cannot bear at once. Resolve to do, or suffer.
  *Are.* If my fortunes be so good to let me fall
Upon thy hand, I shall have peace in death.
Yet tell me this, will there be no slanders,
No jealousies in the other world, no ill there?
  *Phi.* No.
  *Are.* Shew me then the way.
  *Phi.* Then guide
My feeble hand, you that have power to do it,
For I must perform a piece of justice. If your youth
Have any way offended Heaven, let prayers
Short and effectual reconcile you to it.
  *Are.* I am prepared.
                    *Enter a* Country-fellow. [*Cf. 118.1–124.1*]
  *Coun.* I'le see the King if he be in the Forest, I have hunted him these two hours, if I
should come home and not see him my Sisters would laugh at me; I can see nothing but
people better horst than my self, that outride me; I can hear nothing but shouting. These
Kings had need of good brains, this whooping is able to put a mean man out of his wits.
There's a Courtier with his sword drawn, by this hand upon a woman, I think.
  *Phi.* Are you at peace?
  *Are.* With Heavens and Earth.
  *Phi.* May they divide thy soul and body?
  *Coun.* Hold dastard, strike a Woman! 'th'art a craven I warrant thee, thou wouldst be loth
to lay half a dozen of venies at wasters with a good fellow for a broken head.
  *Phi.* Leave us good friend. <*cont.*>

*Phil.* How? What Wound? Where?                                    175
*Ara.* O, touch me gently, there:
I hope 'twill give me ease in t' other World,
For I could never yet find any here.
    *Phil.* My cruel Stars, what have you brought upon me!
Now I defy you all to do your worſt.                               180
    *Ara.* But tell me, pray, are there no Jealousies,
No Slanders, where I'm going? No ill there?
    *Phil.* O, say no more, but help to ſtop thy Wound;
It was not meant to thee, but to the Boy;
That vile, ungrateful Boy.                                         185
    *Ara.* Would you not then have kill'd me? Pray say no,
Whate'er you meant.
    *Phil.*            Can I hear this, and live?
Why would you make me mad? Force me to do
I know not what, and hurt you? Why would you
Disgrace me thus? Why did you love the Boy?                        190
(Curse on th' unhappy Hour when I was born!)
How could you find i' your Heart to use me so?
    *Ara.* Alas, my Soul doats only upon you,
And can love nothing else, whate'er you do.

Enter Clown.

    *Clown.* Hey day! What have we here?
    *Phil.*                Ha! What art thou?            195
    *Clown.* Gods uds, Courtier with his naked Sword upon a
Woman! I think the Rogue has hurt her too; I'm sure she bleeds.
By'r leave, fair Lady, who has hurt you so?
    *Phil.* Good honeſt Friend, pursue thy own Affairs.
    *Clown.* Friend me no Friends; I'll know who hurt the Woman.   200
    *Phil.* Nay leave us, Sirrah, or thou shalt repent it.
    *Clown.* Say'ſt thou so, Boy, I will try that i'faith.
    *Phil.* Slave, doſt thou dare me thus?

---

    *Are.* What ill bred man art thou, to intrude thy self
Upon our private sports, our recreations?
    *Coun.* God 'uds, I understand you not, but I know the Rogue has hurt you.
    *Phi.* Pursue thy own affairs: it will be ill
To multiply bloud upon my head; which thou wilt force me to.
    *Coun.* I know not your Rhetorick, but I can lay it on if you touch the woman.
[They fight.
    *Phi.* Slave, take what thou deservest.

(*They Fight.*)

*Ara.*                   Heav'ns guard my Lord.

[*Clown falls.*]

*Phil.* The Gods take part against me sure, this Boor

[*Noise within.*]

Could ne'er have hurt me else. Here's People coming.      205
What shall I do? Alas, what shall I think?
I heard her pray for me when I was fighting.
Perhaps she may be injur'd. O my Fate!
I either am dishonour'd, or a Wretch
To be despis'd; the very worst of Men.      210

[*Noise again.*]

*Ara.* Fly, fly, my Lord, or your dear Life is lost.
*Phil.* D' ye think I'll leave you thus to save my Life?
*Ara.* Do it then pray, *Philander*, to save mine;
For if you stay indeed I'll bleed to Death;
It is not hard to do: And yet methinks      215
My Wound is nothing now y' are sorry for't.
As soon as you are safe I shall be well.
*Phil.* But I must never hope to be so more.
Kill me, and pardon me; 'tis all I beg.
Farewel then; if thou'rt true, I'll kill my self;      220
And tho' thou should'st deserve the worst of Thoughts,
However, I forgive thee all thy Faults.          [*Exit.*

Enter Thrasomond, Cleon, Agremont, Adelard,
*and Woodmen.*

*Thras.* What art thou?
*Clown.* Almost kill'd I am for a foolish Woman; a Knave has
hurt her.      225
*Thras.* The Princess, Gentlemen! where's the Wound, Madam?
Is it dangerous?

203.2–204 *Clown . . . Phil.*] *Coun.* Oh do you breath?
    *Phi.* I hear the tread of people: I am hurt.
204–22 sure . . . *Exit*] could this Boor
Have held me thus else? I must shift for life,
Though I do loath it. I would find a course,
To lose it, rather by my will than force.          *Exit* Phil.
    *Coun.* I cannot follow the Rogue. I pray thee wench come and kiss me now.

*Ara.* He has not hurt me.

*Clown.* I say she lyes; he has hurt her in the Side: Look else.

*Thras.* O sacred Spring of innocent Blood!                    230

*Cleon.* 'Tis above Wonder who should do this.

*Ara.* I feel it not.

*Thras.* Speak, Villain; who has hurt the Princess?

*Clown.* Is it the Princess?

*Cleon.* I.                                                        235

*Clown.* Then I have seen something yet.

*Thras.* But who has hurt her?

*Clown.* I told you a Rogue: I ne'er saw him before.

*Thras.* Madam, who did it?

*Ara.* Some dishonest Wretch: Alas I know him not, and do    240
forgive him.

*Clown.* He's hurt too, he cannot go far: I made my Father's old
Fox fly about his Ears.

*Thras.* How will you have me kill him?

*Ara.* Not at all; 'tis some distracted Fellow.                   245

*Thras.* By this Hand I'll leave ne'er a piece of him bigger than
a Nut, and bring him all in my Hat.

*Ara.* Nay, good Sir, if you do take him, bring him to me
Alive; and I'll invent some Punishment
For him, great as his Fault.

*Thras.*                    I will.

*Ara.*                                        But swear.          250

*Thras.* Why then i'fecks I will. Wait you upon
The Princess: Woodmen, lead off this poor Man.
Come, Gentlemen, let us pursue our Chase.

> [*Exeunt* Thras. Cleon, Agr. Adel. 1 Wood. *and* Araminta.

*Clown.* I pray you, Freind, let me see the King.

*2 Wood.* That you shall, and receive Thanks.                     255

*Clown.* If I get clear with this, I'll go no more to gay Sights in
haste.                                              [*Exeunt.*

---

229 I say] I'faith      he has] has      Side] breast      231 do] dare      232 feel] felt
238 before] ~, I          240 not, and] not, | And          248 Sir, if] Sir; | If      him] ~ quick
249 Alive . . . some] And I will study for a          250 For him, great] Great          251–3 Why
. . . Chase] By all my love I will: Woodmen conduct the Princess to the King, and bear that
wounded fellow to dressing. Come Gentlemen, we'l follow the chase close.          253.1 Thras
. . . Araminta] Are. Pha. Di. Cle. Thra. *and* 1 Woodman          256–7 no . . . haste] see no
more gay sights

*Enter* Endymion.

*End.* A Heaviness near Death sits on my Brow,
And I muſt sleep; bear me, thou gentle Bank
For ever if thou wilt; you sweet ones all,                           260
Let me unworthy press you; I could wish,
I rather were a Coarse ſtrew'd o'er with you
Than quick above you: Dulness shuts my Eyes,
And I am giddy: O, that I could take
So sound a Sleep as I might never wake.                               265

*Enter* Philander.

*Phil.* Whither shall I go now, or rather why
Should I go any farther? True, I'll end
My Journey here. What should I travel for
With such an odious, tiresom Load upon me,
As now, alas, my Life is grown? And which                            270
I muſt not hope to save whate'er falls out:
For if she's false, I'm sure I cannot live;
And if she should prove true, I'd scorn to do't,
After the Injuries I've basely done her.
Oh why should we thus madly be inclin'd                              275
To think the worse of those we love the moſt?
Ye Gods, it is too great a Tyranny to plague
Mankind at once with Love and Jealousie.
Who's this? *Endymion* sleeping? 'Tis unjuſt
Thy Sleep should be so sound, and mine, whom thou                    280
Haſt wrong'd, so broken. I hope he will not wake:
I'm very loth to kill him, but I feel

263  my] mine          265  as] that          266–78 Whither . . . Jealousie]
I have done ill, my conscience calls me false,
To strike at her, that would not strike at me:
When I did fight, me thought I heard her pray
The gods to guard me. She may be abus'd,
And I a loathed villain: if she be,
She will conceal who hurt her; He has wounds,
And cannot follow, neither knows he me.
279–80 'Tis . . . should] If thou beest
Guilty, there is no justice that thy sleep          [*Cry within.*
Should
280–1 thou | Hast] thou hast          281 wrong'd, so] wrong'd, | So          281–302 I . . . deserv'st]
Hark I am pursued: you gods
I'le take this offer'd means of my escape: <*cont.*>

Something within me that would force me to 't:
If I should but once more behold his Eyes,
They are the Cause of all my Miseries.                                      285
Yet she did vow to me she loves him not;
But who is he dares truſt to Women's Tongues?
They are so us'd to talk before they think,
They know not how to mean one Word they say.
I'm sure I saw him take her in his Arms;                                    290
And he deserves to lose his Life for that.

                      [Endymion *wakes*.]

    *End.*  I cannot sleep, my Heart's too full of Grief;
No sooner are my Eye-lids clos'd, but ſtraight
Methinks I see *Philander* in a Rage,
Ready to ſtrike me dead. Sure there he ſtands:                              295
It muſt be he, for none was ever like him:
I cannot bear his Hatred any longer;
I'll speak, tho' he should kill me for't. Can you
My Lord, be angry with me ſtill?
    *Phil.*                       Forbear;
If thou com'ſt near thou wilt compel me to                                 300
An Aſt I would avoid.
    *End.*            Pray hear me firſt.
    *Phil.* Begone.
    *End.*      I can't.
    *Phil.*          Then take what thou deserv'ſt.

                          [*Wounds him*.]

    *End.* Bleſt be that Hand: Again, for Pity's Sake.
    *Phil.* My Legs now fail me quite with Loss of Blood;
Take your Revenge; I'll teach you Cruelty:                                  305

They have no mark to know me, but my wounds,
If she be true; if false, let mischief light
On all the world at once. Sword, print my wounds
Upon this sleeping boy: I ha' none I think
Are mortal, nor would I lay greater on thee

303  Blest] Oh death I hope is come, blest    Hand: Again] hand, | It meant me well; again
304–8  My . . . *without*] I have caught my self,             [Phi. *falls.*
The loss of bloud hath stayed my flight. Here, here,
Is he that stroke thee: take thy full revenge,
Use me, as I did mean thee, worse than death:
I'le teach thee to revenge this luckless hand
Wounded the Princess, tell my followers
Thou didst receive these hurts in staying me,
And I will second thee: Get a reward.

It was this luckless Hand that hurt the Princess.
Tell my Pursuers, you receiv'd your Wound
In ſtaying me, and I will second it.          [*Noise without.*
   *End.* Oh, fly, and save your self, my Lord.
   *Phil.*                     How's this?
Would'ſt thou I should be safe?
   *End.*                     Else it were vain                    310
For me to live: The Wound you gave me has
Not yet bled much; reach me that noble Hand,
I'll help to cover you.
   *Phil.*           Art thou then true?
   *End.* Or let me perish loath'd; Come, my good Lord,
Creep in among these Bushes; who does know,                   315
But that the Gods may save your precious Life?
   *Phil.* Then shall I die for Grief, if not for this,
That I have wounded thee; what wilt thou do?
   *End.* Shift well enough for one, I warrant you.
   *Within.* Follow, follow; that way they went.                320
   *End.* With my own Wound I'll bloody my own Sword,
I need not counterfeit to fall; Heav'n knows,
That I can ſtand no longer.

     *Enter* Thrasomond, Cleon, Agremont, *and* Adelard.

   *Thras.* I'm sure,
To this Place we have track'd him by his Blood.                  325
   *Agr.* Yonder creeps one away.
   *Cleon.* Stay, what are you?
   *End.* A wretched Creature, wounded in these Woods
By Beaſts; relieve me, if your Names be Men,
Or I shall perish.
   *Cleon.*           This is he, my Lord,                     330
Upon my Soul, that hurt her; 'tis the Boy
That serv'd her.
   *Thras.*           O thou damn'd in thy Creation,
What Cause hadſt thou to hurt the Princess? speak.

309 Oh, fly] Fly, fly my Lord     self, my Lord] self          311–12 The . . . yet] These little
wounds I have, | Ha' not          313 then true] true to me          315 among these] amongst
those          316 precious Life] (much lov'd) breath          317 shall I] I shall          319 well . . .
you] for my self well: peace, I hear 'em come          320 Follow] ~, follow          321 Wound]
wounds          324–5 I'm . . . To] To          326 Yonder] ~, my Lord,          327 Stay] ~ Sir
332 That] ~ wicked boy that          333 hadst thou] could'st thou shape     Princess? speak.]
Princess?

*End.* Then I'm betray'd.
*Cleon.*                         No, apprehended, Sir.
*End.* Well, I confess the Fact, urge it no more.                    335
I set upon the Princess, and design'd
Her Death: For Charity, let fall at once
The Punishment you mean, and do not load
This weary'd Flesh with Tortures.
    *Thras.*                         I will know
Who hir'd thee to this.
    *End.*                My own Revenge.                              340
    *Thras.* Revenge! for what?
    *End.*                         It pleas'd her to receive
Me for her Page, and when my Fortunes ebb'd,
(As Rivers being unsupply'd grow dry)
And Men ſtrid o'er them carelesly; She pour'd
Her welcome Graces on my Wants, and swell'd          345
My Streams so high, that they o'erflow'd their Banks.
Threatning Deſtruction to whoe'er durſt cross 'em.
But then as swift as Storms rise at Sea,
She caſt her fiery Eyes like Lightning on me,
And in an inſtant blaſted all my Hopes;               350
And left me worse, and more contemn'd by far
Than other little Brooks, because I had
Been great: In short I knew I could not live,
And therefore did desire to die reveng'd.
    *Thras.* I'll torture ye i'fecks.
    *Agr.*                         Come lead him hence.      355

334 I'm] I am   No . . . Sir] Betrayed! no, apprehended   335–6 Well . . . design'd] I
confess; | Urge it no more, that big with evil thoughts
I set upon her, and did take my aim
339 weary'd] weary   339–40 know | Who] know who   340 this] ~ deed   My]
Mine   342 for] as   343–4 (As . . . And] That   344 pour'd] did showr
345 my . . . swell'd] me, and did swell   346 Streams . . . that] fortunes, till
o'erflow'd] overflow'd   347–8 Destruction . . . then] the men that crost 'em; when
348 swift as] swift | As   rise] arise   348–51 Sea . . . left] sea, she turn'd her eyes
To burning Suns upon me, and did dry
The streams she had bestowed, leaving
351 worse, and] worse | And   351–2 contemn'd . . . Than] contemn'd than
352 Brooks, because] brooks, | Because   352–3 had | Been] had been   353 knew
I] ~ | ~   353–4 live, | And] live, and   354 desire to] desire | To   355 I'll . . .
Come] If tortures can be found,
Long as thy natural life, resolve to feel
The utmost rigour.                    [Philaster *creeps out of a bush.*
    *Cle.* Help to

[Philander *creeps out.*]

*Phil.* Turn back, you Ravishers of Innocence:
Know you the Price of that you bear away
So rudely?

*Adel.*  Who is this?

*Cleon.*                  The Lord *Philander.*

*Phil.* 'Tis not the Treasure of all Kings in one,
The Wealth of *Tagus*, nor the Rocks of Pearl                    360
That pave the Court of *Neptune*, can weigh down
This Virtue: It was I that hurt the Princess.
Place me some God upon a Pyramis,
Higher than Hills of Earth, and lend a Voice
Loud as your Thunder to me; that from thence                      365
I may declare to all the under World
The Worth that dwells in him.

*Thras.* Who's this?

*End.* My Lord, some Man that's weary of his Life.

*Phil.* Leave these untimely Courtesies, *Endymion*.              370

*End.* Alas, he's mad; come, will you lead me on?

*Phil.* By all the Oaths that Men ought moſt to keep,
And Gods do punish moſt when they are broken,
He touch'd her not. Take heed, *Endymion*,
How thou doſt drown the Virtues thou haſt shewn              375
With Perjury: By all that's good, 'twas I;
You know she ſtood betwixt me and my Right.

*Agr.* It was *Philander.*

*Cleon.*                  'Tis a brave Boy.

*Adel.*                                      I fear,
We were all deceiv'd.

*Phil.* Have I no Friend here?

*Cleon.*                  Yes.

*Phil.*                                      Pray shew it then,       380
Somebody lend a Hand to draw me near him?
Would you have Tears shed for you when you die?

---

355.1 Philander . . . out] *Precedes 355b in 79fc*    357 Know you] ~ ye    357–8 away |
So] away so    358 Who is this] Who's that    The] 'Tis the    362 This] That
366 declare] discourse    368 Who's] How's    369 Man . . . Life] man | Weary of
life, that would be glad to die    373 they are broken] men do break    377 Right]
right. | *Pha.* Thy own tongue be thy judge    378 'Tis] Is't not    Boy. | *Adel.*] boy? |
Well Sirs,    378–9 fear, | We] fear we    380 Pray . . . then] Then shew it
381 Somebody] Some good body    me near him] us nearer

Then lay me gently on his Neck, that there
I may weep Floods, and breath my Spirit out.
'Tis not the Wealth of *Plutus*, nor the Gold　　　　　385
Lock'd in the Heart of Earth, can buy away
This armful from me: You hard-hearted Men,
More ſtony than these Mountains, can you see
Such pure Blood drop, and not cut off your Flesh
To ſtop it with? Queens ought to tear their Hair　　　390
To bind these Wounds, and bathe them with their Tears.
If I had Strength, I'd pluck my Heart out. Oh,
*Endymion!* Thou that art the Wealth of poor
*Philander*, and that I have us'd so ill;
Pray let my Crimes be punish'd as they ought,　　　　395
And don't forgive me, I deserve it not.

　　　　　　　*Enter King, &c.*

*King.* What is the Villain ta'en?
*Thras.*　　　　　　　　　Both these confess
The Deed.
　*Phil.*　Sir, queſtion it no more, 'twas I.
*King.* The Fellow that did fight with him will tell.
*Ara.* Ay me! I know he will.
*King.*　　　　　　　You know him sure.　　　　400
*Ara.* No, Sir; if it was he, he was disguis'd.
*Phil.* I was so. Oh why am I not yet dead?
*King.* Thou vain, ambitious Fool; thou that haſt laid
A Train for thy own Life; now I do mean
To do; I'll leave to talk: Bear him to Prison.　　　　405
　*Ara.* Sir, they did plot together to take hence
This harmless Life; should it pass unreveng'd,

383 gently] gentle　　384 my Spirit out] out my spirit　　387 me] ~,
　　　　　　this had been a ransom
To have redeem'd the great *Augustus Cæsar*,
Had he been taken
389 Such] ~ clear　　cut off] cut　　390 it . . . Queens] his life? To bind whose better
wounds, | Queens　　390–3 Hair . . . *Endymion!*] hair, and with their tears, | Bath 'em.
Forgive me,　　393–6 poor . . . not] poor *Philaster*　　396.1 &c] Arethusa *and a*
Guard　　397 What is] Is　　397–8 Both . . . Deed] Sir, here be two confess the
deed; but say it was *Philaster*　　398 Sir, question] Question　　'twas I] it was　　399 tell]
~ us　　400 You . . . sure.] Did not you know him?　　401 No, Sir] Sir
402 why . . . dead] my stars! that I should live still　　403 Thou vain] Thou　　Fool;
thou] fool; | Thou　　403–4 laid | A] laid a　　404 Life; now] life; | Now
404–5 mean | To] mean to

I should to Earth go weeping; grant me then
(By all the Love a Father bears his Child)
Their Cuſtody, and that I may appoint                         410
Their Tortures, and the Way they are to die.
    *King.* 'Tis granted; take 'em to you with a Guard.
Come, Princely *Thrasomond*, this Business paſt,
We may with more Security go on
To our intended Match.                                        415
                    *[Exeunt all but* Cleon *and* Agremont.
    *Agr.* This Aćtion of *Philander*, I'm afraid,
Will lose the People's Hearts.
    *Cleon.*                   No; fear it not:
Their Subtilty will think it but a Trick.

               *Enter* Adelard.

    *Agr.* How are his Wounds?
    *Adel.*                   They are but Scratches; it
Was only Loss of Blood that made him faint.                   420
    *Cleon.* Come, let's go see him.
    *Adel.*                   No, not yet; The King
Has told the Princess he'll be with her ſtraight,
And that he will examine there *Philander*,
About this Plot; and his Confederates.
    *Cleon.* Sure if he had a Plot, he'd tell us on't.          425
But what a Devil made him hurt the Princess,
I can't imagine what all this should mean.

        *The End of the Fourth Aćt.*

410 Custody] custodies     411 and . . . die] their death.
    *Di.* Death? soft, our Law will not reach that, for this fault     414–15 on | To our] on
to your     415.1–417 *Exeunt* . . . No] *Cle.* I pray that this action lose not *Philaster* the
hearts of the people. | *Di.*     417–18 not: | Their] not, their     418 Subtilty] overwise heads
418.1–427.1 *Enter . . . Act] Exeunt Omnes*     427.1 *The . . . Act.] Not in 79fc.*

## Act V. Scene I.

### Philander, Araminta, Endymion.

*Ara.* Nay, dear *Philander*, pray lament no more.
*End.* For Heavens sake give o'er; we're very well.
*Phil.* Oh *Araminta*, oh *Endymion*, leave
To be thus kind; I shall be shut from Heav'n,
As now from Earth, if you continue so.                              5
I am a Man that have abus'd a pair
Of the moſt truſty ones Earth ever bore:
Can it ſtill bear us all? Forget me, pray,
Think that so great a Wretch could not be born,
As was *Philander*. And for thee, my Boy,                          10
I shall declare Words that will mollifie
The Hearts of Beaſts, to spare thy Innocence.
    *End.* Alas, my Lord, my Life is not a Thing
Worthy your noble Thoughts: 'Tis not a Life,
'Tis but a Piece of Childhood thrown away.                         15
Should I outlive you, I should then outlive
Virtue and Honour; And when that Day comes,

0.1 Philander . . . Endymion] *Enter* Dion, Cleremont, *and* Thrasiline.
    *Thra.* Has the King sent for him to death?
    *Di.* Yes, but the King must know, 'tis not in his power to war with Heaven.
    *Cle.* We linger time; the King sent for *Philaster* and the Headsman an hour ago.
    *Thra.* Are all his wounds well?
    *Di.* All they were but scratches; but the loss of bloud made him faint.
    *Cle.* We dally Gentlemen.
    *Thra.* Away.
    *Di.* We'l scuffle hard before he perish. [*Cf. 94–100.*]                    [*Exeunt.*
                              *Enter* Philaster, Arethusa, *and* Bellario
1–2 pray . . . very] grieve not, we are well.
    *Bell.* Nay good my Lord forbear, we are wondrous
3–4 leave | To] leave to      4 be thus] be      kind; I] ~: | ~      shut] shot      4–5 Heav'n,
| As] Heaven, as      5 Earth, if] Earth, | If      5–6 so. | I] ~; ~      6 Man . . .
abus'd] man, | False to      6–7 pair | Of] pair of      7 ones Earth ever] ones | That
ever earth      7–8 bore: | Can] bore, can      8 it still] it      8–10 all . . . *Philander*]
all? | Forgive and leave me, but the King hath sent
To call me to my death, Oh shew it me,
And then forget me
11 declare Words that] deliver words      16 outlive you] out-live      should] shall

If ever above once I close these Eyes,
May I live spotted for my Perjury.
  *Ara.* And I the miserableſt Maid alive,     20
Do, by the Honour of a Virgin, vow
Never to quit you.
  *Phil.*   Make me not so hated:
People will tear me, when they find you true
To such a Wretch as me: I shall die loath'd.
Enjoy your Kingdoms peaceably, whilſt I     25
For ever sleep forgotten with my Faults.
Every juſt Servant, every Maid in Love
Will have a Piece of me, if you be true.
  *End.* A piece of you? He muſt be one not born
Of Woman, that can cut it, and look on.     30
  *Phil.* Take me in Tears betwixt you; for my Heart
Will break with Shame and Sorrow.
  *Ara.*     Grieve no more.
  *Phil.* Pray tell me now, if you had wrong'd me basely,
And found your Life no Price compar'd to mine?
What is't you would have done?
  *End.*     'Twas a Miſtake.     35
  *Phil.* What if it were?
  *End.*    We would have ask'd your pardon.
  *Phil.* And hope t' enjoy it too?
  *Ara.*    Enjoy it? Yes.
  *Phil.* Would you indeed? Be plain.
  *End.*     We would, my Lord.
  *Phil.* Forgive me then.
  *Ara.*    So, so, 'tis well. Are all
Things ready for our Marriage?

18 above . . . Eyes] I should close these eyes but once  19 Perjury] perjury, | And waste
my limbs to nothing  20 miserablest . . . alive] woful'st maid as ever was,
Forc'd with my hands to bring my Lord to death
21–2 vow . . . you] swear, | To tell no hours beyond it  22 so hated] hated so. | *Are.*
Come from this prison, all joyful to our deaths. | *Phi.*
24 me] I  28 true] ~. | *Are.* My dear Lord say not so  29 you? He] ~? | ~ must
be one] was  29–30 born | Of] born of  30 Woman] women  31 you; for]
you, | For  31–2 Heart | Will] heart will  32 Grieve] Why 'tis well. | *Bell.* Lament
33 Pray . . . if] What would you have done | If  33–4 basely, | And] basely, and had
34 found your] found | My  34–5 mine . . . done] yours? For love Sirs, | Deal with me
truly  35 a Mistake] mistaken, Sir  36 What] Why  We] Then Sir we  your]
you  37 And] ~ have  it too] it  Yes] I  39–41 so, 'tis . . . *Exit*] so. | *Bell.* 'Tis
as it should be now.

*End.* I'll go see; 40
Learn all to love without Design from me. [*Exit.*
  *Phil.* Lead to my Death.
  *Ara.* I hope not so; at leaſt
Thus much I'm sure of, that I won't outlive you:
And that I might the better claim a Right
To end my Days with yours, I have a Prieſt 45
Ready to join our Hands and Hearts together.
  *Phil.* Can there be yet a new Invention found
Still more to shame *Philander?* I muſt now
Fly from her Love, or be her Murderer.
  *Ara.* What means this Pause? Why won't you speak to me? 50
  *Phil.* I know not which is worſt; O my dear Soul,
I dare not truſt your Father's Cruelty;
He is grown hot and speedy in his Rage.
And now I'm Maſter of my self again,
It is not in my Power to do you harm. 55
  *Ara.* Nothing can harm me but your want of Love,
I dread your Coldness, not his Heat nor Rage.
  *Phil.* Ay, but his Hatred againſt me is such,
He would deſtroy you too if you were mine.
  *Ara.* What if he did; I should take Pleasure in't, 60
Had I but you, *Philander,* in my Arms.
  *Phil.* Dear *Araminta,* press me not so far;
Try not my Passion with too ſtrong a Teſt;
Lovers can never very long be wise;
They go too faſt to keep a ſteddy Pace, 65
And mind with too much Violence present things
To take their Measures right of what's to come:
If you inflame me more, my Love will grow
So wild, I shall not have one cool Thought left,
And then I shall undo thee.
  *Ara.* No, you'll make 70
Me bleſt; of all the Race of Womankind
Moſt happy.
  *Phil.* But yet I ——
  *Ara.* What?
  *Phil.* I'm afraid.

---

42–99.1 *Ara . . . Guard*] [*Exeunt.* | *Enter* King, Dion, Cleremont, *and* Thrasiline.

*Ara.* Do not torment me thus, if 'tis for Love
Of me you are so; mark what I shall say;
For Heav'n ne'er yet declar'd a greater Truth;            75
Marry me ſtraight, before my Father comes,
(And you forget how soon he will be here,)
Or, by your Life, which I prize more than mine,
I'll kill my self.
    *Phil.*            Nay, then I muſt obey:
And pardon me, my deareſt *Araminta*,            80
If I, at such a Time of Joy as this,
Can yet have Griefs about me; but I have,
To find that I'm outdone, tho' by thy self,
So far in all the kindeſt Proofs of Love.
    *Ara.* Ah, could my Death to the whole World proclaim,            85
How I love more than you; my Pride would be
So great in having it divulg'd that I
Should scarce (I am afraid) accept of Life,
Tho' to enjoy you ſtill.
    *Phil.*            Come then, my dear,
Let's talk no more, but love, love till we die.            90
    *Ara.* Let's kill our selves with loving furiously,
And so prevent my Father's future Crimes.            [*Exeunt.*

        *Enter* Cleon, Agremont, Adelard.

    *Cleon.* But are you sure the King has sent for him?
    *Adel.* Yes; to the Scaffold; but the King muſt know,
It is in vain for Kings to war with Heav'n.            95
    *Cleon.* You told us tho' the King would hear this Faƈt
Examin'd in the Chamber of the Princess.
    *Adel.* He meant so once, now he has chang'd his Mind.
    *Cleon.* Come then, we'll scuffle hard before he perish.

        *Enter King and a Guard.*

    *King.* Gentlemen, who saw Prince *Thrasomond*?            100
    *Agr.* He's gone and please your Majeſty, to view the City, and
the new Platform, with some Gentlemen attending on him.
    *King.* Is the Princess ready to bring her Prisoners out?
    *Adel.* I'll go see.

---

93–99 *Begins scene in 79fc.*        100 Prince *Thrasomond*] the Prince        101 He's . . .
view] So please you Sir, he's gone to see    City, and] City, | And        102 Gentlemen
attending] Gentlemen | Attending        103 ready to] ready | To        Prisoners] prisoner
104 I'll go see] She waits your Grace

*King.* Tell her, we ſtay.                                           105
*Cleon.* King, you may be deceiv'd yet;
The Head you aim at coſt more setting on
Than to be loſt so slightly.

*Enter* Messenger.

*Mess.* Where's the King?
*King.* Here.                                                       110
*Mess.* Haſte, Sir, to your Strength, and save your self,
The City's in a Mutiny, fearing for Lord *Philander.*
*King.* Bid 'em go hang themselves.
*Cleon.* O, brave Countrymen!
Mutiny, my fine dear Countrymen, Mutiny!                            115
Now my brave valiant Foremen, shew your Weapons,
In Honour of your Miſtresses.

*Enter* Philander, Araminta, *and* Endymion.

*King.* How comes Philander thus to be unbound?
*End.* He is as faſt as Wedlock, Sir, can bind him.

108  slightly] ~: If it must off
Like a wild overflow, that soops before him
A golden Stack, and with it shakes down Bridges,
Cracks the strong hearts of *Pines*, whose Cable roots
Held out a thousand Storms, a thousand Thunders,
And so made mightier, takes whole Villages
Upon his back, and in that heat of pride,
Charges strong Towns, Towers, Castles, Palaces,
And layes them desolate: so shall thy head,
Thy noble head, bury the lives of thousands
That must bleed with thee like a sacrifice,
In thy red ruines.
108.1–117 *Enter . . .* Mistresses] *follows 164.a in 79fc*        117.1 Endymion] Bell. *in a Robe*
*and Garland*        118–23 comes . . . together] now, what Mask is this?
   *Bell.* Right Royal Sir, I should
Sing you an Epithalamium of these lovers,
But having lost my best ayres with my fortunes,
And wanting a celestial Harp to strike
This blessed union on, thus in glad story
I give you all. These two fair Cedar-branches,
The noblest of the Mountain, where they grew
Straightest and tallest, under whose still shades
The worthier beasts have made their layers, and slept
Free from the *Syrian* Star, and the fell Thunder-stroke,
Free from the Clouds, when they were big with humour,
And delivered in thousand spouts, their issues to the earth:
O there was none but silent quiet there! *<cont.>*

*King.* What means this Riddle?
*Ara.*                    He's my Husband, Sir.                    120
*King.* Your Husband, say you? Call the Captain in,
That guards the Citadel; there you shall have
Your Nuptial Joys together: Hear, you Gods,
From this Time do I shake all Title off
Of Father to this Woman, this base Woman;                    125
And what there is of Vengeance in a Lion
Caſt among Dogs, or robb'd of his dear young;
The same inforc'd more terrible, and with
A greater Rage, expeſt from me.
      *Ara.*                    Sir, by
That little Life I've left to swear by, there                    130
Is nothing that can ſtir me from my self:
What I have done, I never shall repent of,

Till never pleas'd fortune shot up shrubs
Base under brambles to divorce these branches;
And for a while they did so, and did raign
Over the Mountain, and choakt up his beauty
With Brakes, rude Thornes and Thistles, till thy Sun
Scorcht them even to the roots, and dried them there:
And now a gentle gale hath blown again
That made these branches meet, and twine together,
Never to be divided: The god that sings
His holy numbers over marriage beds,
Hath knit their noble hearts, and here they stand
Your Children mighty King, and I have done.
      *King.* How, how?
      *Are.* Sir, if you love it in plain truth,
For there is no Masking in't; This Gentleman
The prisoner that you gave me is become
My keeper, and through all the bitter throws
Your jealousies and his ill fate have wrought him,
Thus nobly hath he strangled, and at length
Arriv'd here my dear Husband.
      *King.* Your dear Husband! call in
The Captain of the Cittadel; There you shall keep
Your Wedding. I'le provide a Mask shall make
Your Hymen turn his Saffron into a sullen Coat,
And sing sad Requiems to your departing souls:
Bloud shall put out your Torches, and instead
Of gaudy flowers about your wanton necks,
An Ax shall hang like a prodigious Meteor
Ready to crop your loves sweets.

127 among] amongst        128–9 and . . . expect] more mighty, | Expect        129–30 Sir,
by | That] Sir, | By that        130 I've] I have        130–1 by, there | Is] by, | There's
132 never . . . of] have done without repentance

For Death can be no Bug-bear now to me,
Since *Thrasomond* is not to be my Headsman.
    *Cleon.* Sweet Peace upon thy Soul, thou worthy Woman,     135
Whene'er thou dy'ſt; for this Time I'll excuse thee,
Or be thy Prologue.
    *Phil.*         Sir, let me speak next;
And let my dying Words persuade you more
Than my dull Life has done: If you design,
Or wish a Wrong to her sweet Innocence,     140
You are a Tyrant, and a Savage one;
The Memory of all your better Deeds
Shall be in Water writ, but this in Marble:
No Chronicle shall speak you, tho' your own,
But for the Shame of Men; No Monument     145
(Tho' high and big as *Pelion*) shall be able
To cover this base Murther: Make it rich
With Brass, with pureſt Gold, and shining Jasper,
Like Pyramids, and lay on Epitaphs,
Such as make great Men Gods; my little Marble     150
(That only cloaths my Ashes, not my Faults)
Shall far outshine it: And for After-issues,
Think not so madly of the heav'nly Wisdoms,
That they will give you more for your mad Rage
To cut off thus, unless it be some Snake,     155
Or something like your self, that in his Birth
Shall ſtrangle you: Think of my Father, King,
There was a Fault; but I forgive it; let
That Sin persuade you to be careful of

133 now to] unto     134 Since . . . be] So long as *Pharamond* is not     135 Woman]
maid     138 persuade you more] be better with you     139 Life has done] living
actions     139–40 design . . . Innocence] aime | At the dear life of this sweet Innocent
141 You are] Y'are     one] Monster     142 The Memory of] Your memory shall be as
foul behind you
As you are living
149 Pyramids, and] the Pyramids,     155 off thus] off     155–6 Snake, | Or] Snake,
or     156 something like] something | Like     156–7 Birth | Shall] birth shall
157 you: Think of] you. | Remember     157–8 King, | There] King; there     158 Fault;
but] fault, | But     158–59 let | That] let that     159–64 you . . . happy] you | To love
this Lady. If you have a soul,
Think, save her, and be saved, for my self,
I have so long expected this glad hour,
So languisht under you, and daily withered,
That heaven knows it is my joy to dye, <*cont.*>

Your matchless Daughter; spare but her dear Life,          160
And I'll surrender you my own with Joy;
Tho' I confess I now could wish to live,
For I in her have all this World can give
To make me happy.

*Enter another* Messenger.

*Mess.*          Arm, Sir, quickly, or
'Twill be too late; the City's up in Arms,          165
Led by an old gray Ruffian that has seiz'd
Upon Prince *Thrasomond*, and swears he'll kill
Him, if *Philander* be not ſtraight releas'd.
*King.* A thousand Devils take 'em.
*Cleon.* A thousand Blessings on 'em, and on all          170
Will take their Parts; I'm sure that I'll make one.
*King.* Come, to the Citadel; I'll see these safe,
                              [*Ex. with* Philander *and* Araminta.]
And then cope with these Burghers. Let the Guard,
And all the Gentlemen, give ſtrong Attendance.          [*Exit.*

*Manent* Cleon, Agremont, Adelard.

*Agr.* The City up! this was above our Wishes.          175
*Cleon.* I, and the Marriage too; now by my Life

I find a recreation in't.
                              *Enter a* Messenger. [*Cf. 108.1–117.*]
*Mess.* Where's the King?
*King.* Here.
*Mess.* Get you to your strength,
And rescue the Prince *Pharamond* from danger,
He's taken prisoner by the Citizens,
Fearing the Lord *Philaster.*
*Di.* Oh brave followers;
Mutiny, my fine dear Country-men, mutiny,
Now my brave valiant foremen, shew your weapons
In honour of your Mistresses.
                              *Enter another* Messenger.

164–71 Arm . . . one] Arm, arm, arm.
    *King.* A thousand devils take 'em.
    *Di.* A thousand blessings on 'em.
    *Mess.* Arm O King, the City is in mutiny,
Led by an old Gray Ruffin, who comes on
In rescue of the Lord *Philaster.*          [*Exit with* Are. Phi. Bell.   [See *EN*]
172 Come] Away          these] them          172–172.1 safe . . . Araminta] safe          174 *Exit*]
*Ex. King*          176 too; now] too;

This noble Lady has deceiv'd us all:
A Plague upon my self, a thousand Plagues,
For having such unworthy Thoughts of her
Dear Honour. Oh, how I could beat my self?      180
Preethee beat me, and I'll beat thee again,
For we had both one Thought.
  *Agr.*            No, 'twill lose time.
  *Cleon.* Are your Swords sharp? Well my dear Countrymen,
what d'ye lack? if you continue and fall not back upon the firſt
broken Shin, I'll have you chronicled and chronicled, and cut and    185
chronicled, and all to be prais'd, and sung in Sonnets and new
Ballads, that all Tongues shall troul you in *Sæcula Sæculorum*, my
kind Can-carriers.
  *Adel.* What if a Toy take 'em in th' Heels now, and they run
all away, and cry the Devil take the hindmoſt?      190
  *Cleon.* Then the same Devil take the foremoſt too, and souce
him for his Breakfaſt; if they all prove Cowards, my Curses fly
amongſt them, and be speeding. May they have Murrains reign,
to keep the Gentlemen at home unbound in easie Freeze: May the
Moths branch their Velvets, and their Silks only be worn before    195
sore Eyes. May their false Lights undo 'em, and discover Presses,
Holes, Stains and Oldness in their Stuffs, and make 'em Shop-rid.
May they keep Whores and Horses, and break; and live mew'd up
with Necks of Beef and Turneps. May they have many Children,
and all ugly like the Fathers. May they know no Language, but    200
that Gibberish they prattle to their Parcels, unless it be the
*Gothick Latin* they write in their Bonds, and may they write that
false, and lose their Debts.

*Enter* King.

  *King.* A Vengeance take 'em, what a Hum they make!

177–8 all: | A] all, a      178–9 Plagues, | For] plagues, for      179–80 her | Dear] her
dear     180 Oh, how] O     180–1 self? | Preethee] self, or do you     181–2 thee
again, | For] you, for     182 both] all     'twill] no, ~ but     183 Are] You say true, ~
184 d'ye] ye     186 new] bath'd in ~ brave     187 in] *in*     189 in th'] i'th'
191 souce] sowce     197 'em] them     200 all ugly] none     200 Fathers] Father
202 *Gothick*] goarish     203.1 *Enter*] ~ *the*     204–8 A . . . once.] Now the vengeance
of all the gods confound them; how they swarm together! what a hum they raise; Devils
choak your wilde throats; If a man had need to use their valours, he must pay a Brokage for it,
and then bring 'em on, they will fight like sheep. 'Tis *Philaster*, none but *Philaster* must allay
this heat: They will not hear me speak, but fling dirt at me, and call me Tyrant. Oh run dear
friend, and bring the Lord *Philaster*: speak him fair, call him Prince, do him all the courtesie
you can, commend me to him. Oh my wits, my wits!     [*Exit* Cle.

They swarm like Bees, and (like 'em) buz together:     205
They have no Sense of any thing but Noise,
And therefore will not hear, but bawl ſtill all
At once.
    *Cleon.* Oh my brave Countrymen! as I live I will not buy a Pin
from out your Walls for this; nay you shall cozen me too, and     210
I'll thank you for't.
    *King.* There is no ſtopping them, they're grown so ſtrong,
Except they see *Philander*; one kind Look
Of his would send them home as tame as Sheep:
To me they're fierce as Lions, and they've Reason.     215
Why should I hope for Help in my Diſtress,
That ne'er could pity any one alive?
We think our selves so far above Mankind,
That 'tis beneath us to be juſt or grateful.
Alas, my Faults are numberless.
    *Cleon.*           Yes, and     220
Your Virtues are so too; for you have none.
    *King.* I see I muſt release him now: It goes
Againſt my Heart to do a virtuous Aƈt;
But there's no Remedy. Who's there? Go bring
*Philander* hither.
    *Cleon.*      What can all this mean?     [*Exit* Adelard.    225
    *King.* Ah, if we Princes did consider well,
We are but Men as frail as others are,
As subjeƈt to Misfortunes, and as mortal;
That if the Powers above have made us great,
'Tis that we should with Juſtice rule their People;     230
That Nations were not born to make us Sport,
But we to make them glorious, safe, and happy;
All our Concerns the Gods would favour more,
And Men would all such Kings like Gods adore.

Enter Agremont and Philander.

---

210 from out] out of    me too] me       211 for't] and send you Brawn and Bacon, and soil
you every long vacation a brace of foremen, that at *Michaelmas* shall come up fat and kicking
212–34 There . . . adore] What they will do with this poor Prince, the gods know, and I fear.
    *Di.* Why Sir: they'l flea him, and make Church Buckets on's skin to squench rebellion,
then clap a rivet in's sconce, and hang him up for a sign.
234.1 and] *with*

O, worthy Sir, forgive me; do not make                                    235
Both my Offences, and your Wrongs combine
To bring on greater Dangers; be your self,
Still sound amongſt Diseases; If I've done
You Injury, I'll make you now amends;
Calm but the People, and my Daughter's yours;                             240
Take her, and with her my Repentance, Sir,
My Wishes, and my Prayers: You shall be,
What you were born to be, King of this Land.
Do not miſtruſt me; if the leaſt untruth
Falls from me now, may I be ſtruck with Thunder.                          245
    *Phil.*  I will not do your Majeſty the Wrong
To doubt your Word; let but the Princess, and
The Boy be free, and I will ſtand alone
The Shock of all this Rabble; which I'll quell,
Or perish in th' Attempt.
    *King.*            Your Word already                 250
Has done that: Go, fetch 'em hither ſtraight.
    *Phil.*  Then thus I take my Leave, kissing your Hand,
And truſting to your Royal Promise, Sir.
Be not diſturb'd: I'll bring you back the Peace
You wish for.
    *King.*    All the Gods attend upon you.    [*Exeunt.*  255

---

236 Both . . . combine] Your miseries and my faults meet together    237 on] a
Dangers] danger        238–41 If . . . and] I have wrong'd you,
And though I find it last, and beaten to it,
Let first your goodness know it. Calm the people,
And be what you were born to: take your love,
And
241–2 Sir, | My] and my        242 Wishes, and] wishes, | And all    242–5 You . . . may]
by the gods my heart speaks this:
And if the least fall from me not perform'd,
May
245–51 I . . . straight] Mighty Sir,
I will not do your greatness so much wrong,
As not to make your word truth; free the Princess,
And the poor boy, and let me stand the shock
Of this mad Sea breach, which I'le either turn
Or perish with it.
    *King.*    Let your own word free them
253–5 trusting . . . for] hanging on your Royal word: be Kingly,
And be not moved Sir, I shall bring your peace,
Or never bring my self back
255 attend upon you] go with thee    *Exeunt*] ~ *Omnes*

*Enter an old Captain and Citizens with* Thrasomond.

*Cap.* Come, my brave *Myrmidons*, let's fall on, let our Caps
swarm, my Boys, and your nimble Tongues forget your Mother
Gibberish of *What do you lack*, and set your Mouths up, Children,
till your Palates fall frighted half a Fathom paſt the Cure of Bay
Salt and gross Pepper, and then cry *Philander*, brave *Philander*, let    260
*Philander* be deeper in requeſt, my Ding-dongs, my pair of dear
Indentures, King of Clubs, than your cold Water Chamlets, or
your Paintings spitted with Copper; let not your haſty Silks, or
your branch'd Cloth of Bodkin, or your Tissues, dearly belov'd of
Spice Cake and Cuſtard, your *Robin Hoods* and *Johns*, tie your    265
Affe&#x010D;tions in Darkness to your Shops; no, dainty Duckers, up
with your three-pil'd Spirits, your wrought Valours, and let your
uncouth Choler make the King feel the Measure of your
Mightiness. *Philander*, cry, my Rose-Nobles, cry.
*All.* *Philander, Philander.*    270
*Cap.* How do you like this, my Lord Prince? These are mad
Boys, I tell you these are things that will not ſtrike their Topsails
to a Foiſt, and let a Man of War, an *Argosie*, hull and cry Cockles.
*Thras.* Why, you rude Slaves, do you know what you do?
*Cap.* My pretty Prince of Puppets, we do know,    275
And give your Greatness warning that you talk
No more such Bugs Words, or that solder'd Crown
Shall be scratch'd with a Musquet: Dear Prince *Pepin*,
Down with your noble Blood, or as I live
I'll have you coddled. Let him loose, my Spirits;    280
Make a round ring with your Bills, my He&#x010D;tors,
And let us see what this trim Man dares do.
Now, Sir, have at you; here I hit you,
And with this swashing Blow, (do you sweat Prince?)
I could hulk your Grace, and hang you up cross-legg'd,    285

256-7 Caps swarm] caps | Swarm     257 and your] and you     257-8 Mother
Gibberish] mothers | Gibberish     258 Mouths up] mouths | Up     259 a Fathom] ~
| ~     260 Pepper, and] Pepper. | And    *Philander*, let] *Philaster*, Let     261 Ding-
dongs, my] ding-dongs, | My     pair] pairs     262 Clubs, than] Clubs, | Than
263 Paintings spitted] paintings | Spitted    Silks, or] Silks, | Or     264 Tissues, dearly]
Tishues, | Dearly     265 Spice] spiced    Custard, your] Custard, | Your    *Hoods*]
hoods scarlets     266 Affections in] affections | In    Duckers, up] Duckers, | Up
267 Valours, and] valours. | And     268 uncouth Choler] un-cut Coller    feel the] feel
| The     269 *Philander*, cry] *Philaster*. | Cry     274 Slaves] slave     278 *Pepin*]
Pippen     280 loose] lose     281 Make] ~ us     283 hit you] it     284 sweat]
swear

Like a Hare at the Poulterer's, and do this with this Wiper.

*Thras.* You will not see me murder'd, wicked Villains?

*1 Cit.* Yes indeed will we, Sir, we have not seen one so this great while.

*Capt.* He would have Weapons, would he? Give him a Broad- 290
side, my brave Boys, with your Pikes; branch me his Skin in
Flowers like a Satin, and between every Flower a Mortal Cut;
your Royalty shall ravel; jagg him Gentlemen. I'll have him cut to
the Kell, and down the Seams. Oh for a Whip to make him
Galoon Laces: I'll have a Coach Whip.                    295

*Thras.* O, spare me, Gentlemen.

*Cap.* Hold, hold; the Man begins to fear, and know himself,
he shall, for this time, only be seal'd up with a Feather thro' his
Nose, that he may only see Heav'n, and think whither he's a going;
Nay (beyond Sea, Sir,) we will proclaim you:                    300
You would be King?
Thou tender Heir apparent to Church Ale,
Thou slight Prince of single Sarcenet;
Thou Royal Ring-tail, fit to fly at nothing
But poor Men's Poultry, and have every Boy                    305
Beat thee from that too with his Bread and Butter.

*Thras.* Gods keep me from these Hell-Hounds.

*2 Cit.* Shall's geld him, Captain?

*Capt.* No, you shall spare his Dowcets, my dear Donsels,
As you respect the Ladies, let them flourish:                    310
The Curses of a longing Woman kills
As speedily as a Plague, Boys.

*1 Cit.* I'll have a Leg, that's certain.

*2 Cit.* I'll have an Arm.

*3 Cit.* I'll have his Nose, and at my own Charge                    315
Build a College, and clap't upon the Gate.

*4 Cit.* I'll have his little Gut to String a Kit with;
For certainly a Royal Gut will sound
Like Silver.

---

286 the Poulterer's] a Poulters        288 this] a        292 and] then        294 Whip to]
whip | To        295 Laces: I'll] Laces, | I'le        297–8 himself, he] himself, | He
298 up with] up | With        299 see Heav'n] ~ | ~    he's a] he's        300–1 you, |
You] you, you        302 to] ~ a        303 slight] sleight        311–12 kills | As] kill as
312 speedily] speedy        315 my] mine        315–16 Charge | Build] charge build
318–19 sound | Like] sound like        319 Silver] silver. | *Pha.* Would they were in thy
belly, and I past my pain once

*5 Cit.* Good Captain, let me have his Liver to feed Ferrets.    320
*Cap.* Who will have Parcels else? Speak.
*Thras.* Good Gods, consider me; I shall be tortur'd.
  *1 Cit.* Captain, I'll give you the trimming of your Hand-
Sword, and let me have his Skin to make false Scabbards.
  *2 Cit.* He had no Horns, Sir, had he?    325
*Cap.* No, Sir, he's a Pollard. What would'ſt thou do with Horns?
  *2 Cit.* Oh! if he had, I would have made rare Hafts and
Whiſtles of them, but his Shin Bones, if they be sound, will serve
me well enough.

Enter Philander.

*All.* Long live *Philander!* the brave Prince *Philander.*    330
  *Phil.* I thank you, Gentlemen, but why are these
Rude Weapons brought abroad to teach your Hands
Uncivil Trades?
  *Cap.*        My Royal Rosicleer,
We are thy Myrmidons, thy Guards, thy Roarers;
And when this noble Body is in durance,    335
Thus do we clap our muſty Murriay on,
And trace the Streets in terror. Is it Peace,
Thou *Mars* of Men? Is the King sociable,
And bids thee live? Art thou above thy Foe, Man?
And free as *Phœbus?* Speak; if not, this Stand    340
Of Royal Blood shall be a broach, a tilt, and run
Ev'n to the Lees of Honour.
  *Phil.* Hold, and be satisfy'd, I am my self,
Free as my Thoughts are, by the Gods I am.
  *Cap.* Art thou the dainty Darling of the King?    345
Art thou the *Hylas* to our *Hercules?*
Do the Lords bow, and the regarded Scarlets,
Kiss their gam'd Goles, and cry we are your Servants?
Is the Court navigable, and the Presence ſtuck
With Flags of Friendship? If not we are thy Caſtle,    350
And this Man sleeps.
  *Phil.* I am what I desire to be, your Friend,
I am what I was born to be, your Prince.

---

325 *2 Cit.*] 2      327 *2 Cit*] *Cit*      328 them] 'em    will] shall      329 me well
enough] me      334 Guards] Guard      335 this] thy      336 Murriay] Murrions
339 Foe, Man] foemen      341 a . . . tilt] abroach, atilt      348 gam'd Goles] Gumd
gols      349 stuck] struck

And what, Sir, say you now?

*Thras.* For God's Sake set me firſt free, and I'll say any thing;    355
I am so afraid I know not what to say.

*Phil.* I do pity thee. Friends, discharge your Fears,
Deliver me the Prince. I'll warrant you,
I shall be old enough to find my Safety.

*Cap.* Prince, by your leave, I'll have a Sursingle,    360
And make you like a Hawk.

*Phil.* Away, away, there is no Danger in him:
Look you, Friends, how gently he leads; upon my Word
He's tame enough, he needs no farther watching:
Good Friends, go to your Houses,    365
And by me have your Pardons and my Love.
And know there shall be nothing in my Pow'r
You may deserve, but you shall have your Wishes.
To give you more Thanks were to flatter you:
Continue ſtill your Love, and for an earneſt,    370
Die with this.

*All.* Long may'ſt thou live brave Prince, brave Prince, brave
Prince.

                        [*Ex.* Philander *and* Thrasomond.

*Cap.* Thou art the King of Courtesy.
Fall off again, my sweet Youths, and every Man trace to his House    375
again, and hang his Pewter up, thence to the Tavern, and bring
your Wives in Muffs; we will have Musick, and red Grape shall
make us dance and reel, Boys.        [*Ex. omnes.*

354–6 And . . . say] *Pha.* Sir, there is some humanity in you,
You have a noble soul, forget my name,
And know my misery, set me safe aboard
From these wild *Canibals*, and as I live,
I'le quit this Land for ever: there is nothing,
Perpetual prisonment, cold, hunger, sickness
Of all sorts, all dangers, and all together
The worst company of the worst men, madness, age,
To be as many Creatures as a woman,
And do as all they do, nay to despair;
But I would rather make it a new Nature,
And live with all those than endure one hour
Amongst these wild Dogs.

357 thee] you       359 Safety] safety. | 3 *Cit.* Good Sir take heed he does not hurt you,
He's a fierce man I can tell you Sir
361 make] Male   Hawk] ~. [*He stirs*    362 him] ~: | Alas he had rather sleep to shake
his fit off    364 needs] need   farther] further    365 Good] ~ my
365–6 Houses, | And] houses and    371 Die with] Drink    375 Youths,] youths,
come Man trace] man | Trace    376 thence] then   to the] to | The    377 have
Musick] ~ | ~   and] ~ the    378 reel] rise   *Ex. omnes*] *Exeunt*

    *Enter King,* Araminta, Melesinda, Alga, Cleon,
    Agremont, Adelard, Endymion, *and Attendants.*

*King.* Is it appeas'd?
*Cleon.* Sir, all is quiet as this Dead of Night,          380
As peaceable as Sleep. The Lord *Philander*
Does bring Prince *Thrasomond* away himself.
  *King.* I will not break a Word that I have giv'n
In promise to him: I have heap'd a World
Of Grief upon his Head, which yet I hope          385
To wash away.

          *Enter* Philander *and* Thrasomond.

*Cleon.*      My Lord is come.
*King.*               My Son,
Blest be the Time that I of Right to call
Such Virtue mine. Now thou art in my Arms,
Methinks I find a Salve to my sick Bosom
For all the Wounds I find there; Streams of Grief      390
I have thrown on thee, but I find much Joy,
That I repent it, issue from my Eyes.
Let them appease thee, take thy Right, take her,
She is thy Right too, and forget to urge
My vexed Soul for what I once have done.          395
  *Phil.* Sir, all is blotted from my Memory:
For you, young Prince of Spain,
Whom I have thus redeem'd, you have full Leave
To make your honourable Voyage home.
And if you would go furnish'd to your Realm          400
With fair Diversion, I do see a Lady
Methinks would gladly bear you Company.
How like you, Sir, this Piece?
  *Alga.* Sir, he likes it well,
For he has try'd it, and found it worth          405

378.1-2 Cleon, Agremont] Cle. Dion    381 The] my    382 Does . . . away] Brings on
the Prince    383 *King.* I] *King.* Kind Gentlemen! | I    a Word that] the least word
387 of Right] have leave    388 my] mine    389 find] have  to . . . Bosom] unto
my breast    390 Wounds I find] stings that dwell    391 I . . . much] That I have
wrought thee, and as much of    392 my] mine    395 for . . . done] with that I did
before    396 all is] is it    397 For] Past and forgotten: ~ you, young] you
399 your] an    401 Diversion] provision    403 you, Sir] you    405 has] hath

His Princely Liking. We were ta'en a bed,
I know your Meaning. I am not the firſt
That Nature taught to seek a handsom Fellow.
Can Shame remain perpetually in me,
And not in others? Or have Princes Salves          410
To cure ill Names, that meaner People want?
 *Phil.* What mean you?
 *Alga.*     You muſt get another Ship
To bear the Princess, and the Boy together.
 *Cleon.* How now?
 *Alga.* Others took me, but I took her and him,          415
As that all Women may be ta'en sometimes,
Ship us all four; we can endure
Weather and Wind alike.
 *King.* Clear then thy self, or call me not thy Father.
 *Ara.* 'Tis false as Heav'n is true, but what Means          420
Is left to clear my self? It lies in your Belief.
My Lords, believe me, and let all things else
Struggle together to dishonour me.
 *End.* O! ſtop your Ears, great King, that I may speak
As Freedom would, then I will call this Lady          425
As base as are her Actions: Hear me, Sir,
Believe your heated Blood when it rebels
Againſt your Reason, sooner than this Lady.
 *Alga.* I vow the Boy acts his Part full well.
 *Phil.* This Lady; I will sooner truſt the Winds          430
Or Seas than her. I say, believe her not.
Why think you if I did believe her Words,
I would outlive 'em!
 *King.* Forget her; since, all is firm between us;
But I muſt requeſt of you one Favour,          435
And will not be deny'd.

408 handsom Fellow] fellow forth  413 bear] clear  415 but] and
417 four] ~ my Lord  419 then] thou  call . . . thy] know not me for  420 'Tis .
. . but] This earth, How false it is?  420–1 Means | Is] means is
421 left to] left for me | To  426 are] be  427 your heated] hour hated
429 I . . . well] By this good light he bears it hansomely  430–1 Winds . . . Seas] wind |
With Feathers, or the troubled Sea with Pearl  431 her. I say] her with any thing
433 'em] ~: honour cannot take
Revenge on you, then what were to be known
But death?
434 her] ~ Sir  firm between] knit | Between  434–5 us; | But] us: but  435 you
one] you | One  435–6 Favour, | And] favour, and
436 not] sadly  deny'd] denied. | *Phi.* Command what ere it be.
 *King.* Swear to be true to what you promise

*Phil.* By all the Powers let it not be the Death
Of her or him, and it is surely granted.
  *King.* Bear away that Boy
To Torture, I will have her clear'd or bury'd.    440
  *Phil.* O give my Promise back, O Royal Sir,
Ask something else, bury my Life and Right
In one poor Grave; but take not from me
My Life and Fame at once.
  *King.* Away with him; his Doom's irrevocable.    445
  *Phil.* Turn all your Eyes on me, here ſtands a Man,
The falseſt and the baseſt of the World.
Set Swords againſt this Breaſt, some honeſt Man,
For I have liv'd to be the moſt accurs'd.
  *End.* Be patient, Sir, I soon will make you easy.    450
I cannot tamely see your Pain for me;
My hapless Fortune much rather I'll reveal.
  *King.* Will he then confess?
  *Cleon.* He seems to say so.
  *King.* Speak then.    455
  *End.* Great King, if you command
This Lord to talk with me alone my Tongue,
Urg'd by my Heart, shall utter all the Thoughts

---

437 all . . . let] the powers above, | Let    437–8 Death | Of] death of    438 him,
and] him, | And    is surely] is    439 that] the    441 give . . . Royal] let me call my
words back, worthy    443–4 take . . . My] do not take away my    445 his Doom's]
it stands    447 of the] of this    449 to . . . accurs'd] till I am pitied,
My former deeds are hateful, but this last
Is pitifull, for I unwillingly
Have given the dear preserver of my life
Unto his Torture: is it in the power    [*Offers to kill himself.*
Of flesh and blood, to carry this and live?
450–2 *End.* Be . . . reveal] *Are.* Dear Sir be patient yet, or stay that hand.
  *King.* Sirs, strip that boy.
  *Di.* Come Sir, your tender flesh will try your constancie.
  *Bell.* O kill me gentlemen.
  *Di.* No, help Sirs.
  *Bell.* Will you Torture me?
  *King.* Hast there, why stay you?
  *Bell.* Then I shall not break my vow,
You know just gods, though I discover all.
453 Will] How's that? ~    he then] he    454 He . . . so] Sir, so he says

My Youth has known, and ſtranger things than these
You hear not often.
    *King.*           Walk aside with him.         460
    *Cleon.* Why speak'ſt thou not?
    *End.*              Know you this Face, my Lord?
    *Cleon.* No.
    *End.* I have been often told
In Court of an *Euphrosyne*, a Lady,
And Daughter to you, between whom and me      465
There was such ſtrange Resemblance, that we Two
Could not be known asunder, dreſt alike.
    *Cleon.* By Heav'n, and so there is.
    *End.* For her Sake,
Who now does spend the Spring Time of her Life    470
In holy Pilgrimage, move the King,
That I may scape this Torture.
    *Cleon.*           But thou speak'ſt
As like *Euphrosyne* as thou doſt look.
How came it to thy Knowlege that she lives
In Pilgrimage?      475
    *End.* I know it not, my Lord, but have heard it,
And do scarce believe it.
    *Cleon.* Oh my Shame! is't possible? Draw near,
That I may gaze upon thee? Art thou she,
Or else her Murderer? Where waſt thou born?    480
    *End.* In *Syracuse.*
    *Cleon.* What's thy Name?
    *End.* *Euphrosyne.*
    *Cleon.* 'Tis she!
Now I do know thee: Oh! that thou hadſt dy'd,    485
And I had never seen thee, nor my Shame!
How shall I own thee? Shall this Tongue of mine
E'er call thee Daughter more?
    *End.* Would I had dy'd indeed; I wish it too,

---

459 has] hath    462 No] ~. | *Bell.* Have you not seen it, nor the like?
    *Di.* Yes, I have seen the like, but readily
I know not where.
464 an] one    465 between] betwixt    me] ~ | (They that would flatter my bad face
would swear)    469 her] ~ fair    470 does] doth    471 move] ~ to    472 speak'st
as] speak'st | As    474–5 lives | In] lives in    476 Lord, but] Lord | But I
476–7 it, | And] it, and    480 wast] wert    484 'Tis] O 'tis just, ~    484–5 she! |
Now] she now    489–90 too, | E'er] too, | And so I must have done by vow, e're

E'er publish'd what I have told;                              490
But that there was no Means
To hide it longer: Yet I joy in this,
The Princess is all clear.
    *King.* What have you done?
    *Cleon.* All is discover'd.                          495
    *Ara.* What is discover'd?
    *Cleon.* Why, my Shame.
It is a Woman, let her speak the reſt.
    *Phil.* How! that again.
    *Cleon.* It is a Woman.                             500
    *Phil.* Bleſt be the Pow'rs that favour Innocence.
    *King.* Lay hold upon that Lady.
    *Phil.* It is a Woman; hark ye, Gentlemen,
It is a Woman! *Araminta*, take
My Soul into thy Breaſt, that could be gone                   505
With Joy! It is a Woman; thou art fair,
And virtuous ſtill to Ages, in despight of Malice.
    *King.* Speak you, where lies his Shame?
    *End.* I am his Daughter.
    *Phil.* The Gods are juſt.                          510
    *Cleon.* I dare accuse none; but before you two
The Virtue of the Age, I bend my Knee
For Mercy.
    *Phil.*    Take it freely; for I know
It was well meant.
    *Ara.* And for me,                                  515
I have the Will to pardon Sins as oft
As any Man has Power to wrong me.
    *Cleon.* Noble and worthy!
    *Phil.*    But, *Endymion*,
(For I muſt call thee ſtill so) tell me why
Thou didſt conceal thy Sex? It was a Fault,                   520
A Fault, *Endymion*, tho' thy other Deeds

490 publish'd what] published | What    490–1 told; | But] told, but    495 discover'd]
~. | *Phi.* Why then hold you me?
    *Di.* All is discovered, pray you let me go.    [*He offers to stab himself.*
    *King.* Stay him.
497–8 Shame. | It] shame, it    501 the] you    503 hark ye] Sir, hark    505 could]
would    512 the] our    514 It . . . meant] Though what thou didst were
undiscreetly done, | 'Twas meant well    516 the Will] a power    518 *Cleon*] *Cle*

Of Truth outweigh'd it. All these Jealousies
Had flown to nothing, if thou hadſt discover'd
What now we know.

    *End.*　　　　　　My Father oft would speak
Your Worth and Virtue with a zealous Praise,　　　　　525
Which as I grew in Age encreas'd a Thirſt
Of seeing of a Man so rais'd above the reſt.
But this was but the Child of Curiosity,
Till Fate one Day brought you to my Father's,
And I was order'd there to entertain you.　　　　　530
Oh spare my Blushes; and yet a Flame so pure
Methinks should cause no Shame.
The only Bliss that ever I propos'd,
Was ſtill to live and be within your Sight.
For this I did delude my noble Father　　　　　535
With a feign Pilgrimage, and dreſt my self
In a Boys Habit, and underſtanding well,
That when I made Discovery of my Sex
I could not ſtay with you, I made a Vow
By all the moſt religious things a Maid　　　　　540
Could call together, never to be known,

524 oft would] would oft　　　525–34 with . . . Sight] and as I did grow
More and more apprehensive, I did thirst
To see the man so rais'd, but yet all this
Was but a Maiden longing to be lost
As soon as found, till sitting in my window,
Printing my thoughts in Lawne, I saw a God
I thought (but it was you) enter our Gates,
My bloud flew out, and back again as fast
As I had puft it forth, and suck't it in
Like breath, then was I call'd away in hast
To entertain you. Never was a man
Heav'd from a Sheep-coat to a Scepter rais'd
So high in thoughts as I, you left a kiss
Upon these lips then, which I mean to keep
From you for ever, I did hear you talk
Far above singing; after you were gone,
I grew acquainted with my heart, and search'd
What stir'd it so, Alas I found it love,
Yet far from lust, for could I have but liv'd
In presence of you, I had had my end
536 feign] feign'd　　　537 a . . . Habit] habit of a boy, and, for I knew
My birth no match for you, I was past hope
Of having you

Whilſt there was Hopes to hide me from Mens Eyes
For other than I seem'd, that I might ever
Abide with you. Then sate I by the Fountain,
Where firſt you took me up.
    *King.*          Search out a Match,      545
Greateſt in our Kingdoms, and I will
Pay thy Dower my self.
    *End.*          Ne'er, Sir, will I
Marry, it is a thing within my Vow:
But if I may have leave to serve the Princess,
To see the Virtues of her Lord and her,      550
I shall have Hopes to live.
    *Ara.*          Yes, *Philander*,
I can't be jealous, tho' you had a Lady
Dreſt like a Page to serve you; nor will I
Suspeѐt her living here. Come live with me,
Live free as I do; she that loves my Lord,      555
Curſt be the Wife that hates her.
    *Phil.* I grieve such Virtue should be laid in Earth
Without an Heir. Hear me, my Royal Father,
Wrong not the Freedom of our Soul so much
To think to take Revenge on this base Woman:    560
Her Malice cannot hurt us; set her free
As she was born, saving from Shame and Sin.
    *King.* Set her at Liberty: But leave the Court:
This is no Place for such. You, *Thrasomond*,
Shall have free Passage, and safe Conduѐt home,    565
Worthy so great a Prince. When you come there,
Remember 'twas your Fault that coſt you her,
And not my purpos'd Will.
    *Thras.* I do confess it, moſt renowned Sir.
    *King.* Laſt join your Hands in one; enjoy *Philander*,    570
This Kingdom that is yours, and after me
Whatever I call mine; my Blessing on you:

542 Hopes] hope    544 Fountain] Fount    546–7 Greatest . . . self ] Within our
Kingdom where and when thou wilt,
And I will pay thy Dowry, and thy self
Wilt well deserve him
551 Hopes] hope    Yes] I    552 I can't] Cannot    557 Virtue] vertues    559 Soul]
souls    560 on this] of that    565 safe] a    567 Fault] faults    cost] lost    569 confess
. . . renowned] confess, | Renowned    571 that] which    572 Whatever] What ever

All happy Hours be at your Marriage Joys,
That you may govern all these happy Lands,
And live to see your plenteous Branches spring.                    575
By what has paſt this Day, let Princes learn
To rule the wilder Passions of their Blood,
For what Heav'n wills can never be withſtood.

574 govern . . . happy] grow your selves over all          575 spring] ~ | Where ever there is
Sun          576 By . . . let] Let          577 To . . . wilder] By this to rule the          578 withstood]
~. [*Exeunt Omnes*

# THE EPILOGUE,

To be Spoken by the GOVERNOUR.

*By the Duke of Buckingham.*

*If by my deep Contrivance, Wit and Skill*
*    Things fall out cross to what I mean them ſtill,*
*You muſt not wonder; 'tis the common Fate*
*Of almoſt all grave Governours of late:*
*And one would swear, as every Plot has sped,*          5
*They thought more with their Elbows than their Head;*
*Yet they go on as brisk, and look as well,*
*As if they had out wisdom'd* Machiavel:
*So Curs will wagg their Tails, and think they've won us,*
*At the same inſtant they make water on us.*          10
*Is't not a shame to see Men should have none,*
*That have such tedious, fulsom Bungling shown;*
*For to go Five Years wrong with Art and Pains,*
*Does shew a moſt prodigious want of Brains;*
*Nay, tho' he ne'er judg'd right, yet there was one* ⎫          15
*Who bragadocied ſtill himself upon*              ⎬
*Being infallible, but he is gone.*              ⎭
*O! 'twas a Thought of vaſt Design and Scope,*    ⎫
*To rail ſtill againſt Popery and Hope,*        ⎬
*He might presume to be himself a Pope:*        ⎭          20
*Tho' he might any thing presume to be*
*That could deceive Fops so infallibly;*
*The moſt egregious of all Scribes could tell*
*There never was such an* Achitophel:
*And true Admirers of his Parts and Glory,*          25
*Will doubtless have a juſt Renown in Story.*
*Ten Guineas that Lord paid for't, as Fame goes,*  ⎫
*Above ten times its worth the World knows;*    ⎬
*But he'll be better paid yet, I suppose.*        ⎭
*They were a matchless pair, the one to plot,*          30
*The other to extol ſtill what was not.*
*Yet faith the little Lord, when hence he ran,*
*Did compass one thing like an able Man:*
*For since he could not living aƈt with Reason,*
*'Twas shrewdly done of him to die in Season.*          35

0.1 GOVERNOUR] ~ in *Philaster 15wgv*      11 not a shame] *o4mw*; not *15wgv*

# Untitled Verse Play Fragment

## ['*Theodorick*']

## INTRODUCTION

This untitled fragment of a drama loosely based on the history of the Ostrogoth king Theodoric the Great (*c.*454–526) is found in the Jersey MS, written from the reverse end to the Commonplace book entries. It would seem to have been intended as a tragicomedy of the Fletcherian or Massingerian kind, which was to conclude with the death of the tyrant Odoacer, the reconciliation of the Visigoths under Euric with the Ostrogoths under Theomirus, and the marriage of Theodoric to Amalasonta. The fact that the piece is in blank verse rather than rhyme suggests that it may have been written either before Orrery's dramatic reforms of the early 1660s or after the move away from rhyme as the favoured medium for serious drama in the late 1670s. The earlier date is much more likely. The idea of a highly born nobleman entering enemy territory in disguise in order to win the hand of the daughter of a hostile leader has a specious symmetry with Buckingham's wooing of Mary Fairfax and may have been suggested by it. If so, the promoted secretary, Arsames (I. 79–81), could have been intended as a compliment to Cowley, who had performed that office for the queen. A Civil War context is suggested by the fragment's picture of a nation divided into warring parties that only love or enlightened statesmanship could reunite. If Odoacer and his faction was meant, in a more precise allegory, to represent Cromwell and the Independents, the divided Goths could represent English and Scots, Anglicans and Presbyterians, or even Protestants and Catholics.

The dating question is complicated by that of whether the play was intended for presentation on the pre-1641-style open stage or whether the writer envisaged wing-and-shutter scenery, which was not in general use in England before the reopening of the theatres after the Restoration. The opening direction of Act II, 'The scene a Tent hung with mourning, and a rich herse in it', suggests the post-1660 practice; however, the effect would not have been impossible under the earlier system if hearse, actors, and drapery were revealed together in a discovery space. (The hearse in IV. i. of *The Rehearsal* is carried on, not discovered.) The absence of any corresponding direction from the beginning of Act I and the immediate identification of the scene in the dialogue supports an open-stage interpretation, but not conclusively. A more important clue may be the use of the phrase 'The scene a . . .' at the head of the Act II direction, of which the LION archive offers no example prior to Flecknoe's *Love's Dominion* of 1654, a play which clearly envisages perspective scenery.[1]

Themes from the history of the ancient Gothic nation had become fashionable in mid-seventeenth-century Europe owing to the cultural prestige of Queen Christina of Sweden, the inhabitants of whose realm regarded themselves as descended from the Goths prior to their southward migration and division into western and eastern branches. Grotius's *Historia Gotthorum, Vandalorum et Langobardorum* (Amsterdam, 1655) was compiled under her patronage. Another indirect tribute to Christina was Georges Scudéry's epic *Alaric, ou Rome vaincue* (1654), though this, being set before the time of Theodoric, mentions him only once, in a Sybil's prophecy (ll. 9508–10).[2] It is possible that some French treatment, either in dramatic form or as an episode in a romance, underlies the present work. British interest in the northern peoples is further illustrated by the appearance in 1658 of *A Compendious History of the Goths, Swedes, and Vandals, and other Northern Nations written by Olaus Magnus*, translated from his *Gentium septentrionalium historia*, originally published in 1554. This, however, is a work of social, not political, history that would have been of little use to the author of *Theodorick*. The history of another Germanic tribe of the post-imperial period, the Lombards, had been drawn on, in a totally unhistorical way, in Davenant's *Gondibert* (1651).

The principal ancient accounts of the reign of Theodoric available in the mid-seventeenth century were those of Jordanes' *De Getarum sive Gothorum origine et rebus gestis* and of Procopius in Book 5 of *The History of the Wars*, both of which were included (the latter in a Latin translation) in Grotius's compilation. The situation which *Theodorick* takes as the starting point for its imaginative embroidery belonged to the short period between the young Theodoric's return from a long soujourn as a hostage in Constantinople and the death in 474 of his father Theodemir. A sug-

---

[1] (London, 1654), 1. This also applies to the form without the article.

[2] *Alaric, ou Romæ vaincue*. Introduction et notes à la *Preface* par Rosa Galli Pellegrini. Établissement du texte, résumé et notes par Cristina Bernazzoli (Fasano: Schena–Didier Érudition, 1998), 461.

gestion for his cruel deception of his parents may have come from Jordanes' brief reference to an attack by him on rival Goths being conducted 'inscio patre' (Grotius, 694). The casually opportunistic attitude of the author towards historical fact is evident from the names of the characters. Euric (d. 485) was king of a Visigothic state whose capital was Tolosa (mod. Toulouse). Since the play is set in the 'cheife citty' of the Visigoths (I. 74–6), and this city is situated in transalpine Gaul (I. 180, 284), Toulouse was presumably in the author's mind; however, Theodoric did not gain control of these lands until long after the death of Euric. The real Theodoric's mother, Erelieva, was the concubine, not the wife, of Theodemir: the name Fredegonda has been borrowed from the murderous queen of the Franks who lived from 543 to 597. Amalasonta (for Amalasunta), the name of Theodoric's beloved in the play, was actually that of his daughter, who succeeded him as regent for her son Athalaric. Her mother was Theodoric's wife Audefleda, a Frankish princess—his earlier children were by a concubine. Totilas was the name of a later king of the Goths who reigned from 541 to 552. Thorismond was the name of both an Ostrogoth king three before Theodoric and a Visigoth king of Toulouse, two before Euric.[3] The name Liberius was borrowed from a fourth-century pope. Arsames was a Persian royal name, here used quite inappropriately. Eudoxia, represented as the daughter of the Roman emperor Valentinian III (d. 455), has been given the name of his wife, possibly via the retelling of the story in the *Seconde partie* of D'Urfé's *Astrée* (1610) or Fletcher's slightly later *Valentinian*.[4] 'Eugubin the great Astrologer' (I. 158) derives from a misunderstanding of the name given to a collection of tables in a then still undeciphered language discovered at Gubbio in Italy in 1444, which were mistakenly believed to be prophecies. The name Astolpho (II. 5) is purloined from Ariosto's *Orlando furioso*. The author, in other words, drew a few names and basic historical facts from accounts of the period around 500 without much concern for niceties of chronology or ethnicity, and invented the rest from the stock materials of Romance narrative.

[3] Grotius, 44, 47. It is interesting that Buckingham should have used the name Thrasamond in *The Restauration* for a Prince of Spain, also occupied at one time by the Visigoths. A Thrasimund, king of the north African Vandal state from 496 to 523, was related by marriage to Theodoric.

[4] For 17th-c. versions of the story, see Harold Love, 'The rapes of Lucina', in Michael Bristol and Arthur Marotti (eds.), *Print, Manuscript and Performance: The Changing Relations of the Media in Early Modern England* (Columbus, Ohio: Ohio State University Press, 2000), 200–14. For the historical Eudoxia, see Procopius 2. 39, 41.

The protasis of the play is effective, and its truncation after little more than one act is regrettable. On the assumption that it was by the same author as the commonplace book entries contained in the source, we are inclined to suspect Martin Clifford but can not rule out Buckingham, especially as he had a genuine talent for the stage which is nowhere evident in Clifford's known writings. Certainly the play seems in a significant way *to do* with Buckingham.

## Dramatis Personae[5]

*Theomirus*, king of the Danubian Ostrogoths
*Theodorick*, his son, in love with Amalasonta
*Euric*, king of the Gallic Visigoths and father of Amalasonta
*Liberius*, a Roman nobleman, friend to Theomirus and Euric
*Totilas*, companion to Theodorick
*Arsames*, counsellor to Theomirus
Gentleman attending Liberius
Two captains, followers of Euric
Lords attending Theomirus

*Fredegonda*, wife of Theormirus and mother of Theodorick
*Eudoxia*, daughter to the Roman emperor, Valentinian

Scene: Tolosa (Toulouse)

---

[5] This list has been supplied by the editors.

# 'Theodorick'

Actus primus Scena prima

Liberius. Theodoric. Totilas.

*Lib.* Now Sir you'r welcome to my house,
And what you finde, (as much I feare you will,)
Deficient in your entertainment here,
Be pleasd t' impute to the true cause of it,
The troubles and disorders of the time.                                    5
You may for my good freind Arsames sake
Claime all the kindenes which this place affords,
And even without the ſtrength of that pretence
Do well deserve more then a common welcome
Who from the great beseigers flourishing campe                        10
Come to partake the hungry hospitality
Of a towne beseiged.
       *Theodorick.*          That honour I haue had Sir
In waiting on you home from your captivity
Does without any new additions
More then reward my iourny.
       *Lib.*                    I muſt beg                               15
your leave for a short while, t' acquaint the King
with my returne; Bee pleasd to use this house
iuſt as your owne; I shall within give order
that you may finde it such, and presently
attend you here againe.
       *Theod.*                 Sir, I beseech you                        20
not to let my consideration hinder
the leaſt of your occasions.                        Exit Liber.
                    How now Totilas?
Thou seemſt to be amazd, what doſt thou thinke on?
       *Totilas.* I thinke Sir that wee dreame, and would bee glad
to finde ourselves awake at home againe,                               25
for what can bee more wilde, or more unlike

a truth? then that the Prince Theodoric
should in a day of danger, and of honour,
withdraw his head crownd with so many lawrells?
afflict his father, and a warlike Nation       30
that loves him more then life, or victory,
with a beleife that hee is slayne, and then
as if hee longd to bee so, cast himselfe
disguisd into an Enemyes towne slightly,
whilst 'tis beseiged, and ready to bee taken       35
by his owne Army; If I bee not Sir
distracted quite when I beleive all this,
I am afraid you are so when you do it.
Your Highnes will excuse this liberty
Extorted from my greife, and my affection,       40
for I shall serve you in this course as faithfully
as if I likd it.
    *Theod.*     Pray no more of Highnes
Accustome not your toung here to those titles.
Ah Totilas, thou dost reproach mee iustly.
The only small remainder of my reason       45
Is that I know I'me mad.
    *Tot.*             You promisd Sir,
assoone as wee arrived here you would give mee
such forcing reasons for this strange adventure
as should convince mee that 'twas necessary.
    *Theo.* I undertooke a thing which is I feare       50
more then I can performe, for the necessity
can scarce bee seene but by the man that feels it.
The cause methinks in generall you should guesse at:
for sure there are not two things in the world
that can produce so wilde a resolution.       55
    *Totilas.* Not one within the compasse of my guessing.
    *Theod.* You'r dull of apprehension if you must
bee told that it was Love.
    *Tot.* That's stranger still, you must bee in love Sir
with a man or Horse for yet I'm confident       60
you never saw a woman of this citty.
    *Theo.* But one that ere I markt and that but once too,
yet shee has don the busines of my fate,
which was to make mee eminently miserable.
With one slight looke, one transitory glance       65

more sure then all the reſt of womankinde,
continually placed naked in my sight
could ever have effeɕted it.  oh Totilas
you muſt not laugh, nor wonder at these follyes,
for they'r the worke of violent deſtiny.                         70
    *Totil.*  Wonder I muſt Sir till you please t' explayne
a little more the ſtory.
    *Theod*              Take it all then.
When like a sudden and resiſtles ſtorme
Wee fell upon this kingdome of the Visigots,
And had beseiged Euric, and all his Court                        75
In theyr cheife citty here, ere hee was scarce
awakend with th' alarme,
Arsames whom you know I dearly lovd,
And who had long bin my owne secretary,
Ere I preferd him to my Royall father:                           80
Was sent Embassador into the Towne
With proffers of a peace upon some termes
And a cessation was through both our quarters
Proclaymd till his returne. Before hee parted,
discoursing with him long about his embassy,                     85
I fell into an earneſt curiosity
of seing our brave enemy myselfe:
His flourishing Court, (and to confesse the bottome)
His daughter cheifly the faire Amalazonta,
The fame of whose young beauty had assaulted mee,                90
even on the fartheſt banks of our owne Iſter.
In breife my wilfull passion over ruled,
the kindenes, and the Counsells of Arsames
And with him I came hither in disguise
as a young gentleman of his company,                             95
(You were behinde, as I remember then
in Germany with my Pannonian
regiment, or else you should have bin
of that adventure, as you now are of this).
    *Toti.*  The face of your misfortune now begins         100
to appearc to mcc at a diſtance.
    *Theod.*             You shall presently
see it in all its gyantlike dimensions.
The treaty came to nothing, but Arsames
resolvd to breake of civilly and fairly,

and for my sake desired at his departure                               105
that hee might kisse the Princesse hands. They lead us
to her apartment ſtraigt and my Arsames
for better satisfaction of my fancy
drew out the visit into greater length
Then such formalityes, and such a tyme                                 110
use to allow, Ah mee! There Totilas
you loſt forever your Theodorick.
  *Totilas.* The sequel I can easily conceive
You fell in love with her.
  *Theo.*      So far thou mayeſt.
But how in love thou canſt no more conceive,                           115
then thou conceiveſt the nature of infinity,
there's nothing but negations can expresse it,
that 'twas a love unlike all loves before.
  *Tot.* And what should hinder you from marying her?
Sure nature nere cut out a iuſter paire.                               120
You'r heyre to one, shee to another kingdome,
Two kingdomes of one Nation though long separated
By diſtant lands, and now at laſt by warre,
Your births, your fortunes, and your ages equall,
Her beauty, and your courage fitly matchd,                             125
Insuperable both, and usd to conqueſt.
Even at the firſt impression you are both
Methinks like 2 iuſt tallyes of one nation,
Divided only, to bee ioynd againe
And have the same marks set upon you both.                             130
  *Theod.* There is so much of truth in what y' observe
(Vnles in that one part which flatters mee)
And both the birth and ſtrength too of my passion,
(which like a miracle depended not
Vpon the ripening progresses of tyme)                                  135
Appeard to bee so much the worke of heaven
That fild with cheerfull projects I returnd
And with my utmoſt art, and ſtrongeſt zeale
Proposd it to my father.
  *Tot.* And could hee bee averse sir to a thing                140
Which you desird, and reason too advisd?
  *Theod.* So ſtrangely, so irrationally averse
That by his great, and sacred ſtygian oath
The soules of all his anceſtors hee Swore

That hee would nere consent to such a mariage                      145
Or owne mee for the heyre of his dominions
If I persued it.
    *Tot.*      What can bee his reasons?
    *Theo.*  Firſt Totilas you know my fathers temper
Who though hee bee endowed with many excellencyes
is hurried by his passions like a tempeſt                          150
And then as ſtubborne in them as a rocke.
Next hee hates Euric more then Odoacer
For ioyning in a league with him t' oppose
Our lovd designe of conquering Italy.
And thirdly which I finde to move him moſt                         155
H'as set his heart and faith on some prediȼtions
Drawne from the scheme of my nativity
By Eugubin the great Aſtrologer
Whom never ſtar in heaven had yet deceivd.
But Ile deceive his cunning, and theyr ſtrength,                   160
If they allot mee any wife but this.
    *Tot.*  What does hee say Sir those prediȼtions are?
    *Theo.*  That I shall marry a great Roman Lady,
And bee the founder of a Gothique empire
ore Rome and Italy.                                                165
    *Tot.*  I know not for the mariage, for the reſt
Methinks the byasse of fatality
Is ſtrongly set that way; the eaſterne emperour
has given it to your father, and invited him
T'expell from thence the Tyrant Odoacer,                           170
Hee promises assiſtance, and your father
Already like a deluge from his Iſter
With an impetuous course of violent conqueſt
Has broke a passage through all Germany
Into the Gaules, if you can here but force                         175
Those other powerfull Nations of the Goths
To ioyne in the attempt what can resiſt you.
    *Theo.*  Alas! though all the world should joyne with us
Vnles Amalasonta joyne with mee too
Theodorick muſt nevcr passe the Alpes.                             180
But to proceed: finding the King immoveable,
And toucht with his paternall coniurations
Never to marry any but a Roman
I summond all the forces of my Soule

And all the early glories of my youth 185
Cald to assist mee, I severely chid
That courage which had carried mee so oft
Through dreadfulst dangers to so many conquests,
For sinking now so basely at the sight
Of one faire object, Totilas I struggled 190
And fought with all my might for liberty:
But was orecome at last, disarmd and captivd
(As now you see mee) by my fatall passion.
   *Totil.* I weepe to see it Sir.
   *Theod.*              Some few nights after
wee fell upon the citty in two quarters, 195
The King in person on the monasterye,
And I attaqued by boats the westerne suburbs
That ly upon the River, wee were both
Repulsd with losse, but mine was much the greater.
At first wee forc't our landing very stoutly 200
And beat theyr guards up to the market place
But there orewhelmd with numerous fresh supplyes
Brought up by Euric wee were quite defeated.
With much adoe in darknes and confusion
The enemy still pressing at our backs 205
Wee got t' our boats, but that which I was in
Opprest by numbers of our flying soldiers
Just as it put from shore suncke to the bottome,
And few escaped; I with much difficulty
Swam safely ore, and found out a small cottage 210
Just at my landing to refresh myselfe.
   *Tot.* The great escapes Sir you have often made
Out of the iawes nay from the very bowells
of monstrous dangers makes you I feare too apt
to venture upon new. 215
   *Theod.* It was a very new one (I confesse)
Which I resolvd on then, to let the world
Beleive that I was drownd, and then get hither
As now you see mee; for this end I told
My Host that I was one of Euricks Captaynes 220
Engaged in this distres by severall accidents:
And from him partly out of love to's Prince
But more to mony which I gave him liberally
I presently procurd a peasants habit

And burnt my owne there.

  *Tot.*      You begin to enter    225
into my knowledge now for in that habit
you found mee at my quarters newly arrived,
and sent mee for Arsames.

  *Theo.*      Him you know
how I persuaded, or how rather forced
T'obtayne the Count Liberius his freedome    230
(Which waighty grounds of ſtate made very reasonable)
And recommend mee to him at his parting
As a considerable Roman gentleman
and bound for Italy to passe along with him.

  *Tot.* Thus far tis don; the ends for which you do it  235
are yet obscure to mee.

  *Theod.*    If I should say
To see Amalasonta once agayne,
When you have seen her too, you will confesse
That were enough, but my designe goes further
To tell her who I am, and what my busines    240
To caſt my fortune liberty and life
franckly into her hands.
And as befits one totally subdued
To yeild myselfe to mercy, and not ſtand
On composition.

  *Tot.*    And do you thinke Sir this    245
an undertaking grounded well?

  *Theod.*      Faith, Totilas
tis not so very wilde as it appears.
Firſt shee can never want the generosity
not to betray mee, Next the present ſtate
both of herselfe, her father, and her country   250
Though it can never make mee to deserve her
Makes mee perhaps the fitteſt Husband for her
that's now alive. And if the thing were donne
(Ah Totilas, if don but any way)
My father muſt at laſt comply with it.    255
And is perhaps become more tractable
Since the opinion of my death has tam'd
His ſtubbornesse, and spoild the reputation
Of his vaine prophecyes.

  *Totil.* Pray heaven it may succeed.

*Theo.*                          Why, if it do not                    260
I shall but little feare the consequence
Of any other mischeifs.

Enter a Gentleman.

*Gentle.* My Lord, the Count appointed mee t' attend here
for your commands Sir till himselfe returne.
*Theo.* I shall have no occasion for your trouble.          265
But pray Sir give mee leave to ask you a queſtion.
May a ſtranger have the honour here to see
the Princesse?
*Tot.*      You are very aprupt Sir
*Theod.*                      I am so.   (to the gentleman)
My ſtay Sir here is like to bee so short,
that I'm afraid it will bee difficult                         270
In such a time of busines, and of trouble
To see, and pay my duty to the Princesse
Before I part.
*Gentle.*      Shee's a young Lady Sir,
Who well deserves a ſtrangers curiosity
To see, and to discourse with, for which purpose          275
No man can introduce you to her company
With more advantage then my Lord the Count,
For the young Sir his son Thorismond
Is the man designd to marry her.
*Theod.*                      To marry her?
The Devill hee is, to marry Amalasonta?            280
*Gentle.* Why Sir there's no such ſtrangenes in the match
For though my Lord a subieƈt bee to Euric
Yet hees a Prince himselfe, and Count of Narbonne
(Once capitall of all this part of Gaul)
And a Patrician Roman; besides this                     285
They have bin bred together, have long lovd
For Lovers who are yet so very young
And nature sure intended they should so
For yet shee never joynd a lovelier couple.
*Theodoric.* But does the Princes then love this young
                              Thorismond?                290
*Gent.* There are great reasons to beleive shee dos.
And wee Sir who depend upon this family
Are flatterd with a hope that they are contraƈted.

*Theod.* Contracted too? By heaven Ile kill him Totilas.
*Tot.* Sir you undo yourselfe.                                          295
*Theod.* Contracted too? sure you'r mistaken Sir.
*Gentlem.* I was not there Sir, when they say 'twas donne.
Nor is it yet declared; but Sir I hope
you whom my Lord accounts to bee his freind,
are not at all displeasd                                               300
at this good fortune of his family.
    *Theo.* Displeasd? I'm ravisht at it, (I betray myselfe).
Ile walke Sir if you please a turne or two
in the next gallery, and there please myselfe
a while, with thinking on this happines                                305
like to befall our noble freind the Count.
                                                 Exit.

    *Gentlem.* Hee seems to bee disturbd Sir on the suddaine.
I hope I have said nothing that offends him.
    *Tot.* (I feare h' has ruind all) There's nothing lesse Sir;
but the truth is, if both my Lord, and I,                              310
bee not distracted quite, wee escape fairly,
For wee have neither of us slept this weeke.
    *Gentlem.* His looks methinks confirme it,
pray bee t' entreat Sir to take a little rest
in the next chamber there, Ile see it ready.                           315
                                                 Exit.

    *Totil.* It will bee very seasonable, Oh heavens!
What dos become of man when Hee's in love.
                                                 Exit.

               Enter Euric. Eudoxia. Liberius.

    *Eur.* You cannot doubt Liberius of your welcome;
Since I have lately given the strongest proofes
Of my esteeme, both of yourselfe and family;                           320
By Approbation of your sons affection
To her who is my only ioy and interest
My daughter and sole heire Amalasonta.
Againe you'r welcome, but how got you off
From such a hard and angry enemy                                       325
as Theomirus?
    *Lib.*        All I know is this Sir.
The third day after I was taken Prisoner,
Arsames, (who had bin my old acquaintance

When sixteen years agoe your Maiesty
sent mee embassador into Pannonia)—        330
   *Euric.* That was a time Liberius (as I take it)
When Theomirus was not in estate
To trouble all the world, as now hee dos.
   *Liber.* Far from it Sir, for Odoacer then
Passed through his land like a destroying angell        335
With flight before, and slaughter round about him,
And desolation ever in his reare.
   *Euric.* Just so will Theomirus passe through mine
Vnlesse wee stop him here, and cheque his fury.
But pray go on, Arsames, you were saying—        340
   *Liber.* Came to conduct mee to the King his Master,
Who though I found him drownd in the fresh gall
Of a sons losse, (his brave and only son)
Received mee with extreme civility
And after great professions of old kindenes        345
Told mee I was at freedome to returne,
when ere I pleasd.
   *Eur.*           And for that liberty
Did he impose upon you no conditions?
   *Lib.* I told him that I hoped hee did not do mee
So great, and so unusuall a favour        350
But with intent at the same tyme of charging mee
With some commissions to your Maiesty
Which might renew the ancient peace, and freindship
And reunite the nation of the Goths.
   *Eur.* And how did that take with him?
   *Lib.*                Not at all.        355
Hee said hee owd to mee that courtesy,
As his old freind, and as a noble Roman
(Which Nation hee was come to free and serve)
And that those titles should not bee extinguishd
In his affection, by my being now        360
A subiect to his enemy, as for Euric
I shall (said hee) seeke nothing else from him,
But my revenge, since hee and his faire daughter
(But why hee added Daughter Ime amazd)
Have robd mee of my deare and only son.        365

                  Enter a Captayne.

*Euric.* My daughter? How now?

*Capt.*                        May it please your Maiesty.
The enemy was seene last night
With a strong body of two thousand horse
At least, as our men guesse them, on this side
The River at——

*Eur.*                        Impossible, how could                        370
they passe?

*Eudoxia.* Ah mee—the Princesse Sir—pray heaven
shee has escap'd them! the poore Princesse—

*Eur.* Though I beleive it but a false alarme
The very sound and name of it affrights mee.
How do you know it?

*Capt.*                        May it please your Maiestye                        375
Our scouts were taken by the enemy
And one of them escapd to us agen
After h' had marcht two miles along with them.

*Eur.* Where is hee?

*Capt.*                        Hee's upon my guard at the Southgate.

*Euric* Go fetch him presently.                        380

*Libe.* But I beseech you Madame, why are you
Concernd so for the Princesse at this news?

*Eudoxia.* Alas my Lord! the King this very morning
Has sent away the Princesse with a party
But of five hundred horse, and the young Count                        385
Your son commands them.

*Eur.*                        Ah!
Tis very neare the place where shee's to passe.
I thought that quarter as secure at present
As my owne palace. Is the Captaine yet
come back?

*Gent.* Hee's yet, and't please your Maiesty                        390
scarce downe the stayres.

*Euric.*                        You know Liberius,
From the first day o'th seige 'twas my designe
To send away my daughter to Narbone.
But whilest the Enemyes Horse commanded all
the passages, I durst not venture it.                        395
Since Theodoricks death,
And theyr great losses in that last assault
They drew from thence, and passd againe the River

To theyr maine body, upon this security  
(And having ſtrongly fortifyed the place        400  
On this syde of the foord) I chose laſt night  
As a safe season for my daughters iourney.  
And with a convoy of five hundred horse  
Truſted her to the conduct of her lover  
Your Thorismond. I little thought Liberius        405  
I had given him an employment of such danger,  
as it (I feare) may prove.  
    *Lib.*              If shee bee safe  
There is no danger, nor no death for him  
Which in her service Sir can bee unwelcome  
Either to him or mee, but I admire        410  
Madame what counsell, or what accident  
Has parted you from your deare freind the Princesse  
In this adventure.  
    *Eudox.*        It has coſt mee already  
many a teare my Lord, and will do more,  
If any thing of danger, or misfortune        415  
(Which heaven avert) should happen to the Princesse  
And I not have my share int, but the King  
was pleasd to order't soe.  
    *Eu.*            Eudoxia  
is a Roman Lady and the daughter  
Of Valentinian the Emperour        420  
So far from any cause of apprehension  
Even in the worſt event from Theomirus  
That I have kept her here for my owne intereſt  
As the moſt likely person to obtaine  
Some favour from him, if wee should bee forcd        425  
At laſt to the necessity of asking it.  

               Enter another Captayne.  

Oh, now wee shall have newes Here's one went with them.  
    *Capt.* I beseech your Maieſty—  
    *Eud.* Oh Lord! wee'r ruind; in this fellows looks  
I see his news already.  
    *Eur.*           Prithee speake man.        430  
What ere it bee, what is my daughter safe?  
Or taken? speake.

*Capt.*              Not taken yet I hope,
but in the utmoſt danger Sir of being so
Vnles your Maieſty releive her inſtantly,
I hope your Maieſty will not bee offended                              435
At mee for being forcd to bee the Messenger
Of such unwelcome tydings.
  *Eur.*                         Now a curse
on all thy excuses! tell mee plaine and quickly
the matter; or <u>Ile sinke thee here to Hell.</u>
  *Capt.*  Tis thus Sir                                      440
When wee were got iuſt beyond vicus albus
A little before break of day, a party
or rather army of the Enemyes horse
Having it seems met with our scouts, and taken them
From the wood side fell suddenly upon us.                              445
After an howres dispute with no small slaughter
Theyr numbers, and theyr fortune Sir prevaild.
In breife they totally defeated us
But the young Count who during the whole fight
Had acted to th' amazement of us all                                  450
With his owne troope, and some few other officers
Caſting themselves about the Princesse person
Made theyr retreat good to the neighboring village
From whence they sent mee Sir to beg your Majeſtys
speedy releife.
  *Euric.*      I feare 'twill bee too late.                 455
  *Lib.*  Lets therefore loose no tyme.
  *Capt.*                         They'r all resolvd Sir
Either to save the Princesse till you come
Or perish in the endeavour.
  *Eur.*  If they defend themselves but two howres longer
They shall have good companions what ere                              460
theyr fortune bee. Come gentlemen—Eudoxia
Wee shall not want your prayers to succour us.

            Exeunt.

  *Eud.*  Not till I want the use of voice, and sense
But I perceive my greife, and feare too ſtrong
For either of those two to hold out long.                            465

            Exit.


      Finis Actus primi

## Second Act.

The scene a Tent hung with mourning, and a rich herse in it.
Theomirus and Fredegonda setting at both ends of it. Arsames, and
other Lords ſtanding about it.

*Theomi.* It is enough; here end wee all the noise
And all the female glories of our sorrow
Tis tyme now to begin the manly part,
Resentment, and revenge, Arsames—
    *Arsam.*                  Sir
    *Theom.* No news yet from Aſtolpho?
    *Ars.*              The laſt was Sir,       5
That hee paſt over safe and undiscoverd,
At the three mills, and from thence inſtantly
With fiftteen hundred horse marcht to possesse
The quarters which your Maieſty appointed,
The reſt and all the foote hee left behinde      10
To fortify the landing place, and make
A bridge there of the boats in which hee paſt.
    *Theom.* Since Euric has thus rashly ſtopt the current
Of my revenge on cruell Odoacer
It shall oreflow, and drowne Him and his Country.      15
His envy has prevaild 'gainſt my ambition,
(For that with my Theodorick is sunke,
No carkas of it left, to shew it was.)
But hee shall finde harder, and tougher worke
To grapple with my greife, and with my anger.      20
    *Fredegonda.* That hope Sir now (the effect of which heavens
And your encensed courage promises)            iuſtice
Is all that keeps mee patiently alive
After my childrens death, our youngeſt ioy
Was in his cradle barbarously murthered      25
By the wild rage of Odoacers troops
In theyr inhumane passage through our Country
And Euric too who of Princes living
Ought moſt to have assiſted our revenge
Has fatally by his unlucky daughter      30
And wilfully by his owne ſtubborn malice
Obſtructed our fair way to that and glory,
Has robd us cruelly of all the comfort

By Odoacer left, all that could make
Our labours pleasant, and successes usefull                    35
The Heyr to both, our deare Theodorick.
O my Theodorick! oh wee have loſt
Not thy life only, but thy very death too,
And vainly mourne here ore thy empty tombe
without thy body—
    *Theom.*        Fredegond, no more            40
The heat of this affliction has enough
Softned the noble metall of our courage,
Tis time to ſtrike it into forme and edge
And harden it againe; lets to the busines.
My Lords draw nigh, for you muſt bee             45
Both witnesses, and partners of my vowes.
I sweare (and touch like a religious altar
This sacred herse) I sweare by all that's holy
By all the soules of my dead Anceſtors
And by thy soule Theodoricke, who shouldſt      50
If nature had not dealt unkindely with thee
Have lived to sweare by mine
Never to end, or ceas this war with Euric;
Till the unbounded quarrell bee decided
Either by his deſtruction or mine owne.          55
And if kind heaven so favour my iuſt vengeance
As to deliver him into my hands
Or any of his family, I swear
To sacrifice them here that very day
Vpon this tombe which wants the corps it ought   60
To have, and shall bee other wise supplyed.
And leaſt the execution of this oath
By my untimely death should bee prevented
you Fredegond, and you my Lords shall sweare
To see it well, and faithfully performd          65
Come neare, and lay your hands upon the Hearse.
    *All.* Wee sweare the same.
              (Fredegond embraces the herse)
    *Fred.*          O my Theodorick!
    *Theom.* Hold Fredegond; such ineffectuall passion
Does scandalize this noble sacrament
Which is ordaind for bloud, and not for  tears    70

            *[Text ends here.]*

# EXPLANATORY NOTES AND CRITICAL APPARATUS

# *Explanatory Notes*

## THE CHANCES

These notes draw with gratitude on the very full annotations given in James Patrick Fowler's thesis edition (Shakespeare Institute, University of Birmingham, 1978), which also considers numerous specialized issues of derivation and idiom which were not appropriate for inclusion in the present edition.

### *Prologue*

In Sarah Cowper's Commonplace Book (Hertfordshire Archives and Local Studies MS D/EP F37), 355, this appears as 'The Epilogue to the Same' (i.e. *The Chances*), with a marginal attribution to 'M. C.' [Martin Clifford]. There can be no doubt that Cowper believed that Clifford, a close friend and neighbour, was the author. What is uncertain is whether she received a copy from him during his lifetime or whether it was found among his papers after his death, in which case Buckingham would have to remain in consideration. For the relationship of Clifford and Buckingham see the General Introduction. The text of this version, which varies in several readings from the printed one, is at ll. 251 below in the Commonplace Book. Restoration adaptations of Fletcherian plays by Durfey, Motteux, Powell, Rochester, and Settle all acknowledge this derivation in their prologues as an attraction of the work about to be performed; however, in this case neither the prologue nor the epilogue makes any such acknowledgement, suggesting that they need not have been written specifically for *The Chances*. In its style and brevity the prologue is typical of the 1660s.

17–18. In both lines 'ill' is an adverb.

### *Dramatis personae*

*1682* has no such list. The earliest to appear, here reproduced with appropriate alterations, is that of the 1692 quarto 'for *R. Bently*', which was taken verbatim from *79ct* and therefore is not even accurate.

*2 Constantia, a Whore to old Antonio.* We have retained the phraseology of *47ct* as repeated in *1692*, but in Buckingham's form of the play, though 2 Constantia has been 'sold' to Antonio by her mother, Antonio has apparently proved impotent and her degree of sexual experience is left discreetly vague.

*I. i*

5. *Of . . . where.* In their search, described in ll. 19–38, for Constantia.

6. *eat Bell-ropes.* Cf. Samuel Butler, 'A churchwarden': 'He eats up the Bell-Ropes like the Ass in the Emblem, and converts the broken Glass-Windows into whole Beer-Glasses of Sack' (Samuel Butler, *Characters*, ed. Charles W. Daves (Cleveland, Ohio: Press of Case Western Reserve University, 1970), 169 and n.). The same joke is used in Fletcher and Massinger's *The Spanish Curate*, II. i. 60–1 (*BF*, x. 319–20).

17. *thank . . . Surgeon.* For treating the pox.

19. *invisible Woman.* Either 1 or 2 Constantia, who is known to them only by repute and cannot be located.

27. *malt.* As the raw material of beer.

40. *souls.* Punning on 'soles'.

43. *Bell-man.* A town crier who walked the streets, ringing a bell and making announcements.

54. *next Fame.* The next woman whose beauty is praised to them.

62. *devotions.* Characterizing Frederick as the more serious of the pair. The landlady confuses these roles when she accuses John of having conceived a child in the course of devotions (I. ix. 30).

*I. ii*

24–31. Fowler records a close parallel in Fletcher's *The Humorous Lieutenant*, III. vii. 61–5 (*BF*, v. 363):

> I am not greedy of your lives and fortunes,
> Nor do I gape ungratefully to swallow ye,
> Honour the spur of all illustrious natures,
> That made you famous Souldiers, and next Kings,
> And not ambitious envy strikes me forward . . .

29. *Honour, Honour.* The second occurrence is extra-metrical.

38–9. Fletcher's text, with its repetition of 'stormes', is corrupt here; perhaps the second occurrence should have been some word such as 'gulf'. Buckingham's metrical intentions are not certain: the editors offer a possible solution to the anomalous hexameter.

48. *our Rests.* A rest was a stake in gambling.

*I. iii*

1. *Naples.* Changed from Fletcher's Bologna, possibly because Naples was under Spanish control, whereas Bologna was part of the Papal dominions. As a result

John and Frederick can no longer be presented as students attending Bologna's famous university in order to study 'Morall Philosophy'. Ferrara, the seat of the duke, is close to Bologna but distant from Naples.

17. *Fabritio*. Taken over from Fletcher; however, Fabritio does not actually appear.

*I. iv*

4. *in and in*. Cf. *Commonplace Book*, 157:15 and n. Percy notes that this was 'a game formerly in use, and play'd with four dice in a box' and that it 'furnished a favorite Equivoque to our old writers' (p. 122). Charles Cotton gives careful instructions on how to cheat at this game. See *Games and Gamesters of the Restoration*, ed. Cyril Hughes Hartmann (London: Routledge and Sons, 1930), 80–1.

7. *boot-haleing*. Marauding, pillaging (*OED*).

*I. vi*

9. *Arras work*. Either the conceiving of the child is compared to the weaving of a figure in a tapestry or it took place behind the shelter of one, as in Dryden's *The Wild Gallant*, IV. ii. 81–2 (*Works*, viii. 67). For sex behind an arras see also Massinger, *The Duke of Milan*, III. ii. 41–3 (*The Plays and Poems of Philip Massinger*, ed. Philip Edwards and Colin Gibson, 5 vols. (Oxford: Clarendon Press, 1976), i. 260); and Fletcher and Shakespeare, *The Two Noble Kinsmen*, IV. iii (*Complete Works*, l. 2170).

10. *Infidel*. Because unbaptized, as at *Paradise Lost*, I. 582.

11. *good white bread*. A vocative, addressed to the child. The image, like the more recent 'a bun in the oven', reflects the belief of early medicine that gestation was a form either of cooking or fermentation. The influence of these two images, as they applied to digestion, is described in Rachel Laudan, 'Birth of the Modern Diet', *Scientific American* (Aug. 2000), 62–7. Cf. Dryden, 'Of the Pythagorean Philosophy. From Ovid's Metamorphoses Book XV ', ll. 326–9:

> Then Nature's Hand (fermented as it was)
> Moulded to Shape the soft, coagulated Mass;
> And when the little Man was fully form'd,
> The breathless Embryo with a Spirit warm'd.

15. *Quiddits*. From Latin *Quidditas*, pl. *Quidditates*, a term of Scholastic philosophy expressing the essence or 'whatness' of a thing; here used for the arcane duplicities of women.

16. *bumfidled*. Humiliated. A term of unstable meaning. 'Bum-fiddle' as a noun is sometimes used of the buttocks or anus, and the verb for activities involving that

part. If the 'fiddle' is musical, the root sense may be of insulting someone by fart-ing, but this is far from certain. In Orrery's *Mr Anthony* (1669), IV. 581, it is used of beating a fiddler (*The Dramatic Works of Roger Boyle, Earl of Orrery*, 2 vols., ed. William Smith Clark II (Cambridge, Mass.: Harvard University Press, 1937), ii. 563).

17. *card of five*. Alluding to the game 'five-cards', Cotton's rules for which are given by Hartmann, *Games and Gamesters*, 59. The 'card of five' would be the five of trumps, also known as the 'five fingers', which was the highest-scoring card in the pack.

23. *Butter-prints*. Butter-pats made with a wooden mould.

29. *Candles*. Possibly in error for 'caudles'—nourishing gruels given to infants. The emendation is accepted by Fletcher's editors; however, Fowler defends 'can-dles' as equally appropriate.

## I. vii

1. *beaten all the Purlews*. Strictly grounds surrounding a forest, purlieu had be-come a general term for outskirts or outlying parts. To 'beat' in this sense was to search them for game. To beat or hunt the purlieus was a metaphor for sexual ad-venturism, as at Dryden, *Amphytrion*, I. i. 46–9: 'he is weary of hunting in the spa-cious Forest of a Wife, and is following his Game *incognito*, in some little Purliew' (*Works*, xv. 232).

## I. viii

2. *dance without a fiddle*. Here with the implied meaning 'as the result of beat-ing them' or possibly with the beating legs in mind of those executed by hanging. But the phrase could also be used as a synonym for 'to experience joy' as at Dryden, *The Spanish Friar*, IV. i. 203 (*Works*, xiv. 164) and Crowne, *The English Frier*, IV. i. 8 (*The Comedies of John Crowne*, ed. B. J. McMullin (New York: Garland, 1984), 545). Cf. also Etherege, *The Man of Mode*, II. ii. 144–5: 'What dancing the Gallop-ing Nag without a Fiddle?' where it is used of Loveit's annoyance, following the stage direction '(Offers to catch her by the hand, she flings away and walks on)' (*The Plays of Sir George Etherege*, ed. Michael Cordner (Cambridge: Cambridge University Press, 1982), 249).

7–8. *Almanacks . . . Month*. Times when phlebotomy would benefit a patient were determined by astrology. Cf. *Richard II*, I. ii: 'Our doctors say, this is no time to bleede' (*Complete Works*, l. 157).

14. *far o'th' Bow Hand*. A common expression for an incorrect guess or supposi-tion. Its origin lay in archery, where it was used for a shot that went too far to the left, the bow-hand side.

17. *Old tough Andrew.* A highly reputed broadsword, from the maker's name 'Andrea Ferrara' (*OED*).

22. *audit's lost.* Fowler, following Fletcher's editors, emends to 'audit's cast'; however, this is to treat the text as Fletcher's, not as Buckingham's by appropriation.

*five and fifty.* Not only Antonio's presumed age but a high-scoring hand at the card game of Primero (Fowler).

*I. ix*

10. *Alligant.* A red wine imported from the Spanish city of Alicante.

11. *Linsey-wolsey.* An inferior cloth made from a mixture of linen and wool.

*Hasty-Puddings.* A paste made of flour boiled with milk or water; also applied to oatmeal porridge.

23. *lye beyond all Falconers.* About the success of their birds in catching prey.

29–33. The repeated questions suggest a distant recollection by Fletcher of the 'silkworm' speech in *The Revenger's Tragedy*, ed. R. A. Foakes (London: Methuen, 1966), III. v. 69–82.

35.1. Fowler notes that Buckingham has systematically allocated Peter to John and Anthony to Frederick. Fletcher's allocation would have been determined by availability at a time when minor parts were invariably doubled.

52. *Lodge.* So *47ct.* Fowler suggests that Fletcher might originally have written 'Lodgd'.

*Now . . . Signior.* 'She affects to weep.' (SD deduced and added by Percy, p. 131).

86–9. John divides the jewels between himself and the landlady.

*I. x*

27. *Sugar-sops, and Syrops.* Food given to invalids and the dying, who were unable to take normal nourishment. Sugar was still a luxury at this period.

*I. xi*

48. *clap on proof.* Her prayers will protect him as well as if they were a suit of proof armour.

53. *Sea-Cards.* The markings of a mariner's compass.

*II. i*

14. *Quietus est.* 'He is at rest', i.e. dead.

15. *small guts*. The small as opposed to the large intestine.

*feez'd*. The root sense of the verb is 'drive away' or 'put to flight'; here, colloquially, 'he has done for me'.

23. *thank's good Coat*. In Cervantes a breastplate. For duels it was customary to search the participants to make sure they were not wearing any form of protection.

55. *Bat-fowling*. Hunting birds when they are roosting by night; here with the apparent sense of pursuing women of the night. The *OED* suggests that the original etymology was not from the nocturnal flying animal, but bats as a term for clubs (as with cricket and baseball bats).

73. *Answer the Parish*. The parish vestry, as the body responsible for local administration, would hold him responsible for the infant in order to avoid the expense of caring for it falling upon the ratepayers.

82. *militant Girle*. Continuing the pun on 'infantry' in l. 67.

121. *dog trick*. A mean or malicious deception. Cf. 'dog tired', 'dog trot', 'dog watch'. Also at IV. iv. 128.

## II. ii

12. *An admirable Voyce*. The most likely point at which the song mentioned by Pepys, 'All night I weep', might have been interpolated. The Beaumont and Fletcher 1647 folio has no song at this point. The *79fc* folio introduces one beginning 'Mercilesse Love, whom nature hath deny'd', which is emphatically Caroline, not Carolean in style. A song by Sir Robert Howard, 'Wasted with sighs I sigh'd or pin'd', preserved in a setting by John Eccles (?1668–1735), is also associated with the play and putatively with this scene (see p. 20).

20. *Basco*. Apparently intended for modern Italian and Spanish 'basta', meaning 'enough' or 'stop'. Fletcher uses the form 'basto' in *The Pilgrim*, III. iii. 68 and *Rule a Wife and Have a Wife*, II. ii. 9.

29. *Exit ambo*. Both exit. The correct Latin form would be the plural *exeunt*, which is also the more frequently encountered in stage directions of the period.

52. *Marmalad*. Then made from quinces, not oranges.

57–8. *the Devil . . . suffer*. The Anglican Litany from the 1662 *Book of Common Prayer* includes a plea for deliverance from 'all fornication, and all other deadly sin; and from all the deceits of the world, the flesh and the devil'. The ceremony of baptism from the same source includes a prayer for the baptized person to have power and strength against 'the devil, the world, and the flesh'. To make sense of the lines one has either to emend 'What' to 'That' or follow some earlier editors of Fletcher in making John break off his intended sentence with 'World'.

60. *Pack-Saddle*. A jocular excuse for an inconvenient appearance. Percy (p. 153) identifies the phrase as the punchline of a traditional joke in which a lover has

been discovered by his mistress's husband among a pile of saddles. Alternatively, John may refer to himself as a metaphorical burden to Frederick, the more usual association of pack saddles.

110. *Art thou an Ass?* Some editors of Fletcher insert 'not' after 'thou' to preserve the parallelism and improve the metre.

119. *unslack'd with Service.* Sexual performance, as in Middleton and Rowley, *The Changeling*, where the word recurs sixteen times, mostly with this implication. Heracles, in one version of the Greek legend, impregnated the fifty daughters of Thespius in a single night. The *47ct* reading is 'unslak'd'.

123. *spiced.* Overscrupulous.

133. *Cod-piece-point.* The codpiece (covering the penis) may still have been worn in parts of Spain in Buckingham's time, but had vanished from England. It was attached by means of 'points' in the sense of a string with a tag at its end. In l. 9 of 'A history of insipids' (1674), Henry VIII is called 'Harry with the codpiece' (*POAS-Yale*, i. 244). Wycherley's *The Gentleman Dancing-Master* (1672) satirizes archaic Spanish dress in the character of Don Diego.

142. *hay pity.* It is unclear whether 'hay' is a dialectical form, a contraction ('ha' ye'), or a misprint.

## II. iii

10. *Hernanda.* Fowler restores Fletcher's 'Hernando', this being the 'correct masculine form of the name'.

69. *loose i'th' hilts.* As the blade of a sword might loosen itself from its hilt.

## III. i

13. *at livery.* Available for hire.

14. *How Now?* 'He finds her weeping' (Percy, p. 164).

21. *a Mawkin, a flirt Gillian.* A loose woman. 'Maukin' is a version of Magdalene. 'Flirt-gill' or 'flirt Gillian' was the original form of the later 'gill-flirt'. In Fletcher, but not the present version, the landlady's name is given as Gillian.

37. *as they say.* Possibly half remembering *Hamlet*, ll. 1614–15: 'who would these fardels beare / To grunt and sweat vnder a wearie life . . .'.

45. *Devil's Matins.* A 'service of Satanic worship' (*OED*).

49. *Gentlemen.* An annotator of *MoU* has plausibly emended to 'Gentlewomen'.

51. *Beast.* Replacing Fletcher's 'Boast'.

65. *ropery*. Used here in the sense of 'roguery' but an independent word, perhaps suggested by the coiling or twisting of ropes. Cf. *Romeo and Juliet*, l. 1200: '*Nurse*. I pray you sir, what sawcie merchant was this that was so full of his roperie?'

74a.1. The Landlady's return patches a large excision from *47ct*. Some business would be required: perhaps John mimics the Landlady.

75–6. *though hills . . . met Seas*. An addition by Buckingham from Jonson's *Catiline his Conspiracy* (1616), I. i. 74–5. Fowler, in 'Catiline quoted in *The Chances*', *N&Q*, 231 (1986), 467–9, points out that Charles Hart played both Catiline and Don John and was thus 'prepared to burlesque his own tragic style of delivery when occasion demanded it'. There is a parallel instance in Southerne's *The Maid's Last Prayer*, III. i. 83–4, where Doggett as Lord Malapert addressed Elizabeth Barry as Lady Malapert with lines spoken to her by Betterton in Otway's *The Orphan*. The passage from *Catiline* was a favourite, also echoed in Cowley's *The Guardian* and *The Cornish Comedy* (1696). The monologue of Sulla's ghost, to which this is a reply, was used as the basis of a satire on Buckingham, 'A Dialogue betweene the Duke of Buckingham and his fathers Ghost' (see App. II, ii. 304). Another satire of the time, 'Mrs Nelly's Complaint', invokes the scene in its opening line, 'If Sylla's ghost made bloody Catiline start' (*Court Satires of the Restoration*, ed. John Harold Wilson (Columbus, Ohio: Ohio State University Press, 1976), 97–101). Buckingham had supported a revival of *Catiline* by the King's Company in December 1668.

95. *I must go on though general Massacrees*. Possibly another quotation, though if it is, the source has not proved traceable. The 'though' is from *47ct*, and, if not an error, may indicate a familiar speech broken off, perhaps from a lost play popular in Fletcher's time.

110. *strait a Horse-back*. As they are to travel out of town to the duke's castle.


*III. ii*

6. *the Tune of John Dory*. For the melody see Claude M. Simpson, *The British Broadside Ballad and its Music* (New Brunswick, N.J.: Rutgers University Press, 1966), 399. The ballad describes how a French privateer, captained by a Genoese, Giovanni Doria, was defeated in a sea fight by a Cornish captain named Nicholl.

14. *Barley water*. Fowler cites John Woodall, *The Surgion's Mate* (London, 1617), sig. T3$^r$ on barley water being substituted for wine in the treatment of wounds.

16. *rotten Roots*. In Fletcher 'rotten ends of rooks'.

17. *Pericraniums and Pia-maters*. Both terms were loosely used for parts of the brain. In the terminology of the time, the pericranium was a membrane covering the skull under the skin and the *pia mater* a second membrane covering the surface of the brain.

19–20. *the man i'th' Almanack . . . Aries place*. Almanacs would frequently contain an illustration of a naked male figure with the stomach opened to show the intestines, surrounded by the signs of the zodiac, each of which was connected to a particular limb or organ. See Bernard Capp, *English Almanacs 1500–1800* (Ithaca, N.Y.: Cornell University Press, 1979), 204–5 and plate following 256.

20. *Aries place.* Aries stood for the head and face, which were so labelled in the almanacs. It was associated with anger. There may be a secondary allusion to the horns of cuckoldry.

21. *open'd.* Having his veins opened to let blood or his wound opened for inspection.

22. *brimmer.* A glass filled to the brim.

31. *Presently.* In its early sense of immediately.

## III. iii

4–7. The terminology is from hawking. John is a young hawk, Frederick an older one who has lost some of his abilities but, when he is not too tired, will still attack a target.

7. *Tarmont.* Possibly a form of 'Tarmagant' in its original sense as a violent deity, supposedly worshipped by Mahommedans, and here applied to Don John.

8. *Jenkin.* A diminutive or familiar form of John.

*the dog-days.* The hottest time of the year, corresponding in ancient times to the rising of the extremely bright dog star, Sirius. The analogy here is with sexual heat.

17. *bearing cloath.* A child's christening robe.

## III. iv

38. *contracted before Heaven.* In a private ceremony that would at that period have had the force of law.

56. *the man . . . all's well.* Quoting Puck's expression in *A Midsommer Night's Dreame*, l. 1441. There is a further echo at V. iv. 139. The phrase had become proverbial, and is used by Behn in *The False Count*, V. i and *The Feign'd Curtizans*, V. i. 32–3; by Susannah Centlivre in *The Artifice*, V. i [(London, 1723), 103]; and by Edward Ravenscroft in *The Canterbury Guests*, V. i [(London, 1695), 55].

94. *to my own Ass.* In Fletcher without the 'to'. Buckingham has misunderstood the construction.

113. *A young Gentleman.* A red herring as far as Buckingham's plot is concerned. In Fletcher the alternative Constantia is a common prostitute who plots with Antonio's musician, Francisco, to steal the money. Her speech prefix is simply 'Whore' and she only appears, briefly, in one scene.

127. *Dog-trick.* See note on II. i. 121.

*III. v*

14. *Water-Conjurer.* Either a practitioner of Hydromancy, like Glendower in *1 Henry IV*, l. 1530, who claims a power to 'cal spirits from the vasty deepe', or, as Fowler suggests, a 'tempestarius' who, like Prospero in *The Tempest*, could control the weather.

15. *Duck and Drake.* A game in which flat stones are made to bounce from the surface of a pond before sinking, often used as a metaphor for squandering wealth in irresponsible gambling.

18–19. *blear-ey'd people with red heads, and flat noses.* If the reference is not to a particular individual of Fletcher's day (perhaps an actor who played such parts), the description may be meant to characterize such conjurers as Scots or Irish. Red hair was associated with Judas.

*IV. i*

The mother's prolixity in this scene is a *lazzo* derived from the Greek new comedy via Plautus and Terence in which the bearer of important tidings talks incessantly while deferring the actual point. Shakespeare adapts it for the nurse in *Romeo and Juliet*, II. iv (*Complete Works*, ll. 1288–1348).

9. *depatriate.* Not a Malapropism, as the word is used correctly, but certainly pretentious. The inappropriate use of recondite vocabulary had been satirized in ancient times in Lucian's *Lexiphanes* and more recently in a passage closely imitated from it in Jonson's *The Poetaster*, V. iii. The word may have had a cult significance for those royalists who, like Buckingham, had gone into exile during the civil wars while the more tepid supporters of the Crown chose to stay at home.

24. *Protest I care not.* For 'I protest I care not', an attested seventeenth-century usage, especially at the beginning of sentences. Cf. Stapylton, *The Slighted Maid*, II. i:

*Me.* What would you say?
*Per.* Protest, I know not what: ((London, 1663), p. 25),

and Dryden, *Cleomenes*, IV. i. 73 (*Works* , xvi. 129)

*Ptolo.* 'Protest I thought em honest; are they not?

Also at V. iii. 6 below.

*demarches.* Literally 'gait' or 'walk'; metaphorically, 'mode of thought'.

43–4. *sinning without pleasure . . . that should cause it.* A literal reading of this passage might suggest that Constantia was still a virgin and that her 'sinning' had only taken the form of agreeing to let the impotent Antonio sin with her if he could. But the comic emphasis is surely on the denial of pleasure rather than on the experience of remorse. In her subsequent encounter with John Constantia presents herself as sexually confident and putatively experienced.

55. *the Fiddles are here.* Montague Summers, *The Restoration Theatre* (London: Routledge & Kegan Paul, 1934), 110–11, proposes that the mother was referring to the theatre's music room, which he believed was located in the proscenium arch directly above the stage. Dance music for fiddles was normally performed in Restoration comedy by a reduced ensemble of two violins and a bass viol. See Harold Love, 'The Fiddlers on the Restoration Stage', *Early Music*, 6 (1978), 391–9 and Curtis Price, 'Restoration Stage Fiddlers and their Music', *Early Music*, 7 (1979), 315–22.

## *IV. ii*

9.1. *Musick.* Here probably in the specialized sense of an ensemble of musicians (*OED* 5). Theophilus Cibber records disapprovingly how, on hearing the music, Garrick used to 'give you a Touch of a Hornpipe in the Middle of the Street' (see above, p. 30).

12. *masked.* Prostitutes wore and were identified by 'vizard-masks' that covered the upper portion of the face.

13. *12 score distance.* 'Twelve score' (240) was once used in a variety of contexts to suggest a considerable number. It was also the number of pence in an old pound. As a measure of distance in yards it was a traditional range for shooting with a bow or a gun.

55–84. *Come pray . . . let me try.* John Harold Wilson, *Nell Gwyn: Royal Mistress* (London: Frederick Muller, 1952), 60, connects this passage with one in the preface to Lee's *The Princess of Cleve* (perf. 1682? pub. 1689):

. . . for when they expected the most polish'd Hero in Nemours, I gave 'em a Ruffian reeking from Whetstone's-Park. The fourth and fifth Acts of the Chances, where Don John is pulling down; Marriage Alamode, where they are bare to the Waste; the Libertine, and Epsom-Wells, are but Copies of his Villany. (*The Works of Nathaniel Lee*, ed. Thomas B. Stroup and Arthur L. Cooke, 2 vols. (Metuchen, N.J.: Scarecrow, 1954–5), ii. 153)

Fowler regards Lee's reference as to the general tenor of John's behaviour rather than to any particular act of undressing, but it is possible that John made some gesture towards disrobing at this point.

94. *so just of my humour.* Establishing John and 2 Constantia as precursors of the 'gay couple' comedy created by Dryden and other dramatists for the King's Company in the 1660s (see Smith, *Gay Couple*, ch. 3). The parts were initially taken by Charles Hart and Nell Gwyn (see pp. 16–18, above).

## *IV. iii*

72. *thy Genius lies another way.* The distinction between the sentimental and the practical lover is taken up in a number of Restoration comedies, most notably with Vainlove and Bellmour in Congreve's *The Old Batchelour.*

## IV. iv

A 'French' not an English scene as there is no change of place or time nor alteration of flat scenes.

30. *she is so willing.* Fowler points to two further instances of this joke in plays by Fletcher, *The Faithful Shepherdess*, III. i. 212–13 and *The Captain*, I. iii. 191–2.

64. *Bilbo.* A fine sword forged at Bilboa in Spain.

## V. i

0.1. *Constables.* Fowler emends to 'Constable' since there is only one referred to in the text. What is portrayed is the arrival of the watch headed by a constable.

## V. ii

14. *is it you my Dear?* Fowler suggests that 1 Constantia would be wearing a vizard mask in this scene, but see the note to IV. ii. 12, above. Her wearing a hood to avoid recognition seems more likely.

45. *the fiercest Enemy I have.* Introduced opportunistically without preparation. Only Antonio's general character supports it. The line would have come more persuasively from 2 Constantia.

## V. iii

6. *Protest, Madam.* See note on IV. i. 24.

15. *Meniarderies of a bonne mine.* Anticipating the fun had with Melantha's pretentious use of French phrases in Dryden's *Marriage A-la-Mode* (1671). The term 'meniarderie' is not recorded—possibly it is a phonetic spelling of 'mignarderie' ('delicacy, daintiness'). *Bonne mine* means 'good bearing or appearance'. It is also used at *The Country Gentleman*, I. i. 34 and *passim*.

23. *strange.* OED 'strange', v. 7: 'To be surprised, wonder'.

35. *that other Woman.* Another underprepared plot element.

84. *I do not know Antonio.* Either a lie or an authorial loose end: see IV. iv. 56, 'Who's this? *Antonio?*' uttered in Frederick's presence.

## V. iv

141. *that all shall be well.* Repeating an allusion to *A Midsommer Night's Dreame*, l. 1441, made at III. iv. 56.

180–2. *Consummation . . . consummate.* The passage plays on three senses of the word and of its Latin originals *consummatio* and *consummare*. The duke is speaking of a 'summing up' or 'bringing together' of joys, John of the inauguration of his sexual relationship with 2 Constantia, and Constantia of a completion or terminating of joys. The 'summing' is thus (1) a cumulation; (2) a bringing to a climax; and (3) arrival at the end of a series.

*Epilogue*

In Sarah Cowper's Commonplace Book (Hertfordshire Archives and Local Studies MS D/EP F37) this appears in a variant version as 'A Prologue to the two last Acts of the Chances' and is marginally attributed to ' M.C.' [Martin Clifford]. See note on prologue. The text of this version is at ii. 250 below.

1–6. These lines anticipate the strategy of the 'Thunder and Lightning' passage in *The Rehearsal*, I. i.

2. *fag end.* Originally the last, inferior piece of a rope or bolt of cloth.

15. *a Box.* Referring here to the cost of a place in the box tier, which was normally 4*s*.

20. *Nel.* Nell Gwyn, who is named as 2 Constantia in a manuscript cast that implies performance in the spring or summer of 1664. For her probable availability at that time, see the Introduction, pp. 16–18. Wilson, *All the King's Ladies*, 147, writing before the discovery of the manuscript cast, offered the conjecture that Gwyn took this part in the original production of *The Chances*, for which he accepted the traditional 1667 date. She left the stage for good early in 1671 to become the king's mistress. For her life see Wilson's *Nell Gwyn, Royal Mistress*.

## SIR POLITICK WOULD-BE

The Finch and Joliat edition of *Sir Politick Would-be* (Geneva: Droz, 1978) was the first to be abundantly annotated. Its contribution to the elucidation of the text is gratefully acknowledged and has been drawn on in the present version, which attempts nonetheless to tackle a number of difficulties or apparent puzzles in its own way. Des Maizeaux's notes of 1726—varying slightly from what he provided in 1705 —are treated as an integral part of the text. René de Planhol's modernized *Œuvres de Saint-Évremond*, 3 vols. (Paris: Cité des Livres, 1927) with *Sir Politick Would-be* at ii. 221–347, ignores and omits all but one of Des Maizeaux's notes on the play and has no others. Bishop Percy's edition, probably planned in the 1760s (though evidently not typeset until the 1790s and never actually published) adds two suggestions to Des Maizeaux's, which are given below. The editor of the French text and its translator into English have collaborated in the writing of these notes. The expert advice of Moira Goff of the British Library on the various dances mentioned in Scenes iv and v of Act IV is acknowledged with thanks. Suggestions and additions provided by the general editors have also been gratefully incorporated, since they help in the difficult process of catering for French and English audiences.

The first line number for a note refers to the French text in volume 1. The second line number (given in parentheses) refers to the English translation provided in volume 2, Appendix V (ii. 341–99).

## *ACTEURS*

1 (1). *Sir Politick Would-be.* The name is borrowed from Jonson's *Volpone*, one of the relatively few English texts known to Saint-Évremond, at least by report (see 'De la comédie angloise' in *Œuvres en prose*, ed. René Ternois (Paris: Didier, 1962–9), iii. 55–60). However, it would be rash to argue for any sort of close identification with the earlier character, and the idea that Henry Bennet, later Earl of Arlington, was the satirical target of Saint-Évremond and of his friends (see ibid. iii. 33) is mere supposition. Indeed Quentin Hope (*Saint-Evremond and his Friends* (Geneva: Droz, 1999), 255–7) strongly denies the possibility.

6 (5). *Le Marquis de Bousignac.* This character is generally thought to be a teasing caricature of Saint-Évremond's friend Philibert de Gramont (1621–1707), the eponymous protagonist of Anthony Hamilton's *Mémoires de la vie du comte de Gramont* (Cologne, 1713). The text preserves—even more fitfully in 1726 than in 1705—some of the Gascon pronunciations that go with the role. On Saint-Évremond's connection with Gramont see Hope, 243–51.

16 (13). *faux Caton.* Both the elder (234–149 BCE) and the younger (95–46 BCE) Cato were regarded as models of Roman civic virtue and fervent supporters of republican values. The reference here is probably to the elder, famed for his rigorous conduct in the office of censor and his repeated advocacy of the destruction of Carthage.

19 (16). *Pamfilino.* Finch and Joliat (*Sir Politick Would-be* (Geneva: Droz, 1978) pp. 115–16) link this name with that of Buckingham's host in Rome before 1647: Count Pamphili, nephew of Innocent X. One of the problems of the play's genesis is the extent to which it draws on the memories of Saint-Évremond's friends and collaborators as expressed in conversation.

*Illustration facing the beginning of I. i*

The scene depicted by Bernard Picart—in 1724, presumably for the 1726 edition—is Mme de Riche-Source dancing the saraband (IV. iv. 102–22). The same scene is illustrated in the 1706 Amsterdam edition—the second one authorized by Des Maizeaux—by a different artist, who does not sign a composition that is less faithful to the details set out in the play. The illustration is absent from the other authorized editions (1705 and 1711) that preceded 1726.

*I. i*

42 (42). *le Senat*. Riche-Source's prediction is at bottom a fantasy. Over the centuries Venetian attitudes to foreigners, including *condottieri*, fluctuated, but, while election to the broadly based Great Council sometimes happened, access to higher offices, including the Senate, seems to have been the preserve of the native-born patriciate. On these complex questions see Frederic C. Lane, *Venice: A Maritime Republic* (Baltimore, Md.: Johns Hopkins University Press, 1973); Michael Mallett, 'Venice and its Condottieri, 1404–54', in J. R. Hale (ed.), *Renaissance Venice* (London: Faber and Faber, 1973), 121–45; and James S. Grubb, 'Elite Citizens', in John Martin and Dennis Romano (eds.), *Venice Reconsidered: The History and Civilization of an Italian City-state* (Baltimore, Md.: Johns Hopkins University Press, 2000), 339–64.

48 (47–8). *le Pays orageux*. At the supposed time of the play France was enduring the last stage of its wars of religion in the Huguenot defence of La Rochelle. These were followed at mid-century by the wars of the Fronde.


*I. ii*

20 (19). *Circulation*. See below, II. iv. 46. and *passim*.


*I. iii*

11 (11). *Madame vôtre femme*. Finch and Joliat note analogies between this passage and two speeches by Sir Politick Would-be in *Volpone*, IV. i. There is also a reference to Machiavelli and Bodin (see V. i. 16 below).

49–51 (47–9). *de ces choses . . . qu'elles sont trouvées*. A thought best known from Pope's formulation in *An Essay on Criticism*:

> True *wit* is *Nature* to Advantage dresst;
> What oft was *Thought*, but ne'er so well *Exprest*. (i. 297–8)

Pope acknowledged a loose anticipation in Quintilian, *Institutio Oratoria*, 8. 3. 71; however, the closest parallel cited by the Twickenham editor is from Boileau writing in 1701 (*Pastoral Poetry and An Essay on Criticism*, ed. E. Audra and Aubrey Williams (London: Methuen, 1961), 272–3).

52 (51). *douze cens ans*. Which would correctly fix the migration of the Veneti to the area in the fifth century, though it was not until the ninth that they occupied the present site of the city.

57 (54). *la Porte*. Pierre Richelet's *Dictionnaire françois* (Geneva, 1679–80) defines this as 'la Cour du Grand Seigneur' (ii. 191). It is the Sublime Porte of English usage.

65 (63). *pigeons*. See note on II. ii. 75.

79–80 (77). *Beaucoup de gens en ont pour les siéges.* Buckingham had studied the technical aspect of siegecraft in Paris. See note on II. i. 54. However, it has to be remembered that Saint-Évremond was a professional soldier for nearly three decades, that he served under Condé and Turenne, both of whom he knew very well, and that his last commission—as early as 1652—was as a *maréchal de camp*, a rank variously rendered as brigadier-general or major-general. This background adds piquancy—and authority—to the discussions of military matters in the play.

96 (93). *Antipodes.* The word is defined by Richelet (i. 33) as 'Ceux qui marchent sous l'émisphére qui nous est oposé'. In modern French the uses are wider.

123–4 (117). *retranchemens.* Richelet (ii. 312) suggests 'Sorte de *fortification* & d'ouvrage qu'on fait pour se retrancher contre l'ennemi', i.e. defensive works within others, such as traverses, parapets, or projecting walls within ditches or trenches.

128 (129). *Philippe II.* Sir Politic ignores the counter-example of the armada, committed by Philip to the direction of the Duke of Medina-Sidonia.

160 (152). *en bonne intelligence.* This was true of the time of writing but not of the supposed time of the action, when the two nations were actually at war, with the British giving active military support to the Huguenots.

176 (168). *il est souvent indisposé.* Unintentionally conceding one of Sir Politick's main arguments for multiple dogeships.

## I. iv

16 (15). *Les rivieres les plus profondes.* A proverbial commonplace for which many parallels could be cited. Cf. Anne Wharton, 'Elegie on John, Earle of Rochester' (1680), ll. 1–2.

> Deep Waters silent roul, so greifs like mine
> Tears neuer can relieve, nor words define.

(*The Surviving Works of Anne Wharton*, ed. G. Greer and S. Hastings (Stump Cross, Essex: Stump Cross Books, 1997), 140.)

46 (43). *je veux de belles Putains.* Finch and Joliat compare this expression, which would be surprising in a classical French text, with Buckingham's plain speaking.

52–3 (49–50). *chez des Flores & des Laïs.* Generic names for prostitutes. Flora was the Roman goddess of flowers, whose festival, celebrated in April, was associated with sexual licence. Lais was the name of two celebrated courtesans of ancient Corinth.

70 (67). *le charme de la vûë.* One of the ways in which Italian cuisine asserted its superiority in this period was in the presentation of grand formal meals. Alongside cooking classics like Bartolomeo Scappi's *Opera* (Venice, 1570; repr. with introduction by Giancarlo Roversi, Sala Bolognese: Arnaldo Forni, 1981) there was a literature emphasizing the aesthetics of display.

80 (76–7). *plier le linge.* Table linen was also slow in reaching northern Europe.

85–6 (82). *une chose si surprenante.* The recipe is noted by Finch and Joliat as occurring in *Epulario, or, the Italian banquet* (London, 1598—STC 10433), a work that first appeared in Italian in Venice in 1549.

90–1 (86). *l'ornement de nos Salades.* Not practised in France or in England at this period.

*II. i*

10 (11). *Duc de Buckingham.* George Villiers, first Duke of Buckingham (1592–1628). If an actual cousin was glanced at, he can not now be identified.

35 (34–5). *Monsieur de Montmorency.* Henri II de Montmorency (1595–1632), appointed *maréchal* in 1630, executed two years later for his part in the rebellion of Gaston d'Orléans.

39 (38). *la naissance de Monsieur son fils.* George Villiers, second Duke of Buckingham, was born on 30 January 1628. The action of the play is therefore set at the beginning of the life of one of its claimed authors. Readers are left to cope with a mixture of flattery and self-referentiality.

41–2 (41). *il n'y a que la main.* Which should first offer the hand on meeting and which receive it.

54 (52). *logemens.* Richelet (i. 473) offers '*Logement. Terme de Guerre.* Retranchement qu'on fait lorsqu'on a gagné la contrescarpe, ou quelque autre poste pour empêcher les ennemis de regagner ce qu'on a pris sur eux'. A technical term for the occupation and retention of positions, from the science of siege warfare, which Buckingham had studied in Paris with the distinguished mathematician, Gilles Personne de Roberval, and which was also professionally familiar to Saint-Évremond.

55 (53). *Monsieur de Vignoles.* Des Maizeaux's note does not say which member of the Vignolles family is meant. Almost certainly it was an officer known to Saint-Évremond himself or to members of his circle. The most likely candidates are Paul de Vignolles (1566–1660), sieur de Montredon, who was still on active service in his seventies, Bertrand de Vignolles (1565–1636), sieur de Casaubon et de Preschet, baron, then marquis, de Vignolles, and Jacques de Vignolles (1609–1686), sieur de Prades, father of the scholarly pastor, Alphonse de Vignolles (1649–1744). See Eugène and Émile Haag, *La France protestante*, 10 vols. (Paris and Geneva: Cherbuliez, 1846–59), ix. 497–503. The second held many high posts and was several times wounded. In 1628 he was the principal *maréchal de camp* in Louis XIII's army at the siege of La Rochelle. For an extended list of his military service and responsibilities, see Père Anselme, et al., *Histoire généalogique et chronologique de la Maison royale de France*, 3rd ed., 9 vols. (Paris: Compagnie des Libraires Associés, 1726–33), ix. 145.

136–7 (129–30). *la perte de la Guienne.* Or Aquitaine, the duchy around Bordeaux, which by the second marriage of Eleanor of Aquitaine to the future King Henry II of England in 1152 became English until the end of the Hundred Years War. In the seventeenth century it was part of the *gouvernement* of Guienne and Gascony, a sensitive area during the civil wars of the Fronde.

145 (138–9). *Ah! Monsieur, qu'on nous haït!* An example of violence in London involving the French is provided by the murderous affray in October 1661—not long before Saint-Évremond's second arrival in England—when Louis XIV's ambassador and his Spanish colleague fought over precedence at the formal entry of the Swedish envoy. The affair is recounted in detail in Saint-Évremond's *Lettres*, ed. René Ternois (Paris: Didier, 1967–8), i. 76–7. Various Frenchmen were accused of having helped spread the great fire of 1666 and one, Robert Hubert, was executed. See Neil Hanson, *The Dreadful Judgement: The True Story of the Great Fire of London* (London: Doubleday, 2001), 263–302.

## II. ii

58 (51). *Avec l'Algebre on fait tout.* Finch and Joliat claim this as an old Venetian saying and point to Luca [Pacioli] de Burgos' *Somma di aritmetica, geometria, proporzioni e proporzionalità* (Venice, 1494—Goff L-315) as the first printed book to treat the subject. From Richelet (i. 24) and Randle Cotgrave (*A Dictionarie of the French and English Tongues* (London, 1611); facsim. repr. (Columbia, S.C.: University of South Carolina Press, 1950), sig. D2$^v$) it is clear that the word was currently used in something approaching its modern sense.

75 (67). *quelque chose d'approchant.* The vagueness is a little odd given the long history of the use of 'pigeons messagers'. See Diderot's *Encyclopédie*, xii (1765), 610–14, with a reference to the recourse to carrier pigeons by the Protestants at the sieges of Harlem and Leiden in 1574 and 1575. Their homing abilities were already understood in Roman times.

## II. iv

20 (19). *Plutarque de Cheronée.* The 1705 edition adds a shoulder-note '*De la Version d*'Amyot'. However, Finch and Joliat failed to find the alexandrine in Amyot's much-reprinted sixteenth-century translation of Plutarch. The central position the Greek writer occupied in the reading tradition of the *honnête homme*—from Montaigne to Saint-Évremond—is well treated in Jean-Marc Chatelain's *La Bibliothèque de l'honnête homme: Livres, lecture et collections en France à l'âge classique* (Paris: Bibliothèque nationale de France, 2003). In fact, the line appears as the epigraph to Montaigne's essay ' Du parler prompt ou tardif ' (I. x), having its origin as line 14 of Sonnet XIV of Étienne de La Boétie's *Vers françois* (Paris: Fédéric Morel, 1572), fol. 16$^v$. Montaigne had arranged for the publication of the works of his friend and even included 29 sonnets in editions of his own *Essais* between 1580 and

1588. If Sir Politick is bluffing, his creator is well aware of the fact; but a lapse of memory seems more likely. What is more curious is that Des Maizeaux did not spot the error. Montaigne's contrast between spontaneous and carefully prepared eloquence provides an ironic context for the play. In the seventeenth century, editions of both Montaigne and Plutarch were fitted out with copious shoulder-notes and indexes for the convenience of seekers of moral examples and *sententiae*.

46 (47). *la Circulation.* Harvey's discovery of the circulation of the blood, referred to at 67 below, was enthusiastically seized upon by economic theorists as a metaphor for the functioning of fiscal systems. See on this Ludovic Desmedt, 'Money in the 'Body Politick': The Analysis of Trade and Circulation in the Writings of Seventeenth-century Political Arithmeticians', *History of Political Economy*, 37 (2005), 79–101. Dryden alludes to the parallel in *Annus Mirabilis*, ll. 5–8. Anthony Aspromourgos of the University of Sydney has kindly supplied the following explanation of its meaning in the putative context of 1628. The dominant economic motif of the dialogue is 'circulation', frequently repeated, along with the closely connected idea of 'channel'. Circulation *is* Mr. de Riche-Source's scheme, and Sir Politick Would-be is moved to call it *'the Science'* of circulation. Riche-Source's very incoherent supposition is that Eastern princes have blocked monetary circulation, because Europe exchanges gold for Eastern wares, thereby draining gold to the East. (Even if true, since this exchange process is apparently voluntary, why the Eastern princes should be blamed is not clear.) The solution is not explained, beyond 'unblock our channels'; but in any case, Sir Politick is supposed to have carriage of this, either by negotiation (treaties) or war. (The latter option seems to run into a problem of chicken and egg, since the point of departure of the dialogue is that money, which is lacking owing to blocked circulation, is the prerequisite for waging war.) Riche-Source just vaguely describes a happy movement of gold around the world, from Europe to the East and back again, and so on, with no statement of a genuine policy or process whereby the flow of gold to the East would be altered. There is a reference to 'barriers' being removed; but what are they? Short of theft or conquest, a systematic flow of gold-money from Europe to Asia could only be due to a deficit in the European balance of trade (plus other international transactions) with the East, for the aggregate of all *other* commodities exchanged between them—the gold flow making up the difference and balancing the transactions in total. How the unblocking would alter this is unexplained. By the end of the dialogue one is unsurprised by Riche-Source's earlier comment that 'ordinary minds' have not been able to understand his scheme. The parody is most probably aimed at Edward Misselden (*fl.* 1608–54), author of *Free Trade. Or, The Meanes to make Trade Florish* (London, 1622—STC 17986) and *The Circle of Commerce. Or the Ballance of Trade, in Defence of Free Trade* (London, 1623; STC 17985). The latter was one of the more significant seventeenth-century English mercantilist tracts. Beyond the heavy-handed use of the circle metaphor, there is an allusion at lines 111–13 (104–5) to free trade in this scene ('la Circulation est du droit des gens; que vouloir l'empêcher, c'est interesser les Nations, & aller contre la liberté

naturelle de tous les peuples'). While mercantilist literature tended to favour government regulation and restriction, Misselden is an example of the presence also of a somewhat more liberal element in that literature. Nevertheless, as an official and negotiator for English trading companies, he advocated exclusive trading rights. In these capacities, he spent a decade in Holland and represented the East India Company—perhaps echoed in the dialogue's reference at lines 130–1 (122) to 'the English and Dutch, who trade in the Indies'. On Misselden, see Douglas Vickers, 'Misselden, Edward', in *The New Palgrave: A Dictionary of Economics*, ed. John Eatwell, Murray Milgate and Peter Newman, 4 vols. (London: Macmillan, 1987), iii. 480–1, and the *ODNB* entry.

60–1 (61). *le Mogol.* In 1628, the approximate date for the action of this play, the Sultan and the Shah were actually at war. Shah Jahan, the Great Mogul, would not begin construction of the Taj Mahal with the assistance of Italian craftsmen until 1631.

67 (67–8). *la circulation du sang nouvellement découverte.* William Harvey's *Exercitatio anatomica de motu cordis et sanguinis* was published in Frankfurt in 1628. See the note on l. 46 above.

120–1 (118). *brûler tous les vaisseaux de l'Orient.* As a form of economic warfare, a goal brilliantly achieved in 1666 by Buckingham's friend Sir Robert Holmes when he destroyed a substantial part of the Dutch merchant fleet at the islands of Vlie and Ter Schelling.

## III. i

16 (15). *vos Horloges.* By the period of the play mechanical clocks were three centuries old in Germany, but much older in China. On their place in history see James Jesperson and Jane FitzRandolph, *From Sundials to Atomic Clocks: Understanding Time and Frequency*, 2nd edn. (Gaithersburg, Md.: National Institute of Standards and Technology, 1999).

24 (23). *Cabinets.* The word is defined essentially by the *Dictionnaire de Trévoux* (1771 edn., 129–30) as 'Le lieu le plus retiré dans le plus bel appartement des palais, des grandes maisons'. Figurative meanings extend this complex term considerably.

30 (29). *Mort-nom-sang-Dieu.* The French text reads 'non', but this is evidently a slip for 'nom', a word frequent in oaths (e.g. nom de chien! nom de Dieu!). Josias von Rantzau (1609–50), a member of an old noble family from Schleswig-Holstein, was in Swedish and Imperial service before joining the French army in 1635 and becoming a Marshal of France ten years later.

45–6 (43). *espirituelle.* A typical Gasconism. See Desgrouais, *Les Gasconismes corrigés* (Toulouse: Vve Douladoure, 1801), 142–3. Between the 1705 and 1726 editions a similar regional form, *Estatuës*, was corrected to *Statuës* in the next scene (III. ii. 184–5 (159)).

*III. ii*

46 (42). *Itineraire.* Guides or *itineraria*, in vernacular languages or in Latin, were already quite common in seventeenth-century Europe.

49–50 (45). *Album Amicorum.* According to the *Dictionnaire encyclopédique du livre*, i (2002), 48, the expression *album amicorum* was introduced into France in 1662 (i.e. about the time *Sir Politick Would-be* was written). However, it is not altogether accurate to say the custom originated in Germany in the seventeenth century. Cf. *Abraham Ortelius album amicorum*, ed. Jean Puraye, in *De Gulden Passer*, 45 (1967), 1–125 and 46, nos. 1–3 (1968), 1–99.

85 (76–7). *quel tems avez-vous pour dîner.* Dinner, taken in the early afternoon, was the main meal of the day in Britain and France.

95–6 (85). *les Horloges, qui font passer les douze Apôtres avant que de sonner.* Like the famous Orloj in Prague (1410) and the clock of Strasbourg Cathedral in France (1352).

132 (119). *l'Epitaphe de Talbot.* Despite Des Maizeaux's note the monument is that of Edward Talbot, eighth Earl of Shrewsbury, who died in 1617. See the detailed description in [Jodocus Crull], *The Antiquities of St. Peter's, or the Abbey-Church of Westminster*, 2nd edn. (London, 1715), 30–3.

132–4 (120–1). *le Portrait de Henri VIII, à White-Hall avec la Procession entrant dans Boulogne.* The vast old Palace of Whitehall, where Saint-Évremond lived for a time, was largely destroyed by fire in 1697. Various works by Holbein or done under his supervision were there, not all of which have survived.

134 (121). *les Lions de la Tour.* The fame of the Royal Menagerie in the Tower of London was not always deserved. When Count Camillo Zambeccari visited it in 1682 (see the typescript translation of his 'Viaggio a Londra' in the De Beer Collection, University of Otago Library, MS 54, p. 19) he found 'no animals at all, except for a very old, very large lioness, who lives in company with a little dog which has never barked owing to some disease. There is also an eagle, a wolf, and a small but handsome tiger-leopard.' For another allusion to the lions, see *The Country Gentleman*, I. i. 23.

140–1 (126). *la Cérémonie de Mylord Maire.* Apart from the animal fights, sporting contests, and speeches of condemned men, not all of which drew the attention of the somewhat more fastidious Count, there was the annual Lord Mayor's Procession, described by Zambeccari as 'perhaps . . . the outstanding celebration in the whole country' (p. 15).

141 (127). *les Enseignes des Cabarets.* Finch and Joliat point to a satirical/facetious piece in *The Spectator* (no. 28, 2 April 1711) on street signs. The wider interest of historians is indicated by Peter W. M. Blayney, *The Bookshops in Paul's Cross Churchyard* (London: The Bibliographical Society, 1990) and David Garrioch,

'House Names, Shop Signs, and Social Organization in Western European Cities, 1500–1900', *Urban History*, 21 (1994), 18–46.

152–3 (137–8). *les fossés faits par le Diable pareillement à New-Market.* Bishop Percy's version (p. 319) adds a note 'Le *Devil's Ditch*'. This celebrated embankment dates from Anglo-Saxon times.

154–5 (139). *la Lanterne du déloyal Gui Faux.* This detail is inconsistent with 1628 as the ostensible year of the action of the play. The lantern was presented to the University of Oxford by Robert Heywood in 1641 and exhibited in the Bodleian Library until 1887, when it was transferred to the Ashmolean Museum. See William Dunn Macray, *Annals of the Bodleian Library Oxford*, 2nd edn. (Oxford: Clarendon Press, 1890), 93–4, 478.

183–4 (163–4). *une Disgrace qui arrive à la Cour pour une belle action.* The complaint, though vague, is quite pointed. If an instance of injustice felt by Saint-Évremond is needed, it could lie in his imprisonment in the Bastille in 1658 after Turenne's success in the battle of the Dunes. Mazarin's jealousy of the great general would be enough for the Cardinal to move against an admittedly indiscreet subordinate. In the end Saint-Évremond owed his release to the intervention of his friend Créqui. See Hope, 77–8.

205 (185). *La Cour n'est pas une mauvaise école.* Finch and Joliat compare this assertion with Saint-Évremond's 'Observations sur la maxime qui dit qu'il faut mépriser la Fortune et ne se point soucier de la Cour' (*Œuvres en prose*, ii. 146–54). Bousignac's views are justly seen as a comic reflection of his creator's more complex attitudes.

240 (218). *l'Ordinaire le plus proche de White-Hall.* While our English translation has tavern for 'ordinaire', the term 'ordinary' was coming into use in England at this period for a public *table d'hote*, such as Chatelin's, so often referred to in Restoration comedies, and it may be this that was intended.

285 (263). *l'Alcibiade de nos jours.* The compliment may seem a little incongruous as well as exaggerated, but it has to be remembered that Saint-Évremond was working in a tradition that viewed Alcibiades positively. See his own references (*Œuvres en prose*, iii. 78, 276) or Montaigne's 'Des plus excellens hommes' (*Essais*, ii. 36). Otway's treatment in his *Alcibiades* of 1675, dedicated to Buckingham's friend Charles Sackville, Earl of Middlesex and later Dorset, is more ambiguous but still praises the renegade Athenian as a 'noble generous Youth' (I. i. 211).

*III. iii*

21–2 (19–20). *L'Amour, comme dit à propos un Ancien, a les clefs de toutes les portes.* A phrase so hackneyed as to have no determinable origin, ancient or otherwise. George Colman the younger naturalized it in the title of his 1803 comedy *Love Laughs at Locksmiths*.

*III. iv*

50 (50). *Physionomie.* The ability to read characters from faces was at that time regarded seriously as a science, with Giambattista della Porta's *De humana physiognomia* (Vico Equense, 1586) its principal textbook. Charles II was a keen student of Porta. However, in French the word was being detached from its association with physiognomy even before the seventeenth century.

*III. v*

15–16 (16). *la petite Suzon.* We interpret this to mean that the elegant Mme de Riche-Source was either the daughter of a professional dancer or that at the age of eight she behaved like one. In a paper to the Interdisciplinary Dance Conference in Ghent, Belgium, in April 2000 on 'Budding attractions: daughters of professional dancers and the sarabande in Louis XIV's court', Rose Pruiksma reported that these young girls, styled 'La petite' followed by the name of the parent, would perform the saraband at royal balls. For an instance see note on IV. iv. 108. We have not found any performer with a stage name of 'Suzon' in this period in the standard reference source, Georges Mongrédien and Jean Robert, *Les Comédiens français du XVIIe siècle: Dictionnaire biographique: suivi d'un inventaire des troupes (1590–1710) d'après des documents inédits*, 3rd edn. (Paris: Centre National de la Recherche Scientifique, 1981).

19 (19–20). *Madame la Princesse de Conti.* In 1628 this has to be Louise-Marguerite de Lorraine, the former Mlle de Guise (1577–1631), widow of François de Bourbon, prince de Conti (1558–1614). A dubious reputation and a close link with François de Bassompierre (1579–1646) and with Marie de Médicis earned her the enmity of Richelieu and, ultimately, banishment from Paris.

29 (29). *un Ambigu.* Richelet (i. 27) defines this as 'Festin où la viande & le fruit sont ensemble'.

30 (30). *Cadeaux.* Richelet (i. 102) notes for this use 'Grand repas. Au lieu de *cadeau*, dans ce sens, on dit d'ordinaire *fête*', thus confirming a certain prejudice against a word perceived as old-fashioned and bourgeois. *Cotterie* (l. 27 [26]) is similarly tainted, as is suggested in Saint-Évremond's own *Académiciens* (*La Comédie des Académistes . . . et Les Académiciens*, ed. Paolo Carile (Milan: Cisalpino-Goliardica, 1976), ll. 609–12):

> Qu'au milieu des cités la vaine cotterie,
> Au prodigue cadeau soit toujours assortie,
> Et que dans le repas, ainsi que dans l'amour,
> Ils demeurent bourgeois, éloignés de la Cour.

39–40 (39). *Mascarade.* Cotgrave (sig. 3F1ᵛ) suggests '*A Maske, or Mummerie*'. Richelet (ii. 21) has 'Divertissement agréable, & ingénieux de carnaval, où l'on se masque'.

75 (73). *Galantises.* Older form of *galanterie.* It was used widely in the sixteenth century. See E. Huguet, *Dictionnaire de la langue française du seizième siècle* (Paris: Didier, 1925–73), iv. 253–4.

*IV. iii*

31 (30). *Cardinal de Richelieu.* Armand-Jean Du Plessis de Richelieu (1585–1642), the autocratic and always well-informed principal minister of France during the reign of Louis XIII.

*IV. iv*

0.1 (0.1). *On leve un Rideau, & on voit la Sale du Bal.* English practice at the time for 'discovering' an interior would have been to draw aside shutters (painted flats meeting in the centre of the stage) along grooves in the floor. The absence of stage directions from the script is striking. On 17th-c. French scene change practices, see T. E. Lawrenson, *The French Stage and Playhouse in the XVIIth Century,* rev. edn. (New York: AMS Press, 1986), 211–17. For discussion of the mid-stage curtain, see pp. 162 and 165.

15 (16). *grandement cromatique.* Not quite in the modern musical sense, but implying the consistent use of accidentals foreign to a piece's stated mode or scale. The *Piéce ridiculement grave* may have been a ricercare or fantasia, a genre much disparaged at the court of Charles II but in fact highly esteemed at that of Charles I. Antonio Ferrabosco II's two Hexachord Fantasias are striking examples of English 'chromatic' writing in this form (ed. David Pinto (St Albans: Corda, 1992)).

17 (20). *une Pavane.* Richelet (ii. 137) records, rather unhelpfully, 'C'est une sorte de branle ancien'. The 1771 edition of the *Dictionnaire de Trévoux* (vi. 604) is much more precise: 'Danse grave venue d'Espagne, où les danseurs font la roue l'un devant l'autre, comme les paons font avec leur queue, d'où lui est venu ce nom. . . . C'étoit autrefois une danse sérieuse que les Gentilshommes dansoient avec la cape & l'épée; les gens de Justice avec leurs longues robes; les Princes avec leurs grands manteaux; & les Dames avec les queues de leurs robes abaissées & traînantes. On l'appeloit le *grand bal,* parce que c'étoit une danse majestueuse & modeste. Il s'y faisoit plusieurs assiettes de piés, passades & fleurets, & des découpemens de piés, pour en modérer la gravité, dont la tablature est décrite dans Thoinot Arbeau, en son *Orchésographie.* Elle est suivie ordinairement de la gaillarde. Ce mot est commun aux Langues Italienne, Espagnole & Françoise. Cette danse triste & sérieuse n'est plus en usage.' Another etymology derives the name from Padua. For the history of the dance see Alan Brown's article in *New Grove Dictionary of Music,* xix. 249–52.

The pavan and the later dances mentioned were associated both with formal balls and *ballets de cour* at the French and English courts, which the scene seems to be burlesquing. Saint-Évremond was presumably familiar with both balls and ballets at these courts. Buckingham must have been acquainted with those at the English court, but it may be worth noting that he danced in at least one French *ballet de cour*, *Le Ballet de la nuit* given at the Louvre in 1653. He appeared in the sixth *entrée* in part 1, among 'Des Bandis qui volent vn Mercier sur le chemin'; the first *entrée* in part 4, 'representant le Feu'; and the seventh *entrée* in part 4, among 'Amoureux transis' (who also included James, Duke of York). See Isaac de Benserade, *Ballets pour Louis XIV*, présentés et annotés par Marie-Claude Canova-Green (Toulouse: Société de littératures classiques, 1997), i. 107, 144, 150.

The formal balls given at Louis XIV's court were described many years later in chapter 16 of Pierre Rameau's *Le Maître à danser* (Paris, 1725), 49–54. According to Rameau, these balls began with branles (for several couples together, the first of which was led by the king and queen), followed by 'danses à deux', i.e. courantes. The branles were led, and then the courantes danced in strict order of rank. There are very few earlier references to French court balls, and apparently none before the 1680s: see Rebecca Harris-Warrick, 'Ballroom Dancing at the Court of Louis XIV', *Early Music*, 14 (1986), 45–6. However, there was a ball scene in *Le Ballet de la nuit*, in the fourth *entrée* in part 2: 'Toute la Compagnie estant arriuée, le Bal se commence par plusieurs sortes de danses, courantes figurées, & bransles à la vieille mode' (see Benserade, i. 119). This seems to indicate that the dances (if not their order) described by Rameau did form part of French court balls much earlier in the reign of Louis XIV.

According to Pepys, balls at the English court in the early years of Charles II followed the same pattern. He describes one that took place at Whitehall on 31 December 1662, which began with 'the Bransle' led by the king with the Duchess of York, followed by the Duke and Duchess of Buckingham, and so on, after which the king 'led a lady a single Coranto' followed in turn by other lords and ladies. Similarly, he records another ball at Whitehall on 15 November 1666, which began with 'Bransles' and continued with 'Corants' and 'now and then a French Dance'. See *Diary of Samuel Pepys*, iii. 300–1 and vii. 371–2. There was no English equivalent to the *ballets de cour* mounted regularly at the French court (except for the masque *Calisto*, given in 1674), but Pepys does mention a masquerade at court on 3 February 1665 and another source says that the dancers represented different nations (*Diary*, vi. 29 and n. 6).

41 (42). *la Pyrrhique*. The *Dictionnaire de Trévoux* (vii. 66) gives 'Sorte de danse des Grecs: on tient qu'elle fut inventée par Pyrrhus fils d'Achille. On dansoit en frappant des boucliers avec les armes, au son des instrumens.' There are descriptions of performances from both the sixteenth and eighteenth centuries.

47–8 (48). *aux Créquis & aux Bassompierres*. As is clear from Saint-Évremond's works and letters, he had a close friendship with Charles de Créqui (1623–87), *maréchal de France*. Bassompierre was a distant family connection. See Hope, *Saint-Évremond and his Friends*, passim.

52 (53). *les Branles.* Richelet (i. 92) states '*Terme de maître à dancer.* Dance où plusieurs dancent en rond, se tenant par la main' whereas the *Dictionnaire de Trévoux* (ii. 42–3) sets out a long description of a dance—with many named sequences —that traditionally began and ended balls at the French and English courts (see note on IV. iv. 17). See also Rameau's *Maître à danser,* 51, and *Diary of Samuel Pepys,* iii. 300 and vii. 372.

58 (59). *son Branle simple, le Gai, le Poitou, & le Montirandé.* All four of these branles are mentioned in Marin Mersenne's *Harmonie universelle, contenant la théorie et la pratique de la musique* (Paris, 1636—facsimile repr., Paris: CNRS, 1963), 'Traitez de la voix, et des chants', 167–8.

60 (61). *Courantes.* By 1650 two types of this dance co-existed, both triple-metre, the faster Italian 'corrente' and the slower French 'courante'. Here the reference is probably to the French version, which had emerged as the most important dance at court balls under Louis XIV. Rameau (*Maître à danser,* 52) states that the courante was the dance in which the king excelled. Much earlier Mersenne (*Harmonie universelle,* 'Traitez de la voix, et des chants', 165) describes it as 'la plus frequente de toutes les dances pratiquées en France & se dance seulement par deux personnes à la fois', although his musical examples resemble the Italian rather than the French version. The French courante was musically demanding, and Pepys refers to a disagreement about 'the law of dancing Corant' (23 April 1665, see *Diary,* vi. 88). There is a coranto joke in *The Rehearsal,* V. i. 67–72.

81 (82). *les vingt-quatre. Dictionnaire de Trévoux* (viii. 412): 'On dit les *Vingt-quatre,* absolument, en parlant de la grande bande des Violons du Roi, qui est composée de ce nombre.' For the history of this famous ensemble, see John Spitzer and Neal Zaslaw, *The Birth of the Orchestra: History of an Institution 1650–1815* (Oxford: Oxford University Press, 2004), 70–6 and *passim.*

85 (86). *d'une Vignone, & d'une Belleville.* The *Vignone* was the title of a well-known tune for a courante. See Alis Dickinson, 'The Courante "La Vignonne": In the Steps of a Popular Dance', *Early Music,* 10 (1982), 56–62. There is perhaps some link to the lutenist and composer Jérôme Vignon, active in Paris in the 1640s and 1650s. The *Belleville* is presumably also a popular tune for a courante, perhaps linked to the dancer, violinist, and composer Jacques de Belleville, active in France in the early seventeenth century, when he composed music and created dances for several *ballets de cour* for Louis XIII, including *Ballet de la délivrance de Renaud* (1617) and the *Ballet de Tancrède* (1619). See the articles on Vignon and Belleville in *New Grove Dictionary of Music.*

105 (106). *la Sarabande.* Richelet (ii. 345): 'C'est une sorte de dance grave, qui, à ce qu'on croit, vient d'Espagne comme il paroît par le mot *çarabanda.*' The French, then, opted for the 'slow and serious' conception of this dance, rather than its 'lively and licentious' Spanish character. The use of the guitar and of castanets distinguished certain performances of the saraband, which occurred both in *ballets de cour* and in the ballroom. The present solo belongs rather to the former.

108 (109). *la petite Suzon.* See note on III. v. 15–16. The information that child dancers using this title danced at balls under Louis XIV provides an explanation for the presence of the bourgeois Mme de Riche-Source at court. In the play's chronology this would have been early in the reign of Louis XIII instead of four decades later; however, we have an illustration of Ribera dancing the saraband with castanets in the *Ballet de la nuit* in 1653. It is noted but not shown that he was accompanied by four little girls, his own daughter among them. See Marie-Fran-çoise Christout, *Le Ballet de cour au xviie siècle* (Geneva: Editions Minkoff, 1987), 118. This was precisely the ballet in which Buckingham danced at the Louvre (see note to IV. iv. 17).

*V. i*

8–9 (7–8). *je tiens qu'on peut mentir pour le Bien de la chose publique.* Bishop Percy adds the note 'Plaisanterie de Sir Henrie Wotton, *Legatus est Vir bonus peregre missus ad mentiendum Reipublicæ Causâ.*' The celebrated circumstances of Wotton's inscription of this sentence in an Augsburg *album amicorum* in 1604 are recounted in the *Oxford Dictionary of National Biography* article on this longtime envoy to Venice (lx. 379–80).

16 (16). *de Nicolas Machiavel, & de François Bodin.* It has already been noted (I. iii. 11) that a reference to Machiavelli and Bodin occurs in a speech of Sir Politick Would-be in *Volpone* (IV. i). Although one could relate Sir Politick's defence of lying for the good of the State to Machiavellian tradition, Percy's quotation from Wotton makes this unnecessary. The mention of *François* rather than *Jean* Bodin is puzzling. Is it a misprint (*de François* instead of *du François* = of the Frenchman) or a simple lapsus on the part of Saint-Évremond? Or is an error being attributed to Sir Politick? It is not clear whether Saint-Évremond was familiar with Bodin's political thought, however relevant this may be to the discussions lying behind the play's grand schemes. Certainly there is no mention of the author of the *République* (1576) in the *Lettres* or in the *Œuvres en prose.* Similarly we do not know whether Bodin's *Réponse aux paradoxes de M. de Malestroit* (1566) on inflation is an effective part of the documentation for Riche-Source's project, as Finch and Joliat half seem to suggest.

*V. ii*

36 (34–5). *deux sortes de Folie.* Reflecting the traditional British division of the mentally affected into 'fools' and 'mad'.

*V. v*

28 (25). *à Hambourg, à Lubec, à Dantzic.* It is perhaps not without significance that, after Sir Politick Would-be and M. de Riche-Source have decided to involve

the Venetian Republic and the civic authorities of London and Paris in their schemes (II. iv), three Hanseatic free-trading cities within the Holy Roman Empire should be proposed as destinations for a return to northern Europe. The anti-authoritarian bias may well be deliberate, at least on the part of Saint-Évremond.

## THE COUNTRY GENTLEMAN

These notes draw (with the kind permission of the University of Pennsylvania Press) on those in the 1976 edition by Arthur H. Scouten and Robert D. Hume and also on a list of suggested corrections and additions to that edition published by Bernard Richards in *Notes and Queries*, 224 (1979), 438–9.

*Persons in the Play*

*Mistress Finical.* She is addressed as 'Mistress Finical Fart' in a sardonic speech by Sir Richard Plainbred (I. i. 391). ' Fart' may, however, be merely his irritated and disrespectful joke at her expense. He employs the word again (in a different context) at V. i. 421.

*Sir Cautious Trouble-all.* A satiric portrait of Sir William Coventry. See the Introduction, p. 231 ff.

*Sir Gravity Empty.* A satiric portrait of Sir John Duncomb. See the Introduction, p. 232.

*Act I*

0.1. *Enter.* The implicit location here (as in Acts II, III, and V) is the parlour of the house in London in which Mrs Finical rents out relatively posh accommodations.

1. *Nay.* An exclamation here without any sense of negation (*OED*, 1.c).

6. *person.* A man or woman of distinction or importance (*OED*, II.2.c.). Cf. Dryden, *The Assignation* (1672), I. i. 11–12: 'a man of my parts . . . is a person' (*Works*, xi. 327). Mrs Finical uses the expression again at I. i. 154 and 158. Interestingly, Trim makes use of it of himself in all seriousness at I. i. 300.

15. *my father was kild.* By implication 'at a Civil War battle, on the Royalist side', a formulaic assurance of respectability in the early Restoration period.

*kild.* Spelt thus rather than 'killd', which is the way it appears to be written at first glance. This is the first of numerous instances in which the copyist has written a single l with upstroke from the previous letter separated from the downstroke, creating a kind of inverted V.

17. *Countrey Gentleman.* Even in 1669 (before the full development of what we now regard as the characteristic ideology and values of Carolean comedy) making a plain country gentleman the exemplary hero of a 'London' play was a rather extraordinary thing to do. Most 'country' figures in English comedy 1660–1710 are comic butts or at best figures of fun.

18–19. *this Town.* The ideological hostility of this play to the amusements of fashionable London runs counter to most of the norms of Carolean comedy. Witwouds may affect what they do not understand, or imitate ineptly, but few comedies of any kind seriously question or criticize Truewit culture. Wycherley's *The Plain-Dealer* (1676) is an obvious exception.

23. *Lyons.* Sir Richard could have seen lions in the Tower of London menagerie, kept from Norman times to 1834 (*Encyclopædia Britannica*, xxvii. 110). They are remarked upon in the opening scene of Shadwell's *Epsom-Wells* (*Complete Works*, ii. 107). For another allusion to the lions, see *Sir Politick Would-be*, III. ii. 134.

26. *affect.* Have a liking for.

34. *bonne mine.* A characteristically pretentious French expression from Mrs Finical, literally meaning 'with a fine look' but figuratively 'with a fancy expression'. See also *The Chances*, V. iii. 15 and n.

37. *Townsend.* Exactly what Trim means by the town's end is not clear, but he has sent a servant to meet Sir Richard and his party and guide them into the city—presumably out on the Oxford road towards Brentford, where the Plainbreds started that morning (see I. i. 358).

40. *dyet be drest.* Mrs Finical is asking whether she (or more precisely, her servants) will be responsible for cooking for Sir Richard and his establishment. The alternative (raised at I. i. 360–1) would be to get food sent from an 'ordinary' or cook-shop.

51. *the last Bill.* The conversation makes plain that Vapor and Slander have not yet paid Trim for past goods and services. He says angrily at II. i. 127 'They owe me money.'

53. *Felo-de-se.* Suicide.

62. *subsidy way.* A reference to the unpopular revival of the old Tudor 'subsidy' taxes, tried with mediocre success by Charles II between 1663 and 1671. See David Ogg, *England in the Reign of Charles II*, 2 vols., 2nd edn. (Oxford: Clarendon Press, 1956), ii. 434–6.

65. *periwigs.* A periwig is an artificially constructed head of hair (often made of real hair), a fashionable headdress for men in the seventeenth century and long retained by judges and barristers as part of their professional costume. Good ones could be extremely expensive. Pepys says on 29 March 1667, 'to a periwig-maker's . . . and there bought two periwigs, mighty fine; indeed, too fine I thought for me;

but . . . I did buy them, £4 10s. the two.' The not-very-fashionable Jonathan Swift reports in the *Journal to Stella* that he paid 3 guineas for a periwig (15 January 1710/11).

69. *Tyburn*. The site of the Middlesex gallows from the twelfth century to 1783, at the junction of the present Edgware and Bayswater Roads near the current site of Marble Arch. Felton (assassin of Buckingham's father) was hanged there in 1628. Cromwell's skeleton was exhibited there in 1661. Executions were public performances and treated as a kind of holiday spectacle.

104–6. *basons . . . letst bloud*. 'By 32 Henry VIII. c. 42' barbers 'were united with the company of surgeons, it being enacted that the barbers should confine themselves to the minor operations of blood-letting and drawing teeth'. Barbers and surgeons were not separated into distinct corporations until 1745 (18 George II. c. 15). The basin was used to receive the blood (*Encyclopædia Britannica*, iii. 386).

108. *Citterne*. A cittern is a wire-strung chordophone played with a plectrum. The scroll at the end of the neck was often in the form of a carved head. The *OED* notes that it was 'Commonly kept in barbers' shops for the use of the customers'.

109. *Pole*. Barber's pole.

123. *Bo Garson. Beau garçon* (French). Cf. *The Rehearsal*, 'Why, for a *Beau Gerson*' (I. ii. 34:18) and 'Advice to a Paynter, to Draw the Delineaments of a Statesman, and his Underlings', l. 20 and n.

128. *these wealthy as Indian Vessels*. T. W. Craik (*Notes and Queries*, 224 (1979), 437–8) suggests that 'as' may be a scribal error, and that the passage should read 'these wealthy Indian Vessels', 'a metaphor and not a simile'. Trade with India was proving exceedingly lucrative in the 1660s. It had been a Portuguese monopoly in the sixteenth century, but England and the Netherlands broke their hold and competed fiercely for dominance in the seventeenth. The English East India Company was incorporated by a royal charter granted by Queen Elizabeth in 1600. Trade in spices and other goods proved hugely profitable in the Restoration period, attracting 'interlopers' as well as aggressive competition from the Dutch, but a vessel that returned fully laden from India was the next best thing to a Spanish treasure ship.

131. *Privateers*. A privateer is 'An armed vessel owned and officered by private persons, and holding a commission from the government . . . authorizing the owners to use it against a hostile nation, and especially in the capture of merchant shipping' (*OED*).

132. *no purchas no pay*. *Purchas* in this sense means a prize or booty taken by a privateer (*OED*, II. 8). Vapor means that Trim will receive nothing unless they marry the heiresses.

133. *See where he coms*. Bernard Richards suggests that this is a joking allusion to *Hamlet*, I. i ('looke where it comes', l. 37 in the *Complete Works*); however, the phrase occurs in over sixty other seventeenth-century plays (LION).

139. *garnitures.* Ornaments or trimmings added to dress.

142. *O blesse me here's breeding.* Because he has addressed her with the honorific 'Madam' rather than 'Mistress'.

168. *kyther.* The phrase 'quoth he', with sarcastic force. Buckingham uses the expression 'quoth a!' in *The Rehearsal*, I. ii. 83 and V. i. 71.

196. *Caballing.* Petty plotting, intriguing. The earliest example in the *OED* is from 1680. The earliest LION instance is from V. i of Sir Francis Fane, *Love in the Dark* (1675).

214. *undertakers.* Men engaged in nefarious enterprises to influence the actions of Parliament, especially concerning money bills (*OED*, 4.b). Ironically, Howard was considered one of them. See Pepys, 14 Feb. 1668: 'The House is . . . quite mad at the "Undertakers", as they are commonly called, Littleton, Lord Vaughan, Sir R. Howard and others.'

233. *doubt.* Fear (*OED*, II.5).

244. *Marry come up.* An expression of amused surprise or contempt. See Cowley's *Cutter of Coleman-Street* (1661; pub. 1663): 'marry come up; Wo'nt one o' my choosing serve your turn?' (I. ii, p. 2). Cf. 'hoity-toity'.

250. *harefinders.* Men whose business it is to espy a hare on the hunting field. Cf. Shadwell, *The Virtuoso* (1676): 'You stare about like a Hare-finder' (*Complete Works*, iii. 144).

257–8. *tinkling cymbal.* A biblical allusion, rare in comedy at this time. See 1 Corinthians 13: 1.

261. *ale.* Here any fermented liquor made from malt, water, and yeast. Relatively tasteless in its pure form, it could be flavoured in a number of ways. Beer is ale flavoured with hops, and at the time of the play was still a minority preference. See Oscar A. Mendelsohn, *Drinking with Pepys* (London: Macmillan, 1963), 28–39. Ale would be very English, old-fashioned, and lower-class in the view of French-orientated wine-drinkers. Sir Richard's preference makes a patriotic/ideological point.

266. *flanting pinner.* A coif whose flaps are waving. See Pepys, 18 Apr. 1664: 'Lady Castlemayne . . . in Yellow satin and a pinner on'.

278. *Jewes harp.* 'A generic term for a type of mouth-resonated instrument consisting of a flexible tongue, or lamella, fixed at one end to a surrounding frame' (*New Grove Dictionary of Music and Musicians* (1980), ix. 645–6). The origin of the name is unclear and the instrument has no demonstrable association with the Jewish people. Jew's harps appear to have been used in western Europe 'at least since Gallo-Roman times'.

280–1. *soft checquerd apron.* Evidently the customary attire of a barber.

282–4. *If thy friends . . . past breeding.* The comment about Worthy's dead friends does not make sense to us unless she just means that Worthy's education has not made him well bred. The remark about breeding is evidently a pun in contrast to the usage in line 286.

305. *Maudlin.* Tearful (in allusion to the many pictures in which the Magdalen was represented weeping—*OED*).

307. *imbost.* Foaming at the mouth from rage or exhaustion; it may also mean 'ambushed'. See Otway, *Caius Marius* (1680): 'Was ever Lion thus by Dogs emboss'd?' (IV. ii, p. 45) and an *OED* citation from 1654: 'As Mules and Horses, who are imboss'd, foame and chafe the more'.

334. *gether.* Quotha. See 'kyther' at line 168 above.

351. *the Terme.* The law courts in London held four sessions each year: autumn (Michaelmas), winter (Hilary), Easter (spring), and Trinity (early summer). Country gentry often came to town for sessions of Parliament or for one or more of the court terms.

354. *printed curtesie.* Mrs Finical's high-flown speech is stolen from a printed handbook. Cf. the allusion to *The Academy of Complements*, III. i. 376.

358. *Branford.* i.e. Bra(i)nford (Brentford), a location prominent in *The Rehearsal* two years later because it is the scene of Bayes's play. See page 630, below. Brentford is about eight miles west of the present-day Charing Cross—not a negligible stage in the journey, but not a long one.

360–1. *Jerro's, Shatlings, or La frondes.* Fashionable French eating-houses ('ordinaries') in London. Chatelin's and Lafronde's are coupled in allusions in Dryden and Newcastle's *Sir Martin Mar-all* (1667; *Works*, ix. 256), Shadwell's *The Sullen Lovers* (1668; *Complete Works*, i. 37), and Sedley's *The Mulberry Garden* (1668; 48). Pepys ate at Chatelin's on 13 March 1668 (complaining bitterly about paying 8s. 6d. per head—a startling price) and again on 23 April. He refers to it as 'the French house in Covent-garden'.

364. *cotelets* (and *Catlotti* in line 375). Variants of the French *côtelette*.

*amlets.* Omelettes.

370. *stink of beef.* Beef (and in particular, roast beef) had long formed an important part of the English diet and hence in popular lore of the English character. The patriotic devotion to roast beef, and its association with the greatness of 'Old England' are vividly expressed in Richard Leveridge's 'A Song in Praise of Old English Roast Beef', which was immensely popular in the eighteenth century. 'When mighty Roast Beef was the Englishman's Food, / It ennobl'd our Veins & enriched our Blood; / Our Soldiers were brave, and our Courtiers were good. / . . . But since we have learn'd from all Conquering France / To eat their Ragouts, as well as to dance, / We are fed up with nothing but vain Complaisance.' See Richard Leveridge, *Complete Songs*, intro. by Olive Baldwin and Thelma Wilson (London: Stainer and Bell, 1997), 152. The name 'Beef-eaters' for the Yeomen of the Guard was reportedly coined in 1669 by Count Cosimo, Grand Duke of Tus-

cany, on a visit to London (*Encyclopædia Britannica*, xxviii. 917). Sir Richard Plain-bred's enthusiasm for beef and hostility towards French cuisine is a prejudice roundly satirized by Shadwell in Act I of *Epsom-Wells* (1672), where Clodpate (a 'discontented Fop, an immoderate Hater of *London*, and a Lover of the Country above measure, a hearty true *English Coxcomb*') says 'I am drunk once a week at my Lord Lieutenant's, and at my own house spend not scurvy French kick-shaws but much Ale, and Beef, and Mutton, the Manufactures of the Country' (*Complete Works*, ii. 112)—an attitude held in contempt by the gentry of the play.

372. *we cannot sell our beef.* Buckingham had ardently supported the Irish Cattle Bill of 1666, a measure designed to protect landowners such as Sir Richard from one source of competition. Pepys described it as 'a thing, it seems, carried on by the Westerne parliament-men, wholly against the sense of most of the rest of the House' (*Diary* vii. 313–4; 7–8 October).

383. *stave and tale.* To intervene and separate the participants in a bear-baiting or bull-baiting (here Sir Richard) with sticks and pulling the tails of the dogs (*OED*, *stave*, 6.c. and *tail*, v.I.2). Cf. Scott's *Quentin Durward*, ch. 33: 'soon have throttled him, had not the Duke called out—'Stave and tail! . . . take them off him'.

393. *kennell rakers.* Scavengers, specifically those sifting the contents of the central gutter in a street, which at this time served as an above-ground sewer. The *OED* notes that 'kennel-raker' is used both literally and 'as a term of abuse'.

396. *mumpe.* Exaggerated movement of the lips in pronouncing the word.

405. *sack.* From *vin sec*, dry wine imported from Spain and the Canaries and popular in England by the middle of the sixteenth century—hence an old established drink that Sir Richard does not hesitate to call for.

408–10. *Bourdeaux, Burgundie, Bourgoigne, vin de Champaigne, Sillery, Hermitage, O Brian, Piedmont, Port a Port, Peralta Escevas vin d'Ay.* Champagne had only recently been introduced into England. The earliest example of the word in the *OED* is from Butler's *Hudibras* (1664), and the first *OED* entry for *Sillery* is from Shadwell's *The Woman-Captain* (1679). Although *Vin d'Ay* had been made since 1600, these early champagnes were not yet effervescent. They were exported to England in casks; only after champagne began to be fermented in corked bottles did it become a sparkling wine. *Sillery* was a 'still' champagne from the vineyards of the Marquis de Sillery, below Rheims. The Duke of Bedford's first purchase, in 1664, makes no mention of glass bottles. Instead, the steward lists 'three . . . casks, of sillery'. The steward continued receiving it by the hogshead in 1669 and 1670: not until 1676 did it come bottled. Allusions to champagne in English comedy after 1676 begin to mention the sparkling quality of the wine. See Gladys Scott Thomson, *Life in a Noble Household, 1641–1700* (London: Cape, 1937), ch. 10, and Roger Dion, *Histoire de la vigne et du vin en France des origines au xixe siècle* (Paris: n.p., 1959), 628–43. In Rochester's(?) 'Timon' we find 'French Kickshaws, Cellery, and Champoone, / Ragous, and Fricasses' (ll. 73–4). *Hermitage* is a Côtes du Rhône wine; *O Brian* is Haut Brion, a Bordeaux wine. *Peralta* is a seventeenth-century wine from Valencia; *Escevas* or *Sciveses* is Esquivias, a wine from the region of Toledo. Both of these Spanish wines are mentioned by the boaster Friendall in Southerne's *The Wive's Excuse* (1691): 'the Peralta . . . the Schiveas' (IV. i. 9–10). On the topic generally, see Oscar A. Mendelsohn, *Drinking with Pepys* (London: Macmillan, 1963).

414. *vogue names.* The *OED* lists this as the earliest adjectival use of 'vogue'.

415. *well boyld ale.* The traditional infusion mashing process involves mixing malted barley and water to create the wort, which is then drawn off and boiled.

421–2. *this Town.* Isabella's negative attitude towards London is in striking contrast to that of most women arriving from the country, whether fine lady (Harriett in *The Man of Mode*) or innocent (Margery in *The Country-Wife*).

434. *hip shotten.* As with a dislocated hip-joint (i.e. unnatural).

434–5. *paint and patches.* On the use of cosmetics, see the note concerning I. ii. 175 of *The Rehearsal* (645, below). 'Painting' was a relatively recent development: John Evelyn says in 1654 'I now observed how the Women began to paint themselves, formerly a most ignominious thing, & used onely by prostitutes' (*Diary*, iii. 97).

## Act II

7. *Strapado.* A form of torture in which the victim's hands were tied behind his back and he was hoisted by them on a pulley and let halfway down with a jerk.

10–11. *Labyrinthious.* A coined word evidently signifying surprise and confusion. Cf. Milton, 'Into perplexity and new amaze' (*Paradise Regained*, 1671, ii. 38).

16. *litle Archer.* Cupid.

18. *tœdious.* Tedious. The *OED* does not include this form of the word, but gives an example from 1663 under 'tedium': 'deceive the tædium of a winter night'. This is the sort of verbal ostentation for which Shadwell ridiculed Sir Robert Howard in *The Sullen Lovers*. Both here and at III. 81 we read 'tœdious' rather than 'tædious', but the latter is much the more common form, derived from the Latin 'taedium'.

33. *labels of several French names sewd to the Corks.* Labels affixed to the bottle were a slightly later development. See *Wine Labels: 1730–2003—A Worldwide History*, ed. John Salter (London: Antique Collectors' Club, 2004).

39. *cousend.* Cheated. Cf. Howard and Dryden's *The Indian-Queen*, 'Be cousen'd by thy guilty honesty' (I. i. 110; *Works*, viii. 188).

50. *divell a word . . . get out.* The basic situation in Goldsmith's *She Stoops to Conquer* a century later.

51. *whitepots.* A custard or milk-pudding, made chiefly in Devonshire.

54.1. *hoods*. At this time women often wore hoods (rather than hats) as a means of keeping their head and shoulders warm and dry in bad weather. They were often attached to capes for travelling.

66.2. *Enter Trim . . . and stops*. Not a full entrance in view of the characters already on stage. Three lines later he is eavesdropping; at line 99 he has an aside; at 113.2 he 'peeps after' the fops when they leave.

112. *are gon*. Meaning 'far gone in love'. This speech and the next one are asides, since Kate and Lucy have not left the stage and are clearly not meant to hear these sentiments.

113. *chaldese*. To cheat or trick. The first example in the *OED* is from Butler's *Hudibras* (1664). Cf. 'Chaldeans' at III. i. 209.

125–6. *snailes in painted shells*. The expression 'painted Snails' is used of mercenary suitors in Killigrew's *The Parson's Wedding*, in Thomas Killigrew, *Comedies and Tragedies* (London, 1664), 149.

131.1. *makes legs*. 'To perform a bodily movement or gesture, e.g. one expressive of respect or of contempt'; in this case probably to 'make an obeisance, a salaam' (*OED*, 'make', v.1 57.c).

134. *advance*. Trim tells his daughters to come forward.

137. *merchants*. The application of this term to Sir Cautious and Sir Gravity is odd. In the finished form of the play they are definitely pretenders to government rather than mercantile 'business'. This reference might be a remnant of an earlier draft or alternatively a snide suggestion that they are wealthy cits pretending to parliamentary influence that they do not really possess. Behn uses the name 'Sir Cautious' for a city knight in *The Luckey Chance* (1686). We may wonder whether Howard designed them as cits and Buckingham then rejigged them as politicians.

182. *What are these Ladies?* Cautious is asking whether Isabella and Philadelphia are gentlewomen.

187. *Caball*. A clique or faction engaged in secret intrigue. This is *not* an allusion to 'the Cabal' (Clifford, Arlington, Buckingham, Ashley, and Lauderdale), the uneasy ministerial alliance that dominated Charles's government from roughly 1668 to 1673, on which see Maurice Lee, Jr., *The Cabal*.

211. *not long*. The text appears to be corrupt here. The sense is that if Isabella and Philadelphia do not leave they will quickly betray their identity to Cautious and Trouble-all.

227. *I study all humours*. A joke: Sir Cautious is himself a 'humours' character, a butt in the Jonsonian tradition.

233–4. *conjure power within my circle*. This refers to magicians doing their conjuring within circles and (as Bernard Richards suggests) 'obliquely prefigures the table with a hole in it' displayed in Act III.

237. *admire.* Wonder, or are surprised. Empty's response indicates that he takes the word in its modern sense.

238. *Ne'r stirre.* A mild expletive. It is used six times in this play, twice by Empty and four times by Vapor and Slander. Harold Brooks suggested to Robert D. Hume that the phrase was earlier a Puritan asseveration or substitute for profanity, citing a verse from Alexander Brome: 'Gods nigs and ne'er stir, sir, has vanquished God damn me.' Two years later the phrase appears in Elizabeth Polwhele's comedy *The Frolicks* where two characters faced with a tavern reckoning respond as follows:

> *Sir Gregory.* I never will be bafled so again.
> *Zany.* Ne'er stir, if henceforth I do not . . . . (III. 73–4)

Cf. also Rochester's 'To the Postboy', l. 15 (*Works*, 43).

280. *ambo.* The two (Latin).

281. *how true their names are.* With the exception of the four young women, all of the principals in this play have 'telling' names, whether positive (Worthy and Lovetruth) or descriptive (Trim and Sir Richard Plainbred) or derogatory (Mistress Finical, Vapor, Slander, and the pretentious men of business).

289. *cryd smal coal.* Charcoal or small pieces of coal, hawked in the streets of London for cooking and heating—obviously a very dirty occupation.

296. *Trim is made for ever.* Trim—though an ally of the heroes and heroines in the play—is satirized here. He is anxious to marry his daughters for his own advantage, and simply orders them to ' be obedient' in overriding Lucy's protest (ll. 297–300).

306. *all saturday night.* So that customers would be clean-shaven for church the following day. Barbers could not work on the sabbath.

321. *Snapfinger.* A barber. Mrs Finical uses this expression again at IV. i. 52. Cf. *Scoggin's Iestes* (1616): 'they say in our country that he is a foole that cannot snap with his finger and thumbe . . . as Berbars vse to do with their hands when they wash a mans face' (F1r).

326. *Billingsgate Corporation.* A joking reference to the scurrilous, vituperative invective to be found in the famous Billingsgate Fish Market near Lower Thames Street—cf. 'speak like a fishwife'. A market was on the site by 1016, but it was not officially chartered as a fishmarket until a Parliamentary Act of 1698.

329. *case-shot.* 'A collection of small projectiles put up in cases to fire from a cannon; canister shot' (*OED*).

331. *chain bullet.* Better known as 'chain shot', linked projectiles used in naval warfare to destroy a ship's rigging.

336. *runnet.* Rennet; anything used to curdle milk.

338. *Chops.* Jaws.

339. *moon's in Cancer . . . antient Poet.* The conjunction of the moon, Saturn, and Jupiter in May 1385 bringing a great downpour of rain. See Chaucer's *Troilus and Criseyde*, iii. 624–5: 'The bente moone with hire hornes pale, / Saturne, and Jove, in Cancro joyned were.'

346. *ambergrease.* Ambergris. 'A wax-like substance of marbled ashy colour, found floating in tropical seas, and as a morbid secretion in the intestines of the sperm-whale. It is odoriferous and used in perfumery' (*OED*).

351–2. *cucking stoole.* A chair to which a person was bound when being punished by 'ducking'. The *OED* gives an example from 1633: 'committed . . . to be duck'd in a Cucking-Stool at Holborn Dike'.

352. *kennell water.* Liquid waste from the central gutter of a city street. Cf. I. i. 393 and note above.

358. *totterd.* Bernard Richards suggests plausibly that what is meant is not *OED* 1 (tattered) but rather *OED* 2, 'in a tottering condition'. Mrs Finical has wept so copiously that her starched pinner has gone limp and soggy, and hence needs to be restarched and ironed.

363. *looshe.* A variant of the colloquial expression lush, lusche, lousche, etc. To run or dash. Delivered here as an imperative, it is equivalent to the modern 'scoot!' or 'scram!'

395. *hanted.* Haunted.

416–17. *praises of Queen Elizabeth, or deep mouthd hounds.* Exemplary figure though Sir Richard is, his enthusiasm for Old England and country pursuits is being teased here. Buckingham was himself, of course, a great hunter, and a fanatical enthusiast for hunting dogs.

425. *Organda.* Urganda la Desconocida, a fairy in the romance *Amadis de Gaule*.

444. *chang'd your religion.* Found a series of different women attractive.

466. *glasing.* Perhaps mornings glazed by frost or by the sun on dew.

486.1. *hats tuckt up.* This refers to a change in haberdashery fashions. After 1660, brims became wider and were turned up at the sides—an innovation that evidently offends Sir Richard. For illustrations, see R. Turner Wilcox, *The Mode in Hats and Headdress* (New York: Scribner's, 1948).

498. *Sir Rude be.* Rudesby, as in *Twelfe Night*, line 1916: 'Rudesbey be gone' (IV. i).

506. *bore cats.* Archaic form of 'tomcat'.

523. *too hasty for chancery suits.* The longueurs and inefficiency of the Court of Chancery were notorious two centuries before Dickens ridiculed them in *Bleak House*. Isabella is saying that they will sit indefinitely on Worthy and Lovetruth's 'Depositions' before arriving at any decision.

*Act III*

2. *men of buisnes.* This phrase is used twice in the opening lines of *The Rehearsal*, where it has no obvious function (I. i. 10 and 16). With this phrase are used 'grave' and 'troubling one another'. Possibly a private allusion to *The Country Gentleman* included for the delectation of insiders.

20. *windlesse.* Decoy or ensnare (*OED*).

26. *alone, and yet by way of Dialogue.* A sardonic allusion to Dryden's *An Essay of Dramatick Poesie*, probably published early in 1668, in which Sir Robert Howard is represented by Crites in a rather derogatory way. The fairest account of the resulting squabble between Dryden and Howard is probably that by Oliver, *Sir Robert Howard, 1626–1698*, ch. 6. For the documents in the dispute, see D. D. Arundell, *Dryden and Howard, 1664–1668* (Cambridge: Cambridge University Press, 1929).

43–4. *nick 'em all.* Cf. *The Rehearsal* (1675 version), 'I'll nick 'em' (I. ii. 34:15).

46. *oyster Table.* Specially used for the consumption of oysters in the seventeenth and eighteenth centuries. Before 1700, the word *table* (in this sense) meant the tabletop only. Hence Sir Cautious's servant John could easily be sent to fetch the 'oyster table'. It was presumably mounted on trestles. Henry Hastings (1551–1650) owned one, which was kept at the lower end of his parlour. It 'was in constant use twice a day all the year round, for he never failed to eat oysters before dinner and supper, the neighbouring Town of Poole supplied him with them'. See Percy Macquoid and Ralph Edwards, *The Dictionary of English Furniture From the Middle Ages to the Late Georgian Period*, 3 vols. (New York: Scribner's, 1924–7), iii. 209. A manuscript published in 1860 mentions a round oyster table, kept in 'The Parlor' (*OED*), but the only definition the *OED* offers is 'a table inlaid with mother-of-pearl'. The central hole clearly postulated by Buckingham was presumably intended for the disposition of shells. In appearance, what Buckingham had in mind was probably very like two semi-circular 'wine tables' set together (see Macquoid and Edwards, iii. 286–7, figs. 4 and 5).

48. *U 'ds.* A minced form of 'God's'. Ud's so (or 'ods' or 'ads') is a common expletive in late seventeenth-century comedy.

54. *Table for buisnes.* Sir William Coventry actually had such a table and delighted in showing it off to visitors, Pepys among them. See the Introduction, p. 247. Bernard Richards has suggested (rather speculatively, in our opinion) that 'sexual innuendo' attaches to the 'Table for buisnes'. He believes that 'gestural allusions to the hole' would make it 'a sort of primitive lavatory'.

62–3. *Spanish papers . . . French papers.* In real life, Coventry, as the junior secretary of state, would only have been concerned with northern Europe, leaving the south and Ireland to his colleague, Arlington. See G. E. Alymer, *The Crown's Servants* (Oxford: Oxford University Press, 2002), 15–16.

81. *tœdious.* Complicated.

83–4. *newes books or Gazets.* On manuscript newsletters, see page 620; on the recently founded *London Gazette*, see p. 443 in vol. II.

86. *Sookers.* Truncated form of 'Gadsookers', a expletive which appears seven times in variant spellings in *The Rehearsal,* including 'Zookers' (IV. i. 102).

94. *light.* Lit.

102–3. *goes to dinner . . . at twelve.* Probably meant to seem odd or worse. To judge from Pepys, government functionaries tended to dine about 2 p.m., comfortably in advance of the commencement of theatrical performances, which started at 3.30 in the 1660s (see the prologue to Dryden's *The Wild Gallant*).

112. *Whife.* Possibly the copyist's error for 'while'; however, the fact that this extremely rare form occurs four times on p. 6 of Sir Robert Howard's *The Surprisal* (performed in 1662; published in *Four New Plays* (London, 1665)) suggests that it may have had a function similar to that of *OED* 'whifflow', i.e. as a nonsense word used when the correct term could not be remembered or none existed (cf. 'thingy', 'thingummyjig'). In *The Surprisal* the reference is to an article of clothing:

Tayl. A Port hole is, as the vulgar have it, a kind of Slit; but in *France* it is call'd Porthole, and is made with a whife down Here, and a whife down there; they are very chargable.

Clearly the intended word was not modern 'wife'. In the present scene, the reference is to the rotating part of a stool.

127. *Pendennis.* A castle in Falmouth, Cornwall.

128. *Roan.* Rouen.

129. *Marybone.* Marylebone, a north-western borough of London, bounded by Hampstead to the north, St Pancras on the east, Westminster to the south, and Paddington to the West. Today it comprises much of Regent's Park and the northern part of the Oxford Street shopping district.

130. *The Brill.* Brielle (Den Briel) in Holland. Since Sir Gravity is responsible for foreign names, the reference is *not* (as the 1976 editors suggested) to that area of London between Euston Road and old St Pancras Church, later called 'Somers Town'.

131. *Harrow oth' Hill.* Harrow-on-the-Hill is a town in Middlesex, twelve miles WNW of St Paul's Cathedral in London. The name is from an isolated hill some 345 feet in height. At this time it was already associated with the celebrated public school, founded in 1571.

133. *Petty France.* In Westminster, just south of St James's Park. Putney, Chelsea, and Petty France are grouped in *The Rehearsal*, V. i. 194–202.

138. *The Vly.* The channel between Vlieland and Terschelling in Holland. On 9 August 1666 English warships under the command of Sir Robert Holmes found and destroyed a large fleet of Dutch merchantmen anchored there. Pepys records: 'called up by a letter from Sir W. Coventry; which . . . tells me how we have burned 160 ships of the enemy within the Fly' (15 August 1666).

140. *Grand Caire.* The French name for Cairo.

141. *Ware.* A market town in Hertfordshire on the river Lea, twenty-two miles north of London.

143. *Combe.* Combe and Coombe appear in many place-name combinations in England, but this is most probably a reference to Coombe in Surrey.

145. *Cam.* A small town in Gloucestershire located about halfway between Bristol and Gloucester.

146–53. *Naples . . . Gilford.* At this point Cautious and Empty abandon their match of *bouts rimés* and screech out names simultaneously, spinning ever faster.

151. *Bristow.* Variant spelling of Bristol.

152. *Cullen.* Cologne.

153. *Gilford.* Guildford, in Surrey.

153.1. *admires.* Views with wonder or surprise. Cf. *Spectator*, no. 575 (1714): 'How can we sufficiently admire the Stupidity or Madness of those Persons?'

156. *Juglers.* Some slapstick business is implied as Empty tries to extricate himself from the hole in the table he is occupying.

169. *salve.* A solution of a difficulty. The *OED* (*n.*4) gives two examples from 1651.

193. *exorbitancy.* An aberration. Cf. Milton, *Eikonoklastes* (1649): 'That planetary motion, that . . . exorbitancy'. Bernard Richards points out that a pun attaches to this usage: 'the entry of Sir Richard has interrupted them' and hence at line 193 'Empty is literally exorbitant—he is *out of* his sphere, or "orb" of business, the table being circular, and about to move into another motion.'

195. *dark roome.* 'Formerly considered a proper place of confinement for a madman' (*OED*). Cf. Shakespeare, *Comedy of Errors*, IV. iv (*Complete Works*, l. 1285), *As You Like It*, III. ii (l. 1532), and *Twelfe Night*, ll. 1609, 1931–2065, 2238.

205. *thy preferment.* Sir Cautious and Sir Gravity intimate that they will obtain a government post or even a sinecure for Trim if he helps them marry the heiresses. Such commentary on government corruption could get playwright and players in trouble. In 1667 *The Change of Crownes* (by Howard's brother, Edward) provoked the king's wrath. Particular exception was taken to Asinello, a country gentleman come up to court to buy a place. On this imbroglio, see Pepys, 15–16 April 1667. The play was suppressed and not printed, but survived in manuscript and was edited and published by Frederick S. Boas in 1949.

209. *Chaldeans.* By implication, dupes. The *OED* says that a Chaldean is 'A native of Chaldea, *esp.* (as at Babylon) one skilled in occult learning, astrology, etc.', hence by extension one who cheats as a seer, soothsayer, or astrologer, or is cheatable by such devices. Cf. use as a verb at II. i. 113.

212–13. *love . . . buisnes.* A sarcastic reference to the Love and Honour conflicts suffered by characters in the rhymed heroic dramas popular at this time, to be the object of Buckingham's satire in *The Rehearsal* two years later.

221. *nickt.* Hit the mark, guess correctly (*OED*, *v.*2 10). First used this way by Massinger in 1624.

240–1. *Coventgarden Church.* St Paul's Church, built in the 1630s to a design by Inigo Jones. It still forms the western side of what used to be called 'the Square' or 'the Marketplace'. This is our clearest hint of the neighbourhood in which Mrs Finical's house is located. The promiximity of the market notwithstanding, the Covent Garden Piazza was a very fashionable place to live in the late seventeenth century. See Walter Thornbury and Edward Walford, *Old and New London: A Narrative of Its History, Its People, and Its Places*, 6 vols. (London: Cassell et al., 1873–78), iii. 240–1.

244. *plainly bred.* Both the truth and a pun on their supposed name.

298. *in the straw.* In childbed.

299. *tendance.* Aphetic form of *attendance.* Cf. Milton, *Paradise Lost*, viii. 47: 'toucht by her fair tendance'.

321. *a duell.* On duelling and attitudes towards duels at this time see V. G. Kiernan, *The Duel in European History: Honour and the Reign of Aristocracy* (Oxford: Oxford University Press, 1988); Markku Peltonen, *The Duel in Early Modern England: Civility, Politeness and Honour* (Cambridge: Cambridge University Press, 2003); and Jennifer A. Low, *Manhood and the Duel: Masculinity in Early Modern Drama and Culture* (New York: Palgrave Macmillan, 2003). Law (seldom enforced with rigour) and religious dictates were at odds with social practice.

331. *Mam.* Ma'am. The first example in the *OED* is from III. i. 95 of Dryden's *An Evening's Love*, performed in 1668 but not printed until 1671 (*Works*, x. 251). The passage implies that Dryden is deliberately introducing a new form of 'madam' into the language.

339. *su saw.* Probably a variant of 'see saw': the fops are walking affectedly.

376. *schoole of Complements.* *The Academy of Complements* (1639), often reprinted, which made 'genteel' conversation available for use by affected English snobs. Cf. Sir Richard's snippy comment about Mrs Finical's use of a 'printed curtesie' at I. i. 354.

385. *resentment.* Feeling or emotion, a meaning now obsolete but common in the later seventeenth century without pejorative connotation. The *OED* cites an example from 1658: 'ravishing refreshing resentments' (4.a).

407–8. *beaus eus*. Beaux yeux (French). The modern phrase is 'make eyes'.

414. *ridicule*. Evidently pronounced affectedly as a French word.

440. *sea-fight … Turk*. Algier and Tangier pirates (invariably referred to as 'Moors' in this period) had been making trouble in the Mediterranean. In October 1668 a fleet under Sir Thomas Allin had made a successful 'show of force' in a minor fleet action. Continued depredations kept the subject topical through 1669. However, the reference here seems likely to be to the famous siege of Candia in Venetian Crete by the Turks, which reached its crisis in 1669. Foreign Christian volunteers were involved in the city's defence.

488. *murray*. i.e. murrey. Purple-red or blood colour.

500. *blatant Beast*. See Spenser, *The Faerie Queene*, V, 12:37.

651–2. *sparkling canary*. A light, sweet wine from the Canary Islands. Evidently long enough established in English custom to be acceptable to Sir Richard. Shakespeare mentions it in *Twelfe Night*, I. iii (*Complete Works*, l. 179): 'Thou lack'st a cup of Canarie'.

672. *bug's*. An imaginary monster of the sort used to frighten children. Cf. 'bogy'. ' Bugaboo' in American English.

674. *news books*. The newsbook was a regularly issued (often weekly) pamphlet, which is the most significant forerunner of the newspaper. For its early history see Joad Raymond, *The Invention of the Newspaper: English Newsbooks 1641–1649* (Oxford: Clarendon Press, 1996). Newspapers were barely in their infancy in 1669. The government's official *Gazette* was founded in 1665. No daily paper appeared in England until the *Daily Courant* was started in 1702. See James Sutherland, *The Restoration Newspaper and its Development* (Cambridge: Cambridge University Press, 1986). Philadelphia may have been thinking of fledgling newspapers and MS newsletters circulated from scriptoria (on which see Love, *Scribal Publication*, esp. 9–22), though these were not books as such.

691. *if you encroach*. By implication, Worthy and Lovetruth try to kiss Isabella and Philadelphia, but are repulsed and have to settle for kissing their hands (ll. 692–6).

695. *our Gloves*. The manuscript reads 'our by loves' which could be a pun or a scribal error for ' by laws'. Discourse among this group is heavily marked by legal terminology. We have, however, adopted an emendation offered by T. W. Craik, who suggests that 'the scribe misread a capital G with a curved tail … as "by", and that the correct reading is "Fy, fy you spoyle our Gloves", a remark suitable to the stage action' (*Notes and Queries*, 224 (1979), 437–8).

*Act IV*

0.1. *S.D.* A discovery scene. A set of shutters is drawn off to 'discover' Isabella and Philadelphia talking in their room.

22. *Forefend.* (Heaven) forbid, prevent, avert.

44. *Walloon.* A person 'of the race, of Gaulish origin and speaking a French dialect, which forms the chief portion of the population of the south-eastern provinces of Belgium' (*OED*). Trim's joke is explained in the rest of his sentence: Mrs Finical wishes to seem 'a Frenchifyd Lady' but gets no closer than seeming a Walloon.

64. *assiduary.* Assiduously. Not recorded in the *OED*.

69. *jentiest.* i.e. 'jauntiest'.

*Bo-garsons.* Beaux garçons—'pretty boys' with both positive and negative connotations.

70. *illustrat.* To shed lustre upon (*OED* 4—rare or obsolete).

97. *When we quarter our Coat.* When the arms of the female line are added to the coats of arms of their husbands.

109. *present.* To offer compliments or convey greetings (*OED*, v. II. 11. c.).

116. *trowling.* An obsolete form of *trolling* or *troll*: to move nimbly, as the tongue in speaking (*OED*, II.4). Cf. Milton, *Paradise Lost*, XI. 620: 'To sing, to dance, To dress and troule the Tongue'.

195. *flye-blowes.* A fly-blow is 'the egg deposited by a fly . . . or the maggot proceeding therefrom' (*OED*).

243. *red Lyon.* A favourite place for duels was behind the Red Lyon Inn, near Lamb's Conduit, about three blocks east of what is now Russell Square. Cf. Durfey's epilogue to *Madam Fickle* (1676): 'Meet me to morrow in *Lambs-Conduit Fields*.'

250. *place appointed.* This passage has unintended ironic overtones: Buckingham himself had failed to show up for a duel in 1666, claiming that he had misunderstood the place named by the Earl of Ossory. On this episode, see Wilson, *Buckingham*, 60–3.

269. *Irish footmen.* Bernard Richards states that 'It was a literary and a social tradition that the Irish provided good fast footmen', quoting John Clavell, *The Sodder'd Citizen* (Malone Society, 1936): 'nor / My sweatie Lackies runn o'the winde side, / Nor shall they be dull, Country footpost fellowes, / But of the swiftest Irishe' (ll. 734–7).

279.1. *going out.* The fops start to leave the stage, but their escape is prevented.

*coranto*. The Italian 'running' dance corresponding to the French courante. The word is discussed in *The Rehearsal*, V. i. 67–71 (and see note). See also the note to *Sir Politick Would-be*, IV. iv. 60.

283. *to the book*. That is, the fops must stay and give testimony (jokingly implied here to be upon oath).

310. *Ladies chamber*. The reference here (and those in ll. 314, 387, and 401) all strongly indicate that the setting of Act IV is a room in Mrs Finical's house belonging to Isabella and Philadelphia, not a more public space.

316–17. *Grays inn walks*. A popular meeting place that was also a sanctuary area from being arrested for debt.

327. *Mandrakes*. In figurative seventeenth-century usage, a mandrake is 'an unpleasant or unwanted person or thing ; something to be rooted up, a pestilential growth' (*OED*, I.1.b). The shape of the root (forked and resembling a human figure) has contributed to a rather garbled folklore. Mandrakes were thought to grow under the feet of a hanged man (hence around gallows) and to scream when pulled up. Mandrake was used as an aphrodisiac and as a charm for pregnancy (*Encyclopedia Mythica*). Cf. note on *A Hue-and-Cry*, l. 13 (vol. II. 444).

339. *Knights errant*. Bernard Richards points out a double meaning: chivalric knights (in an ironic sense) and knights who are astray, wandering, erring in conduct (*OED* 9 and 10).

341. *crosse Bill*. A countersuit filed in Chancery by a defendant against the plaintiff.

342. *Parrat*. Parrot.

373. *Quarterstaff*. 'A stout pole, from six to eight feet long and tipped with iron, formerly used as a weapon by the English peasantry' (*OED*)—i.e. not a weapon for a gentleman.

*sharpes*. Fighting in earnest with unbated swords, in contradistinction to fencing. Cf. Shadwell, *Epsom-Wells* (1672), Act I: 'Since they were so much too hard for us at Blunts; we were fools to go to sharps with them' (*Complete Works*, ii. 116).

394. *skonces*. An obsolete form of *sconce*, a jocular term for the head (*OED*).

399 (s.d.). *draw*. Both Worthy and Lovetruth draw their swords.

409. *loonging*. Lunging.

420–1. *to shew you the movement of a Courant*. See also the notes to IV. 279.1 and to *Sir Politick Would-be*, IV. iv. 60. The courant was the most important of the ballroom dances performed at the French court during the late seventeenth century and a favourite of Louis XIV, who excelled in it himself. See Pierre Rameau, *Le Maitre a Danser* (Paris: chez Jean Villette, 1725), 110–11 ('Discours sur la Courante en general'), and Régine Astier, 'Louis XIV, "Premier Danseur"', in David Lee Rubin (ed.), *Sun King: The Ascendancy of French Culture during the Reign of Louis XIV* (Washington, DC: Folger Shakespeare Library, 1992), 73–102 at 78–9. The

Courant was a formal ball dance for a man and a woman, with particular steps and figures. Part of the joke is having it danced by two men (who are presumably doing it badly). We are indebted to Moira Goff for the substance of this note. And see the next note.

428. *Chicken a Chicken a trayn-tro.* The editors have no satisfactory, documented explanation for this phrase. We offer the speculation that it could be fractured French instructions on doing the dance, e.g. 'chacun à chacun . . . r'entrer'. Such mockery of French would be in character for Sir Richard. Moira Goff points out to us that the fops are attempting to demonstrate an elegant court dance, but Sir Richard apparently takes it for some kind of English country dance. His terminology is not to be found in either John Playford's *The English Dancing Master* (1651) and the seven subsequent editions published as *The Dancing Master* by 1686 or in Raoul Auger Feuillet's *Recueil de contredances* (Paris: Chez l'Auteur, 1706).

439. *foot ball.* Various forms of the games now known as football (European style) and rugby have been played in England since at least the fifteenth century, the games involving (as the *OED* sedately observes) a ball consisting 'of an inflated bag or bladder enclosed in a leather case'. A quotation from 1663 refers to 'Football' as a 'boysterous sport or game'. Sir Richard seems to regard it as a healthy, manly, country pursuit, but in the early modern period as now it could be quite rough. In 1531 Elyot speaks of 'Foote balle, wherein is nothinge but beastly furie and extreme violence' (*Governour*, I. xxvii).

446. *ridicule.* Ridiculous. Sir Richard's objection is to the Frenchified version of a word with a long-standing English form. The pseudo-French usage was not just a joke: the *OED* quotes examples from 1672 and 1674, the former from Marvell's *Rehearsal Transpros'd*. Slander has already used the term at III. 414.

468. *beacons fir'd.* Signalling an invasion.

487. *collogue.* To wheedle or flatter (Dr Johnson).

534. *bon mines.* Cf. I. i. 34.

570. *grin.* In this sense, 'a forced or unnatural smile, or . . . the broad smile indicative of unrestrained or vulgar merriment, clownish embarrassment, stupid wonder or exultation, or the like' (*OED*).

576. *mump.* 'To grimace; to force the lips into a grimace or grin; to convey a thought or meaning indirectly by one's facial expression'. In some cases more specifically 'to assume a demure, melancholy, or sanctimonious expression; to be silent and sullen; to sulk, mope' (*OED*).

581. *winch.* An obsolete form of *wince*. See *Hamlet*, lines 1958–9: 'let the gauled Iade winch' and Congreve, *The Old Batchelour*, V. ii. 46: 'Only touch'd a gall'd beast till he winch'd'.

582. *more teeth, then thou hast drawn.* Extracting decayed teeth was among the functions of a barber at this time.

592. *brown bread, small beere.* These are cheap rather than luxury goods.

*Act V*

16. *exit.* Mrs Finical must leave to let Isabella and Vapor talk, though there is no exit marked in the manuscript.

24. *sentiments.* Resentment, though the context suggests the late eighteenth-century meaning of 'hurt feelings'.

89. *launces.* Launches, throws out.

123.1. *at several doors.* Slander and Philadelphia enter at different doors, presumably on opposite sides of the stage. On proscenium doors in the 1660s theatres, see Summers, *The Restoration Theatre*, 126–44.

175. *puppets.* Shown regularly at Charing Cross by Anthony Devoto in the later 1660s and early 1670s. See George Speaight, *The History of the English Puppet Theatre*, 2nd edn. (Carbondale, Ill.: Southern Illinois University Press, 1990), 75–6.

179. *Ordinaryes.* His meals—specifically, public meals provided at a fixed price in an eating house or tavern (*OED* 14.a).

189–90. *Rodomontados … Gascoignes.* His vainglorious boasts exceed those of a native of Gascony, a province of France notorious for braggarts and boasters.

242. *black spiritual Baylif.* A clergyman dressed in black.

281. *allies.* Alleys.

312. *Heralds.* In this sense, an office in the College of Arms, also known as the Heralds' College (a royal corporation founded in 1484 by Richard III), consisting of the Earl Marshall, kings of arms, heralds, and pursuivants, exercising jurisdiction in armorial matters and granting rights to coats of arms. In 1703 Vanbrugh's friends wangled his appointment as Clarenceux King of Arms in the College, a post he was to occupy with profit until he sold it for £2,400 in 1725.

314. *rose.* The arms of the Worshipful Company of Barbers granted in 1569 are described as follows: 'Quarterly, first and fourth, Sable a Chevron between three Fleams Argent, second and third, Per pale of the second and Vert on a Spatter also Argent a Tudor rose proper crowned Or; on a Cross Gules dividing the quarters a Lion passant guardant Gold' (reproduced at www.heraldicmedia.com). Bernard Richards suggests a complicated and perhaps implausible joke here. 'Surely not a flower but a hose with a sprinkler on the end—the kind a barber would use for rinsing soap suds off customers. . . . There *is* no "gentiler flower" than the rose.' The *OED* definition (17) of this sort of 'rose' is 'A perforated metal cap or nozzle attached to the spout of a watering-pot, etc., to distribute water in fine sprays'. The earliest example quoted is from 1706.

323. *Brawn.* Boar-flesh, though some of the *OED* quotations around this time specify other animals.

325. *riggles.* Wriggles (*OED*, v. 6. a): cut with a wriggly or sinuous pattern. Cf. Jonson, *The Alchemist*, IV. iii: 'a collar of brawne, cut downe Beneath the souse, and wriggled with a knife'. *Ben Jonson*, ed. C. H. Herford and Percy Simpson, vol. v (Oxford: Clarendon Press, 1937), 369.

365. *in former times.* A good example of cultural primitivism of the sort analysed in the opening part of Lois Whitney's *Primitivism and the Idea of Progress in English Popular Literature of the Eighteenth Century* (Baltimore, Md.: Johns Hopkins Press, 1934).

370. *mouth made.* A grimace. The sense is that all a town-dweller gets now is an obsequious ritualistic remark and a disbelieving facial movement in place of real concern and respect.

374. *importunat.* Urgent, pressing. The usage was archaic by 1669, though the *OED* quotes Clarendon using the word in this sense in 1674.

387. *Sackposset.* Hot milk curdled with ale, wine, or other liquor, with sugar and spices. It served both as a celebratory delicacy and as a medicinal remedy (*OED*). It was traditional for a sack posset to be offered to newly-weds before they retired to bed. Cf. Delarivier Manley's *The Lost Lover* (1696), III. ii: 'Be-gad, I long for the Sack-posset, and throwing the Stocking; that was the Fashion when I was married' (p. 21).

445–7. *you have such fames, . . . spoyle my Boyes.* Sir Richard's remark seems to underline what the reader may already have suspected—that the two 'fops' are a gay couple in the present-day rather than the John Harrington Smith sense of that phrase.

455. *repayrd.* Since Vapor and Slander have not been married off to a pair of whores, they are back in their original, unimpaired condition, and can sneer at Sir Cautious.

457. *Juno.* The Roman goddess, popularly viewed as goddess of marriage and the jealous consort of Jupiter.

486. *noble Company.* The authors have managed to bring every character in the cast on stage in the course of Act V, with the exception of Mrs Finical's maid and the servant John.

487. *Countrey Gentlemen.* This may be the intended title of the play; no other indication of a title is contained in the manuscript.

## The Rehearsal

The following list records the plays cited in the Explanatory Notes as sources or parallels for the 1672 and 1675 versions. Plays are listed in alphabetical order by title. Major target sources in the 1672 version are marked with an asterisk (*). Titles listed in 'Plays Named in this KEY' in 1704 are marked with a dagger (†).

*Aglaura*, by Sir John Suckling (1637; pub. 1638)

*All Mistaken*, by James Howard (1665? pub. 1672)

†*The Amorous Prince*, by Aphra Behn (Feb. 1671; pub. 1671)

†*The Assignation*, by John Dryden (c. Nov. 1672; pub. 1673)[1]

*The Bastard*, anon.; sometimes attributed to Cosmo Manuche (date and performance history unknown; pub. 1652)

*Bellamira*, in two parts, by Thomas Killigrew (wr. c.1652; unacted; pub. 1664)

*The Black Prince*, by Roger Boyle, Earl of Orrery (1667; pub. 1669)

*The Blind Lady*, by Sir Robert Howard (unacted; pub. 1660)

*Cambises*, by Thomas Preston (c.1560; pub. c.1569)

*Cambyses King of Persia*, by Elkanah Settle ( Jan. 1671; pub. 1671)

*The Carnival*, by Thomas Porter (c.1663; pub. 1664)

*Catiline*, by Ben Jonson (1611; pub. 1611)

*The Cheats*, by John Wilson (1663; pub. 1664)

*Cicilia and Clorinda*, in two parts, by Thomas Killigrew (wr. c.1650; unacted; pub. 1664)

*The Committee*, by Sir Robert Howard (1662; pub. in *Four New Plays*, 1665)

*†*The Conquest of Granada*, by John Dryden (in two parts, Dec. 1670–Jan. 1671; pub. 1672)

*The Country Gentleman*, by Sir Robert Howard and Buckingham (banned in Feb. 1669; not printed but survived in MS; first pub. 1976)

*The Cruelty of the Spaniards in Peru* (1658; pub. 1658)

*The Damoiselles a la Mode*, by Richard Flecknoe (unacted? pub. 1667)

*Don Juan*, by Molière (1665; pub. 1682 in French)

*The Duke of Lerma*, by Sir Robert Howard (1668; pub. 1668)

*†*The English Mounsieur*, by James Howard (1663; pub. 1674)

*The English Rogue*, by Thomas Thomson (c.1660–68; perhaps privately acted at an unknown date; pub. 1668)

*Erminia*, by Richard Flecknoe (unacted; pub. 1661)

*An Evening's Love*, by John Dryden (1668; pub. 1671)

*The Faithfull Virgins*, by Elizabeth Polwhele (staged at Lincoln's Inn Fields c.1670? not printed; survived in MS)

*The Forc'd Marriage*, by Aphra Behn (1670; pub. 1671)

---

1 Referred to in the *Key* by its subtitle, *Love in a Nunnery*.

*The Frolicks*, by Elizabeth Polwhele (1671; possibly staged; survived in MS; first pub. 1977)

*The Generall*, by Roger Boyle, Earl of Orrery (wr. 1661; perf. 1664; not printed but survived in MS; pub. 1937)

\**Henry VIII*, by Shakespeare and John Fletcher (1613; pub. 1623)

*Heraclius*, by Corneille, trans. Sir Thomas Clarges (1664; not pub.; lost)

*The History of Charles VIII of France*, by John Crowne (Nov. 1671; pub. 1672)

*The Humorous Lieutenant*, by John Fletcher (1619–25; pub. 1647)

*The Imperial Tragedy*, by Sir William Killigrew (1669; pub. 1672)

\**The Indian Emperour*, by John Dryden (1665; pub. 1667)

*The Indian-Queen*, by Sir Robert Howard and John Dryden (1664; pub. in Howard's *Four New Plays*, 1665)

*The Jews Tragedy*, by William Hemming (wr. 1620s or 1630s; no performance history known; pub. 1662)

*King Henry the Fifth*, by Roger Boyle, Earl of Orrery (1664; pub. 1668)

†*The Lost Lady*, by Sir William Berkeley (1637; pub. 1638)

†*Love and Honour*, by Sir William Davenant (1634; pub. 1649)

*Love in its Extasy*, by William(?) Peaps (*c*.1634; unacted; pub. 1649)

*Love's Kingdom*, by Richard Flecknoe (acted at LIF at an uncertain date before 1664; pub. 1664)

*Love's Mistress*, by Thomas Heywood (1634; pub. 1636)

*The Man's the Master*, by Sir William Davenant (1668; pub. 1669)

*The Mariage Night*, by Henry or Lucius Cary (1663; pub. 1664)

\*†*Marriage A-la-Mode*, by John Dryden (Dec. 1671; pub. 1673)

*The Merry Wives of Windsor*, by Shakespeare (1597; pub. 1602)

*A Midsommer Night's Dreame*, by Shakespeare (*c*.1596; pub. 1600)

*Money is an Ass*, by Thomas Jordan (*c*.1635; pub. 1668)

*Mustapha*, by Roger Boyle, Earl of Orrery (1665; pub. 1668)

*The Obstinate Lady*, by Aston Cokain (wr. pre-1642; unperformed? pub. 1657)

*Orgula*, by Leonard Willan (unacted? pub. 1658)

†*Ormasdes*, by Sir William Killigrew (unacted? pub. 1665 in *Three Plays*)[2]

†*Pandora*, by Sir William Killigrew (*c*.1662–3? pub. 1665 in *Three Plays*)

†*The Playhouse to be Let*, by Sir William Davenant (1663; pub. 1673)

*The Politician Cheated*, by Alexander Green (unacted; pub. 1663)

*Pompey the Great*, from Corneille, trans. Edmund Waller, et al. (1664; pub. 1664)

*The Poor Scholar*, by Robert Neville (unacted? pub. 1662)

*The Rewards of Virtue*, by John Fountain (unacted; pub. 1661)

*The Rival Friends*, by Peter Hausted (1632; pub. 1632)

*The Rival Ladies*, by John Dryden (1664; pub. 1664)

*The Roman Empress*, by William Joyner (1670; pub. 1671)

*The Roman Generals*, by John Dover (unacted; pub. 1667)

---

[2] Referred to in the *Key* by its subtitle, *Love and Friendship*.

*The Secret*, by 'Ellis' (acted at LIF *c*.1663–4? not pub.; lost)[3]

†*Secret-Love*, by John Dryden (1667; pub. 1668)[4]

\*†*The Siege of Rhodes*, 2 parts, by Sir William Davenant (Part 1 1656; pub. 1656; LIF versions staged 1661 and pub. 1663)

*The Siege of Urbin*, by Sir William Killigrew (*c*.1665; unacted? pub. 1666)

*Sir Francis Drake*, by Sir William Davenant (1658; pub. 1659)

*The Six Days Adventure*, by Edward Howard (March 1671; pub. 1671)

\* †*The Slighted Maid*, by Sir Robert Stapylton (1663; pub. 1663)

*The Spanish Tragedy*, by Thomas Kyd (*c*.1587; pub. *c*.1592)

*The Stepmother*, by Sir Robert Stapylton (1663; pub. 1664)

*The Sullen Lovers*, by Thomas Shadwell (1668; pub. 1668)

*The Surprisal*, by Sir Robert Howard (1662; pub. in *Four New Plays*, 1665)

\* *The Tempest*, revision of Shakespeare by Sir William Davenant and John Dryden (1667; pub. 1670)

*Thomaso*, by Thomas Killigrew (1654; unperformed; pub. 1664)

*To Love Only for Love's Sake*, translation of Mendoza's *Querer por solo querer* by Sir Richard Fanshawe (1654; pub. 1670)

*The Tragedy of Ovid*, by Aston Cokain (unacted? pub. 1662)

*Trappolin Supposed a Prince*, by Aston Cokain (1633; pub. 1658)

*Tryphon*, by Roger Boyle, Earl of Orrery (1668; pub. 1669)

\*†*Tyrannick Love*, by John Dryden (1669; pub. 1670)

*The Ungrateful Favourite*, anon., possibly by Robert Southland (unacted; pub. 1664)

†*The United Kingdoms*, by Henry Howard (*c*.1663; not pub.; lost)

*The Usurper*, by Edward Howard (1664; pub. 1668)

*The Variety*, by William Cavendish and James Shirley (*c*.1641; pub. 1649)

*The Vestal-Virgin*, by Sir Robert Howard (*c*.1664; pub. in *Four New Plays*, 1665)

†*The Villain*, by Thomas Porter (1662; pub. 1663)

*The Virgin Widow*, by Francis Quarles (*c*.1640; privately acted; pub. 1649)

†*The Wild Gallant*, by John Dryden (1663; pub. 1669)

*The Womens Conquest*, by Edward Howard (1670; pub. 1671)


*Prologue*

2. *Posie made of Weeds.* Crane (p. 80) cites George Gascoigne's preface to his *Posies* (1575): 'Floures to comfort, Herbes to cure, and Weedes to be avoyded.'

5. *Would some of 'em were here.* Although the Third Dutch War was not declared until March 1672, gentleman-officers were already leaving town by the beginning of December, as allusions in the prologues to Crowne's *The History of Charles VIII of France* and Dryden's *Marriage A-la-Mode* prove.

---

[3] Revision of Shirley's *The Court Secret*? See Milhous and Hume, 'Lost Plays', no. 11.
[4] Referred to in the *Key* by its subtitle, *The Maiden Queen.*

7–9. *Here . . . There.* In comedy and tragedy, respectively.

10. *King Cambyses vain.* Crane (p. 80) cites both Falstaff's speech in II. v. of *1 Henry IV* with its well-known reference to the ranting hero of Thomas Preston's *Cambises* (pub. *c.*1569) and Settle's noisy *Cambyses King of Persia* (1671). Wishing to speak 'in passion', Shakespeare's Falstaff proposes to do so 'in king Cambises' vaine' (*Complete Works*, l. 1317).

15. *Critiques.* Probably in the sense of 'One who pronounces judgement on any thing or person; *esp.* one who passes severe or unfavourable judgement; a censurer, fault-finder, caviller' (*OED*). The 'critics in the pit' soon became a theatrical commonplace (see Danchin's index). The wits and 'men of fashion' (or would-be such) congregated in the pit when new plays were performed and sometimes indulged in dismissive and disruptive heckling. Pepys reports on 4 October 1664 at Orrery's *The Generall*, 'I happened to sit next to Sir Ch. Sidly; who I find a very witty man, and did at every line take notice of the dullness of the poet and badness of the action' (*Diary*, v. 288), and at *The Maid's Tragedy* on 18 February 1667 he found Sedley's 'exceptions against both words and pronouncing was very pretty' (*Diary*, viii. 72). A famous, spurious, much-quoted, and paraphrased anecdote about Buckingham attributes such behaviour to him, not altogether implausibly:

In one of Dryden's plays there was this line, which the actress endeavoured to speak in as moving and affecting a tone as she could:

My wound is great, because it is so small!

and then she paused and looked very much distressed. The Duke of Buckingham, who was in one of the boxes, rose immediately from his seat and added in a loud, ridiculing voice:

Then 'twould be greater, were it none at all!

which had so strong an effect on the audience (who before were not very well pleased with the play) that they hissed the poor woman off the stage, would never bear her appearance in the rest of her part, and (as this was the second time only of its appearance) made Dryden lose his benefit night. (Spence, *Anecdotes*, no. 665)

This story is reported by Horace Walpole in *A Catalogue of the Royal and Noble Authors of England* (Strawberry Hill, 1758), ii. 74–5, and is embroidered by Malone in his edition of Spence (1820), 103–4, but there is no such line in any of Dryden's printed plays, and his numerous enemies would surely have seized on the episode had it actually occurred. G. Thorn-Drury finds the whole tale 'highly improbable', and cites early versions of the anecdote that involve neither Dryden nor Buckingham. See 'Some Notes on Dryden', *Review of English Studies*, i (1925), 79–83, 187–97, 324–30, at 81–2). Osborn agrees (Spence, *Anecdotes*, i. 275–6). For a catalogue of references to what a prologuer calls 'the rude disturbers of the Pitt' (Danchin, iii. 204), see Summers, *Restoration Theatre*, 67–76. The falsity of the anecdote just quoted aside, Buckingham had played the pit critic himself and knew that they were to be feared. See also I. ii. 105 and note.

16. *Rook . . . hedg'd in my Bet.* A swindler who has bet on both sides. Summers (*Rehearsal*, p. 75) elaborates: 'If the critics laugh Lacy will have attained his object; if they take the play quite seriously he will turn tragedian forthwith.'

18. *high-flyers*. A slang term with a great variety of meanings; here evidently signifying pretentious, over-ambitious playwrights like Bayes.

27. *John Lacy*. One of the principal actor-sharers in the King's Company from 1660 until his death in 1681. Percy's *New Key* quotes Langbaine's rapturous encomium at length (p. 377). Lacy took such parts as Falstaff in *The Merry Wives of Windsor* and the title role in *The Humorous Lieutenant*. Langbaine comments that 'He was so well approv'd of by King *Charles* the Second, an undeniable Judge in Dramatick Arts, that he caus'd his Picture to be drawn, in three several Figures in the same Table. *viz*. That of *Teague* in the *Committee*, Mr. *Scruple* in *The Cheats*, and *M. Galliard*, in *The Variety*: which piece is still in being in *Windsor-Castle*. Nor did his Talent wholly ly in Acting, he knew both how to judge and write Plays' (*Lives and Characters*, 317). On the 'triple portrait', see *Biographical Dictionary*, ix. 102–4. Anecdotal evidence suggests that Lacy took the part of Bayes and was personally instructed in the part by Buckingham (Spence, *Anecdotes*, i, no. 667).

*The Actors Names*

Lack of a full cast list is extremely frustrating, especially because the play offers wonderful opportunities for jokes of the sort later exploited in *The Female Wits* and in Molière's *L'Impromptu de Versailles*. The 'Players' who appear in I. ii and V. ii and iii are manifestly appearing as themselves, and Bayes's complete inability to remember the names of his performers is the more telling if he is insulting Charles Hart, Michael Mohun, and other principals in the company. We have, of course, no way of knowing how many of these people participated in the original production. The known performers are as follows: Bayes—John Lacy (prologue and anecdote); Thunder—William Cartwright (I. ii. 161), who also doubled the first or second King (V. i. 100); Gentleman Usher *or* Physician—Abraham Ivory (I. ii. 190), who is also one of the fighters at V. i. 310; Amaryllis—Anne Reeves (anecdote). Jo Hayns, George Shirley, and John Littlewood apparently participated as dancers and perhaps doubled in other capacities. See V. iii. 31–2 and 'A New Ballad to an Old Tune Call'd Sage Leafe'. (Text in App. II, ll. 308.) Shirley's name was added as a character (l. 15) in *Q4*.

22–5. *Four Cardinals . . . Serjeants at Arms*. These four entries are bracketed and described as 'Mutes' in 1675 in *Q3*. Crane (p. 3) speculates, plausibly enough, that the last three appear 'in the grand scene at the beginning of Act V'.

35. *Brentford*. This is the scene of Bayes's play; the action of Buckingham's play takes place in and just outside the King's Company's Bridges Street Theatre in London—the venue of the original production. D. F. Smith (*Plays about the Theatre*, p. 11) suggests that Brentford is a hit at I. i. of Davenant's *The Playhouse to be Let* (1663), where the chief player says 'We'll let this Theatre and build another, where, At a cheaper rate, we may have Room for Scenes. *Brainford*'s the place!' Brentford was a trading community on the river Brent, some eight miles west of

Charing Cross. Stocker (p. 19) points out that Brentford 'had been the site of an important battle during the Civil War [in 1642], the high-watermark of the king's advance on London'—a temporary success for the royalists, before they were repulsed at Turnham Green. At least as pertinently, it was the site of a battle for dominion in England between Edmund Ironside and Canute in 1016. One possible reason for the choice of the place name is its connection with Buckingham's hated rival the Earl of Arlington, who came from those parts and the source of whose title was a small village of that name near Brentford. The town and its famous inn, The Three Pigeons, had an unsavoury reputation as a venue for assignations, as in Thomas Ravenscroft's Jacobean catch, 'Goe no more to Brainford, vnlesse you loue a Punke . . .', *Pammelia* (London, 1609), no. 24.

*I. i*

0.1. The setting is evidently a street in the neighbourhood of the Bridges Street Theatre. In 1671 the King's Company might just have played this scene against the proscenium; by the early eighteenth century, London productions would probably have put up a wing-and-shutter 'street' scene.

0.2. *Johnson and Smith*. The two gentlemen who serve as Buckingham's mouthpieces in his systematic rubbishing of Bayes are anything but identical. Johnson is a Londoner; Smith is a 'Country' person. Johnson's name may well be meant to call Ben Jonson to mind. Stocker (pp. 21–2) observes that 'Like Sir Richard Plainbred in *The Country Gentleman*, Smith in this play represents oldfashioned patriotic virtue as enshrined in the country party. His surname characterizes his common sense, his Christian name (Frank) his honesty. His frank criticism lies in political opposition to Bayes'/Dryden's frenchified parlance (a similar contrast to that in *Country Gentleman*), associating him with country patriotism against the Court's pro-French policy.' Within this play, the two wits are essentially exemplary 'critiques' taken from the pit and placed on stage. (Paul D. Cannan points out to us that 'this is similar to what Jonson does in *Every Man Out of His Humour*, when he has Cordatus and Mitis provide critical commentary on stage after each scene'.) As Stocker observes, Smith carries 'the larger political burden of the critique' while Johnson, who represents 'the old plain way' (I. ii. 9 and 88), is the principal spokesman in literary matters. 'Smith and Johnson' are often invoked by name as a kind of gold standard of judgement, as in Pope's couplet in his verse epistle to Cromwell: 'Who are to me both *Smith* and *Johnson* / So seize them Flames, or take them *Tonson*' (*The Correspondence of Alexander Pope*, ed. George Sherburn, 5 vols. (Oxford: Clarendon Press, 1956), i. 26).

5. *Country*. Here and elsewhere in his work, Buckingham draws a sharp distinction between town and country outlooks, generally to the disadvantage of the town. Here country stands for good sense, town for foolishness and affectation.

16. *men of Business*. In Restoration parlance, politicians or would-be politicians; meddlers in government affairs. Possibly a glancing allusion to Sir Cautious Trou-

ble-all and Sir Gravity Empty (Sir William Coventry and Sir John Duncomb), the 'men of business' satirized in Sir Robert Howard and Buckingham's *The Country Gentleman* (banned in March 1669). See above, 231ff.

17. *grave lookers*. Perhaps another delicate allusion to the grave 'men of business' in *The Country Gentleman*. The word 'grave' appears frequently in the Buckingham corpus, never in a complimentary sense.

28. *many new Plays*. A comment that makes better sense in the context of 1664–65 than 1671–72. Seventeen new plays were staged professionally in London in 1663, and eighteen in 1664. Nine were staged in 1669, ten in 1670, and eleven in 1671. Few of them seem likely to have met with Buckingham's approval at either time, but he probably found particularly objectionable such plays as Orrery's *The Generall* (1664), Howard and Dryden's *The Indian-Queen* (1664), Dryden's *Tyrannick Love* (1669), and Dryden's *The Conquest of Granada* (1670–71).

29. *Country-wits commend 'em*. We are not aware of any particular target for this gibe.

33. *Blade* [*Virtuosi* in 1675]. A blade is a rake. A virtuoso is a learned person or savant; in this context, a dilettante or trifler.

*your frank Persons*. The use of 'frank' is probably a joke, the in light of the insistence on 'Frank' as Smith's Christian name at lines 1 and 24, and 71 and 77 in II. i.

34–5. *scorn to imitate Nature . . . elevate and surprise*. Elevation of thoughts and words was one of Dryden's consistent preoccupations. In the *Essay of Dramatick Poesie* Neander defends the use of rhyme because it conduces to thoughts that are 'higher then nature' (*Works*, xvii. 75), and in the preface to *Tyrannick Love* Dryden comments that 'By the Harmony of words we elevate the mind to a sense of Devotion' (*Works*, x. 109). What Dryden has in mind—obviously anathema to Buckingham—is something like the sublime, and he adopts that terminology after the appearance of Boileau's translation of Longinus in 1674.

43.1 *Bayes*. In 1671 an obvious allusion to Dryden, appointed Poet Laureate in 1668 after Davenant's death. In the lost '1665' version, perhaps a hit at Davenant, though the introduction to the 1704 *Key* says that the poet's name was originally Bilboa (a hit at Sir Robert Howard). Even in 1671 Bayes is to some degree a composite figure, though after Dryden became Poet Laureate the name applied quite specifically to him because of the association with the bay leaves traditionally woven into a garland to crown a poet (*OED*).

58. *thy last Play*. In 1671 Dryden's last new play was *The Conquest of Granada*, staged in two parts in December 1670 and January 1671.

59. *the Plot*. Dryden made plain his low estimation of plot in his preface to *An Evening's Love* (pub. 1671): 'little Criticks do not well consider what is the work of a Poet, and what the Graces of a Poem: The Story is the least part of either' (*Works*, x. 212).

62. *a new one*. Perhaps with a secondary allusion to Dryden's *Marriage A-la-Mode*, which was in final rehearsals at the time of the premiere of *The Rehearsal*.

*a Virgin*. Crane (p. 81) speculates that this is a vestigial reference to Sir Robert Howard's *The Vestal-Virgin* (performed *c.* November 1664?), but more probably the phrase was meant to indicate that Bayes's new play (i.e. *Marriage A-la-Mode*) had not yet been publicly performed.

63–4. *never yet been blown upon . . . all new Wit*. A take-off on Neander's speech in *Of Dramatick Poesie*: 'There is scarce an Humour, a Character, or any kind of Plot, which they have not blown upon. . . . This therefore will be a good Argument to us either not to write at all, or to attempt some other way. There is no bayes to be expected in their Walks.' *Works*, xvii. 73, giving the 1668 reading. See Richard Elias, '"Bayes" in Buckingham's *The Rehearsal*', *English Language Notes*, 15 (1978), 178–81. Elias points out that 'blown upon' in seventeenth-century usage meant 'to make public', or 'to make stale or hackneyed', with an underlying connotation of sexual defloration. In the 1683 edition Dryden changed 'blown upon' to 'us'd'.

65. *how that took*. Dryden's *The Conquest of Granada* was by all accounts a great success.

67. *any Play in Europe*. The *Key* (p. 1) annotates as follows: '"*In fine, it shall Read, and Write, and Act, and Plot, and Shew; Ay, and Pit, Box, and Gallery it, I Gad, with any Play in* Europe." The usual Language of the Honourable Edward Howard Esq. at the Rehearsal of his Plays.' Edward Howard was author of *The Usurper* (acted 1664; pub. 1668), a pretentious semi-heroic play, *The London Gentleman* (Stationers' Register 1667; lost); *The Womens Conquest* (1670), and *The Six days Adventure* (1671). The quartos of the last two are prefaced by lengthy, pompous (but not uninteresting) critical essays that probably annoyed Buckingham. Edward Howard is caricatured as Ninny ('A conceited Poet') in Shadwell's *The Sullen Lovers* (1668). Rochester applied the name to Sir Carr Scroope in 'On Poet Ninny' (*Works*, 107–8).

*morning . . . Rehearsal*. According to *The Female Wits* (1696; pub. 1704), 1, rehearsals started at 10 a.m. and concluded in time to let the actors eat dinner before the day's show. In 1671 the public performance probably started at 3.30; certainly not after 4.00. The earlier time is specified in the 1663 prologue to Dryden's *The Wild Gallant*, in *Works*, viii. 4. Compare the reference at V. iii. 2–3.

67–8. *in their habits*. A dress rehearsal. Ordinary rehearsals were held without costumes. See *The Female Wits*, p. 13: 'why what's the Whim, that we must be all dress'd at Rehearsal, as if we play'd?'

68. *and all that*. Bayes uses this phrase over and over again in the course of the play (sixteen times in all), often in conjunction with his '——a——' noise. In *Spectator*, no. 80 (1 June 1711) Steele comments jokingly on this characterization device, 'And what a poor Figure would Mr. *Bayes* have made without his *Egad and all*

*That?*' Bayes uses the ejaculation 'i gad' seventy-seven times in the *Q1* text and 105 times in the *Q3* text.

78. *Drama Common places*. Against line 77 ('this is my book') an annotator has written 'Dryden' (U of PA-1683). We are not aware of any specific target for this passage, nor for the coffee-house table book and digest of classical authorities later in this scene. Winn (James Anderson Winn, *John Dryden and His World* (New Haven, Conn.: Yale University Press, 1987), 44) points out that at Westminster School, Busby, 'By encouraging his students to collect useful written material', helped them 'to keep notebooks listing striking words and apt phrases' useful in their compositions and 'helped men like Dryden establish the habit of note-taking'. The 'Buckingham' Commonplace Book is a compilation of this kind. Hugh Ormsby-Lennon speculates that Swift's *Polite Conversation* grew out of his keeping just such a 'book of Drama Common places' in the 1690s. See 'Commonplace Swift', in Hermann J. Real and Helgard Stöver-Leidig (eds.), *Reading Swift: Papers from The Third Münster Symposium on Jonathan Swift* (Munich: Wilhelm Fink Verlag, 1998), 13–44 at 37–8. In *Tatler*, no. 22 (31 May 1709) Steele gives an extended joking description of a 'very Sad' tragedy that he will be able to write in short order by tacking together bits from 'my Book of Common Places'. On the practice of compiling commonplaces, see Ann Moss, *Printed Commonplace-Books and the Structuring of Renaissance Thought* (Oxford: Clarendon Press, 1996).

85. *these my Rules*. The *Key*, pp. 1–2, annotates with a passage from the prologue to *Secret-Love*:

> He who writ this, not without pains and thought
> From *French* and *English* Theaters has brought
> Th' exactest Rules by which a Play is wrought:
>
>    .    .    .    .    .    .    .    .
>
> The Unities of Action, Place, and Time;
> The Scenes unbroken; and a mingled chime
> Of *Johnsons* humour, with *Corneilles* rhyme. (*Works*, ix. 119)

Dryden's view of the 'rules' was not in fact particularly prescriptive at any time in his career. He always felt that servile obedience to critical precepts kills beauties. He admitted that rules might help judgement follow nature, but held that they could not in themselves produce good writing and that they might legitimately be violated for the sake of a greater beauty. For a catalogue of allusions in his criticism, see H. James Jensen, *A Glossary of John Dryden's Critical Terms* (Minneapolis, Minn.: University of Minnesota Press, 1969), 103–4.

88. *Regula Duplex*. Twofold rule (Latin).

*Verse into Prose, or Prose into verse*. Percy's *New Key*, pp. 379–80, annotates as follows: 'Take an instance from the Prologue to the *Maiden Queen* [i.e. Dryden's *Secret-Love*], stanz. 4.

> Plays are like Towns, which howe're fortifi'd
> By Engineers, have still some weaker side
> By the o'erseen Defendant unespy'd. (*Works*, ix. 119)

This is transversed from the preface to *Ibrahim, or The Illustrious Bassa, a Romance translated from the French.* Lond. 1652, folio. "It is of works of this nature, as of a place of war, where notwithstanding all the care the engineer hath brought to fortify it, there is always some weak part found, which he hath not dreamed of." See Langbaine, p. 169.' Percy goes on to refer the reader to 'Mr. Hurd's ingenious *Letter on the marks of Imitation*' for 'more examples of this kind of theft' (unrelated to *The Rehearsal*), and to point out a source in Bacon's *Essays* for a passage in Lee's *Lucius Junius Brutus* (1680).

91. *nothing more easie.* An annotator has written 'Dryden' against this line (U of PA-1683).

94. *Transverse it.* Langbaine (*Account*, 169) comments snidely on Dryden's 'making use of *Bayes*'s Art of Transversing, as any One may observe by comparing the Fouth *Stanza* of his First Prologue [to *Secret-Love*] with the last Paragraph of the Preface to *Ibrahim*' (the French romance by Madeleine de Scudéry, 1641). On Dryden's considerable borrowings from prose sources in 'the serious actions' of his early tragicomedies, see Leslie Howard Martin, 'Dryden and the Art of Transversion', *Comparative Drama*, 6 (1972), 3–13.

97. *Transprosing.* Summers (*Rehearsal*, p. 80) notes that the author of 'On the Duke of Bucks' turns the idea against Buckingham himself:

> With transcribing of these, and transversing those,
> With transmitting of Rhyme, and transversing Prose,
> He hath drest up his Farce with others Mens Clothes.
> *Poems on Affairs of State* (1703), ii. 216–17

(For the text of the 'Sage Leafe' version, see App. II, 11. 306.) Within a year or so of the performance of Buckingham's satire, Andrew Marvell picked up the transformation conceit in his *The Rehearsal Transpros'd* (1672), a bitingly effective reply to Samuel Parker's *Discourse of Ecclesiastical Politie* (1669), and two successor works. The concept is turned directly against Dryden by Matthew Prior and Charles Montague in *The Hind and the Panther Transvers'd To the Story of The Country-Mouse and the City-Mouse* (1687). The idea is borrowed jokingly in *Tatler*, no. 194 (6 July 1710): 'I shall transprose it, to use Mr. *Bays*'s Term.'

105. *Coffee-house.* The U of PA-1683 annotator has written 'Dryden' against this line. Dryden's standing as literary patriarch in Will's Coffee House late in his life is well known (Spence, *Anecdotes*, i. nos. 68 and 664). In the 1660s and 1670s, however, coffee-houses were a more dubious resort. As late as 1675 the government issued a proclamation suppressing them. See Pepys, x. 71 (*Companion* volume). Dryden's association with Will's can be documented from very early. On 3 February 1664 Pepys wrote:

In Covent-garden tonight . . . I stopped at the great Coffee-house there, where I never was before—where Draydon the poet (I knew at Cambrige) and all the wits of the town, and Harris the player and Mr. Hoole of our college; and had I had time then, or could at other times, it will be good coming thither, for there I perceive is very witty and pleasant discourse. (*Diary*, v. 37)

In 1682 in 'The Medal of John Bayes' Shadwell says 'You who would know him better, go to the Coffee-house (where he may be said almost to inhabit) and you shall find him holding forth to half a score young fellows.' On coffee-house culture, see Aytoun Ellis, *The Penny Universities: A History of the Coffee-Houses* (London: Secker & Warburg, 1956), Bryant Lillywhite, *London Coffee Houses: A Reference Book of Coffee Houses of the Seventeenth, Eighteenth and Nineteenth Centuries* (London: Allen and Unwin, 1963), and Steven C. A. Pincus, '"Coffee Politicians Does Create": Coffeehouses and Restoration Political Culture', *Journal of Modern History*, 67 (1995), 807–34. Summers (*Rehearsal*, p. 80) remarks on Sir Walter Scott's 'vivid picture of Dryden' at Will's Coffee House in *The Pirate* (1822). See *The Pirate*, ed. Mark Weinstein and Alison Lumsden (Edinburgh: Edinburgh University Press, 2001), esp. 113, 116, 131–3 (chs. 12 and 14 in the continuous numeration). Scott had edited the works of Dryden in eighteen volumes (1808).

111. *the world's unmindful.* Attitudes towards appropriation from sources (which often seems like outright plagiarism by later standards) were changing rapidly in the later seventeenth century. Buckingham's views of Dryden's practice anticipate those of Langbaine in *An Account of the English Dramatick Poets* (1691), where Dryden is lambasted as a 'plagiary'. On such issues, see Kewes, *Authorship and Appropriation*.

118. *when I have any thing to invent.* The U of PA-1683 annotator has written 'Dryden' against this line.

120–2. *Perseus, Montaigne, Seneca's Tragedies, Horace, Juvenal, Claudian, Pliny, Plutarch's lives.* Persius (CE 34–62), a Roman satirist; Montaigne (1533–92), French essayist; Seneca (*c.*3 BCE – CE 65), Roman philosopher and playwright; Horace (65–8 BCE), Roman writer of satires, verse epistles, and odes; Juvenal (*c.* CE 55–60 to *c.*127), Roman satirist; Claudius Claudianus (*fl. c.* CE 400), Roman poet; Pliny (the younger? CE *c.*61–*c.*112), orator and epistle writer; Plutarch (*c.* CE 46–*c.*120), biographer. None of these writers was particularly apropos to Dryden's published work in 1671, though in the eighties and nineties he was to become a noted translator of and commentator upon classical authors. Buckingham's point seems to be to suggest classical pretentions that neither Bayes nor Dryden can sustain.

I. ii

0.1. *Enter three Players.* The scene changes to the stage of the King's Company's Bridges Street theatre.

2. *without book.* In the seventeenth century, actors normally learnt their parts from 'sides' rather than from a complete manuscript or printed copy of the play. The prompter or his clerk copied out each part with the end of each preceding speech to serve as cue. Hardly any exemplars survive, but Trico's part (taken by

Matthew Medbourne) in George Ruggle's *Ignoramus* (Duke's Company, 1662) is preserved in the Harvard Theatre Collection and has been printed by Edward A. Langhans, in *Restoration Promptbooks* (Carbondale, Ill.: Southern Illinois University Press, 1981), 509–13. Actors got some sense of the overall shape and meaning of a new play by hearing the author read it aloud to the company before the start of rehearsals. For an example of a performer responding to the cues while learning a role, see the quotation from Pepys in the note at II. i. 29.

5. *what humour*. Also a puzzle for Thomas Doggett in his visit to Dryden to discuss his part in *Love Triumphant* (*Letters*, 54).

8. *new way of writing*. Writers in the 1660s were conscious of the need for experimentation and proud of their innovations. In his *Essay of Dramatick Poesie* (pub. 1668) Dryden has Neander insist at length on the impossibility of competing directly with Shakespeare, Fletcher, and Jonson:

> They are honour'd, and almost ador'd by us, as they deserve; neither do I know any so presumptuous of themselves as to contend with them. . . . We acknowledge them our Fathers in wit, but they have ruin'd their Estates themselves before they came to their childrens hands. There is scarce an Humour, a Character, or any kind of Plot, which they have not us'd. . . . This therefore will be a good Argument to us either not to write at all, or to attempt some other way. (*Works*, xvii. 72–3)

Percy's *New Key* (p. 378) quotes from Orrery's *Dramatic Works* of 1739 'a Letter of Roger Boyle's Earl of Orrery, which shews from what quarter, and by whose incouragement this new manner of writing was adopted':

> I have now finished a Play in the French Manner; because I heard the King declare himself more in favour of their Way of Writing than ours: My poor Attempt cannot please his Majesty, but my Example may incite others who can: Sir William Davenant will have it acted about Easter. And as it is wrote in a new Way, he may possibly take Confidence to invite the King to see it. (Orrery, *Dramatic Works*, ed. Clark, i. 34)

The 1739 *Dramatic Works* mistakenly identifies the play as *The Black Prince*, but the reference is evidently to *King Henry the Fifth*, staged by the Duke's Company with great success in August 1664. Obviously this letter was not available to Buckingham in 1671, but Orrery's boasts about writing 'in a new way' may well have caught his attention.

13–14. *Scenes, Cloaths and Dancing*. Buckingham's dig here actually echoes Dryden's complaint in the prologue to *The Rival Ladies*:

> You now have Habits, Dances, Scenes, and Rhymes;
> High Language often; I, and Sense, sometimes. (*Works*, viii. 103)

The hostile reference to scenery is probably a remnant of the Ur-*Rehearsal*. The King's Company was slow and reluctant in its response to Davenant's introduction of changeable scenery in a public theatre. Only under pressure of public preference and bad receipts did they raise the capital to build a scenic theatre. Bridges Street opened in May 1663.

18–19. *Mr.——a——*. There is no evidence that inability to remember actors' names was characteristic of Dryden or Sir Robert Howard, and it could hardly have been true of Davenant (principal owner and manager of the Duke's Company), but Bayes is definitely characterized by failure to remember names and his '——a——' is reiterated in a way clearly meant to be comic in itself. Other instances of inability to remember actors' names occur at III. ii. 80, IV. i. 230–1, V. i. 222–3, and V. iii. 4. Bayes openly expresses his contempt for actors ('these Players are such dull persons') at III. ii. 244–5 but is capable of blanking even on Smith's name at IV. i. 89–90.

29–30. *Amarillis . . . Armor.* We cannot identify a particular target for this bad pun. Buckingham may just be teasing the artificial naming conventions of contemporary drama.

32. *my Mistress.* 'The Part of *Amaryllis* was Acted by Mrs. *Ann Reeves*, who, at that time, was kept by Mr. *Bayes*' (*Key*, p. 2). Crane (p. 82) points out that no confirmatory evidence has ever been discovered for this claim, though it is not *ipso facto* implausible. Anne Reeves was active with the King's Company 1670–5, after which she disappeared. She took the part of '*Esperanza*, slave to the Queen' in *The Conquest of Granada.* Her connection with Dryden is amply suggested by contemporary gossip. The song 'Farewel dear *Revechia*' in the *Covent Garden Drollery*, 'Collected by A.B.' (London, 1672), is either by Dryden or (perhaps more probably) meant to seem as if it were. See *Covent Garden Drollery*, ed. G. Thorn-Drury (London: Dobell, 1928). Thorn-Drury (pp. 135–7) strenuously denies the plausibility of Reeves performing the part of Amaryllis, but his position seems largely founded on Victorian presumptions. In a violently hostile satire, 'The Medal of John Bayes' (1682), Shadwell says in the prefatory epistle 'His prostituted *Muse* will become as common for hire, as his Mistress *Revesia* was, upon whom he spent so many hundred pounds; and of whom (to shew his constancy in Love) he got three Claps, and she was a Bawd' (*Complete Works*, v. 248). The truth of any of this is undeterminable. Allusions *c.*1675–6 suggest that Reeves eventually entered a foreign nunnery. John Harold Wilson (*All the King's Ladies*, 184) repeats Clifford Leech's speculation that the author of a 1745 *Gentleman's Magazine* story about his eating tarts with Dryden and Madam Reeve at the Mulberry-Garden was Thomas Southerne (*Notes and Queries*, 164 (10 June 1933), 401–3), but this is implausible: Southerne would have been only 13 years old in 1672. On Anne Reeves see Winn, *John Dryden*, Appendix D ('Facts and Questions about Anne Reeves'), 532–9.

34:2. *I have talkt bawdy to her already.* 'Mr. Dryden was remarkable for this. See Ld Rochester's imitation of Hor. Lib. I. Sat. 10. "Dryden, in vain &c.—"' (Percy's *New Key*, p. 380). The passage is quoted in the note to 34:25–6 ('I am not able . . .'). The U of PA-1683 annotator has duly written 'Dryden' in the margin against this phrase.

34:6–7. *if, before vie you put Mon instead of Ma, you make it bawdy.* Crane (p. 82) points out that the phrase thus becomes 'mon vit' (a vulgar term for the penis).

34:10. *Adieu bel Esperansa de mavie.* 'Good-bye beautiful hope of my life', playing in French and on Mrs Reeves's character name in *The Conquest of Granada* ('hope' in Spanish). She replies 'Dream about my life, Sir' to which he ripostes,

'No, no, Madam, dream of me.' Bayes seems notably ineffectual as a womanizer—as no doubt Dryden did to Buckingham.

34:16. *kept by another woman, in the City.* We are unable to identify any basis for this gibe, but probably the point is that Bayes is kept by a cit's wife, which was exceedingly *infra dig.* The U of PA-1683 annotator has written 'Dryden' in the margin.

34:18. *Beau Gerson.* i.e. 'beau garçon' (gigolo). See also *The Country Gentleman,* I. i. 123 (and note) and 'Advice to a Paynter to draw the Delineaments of a Statesman, and his Underlings', line 20 and note.

*ifackins.* In faith.

34:24. *toil like a Horse.* This may well be a snide allusion to Dryden's comparison of the poet's position with that of a husband trying to satisfy his wife in bed in the prologue to *An Evening's Love:*

> When first our Poet set himself to write,
> Like a young Bridegroom on his Wedding-night.
> He layd about him . . .
> But now his Honey-moon is gone and past,
> Yet the ungrateful drudgery must last:
> And he is bound, as civil Husbands do,
> To strain himself, in complaisance to you:
> To write in pain, and counterfeit a bliss . . . . (*Works,* x. 214)

34:25–6. *I am not able to say you one good thing.* Dryden himself said in his 'Defence of an Essay of Dramatique Poesie' that 'My Conversation is slow and dull, my humour Saturnine and reserv'd: In short, I am none of those who endeavour to break Jests in Company, or make reparties' (*Works,* ix. 8), but Shadwell's satiric portrait of Dryden as Drybob in *The Humorists* (1670) suggests that his contemporaries thought otherwise. Shadwell has Drybob say 'I do say as many fine things in a year, as e'r a Wit of 'em all' (Shadwell, *Complete Works,* i. 204). Dryden's modern biographer finds that 'Shadwell's implication that Dryden actually valued himself on his skill at repartee was solidly based' (Winn, *John Dryden,* 223). In 1671 Dryden had become temporarily friendly with Rochester (to whom he dedicated *Marriage A-la-Mode* in 1673, with fulsome thanks for 'the favour, of being admitted into your Lordship's Conversation', *Works,* xi. 221). Rochester, however, does not seem to have been impressed by Dryden's attempt to emulate the wit of his betters. Praising 'refin'd Etheridge' in 'An Allusion to Horace' (1676?), Rochester said

> Dryden in vain tryd this nice way of Witt,
> For he to be a tearing Blade thought fitt.
> But when he would be sharp he still was blunt:
> To frisk his frolick fancy hee'd cry Cunt;
> Wou'd give the Ladyes a drye bawdy bobb,
> And thus he gott the name of Poet Squobb. (ll. 71–6; *Works,* 73)

Obviously few members of the public would have known whether Dryden was a brilliant wit and conversationalist; Buckingham's unkind dig was intended for insiders.

35–6. *very ridiculous*. An odd desideratum for a work presumably intended as a heroic drama in the style of Dryden.

38. *let's sit down*. Bayes and his guests presumably sit down in chairs provided for the rehearsal and placed at the side of the forestage, or possibly in a stage box.

*chief hindge*. 'H Howard United Kingdomes' has been written against this line by the U of PA-1683 annotator. Buckingham's reiterated hits at this failed and unpublished play (staged *c*.1663?) have a personal background explained in 'The Publisher to the Reader' in the 1704 *Key*:

> Our *most noble Author*, to manifest his just Indignation, and hatred of this Fulsom new-way of Writing, used his utmost Interest and Endeavours to Stifle it at its first appearing on the Stage, by engaging all his Friends to Explode and Run down these Plays, especially the *United Kingdoms*; which had like to have brought his Life in danger.
> The Author of it being Nobly born, of an antient and numerous Family, had many of his Relations and Friends in the *Cock-Pit*, during the Acting it; some of 'em perceiving his *Grace* to head a Party, who were very active in Damning the Play, by Hissing and Laughing immoderately at the strange Conduct thereof; there were Persons laid wait for him, as he came out; but there being a great Tumult and Uproar in the House, and the Passages near it, he escap'd: But he was Threaten'd hard. . . . After this, our *Author* endeavour'd by Writing, to expose the *Follies* of these new-fashion'd Plays in their proper Colours. (pp. x–xi)

On this passage Percy comments (*New Key*, p. 381): 'Bayes's obscure and perplexed account of his plot is very much in the manner of the Preface to *Orgula, or the Fatal Error*: By way of specimen take the author's very profound definition of poesy: "Poesy only is an art of lively representation of bodies natural simply without reference to other, or compositively with circumstance to their mutual communities, either natural or civil. Real in respect of their precedent, present or future condition: or imaginary in relation of their possibility", etc.' *Orgula*, by 'L.W.' [Leonard Willan], was published in 1658. There is no record of performance, but the play contains a number of features alluded to derisively in *The Rehearsal*. It opens with a funeral; a revolution is brought about by an army in disguise; it contains a key whispering scene.

42. *two Kings*. 'Supposed to be the two Brothers, the King and the Duke' (*Key*, p. 2). The author of the *Key* says, concerning the opening of Act IV: 'Coll. *Henry Howard* . . . made a Play, call'd the *United Kingdoms*, which . . . had also two Kings in it. This gave the Duke a just occasion to set up two Kings in *Brentford*, as 'tis generally believ'd; tho' others are of Opinion, that his Grace had our two Brothers [King Charles II and James, Duke of York] in his thoughts' (p. 17). If Buckingham was indeed aiming at the king and the Duke of York, then he certainly needed plausible secondary targets to cover his audacity. Summers (*Rehearsal*, p. 83) suggests Mahomet Boabdelin and his traitorous brother Prince Abdalla in *The Conquest of Granada*. Stocker (p. 24) suggests that in political terms the two kings are designed as a comic rendering of 'the political cross-currents provoked by James' power as

the active heir-presumptive, and the resultant factional interest'. Historically, a reference may be intended to the dual kingship of ancient Sparta. Buckingham's view of Charles and James was far from worshipful. He terms Charles a 'dull Blockhead' and an 'Ugly, perjur'd Rogue' in 'The Cabbin-Boy'. Burnet reports that 'The Duke of *Buckingham* gave me once a short but severe character of the two brothers. It was the more severe, because it was true: The King (he said) could see things if he would, and the Duke would see things if he could' (*History*, i. 169).

43. *I love to write familiarly.* Hardly true of either Dryden or Davenant in either geographic setting or subject matter, but characteristic of Dryden's prose style and dedications.

62. *Prologue and an Epilogue.* 'See the two Prologues to the *Maiden Queen* [i.e. *Secret-Love*]' (*Key*, p. 2). Dryden provides an eighteen-line prologue, after which 'The Prologue goes out, and stayes while a Tune is play'd, after which he returns again', says 'I had forgot one half I do protest, / And now am sent again to speak the rest' and thereupon delivers a 'Second Prologue' with thirty-eight additional lines (*Works*, ix. 119–21). *The Rival Ladies* (1664) also employs a double prologue in which after twenty-three lines 'A Second Prologue Enters' and speaks another thirteen.

62–3. *Prologue and an Epilogue, which may both serve for either.* This passage is alluded to in *Spectator*, no. 341 (1 April 1712).

65. *Artificial.* 'Well contrived'.

68. *two ways of making very good Prologues* ['by insinuation' and 'in terrorem']. Percy's *New Key*, pp. 382–3, notes that 'Mr. Dryden's plays afford instances of both kinds', quoting the prologue and epilogue to *The Wild Gallant* as instances of civility and insinuation, and the 'little Hectors of the pit' passage in the prologue to *Secret-Love* as an example of the *in terrorem* sort. Percy mentions the prologue to *The Rival Ladies* as another instance of the threatening mode.

72. *keep a hank upon.* i.e. a restraining hold.

74–5. *I come out.* Odd, because playwrights did not deliver prologues. Rutelli (*La Prova téatrale* [*The Rehearsal*], ed. Romana Rutelli (Napoli: Liguori, 1994) [facing English and Italian texts]), 229, cites Jonson's *Poetaster* as a prior case where 'un personaggio che parlava a nome dell'autore tendeva a stabilire un dialogo fra *stage* e *audience*'.

75. *long black Veil, and a great huge Hang-man.* Percy's *New Key*, pp. 383–4, comments that 'we must not expect to find here the exact resemblance of any thing that was ever really exhibited on the stage: but only a general satire on the modern Prologues and Epilogues . . . [which] often abound with conceits as strange, as this of the Hangman's cutting off the Poet's head'. The author then quotes at length the astrological conceit in the 1663 prologue to Dryden's *The Wild Gallant*. The hang-man passage is alluded to in *Tatler*, no. 6 (23 April 1709).

79. *clapping.* Percy's *New Key*, p. 385, notes that 'In the Epilogue to the *English Rogue* the author is so sure of his play's being clapped, that he puts it in the margin as a stage direction.' Thomas Thomson's *The English Rogue* was published in 1668 and may have been privately performed at an unknown date.

88. *the old plain way.* Buckingham's attitude towards fashion in drama is strongly reminiscent of Sir Richard Plainbred's detestation of fashionable French food and wine in *The Country Gentleman* (see particularly I. i. 360–75 and 404–16). Buckingham was fond of this phrase, using it in *The Chances*, IV. iii. 73–4 and at I. ii. 9 in the present play. In the political context of *c.*1670 it amounted to political code, appealing to 'country party' ideology. Bayes says that he is writing not for the country party but for some persons of quality (i.e. Frenchified courtiers and town fops)—a snide but not wholly inaccurate characterization of Dryden.

88–9. *I write for some persons of Quality.* Percy's *New Key*, p. 385, quotes the preface to *Tyrannick Love* (pub. 1670): 'I was moved to write this Play by many reasons: amongst others, the Commands of some Persons of Honour . . . were daily sounding in my ears, &c' (*Works*, x. 109), and also refers the reader to the Dedication of Dryden's *The Assignation* (pub. spring 1673), in which he flaunts his friendship with Sir Charles Sedley and 'Great Persons of our Court . . . who have taken care of me, even amidst the Exigencies of a War'.

90. *Flame and Power in writing.* ''Tis an irregular piece . . . written with more Flame than Art' (*Works*, ix. 25), Dedication to *The Indian Emperour* (pub. 1667), cited in Percy's *New Key*, p. 385.

94. *I gad.* '*I Gad, I vow to Gad, and all that* is the constant Stile of *Failer* in The *Wild Gallant.*' See the *Key*, p. 3 and Percy's *New Key*, p. 387, which cite in particular 'this short Speech, instead of many'. '*Failer.* Really Madam, I look upon you as a person of such worth and all that, that I Vow to Gad, I honour you of all persons in the World; and though I am a person that am inconsiderable in the World, and all that Madam, yet for a person of your worth and excellency I would—.' (*Works*, viii. 33).

95. *a hundred sheets of papyr.* 'There were Printed papers given the Audience, before the Acting the *Indian* Emperor: telling them, that it was the Sequel of the *Indian* Queen, part of which Play was written by Mr. *Bayes*, &c.' (*Key*, p. 3). Narcissus Luttrell's annotated copy of *Q3* says much the same thing (Boston Public Library, Mass., G.3967.19). What is evidently the gist of this handout is printed in the front matter of the 1667 quarto of *The Indian Emperour*. See *Works*, ix. 27–8.

96–7. *two or three dozen of my friends.* No organized professional claque is known in the Carolean theatres, but the small total audience pool in London and the system of authors' 'third days' must have encouraged organized applause (and disapprobation as well).

102. *engage 'em to clap.* 'Ned Howard' is written against this line by the U of PA-1683 annotator.

105. *Critiques.* Faultfinders. Dryden's many sneering references to 'little critics' are catalogued by Jensen (p. 36). In the second prologue to *Secret-Love*, for example, he attacks 'the little Hectors of the Pit' and the 'peevish Critick' who is 'cheaply witty on the Poets cost' (*Works*, ix. 120). Cf. note on the prologue, line 15.

106. *Hobby-horses.* Either in the sense of *OED* 3.a ('a frivolous or foolish fellow, jester, buffoon') or 4 (a stick with a wooden horse's head 'which children bestride as a toy horse'). See also V. i. 287.1–2.

116–17. *choice female spirits.* Summers (*Rehearsal*, p. 86) glosses this as an allusion to Lady Castlemaine, to whom Dryden wrote some complimentary verses: 'To the Lady Castlemaine, upon Her Incouraging His First Play' (*Works*, i. 45–6). These verses, however, were not published until 1674.

122. *certain tyes.* 'He Contracted with the King's Company of Actors, in the Year 1668, for a whole Share, to write them four Plays a year' (*Key*, p. 3). For some details of the agreement, calling for *three* plays per annum, see James M. Osborn, *John Dryden: Some Biographical Facts and Problems*, rev. edn. (Gainesville, Fla.: University of Florida Press, 1965), 200–7. When Dryden defected to the Duke's Company in 1678, the King's Company actors protested that 'his share & a quarter' had brought him '3 or 4 hundred pounds *Communibus annis*', probably a considerable exaggeration (ibid., 204).

131. *Thunder and Lightning.* Percy's *New Key* (pp. 389–90) states inaccurately that 'It was customary in the D. of Buckingham's time to have the Prologue spoken by some allegorical personage', instancing Night in Thomas Jordan's *Money is an Ass* (*c.*1635; pub. 1668), Venus-Phœbus-Thetis in Peter Hausted's *The Rival Friends* (1632), the prologue to Richard Flecknoe's *Love's Kingdom* (1664), and Cupid in Thomas Heywood's *Love's Mistress* (1634). Allegorical speakers of prologues were, however, unusual.

135. *non pareillo.* (Mangled Franco-Italian.) i.e. nonpareil (matchless, peerless) in modern English.

136. *Prologue to be Dialogue.* Percy's *New Key*, p. 388, comments disparagingly on the vogue for prologues and epilogues in 'the form of low, pert, flashy Dialogues', citing particularly Dryden's prologue for *The Rival Ladies* (1664), Davenant's epilogue for *The Man's the Master* (1668), and Sir Robert Howard's prologue for *The Duke of Lerma* (1668)—the latter spoken by Nell Gwyn and Elizabeth Knepp. Downes, *Roscius Anglicanus*, 66, implies that Davenant's epilogue was a great hit. Summers (*Rehearsal*, p. 88) points also to Orrery's prologue for *Tryphon* (1668), spoken by the low comedians Nokes and Angel, and the prologue to *The Indian-Queen*, spoken by an Indian boy and girl, awakened 'under two Plaintain-Trees' by martial music. Rutelli, *La Prova téatrale*, 230, cites as an extreme example the epilogue to Molière's *L'École des Femmes*, which is spoken and sung by 'una dozzina di personaggi'.

142–3. *at that lock.* i.e. such a hold on them (wrestling terminology).

148. *So Boar and Sow*. 'In Rediculé of this',

> So, two kind Turtles, when a storm is nigh,
> Look up; and see it gath'ring in the Skie:
> Each calls his Mate to shelter in the Groves,
> Leaving, in murmures their unfinish'd Loves.
> Perch'd on some dropping Branch they sit alone,
> And Cooe, and hearken to each others moan.
>
> > *Conquest of Granada*, Part 2, I. ii. 128–33
> > (cited in the *Key*, p. 4). See *Works*, xi. 115.

Against this line the U of PA-1683 annotator wrote 'Dryden'.

158. *profecto*. Certainly (Latin).

159.1 *Enter Thunder and Lightning*. As the *Key* (pp. 4–5) observes, this exchange is a parody of the 'Song in Dialogue' in III. i of Stapylton's *The Slighted Maid* (1663):

> *Evening.* I am an Evening dark as Night,
> Jack-with-the Lantern bring a Light—
> > *Jack.* Whither, whither, whither?          [within.
> > *Evening.* Hither, hither, hither.
> > *Jack.* Thou art some pratling Eccho, of my making:
> > *Evening.* Thou art a Foolish Fire, by thy mistaking:
> I am the Evening that creates thee.
> > *Enter* Jack *in a black Suit border'd with* Glow-worms, *a*
> > *Coronet of Shaded Beams on his head, over it a Paper*
> > *Lantern with a Candle in't.*
> > *Jack.* My Lantern and my Candle waits thee.
> > *Evening.* Those Flajolets that we heard play,
> Are Reapers who have lost their way;
> They Play, they Sing, they Dance a-Round,
> Lead them up, here's Faery-ground.
> > *Chorus.*
> Let the Men ware the Ditches,
> Maids, look to your Breetches,
> We'l scratch them with Briars and Thistles:
> When the Flajolets cry.
> We are a-dry;
> Pond-water shall wet their Whistles. (pp. 48–9)

Dryden shared Buckingham's contemptuous view of Stapleton's play, referring to it dismissively in 'The Grounds of Criticism in Tragedy' in 1679 (*Works*, xiii. 230), in a prologue of 1684 (Danchin, iv. 533), and again in *A Parallel of Poetry and Painting* in 1695 (*Works*, xx. 69).

160. *I am the bold Thunder*. This passage is evidence that authors in this period directed actors specifically in line delivery. (For discussion, see Milhous and Hume, *Producible Interpretation*, ch. 2.) For another instance of instruction on line delivery, see III. ii. 48. Whether Dryden attempted to instruct performers in line delivery, or did it well, may be doubted. Cibber says that when Dryden 'brought his Play of

*Amphytrion* to the Stage, I heard him give it his first Reading to the Actors, in which, though it is true he deliver'd the plain Sense of every Period, yet the whole was in so cold, so flat, and unaffecting a manner, that I am afraid of not being believ'd when I affirm it' (*Apology*, i. 113). See also Love, 'Roger L'Estrange's Criticism of Dryden's Elocution'. For evidence that Davenant gave actors very specific instruction (ostensibly passing on stage tradition straight from Shakespeare), see Downes, *Roscius Anglicanus*, 51–2, 55. 'I am the bold Thunder' is quoted in *Spectator*, no. 36 (11 April 1711). The line is significantly quoted in John O'Keefe's *Wild Oats* (1791).

161. *Cartwright.* William Cartwright (*c.*1606–86). See *Biographical Dictionary*, iii. 89–93. A big, burly man (to judge from his portrait), Cartwright was a sharer, and one of the King's Company's principal actors from its re-establishment in 1660 to its dissolution in 1682. Cartwright's Falstaff was commended by Pepys (2 November 1667), and his many roles in Dryden's plays led the authors of the *Biographical Dictionary* to the conclusion that he was 'one of Dryden's favorites'.

165. *brisk Lightning, I.* The list of names at the outset of the play and line 169 in this passage show that Lightning was definitely played by a woman. Depending on the casting, various sorts of jokes could have been intended.

168. *Hector.* In its subsidiary sense of a street ruffian or bully.

169. *Helen . . . Hector.* In Homer's *Iliad*. Helen's leaving her husband Menelaus in favour of Prince Paris was the cause of the Trojan war, and hence of the death of Paris's older brother Hector, killed by Achilles.

171. *I fire the Town.* The phrase would have had an enhanced impact in a city that itself had been so recently 'fired'. Percy's *New Key* (p. 391) annotates with a passage from Sir Aston Cokain's *The Tragedy of Ovid* (pub. 1662), Act I. Scene iii, with Hymen, Cupid, and Venus singing:

> *Ven.* I smiled with eies, that darted rayes
> Of sweet desire on either's face.
> *Cupid.* And I such shafts did put in use
> As only they themselves could cure.
> *Hym.* And I Love's best Physitian, quickly found
> Each others hand might heal each others wound. (p. 16)

175. *paint on their faces.* The use of cosmetics was of course standard for actresses and common among Carolean court ladies, but decidedly shocking to the bourgeois. John Evelyn denounces the use of make-up in his *Diary*, iii. 97 (11 May 1654). Diana Dethloff, 'Portraiture and Concepts of Beauty in Restoration Painting', in Catharine MacLeod and Julia Marciari Alexander (comps. and eds.), *Painted Ladies: Women at the Court of Charles II* (London: National Portrait Gallery, 2001), 35 n. 42, notes that 'the use of make-up . . . was particularly associated with prostitutes' (citing Evelyn). When Pepys visited the women's dressing room at Bridges Street on 5 October 1667 he saw Nell Gwyn and Elizabeth Knepp preparing to perform and commented 'But Lord, to see how they were both painted would make a man mad—and did make me loath them' (viii. 463). Pepys's dislike

of cosmetics was strong. On 16 September his wife took him to dinner at Mrs Pierce's, 'where I find her painted (which makes me loathe her)' (viii. 439).

176. *Peter.* Vermillion—i.e. rouge (Summers, *Rehearsal*, p. 92).

183. *Feather.* Worn in the hat.

190. *Ivory.* '*Abraham Ivory* [*d.* 1680?] had formerly been a considerable Actor of Womens Parts; but afterwards stupified himself so far, with drinking strong waters, that, before the first Acting of this Farce, he was fit for nothing, but to go of Errands: for which, and meer Charity, the Company allow'd him a Weekly Salary' (*Key*, p. 5). Almost nothing else is definitely known of him. See *Biographical Dictionary*, viii. 107. The establishment 'two doors off' was presumably a tavern.

## II. i

2. [*Spits.* As an after-effect of the tobacco?

5. *begin . . . with a whisper.* '*Drake Sen.* Draw up our Men; and in low Whispers give our Orders out. *Play House to be let*, P. 100. See the Amorous Prince, *Page.* 20, 22, 39, 69: where you will find, all the chief Commands, and Directions, are given in Whispers' (*Key*, p. 6). Crane (p. 85) points out other instances of whispering: *Orgula*, II. ii; *Mustapha*, IV. i; *The Womens Conquest*, V. i; and *Marriage A-la-Mode*, I. i. Percy's *New Key* (pp. 394–5) adds *The Politician Cheated*, Act V, p. 48, and Sir William Killigrew's *Pandora* 'in which there is hardly a scene without whispering', quoting Act III, p. 45, in particular.

7.1. *Gentleman-Usher.* A genteel doorkeeper and factotum. The position required more breeding than brains or energy. Charles II's household included four '*Gentlemen Ushers of the Privy-Chamber*', who were to 'wait, one at a time, in the Privy-Lodgings' attended by twelve '*Gentlemen of the Privy Chamber in Ordinary*' (rotated each quarter year) and eight '*Gentlemen-Ushers, Quarter-Waiters in Ordinary*' who were to 'wait also in the Presence-Chamber, and are to give Directions in the absence of the Gentlemen-Ushers', supervising the 'Daily Waiters', 'Grooms', and 'Pages' of the Royal Household. See Edward Chamberlayne, *Angliæ Notitia; or, The Present State of England*, 5th edn. ([London], 1671), Part 1, pp. 175, 178–9. Buckingham was, of course, thoroughly familiar with the intricacies of the Royal Household, its personnel, hierarchies, and pecking orders. In 1671 he was one of its three most senior officials. Chamberlayne says 'The Third Great Officer of the *Kings Court*, is the *Master of the Horse* . . . . This Great Officer hath now the ordering and disposal of all the *Kings Stables*, and *Races*, or *Breed of Horses*. . . . He hath also the power over *Escuiries*, and *Pages*, over the *Footmen*, *Grooms*, *Riders* of the *Great Horses*, *Farriers*, *Smiths*, *Coachmen*, *Sadlers*, and all other *Trades* working to the *Kings Stables*. . . . He hath the Charge of all *Lands* and *Revenues*, appointed for the *Kings* breed of Horses. . . . This Great Honor is now enjoyed by *George* Duke of *Buckingham*. His yearly Fee is £666 16s. 4d. and a Table of Sixteen dishes each Meal' (ibid. 163–4).

15. *let's imbrace.* 'H Howard' is written against this line by the U of PA-1683 annotator.

29. *Tyring-room.* Little is known of the nature, location, and amenities of dressing rooms in seventeenth-century theatres. At what date principals started to get private or semi-private quarters is unclear. Pepys inspected 'all the tiring roomes' when he saw Bridges Street Theatre in process of alterations in March 1666 (*Diary*, vii. 76–7). On 22 May 1667 he reports that 'Knipp spied me out of the tiring-room and came to the pit door' (viii. 232), and on 5 October that year he says:

to the King's House [Bridges Street Theatre]; and there going in, met with Knipp and she took us up into the Tireing-rooms and to the women's Shift, where Nell was dressing herself . . . and so walked all up and down the House above, and then below into the Scene-room, and there sat down and she gave us fruit; and here I read the Qu's to Knepp while she answered me, through all her part of *Flora's Figarys*, which was acted today. (viii. 463)

Depositions in a murder case of June 1685 suggest that at Drury Lane the dressing rooms were on at least two levels on either side of the stage. Elizabeth Barry's dressing room was up a flight of stairs and had its own fireplace. See R. Jordan, 'Observations on the Backstage Area in the Restoration Theatre', *Theatre Notebook*, 38 (1984), 66–8, and Judith Milhous and Robert D. Hume, 'Murder in Elizabeth Barry's Dressing Room', *Yale University Library Gazette*, 79 (2005), 149–74. We presume that Buckingham's reference to the 'Tyring-room' was to non-private space used by lesser members of the company.

33. *Clouds, do hover o'er our heads.* Percy, *New Key* (pp. 392–3), thinks it 'not impossible but this may be in part intended to ridicule the following lines of a play attributed to Lord Digby.

> *Francisca.* Since the black Cloud, that threatn'd you last night
> With such a storm, is luckily blown over,
> Without a sprinkling; I hope, Madam, you
> Will imitate the fates, and grow Serene
> From all those Clouds, which so much threatn'd others.

*Elvira*, A[ct].3. p.36 [*recte* 33].' Percy's *New Key* also cites a passage in Edward Howard's *The Usurper* (1664; pub. 1668):

> it is
> Within your choise, timely to scatter all
> Those hovering Clouds that may involve you in
> Too late Repentance. (p. 28)

34. *grasp'd but by the eye of reason.* Percy's *New Key* (p. 393) comments that this 'proper ridicule on . . . forced and unnatural metaphors' cannot be 'exactly' paralleled in plays of the time, 'but it would be easy to glean innumerable instances, as harsh, confused and absurd as the above'. The 'specimens' Percy cites from Neville's *Poor Scholar* seem remote indeed.

38–9. *if Lorenzo ... the great Gods can tell.* 'How far the King's jealousy may work / Upon him, none but the Gods can tell.' *The Ungrateful Favourite*, Act II, scene iv, p. 27 (cited in Percy's *New Key*, pp. 393–4).

59–60. *despise your Johnson, and Beaumont.* An allusion to Dryden's rather arrogant epilogue to Part 2 of *The Conquest of Granada*:

> ... *Jonson* did Mechanique humour show,
> When men were dull, and conversation low.
> Then, Comedy was faultless, but 'twas course. ...
>
> .    .    .    .    .    .    .    .
>
> Fame then was cheap, and the first commer sped;
> And they have kept it since, by being dead. (*Works*, xi. 201)

Response to this ill-considered rhetoric was sufficiently hostile that Dryden felt obliged to add 'A Defence of the Epilogue' when *The Conquest of Granada* was published in 1672. As of 1671 Ben Jonson and 'Beaumont and Fletcher' were widely regarded as the greatest of English dramatists. Bayes's sneer would have had the same effect as denigrating Shakespeare in the time of Garrick's later career—or to-day.

61. *out of my own fancie.* An allusion to Dryden's heavy emphasis on unfettered fancy in his prologue for *Tyrannick Love*:

> ... our Poet in his conjuring,
> Allow'd his Fancy the full scope and swing.
> But when a Tyrant for his Theme he had,
> He loos'd the Reins, and bid his Muse run mad. (*Works*, x. 114)

This notion of fancy culminated, after the premiere of *The Rehearsal*, in Dryden's Preface to *The Conquest of Granada*. At times his position on creative imagination is almost Coleridgean. See John M. Aden, 'Dryden and the Imagination: The First Phase', *PMLA* 74 (1959), 28–40. After 1672 Dryden quickly retreated from this position and adopted the more usual compromise view of fancy/imagination needing to be checked by judgement. See Robert D. Hume, 'Dryden on Creation: "Imagination" in the Later Criticism', *RES*, NS 21 (1970), 295–314.

62. *Sir John Suckling.* Renowned cavalier poet (1609–42) and author of *Aglaura*, *Brennoralt*, and *The Goblins*, plays still popular in the 1660s. His poetry enjoyed a high reputation in the Restoration, and Bayes's boast would have shocked the audience. Etherege gives Dorimant a fragment of Suckling's verse to quote in III. iii of *The Man of Mode* (1676), a sign of high favour in his eyes, and perhaps by implication in Rochester's ('See how unregarded now / That piece of Beauty passes'). As late as 1700 Congreve names Suckling and quotes him several times in IV. i of *The Way of the World*.

63. *a better Poet than he.* 'Ned: Howard' is written against this line by the U of PA-1683 annotator.

66. *Polititians.* From its inception in the 1580s the word 'politician' was two-edged, implying knowledge of or engagement in business of state, but also 'chiefly in a sinister sense, a shrewd schemer; a crafty plotter or intriguer' (*OED*, 1 and 2).

77. *Wintershull.* 'Mr. *William Wintershull* was a most Excellent, Judicious Actor, and the best Instructor of others: He Dy'd in *July*, 1679' (*Key*, p. 6). Wintershall was one of the King's Company's principal sharing actors from its re-establishment in 1660. He took such parts as the king in *The Maid's Tragedy*, Subtle in *The Alchemist*, and the king in *The Humorous Lieutenant*. He had performed in plays satirized in *The Rehearsal*, taking Don Alonzo in *An Evening's Love* and Selim in both parts of *The Conquest of Granada*. See *Biographical Dictionary*, xvi. 191–4.

81. *good language.* Refinement of language was something of an *idée fixe* with Dryden. In the epilogue to Part 2 of *The Conquest of Granada* he says:

> Wit's now ariv'd to a more high degree;
> Our native Language more refin'd and free.
> Our Ladies and our men now speak more wit
> In conversation, than those Poets writ. (*Works*, xi. 201)

Buckingham's sneer at his harrangues on the subject seems to look ahead to Dryden's rather unfortunate 'Defence of the Epilogue', published in 1672. Dryden remained undaunted, however, and his 1673 dedication of *Marriage A-la-Mode* to Rochester makes much of 'the favour, of being admitted into your Lordship's Conversation'. See also the note on I. ii. 34:25–6.

87. *Foppery.* The modern sense of 'fop' as one 'vain of his appearance, dress, or manners; a dandy, an exquisite' (*OED* 3) was very new in the 1670s. Neither Dryden nor any of the other playwrights who contributed to the character of Bayes is known to have dressed or behaved in a fashion anticipating Sir Fopling Flutter or Lord Foppington. Buckingham may be using 'Foppery' in its earlier sense of 'foolishness, imbecility, stupidity, folly' (*OED*).

87:7. *ifackins.* In faith.

87:11. *I write standing.* We have no information as to whether this was actually Dryden's practice. Buckingham may have put it in just because he found the idea fatuous. According to Charles Gildon, Otway acted out his lines as he composed them:

the Poet should endeavour . . . to imitate with his own Body the Gestures and Actions of those Dramatic Persons, to whom he is about to give Words and Sentiments proper to the Passions they are possess'd with; to which I must add, that he should likewise imitate the Voice and the Utterance; all which join'd together will fix in his Soul the Passion and Characters he is writing, and by that means he can never miss drawing them according to Nature. This was the Method that *Otway* follow'd, as I have been assur'd by an intimate Acquaintance of his; and to this Method I must in great measure attribute his admirable touching of the Passions. (*Complete Art of Poetry*, i. 258.)

Otway's playwriting career commenced *c.* September 1675, too late to make him the model for this jibe, but Buckingham would certainly have found his modus operandi silly.

87:14–15. *Sonnets to Armida*. This is one of two allusions added in *Q3* to a song, 'Farewell fair *Arminda*', said by the *Key* (pp. 13–14) to have been 'made by Mr. *Bayes* [i.e. Dryden] on the Death of Captain *Digby*, Son of *George* Earl of *Bristol*, who was a passionate Admirer of the Dutchess . . . *Dowager* of *Richmond*, call'd by the Author, *Armida*: he lost his Life in a Sea fight, against the *Dutch*, the 28*th* of *May*, 1672'. The piece was first published in *The Covent Garden Drollery* in 1672 and reprinted almost immediately in the *Westminster* and *Windsor* drolleries and in *New Court Songs*. Music by Robert Smith appeared in *Choice Songs and Ayres*, First Book (1673). Summers accepted the attribution to Dryden in his edition of *The Rehearsal* (p. 110), but Thorn-Drury says in his edition of the *Covent Garden Drollery* that 'Except in so far as an inference may be drawn from what appears in *The Rehearsal*, which may, of course, be due to mistake, wilful or otherwise, there is not the ghost of a suggestion to be found elsewhere to connect Dryden with this song' (p. 127). Simpson discusses the entangled history of this piece and its variants, but says of this version merely 'perhaps by Dryden' (*British Broadside Ballad*, 62–3, 182). The editors of Dryden's *Works* have ignored the piece. Cf. note on III. i. 81:13–22 below.

87:15. *Stew'd Prunes*. Perhaps a lifelong taste of Dryden's. In a letter of 30 August 1693 to Jacob Tonson Dryden asks him to pass on a message requesting Dryden's wife to buy 'a Sieve full' of 'Damsins . . . to preserve whole, & not in Mash'. See Dryden, *Letters*, 58. Very possibly, this is an accurate hit meant to amuse some knowledgeable insiders while serving to ridicule Bayes for the larger audience. The phrase also, however, had a sexual connotation, as at II. i. in *Measure for Measure* (lines 492–7 in the *Complete Works* edition).

87:16. *I ever take Phisic*. Percy's *New Key* (p. 395) quotes a passage from Charles Lamotte, *An Essay upon Poetry and Painting* (London: F. Fayram, 1730), 103, who quotes *The Rehearsal* and says: 'I once thought that this was pure Waggery, and Banter of the Author of that diverting Play. But I have been told since by a Person of good Credit, and who was acquainted with Mr. *Dryden* [perhaps Southerne, if the anecdote is not fabricated?] that it was actually true; and that when he was about any considerable Work, he used to purge his Body, and clear his Head, by a Dose of Physick.' Osborn, *John Dryden: Some Biographical Facts and Problems*, 177, suggests that Lamotte was merely repeating anecdotal evidence deriving from *The Rehearsal*. For what the evidence may be worth, Shadwell elaborates the charge in 1682 in the prefatory epistle to 'The Medal of John Bayes':

> the great Subject of his Discourse shall be . . . What Diet he uses for *Epick* what for *Comick*. . . .' 'Tis not two years since he consulted with an Eminent and Learned Physician of this Town; telling him, he was obliged to write a Play, and finding himself very dull, desired he would prescribe him a Diet, and course of Physick fit for his Malady: the Dr. merrily asked him Whether 'twas *Comedy* or *Tragedy* he designed? he answered, *Tragedy*; the Dr. replyed, The Steel Diet was most proper for *Tragedy*; whereupon the Poet desired to have it prescribed, and did undergo it for six weeks. (*Complete Works*, v. 248)

On the likelihood of Dryden's letting blood and purging his belly, see Hugh Ormsby-Lennon, 'Radical Physicians and Conservative Poets in Restoration England: Dryden among the Doctors', *Studies in Eighteenth-Century Culture*, 7 (1978), 389–411, who concludes that Buckingham's satire and the anecdotal evidence about Dryden are 'not only consonant with the theory of medicine that can be gleaned from his writings, but also with the accepted medical practice of his age' (p. 391).

87:22. *Experto crede Roberto.* 'Believe Robert, who knows' (Latin). A traditional Latin tag. Crane (p. 86) identifies it as a Vergilian echo (*Aeneid*, II. 283–4); but in a later note reports that the phrase appears in Robert Burton's satirical preface to *The Anatomy of Melancholy* ('Burton and Buckingham', *Notes and Queries*, 229 (1984), 229). *Stevenson's Book of Quotations*, 10th edn. (London: Cassell, 1967), 594:12, describes it as an 'anonymous medieval line' whose full form is 'Quam subito, quam certo, experto crede Roberto'. Their translation is 'How suddenly and how certainly [it will come] believe the experienced Robert'. See also Karl Beyer, *Nota bene! Das lateinische Zitatenlexikon* (Darmstadt: Wissenschaftliche Buchgesellschaft, 1999), 146. In some versions the name is Ruperto. Perhaps originally in the Ur-*Rehearsal* as a swipe at Sir Robert Howard, though omitted from the 1671 version when Buckingham and Howard were close political allies. If Howard was the target, the phrase had added sting after his appearance as the know-all Sir Positive At-all in Shadwell's *The Sullen Lovers* (1668).

87:23. *never take snuff, when you write.* The *Key* states that Dryden 'was a great taker of Snuff: and made most of it himself' (p. 6). He was certainly a user of snuff by *c*.1698 when he wrote to Tonson in an undated letter 'I desire you to make sure of the three pounds of snuff, the same of which I had one pound from you' (*Letters*, 99).

87:25. *sparkishest.* Here used positively to mean the wittiest, the most elegant. 'Spark' was a modish term for witty socialites, but rapidly acquiring negative connotations, as witness Sparkish in Wycherley's *The Country-Wife* (1675).

87:26. *Gresham Colledge.* Originally the house of Sir Thomas Gresham in Bishopsgate Street, who willed it to the Mercers' Company as a site for learned lectures. It was the venue of the early meetings of the Royal Society, to which Dryden was elected on 19 November 1662 and from which he was expelled for non-payment of dues in 1666. On Dryden's association with it, see Winn, *John Dryden*, 129–36, and Michael Hunter, 'The Social Basis and Changing Fortunes of an Early Scientific Institution: An Analysis of the Membership of the Royal Society, 1660–1685', *Notes and Records of the Royal Society of London*, 31 (1976), 9–114 at 88.

*II. ii*

0.1. *hand in hand.* Buckingham's primary targets were almost undoubtedly Charles and James, but Gaston Hall points out to us that Buckingham could also have had an eye on the devoted brother princes in Corneille's *Rodogune* (1644).

1. *the two Kings.* 'H Howard United Kingdoms' is written against this line by the Uof PA-1683 annotator.

7. *sweet-heart*. Percy's *New Key* (p. 396) points out that 'Dear Heart' is the favourite and oft-repeated expression of Burr (a soldier just returned from the Low Countries) in Dryden's *The Wild Gallant*.

15–18. *Mon foy . . . Pardonnes moy . . . breeding*. 'My faith . . . pardon me' (French). Correctly, 'Mon foy' would be 'ma foi'. At *Q3* I. i. 34:3–6 Bayes asserts that the use of a wrong gender in French was a way of indicating an improper meaning. Alternatively, it may in this case have been a joke at the expense of ignorant linguistic pretentiousness. That a further joke at the expense of mispronunciation was intended is unlikely since (1) the spelling 'oy' for 'oi' was still current in the French of the time; and (2) the modern 'wa' pronunciation was not yet established. Abel Boyer's *The Compleat French-Master, for Ladies and Gentlemen* (London, 1694), p. 6 explains the matter thus: '*Oi* and *Oy*, sound sometimes like *Oai* as in *Foin* Hay, *Foy* Faith, *Loy* Law; but is usually pronounced like *Ai*, as, *Connaitre* to know, *Anglois* English.' Much as 'mon vie' in the earlier passage would have been heard as 'mon vit' (penis), so 'mon foi', Wallace Kirsop has pointed out to us, would have been heard as 'mon foie' (liver). The Frenchified lingo of the two kings may be an allusion to the extended period Charles and James spent in exile in France, or to their having a French mother.

17. *I Makes*. Summers (*Rehearsal*, p. 96) notes that Otto Jespersen cites this passage as an instance of vulgarism in his *Growth and Structure of the English Language* (1905), 10th edn. (Chicago, Ill.: University of Chicago Press, 1982), 192.

21. *hand in hand*. Percy's *New Key* (pp. 396–7) annotates with some rather remote parallels from *Mr Anthony* and *Love in Its Extacy*. Summers (*Rehearsal*, p. 95) more plausibly suggests parody of the encounter between Mustapha and Zanger in III. iii (not 'Act IV') of *Mustapha*, at the end of which '*They embrace: Exeunt*' (Orrery, *Dramatic Works*, i. 265).

23. *crust for your Rogue Critiques*. 'Ned: Howards own words' has been written against this line by the U of PA-1683 annotator. 'Crust' apparently implies something hard to chew.

25. *rub their gums*. In modern idiom, 'give them something to chew on'. And see *OED* s.v. 'gum', 5 (compounds): 'gum-rubber' and 'a crust of bread is the best gum-stick'. It was customary to rub the gums of teething infants.

26. *the Play I told you of*. Not a very clear reference, but apparently either an allusion to II. ii. 3–4 ('to shew you a whole Play, written all just so') or a blind reference to something in the Ur-*Rehearsal* that had been removed from the extant text.

30 (and 26:1–8). *They refus'd it*. There is no recorded instance of a play by Dryden being refused, but other authors were less fortunate. For Percy's comments in the *New Key* on Flecknoe's plaints, see the note to II. ii. 47 below. In the mid-1670s Dryden's *The State of Innocence* (pub. 1677) failed to get produced at Drury Lane, but this was evidently on account of the King's Company's lacking the money to do a competitive staging of an elaborate semi-opera, a kind of work the Drury Lane theatre was not well suited for in any case.

33. *the rudest, uncivilest persons.* Pepys comments as early as 23 February 1661: 'I see the gallants do begin to be tyred with the Vanity and pride of the Theatre-actors, who are endeed grown very proud and rich' (*Diary*, ii. 41).

45–6. *the best things in Christendom.* Parodying an indecent toast referred to in 'Timon', ll. 109–10: 'Mine Host, drinkes to the best in Christendome, / And decently my Lady quits the Roome' (Rochester, *Works*, 261). It is used to point to Dryden in a passage from Roger L'Estrange's *Observator* of 2 June 1686: 'He did, really, *Spoyle the Best Things in the World*, in his way of Mouthing them' (iii, no. 179, p. 1).

47–8. *peremptoriness of these fellows.* Percy's *New Key* (pp. 397–8) quotes the preface to Richard Flecknoe's *Damoiselles a la Mode* (pub. 1667) as a parallel expression of authorial indignation at having scripts refused by the players. 'For the Acting it, those who have the Governing of the Stage, have their Humours, and wou'd be intreated; and I have mine, and w'ont intreat them; and were all Drammatick Writers of my mind, they shou'd wear their old *Playes* Thred-bare, e're they shou'd have any *New*; till they better understood their own Interest, and how to distinguish betwixt good and bad' (sig. A4ʳ).

49. *the Nursery.* The company of actors in training, which operated under licence from the two patent theatres. See Hotson, ch. 4. Founded in the spring of 1664, the nursery led a chequered existence in several locations but appears to have collapsed and disappeared by the mid-1670s. Dryden refers sourly to the nursery in *Mac Flecknoe*, lines 74 ff:

> Near these a Nursery erects its head,
> Where Queens are form'd, and future Hero's bred;
> Where unfledg'd Actors learn to laugh and cry,
> Where infant Punks their tender Voices try,
> And little *Maximins* the Gods defy.
> Great *Fletcher* never treads in Buskins here.
> Nor greater *Johnson* dares in Socks appear. (*Works*, ii. 56)

The gibe at the hero of his own *Tyrannick Love* is striking. Performance standards were apparently dismal. Pepys reports his first visit to the Nursery on 24 February 1668: 'the house is better and the Musique better then we looked for and the acting not much worse, because I expected as bad as could [be]; and I was not much mistaken, for it was so' (ix. 89–90).

*mump your proud Players.* 'Mump' means cheat or disappoint. 'Dryden' is written against this line by the U of PA-1683 annotator (a somewhat implausible annotation, as Dryden could hardly have afforded to decamp to the Nursery).

49:3. *a Knight.* Sir William Killigrew, Lord Chamberlain to the Queen. See the note on 'falls asleep' at II. iii. 9. Sir William's plays were easy targets for satire, but perhaps his prominence at Court made him seem a worthwhile target. For an account of him, see J. P. Vander Motten, *Sir William Killigrew (1606–1695): His Life and Dramatic Works* (Ghent: Rijksuniversiteit, 1980).

*II. iii*

1. *How strange a captive.* 'Sir Will Killigrew' is written against this line by the Uof PA-1683 annotator.

6. *Blazing Comet.* Perhaps a topical allusion left over from the Ur-*Rehearsal*, but one that retained its general point. Apropos of line 6, we note that there are four references to comets in Killigrew's *The Imperial Tragedy*, acted by the Nursery Company in 1669. A major comet was visible in London in November and December 1664. Pepys and Evelyn both saw the comet in late November and comment regularly on discussion of it. See particularly Pepys's comment on 15 December (when he wrote a letter to Lord Sandwich about it) and Evelyn's remarks on 14 December 1664 and 18 January 1665. Robert Hooke presented a lecture at Gresham College on 1 March 1665 (reported by Pepys that day) in which he argued 'that this is the very same Comett that appeared before in the year 1618, and that in such a time probably it will appear again—which is a very new opinion'. For contemporary commentary, see J. B., *The Blazing Star: or, A Discourse of Comets, Their Natures and Effects* (London, 1665). The author emphasizes the association of comets with 'the most horrid apprehensions' of the fall of kings, conquest, and change of government, providing a long list of dates and events from Roman times onwards (pp. 2–3, 6–12). S. Danforth's *An Astronomical Description Of the late Comet or Blazing-Star* (orig. pub. in New England in 1665; rpt. in London in 1666) prints an epigraph from Joshua Sylvester's 1621 translation of Du Bartas:

> There, with long bloody hair, a blazing-star
> Threatens the World with Famine, Plague and War.
> To Princes, deaths; to Kingdomes, many crosses.
> To all estates inevitable losses.
> To Heardsmen, Rots; to Plowmen haplesse seasons.
> To Saylors, storms; to Cities, civil treasons.

The introduction 'To the Reader' concludes: '*As for the Judicatory part, every man is left to his own opinion; mine being,* That God hath sent it as an Herauld, to proclaim great and wonderful mutations to happen in the World.' For a catalogue of the sorts of horrors portended by comets, see John Gadbury, *De cometis* (London, 1665). For a contextual account of 'The Comet of 1664', see Donald K. Yeomans, *Comets: A Chronological History of Observation, Science, Myth, and Folklore* (New York: John Wiley & Sons, 1991), ch. 4. The 1664 comet was widely believed to have portended the London plague of 1665 and the Great Fire of 1666. In *Paradise Lost* (first published in 1667), Milton describes Satan's confrontation with Death before the gates of hell:

> . . . on th' other side
> Incens't with indignation *Satan* stood
> Unterrifi'd, and like a Comet burn'd
> That fires the length of *Ophiucus* huge
> In th' Artic Sky, and from his horrid hair
> Shakes Pestilence and War. (Book ii, ll. 706–11).

The association of comets with war goes back at least to the *Iliad*. The particular phrase here, 'blazing Comet', is used by Elkanah Settle in Act V, Scene iii of *Cambyses* ( January 1671): 'I'le mount into the Sky, / And hang a blazing Comet in the Air' (p. 84). We are indebted to Paul D. Cannan for this reference.

9. *fall asleep* (and 49:1–2 in the 1675 text: *falls a sleep, making love to his Mistress . . . in a late Play*). This is identified by the *Key* (p. 7) as a reference to *The Lost Lady*, by Sir Robert Stapylton [error for Sir William Berkeley]. Percy says 'The play here meant is [Don Antonio de Mendoza's] *Querer por solo querer* : To love only for love's sake, a Dramatic Romance paraphrased from the Spanish by Sir Richard Fanshaw. The Duke calls it *a late play* for tho' written in 1654, it was not published till 1671 [*recte* 1670]. The passage had in view is in Act I. pag. 19. where Felisbravo king of Persia, travelling in search of his mistress Zelidaura queen of Tartaria (whom, it seems, he had never seen) retires into a wood to shun the noontide heat, and pulling out his mistress's picture, amid some passionate rants, very fairly falls asleep over it' (*New Key*, pp. 398–9). Summers follows the *Key*; Crane follows Percy. The allusion, however, is almost undoubtedly to Sir William Killigrew's *Ormasdes* (pub. 1665). In Act V Ormasdes interrupts his love-making to 'try to get a little Rest'. See J. P. Vander Motten, 'A Misunderstood Allusion in Buckingham's *The Rehearsal*?', *Notes and Queries*, 227 (1982), 516–18. Killigrew's play was performed *c.*1664 (while Fanshawe's remained unproduced), and Ormasdes actually falls asleep 'making love to his Mistress', not just to her picture. The reference to sleep in *Q1* could be to either Killigrew's play or Fanshawe's (whose translation from Spanish was published in 1670 and reissued the next year), but if the reference is a carry-over from the 1665 version, then Killigrew was definitely the target. The added passage in *Q3* was probably occasioned by the reprinting of *Ormasdes* in Killigrew's *Three New Playes* of 1674.

11. *swop*. Suddenly, abruptly (as in the expression, 'at one fell swoop'). Cf. *Macbeth*, line 1767 in the *Complete Works*.

11–12. *make a simile*. 'This rule is most exactly observed in Dryden's *Indian Emperor*, Act IV. sc. 4—Upon a sudden and unexpected misfortune, Almeria thus expresses her surprize and concern.

> All hopes of safety and of love are gone:
> As when some dreadful Thunder-clap is nigh,
> The winged Fire shoots swiftly through the Skie,
> Strikes and Consumes e're scarce it does appear,
> And by the sudden ill, prevents the fear.'

Percy's *New Key*, pp. 399–400. (*Works*, ix. 89.)

17–24. *As some tall Pine . . . tears.* The *Key* (pp. 7–8) says '*In imitation of this Passage.*

> As some fair tulip, by a storm opprest,
> Shrinks up; and folds its silken arms to rest;
> Bends to the blast, all pale and almost dead,

> While the loud wind sings round its drooping head:
> So, shrowded up your beauty disappears;
> Unvail my Love; and lay aside your fears.
> The storm that caus'd your fright, is past and done.

*Conquest of Granada*, Part. 1. p. 55.' (*Works*, xi. 91.)

40–1. *last Scene before the Dance.* A great many Carolean comedies conclude with a dance (as *The Rehearsal* does). Bayes seems here to be suggesting that tragic and heroic plays should also end with a dance.

42–3. *without ever opening the Plot at all.* Percy's *New Key* (pp. 400–1) cites Sir Robert Howard's *The Blind Lady* (pub. 1660; unperformed) and Killigrew's *Thomaso* (pub. 1664; unperformed), and quotes Porter's *The Carnival* (1663; pub. 1664), Act III, p. 31:

> *Lorenzo.* It was a very dainty Masque; for all
> The Company were kept in suspence till the last, and
> Did never comprehend what we meant.

*II. iv*

1–2. *lay our heads together.* Summers (*Rehearsal*, p. 100) cites discussion between Osmyn and Benzayda, and later between Almanzor and Lyndaraxa in Part 2 of *The Conquest of Granada*, as evidence of 'Dryden's partiality for scholastic logic and argument in verse', going on to quote the 'Defence of an Essay of Dramatique Poesie': 'I am of opinion that they cannot be good Poets who are not accustomed to argue well' (*Works*, ix. 12). The Uof PA-1683 annotator, however, wrote 'Sr Wm Coventry Sr John Duncomb' against this line—i.e. the 'men of business' in How-- ard and Buckingham's *The Country Gentleman.* If accurate, this was strictly an in-joke, but the annotator's knowledge of the content of a suppressed and unpublished play is interesting in itself. Crane (pp. 87–8) says that 'The hesitation between the Gentleman-Usher and the Physician in this scene recalls the dialogue between Zoranzo and Amphelia in *All Mistaken*, V. i, each unwilling to confess to loving another, and each urging the other to speak first.' The passage reads:

> *Zoranzo.*          . . . pray tell me
> What you mean.
> *Amphelia.* I cannot, first do you begin.
> *Zo.* Nor I.
> *Amph.* Let us tell both together, then, that one
> May not blame the tother.
> *Zo.* Agreed, are you ready now to speak,
> *Amph.* Yes, oh no I am not,—well now I am,
> Are you?
> *Zo.* Yes, I am, begin. (p. 58)

5. *a pipe of Tobacco.* The point of Bayes's fondness for tobacco (cf. I. ii. 192–3) is not clear, though evidently Buckingham was not of Sherlock Holmes's mind about

it. The use of tobacco for both medicinal and recreational purposes remained controversial in the Restoration. See, for example, Tobias Venner, *Via Recta ad Vitam Longam*, 4th edn. (London, 1660), which contains his *A Brief and accurate Treatise concerning The taking of the Fume of Tobacco*, 'In which the immoderate, irregular, and unseasonable use thereof is reprehended, and the true nature and best manner of using it, perspicuously demonstrated'. Buckingham's apparently intense dislike of smoking is expressed in *The Militant Couple*, lines 55, 121, 148–50.

5. *I whew it away*. 'Whew' can mean 'whistle' or 'hurry away' (*OED*). *Q3* reads 'I feague it away'. Summers (*Rehearsal*, p. 100) glosses this as 'beat or drive', but the *OED* suggests 'to set in motion briskly', or figuratively 'to agitate a point in one's thoughts'. The point seems to be to blow away the problem in tobacco smoke.

9–10. *I divide thus . . . whether they heard or no*. Percy's *New Key*, p. 401, quotes at length from a speech by Balthazar in Act II of Kyd's *The Spanish Tragedy* (c.1587) as a parallel, but the connection seems strained and the only record of performance for Kyd's play in this period is at the Nursery (seen by Pepys, 24 February 1668). Division in this sense was a standard technique of formal disputation, as practised in the universities, and of the Anglican sermon, in which the preacher was expected to divide the words of the text thematically at the commencement of the discourse.

15. *Videlicet*. 'To wit' or 'namely' (Latin).

17:17–18. *Susurrare . . . Quomodo*. The Usher's Latin is again correct. We see no point to the passage beyond pedantry.

30.1–2. *sit down in the two great chairs upon the Stage*. Percy's *New Key* (pp. 402–3) says: 'This is a fine ridicule on some of the Revolutions in modern plays. But perhaps is particularly levelled at Sir Will. Killegrew's *Emperial Tragedy*, where an Emperor of Greece dethrones his colleague only by turning him out of his chair; which is performed in the following easy and concise manner.

> *The scene shews Zeno set in council with Basiliscus, Senators, Attendants, &c.*
> Zeno. Rise, rise Basiliscus, and quit that seat—
> *Basiliscus rises. (without speaking a word.)*
> What do you stop? Remove and stand below.
> My Lords you see how Empires are expos'd
> To change, &c. (Act I. Sc. 5).

And then like that of Brentford, tho' this is so silent a change of government, there follows some fighting afterwards, but it is not till the next act but one.—See also Dryden's *Maiden Queen* [*Secret-Love*], where is a Revolution brought about as easily as that of the two Kings of Brentford. Compare Act IV. Scen. 1. Scen. 2. and Act V. Sc. 1.' *The Imperial Tragedy* was published in 1669, apparently after being acted at the Barbican Nursery.

30.2. *two great chairs upon the Stage*. Presumably set in place before the action moved to the stage of the Bridges Street Theatre at the beginning of I. ii.

31–2. *State's . . . topsi-turvy.* This crack was probably directed particularly against *Marriage A-la-Mode.* 'Such easy turns of State, are frequent in our Modern Plays; where we see Princes Dethron'd, and Governments Chang'd, by very feeble Means, and on slight Occasions: Particularly, in *Marriage a la Mode* ; a Play, writ since the first Publication of this Farce. Where (to pass by the Dulness of the State-part, the obscurity of the Comic, the near Reasemblance *Leonidas* bears to our Prince *Pretty-man*, being sometimes a King's Son, sometimes a Shepherds; and not to question how *Amalthea* comes to be a Princess, her Brother, the King's great Favourite, being but a Lord) 'tis worth our while to observe, how easily the Fierce and Jealous Usurper is Depos'd, and the Right Heir plac'd on the Throne: as it is thus Related, by the said Imaginary Princess.

> *Amalthea.* Oh, Gentlemen, if you have loyalty,
> Or courage, show it now: *Leonidas*
> Broke on the sudden from his Guards, and snatching
> A sword from one, his back against the Scaffold,
> Bravely defends himself; and owns aloud
> He is our long lost King, found for this moment;
> But, if your valours help not, lost for ever.
> Two of his Guards, mov'd by the sense of virtue,
> Are turn'd for him, and there they stand at Bay
> Against an host of foes.

*Marriage al a Mode*, p. 69 [*Works*, xi. 311]. This shows Mr. *Bayes* to be a Man of Constancy, and firm to his Resolution, and not to be laugh'd out of his own Method: Agreeable to what he says in the next Act. *As long as I know my things are Good, what care I what they say?*' (*Key*, pp. 8–10). Stocker (pp. 18–19) suggests an allusion to the Restoration of 1660: 'A favorite theme of conservative writers was that the . . . Restoration had been a bloodless revolution. . . . Since Bayes is portrayed as a plagiarist, it should not surprise us that he owes his "novel" portrait of revolution to events themselves.'

32. *topsi-turvy.* 'H Howard' has been written against this line by the Uof PA-1683 annotator.

37.2. *Shirley.* The use of the actor's (rather than the unidentified character's) name is curious. George Shirley was a minor actor-dancer active with the King's Company from *c.*1668 to 1674. He played such roles as Pedro in Corye's *The Generous Enemies* (1671) and Sanco-panco in Duffett's(?) *The Amorous Old Woman* (1674). Buckingham seems unlikely to have written a part specially for him, and there is no other evidence suggesting that *Q1* was set from a prompt copy. For the little known of Shirley, see *Biographical Dictionary*, xiii. 364.

38–9. *hey day! . . . nor what to say.* The *Key* (p. 10) quotes *Love and Friendship* (p. 46): 'I know not what to say, or what to think! / I know not when I sleep, or when I Wake!' and *Pandora* (p. 46): 'My Doubts and Fears, my Reasons do dismay: / I know not what to do, or what to Say.' Crane (p. 88) cites James Howard's *All Mistaken* (spring 1665? pub. 1672): 'Hey Day, hey day, I know not what / To do, or say.' Percy's *New Key* (pp. 404–5) quotes similar lines from Flecknoe's *Erminia* (pub. 1661), I. vi; Cokain's *Trappolin Supposed a Prince* (1633; pub. 1658), III. i; Sir William Killigrew's *Ormasdes* (1664; pub. 1665), V, p. 77; and *Pandora* (1663; pub. 1665), V, p. 46.

39:3. *I under writ his Part . . . to set off the rest*. Percy's *New Key*, p. 405, quotes a passage from Dryden's preface to *Tyrannick Love*: 'The part of *Maximin*, against which these holy Criticks so much declaim, was designed by me to set off the Character of S. *Catharine*' (*Works*, x. 110). Obviously Maximin is over-, not under-written, adding a nice twist to Buckingham's joke. The U of PA-1683 annotator wrote 'Dryden' against this line.

*end of scene*. We suggest that '*the two great chairs*' were struck at this point.

## II. v

0.1. *at one door*. All late seventeenth-century theatres had at least one perma-nent, practicable ante-proscenium door on each side of the stage. A majority of entrances and exits were through these doors, though passages between the wings and shutters were also used. In this case, the opposing forces evidently entered through the doors on opposite sides of the forestage.

1–5. *Stand . . . Fall on*. Percy's *New Key* (p. 405) quotes challenges from Porter's *The Villain* (1662), IV, p. 62; *Secret-Love*, IV. i (*Works*, ix. 169); and Behn's *The Forc'd Marriage* (1670), II. vi, of which the last seems most pertinent:

> *Phillander*. Who's there?
> *Pisaro*. A man, a friend to the General.
> *Phillander*. Then thou'rt an enemy to all good men . . . *they fight*.

7–9. *dead men . . . rise up presently . . . and fall a Dancing*. Dryden alludes sar-castically to such an occurrence in his prologue to *The Rival Ladies* (1664): 'And for Surprize, two Bloody-minded Men / Fight till they Dye, then rise and Dance again' (cited in Percy's *New Key*, p. 406). The editors of the *Works* (viii. 279) report that 'The play satirized has never been identified.' Against line 7 the U of PA-1683 annotator has written 'Sir Robert Howard'. The passage is satirically applied in *Tatler*, no. 257 (30 November 1710).

10 (and 28). *Effaut flat*. 'The fuller name (F *fa ut*) of the note F, which was sung to the syllable *fa* or *ut* according as it occurred in one or other of the Hexachords (imperfect scales) to which it could belong' (*OED*, citing this passage). For the derivation of the syllabic names of the degrees of the scale, see Thomas Morley, *A Plain and Easy Introduction to Practical Music*, ed. R. Alec Harman (London: Dent, 1952), 11. Curtis Alexander Price, *Henry Purcell and the London Stage* (Cambridge: Cambridge University Press, 1984), 50, says that

In the late seventeenth century . . . 'F fa ut flat' meant simply the key of 'F with a flat third', that is F minor, the favourite for ghosts, witches, and the like, and not at all inappropriate for this bizarre dance. The point is not that Bayes is ignorant of music theory, but that the dance, which he has composed himself, is rhythmically confusing. . . . The pantomime playwright is shown to be a competent, even learned, theoretician and a bungling practitioner.

11. *The Musick play.* Music for 'A Dance in the Rehearsal' (treble part only) survives in Royal College of Music MS 1172, fo. 19. Curtis Price advises us that musical style and location within the manuscript suggest a mid-1690s date. Because the piece is short and for violin only, it is evidently not the 'Grand Dance' in V. i or the final dance. It would be appropriate here or at III. ii. 234.

14–15. *Angels in Harry the Eight, or the fat Spirits in The Tempest.* An allusion to the fancy staging in Davenant's production of the Shakespeare–Fletcher *Henry the Eighth* at Lincoln's Inn Fields in December 1663, in particular to the vision of spirits seen by the dying Queen Katherine in IV. ii (*Complete Works*, following line 2154) and to III. ii of the Dryden–Davenant *Tempest* (1667; pub. 1670), where we find the following:

> *Enter eight fat Spirits, with* Cornu-Copia *in their hands.*
>
> *Alonzo.* Are these plump shapes sent to deride our hunger?
>
> *Gonzalo.* No, no: it is a Masque of fatten'd Devils, the Burgo-Masters of the lower Region. ([*The Spirits*] *Dance and vanish.*) O for a Collop of that large-haunch'd Devil Who went out last!' (*Works*, x. 51–2.)

Whether because of Buckingham's ridicule or for some other reason, the fat spirits were omitted from the 1674 operatic revision of *The Tempest*, a change which puzzled Percy (*New Key*, p. 406).

19–20. *I sate up two whole nights.* Summers (*Rehearsal*, p. 107) cites (without source) an anecdote from many years later to the effect that Bolingbroke called one morning to find that Dryden had sat up all night composing his *Ode on St. Cecilia's Day.*

20. *composing this Air.* This appears to be a flight of satiric fancy on Buckingham's part. We are not aware of any playwright in the 1660s who claimed to be able to compose music, apart from Shadwell (see his *Complete Works*, v. 384) and Flecknoe, who composed two operas, now lost, in the style of Monteverdi (*New Grove*).

26. *I have broke my Nose.* Traditionally identified as a residual 'hit at D'Avenant, who had lost his nose by venereal disease' (Smith, *Plays about the Theatre*, 16). However, George McFadden has shown that 'Buckingham copied the "broken nose incident" from an episode in Molière's *Dom Juan* where Sganarelle, showing himself off in a doctor's robe, takes a leap upward, falls, and breaks his nose.' McFadden also argues very convincingly that the patch Bayes then puts on his nose is a crack at Henry Bennet, Earl of Arlington, Secretary of State in the Cabal ministry. See 'Political Satire in *The Rehearsal*'.

30. *tenter-hooks.* 'Hooks or bent nails set in a close row' (*OED*) along the edges of cloth stretched out tight—in this instance the green baize used to cover the stage. Whether at this date green baize was used for all plays or only for tragedy is

not clear. Its use for all performances of tragedy persisted in some form well into the nineteenth century. See Summers, *Restoration Theatre*, 269–70.

32. *a wet piece of brown papyr.* As a bandage. 'Wet brown paper was the 18th century adhesive tape' (explanatory note in *Walpole's Correspondence*, xliii. 257). By McFadden's plausible reading, an allusion to Buckingham's great political rival, the Earl of Arlington. An illustration of this scene is printed as a frontispiece to *The Rehearsal* in vol. ii of the 1715 *Works* and is reproduced by Dane Farnsworth Smith in *Plays about the Theatre* (opposite p. 34). It shows Bayes wearing an elegant black patch of the sort affected by Arlington. See his portrait in Maurice Lee, Jr., *The Cabal*, following p. 150. And see the Introduction above, p. 350.

### III. i

1–2. *to end every Act with a Dance.* Very probably, as Percy's *New Key* (p. 407) observes, a dig at Davenant's *Sir Francis Drake* and *The Cruelty of the Spaniards in Peru* (both of 1658), 'where every entry or scene begins and ends with a Dance'. These plays were revived as the third and fourth acts of *The Play-house to be Let* (1663). Buckingham may also have *The Siege of Rhodes* in view, 'where every entry or act concludes with a ludicrous song, which might very consistently in the representation be accompanied by a jig' (Percy's *New Key*, p. 407). *The Siege of Rhodes* was mounted in a public production for the opening of Lincoln's Inn Fields in June 1661 and remained popular for some years. Crane (p. 88) cites dances in *The Indian-Queen* (III. i), *The Indian Emperour* (IV. iii), *Tyrannick Love* (IV. i), and *1 Conquest of Granada* (III. i). *The Rehearsal* by no means put an end to such use of dances. Summers (*Rehearsal*, p. 109) points to Settle's *The Empress of Morocco* (1673), in which Act II concludes with a 'Moorish dance performed "about an artificial palm tree", of which entertainment there is a curious copper-plate in the illustrated first quarto'.

7. *upon my own wings.* 'Drydens Wild Gallant' has been written against this line by the U of PA-1683 annotator.

10 (and 24.1:2 in the 1675 additions). *Orange stuck with Cloves.* Bayes evidently means some kind of pomander—'A mixture of aromatic substances, usually made into a ball, and carried in a small box or bag in the hand or pocket, or suspended by a chain from the neck or waist, esp. as a preservative against infection. . . . The case . . . often in the shape of an apple or orange' (*OED*). Used as an air freshener. The point is that it takes a lot of cloves (according to Bayes, his scene has a lot of drolleries). Shakespeare has a reference to 'A Lemmon . . . Stucke with Cloues' in *Loves Labour's Lost*, V. ii (*Complete Works*, ll. 2393–4).

14. *Pretty-man, and Tom Thimble.* The *Key* (p. 11) refers the reader to '*Failer*, and *Bibber*, his *Taylor*, in the *Wild Gallant*' (see *Works*, viii. 10–11).

15. *prize.* i.e. a fencing match for a prize.

26. *nine Taylors make but one man.* Proverbial (Tilley, T23).

27–8. *for thy self, trow we?* 'What, is my Master mad trow?', *The Wild Gallant*, Act III. ii, cited in Percy's *New Key*, 408 (*Works*, viii. 47).

35. *by the day.* A journeyman worked on a daily contract (cf. French *journée*).

37. *sits but cross-leg'd.* That is, she works with the tailors as one of them, but there is a secondary implication: the 'night work' will not involve sex if she keeps her legs crossed.

39. *Coronation-suit.* The belated coronation of Charles II finally occurred on 23 April 1661. See Pepys, *Diary*, ii. 83–7. The tailor implies that he was worried about whether Pretty-man would pay him. Even clothes ordered by those who were merely onlookers could have been quite expensive. The king's coronation clothes cost the startling sum of £2,027. See Diana de Marly, *Costume on the Stage 1600–1940* (London: Batsford, 1982), 35.

47. *bob for the Court.* The *Key* (p. 11) cites a speech in Dryden's *The Wild Gallant*: 'Nay, if that be all, there's no such hast: the Courtiers are not so forward to pay their Debts' (*Works*, viii. 19). This seems to miss the point of Buckingham's sneer at Dryden's rather jejeune satiric thrust. A 'bob' is a taunt. There may also be a wider political allusion to the slowness of the Exchequer to pay debts and salaries, a forerunner of the 'Stop of the Exchequer' of 2 January 1672 (Hutton, *Charles the Second*, 284).

49:1. *pay, upon pay.* Percy's *New Key*, p. 409, points out a similar piece of word-play upon 'forbearance' in *The Wild Gallant*, II. i (see *Works*, viii. 24).

50. *nothing but words.* The *Key* (pp. 11–12) quotes an exchange in *The Wild Gallant*, 12:

> *Failer.* . . . Take a little *Bibber*,
> And throw him in the river,
> And if he will trust never,
> Then there let him lie ever.
> *Bibber.* Then say I:
> Take a little *Failer*,
> And throw him to the Jailour.
> And there let him lye,
> Till he has paid his Tailor. (*Works*, viii. 24)

53. *the Wars come on.* Appropriate either in 1665 (as an allusion to the Second Dutch War) or in 1671 (to the Third Dutch War).

57. *top his part.* 'A great Word with Mr. *Edward Howard*' (*Key*, p. 12). The U of PA-1683 annotator, however, has written 'Sr Ro: Howard' against this line. The *OED* (15) quotes this line with the definition, 'To play one's part to its utmost possibilities or to perfection; also, to transcend the character assigned to one'.

59–60. *an Angel for the King's evil, with a hole bor'd through you.* Scrofula ('the King's Evil') was thought to be curable by the touch of the king, a practice continued into the eighteenth century. After the 'touch' a gold coin called an 'Angel' (originally an 'Angel-noble') was hung round the patient's neck as a talisman. The coin had as its device the Archangel Michael standing upon and piercing a dragon in imitation of the French *angelot*. The coin was created in 1465 and not minted after the reign of Charles I. Its value varied from 6*s*. 8*d*. to 10*s*. It was replaced for ceremonial purposes by a medal (with a hole bored through it) known as a touch-piece (*OED*).

62. *up to the hilts*. Continuing the fencing metaphor. Cf. line 15.

69–70. *what . . . is the Plot good for, but to bring in fine things*. Dryden's rather cavalier view of plots is frequently expressed in his criticism. Percy's *New Key* (p. 410) quotes his response to criticism of the final scene of *Secret-Love*, where he allows Celadon and Florimell to indulge in extended banter 'while the great action of the *Drama* is still depending'. 'This I cannot otherwise defend, than by telling you I so design'd it on purpose to make my Play go off more smartly' (preface). See *Works*, ix. 117.

78–9. *'Tis not their talk shall stop me*. Percy's *New Key* (p. 410) quotes the Duchess of Newcastle's preface to her plays (1668), where she says that the malice of her envious detractors cannot hinder her from writing and from publishing what she writes.

79. *at that lock*. That way, in that grip (wrestling terminology; compare the usage at I. ii. 142–3).

80–1. *what care I what they say?* Dryden takes very much this attitude a year later in his dedication to *The Assignation* when he dismisses attacks by his 'little Critiques': 'I have neither concernment enough upon me to write any thing in my own Defence, neither will I gratifie the ambition of two wretched Scriblers, who desire nothing more than to be Answer'd' (*Works*, xi. 322).

81:1–2. *'Sbud, would it were in their Bellies*. David M. Vieth has suggested that this is 'a conspicuous allusion to *1 Henry IV*', in Act III. iii of which Bardolph and Falstaff have this interchange (under different names in the *Complete Works* old-spelling version (lines 1969–70):

> *Rossill.* Zbloud, I would my face were in your belly.
> *Sir Iohn.* Godamercy, so should I be sure to be hartburnt.

Vieth says (with considerable exaggeration, in our view) that 'Nearly every Restoration theatregoer', hearing Bayes's speech, 'must have recognized the allusion to Shakespeare's very popular play.' 'Bayes and Bardolph: An Unnoticed Allusion in Buckingham's "The Rehearsal"', *Notes and Queries*, 223 (1978), 25–6. Buckingham may have been amused by Shakespeare's line and used it deliberately, but we doubt that many playgoers caught the allusion, or were meant to do so, or that it had any particular point. For a later echo, see Southerne, *The Wive's Excuse*, I. i. 134–5.

81:4. *after she was dead*. Probably satire on a passage in Dryden's *Marriage A-la-Mode*, Act I, where a letter in the hand of Polydamas's long-lost wife is said to report that 'she dy'd in childbed' (*Works*, xi. 236–7). See John Reichert, 'A Note on Buckingham and Dryden', *Notes and Queries*, 207 (1962), 220–1. Cf. III. ii. 35–6.

81:10. *by a fall*. The U of PA-1683 annotator wrote 'Dryden' against this line.

81:13–22. *Farewel, fair Armida*. As the *Key* (pp. 12–14) and most subsequent annotators through Crane observe, this is a parody of the second stanza of a poem first printed in the *Covent Garden Drollery* in 1672, long (mis?)attributed to Dryden on flimsy authority (see note on II. i. 87:14–15 above):

> Farewell fair *Arminda*, my joy and my griefe,
> In vain I have lov'd you, and hope no reliefe;
> Undone by your vertue, too strict and severe,
> Your Eyes gave me Love, and you gave me Despaire.
> Now call'd by my Honour, I seek with content,
> The Fate which in pitty, you would not prevent:
> To languish in Love, were to find by delay,
> A death that's more welcome the speedyest way.
>
> Or Seas, and in Battles, in Bullets and Fire,
> The danger is less, then is hopeless desire;
> My Death's-wound you gave though far off I bear,
> My fall from your fight, not to cost you a Tear.
> But if the kind Flood, on a Wave should convey,
> And under your Window, my Body would lay!
> The wound on my breast, when you happen to see,
> You'l say with a sigh—it was given by me. (pp. 16–17)

For the melody, see Simpson, *British Broadside Ballad*, 182–3.

81:23. *fast as hops*. Proverbial (Tilley, H595).

83–4. *interlard your Plays with Songs, Ghosts and Idols*. Q3 substitutes 'Dances' for 'Idols'. Buckingham is generally hostile to the introduction of song and dance in serious drama, and plainly found ghosts ridiculous. The conversation between Almanzor and his mother's ghost in Part 2 of *The Conquest of Granada*, IV. iii. 95–142 is ridiculed at IV. i. 56–7. Dryden answers objections to ghosts and magic at some length in 'Of Heroique Playes':

an Heroick Poet is not ty'd to a bare representation of what is true, or exceeding probable: but . . . he may let himself loose to visionary objects, and to the representation of such things, as depending not on sence, and therefore not to be comprehended by knowledge, may give him a freer scope for imagination. 'Tis enough that in all ages and Religions, the greatest part of mankind have believ'd the power of Magick, and that there are Spirits, or Spectres, which have appear'd. This I say is foundation enough for Poetry. . . . Some men think they have rais'd a great argument against the use of Spectres and Magique in Heroique Poetry, by saying, They are unnatural: but, whether they or I believe there are such things, is not material, 'tis enough that, for ought we know, they may be in Nature: and what ever is or may be, is not, properly, unnatural. (*Works*, xi. 12–13)

On the prevalence of songs in late seventeenth-century drama, see Curtis A. Price, *Music in the Restoration Theatre* (Ann Arbor, Mich.: UMI Research Press, 1979), and Day and Murrie, *English Song-Books, 1651–1702*. A record of verbal and some musical texts is available on-line through the *Restoration Theatre Song Archive*, compiled by Anthony Butler. Dances conclude a very large number of comedies in this period, extending well into the eighteenth century. Summers (*Rehearsal*, pp. 111–12) notes Edward Howard's sarcastic allusion to the 'Scenes, Machines, Habits, Jiggs and Dances' in current plays in his critical preface to *The Womens Conquest* (pub. 1671) and in his first prologue for that play a mocking promise of 'sixteen Mimics . . . with two and thirty Dances and Jiggs à la mode'.

85. *Pit, Box and Gallery.* 'Mr. *Edward Howard*'s words' (*Key*, p. 14). The phrase is also used at I. i. 66.

87. *I don't flatter.* 'Ned Howard' has been written against this line by the Uof PA-1683 annotator.

96. *Clara voyant.* Clear-sighted (mangled French).

*III. ii*

0.1. *the two Usurpers.* 'The two Kings in *Granada*' (Q1701, 20).

1. *Volscius the great.* The rationale for the choice of name is not clear, but Gaston Hall suggests to us that the name derives from the Volsci, a tribe who were an important early rival to the Romans but were eventually defeated and assimilated (the subject of *Coriolanus*).

3–4. *I fear some ill . . . wrung.* 'Ellis' has been written against these lines by the Uof PA-1683 annotator. 'Ellis' is mentioned at three other points by this annotator, but he is otherwise unknown except for a reference in a single line of the '1668' 'Session of the Poets' (written in 1664):

> Ellis in great discontent went away,
>     Whilst D'Av'nant against Apollo did rage,
> Because he declar'd *The Secret* a play
>     Fitting for none but a mountebank's stage.

(*POAS-Yale*, i. 335.) On the problems posed by this passage, see Milhous and Hume, 'Lost English Plays, 1660–1700', no. 11. *The Secret* might be an adaptation of James Shirley's *The Court Secret*. The play was evidently mounted at Lincoln's Inn Fields without success *c.*1663–64.

10. *whatsoe'er it be.* The *Key* (p. 14) cites an exchange from Behn's *The Amorous Prince*, 39:

> *Alberto. Curtius*, I've something to deliver to your ear.
> *Curtius.* Any thing from *Alberto* is welcome.

17–20. *the fair person . . . Upon her precious life.* Percy's *New Key* (p. 412) quotes a passage from I. iv of *Love in its Extasy*:

> The woeful princess—knowing
> That she could not live without your anger,
> Which to her was the worst of miseries,
> Threw her dejected body into the hideous stream.

26. *Piccadillè.* Piccadilly. By the nineteenth century, Piccadilly was the most famous street in the West End of London, a major shopping and entertainment centre. In 1671 it was very much in its infancy. The *Survey of London* comments that

The origin of the name 'Piccadilly' has been the subject of antiquarian discussion for over three hundred years. . . . Piccadilly has for centuries been one of the two most important highways leading to the metropolis from the west; unlike Oxford Street there is, however, no evidence that a Roman road ran along Piccadilly. . . . Its importance must have increased after the western section of the highway from Hyde Park Corner to Charing Cross had been stopped up for the formation of Green Park in 1668. (xxix. 251)

The term 'Piccadilly' was originally applied in the mid-seventeenth century to a range of houses east of Windmill Street and gradually extending to Swallow Street. As of 1720 Strype could apply the term to the whole stretch of territory to St James's Street. In 1671 what we now think of as the eastern end of Piccadilly had become an area of ill-regulated speculative building, which occasioned the Royal proclamation of 7 April 1671 against unlicensed building. The *Survey* notes that building on what is now Great Windmill Street 'threatened to pollute the springs supplying water to Whitehall. This proximity to the centre of government seems to have brought the area under particularly anxious notice' (xxxi. 7, 41). The name may derive from 'pickadil' ('the round hem, or the several divisions set together about the skirt of a Garment', which gave rise to the name of a tavern near St James 'because it was then the outermost or skirt house of the Suburbs that way') or from a house of that name built by a tailor who 'got most of his Estate by Pickadilles, which in the last age were much worn in England' (xxxi. 32, 33–4). Why Buckingham gave the name a French spin we do not know. The replacement form given in *Q2* and *Q3* may be meant to suggest a pun on peccadillo (a small or trivial sin).

28. *Dead! is that possible?* 'Sr Wm Killegrew' has been written against this line by the U of PA-1683 annotator.

29. *O ye Gods!* 'O! ye Gods! is a constant exclamation in Thomas Killigrew's plays. It is also noticeably frequent in Joyner's *The Roman Empress* (1671), and Settle's ranting *Cambyses, King of Persia* (1666 [*recte* 1670–71]). Cf. Hemmings' *The Jew's Tragedy* (4to 1662), "Is it possible! O! ye gods!"—Act i' (Summers, *Rehearsal*, p. 112). Percy's *New Key* (p. 413) refers readers to these plays, but also to Cokain's *The Obstinate Lady* (pre-1642; pub. 1657; no known history of performance), 326.

35–6. *she's not dead neither.* A parody of a mistake in I. i of Dryden's *Marriage A-la-Mode* (*Works*, xi. 236–7). Cf. III. i. 81:4.

41. *What shout Triumphant's that?* 'What means that shout?' *Ungrateful Favourite*, V. iv, p. 82 (cited in Percy's *New Key*, p. 413). This seems more a commonplace than a satiric allusion. Against this line the U of PA-1683 annotator has written 'Ellis'.

42. *Shie.* Obsolete form of 'shy'.

46. *A forward Exit to all future end.* 'Fortune and Resolution both intend / This great beginning to some glorious End.' *The Roman Generals*, I. i (cited in Percy's

*New Key*, p. 460). Against this line the Uof PA-1683 annotator has written 'Ned Howard'.

48. *you must lay the accent.* An instance of Bayes instructing an actor in line delivery.

58. *Tell me who set thee on.* Percy's *New Key* (p. 413) misquotes Sir Robert Howard's *The Surprisal*, IV. i (*Four New Plays*, p. 41), a passage that actually reads:

> Who hir'd you to that damn'd act
> Of murthering the generous *Cialto?*

60. *to kill whom?* Against this line the Uof PA-1683 annotator has written 'Ellis'.

61–9. *Prince Pretty-man . . . drag him hence.* Percy's *New Key* (p. 414) quotes a tangentially relevant interrogatory passage from Howard's *The Blind Lady*, V. ii, p. 122, and one rather more apropos from Stapylton's *The Slighted Maid*, III, pp. 46–7:

> *Decio.* . . . who play'd at Cards with you?
> *Pyramena.* None but my Lord *Iberio* and I plai'd.
> *Dec.* Who waited?
> *Pyr.* No Body.
> *Dec.* No Page?
> *Pyr.* No Page.
> *Dec.* No Groom?
> *Pyr.* No Groom; I tell you no body.
> *Dec.* What, not your Woman?
> *Pyr.* Not my Woman.

Crane (p. 90) says that 'the interrogation episode parodies *Marriage A-la-Mode*, I. i, where Hermogenes, the foster father of Leonidas, is questioned by Polydamas; in the same scene the rack is much in evidence, and it duly makes its appearance here'. But the verbal parallels are not close, and most clear allusions to *Marriage A-la-Mode* do not make their appearance until *Q3*. Summers (*Rehearsal*, p. 113) points out a reference to a rack in IV. ii of Howard's *The Surprisal*. The rack also figures in Fletcher's *The Double Marriage*, which had probably been revived recently since there is a prologue for it in the 1672 *Covent Garden Drollery*.

73. *you have a several design for every Scene.* Percy's *New Key* (p. 414) refers the reader to Dryden's preface to *Secret-Love*, but the parallel seems remote.

84. *rous.* 'With a bounce or bang' (*OED*, citing this passage), or perhaps more probably 'rouse' [raus], 'to scold; upbraid', cognate with Scottish *roust*, to shout, roar (*Macquarie Dictionary*), still heard in Australia.

90. *Bring in my Father.* Percy's *New Key* (p. 415) quotes a passage from *Abedelazer*, I. ii: 'Where is the body of my Royal Father . . .' (*The Works of Aphra Behn*, ed. Janet Todd, 7 vols. (London: Pickering & Chatto, 1992–6), v. 254). Behn's play was not performed until 1676 (pub. 1677). The passage is not close in any case, but this is an instance of a loose parallel, not a hit at a direct source. More to the point are the doubts expressed at the time about the paternity of two of the acknowl-

edged sons of Charles II, Don Carlos (the Earl of Plymouth, a recent arrival at court), and James Scott, Duke of Monmouth, who was alleged to be the son of Col. Robert Sidney (*POAS-Yale*, i. 170).

91. *a Fisherman*. 'Leonidas, the rightful prince, is concealed amongst fishermen in *Marriage A-la-Mode*, and his various turns of fortune, obscure, raised to royalty, banished, and finally found to be truly royal are parodied in Prince Pretty-man's career, just as Pretty-man's style of speech mocks the heroic manner' (Crane, p. 90). Stocker observes (p. 25) that Prince Pretty-man's '"Fisherman" parent is a jokey reference to Charles' fondness for fishing'. Malone observes that Dryden liked to fish, instancing his letter to Tonson of 13 September [1693] in which he remarks that he had been able to feed some guests because he had 'taken a very lusty pike that day' (*Letters*, 60). See *Critical and Miscellaneous Prose Works of John Dryden*, ed. Malone, i. 520. Gaston Hall kindly points out to us that the whole business of Prince Pretty-man and his fisherman father closely parallel parts of Corneille's 'comédie héroïque' of 1650, *Don Sanche d'Aragon* (especially V. vi–vii), which constitute a parallel or possibly a source for both Dryden and Buckingham. In Corneille's play, Carlos (the unknown knight thought to be a fisherman's son) proves to be the king of Aragon and hence the proper fiancé of the queen of Castile, who already loves him.

95. *The being of a Son*. Against this line (or possibly the next one) the U of PA-1683 annotator has written 'Ellis'.

109–10. *taken in a Cradle by a Fisherman*. Percy's *New Key* (pp. 415–16) describes this as 'proper ridicule on that common thread-bare incident in modern Tragedies of representing some personage thro' a great part of the play, as one of low birth, and then of a sudden discovering him or her to be the concealed son or daughter of a king, &c.' As an example, the author offers John Fountain's *The Rewards of Virtue* (unacted; pub. 1661) in which Parthenia interrupts the execution of Urania with the announcement that she 'is / A princess born—Her father was a king' (Act V, p. 79). But the allusion is most probably a direct hit at Leonidas in *Marriage A-la-Mode*.

123. *he is not thy Sire who thee conceal'd*. Percy's *New Key* (pp. 416–17) quotes at length a passage from Act V of James Howard's *All Mistaken* in which Ortellus informs the Duke that he secretly conveyed away the Duke's lost sister when she was 3 years old and had her raised elsewhere, after which the Duke goes into violent raptures at the discovery:

> *Artabella*, is my sister, how
> Blest a sound is sister to my Eares?
> I'le give command, no other word but
> Sister shall be spoke throughout My
> Dukedom; . . .
>
> .   .   .   .   .   .
>                    I'le
> Have the name ingrav'd in Gold on

Every Post and Pillar in the Streetes,
And passers by, shall worship it. (p. 66)

126. *the Plot thickens.* This phrase was to become a cliché, especially common in the twentieth-century detective story: we note forty-four instances in the literary texts in LION, several with specific allusion to *The Rehearsal.* On the phrase, see Eric Partridge, *A Dictionary of Catch Phrases,* 2nd edn., rev. Paul Beale (London: Routledge, 1985), 245.

128. *sometimes a Prince.* Stocker (p. 25) suggests that Prince Pretty-man's ambiguous status can be read as an allusion to Charles's handsome bastard son, the Duke of Monmouth. A closer analogy would be with Charles's long absent 'Spanish' son, Charles Fitzcharles, Earl of Plymouth, who staged a dramatic reappearance at about this time (see Hutton, *Charles the Second,* 125, 337–8).

131–2. *blackest Ink of Fate . . . she made a blot.* Percy's *New Key* (pp. 417–18) comments: 'In ridicule of that common-place Cant about the book of Fate, &c. so frequent in modern plays' and cites examples. 'Good Heav'n, thy book of fate before me lay, / But to tear out the journal of this day' (*Conquest of Granada,* III. i; *Works,* xi. 58); 'Fate grew pale lest he should win the Town, / And turn'd the Iron leafs of its dark Book / To make new dooms; or mend what it mistook' (*Tyrannick Love,* I. i; *Works,* x. 124).

139. *going out of Town.* This scene is a parody of IV. i in James Howard's *The English Mounsieur* in which Mr Comely, 'in a Riding Garb', is preparing to leave town, but meets Elsbeth Pritty (a country innocent) and falls violently in love with her, much to the amusement of the London ladies. And see the note on 'quit this *Urban* throng' at III. ii. 165. Travelling clothes (prominently figuring boots) were a costume convention going right back to the Elizabethan theatre. See Alan C. Dessen, *Elizabethan Stage Conventions and Modern Interpreters* (Cambridge: Cambridge University Press, 1984), 39–40. 'On the humor in Mr [——] Howards Play' (Bodleian MS Eng. Poet e.4, pp. 198–9) strongly implies that Comely was acted by Edward Kynaston. We print the passage among Buckingham's poems (below, II. 10).

144. *the Army, that lies conceal'd for him.* Percy's *New Key* (p. 418) cites a passage from *The Ungrateful Favourite,* III. iii: '. . . some other troops, / That lie concealed in a place remote / Expecting a fit opportunity / Upon advantage to disclose themselves'.

145. *Knights-bridge.* Today a posh district just west of Hyde Park Corner, but in 1671 on the outskirts of London.

148.1–2. *Enter . . . with a Riding-Cloak and Boots.* Against this stage direction or the next line the Uof PA-1683 annotator has written 'James Howard'.

149. *you are cruel, thus to leave the Town.* 'Why, can you ever leave this Town?' *The English Mounsieur,* 37 (cited by Percy's *New Key,* p. 422).

152. *Have held the honour of your company.* Percy's *New Key* (pp. 418–19) finds 'no parallel to the phrase', but quotes 'I still shall court the honour of your presence' (*The Villain*, II, p. 24) to illustrate those passages 'which approach nearest to it'. Crane (p. 91) says that the phrase 'recalls' the passage in Porter's play, but it does not seem to us a genuine allusion. The phrase is essentially a commonplace; the joke is that Bayes should be so pleased with it.

158. *Bayes. I, I, he's a little envious; but . . . Come.* Crane (p. 91) points out that 'The masculine pronoun used by Bayes makes no sense, since the comment concerns an actress.' He suggests that 'a speech heading may have dropped out', and that lines 156–8 should read as follows:

> *Johnson.* I assure you Sir, I admire it extreamly:
> [*Aside to Smith.*] I don't know what he does.
> *Smith.* I, I, he's a little envious; but 'tis no great matter.
> *Bayes.* Come.

Alternatively, 'he' could be taken with reference to some piece of by-play by Smith or by one of the actors prior to Bayes's 'Godsookers'.

160. *poor us.* In V. ii of *The Indian Emperour* Cydaria laments the death of her father, Montezuma; 'He's gone, he's gone, / And leaves poor me defenceless here alone.' (Pointed out by Summers, *Rehearsal*, p. 115; see *Works*, ix. 107.)

165. *quit this Urban throng.* The *Key* (pp. 14–15) glosses with three passages from James Howard's *The English Mounsieur*: 'Let my Horses be brought ready to the door, for I'le go out of Town this Evening' (p. 36); 'Into the Country I'le with speed, / With Hounds and Hawks my fancy feed!' (p. 38); 'Now i'le away, a country life / Shall be my Mistriss and my Wife' (p. 39).

167. *keep an Army thus conceal'd.* Stocker (p. 19) suggests allusion to Charles II's Life Guards, a considerable force that was a standing army in all but name.

170. *Inn-keepers.* Owing to shortage of barracks, soldiers at this time were frequently billeted at inns and private households.

180. *how frail are all.* Against this line the Uof PA-1683 annotator has written 'James Howard'.

180–2. *Bless me! . . . secure from Love.* This is part of the satire on Comely in *The English Mounseiur*, but, as Crane points out (p. 91), it is relevant to Almanzor's falling in love with Almahide in Part 1 of *The Conquest of Granada*, III. i, and to Maximin's succumbing to love for St Catharine in *Tyrannick Love*, II. i.

183. *to ask her name.* 'And what's this maids name', *The English Mounsieur*, 40 (cited by *Key*, p. 15).

189. *Can vulgar Vestments.* The great Volscius falling in love with a lower-class girl may have been suggested by a passage in Machiavelli's *Discorsi*, III. xxvi, about a civil war in Ardea (a town of the Volsci) in which a pleb and a patrician both fall desperately in love with the same plebian girl (a possibility suggested to us by Gaston Hall).

190. *Morning pictur'd in a Cloud*. 'I bring the Morning pictur'd in a Cloud', *The Siege of Rhodes*, Part 1, 10 (cited by *Key*, p. 15). Percy's *New Key* (p. 423) adds: 'This curious flower seems to be transplanted from a play of Sir William Barclay's called the *Lost Lady*, Act 2, sc. ult. . . . *Cleon*. From what part of the town came this fair day / In a cloud that makes you look so chearfully?' Berkeley's play was in the King's Company's repertory in 1660–61.

196. *Volscius in love?* 'Mr. *Comely*, in Love?' *The English Mounsieur*, 45 (cited by *Key*, p. 15). In James Howard's play Lady Wealthy and her friends roar with laughter when they discover that the elegant Comely has succumbed to love. Even more amusingly, he has fallen for 'a Country Farmer's daughter' (p. 46).

203–4. *Love and Honour*. The hero's conflict between love and honour is the great cliché of rhymed heroic drama in the 1660s and 1670s. The passage is directed against Davenant, Orrery, and Dryden, but their imitators—particularly Settle and Crowne—embraced the trope with enthusiasm. Crane (p. 91) quotes a passage from Sir Richard Fanshawe's translation of Mendoza's *Querer por solo querer*, III. i (pub. 1670):

> LOVE, and HONOUR, pull *two* ways;
> And I stand doubtful *which* to take:
> To *Arabia*, Honour says,
> *Love* says, no; thy stay *here* make.

204. *An ancient Author*. 'Sir *William D'Avenant*'s Play of Love and Honour' (*Key*, p. 16).

205.1 [1675 addition]. *over acts the Part*. 'To act or render (a part) with exaggerated or unnecessary action or emphasis; to overdo in action' (*OED* 2), citing Massinger's *Believe as you list* (1631) in this sense.

206. *my passion made me Cupid's scoff*. Percy's *New Key* (pp. 423–4) calls this 'a general satire on that common-place cant about Love and Honour, so frequent in modern plays', but finds it 'more immediately levelled at Quarles's *Virgin Widow*', which it quotes at great length from Act II. However, the parallels seem remote and there is no evidence that Quarles's play (*c.*1641? pub. 1649; never publicly acted?) was performed in the Carolean period. Against this line the U of PA-1683 annotator has written 'James Howard'. This passage does seem to continue the send-up of *The English Mounsieur*. See also ll. 10 below for the version printed with Buckingham's poems.

207. *This hasty Boot is on, the other off*. 'How shall I this avoid, or gain that Love?', Percy's *New Key*, p. 425, quoting *Tyrannick Love*, Act III (*Works*, x. 141). The connection seems tenuous at best. For a parallel of sorts in the context of primogeniture, see Commonplace Book 18:1 (Jersey version). Byplay with boots is found in *Richard II*, V. ii.

219. *Love says, nay*. 'But Honour says, not so' (*Siege of Rhodes*, Part 1, 19, cited by the *Key*, p. 16). A commonplace by the later 1660s: see the note on ll. 203–4,

above. Percy quotes general parallels from *Hero and Leander* (IV, p. 32), *Querer por* (III, p. 140), and *Roman Generals* (II, p. 19) (*New Key*, pp. 425 and 460).

227.1. *one Boot on, and the other off.* A famous scene, alluded to by Congreve in his epilogue for Southerne's *Oroonoko* (1695): 'Like Volscius, hip-hop in a single Boot'. And see the note on l. 207, above.

232:5. *Petticoat, and the Belly ake.* The U of PA-1683 annotator has written 'Drydens Mock-Astrologer' against this line. The *Key* (p. 16) notes that this swipe at Dryden—added after the premiere of *The Assignation* (November 1672)—refers to the scene in IV. i in which Prince Frederick runs to a chair and sits on some ladies' 'Masking-habits' to hide them and feigns 'A most violent griping' in order to distract his father and send him off in search of 'Physitians' (*Works*, xi. 366–8).

232:19–20. *I made 'em all talk baudy.* An allusion to the witty sexual exchanges in *Marriage A-la-Mode* and *The Assignation*, though in fact neither is particularly bawdy; not really true of Dryden even when this passage was published in 1675. Only in *The Kind Keeper, or Mr Limberham* (1678) did he write a genuinely bawdy play. This passage is a more general comment on the rising tide of Carolean sexcomedy, which was to reach its peak between 1675 and 1678 in such plays as Wycherley's *The Country-Wife*, Etherege's *The Man of Mode*, Shadwell's *The Virtuoso*, and Behn's *Sir Patient Fancy*.

232:20. *downright baudry upon the Stage.* The U of PA-1683 annotator wrote 'Dryden' against this line.

232:26.1. *puts 'em out with teaching 'em.* The particular joke here is that John Lacy, who created the part of Bayes, was an expert choreographer and dancing master. Pepys rhapsodizes over his performance of the dancing master in Cavendish's *The Variety* (*Diary*, 21 May 1662).

247. *is the Funeral ready?* Against this line the U of PA-1683 annotator has written 'Tom Porter'.

249. *the Lance fill'd with Wine?* In preparation for the burlesque of a scene in *The Villain* at IV. i. 190 below.

258–9. *what care I for my money?* Sarcastic if meant to be applied to Dryden, who earned his living by his pen and was notoriously a hard bargainer. Davenant too was professional and business-like, not a gentleman amateur who need not worry about mere money.

*IV. i*

3. *a Funeral.* See IV. i. 68.1 below.

5–6. *A person of Honour.* Col. Henry Howard, son of the Earl of Berkshire (see IV. i. 68 ff.).

*15–16. I have design'd a Conquest . . . a whole week.* Dryden's *The Conquest of Granada* in two parts (ten acts), first acted by the King's Company in December 1670 and January 1671. It proved a considerable success. Against these lines the U of PA-1683 annotator has written 'Dryden'.

*17. Drum, Trumpet . . . Battel.* Identified by the *Key* (p. 18) as a hit at the battles in Part 2 of *The Conquest of Granada.* Dryden defended his practice in 'Of Heroique Plays', prefixed to *The Conquest of Granada* when the play was published in 1672. 'To those who object [to] my frequent use of Drums and Trumpets; and my representations of Battels, I answer, I introduc'd them not on the *English* Stage, *Shakespear* us'd them frequently: and, though *Jonson* shows no Battel in his *Catiline,* yet you hear from behind the Scenes, the sounding of Trumpets, and the shouts of fighting Armies. But, I add farther; that these warlike Instruments, and, even the representations of fighting on the Stage, are no more than necessary to produce the effects of an Heroick Play' (*Works,* xi. 13–14). For a mocking account of battle scene representation in English plays, see *Spectator,* no. 42 (18 April 1711).

*22. Rule of Romance.* The French romances of La Calprenède, de Scudéry, and others were usually published in multiple volumes—e.g. *Cléopatre* (12 vols.) and *Clélie* (10 vols.). Bayes is proposing to write plays on the same grandiose scale.

*30–1. five Plays to one Plot.* Perhaps a sneer at Dryden's ostentatious disdain for plot in his preface to *An Evening's Love* (pub. 1671): 'little Criticks do not well consider what is the work of a Poet, and what the Graces of a Poem: The Story is the least part of either: I mean the foundation of it, before it is modell'd by the art of him who writes it' (*Works,* xi. 212). However, Percy's *New Key* (p. 428) takes the 'five Playes' passage as ridicule of 'the absurd custom of writing plays in several parts', instancing *The Siege of Rhodes;* Killigrew's *Bellamira, Thomaso,* and *Cicilia and Clorinda;* and especially *The Conquest of Granada.* Killigrew's plays were not staged.

*36–7. begin upon a Monday.* We are puzzled by this statement. So far as we know, Monday was not a good day for a premiere. Perhaps this is yet another instance of Bayes's fatuity.

*42. The third week.* An author's pay for a new play was the net profits of the third night (plus any payment from a publisher). After about 1690 a sixth night benefit was also allowed, if the play had so long an initial run. As Downes makes clear, ten or more consecutive performances constituted exceptional success for a new play. In this case, of course, Bayes's payment from the theatre would be only the profit of the third night, no matter how long the run.

*55. my five whole Plays.* Against this line or the next the U of PA-1683 annotator has written 'Dryden'.

*56–7. Mother had appear'd to him like a Ghost.* 'This refers to the IVth Act of the *Conquest of Granada,* Part 2d. Where Almanzor having passionately loved Almahide thro' the whole first part, and thro' the former scenes of this, is upon the point of entering his mistress's bed-chamber, when "as he goes to the door, the ghost of his mother meets him" [*Works*, xi. 167–9]. And tho' neither the hero nor his mistress actually kill themselves after it, yet both of them talk of it.' (Percy's *New Key*, p. 429)

59. *she kills her self.* Cf. *The Conquest of Granada*, Part 2, IV. iii:

> Almahide. You've mov'd my heart, so much, I can deny
> No more; but know, *Almanzor*, I can dye.
> Thus far, my vertue yields . . . . [*Going to stab herself.* (*Works*, xi. 173)

68.1. *a Funeral.* The *Key* (p. 17), glosses as follows: 'Coll. *Henry Howard*, Son of *Thomas* Earl of *Bark-shire*, made a Play, call'd the *United Kingdoms*, which began with a Funeral; and had also two Kings in it. This gave the Duke a just occasion to set up two Kings in *Brentford*, as 'tis generally believ'd; tho' others are of Opinion, that his Grace had our two Brothers in his thoughts [i.e. King Charles II and James Duke of York; cf. I. ii. 42, above]. It was Acted at the Cock-pit in *Drury Lane*, soon after the Restoration; but miscarrying on the Stage, the Author had the Modesty not to Print it; and therefore the Reader cannot reasonably expect any particular Passages of it. Others say that they are *Boabdelin* and *Abdalla*, the two contending Kings of *Granada*, and Mr. *Dryden* has in most of his serious Plays two contending Kings of the same Place.' Other funerary displays may be found in early Carolean plays. Elizabeth Polwhele's *The Faithfull Virgins* (Duke's Company, *c.*1670) opens with Meranthe and Umira keeping vigil over a hearse (Bodleian MS Rawl. poet 195, fos. 49–78; not printed). I. ii of L[eonard] W[illan]'s *Orgula* (pub. 1658; not produced) presents 'Castrophilus *Funeral Triumph*' (p. 3). A funeral appears in the second scene of Shakespeare's *Richard III* and in I. i. of *1 Henry VI*. Rights to this play were formally assigned to the King's Company in January 1669 (TNA PRO LC 5/12, pp. 212–13) and a prologue for it was printed in *The Covent Garden Drollery*, 13–14, in 1672, so it was (or had recently been) in the current repertory.

79. *Lardella.* Ridiculous for its suggestion of lard and therefore kitchen maids, much as Drawcansir suggests a tapster.

82. *a wave for her winding-sheet.* The *Key* (p. 18) quotes IV. iii of Part 2 of *The Conquest of Granada*, a speech by the ghost of Almanzor's mother:

> On Sea's I bore thee, and on Sea's I dy'd.
> I dy'd; and for my Winding-sheet, a Wave
> I had; and all the Ocean for my Grave. (*Works*, xi. 168)

84. *Behold the Tragick issue of our Love.* 'Let me intreat / The issues of our love', *The Ungrateful Favourite*, III. iv, p. 42 (Percy's *New Key*, p. 430).

91. *Drawcansir.* A burlesque of heroic play superheroes, and in particular of Almanzor in *The Conquest of Granada*. 'In his essay *Of Heroique Playes*, Dryden attempted to counter contemporary charges against Almanzor that he was a despiser of kings, that he changed sides to suit himself, and that he spoke and acted with ludicrous extravagance and incredible success. All these criticisms of Dryden's hero are reflected in Buckingham's treatment of Drawcansir' (Crane, pp. 92–3). Stocker

(p. 29) argues for a particular real-life identification with the notorious Colonel Thomas Blood: 'In the person of Drawcansir—soldier of fortune, renegade, boaster, bloodthirsty villain, insensible of and untouched by "justice"—we should recognise a portrait of Blood, who was all these things. In Drawcansir's theft of the kings' "Boles" there is a comic re-enaction of Blood's recent theft of Charles' orb from the Crown Jewels, and both of them get away with it. Drawcansir is a brilliant exploitation of this *miles gloriosus* of real life.' We find this reading strained. Another possible model would be the king's irascible cousin Prince Rupert of the Rhine, a civil-war hero who had settled in London and taken an actress, Margaret Hughes, as his de facto wife.

92–3. *snubs up Kings.* The U of PA-1683 annotator has written 'Dryden' against this line.

99–100. *singly beating of whole Armies, above all your moral vertues.* 'I have form'd a Heroe, I confess, not absolutely perfect, but of an excessive and overboyling courage: but *Homer* and *Tasso* are my precedents. Both the *Greek* and the *Italian* Poet had well consider'd that a tame Heroe who never transgresses the bounds of moral vertue, would shine but dimly in an Epick poem.' Dedication of *The Conquest of Granada* to the Duke of York (*Works*, xi. 6). Cited in Percy's *New Key* (pp. 430–1). In this case Dryden takes after Mr Bayes, since Buckingham's mockery was in the 1671 *Rehearsal* before Dryden's dedication was published.

104–5. *I must use my Spectacles.* Dryden is not known to have used spectacles prior to 1672—but he may have done so. This may be a sight gag left from the 1665 version alluding to Davenant, perhaps with reference to a well-known anecdote about the inadequacy of his nose (attenuated by treatment for the pox) to support spectacles. See Arthur H. Nethercot, *Sir William D'avenant* (1938; repr. New York: Russell and Russell, 1967), 92–3, 101–2, and 1967 'Addenda' following p. vii, particularly for 99 ff. Winn, however (*John Dryden*, 230 and 579 n. 60), points out that as early as 1674 in *Notes and Observations on the Empress of Morocco Revised* Elkanah Settle says of Dryden 'But why his *Eyes* should be so dimm or his *Spectacles* so dull, as to let such [errors] as these slip . . . .' (p. 54), implying that by then Dryden was known to be wearing spectacles.

106–7. *pin'd on her Coffin.* Pinning elegies onto the hearse-cloths of the distinguished dead was a long-established custom. See Alastair Bellany, 'A Poem on the Archbishop's Hearse: Puritanism, Libel and Sedition after the Hampton Court Conference', *Journal of British Studies*, 34 (1995), 137–64.

115. *Humble Bee.* 'A large wild bee, of the genus *Bombus*, which makes a loud humming sound' (*OED*). The point seems to be mockery of a female poet, likening her love verses to the humming of a bee.

118–19. *transmigration of the soul.* A pretentious allusion to Pythagoras's doctrine of metempsychosis.

121. *King Phys.* The name may be a play on 'fizzle', which at this time could mean 'to break wind without noise' (*OED*). Thus translated, the letter is titled 'To my dear cousin, King Fart'. We are indebted to Don-John Dugas for this suggestion.

129. *Since death my earthly part will thus remove.* The *Key* (pp. 18–20) quotes a passage from *Tyrannick Love* 'In Ridicule of this'. Berenice is addressing her lover, Porphyrius, in III. i:

> My earthy part—
> Which is my Tyrants right, death will remove,
> I'le come all Soul and Spirit to your Love.
> With silent steps I'le follow you all day;
> Or else before you, in the Sun-beams, play.
> I'le lead you thence to melancholy Groves,
> And there repeat the Scenes of our past Loves.
> At night, I will within your Curtains peep;
> With empty arms embrace you while you sleep.
> In gentle dreams I often will be by;
> And sweep along, before your closing eye.
> All dangers from your bed I will remove;
> But guard it most from any future Love.
> And when at last, in pity, you will dye,
> I'le watch your Birth of Immortality:
> Then, Turtle-like, I'le to my Mate repair;
> And teach you your first flight in open Air. (*Works*, x. 146)

139. *I will pass.* Against this line the U of PA-1683 annotator has written 'Dryden'.

147. *a pick-a-pack.* Piggyback (*OED*).

148. *tuant.* Biting, trenchant (French). The same piece of affected gallicism is used in Shadwell's *Bury-Fair*, II. i (*Complete Works*, iv. 313, 324).

162.1. *Enter Pallas.* The stage direction at line 194 probably implies that she was 'flown' in and out as befitted a goddess. Stocker (p. 26) suggests that 'Pallas herself personates Barbara Villiers. Formerly Lady Castlemaine, she received the title of Duchess of Cleveland in 1670. . . . In the same year her children were ennobled. Lely's famous series of portraits of Court beauties had represented Barbara as Pallas / Minerva.' For the portrait, see MacLeod and Alexander, *Painted Ladies*, 64, and Oliver Millar, *The Tudor, Stuart and Early Georgian Pictures in the Collection of Her Majesty The Queen*, 2 vols. (London: Phaidon, 1963), no. 257 and plate 109. Pepys saw what are now known as the 'Windsor Beauties' on 21 August 1668 (*Diary*, ix. 284). On 4 February 1668 Lady Castlemaine played a virtuous maiden in an amateur court performance of Katherine Philips's translation of *Horace* wearing the Crown jewels, 'taken from the Tower for her'. John Evelyn was offended. See *The London Stage*, Part 1, 128–9.

163–7. *Hold, stop . . . Lardella lives.* See *Cambyses*, Act V, p. 80: '*Mandana.* Now Executioner. *Osiris.* Hold, you mistake, Osiris lives.' (Cited in Percy's *New Key*, p. 432.)

172.1. *The Coffin opens.* This is the sort of trick property that Downes enjoyed so much in the 1674 'operatic' version of *The Tempest*, where there is a scene 'with a Table Furnisht out with Fruits, Sweet meats, and all sorts of Viands' that flies away out of reach (*Roscius Anglicanus*, 74).

173. *the very Funeral.* Against this line the U of PA-1683 annotator has written 'Tom Porter'.

175:2. *a Dance, for joy.* Crane (p. 93) points out a dance for joy at the arrival of Sir Francis Drake in *The Play-house to be Lett*, III, entry II, and another in entry VI [*recte* V]. In the former, four Indians 'dance for joy of the arrival of Sir Francis Drake', and when Drake rescues a bride and bridegroom, 'the Bridegroom' enters dancing with castanets 'to express the joy he receives for his liberty'.

178. *to elevate your expectation.* Elevation of style was an *idée fixe* of Dryden's, appearing, for example, in *An Essay of Dramatick Poesie* and the preface to *Tyrannick Love.* See note to I. i. 34–5.

183. *supple Statues.* Percy's *New Key* (pp. 432–3) offers as a 'contrast' a line from II. ii of Sir Robert Howard's *The Blind Lady*: 'If you deny, I'll grow a fixed Monument, Still to upbraid your rigour' (Howard, *Poems*, 1660, p. 59). Against this line the U of PA-1683 annotator has written 'Sr W D'avan't'. If there were any record of a Carolean revival of Shakespeare's *A Winter's Tale*, we would suspect allusion to a Duke's Company production of that play.

188. *Lo, from this conquering Lance.* 'See the Scene in the *Villain* . . . [III. i, pp. 47ff.]. Where the Host [turned out of his tavern] furnishes his Guests with a Collation out of his Cloaths; a Capon from his Helmet, a Tansey out of the lining of his Cap, Cream out of his Scabbard, &c.' (*Key*, pp. 20–1). Against this line the U of PA-1683 annotator has written 'Tom Porter'.

194. *What man . . . dares disturb our feast?* Against this line the U of PA-1683 annotator has written 'Dryden'.

196. *dares yet drink on.* The *Key* (p. 21) quotes an exchange from IV. iii of Part 2 of *The Conquest of Granada*:

> *Almahide.* Who dares to interrupt my private Walk?
> *Almanzor.* He who dares love; and for that love must dy,
> And, knowing this, dares yet love on, am I. (*Works*, xi. 170)

200:1–2. *the Second Dare, and print Must in the place on't.* The *Key*, p. 22, quotes this passage and says somewhat cryptically, 'It was at first, *Dares dye*', again citing IV. iii of Part 2 of *The Conquest of Granada*. Crane (p. 94) points out that Buckingham thus underlines his pointing up of the absurdity of Dryden's line.

204. *gent.* 'Well-bred, polite' (*OED*, citing this passage).

207. *my Boles away*. The *Key* (p. 22) quotes from Part 1 of *The Conquest of Granada*, Act V: '*Almanzor*. I will not now, if thou wouldst beg me, stay; / But I will take my *Almahide* away' (*Works*, xi. 90). Stocker (p. 29) suggests particular allusion to Colonel Blood's theft of the Crown jewels in 1671 (and see note at IV. i. 92).

210. *grum*. Surly.

210–13. *Though, Brother, this grum . . . pow'r to drink*. The *Key*, pp. 22–3, quotes what seems at best a remote parallel from V. i of Part 1 of *The Conquest of Granada* :

> *Almanzor*. Thou darst not marry her while I'm in sight;
> With a bent brow thy Priest and thee I'le fright,
> And in that Scene
> Which all thy hopes and wishes should content,
> The thought of me shall make thee impotent. (*Works*, xi. 91)

215. *because I dare*. The *Key* (p. 23) cites Part 2 of *The Conquest of Granada*, II. iii: 'Spight of my self I'le Stay, Fight, Love, Despair; / And I can do all this, because I dare' (*Works*, xi. 134).

228. *Roman Cloaths*. Buckingham apparently found attempts at historical costume ridiculous, though not all members of the audience agreed. Katherine Philips reports that when *Pompey the Great* by Waller et al. was staged *c*. January 1664 it was 'acted in English habits . . . Caesar was sent in with his feather & Muff, till he was hiss'd off ye Stage' (*London Stage*, Part 1, 74). We have no record of how Philips's own *Pompey* was costumed. When the Duke's Company mounted Sir Thomas Clarges's adaptation of Corneille's *Heraclius* (8 March 1664) Pepys found 'The guarments like Romans very well'. Crane (p. 94) suggests allusion to the 1668 King's Company revival of Jonson's *Catiline*, whose costumes drew admiring comments from Pepys (19 December), though this allusion to Roman dress seems likelier to date from the 1665 Ur-*Rehearsal*. On stage conventions for Roman dress, see de Marley, *Costume on the Stage*, ch. 1.

230. *I'l write no more*. Against this line the U of PA-1683 annotator has written 'Dryden'.

## IV. ii

3. *both fall out*. Reversing the usual quarrel between rival lovers. Crane (p. 94) suggests that the debate between Prince Pretty-man and Volscius 'recalls . . . the dialogue between Zanger and Achmat in *Mustapha*, II. ii'.

10. *Lend thy attention*. Against this line the U of PA-1683 annotator has written 'Dryden'.

13. *love in thy breast is not love in mine*. Percy's *New Key* (p. 436) quotes *Abdelazer*, Act V (Behn, *Works*, v. 306):

> Love in my Soul! is not that gentle thing
> It is in other breasts; instead of Calms

It ruffles mine into uneasie Storms.

This is a parallel, not an allusion, since *Abedelazer* postdates even the 1675 *Rehearsal*.

17. *I love reasoning in verse.* 'See the Heroic Plays of Lord Orrery, Mr. Dryden, &c, &c, particularly where they pretend to reason *pro* and *con*' (Percy's *New Key*, p. 436). Orrery was especially fond of versified reasoning scenes. As Crane points out (p. 94), this particular debate is reminiscent of the dispute between Zanger and Achmet in II. ii of *Mustapha*, where each describes love's effect on him.

24. *Contending with the pow'rful God of Love?* Percy's *New Key* (p. 436) cites a rather remote parallel: 'How powerful is thy deity, O love!' *The Siege of Urbin*, V, p. 51.

29. *her bright flames make all flames else look pale.* 'All other flames but his I did deride.' *The Black Prince*, I, p. 5 (cited in Percy's *New Key*, p. 437).

32. *ador'd with Sacrifice.* Percy's *New Key* (p. 437) cites two parallels: 'My heart's engag'd by Sylviana's eyes / To waste itself in daily sacrifice' (*The Siege of Urbin*, II, p. 16), and *Ormasdes*, V, p. 90:

> Ormasdes' heart shall into incense turn,
> And in bright flames before this altar burn.
> So long as my fair Saint does not despise
> To look upon so mean a sacrifice.

34. *The Body they consume as well as Soul.* Probably a parody of a passage in *Ormasdes*, III, p. 53: 'What a strange heat I feel, that always burn, / Yet do not waste, cannot to ashes turn.' Cited in Percy's *New Key*, p. 437.

46. *beauty in a Fly.* Cf. Commonplace Book, 15:6 and n.

59. *un-god themselves to see.* The *Key* (p. 24) quotes Maximin in *Tyrannick Love*, III. i:

> Thou ly'st:—there's not a God inhabits there,
> But for this Christian would all Heav'n forswear.
> Ev'n *Jove* would try more shapes her Love to win: ⎤
> And in new birds, and unknown beasts would sin; ⎬
> At least, if *Jove* could love like *Maximin*. ⎦
>                    (*Works*, x. 136)

61–2. *Gods be so uncivil . . . Devil.* The *Key* (pp. 24–5) quotes three passages from *Tyrannick Love*: 'Some God now, if he dares, relate what's past: / Say but he's dead, that God shall mortal be' (Act I; *Works*, x. 123). 'Provoke my rage no farther, lest I be / Reveng'd at once upon the Gods and thee' (Act I; *Works*, x. 125). 'What had the Gods to do with me or mine?' (V.i; *Works*, x. 187).

68. *transcend the joys of Heav'n in Hell.* Percy's *New Key* (pp. 439–40) comments: 'There is a rant not unlike this in *Love in its Extasy*. "Desdonella. I must assume some other shape / Before thou can'st behold me. Bermudo. Take any, gra-

cious goddess, I may see thee: / Cou'dst thou assume the devil's 'twould be lovely."
Act 3. sc. 2.'

69–70. *I have lost my peruke.* A sight gag of some sort is indicated here. Evidently Bayes's capering as he revels in Prince Pretty-man's rant occasions the loss of the peruke and exposes him to ridicule. Crane (p. 95) points out the identification of Hermogenes when '*his Perruke falls off*' at I. i. 357.1 in *Marriage A-la-Mode* (*Works*, xi. 239).

73:4–5. *creep servily after Sense.* A direct and particular hit at Dryden. The U of PA-1683 annotator wrote against this line, 'Drydens own Words in a prologue'. The *Key* (p. 25) quotes from the prologue to *Tyrannick Love*:

> Poets, like Lovers, should be bold, and dare,
> They spoil their business with an over-care.
> And he who servilely creeps after sence,
> Is safe, but ne're will reach an Excellence. (*Works*, x. 114)

Although *Tyrannick Love* (acted in June 1669) was published in 1670, Buckingham (or whoever did the additions to the *Rehearsal*) did not insert this passage until the 1675 version. Dryden specifically defended this passage in his preface and extended his defence in the edition of 1672. 'For the little Critiques who pleas'd themselves with thinking they have found a flaw in that line of the Prologue, (And he who servilely creeps after sence, is safe, &c.) as if I patroniz'd my own nonsense, I may reasonably suppose they have never read Horace [*Ars poetica*, 28]. Serpit humi tutus, &c. are his words: He who creeps after plaine, dull, common sence, is safe from committing absurdities; but, can never reach any heighth, or excellence of wit.' (*Works*, x. 112–13)

74. *the subject is too great for Prose.* A gibe at Neander's defense of verse (and rhyme in particular) in Dryden's *Essay of Dramatick Poesie*. Dryden further defended the use of 'Heroique verse' in 'serious Playes' in 'Of Heroique Playes' in 1672.

80. *let down the Curtain.* For most plays in the late seventeenth century the curtain was raised at the end of the overture and lowered at the conclusion of Act V (see Summers, *Restoration Theatre*, 97). This passage is probably a jab at Orrery's frequent use of the curtain, especially in *Henry the Fifth* (1664). The action here continues seamlessly into the fifth act with Bayes, Smith, and Johnson on the forestage in front of the proscenium arch.

*V. i*

1–2. *the greatest Scene that ever England saw.* Percy's *New Key* (pp. 441–2) calls this 'ridicule of the pompous processions so much affected upon the stage', and cites examples from *The Duke of Lerma*, *The Mariage Night*, and Orrery's *Henry the Fifth*, but Buckingham seems here to name his own target later in Bayes's speech: 'that great Scene in *Harry* the Eight' (l. 5). In II. iv. of Shakespeare and Fletcher's *Henry VIII* (lavishly staged at Lincoln's Inn Fields in December 1663) there are four bishops, one archbishop, and two cardinals. (Bayes is proud of having upped the ante by replacing two of the bishops with additional cardinals.) Downes expresses extravagant admiration for this production, 'being all new Cloath'd and new Scenes' (*Roscius Anglicanus*, 55–6). The 1675 edition of *The Rehearsal* clouds the directness of this reference, though *Henry VIII* was at least occasionally revived. Pepys attended a performance on 30 December 1668 and Nell Gwyn saw it in November 1675.

8. *Hats . . . Caps*. Percy's *New Key* (p. 442) worries this reference at length, but no clear allusion has yet been found, and probably none will be, since the reference is evidently to costuming, something rarely specified in printed texts.

20–1. *he is his son*. 'Such a discovery is made in the like abrupt manner in the *Roman Empress*. "Arsenius has let me know / Of late a secret, which will raise your wonder, / How Florus is his son" . . . Act 3. pag. 34' (Percy's *New Key*, p. 442).

27. *what sound is this invades our ears?* The *Key* (p. 26) cites *The Siege of Rhodes*: 'What various Noises do mine ears invade? / And have a Consort of confusion made?' (Entry I, p. 2.) Percy's *New Key* (p. 443) notes a similar query in *The Indian-Queen*, I. i, where Acacis asks, 'What noise is this invades my ears?' (*Works*, viii. 189.) Percy's *New Key* (p. 460) adds: 'Grave Senators! I bear / News, which with terrour will invade your Eare' (*The Roman Generals*, III, p. 32). What special (musical?) sound effect was used in the theatre is not clear. Allusion may also have been intended to a much ridiculed line by Dryden, 'An horrid Stillness first invades the ear' (*Astræa Redux*, l. 7).

28. *Musick of the moving Spheres*. Presumptively created by the movement of heavenly bodies around the earth in Ptolemaic astronomy.

30–2. *triumphant Carr . . . Virgin Vests*. Percy's *New Key* (p. 443) quotes 'Her spotless soul in white, ascends / In a clear chariot drawn by virgins' from (Cosmo Manuche's?) *The Bastard* (pub. 1652), IV, p. 58. There is no evidence that this play was on the stage during the Carolean period, but the costuming implication is probably valid.

37.1–2. *descend in the Clouds*. Percy's *New Key* (pp. 443–4) points out the opening of Act II of Orrery's *The Black Prince* (1667) in which clouds lead men and women on stage and float them off again while they sing '*in Dialogue and Chorus*'. And see the note to lines 39 and 40.

37.3–4. *Fidlers . . . in green* (and 68. *Fidlers are all in green*). The significance of green is not clear to us, but it was evidently unusual and hence regarded as ridiculous. How musicians were normally dressed we cannot be certain, but possibly allusion is being made here to a particular instance of special costuming. On 25 January 1663[/4] the Lord Chamberlain ordered that the King's Company be given £40 worth of silk 'to cloath the Musick for the play called the Indian Queene' (TNA PRO LC 5/138, p. 15). Whether the theatres' musicians always wore silk 'Habbitts' of the sort specified in a warrant to the Great Wardrobe on 20 March

1664[/5] is not clear (PRO LC 5/138, p. 45). A similar warrant of 18 January 1668[/9]
specifies that the Great Wardrobe is to 'make upp Habitts of severall coloured rich
Taffataes, for Twenty ffowre violins like Indian Gownes, but not so full with short
sleeves to the Elbowe, and trymmed with Tynsell about the Neck, and bottome,
and att the Sleeves, after the same manner and fashion as formerly' (PRO LC 5/62,
fo. 52ᵛ).

    39. *modern Spirits.* Probably a snide reference to Dryden's Nakar and Damilcar
in *Tyrannick Love,* 'Spirits' who '*descend in Clouds, and sing*' (*Works*, x. 148–51).

    40. *Haste, brother King, we are sent from above.* A direct parody of a cloud-song
by Dryden. The *Key* (pp. 26–8) refers the reader to *Tyrannick Love,* IV. i, which
reads:

> Nakar *and* Damilcar *descend in Clouds, and sing.*
>    *Nakar.* Hark, my *Damilcar*, we are call'd below!
>    *Dam.* Let us go, let us go!
> Go to relieve the care
> Of longing Lovers in despair!
>    *Nakar.* Merry, merry, merry, we sail from the East
> Half tippled at a Rain-bow Feast.
>    *Dam.* In the bright Moon-shine while winds whistle loud,
> Tivy, tivy, tivy, we mount and we fly,
> All racking along in a downy white Cloud:
> And lest our leap from the Skie should prove too far,
> We slide on the back of a new-falling Star.
>    *Nakar.* And drop from above,
> In a Gelly of Love!
>    *Dam.* But now the Sun's down, and the Element's red,
> The Spirits of Fire against us make head!
>    *Nakar.* They muster, they muster, like Gnats in the Air:
> Alas! I must leave thee, my Fair;
> And to my light Horse-men repair.
>    *Dam.* O stay, for you need not to fear 'em to night;
> The wind is for us, and blows full in their sight:
> And o're the wide Ocean we fight!
> Like leaves in the Autumn our Foes will fall down;
> And hiss in the Water——
>    *Both.* And hiss in the Water and drown!
>    *Nakar.* But their men lye securely intrench'd in a Cloud:
> And a Trumpeter-Hornet to battel sounds loud.
>    *Dam.* Now Mortals that spie
> How we tilt in the Skie
> With wonder will gaze;
> And fear such events as will ne're come to pass!
>    *Nakar.* Stay you to perform what the man will have done.
>    *Dam.* Then call me again when the Battel is won.
>    *Both.* So ready and quick is a Spirit of Air

> To pity the Lover, and succour the fair,
> That, silent and swift, the little soft God
> Is here with a wish, and is gone with a nod. (*Works*, x. 148–9)

Curtis Price observes that 'The original setting of "Haste, brother King", if there ever was one, is lost. Buckingham almost certainly made his paraphrase so that it could be sung to the original duet; to use this music as the vehicle for its own ridicule would certainly be in keeping with *The Rehearsal*'s own parasitic verse.' Price also points out that Purcell's setting of 'Hark, my Damilcar' in *Tyrannick Love* (done for a revival of 1694?) was later pressed into service for the parody in *The Rehearsal* (*Henry Purcell*, 50–53).

41. *Let us move.* Against this line the U of PA-1683 annotator has written 'Dryden'.

51. *Pigs Petty-toes.* Pigs' feet (a delicacy).

53. *Ollio.* A medley, miscellany, potpourri—from the Spanish/Portuguese stew comprising a great variety of ingredients (*OED*).

55. *storm a whole half-moon-pye.* In seventeenth-century military terminology demilunes (half-moons) were protective outworks (Crane, p. 97).

62. *Maggots in Filberds.* We are aware of no special significance to vermin in hazelnuts beyond low burlesque.

64. *We'l firk.* We'll be frisky, lively. A term with sexual and possible homoerotic overtones. See Middleton's *A Game at Chess*, III. ii. 34–7, in *Women Beware Women and Other Plays*, ed. Richard Dutton (Oxford: Oxford University Press, 1999), 280 and 440.

67. *Coranto.* The Italian counterpart of the French *courante*. Cf. note on *Sir Politick*, IV. iv. 60.

69–70. *no Coranto . . . a Tune, that's a great deal better.* The editors propose use of 'When the King enjoys his own again' or a similar patriotic ditty. See Simpson, *British Broadside Ballad*, 764–8.

82. *whoop . . . holla.* This passage is quoted in the *OED* ('whoop' 1) to illustrate the sound made in 'incitement, summons, exultation, defiance, intimidation, or mere excitement'.

82.1. *phillips his finger.* Precise meaning uncertain. 'Fillip' can mean to tap sharply with the nail joint of the finger, or to snap a finger against the thumb (*OED*). Whether Bayes is making an appropriately careless gesture, snapping his finger, or tapping in time with the music we cannot be certain.

84. *a Conjurer.* The *Key* (p. 27) refers the reader to *Tyrannick Love*, IV. i, where the conjurer Nigrinus raises the spirits of Nakar and Damilcar (*Works*, x. 147–8). Summers (*Rehearsal*, p. 139) points also to the necromancer Ismeron in Act III of *The Indian-Queen*. Buckingham's joke is of course that Dryden is even worse than Bayes, for unlike Bayes Dryden did not think better of employing a conjurer in *Tyrannick Love*. Buckingham must also have recalled the introduction of the con-

jurer Peter Vechio to resolve the plot in Act V of Fletcher's *The Chances*, an element that he banished from his own adaptation.

93–4. *people in Clouds speak plain?* In a jokey letter to Congreve from Switzerland (1 August 1702) Joseph Addison says 'the Rehearsal will tell you that people in clouds must not be confined to Speak sense'. *William Congreve: Letters & Documents*, ed. John C. Hodges (New York: Harcourt Brace, 1964), 211. Addison incorporated this letter in *Tatler*, no. 93 (12 November 1709). In *Spectator*, no. 419 (1 July 1712), Addison again alludes to this passage: 'I do not say with Mr. Bays in the *Rehearsal*, that Spirits must not be confined to speak Sense.'

94. *fancie, at its full range.* Yet another jab at the 'loos'd the Reins, and bid his Muse run mad' passage in the prologue to *Tyrannick Love*. Cf. note on II. i. 61 above.

99. *first, let's have a Dance.* Percy's *New Key* (pp. 445–6) cites a passage in Davenant's *The History of Sir Francis Drake*, Entry V: '*Drake*. March on—*Pedro.*—Ere yet our van shall far advance, / Know, Diegos, you must dance; / Strike up, strike up, in honour of the king.' Percy's *New Key* also suggests allusion to IV. i, p. 57 of *The Womens Conquest*, where prisoners of war desire to present a conquering king 'with a dance, after the Manner of their country'. Echoed in 'Rochester's Farewell' (1680) in a description of a court ball: 'Well, since he must, he'll to Tangier advance; / It is resolv'd, but first let's have a dance!' (*POAS*-Yale, ii. 221).

100. *Cartwright.* See note at I. ii. 161 above. Cartwright evidently performed one of the two kings.

102. *done as if it were the effect of thought.* Another instance of line reading as taught by Bayes.

107. *grand Dance.* This probably implies a dance involving all the performers on the stage and dressing the whole of the stage, as opposed to one performed by a few actors and watched by others. Buckingham might have been recognizably satirizing an entertainment done at the Inns of Court. The dance could have been done straight but may have been contrived to look silly or to degenerate into confusion. Bayes's pride in the dance suggests satire. In 1676 Wycherley has Manley refer sarcastically to behaviour of the gentry in Westminster-Hall and Whitehall when he says 'they seem to rehearse *Bays's* grand Dance'. See *The Plays of William Wycherley*, ed. Arthur Friedman (Oxford: Clarendon Press, 1979), 387.

110. *Inns of Court.* i.e. the dance parodies the sort of revels held at the Inns of Court. See Bartholow V. Crawford, 'The Dance of the Kings', *Philological Quarterly*, 2 (1923), 151–3. There was a particular dance, traditional to the Inner Temple, that involved circling three times, hand in hand, round a fire to the music of an 'ancient song'. Buckingham was admitted as a member of the Society of the Inner Temple in 1661. See Thornbury and Walford, *Old and New London*, i. 161, 164.

122. *five Guineys.* Percy's *New Key* (pp. 446–7) cites a passage in Sir William Killigrew's *The Imperial Tragedy*, III, p. 24. 'This gold accept it / As a small testimony of my love. / Castor, pray see it be distributed.' Percy also refers to I. ii of

*The Spanish Tragedy* ('We will bestow on every soldier / Two duckets, and on every leader ten'), though this play was apparently performed only at the Nursery in the Carolean period.

123–4. *five more . . . just ten . . . We have not seen so much the Lord knows when.* By no means a negligible sum of money in 1671, but not much of a payment for even a small army. The 'wrangling for the gold' reported at line 131 is obviously a snide comment about failure to pay those in the employment of the kings, a sore subject in the reign of Charles II. Failure to pay English soldiers and sailors was a long-standing scandal. See, for example, remarks by Pepys on 27 March 1662 and 25 June 1667. Pepys remarks glumly on the latter date the unpaid seamen 'would, if they could, go over [and] serve the King of France or Holland rather then us' (viii. 291)—as indeed 3,000 sailors were discovered to have done when a commission enquired into military grievances in the summer of 1667, though it was a capital offence. See Ogg, *England in the Reign of Charles II*, i. 261–2.

128–32. *dreadful noise . . . handy-blows.* The *Key* (pp. 27–8) refers the reader to Part 2 of *The Conquest of Granada*, I. ii:

> *Boabdelin.* What new misfortune do these Cries presage?
>
> . . . . . . . . .
>
> *Sec. Mess.* Haste all you can their fury to asswage:
> You are not safe from their rebellious rage.
> *Third Mes.* This Minute if you grant not their desire
> They'll seize your Person and your Palace Fire. (*Works*, xi. 111, 113)

Percy's *New Key* (p. 447) quotes *The Spanish Tragedy*, Act I: 'While they maintain hot skirmish too and fro, / Both battailes joyne and fall to handie blowes' (London, 1592), sig. A4ʳ.

129. *Haste hence, great Sirs.* Percy's *New Key* (p. 447) quotes *The Indian-Queen*: 'Make haste, Great Sir'. See Dryden, *Works*, viii. 192.

130. *the event of war no mortal knows.* '. . . th' events of all things doubtful are, / And, of Events, most doubtful those of Warre', *The Conquest of Granada*, Part I, Act IV (Percy's *New Key*, p. 447). See *Works*, xi. 70.

132:1. *a pretty kind of a Stanza.* Crane points out (p. 98) that the quatrain is used in II. i of *The Indian-Queen*, and that Dryden praises the form in his letter to Sir Robert Howard prefacing *Annus Mirabilis* (1666). See *Works*, i. 51. This comment on the preceding quatrain was introduced in *Q3*, probably a hint that the audience had missed Buckingham's point.

135. *our Cabinet.* Probably either 'council-chamber' (*OED* 7.a) or a private, secret place (*OED* 10).

155. *a battel before Ladies.* Gentlemen did not fight before ladies. See, for example, *The Country Gentleman*, Act IV, lines 310 and 401. Crane (p. 98) cites Bottom's explanatory prologue in *A Midsummer Night's Dream* as an instance of reassuring the ladies before theatrical bloodshed.

158-9. *long relation of Squadrons.* i.e. to have mere reportage of off-stage fighting.

161-2. *sum up my whole battel.* Against this line the Uof PA-1683 annotator has written 'Sr Wm Davenant Seige of Rhodes'. Probably, as Summers suggests (*Rehearsal*, p. 141), a swipe at Entry V in Part 1 of *The Siege of Rhodes*, where Davenant had to work within severe staging limitations, but generally applicable to Dryden's penchant for military show. Dryden's defence of his practice is discussed by E. Nelson James in 'Drums and Trumpets', *Restoration and Eighteenth Century Theatre Research*, 9/2 (1970), 46-55, and 10/1 (1971), 54-7.

168. *Cap-a-pea.* i.e. *cap-à-pied* (from head to foot) [French].

169. *a scarlet Ribbon.* Presumably representing blood, which was usually handled more realistically with sheep's blood in a bladder or a sponge to splash on victims. See Summers, *Restoration Theatre*, 201-2.

172. *Buckler.* A small round shield.

174-5. *Recitativo.* Recitative in modern English, i.e. sung declamation in speech rhythm. In its 1656 version *The Siege of Rhodes* was given 'in *Recitative* Musick', as the title page states—a device adopted to help evade the parliamentary ban on spoken drama. The public theatre adaptation mounted at Lincoln's Inn Fields in 1661 was an ordinary blank verse tragedy, but the notion of musical battle evidently tickled Buckingham too much for him to pass up the opportunity for mockery. Saint-Évremond may have been thinking of this passage when he wrote that 'the Duke of *Buckingham* says he will support it [opera] as long as they sing: *Hola, Ho &c! Captain of the Guard, Summon Monsieur So-and-So!*' (*The Letters of Saint Evremond*, ed. John Hayward (London: Routledge, 1930), 161).

188.1-2. *Enter . . . the General . . . a Lute in his hand.* The *Key* (p. 28) comments: 'There needs nothing more to explain the meaning of this Battel, than the perusal of the first Part of the Siege of *Rhodes*, which was perform'd in *Recitative Musick*, by seven Persons only: And the passage out of the *Play-house to be Let*.' By this last comment the author probably means a passage spoken by the Musician:

> Recitative Musick is not compos'd
> Of matter so familiar, as may serve
> For every low occasion of discourse.
> In Tragedy, the language of the Stage
> Is rais'd above the common dialect,
> Our passions rising with the height of Verse;
> And Vocal Musick adds new wings to all
> The flights of Poetry.
>
> (Act I of *The Play-house to be Let*; Davenant, 1673 *Works*, 72)

188:2. *I'l make it, too, a Tragedy, in a trice.* This passage is probably a vestige of the 1665 version: there was a decided vogue for alternate endings c.1664. The best-known example is James Howard's happy-ending *Romeo and Juliet* (lost, but described by Downes, *Roscius Anglicanus*, 53). Sir Robert Howard's *The Vestal-Virgin* was performed by the King's Company, probably *circa* late autumn 1664. Edmund

Waller's alternative ending for Beaumont and Fletcher's *The Maid's Tragedy*, though not published until 1690, was probably written about this time. See Robert D. Hume, 'The Maid's Tragedy and Censorship in the Restoration Theatre', *Philological Quarterly*, 61 (1982), 484–90. The *Key* (p. 28) notes that *Aglaura* and *The Vestal-Virgin* 'are so contriv'd by a little alteration towards the latter end of them, that they have been Acted both ways, either, as Tragedies, or Comedies'. *Aglaura* was popular in the 1660s, but Buckingham is unlikely to have been directly ridiculing the work of Suckling, whom he admired. Percy's *New Key* (p. 448) also points to Sir William Killigrew's *Pandora* (staged by the Duke's Company *c*.1663).

189. *Villain, thou lyest.* Percy's *New Key* (p. 449) quotes this phrase from *The Spanish Tragedy*, III. xiiA, *The Forced Marriage*, II. vii, and *The Surprisal*, IV. iii. This is of course a commonplace: 'to give the lie' is a challenge.

190. *Arm, arm, Gonsalvo, arm.* 'The Siege of *Rhodes* begins thus. *Admiral.* Arm, arm, *Valerius*, arm' (*Key*, p. 28).

192. *Musquetiers.* Obsolete form of 'musketeers'. Infantry armed with muskets, which were originally a 'matchlock' weapon, distinguished from 'firelock' weapons discharged with a sparking device.

192–7. *Acton . . . Chelsey . . . Putney . . . Hammersmith.* The suburban locations on the western fringes of London parody the fondness of writers of heroic plays for exotic settings. Buckingham's enjoyment of mock-geography is evident in Act III of *The Country Gentleman* in the 'contest' between Sir Cautious Trouble-all and Sir Gravity Empty. Locations have been annotated with reference to Kenneth J. Panton, *Historical Dictionary of London* (Lanham, Md.: Scarecrow Press, 2001).

192. *Acton.* An agricultural settlement some 6.5 miles west of Charing Cross. A centre of royalist support during the Civil War.

193. *Draw down the Chelsey Curiasiers.* These instructions for disposing the troops parody the Third Entry of Part 1 of *The Siege of Rhodes*:

> *Solyman. Pirrhus,* Draw up our Army wide!
> Then from the Gross two strong Reserves divide;
> And spread the Wings;
> As if we were to Fight,
> In the lost *Rhodians* sight,
> With all the Western Kings!
> Each Wing with *Janizaries* line;
> The Right and Left to *Haly*'s Sons assign;
> The Gross to *Zangiban.*
> The Main Artillery
> With *Mustapha* shall be:
> Bring thou the *Rear*, we lead the *Van.*
>
> (Davenant, *Works*, 10; cited in *Key*, p. 29.)

193. *Chelsey.* On the north bank of the Thames, two miles south-west of Charing Cross. A haunt of the aristocracy.

*Curiasiers.* A *cuirassier* is a horse soldier 'wearing a cuirass, a piece of heavy (originally leather) armour for the body, reaching down to the waist and consisting of breast and back plates buckled or fastened together' (*OED*).

195. *Putney.* On the south bank of the Thames, 5.5 miles west of Charing Cross. An upmarket area by the time of Henry VIII.

*Pikes.* Pikemen, infantry carrying pikes, a weapon consisting of a long wooden shaft with a pointed head of iron or steel (superseded in the eighteenth century by the bayonet attached to a gun). The regulation arms prescribed for pikemen in 13–14 Charles II, cap. iii and 15 Charles II, cap. iv included 'a pike of ash not less than 16 feet long, with back, breast, headpiece, and sword'. Ogg, *England in the Reign of Charles II*, i. 252.

*Pikes, now meet their Peers.* The *Key* (pp. 29–30) glosses with a passage from *The Play-house to be Let*, 72: 'More Pikes! more Pikes! to reinforce / That Squadron, and repulse the Horse.' The pikemen would plant the feet of their weapons in the earth, forming an impenetrable barrier against cavalry.

196. *Chiswickians.* From a residential area six miles west of Charing Cross on the north bank of the Thames with a ford to the southern shore. A major supplier of fruits and vegetables for London.

197. *Hammersmith.* On the north bank of the Thames, about five miles west of Charing Cross. A principal source of market garden products and flowers from the fifteenth century.

198. *Mortlake.* On the south bank of the Thames between Barnes and Kew. It was a centre for market garden products, brewing, tapestry, and pottery.

199. *Fulham.* A town on the north bank of the Thames about four miles south-west of London. By 1500 its alluvial soil had made it a major supplier of vegetables for the London markets and it remained primarily agricultural into the nineteenth century.

200. *Twick'nam.* A village ten miles south-west of Charing Cross, well outside London until the middle of the nineteenth century. Its principal businesses were agriculture, fishing, and ferry services.

202. *Petty-France.* Just beyond the city wall to the north of Broad Street and west of St Botolph, Bishopsgate, with a passage to Moorfields. Named for French cloth merchants who lived there in the sixteenth century. See Henry A. Harben, *A Dictionary of London* (London: Herbert Jenkins, 1918), 472. Summers (*Rehearsal*, p. 143) points out that Defoe refers in his *Journal of the Plague Year* to a passage leading from Petty France into Bishopsgate churchyard (still in existence). See Daniel Defoe, *A Journal of the Plague Year*, ed. Paula R. Backscheider (New York: Norton, 1992), 24.

202–3. *Horse . . . Shall try their chance.* Percy quotes a remote parallel from *The Siege of Rhodes*, Entry V, p. 23: 'Horse, horse! . . . Wheel, wheel, from their reserves, and charge our own!' (*New Key*, p. 451).

204. *Sedge.* 'Various coarse grassy, rush-like or flag-like plants growing in wet places' (*OED*).

205. *Stand: give the word.* Percy's *New Key* (p. 451), quotes *The Siege of Rhodes*, Part 2, Act V, p. 59: 'Stand . . . *Ianthe* is the Word.' This is not satire but merely military procedure.

209–10. *give fire . . . mine ire.* The *Key* (pp. 30–1) glosses the general's orders with a passage from Part 1 of *The Siege of Rhodes*, Fifth Entry:

> *Mustapha.* Point well the Cannons and play fast!
> Their fury is too hot to last.
> That Rampire shakes, they fly into the Town.
> *Pirrhus.* March up with those Reserves to that Redout!
> Faint slaves! the *Janizaries* reel!
> They bend, they bend! and seem to feel
> The Terrours of a Rout.
> *Musta.* Old *Zanger* halts, and re-inforcement lacks!
> *Pir.* March on!
> *Musta.* Advance those Pikes, and charge their Backs!

(Davenant, *Works*, 20).

211. *Pursue, pursue; they fly.* Percy's *New Key* (p. 452) quotes *The History of Sir Francis Drake*, Entry VI: 'They fly, they fly . . . Follow, follow, follow!' This is merely a commonplace.

215. *Brentford.* See annotation under 'The Actors' Names' (p. 630, above).

220. *By an Eclipse.* Eclipses (especially solar eclipses) were feared in the seventeenth century and were much commented upon by astrologers. See, for example, *Eagle 1666. A new Almanack and Prognostication for the Yeare of our Lord God 1666* (York, 1666), whose title page calls particular attention to a forthcoming eclipse, and John Gadbury, *Vox Solis: or, An Astrological Discourse of the Great Eclipse of the Sun, which happened on June 22. 1666* (London, 1667). The association of sun with king at the time lent solar eclipses an especially ominous quality. See, for example, concerning Charles I, *The Great Eclipse of the Sun, or Charles his Waine Over-Clouded* (London, 1644) and the pamphlet controversy over the significance of the eclipse of 29 March 1652. For a good summary of contemporary views of eclipses, see Ann Geneva, *Astrology and the Seventeenth-Century Mind: William Lilly and the Language of the Stars* (Manchester: Manchester University Press, 1995).

228. *O Moon.* Percy's *New Key* (p. 452) points out that 'In like manner Daphne addresses a Laurel tree, in the *Stepmother*' (III, p. 43).

239. *may as well suppose.* Against this line the U of PA-1683 annotator has written 'Sr Robert Stapleton'.

245. *Slighted Maid.* Sir Robert Stapylton's *The Slighted Maid*, staged with success at Lincoln's Inn Fields in 1663 and published later that year. In Act V there is a long 'Song in Dialogue' between Aurora and Phœbus (ll. 80–2) directly parodied in Buckingham's interchange between Luna and Orbis in lines 266–85. Aurora enters 'in a black Veil' (cf. l. 270); night and day are contrasted (cf. l. 269); 'Mount Vesuvio' is mentioned (cf. l. 281) as is 'Lipary wine' (l. 284).

255–6. *Earth, Sun, and Moon . . . dance.* This dance is used as a satirical application in *Spectator*, no. 3 (3 March 1711).

256. *Moon, come out upon the Stage.* Crane (p. 99) observes that 'Moonshine is figured forth equally dramatically' in III. i of Shakespeare's *A Midsummer Night's Dream* (*Complete Works*, ll. 830–42). This play was at least briefly in the repertory of the King's Company. The only recorded performance in the 1660s was seen by Pepys on 29 September 1662. He noted that he had never seen it before, 'nor shall ever again, for it is the most insipid ridiculous play that ever I saw in my life' (*Diary*, iii. 208). Buckingham very likely agreed with him.

*the Hey.* An old country dance (Hey go-bet in the sixteenth century). Summers (*Rehearsal*, p. 147) says that the name may be 'derived from the French, haie = a hedge, the dancers, who stood in two rows, being compared to hedges. It seems to have been a kind of reel, and Thoinot Arbeau (pen-name of Jehan Tabourot) describes one of the passages-at-arms in the Buffons or Matassins as the "Passage de la Haye". This was solely danced by men who imitated a combat.' As early as Shakespeare's *Love's Labour's Lost*, V. i (*Complete Works*, l. 1749), Dull is ridiculed for liking 'the hey'. Bayes's choice is being mocked: this is no longer a fashionable dance at court. 'The Hey involves three or more persons going in opposite directions, passing one another alternately by the right and left shoulders, with or without joining hands, until all dancers have either returned to their original places or arrived at a new place in accordance with the choreographic plan.' *International Encyclopedia of Dance*, ed. Selma Jeanne Cohen, 6 vols. (New York: Oxford University Press, 1998), iii. 361.

263–4. *sell the Earth a Bargain.* To answer an innocent question with a vulgarity. Summers (*Rehearsal*, pp. 147–8) cites allusions and illustrations in Dryden's attack on Shadwell's *The Virtuoso* in lines 181–2 of *Mac Flecknoe* ('Where sold he Bargains, Whip-stitch, kiss my Arse, / Promis'd a Play and dwindled to a Farce'), Dryden's prologue to *The Prophetess* (1690), Lee's prologue to *The Rival Queens* (1677), and Young Ranter in John Crowne's *The English Frier* (1690).

264–5. *Tune of Tom Tyler.* An old country dance (mentioned by Simpson, *British Broadside Ballad*, 645).

265.1–86. *Enter Luna . . . Eclipse.* Cf. Commonplace Book 150:7.

268. *What calls Terra firma, pray?* A direct burlesque of the opening of Stapylton's 'Song in Dialogue':

*Aurora. Phœbus?*
*Phœbus.* Who calls the World's great Light?
*Aurora. Aurora*, that Abhors the Night.
(*The Slighted Maid*, 80; cited in the *Key*, p. 31).

271. *shew her tail.* Literally, display her buttocks, but with the vulgar overtone of showing her genitalia (*OED* 5c). One notion of 'selling a bargain' was to invite a question that could be answered with 'Kiss my arse'.

271.1 (*Q3* addition). *Tune of Robin Hood.* An old country tune particularly associated with May Day revels (Summers, *Rehearsal*, p. 148). See Simpson, *British Broadside Ballad*, 610.

280–1. *To morrow . . . On Mount Vesuvio.* 'The burning Mount *Vesuvio*', *The Slighted Maid*, 81 (*Key*, p. 31). Vesuvio is the volcano near Naples, famous for its eruption in CE 79.

282 (addition in *Q3*). *To the Tune of Trenchmore.* A lively, merry dance tune, popular from the mid-sixteenth century (Simpson, *British Broadside Ballad*, 716–18).

284. *nothing but Lipary wine.* 'Drink, drink, wine, *Lippari-wine*', *The Slighted Maid*, 81 [*recte* 83] (*Key*, p. 32). The Lipari islands are north of Sicily.

287.1–2. *Hobby-horses.* Here wickerwork figures of horses fastened about the waists of the performers. Often used by morris dancers and by visiting commedia dell'arte troupes. Dryden sneers at their use by 'Th' *Italian* Merry-Andrews' in his 1673 epilogue to the University of Oxford:

> Th' *Italian* Merry-Andrews took their place,
> And quite Debauch'd the Stage with lewd Grimace;
> Instead of Wit, and Humours, your Delight
> Was there to see two Hobby-horses Fight,
> Stout *Scaramoucha* with Rush Lance rode in,
> And ran a Tilt at Centaure *Arlequin.* (Danchin, ii. 549).

Summers (*Rehearsal*, p. 148) points out their use with jockeys in Edward Howard's *The Man of Newmarket* (1678).

287.4. *telling them when to shout.* Another instance of Bayes exercising a directorial function.

290–1. *Let petty Kings . . . I slay both friend and foe.* Percy's *New Key* (p. 455) comments: 'Almanzor in the *Conquest of Granada* is perpetually shifting sides: He is now for Boabdelin . . . then for Abdallah . . . presently he turns to Boabdelin again . . . &c &c &c.'

294–5. *If they had wings . . . I would pursue, and beat 'em, through the skie.* Percy's *New Key* (p. 455) quotes Maximin: 'And shoving back this Earth on which I sit, / I'll mount—and scatter all the Gods I hit' (*Tyrannick Love*, V. i; *Works*, x. 189).

296–7. *And make . . . more dreadful is, than he.* As in *The Conquest of Granada*, Part I, I. i:

> *Arcos.* My King his hope from heavens assistance draws.
> *Almanz.* The *Moors* have Heav'n and me t' assist their cause.
> (*Works*, xi. 35).

Cited in Percy's *New Key* (p. 456), which also refers to Maximin's 'Look to it, Gods' speech in Act V. i of *Tyrannick Love* (*Works*, x. 188).

299. *your Hector, your Achilles.* Dryden himself says of Almanzor—a year later —that 'The first Image I had of him was from the *Achilles* of *Homer*, the next from *Tasso's Rinaldo*' ('Of Heroique Playes', *Works*, xi. 14).

303. *how shall all these dead men go off?* Stage convention dictated that bodies be hidden by closing shutters or dropping the curtain if they were not carried off. Bayes has evidently littered the forestage with dead bodies without preserving anyone to clear the stage. Having them get up and walk off is an obvious allusion to the end of *Tyrannick Love*. As the *Key* (p. 32) explains, '*Valeria*, Daughter to *Maximin*, having kill'd her self for the Love [of ] *Porphyrius*, when she was to be carry'd off by the Bearers, strikes one of them a Box on the Ear, and speaks to him thus—'

> Hold, are you mad? you damn'd confounded Dog,
> I am to rise, and speak the Epilogue. (*Works*, x. 192)

Valeria was acted by Nell Gwyn. This metatheatrical device seems to have delighted the audience, and the speech is often quoted by eighteenth-century anecdotalists.

309. *Rise, Sirs, and go about your business.* Wilkinson reports a bit of added dialogue at this point:

*Bayes.* Dead men!
*Dead Men.* Halloo!
*Bayes.* Are you all dead?
*Dead Men.* Aye, Aye.
*Bayes.* Why then you that are foot-soldiers get up and walk off, and you that are horsemen get up and ride off. (*Wandering Patentee*, iv. 123)


*V. ii*

6:1. *3 or 4 Play.* Perhaps here the collective group rather than individuals identified as 3 Player and 4 Player.

7. *The Argument.* This capsule account of Act V is obviously a dramaturgical convenience here, but such synopses might actually have proved helpful to actors who did not get complete scripts.

9. *consents to marry him.* Against these lines the Uof PA-1683 annotator has written 'Harry Savile but never acted'. Nothing is known of playwriting by the diplomat Henry Savile (1642–87), a close friend and correspondent of Rochester's who had carried Sir William Coventry's challenge to Buckingham in 1669. On Savile, see *Savile Correspondence: Letters to and from Henry Savile, Esq.*, ed. W. Durrant Cooper (London: Camden Society, 1858), i–xxiv, and John Harold Wilson, *The Court Wits of the Restoration* (Princeton, N.J.: Princeton University Press, 1948), 214–15 and *passim*. Wilson believed that the annotation means that 'the pas-

sage beside which his name appears was written by Savile, but cut out in the per-formance' (personal letter to A. H. Scouten, 28 November 1975). This strikes us as far-fetched.

13–14. *Cloris . . . drowns her self.* Percy's *New Key* (p. 458) suggests that Bucking-ham took 'the hint of this' from IV. ii of *The Amorous Prince*, where Curtius's sister Cloris is reported (falsely) to have drowned herself.

### V. iii

2–3. *go to dinner.* i.e. to eat prior to the afternoon performance. See the note on I. i. 67.

18. *the other House.* The fancy new Dorset Garden Theatre, just opened by the rival Duke's Company in November 1671.

19. *the Book.* The promptbook, which was vital to the coordination of a perform-ance in a changeable scenery theatre. For facsimiles of major exemplars and discus-sion of such promptbooks from this period, see Langhans, *Restoration Promptbooks*.

19–20. *you'l disappoint the Town, that comes to see it acted here, this afternoon.* This implies that what we have seen is a final dress rehearsal prior to the premiere the same day. There is poetic licence here: some of what is shown should definitely have been done at an earlier stage in getting up the production. Buckingham is un-derlining the point that the actors are clueless as to the meaning of Dryden's plays, even when giving public performances.

23. *what care I for the Town?* Against this line the U of PA-1683 annotator has written 'Ned Howard'. Cf. III. i. 80 and III. ii. 258–9.

25. *Lampoon and print 'em too.* Lampoons were often circulated among in-groups in manuscript. Bayes is threatening to do that, but also to publish his sat-ires. On the genre, see Harold Love, *English Clandestine Satire 1660–1702* (Oxford: Oxford University Press, 2004).

26. *what a Satyrist I am.* Neither Dryden nor any of the other contributors to the character of Bayes was publicly known as a satirist in 1671, though Dryden was said to have lampooned a nobleman while a student at Cambridge. Insofar as Dry-den was the immediate target, Buckingham very likely meant this as a joke, though if so he was to prove a better prophet than he could have imagined. Buckingham is probably best known today via Dryden's unflattering portrait of him as Zimri in *Absalom and Achitophel* (1681).

29. *Bills for another Play.* In the era before daily newspapers, the principal mode of theatrical advertising was the 'Great Bills' displayed on posts outside the theatre and other places in the city. On 24 March 1662 Pepys reports 'I went to see if any play was acted, and I find none upon the post, it being passion weeke' (*Diary*, iii. 51).

31–2. *Haynes and Shirley.* Jo Hayns (1646?–1701) was known mostly as an irresponsible buffoon and prankster, but he was a popular speaker of prologues and epilogues and an excellent dancer. Tobyas Thomas's *The Life Of the Late Famous Comedian Jo. Hayns* (1701)—a thoroughly unreliable compilation of anecdotes— conveys some sense of his chequered career. For a judicious modern reconsideration, see *Biographical Dictionary*, vii. 7–17. On George Shirley, see the note to II. iv. 37.2, above.

34.1–35. *Dance ... let's go away to dinner.* Percy's *New Key* (pp. 458–9) points out the close resemblance of the finale of *The English Rogue*: '(*They Dance*). *Avaritius.* Well now, lets in to dinner.'

*Epilogue*

3. *a plotting Age.* Stocker (pp. 16–17) observes that even before 1678 and the Popish Plot this was absolutely true: 'Selected highlights include White's Plot and Venner's Rising in 1660, the Wildman Plot of 1661, the Tong Plot of 1662, the abortive Northern rebellion and the Dublin Plot of 1663, the republican design in 1665, the alleged conspiracy behind the Fire of 1666, a major Presbyterian rebellion in Scotland in 1666, the Yorkshire skirmish of 1667, the Bawdy House Riots in London and provincial sectarian disturbances in 1668, followed by serious Nonconformist unrest throughout 1670. . . . Buckingham's own arrest in 1667 and the Coventry scandal [of 1669] were followed in the Winter of 1670 by an attempt to assassinate the Duke of Ormonde and the attack on Sir John Coventry by Monmouth's thugs. In 1671 these were followed by the Blood scandal.' The phrase is echoed in Behn's prologue to *The Feign'd Curtizans* (1679), line 1, and that to Durfey's *Sir Barnaby Whigg* (1681), l. 2.

18–19. *not all Rhyme ... these ten years.* A bit of an exaggeration in 1671. Rhymed heroic plays were made popular by Howard and Dryden's *The Indian-Queen* (January 1664) and Orrery's *The Generall* and *Henry the Fifth*, staged late the following summer.

## The Restauration

Because the present edition is one of Buckingham, not Beaumont and Fletcher, the notes have been restricted to matters of basic comprehension and to issues arising out of the process of revision. They do not attempt to cover other matters of interest arising from the original *Philaster*, which would have required attention to revisions prior to *79fc*, ancient sources, and echoes of other dramatists. For a fuller consideration of these topics, readers are referred to modern scholarly editions, especially that by Andrew Gurr for the Revels Plays series (London: Methuen, 1969; repr. Manchester University Press, 2003), to which we are deeply indebted. In the few cases where a longer note on a reading from the original play has been attempted, it is because it concerns a matter on which existing scholarship can be extended. Readers should be mindful of the statement of *15wgv* that Buckingham had not completed his revisions at the time of his death. We suspect that some of the original play's references would have been mysterious even to him, let alone any supplementary reviser, or understood in other senses than those of the Jacobean era. Some of these references would probably have been removed or replaced if Buckingham had lived to complete his revision (assuming it to be his, or primarily his).

### Prologue

The prologue acknowledges the failure of Buckingham's attempts to remain at the heart of British political life through his association with the Whig opposition. By 1683 the political pendulum had swung to the Tory side. The frankness and intimacy of this 'stage oration' suggests that it may have been intended for a performance at the court theatre, with the author clearly visible to the audience, rather than at one of the public theatres.

3. *our Friend.* Buckingham himself.

17. *all the Polls.* 'Polls' is used by Buckingham at line 30 of 'An epitaph upon Thomas Late Lord Fairfax', and elsewhere, as a cant word for politicians. If the more recent sense of 'elections' is intended, it may be with reference to the hotly contested shrieval ones, held and reheld during the summer of 1682 (*POAS-Yale*, iii. 207–16).

### Dramatis personae

For reasons best known to himself, the adapter chose to alter the names of all the characters. Most of these changes appear arbitrary and inconsequential but a few help in clarifying dramatic meaning. Alternatively, this may have been part of an attempt to evade copyright difficulties by distancing the play from its original.

*Philander.* A common pastoral name in the period. Its meaning is 'lover of mankind', whereas 'Philaster' (hardly less common) means 'one in love with a star', with a half-echo of Sidney's Astrophel. The sense of modern 'philandering' derives from the alternative meaning of a man devoted to love and is not found before the eighteenth century.

*Thrasomond.* Apparently a compound of the preceding Pharamond with Thrasiline, the original name of the second gentleman; however, a similar name, 'Thorismond', is used in *Theodorick*.

*Cleon.* Perhaps similarly contracted from 'Cleremont', the original name of the first gentleman; yet the character's forthright personality and willingness to use underhand tactics recall the Athenian demagogue of that name (d. 422 BCE.). Perhaps Buckingham had read Thucydides. The 'Dion' of *Philaster* received his name from another turbulent statesman, this time from Sicily. Gurr (pp. liv–lv) suggests that his altercation with the king in Fletcher's IV. iv (IV. i. 69–102 below) may have been meant to suggest James I's confrontation with Sir Edward Coke on 13 November 1608 over whether the king could regard himself as standing above the law or the law was above the king. In 1683 this question was still pressingly open.

*A Spaniard.* This small comic part, the performer of which is also entrusted with the delivery of the epilogue, may have been created for Jo Hayns, a specialist in prologues and epilogues, who accompanied Buckingham on his embassy to France in 1670 and succeeded Lacy as Bayes in *The Rehearsal.*

*Araminta.* A fashionable woman's name of the Restoration period: Congreve uses it for a leading character in *The Old Batchelour* (1693) and Vanbrugh likewise in *The Confederacy* (1705). The change of name loses the connection with Sicily, and specifically Syracuse, of the original Arathusa (altered to 'Arethusa' in later editions of *Philaster*).

*Melesinda.* The name had some popularity in seventeenth-century Britain as an up-market form of Millicent, both being derived from the Old German Amala-suintha, the correct historical form of the name of the heroine of *Theodorick.* Dryden assigned it, incongrously, to the wife of Morat in *Aureng-Zebe* (1676). Curiously, it recurs in Tom Brown's 'Melesinda's misfortune on the burning of her smock' (dated 1690 in *The Remains of Mr Tho. Brown, Serious and Comical, in Prose and Verse* (London: Sam. Briscoe et al., 1720), 7–10), as part of a narrative in which the title character dreams of a night spent in the arms of a lover named Philander.

*Alga.* From a Greek root meaning pain (cf. 'neuralgia'). Buckingham may have imagined that the original 'Megra' had a similar meaning because of its similarity to English 'megrim', cognate with modern migraine. 'Aglaia', the name of one of the three Graces (see next), may also have been an influence. The modern connection with aquatic flora is not intended.

*Euphrosyne . . . Endymion.* Two Greek mythological names. The first, famously used by Milton in l. 12 of 'L'Allegro', was that of one of the three classical Graces, representing beauty and joy. The second is that of a young man placed by the moon goddess in a perpetual slumber. The replaced 'Eufrasia' is a version of Greek 'euphrasia' meaning eloquent or considerate (Gurr, p. 30, prefers 'mind-gladdening'). The male name 'Bellario', by contrast, is a stock romance name suggesting physical beauty.

*I. i*

3. *deny Admission.* At the Stuart courts, access to the presence chamber for the purpose of 'waiting' on the monarch was open to all persons of suitable social status. Certain rules applied, however, among which were to avoid direct eye contact with the sovereign and never to turn one's back on royalty.

14. *Sicily and Calabria.* In Buckingham's time parts of a single kingdom, that of the Two Sicilies. Similarly, Britain was composed of the two independent kingdoms of England and Scotland, united in the person of their sovereign.

24. *I drew my self.* As part of the invading Calabrian army.

38–9. *keep his own People in Awe.* Sicily came under Spanish rule in 1296 and remained so, with intermissions, until 1860. During that period it was the site of many intense military struggles from which the side aligned with Spain normally emerged victorious. In Settle's revision of the play, Philaster himself is made a Spanish prince.

43. *a standing Army.* England had last been under military rule in the later stages of the Interregnum. There was strong hostility to the idea of a large army being maintained in peacetime, both for reasons of expense and for fear it would be used as an instrument of tyranny. James II's attempt to establish such an army was one of the reasons for his overthrow. The issue was also a pressing one in 1715 when the adaptation was published.

48. *destroyed her own.* With venereal disease.

52. *Governour.* A tutor who travelled with his charge.

75. This overlong line may have been intended as a hemistich followed by a regular pentameter. Because in so radical a compression it is hard to judge which metrical effects were intended and which fortuitous, we have retained the line-division of the copy-text.

95. *15wgv*'s full stop at the end of this line may have been meant to illustrate the incomprehension described at lines 132–3 but is more likely to have been a printer's error.

97. *free Trumpet.* Apparently a stock phrase close in effect to the modern 'blow one's own trumpet'. Professional trumpeters in Beaumont and Fletcher's time performed only with other trumpeters and the essential drums. Most were employees of royal or noble persons or members of military units. A free trumpeter was therefore a rarity.

113. *fenc'd.* In shortening *Philaster*'s 'defenced' to a monosyllable, the revision opens the alternative meaning 'surrounded with a [metaphorical] fence'.

114. *Travels.* Travails.

129. *Constable.* The parish official responsible for apprehending malefactors and maintaining order at night at the head of his watch.

155. *made fertile.* Metaphorically with their faith, but also physically with their blood and bodies.

161. *a Tooth-drawer.* Proverbial at a later date for a very thin person, though, as Gurr points out, *Philaster*'s Pharamond is twice described as fat. Pulling teeth required strength as well as dexterity.

165. *drunken Cloud.* By imbibing moisture from the earth.

167. *tainted.* Distraught or demented, as in *Twelfe-night*, l. 1489 (III. iv).

169. *general Purge.* By depriving him of his inheritance.

181–3. Referring to Alexander the Great.

187. *bellied*. Short for 'big-bellied'; like a toad with its belly distended with air.

190. *better temper'd*. In the Galenic sense of having his constituent elements in a state of disproportion.

197. [*Whisper*. Cf. *The Rehearsal*, II. i. 6–54.

198. *strong Atlas*. Who carried the world on his shoulders.

205. *Elder Gun*. 'A pop-gun made of a hollow shoot of elder' (*OED*).

230. This line, uncued in *15wgv* and assigned to Dion in *Philaster*, is here given to Dion's counterpart Cleon. The king could not speak it as he had already exited, and Philander is preoccupied in dumb-show with his labouring fancy.

246. *Male Dragons*. Taken over from *Philaster*, but not found elsewhere and possibly corrupt.

263.1. Although it is not specifically marked, there is an implied change of scene here to 'the Chamber of the Princess' (l. 425). Whereas on the pre-1642 stage there was no need to distinguish one venue visually from another, a Restoration dramatist was expected to make this evident by drawing on or drawing off wings and shutters. Such changes also emphasize that a lapse of time has taken place between events, something that had to be deduced from dialogue and action in Beaumont and Fletcher's time.

291–310. Buckingham has suppressed a striking passage in which Philaster is led to believe that Arethusa desires his death so that her dowry will not be compromised by his claim on Sicily, giving more force to ll. 309–12 in his case and to ll. 321–7 in hers. By contrast, the declaration of love that follows is expanded so as offer greater scope to a Restoration star actress.

339. Either some text was lost at this point or the revision was not complete.

420. *Blast*. Metaphorically, either one who blasts airily and insubstantially through boasting or one whose impact is restricted to a brief initial flash. The earlier 'free trumpet' image suggests the first of these.

*thou*. Here, Philander's switch from 'you' to 'thou' is insulting, as he is addressing Thrasomond as if he were a child or a domestic; however, his addressing Endymion as 'thou' in II. i. 1 and subsequently is appropriate and affectionate.

431. *thus, thus*. Perhaps accompanied by a squeezing action; however, the electronic LION archive shows that duplicated 'thus' was surprisingly common in texts of this period.


## II. i

14. *prefer*. In the technical sense of gaining advancement at court.

60. Buckingham's complete suppression of the two delightful comic exchanges that follow *Philaster*'s exit in the original can hardly be for any deficiency in wit or erotic

suggestiveness. Cutting the scene between Pharamond and Megra was made necessary by Pharamond's part having been reworked as a low comedy one and hers as a conventional villainess. Galatea/Melesinda's demotion to a bit part may have resulted from the King's Company of the early 1680s lacking an actress capable of doing justice to the role, or perhaps witty virtue was no longer interesting to audiences. However, neoclassical ideals of dramatic economy also demanded the removal of a scene that existed largely for its own sake and was of so little consequence for the advancement of the action that it could be covered by five lines of dialogue (ll. 77–81).

60.1. As at I. i. 263.1, there is an implied change of scene here to Araminta's chamber.

65. *sad.* Here, 'sober', 'reserved'.

71. *strain'd a Point.* Metaphorically, from the practice of securing clothes with points and laces.

82. *into the Presence.* The presence chamber at court, where courtiers 'waited' in attendance on the sovereign.

124.1. The scene has changed again, this time to the front of Alga's lodgings.

141. *undeserving.* For *15wgv*'s obviously wrong 'understanding'.

153. *Alga's Lodgings.* The scene has been changed from Pharamond's own lodgings to permit the comic turn of his frustrated escape and being brought on in his drawers. In *Philaster* he displays gallantry in refusing entry to the king's party.

162–3. Possibly intended as a single verse line; however, these characters generally interject in prose.

172. *Alga.* Where this speech was spoken from is not specified in *15wgv*. Alga leaves the stage at line 130 and re-enters at line 189.1. Fletcher's text says 'Megra *above*' when she delivers these lines prior to her re-entrance. The Buckingham version clearly pictures her 'above' the king and his retinue: he says 'Come down' at line 178 and 'Will you come down?' at line 184. At Drury Lane or Dorset Garden in the 1680s this passage could have been staged with Agra appearing in a practicable window in a wing or shutter. The likelihood, however, is that she would simply have shown herself in one of the side boxes above the proscenium doors that were on both sides of the forestage. For a plausible pictorial representation, see Richard Leacroft, *The Development of the English Playhouse* (London: Eyre Methuen, 1973), 95 (Fig. 63).

187. *If this Geer holds.* A stock phrase with the general meaning 'if these happenings continue' (Gurr). Used also in *The Chances*, at III. i. 11.

193. *Painter and Apothecary.* Because her face is painted and her body diseased.

206–7. *her Haunts, Her Layes and Leaps.* Comparing her to a deer, but with a sexual second meaning on each word. The language of the deer hunt recurs extensively in Acts IV and V.

225–6. *nine Worthies.* Nine legendary leaders in war, namely Joshua, Judas Maccabaeus, David, Alexander, Hector, Julius Caesar, Charlemagne, Godfrey of Bouillon, and King Arthur.

226. *ride astride.* In the male way rather than side-on. Cf. Rochester, 'A Letter from Artemiza in the Towne to Chloe in the Countrey', ll. 1–2:

> Chloe, in Verse by your commande I write;
> Shortly you'l bid mee ride astride, and fight.

### III. i

5. *Bravery.* 'Model, paragon' (Gurr).

17–21. Heard in 1660 or later, these lines would have seemed prophetic of Charles II's predicament during the final years of his exile. In 1683 the more striking association would have been with Monmouth.

69. *Set Hills on Hills.* As did the giants when they stormed heaven, piling Pelion on Ossa and both upon Olympus.

74. *She is my Mistress.* i.e. Truth. The sense is clearer in *Philaster*.

91. *all Women.* For infidelity.

113. *ill temper'd.* Cf. I. i. 190 n.

115. *four several Corners.* As they are often illustrated in early maps.

132–3. i.e. Cleon is these things.

150. *this unto you.* The letter mentioned at l. 158.

159. *Adamant.* Here apparently diamonds, but often applied to other hard things and to magnets.

226. *Bulls of Brass.* As in the legendary bull of Phalaris, a torture apparatus in which the cries of the trapped victim resembled the bellowing of bulls.

239–40. Buckingham has extracted a heroic couplet that was latent but deliberately avoided in *Philaster*.

285. *bathe.* Bathing was then a medical treatment rather than a means to personal cleanliness, which was little regarded.

300. *Service.* With its common sexual double meaning.

323. *Batt'ry.* Of artillery.

327. *Chrystals.* Her eyes.

337–45. Buckingham's rewriting of this short speech shows how much his ear was guided by the Restoration practice of declaiming to a 'tone' and by the preference of actresses for uncomplicatedly affective language. The two kinds of musical performance distinguished in the original—singing elegies and playing the lute to induce sleep—are elided into one, and the complex imagery discarded as dramatically irrelevant.

370.  *sad Bell.* The church bell rung to announce a death or for a funeral.

375.  A crucial addition in that it implicates Philander himself in the promulgation of false evidence.

386.  *Both heal and poison.* A squashed scorpion was believed to be an antidote to its own sting.

433–7.  An obscure comparison in which Araminta compares herself to Hecuba or Cassandra at the fall of Troy, or perhaps Helen as the victim of the smooth-talking Paris.

441–5.  Alluding to the legend in which Diana turned the hunter Actaeon into a stag and let him be torn to pieces by his own hounds.

*IV. i*

The act is designed to be played against an unchanged pair of flat scenes representing a forest. This may be one reason for the suppression of the scene-setting opening passage in *Philaster*, which in the non-pictorial theatre of 1611 had the function of establishing locale by verbal means. However, by 1683 deer-hunting from stands with bows and arrows was no longer fashionable and probably not even understood. When the deer was hunted it was on horseback with hounds. Buckingham himself was a fox, not a stag, hunter.

1–12.  Modelled on Juvenal 6: 1–10. The vestigial rhymes suggest that the lines might have originated as part of an earlier stanzaic translation.

13–14.  The theme of Horace, *Carm.* 1. 22.

78–9.  *thou, Thou Traytor.* The insulting use of 'thou'.

85–7, 97.  Recollecting Horace, *Carm.* 1. 10. 9–12?

118.1.  On the title page of *Philaster Q1*, 'a Countrey Gentellman' and on his entrance in the text 'a Country Gallant'. In *Q2* and subsequent editions he is 'a Country Fellow', and only in *The Restauration* a 'Clown'. The fact that he rides a horse (ll. 121–2) and wears a sword indicates regional gentry status. Once again an event is prepared by Buckingham that, in *Philaster*, is introduced as a complete surprise.

152.1.  *Runs . . . Araminta.* This, the most important of Buckingham's changes, satisfies objections to Philaster's wounding of Arethusa by making it an accident; however, it also requires the suppression of her masochistic acceptance of her death at the hands of her lover and her irritation at the countryman for interrupting this ritual of honour by saving her.

155.  *Æolus.* As in *Aeneid*, 1. 132 ff.

169. *transform'd themselves.* As Zeus did into animals and birds on numerous occasions in order to seduce mortal women.

175–6. These lines taken together would scan as a pentameter composed of two spondees and three iambs. We have left it as a tetrameter rhymed couplet, with a further half-rhyme at l. 178 hinting at a vestigial stanzaic pattern like that at ll. 1–12.

194.1. *Enter Clown.* See note on 118.1.

194.1–203.1. The overthrowing of the Clown, who in *Philaster* defeats and drives away his opponent, may be the effect of stricter ideas of dramatic decorum as much as of aristocratic fellow-feeling; but it also reflects hierarchies within the acting profession, following its transition from a sharer to a managerial system, in which the beplumed specialist performer of heroic roles regarded himself as socially superior to the low comedian.

196. The truncated syntax suggests corruption.

211–22. Philaster's antiheroic exit is remedied here by a parting exchange between the lovers. In the original Arethusa is ungallantly left exposed to the sexual advances of the countryman.

229. Moving the Clown's last two words to l. 230 would produce regular blank verse; but his medium is prose.

239–41. Again, scannable as two regular blank verse lines; but the surrounding speeches are in prose.

242–3. *old Fox.* An ancient but reliable sword, as might have been worn by Major Oldfox in Wycherley's *The Plain-Dealer.*

251. *i'fecks.* A feeble oath by contrast with *Philaster*'s 'By all my love', marking Buckingham's reformulation of Thrasomond as a buffoon.

260. *sweet ones.* The flowers on the bank, recalling I. i. 381–6.

279. An evocation of the original myth in which Endymion's sleep is perpetual.

302.1. Buckingham softens the wounding of Endymion by having it done to his face, after dialogue and as the result of jealous anger, rather than in his sleep as a device to make him appear guilty of the attack on the princess. Philaster assumes that if Arethusa really loves him she will deny that he was her attacker and do nothing to prevent the blame falling upon the innocent Bellario.

360. *Wealth of Tagus.* Because its sands contained alluvial gold.

366. *under World.* Not the infernal regions but the world as seen from a great height.

385. *Plutus.* The god of wealth.

400. *Ay me . . . will.* Araminta would have denied the fact if there had not been another witness.

*V. i*

1–92. While this passage could have been set in a generalized stateroom which could then be reoccupied by the king and his courtiers, it would make better sense to place it in the princess's chamber, with a change of scene following the exit.

30. *cut it.* Even the executioner would not be able to look at where his axe was to fall.

42–92. This substantial addition both prepares for the marriage procession, which comes as a complete surprise in *Philaster*, and allows for the invention of fresh Beaumontian points of honour to replace those stripped from Act IV. In this respect it is competent pastiche; however, Philander's casuistically motivated reluctance has more than a hint of Prince Pretty-man about it.

108. Just as Buckingham had abandoned the original masque-like conclusion to *The Chances*, he also suppresses a masque-influenced episode from *Philaster* as irrelevant to Restoration theatrical tastes and impeding the progress of the action. The densely imagistic passages from the speeches of Cleon and the king are removed with this episode as failing to accord with a 'modern' desire that dialogue should be immediately intelligible.

111–17. In *Philaster* this messenger enters immediately before the other at the point corresponding to V. i. 164.

134. *Headsman.* Gurr suggests a pun on headsman as (1) an executioner; (2) one who takes a maidenhead. Or simply husband.

135–7. He will excuse her from his false allegation if he lives long enough to do so.

163. *World. 15wgv*'s 'Word' is a clear error.

164–74. By placing the first messenger's speech at 108.1–17, Buckingham once again abandons the aesthetic of surprise, attacked in *The Rehearsal*, for one in which effects are signalled in advance (cf. note on ll. 42–92 above). The symmetry of two messengers entering in succession may also have been too stagy for Restoration tastes. The exit of Arethusa, Philaster and Bellario seems to be misplaced by one line in *79fc*.

183–203. Cleon's speeches anticipate the rhetoric of the captain in urging the citizens to rebel. The participants in the uprising are represented as cheating tailors and haberdashers, bankrupts in hiding from bailiffs, and usurers, in that order. They are addressed in a style anticipating that of the nonsensical speeches cultivated by the later 'Order of the Fancy', discussed in Timothy Raylor, *Cavaliers, Clubs and Literary Culture: Sir John Mennes, James Smith, and the Order of the Fancy* (Newark, Del.: University of Delaware Press, 1994). The order stood in a line of descent from the Mermaid club to which Beaumont may have delivered his 'grammar lecture'.

184. *what d'ye lack?* A common street cry used by pedlars.

185. *cut.* Illustrated in woodcuts.

187. *in Sæcula Sæculorum.* The concluding phrase of the Lord's prayer and other liturgical texts in Latin, translated in the Anglican liturgy as 'for ever and ever'. Anomalous, since the 'Sicilians' are elsewhere represented as classical pagans, swearing by the gods.

191-2. *souce him for his Breakfast.* Eat him for breakfast pickled in brine.

193. *Murrains.* Epidemic diseases.

194. *in easie Freeze.* Wearing plain woollen clothes, rather than expensive suits from tailors.

195. *branch their Velvets.* Emboss with a pattern, in this case destructively.

195-6. *before sore Eyes.* Which would not appreciate their fineness. Alternatively as a mask to protect sore eyes from light.

196. *false Lights.* Windows darkened so that imperfections in the cloth will not be visible.

196. *Presses.* Marks made by pressing; creases.

197. *Shop-rid.* Unsaleable from being too long in the shop.

198. *break.* Become bankrupt and either seek sanctuary or remain perpetually indoors, eating the cheapest food, so as not to be arrested by bailiffs. The life of such fugitives is represented in Shadwell's *The Squire of Alsatia* (1688).

202. *Gothick Latin.* Barbarous legal Latin. *79fc's* 'goarish' is a misprint for an earlier 'goatish'.

203.1. *Enter King.* From trying to pacify the 'Burghers'.

210. *from out your Walls.* By Beaumont and Fletcher's time, and more so Buckingham's, the city livery companies, which enforced anti-competitive regulations within the ancient walls of London, were experiencing competition from retailers in the rapidly extending suburbs, over which they had no control. A smart shopper would explore both possibilities.

*cozen.* Cheat.

212-20. Buckingham suppresses the king's account of having dirt flung at him, allowing him a moment of remorse not present in the original.

225. Adelard is sent, but at 234.1 it is Agremont who returns—one of several indications of the unfinalized nature of the revision. Given Agremont's total ignorance of court affairs at I. i. 1-43, it is hard to see him as a trusted official.

234.1. *Agremont.* See 225 n.

255.1. The scene changes here to a street.

256. *Myrmidons.* The citizens are jokingly compared with the soldiers of Achilles in the *Iliad*, originally created from ants.

258. *What do you lack.* See above, V. i. 184-5 n.

259–60. *Bay Salt.* Sea salt, made through evaporation, as opposed to rock salt, which was mined.

261. *Ding-dongs.* Gurr suggests 'Cockneys, born in sound of the bells of St Mary-le-Bow' (p. 106); however, the sense of a 'ding-dong battle' may also be present, or of clumsy soldiers continually banging their armour.

262. *Indentures.* Apprentices were legally indentured to serve their masters for seven years. 'Pairs' because each party retained a copy.

*Clubs.* The weapon of apprentices, who could not wear swords.

262–4. *cold Water Chamlets . . . Tissues.* Specialized kinds of cloth used by tailors.

265. *Robin Hoods and Johns.* Punning on the legendary outlaws and types of clothing. *79fc*'s 'scarlets' refers to their companion, Will Scarlett.

267. *three-pil'd.* On the analogy of the thick pile or nap of the most expensive velvet. 'Valours', 'Choler', and 'Measure' continue the tailoring analogy.

269. *Rose-Nobles.* A coin worth a third of a pound, stamped with a rose.

272–3. *strike their Topsails to a Foist.* Pay homage to an inferior barge or galley. Ships of the British navy insisted on being so saluted.

273. *hull and cry Cockles.* Be converted into a fishing boat selling shellfish. To 'hull' was to drift with the tides. The analogy is with Philander.

277. *solder'd Crown.* Because (1) his royal status was not legitimate; (2) the crown of his head had been treated for scab or syphilitic sores.

278. *Pepin.* A rehistorization of the original's 'Pippin' but one that also removes the pun on apples. Pepin was the father of Charlemagne.

280. *coddled.* Boiled, as was done with eggs and apples.

281. *Bills.* Bladed weapons mounted on a staff.

285. *hulk.* Eviscerate.

286. *Wiper.* His sword. Gurr suggests a comparison with a pull-through used to clean muskets; however, a sword used with a swishing motion was sometimes said to 'wipe'.

291. *branch.* See V. i. 195–6 n.

292–3. *like a Satin . . . ravel.* Another tailoring metaphor.

293–4. *cut to the Kell.* A membrane (caul) covering the intestines of a deer.

295. *Galoon Laces.* Narrow braided trimmings resembling ribbons, associated with gallants.

298–9. *seal'd up with a Feather thro' his Nose.* Techniques used to restrict the vision of falcons while they were being trained for hunting. To 'seal' was to sew up part of the eyelids.

302. *Heir apparent to Church Ale.* Church ales were traditional parish money-raising functions often accompanied by licentious revelry. By Fletcher's time there was a strong Puritan-led move to suppress them. The captain suggests that Thrasomond was conceived during one.

303. *Sarcenet.* A light silk only useful for linings.

304. *Ring-tail.* An inferior species of falcon, of little use as a hunting bird.

305. *poor Men's Poultry.* With a derogatory reference to Alga.

306. *Bread and Butter.* Then food for infants, as in Prior's 'On Fleet: Shepheard's takeing away a child's bread and butter'.

309. *Dowcets.* The stag's testicles, which were regarded as a delicacy. The following lines continue the analogy of a deer being divided among hunters after a kill.

*Donsels.* Little dons, or squireens.

316. *Build a College.* Possibly a joke at the expense of Brasenose College, Oxford, or Gresham College in Bishopsgate. The reference was taken over from Fletcher. Brasenose had been founded as far back as 1509; Gresham College was established in 1597, so might have come to the mind of an early seventeenth-century Londoner.

317. *Kit.* A 'kit' was a small rebec or violin used by dancing masters and in Beaumont and Fletcher's time would have been strung with gut. Brass strings were used for plucked chordophones of the cittern and bandora families. Wound strings, with loops of metal wire covering a gut core, were coming into use for the lower courses of some gut-strung instruments and may be what the citizen is thinking of. Alternatively the reference may be to the chink of silver coins.

323. *give you the trimming.* Identifying the speaker as a fellmonger.

324. *false Scabbards.* Literally a decorative outer covering for the scabbard; also, given the context, possibly a reference to primitive condoms of the kind found in 1985 at Derby Castle.

326. *Pollard.* A stag that has lost its antlers.

328. *if they be sound.* i.e. not decayed by venereal disease.

333. *Rosicleer.* The hero of a popular chivalric romance, the *Espejo de Príncipes*, popular in English in a translation by Margaret Tyler as *The Mirror of Princely Deeds and Knighthoods*. There are also jokes about him in *The Knight of the Burning Pestle*.

335. *this.* Erroneously for 'thy', though the change could be justified by the captain gesturing towards Philander.

336. *Murriay.* Erroneously for the 'murrions' (a simple military helmet) of earlier editions.

340–1. *this Stand Of Royal Blood*. Since the captain appears to be referring to himself, 'loyal' would be more appropriate than 'royal'. A stand was a kind of barrell.

346. *Hylas*. A boy beloved by Hercules, when he sailed with the Argonauts, who was stolen from him by water nymphs.

347. *Scarlets*. Wearers of scarlet robes of office.

348. *gam'd Goles*. An obscure phrase in *Philaster* made even more obscure in *The Restauration*. The reference is to courtiers kissing their hands to the king. In *Philaster* the hands are 'Gum'd' (i.e. perfumed). The replacement, 'gam'd', indicates crippled (as in 'gammy leg').

349. *navigable*. Like a sea or strait.

351. *this Man sleeps*. Either Thrasomond or the king dies.

355–6. Replacing thirteen lines of intricate Jacobean wit from Thrasomond, who is again reduced to a poltroon, to be addressed at l. 357 as 'thee' rather than the original 'you'.

360. *Sursingle*. A strap, particularly the girth-strap of a saddle, but here apparently for a strap used to confine a falcon.

361. *make*. Returning *79fc*'s 'male' to the reading of the early editions; but to 'male' (cover with a hood) was a valid piece of hawking terminology (Gurr, p. 112).

364. *watching*. As a hawk was tamed by being prevented from sleeping.

371. *Die with this*. Play dice with this money (which he gives them). In *Philaster*, 'Drink this'.

376. *Pewter*. Their armour. The fact that they wore it together with helmets (murrions) indicates that they were the Trained Bands, not an undisciplined rabble. Beaumont had earlier poked fun at this body in *The Knight of the Burning Pestle*, V. ii.

377. *in Muffs*. Gurr identifies this as a new winter fashion in Beaumont and Fletcher's time. Muffs are often mentioned as being worn by prostitutes.

378.1. Another unmarked scene change, this time back to the palace.

480. *Murderer*. In the superstititous sense that, having killed her, he has taken on her appearance.

524–34. The omission of the tender opening to Euphrasia's speech, describing her first encounter with Philaster, reflects a general tendency in the revision away from lyrical evocation of interiority to an externalized representation of the 'passions' through their outward physical signs.

500. Cleon is given an exit here in *15wgv* although he still has lines to deliver. At the corresponding point in *79fc* he threatens to kill himself.

558. *Without an Heir*. Remedied in Settle's version by marrying Euphrasia to Thrasiline.

*Epilogue*

5. *every Plot.* Among others the Popish Plot, the Meal Tub Plot, and the Rye House Plot. Cf. note to l. 3 of the Epilogue to *The Rehearsal*, p. 694 above.

6. *with their Elbows.* As used for jostling others aside.

13. *Five Years wrong.* A personal apology for Buckingham's period of adherence to the Whig cause?

15. *there was one.* The Whig leader and Buckingham's former political colleague, Anthony Ashley Cooper, first Earl of Shaftesbury.

19–20. *Popery . . . Pope.* Anticipating Burke's quip that the French reformers of the revolutionary period had 'learnt to talk against monks with the spirit of a monk'.

23–31. Alluding initially to Dryden's *Absalom and Achitophel*, in which Achitophel represented Shaftesbury. The reference reveals no resentment over the rough handling of Buckingham as Zimri in that poem. The 'most egregious of all Scribes' need not necessarily be Dryden, but could represent some author who had been hired by Shaftesbury to defend him against Dryden's attack. One possibility would be Elkanah Settle, whose *Absalom Senior* was in print by 6 April 1682 (text in *POAS-Yale*, iii. 106–73). *Heraclitus ridens* of 10 January 1682 alleges that Settle had agreed to write the poem for 'a few guineas'. Buckingham is himself praised in it at ll. 1290–1307. In this case 'egregious' and 'have a just Renown' would need to be taken ironically. However, the simplest reading of these lines is as a defence of Shaftesbury against the inaccuracy of Dryden's portrait (l. 24), a justification of his 'true Admirers' (ll. 25–6), and an accusation that Dryden's poem had been commissioned by an unspecified lord (the Earl of Mulgrave?) for 10 guineas. The ambiguity of the passage is no doubt carefully calculated.

30–1. *matchless pair.* The 'matchless pair', resembling Beaumont and Fletcher themselves in their division of labour, would here be Dryden and his unnamed patron.

32. *when hence he ran.* Shaftesbury had died in exile in Holland on 21 January 1683.

## Untitled Play Fragment ['Theodorick']

*Act I*

10. *great beseigers . . . campe.* The camp of the Ostrogoths under Theomirus.

22. *Totilas.* For this and other names, see the Introduction, p. 560ff.

30. *a warlike Nation.* The Ostrogoths or eastern Goths, who were encouraged by the Byzantines to migrate into Italy and ruled it until, after the death of Theodoric, they were conquered in their turn by the Byzantine generals Belisarius and Narses.

76. *theyr cheife citty.* Toulouse (see the Introduction, p. 561ff).

79. *my owne secretary.* The historical Theodoric employed Cassiodorus in this role. Possibly an allusion to Cowley's work as a messenger for the exiled court. Buckingham had been his patron since their Cambridge years.

89. *Amalazonta.* The 'z' spelling, only used once, may have been meant to suggest 'Amazon'. Chapters 7–9 of Jordanes' history (Grotius, 619–23) are concerned with the Amazons, whom he regarded as Goths.

91. *our owne Ister.* The Danube.

97. *Pannonian.* Referring to the region of modern Hungary, from which the wandering Ostrogoths, having beaten off the Huns, launched their assaults on Thrace and later Italy.

117. *negations.* Cf. Hobbes, *Leviathan*, I. iii: 'Whatsoever we imagine, is *Finite*. Therefore there is no Idea, or conception of anything we call *Infinite*. . . . When we say any thing is infinite, we signifie onely that we are not able to conceive the ends, and bounds of the thing named; having no Conception of the thing, but of our own inability' (ed. C. B. Macpherson (Harmondsworth: Penguin, 1968), 99).

120–30. These lines, as well as being appropriate to the sundered Gothic nation, are clearly applicable to the political situation of Britain during the Interregnum and by extension to Buckingham's wooing of Mary Fairfax.

128. *2 iust tallyes of one nation.* An agreement or loan in early times was often sealed by the breaking of a token, with one half retained by each party.

143. *stygian.* As if sworn on the Styx, the principal river of the classical underworld. Zeus made his most sacred oaths in this way.

152. *Odoacer.* Ruler of Italy from 476 to 493, when he was finally overcome and killed by Theodoric. He rose to power with the support of Germanic troops in the service of the empire.

158. *Eugubin the great Astrologer.* Either a mistake or a joke. The Eugubine or Iguvine tables were seven carved tablets in Etruscan script discovered at Gubbio (Lat. Iguvium) in 1444. They were not deciphered until 1841, when it was established that their language was Umbrian, a relative of Latin, and their content liturgical. The fame of the Etruscans as soothsayers had encouraged earlier speculation that they contained prophecies.

163. *a great Roman Lady.* A possible allusion to an offer made by Charles II late in 1659 to marry Rome-born Hortense Mancini, which was declined by her uncle, Cardinal Mazarin. She was later to be Charles's mistress. The historical Theodoric married a Frankish princess. The reference hints at a plot twist invovling Eudoxia, though its nature is undeterminable.

164–5. The historical Theodoric established the empire exactly as predicted, though in deference to Byzantine sensibilities he used the title 'rex' (king) rather than emperor.

168. *the easterne emperour*. Zeno, Gibbon's 'base Isaurian', who reigned from 474 to 491. He encouraged the Ostrogoths to expand into Italy in order to divert their attention from Greece.

175. *Into the Gaules*. Southern France was then under the control of Visigoth invaders from Spain, who had established their capital in Toulouse in 412. The writer places the scene of the action in this region.

176. *Those other powerfull Nations of the Goths*. A number of lesser Germanic tribes had attached themselves to the Visigoths and Ostrogoths but only those two counted as powerful. Victory over Euric would unite the Goths against Odoacer.

196. *monasterye*. If the author is thinking of seventeenth-century Toulouse rather than ancient Tolosa, the reference may be to the impressive medieval monastery of the Augustinians, now a museum.

197–8. *the westerne suburbs | That ly upon the River*. Old Toulouse (Tolosa) stood on the right (eastern) bank of the Garonne, with its western suburbs closest to the water.

259. *prophecyes*. See ll. 156–61.

283–5. *Count of Narbonne . . . Patrician Roman*. Narbonne had been a Roman colony since 118 BCE.

358. *was come to free and serve*. This was certainly the ideal of Theodoric, who prevented the Goths from oppressing their Roman fellow subjects and tolerated their heretical Trinitarianism (as he regarded it).

369–70. *on this side | The River*. The Ostrogoths are imagined as attacking from the west or Spanish direction.

420. *Valentinian the Emperour*. See the Introduction, p. 558ff.

441. *vicus albus*. Literally the white village, perhaps meant to suggest the modern Albi, north-east of Toulouse, after which the Albigensians were named.

*Act II*

0.1. *a Tent hung with mourning, and a rich herse in it*. See the Introduction, p. 558.

7. *the three mills*. Again suggesting that the author has a remembered topography in mind. 'Les trois moulins' is a common French place name.

24–5. *our youngest ioy . . . murthered*. Possibly an allusion to Buckingham's younger brother, Francis Villiers, who died fighting against the Parliamentarians on 7 July 1648.

27. *inhumane passage*. Unhistorical. Odoacer's generally temperate rule (476–93) anticipated the conciliatory policies of Theodoric. An allusion may be intended to Cromwell's oppression of Ireland.

# Transmissional Histories

## THE CHANCES

Fletcher's play was first printed in *Comedies and Tragedies written by Francis Beaumont and John Fletcher* (London, 1647), henceforth *47ct*. Fowler has established that it was this edition, not the second folio of 1679, that was Buckingham's source.[1] The standard scholarly edition is that of George Walton Williams in *The Dramatic Works in the Beaumont and Fletcher Canon*, gen. ed. Fredson Bowers (Cambridge: Cambridge University Press, 1966–96), iv. 541–645. Buckingham's revision first appeared as a quarto (Wing F1338) dated 1682.

THE | CHANCES, | A | COMEDY: | 𝔄𝔰 𝔦𝔱 𝔴𝔞𝔰 𝔄𝔠𝔱𝔢𝔡 | AT THE | THEATER ROYAL. | [rule 114 mm] | Corrected and Altered by a PERSON | of HONOUR. | [rule 115 mm] | *LONDON,* | Printed for *A. B.* and *S. M.* and Sold by | *Langley Curti<lig.>s* on *Ludgate Hill*, 1682.

Foolscap 4⁰: *A*² B—I⁴ $2 (–*A*1, *A*2)

Pag. [4] 1–9, 15, 11–14, 10, 16–63, [1]

*A*1ʳ tp *A*1ᵛ blank *A*2ʳ PROLOGUE. *A*2ᵛ blank B1ʳ [double rule 117 mm] The Chances. [single rule 117 mm] ACT I. SCENE I. [single rule 117 mm] I4ʳ EPILOGUE. I4ᵛ blank

S. M. is Samuel Magnes, who, on the evidence of publication dates, seems to have acquired ownership of a body of Beaumount and Fletcher copyrights around 1680 jointly with Richard Bentley. The pair were also responsible for the second edition of *The Chances* in 1692 (Wing 1339) and the fourth edition of *The Rehearsal* in 1683. Since no 'A. B.' then operating in the trade is a plausible suspect, it is likely that the initials are an error for 'R. B.'. There is no *Stationers' Register* or *Term Catalogue* entry for the edition. Quarto reprints of 1692 (Wing F1339) and 1705 and the octavo of 1710 are without authority and their variants are not listed in the present edition.[2] The copy-text for the present edition is the Monash University Library copy of *Q1* (*Sw Pam. 820.3 F613 A6/C). This has been collated, using transparencies, with Bodleian Library Mal. 66(7); British Library 11773.g.8; Cambridge University Library Brett-Smith 988; Folger Shakespeare Library F1338; Harvard University,

---

[1] 'Chances', pp. 155–7.

[2] Fowler (p. 152) has established that *Q3* and *O1* were both set from *Q2* and *15wgv* from *Q3*. We concur in his judgement that *Q2* 'supplies no reading which suggests an independent source of authority'.

Houghton Library *EC.F6353.682c; Huntington Library D/F/1338/111967; and Yale University, Beinecke Library Ij B862 882c. The only press variant affecting text is a font-correction first noted by Fowler:

Sheet C, inner forme
*Corrected*: British Library, Cambridge, Monash, Yale
*Uncorrected*: Bodleian, Folger, Huntington
Cr$^v$, l. 20: and his] *and his*

It is surprising that a play that had been in the active repertory for nearly two decades should only at this late date have made its way to the press. One possibility is that the prior owners of the copyright in Fletcher's version had been unwilling to authorize an edition until after the publication of the 1679 second folio (Wing B1582); another possibility, not necessarily exclusive of the first, is that the quarto was a fund-raising activity by members of the King's Company, by then in terminal decline and deprived by retirement of the services of its Don John, Charles Hart, or even by Hart himself. However, the text, which is of good quality, gives no obvious signs of playhouse provenance and must therefore have been set from an independent manuscript (scribal or authorial) or, as Fowler proposes, a marked-up copy of *47ct* with MS supplementation.[3] The quarto has been carefully set and printed but lacks the usual preface and dedication or an author's name. Both omissions are explained by Buckingham's rank, in which he gave precedence only to dukes of the royal blood. In addition, at this crucial stage of his political career, he would hardly have wished to risk the damage that such a light-hearted publication might have done to his laboriously constructed status as an elder statesmen of the Whig cause. His name was first publicly associated with it by Gerard Langbaine in *Momus Triumphans* (London, 1688 [1687]), p. 8, who lists the title under Fletcher with a footnote: 'Altered by the Duke of Buckingham, and Printed in Quarto. Lond. 1682'. The duke's name appeared on the title page of the 1692 quarto in the form 'By his Grace the Duke of BUCKINGHAM; Author of the REHEARSAL'. Yet there is no reason to doubt that the edition appeared with his approval: it would have been a bold bookseller who would have risked the wrath of so powerful and vindictive a personage. In addition, Langley Curtis, the only stationer named on the title page, was himself a fervent Whig, publishing from a shop whose sign was the head of Sir Edmund Berry Godfrey, the Popish Plot martyr. Only the extent of Buckingham's personal involvement in the publication process remains uncertain.

*Emendations to Copy-text*

Dramatis Personæ. *From 1692 with substantive corrections*    Naples] Bolognia        Boy.] ~.
| Peter Vecchio *a Teacher of Latin and Musick, a reputed Wizard. [deleted because the character is omitted    from    the    Buckingham    version]*    Mother. . .Constantia]    *Bawd Characters not listed in 1692 have been added by the editors in angle brackets.*

---

3 Pp. 156–7, 159–60. We accept that the play was probably composed in this way but doubt that this was the form of the actual printer's copy.

I. ii. 5 Too] To        38–9 everlasting | Ruine, yet] everlasting ruine, | Yet
I. iii. 14 play.] ~'        25–6 Peace: | Goodnight] Peace: goodnight
I. vi. o.1 SCENE] ~.        36 leave] <*turned* l>eave
I. vii. 1 home: I] ~: | ~        3 him:] ~' <*space before 'to'*>        5 Leaks] Laks        26 Into]
        into        29 takes you] takes | You
I. viii. 14 cry] try
I. ix. 82 Nurses.] ~ ₳        98 *Exit.*] *Exit*₳
I. x. o.1 SCENE] ~.        20 Ocean,] ~.        38 in't: What's] ~: | ~
I. xi. 47 ye.] ~,

II. i. 21 *Petr.*] *Peter.*        67–8 Infantry, | A] Infantry, a        104 him.] ~,        116–17 her?
        | What] her? what        128 *Jo.* I] I        133 *Fre.*] *Free.*
II. ii. o.1 SCENE] ~.        17a.1 *Enter*] *Fnter*        30 *Fred.*] *Pred.*        40 Meditations.] ~₳
        77 Now may] Nowmay        83 honest, this] honest, | This        99 *SD*
        *marginal at 100 following 'there?'*        100 there? Stand] ~ [*Knock within.* | ~
        102–3 without, would speak | With] without, | Would speak with        108 How]
        *Fred.* ~        135–6 for't: | How] for't: how        143 me first:] me: first
        155 not, nor] nor, not
II. iii. o.1 SCENE] ~.        71 slip.] ~₳

III. i. 37 (And as they say am] ₳~ ~ ~ ~ (~        77–8 me, | I'll] ~, ~        78–9 will. | Go] ~.
        ~        82 that I] ~ | ~        86 face] ~.        104 *Fre.* I] I        105 And] *Fre.* ~
        119 So, now] So, | Now
III. iv. 58–9 Gentlemen. | I] ~. ~        59 ye: May] ~: | ~        86 Face] ~.        92–99a *As*
        *prose in Q. Verse lineation editorial*        {93 Was] was        94 And] and
        96 Better] better        97 In] in        98–9 me | Consider] me consider}        102–
        37 *As prose in Q. Verse lineation editorial.*        {103 In] in        104 Just] just
        106 Her] her        110 So] so        116 As] as        119 Must] must
        120 Come] come        126 To] to        127 'Tis] 'tis        129 Where] where
        131 Let's] let's        132 Our] our        133 And] and        135 But] but
        136 We] we}        139–40 be | As] be as        141–2 any | Other] any other
III. v. o.1 SCENE] ~.

IV. i. 12 learn] learn
IV. ii. 29 Lady.] ~₳
IV. iii. 15.1 SD editorial
IV. iv. 28 by] hy        29 and] aud        65 lock] Iock        75 Sir,] ~.

V. i. 9 is—] ~₳
V. ii. 24 Ladyship] Ladyshp        47 hard — She'll] ~ — | ~        48 her. A] ~. | ~
V. iii. 2 she's] she₳s

Ambiguous hyphenation

No end-of-line hyphens in Q have been judged as possessing a word-dividing function;
however, the following end-of-line hyphens in the present edition occur within the line in Q:

III. v. 10–11 Master-piece  v. 14–15 Water-Devils  IV. iii. 73–4 down-right

## Sir Politick Would-be

*Editions Collated*

Brief descriptions are provided below of the two editions that have credible textual authority and that have consequently been collated. Although the small number of exemplars inspected precludes overambitious claims about ideal copies, in the editor's experience there seems little likelihood of unrecorded variation.

A. OEUVRES | MESLÉES | de M$^R$. | *DE* SAIN*T*-EVREMON*D*, | Publiées fur les Manuſcrits de l'Auteur. | TOME PREMIER. | A LONDRES, | Chez *JACOB TONSON* Marchand Libraire, | à *Grays-Inn-Gate.* | [rule: 52.5 mm] | M D CC V.

*Coll*: 4°, π² a–d⁴ A–3M⁴ 3N–3O²

In this first of two volumes, *Sir Politick Would-be* runs from sig. 2I4$^r$ to sig. 2X4$^v$, and is therefore paginated [251–2] 253–348. The 'ERRATA du premier Tome' are listed on sig. d4$^v$.

The copy examined at the National Library of Australia (RBq/CLI/3694) was formerly in the collection of the Cliffords of Ugbrooke. The copy reproduced in the Finch and Joliat facsimile edition is not identified.

B. [in black and red] OEUVRES | DE MONSIEUR | DE | SAINT-EVREMOND, | Publiées fur fes Manuſcrits, | AVEC | LA VIE | DE L'AUTEUR; | PAR MR. DES MAIZEAUX | *Membre de la Societé Royale.* | Quatriéme Edition, revûë, corrigée & augmentée. | Enrichie de Figures gravées par B. Picart le Romain. | TOME SECOND. | [orn. with allegorical figures representing the arts and sciences—50 × 74 mm] | *A AMSTERDAM,* | Chez CÓVENS & MORTIER. | M. DCC. XXVI.

*Coll*: 12°, *² A–T¹² V⁸

In this second volume of five, *Sir Politick Would-be* runs from sig. I6$^r$ to sig. Q5$^r$ and is paginated [203] 204–369. The leaf with the engraved plate representing the end of IV. iv is inserted between I6 and I7, facing page 205.

Two copies were examined: British Library 95.k.7 (from the King's Library) and Harris Manchester College, Oxford Y 1726/22 (2). In addition photocopies were consulted from copies at Harvard, the Library Company of Philadelphia, and the University of Texas, Austin.

W. K.

*Emendations to Copy-text*

Acteurs. 2 RICHE-SOURCE] RICHE-SOURCE    *d'Affaires*ₐ] ~,          6 *Gascon*ₐ] ~,
15 TANCREDE] TANCRREDE

I. i. 52 ce] ee

I. ii. 4 facilement] faeilement

I. iii. 22n c'est-à-dire] c'est-à dire          72 Bosnie] Bossine          80-1 pour les retraites, &
un principalement] *om.*
I. iv. 47 Nord!] ~ *l*

II. ii. 53-6 *copy-text has opening quotation marks at start of each new line*          {53 "Que] „ ~
devenir] de-/„ venir          54 besoin] „ ~          55 se] „ ~          la] „ ~          56 tout."]
~·ₐ}          73 Bosnie] Bossine
II. iv. 87 suffira] susfira          105.1 SIR POLITICK] MR. DE RICHE-SOURCE          152.1 RICHE]
RICHF

III. i. 30 nom] non
III. ii. 63 ont] out          98 Chefs-d'œuvres-là] Chefs-d'œuvres là          119 connu là] connu-
la
III. iii. 0.3 POLITICK.] ~,          26 blâmer] blâme
III. iv. 10 mais] mas          12 que] qne
III. vii. 14 de] des

IV. ii. 58 Vôtre] Vôttre
IV. iv. 19 *A*] A          58 *Montirandé*] *Montivande*

V. ii. 5 disent] disens

*Collation of Substantive Variants*

Copy-text: 1726
Collated text: 1705 (Errata list contains *corrected* readings)

*Acteurs.* 2 *d'Affaires*ₐ *François*] *ed*; *d'Affaires*ₐ François *05sp*; ~, ~ *26sp*          6 *Gascon*ₐ] *ed*;
Gasconₐ *05sp*; ~, *26sp*

I. i. 0.2 *note marginal and in italics in 05sp*          {Le] *Le dernier 05sp*          Voyez . . . 1662.] *om.*
*05sp*}          26 compte] conte *05sp*          28 de quoi] dequoi *05sp*
49 à] un fort *05sp*          58 comptéₐ] conté, *05sp*
I. iii. 14 que j'ai faites] miennes *05sp*          17 &] comme aussi *05sp*          22 *note marginal and*
*in italics in 05sp*          {FOX; (c'est-à-dire, LE RENARD)] *FOX, 05sp*}          23 mal-
habile-homme] mal-habile homme *05sp*          67 surprend?] ~! *05sp*          72 Bosnie]
*ed.*; *Bossine 05sp*; Bossine *26sp*          78 dirai] ~ à vous *05sp*          80-1 pour les
retraites, & un principalement] *05sp*; *om. 26sp*          95 qu'ils] qu'il *05sp*          99 vais]
vai *05sp*          101 ça] ç'a *05sp*          112 considere] ~ encore *05sp*          123 foible, je
donne ordre] foible; Ordre *05sp*          130 II!] *II. 05sp*          135 guerre] Guerre, *05sp*
I. iv. 30 avez] ~, je m'assûre, *05sp*          103 délicatement] ~ cela *05sp*          104 non] ~ pas
*05sp*          116.1 *seul*] *après que* TANCREDE *est parti 05sp*          123 ferois bien de
n'avoir] ne veux *05sp*

II. i. 46 Enfin,] Tant y a, que *o5sp*    73 brutaux] Brutaux-là *o5sp*    sortie] Sourtie
*o5sp*    75 Ah] Jesus *o5sp*    77 compte] conte *o5sp*    82 mais] ~, à dire
vrai, *o5sp*    collet] coullet *o5sp*    87 le] mon *o5sp*    88 fut] sut *o5sp*
102 Par-Dieu] Par-/bieu *o5sp*    110 m'oubliger] m'obliger *o5sp*
112 Paris.] *Paris?* *o5sp*    128 j'allai] je vins *o5sp*    166 a fait] en a usé *o5sp*

II. ii. 10 quelques] quelque *o5sp*    25 de quoi] dequoi *o5sp*    31 *une*] *un o5sp*
49 qu'ensuite] qu'en suite *o5sp*    53–6 *quoted passage in italics without quotation
marks o5sp*    68 *faire*] *foire o5sp*    73 Bosnie] *ed.*; Bossine *o5sp*, *26sp*
102 d'un] ~ si *o5sp*

II. iv. 20 Cheronée] *1705 adds marginal note 'De la Version d'*Amyot'.    87 suffira] *o5sp*;
susfira *26sp*    105.1 SIR POLITICK] *o5sp*; MR. DE RICHE-SOURCE *26sp*
152 secret.] Secret. Adieu. *o5sp*

III. i. 7 Vous] Par-Dieu vous *o5sp*    22 Couyouneries] Couyonneries *o5sp*    30 nom]
*ed.*; non *o5sp*, *26sp*

III. ii. 63 ont] *o5sp*; out *26sp*    76 compter] conter *o5sp*    119 connu là] *o5sp*; connu-
la *26sp*    137 choses] ~ dignes *o5sp*    152 *note omitted in o5sp*
159 on] il *o5sp*    184–5 Statuës] Estatuës *o5sp*    209 civilité] Civilité;
beaucoup *o5sp*    229 creveriez] ~, morbieu! *o5sp*    262 Ce] le *o5sp*
274 petites] petite *o5sp*

III. iii. 25 compte] conte *o5sp*    26 blâmer] *o5sp*; blâme *26sp*

III. iv. 10 mais] *o5sp*; mas *26sp*    35 Des] Ces *o5sp*    65 dès] dez *o5sp*    76 que]
*om. o5sp*    88 Dès] Dez *o5sp*

III. v. 9 femmes des] Femmes de *o5sp*    48 mesure] mesures *o5sp*    56 courtoise]
courtoisie *o5sp-uncorr*

III. vii. 2 fait le] fait, *o5sp*    Mylord] ~ *Tancrede o5sp*    11-12 *Beau-Monde*] beau
Monde *o5sp*    14 de] *o5sp*; des *26sp*    27 Le Mylord] Mylord *Tancrede o5sp*

IV. i. 1 se] *om. o5sp-uncorr*    19 le Mylord] Mylord *Tancrede o5sp*    64.1 MARQUIS,
*à* L'ALLEMAND] MARQUIS *o5sp*

IV. ii. 5 mais] *om. o5sp-uncorr*    6 trouverez] trouvrez *o5sp*    26 son] *om. o5sp*
59 *loger dans les cûrs*] *not in italics in o5sp*    70 Bal?] ~. *o5sp*

IV. iii. 11 *loger . . . Palais*] *not in italics in o5sp*    12 *enrichit . . . zele*] *not in italics in o5sp*
12-13 *garnit de fidelité*] *not in italics in o5sp*    22-3 *mis aux pieds*] *not in italics in o5sp*
24 magnifique] manifique *o5sp*
IV. iv. 0.5–0.6 LES DEMOISELLES *se disant*] & *les* FILLES *faisant les o5sp*
12 avant] ~ que *o5sp*    16 voudroit me] me voudroit *o5sp*    58 *Montirandé*] *ed.*;
*Montivandé o5sp*; *Montivande 26sp*    87 dansez] dancerez *o5sp*    112 la petite
Suzon] *la Petite Suzon o5sp*    116 y] n'y *o5sp*    119 Mesdames.] ~? *o5sp*

IV. v. 10 eu] ~ le *o5sp*    55 Adieu] ~, Madame *o5sp*    62 toute] tout *o5sp*

V. i. 0.3 AGOSTINO] LES QUATRE SENATEURS, ~ *o5sp*    AZARO] ASARO *o5sp*
60 dis-je.] ~? *o5sp*

V. ii. 3 ils . . . ils] ils . . . il *o5sp*    24 à] a *o5sp-uncorr*    46 ils] il *o5sp*

V. iii. 36 falloit] saloit *o5sp*

V. v. 13 pourrons] ~. Adieu *o5sp*

## The Country Gentleman

This play survives only in Folger V.b. 228, a scribal manuscript probably made about a quarter-century after the suppression of the play in 1669. For description of the manuscript and the textual policy adopted with regard to it, see the Introduction (p. 254). Here we supply merely a list of corrections of obvious errors and a few editorially supplied stage directions.

I. 99 *aside*] *eds.*      247 Ladyship's] La^p      336.2 Philadelphia] Philadelpha
340 Worthy, and] ~, & and      355 *aside*] *eds.*

II. 21 now] ~ now      29 What] W      39 *aside*] *eds.*      44 *aside*] *eds.*
55 Slife] Slifle      69 *heares*] hearers      121–2 cast | whores]
castwhores      189 daughters] daugters      419 utmost] ut most
517 *exit* Finical] *eds.*

III. 110 you a] you      154 *Empty*] *the copyist wrote 'S^r Rich' and then wrote*
*'Empty' above it and 'Emp' beside it.*      198 This is] This
265 contrive] continue      272 Trouble] trouble      300 should] shou
329 you] *careted in a later hand*      427 had as] had a      494.1 *Enter*
Trim] *eds.*      515 *exeunt* Mrs. Finical *and* Trim] *eds.*      558 did it] did
655 *Exeunt* Sir Richard *and* Trim.] *eds.*      695 our Gloves] our by loves
*eds. (see Explanatory Note)*      696–697.1 *not written as a couplet in the MS,*
*but with s.d. bracketed to the right*

IV. 47 intelligibly] properly *cancelled, with 'intelligibly' written beside it*
125–6 to be] to      126 *exit Trim.*] *eds.*      252 a long] along
272 the] they      280 Servant] Serant      292 we] why
317 him on] on      414 preservd] preserd      418 'em.] 'em_∧
469 Mistress] M^r      599 then] them

V. 16 *exit* Finical.] *eds.*      83 *Vap.* Friend!] Friend!      90 dance and]
dance      124 *Exit* Finical] *eds.*      201 your] you      217 And] An
298 *MS has redundant speech tag after s.d.*      336 forget] for get      476–
7 *To* Cautious *and* Empty] *eds.*

*Record of indeterminate copy-text end-of-line hyphenation*
I. 18 extraordinary] extra-|ordinary
II. 227 constitutions] consti-|tutions
V. 361 word-breaking] word-|breaking

*Record of indeterminate edition end-of-line hyphenation*
III. 486–7 sea-|coal] sea-coal
V. 361–2 word-|breaking] word-|breaking

## The Rehearsal

As has already been made clear, the versions of *The Rehearsal* which are of primary interest are those contained in the first edition (*Q1*) of 1672 (Wing B5324) and the heavily revised third edition (*Q3*) of 1675 (Wing B5326). *Q2* (1673) contains two short added passages and some minor corrections. The other lifetime editions, *Q4* (1683) and *Q5* (1687), and the first posthumous edition, *Q6* (1692), have been freshly collated for this edition; but, since in the judgement of the editors their variant readings are entirely of compositorial origin, their variants have not been listed in our apparatus, and are only referred to in a handful of cases where they supply an interesting speculative correction. An extensive, though not complete, listing of the *Q4–5* variants is available for consultation in the apparatus of D. E. L. Crane's edition.[4] Crane's conclusion, with which we concur, is that the post-1675 text is 'almost entirely stable, though with some sophistication' (p. xv). *Q4* and *Q6* are both set from *Q3*. *Q5* is set from *Q4*.

The present edition differs from all its modern predecessors by taking *Q1* as its copy-text rather than *Q3*. The 1675 additions and revisions are given at the foot of the page, where they can easily be consulted and in a type size that facilitates eye movement between the main text and the undertext. Our reading text is, therefore, the earliest performed version, not the subsequent *textus receptus*. One reason for adopting this course was uncertainty over responsibility for the 1675 revisions (a matter already raised): in a text meant to appear as part of an edition of Buckingham there was a clear case for preferring the version likely to contain the highest proportion of his unaided work; but we also maintain that the earlier version was more effective as a script for the theatre than the 1675 one. By no means all the additions match the wit and inventiveness of the original and in a modern stage performance *Q1* would be the least likely of the two to outstay its welcome. In addition scholarly readers, for whom this edition is primarily intended, will get a clearer sense of the evolution of the work by reading forward from the *Q1* to the *Q3* version of passages than they would have done by being forced to attempt the more difficult reverse process. Both our choice of source text and the way in which the variants are presented are meant to facilitate a direct apprehension of the process of change across the three substantive editions. A final reason for preferring *Q1* is Greg's principle of privileging the source which was most likely to preserve the author's accidentals.[5] While this was not our main reason for choosing as we did, it does allow us to retain distinctive spellings which may prove to have attributional significance for this collaborative and highly contested work. Readings from *Q2* and

---

[4] George Villiers, Duke of Buckingham, *The Rehearsal*, ed. D. E. L. Crane (Durham: University of Durham), 67–76.

[5] W. W. Greg, 'The Rationale of Copy-Text', *Studies in Bibliography*, 3 (1950–1), 19–36 and *Collected Papers* (Oxford: Clarendon Press, 1966), 374–91.

*Q3* have been introduced to the edited text only when they were clear corrections of errors in *Q1*.

*Q1* was published by the bookseller Thomas Dring, a leading play-publisher of the time whose name also appears on all the other quartos except the fourth, which was published by Richard Bentley and Samuel Magnes, the publishers of *The Chances*. The printer, identified only as 'J. M.', may have been the experienced play printer John Macock or the illustrious Joseph Moxon. We have been unable to find other work bearing the distinctive title page ornament (see the facsimile of the title page at p. 335). The edition was entered in the Stationers' Register to Thomas Dring and William Cademan on 19 June[6] and is listed in the Term Catalogue for Trinity Term, published on 24 June 1672. As one would expect from Buckingham's elevated position in the state at the time of publication, the setting was done with respectful care. The composition is virtually free from obvious errors and shows a high level of competence in its distinguishing of verse passages from prose and its indentation of stage directions, a number of which have been given an inverted pyramidal shape (an effect retained in the present edition). If these were features of the manuscript, carefully imitated by the printer, that manuscript must have been the work of a skilled professional scribe. Presswork and choice of paper stock were done with less care, with the result that most surviving copies are disfigured by bleedthrough. The compositor (there is no evidence that more than one was used) worked with a high level of fidelity from a manuscript written by a scribe with a preference for the unusual spelling 'papyr' for 'paper' (nine instances spread across all five acts). That this is not a compositorial spelling is suggested by the enormous LION electronic archive, which contains no examples at all from other seventeenth-century printed plays and only four from poetry, all of which are pre-1650. The collation is as follows.

THE | REHEARSAL, | As it was Acted at the | Theatre-Royal. | [rule 112 mm] | [Triangular orn. 34 mm by 34 mm] | [rule 114 mm] | *LONDON,* | Printed for *Thomas Dring,* at the *White-Lyon,* | next *Chancery-lane* end in *Fleet- | ſtreet.* 1672.

Foolscap 4°: *A*² B–H⁴ $2 (–*A*1, *A*2)

Pagination: [4] 1–50, 53, 51, 52, 54 [2]

*A*1ʳ tp; *A*1ᵛ blank; *A*2ʳ PROLOGUE. *A*2ᵛ The Actors Names. B1ʳ [row of 26 printer's flower ornaments 115 mm] | THE | REHEARSAL. | [rule 110 mm] H4ʳ EPILOGUE. | H4ᵛ blank

Page numbers are central at the top within curved brackets. There are no page headlines.

[6] *A Transcript of the Registers of the Worshipful Company of Stationers; from 1640–1708,* 3 vols. (London: privately printed, 1913–14), ii. 444.

The following copies were compared for press variants, using either letter-by-letter comparison or coloured transparencies laid on the pages: British Library (1) 11773.e.15, (2) C 34.i.1 and (3) 841.d.8 [H4 supplied from 8th edn., 1711]; Bodleian Library Malone 123(1); Cambridge University Library Brett-Smith 991; Folger Library B5323; Houghton Library, Harvard University EC65 B8565 672r; Huntington Library 131122; University of Leeds, Brotherton Collection Lt BUC; Beinecke Library, Yale University Ij B852 672.

Only one press variant affecting text was found.
Sheet F: inner forme
*Corrected:* BL1, BL3, Bodleian, CUL, Folger, Huntington, Leeds
*Uncorrected:* BL2, Yale
F2ᵛ line 35    Enter] Entes

The second edition, which appeared in the following year, incorporated some minor corrections and two significant additions.

THE | REHEARSAL, | As it was Acted at the | Theatre-Royal. | [rule 111 mm] | [Triangular ornament 34 mm by 34 mm] | [rule 110 mm] | *LONDON,* | Printed for *Thomas Dring,* at the *White-Lyon,* | next *Chancery-lane* end in *Fleet-* | *ſtreet.* 1673.
     Foolscap 4°: *A*² B–H⁴ $2 (–*A*1, *A*2)
     Pagination: [4] 1–54 [2]
*A*1ʳ tp; *A*1ᵛ blank; *A*2ʳ PROLOGUE. *A*2ᵛ The Actors Names. B1ʳ [row of 20 ornaments 109 mm] | THE | REHEARSAL | [rule 112 mm] H4ʳ EPILOGUE. | H4ᵛ blank
     Page headline: *The Rehearsal.*

The title page ornament and typography are the same as those used for the first edition but the page is definitely a resetting. This edition is represented by Monash University Library 820.4 A . . . 2 PLA v. 9. Variants have been checked against Harvard *EC65 B8565/672rb.
     The third edition of 1675 (*TC* of 15 February 1675), set from a marked-up *Q2* and additional MS leaves, offers a revised text incorporating very numerous interpolations and revisions.

THE | REHEARSAL, | As it is now Acted at the | Theatre-Royal. | [rule 112 mm] | The third Edition with Amendments and | large Additions by the Author. | [rule 111 mm] | *LONDON,* | Printed for *Thomas Dring,* at the *Harrow* at the | Corner of *(hancery-lane* in *Fleet-* | *ſtreet,* 1675.
[Note: The first letter of 'Chancery' is an initial bracket, not a capital C.]
     Foolscap 4°: *A*² B–H⁴ I² $2 (–*A*1, *A*2, *I*2)
     Pagination: [4] 1–27, 27–8, 30–1, 31, 33–59, 60

*A*1ʳ tp; *A*1ᵛ blank; *A*2ʳ PROLOGUE. *A*2ᵛ *The Aɛtors Names.* B1ʳ  THE |
Rehearſal. | [rule 113 mm] I2ᵛ EPILOGUE.

The text was in this case rather carelessly set, though an attempt was made to preserve the patterned typography of the earlier editions. Some of the edition's many
indifferent variants are likely to be errors.

In establishing a text for the sections of *Q3* reproduced in our apparatus, we
have been guided by Crane's collations of nine copies, which identified press
correction in Sigs A/I inner and outer and F outer.[7] Crane did not, however, list
the actual variants as they were not of significance for the establishment of the text.
We have recollated two of his copies—National Library of Scotland and Folger
B5326, copy 2—which between them contain all three variant states, and an additional  copy from the Macdonald Collection in the Fisher Library of the University of Sydney. Variants and additions have also been proofread against Harvard
University, Houghton Library *EC65 B8565 672rc and Beinecke Library, Yale University, Yale Plays 389, a copy formerly owned by the Restoration beauty Grace
Anstruther. The variants are as follows. Since they do not refer to the copy-text,
they are identified by their *Q3* page lineation, counting down from the first line of
text.

Half-sheet A, outer forme [A1ʳ, A2ᵛ]
*Corrected:* Macd., NLS
*Uncorrected:* Folger2
A1ʳ Amendments] a mendments
    *Wrong fount 'A' replaced in 'Author'*
A2ᵛ Cordelio] *Cordelie*
Half-sheet A, inner forme [A1ᵛ, A2ʳ]
    *Corrected*: Macd., NLS
    *Uncorrected*: Folger2
A2ʳ 18 whom] whome
Half-sheet I, outer forme [I1ʳ, I2ᵛ]
    *Corrected*: Macd., NLS
    *Uncorrected*: Folger2
I1ʳ 6 boast] bost        14 make] moke        25 your] you        37 *Bayes*] *Baes*
I2ᵛ 11 presage] pres     19 Influence] Iefluence        20 this prove] thisprove
Half-sheet I, inner forme
    *Corrected:* Macd., NLS
    *Uncorrected*: Folger2
I2ʳ 4 proud] pround      9 good‚] ~,        11 afternoon] after noon        16 care
    I] care 1
I1ᵛ 26 away] a way

7 See Crane, pp. xv–xvi, 69.

Sheet F, outer forme
  *Corrected*: Folger2, Macd.
  *Uncorrected*: NLS
F2ᵛ 2 upon] unpon       5 It] I       6 I] It       14 fulſom] foulſom       17 be]
  ~ the          36 Lance] lance
F3ʳ 1 then, I'l] then I 1       18 B*ayes.*] ~ₐ       20 S*cholar*] Scholar
F4ᵛ 4 true] ttue

All these corrections appear to be proofreader's revises made without consultation of copy.
  As stated above, the text of *Q4* yields no evidence of authorial correction. However, at III. ii. 256 the words 'Fame and', which are present in *Q1*, *Q2*, *Q4* and *Q5*, are missing from *Q3* and *Q6*. This may represent either a correction to the copy of *Q3* used in the setting of *Q4* or indicate that the *Q4* compositor was preserving a currently unrecorded state of sig. F, outer forme of *Q3*. Our undertext contains a full record of the variants of *Q2* and *Q3*. The few editorial emendations to the text of *Q1* are also recorded in the separate list of 'Emendations to the copy-text'. Other relevant textual evidence is discussed in the explanatory notes.


*Editorial emendations to Q1*

The Actors Names 14–5 *Thimble.* | Shirley.] *Q4 addition*; *Thimble.*       24 Judges.] ~:

I. i. 121 Pliny,] *Comma sort upside down in Q.*

I. ii. 0.1 *New scene number editorial.*       7 1 *Play.*] 1.       49 understood.)] ~.ₐ
  150 Chestnut] Chesnunt       166 nimble. The] ~. | ~

II. i. 19 Physician] Physicians

II. v. 39 *Exeunt*] Exeumt

III. i. 13 gad. [*Reads*—] ] gad. [*Reads*— <*SD right justified*>       13–14 Enter . . . Taylor.]
  *On separate line with roman and italic reversed as if SD.*

III. ii. 26 went,] ~.       52 *Bayes.*] ~,       131 Lot,] ~.

IV. i. 48 two] to       104 *coffin.*] ] ~.ₐ | <*SD right justified in Q.*>       136 [*After a pause.*]] After a pause <*as if part of dialogue*>       145 your] you

V. i. 12–13 you, | Must] you, must       13–14 Son; | Let] Son; let       14–15 –*man* | First]
  –*man* first       15–16 preheminence, | In] preheminence, in       16–17 good, |
  May] good, may       145 *Johns.*] *John.*       220 let] Iet

V. ii. 0.1 *New scene editorial*       6.1 *The . . . Act* <*right justified in Q.*>

V. iii. 0.1 *New scene editorial.*       5.1 *Player*] Players again       19 good] ~,       34 2
  Play] 2 *Bayes*


*Editorial emendations to passages from Q3 quoted as undertext*

II. i. 87:0 Foppery.] ~,

II. ii. 26:1 but it] but [ ]t

II. iv. 17:23  *Bayes.* Pray] *Bayes* pray          39:4  *Johns.*] ~,
III. i. 81:7  Devil that] *Crane*; that Devil
III. ii. 201:4  *Smith.*] ~‸          232:21  ha; but] ha; hut
IV. ii. 73:2  scaning—] ~‸


*Record of indeterminate copy-text end-of-line hyphenation*

I. ii. 122  cannot] can-|not *Q1*
III. ii. 55  something] some-|thing *Q1*          232:14  Belly-ake] Belly-|ake *Q3*
IV. i. 82  winding-sheet] winding-|sheet *Q1*
V. i. 287.1–287.2  Hobby-|horses] Hobby-|horses *Q1*
V. iii. 34  Tyring-room] Tyring-|room *Q1*


*Record of indeterminate edition end-of line hyphenation*

I. i. 102–3  Table-|Book] Table-Book *Q1*          129–30  Play-|house] Play-house *Q1*
I. ii. 104–5  now-|a-days] now-a-days *Q1*
II. i. 4–5  some-|thing] something *Q1*          8–9  Gentle-|man-Usher] Gen-|tleman-Usher *Q1*
II. iv. 3–4  some-|times] sometimes *Q1*
III. ii. 167–8  *Knights-|bridge*] *Knights-bridge Q1*
IV. i. 48–9  Gentle-|men] Gentlemen *Q1*
V. i. 287.1–287.2  *Hobby-|horses*] *Hobby-|horses Q1*
V. iii. 14–15  cross-|grain'd] cross-grain'd *Q1*


## The Restauration: or, Right will Take Place

The only substantive source for the main text of this work is at i. 1–80 of the third edition of the *Miscellaneous Works*, which was published in 1715 by Samuel Briscoe as *The Works of his His Grace, George Villiers, Late Duke of Buckingham* (*15wgv*). The format is as follows:

Crown octavo in 8s and 4s: A⁸ B–E⁸ F–G⁴ H–M⁸ N⁴ O–Dd⁸

of which *The Restauration* occupies A1ʳ to G4ᵛ. There are engraved plates preceding A1 and following A8, G4, and K1, the second of which is a scene from *The Restauration*. The prologue and epilogue had earlier appeared in the 1704 *Miscellaneous Works* (*04mw*), i. 9–13. The version here given is that of *15wgv*. Because (1) the revision was so radical at the verbal level; (2) so much of the predecessor play was cut; and (3) many obvious corruptions were corrected, we cannot say with confidence which edition or editions of *Philaster* provided the textual basis for the revision. If Buckingham did indeed commence work after the collapse of his public career in the early 1680s, we would expect him to have used either the current edition of the quarto, Wing B1599 (*Dramatic Works Q8*), or its direct descendant,

*Fifty Comedies and Tragedies* (London, 1679), 21–40 (*79fc*), the first collected edition to contain the play. Sufficient variant readings originating in either *Q8* or *79fc* survive to suggest that one of these two was a primary source, though perhaps not the exclusive one.[8] These two texts also preserve a number of readings that originated in *Q4* (1634), including the striking '*Nemesis*' for 'the just gods' at I. i. 193. In cases where an error originating in *Q8* or *79fc* has been emended in *15wgv* so as to accord with an earlier edition, there is no way of telling whether this was done speculatively or through consultation. In most cases *Q8* and *79fc* also agree with the version in volume 1 of *The Works of Mr. Francis Beaumont, and Mr. John Fletcher* (London: Tonson, 1711) (*11wfb*), which was set from *79fc* but 'Revis'd and corrected' by Gerard Langbaine the younger. A case might be made for pages from *11wfb* having been marked up to serve as printer's copy for *15wgv*; but in our view the sheer density of change would have made this impractical. We assume that Buckingham's working draft took the form of a new manuscript, and that a further transcript may have been prepared to serve as press copy. After consideration, *79fc* has been chosen to represent the comparison text for the adaptation. Since there is very little substantive variation between the three late editions specified, the reader's understanding of the process of revision would not be significantly affected by a mistaken editorial choice. The 1715 edition is relatively free of obvious errors and seems to have been printed with some care.

The following copies have been compared for press variants: British Library 122 71 c 33 (*BL1*) and 1340 l 20 (*BL2*); Cambridge University Library 7000 d 410 (*C*); copy owned by Robert D. Hume (*H*); Bodleian Library Vet. A4 e 625 (*O*); Pennsylvania State University Library PR3328.B5 (*P*).

No variants affecting text were discovered. On C1ʳ the page number reads '71' in *BL2*, *C* and *O* and '17' in *BL1*, *H* and *P*. The plate of a scene from IV. i. following A8 is missing from *P*. A plate of Aphra Behn has been wrongly inserted following C6 in *BL1*.

The footnotes list all substantive variants between *15wgv* and *79fc*, including the complete text of extensive omitted passages; however, the changes made by Buckingham to the names of characters are not treated as substantive, meaning that they are only listed when they occur naturally as part of a larger phrasal variant. Nor, for this play, are changes to the wording of act and scene headings recorded. The act headings for *79fc* follow the pattern '*Actus primus. Scena prima.*'; those of *15wgv* 'ACT I. SCENE I.' There are no scene divisions in either case within the acts. It must be remembered that *79fc* differs in many readings from *Q2*, which is the copy-text for modern editions of *Philaster*. The present edition is not concerned with this earlier textual history except for its relevance to the determining of the immediate source text. Verse lines distributed between more than one

---

[8] For instance at I. i. 129 [also *Q7*], 222; I. ii. 114; II. iv. 184; IV. iv. 1, 3, 14; IV. vi. 106; V. iii. 138; V. iv. 39, 54, 106; and V. v. 34 (*Dramatic Works*, i. 515–40).

speaker have been supplied with the appropriate indentation. Any actual relineation of verse set as prose, of mislineated verse, or of prose set as verse is specified in the list of emendations to the copy-text, with a few dubious cases discussed in the Explanatory Notes. We have been concerned in these cases with Buckingham's presumed intentions, which in a number of cases probably differed from those of Beaumont and Fletcher, criteria for what constituted an acceptable verse line having become more rigorous by the 1680s than they were in Jacobean times. There have also been cases where we have judged that short passages scannable as verse but occurring in a prose context should be lineated as prose. Such decisions are unavoidably speculative and readers are under no obligation to observe them when their ears suggest better solutions.

As in the case of *The Chances* the lemma of the page footnotes is the reading of *15wgv*, which in cases where the text has been editorially emended will differ from that of the edition text. The immediately following list details all such emendations, other than those classified as silent in the General Introduction.

*List of editorial emendations*

*Prologue.* See Explanatory Notes, p. 579.

I. 4 Gentlemen] Gentleman        13 Kingdoms] Kingdom        18 especially]
especilaly        91–2 Sir, | Your] Sir, your        95 leave,] ~.        160 Veins.
The] ~. | ~        169 now he] now | He 170 Gentlemen, by] Gentlemen, | By
171 Name out] Name | Out        187 Commendations —] ~.
197 then] them        208 and] ~ and        230 *Cleon.* I] I        231 See] *Cleon.* ~
287–8 well. —— | What] ~. —— ~        405 him.] ~,        415–6 name | The] name the

II. 39 stay,] stay.        45 Trust₄] ~.        137 crossly] crosfly
141 undeserving] understanding        161.1 *Cloak.*] ~,        234 Gentlemen.] ~,

III. 32 best.] ~,        61 thought] thonght        181 off] of        423 of] ~ of

IV. 18 last] lasts        32 nothing] noting        54 or to the] or the to        58 himself!]
himself?        197 I'm] I' m        226–7 Madam? Is] ~ | ~        252 off] of
323.1 Adelard.] ~,        397–8 confess | The] confess the

V. 1 more.] ~₄        35 is't] Is't        39b–40a well. Are all | Things] ~ | ~ ~
things        163 World] Word        171 I'll] I ll        196 false] falfe
221 none.] ~:        253 Sir.] ~,        256–7 Caps swarm] Caps | Swarm        256–
73 *Mislineated as verse in 79fc*        257–8 Mother <|> Gibberish] ~ | ~
258 Mouths up] Mouths | Up        259 a Fathom] ~ | ~        260 Pepper, and]
Pepper, | And        *Philander*, let] *Philander*, | Let        261 Ding-dongs, my] Ding-
dongs, | My        262 Clubs, than] Clubs, | Than 263 Paintings spitted] Paintings |
Spitted        Silks, or] Silks, | Or        264 Tissues, dearly] Tissues, | Dearly
265 Custard, your] Custard, | Your        266 Affections in] Affections | In
Duckers, up] Duckers, | Up        267 Valours, and] Valours, | And
268 feel the] feel | The        269 *Philander*, cry] *Philander*, | Cry        272 Boys,
I] ~, | ~        272–3 Top-sails <|> to] Topsails | To        279 with] ~ with
297–8 himself, he] himself, | He        298 up with] up | With        299 see Heav'n]

~ | ~        300–1 you: | You] ~, ~        311–12 kills | As] kills as        315–6 Charge |
Build] Charge build        318–19 sound | Like] sound like        340 *Phœbus*] *Phœbus*
360 Sursingle] Surfiagle        365–6 Houses, | And] Houses, and        430–1 Winds |
Or] ~ ~        431 Seas than] Seas | Than        472–3 speakst | As] speakst as
475 Pilgrimage?] ~;        500 Woman.] ~. [*Exit.*        539 you,] you.

*Epilogue* 11  *not a shame*] not


*Record of indeterminate copy-text end-of-line hyphenation*

II. i. 233 nothing] no-|thing *15wgv*        IV. i. 58 cannot] can-|not *15wgv*        V. i. 270
Topsails] Top-|sails *15wgv*


*Record of indeterminate edition end-of-line hyphenation*

I. i. 160 Out-|landish] Out-landish  *15wgv*        V. i 290 Broad-|side] Broadside *15wgv*
323–4 Hand-|Sword] Hand-Sword


## UNTITLED PLAY FRAGMENT ['THEODORICK']

This incomplete, untitled blank-verse tragedy is entered on pages 1–37 *retro* of the
Jersey MS of the Commonplace Book and was recopied from that source into the
Princeton MS. It is not present in the Cowper (HALS) MS. The hand is that of
the scribe of the Commonplace Book, who was neither Clifford nor Buckingham.
The scribe had difficulty in determining the intended verse lineation, and at the
following places has entered verse speeches in unlineated or mislineated form:

I. i. 15–20a, 24–38, 40–42a, 46b–55, 57–72a, 76–7, 83–7, 90–112, 115–18, 168–9, 194b–5,
213–15, 225b–9, 235–6a, 245b–50, 252–3, 263–4, 267–8a, 269–70, 299–301, 303–6, 309–
11, 314–15, 325–6a, 346–7a, 370b–72, 389–91a, 394–5, 406–7a, 417–19, 437b–9, 454–5a,
460–61

Line division within these sections is editorial; however, MS majuscules and
minuscules have not been altered. Inconsistencies in speech prefixes are those of
the original; however, punctuation following SPs (frequently in the form of a
solidus) has been regularized to a full stop. Missing SPs have been supplied at lines
212 and 366. Abbreviations, except in stage directions, are silently expanded and
attendant stops of abbreviation, when present, silently suppressed. With the exception of a single substantive emendation in I. i. 395, other editorial change has been
restricted to the addition of final full stops in essential cases and the addition, or
modification, of a small number of other punctuation marks. All such changes are
listed below.

*Emendations to the copy-text*

I. 0.1 Actus . . . prima] Act: j: Sce: jᵃ  40 affection,] ~.  55 resolution.] ~ₐ
77 alarme,]  ~.  82 termes]  ~.  84 returne.]  ~ₐ
89 Amalazonta,] ~.  93 Arsames]  ~.  99 this)]  ~ₐ
106 hands.] ~ₐ  121 kingdome,] ~.  123 warre,] ~.  124 equall,]
~,] ~.  125 matchd,] ~.  138 zeale] ~.  147 it.] ~ₐ  150 tempest] ~.
152 Odoacer] ~.  178 us] ~.  181 proceed:] ~.  193 passion.] ~ₐ
211 myselfe.] ~ₐ  212 *Tot.* The] The  236 mee.] ~ₐ
245 composition.] ~ₐ  259 prophecyes.] ~ₐ  260 succeed.] ~ₐ
264 returne.] ~ₐ  268 so.] ~ₐ  278 Thorismond] Torismond *uncorr.*
284 Gaul)] ~.  295 yourselfe.] ~ₐ  298 declared;] ~.  306 Count.] ~ₐ
317.1 Eudoxia.] ~ₐ  330 Pannonia)] ~ₐ  333 dos.] ~ₐ  340 saying—
] ~ₐ  342 drownd] galld *uncorr.*  347 pleasd.] ~ₐ  353 freindship] ~.
354 Goths.] ~ₐ  366 *Capt.* May] May  387 passe.] ~ₐ  391 stayres.]
~ₐ  395 venture it] venture  398 River] ~.  418 *Eu.*] Eud. *uncorr.*
433 so] ~.  439 *Underlining   so   in   MS.*  447 prevaild.] ~ₐ
455 releife.] ~ₐ  465.2 Finis Actus primi] Fin: Act j

II. 15 Country.] ~ₐ  16 has] ~ envy has  22 promises)] ~ₐ  32 glory,]
~.  38 too,]  ~.  61 supplyed.]  ~ₐ  66 Hearse.]  ~ₐ
67 Theodorick!] ~ₐ  67.1 (Fredegond . . . herse)] ₐ ~ . . . ~ₐ

# Bibliography

This bibliography covers printed sources cited in volume 1. It does not incorporate all the plays cited as sources or parallels to *The Rehearsal*, a separate list of which may be found above at p. 626.

*Abraham Ortelius album amicorum*, ed. Jean Puraye, in *De Gulden Passer*, 45 (1967) 1–124 and 46 nos. 1–3 (1968), 1–99.

Addison, Joseph, and Steele, Richard, *The Spectator*, ed. Donald F. Bond, 5 vols. (Oxford: Clarendon Press, 1965).

—— *The Tatler*, ed. Donald F. Bond, 3 vols. (Oxford: Clarendon Press, 1987).

Aden, John M., 'Dryden and the Imagination: The First Phase', *PMLA* 74 (1959), 28–40.

Aercke, Kristiaan P., 'An Orange Stuff'd with Cloves: Bayesian Baroque Rehearsed', *English Language Notes*, 25/4 (1988), 33–45.

Alymer, G. E., *The Crown's Servants* (Oxford: Oxford University Press, 2002).

Ambrosini, Federica, 'Toward a Social History of Women in Venice from the Renaissance to the Enlightenment', in John Martin and Dennis Romano (eds.), *Venice Reconsidered: The History and Civilization of an Italian City-State, 1297–1797* (Baltimore, Md. and London: Johns Hopkins University Press, 2000), 420–53.

*Annals of English Drama, 975–1700*, ed. Alfred Harbage; 2nd edn. rev. S. Schoenbaum (London: Methuen, 1964); 3rd edn. rev. Sylvia Stoler Wagonheim (London: Routledge, 1989).

Anon., *Authentick Memoirs of the Life of that Celebrated Actress Mrs. Ann Oldfield*, 3rd edn. (London: Booksellers and Pamphletsellers of London and Westminster, 1730).

Anon. (ed.), *A Collection of the most esteemed Farces and Entertainments Performed on the British Stage* (Edinburgh: C. Elliot, 1788).

Anon. ['A Gentleman of Oxford'], *The Devil upon Crutches In England, or Night Scenes in London* (London: Philip Hodges, 1755).

Anon., *Eagle 1666. A new Almanack and Prognostication for the Yeare of our Lord God 1666* (York: 1666 [Wing A1648B]).

Anon., *The Friendly Vindication of Mr. Dryden From the Censure of the Rota by His Cabal of Wits* (Cambridge: 1673 [Wing F2229]).

Anon., *The Great Eclipse of the Sun, or Charles his Waine Over-Clouded* (London: 1644 [Wing G1888]).

Anon., *A Letter from Mons. de Voltaire to the Author of the Orphan of China* (London: I. Pottinger, 1759). Not by Voltaire. See the printed catalogue of the Bibliothèque nationale de France, vol. 214/2, cols. 776–7.

Anon., *A Letter to Mr. Garrick on the Opening of the Theatre* (London: J. Coote, 1758).

Anon., *The New Key to the Rehearsal* (London: Printed for S. Briscoe and Sold by J. Morphew and A. Dod, 1717). [Actually just a reprint of the original 1704 edition, title notwithstanding.]

Anon., *Poems on Affairs of State*, vol. ii (London: 1703).

Anon. [Thomas Middleton?], *The Revenger's Tragedy*, ed. R. A. Foakes (London: Methuen, 1966).

Anselme, Père, et al., *Histoire généalogique et chronologique de la Maison royale de France*, 3rd edn., 9 vols. (Paris: Compagnie des Libraires Associés, 1726–33).

Arundell, D. D., *Dryden and Howard, 1664–1668* (Cambridge: Cambridge University Press, 1929).

Ashley, Maurice, *John Wildman: Plotter and Postmaster* (New Haven, Conn.: Yale University Press, 1947).

Astier, Régine, 'Louis XIV, "Premier Danseur"', in David Lee Rubin (ed.), *Sun King: The Ascendancy of French Culture during the Reign of Louis XIV* (Washington, DC: Folger Shakespeare Library, 1992), 73–102.

Aubrey, John, *'Brief Lives', chiefly of Contemporaries, set down by John Aubrey, between the Years 1669 & 1696*, ed. Andrew Clark, 2 vols. (Oxford: Clarendon Press, 1898).

Avery, Emmett L., 'The Stage Popularity of *The Rehearsal*, 1671–1777', *Research Studies of the State College of Washington*, 7 (1939), 201–4.

Baker, David Erskine, *The Companion to the Play-House*, 2 vols. (London: T. Becket et al., 1764).

Baker, Sheridan, 'Buckingham's Permanent *Rehearsal*', *Michigan Quarterly Review*, 12 (1973), 160–71.

Balderston, Katharine C. (ed.), *Thraliana*, 2 vols. (Oxford: Clarendon Press, 1942).

Bawcutt, N. W. (ed.), *The Control and Censorship of Caroline Drama: The Records of Sir Henry Herbert, Master of the Revels 1623–73* (Oxford: Clarendon Press, 1996).

Beal, Peter, *Index of English Literary Manuscripts*, ii, pt. 2: *Lee–Wycherley* (London: Mansell, 1993).

Beaumont, Francis, and Fletcher, John, *Comedies and Tragedies Written by Francis Beaumont And John Fletcher Gentlemen* (London: 1647 [Wing B1581]).

—— —— *Fifty Comedies and Tragedies. Written by Francis Beaumont And John Fletcher, Gentlemen* (London: 1679 [Wing B1582]).

—— —— *The Works of Mr. Francis Beaumont and Mr. John Fletcher*, 7 vols. (London: Tonson, 1711).

—— —— *The Works of Beaumont and Fletcher*, ed. Alexander Dyce, 11 vols. (London: Edward Moxon, 1843–6).

—— —— *The Dramatic Works in the Beaumont and Fletcher Canon*, gen. ed. Fredson Bowers (Cambridge: Cambridge University Press, 1966–96).

Behn, Aphra, *The Works of Aphra Behn*, ed. Janet Todd, 7 vols. (London: Pickering & Chatto, 1992–6).

Bellany, Alastair, 'A Poem on the Archbishop's Hearse: Puritanism, Libel and Sedition after the Hampton Court Conference', *Journal of British Studies*, 34 (1995), 137–64.

Benserade, Isaac de, *Ballets pour Louis XIV*, présentés et annotés par Marie-Claude Canova-Green (Toulouse: Société de littératures classiques, 1997).

Bentley, Gerald Eades, *The Jacobean and Caroline Stage*, 7 vols. (Oxford: Clarendon Press, 1941–68).

Beyer, Karl, *Nota bene! Das lateinische Zitatenlexikon* (Darmstadt: Wissenschaftliche Buchgesellschaft, 1999).

B., J., *The Blazing Star: or, A Discourse of Comets, Their Natures and Effects* (London: 1665 [Wing B94]).

Blayney, Peter W. M., *The Bookshops in Paul's Cross Churchyard* (London: The Bibliographical Society, 1990).

Bond, David, 'Nell Gwyn's Birthdate', *Theatre Notebook*, 40 (1986), 3–9.

Boswell, James, *Boswell's Life of Johnson*, ed. George Birkbeck Hill, rev. L. F. Powell, 6 vols. (Oxford: Clarendon Press, 1934–50).

Bouwsma, William, 'Venice, Spain, and the Papacy: Paolo Sarpi and the Renaissance Tradition', in Eric Cochrane (ed.), *The Late Italian Renaissance, 1525–1630* (London: Macmillan, 1970), 366–7.

Boyle, Roger, Earl of Orrery, *The Dramatic Works of Roger Boyle, Earl of Orrery*, ed. William Smith Clark II, 2 vols. (Cambridge, Mass.: Harvard University Press, 1937).

*The British Theatre . . . Printed under the Authority of the Managers from the Prompt Books. With Biographical and Critical Remarks by Mrs. Inchbald*, ed. Elizabeth Inchbald, 25 vols. (London: Longman et al., 1808).

Brown, Gillian Fansler, "'The Session of the Poets to the Tune of Cook Lawrel': Playhouse Evidence for Composition Date of 1664', *Restoration and Eighteenth Century Theatre Research*, 13/1 (May 1974), 19–26, 62.

Brown, Laura, *English Dramatic Form, 1660–1760* (New Haven, Conn.: Yale University Press, 1981).

Brown, Patricia Fortini, *Private Lives in Renaissance Venice: Art, Architecture, and the Family* (New Haven, Conn. and London: Yale University Press, 2004).

Brown, Thomas (ed.), *Miscellanea Aulica: or, a Collection of State-Treatises, Never before publish'd*, . . . *Faithfully Collected from their Originals, by Mr. T. Brown* (London: J. Hartley et al., 1702).

—— *The Remains of Mr Tho. Brown, Serious and Comical, in Prose and Verse* (London: Sam. Briscoe et al., 1720).

Browning, Andrew, *Thomas Osborne, Earl of Danby and Duke of Leeds, 1632–1712*, 3 vols. (Glasgow: Jackson, Son & Co., 1944–51).

Burghclere, Winifred, Lady, *George Villiers, Second Duke of Buckingham, 1628-1687: A Study in the History of the Restoration* (London: John Murray, 1903; repr. New York: Kennikat Press, 1971).

Burgos, Luca [Pacioli] de, *Somma di aritmetica, geometria, proporzioni e proporzionalità* (Venice: 1494).

Burnet, Gilbert, *Bishop Burnet's History of His Own Time*, 2 vols. (London: Thomas Ward, 1724–34).

Burnim, Kalman A., and Highfill, Jr. Philip H., *John Bell, Patron of British Theatrical Portraiture: A Catalog of the Theatrical Portraits in his Editions of Bell's Shakespeare and Bell's British Theatre* (Carbondale, Ill.: Southern Illinois University Press, 1998).

Butler, Douglas R., 'The Date of Buckingham's Revision of *The Chances* and Nell Gwynn's First Season on the London Stage', *Notes and Queries*, 227 (1982), 515–16.

Butler, Samuel, *Characters*, ed. Charles W. Daves (Cleveland, Ohio: Press of Case Western Reserve University, 1970).

Canfield, J. Douglas, *Tricksters and Estates: On the Ideology of Restoration Comedy* (Lexington, Ky.: University Press of Kentucky, 1997).

—— *Heroes and States: On the Ideology of Restoration Tragedy* (Lexington, Ky.: University Press of Kentucky, 2000).

Cannan, Paul D., *The Emergence of Dramatic Criticism in England: From Jonson to Pope* (New York: Palgrave, 2006).

Capp, Bernard, *English Almanacs 1500–1800* (Ithaca, N.Y.: Cornell University Press, 1979).

Cartwright, Julia, *Madame: A Life of Henrietta, Daughter of Charles I and the Duchess of Orleans* (New York: Scribner's, 1894).

Cervantes Saavedra, Miguel de, *Les novvelles de Miguel de Cervantes Saavedra*, trans. F. de Rosset and Sr. d'Audiguier (Paris: 1615).

—— *Exemplarie Novells* 'Turned into English by Don Diego Puede-Ser' [James Mabbe] (London: 1640 [Wing STC 4914]). Reissued as *Delight in Severall Shapes* (London: 1654 [Wing C1770]).

Chamberlayne, Edward, *Angliæ Notitia; or, The Present State of England*, 5th edn. (London: 1671 [Wing C1823]).

Chambers, Ephraim, *Cyclopaedia*, 4 vols. (London: 1783).

Chapman, Hester W., *Great Villiers: A Study of George Villiers Second Duke of Buckingham 1628–1687* (London: Secker & Warburg, 1949).

Chatelain, Jean-Marc, *La Bibliothèque de l'honnête homme: Livres, lecture et collections en France à l'âge classique* (Paris: Bibliothèque nationale de France, 2003).

Child-Villiers, Margaret Elizabeth, Countess of Jersey, untitled review article quoting extensively from the 'Jersey' version of the commonplace book, *Quarterly Review*, 187 (Jan.–Apr. 1898), 86–111.

Christout, Marie-Françoise, *La Ballet de cour au xvii^e siècle* (Geneva: Éditions Minkoff, 1987).

Cibber, Colley, *A Letter from Mr. Cibber, to Mr. Pope* (London: W. Lewis, 1742).

—— *An Apology for the Life of Mr. Colley Cibber, Written by Himself*, ed. Robert W. Lowe, 2 vols. (London: Nimmo, 1889).

—— *The Plays of Colley Cibber*, ed. Timothy J. Viator and William J. Burling, (Madison, NJ: Fairleigh Dickinson University Press, 2001).

Cibber, Theophilus, *Two Dissertations on the Theatres* (London: Printed for the Author, To be had of Mr Griffiths [bookseller], 1756).

Clavell, John, *The Sodder'd Citizen* (London: Malone Society, 1936).

Clinton-Baddeley, V. C., *The Burlesque Tradition in the English Theatre after 1660* (1952; repr. New York: Blom, 1971).

Cohen, Selma Jeanne (ed.), *International Encyclopedia of Dance*, 6 vols. (New York: Oxford University Press, 1998).

Congreve, William, *William Congreve: Letters & Documents*, ed. John C. Hodges (New York: Harcourt Brace, 1964).

*The Conway Letters*, ed. Marjorie Hope Nicolson, rev. edn. Sarah Hutton (Oxford: Clarendon Press, 1992).

Cotgrave, Randle, *A Dictionarie of the French and English Tongues* (London: 1611); facsim. repr. (Columbia, SC: University of South Carolina Press, 1950).

*Court Satires of the Restoration*, ed. John Harold Wilson (Columbus, Ohio: Ohio State University Press, 1976).

*Covent Garden Drollery*, 'Collected by A.B.' (London: 1672 [Wing C6624A]).

*Covent Garden Drollery*, ed. Montague Summers (London: Fortune Press 1927).

*Covent Garden Drollery*, ed. G. Thorn-Drury (London: Dobell, 1928).

Cowley, Abraham, *The English Writings of Abraham Cowley*, ed. A. R. Waller, 2 vols. (Cambridge: Cambridge University Press, 1905–6).

Craik, T. W., 'Two Emendations in the Text of Howard's and Villiers's *The Country Gentleman*', *Notes and Queries*, 224 (1979), 437–8.

Crane, D. E. L., 'Burton and Buckingham', *Notes and Queries*, 229 (1984), 229.

Crawford, Bartholow V., 'The Dance of the Kings', *Philological Quarterly*, 2 (1923), 151–3.

Crowne, John, *The Comedies of John Crowne*, ed. B. J. McMullin (New York: Garland, 1984).

[Crull, Jodocus], *The Antiquities of St. Peter's, or the Abbey-Church of Westminster*, 2nd edn. (London: J. Nutt et al., 1715).

Curll, Edmund, and Oldys, William (?), *The History of the English Stage* (London: E. Curll, 1741).

Danby, Jennifer Renee, 'The Faces of Masculinity and Femininity on the Early Restoration Stage: A Study of Five Actors' (Ph.D. diss.; City University of New York, 2004).

Danforth, S., *An Astronomical Description of the late Comet or Blazing-Star* (1665; rpt. London: Peter Parker, 1666 [Wing D174]).

Davies, Thomas, *Dramatic Miscellanies*, 3 vols. (London: For the Author, 1784).

—— *Memoirs of the Life of David Garrick*, 4th edn., 2 vols. (London: Printed for the Author, 1784).

—— *Memoirs of the Life of David Garrick Esq.*, ed. Stephen Jones, 2 vols. (London: Longman et al., 1808).

Day, Cyrus Lawrence, and Murrie, Eleanore Boswell, *English Song-Books 1651–1702* (London: Printed for the Bibliographical Society at the University Press, Oxford, 1940 for 1937).

Defoe, Daniel, *Review*, 28 March 1712.

—— *A Journal of the Plague Year*, ed. Paula R. Backscheider (New York: Norton, 1992).

de Marly, Diana, *Costume on the Stage 1600–1940* (London: Batsford, 1982).

Dennis, John, *The Critical Works of John Dennis*, ed. Edward Niles Hooker, 2 vols. (Baltimore, Md.: Johns Hopkins Press, 1939–43).

Desgrouais, M[ons.], *Les Gasconismes corrigés* (Toulouse: Vve Douladoure, 1801).

Des Maizeaux, Pierre, *The Life of Monsieur de St. Evremond* (London: printed in the year 1714).

Desmarets de Saint-Sorlin, Jean, *Les Visionnaires*, ed. H. Gaston Hall, 2nd edn. (Paris: Société des Textes français modernes, 1995).

Desmedt, Ludovic, 'Money in the 'Body Politick': The Analysis of Trade and Circulation in the Writings of Seventeenth-century Political Arithmeticians', *History of Political Economy*, 37 (2005), 79–101.

Dessen, Alan C., *Elizabethan Stage Conventions and Modern Interpreters* (Cambridge: Cambridge University Press, 1984), 39–40.

Dethloff, Diana, 'Portraiture and Concepts of Beauty in Restoration Painting', in Catharine MacLeod and Julia Marciari Alexander (comps. and eds.), *Painted Ladies: Women at the Court of Charles II* (London: National Portrait Gallery, 2001), 24–35.

Dickinson, Alis, 'The Courante "La Vignonne": In the Steps of a Popular Dance', *Early Music*, 10 (1982), 56–62.

Dion, Roger, *Histoire de la vigne et du vin en France des origines au xixe siècle* (Paris: n.p., 1959).

Downes, John, *Roscius Anglicanus, or an Historical Review of the Stage* (1708), ed. Judith Milhous and Robert D. Hume (London: Society for Theatre Research, 1987).

*Dr Johnson by Mrs Thrale*, ed. Richard Ingrams (London: Chatto & Windus, 1984).

Dryden, John, *The Critical and Miscellaneous Works of John Dryden*, ed. Edmond Malone, 4 vols. (London: Cadell and Davies, 1800).

—— *The Letters of John Dryden*, ed. Charles E. Ward (Durham, NC: Duke University Press, 1942).

—— *The Works of John Dryden*, gen. eds. H. T. Swedenberg and others, 20 vols. (Berkeley and Los Angeles, Calif.: University of California Press, 1956–2000).

Durfey, Thomas, *New Opera's* (London: Chetwood, 1721).

E., B. Gent., *A New Dictionary of the Terms Ancient and Modern of the Canting Crew* (London: [1699] [Wing E4]).

Echard, Laurence, *History of England*, 2 vols. (London: Tonson, 1720).

Elias, A. C. Jr., 'Swift's *Don Quixote*, Dunkin's *Virgil Travesty*, and other New Intelligence: John Lyon's "Materials for a Life of Dr. Swift"', 1765', *Swift Studies*, 13 (1998), 27–104.

Elias, Richard, '"Bayes" in Buckingham's *The Rehearsal*', *English Language Notes*, 15 (1978), 178–81.

Ellis, Aytoun, *The Penny Universities: A History of the Coffee-Houses* (London: Secker & Warburg, 1956).

*The Ellis Correspondence: Letters Written during the Years 1686, 1687, 1688, and Addressed to John Ellis, Esq.*, 2 vols. (London: Henry Colburn, 1829).

Etherege, Sir George, *The Plays of Sir George Etherege*, ed. Michael Cordner (Cambridge: Cambridge University Press, 1982).

Evelyn, John, *The Diary of John Evelyn*, 6 vols., ed. E. S. de Beer (Oxford: Clarendon Press, 1955).

Evershed-Martin, Leslie, *The Impossible Theatre: The Chichester Festival Theatre Adventure* (London and Chichester: Phillimore, 1971).

Feuillet, Raoul Auger, *Recueil de contredances* (Paris: Chez l'Auteur, 1706).

Fiske, Roger, *English Theatre Music in the Eighteenth Century* (1973; rev. edn. London: Oxford University Press, 1986).

Fletcher, John, *The Chances: A Comedy; As it is Acted at the Theatre-Royal in Smock-Alley* ed. for production by Thomas Sheridan (Dublin: J. Esdall, 1751).

—— *Philaster or, Love Lies a-Bleeding*, ed. Andrew Gurr (1969; repr. Manchester: Manchester University Press, 2003).

—— *The Chances*, ed. George Walton Williams, in *The Dramatic Works in the Beaumont and Fletcher Canon*, gen. ed. Fredson Bowers, vol. iv (Cambridge: Cambridge University Press, 1979).

Forsythe, Robert Stanley, *The Relations of Shirley's Plays to the Elizabethan Drama* (1914; repr. New York: Blom, 1965).

Fowler, James Patrick, '*The Chances* adapted by George Villiers second Duke of Buckingham from the Comedy by John Fletcher' (Ph.D. thesis; Shakespeare Institute, University of Birmingham, 1978).

—— 'Catiline quoted in *The Chances*', *Notes and Queries*, 231 (1986), 467–9.

Gadbury, John, *De cometis* (London: 1665 [Wing G81]).

—— *Vox Solis: or, An Astrological Discourse of the Great Eclipse of the Sun, which happened on June 22. 1666* (London: 1667 [Wing G100A]).

*Games and Gamesters of the Restoration*, ed. Cyril Hughes Hartmann (London: Routledge, 1930).

Garrick, David, *The Letters of David Garrick*, ed. David M. Little and George M. Kahrl, 3 vols. (London: Oxford University Press, 1963).

—— (reviser), *The Chances. A Comedy*, in *The Plays of David Garrick*, 7 vols., ed. Harry William Pedicord and Fredrick Louis Bergmann (Carbondale, Ill.: Southern Illinois University Press, 1980–2).

Garrioch, David, 'House Names, Shop Signs, and Social Organization in Western European Cities, 1500–1900', *Urban History*, 21 (1994), 18–46.

Genest, John, *Some Account of the English Stage from the Restoration in 1660 to 1830*, 10 vols. (Bath: Carrington, 1832).

Geneva, Ann, *Astrology and the Seventeenth-Century Mind: William Lilly and the Language of the Stars* (Manchester: Manchester University Press, 1995).

Gildon, Charles, *The Lives and Characters of the English Dramatick Poets* (London: [1699] [Wing L376]).

—— *A New Rehearsal, or Bays the Younger* (London: J. Roberts, 1714).

—— *The Complete Art of Poetry*, 2 vols. (London: Charles Rivington, 1718).

Goldgar, Anne, *Impolite Learning: Conduct and Community in the Republic of Letters, 1680–1750* (New Haven, Conn. and London: Yale University Press, 1995).

Granville, George, *The Jew of Venice* (London: Ber. Lintott, 1701).

Greg, W. W., *A Bibliography of the English Printed Drama to the Restoration*, 4 vols. (London: Bibliographical Society, 1939–59).

Grey, Anchitell, *Debates of the House of Commons, from the Year 1667 to the Year 1694*, 10 vols. (London: D. Henry et al., 1763).

Grubb, James S., 'Elite Citizens', in John Martin and Dennis Romano (eds.), *Venice Reconsidered: The History and Civilization of an Italian City-State* (Baltimore, Md.: Johns Hopkins University Press, 2000).

*The Gyldenstolpe Manuscript Miscellany of Poems by John Wilmot, Earl of Rochester, and Other Restoration Authors*, ed. Bror Danielsson and David M. Vieth (Stockholm: Almquist and Wiksell, 1967).

Haley, K. H. D., *The First Earl of Shaftesbury* (Oxford: Clarendon Press, 1968).

Hall, H. Gaston, *Richelieu's Desmarets and the Century of Louis XIV* (Oxford: Clarendon Press, 1990).

Hamilton, Anthony, *Mémoires de la vie du comte de Gramont* (Cologne: 1713).

Hanson, Neil, *The Dreadful Judgement: The True Story of the Great Fire of London* (London: Doubleday, 2001).

Harbage, Alfred, 'Elizabethan-Restoration Palimpsest', *Modern Language Review*, 35 (1940), 287–319.

Harben, Henry A., *A Dictionary of London* (London: Herbert Jenkins, 1918).

Harris, Brice, *Charles Sackville, Sixth Earl of Dorset, Patron and Poet of the Restoration* (Urbana, Ill.: University of Illinois Press, 1940).

Harris-Warrick, Rebecca, 'Ballroom Dancing at the Court of Louis XIV', *Early Music*, 14 (1986), 41–9.

Hayman, Ronald, *The First Thrust: The Chichester Festival Theatre* (London: Davis-Poynter, 1975).

Hazlitt, William, *A View of the English Stage; or, A Series of Dramatic Criticisms* (London: R. Stodart et al., 1818).

—— *The Complete Works of William Hazlitt*, ed. P. P. Howe after the edition of A. R. Waller and Arnold Glover, 21 vols. (London: Dent, 1930–3).

Hensman, Bertha, *The Shares of Fletcher, Field and Massinger in Twelve Plays of the Beaumont and Fletcher Canon*, 2 vols. (Salzburg Studies in English Literature; Salzburg: Institut für Englische Sprache und Literatur, Universität Salzburg, 1974).

Highfill, Philip H., Jr., Burnim, Kalman A., and Langhans, Edward A., *A Biographical Dictionary of Actors, Actresses, Musicians, Dancers, Managers & Other Stage Personnel in London, 1660–1800*, 16 vols. (Carbondale, Ill.: Southern Illinois University Press, 1973–93).

*Historical Manuscripts Commission*, Sixth Report (London: 1877).

—— *Ormonde*, NS V (London: 1908).

Hobbes, Thomas, *Leviathan*, ed. C. B. Macpherson (Harmondsworth: Penguin, 1968).

Hope, Quentin M., *Saint-Evremond and his Friends* (Geneva: Droz, 1999).

Hotson, Leslie, *The Commonwealth and Restoration Stage* (Cambridge, Mass.: Harvard University Press, 1928).

Howard, Edward, *The Change of Crownes*, ed. Frederick S. Boas (London: Royal Society of Literature, 1949).

Howard, James, *The English Mounsieur* (pub. 1674), intro. by Robert D. Hume (Los Angeles, Calif.: Augustan Reprint Society, 1977).

Howard, Sir Robert, and Villiers, George, Second Duke of Buckingham, *The Country Gentleman*, ed. Arthur H. Scouten and Robert D. Hume (Philadelphia, Pa.: University of Pennsylvania Press, 1976).

Howarth, R. G., 'Edward Phillips's "Compendiosa Enumeratio Poetarum"', *Modern Language Review*, 54 (1959), 321–8.

Hoy, Cyrus, 'The Shares of Fletcher and his Collaborators in the Beaumont and Fletcher Canon (I)', *SB* 8 (1956), 129–46.

Hughes, Derek, *English Drama, 1660–1700* (Oxford: Clarendon Press, 1996).

Huguet, Edmond, *Dictionnaire de la langue française du seizième siècle*, 7 vols. (Paris: Didier, 1925–73).

Hume, Robert D., 'Dryden on Creation: "Imagination" in the Later Criticism', *RES* NS 21 (1970), 295–314.

—— 'The Date of Dryden's *Marriage A-la-Mode*', *Harvard Library Bulletin*, 21 (1973), 161–6.

—— *The Development of English Drama in the Late Seventeenth Century* (Oxford: Clarendon Press, 1976).

—— '*The Maid's Tragedy* and Censorship in the Restoration Theatre', *Philological Quarterly*, 61 (1982), 484–90.

—— 'Dr. Edward Browne's Playlists of "1662": A Reconsideration', *Philological Quarterly*, 64 (1985), 69–81.

—— 'The Politics of Opera in Late Seventeenth-Century London', *Cambridge Opera Journal*, 10 (1998), 15–43.

—— 'Editing a Nebulous Author: The Case of the Duke of Buckingham', *The Library*, 7th ser., 4 (2003), 249–77.

Hunter, Michael, 'The Social Basis and Changing Fortunes of an Early Scientific Institution: An Analysis of the Membership of the Royal Society, 1660–1685', *Notes and Records of the Royal Society of London*, 31 (1976), 9–114.

Hutton, Ronald, *Charles the Second, King of England, Scotland, and Ireland* (Oxford: Oxford University Press, 1989).

Hyde, Edward, Earl of Clarendon, *The Life of Edward, Earl of Clarendon . . . Written by Himself* (Oxford: Oxford University Press, 1857).

*Index to the London Stage 1660–1800*, ed. Ben Ross Schneider, Jr. (Carbondale, Ill. Southern Illinois University Press, 1979).

Jacob, Giles, *The Poetical Register: or, the Lives and Characters of the English Dramatick Poets* (London: E. Curll, 1719).

James, E. Nelson, 'Drums and Trumpets', *Restoration and Eighteenth Century Theatre Research*, 9/2 (1970), 46–55, and 10/1 (1971), 54–7.

Jensen, H. James, *A Glossary of John Dryden's Critical Terms* (Minneapolis, Minn.: University of Minnesota Press, 1969).

Jespersen, Otto, *Growth and Structure of the English Language* (1905), 10th edn. (Chicago, Ill.: University of Chicago Press, 1982).

Jesperson, James, and FitzRandolph, Jane, *From Sundials to Atomic Clocks: Understanding Time and Frequency*, 2nd edn. (Gaithersburg, Md.: National Institute of Standards and Technology, 1999).

Jones, J. R., *The First Whigs: The Politics of the Exclusion Bill Crisis 1678–1683* (Oxford: Oxford University Press, 1961).

Jones, Stephen, *Biographica Dramatica*, 4 vols. (London: Longman et al., 1812).

Jonson, Ben, *Ben Jonson*, ed. C. H. Herford and Percy Simpson, 11 vols. (Oxford: Clarendon Press, 1925–52).

—— *Volpone*, ed. Philip Brockbank (London: Benn, 1968).

Kewes, Paulina, *Authorship and Appropriation: Writing for the Stage in England, 1660–1710* (Oxford: Clarendon Press, 1998).

Keynes, J. M., *Essays in Biography*, 2nd edn., ed. Geoffrey Keynes (London: Heinemann, 1951).

*A Key to the Rehearsal*, (London: S. Briscoe, 1704), included in vol. ii of the Buckingham *Miscellaneous Works* of 1704–5.

Kiernan, V. G., *The Duel in European History: Honour and the Reign of Aristocracy* (Oxford: Oxford University Press, 1988).

Killigrew, Thomas, *Comedies and Tradegies* (London: 1664).

Kinservik, Matthew J., 'Garrick's Unpublished Epilogue for Catherine Clive's *The Rehearsal: or, Bays in Petticoats* (1750)', *Études anglaises*, 49 (1996), 320–6.

Kretschmayr, Heinrich, *Geschichte von Venedig*, 3 vols. (Gotha and Stuttgart, 1905–34; repr. Aalen: Scientia Verlag, 1964).

Labarre, E. J., *Dictionary and Encyclopædia of Paper and Paper-Making* (London: Oxford University Press, 1952).

La Boétie, Étienne de, *Vers françois* (Paris: Fédéric Morel, 1572).

Lamb, Charles, *Elia* (London: Taylor and Hessey, 1823).

Lamotte, Charles, *An Essay upon Poetry and Painting* (London: F. Fayram, 1730).

Lane, Frederic C., *Venice: A Maritime Republic* (Baltimore, Md.: Johns Hopkins University Press, 1973).

Langbaine, Gerard, *An Account of the English Dramatick Poets* (Oxford: 1691 [Wing L373]).

Langhans, Edward A., *Restoration Promptbooks* (Carbondale, Ill.: Southern Illinois University Press, 1981).

—— *Eighteenth Century British and Irish Promptbooks: A Descriptive Bibliography* (Westport, Conn.: Greenwood, 1987).

Laudan, Rachel, 'Birth of the Modern Diet', *Scientific American* (Aug. 2000), 62–7.

Lawrenson, T. E., *The French Stage and Playhouse in the XVIIth Century*, rev. edn. (New York: AMS Press, 1986).

Leacroft, Richard, *The Development of the English Playhouse* (London: Eyre Methuen, 1973).

Lee, Maurice, Jr., *The Cabal* (Urbana, Ill.: University of Illinois Press, 1965).

Lee, Nathaniel, *The Princess of Cleve* (London: 1689 [Wing L861]).

—— *The Works of Nathaniel Lee*, ed. Thomas B. Stroup and Arthur L. Cooke, 2 vols. (Metuchen, N.J.: Scarecrow, 1954–5).

Leech, Clifford, 'Thomas Southerne and *On the Poets and Actors in King Charles II's Reign*', *Notes and Queries*, 164 (June 1933), 401–3.

Leigh, Richard (?), *The Censure of the Rota* (Oxford: 1673 [Wing L1018]).

Leveridge, Richard, *Complete Songs*, intro. by Olive Baldwin and Thelma Wilson (London: Stainer and Bell, 1997).

Lewis, Peter, '*The Rehearsal*: A Study of its Satirical Methods', *Durham University Journal*, NS 31 (1970), 96–113.

*The Life and Times of Anthony Wood*, 5 vols., ed. Andrew Clark (Oxford: Oxford Historical Society, 1891–1900).

Lillywhite, Bryant, *London Coffee Houses: A Reference Book of Coffee Houses of the Seventeenth, Eighteenth and Nineteenth Centuries* (London: Allen and Unwin, 1963).

Loftis, John, Southern, Richard, Jones, Marion, and Scouten, A. H., *The Revels History of Drama in English*, v: *1660–1750* (London: Methuen, 1976).

*The London Encyclopædia*, ed. Ben Weinreb and Christopher Hibbert (London: Macmillan, 1983).

Love, Harold, 'The Fiddlers on the Restoration Stage', *Early Music*, 6 (1978), 391–9.

—— 'Shadwell, Rochester and the Crisis of Amateurism', in Judith Slagle (ed.), *Thomas Shadwell Reconsider'd*, published as *Restoration*, 20 (1996), 119–34.

—— *Scribal Publication in Seventeenth-Century England* (Oxford: Clarendon Press, 1993); repr. as *The Culture and Commerce of Texts: Scribal Publication in Seventeenth-Century England* (Amherst, Mass.: University of Massachusetts Press, 1998).

—— 'The Rapes of Lucina', in Michael Bristol and Arthur Marotti (eds.), *Print, Manuscript and Performance: The Changing Relations of the Media in Early Modern England* (Columbus, Ohio: Ohio State University Press, 2000), 200–14.

—— 'Roger L'Estrange's Criticism of Dryden's Elocution', *Notes and Queries*, 246 (2001), 398–400.

—— 'Vocal Register in Behn's *Love-Letters between a Nobleman and his Sister*', *English Language Notes*, 41 (2003), 44–53.

—— *English Clandestine Satire 1660–1702* (Oxford: Oxford University Press, 2004).

Low, Jennifer A., *Manhood and the Duel: Masculinity in Early Modern Drama and Culture* (New York: Palgrave Macmillan, 2003).

McFadden, George, 'Political Satire in *The Rehearsal*', *Yearbook of English Studies*, 4 (1974), 120–8.

McKenna, Antony, 'Aubigny, Ludovic Stuart, seigneur d", in *Dictionnaire de Port-Royal*, ed. Jean Lesaulnier and Antony McKenna (Paris: H. Champion, 2004), 127–8.

McMullan, Gordon, *The Politics of Unease in the Plays of John Fletcher* (Amherst, Mass.: University of Massachusetts Press, 1994).

Macquoid, Percy, and Edwards, Ralph, *The Dictionary of English Furniture from the Middle Ages to the Late Georgian Period*, 3 vols. (New York: Scribner's, 1924–7).

Macray, William Dunn, *Annals of the Bodleian Library Oxford*, 2nd edn. (Oxford: Clarendon Press, 1890).

Magalotti, Lorenzo, *Lorenzo Magalotti at the Court of Charles II: His 'Relazione d'Inghilterra' of 1668*, ed. and trans. W. E. Knowles Middleton (Waterloo, Ont.: Wilfred Laurier University Press, 1980).

Maguire, Nancy Klein, 'Tragicomedy', in Deborah Payne Fisk (ed.), *The Cambridge Companion to English Restoration Theatre* (Cambridge: Cambridge University Press, 2000), 86–106.

Mallett, Michael, 'Venice and its Condottieri, 1404–54', in J. R. Hale (ed.), *Renaissance Venice* (London: Faber and Faber, 1973), 121–45.

Markham, Clements R., *Life of Robert Fairfax of Steeton . . . compiled from Original Letters and other Documents* (London: Macmillan, 1885).

Markley, Robert, *Two Edg'd Weapons: Style and Ideology in the Comedies of Etherege, Wycherley, and Congreve* (Oxford: Clarendon Press, 1988).

Marshall, Alan, *The Age of Faction* (Manchester: Manchester University Press, 1999).

Martin, Leslie Howard, 'Dryden and the Art of Transversion', *Comparative Drama*, 6 (1972), 3–13.

Marvell, Andrew, *An Account of the Growth of Popery, and Arbitrary Government in England* (Amsterdam: 1677 [Wing M860A]).

—— *The Poems and Letters of Andrew Marvell*, 2 vols., ed. H. M. Margoliouth, rev. Pierre Legouis and E. E. Duncan-Jones (Oxford: Clarendon Press, 1971).

Massinger, Philip, *The Plays and Poems of Philip Massinger*, ed. Philip Edwards and Colin Gibson, 5 vols. (Oxford: Clarendon Press, 1976).

Masten, Jeffrey, 'Beaumont and/or Fletcher: Collaboration and the Interpretation of Renaissance Drama', *ELH* 59 (1992), 337–56.

—— 'Playwrighting: Authorship and Collaboration', in John D. Cox and David Scott Kastan (eds.), *A New History of Early English Drama* (New York: Columbia University Press, 1997), 357–82.

—— *Textual Intercourse: Collaboration, Authorship, and Sexualities in Renaissance Drama* (Cambridge: Cambridge University Press, 1997).

Melton, Frank T., 'Absentee Land Management in Seventeenth-Century England', *Agricultural History*, 52 (1978), 147–59.

—— 'A Rake Refinanced: The Fortune of George Villiers, Second Duke of Buckingham, 1671–1685', *Huntington Library Quarterly*, 51 (1988), 297–318.

Mendelsohn, Oscar A., *Drinking with Pepys* (London: Macmillan, 1963).

Mersenne, Marin, *Harmonie universelle, contenant la théorie et la pratique de la musique* (Paris: 1636; facsimile repr., Paris: CNRS, 1963).

Middleton, Thomas, *Women Beware Women and Other Plays*, ed. Richard Dutton (Oxford: Oxford University Press, 1999).

Mignon, Elizabeth, *Crabbed Age and Youth: The Old Men and Women in the Restoration Comedy of Manners* (Durham, NC: Duke University Press, 1947).

Milhous, Judith, 'An Annotated Census of Thomas Betterton's Roles, 1659–1710', *Theatre Notebook*, 29 (1975), 33–43, 85–94.

—— 'Elizabeth Bowtell and Elizabeth Davenport: Some Puzzles Solved', *Theatre Notebook*, 39 (1985), 124–34.

—— and Hume, Robert D., 'Lost English Plays, 1660–1700', *Harvard Library Bulletin*, 25 (1977), 5–33.

—— —— 'Attribution Problems in English Drama, 1660–1700', *Harvard Library Bulletin*, 31 (1983), 5–39.

—— —— *Producible Interpretation: Eight English Plays, 1675–1707* (Carbondale, Ill.: Southern Illinois University Press, 1985).

—— —— 'Murder in Elizabeth Barry's Dressing Room', *Yale University Library Gazette*, 79 (2005), 149–74.

Millar, Oliver, *The Tudor, Stuart and Early Georgian Pictures in the Collection of Her Majesty the Queen*, 2 vols. (London: Phaidon, 1963).

Misselden, Edward, *Free Trade. Or, The Meanes to make Trade florish* (London: 1622 [STC 17986]).

—— *The Circle of Commerce. Or the Ballance of Trade, in Defence of Free Trade* (London: 1623 [STC 17985]).

Mizener, Arthur, 'George Villiers, Second Duke of Buckingham: His Life and a Canon of His Works' (Ph.D. diss.; Princeton University, 1934).

Mongrédien, Georges, and Robert, Jean, *Les Comédiens français du XVIIe siècle: Dictionnaire biographique: suivi d'un inventaire des troupes (1590–1710) d'après des documents inédits*, 3rd edn. (Paris: Centre National de la Recherche Scientifique, 1981).

Morley, Thomas, *A Plain and Easy Introduction to Practical Music*, ed. R. Alec Harman (London: Dent, 1952).

Moss, Ann, *Printed Commonplace-Books and the Structuring of Renaissance Thought* (Oxford: Clarendon Press, 1996).

Mottley, John (?), *A Compleat List Of all the English Dramatic Poets*, attached to Thomas Whincop's *Scanderbeg* (London: W. Reeve, 1747).

Murphy, Arthur, *The Life of David Garrick, Esq.*, 2 vols. (London: J. Wright and J. F. Foot, 1801).

Murray, Nicholas, *World Enough and Time: The Life of Andrew Marvell* (New York: St. Martin's Press, 2000).

Nethercot, Arthur H., *Sir William D'avenant* (1938; repr. New York: Russell and Russell, 1967).

Nichols, John, *Literary Anecdotes of the Eighteenth Century*, iii (London: Printed for the Author, 1812).

Nicoll, Allardyce, *A History of English Drama, 1660–1900*, rev. edn., 6 vols. (Cambridge: Cambridge University Press, 1952–9).

Ogg, David, *England in the Reign of Charles II*, 2 vols., 2nd edn. (Oxford: Clarendon Press, 1956).

Oliver, H. J., *Sir Robert Howard (1626–1698): A Critical Biography* (Durham, NC: Duke University Press, 1963).

Ollard, Richard, *Man of War: Sir Robert Holmes and the Restoration Navy* (1969; London: Phoenix Press, 2001).

O'Neill, John H., *George Villiers, Second Duke of Buckingham* (Boston: Twayne, 1984).

Ormsby-Lennon, Hugh, 'Radical Physicians and Conservative Poets in Restoration England: Dryden among the Doctors', *Studies in Eighteenth-Century Culture*, 7 (1978), 389–411.

—— 'Commonplace Swift', in Hermann J. Real and Helgard Stöver-Leidig (eds.), *Reading Swift: Papers from the Third Münster Symposium on Jonathan Swift* (Munich: Wilhelm Fink Verlag, 1998), 13–44.

Osborn, James M., *John Dryden: Some Biographical Facts and Problems*, rev. edn. (Gainesville, Fla.: University of Florida Press, 1965).

Panton, Kenneth J., *Historical Dictionary of London* (Lanham, Md.: Scarecrow Press, 2001).

Partridge, Eric, *A Dictionary of Catch Phrases*, 2nd edn., rev. Paul Beale (London: Routledge, 1985).

Patterson, Annabel, '*The Country Gentleman*: Howard, Marvell, and Dryden in the Theater of Politics', *Studies in English Literature*, 25 (1985), 491–509.

Peltonen, Markku, *The Duel in Early Modern England: Civility, Politeness and Honour* (Cambridge: Cambridge University Press, 2003).

Pepys, Samuel, *The Diary of Samuel Pepys*, ed. Robert Latham and William Matthews, 11 vols. (London: Bell, 1970–83).

Percy, Thomas (later Bishop of Dromore), Unfinished edition of 'The Works of Villiers, Duke of Buckingham'. Started in the early 1760s. Most of the introductions, texts, and notes were printed, but the sheets were destroyed in a warehouse fire of 1808. Partial copies survive in British Library C39.g.18–19 and 643.e.10(2), Bodleian Percy 39 and 92, Bodleian Vet. A5d.1797/1–2, the Northampton Record Office, and the Queen's University Library, Belfast.

—— *The Correspondence of Thomas Percy and Thomas Warton*, ed. M. G. Robinson and Leah Dennis (Baton Rouge, La.: Louisiana State University Press, 1951).

Pincus, Steven C. A., '"Coffee Politicians Does Create": Coffeehouses and Restoration Political Culture', *Journal of Modern History*, 67 (1995), 807–34.

—— *Protestantism and Patriotism: Ideologies and the Making of English Foreign Policy, 1650–1668* (Cambridge: Cambridge University Press, 1996).

Playford, John, *The English Dancing Master* (London: 1651 [Wing P2477]).

*Plays of the Year*: 25, ed. J. C. Trewin (London: Elek, 1963).

Podewell, Bruce, 'Thomas Betterton's Roles', *Theatre Notebook*, 32 (1978), 89–90.

*Poems on Affairs of State: Augustan Satirical Verse, 1660–1714*, gen. ed. George deF. Lord, 7 vols. (New Haven, Conn.: Yale University Press, 1963–75).

Pope, Alexander, *The Correspondence of Alexander Pope*, ed. George Sherburn, 5 vols. (Oxford: Clarendon Press, 1956).

—— *Pastoral Poetry and An Essay on Criticism*, ed. E. Audra and Aubrey Williams (London: Methuen, 1961).

Potts, Denys, *Saint-Evremond: A Voice from Exile. Newly Discovered Letters to Madame de Gouville and the Abbé de Hautefeuille (1697–1701)* (Oxford: Legenda, 2002).

Powell, Violet, *Margaret, Countess of Jersey: A Biography* (London: Heinemann, 1978).

Price, Curtis, 'Restoration Stage Fiddlers and their Music', *Early Music*, 7 (1979), 315–22.

—— *Music in the Restoration Theatre* (Ann Arbor, Mich.: UMI Research Press, 1979).

—— *Henry Purcell and the London Stage* (Cambridge: Cambridge University Press, 1984).

*The Prologues and Epilogues of the Restoration 1660–1700*, ed. Pierre Danchin, 7 vols. (Nancy: Presses Universitaires de Nancy, 1981–8).

Rameau, Pierre, *Le Maître a danser* (Paris: chez Jean Villette, 1725).

Raylor, Timothy, *Cavaliers, Clubs and Literary Culture: Sir John Mennes, James Smith, and the Order of the Fancy* (Newark, Del.: University of Delaware Press, 1994).

—— 'Newcastle's Ghosts: Robert Payne, Ben Jonson, and the "Cavendish Circle"', in Claude J. Summers and Ted-Larry Pebworth (eds.), *Literary Circles and Cultural Communities in Renaissance England* (Columbia, Mo.: University of Missouri Press, 2000), 92–114.

Raymond, Joad, *The Invention of the Newspaper: English Newsbooks 1641–1649* (Oxford: Clarendon Press, 1996).

Reed, Isaac, *Biographica Dramatica*, 2 vols. (London: Mess. Rivingtons et al., 1782).

Reichert, John, 'A Note on Buckingham and Dryden', *Notes and Queries*, 207 (1962), 220–1.

Reresby, Sir John, *Memoirs of Sir John Reresby*, ed. Andrew Browning, 2nd edn. with a new preface and notes by Mary K. Geiter and W. A. Speck (London: Royal Historical Society, 1991).

*Restoration Drama: An Anthology*, ed. David Womersley (Oxford: Blackwell, 2000).

Reynolds, Frederick, *Don John; or the Two Violettas, A Musical Drama, in three acts; founded on Beaumont and Fletcher's Comedy of The Chances* (London: John Miller, 1821).

—— *The Life and Times of Frederick Reynolds. Written by Himself.* 2 vols., 2nd edn. (London: Henry Colburn, 1827).

Richards, Bernard, 'Corrections and Additions to A. H. Scouten's and R. D. Hume's Edition of Sir Robert Howard's and George Villiers's *The Country Gentleman*', *Notes and Queries*, 224 (1979), 438–9.

Richelet, Pierre, *Dictionnaire françois* (Geneva: 1679–80).

Robinson, K., 'Two Casts Lists for Buckingham's "The Chances"', *Notes and Queries*, 224 (1979), 436–7.

Rulfs, Donald J., 'Beaumont and Fletcher on the London Stage 1776–1833', *PMLA* 63 (1948), 1245–64.

Rymer, Thomas, *The Critical Works of Thomas Rymer*, ed. Curt A. Zimansky (New Haven, Conn.: Yale University Press, 1956).

Sackville, Charles, *The Poems of Charles Sackville, Sixth Earl of Dorset*, ed. Brice Harris (New York: Garland, 1979).

Saint-Évremond, Charles de Saint-Denis, Sieur de, *Œuvres meslées*, 2 vols. (London: Tonson, 1705).

—— *Œuvres*, 5 vols. (Amsterdam: Chez Cóvens and Mortier, 1726).

—— *Œuvres de Saint-Évremond*, ed. René de Planhol, 3 vols. (Paris: Cité des Livres, 1927).

—— *The Letters of Saint Evremond*, ed. John Hayward (London: Routledge, 1930).

—— *Œuvres en prose*, ed. René Ternois, 4 vols. (Paris: M. Didier, 1962–9).

—— *Lettres*, ed. René Ternois, 2 vols. (Paris: M. Didier, 1967–8).

—— *La Comédie des Académistes* & *Les Académiciens*, ed. Paolo Carile (Milan: Cisalpino-Goliardica; Paris: Nizet, 1976).

—— and Buckingham and Daubigny, *Sir Politick Would-be*, ed. Robert Finch and Eugène Joliat (Geneva: Droz, 1978).

—— *Les Opéra*, ed. Robert Finch and Eugène Joliat (Geneva: Droz, 1979).

Salter, John (ed.), *Wine Labels: 1730–2003—A Worldwide History* (London: Antique Collectors' Club, 2004).

Saslow, Edward L., 'The Rose Alley Ambuscade', *Restoration*, 26 (2002), 27–49.

Savile, George, *The Works of George Savile, Marquis of Halifax*, 3 vols., ed. Mark N. Brown (Oxford: Clarendon Press, 1989).

Savile, Henry, *Savile Correspondence: Letters to and from Henry Savile, Esq.*, ed. W. Durrant Cooper (London: Camden Society, 1858).

Scappi, Bartolomeo, *Opera* (Venice, 1570; repr. with introduction by Giancarlo Roversi, Sala Bolognese: Arnaldo Forni, 1981).

Scott, Sir Walter, *The Pirate*, ed. Mark Weinstein and Alison Lumsden (Edinburgh: Edinburgh University Press, 2001).

Scudéry, Georges, *Alaric, ou Rome vaincue* (1654), ed. Rosa Galli Pellegrini and Cristina Bernazzoli (Fasano: Schena–Didier Érudition, 1998).

Settle, Elkanah, *A Supplement to The Narrative* (London: 1683 [Wing S2720]).

Shadwell, Thomas, *The Complete Works of Thomas Shadwell*, ed. Montague Summers, 5 vols. (London: Fortune Press, 1927).

Shakespeare, William, *The Complete Works*, ed. Stanley Wells and Gary Taylor (Oxford: Clarendon Press, 1986) [old spelling version].

Sheldon, Esther K., *Thomas Sheridan of Smock-Alley* (Princeton, N.J.: Princeton University Press, 1967).

Simpson, Claude M., *The British Broadside Ballad and its Music* (New Brunswick, N.J.: Rutgers University Press, 1966).

Smith, Dane Farnsworth, *Plays about the Theatre in England from* The Rehearsal *in 1671 to the Licensing Act in 1737* (New York: Oxford University Press, 1936).

—— and Lawhon, M. L., *Plays about the Theatre in England, 1737–1800* (Lewisburg, Pa.: Bucknell University Press, 1979).

Smith, John Harrington, *The Gay Couple in Restoration Comedy* (Cambridge, Mass.: Harvard University Press, 1948).

A Society of Gentlemen, [James Boswell?], *A View of the Edinburgh Theatre during Summer Season, 1759* (London: A. Morley, 1760).

Sorelius, Gunnar, *'The Giant Race before the Flood': Pre-Restoration Drama on the Stage and in the Criticism of the Restoration* (Studia Anglistica Upsaliensia, 4; Uppsala: Almqvist & Wiksell, 1966).

Speaight, George, *The History of the English Puppet Theatre*, 2nd edn. (Carbondale, Ill.: Southern Illinois University Press, 1990).

Spence, Joseph, *Observations, Anecdotes, and Characters of Books and Men*, ed. James M. Osborn, 2 vols. (Oxford: Clarendon Press, 1966).

Spitzer, John, and Zaslaw, Neal, *The Birth of the Orchestra: History of an Institution 1650–1815* (Oxford: Oxford University Press, 2004).

Sprague, Arthur Colby, *Beaumont and Fletcher on the Restoration Stage* (Cambridge, Mass.: Harvard University Press, 1926).

Spurr, John, *England in the 1670s: 'This Masquerading Age'* (Oxford: Blackwell, 2000).

['Stationers' Register'], *A Transcript of the Registers of the Worshipful Company of Stationers; from 1640–1708*, 3 vols. (London: privately printed, 1913–14).

Stern, Tiffany, *Rehearsal from Shakespeare to Sheridan* (Oxford: Clarendon Press, 2000).

Stocker, Margarita, 'Political Allusion in *The Rehearsal*', *Philological Quarterly*, 67 (1988), 11–35.

Stone, George Winchester, Jr., and Kahrl, George M., *David Garrick, A Critical Biography* (Carbondale, Ill.: Southern Illinois University Press, 1979).

Summers, Montague, *The Restoration Theatre* (London: Kegan Paul, Trench, Trubner & Co., 1934).

—— *The Playhouse of Pepys* (London: Routledge and Kegan Paul, 1935).

*Survey of London*, vol. xxix: *The Parish of St. James Westminster*, Part One: South of Piccadilly, ed. F. H. W. Sheppard (London: Athlone Press, 1960).

Sutherland, James, *The Restoration Newspaper and its Development* (Cambridge: Cambridge University Press, 1986).

Tarantino, Giovanni, *Martin Clifford 1624–1677: Deismo e tolleranza nell'linghiterra della Restaurazione* (Florence: Leo S. Olschki Editore, 2000).

*The Term Catalogues, 1668–1709*, ed. Edward Arber, 3 vols. (London: privately printed, 1903–6).

Thomas, Tobyas, *The Life of the Late Famous Comedian, Jo. Hayns* (London: J. Nutt, 1701).

Thomson, Gladys Scott, *Life in a Noble Household, 1641–1700* (London: Cape, 1937).

Thornbury, Walter, and Walford, Edward, *Old and New London: A Narrative of Its History, Its People, and Its Places*, 6 vols. (London: Cassell, Petter, & Galpin, 1873–8).

Thorn-Drury, G., 'Some Notes on Dryden', *RES* 1 (1925), 79–83, 187–97, 324–30.

Tilley, Morris Palmer, *A Dictionary of the Proverbs in England in the Sixteenth and Seventeenth Centuries* (Ann Arbor, Mich.: University of Michigan Press, 1950).

Vander Motten, J. P., *Sir William Killigrew (1606–1695): His Life and Dramatic Works* (Ghent: Rijksuniversiteit, 1980).

—— 'A Misunderstood Allusion in Buckingham's *The Rehearsal*?', *Notes and Queries*, 227 (1982), 516–18.

Venner, Tobias, *Via Recta ad Vitam Longam*, 4th edn. (London: 1660 [Wing V196]) [contains his *A Brief and accurate Treatise concerning The taking of the Fume of Tobacco*].

Vickers, Douglas, 'Misselden, Edward', in *The New Palgrave: A Dictionary of Economics*, John Eatwell, Murray Milgate, and Peter Newman (eds.), 4 vols. (London: Macmillan, 1987), iii. 480–1.

Vieth, David M., *Attribution in Restoration Poetry: A Study of Rochester's 'Poems' of 1680* (New Haven, Conn.: Yale University Press, 1963).

—— 'Bayes and Bardolph: An Unnoticed Allusion in Buckingham's "The Rehearsal"', *Notes and Queries*, 223 (1978), 25–6.

Villiers, George, Second Duke of Buckingham, *The Rehearsal, As it was Acted at the Theatre-Royal* (London: 1672 [Wing B5323]).

—— *The Chances, a Comedy: As it was Acted at the Theater Royal. Corrected and Altered by a Person of Honour* (London: 1682 [Wing F1338]).

—— *Miscellaneous Works, Written by His Grace, George, Late Duke of Buckingham. Collected in One Volume from the Original Papers* (London: J. Nutt, 1704).

—— *Miscellaneous Works, Written by His Grace, George, Late Duke of Buckingham.* The Second Edition. (London: Printed for S. Briscoe and Sold by J. Nutt, 1704).

—— *The Second Volume of Miscellaneous Works, Written by George, Late Duke of Buckingham . . . Collected and Prepar'd for the Press, by the Late Ingenious Mr. Tho. Brown* (London: Printed for Sam. Briscoe, and Sold by J. Nutt, 1705).

—— *The Rehearsal: a comedy. Written To expose some plays then in vogue, and their authors: With a key and remarks, necessary to illustrate the most material passages, of this piece, and to point out the authors, and writings here exposed* (London: H. Hills, 1709).

—— *The Works of His Grace, George Villiers, Late Duke of Buckingham*, 2 vols. The Third Edition with large Additions, adorn'd with Cuts (London: printed for S. Briscoe, and sold by Fardinando Burleigh, 1715).

—— *The Chances. A Comedy, As altered from Beaumont and Fletcher, by his grace The Duke of Buckingham. Distinguishing also the Variations of the Theatre, as performed at the Theatre-Royal in Drury-Lane. Regulated from the Prompt-Book, by Permission of the Managers, By Mr. Hopkins, Prompter* (London: John Bell, 1777).

—— *The Rehearsal*, ed. Edward Arber (London: Alex. Murray & Son, 1868).

—— *The Rehearsal*, ed. Montague Summers (Stratford-upon-Avon: Shakespeare Head Press, 1914).

—— *The Rehearsal*, ed. D. E. L. Crane (Durham: University of Durham, 1976).

—— 'The Chances Adapted by George Villiers, second Duke of Buckingham from the Comedy by John Fletcher', ed. James Patrick Fowler (Ph.D. thesis; Shakespeare Institute, University of Birmingham, 1978).

—— *Buckingham: Public and Private Man: The Prose, Poems and Commonplace Book of George Villiers, Second Duke of Buckingham (1628–1687)*, ed. Christine Phipps (New York: Garland, 1985).

—— *La Prova téatrale* [dual-language edition of *The Rehearsal*], ed. Romana Rutelli (Naples: Liguori, 1994).

Waller, Edmund, *The Maid's Tragedy Altered. With Some Other Pieces* (London: 1690 [Wing W502]).

Walpole, Horace, *A Catalogue of the Royal and Noble Authors of England*, vol. ii (London: Strawberry Hill, 1758).

—— *The Yale Edition of Horace Walpole's Correspondence*, ed. W. S. Lewis, et al., 48 vols. (New Haven, Conn.: Yale University Press, 1937–83).

Wanko, Cheryl, 'Colley Cibber's *The Rival Queans*: A New Consideration', *Restoration and Eighteenth Century Theatre Research*, 2nd ser., 3/2 (1988), 38–52.

Wharton, Anne, *The Surviving Works of Anne Wharton*, ed. G. Greer and S. Hastings (Stump Cross, Essex: Stump Cross Books, 1997).

Whitney, Lois, *Primitivism and the Idea of Progress in English Popular Literature of the Eighteenth Century* (Baltimore, Md.: Johns Hopkins Press, 1934).

Wilcox, John, *The Relation of Molière to Restoration Comedy* (New York: Columbia University Press, 1938).

Wilcox, R. Turner, *The Mode in Hats and Headdress* (New York: Scribner's, 1948).

Wilkinson, Tate, *The Wandering Patentee; or, A History of the Yorkshire Theatres, from 1770 to the Present Time*, 4 vols. (York: For the Author, 1795).

Willson, Robert F., 'Bayes versus the Critics: *The Rehearsal* and False Wit', in *'Their Form Confounded': Studies in the Burlesque Play from Udall to Sheridan* (The Hague: Mouton, 1974).

Wilmot, John, Earl of Rochester, *The Letters of John Wilmot, Earl of Rochester*, ed. Jeremy Treglown (Oxford: Blackwell, 1980).

—— *The Works of John Wilmot, Earl of Rochester*, ed. Harold Love (Oxford: Oxford University Press, 1999).

Wilson, Edward M., 'Did John Fletcher Read Spanish?', *Philological Quarterly*, 27 (1948), 187–90.

Wilson, John Harold, *The Influence of Beaumont and Fletcher on Restoration Drama* (Columbus, Ohio: Ohio State University Press, 1928).

—— *The Court Wits of the Restoration* (Princeton, N.J.: Princeton University Press, 1948).

—— *Nell Gwyn: Royal Mistress* (London: Frederick Muller, 1952).

—— *A Rake and His Times: George Villiers 2nd Duke of Buckingham* (New York: Farrar, Straus and Young, 1954).

—— *All the King's Ladies: Actresses of the Restoration* (Chicago, Ill.: University of Chicago Press, 1958), 146–7.

Winn, James Anderson, *John Dryden and His World* (New Haven, Conn.: Yale University Press, 1987).

*The Wits or, Sport upon Sport*, ed. John James Elston (Ithaca, N.Y.: Cornell University Press, 1932).

Wood, Anthony a, *Athenæ Oxonienses*, 4 vols., ed. Philip Bliss (London: F. C. and J. Rivington et al., 1813–20).

Woods, Leigh, *Garrick Claims the Stage* (Westport, Conn.: Greenwood, 1984).

Wycherley, William, *The Plays of William Wycherley*, ed. Arthur Friedman (Oxford: Clarendon Press, 1979).

Yardley, Bruce, 'George Villiers, Second Duke of Buckingham, and the Politics of Toleration', *Huntington Library Quarterly*, 55 (1992), 317–37.

Yeomans, Donald K., *Comets: A Chronological History of Observation, Science, Myth, and Folklore* (New York: John Wiley & Sons, 1991).

# *INDEX*
## to the Introductions and Explanatory Notes
Coverage is principally of seventeenth- and eighteenth-century (and earlier)
persons and books. Incidental references are omitted.